World Civilizations

FIFTH EDITION

WORLD

FIFTH EDITION

CIVILIZATIONS

Their History and Their Culture

EDWARD McNALL BURNS

AND

PHILIP LEE RALPH

W·W·NORTON & COMPANY·INC·NEW YORK

Including material from WESTERN CIVILIZATIONS by
Edward McNall Burns. Copyright 1973, 1968, 1963,
1958, 1954, 1949, 1947, 1941

Library of Congress Cataloging in Publication Data

Burns, Edward McNall, 1897-
   World civilizations.

   "Including material from Western civilizations, by
Edward McNall Burns."
   Includes bibliographies.
   1. Civilization—History. I. Ralph, Philip Lee,
1905-   joint author. II. Title.
CB59.B8 1974b   901.9   73-21555
ISBN 0-393-09276-3

CARTOGRAPHY BY HAROLD K. FAYE

PRINTED IN THE UNITED STATES OF AMERICA

1   2   3   4   5   6   7   8   9   0

To our Students

Contents

Preface

Part One THE DAWN OF HISTORY

Part Five THE EARLY MODERN WORLD,
1400–1789

XV

Maps

MAPS IN BLACK AND WHITE

xxiii

Preface

The time has long since passed when modern man could think of the world as consisting of Europe and the United States. Western culture is, of course, primarily a product of European origins. But it has never been that exclusively. Its original foundations were in Southwestern Asia and North Africa. These were supplemented by influences seeping in from India and eventually from China. From India and the Far East the West derived its knowledge of the zero, the compass, gunpowder, silk, cotton, and probably a large number of religious and philosophical concepts. Especially in recent times the East has increased in importance. The exhaustion of Europe by two World Wars, the revolt of the colored races against Caucasian domination, and the struggle for the world between the Communist powers and the United States have made every part of the earth of vital importance to every other. If peace is indivisible, so are prosperity, justice, and freedom; so, in fact, is civilization itself.

The purpose of this work is to present a compact survey of man's struggle for civilization from early times to the present. No major area or country of the globe has been omitted. Europe, the Commonwealth of Nations, the Middle East, Southeast Asia, Africa, India, China, Japan, and North, Central, and South America have all received appropriate emphasis. Obviously, the history of none of them could be covered in full detail. The authors believe, however, that a broad view of the world as a whole is necessary to understand the basic problems of any of its parts. This thesis acquires additional validity as the nations increase in interdependence. Perspective in history becomes more and more urgent as the momentous problems of our own generation press for solution. If there is any basic philosophical interpretation underlying the narrative, it is the conviction that most of human progress thus far has resulted from the growth of intelligence and respect for the rights of man, and that therein lies the chief hope for a better world in the future.

As its title indicates, this work is not exclusively or even primarily a political history. Political events are recognized as important, but they are not the whole substance of history. In the main, the facts of political history are subordinated to the development of institutions and ideas or are presented as the groundwork of cultural, social, and economic movements. The authors consider the effects of the Industrial Revolutions to be no less important than the Napoleonic Wars. They believe it is of greater value to understand the significance of Buddha, Confucius, Newton, Darwin, and Einstein than it is to be able to name the kings of France. In accordance with this broader conception of history, more space has been given to the teachings of John Locke and John Stuart Mill, of Mahatma Gandhi and Mao Tse-tung, than to the military exploits of Gustavus Adolphus or the Duke of Wellington.

The first edition of *World Civilizations* was published in 1955, the second in 1958, the third in 1964, and the fourth in 1969. A major objective of the present edition is to take account of the numerous discoveries and reinterpretations that have resulted from recent historical research. Another equally important objective is to bring into clear focus the realities of the contemporary world—the ascendancy of rival superpowers, the struggles and aspirations of emerging nations of the Third World, the threat to the human environment posed by a population explosion and the depletion of natural resources, and the promise inherent in scientific and cultural innovation.

This edition of *World Civilizations* is not a mere enlargement of the previous edition; much new material has been added but substantial portions of the old material has been eliminated or condensed. In this vein the two chapters of the previous edition dealing with the Mesopotamian and Persian civilizations have been combined, as have those on the First and Second Industrial Revolutions. The chapter on the United States has been merged with material on the maturing of the European democracies, and a new chapter added, tracing the roots of the political and social revolutions of our time. Three chapters have been expanded to reflect events and trends of the late 1960's and early 1970's. The most significant innovation in the present edition is the expanded treatment of the history of Africa, contributed by Professor Richard W. Hull of New York University. Besides revising the material on Africa in Chapter 38, Professor Hull has added new sections at appropriate points throughout the text, providing a compact but enlightening account of the peoples and the major civilizations of the African continent. All of the chapters on non-Western areas, and the accompanying reading lists, have been thoroughly revised. Some portions have been condensed to allow room for full treatment of recent and crucial developments in China, Japan, the Indian subcontinent, and Southeast Asia. The chapter on Latin America contains a more intensive analysis than heretofore of the problems and prospects of that too generally neglected area.

The fifth edition of *World Civilizations* has been redesigned for easier reading and to accommodate literally hundreds of new illustrations, from archives both Western and non-Western. The color plates have been retained and improved in clarity and brightness. The new edition is published in both a one-volume and a two-volume format. Available for use with either is a Teacher's Manual and a new Study Guide, which, as its most distinctive feature, includes numerous extracts from original sources.

In preparing this revision the authors have benefited from the assistance and counsel of many individuals whose services no words of appreciation can adequately measure. The list would include not only various specialists but also teachers and students who have used the text in their courses. The authors owe a debt of gratitude to demanding but kindly editors who have worked with them over the years, and, above all, are indebted to their wives, for their aid with laborious tasks and for their patience and understanding.

Edward McNall Burns
Philip Lee Ralph

World Civilizations

PART I

The Dawn of History

No one knows the place of origin of the human species. There is evidence, however, that it may have been south central Africa or possibly central or south central Asia. Here climatic conditions were such as to favor the evolution of a variety of human types from primate ancestors. From their place or places of origin members of the human species wandered to southeastern and eastern Asia, northern Africa, Europe, and eventually, to America. For hundreds of centuries they remained primitive, leading a life which was at first barely more advanced than that of the higher animals. About 5000 B.C. a few of them, enjoying special advantages of location and climate, developed superior cultures. These cultures, which attained knowledge of writing and considerable advancement in the arts and sciences and in social organization, began in that part of the world known as the Near Orient. This region extends from the western border of India to the Mediterranean Sea and to the farther bank of the Nile. Here flourished, at different periods between 5000 and 300 B.C., the mighty empires of the Egyptians, the Babylonians, the Assyrians, the Chaldeans, and the Persians, together with the smaller states of such peoples as the Cretans, the Sumerians, the Phoenicians, and the Hebrews. Farther east, in the Indus River valley, another high civilization appeared by 3000 B.C. In other parts of the world the beginnings of civilization were retarded. There was nothing that could be called civilized life in China until about 2000 B.C. And, except on the island of Crete, there was no civilization in Europe until more than 1000 years later.

A Table of Geologic Time

TIME	ERA	PERIOD	EPOCH	CHARACTERISTIC FORMS OF LIFE	CULTURE PERIODS	CHARACTERISTIC ACHIEVEMENTS
3 billion years ago	Precambrian	Early Precambrian				
510 million years ago	Precambrian	Late Precambrian		One-celled organisms First invertebrates: worms, algae		
	Paleozoic	Cambrian		Mollusks, sponges		
	Paleozoic	Ordovician		Insects, first vertebrates		
	Paleozoic	Silurian		Corals, sharks, seaweed		
	Paleozoic	Devonian		Lungfish, crustaceans		
	Paleozoic	Carboniferous Pennsylvanian Mississippian		Earliest amphibians Large amphibians Ferns		
180 million years ago	Paleozoic	Permian				
	Mesozoic	Triassic		Giant reptiles Diversified reptiles, birds		
	Mesozoic	Jurassic		Marsupials, bony fishes Trees		
90 million years ago	Mesozoic	Cretaceous				
	Cenozoic	Tertiary	Paleocene	Early mammals, first primates		
	Cenozoic	Tertiary	Eocene	Primitive apes, ancestors of monkeys		
	Cenozoic	Tertiary	Oligocene			
	Cenozoic	Tertiary	Miocene	Ancestors of great apes		
	Cenozoic	Tertiary	Pliocene	Ancestors of man, modern mammals		
	Cenozoic	Tertiary		Early human species, other primates	Lower Paleolithic	Spoken language, knowledge of fire, burial of dead, stone tools and weapons
500,000 years ago	Cenozoic	Quaternary	Pleistocene	Present-day animals and races of men		
	Cenozoic	Quaternary	Recent		Upper Paleolithic	Needles, harpoons, fishhooks, dart throwers, magic, art, social organization, cooking of food
	Cenozoic	Quaternary			Neolithic	Agriculture, domestication of animals, pottery, houses, navigation, institutions
7000 years ago	Cenozoic	Quaternary			Civilized man	Bronze, iron, writing, technology, science, literature, philosophy, etc.

CHAPTER 1

The Earliest Beginnings

As we turn to the past itself . . . we might well begin with a pious tribute to our nameless [preliterate] ancestors, who by inconceivably arduous and ingenious effort succeeded in establishing a human race. They made the crucial discoveries and inventions, such as the tool, the seed, and the domesticated animal; their development of agriculture, the "neolithic revolution" that introduced a settled economy, was perhaps the greatest stride forward that man has ever taken. They created the marvelous instrument of language, which enabled man to discover his humanity, and eventually to disguise it. They laid the foundations of civilization: its economic, political, and social life, and its artistic, ethical, and religious traditions. Indeed, our "savage" ancestors are still very near to us, and not merely in our capacity for savagery.
—Herbert J. Muller, *The Uses of the Past*

I. THE MEANING OF HISTORY

Broadly defined, history is a record and interpretation of man's achievements, hopes and frustrations, struggles and triumphs. This conception has not always been the prevailing one. At one time history was quite generally regarded as "past politics." Its content was restricted largely to battles and treaties, to the personalities and policies of statesmen, and to the laws and decrees of rulers. But important as such data are, they do not constitute the whole substance of history. Actually, history comprises a record of all of man's accomplishments in every sphere, whether political, economic, intellectual, or social. It embraces also a chronicle of his dreams and ideals, his hopes, triumphs, and failures. Perhaps most important of all, it includes an inquiry into the causes of the chief political and economic movements, a search for the forces that impelled man toward his great undertakings, and the reasons for his successes and failures.

History defined

3

Whether history is a science, and whether it can be used as an instrument for predicting the future, are questions that do not yield conclusive answers. With regard to the first, about all we can say is that both the study and the writing of history should be made as scientific as possible. This means that the scientific attitude should be brought to bear upon the solution of all of history's problems, be they political, intellectual, moral, or religious. As the American philosopher, the late John Dewey, pointed out, the scientific attitude demands a skeptical and inquiring approach toward all issues and a refusal to form conclusive judgments until all available evidence has been amassed and examined. Obviously, this approach rules out such conceptions of history as the patriotic, the racial, or the providential. Scientific history cannot be made to serve the purposes of national greatness, race supremacy, or the doctrine of a Chosen People.

History as a
chart for the
future

The value of history as a chart for the future has tormented the minds of philosophical historians for scores of centuries. The father of scientific history, Thucydides, who lived in Athens in the fifth century B.C., asserted that events do "repeat themselves at some future time—if not exactly the same, yet very similar." The British essayist Thomas Carlyle and the American philosopher William James saw in the stimulating genius of eminent individuals the motivating force of historical progress. What would have been the future of Germany, James asked, if Bismarck had died in his cradle, or of the British Empire if Robert Clive had shot himself, as he tried to do at Madras? Great stages of civilization could be accounted for only by an exceptional concourse of brilliant individuals within a limited time. But James offered no theory as to the conditions likely to produce such a concourse.

The most elaborate hypothesis in modern times concerning inevitability in history was developed by Karl Marx in the nineteenth century. Marx taught that individuals are mere instruments of forces more powerful than they. These forces, he contended, are exclusively economic and are grounded in changes in modes of production. Thus the change from a feudal economy to a commercial and industrial economy brought into existence the capitalist epoch and the rule of the bourgeois class. In time capitalism would be superseded by socialism, and, finally, by communism. The course of history was consequently predetermined, and future changes would succeed one another in the same mechanical fashion as they had in the past.

Although the theories of Marx have attracted considerable attention, they cannot be accepted as gospel by scientific historians. The motivation of human events is too complex to be forced into a single pattern. It is impossible to predict the future in terms of a single theory or thesis. No crystal ball exists which will enable anyone to foretell with certainty that every revolution must be followed by counterrevolution, that every war begets new wars, or that progress is an inescapable law. Greed is undoubtedly a powerful motive for human action, but this does not mean that economic causation must be accepted as a universal rule. Fear is also a powerful motive, in somes cases overbalancing greed. Other psychological motives, including sex and the lust for power, likewise play a part in the determination of human actions. In short, no one explanation will suffice, and a vast amount of research will be necessary before there can be any assurance that all the possible driving forces have been discovered.

One final question remains. Is history a unilinear process, an unbroken stream of progress toward higher and nobler achievements? Or is it simply a process of change marked by a general trend of advancement but with many interruptions and setbacks? Scarcely a historian would deny that some ideas and discoveries have come down through the centuries with no change except in the direction of improvement. This would be true of much of the mathematics of the ancient Egyptians, the Babylonians, and the Greeks. But other examples illustrate the opposite. Aristarchus of Samos, in the third century B.C., propounded a heliocentric theory. It was superseded, largely for religious reasons, about 400 years later by the geocentric theory. It was not reaffirmed until the time of Copernicus in the sixteenth century A.D. Although Hellenistic physicians came close to a discovery of the circulation of the blood, knowledge of their achievement lay buried for 1500 years and had to await rediscovery in the seventeenth century by Sir William Harvey, the English physician and anatomist. As with individual accomplishments, so with whole cultures. The first three millennia of written history were strewn with the wreckage of fallen empires and extinct civilizations. Egypt, Mesopotamia, Persia, Greece, and Rome fell prey one after the other to external conquest, internal conquest, or a combination of both. Many elements of the old cultures survived, but they were frequently modified or woven into quite different patterns. As Lincoln said, we cannot escape history, and the influence which history presses upon us is more complicated than we usually suspect.

2. HISTORY AND PREHISTORY

It is the custom among many historians to distinguish between historic and prehistoric periods in the evolution of human society. By the former they mean history based upon written records. By the latter they mean the record of man's achievements before the invention of writing. But this distinction is not altogether satisfactory. It suggests that human accomplishments before they were recorded in characters or symbols representing words or concepts were not important. Nothing could be farther from the truth. The foundations, at

5

least, of many of the great accomplishments of modern technology, and even of social and political systems, were laid before human beings could write a word. It would seem preferable, therefore, that the whole period of man's life on earth should be regarded as historic, and that the era before the invention of writing be designated by some term such as "preliterate." The records of preliterate societies are, of course, not books and manuscripts, but tools, weapons, fossils, utensils, carvings, paintings, and fragments of jewelry and ornamentation. These, commonly known as "artifacts," are often just as valuable as the written word in providing knowledge of a people's deeds and modes of living.

The entire span of human history can be divided roughly into two periods, the Age of Stone and the Age of Metals. The former is identical with the Preliterate Age, or the period before the invention of writing. The latter coincides with the period of history based upon written records. The Preliterate Age covered at least 95 per cent of man's existence and did not come to an end until about 5000 B.C. The Age of Metals practically coincides with the history of civilized nations. The Age of Stone is subdivided into the Paleolithic, or Old Stone Age, and the Neolithic, or New Stone Age. Each takes its name from the type of stone tools and weapons characteristically manufactured during the period. Thus during the greater part of the Paleolithic Age implements were commonly made by chipping pieces off a large stone or flint and using the core that remained as a hand ax or "fist hatchet." Toward the end of the period the chips themselves were used as knives or spearheads, and the core thrown away. The Neolithic Age witnessed the supplanting of chipped stone tools by implements made by grinding and polishing stone.

Fist Hatchet

3. THE CULTURE OF LOWER PALEOLITHIC MEN

The Paleolithic period can be dated from roughly 1,750,000 B.C. to 10,000 B.C. It is commonly divided into two stages, an earlier or

The earliest Stone Age men

Lower Paleolithic and a later or Upper Paleolithic. The Lower Paleolithic was much the longer of the two, covering about 75 per cent of the entire Old Stone Age. During this time at least four species of men inhabited the earth. The oldest was apparently a creature whose skeletal remains were found in 1960–1964 by Louis S. B. Leakey in what is now Tanzania, East Africa. Leakey named this creature *Homo habilis*, or "man having ability." Estimated to be at least 1,750,000 years old, the remains included parts of the skull, hands, legs, and feet. That *Homo habilis* was a true ancestral human being is indicated by evidence that he walked erect and that he used crude tools. It must not be supposed, of course, that these tools represented any high degree of manufacturing skill or inventive talent.

For the most part, they consisted of objects taken from nature:

The Skull (left) of a Young Woman of the Species Homo habilis, believed to have lived in Tanzania, East Africa, about 1,750,000 years ago. On the right is the skull of a present-day African. Though *Homo habilis* was smaller than a pygmy, the brain casing was shaped like that of modern man.

bones of large animals, limbs from trees, and chunks of stone, perhaps broken or crudely chipped.[1]

Two other early inhabitants of the Lower Paleolithic were Java man and Peking man. Java man was long thought to be the oldest of manlike creatures, but it is now generally agreed that the date of his origin was about 500,000 B.C. His skeletal remains were found on the island of Java in 1891. The remains of Peking man were found in China, about forty miles southwest of Peking between 1926 and 1930. Since the latter date, fragments of no fewer than 32 skeletons of the Peking type have been located, making possible a complete reconstruction of at least the head of this ancient species. Anthropologists generally agree that Peking man and Java man are of approximately the same antiquity, and that both probably descended from the same ancestral type.

During the last 25,000 years of the Lower Paleolithic period a fourth species of ancient man made his appearance. He was Neanderthal man, famous as an early cave man. His skeletal fragments were first discovered in the valley of the Neander, near Düsseldorf, northwestern Germany, in 1856. Since then numerous other discoveries have been made, in some cases complete skeletons, in such widely separated regions as Belgium, Spain, Italy, Yugo-

Java Man

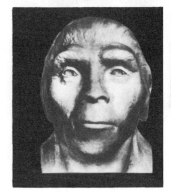

Peking Man

[1] In 1972, near Lake Rudolf in East Africa, the remains of another manlike species were found. They were estimated to be between 2.5 and 3 million years old. The size of its brain cavity seemed to justify the species' being called the predecessor of *Homo habilis.*

7

Neanderthal Man

Lower Paleolithic Carving Tool and Side Scraper

slavia, Russia, and Palestine. So closely did Neanderthal man resemble modern man that he is classified as a member of the same genus, the genus *Homo*. The resemblance, however, was by no means perfect. Neanderthal men, on the average, were only about five feet, four inches in height. They had receding chins and heavy eyebrow ridges. Although their foreheads sloped back and their brain cases were low-vaulted, their average cranial capacity was slightly greater than that of modern Caucasians. What this may have signified with respect to their intelligence cannot be determined.

The knowledge we possess of the culture of Lower Paleolithic men is scanty indeed. The skills they achieved and the learning they acquired must have been pitiful in quantity even when compared with the accomplishments of modern primitive men. Yet Neanderthal man and his successors were not mere apes, forgetting in a moment the chance triumphs they had made. They undoubtedly had the capacity for speech, which enabled them to communicate with their fellows and to pass on what they had learned to succeeding generations. We are justified in assuming also that they possessed reasoning ability, however crudely it may have been developed. Practically from the beginning, therefore, they were probably tool-using creatures, employing their wits to fashion implements and weapons. Perhaps at first these would be nothing but limbs broken from trees to be used as clubs. Eventually it was discovered that stones could be chipped in such a way as to give them cutting edges. Thus were developed spearheads, borers, and much superior knives and scrapers. Indications have been found also of a degree of advancement in nonmaterial culture. In the entrances to caves where Neanderthal man lived, or at least took refuge, evidence has been discovered of flint-working floors and stone hearths where huge fires appear to have been made. These would suggest the origins of co-operative group life and possibly the crude beginnings of social institutions. More significance may be attached to Neanderthal man's practice of bestowing care upon the bodies of his dead, interring with them in shallow graves tools and other objects or value. Perhaps this practice indicates the development of a religious sense, or at least a belief in some form of survival after death.

4. UPPER PALEOLITHIC CULTURE

About 30,000 B.C. the culture of the Old Stone Age passed from the Lower Paleolithic stage to the Upper Paleolithic. The Upper Paleolithic period lasted for only about 200 centuries, or from 30,000 to 10,000 B.C. A new and superior type of human being dominated the earth in this time. Biologically these men were closely related to modern man. Their foremost predecessors, Neanderthal men, had ceased to exist as a distinct variety. What became of the Neanderthalers is not known.

Cro-Magnon man: physical characteristics

8

The name used to designate the prevailing breed of Upper Paleolithic men is Cro-Magnon, from the Cro-Magnon cave in Dordogne, France, where some of the most typical remains were discovered. Cro-Magnon men were tall, broad-shouldered, and erect, the males averaging over six feet. They had high foreheads, well-developed chins, and a cranial capacity about equal to the modern average. The heavy eyebrow ridges so typical of earlier species were absent. Whether Cro-Magnon men left any survivors is a debatable question. They do not seem to have been exterminated but appear to have been driven into mountainous regions and to have been absorbed ultimately into later breeds.

Cro-Magnon Man

Upper Paleolithic culture was markedly superior to that which had gone before. Not only were tools and implements better made, but they existed in greater variety. They were not fashioned merely from flakes of stone and an occasional shaft of bone; other materials were used in abundance, particularly reindeer horn and ivory. Examples of the more complicated tools included the bone needle, the fishhook, the harpoon, the dart thrower, and, at the very end, the bow and arrow. That Upper Paleolithic man wore clothing is indicated by the fact that he made buttons and toggles of bone and horn and invented the needle. He did not know how to weave cloth, but animal skins sewn together proved a satisfactory substitute. It is certain that he cooked his food, for enormous hearths, evidently used for roasting flesh, have been discovered. In the vicinity of one at Solutré, in southern France, was a mass of charred bones, estimated to contain the remains of 100,000 large animals. Although Cro-Magnon man built no houses, except a few simple huts in regions where natural shelters did not abound, his life was not wholly nomadic. Evidences found in the caves that were his usual homes indicate that he must have used them, seasonally at least, for years at a time.

Upper Paleolithic culture: material goods

With respect to nonmaterial elements there are also indications that Upper Paleolithic culture represented a marked advancement. Group life was now more regular and more highly organized than ever before. The profusion of charred bones at Solutré and elsewhere probably indicates cooperative enterprise in the hunt and sharing of the results in great community feasts. The amazing workmanship displayed in tools and weapons and highly developed techniques in the arts could scarcely have been achieved without some division of labor. It appears certain, therefore, that Upper Paleolithic communities included professional artists and skilled craftsmen. In order to acquire such talents, certain members of the communities must have gone through long periods of training and given all their time to the practice of their specialties.

Upper Paleolithic Fish Hook

Substantial proof exists that Cro-Magnon man had highly developed notions of a world of unseen powers. He bestowed more care upon the bodies of his dead than did Neanderthal man, painting the

9

Upper Paleolithic Engraving and Sculpture. The two objects at the top and upper right are dart throwers. At the lower left is the famous Venus of Willendorf.

corpses, folding the arms over the heart, and depositing pendants, necklaces, and richly carved weapons and tools in the graves. He formulated an elaborate system of sympathetic magic designed to increase his supply of food. Sympathetic magic is based upon the principle that imitating a desired result will bring about that result. Applying this principle, Cro-Magnon man made paintings on the walls of his caves depicting the capture of reindeer in the hunt. At other times he fashioned clay models of the bison or mammoth and mutilated them with dart thrusts. The purpose of such representations was quite evidently to facilitate the very results portrayed and thereby to increase the hunter's success and make easier the struggle for existence. Possibly incantations or ceremonies accompanied the making of the pictures or images, and it is likely that the work of producing them was carried on while the actual hunt was in progress.

The supreme achievement of Cro-Magnon man was his art—an achievement so original and resplendent that it ought to be counted among the Seven Wonders of the World. Nothing else illustrates so well the great gulf between his culture and that of his predecessors. Upper Paleolithic art included nearly every branch that the material culture of the time made possible. Sculpture, painting, carving, and engraving were all represented. The ceramic arts and architecture were lacking; pottery had not yet been invented; and the only buildings erected were of simple design.

The art *par excellence* of Cro-Magnon man was painting. Here were exhibited the greatest number and variety of his talents—his discrimination in the use of color, his meticulous attention to detail, his capacity for the employment of scale in depicting a group, and above all, his genius for naturalism. Especially noteworthy was the painter's skill in representing movement. A large proportion of murals depict animals running, leaping, browsing, chewing the cud, or facing the hunter at bay. Ingenious devices were often employed to give the impression of motion. Chief among them was the drawing or painting of additional outlines to indicate the areas in which the legs or the head of the animal had moved. The scheme was so shrewdly executed that no appearance whatever of artificiality resulted.

Cave-man art throws a flood of light on many problems relating to primitive mentality and folkways. To a certain extent it was undoubtedly an expression of a true aesthetic sense. Cro-Magnon man did obviously take some delight in a graceful line or symmetrical pattern or brilliant color. The fact that he painted and tattooed his body and wore ornaments gives evidence of this. But his chief works of art can scarcely have been produced for the sake of creating beautiful objects. Such a possibility must be excluded for several reasons. To begin with, the best of the paintings and drawings are usually to be found on the walls and ceilings of the darkest and most inaccessible parts of the caves. The gallery of paintings at Niaux, for instance, is more than half a mile from the entrance of the cavern. No one could see the artists' creations except in the imperfect light of torches or of primitive lamps, which must have smoked and sputtered badly, for the only illuminating fluid was animal fat. Furthermore, there is evidence that Cro-Magnon man was largely indifferent toward his work of art after it was finished. Numerous examples have been found of paintings or drawings superimposed upon earlier ones of the same or of different types. Evidently the important thing was not the finished work itself, but the act of making it.

For Paleolithic man, art was a serious business. The real purpose of nearly all of it was apparently not to delight the senses but to

The Venus of Laussel

Significance of Upper Paleolithic art

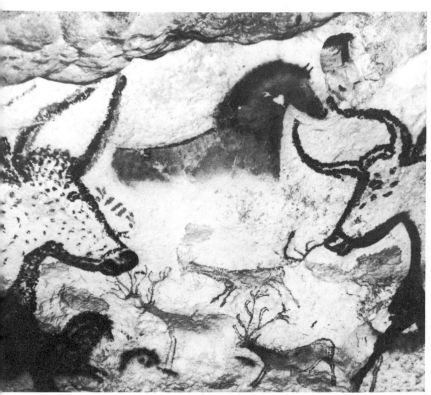

Cave Drawings at Lascaux, France. On the left are characteristic examples of the realism of Cro-Magnon man's art. On the right, a view of the entrance to the caves.

make easier the struggle for existence by increasing the supply of animals useful for food. The artist himself was not an aesthete but a magician, and his art was a form of magic designed to promote the hunter's success. In this purpose lay its chief significance and the foundation of most of its special qualities. It suggests, for example, the real reason why game animals were almost the exclusive subjects of the great murals and why plant life and inanimate objects were seldom represented. It aids us in understanding Cro-Magnon man's neglect of finished paintings and his predominant interest in the process of making them.

Art an aid in the struggle for existence

Upper Paleolithic culture came to an untimely end about 10,000 B.C. Internal decay, exemplified by the decline of art, seems to have been one of the causes. A more obvious and doubtless more effective cause was partial destruction of the food supply. As the last great glacier retreated farther and farther northward, the climate of southern Europe became too warm for the reindeer, and they gradually migrated to the shores of the Baltic. The mammoth, whether for the same or for different reasons, became extinct. Representatives of the magnificent Cro-Magnon breed probably followed the reindeer northward, but apparently they did not continue their cultural achievements.

The end of Upper Paleolithic culture

5. NEOLITHIC CULTURE

The last stage of preliterate culture is known as the Neolithic period, or the New Stone Age. The name is applied because stone weapons and tools were now generally made by grinding and polishing instead of by chipping or fracturing as in the preceding periods. The bearers of Neolithic culture were new varieties of modern man who poured into Africa and southern Europe from western Asia. Since no evidence exists of their later extermination or wholesale migration, they must be regarded as the immediate ancestors of most of the peoples now living in Europe.

The meaning of the term Neolithic

It is impossible to fix exact dates for the Neolithic period. The culture was not well established in Europe until about 3000 B.C., though it certainly originated earlier. There is evidence that it existed in Egypt as far back as 5000 B.C., and that it probably began at an equally early date in southwestern Asia. There is also variation in the dates of its ending. It was superseded in the Nile valley by the first literate civilization soon after the year 4000.[2] Except on the island of Crete it did not come to an end anywhere in Europe before 2000, and in northern Europe much later still. In a few regions of the world it has not terminated yet. The natives of some islands of the Pacific, the Arctic regions of North America, and the jungles of Brazil are still in the Neolithic culture stage except for a few customs acquired from explorers and missionaries.

The varying dates of the Neolithic stage

In many respects the New Stone Age was the most significant in the history of the world thus far. The level of material progress rose to new heights. Neolithic man had a better mastery of his environment than any of his predecessors. He was less likely to perish from a shift in climatic conditions or from the failure of some part of his food supply. This decided advantage was the result primarily of the development of agriculture and the domestication of animals. Whereas all of the men who had lived heretofore were mere food-gatherers, Neolithic man was a *food-producer*. Tilling the soil and keeping flocks and herds provided him with much more dependable food resources and at times yielded him a surplus. These circumstances made possible a more rapid increase of population, promoted a settled existence, and fostered the growth of institutions. Such were the elements of a great social and economic revolution whose importance it would be impossible to exaggerate.

The Neolithic revolution

The new culture also derives significance from the fact that it was the first to be distributed over the *entire* world. Although some earlier cultures, especially those of Neanderthal and Cro-Magnon men, were widely dispersed, they were confined chiefly to the accessible mainland areas of the Old World. Neolithic man penetrated into every habitable area of the earth's surface—from Arctic wastes

The wide diffusion of the Neolithic culture

[2] All dates in Egyptian history prior to 2000 are approximations and may represent a margin of error of several centuries.

to the jungles of the tropics. He apparently made his way from a number of centers of origin to every nook and cranny of both hemispheres. He traveled incredible distances by water as well as by land, and eventually occupied every major island of the oceans, no matter how remote.

The historian would have difficulty in overestimating the importance of the Neolithic migrations. The net result was that they distributed a similar pattern of culture over the entire world. The few elements of earlier cultures which had managed to survive were almost completely inundated. Their disappearance means that we now have no way of discovering more than a small part of what went on in Paleolithic man's mind—whether he believed that government is an evil or that private property is sacred or that the world was created out of nothing. The fact that we find particular notions in the primitive mind of today does not prove that they are inseparable from the blood and sinew of the species, for it is necessary to remember that all existing primitive races are the beneficiaries or the victims of a common heritage.

Importance of the Neolithic migrations

Migration over long distances was not the only example of Neolithic man's achievements. He developed the arts of knitting, of spinning, and of weaving cloth. He made the first pottery and knew how to produce fire artificially by friction. He built houses of wood and sun-dried mud. Toward the end of the period he discovered the possibilities of metals, and a few implements of copper and gold were added to his stock. Since nothing was yet known of the arts of smelting and refining, the use of metals was limited to the more malleable ones occasionally found in the pure state in the form of nuggets.

New tools and technical skills

But the real foundation stones of the Neolithic culture were the domestication of animals and the development of agriculture. Without these it is inconceivable that the culture would have attained the complexity it did. More than anything else they made possible a settled mode of existence and the growth of villages and social

Neolithic Dwellings. Examples shown are restorations of Swiss lake dwellings. They were commonly erected on poles or stilts for purposes of defense.

institutions. The first animal to be domesticated is generally thought to have been the dog, on the assumption that he would be continually hanging around the hunter's camp to pick up bones and scraps of meat. Eventually it would be discovered that he could be put to use in hunting, or possibly in guarding the camp. After achieving success in domesticating the dog, Neolithic man would logically turn his attention to other animals, especially to those he used for food. Before the period ended, at least five species—the cow, the dog, the goat, the sheep, and the pig—had been made to serve his needs. Not all of them in all parts of the world, however. The Neolithic tribes of the New World domesticated no animals at all, except the hairless dog in some parts of Mexico, the llama and the alpaca in the Andean highland, and the guinea pig and the turkey in a few other regions.

The exact spot where agriculture originated has never been positively determined. All we know is that wild grasses which were probably the ancestors of the cereal grains have been found in a number of places. Types of wheat grow wild in Asia Minor, in the Caucasus, and in Mesopotamia. Wild ancestors of barley have been reported from North Africa, from Persia, from Asia Minor, and from Turkestan. Though it is probable that these were the first crops of Neolithic agriculture, they were by no means the only ones. Millet, vegetables, and numerous fruits were also grown. Flax was cultivated in the Old World for its textile fiber, and in some localities the growing of the poppy for opium had already begun. In the New World maize (Indian corn) was the only cereal crop, but the American Indians cultivated numerous other products, including tobacco, beans, squashes, pumpkins, and potatoes.

Historically, the most important feature of Neolithic culture was probably the development of institutions. An institution may be defined as a combination of group beliefs and activities organized in a relatively permanent fashion for the purpose of fulfilling some group need. It ordinarily includes a body of customs and traditions, a code of rules and standards, and physical extensions such as buildings, punitive devices, and facilities for communication and indoctrination. Since man is a social being, some of these elements probably existed from earliest times, but institutions in their fully developed form seem to have been an achievement of the Neolithic Age.

One of the most ancient of human institutions is the family. Sociologists do not agree upon how it should be defined. Historically, however, the family has always meant a more or less permanent unit composed of parents and their offspring, which serves the purposes of care of the young, division of labor, acquisition and transmission of property, and preservation and transmission of beliefs and customs. The family is not now, and never has been, exclusively biological in character. Like most institutions, it has evolved through a

Importance of agriculture and the domestication of animals

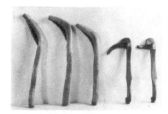

Neolithic Flint Sickles

The beginning of agriculture

The nature of institutions

Definition of the family

15

long period of changing conventions which have given it a variety of functions and forms. The family during Neolithic times appears to have existed in both polygamous and monogamous forms.

A second institution developed in more complex form by Neolithic man was religion. On account of its infinite variations, it is hard to define, but perhaps the following would be accepted as an accurate definition of the institution in at least its basic character: "Religion is everywhere an expression in one form or another of a sense of dependence on a power outside ourselves, a power which we may speak of as a spiritual or moral power." [3] Modern anthropologists emphasize the fact that early religion was not so much a matter of belief as a matter of rites. For the most part, the rites came first; the myths, dogmas, and theologies were later rationalizations. Primitive man was universally dependent upon nature—on the regular succession of the seasons, on the rain falling when it should, on the growth of plants and the reproduction of animals. Unless he performed sacrifices and rites these natural phenomena, according to his notion, would not occur. For this reason he developed rainmaking ceremonies in which water was sprinkled on ears of corn to imitate the falling of the rain. The ceremonial dances of the American Indians often had a similar import. The members of a whole village or even a whole tribe would attire themselves in animal skins and mimic the habits and activities of some species they depended upon for food. They apparently had a vague feeling that by imitating the life pattern of the species they were helping to guarantee its continuance.

But there was also another element conspicuously present in primitive religion. This was the element of fear. Modern primitive men, at least, live in an almost constant state of alarm and dread. As an old Eskimo medicine man said to the explorer Knud Rasmussen: "We do not believe; we fear." [4] Everything strange and unfamiliar is fraught with danger. The savage fears not only sickness and death but also hunger, drought, storms, the spirits of the dead, and the animals he has killed.

It follows that a large part of primitive man's religion consists of ceremonial precautions to ward off evil. For example, no savage will risk swimming across a dangerous river without first endeavoring by prayers or incantations to win its favor. An Eskimo who has killed a polar bear must present it with tools and weapons pleasing to it; if the bear is a female, women's knives and needle cases are given. Bestowal of these gifts is considered necessary to appease the wrath of the bear's soul and keep it from wreaking damage. In West Africa, the hunter who has killed a hippopotamus disembowels it, strips himself naked, crawls inside the carcass, and bathes his entire

The nature of primitive religion; rites and ceremonies

The element of fear

Ceremonies to ward off evil

[3] A. R. Radcliffe-Brown, *Structure and Function in Primitive Society*, p. 157.
[4] Lucien Lévy-Bruhl, *Primitives and the Supernatural*, p. 22.

body with the animal's blood. Throughout the procedure he prays to the spirit of the hippo that it will bear him no ill-will for having killed it, and that it will not incite other hippopotami to attack his canoe in revenge.[5]

Still another of the great institutions to be developed by Neolithic man was the state. By way of definition, the state may be described as an organized society occupying a definite territory and possessing an authoritative government independent of external control. The essence of the state is sovereignty, or the power to make and administer laws and to preserve social order by punishing men for infractions of those laws. A state must not be confused with a nation. The latter is an ethnic concept, used to designate a people bound together by ties of language, customs, or racial origin or by common memories or a belief in a common destiny. A nation may or may not occupy a definite territory and does not possess the element of sovereignty. It may not even have an independent government, as for example, the Poles during the long period when they were under Austrian, German, and Russian rule. At the present time most nations are also states, but this condition has resulted largely from the breaking up of empires in the twentieth century.

The state defined

Except in time of crisis, the state does not exist in a very large proportion of preliterate societies—a fact which probably indicates that its genesis was rather late in the Neolithic culture stage. Most primitive communities have no permanent system of courts, no police agencies, and no governments with coercive power. Custom takes the place of law, the blood-feud is the mode of administering justice, and there is very little conception of crime against the community. To primitive man, offenses are mostly what we call "torts," or private wrongs between individuals or families, in the punishment of which no public authority takes part. The acceptance of *wergeld*, or blood-money, is a common practice, and even felonies such as murder are regarded merely as offenses against the victim's family. Since the family of the victim has been deprived of a valuable member, the proper satisfaction is a money payment. If this is not offered, the family may retaliate in kind by killing the offender or a member of the offender's family.

Absence of the state in many primitive societies

The origin of the state was probably the consequence of a variety of factors. We are certainly justified in assuming the development of agriculture to have been one of the most important. In sections like the Nile valley, where a large population lived by cultivating intensively a limited area of fertile soil, a high degree of social organization was absolutely essential. Ancient customs would not suffice for the definition of rights and duties in such a society, with its high standard of living, its unequal distribution of wealth, and its wide scope for the clash of personal interests. New measures of so-

A variety of causes of the origin of the state

---

[5] Lucien Lévy-Bruhl, *How Natives Think*, p. 238.

cial control would become necessary, which could scarcely be achieved in any other way than by setting up a government of sovereign authority and submitting to it; in other words, by establishing a state.

A number of ancient states evidently owed their origin to war activities. That is, they were founded for purposes of conquest, for defense against invasion, or to make possible the expulsion of an invader from the country. The Hebrew monarchy seems to have been a product of the first of these reasons. With the war for the conquest of Canaan none too successful, the Hebrew people besought their leader Samuel to give them a king, that they might be "like all the nations" with a powerful ruler to keep them in order and to lead them to victory in battle. One has only to observe the effects of modern warfare, both offensive and defensive, in enlarging the powers of government to see how similar influences might have operated to bring the state into existence in the first place.

Origin of the state in military causes

Other factors undoubtedly contributed to the origin of states in various areas. A likelihood exists that one of these was religion. Medicine men, or shamans, frequently exercise a kind of sovereignty. Though they may command no physical force, their power to impose religious penalties and to strike terror into the hearts of their followers gives them a degree of coercive authority. In all probability some of them made themselves kings. It is conceivable that in other cases the state arose from the natural expansion of group life, with its resulting complexities and conflicts. As the population increased in limited areas, customary law and family administration of justice proved inadequate, and political organization became necessary as a substitute. In the domain of politics as in every other sphere concerned with social origins, no one explanation can be made to accommodate all the facts.

Other causes

6.   CULTURES AND CIVILIZATIONS

The stages of man's advancement described thus far have been referred to as *cultures*. This word is commonly used to designate societies or periods which have not yet attained to a knowledge of writing and whose general level of achievement is comparatively primitive. But the term has other meanings. It is sometimes applied to intellectual and artistic accomplishments, to literature, art, music, philosophy, and science. It is employed by some historians to designate the whole complex pattern of ideas, achievements, traditions, and characteristics of a nation or empire at a particular time.

Culture defined

The term *civilization* also carries a variety of meanings. The German philosopher of history Oswald Spengler referred to civilizations as decadent phases of highly developed cultures. When a great people or empire was in its prime, he characterized its social and intellectual pattern as a culture. When it passed its prime and became ossified and stagnant, he described it as a "civilization." The noted British historian, Arnold J. Toynbee, also sees world history as a succession of cultural units. But he designates each of the primary ones, throughout its development, as a "civilization." He distinguishes between civilizations and "primitive societies" largely on a quantitative basis. The latter are "relatively short-lived, are restricted to relatively narrow geographical areas, and embrace relatively small numbers of human beings." [6]

The meaning of civilization

The term *civilization* has still another meaning. Since each culture has peculiar features of its own, and since some cultures are more highly developed than others, we can speak quite properly of a civilization as an advanced culture. We can say that a culture deserves to be called a civilization when it has reached a stage in which writing has come to be used to a considerable extent, some progress has been made in the arts and sciences, and political, social and economic institutions have developed sufficiently to conquer at least some of the problems of order, security, and efficiency in a complex society. This is the sense in which the term will be used throughout the remainder of this book.

Civilizations as advanced cultures

7. FACTORS RESPONSIBLE FOR THE ORIGIN AND GROWTH OF CIVILIZATIONS

What causes contribute to the rise of civilizations? What factors account for their growth? Why do some civilizations reach much higher levels of development than others? Inquiry into these questions is one of the chief pursuits of social scientists. Some decide that factors of geography are the most important. Others stress economic resources, food supply, contact with older civilizations, and so on. Usually a variety of causes is acknowledged, but one is commonly singled out as deserving special emphasis.

Origin and growth of civilizations variously explained

Probably the most popular of the theories accounting for the rise of advanced cultures are those which come under the heading of geography. Prominent among them is the hypothesis of climate. The climatic theory, advocated in days past by such notables as Aristotle and Montesquieu, received its most eloquent exposition in the writings of an American geographer, Ellsworth Huntington. Huntington acknowledged the importance of other factors, but he insisted that no nation, ancient or modern, rose to the highest cultural status except under the influence of a climatic stimulus. He described the ideal climate as one in which the mean temperature seldom falls below the mental optimum of 38 degrees or rises above the physical optimum of 64 degrees. But temperature is not alone important. Moisture is also essential, and the humidity should average about 75 per cent. Finally, the weather must not be uniform: cy-

Geographic theories: the climatic hypothesis

[6] D. C. Somervell (ed.), A. J. Toynbee's *A Study of History*, I, 35.

clonic storms, or ordinary storms resulting in weather changes from day to day, must have sufficient frequency and intensity to clear the atmosphere every once in a while and produce those sudden variations in temperature which seem to be necessary to exhilarate and revitalize man.[7]

Much can be said in favor of the climatic hypothesis. Certainly some parts of the earth's surface, under existing atmospheric conditions, could never cradle a superior culture. They are either too hot, too humid, too cold, or too dry. Such is the case in regions beyond the Arctic Circle, the larger desert areas, and the jungles of India, Central America, and Brazil. Evidence is available, moreover, to show that some of these places have not always suffered under climate so adverse as that now prevalent. Various inhospitable sections of Asia, Africa, and America contain unmistakable traces of more salubrious days in the past. Here and there are the ruins of towns and cities where now the supply of water seems totally inadequate. Roads traverse deserts which at present are impassable. Bridges span river beds which have had no water in them for years.

The best-known evidences of the cultural importance of climatic change are those pertaining to the civilization of the Mayas. Mayan civilization flourished in Guatemala, Honduras, and on the peninsula of Yucatan in Mexico from about 400 to 1500 A.D. Numbered among its achievements were the making of paper, the invention of the zero, the perfection of a solar calendar, and the development of a system of writing partly phonetic. Great cities were built; marked progress was made in astronomy; and sculpture and architecture were advanced to high levels. At present most of the civilization is in ruins. No doubt many factors conspired to produce its untimely end, including deadly wars between tribes, but climatic change was also probably involved. The remains of most of the great cities are now surrounded by jungles, where malaria is prevalent and agriculture difficult. That the Mayan civilization or any other could have grown to maturity under conditions like these is hard to believe.

Related to the climatic hypothesis is the soil-exhaustion theory. A group of modern conservationists has hit upon this theory as the sole explanation of the decay and collapse of the great empires of the past and as a universal threat to the nations of the present and future. At best it is only a partial hypothesis, since it offers no theory of the birth or growth of civilizations. But its proponents seem to think that almost any environment not ruined by man is capable of nourishing a superior culture. The great deserts and barren areas of the earth, they maintain, are not natural but artificial, created by man through bad grazing and farming practices. Conservationists discover innumerable evidences of waste and neglect that have

Evidence in favor of the climatic hypothesis

The Mayan civilization

The soil-exhaustion theory

[7] Ellsworth Huntington, *Civilization and Climate*, 3d ed., pp. 220–23.

wrought havoc in such areas as Mesopotamia, Palestine, Greece, Italy, China, and Mexico. The majestic civilizations that once flourished in these countries were ultimately doomed by the simple fact that their soil would no longer provide sufficient food for the population. As a consequence, the more intelligent and enterprising citizens migrated elsewhere and left their inferiors to sink slowly into stagnation and apathy. But the fate that overtook the latter was not of their making alone. The whole nation had been guilty of plundering the forests, mining the soil, and pasturing flocks on the land until the grass was eaten down to the very roots. Among the tragic results were floods alternating with droughts, since there were no longer any forests to regulate the run-off of rain or snow. At the same time, much of the top soil on the close-cropped or excessively cultivated hillsides was blown away or washed into the rivers to be carried eventually down to the sea. The damage done was irreparable, since about 300 years are required to produce a single inch of top soil.

The most recent hypothesis of the origin of civilizations is Toynbee's adversity theory. According to this theory, conditions of hardship or adversity are the real causes which have brought into existence superior cultures. Such conditions constitute a *challenge* which not only stimulates men to try to overcome it but generates additional energy for new achievements. The challenge may take the form of a desert, a jungle area, rugged topography, or a grudging soil. The Hebrews and Arabs were challenged by the first, the Indians of the Andean Highland by the last. The challenge may also take the form of defeat in war or even enslavement. Thus the Carthaginians, as a result of defeat in the First Punic War, were stimulated to conquer a new empire in Spain; centuries later, Oriental captives enslaved by the Romans strengthened and propagated their religious heritage until Rome itself succumbed to it. In general it is true that the greater the challenge, the greater the achievement; nevertheless, there are limits. The challenge must not be too severe, else it will deal a crushing blow to all who attempt to meet it.

The adversity theory of Arnold J. Toynbee

8. WHY THE EARLIEST CIVILIZATIONS BEGAN WHERE THEY DID

Which of the great civilizations of antiquity was the oldest is still a sharply debated question. The judgment of some scholars inclines toward the Egyptian, though a larger body of authority supports the claims of the Tigris-Euphrates valley. These two areas were geographically the most favored sections in the general region of the so-called Fertile Crescent. The Fertile Crescent is that wide belt of productive land which extends northwestward from the Persian Gulf and then down the Mediterranean coast almost to Egypt. It

The Nile and the Tigris-Euphrates

21

forms a semicircle around the northern part of the Arabian desert. Here larger numbers of artifacts of undoubted antiquity have been found than in any other sections of the Near Orient. Furthermore, progress in the arts and sciences had reached unparalleled heights in both of these areas as early as 3000 B.C., when most of the rest of the world was steeped in ignorance. If the foundations of this progress were really laid elsewhere, it seems strange that they should have disappeared, although of course there is no telling what the spade of the archaeologist may uncover in the future.

Of the several causes responsible for the earliest rise of civilizations in the Nile and Tigris-Euphrates valleys, geographic factors would seem to have been the most important. Both regions had the notable advantage of a limited area of exceedingly fertile soil. Although it extended for a distance of 750 miles, the valley of the Nile was not more than ten miles wide in some places, and its maximum width was thirty-one miles. The total area was less than 10,000 square miles, or roughly the equivalent of the State of Maryland. Through countless centuries the river had carved a vast canyon or trench, bounded on either side by cliffs ranging in height from a few hundred to a thousand feet. The floor of the canyon was covered with a rich alluvial deposit, which in places reached a depth in excess of thirty feet. The soil was of such amazing productivity that as many as three crops per year could be raised on the same land. This broad and fertile canyon constituted the cultivable area of ancient Egypt. Here several million people were concentrated. In Roman times the population of the valley approximated seven million, and probably it was not much smaller in the days of the Pharaohs. Beyond the cliffs there was nothing but desert—the Libyan desert on the west and the Arabian on the east.

In the Tigris-Euphrates valley similar conditions prevailed. As in Egypt, the rivers provided excellent facilities for inland transportation and were alive with fish and waterfowl for a plentiful supply of protein food. The distance between the Tigris and Euphrates rivers at one point was less than twenty miles, and nowhere in the lower valley did it exceed forty-five miles. Since the surrounding country was desert, the people were kept from scattering over too great an expanse of territory. The result, as in Egypt, was the welding of the inhabitants into a compact society, under conditions that facilitated a ready interchange of ideas and discoveries. As the population increased, the need for agencies of social control became ever more urgent. Numbered among such agencies were government, schools, legal and moral codes, and institutions for the production and distribution of wealth. At the same time conditions of living became more complex and artificial and necessitated the keeping of records of things accomplished and the perfection of new techniques. Among the consequences were the invention of writing, the practice of smelting metals, the performance of mathematical operations,

A limited area of fertile soil in the Nile valley

A similar condition in Mesopotamia

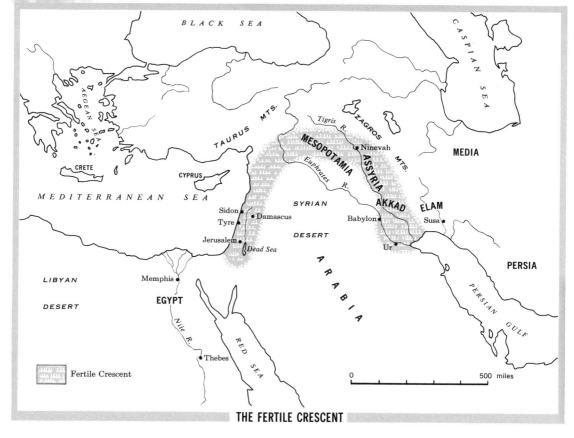

THE FERTILE CRESCENT

and the development of astronomy and the rudiments of physics. With these achievements the first great ordeal of civilization was passed.

Climatic influences also played their part in both regions. The atmosphere of Egypt is dry and invigorating. Even the hottest days produce none of the oppressive discomfort which is often experienced during the summer seasons in more northern countries. The mean temperature in winter varies from 56 degrees in the Delta to 66 degrees in the valley above. The summer mean is 83 degrees and an occasional maximum of 122 is reached, but the nights are always cool and the humidity is extremely low. Except in the Delta, rainfall occurs in negligible quantities, but the deficiency of moisture is counteracted by the annual inundations of the Nile from July to October. Also very significant from the historical standpoint is the total absence of malaria in Upper Egypt, while even in the coastal region it is practically unknown. The direction of the prevailing winds is likewise a favorable factor of more than trivial importance. For more than three-quarters of the year the wind comes from the north, blowing in opposition to the force of the Nile current. The effect of this is to simplify immensely the problem of transportation. Upstream traffic, with the propulsion of the wind to counteract the force of the river, presents no greater difficulty than down-

Climatic advantages in Egypt

23

stream traffic. This factor in ancient times must have been of enormous advantage in promoting communication among a numerous people, some of whom were separated by hundreds of miles.

Climatic conditions in Mesopotamia do not seem to have been quite so favorable as in Egypt. The summer heat is more relentless; the humidity is somewhat higher; and tropical diseases take their toll. Nevertheless, the torrid winds from the Indian Ocean, while enervating to human beings, blow over the valley at just the right season to bring the fruit of the date palm to a full ripeness. More than anything else the excellent yield of dates, the dietary staple of the Near Orient, encouraged the settlement of large numbers of people in the valley of the two rivers. Finally, the melting of the snows in the mountains of the north produced an annual flooding of the Babylonian plain similar to that in Egypt. The effect was to enrich the soil with moisture and to cover it over with a layer of mud of unusual fertility. At the same time, it should be noted that water conditions in Mesopotamia were less dependable than in Egypt. Floods were sometimes catastrophic, a factor which left its mark on the development of culture.

The importance
of scanty rainfall
as a spur to
initiative

Most significant of all of the geographic influences, however, was the fact that the scanty rainfall in both regions provided a spur to initiative and inventive skill. In spite of the yearly floods of the rivers there was insufficient moisture left in the soil to produce abundant harvests. A few weeks after the waters had receded, the earth was baked to a stony hardness. Irrigation was accordingly necessary if full advantage was to be taken of the richness of the soil. As a result, in both Egypt and Mesopotamia elaborate systems of dams and irrigation canals were constructed as long ago as five thousand years. The mathematical skill, engineering ability, and social cooperation necessary for the development of these projects were available for other uses and so fostered the achievement of civilization.

Uncertainty as
to which civiliza-
tion was older

Which of the two civilizations, the Egyptian or the Mesopotamian, was the older? Until recently most historians appeared to take it for granted that the Egyptian was the older. They based their assumption upon the conclusions of two of the world's most renowned Egyptologists, James H. Breasted and Alexandre Moret. Between the two world wars of the twentieth century, however, facts were unearthed which seemed to prove a substantial Mesopotamian influence in the Nile valley as early as 3500 B.C. This influence was exemplified by the use of cylinder seals, methods of building construction, art motifs, and elements of a system of writing of undoubted Mesopotamian origin. That such achievements could have radiated into Egypt from the Tigris-Euphrates valley at so early a date indicated beyond doubt that the Mesopotamian civilization was one of vast antiquity. It did not necessarily prove, though, that it was older than the Egyptian. For the achievements mentioned were not taken over and copied slavishly. Instead, the Egyptians modified them radically to suit their own culture pattern. On the basis of this evidence, it would seem that the only conclusion which can be safely drawn is that both civilizations were very old, and that to a large extent they developed concurrently.

SELECTED READINGS

· *Items so designated are available in paperbound editions.*

ANTHROPOLOGICAL AND ARCHAEOLOGICAL WORKS

· Boas, Franz, *The Mind of Primitive Man*, New York, 1927 (Free Press, 1965).

Breasted, James H., *The Dawn of Conscience*, New York, 1934. An excellent treatise on the origin of religious and ethical concepts.

———, *History of Egypt*, New York, 1912 (Bantam). Still one of the best.

· Ceram, C. W., *Gods, Graves and Scholars*, New York, 1951. Popular but scholarly.

· Childe, V. G., *Man Makes Himself*, London, 1936 (Mentor, 1952).

· ———, *New Light on the Most Ancient East*, New York, 1934 (Evergreen).

· Dawson, Christopher, *The Age of the Gods*, New York, 1937.

Herskovits, M. J., *Man and His Works*, New York, 1948. One of the best introductions to anthropology.

Lévy-Bruhl, Lucien, *How Natives Think*, London, 1926.

———, *Primitives and the Supernatural*, New York, 1935. A superlative study of primitive "Logic."

· Linton, Ralph, *The Tree of Culture*, New York, 1955 (Vintage, abr.).

MacCurdy, G. G., *Human Origins*, New York, 1924, 2 vols.

Magoffin, R. V. D., and Davis, E. C., *The Romance of Archaeology*, New York, 1929.

· Malinowski, Bronislaw, *Crime and Custom in Savage Society*, New York, 1951 (Littlefield, 1959). The most provocative and valuable study on the subject.

Osborn, H. F., *Men of the Old Stone Age*, New York, 1915.

· Radcliffe-Brown, A. R., *Structure and Function in Primitive Society*, Glencoe, Ill., 1952 (Free Press, 1952). Stimulating and informative.

· Radin, Paul, *Primitive Religion*, New York, 1937 (Dover, 1957).

Renard, Georges, *Life and Work in Prehistoric Times*, New York, 1929.

INTERPRETATIONS OF HISTORY

Butterfield, Herbert, *History and Human Relations*, New York, 1952.

· Clough, Shepard B., *The Rise and Fall of Civilization*, New York, 1951 (Columbia University Press, 1961).

· Fox, Edward W., *History in Geographic Perspective*, New York, 1971 (Norton Library).

Kahler, Erich, *The Meaning of History*, New York, 1964.

· Muller, H. J., *The Uses of the Past*, New York, 1952 (Galaxy).

· Nevins, Allan, *The Gateway to History*, New York, 1938 (Anchor, rev.).

· Somervell, D. C., ed., A. J. Toynbee, *A Study of History*, New York, 1947–57, 2 vols. (Galaxy, 6 vols.). An excellent abridgment of a monumental work.

Spengler, Oswald, *The Decline of the West*, 1-vol. ed., New York, 1934. The gist of his philosophy is contained in the Introduction.

25

Ancient Civilizations of the East and West

4000 B.C.	POLITICAL	CULTURAL
	Pre-dynastic period in Egypt, *ca.* 4000–3100	Solar calendar in Egypt, *ca.* 4000

	POLITICAL	CULTURAL
	Sumerian supremacy in Mesopotamia, *ca.* 4000–2000	Egyptian hieroglyphic writing, *ca.* 3500
		Development of irrigation, mathematics, rudimentary astronomy in Egypt and Mesopotamia, *ca.* 3500–2500
	Old Kingdom in Egypt, *ca.* 3100–2200	Cuneiform writing, *ca.* 3200
		Invention of principle of alphabet in Egypt, *ca.* 3000
3000 B.C.	Minoan-Mycenaean civilization, *ca.* 3000–1000	Construction of great pyramids in Egypt, *ca.* 2700
		Philosophy in Egypt, *ca.* 2500
2000 B.C.	Middle Kingdom in Egypt, 2052–1786	
	Aryan invasions of India, 2000–1500	
	Hittite empire, 2000–1200	
	Old Babylonian kingdom, 1950–1650	Code of Hammurabi, *ca.* 1790
	Hyksos conquer Egypt, 1786–1575	
	Kassites conquer Babylonians, *ca.* 1650	Egyptian temple architecture, 1580–1090
1500 B.C.	The Empire in Egypt, 1575–1087	Development of alphabet by Phoenicians, *ca.* 1500
	Shang Dynasty in China, *ca.* 1523–1027	Invention of decimal system and discovery of principle of zero in India, 1500–1000
	Kushitic Kingdom in upper Nile, *ca.* 1500	
	Hebrew conquest of Canaan, *ca.* 1300–900	Realistic sculpture of Assyrians, 1300–600
	Chou Dynasty in China, 1027–249	Composition of the *Vedas*, 1200–800
1000 B.C.	United Hebrew Monarchy, 1025–935	
	Secession of Ten Tribes of Israel, 935	
	Kingdom of Israel, 935–722	
	Kingdom of Judah, 935–586	
	Feudalism in China, 800–250	The *Upanishads*, 800–600
	Kushitic Dynasty in Egypt, *ca.* 750–670	
	Assyrian empire, 750–612	
	Assyrian conquest of Egypt, 670	Division of day into hours and minutes, *ca.* 600
	Chaldean empire, 612–539	Calculation of length of year, *ca.* 600
	Babylonian captivity, 586–539	Deuteronomic Code, *ca.* 600
	Persian empire, 559–330	Confucius, 551?–479?
	Persian conquest of Egypt, 525	Lao-tzu, *ca.* 550
500 B.C.	Persian Empire under Darius, 522–486	Book of Job, *ca.* 500
	Invasion of India by Alexander the Great, 327–326.	Mo Ti, 468?–382?
		Mencius, 373?–288?
	Reign of Emperor Asoka in India, *ca.* 273–232	Zenith of Kushitic civilization at Meruë, 250 B.C.–200 A.D.

Dates are B.C. unless given as A.D.

ECONOMIC	RELIGIOUS	
	Creation and Flood epics in Mesopotamia, *ca.* 4000	**4000 B.C.**
Development of serfdom in Mesopotamia and in Egypt, *ca.* 3500	Egyptian sun worship, *ca.* 3500	
	Ethical religion in Egypt, *ca.* 3000	**3000 B.C.**
	Egyptian belief in personal immortality, *ca.* 2500	
Large-scale industry in Egypt and Crete, *ca.* 2000		**2000 B.C.**
	Demon worship and witchcraft in Babylonia, *ca.* 1900	
Slavery in Egypt, *ca.* 1580		**1500 B.C.**
Introduction of use of iron by Hittites, *ca.* 1500		
	Religious revolution of Ikhnaton, 1375	
World trade of Phoenicians, *ca.* 1000–500	Hebrew worship of Yahweh, *ca.* 1000	**1000 B.C.**
Rise of caste system in India, 1000–500		
	Ten Commandments, *ca.* 700	
	Prophetic Revolution, 800–600	
	Hebrew doctrine of universal monotheism, *ca.* 600	
Slavery in Assyria, *ca.* 750	Astral religion of Chaldeans, 600–500	
	Divination and astrology, 600–500	
Invention of coinage by Lydians, *ca.* 600	Zoroastrianism, *ca.* 600–300	
World trade of Chaldeans, 600–500	Founding of Jainism in India, 599–527	
	Babylonian Captivity of Jews, 586–539	
	Gautama Buddha, *ca.* 563–483	
	Mithraism, *ca.* 300 B.C. 275 A.D.	
Royal Road of Persians, *ca.* 500	Gnosticism, *ca.* 100 B.C.–100 A.D.	**500 B.C.**
Use of iron in China, *ca.* 500	Rise of Christianity, *ca.* 25 A.D.	
Development of coinage in China, *ca.* 400	King Ezana of Ethiopia converted to Christianity, *ca.* 350 A.D.	

CHAPTER 2

The Civilizations of the Nile

How great is that which thou has done, O lord of gods. Thy
plans and thy counsels are those which come to pass throughout.
Thou sentest me forth in valor, thy strength was with me. No
land stood before me, at the mention of thee. I overthrew those
who invaded my boundary, prostrated in their place. . . . It was
ordained because of thy victory-bringing commands, it was given
because of thy kingdom-bestowing power.

> —Utterance of King Ramses III before his father, Amon-
> Re, ruler of the gods, from The Great Inscription in the
> Second Court relief in Medinet Habu temple

Although the Egyptian civilization was not necessarily the oldest in
the ancient world, it was certainly of great antiquity. As we have
seen, its origins went back to at least 4000 B.C. Besides, somewhat
more is known about its accomplishments than about those of most
other peoples. For these reasons the Egyptian civilization may be
considered a kind of archetype or pattern of all the civilizations of
the Near Orient.

I. POLITICAL HISTORY UNDER THE PHARAOHS

The ancient history of Egypt is commonly divided into three
periods: the Old Kingdom, the Middle Kingdom, and the Empire.
Even before the Old Kingdom some cultural beginnings had been
made. A system of laws based upon customs had been developed
and the initial stage of a system of writing. More important was
the invention of the first solar calendar in the history of man. This
calendar was apparently put into effect about the year 4200 B.C. It
was based upon the annual reappearance of Sirius, the "Dog Star,"
and it provided for twelve months of thirty days each, with five
feast days added at the end of the year.

*Stages of
Egyptian history*

29

Character of the
Old Kingdom

The nonmilitaristic
character of the
Old Kingdom

End of the
Old Kingdom

The Middle
Kingdom (2052–
1786 B.C.)

About 3100 B.C. Egypt was combined into a single unit known to historians as the Old Kingdom. From 3100 B.C. to 2200 B.C. six dynasties ruled the country. Each was headed by a "Pharaoh," from the Egyptian "per-o" meaning "great house" or "royal house." He was considered to be the son of the great sun god and he was forbidden to marry outside of his immediate family, lest the divine blood be contaminated. Moreover, his authority was limited by the ancient law. He was not above the law but subject to it. No separation of church and state existed. The Pharaoh's chief subordinates were the priests, and he himself was the chief priest.

The government of the Old Kingdom was founded upon a policy of peace and nonaggression. In this respect it was almost unique among ancient states. The Pharaoh had no standing army, nor was there anything that could be called a national militia. Each subdivision had its local militia, but it was commanded by the civil officials, and when called into active service it generally devoted its energies to labor on the public works. In case of a threat of invasion the various local units were assembled at the call of the Pharaoh and placed under the command of one of his civil subordinates. At no other time did the head of the government have a military force at his disposal. The Egyptians of the Old Kingdom were content for the most part to work out their own destinies and to let other nations alone. The reasons for this attitude are to be found in the protected position of their country, in their possession of land of inexhaustible fertility, and in the fact that their state was a product of cooperative need instead of being grounded in exploitation.

After a solid millennium of peace and relative prosperity the Old Kingdom came to an end about 2200 B.C. Several causes appear to have been responsible: the usurpation of power by the local rulers; the growth of individualism; and the financial burdens imposed upon the people by Pharaohs with grandiose schemes for national development. The period which followed is called the Feudal Age. Save for intervals of order and progress it was marked by anarchy, aggrandizement of the power of the nobles, social revolution of the masses, and invasion by desert and barbarian tribes. It did not end until the rise of the Eleventh Dynasty about 2050 B.C.—an event which ushered in the next great stage in Egyptian history, which is known as the Middle Kingdom.

The government of the Middle Kingdom was notably weaker than that of the Old Kingdom. Dynasties of Pharaohs continued a nominal rule, but extensive authority gravitated into the hands of the subordinates and nobles of lesser rank. In time they, too, were assailed by the masses, with the result that after 2000 B.C. the Pharaohs of the Twelfth Dynasty were able to regain a measure of their former power. The people themselves were rewarded by appointments to government positions and by grants of land and vested rights in particular occupations. The whole population, regardless of birth or rank, appears to have been accorded privileges hitherto reserved for the few. For this reason the government of the Twelfth Dynasty is sometimes referred to as the first democratic kingdom in history. The period of its rule was a golden age of social justice and intellectual achievement, although the forms of theocracy still survived.

With the end of the Twelfth Dynasty, Egypt entered another era of internal chaos and foreign invasion which lasted for more than two centuries, or from 1786 to 1575 B.C. The contemporary records are scanty, but they seem to show that the internal disorder was the result of a counterrevolt of the nobles. The Pharaohs were again reduced to impotence, and much of the social progress of the preceding age was destroyed. About 1750 the land was invaded by the Hyksos, or the "Shepherd Kings," a mixed horde originating in western Asia. Their military prowess is commonly ascribed to the fact that they possessed horses and war chariots, but their victory was certainly made easier by the dissension among the Egyptians themselves. Their rule had profound effects upon Egyptian history. Not only did they familiarize the Egyptians with new methods of warfare; but by providing them with a common grievance in the face of foreign tyranny they also enabled them to forget their differences and unite in a common cause.

The invasion of the Hyksos

Near the end of the seventeenth century the rulers of Upper Egypt launched a revolt against the Hyksos, a movement which was eventually joined by most of the natives of the valley. By 1575 all of the conquerors who had not been killed or enslaved had been driven from the country. The hero of this victory, Ahmose I, founder of the Eighteenth Dynasty, now made himself despot of Egypt. The regime he established was much more highly consolidated than any that had hitherto existed. In the great resurgence of nationalism which had accompanied the struggle against the Hyksos, local patriotism was annihilated, and with it the power of the nobles.

Expulsion of the Hyksos and founding of the Empire

The period which followed the accession of Ahmose is called the period of the Empire. It lasted from 1575 to 1087 B.C., during which time the country was ruled by three dynasties of Pharaohs in succession, the Eighteenth, Nineteenth, and Twentieth. No longer was the prevailing state policy pacific and isolationist; a spirit of aggressive imperialism rapidly pervaded the nation. The causes of this change are not far to seek. The military ardor generated by the successful war against the Hyksos whetted an appetite for further victories. A vast military machine had been created to expel the invader, which proved to be too valuable an adjunct to the Pharaoh's power to be discarded immediately.

Ramses II (XIXth Dynasty)

The first steps in the direction of the new policy were taken by the immediate successors of Ahmose in making extensive raids into Palestine and claiming sovereignty over Syria. With one of the most formidable armies of ancient times the new Pharaohs speedily annihilated all opposition in Syria and eventually made themselves masters of a vast domain extending from the Euphrates to the farther cataracts of the Nile. But they never succeeded in welding the conquered peoples into loyal subjects, and weakness was the signal for widespread revolt in Syria. Their successors suppressed the uprising and managed to hold the Empire together for some time, but ultimate disaster could not be averted. More territory had been annexed than could be managed successfully. The influx of wealth into Egypt weakened the national fiber by fostering corruption and luxury, and the constant revolts of the vanquished eventually sapped the strength of the state beyond all hope of recovery. By the twelfth century most of the conquered provinces had been permanently lost.

The government of the Empire resembled that of the Old Kingdom, except for the fact that it was more absolute. Military power rather than national unity was now the basis of the Pharaoh's rule. A professional army was always available with which to overawe his subjects. Most of the former nobles now became courtiers or members of the royal bureaucracy under the complete domination of the king. The Pharaoh was not yet a divine-right monarch, but the actual extent of his power had begun to approach that of more modern despots.

*The government
of the Empire*

The last of the great Pharaohs was Ramses III, who ruled from 1182 to 1151 B.C. He was succeeded by a long line of nonentities who inherited his name but not his ability. By the middle of the twelfth century Egypt had fallen prey to numerous ills of barbarian invasion and social decadence. Libyans and Nubians were swarming over the country and gradually debasing cultural standards. About the same time the Egyptians themselves appear to have lost their creative talent; their intellects seem to have been led astray by the seductions of magic and superstition. To win immortality by magic devices was now the commanding interest of men of every class. The process of decline was hastened also by the growing power of the priests, who finally usurped the royal prerogatives and dictated the Pharaoh's decrees.

*The last of the
Pharaohs*

From the middle of the tenth century to nearly the end of the eighth a dynasty of Libyan barbarians occupied the throne of the Pharaohs. The Libyans were followed by a line of Ethiopians or Nubians, who came in from the desert regions west of the Upper Nile. In 670 Egypt was conquered by the Assyrians, who succeeded in maintaining their supremacy for only eight years. After the collapse of Assyrian rule in 662 the Egyptians regained their independence, and a brilliant renaissance of culture ensued. It was doomed to an untimely end, however, for in 525 B.C. the country was conquered by the Persians. The ancient civilization was never again revived.

*The downfall
of Egypt*

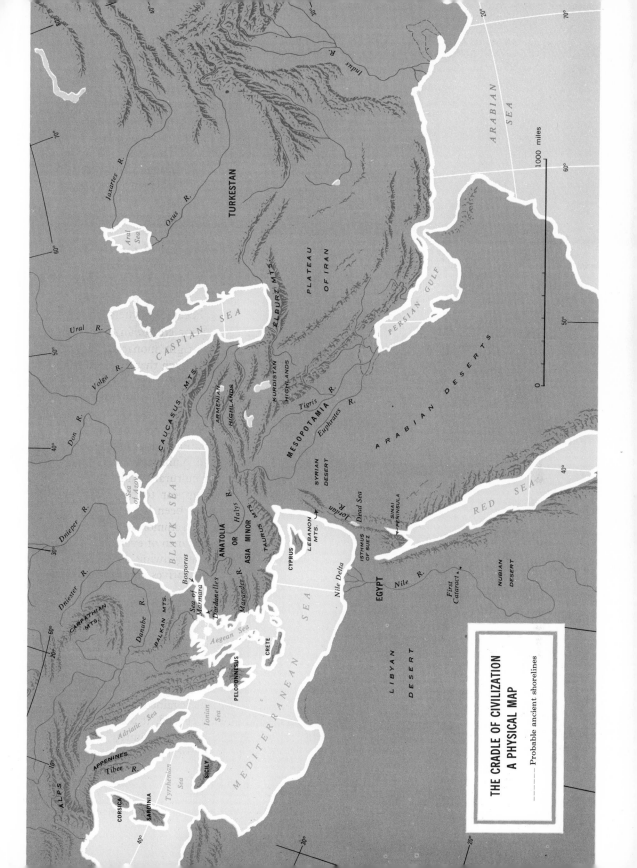

THE CRADLE OF CIVILIZATION
A PHYSICAL MAP

------- Probable ancient shorelines

Egyptian Pottery Jar, *ca.* 3600 B.C. It was filled with food or water and placed in the tomb to provide for the afterlife. (MMA)

An Egyptian Official and His Son. Painted limestone, *ca.* 2500 B.C.

Gold and Inlay Pendant of Princess Sit Hat-Hor Yunet. Egyptian, Twelfth Dynasty.

Farm Hand Plowing. Egyptian tomb figures, *ca.* 1900 B.C.

Jeweled Headdress of Gold, Carnelian, and Glass. Egyptian, 1475 B.C.

Scarab or Beetle-Shaped Charm of a Pharaoh, *ca.* 1395 B.C. The beetle was sacred in ancient Egypt.

Silversmiths Working on a Stand and a Jar. Egyptian, *ca.* 1450 B.C.

A scribe writing on a papyrus roll. Egyptian, *ca.* 1415 B.C.

Painted Wood Shrine Box for Shawabty Figures. *Ca.* 1200 B.C.

Wall painting of an Egyptian house, *ca.* 1400 B.C.

Religion played a dominant role in the life of the ancient Egyptians, leaving its impress upon almost everything. The art was an expression of religious symbolism. The literature and philosophy were suffused with religious teachings. The government of the Old Kingdom was to a large extent a theocracy, and even the military Pharaohs of the Empire professed to rule in the name of the god. Economic energy and material resources in considerable amounts were squandered in providing elaborate tombs and in maintaining a costly ecclesiastical system.

The importance of religion in Egypt

The religion of the ancient Egyptians evolved through various stages from simple polytheism to philosophic monotheism. In the beginning each city or district appears to have had its local deities, who were guardian gods of the locality or personifications of nature's powers. The unification of the country under the Old Kingdom resulted not only in a consolidation of territory but in a fusion of divinities as well. All of the guardian deities were merged into the great sun god Re or Ra. In later times, with the establishment of a Theban dynasty in control of the government, this deity was commonly called Amon or Ammon-Re from the name of the chief god of Thebes. The gods who personified the vegetative powers of nature were fused into a deity called Osiris, who was also the god of the Nile. Throughout Egyptian history these two great powers who ruled the universe, Re and Osiris, vied with each other for supremacy. Other deities, as we shall see, were recognized also, but they occupied a distinctly subordinate place.

The early religious evolution

See color plates at page 64

King Mycerinus and His Queen Salet on his Right. A sculpture of the IVth Dynasty located at Gizeh.

33

Funerary Papyrus. The scene shows the heart of a princess of the XXIst Dynasty being weighed in a balance before the god Osiris. On the other side of the balance are the symbols for life and truth.

During the period of the Old Kingdom the solar faith, embodied in the worship of Re, was the dominant system of belief. It served as **The solar faith** an official religion whose chief function was to give immortality to the state and to the people collectively. The Pharaoh was the living representative of this faith on earth; through his rule the rule of the god was maintained. But Re was not only a guardian deity. He was in addition the god of righteousness, justice, and truth and the upholder of the moral order of the universe. He offered no spiritual blessings or even material rewards to men as individuals. The solar faith was not a religion for the masses as such, except in so far as their welfare coincided with that of the state.

The cult of Osiris, as we have already observed, began its existence as a nature religion. The god personified the growth of vegeta- **The Osiris cult** tion and the life-giving powers of the Nile. The career of Osiris was wrapped about with an elaborate legend. In the remote past, according to belief, he had been a benevolent ruler, who taught his people agriculture and other practical arts and gave them laws. After a time he was treacherously slain by his wicked brother Set, and his body cut into pieces. His wife Isis, who was also his sister, went in search of the pieces, put them together, and miraculously restored his body to life. The risen god regained his kingdom and continued his beneficent rule for a time, but eventually descended to the nether world to serve as judge of the dead. Horus, his posthumous son, finally grew to manhood and avenged his father's death by killing Set.

Originally this legend seems to have been little more than a nature myth. The death and resurrection of Osiris symbolized the recession of the Nile in the autumn and the coming of the flood in the spring. But in time the Osiris legend began to take on a deeper significance. The human qualities of the deities concerned—the paternal solicitude of Osiris for his subjects, the faithful devotion of his wife and son—appealed to the emotions of the average Egyptian, who was now able to see his own tribulations and triumphs mirrored in the lives of the gods. More important still, the death and resurrection of Osiris came to be regarded as conveying a promise of personal immortality for man. As the god had triumphed over death and the grave, so might also the individual who followed him faithfully inherit everlasting life. Finally, the victory of Horus over Set appeared to foreshadow the ultimate ascendancy of good over evil.

Egyptian ideas of the hereafter attained their full development in the later history of the Middle Kingdom. For this reason elaborate preparations had to be made to prevent the extinction of one's earthly remains. Not only were bodies mummified but wealthy men left munificent endowments to provide their mummies with food and other essentials. As the religion advanced toward maturity, however, a less naïve conception of the afterlife was adopted. The dead were now believed to appear before Osiris to be judged according to their deeds on earth.

All of the departed who met the tests included in this system of judgment entered a celestial realm of physical delights and simple pleasures. Here in marshes of lilies and lotus-flowers they would hunt wild geese and quail with never-ending success. Or they might build houses in the midst of orchards with luscious fruits of unfailing yield. They would find lily-lakes on which to sail, pools of sparkling water in which to bathe, and shady groves inhabited by singing birds and every manner of gentle creature. The unfortunate victims whose hearts revealed their vicious lives were condemned to perpetual hunger and thirst in a place of darkness, forever cut off from the glorious light of Re.

The Egyptian religion attained its highest perfection about the end of the Middle Kingdom and the beginning of the Empire. By this time the solar faith and the cult of Osiris had been merged in such a way as to preserve the best features of both. The province of Re as the god of the living, as the champion of good in this world, was accorded almost equal importance with the functions of Osiris as the giver of personal immortality and the judge of the dead. The religion was now quite clearly an ethical one. Men repeatedly avowed their desire to do justice because such conduct was pleasing to the great sun god.

Soon after the establishment of the Empire the religion which has just been described underwent a serious debasement. Its ethical significance was largely destroyed, and superstition and magic gained the ascendancy. The chief cause seems to have been that the long and bitter war for the expulsion of the Hyksos fostered the growth of irrational attitudes and correspondingly depreciated the intellect.

The result was a marked increase in the power of the priests, who
preyed upon the fears of the masses to promote their own advantage. Greedy for gain, they inaugurated the practice of selling
magical charms, which were supposed to have the effect of preventing the heart of the deceased from betraying his real character.
They also sold formulas which, inscribed on rolls of papyrus and
placed in the tomb, were alleged to be effective in facilitating the
passage of the dead to the celestial realm. The aggregate of these
formulas constituted what is referred to as the Book of the Dead.
Contrary to the general impression, it was not an Egyptian Bible,
but merely a collection of mortuary inscriptions.

This degradation of the religion at the hands of the priests into a
system of magical practices finally resulted in a great reformation or
religious revolution. The leader of this movement was the Pharaoh
Amenhotep IV, who began his reign about 1375 B.C. and died or
was murdered about fifteen years later. After some fruitless attempts
to correct the most flagrant abuses, he resolved to crush the system
entirely. He drove the priests from the temples, hacked the names of
the traditional deities from the public monuments, and commanded
his people to worship a new god whom he called "Aton," an ancient
designation for the physical sun. He changed his own name from
Amenhotep ("Amen rests") to Ikhnaton, which meant "Aton is
satisfied." Ikhnaton is the name by which he is commonly known
in history.

*Ikhnaton and His Wife Mak-
ing Offerings to Aton.* A stele
from the XVIIIth Dynasty.

More important than these physical changes was the new set of
doctrines enunciated by the reforming Pharaoh. According to eminent authorities, he taught first of all a religion of universal
monotheism; Aton, he declared, was the only god in existence, the
god not merely of Egypt but of the whole universe.[1] He restored
the ethical quality of the national religion at its best by insisting that
Aton was the author of the moral order of the world and the re-
warder of men for integrity and purity of heart. He envisaged the
new god as an eternal creator and sustainer of all that is of benefit to
man, and as a heavenly father who watches with benevolent care
over all his creatures. Conceptions like these of the unity, righteousness, and benevolence of God were not attained again until the time
of the Hebrew prophets some 600 years later.

The revolution of Ikhnaton was not an enduring success. Because
of its challenge to ancient myths and magical practices it was not
popular with the masses. Moreover, the Pharaohs who followed
Ikhnaton were not inspired by the same devoted idealism. The result
was a revival and a gradual extension of the same old superstitions
that had prevailed before Ikhnaton's reign. For the great masses of the
nation the ethical significance of the religion was permanently lost,

*The results of
Ikhnaton's
revolution*

[1] J. H. Breasted, *A History of Egypt,* p. 376; see also Alexandre Moret,
From Tribe to Empire, pp. 298-300.

and they were thrown back once more to ignorance and priestly greed. Among the educated classes, however, the influence of Ikhnaton's teachings lingered for some time. Although the god Aton was no longer recognized, the qualities he represented continued to be held in high esteem. What happened was that the attributes of Aton were now transferred by the educated minority to Ammon-Re. The traditional solar deity was acclaimed as the only god and the embodiment of righteousness, justice, and truth. He was worshiped, moreover, as a merciful and loving being "who heareth prayers, who giveth the hand to the poor, who saveth the weary." [2]

Adherence by the intelligent few to these noble ideas was not enough to save the religion from complete degeneracy and ruin. The spread of superstition, the popularity of magic, and the paralyzing grip of a degenerate priesthood were far too deadly in their effects to be overcome by exalted doctrines. In the end the whole system of belief and worship was engulfed by formalism and ignorance and by fetishism (worship of magical objects), animal worship, and other magical crudities. The commercialism of the priests was more rampant than ever, and the chief function of the organized religion had come to be the sale of formulas and charms which would stifle the conscience and trick the gods into granting eternal salvation. The tragedy was compounded by the fact that as the religion decayed it exerted a baneful effect upon the rest of the culture. Philosophy, art, and government were so closely linked with religion that all of them went down together.

The return of decay

3. EGYPTIAN INTELLECTUAL ACHIEVEMENTS

The philosophy of ancient Egypt was chiefly ethical and political, although traces of broader philosophic conceptions are occasionally to be found. The idea that the universe is controlled by mind or intelligence, for example, is a notion that appeared from time to time in the writings of priests and sages. Other philosophic ideas of the ancient Egyptians included the conception of an eternal universe, the notion of constantly recurring cycles of events, and the doctrine of natural cause and effect. Few, if any, of Egyptian writers could be classified as "pure" philosophers. They were concerned primarily with religion and with questions of individual conduct and social justice.

The general character of Egyptian philosophy

The earliest examples of Egyptian ethical philosophy were maxims of sage advice similar to those of the Book of Proverbs and the Book of Ecclesiastes in the Old Testament. They went little beyond practical wisdom, but occasionally they enjoined tolerance, moderation, and justice.

The earliest ethical philosophy

[2] J. H. Breasted, *The Dawn of Conscience*, p. 316.

During the Middle Kingdom this practical philosophy was succeeded by a kind of epicureanism. Skepticism regarding the gods now took the place of the lofty religious conceptions of earlier times, and the life of self-indulgence was extolled as the best. Lip service, however, was also paid to the pursuit of a good name by deeds of charity and benevolence.

As political philosophers the Egyptians developed a conception of the state as a welfare institution presided over by a benevolent ruler. This conception was embodied especially in the *Plea of the Eloquent Peasant,* written about 2050 B.C. It sets forth the idea of a ruler committed to benevolence and justice for the good of his subjects. He is urged to act as the father of the orphan, the husband of the widow, and the brother of the forsaken. He is supposed to judge impartially and to execute punishment upon whom it is due; and to promote such an order of harmony and prosperity that no one may suffer from hunger or cold or thirst.

The branches of science which first absorbed the attention of the Egyptians were astronomy and mathematics. Both were developed for practical ends—to compute the time of the Nile inundations, to lay out the plans for pyramids and temples, and to solve the intricate problems of irrigation and public control of economic functions. The Egyptians were not pure sicentists; they had little interest in the nature of the physical universe as such—a fact which probably accounts for their failure to advance very far in the science of astronomy. They perfected a solar calendar, as we have already learned, mapped the heavens, identified the principal fixed stars, and achieved some success in determining accurately the positions of stellar bodies.

The science of mathematics was more highly developed. The Egyptians laid the foundations for at least two of the common mathematical subjects—arithmetic and geometry. They devised the arithmetical operations of addition, subtraction, and division, although they never discovered how to multiply except through a series of additions. They invented the decimal system, but they had no symbol for zero. Fractions caused them some difficulty: all those with a numerator greater than one had to be broken down into a series, each with *one* as the numerator, before they could be used in mathematical calculations. The only exception was the fraction two-thirds, which the scribes had learned to use as it stood. The Egyptians also achieved a surprising degree of skill in mensuration, computing with accuracy the areas of triangles, rectangles, and hexagons. The ratio of the circumference of a circle to its diameter they calculated to be 3.16. They learned how to compute the volume of the pyramid and the cylinder, and even the volume of the hemisphere.

The third branch of science in which the Egyptians did some remarkable work was medicine. Early medical practice was conservative and profusely corrupted by superstition, but a document dating from about 1700 B.C. reveals a fairly adequate conception of scientific diagnosis and treatment. Egyptian physicians were frequently specialists: some were oculists; others were dentists, surgeons, specialists in diseases of the stomach, and so on. In the course of their work they made many discoveries of lasting value. They recognized the importance of the heart and had some appreciation of the significance of the pulse. They acquired a degree of skill in the treatment of fractures and performed simple operations. Unlike some peoples of later date they ascribed disease to natural causes. They discovered the value of cathartics, noted the curative properties of numerous drugs, and compiled the first *materia medica,* or catalogue of medicines. Many of their remedies, both scientific and magical, were carried into Europe by the Greeks and are still employed by the peasantry of isolated regions.

Medicine

In other scientific fields the Egyptians contributed little. Although they achieved feats which rival modern engineering, they possessed but the scantiest knowledge of physics. They knew the principle of the inclined plane, but they were ignorant of the pulley. To their credit also must be assigned considerable progress in metallurgy, the invention of the sundial, and the making of paper and glass. With all their deficiencies as pure scientists, they equaled or surpassed in actual accomplishment most of the other peoples of the ancient Near Orient.

Other scientific accomplishments

The Egyptians developed their first form of writing during the pre-dynastic period. This system, known as the *hieroglyphic,* from the Greek words meaning sacred carving, was originally composed of pictographic signs denoting concrete objects. Gradually certain of these signs were conventionalized and used to represent abstract concepts. Other characters were introduced to designate separate syllables which could be combined to form words. Finally, twenty-four symbols, each representing a single consonant sound of the human voice, were added early in the Old Kingdom. Thus the hieroglyphic system of writing had come to include at an early date three separate types of characters, the pictographic, syllabic, and alphabetic.

The hieroglyphic system

The ultimate step in this evolution of writing would have been the complete separation of the alphabetic from the non-alphabetic characters and the exclusive use of the former in written communication. The Egyptians were reluctant to take this step. Their traditions of conservatism impelled them to follow old habits. Although they made frequent use of the consonant signs, they did not commonly employ them as an independent system of writing. It was left for the Phoenicians to do this some 1500 years later. Nevertheless, the Egyptians must be credited with the invention of the principle of the alphabet. It was they who first perceived the value of single symbols for the individual sounds of the human voice. The Phoenicians merely copied this principle, based their own system of writ-

The principle of the alphabet

ing upon it, and diffused the idea among neighboring nations. In the ultimate sense it is therefore true that the Egyptian alphabet was the parent of every other that has ever been used in the Western world.

4. THE MEANING OF EGYPTIAN ART

*The character
of Egyptian art*

No single interpretation will suffice to explain the meaning of Egyptian art. In general, it expressed the aspirations of a collectivized national life. It was not art for art's sake, nor did it serve to convey the individual's reactions to the problems of his personal world. Yet there were times when the conventions of a communal society were broken down, and the supremacy was accorded to a spontaneous individual art that sensed the beauty of the flower or caught the radiant idealism of a youthful face. Seldom was the Egyptian genius for faithful reproduction of nature entirely suppressed. Even the rigid formalism of the official architecture was commonly relieved by touches of naturalism—columns in imitation of palm trunks, lotus-blossom capitals, and occasional statues of Pharaohs that were not conventionalized types but true individual portraits.

Architecture

In most civilizations where the interests of society are exalted above those of its members, architecture is at once the most typical and the most highly developed of the arts. Egypt was no exception. Whether in the Old Kingdom, Middle Kingdom, or Empire it was the problems of building construction that absorbed the talent of the artist. Although painting and sculpture were by no means primitive, they nevertheless had as their primary function the embellishment of temples. Only at times did they rise to the status of independent arts.

The Pyramids of Gizeh with the Sphinx in the Foreground. The pyramid on the right is the Great Pyramid of Khufu or Cheops.

Detail of the Temple of Karnak. Most of this building has collapsed or been carried away, but the huge pylons and statues give an idea of the massiveness of Egyptian temples.

The characteristic examples of Old Kingdom architecture were the pyramids, the first of which were built at least as early as 2700 B.C. An amazing amount of labor and skill were expended in their construction. The Greek historian Herodotus estimated that 100,000 men must have been employed for twenty years to complete the single pyramid of Khufu at Gizeh. Its total height exceeds 480 feet, and the more than two million limestone blocks it contains are fitted together with a precision which few modern masons could duplicate. Each of the blocks weighs about two and a half tons. They were evidently hewn out of rock cliffs with drills and wedges and then dragged up earthen ramps by gangs of men and pried into place.

The pyramids

The significance of the pyramids is not easy to comprehend. They may have been intended for the economic purpose of providing employment opportunities. Such a theory would assume that the population had increased to overcrowding, and that the resources of agriculture, mining, industry, and commerce were no longer adequate to provide a livelihood for all the people. This theory doubtless had some validity. But for propaganda purposes it was glossed over with a political and religious significance. The construction of the pyramids was held to be an act of faith, the expression of an ambition to endow the state with permanence and stability. As indestructible tombs of the rulers they were believed to guarantee immortality to the people, for the Pharaoh was the embodiment of the national life. It is possible also that they were intended to serve as symbols of sun worship. As the tallest structures in Egypt they would catch the first light of the rising sun and reflect it to the valley below.

Significance of the pyramids

During the Middle Kingdom and the Empire the temple displaced the pyramid as the leading architectural form. The most noted

41

The Temple at Karnak. Hypostyle columns are shown at the left. Details of wall construction on the right.

examples were the great temples at Karnak and Luxor, built during the period of the Empire. Many of their gigantic, richly carved columns still stand as silent witnesses of a splendid architectural talent. Egyptian temples were characterized by massive size. The temple at Karnak, with a length of about 1300 feet, covered the largest area of any religious edifice ever built. Its central hall alone could contain almost any of the Gothic cathedrals of Europe. The columns used in the temples had stupendous proportions. The largest of them were seventy feet high, with diameters in excess of twenty feet. It has been estimated that the capitals which surmounted them could furnish standing room for a hundred men.

The templesAs already mentioned, Egyptian sculpture and painting served primarily as adjuncts to architecture. The former was heavily laden with conventions that restricted its style and meaning. Statues of Pharaohs were commonly of colossal size. Those produced during the Empire ranged in height from seventy-five to ninety feet. Some of them were colored to resemble life, and the eyes were frequently inlaid with rock crystal. The figures were nearly always rigid, with the arms folded across the chest or fixed to the sides of the body and with the eyes staring straight to the front. Countenances were generally represented as impassive, utterly devoid of emotional expression. Anatomical distortion was frequently practiced: the natural length of the thighs might be increased, the squareness of the shoulders accentuated, or all of the fingers of the hand made equal in length. A familiar example of non-naturalistic sculpture was the Sphinx. This represented the head of a Pharaoh on the body of a lion. The purpose was probably to symbolize the notion that the Pharaoh possessed the lion's qualities of strength and courage. The figures of sculpture in relief were even less in conformity with na-

Egyptian sculpture

See color plates at pages 33, 64

42

ture. The head was presented in profile, with the eye fullface; the torso was shown in the frontal position, while the legs were rendered in profile. Such were the general tendencies, but it should be noted that they were not universal. Occasionally the artist succeeded in a partial defiance of conventions, as is evidenced by the production of some highly individual likenesses of the later Pharaohs.

The meaning of Egyptian sculpture is not hard to perceive. The colossal size of the statues of Pharaohs was doubtless intended to symbolize their power and the power of the state they represented. It is significant that the size of these statues increased as the empire expanded and the government became more absolute. The conventions of rigidity and impassiveness were meant to express the timelessness and stability of the national life. Here was a nation which, according to the ideal, was not to be torn loose from its moorings by the uncertain mutations of fortune but was to remain fixed and imperturbable. The portraits of its chief men consequently must betray no anxiety, fear, or triumph, but an unvarying calmness throughout the ages. In similar fashion, the anatomical distortion can probably be interpreted as a deliberate attempt to express some national ideal. The most eloquent device for this purpose was representation of the body of a Pharaoh with the head of a god, but the other examples of non-naturalistic portrayal probably had a similar object.

The meaning of Egyptian sculpture

Egyptian painting developed late and did not have time to become weighted down with a mass of traditions. Religion did exert its influence, but in a positive manner. The best paintings were those created during the reign of Ikhnaton and immediately after. The gospel of the reforming king, with its reverence for nature as the handiwork of God, fostered a revival of realism in art which was particularly evident in painting. As a result, the murals of this period exhibit a decided talent for representation of the striking phenomena of the world of experience. They have particular merit as examples of the portrayal of movement. They caught the instant action of the wild bull leaping in the swamp, the headlong flight of the frightened stag, and the effortless swimming of ducks in the pond.

Queen Hat-shepsut. Limestone statue about 1485 B.C.

5. SOCIAL AND ECONOMIC LIFE

During the greater part of the history of Egypt the population was divided into five classes: the royal family; the priests; the nobles; the middle class of scribes, merchants, artisans, and farmers; and the serfs. During the Empire a sixth class, the professional soldiers, was added, ranking immediately below the nobles. Thousands of slaves were captured in this period also, and these formed for a time a seventh class. Despised by freemen and serfs alike, they were forced to labor in the government quarries and on the temple estates. Gradually, however, they were enrolled in the army and

The principal classes

43

Fishing and Fowling: Wall Painting Thebes, XVIIIth Dynasty. Most of the women appear to belong to the prosperous classes, while the simple garb and insignificant size of the men indicates that they are probably slaves.

even in the personal service of the Pharaoh. With these developments they ceased to constitute a separate class. The position of the various ranks of society shifted from time to time. In the Old Kingdom the nobles and priests among all of the Pharaoh's subjects held the supremacy. During the Middle Kingdom the classes of commoners came into their own. Scribes, merchants, artisans, and serfs rebelled against the nobles and wrested concessions from the government. Particularly impressive is the dominant role played by the merchants and industrialists in this period. The establishment of the Empire, accompanied as it was by the extension of government functions, resulted in the ascendancy of a new nobility, made up primarily of bureaucrats. The priests also waxed in power with the growth of magic and superstition.

The gulf between rich and poor

The gulf that separated the standards of living of the upper and lower classes of Egypt was perhaps even wider than it is today in Europe and America. The wealthy nobles lived in splendid villas that opened into fragrant gardens and shady groves. Their food had all the richness and variety of sundry kinds of meat, poultry, cakes, fruit, wine, beer, and sweets. They ate from vessels of alabaster, gold, and silver, and adorned their persons with expensive fabrics and costly jewels. By contrast, the life of the poor was wretched indeed. The laborers in the towns inhabited congested slums composed of mud-brick hovels with roofs of thatch. Their only furnishings were stools and boxes and a few crude pottery jars. The peasants on the great estates enjoyed a less crowded but no more abundant life.

The basic social unit among the Egyptians was the monogamous family. No man, not even the Pharaoh, could have more than one lawful wife. Concubinage, however, was a socially reputable institution. Women occupied an unusually enviable status. Wives were not secluded, and there is no record of any divorce. Women could own and inherit property and engage in business. Almost alone among Oriental peoples the Egyptians permitted women to succeed to the throne. Another extraordinary social practice was close inbreeding. The ruler as son of the great sun god was required to marry his sister or some other female of his immediate family lest the divine blood be contaminated. There is evidence that many of his subjects followed the identical custom. As yet, historians have been unable to discover any positive traces of racial degeneration produced by this practice, probably for the reason that the Egyptian stock was genetically sound to begin with.

The Egyptian economic system rested primarily upon an agrarian basis. Agriculture was diversified and highly developed, and the soil yielded excellent crops of wheat, barley, millet, vegetables, fruits, flax, and cotton. Theoretically the land was the property of the king, but in the earlier periods he granted most of it to his subjects, so that in actual practice it was largely in the possession of individuals. Commerce did not amount to much before 2000 B.C., but after that date it grew rapidly to a position of first-rate importance. A flourishing trade was carried on with the island of Crete, with Phoenicia, Palestine, and Syria. The chief articles of export consisted of wheat, linen fabrics, and fine pottery. Imports were confined largely to gold, silver, ivory, and lumber. Of no less significance than commerce was manufacturing as a branch of economic life. As early as 3000 B.C. large numbers of people were already engaged in industrial pursuits, mostly in separate crafts. In later times factories were established, employing twenty or more persons under one roof, and with some degree of division of labor. The leading industries were quarrying, shipbuilding, and the manufacture of pottery, glass, and textiles.

Left: *Making Sun-dried Bricks*. Nile mud (generally mixed with chaff or straw) is being worked with a hoe, carried away in buckets and dumped in a pile. Lying on the ground in a row are three bricks, from the last of which a wooden mold, used in shaping them, is being lifted. An overseer with a stick is seated close by. The finished bricks are carried off by means of a yoke across the shoulders. From a wall-painting at Thebes about 1500 B.C.
Right: *Stonecutters Dressing Blocks*. Men with mallets and chisels are dressing down blocks to true surfaces. Below, two of them test the accuracy of the dressed surface. After two edges of the block are determined, a cord is stretched between two pegs to help gauge how much remains to be chiseled away.

Sowing Seed and Working It into the Soil. From a bag which he wears over his left shoulder, the sower casts seed under the feet of cattle yoked to a plow. The plow is here used to harrow the soil. While one laborer guides the cows with a stick, another guides the plow straight and keeps the plow-share in the ground by bearing down on the handles. Sheep are then driven across the field to trample in the seed. From wall paintings at Sheïkh Saïd, about 2700 B.C.

From an early date the Egyptians made progress in the perfection of instruments of business. They knew the elements of accounting and bookkeeping. Their merchants issued orders and receipts for goods. They invented deeds for property, written contracts, and wills. While they had no system of coinage, they had nevertheless attained a money economy. Rings of copper or gold of definite weight circulated as media of exchange. This Egyptian ring-money is apparently the oldest currency in the history of civilizations. Probably it was not used except for larger transactions. The simple dealings of the peasants and poorer townsfolk doubtless continued on a basis of barter.

The Egyptian economic system was always collectivistic. From the very beginning the energies of the people had been drawn into socialized channels. The interests of the individual and the interests of society were conceived as identical. The productive activities of the entire nation revolved around the huge state enterprises, and the government remained by far the largest employer of labor. But this collectivism was not all-inclusive; a considerable sphere was left for private initiative. Merchants conducted their own businesses; many of the craftsmen had their own shops; and as time went on, larger and larger numbers of peasants gained the status of independent farmers. The government continued to operate the quarries and mines, to build pyramids and temples, and to farm the royal estates.

The extreme development of state control came with the founding of the Empire. The growth of a military absolutism and the increasing frequency of wars of conquest augmented the need for revenue and for unlimited production of goods. To fulfill this need the government extended its control over every department of economic life. The entire agricultural land became the property of the Pharaoh. Although large sections of it were granted to favorites of the king, most of it was worked by royal serfs and slaves. The free middle class largely disappeared. The services of craftsmen were conscripted for the erection of magnificent temples and for the manufacture of implements of war, while foreign trade became a state monopoly. As the Empire staggered toward its downfall, the government absorbed more and more of the economic activities of the people.

Except during the reign of Ikhnaton, a corrupt alliance existed between the Pharaohs of the Empire and the priests. Greedy for power and plunder, the members of the ecclesiastical hierarchy supported the kings in their ambitions for despotic rule. As a reward they were granted exemption from taxation and a generous share of the national wealth. War captives were turned over to them in such numbers that they actually held two per cent of the population of the country as temple slaves. They employed a great host of artisans in the manufacture of amulets and funerary equipment, which they sold at tremendous profit to the worshipers. Without question these priestly enterprises meant a serious drain on the national resources and thereby contributed to economic and social decay. Too large a proportion of the wealth of Egypt was being squandered on sterile projects of the church and the state and on the conquest of an empire.

Defects in the economic system

6. THE EGYPTIAN ACHIEVEMENT AND ITS IMPORTANCE TO US

Few civilizations of ancient times surpassed the Egyptian in importance to the modern world. Even the influence of the Hebrews was not much greater. From the land of the Pharaohs came the germ and the stimulus for numerous intellectual achievements of later centuries. Important elements of philosophy, mathematics, science, and literature had their beginnings there. The Egyptians also developed one of the oldest systems of jurisprudence and political theory. They perfected the achievements of irrigation, engineering, and the making of pottery, glass, and paper. They were one of the first peoples to have any clear conception of art for other than utilitarian purposes, and they originated architectural principles that were destined for extensive use in subsequent history.

Egyptian contributions: (1) intellectual and artistic

More significant still were the Egyptian contributions in the fields of religion and individual and social ethics. Aside from the Persians, the dwellers on the banks of the Nile were the only people of the ancient world to build a national religion around the doctrine of personal immortality. Egyptian priests and sages likewise were the first to preach universal monotheism, the providence of God, forgiveness of sins, and rewards and punishments after death. Finally, Egyptian ethical theory was the source from which various nations derived standards of personal and social morality; for it embraced not only the ordinary prohibitions of lying, theft, and murder, but included also the exalted ideals of justice, benevolence, and the equal rights of all men.

(2) religious and ethical

47

Egyptian tomb art. Egypt's Sudanic neighbors were frequently portrayed in Egyptian art.

7. KUSHITIC CIVILIZATION

Egyptian splendor rested in large measure on vast human and physical resources lying beyond its southern periphery. Successive Egyptian dynasties drew heavily on the area known today as the Sudan Republic for laborers and soldiers as well as for precious stones and exotic woods used in the crafting of jewelry and fine furniture. The contributions of these darker-skinned neighbors are vividly recorded in scenes etched on objets d'art found in the tombs of Egypt's Pharaohs.

Foundation of the Kingdom of Kush

The origin of the Negroid southerners, long shrouded in mystery, is beginning to come to light through recent archaeological discoveries. We are now fairly certain that from at least 2200 B.C. food-producing Neolithic groups from the ecologically-deteriorating southern Sahara were dispersing to more fertile parts of Africa. Some migrated to the lower Nile where they joined peoples of Mediterranean and Asian stock in laying the foundations of the so-called New Kingdom of Egypt. Others wandered southward to the upper Nile in a region later known to the Egyptians as "Kush." By 1500 B.C. these black-complexioned Kushites, showing remarkable cultural affinities to late predynastic Egypt, had established their own kingdom. Indeed, this Kingdom of Kush became the first highly advanced, essentially Negroid, civilization in Africa. Its vigorous inhabitants traded actively with Egypt and borrowed extensively from their culture. Within four centuries, the capital at Napata, just south of the Fourth Cataract, had flowered into a major religious center for the worship of the Egyptian god Ammon-Re.

Kushitic Invasion of Egypt

Under their king, Kashta, the Kushites began to take advantage of Egypt's decaying social fabric. In about 750 B.C. Kashta's armies swept into the temple city of Thebes, capital of Upper Egypt. Kashta's son, Piankhy, went on to capture Memphis and to extend Kushitic dominion over Lower Egypt as well. With the entire country in hand, Piankhy assumed the title of Pharaoh and established Egypt's Twenty-Fifth Dynasty.

The rule of the Kushites was short-lived. Their genius at governance was no match for the Iron Age Assyrians who burst into Egypt in 670 B.C. The Kushites quickly retreated to their former homelands along the far reaches of the upper Nile. A new Kushitic power base was established at Meroë, some 120 miles north of modern Khartoum, in the fertile pastures between the river Atbara and the Blue Nile. They may have acquired from the Assyrians the technique of iron-smelting, for Meroë soon became the major iron-working center of ancient Africa and the first black industrial city south of the Sahara.

KUSHITIC CIVILIZATION

Meroë: black Africa's first industrial city

The Kushites made an indelible imprint on numerous Mediterranean civilizations. By the fifth century B.C. their likeness appeared on vases, wall murals, and statues from Cyprus in the eastern Mediterranean to ancient Etruria on the Italian peninsula. They were variously depicted as athletes, dancers, court attendants, and warriors. Greek merchants, active in Egyptian markets, called the Kushites "Ethiopians" meaning "men with burnt faces."

Kushitic impact on Mediterranean civilizations

In 322 B.C. Egypt was conquered by Alexander the Great and became a Greek-ruled kingdom. Thenceforth, via Hellenized Egypt, Kushitic exposure to Mediterranean civilizations increased. A brisk trade with the Greeks and Hellenized Egyptians brought prosperity to Kush and enabled its people to develop distinctive architectural and artistic traditions. Unique stone pyramids cast haunting shadows across the Nile at Meroë; and Meroitic pottery, decorated with incised geometric designs, could compare favorably to the finest produced in the ancient world at that time. Kush reached its zenith between 250 B.C. and 200 A.D. By that time Meroitic hieroglyphs had even begun to replace Egyptian as the literary language.

The flowering of Kushitic civilization 250 B.C.–200 A.D.

The Kushitic window on the non-African world opened still further between 13 A.D. and the third century, when Egypt was under Roman rule. After that, Nile valley trade quickly declined and with it Kushitic civilization. For centuries, the Nile's treacherous cataracts had shielded Kush from northern invasions and permitted its inhabitants to adopt only those aspects of Egyptian, Greek, and Roman culture they found desirable. But with the Nile valley connection weakened, Kush suffered economically and fell vulnerable to desert infiltrators from the west. This made it rather easy in the mid-fourth century for Meroë to be overrun by the armies of neighboring Axum, a rising kingdom in the southeast.

The downfall of Kush

Tantalizing legends suggest that Meroë's royal family migrated to West Africa where they may have contributed to the evolution of new political and cultural institutions. West Africans were less advanced politically and economically even though their trans-Saharan links with North Africa and the Nile extend far into antiquity. Since at least 130 B.C. West Africans supplied the north with gold, slaves, precious stones, and wild animals for sports arenas. An ancient chariot route extended from the Punic settlements on the North African coast through the oases of the Fezzan to the Chad Basin.

Ancient trans-Saharan links

The Kushitic refugees may have followed an even more ancient trail connecting the Nile with the Niger river by way of Fezzan.

8. THE CHRISTIAN KINGDOM OF ETHIOPIA

Unlike landlocked Kush, Axum to the southeast could profit from a fast moving trade with Ptolemaic Egypt via the Red Sea. Axumite seaports were busy entrepôts for interior goods destined for the Mediterranean world, the Persian Gulf, India, and beyond. Egyptian Greek middlemen provided Axumites a window on the eastern Mediterranean while their Arabian counterparts exposed them to the outlets of the Orient.

The Axumites as a people were the product of peaceful mingling of African and Semitic Arabians. The latter had been migrating in small bands toward the rugged Ethiopian highlands since 1000 B.C. With intermarriage came cultural enrichment, so superbly reflected in giant religious obelisks, cut with incredible precision from single blocks of stone. Great strides were also made in agricultural productivity through the introduction of the plow and the art of stone terracing and irrigation.

In the mid-fourth century King Ezana converted to Christianity and declared it the official state religion. Christianity became an effective instrument for the cultural and political unification of the various Axumite chieftaincies into a centralized kingdom called Ethiopia. Monasteries took root in Ethiopia and served as vital centers of learning and cultural transmission. Ethiopian monks translated the Bible into Ge'ez, the indigenous language. In time, the monasteries became economically powerful, as successive emperors endowed them with huge tracts of land. Monasticism as a way of life spread quickly to neighboring Nubian kingdoms, before it had appeared in Christian western Europe.

Ethiopia, centered in mountainous and almost inaccessible highlands, became a natural citadel. In relative seclusion, its inhabitants forged a powerfully stable monarchy and a distinctive Christian culture. Representing one of the world's most stable and enduring civilizations, Ethiopia continued into the twentieth century under essentially the same time-honored institutions and the same royal family.

SELECTED READINGS

· *Items so designated are available in paperbound editions.*

· Alfred, Cyril, *The Egyptians*, New York, 1963 (Praeger).

Breasted, James H., *The Dawn of Conscience*, New York, 1934. An excellent account of the development of religious and ethical concepts.

———, *History of Egypt*, New York, 1912. Still one of the best histories of ancient Egypt.

Clark, J. Desmond, *The Prehistory of Africa*, New York, 1970.

· Cottrell, Leonard, *Life under the Pharaohs*, New York, 1960 (Tempo, 1964).

· Desroches-Noblecourt, Christiane, *Egyptian Wall Paintings*, New York, 1962 (Mentor).

· Edwards, I. E. S., *The Pyramids of Egypt*, Baltimore, 1962 (Penguin).

· Emery, W. B., *Archaic Egypt*, Baltimore, 1961 (Penguin).

· Frankfort, Henri, *et al.*, *Before Philosophy*, Baltimore, 1949 (Penguin). A splendid account of early man's thinking.

Glanville, S. R. K., *The Legacy of Ancient Egypt*, Oxford, 1957.

· Kramer, S. N., *Mythologies of the Ancient World*, New York, 1961 (Anchor).

· Lloyd, Seton, *The Art of the Ancient Near East*, New York, 1962 (Praeger).

Moret, Alexandre, *The Nile and Egyptian Civilization*, New York, 1928. Interesting in its contrast with Breasted.

· Moscati, Sabatino, *The Face of the Ancient Orient*, New York, 1962 (Anchor).

Shinnie, Margaret, *Ancient African Kingdoms*, New York, 1966.

Shinnie, P. L., *Meroë: The Civilization of the Sudan*, New York, 1966.

Shorter, A. W., *Everyday Life in Ancient Egypt*, London, 1932. One of the few works of its kind, therefore valuable.

· Smith, W. S., *Art and Architecture of Ancient Egypt*, Baltimore, 1958 (Penguin).

· Snowden, Frank M., *Blacks in Antiquity*, Cambridge, Mass., 1970 (Harvard).

· Steindorff, G., and Steele, K. C., *When Egypt Ruled the East*, Chicago, 1942 (Phoenix). A useful supplement to Breasted.

· Wilson, J. A., *The Burden of Egypt*, Chicago, 1951. An excellent interpretation. Also available in paperback under the title, *The Culture of Ancient Egypt* (Phoenix).

SOURCE MATERIALS

· Bovill, E. W., *The Golden Trade of the Moors*, 2nd ed., New York, 1970 (Oxford).

Breasted, J. H., *Ancient Records of Egypt*, Chicago, 1929, 5 vols.

· ———, *Development of Religion and Thought in Ancient Egypt*, Gloucester, Mass., 1959 (Torchbook).

Budge, E. A. W., *Osiris and the Egyptian Resurrection*, New York, 1911, 2 vols.

· Pritchard, J. B., ed., *Ancient Near Eastern Texts*, Princeton, 1950 (Princeton University Press).

CHAPTER 3

The Mesopotamian and
Persian Civilizations

If a son strike his father, they shall cut off his fingers.
If a man destroy the eye of another man, they shall destroy
his eye.
If one break a man's bone, they shall break his bone.
If one destroy the eye of a freeman or break the bone of a free-
man, he shall pay one mina of silver.
If one destroy the eye of a man's slave or break a bone of a man's
slave he shall pay one-half his price.
—The Code of Hammurabi, lines 195–199.

The other of the most ancient civilizations was that which began in the Tigris-Euphrates valley at least as early as 4000 B.C. This civilization was formerly called the Babylonian or Babylonian-Assyrian civilization. It is now known, however, that the civilization was not founded by either the Babylonians or the Assyrians but by an earlier people called the Sumerians. It seems better, therefore, to use the name Mesopotamian to cover the whole civilization, even though Mesopotamia is sometimes applied only to the northern portion of the land between the two rivers. The Mesopotamian civilization was unlike the Egyptian in many respects. Its political history was marked by sharper interruptions. Its ethnic composition was less homogeneous, and its social and economic structure gave wider scope to individual initiative.

Origin and comparison with Egypt

The differences in ideals and in religious and social attitudes were perhaps more fundamental. The Egyptian culture was predominantly ethical, the Mesopotamian legalistic. The Egyptian outlook on life, except during the Middle Kingdom, was generally one of cheerful resignation, comparatively free from the cruder superstitions. By contrast, the Mesopotamian view was gloomy, pessimistic, and enthralled by morbid fears. Where the native of Egypt believed in immortality and dedicated a large part of his energy to preparation for the life to come, his Mesopotamian contemporary lived in the present and cherished few hopes regarding his fate beyond the

Religious and social differences

53

grave. Finally, the civilization of the Nile valley embodied concepts of monotheism, a religion of love, and of social equalitarianism; that of the Tigris-Euphrates was more selfish and practical. Its religion seldom evolved beyond the stage of primitive polytheism, and its arts bore few of the natural and personal qualities of the Egyptian.

On the other hand, there were similarities too striking to be ignored. Both civilizations made progress in ethical theory and in concepts of social justice. Both had their evils of slavery and imperialism, of oppressive kings and greedy priests. Both had common problems of irrigation and land boundaries; and, as a result, both made notable progress in the sciences, especially in mathematics. Finally, rivalry among small states led eventually to consolidation and to the growth of mighty empires, especially in the case of Mespotamia.

Similarities

I. FROM THE SUMERIAN TO THE PERSIAN CONQUEST

The pioneers in the development of the Mesopotamian civilization were the people known as Sumerians, who settled in the lower Tigris-Euphrates valley between 5000 and 4000 B.C. Their precise origin is unknown, but they seem to have come from the plateau of central Asia. They spoke a language unrelated to any now known, although their culture bore a certain resemblance to the earliest civilization of India. With little or no difficulty they subjugated the natives already in the lower valley, a mysterious people who were just emerging from the Neolithic stage.

The Sumerians

The new Sumerian empire did not survive long. It was annexed by the Elamites in the twenty-first century and about 1950 B.C. was conquered by a Semitic people known as the Amorites, who had come in from the fringes of the Arabian desert. Since they made the village of Babylon the capital of their empire they are commonly called the Babylonians, or the Old Babylonians, to distinguish them from the Neo-Babylonians or Chaldeans who occupied the valley much later. The rise of the Old Babylonians inaugurated the second important stage of the Tigris-Euphrates civilization. Although most of the Sumerian culture survived, Sumerian dominance was now at an end. The Babylonians established an autocratic state and during the reign of their most famous king, Hammurabi, extended their dominion north to Assyria. But after his time their empire gradually declined until it was finally overthrown by the Kassites about 1650 B.C.

The rise and fall of the Old Babylonians

With the downfall of Old Babylonia a period of retrogression set in which lasted for 600 years. The Kassites were barbarians with no interest in the cultural achievements of their predecessors. Their lone contribution was the introduction of the horse into the Tigris-Euphrates valley. The old culture would have died out entirely had it not been for its partial adoption by another Semitic people who,

The Kassites and the Assyrians

as early as 3000 B.C., had founded a tiny kingdom on the plateau of Assur some 500 miles up the Tigris River. These people came to be called the Assyrians, and their ultimate rise to power marked the beginning of the third stage in the development of the Mesopotamian civilization. They began to expand about 1300 B.C. and soon afterward made themselves masters of the whole northern valley. In the tenth century they overturned what was left of Kassite power in Babylonia. Their empire reached its height in the eighth and seventh centuries under Sargon II (722–705 B.C.), Sennacherib (705–681), and Assurbanipal (668–626). It had now come to include nearly all of the civilized world of that time. One after another, Syria, Phoenicia, the Kingdom of Israel, and Egypt had fallen victims to Assyrian military prowess. Only the little Kingdom of Judah was able to withstand the hosts of Nineveh, probably because of an outbreak of pestilence in the ranks of Sennacherib's army.[1]

Brilliant though the successes of the Assyrians were, they did not endure. So rapidly were new territories annexed that the empire soon reached an unmanageable size. The Assyrians' genius for government was far inferior to their appetite for conquest. Subjugated nations chafed under the cruel despotism that had been forced upon them and, as the empire gave signs of cracking from within, determined to regain their freedom. The death blow was delivered by the Kaldi or Chaldeans, a nation of Semites who had settled southeast of the valley of the two rivers. Under the leadership of Nabopolassar, who had served the Assyrian emperors in the capacity of a provincial governor, they organized a revolt and finally captured Nineveh in 612 B.C.

The downfall of the Assyrians and the rise of the Chaldeans

In 539 B.C. the empire of the Chaldeans fell, after an existence of less than a century. It was overthrown by Cyrus the Persian, as he himself declared, "without a battle and without fighting." The easy victory appears to have been made possible by assistance from the Jews and by a conspiracy of the priests of Babylon to deliver the city to Cyrus as an act of vengeance against the Chaldean king, whose policies they did not like. Members of other influential classes appear also to have looked upon the Persians as deliverers.

Although the Persian state incorporated all of the territories that had once been embraced by the Mesopotamian empires, it included many other provinces besides. It was the vehicle, moreover, of a new and different culture. The downfall of Chaldea must therefore be taken as marking the end of Mesopotamian political history.

2. SUMERIAN ORIGINS OF THE CIVILIZATION

More than to any other people, the Mesopotamian civilization owed its character to the Sumerians. Much of what used to be

Assurbanipal and His Armies Storming the Elamite Capital

[1] Hebrew prophets declared that an angel of the Lord visited the camp of the Assyrians by night and slew 185,000 of them. II Kings 19:35.

ascribed to the Babylonians and Assyrians is now known to have been developed by the nation that preceded them. The system of writing was of Sumerian origin; likewise the religion, the laws, and a great deal of the science and commercial practice. Only in the evolution of government and military tactics and in the development of the arts was the originating talent of the later conquerors particularly manifest.

The Sumerian political system

Through the greater part of their history the Sumerians lived in a loose confederation of city-states, united only for military purposes. At the head of each was a *patesi,* who combined the functions of chief priest, commander of the army, and superintendent of the irrigation system. Occasionally one of the more ambitious of these rulers would extend his power over a number of cities and assume the title of king. Not until about 2000 B.C., however, were all of the Sumerian people united under a single authority of the same nationality as themselves.

The Sumerian economic pattern

The Sumerian economic pattern was relatively simple and permitted a wider scope for individual enterprise than was generally allowed in Egypt. The land was never the exclusive property of the king either in theory or in practice. Neither was trade or industry a monopoly of the government. The temples, however, seem to have fulfilled many of the functions of a collectivist state. They owned a large portion of the land and operated business enterprises. Because the priests alone had the technical knowledge to calculate the seasons and lay out canals, they controlled the irrigation system. The masses of the people had little they could call their own. Many of them were serfs, but even those who were technically free were little better off, forced as they were to pay high rents and to labor on public works. Slavery in the strict sense of the word was not an important institution.

Agriculture was the chief economic pursuit of most of the citizens, and the Sumerians were excellent farmers. By virtue of their

Diorama of a Part of Ur about 2000 B.C. A modern archaeologist's conception. Walls are omitted to show interiors at left.

knowledge of irrigation they produced amazing crops of cereal grains and subtropical fruits. Since most of the land was divided into large estates held by the rulers, the priests, and the army officers, the average rural citizen was either a tenant farmer or a serf. Commerce was the second most important source of the nation's wealth. A flourishing trade was established with all of the surrounding countries, revolving around the exchange of metals and timber from the north and west for agricultural products and manufactured goods from the lower valley. Nearly all of the familiar adjuncts of business were highly developed; bills, receipts, notes, and letters of credit were regularly used.

Agriculture

The most distinctive achievement of the Sumerians was their system of law. It was the product of a gradual evolution of local usage, but it was finally incorporated into a comprehensive code after the middle of the third millennium. Only a few fragments of this law have survived in their original form, but the famous code of Hammurabi, the Babylonian king, is now recognized to have been little more than a revision of the code of the Sumerians. Ultimately this code became the basis of the laws of nearly all of the Semites—Babylonians, Assyrians, Chaldeans, and Hebrews.

Sumerian law

The following may be regarded as the essential features of the Sumerian law:

Essential features of Sumerian law

(1) The *lex talionis*, or law of retaliation in kind—"an eye for an eye, a tooth for a tooth, a limb for a limb," etc.

(2) Semiprivate administration of justice. It was incumbent upon the victim himself or his family to bring the offender to justice. The court served principally as an umpire in the dispute between the plaintiff and defendant, not as an agency of the state to maintain public security, although constables attached to the court might assist in the execution of the sentence.

(3) Inequality before the law. The code divided the population into three classes: patricians or aristocrats; burghers or commoners; serfs and slaves. Penalties were graded according to the rank of the victim, but also in some cases according to the rank of the offender. The killing or maiming of a patrician was a much more serious offense than a similar crime committed against a burgher or a slave. On the other hand, when a patrician was the offender he was punished *more severely* than a man of inferior status would be for the same crime. The origin of this curious rule was probably to be found in considerations of military discipline. Since the patricians were army officers and therefore the chief defenders of the state, they could not be permitted to give vent to their passions or to indulge in riotous conduct.

(4) Inadequate distinction between accidental and intentional homicide. A person responsible for killing another accidentally did not escape penalty, as he would under modern law, but had to pay a fine to the family of the victim, apparently on the theory that chil-

Male Votive Figure, Sumer.
This statue of white gypsum
colored with bitumen shows
the huge staring eyes characteristic of Mesopotamian art.

A religion
neither ethical
nor spiritual

dren were the property of their fathers and wives the property of
their husbands.

Quite as much as their law, the religion of the Sumerians illumi-
nates their social attitudes and the character of their culture. They
did not succeed in developing a very exalted religion; yet it occupied an important place in their lives. To begin with, it was
polytheistic and anthropomorphic. They believed in a number of
gods and goddesses, each a distinct personality with human attributes. Shamash, the sun god; Enlil, the lord of the rain and wind;
and Ishtar, the goddess of the female principle in nature, were only
a few of them. Although the Sumerians had a special deity of the
plague in the person of the god Nergal, their religion was really
monistic in the sense that they regarded all of their deities as capable
of both good and evil.

The Sumerian religion was a religion for this world exclusively; it
offered no hope for a blissful, eternal afterlife. The afterlife was a
mere temporary existence in a dreary, shadowy place which later
came to be called Sheol. Here the ghosts of the dead lingered for a
time, perhaps a generation or so, and then disappeared. No one
could look forward to resurrection in another world and a joyous
eternal existence as a recompense for the evils of this life; the victory of the grave was complete. In accordance with these beliefs the
Sumerians bestowed only limited care upon the bodies of their
dead. No mummification was practiced, and no elaborate tombs
were built. Corpses were commonly interred beneath the floor of
the house without a coffin and with comparatively few articles for
the use of the ghost.

Spiritual content had no place of conspicuous importance in this
religion. As we have seen, the gods were not spiritual beings but
creatures cast in the human mold, with most of the weaknesses and
passions of mortal men. Nor were the purposes of the religion any
more spiritual. It provided no blessings in the form of solace, uplift
of the soul, or oneness with God. If it benefited man at all, it did so
chiefly in the form of material gain—abundant harvests and prosperity in business. At the same time, the religion did, at least, have an
ethical content. All the major deities in the Sumerian pantheon were
extolled in hymns as lovers of truth, goodness, and justice. The goddess Nanshe, for example, was said "to comfort the orphan, to make
disappear the widow, to set up a place of destruction for the
mighty." Yet the same deities who personified these noble ideals
created such evils as falsehood and strife, and endowed every human
being with a sinful nature. "Never," it was said, "has a sinless child
been born to its mother." [2]

A dominant idea in the Sumerian religion was the notion that man
was created in order that he might serve the gods—not merely by
worshipping them, but also by giving them food. This notion was

[2] S. N. Kramer, *History Begins at Sumer,* pp. 106–107.

revealed in the famous Creation and Flood epics, which provided the framework for the much later Hebrew stories in the Old Testament. The Creation epic related the magic triumph of the god Marduk over the jealous and cowardly gods who had created him, the formation of the world out of the body of one of his slain rivals, and finally, in order that the gods might be fed, the making of man out of clay and dragon's blood. The whole account was crude and revolting, with nothing in it to appeal to a spiritual or moral sense. Almost as barbarous was the Sumerian version of the Flood. Grown jealous of man, the gods decided to destroy the whole race of mortals by drowning. One of their number, however, betrayed the secret to a favorite inhabitant of the earth, instructing him to build an ark for the salvation of himself and his kind. The flood raged for seven days, until the whole earth was covered with water. Even the gods "crouched like a dog on the wall." Finally the tumult was stilled and the waters subsided. The favored man came forth from the ark and offered grateful sacrifice. As a reward he was given "life like a god" and translated to "the place where the sun rises."

In the field of intellectual endeavor the Sumerians achieved no small distinction. They produced a system of writing which was destined to be used for a thousand years after the downfall of their nation. This was the celebrated *cuneiform* writing, consisting of wedge-shaped characters imprinted on clay tablets with a square-tipped reed. At first a pictographic system, it was gradually transformed into an aggregate of syllabic and phonetic signs, some 350 in number. No alphabet was ever developed out of it. The Sumerians wrote nothing that could be called philosophy, but they did make some notable beginnings in science. In mathematics, for example, they surpassed the Egyptians in every field except geometry. They discovered the processes of multiplication and division and even the extraction of square and cube root. Their systems of numeration and of weights and measures were duodecimal, with the number sixty as the most common unit. They invented the water clock and the lunar calendar, the latter an inaccurate division of the year into months based upon cycles of the moon. In order to bring it into harmony with the solar year, an extra month had to be added from time to time. Astronomy was little more than astrology, and medicine was a curious compound of herbalism and magic. The repertory of the physician consisted primarily of charms to exorcise the evil spirits which were believed to be the cause of the disease.

Gudea of Lagash. A black diorite statue of the late Sumerian ruler.

As artists, the Sumerians excelled in metalwork, gem carving, and sculpture. They produced some remarkable specimens of naturalistic art in their weapons, vessels, jewelry, and animal representations, which revealed alike a technical skill and a gift of imagination. Evidently religious conventions had not yet imposed any paralyzing influence, and consequently the artist was still free to follow his own impulses. Architecture, on the other hand, was distinctly inferior, probably because of the limitations enforced by the scarcity of

Left: *The Great Ziggurat, or Flat-topped Temple at Ur*. Right: *Fragments of Jewelry Found at Ur in Two Graves of Ladies-in-waiting to the Queen*. The gold jewelry is the oldest in the world.

good building materials. Since there was no stone in the valley, the architect had to depend upon sun-dried brick. The characteristic Sumerian edifice, extensively copied by their Semitic successors, was the *ziggurat*, a terraced tower set on a platform and surmounted by a shrine. Its construction was massive, its lines were monotonous, and little architectural ingenuity was exhibited in it. The royal tombs and private houses showed more originality. It was in them that the Sumerian inventions of the arch, the vault, and the dome were regularly employed, and the column was used occasionally.

3. OLD BABYLONIAN "CONTRIBUTIONS"

The shortcomings of the Old Babylonians

Although the Old Babylonians were an alien nation, they had lived long enough in close contact with the Sumerians to be influenced profoundly by them. They had no culture of their own worthy of the name when they came into the valley, and in general they simply appropriated what the Sumerians had already developed. With so excellent a foundation to build upon, they should have made remarkable progress; but such was not the case. When they ended their history, the state of civilization in the Tigris-Euphrates valley was little more advanced than when they began.

Changes in the system of law

First among the significant changes which the Old Babylonians made in their cultural inheritance may be mentioned the political and legal. As military conquerors holding in subjection numerous vanquished nations, they found it necessary to establish a consolidated state. Vestiges of the old system of local autonomy were swept away, and the power of the king of Babylon was made supreme. Kings became gods, or at least claimed divine origin. A system of royal taxation was adopted as well as compulsory military service. The system of law was also changed to conform to the new condition of centralized despotism. The list of crimes against the state was enlarged, and the king's officers assumed a more active role

60

in apprehending and punishing offenders, although it was still impossible for any criminal to be pardoned without the consent of the victim or the victim's family. The severity of penalties was decidedly increased, particularly for crimes involving any suggestion of treason or sedition. Such apparently trivial offenses as "gadding about" and "disorderly conduct of a tavern" were made punishable by death, probably on the assumption that they would be likely to foster disloyal activities. Whereas under the Sumerian law the harboring of fugitive slaves was punishable merely by a fine, the Babylonian law made it a capital crime. According to the Sumerian code, the slave who disputed his master's rights over him was to be sold; the Code of Hammurabi prescribed that he should have his ear cut off. Adultery was also made a capital offense, whereas under the Sumerian law it did not even necessarily result in divorce. In a few particulars the new system of law revealed some improvement. Wives and children sold for debt could not be held in bondage for longer than four years, and a female slave who had borne her master a child could not be sold at all.

The Old Babylonian laws also reflect a more extensive development of business than that which existed in the preceding culture. That a large middle class traded for profit and enjoyed a privileged position in society is evidenced by the fact that the commercial provisions of Hammurabi's code were based upon the principle of "Let the buyer beware." The Babylonian rulers did not believe in a regime of free competition, however. Trade, banking, and industry were subject to elaborate regulation by the state. There were laws regarding partnership, storage, and agency; laws respecting deeds, wills, and the taking of interest on money; and a host of others. For a deal to be negotiated without a written contract or without witnesses was punishable by death. Agriculture, which was still the occupation of a majority of the citizens, did not escape regulation. The code provided penalties for failure to cultivate a field and for neglect of dikes and canals. Both government ownership and private tenure of land were permitted; but, regardless of the status of the owner, the tenant farmer was required to pay two-thirds of all he produced as rent.

Religion at the hands of the Old Babylonians underwent numerous changes both superficial and profound. Deities that had been venerated by the Sumerians were now neglected and new ones exalted in their stead. They carried no spiritual significance, however, conveying no promise of the resurrection of man from the dead or of personal immortality. The Old Babylonians were no more otherworldly in their outlook than the Sumerians. The religions of both peoples were fundamentally materialistic.

Equally noteworthy was an increase in superstition. Astrology, divination, and other forms of magic took on added significance. A morbid consciousness of sin gradually displaced the essentially

Gold Jewelry from Ur, ca. 3500–2800 B.C.

Changes in religion

61

amoral attitude of the Sumerians. In addition, an increased emphasis was placed upon the worship of demons. Nergal, the god of the plague, came to be envisaged as a hideous monster seeking every chance to strike down his victims. Hordes of other demons and malevolent spirits lurked in the darkness and rode through the air bringing terror and destruction to all in their path. Against them there was no defense except sacrifices and magic charms. If the Old Babylonians did not invent witchcraft, they were at least the first "civilized" people to magnify it to serious proportions. Their laws invoked the death penalty against it, and there is evidence that the power of witches was widely feared. Whether the growth of demonology and witchcraft was a result of the increasing unhealthfulness of the climate of the Tigris-Euphrates valley, or of the needs of a centralized, conquering state to inspire fear in its subjects is a question which cannot be answered; but it is probable that the latter is the chief explanation.

The increase in superstition

There seems to be little doubt that intellectually and artistically the Mesopotamian civilization suffered a partial decline during the period of Babylonian rule. This was not the first instance of cultural retrogression in history, but it was one of the most pronounced. Nothing of great importance was added to the scientific discoveries of the Sumerians, except for advancement in mathematics; they discovered, for example, the solution of quadratic equations. Literature showed some improvement over the earlier writings. A kind of prototype of the Book of Job, the so-called *Babylonian Job,* was written in this period. It relates the story of a pious sufferer who is afflicted he knows not why, and it contains some mature reflections on the helplessness of man and the impenetrable mysteries of the universe. As an example of Oriental philosophy it is not without merit. The graphic arts, on the other hand, definitely deteriorated. The Babylonians lacked the creative interest and talent to

The decline of intellect and the arts

Panel of Glazed Brick, Babylon, Sixth Century B.C. An ornamental relief on a background of earth brown. The lion is in blue, white, and yellow glazes.

surpass the fresh and ingenious carving and engraving of the Sumerians. Moreover, sculpture fell under the domination of religious and political conventions, with the result that originality was stifled.

4. THE METAMORPHOSIS UNDER ASSYRIA

Of all the peoples of the Mesopotamian area after the time of the Sumerians, the Assyrians went through the most completely independent evolution. For several centuries they had lived a comparatively isolated existence on top of their small plateau in the upper valley of the Tigris. Eventually they came under the influence of the Babylonians, but not until after the course of their own history had been partially fixed. As a consequence, the period of Assyrian supremacy (from about 1300 B.C. to 612 B.C.) had more nearly a peculiar character than any other era of Mesopotamian history.

The evolution of Assyrian supremacy

The Assyrians were preeminently a nation of warriors; not because they were racially different from any of the other Semites, but because of the special conditions of their own environment. The limited resources of their original home and the constant danger of attack from hostile nations around them forced the development of warlike habits and imperial ambitions. It is therefore not strange that their greed for territory should have known no limits. The more they conquered, the more they felt they had to conquer, in order to protect what they had already gained. Every success excited ambition and riveted the chains of militarism more firmly than ever. Disaster was inevitable.

A nation of warriors

The exigencies of war determined the whole character of the Assyrian system. The state was a great military machine. The army commanders were at once the richest and the most powerful class in the country. Not only did they share in the plunder of war, but they were frequently granted huge estates as rewards for victory. At least one of them, Sargon II, dared to usurp the throne. The military establishment itself represented the last word in preparedness. The standing army greatly exceeded in size that of any other nation of the Near Orient. New and improved armaments and techniques of fighting gave to the Assyrian soldiers unparalleled advantages. Iron swords, heavy bows, long lances, battering rams, fortresses on wheels, and metal breastplates, shields, and helmets were only a few examples of their superior equipment.

Features of the Assyrian militarism

But swords and spears and engines of war were not their only instruments of combat. As much as anything else the Assyrians depended upon frightfulness as a means of overcoming their enemies. Upon soldiers captured in battle, and sometimes upon noncombatants as well, they inflicted unspeakable cruelties—skinning them alive, impaling them on stakes, cutting off ears, noses, and sex organs, and then exhibiting the mutilated victims in cages for the

Terrorism

63

benefit of cities that had not yet surrendered. Accounts of these cruelties are not taken from atrocity stories circulated by their enemies; they come from the records of the Assyrians themselves. Their chroniclers boasted of them as evidences of valor, and the people believed in them as guaranties of security and power. It is clear why the Assyrians were the most hated of all the nations of antiquity.

The tragedy of Assyrian militarism

Seldom has the decline of an empire been so swift and so complete as was that of Assyria. In spite of her magnificent armaments and her wholesale destruction of her foes, Assyria's period of imperial splendor lasted little more than a century. Nation after nation conspired against her and finally accomplished her downfall. Her enemies took frightful vengeance. The whole land was so thoroughly sacked and the people so completely enslaved or exterminated that it has been difficult to trace any subsequent Assyrian influence upon history. The power and security which military strength was supposed to provide proved a mockery in the end. If Assyria had been utterly defenseless, her fate could hardly have been worse.

Assyrian political and economic achievements

With so complete an absorption in military pursuits, it was inevitable that the Assyrians should have neglected in some measure the arts of peace. Industry and commerce appear to have declined under the regime of the Assyrians; for such pursuits were generally scorned as beneath the dignity of a soldierly people. The minimum of manufacturing and trade which had to be carried on was left quite largely to the Arameans, a people closely related to the Phoenicians and the Hebrews. The Assyrians themselves preferred to derive their living from agriculture. The land system included both public and private holdings. The temples held the largest share of the landed wealth. Although the estates of the crown were likewise extensive, they were constantly being diminished by grants to army officers.

Defects in the economic system

Neither the economic nor the social order was sound. The frequent military campaigns depleted the energies and resources of the nation. In the course of time the army officers became a pampered aristocracy, delegating their duties to their subordinates and devoting themselves to luxurious pleasures. The stabilizing influence of a prosperous and intelligent middle class was precluded by the rule that only foreigners and slaves could engage in commercial activities. Yet more serious was the treatment accorded to the lower classes, the serfs and the slaves. The former comprised the bulk of the rural population. Some of them cultivated definite portions of their master's estates and retained a part of what they produced for themselves. Others were "empty" men, without even a plot to cultivate and dependent on the need for seasonal labor to provide for their means of subsistence. All were extremely poor and were subject to the additional hardships of labor on public works and compulsory military service. The slaves, who were chiefly an urban

Stele or Grave Marker. It shows the deceased being presented to the Sun god on his throne. She is holding her heart in her hand.

Head of Ramses II, 1324–1258 B.C.

Shawabty ("to answer") Figures, *ca.* 1400 B.C. These were put in the tomb to do any degrading work the rich man might be called upon to do in the next world.

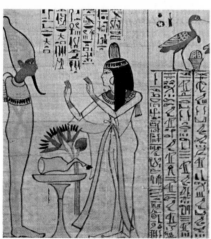

Part of the Egyptian "Book of the Dead." A collection of magic formulas to enable the deceased to gain admission to the realm of Osiris and to enjoy its eternal benefits.

Painted limestone figures, *ca.* 1300 B.C.

A hieroglyphic character for the idea "Millions of Years," 500–330 B.C.

A carved sandstone capital, *ca.* 370 B.C., representing a bundle of papyrus reeds.

Thutmose III as Amon, 1450 B.C. The Pharaoh wears the crown and the beard of the god, and carries a scimitar and the symbol of "life."

Bronze Bull, Symbol of Strength. Arabian, VI cent. B.C.

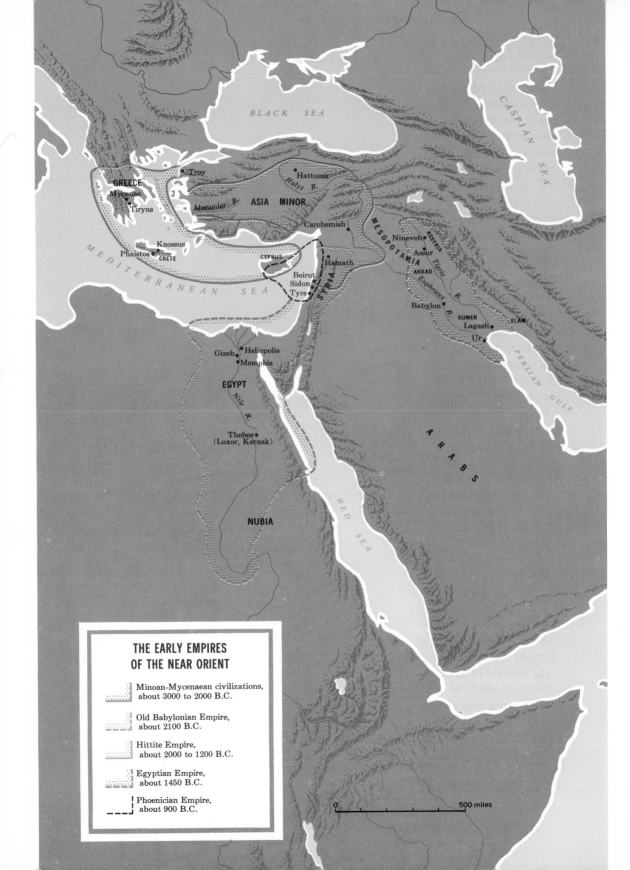

BLACK SEA

CASPIAN SEA

GREECE
Mycenae
Tiryns
Troy
Maeander R.
ASIA MINOR
Hattusas
Halys R.
Carchemish
MESOPOTAMIA
Nineveh
Assur
ASSYRIA
Tigris R.
Phaistos
Knossus
CRETE
CYPRUS
Hamath
SYRIA
Beirut
Sidon
Tyre
AKKAD
Euphrates R.
Babylon
SUMER
Lagash
Ur
ELAM
PERSIAN GULF

MEDITERRANEAN SEA

Gizeh
Heliopolis
Memphis
EGYPT
Nile R.
A R A B S
Thebes
(Luxor, Karnak)
NUBIA
RED SEA

THE EARLY EMPIRES
OF THE NEAR ORIENT

Minoan-Mycenaean civilizations,
about 3000 to 2000 B.C.

Old Babylonian Empire,
about 2100 B.C.

Hittite Empire,
about 2000 to 1200 B.C.

Egyptian Empire,
about 1450 B.C.

Phoenician Empire,
about 900 B.C.

0   500 miles

working class, were of two different types: the domestic slaves, who performed household duties and sometimes engaged in business for their masters; and the war captives. The former were not numerous and were allowed a great deal of freedom, even to the extent of owning property. The latter suffered much greater miseries. Bound by heavy shackles, they were compelled to labor to the point of exhaustion in building roads, canals, and palaces.

Whether the Assyrians adopted the law of the Old Babylonians has never been settled. Undoubtedly they were influenced by it, but several of the features of Hammurabi's code are entirely absent. Notable among these are the *lex talionis* and the system of gradation of penalties according to the rank of the victim and the offender. Whereas the Babylonians prescribed the most drastic punishments for crimes suggestive of treason or sedition, the Assyrians reserved theirs for such offenses as abortion and unnatural vice, probably for the military reason of preventing a decline in the birth rate. Another contrast is the more complete subjection of Assyrian women. Wives were treated as chattels of their husbands, the right of divorce was placed entirely in the hands of the male, a plurality of wives was permitted, and all married women were forbidden to appear in public with their faces unveiled. Here, according to Professor Olmstead, was the beginning of the Oriental seclusion of women.[3]

Assyrian law

That a military nation like the Assyrians should not have taken first rank in intellectual achievement is easily understandable. The atmosphere of a military campaign is not favorable to reflection or disinterested research. Yet the demands of successful campaigning may lead to a certain accumulation of knowledge, for practical problems have to be solved. Under such circumstances the Assyrians accomplished some measure of scientific progress. They appear to have divided the circle into 360 degrees and to have estimated locations on the surface of the earth in something resembling latitude and longitude. They recognized and named five planets and achieved some success in predicting eclipses. Since the health of armies is important, medicine received considerable attention. More than 500 drugs, both vegetable and mineral, were catalogued and their uses indicated. Symptoms of various diseases were described and were generally interpreted as due to natural causes, although incantations and the prescription of disgusting compounds to drive out demons were still commonly employed as methods of treatment.

Scientific achievements

In the domain of art the Assyrians surpassed the Old Babylonians and at least equaled the work of the Sumerians, although in different form. Sculpture was the art most highly developed, particularly in the low reliefs. These portrayed dramatic incidents of war and the hunt with the utmost fidelity to nature and a vivid description of movement. The Assyrians delighted in depicting the cool bravery of

The excellence of Assyrian art

[3] A. T. E. Olmstead, *History of Assyria*, p. 553.

Assyrian Relief Sculpture. This panel depicts Assurbanipal hunting lions.

the hunter in the face of terrific danger, the ferocity of lions at bay, and the death agonies of wounded beasts. Unfortunately this art was limited almost entirely to the two themes of war and sport. Its purpose was to glorify the exploits of the ruling class. Architecture ranked second to sculpture from the standpoint of artistic excellence. Assyrian palaces and temples were built of stone, obtained from the mountainous areas of the north, instead of the mud brick of former times. Their principal features were the arch and the dome. The column was also used but never very successfully. The chief demerit of this architecture was its hugeness, which the Asyrians appeared to regard as synonymous with beauty.

5. THE CHALDEAN RENASCENCE

The Mesopotamian civilization entered its final stage with the overthrow of Assyria and the establishment of Chaldean supremacy.

The Chaldean or final stage in Mesopotamian civilization

This stage is often called the Neo-Babylonian, because Nebuchadnezzar and his followers restored the capital at Babylon and attempted to revive the culture of Hammurabi's time. As might have been expected, their attempt was not wholly successful. The Assyrian metamorphosis had altered that culture in various profound and ineffaceable ways. Besides, the Chaldeans themselves had a history of their own which they could not entirely escape. Nevertheless, they did manage to revive certain of the old institutions and ideals. They restored the ancient law and literature, the essentials of the Old Babylonian form of government, and the economic system of their supposed ancestors with its dominance of industry and trade. Farther than this they were unable to go.

It was in religion that the failure of the Chaldean renascence was most conspicuous. Although Marduk was restored to his traditional place at the head of the pantheon, the system of belief was little more than superficially Babylonian. What the Chaldeans really did was to develop an astral religion. The gods were divested of their limited human qualities and exalted into transcendent, omnipotent beings. They were actually identified with the planets themselves. Marduk became Jupiter, Ishtar became Venus, and so on. Though still not entirely aloof from man, they certainly lost their character as beings who could be cajoled and threatened and coerced by magic. They ruled the universe almost mechanically. While their immediate intentions were sometimes discernible, their ultimate purposes were inscrutable.

Two significant results flowed from these amazing conceptions. The first was an attitude of fatalism. Since the ways of the gods were past finding out, all that man could do was to resign himself to his fate. It behooved him therefore to submit absolutely to the gods, to trust in them implicitly, in the vague hope that the results in the end would be good. Thus arose for the first time in history the conception of piety as submission—a conception which was adopted in several other religions, as we shall see in succeeding chapters. For the Chaldeans it implied no otherwordly significance; one did not resign himself to calamities in this life in order to be justified in the next. The Chaldeans had no interest in a life to come. Submission might bring certain earthly rewards, but in the main, as they conceived it, it was not a means to an end at all. It was rather the expression of an attitude of despair, of humility in the face of mysteries that could not be fathomed.

The second great result which came from the growth of an astral religion was the development of a stronger spiritual consciousness. This is revealed in the penitential hymns of unknown authors and in the prayers which were ascribed to Nebuchadnezzar and other kings as the spokesmen for the nation. In most of them the gods are addressed as exalted beings who are concerned with justice and righteous conduct on the part of men, although the distinction between ceremonial and genuine morality is not always sharply drawn. It has been asserted by one author that these hymns could have been used by the Hebrews with little modification except for the substitution of the name of Yahweh for that of the Chaldean god.[4]

With the gods promoted to so lofty a plane, it was perhaps inevitable that man should have been abased. Creatures possessed of mortal bodies could not be compared with the transcendent, passionless beings who dwelt in the stars and guided the destinies of the earth. Man was a lowly creature, sunk in iniquity and vileness, and hardly even worthy of approaching the gods. The consciousness of sin already present in the Babylonian and Assyrian religions now reached a stage of almost pathological intensity. In the hymns the sons of men are compared to prisoners, bound hand and foot, lan-

The astral religion of the Chaldeans

The growth of fatalism

The development of a spiritual consciousness

The abasement of man

[4] Morris Jastrow, *The Civilization of Babylonia and Assyria*, p. 217.

guishing in darkness. Their transgressions are "seven times seven." Their misery is increased by the fact that their evil nature has prompted them to sin unwittingly.[5] Never before had men been regarded as so hopelessly depraved, nor had religion been fraught with so gloomy a view of life.

Curiously enough, the pessimism of the Chaldeans does not appear to have affected their morality very much. So far as the evidence reveals, they indulged in no rigors of asceticism. They did not mortify the flesh, nor did they even practice self-denial. Apparently they took it for granted that man could not avoid sinning, no matter how hard he tried. They seem to have been just as deeply engrossed in the material interests of life and in the pursuit of the pleasures of the senses as any of the earlier nations. Indeed, it seems that they were even more greedy and sensual. Occasional references were made in their prayers and hymns to reverence, kindness, and purity of heart as virtues, and to oppression, slander, and anger as vices, but these were intermingled with ritualistic conceptions of cleanness and uncleanness and with expressions of desire for physical satisfactions. When the Chaldeans prayed, it was not always that their gods would make them good, but more often that they would grant long years, abundant offspring, and luxurious living.

Aside from religion, the Chaldean culture differed from that of the Sumerians, Babylonians, and Assyrians chiefly in regard to scientific achievements. Without doubt the Chaldeans were the most capable scientists in all of Mesopotamian history, although their accomplishments were limited primarily to astronomy. They worked out the most elaborate system for recording the passage of time that had yet been devised, with their invention of the seven-day week and their division of the day into twelve double-hours of 120 minutes each. They kept accurate records of their observation of eclipses and other celestial occurrences for more than 350 years— until long after the downfall of their empire. The motivating force behind Chaldean astronomy was religion. The chief purpose of mapping the heavens and collecting astronomical data was to discover the future the gods had prepared for the race of men. Since the planets were gods themselves, that future could best be divined in the movements of the heavenly bodies. Astronomy was therefore primarily astrology.

Sciences other than astronomy continued in a backward state. There is evidence that the Chaldeans knew the principle of the zero and laid at least some of the foundations of algebra. Medicine showed little advance beyond the stage it had reached under the Assyrians. The same was true of the remaining aspects of Chaldean culture. Art differed only in its greater magnificence. Literature, dominated by the antiquarian spirit, revealed a monotonous lack of

Chaldean morality

Chaldean achievements in astronomy

Other aspects of Chaldean culture

68 [5] *Ibid.,* pp. 471–74.

originality. The writings of the Old Babylonians were extensively copied and reedited, but they were supplemented by little that was new.

6. THE PERSIAN EMPIRE AND ITS HISTORY

Comparatively little is known of the Persians before the sixth century B.C. Up to that time they appear to have led an obscure and peaceful existence on the eastern shore of the Persian Gulf. Their homeland afforded only modest advantages. On the east it was hemmed in by high mountains, and its coast line was destitute of harbors. The fertile valleys of the interior, however, were capable of providing a generous subsistence for a limited population. Save for the development of an elaborate religion, the people had made little progress. They had no system of writing, but they did have a spoken language closely related to Sanskrit and to the languages of ancient and modern Europe. It is for this reason alone and not because of race that they are accurately referred to as an Indo-European people. At the dawn of their history they were not an independent nation but were vassals of the Medes, a kindred people who ruled over a great empire north and east of the Tigris River.

In 559 B.C. a prince by the name of Cyrus became king of a southern Persian tribe. About five years later he made himself ruler of all the Persians and then developed an ambition for dominion over neighboring peoples. As Cyrus the Great he has gone down in history as one of the most sensational conquerors of all time. Within the short space of twenty years he founded a vast empire, larger than any that had previously existed.

The first of the real conquests of Cyrus was the kingdom of Lydia, which occupied the western half of Asia Minor and was separated from the lands of the Medes only by the Halys River, in what is now northern Turkey. Perceiving the ambitions of the Persians, Croesus, the famous Lydian king, determined to wage a preventive war to preserve his own nation from conquest. He formed alliances with Egypt and Sparta and then consulted the Greek oracle at Delphi as to the advisability of an immediate attack. According to Herodotus, the oracle replied that if he would cross the Halys and assume the offensive he would destroy a great army. He did, but that army was his own. His forces were completely overwhelmed, and his prosperous little kingdom was annexed as a province of the Persian state. Seven years later, in 539 B.C., Cyrus took advantage of discontent and conspiracies in the Chaldean empire to capture the city of Babylon. His victory was an easy one, for he had the assistance of the Jews within the city and of the Chaldean priests, who were dissatisfied with the policies of their king. The conquest of the Chaldean capital made possible the rapid extension of control over

The Persian background

The rise of Cyrus

The conquests of Cyrus

69

the whole empire and thereby added the Fertile Crescent to the domains of Cyrus.

The great conqueror died in 529 B.C., apparently as the result of wounds received in a war with barbarian tribes. Soon afterward a succession of troubles overtook the state he had founded. Like so many other empire builders both before and since, he had devoted too much energy to conquest and not enough to internal development. He was succeeded by his son Cambyses, who conquered Egypt in 525 B.C. During the new king's absence revolt spread throughout his Asiatic possessions. Chaldeans, Elamites, and even the Medes strove to regain their independence. The chief minister of the realm, abetted by the priests, organized a movement to gain possession of the throne for a pretender who was one of their puppets. Upon learning of conditions at home, Cambyses set out from Egypt with his most dependable troops, but he was murdered on the way. The most serious of the revolts was finally crushed by Darius, a powerful noble, who killed the pretender and seized the throne for himself.

Darius I, or the Great, as he has been called by his admirers, ruled the empire from 522 to 486 B.C. The early years of his reign were occupied in suppressing the revolts of subject peoples and in improving the administrative organization of the state. He completed the division of the empire into satrapies, or provinces, and fixed the annual tribute due from each province. He standardized the currency and weights and measures. He repaired and completed a primitive canal from the Nile to the Red Sea. He followed the example of Cyrus in tolerating and protecting the institutions of subject peoples. Not only did he restore ancient temples and foster local cults, but he ordered his satrap of Egypt to codify the Egyptian laws in consultation with the native priests. But in some of his military exploits Darius overreached himself. In order to check the incursions of the Scythians, he crossed the Hellespont, conquered a large part of the Thracian coast, and thereby aroused the hostility of the Athenians. In addition, he increased the oppression of the Ionian Greeks on the shore of Asia Minor, who had fallen under Persian domination with the conquest of Lydia. He interfered with their trade, collected heavier tribute from them, and forced them to serve in his armies. The immediate result was a revolt of the Ionian cities with the assistance of Athens. And when Darius attempted to punish the Athenians for their part in the rebellion, he found himself involved in a war with nearly all the states of Greece.

Darius the Great died while the war with the Greeks was still raging. The struggle was prosecuted vigorously but ineffectively by his successors, Xerxes I and Artaxerxes. By 479 B.C. the Persians had been driven from all of Greece. Though they recovered temporarily possession of the Ionian islands and continued to hold sway as a major power in Asia, their attempt to extend their dominion into

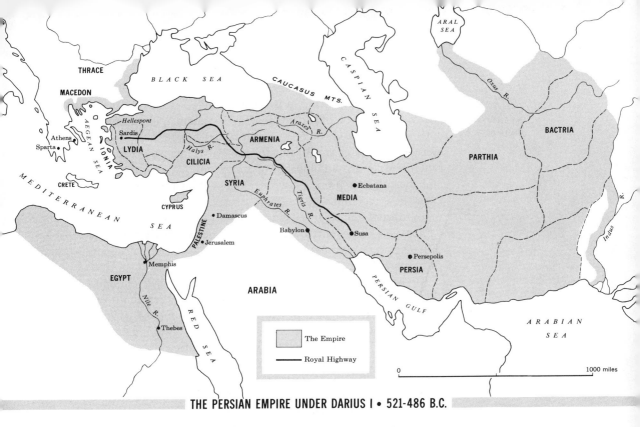

THE PERSIAN EMPIRE UNDER DARIUS I • 521-486 B.C.

Europe had come to an end. The last century and a half of the empire's existence was marked by frequent assassinations, revolts of provincial governors, and barbarian invasions, until finally, in 330 B.C., its independence was annihilated by the armies of Alexander the Great.

Although the Persian government had its defects, it was certainly superior to most of the others that had existed in the Near Orient. The Persian kings did not imitate the terrorism of the Assyrians. They levied tribute upon conquered peoples, but they generally allowed them to keep their own customs, religions, and laws. Indeed, it may be said that the chief significance of the Persian empire lay in the fact that it resulted in a synthesis of Near Eastern cultures, including those of Persia itself, Mesopotamia, Asia Minor, the Syria-Palestine coast, and Egypt.

Significance of the Persian empire

The Persian kings built excellent roads to help hold their empire together. Most famous was the Royal Road, some 1600 miles in length. It extended from Susa near the Persian Gulf to Ephesus on the coast of Asia Minor. So well kept was this highway that the king's messengers, traveling day and night, could cover its entire length in less than a week. Other roads linked the various provinces with one or another of the four Persian capitals: Susa, Persepolis, Babylon, and Ecbatana. Although they naturally contributed to ease of trade, the highways were all built primarily to facilitate control over the outlying sections of the empire.

Persian government

71

7. PERSIAN CULTURE

The eclectic
culture of Persia

The culture of the Persians, in the narrower sense of intellectual and artistic achievements, was largely derived from that of previous civilizations. Much of it came from Mesopotamia, but a great deal of it from Egypt, and some from Lydia and northern Palestine. Their system of writing was originally the Babylonian cuneiform, but in time they devised an alphabet of thirty-nine letters, based upon the alphabet of the Arameans who traded within their borders. In science they accomplished nothing, except to adopt with some slight modifications the solar calendar of the Egyptians and to encourage exploration as an aid to commerce. They deserve credit also for diffusing a knowledge of the Lydian coinage throughout many parts of western Asia.

The eclectic
character of
Persian
architecture

It was the architecture of the Persians which gave the most positive expression of the eclectic character of their culture. They copied the raised platform and the terraced building style that had been so common in Babylonia and Assyria. They imitated also the winged bulls, the brilliantly colored glazed bricks, and other decorative motifs of Mesopotamian architecture. But at least two of the leading features of Mesopotamian construction were not used by the Persians at all—the arch and the vault. In place of them they adopted the column and the colonnade from Egypt. Such matters as interior arrangement and the use of palm and lotus designs at the base of columns also point very distinctly toward Egyptian influence. On the other hand, the fluting of the columns and the volutes or scrolls beneath the capitals were not Egyptian but Greek, adopted not from the mainland of Greece itself but from the Ionian

The Great Palace of Darius and Xerxes at Persepolis. Persian architecture made use of fluted columns, probably copied from the Greeks, and reliefs resembling those of the Assyrians.

Two Reliefs from the Staircase of the Great Palace at Persepolis

cities of Asia Minor. If there was anything unique about Persian architecture, it was the fact that it was purely secular. The great Persian structures were not temples but palaces. They served to glorify not gods, but the "King of Kings." The most famous were the magnificent residences of Darius and Xerxes at Persepolis. The latter, built in imitation of the temple at Karnak, had an enormous central audience-hall containing a hundred columns and surrounded by innumerable rooms which served as offices and as quarters for the eunuchs and members of the royal harem.

8. THE ZOROASTRIAN RELIGION

By far the most enduring influence left by the ancient Persians was that of their religion. Their system of faith was of ancient origin. It was already highly developed when they began their conquests. So strong was its appeal, and so ripe were the conditions for its acceptance, that it spread through most of western Asia. Its doctrines turned other religions inside out, displacing beliefs which had been held for ages.

The religion of the Persians

Although the roots of this religion can be traced as far back as the fifteenth century B.C., its real founder was Zoroaster,[6] who appears to have lived in the early sixth century B.C. From him the religion derives its name of Zoroastrianism. He seems to have conceived it to be his mission to purify the traditional beliefs of his people—to eradicate polytheism, animal sacrifice, and magic—and to establish their worship on a more spiritual and ethical plane. In spite of his reforming efforts many of the old superstitions survived and were gradually fused with the new ideals.

The founding of Zoroastrianism

[6] "Zoroaster" is the corrupt Greek form of the Persian name Zarathustra.

73

Characteristics
of Zoroastrianism:
(1) dualism

In many respects Zoroastrianism had a character unique among the religions of the world up to that time. First of all, it was dualistic—not monistic like the Sumerian and Babylonian religions, in which the same gods were capable of both good and evil; nor did it make any pretensions to monotheism, or belief in a single divinity, as did the Egyptian and Hebrew religions. Two great deities ruled over the universe: one, Ahura-Mazda,[7] supremely good and incapable of any wickedness, embodied the principles of light, truth, and righteousness; the other, Ahriman, treacherous and malignant, presided over the forces of darkness and evil. The two were engaged in a desperate struggle for supremacy. Although they were about evenly matched in strength, the god of light would eventually triumph, and the world would be saved from the powers of darkness.

(2) messianism

Zoroastrianism included such ideas as the coming of a messiah, the resurrection of the dead, a last judgment, and the translation of the redeemed into a paradise eternal. According to the Zoroastrian belief the world would endure for 12,000 years. At the end of 9000 years the second coming of Zoroaster would occur as a sign and a promise of the ultimate redemption of the good. This would be followed in due course by the miraculous birth of a messiah, whose work would be the perfection of the good as a preparation for the end of the world. Finally the last great day would arrive when Ahura-Mazda would overpower Ahriman and cast him down into the abyss. The dead would then be raised from their graves to be judged according to their deserts. The righteous would enter into immediate bliss, while the wicked would be sentenced to the flames of hell. Ultimately, though, all would be saved; for the Persian hell, unlike the Christian, did not last forever.

(3) an ethical
religion

The Zoroastrian religion was definitely an ethical one. Although it contained suggestions of predestination, of the election of some from all eternity to be saved, in the main it rested upon the assumption that men possessed free will, that they were free to sin or not to sin, and that they would be rewarded or punished in the afterlife in accordance with their conduct on earth. Ahura-Mazda commanded that men should be truthful, that they should love and help one another to the best of their power, that they should befriend the poor and practice hospitality. The essence of these broader virtues was perhaps expressed in another of the god's decrees: "Whosoever shall give meat to one of the faithful . . . he shall go to Paradise." The forms of conduct forbidden were sufficiently numerous and varied to cover the whole list of the Seven Cardinal Sins of medieval Christianity and a great many more. Pride, gluttony, sloth, covetousness, wrathfulness, lust, adultery, abortion, slander, and waste were among the more typical. The taking of interest on loans to others of the same faith was described as the "worst of sins," and the accumulation of riches was strongly discountenanced. The restraints which

[7] The name was frequently abbreviated to Mazda.

men were to practice included also a kind of negative Golden Rule: "That nature alone is good which shall not do unto another whatever is not good for its own self." [8]

9. THE MYSTICAL AND OTHERWORLDLY HERITAGE FROM PERSIA

The religion of the Persians as taught by Zoroaster did not long continue in its original state. It was corrupted, first of ·all, by the persistence of primitive superstitions, of magic and priestcraft. The farther the religion spread, the more of these relics of barbarism were engrafted upon it. As the years passed, additional modification resulted from the influence of alien faiths, particularly that of the Chaldeans. The outcome was the growth of a powerful synthesis in which the primitive priestliness, messianism, and dualism of the Persians were combined with the pessimism and fatalism of the Neo-Babylonians.

The fusion of Zoroastrianism with alien faiths

Out of this synthesis gradually emerged a profusion of cults, alike in their basic dogmas but according them different emphasis. The oldest of these cults was Mithraism, deriving its name from Mithras, the chief lieutenant of Mazda in the struggle against the powers of evil. At first only a minor deity in the religion of Zoroastrianism, Mithras finally won recognition in the hearts of many of the Persians as the god most deserving of worship. The reason for this change was probably the emotional appeal made by the incidents of his career. He was believed to have lived an earthly existence involving great suffering and sacrifice. He performed miracles giving bread and wine to man and ending a drought and also a disastrous flood. Finally, he created much of the ritual of Zoroastrianism, proclaiming Sunday as the most sacred day of the week and the twenty-fifth of December as the most sacred day of the year. Since the sun was the giver of light and the faithful ally of Mithras, his day was naturally the most sacred. The twenty-fifth of December also possessed its solar significance: as the approximate date of the winter solstice it marked the return of the sun from his long journey south of the Equator. It was in a sense the "birthday" of the sun, since it connoted the revival of his life-giving powers for the benefit of man.

Mithraism

Exactly when the worship of Mithras became a definite cult is unknown, but it was certainly not later than the fourth century B.C. Its characteristics became firmly established during the period of social ferment which followed the collapse of Alexander's empire, and its spread at that time was exceedingly rapid. In the last century B.C. it was introduced into Rome, although it was of little importance in Italy itself until after 100 A.D. It drew its converts especially from the lower classes, from the ranks of soldiers, foreigners, and slaves. Ultimately it rose to the status of one of the most popular religions

The spread and influence of Mithraism

[8] The quotations in the last paragraph are taken from J. O. Hertzler, *The Social Thought of the Ancient Civilizations*, pp. 149–158.

of the Empire, the chief competitor of Christianity and of old Roman paganism itself. After 275, however, its strength rapidly waned. How much influence this astonishing cult exerted is impossible to say. Its superficial resemblance to Christianity is certainly not hard to perceive, but this does not mean, of course, that the two were identical, or that one was an offshoot of the other. Nevertheless, it is probably true that Christianity as the younger of the two rivals borrowed a good many of its externals from Mithraism, at the same time preserving its own philosophy essentially untouched.

One of the principal successors of Mithraism in transmitting the legacy from Persia was Manicheism, founded by Mani, a high-born priest of Ecbatana, about 250 A.D. Like Zoroaster he conceived it to be his mission to reform the prevailing religion, but he received scant sympathy in his own country and had to be content with missionary ventures in India and western China. About 276 A.D. he was condemned and crucified by his Persian opponents. Following his death his teachings were carried by his disciples into practically every country of western Asia and finally into Italy about 330 A.D. Large numbers of western Manicheans, the great Augustine among them, eventually became Christians.

Manicheism

Of all the Zoroastrian teachings, the one that made the deepest impression upon the mind of Mani was dualism. But Mani gave to this doctrine a broader interpretation than it had ever received in the earlier religion. He conceived not merely of two deities engaged in a relentless struggle for supremacy, but of a whole universe divided into two kingdoms, each the antithesis of the other. The first was the kingdom of spirit ruled over by a God eternally good. The second was the kingdom of matter under the dominion of Satan. Only spiritual" substances such as fire, light, and the souls of men were created by God. Darkness, sin, desire, and all things bodily and material owed their origin to Satan.

*The strict
dualism of the
Manicheans*

The moral implications of this rigorous dualism were readily apparent. Since everything connected with sensation or desire was the work of Satan, man should strive to free himself as completely as possible from enslavement to his physical nature. He should refrain from all forms of sensual enjoyment, the eating of meat, the drinking of wine, the gratification of sexual desire. Even marriage was prohibited, for this would result in the begetting of more physical bodies to people the kingdom of Satan. In addition, man should subdue the flesh by prolonged fasting and infliction of pain. Recognizing that this program of austerities would be too difficult for ordinary mortals, Mani divided the race of mankind into the "perfect" and the "secular." Only the former would be obliged to adhere to the full program as the ideal of what all should hope to attain. To aid the children of men in their struggle against the powers of darkness, God had sent prophets and redeemers from time to time to comfort and inspire them. Noah, Abraham, Zoroaster, Jesus, and Paul were

*The moral implications of
dualism*

numbered among these divine emissaries; but the last and greatest of them was Mani.

The influence of Manicheism is very difficult to estimate, but it was undoubtedly considerable. People of all classes in the Roman Empire, including some members of the Christian clergy, embraced its doctrines. In its Christianized form it became one of the principal sects of the early Church,[9] and it exerted some influence upon the development of the Albigensian heresy as late as the twelfth and thirteenth centuries.

The influence of Manicheism

The third most important cult which developed as an element in the Persian heritage was Gnosticism (from the Greek *gnosis*, meaning knowledge). The name of its founder is unknown, and likewise the date of its origin, but it was certainly in existence as early as the first century A.D. It reached the height of its popularity in the latter half of the second century. Although it gained some followers in Italy, its influence was confined primarily to the Near East.

Gnosticism

The feature which most sharply distinguished this cult from the others was mysticism. The Gnostics denied that the truths of religion could be discovered by reason or could even be made intelligible. They regarded themselves as the exclusive possessors of a secret spiritual knowledge revealed to them directly by God. This knowledge was alone important as a guide to faith and conduct.

The mysticism of the Gnostics

The combined influence of these several Persian religions was enormous. Most of them were launched at a time when political and social conditions were particularly conducive to their spread. The breakup of Alexander's empire about 300 B.C. inaugurated a peculiar period in the history of the ancient world. International barriers were broken down; there was an extensive migration and intermingling of peoples; and the collapse of the old social order gave rise to profound disillusionment and a vague yearning for individual salvation. Men's attentions were centered as never before since the downfall of Egypt upon compensations in a life to come. Under such circumstances religions of the kind described were bound to flourish like the green bay tree. Otherwordly, mystical, and messianic, they offered the very escape that men were seeking from a world of anxiety and confusion.

The combined influence of the several off-shoots of Zoroastrianism

Although not exclusively religious, the heritage left by the Persians contained few elements of a secular nature. Their form of government was adopted by the later Roman monarchs, not in its purely political aspect, but in its character of a divine-right despotism. When such emperors as Diocletian and Constantine I invoked divine authority as a basis for their absolutism and required their subjects to prostrate themselves in their presence, they were really submerging the state in the religion as the Persians had done from the time of Darius. At the same time the Romans were impressed by

Persian Legacy

---

[9] See pp. 334–35

the Persian idea of a world empire. Darius and his successors conceived of themselves as the rulers of the whole civilized world, with a mission to reduce it to unity and, under Ahura-Mazda, to govern it justly. For this reason they generally conducted their wars with a minimum of savagery and treated conquered peoples humanely. Their ideal was a kind of prototype of the *Pax Romana*. Traces of Persian influence upon certain Hellenistic philosophies are also discernible; but here again it was essentially religious, for it was confined almost entirely to the mystical theories of the Neo-Platonists and their philosophical allies.

SELECTED READINGS

• *Items so designated are available in paperbound editions.*

Burn, A. R., *Persia and the Greeks*, New York, 1962.
• Chiera, Edward, *They Wrote on Clay*, Chicago, 1956 (Phoenix).
• Childe, V. G., *What Happened in History*, Baltimore, 1946 (Penguin).
• Contenau, G., *Everyday Life in Babylonia and Assyria*, New York, 1954 (Norton Library). Based on archaeological evidence and well illustrated.
• Cumont, Franz, *The Mysteries of Mithra*, Chicago, 1903 (Dover). A thorough analysis, interestingly presented.
• Frankfort, Henri, *The Birth of Civilization in the Near East*, Bloomington, Ind., 1951 (Anchor). Brief but useful.
• _____, *The Intellectual Adventure of Ancient Man*, Chicago, 1946. Contains evidence of the pessimism of the Mesopotamian peoples.
• Frye, R. N., *The Heritage of Persia*, New York, 1962 (Mentor).
• Ghirshman, Roman, *Iran*, Baltimore, 1954 (Penguin).
• Kramer, S. N., *History Begins at Sumer*, New York, 1959 (Anchor).
• _____, *Sumerian Mythology*, New York, 1961 (Torchbook).
_____, *The Sumerians, Their History, Culture, and Character*, Chicago, 1963.
• Lloyd, Seton, *Foundations in the Dust*, Baltimore, 1955 (Penguin).
• Neugebauer, Otto, *The Exact Sciences in Antiquity*, New York, 1969 (Dover).
Olmstead, A. T. E., *History of Assyria*, New York, 1923. The standard work. Perhaps a little too favorable.
• _____, *History of the Persian Empire (Achaemenid Period)*, Chicago, 1948 (Phoenix). Detailed and complete but somewhat uncritical.
Openheim, A. L., *Ancient Mesopotamia: Portrait of a Dead Civilization*, Chicago, 1964.
• Woolley, C. L., *The Sumerians*, New York, 1928 (Norton Library). A pioneer work, brief and interestingly written.
• _____, *Ur of the Chaldees*, New York, 1965 (Norton Library).
Zaehner, R. C., *The Dawn and Twilight of Zoroastrianism*, New York, 1961.

SOURCE MATERIALS

Barton, G. A., *The Royal Inscriptions of Sumer and Akkad*, New Haven, 1929.
Harper, R. F., ed., *The Code of Hammurabi*, Chicago, 1904.
• Herodotus, *The Persian Wars*, Baltimore, 1954 (Penguin).
Hertzler, J. O., *The Social Thought of the Ancient Civilizations*, New York, 1961, pp. 149–68.
Luckenbill, D. D., ed., *Ancient Records of Assyria and Babylonia*, Chicago, 1926, 2 vols.

CHAPTER 4

The Hebrew Civilization

> I am the Lord thy God, which brought thee out of the land of
> Egypt from the house of bondage.
> Thou shalt have none other Gods before me.
> Thou shalt not make thee any graven image, or any likeness of
> any thing that is in heaven above, or that is in the earth beneath,
> or that is in the waters beneath the earth:
> Thou shalt not bow down thyself unto them, nor serve them: for
> I the Lord thy God am a jealous God, visiting the iniquity of the
> fathers upon the children unto the third and fourth generation of
> them that hate me . . .
> —*Deuteronomy* v. 6–9

Of all the peoples of the ancient Orient, none, with the possible exception of the Egyptians, has been of greater importance to the modern world than the Hebrews. It was the Hebrews, of course, who provided much of the background of the Christian religion— its Commandments, its stories of the Creation and the Flood, its concept of God as lawgiver and judge, and more than two-thirds of its Bible. Hebrew conceptions of morality and political theory have also profoundly influenced modern nations, especially those in which the Calvinist faith has been strong. On the other hand, it is necessary to remember that the Hebrews themselves did not develop their culture in a vacuum. No more than any other people were they able to escape the influence of nations around them.

Importance of the Hebrew civilization

I. HEBREW ORIGINS AND RELATIONS WITH OTHER PEOPLES

The origin of the Hebrew people is still a puzzling problem. Certainly they were not a separate race, nor did they have any physical characteristics sufficient to distinguish them clearly from other nations around them.

Origin of the Hebrews and their name

Most scholars agree that the original home of the Hebrews was the Arabian Desert. The first definite appearance of the founders of the nation of Israel, however, was in northwestern Mesopotamia.

THE HEBREW CIVILIZATION

Hebrew migrations

Apparently as early as 1800 B.C. a group of Hebrews under the leadership of Abraham had settled there. Later Abraham's grandson Jacob led a migration westward and began the occupation of Palestine. It was from Jacob, subsequently called Israel, that the Israelites derived their name. Sometime after 1600 B.C. certain tribes of Israelites, together with other Hebrews, went down into Egypt to escape the consequences of famine. They appear to have settled in the vicinity of the Delta and to have been enslaved by the Pharaoh's government. Around 1300–1250 B.C. their descendants found a new leader in the indomitable Moses, who freed them from bondage, led them to the Sinai Peninsula, and persuaded them to become worshipers of Yahweh, a god whose name is sometimes written erroneously as Jehovah. Hitherto Yahweh had been the deity of Hebrew shepherd folk in the general locality of Sinai. Making use of a Yahwist cult as a nucleus, Moses welded the various tribes of his followers into a confederation, sometimes called the Yahweh Amphictyony. It was this confederation which played the dominant role in the conquest of Palestine, or the Land of Canaan.

The Promised Land

With its scanty rainfall and rugged topography, Palestine as a haven for the Children of Israel left much to be desired. For the most part it was a barren and inhospitable place. But compared with the arid wastes of Arabia it was a veritable paradise, and it is not surprising that the leaders should have pictured it as a "land flowing with milk and honey." Most of it was already occupied by the Canaanites, another people of Semitic speech who had lived there for centuries. Through contact with the Babylonians, Hittites, and Egyptians they had built up a culture which was no longer primitive. They practiced agriculture and carried on trade. They knew the use of iron and the art of writing, and they had adapted the laws of Hammurabi's code to the needs of their simpler existence. Their religion, which was also derived in large part from Babylonia, was cruel and sensual, including human sacrifice and temple prostitution.

Efforts to conquer the Promised Land

The Hebrew conquest of the land of Canaan was a slow and difficult process. Seldom did the tribes unite in a combined attack, and even when they did, the enemy cities were well enough fortified to resist capture. After several generations of sporadic fighting the Hebrews had succeeded in taking only the limestone hills and a few of the less fertile valleys. In the intervals between wars they mingled freely with the Canaanites and adopted no small amount of their culture. Before they had a chance to complete the conquest, they found themselves confronted by a new and more formidable enemy, the Philistines, who had come into Palestine from Asia Minor and from the islands of the Aegean Sea. Stronger than either the Hebrews or Canaanites, the new invaders rapidly overran the country and forced the Hebrews to surrender much of the territory they had already gained. It is from the Philistines that Palestine derives its name.

2. THE RECORD OF POLITICAL HOPES AND FRUSTRATIONS

The crisis produced by the Philistine conquests served not to discourage the Hebrews but to unite them and to intensify their ardor for battle. Moreover, it led directly to the founding of the Hebrew monarchy about 1025 B.C. Up to this time the nation had been ruled by "judges," who possessed little more than the authority of religious leaders. But now with a greater need for organization and discipline, the people demanded a king to rule them and to go out before them and fight their battles. The man selected as the first incumbent of the office was Saul, "a choice young man and a goodly," a member of the tribe of Benjamin.

The founding of the Hebrew monarchy

In spite of his popularity at the start, the reign of King Saul was not a happy one, either for the nation or for the ruler himself. Only a few suggestions of the reasons are given in the Old Testament account. Evidently Saul incurred the displeasure of Samuel, the last of the great judges, who had expected to remain the power behind the throne. Before long there appeared on the scene the ambitious David, who, with the encouragement of Samuel, carried on skillful maneuvers to draw popular support from the king. Waging his own military campaigns, he achieved one bloody triumph after another. By contrast, the armies of Saul met disastrous reverses. Finally the king himself, being critically wounded, requested his armor-bearer to kill him. When the latter would not, he drew his own sword, fell upon it, and died.

The reign of King Saul

David now became king and ruled for forty years. His reign was one of the most glorious periods in Hebrew history. He smote the Philistines hip and thigh and reduced their territory to a narrow strip of coast in the south. He united the Twelve Tribes into a consolidated state under an absolute monarch, and he began the construction of a magnificent capital at Jerusalem. But strong government, military glory, and material splendor were not unmixed blessings for the people. Their inevitable accompaniments were high taxation and conscription. As a consequence, before David died, rumblings of discontent were plainly to be heard in certain parts of his kingdom.

The mighty David

David was succeeded by his son Solomon, the last of the kings of the united monarchy. As a result of the nationalist aspirations of later times, Solomon has been pictured in Hebrew lore as one of the wisest, justest, and most enlightened rulers in all history. The facts of his career furnish little support for such a belief. About all that can be said in his favor is that he was a shrewd diplomat and an active patron of trade. Most of his policies were oppressive, although of course not deliberately so. Ambitious to copy the luxury and magnificence of other Oriental despots, he established a harem of 700 wives and 300 concubines and completed the construction of

Solomon aspires to Oriental magnificence

The Entrance to King David's Tomb on Mount Zion, Jerusalem

sumptuous palaces, stables for 4000 horses, and a costly temple in Jerusalem. Since Palestine was poor in resources, most of the materials for the building projects had to be imported. Gold, silver, bronze, and cedar were brought in in such quantities that the revenues from taxation and from the tolls levied upon trade were insufficient to pay for them. To make up the deficit Solomon ceded twenty towns and resorted to the corvée, or the system of conscripting labor. Every three months 30,000 Hebrews were drafted and sent into Phoenicia to work in the forests and mines of King Hiram of Tyre, from whom the most expensive materials had been purchased.

Solomon's extravagance and oppression produced acute discontent among his subjects. His death in 935 B.C. was the signal for open revolt. The ten northern tribes, refusing to submit to his son Rehoboam, seceded and set up their own kingdom. Sectional differences played their part also in the disruption of the nation. The northern Hebrews were sophisticated and accustomed to urban living. They benefited from their location at the crossroads of Near Eastern trade. While this factor increased their prosperity, it also caused them to be steeped in foreign influences. By contrast, the two southern tribes were composed very largely of pastoral and agricultural folk, loyal to the religion of their fathers, and hating the ways of the foreigner. Perhaps these differences alone would have been sufficient in time to break the nation asunder.

After the secession the ten northern tribes came to be known as the Kingdom of Israel [1] while the two southern tribes were called henceforth the Kingdom of Judah. For more than two centuries the two little states maintained their separate existences. But in 722 B.C. the Kingdom of Israel was conquered by the Assyrians. Its inhabit-

The secession of the Ten Tribes

The fate of Israel and Judah

[1] Or the Kingdom of Samaria, from the name of its capital city.

ants were scattered throughout the vast empire of their conquerors and were eventually absorbed by the more numerous population around them. They have ever since been referred to as the Lost Ten Tribes of Israel. The Kingdom of Judah managed to survive for more than a hundred years longer, successfully defying the Assyrian menace. But in 586 B.C., as we have already learned, it was overthrown by the Chaldeans under Nebuchadnezzar. Jerusalem was plundered and burned, and its leading citizens were carried off into captivity in Babylon. When Cyrus the Persian conquered the Chaldeans, he freed the Jews and permitted them to return to their native land. Few were willing to go, and considerable time elapsed before it was possible to rebuild the temple. From 539 to 332 B.C. Palestine was a vassal state of Persia. In 332 B.C. it was conquered by Alexander and after his death was placed under the rule of the Ptolemies of Egypt. In 63 B.C. it became a Roman protectorate. Its political history as a Jewish commonwealth was ended in 70 A.D. after a desperate revolt which the Romans punished by destroying Jerusalem and annexing the country as a province. The inhabitants were gradually diffused through other parts of the Empire.

The destruction of Jerusalem and annexation of the country by the Romans were the principal factors in the so-called *Diaspora*, or dispersion of the Jews from Palestine. Even earlier large numbers of them had fled into various parts of the Greco-Roman world on account of difficulties in their homeland. In their new environment they rapidly succumbed to foreign influences, a fact which was of tremendous importance in promoting a fusion of Greek and Oriental ideas. It was a Hellenized Jew, St. Paul, who was mainly responsible for remolding Christianity in accordance with Greek philosophical doctrines.

The *Diaspora*

Model of King Solomon's Temple. Significant details are: A, royal gates; B, treasury; C, royal palace; D, people's gate; E, western (wailing) wall; F, priests' quarters; G, courthouse; H, Solomon's porch.

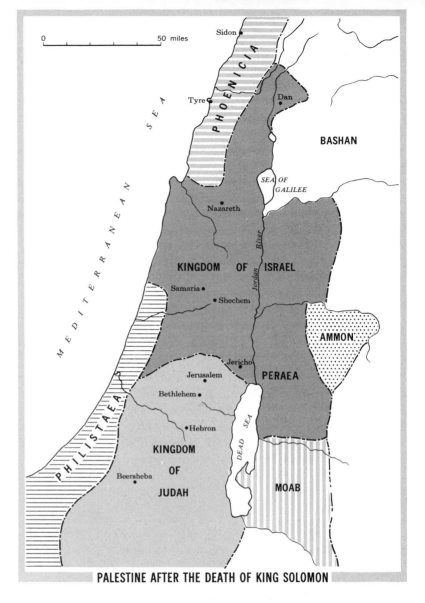

PALESTINE AFTER THE DEATH OF KING SOLOMON

3. THE HEBREW RELIGIOUS EVOLUTION

Reasons for the
varied evolution
of Hebrew
religion

Few peoples in history have gone through a religious evolution comparable to that of the Hebrews. Its cycle of development ranged all the way from the crudest superstitions to the loftiest spiritual and ethical conceptions. Part of the explanation is doubtless to be found in the peculiar geographic position occupied by the Hebrew people. Located as they were after their conquest of Canaan on the highroad between Egypt and the major civilizations of Asia, they were bound to be affected by an extraordinary variety of influences.

At least four different stages can be distinguished in the growth of the Hebrew religion. The first we can call the pre-Mosaic stage, from the earliest beginnings of the people to approximately 1100 B.C. This stage was characterized at first by animism, the worship of spirits that dwelt in trees, mountains, sacred wells and springs, and even in stones of peculiar shape. Diverse forms of magic were practiced also at this time—necromancy, imitative magic, scapegoat sacrifices, and so on. Numerous relics of these early beliefs and practices are preserved in the Old Testament.

Gradually animism gave way to anthropomorphic gods. How this transition occurred cannot be determined. Perhaps it was related to the fact that Hebrew society had become patriarchal, that is, the father exercised absolute authority over the family and descent was traced through the male line. The gods may have been thought to occupy a similar position in the clan or tribe. Apparently few of the new deities were as yet given names; each was usually referred to merely by the generic name of "El," that is, "God." They were guardian deities of particular places and probably of separate tribes. No *national* worship of Yahweh was known at this time.

The second stage, which lasted from the twelfth century B.C. to the ninth, is frequently designated the stage of national monolatry. The term may be defined as the exclusive worship of one god but without any denial that other gods exist. Due chiefly to the influence of Moses, the Hebrews gradually adopted as their national deity during this period a god whose name appears to have been written "Jhwh" or "Yhwh." How it was pronounced no one knows, but scholars generally agree that it was probably uttered as if spelled "Yahweh." The meaning is also a mystery. When Moses inquired of Yahweh what he should tell the people when they demanded to know what god had sent him, Yahweh replied: "I AM THAT I AM: and he said, Thus shalt thou say unto the children of Israel, I AM hath sent me unto you." [2]

During the time of Moses and for two or three centuries thereafter Yahweh was a somewhat peculiar deity. He was conceived almost exclusively in anthropomorphic terms. He possessed a physical body and the emotional qualities of men. He was capricious, on occasions, and somewhat irascible—as capable of evil and wrathful judgments as he was of good. His decrees were often quite arbitrary, and he would punish the man who sinned unwittingly just about as readily as him whose guilt was real.[3] Omnipotence was scarcely an attribute that Yahweh could claim, for his power was limited to the territory occupied by the Hebrews themselves.

The religion of this stage was neither primarily ethical nor profoundly spiritual. Yahweh was revered as a supreme lawgiver and as the stern upholder of the moral order of the universe. According to Biblical account, he issued the Ten Commandments to Moses on top of Mount Sinai. Old Testament scholars, however, do not generally accept this tradition. They admit that a primitive Decalogue may

[2] Exodus 3:13–14.
[3] By way of illustration, he struck Uzza dead merely because that unfortunate individual placed his hand upon the Ark of the Covenant to steady it while it was being transported to Jerusalem. I Chronicles 13:9–10.

have existed in Mosaic times, but they doubt that the Ten Commandments in the form in which they are preserved in the Book of Exodus go back any farther than the seventh century. In any event, it is clear that Moses' God was interested just about as much in sacrifice and in ritualistic observances as he was in good conduct or in purity of heart. Moreover, the religion was not vitally concerned with spiritual matters. It offered naught but material rewards in this life and none at all in a life to come. Finally, the belief in monolatry was corrupted by certain elements of fetishism, magic, and even grosser superstitions that lingered from more primitive times or that were gradually acquired from neighboring peoples. These varied all the way from serpent worship to bloody sacrifices and licentious fertility orgies.

The stage of the prophetic revolution

The really important work of religious reform was accomplished by the great prophets—Amos, Hosea, Isaiah,[4] and Micah. And their achievements represented the third stage in the development of the Hebrew religion, the stage of the prophetic revolution, which occupied the eighth and seventh centuries B.C. The great prophets were men of broader vision than any of their forerunners. Their outlook was progressive; they did not demand a return to some age of simplicity in the past but taught that the religion should be infused with a new philosophy and a new conception of the ends it was supposed to serve. Three basic doctrines made up the substance of their teachings: (1) rudimentary monotheism—Yahweh is the Lord of the universe; He even makes use of nations other than the Hebrews to accomplish his purposes; the gods of other peoples are false gods and should not be worshiped for any reason; (2) Yahweh is a god of righteousness exclusively; He is not really omnipotent, but His power is limited by justice and goodness; the evil in the world comes from man not from God; (3) the purposes of religion are chiefly ethical; Yahweh cares nothing for ritual and sacrifice, but that men should "seek justice, relieve the oppressed, judge the fatherless, plead for the widow." Or as Micah expressed it: "What doth the Lord require of thee, but to do justly, and to love mercy, and to walk humbly with thy God?"[5]

Contrasts with the older religion; political and social aspects

These doctrines contained a definite repudiation of nearly everything that the older religion had stood for. Such, however, was apparently not the intention of the prophets. They conceived it rather as their mission to restore the religion to its ancient purity. The crudities within it they regarded as foreign corruptions. But like many such leaders, they builded better than they knew. Their actual accomplishments went so far beyond their original objectives that

[4] Many Old Testament authorities consider the Book of Isaiah the work of two authors. They ascribe the first part to Isaiah, and the second part, beginning with Chapter 40, to Deutero-Isaiah, or the Second Isaiah. The Second Isaiah is more emphatic than the first in denying the existence of the gods of other peoples. It dates from the period of the Exile.
[5] Micah 6:8.

Remains of an Ancient Synagogue at Capernaum. Capernaum was supposed to have been the scene of many of the miracles attributed to Jesus. Here also he called out Peter, Andrew, and Matthew to be his disciples.

they amounted to a religious revolution. To a considerable extent this revolution also had its social and political aspects. Wealth had become concentrated in the hands of a few. Thousands of small farmers had lost their freedom and had passed under subjection to rich proprietors. If we can believe the testimony of Amos, bribery was so rife in the law courts that the plaintiff in a suit for debt had merely to give the judge a pair of shoes and the defendant would be handed over as a slave.[6] Overshadowing all was the threat of Assyrian domination. To enable the nation to cope with that threat, the prophets believed that social abuses should be stamped out and the people united under a religion purged of its alien corruptions.

The results of this revolution must not be misinterpreted. It did eradicate some of the most flagrant forms of oppression, and it rooted out permanently most of the barbarities that had crept into the religion from foreign sources. But the Hebrew faith did not yet bear much resemblance to modern orthodox Judaism. It contained little of a spiritual character and hardly a trace of the mystical. Instead of being otherwordly, it was oriented toward this life. Its purposes were social and ethical—to promote a just and harmonious society and to abate man's inhumanity to man—not to confer individual salvation in an afterlife. As yet there was no belief in heaven and hell or in Satan as a powerful opponent of God. The shades of the dead went down into Sheol to linger there for a time in the dust and gloom and then disappear.

The religion not yet otherworldly or mystical

The final significant stage in Hebrew religious evolution was the post-Exilic stage or the period of Persian influence. This period may be considered to have covered the years from 539 to about 300 B.C. Perhaps enough has been said already to indicate the character of the influence from Persia. It will be recalled from the preceding

The post-Exilic stage

[6] Amos 2:6. This, of course, was poetic propaganda and may have been slightly exaggerated.

87

chapter that Zoroastrianism was a dualistic, messianic, otherwordly, and esoteric religion. In the period following the Exile these ideas gained wide acceptance among the Jews. They adopted a belief in Satan as the Great Adversary and the author of evil. They developed an eschatology, including such notions as the coming of a spiritual savior, the resurrection of the dead, and a last judgment. They turned their attention to salvation in an afterworld as more important than enjoyment of this life. Lastly, they embraced the conception of a revealed religion. The Book of Ezekiel, for example, was asserted to have been prepared by God in heaven and given to the man whose name it bears with instruction to "eat" it.[7]

4. HEBREW CULTURE

The limitations of the Hebrew genius

In certain respects the Hebrew genius was inferior to that of some other great nations of antiquity. In the first place, it revealed no talent for science. Not a single important discovery in any scientific field has ever been traced to the ancient Hebrews. Nor were they particularly adept in appropriating the knowledge of others. They could not build a bridge or a tunnel except of the crudest sort. Whether it was from lack of interest in these things or whether it was because of too deep an absorption in religious affairs is not clear. In the second place, they seem to have been almost entirely devoid of artistic skill. Their only examples of the glyptic arts were engraved seals similar to those made by the Sumerians and Hittites and used for the purpose of affixing signatures. They had no architecture, sculpture, or painting worthy of mention. The famous temple at Jerusalem was not a Hebrew building at all but a product of Phoenician skill, for Solomon imported artisans from Tyre to finish the more complicated tasks.

Hebrew law

It was rather in law, literature, and philosophy that the Hebrew genius was most perfectly expressed. Although all of these subjects were closely allied with religion, they did have their secular aspects. The finest example of Jewish law was the Deuteronomic Code, which forms the core of the Book of Deuteronomy. Despite claims of its great antiquity, it was probably an outgrowth of the prophetic revolution. It was based in part upon an older Code of the Covenant, which was derived in considerable measure from the laws of the Canaanites and the Old Babylonians.[8] In general, its provisions were more enlightened than those of Hammurabi's code. One of them enjoined liberality to the poor and to the stranger. Another commanded that the Hebrew slave who had served six years should be freed, and insisted that he must not be sent away empty. A third provided that judges and other officers should be chosen by the peo-

[7] Ezekiel 3:1–4.
[8] C. F. Kent, *The Message of Israel's Lawgivers*, p. 24.

ple and forbade them to accept gifts or to show partiality in any form. A fourth condemned witchcraft, divination, and necromancy. A fifth denounced the punishment of children for the guilt of their fathers and affirmed the principle of individual responsibility for sin. A sixth prohibited the taking of interest on any kind of loan made by one Jew to another. A seventh required that at the end of every seven years there should be a "release" of debts. "Every creditor that lendeth aught unto his neighbour shall release it; he shall not exact it of his neighbour, or of his brother . . . save when there shall be no poor among you." [9]

The literature of the Hebrews was by far the best that the ancient Orient ever produced. Nearly all of it now extant is preserved in the Old Testament and in the books of the so-called Apocrypha. Except for a few fragments like the Song of Deborah in Judges 5, it is not really so ancient as is commonly supposed. Scholars now recognize that the Old Testament was built up mainly through a series of collections and revisions (redactions) in which the old and new fragments were merged and generally assigned to an ancient author, Moses, for example. But the oldest of these redactions was not prepared any earlier than 850 B.C. The majority of the books of the Old Testament were of even more recent origin, with the exception, of course, of certain of the chronicles. As one would logically expect, the philosophical books were of late authorship. Although the bulk of the Psalms were ascribed to King David, a good many of them actually refer to events of the Captivity. It seems certain that the collection as a whole was the work of several centuries. Most recent of all were the books of Ecclesiastes, Esther, and Daniel, composed no earlier than the third century B.C. Likewise, the Apocrypha, or books of doubtful religious authority, did not see the light of day until Hebrew civilization was almost extinct. Some, like Maccabees I and II, relate events of the second century B.C. Others including the Wisdom of Solomon and the Book of Enoch were written under the influence of Greco-Oriental philosophy.

Not all of the writings of the Hebrews had high literary merit. A considerable number were dull, repetitious chronicles. Nevertheless, most of them, whether in the form of battle song, prophecy, love lyric, or drama, were rich in rhythm, concrete images, and emotional vigor. Few passages in any language can surpass the scornful indictment of social abuses voiced by the prophet Amos:

> Hear this, O ye that swallow up the needy, even to make the
> poor of the land to fail,
> Saying, when will the new moon be gone, that we may sell
> corn?
> And the sabbath that we may set forth wheat,
> Making the ephah small, and the shekel great,

The Shekel of Ancient Israel. Struck between 141 and 137 B.C., this silver coin is approximately half the weight of a United States silver dollar.

Hebrew literature

Amos' indictment of social abuses

[9] Deuteronomy 15:1–4.

And falsifying the balances by deceit?
That we may buy the poor for silver, and the needy for a pair
of shoes;
Yea, and sell the refuse of the wheat?

The most beautiful of Hebrew love lyrics was the Song of Songs,
or the Song of Solomon. Its theme was quite probably derived from
The Song of an old Canaanite hymn of spring, celebrating the passionate affec-
Songs tion of the Shulamith or fertility goddess for her lover, but it had
long since lost its original meaning. The following verses are typical
of its sensuous beauty:

I am the rose of Sharon
and the lily of the valleys.
As the lily among thorns,
so is my love among the daughters.

. . . .

My beloved is white and ruddy,
the chiefest among ten thousand.
His head is as the most fine gold;
his locks are bushy and black as a raven:
His eyes are as the eyes of doves by the rivers of waters,
washed with milk and fitly set.
His cheeks are as a bed of spices, as sweet flowers;
his lips like lilies, dropping sweet smelling myrrh.

. . . .

How beautiful are thy feet with shoes, O prince's daughter!
The joints of thy thighs are like jewels,
the work of the hands of a cunning workman.

Few authorities would deny that the supreme achievement of the
Hebrew literary genius was the Book of Job. In form the work is a
The Book of drama of the tragic struggle between man and fate. Its central theme
Job is the problem of evil: how it can be that the righteous suffer while
the eyes of the wicked stand out with fatness. The story was an old
one, adapted very probably from the Babylonian writing of similar
content, but the Hebrews introduced into it a much deeper realization of philosophical possibilities. The main character, Job, a man of
unimpeachable virtue, is suddenly overtaken by a series of disasters:
he is despoiled of his property, his children are killed, and his body
is afflicted with a painful disease. His attitude at first is one of stoic
resignation; the evil must be accepted along with the good. But as
his sufferings increase he is plunged into despair. He curses the day
of his birth and delivers an apostrophe to death, where "the wicked
cease from troubling and the weary be at rest."

Then follows a lengthy debate between Job and his friends over the meaning of evil. The latter take the traditional Hebraic view that all suffering is a punishment for sin, and that those who repent are forgiven and strengthened in character. But Job is not satisfied with any of their arguments. Torn between hope and despair, he strives to review the problem from every angle. He even considers the possibility that death may not be the end, that there may be some adjustment of the balance hereafter. But the mood of despair returns, and he decides that God is an omnipotent demon, destroying without mercy wherever His caprice or anger directs. Finally, in his anguish he appeals to the Almighty to reveal Himself and make known His ways to man. God answers him out of the whirlwind with a magnificent exposition of the tremendous works of nature. Convinced of his own insignificance and of the unutterable majesty of God, Job despises himself and repents in dust and ashes. In the end no solution is given of the problem of individual suffering. No promise is made of recompense in a life hereafter, nor does God make any effort to refute the hopeless pessimism of Job. Man must take comfort in the philosophic reflection that the universe is greater than himself, and that God in the pursuit of His sublime purposes cannot really be limited by human standards of equity and goodness.

As philosophers the Hebrews surpassed every other people before the Greeks, including the Egyptians. Although they were not brilliant metaphysicians and constructed no great theories of the universe, they did concern themselves with most of the problems relating to the life and destiny of man. Their thought was essentially personal rather than abstract. Probably the earliest of their writings of a distinctly philosophical character were the Book of Proverbs and the Book of Ecclesiasticus. In their final form both were of late composition, but much of the material they contain was doubtless quite ancient. Not all of it was original, for a considerable portion had been taken from Egypt sources as early as 1000 B.C. The books have as their essential teaching: be temperate, diligent, wise, and honest, and you will surely be rewarded with prosperity, long life, and a good name among men. Only in such isolated passages as the following is any recognition given to higher motives of sympathy or respect for the rights of others: "Whoso mocketh the poor reproacheth his Maker; and he that is glad at calamities shall not be unpunished." [10]

A much more profound and critical philosophy is contained in Ecclesiastes, an Old Testament book, not to be confused with the Ecclesiasticus mentioned above. The author of Ecclesiastes is unknown. In some way it came to be attributed to Solomon, but he certainly did not write it, for it includes doctrines and forms of

[10] Proverbs 17:5.

expression unknown to the Hebrews for hundreds of years after his death. Modern critics date it no earlier than the third century B.C. The basic ideas of its philosophy may be summarized as follows:

(1) Mechanism. The universe is a machine that rolls on forever without evidence of any purpose or goal. Sunrise and sunset, birth and death are but separate phases of constantly recurring cycles.

(2) Fatalism. Man is a victim of the whims of fate. There is no necessary relation between effort and success. "The race is not to the swift, nor the battle to the strong, neither yet bread to the wise . . . but time and chance happeneth to them all."

(3) Pessimism. All is vanity and vexation of spirit. Fame, riches, extravagant pleasure are snares and delusions in the end. Although wisdom is better than folly, even it is not a sure key to happiness, for an increase in knowledge brings a keener awareness of suffering.

(4) Moderation. Extremes of asceticism and extremes of indulgence are both to be avoided. "Be not righteous over much . . . be not over much wicked: why shouldest thou die before thy time?" [11]

5. THE MAGNITUDE OF THE HEBREW INFLUENCE

The nature of the Hebrew influence

The influence of the Hebrews, like that of most other Oriental peoples, has been chiefly religious and ethical. While it is true that the Old Testament has served as a source of inspiration for much of the literature and art of the Renaissance and early modern civilizations, this has resulted largely because the Bible was already familiar material as a part of the religious heritage. The same explanation can be applied to the use of the Old Testament as a source of law and political theory by the Calvinists in the sixteenth century, and by many other Christians both before and since.

Hebrew foundations of Christianity: the beliefs of the Pharisees

But these facts do not mean that the Hebrew influence has been slight. On the contrary, the history of nearly every Western civilization during the past two thousand years would have been radically different without the heritage from Israel. For it must be remembered that Hebrew beliefs were among the principal foundations of Christianity. The relationship between the two religions is frequently misunderstood. The movement inaugurated by Jesus of Nazareth is commonly represented as a revolt against Judaism; but such was only partly the case. On the eve of the Christian era the Jewish nation had come to be divided into three main sects: a majority sect of Pharisees, and two minority sects of Sadducees and Essenes. The Pharisees represented the middle classes and some of the better educated common folk. They believed in the resurrection, in rewards and punishments after death, and in the coming of a political messiah. Intensely nationalistic, they advocated participation in government and faithful observance of the ancient ritual.

[11] For a more complete analysis of the philosophy of Ecclesiastes see Morris Jastrow, *A Gentle Cynic*.

They regarded all parts of the law as of virtually equal importance, whether they applied to matters of ceremony or to obligations of social ethics.

Representing altogether different strata of society, the minority sects disagreed with the Pharisees on both religious and political issues. The Sadducees, including the priests and the wealthier classes, were most famous for their denial of the resurrection and of rewards and punishments in an afterlife. Although temporarily, at least, they favored the acceptance of Roman rule, their attitude toward the ancient law was even more inflexible than that of the Pharisees. The sect of Essenes, the smallest of them all, was possibly the most influential. Its members, who were drawn from the lower classes, practiced asceticism and preached otherworldliness as means of protest against the wealth and power of priests and rulers. They ate and drank only enough to keep themselves alive, held all their goods in common, and looked upon marriage as a necessary evil. Far from being fanatical patriots, they regarded government with indifference and refused to take oaths under any conditions. They emphasized the spiritual aspects of religion rather than the ceremonial, and stressed particularly the immortality of the soul, the coming of a religious messiah, and the early destruction of the world.

The Sadducees and the Essenes

Until recently scholars were dependent for their knowledge of the Essenes almost entirely upon secondary sources. But in 1947 an Arab shepherd unwittingly opened the way to one of the most spectacular discoveries of documentary evidence in world history. Searching for a lost sheep on the western shore of the Dead Sea, he threw a stone that entered a hole in the rocks and made such a peculiar noise that he ran away in fright. He returned, however, with a friend to investigate and discovered a cave in which were stored

The Dead Sea scrolls

The Dead Sea Scrolls. Now on display in an underground vault at the Hebrew University in Jerusalem. The oldest extant examples of Hebrew religious literature, they furnish us with evidence of the activities of the Essenes and mystical and other worldly sects about the beginning of the Christian era.

about fifty cylindrical earthen jars stuffed with writings on leather scrolls. Studied by scholars, the scrolls revealed the existence of a monastic community which flourished from about 130 B.C. to 67 A.D. Its members lived a life of humility and self-denial, holding their goods in common, and devoting their time to prayer and sacraments and to studying and copying Biblical texts. They looked forward confidently to the coming of a messiah, the overthrow of evil, and the establishment of God's kingdom on earth. That they belonged to the same general movement that fostered the growth of the Essenes seems almost beyond question.

All branches of Judaism except the Sadducees strongly influenced the development of Christianity. From Jewish sources Christianity obtained its cosmogony, or theory of the origin of the universe; the Ten Commandments; and a large portion of its theology. Jesus himself, although he condemned the Pharisees for their legalism and hypocrisy, did not repudiate all of their tenets. Instead of abolishing the ancient law, as he is popularly supposed to have done, he demanded its fulfillment, insisting, however, that it should not be made the essential part of religion. To what extent the beliefs and practices of the Christian religion were molded by the more radical Judaism of the Essenes and kindred sects is a question whose answer must await further research. Nonetheless, we know that many early Christians practiced asceticism, regarded government with indifference and the Roman Empire with hostility, held all their goods in common, and believed in the imminent end of the world. These parallels do not mean, of course, that Christianity was a mere adaptation of beliefs and practices emanating from Judaism. There was much in it that was unique; but that is a subject which can be discussed more conveniently in another connection.[12]

The ethical and political influence of the Hebrews has also been substantial. Their moral conceptions have been a leading factor in the development of the negative approach toward ethics which has prevailed for so long in Western countries. For the early Hebrews, "righteousness" consisted primarily in the observance of taboos. Although a positive morality of charity and social justice made rapid headway during the time of the prophets, this in turn was partly obscured by the revival of priestly influence in the period that followed. With respect to political influence, the record is more impressive. Hebrew ideals of limited government, the sovereignty of law, and regard for the dignity and worth of the individual have been among the major formative influences which have shaped the growth of modern democracy. It is now almost universally recognized that the traditions of Judaism contributed equally with the influence of Christianity and Stoic philosophy in fostering recognition of the rights of man and in promoting the development of the free society.

Hebrew influence upon Christianity

Ethical and political influence of the Hebrews

[12] See chapter on The Civilization of the Early Middle Ages.

· *Items so designated are available in paperbound editions.*

· Albright, W. F., *The Archaeology of Palestine*, Baltimore, 1960 (Penguin).

Anderson, B. W., *Rediscovering the Bible*, New York, 1951.

Bertholet, Alfred, *A History of Hebrew Civilization*, London, 1926.

· Chase, Mary E., *Life and Language in the Old Testament*, New York, 1955 (Norton Library).

· Davies, A. P., *The Meaning of the Dead Sea Scrolls*, New York, 1956 (Mentor).

· De Burgh, W. G., *The Legacy of the Ancient World*, 3d ed., New York, 1960 (Penguin). A good survey of the influence of Hebrew thought.

Finegan, Jack, *Light from the Ancient Past*, Princeton, 1946.

Fritsch, C. T., *The Qumrān Community*, New York, 1956. Relates the importance of the Dead Sea Scrolls.

· Frye, R. N., *The Heritage of Persia*, Cleveland, 1963 (Mentor).

· Kenyon, K. M., *Archaeology in the Holy Land*, New York, 1960 (Praeger).

Klausner, Joseph, *The Messianic Idea in Israel*, New York, 1955.

Lods, Adolphe, *Israel from Its Beginnings to the Middle of the Eighth Century*, New York, 1932. Excellent on religious, intellectual, and social history.

· Meek, T. J., *Hebrew Origins*, rev., New York, 1951 (Torchbook).

Oesterley, W. O. E., and Robinson, T. H., *Hebrew Religion, Its Origin and Development*, New York, 1932. One of the best interpretations.

Olmstead, A. T. E., *History of Palestine and Syria*, New York, 1931.

· Orlinsky, H. M., *Ancient Israel*, Ithaca, 1956 (Cornell). Brief but good.

· Roth, Cecil, *The Dead Sea Scrolls*, New York, 1965 (Norton Library). Author contends that the scrolls were not produced by the Essenes but by the Zealots, a warlike sect deeply involved in the rebellion against Rome in 66 A.D.

Smith, J. M. P., *The Moral Life of the Hebrews*, Chicago, 1923.

————, *The Origin and History of Hebrew Law*, Chicago, 1931.

Vaux, Roland de, *Ancient Israel: Its Life and Institutions*, New York, 1962. Especially valuable for archaeological data.

SOURCE MATERIALS

The Apocrypha, Ancient Hebrew writings of doubtful authorship. Not recognized as scriptural by Hebrew and Protestant theologians.

· Gaster, T. H., trans., *The Dead Sea Scriptures in English Translation*. New York, 1964 (Anchor).

The Old Testament, especially the following books and portions of books: Deuteronomy 5, 12–21; Ecclesiastes; Amos; I Samuel 8–31; II Samuel; I Kings 1–12; Job; Proverbs; Isaiah 1–12, 40–66; Micah; Psalms.

Pritchard, J. B., ed., *Ancient Near Eastern Texts Relating to the Old Testament*, rev. ed., Princeton, 1955.

CHAPTER 5

The Hittite, Minoan-Mycenaean, and Lesser Cultures

> But for them among these gods will be bled for annual food:
> to the god Karnua one steer and one sheep;
> to the goddess Kupapa one steer and one sheep;
> to the divinity Sarku one sheep;
> and a Kutupalis sheep to the male divinities.
>
> —Hittite sacrifice formula, translated
> from a hieroglyph by
> H. T. Bossert

A few other ancient cultures of the Near Orient require more than passing attention. Chief among them are the Hittite, Minoan-Mycenaean, Phoenician, and Lydian cultures. The Hittites are important primarily as intermediaries between East and West. They were one of the main connecting links between the civilizations of Egypt, the Tigris-Euphrates valley, and the region of the Aegean Sea. It appears certain also that they were the original discoverers of iron. The Minoan-Mycenaean civilization is significant for its remarkable achievements in the arts and for its quality of freedom and courage for experimentation. Though many of its achievements perished, there is evidence that the Greeks owed to these Aegean peoples a considerable debt. The Greek religion, for example, contained numerous Minoan-Mycenaean elements. Of the same origin were probably the devotion of the Greeks to athletics, their system of weights and measures, their knowledge of navigation, and perhaps also a great many of their artistic traditions. As for the Phoenicians, no one could overlook the importance of their distribution of a knowledge of the alphabet and a primitive commercial law to the surrounding civilized world. The Lydians have gone down in history as the originators of the first system of coinage.

Importance of these cultures

97

1. THE HITTITES AND THE PHRYGIANS

Until about a century ago little was known of the Hittites except their name. They were commonly assumed to have played no role of any significance in the drama of history. The slighting references to them in the Bible give the impression that they were little more than a half-barbarian tribe. But in 1870 some curiously inscribed stones were found at Hamath in Syria. This was the beginning of an extensive inquiry which has continued with a few interruptions to the present day. It was not long until scores of other monuments and clay tablets were discovered over most of Asia Minor and through the Near East as far as the Tigris-Euphrates valley. In 1907 some evidences of an ancient city were unearthed near the village of Boghaz-Keui in the province of Anatolia. Further excavation eventually revealed the ruins of a great fortified capital which was known as Hattusas or Hittite City. Within its walls were discovered more than 20,000 documents and fragments, most of them apparently laws and decrees.

On the basis of these finds and other evidences gradually accumulated, it was soon made clear that the Hittites were once the rulers of a mighty empire covering most of Asia Minor and extending to the upper reaches of the Euphrates. Part of the time it included Syria as well and even portions of Phoenicia and Palestine. The Hittites reached the zenith of their power during the years from 2000 to 1200 B.C. In the last century of this period they waged a long and exhausting war with Egypt, which had much to do with the downfall of both empires. Neither was able to regain its strength. After 1200 B.C. Carchemish on the Euphrates River became for a time the leading Hittite city, but as a commercial center rather than as the capital of a great empire. The days of imperial glory were over. Finally, after 717 B.C., all the remaining Hittite territories were conquered and absorbed by the Assyrians, Lydians, and Phrygians.

The mystery of
the race and
language of the
Hittites

Where the Hittites came from and what were their relationships to other peoples are problems which still defy a perfect solution. As depicted by the Egyptians, some of them appear to have been of a Mongoloid type. All had enormous hooked noses, receding foreheads, and slanting eyes. Most modern scholars trace their place of origin to Turkestan and consider them related to the Greeks. Their language was Indo-European. Its secret was unlocked during World War I by the Czech scholar Bedrich Hrozny. Since then thousands of clay tablets making up the laws and official records of the emperors have been deciphered. They reveal a civilization resembling more closely the Old Babylonian than any other.

Hardly enough evidence has yet been collected to make possible an accurate appraisal of Hittite civilization. Some modern historians refer to it as if it were on a level with the Mesopotamian or even with the Egyptian civilization. Such may have been the case from the material standpoint, for the Hittites undoubtedly had an extensive knowledge of agriculture and a highly developed economic life in general. They mined great quantities of silver, copper, and lead, which they sold to surrounding nations. They discovered the mining and use of iron and made that material available for the rest of the civilized world. Trade was also one of their principal economic pursuits. In fact, they seem to have depended almost as much upon commercial penetration as upon war for the expansion of their empire.

The literature of the Hittites consisted chiefly of mythology, including adaptations of creation and flood legends from the Old Babylonians. They had nothing that could be described as philosophy, nor is there any evidence of scientific originality outside of the metallurgical arts. They evidently possessed some talent for the perfection of writing, for in addition to a modified cuneiform adapted from Mesopotamia they also developed a hieroglyphic system which was partly phonetic in character.

One of the most significant achievements of the Hittites was their system of law. Approximately two hundred separate paragraphs or decrees, covering a great variety of subjects, have been translated. They reflect a society comparatively urbane and sophisticated but subject to minute governmental control. The title to all land was vested in the king or in the governments of the cities. Grants were made to individuals only in return for military service and under the strict requirement that the land be cultivated. Prices were fixed in the laws themselves for an enormous number of commodities—not only for articles of luxury and the products of industry, but even for food and clothing. All wages and fees for services were likewise minutely prescribed, with the pay of women fixed at less than half the rate for men.

On the whole, the Hittite law was more humane than that of the Old Babylonians. Death was the punishment for only eight offenses —such as witchcraft, and theft of property from the palace. Even premeditated murder was punishable only by a fine. Mutilation was not specified as a penalty at all except for arson or theft when committed by a slave. The contrast with the cruelties of Assyrian law was more striking. Not a single example is to be found in the Hittite decrees of such fiendish punishments as flaying, castration, and impalement, which the rulers at Nineveh seemed to think necessary for maintaining their authority.

The art of the Hittites was not of outstanding excellence. So far as we know, it included only sculpture and architecture. The former was generally crude and naïve, but at the same time it revealed a freshness and vigor all too uncommon in the work of Oriental peoples. Most of it was in the form of reliefs depicting scenes of war and mythology. Architecture was ponderous and huge. Temples and palaces were squat, unadorned structures with small, two-columned porches and great stone lions guarding the entrance.

The economic life of the Hittites

The intellectual level of Hittite culture

Hittite law

Humane character of Hittite law

The art of the Hittites

99

Hittite Sculpture. Perhaps the most highly conventionalized sculpture of the ancient world is found in Hittite reliefs.

Hittite religion

Not a great deal is known about the Hittite religion except that it had an elaborate mythology, innumerable deities, and forms of worship of Mesopotamian origin. A sun god was worshiped, along with a host of other deities, some of whom appear to have had no particular function at all. The Hittites seem to have welcomed into the divine company practically all of the gods of the peoples they conquered and even of the nations that bought their wares. The practices of the religion included divination, sacrifice, purification ceremonies, and the offering of prayers. Nothing can be found in the records to indicate that the religion was in any sense ethical.

The importance of the Hittites

The chief historical importance of the Hittites probably lies in the role which they played as intermediaries between the Tigris-Euphrates valley and the westernmost portions of the Near East. Doubtless in this way certain culture elements from Mesopotamia were transmitted to the Canaanites and Hyksos and perhaps to the peoples of the Aegean islands.

2. THE MINOAN-MYCENAEAN CIVILIZATION

A long-forgotten civilization

By a strange coincidence the discovery of the existence of the Hittite and Minoan-Mycenaean civilizations was made at just about the same time. Before 1870 scarcely anyone dreamed that great civilizations had flourished on the Aegean islands and on the shores of Asia Minor for hundreds of years prior to the rise of the Greeks. Students of the *Iliad* knew, of course, of the references to a strange people who were supposed to have dwelt in Troy, to have kidnaped the fair Helen, and to have been punished by the Greeks for this act by the siege and destruction of their city; but it was commonly supposed that these accounts were mere figments of a poetical imagination.

The first discovery of a highly developed Aegean culture center was made not by a professional archaeologist but by a retired German businessman, Heinrich Schliemann. Fascinated from early

100

youth by the stories of the Homeric epics, he determined to dedicate his life to archaeological research as soon as he had sufficient income to enable him to do so. Luckily for him and for the world he accumulated a fortune in Russian petroleum and then retired from business to spend both time and money in the pursuit of his boyhood dreams. In 1870 he began excavating at Troy. Within a few years he had uncovered portions of nine different cities, each built upon the ruins of its predecessor. The second of these cities he identified as the Troy of the *Iliad*, although it has been proved since that Troy was the seventh city. After fulfilling his first great ambition, he started excavations on the mainland of Greece and eventually uncovered two other Aegean cities, Mycenae and Tiryns. The work of Schliemann was soon followed by that of other investigators, notably the Englishman Sir Arthur Evans, who discovered Knossos, the resplendent capital of the Minoan kings of Crete. Up to the present time more than half of the ancient Aegean sites have been carefully searched, and a wealth of knowledge has been accumulated about various aspects of the culture.

The discoveries by Schliemann and others

The Minoan-Mycenaean civilization appears to have originated on the island of Crete, from which it spread to the mainland of Greece and to Asia Minor. In few other cases in history does the geographic interpretation of culture origins fit so neatly. Crete has a benign and equable climate, neither so hot as to make men lazy nor so cold as to require a life of unceasing struggle. While the soil is fertile, it is not of unlimited area; consequently, as the population increased, men were impelled to sharpen their wits and to contrive new means of earning a living. Some emigrated; others took to the sea; but a larger number remained at home and developed articles for export. The latter included, especially, wine and olive oil, pottery, gems and seals, knives and daggers, and objects of skilled craftsmanship. The chief imports were foodstuffs and metals. As a result of such trade, the country became an industrial and commercial nation with pros-

The favorable natural environment of Crete

The Goddess Cybele. A Roman statue depicting the Phrygian goddess on a processional cart drawn by lions.

The glory and
the downfall of
the Minoan-
Mycenaean
civilization

perous cities and extensive contacts with the surrounding civilized world. Added to these factors of a favorable environment were the beauties of nature, which abounded almost everywhere, stimulating the development of a marvelous art.

The Minoan civilization was one of the earliest in the history of the world. As far back as 3000 B.C. the natives of Crete had made the transition from the Neolithic stage to the age of metals and probably to the age of writing. The first peak of advancement was attained under the leadership of the cities of Knossos and Phaistos about 1800 B.C. Recently evidence has been found of the existence of another great city, Kato Zakros, on the east coast of Crete. Here was a huge palace of 250 rooms, with a swimming pool, parquet floors, and thousands of decorated vases. About 1450 B.C. this palace was destroyed by volcanic eruptions followed by violent earthquakes. Other cities probably suffered a similar fate, although Knossos and Phaistos were rebuilt. A new dynasty came to the throne of Crete. A new system of writing was adopted, and a new cycle of civilization began which carried Minoan culture to its greatest heights.

After about fifty years of uncertainty the Minoan-Mycenaean civilization rose to new heights of brilliance and strength. Troy and the cities of Crete were rebuilt, and other great centers were established at Mycenae and Tiryns. Soon afterward Cretan hegemony was extended over the remaining portions of the Aegean world. But the new age of power and splendor was not destined for long duration. The island's resources were substantially depleted, and commerce with Egypt had diminished. In the sixteenth century B.C. a group of barbarian Greeks subsequently known as Achaeans expanded from their original home in the northern Peloponnesus and eventually conquered Mycenae. Gradually absorbing the material culture of the vanquished, they became rich and powerful sea lords. About 1400 B.C. they overwhelmed the city of Knossos, and soon the whole island of Crete passed under their sway. Although they were no longer a primitive people, they seem never to have appreciated the finer aspects of Cretan culture. As a result this period of Mycenaean supremacy was marked by a decline in art and probably in intellect as well. In the thirteenth century the Mycenaeans waged their successful war with the Trojans, but less than 200 years later they themselves fell the victims of barbarian invasion. The new hordes that came in were also Greeks, but they belonged to the group known as Dorians (originally from somewhere on the Balkan peninsula). Their culture was relatively primitive, except for the fact that they had iron weapons. For centuries they had lived on the mainland of Greece, gradually penetrating farther southward. About 1250 B.C. they began their conquest of the Mycenaean cities. Two hundred years later the Minoan-Mycenaean civilization had passed into the limbo of history.

The racial character of the Minoan people has been determined with substantial accuracy. Archaeological data from Crete have been found in sufficient profusion to leave little doubt that its ancient inhabitants were a composite nation. Their ancestors appear to have come from Syria and Anatolia and were closely related to the Hittites and to the earliest invaders of India. At the same time there is evidence—from the fact that their artists depicted them with long heads, short, slender bodies, and dark, wavy hair—that they bore a relationship to the Egyptians. Although they occupied Greek territory, they were not Greeks at all in the historic meaning of that name. The true Greeks, as we shall presently see, were of altogether different ethnic origin.

The Minoan civilization was probably one of the freest and most progressive in all the Near Orient. The ruler was known by the title of Minos, which was roughly the equivalent of Pharaoh (hence the name *Minoan*). That it was a title of divinity is shown by the fact that it was occasionally used as if it referred to a god. But the Minos was no bristling war lord like the Assyrian and Persian kings. He did have a large and efficient navy, but this was for defense against external attack and for the protection of trade, not to overawe the citizens at home.

On the other hand, there was some regimentation of industry. The king was the chief capitalist and entrepreneur in the country. The factories in connection with his palace turned out great quantities of fine pottery, textiles, and metal goods. Although private enterprise was not prohibited, the owners of smaller establishments were naturally at some disadvantage in competing with the king. Nevertheless, numerous privately owned factories did flourish, especially in cities other than the capital, and agriculture and trade were also in private hands. It must be understood that these establishments, both royal and private, were factories in nearly every modern sense of the word. While they did not use power-driven machinery, they were engaged in large-scale production, and there was division of labor and centralized control and supervision of workers. The hundreds of women employed in the royal textile factory worked under the supervision of the queen.

The Aegean people of nearly all classes appear to have led happy and fairly prosperous lives. If slavery existed at all, it certainly occupied an unimportant place. The dwellings in the poorest quarters of great industrial towns such as Gournia were substantially built and commodious, often with as many as six or eight rooms, but we do not know how many families resided in them. If we can judge from the number of inscriptions found in the homes of the common people, literacy was well-nigh universal. Women enjoyed complete equality with men. Regardless of class there was no public activity from which they were debarred, and no occupation which they could not enter. Crete had its female bull fighters and even female

103

Scenes from the Bull Ring, Cretan Painting, about 1500 B.C. Evident are the Cretans' devotion to sport and the skill and agility of their athletes. The body and horns of the bull, however, are exaggerated as are the slenderness of the athletes and their full-face eyes in profile heads.

pugilists. Ladies of the upper strata devoted much time to fashion. Dressed in their tight-fitting bodices and bell-shaped skirts with flounces which would not have been much out of style in nineteenth-century Europe, they vied with each other for attention in the theaters and at public entertainments of numerous kinds.

The love of sports and games

The natives of the Aegean area delighted in games and sports of every description. Chess, dancing, running matches, and boxing rivaled each other in their attraction for the people. The Cretans were the first to build stone theaters where processions and music entertained large audiences.

The Minoan religion

The religion of the subjects of Minos was a medley of strange characteristics. First of all it was matriarchal. The chief deity was not a god but a goddess, who was the ruler of the entire universe—the sea and the sky as well as the earth. Originally no male deity appears to have been worshiped, but later a god was associated with the goddess as her son and lover. Although, like the divine sons in several other religions, he apparently died and rose from the dead, he was never regarded by the Cretans as of particular importance.

The mother goddess

In the second place, the Minoan religion was thoroughly monistic. The mother goddess was the source of evil as well as of good, but not in any morbid or terrifying sense. Though she brought the storm and spread destruction in her path, these served for the replenishment of nature. Death itself was interpreted as the condition prerequisite for life. Whether the religion had any ethical purposes is unknown.

Symbols and sacrifices

Other rather curious features included the worship of animals and birds (the bull, the snake, and the dove); the worship of sacred trees; the veneration of sacred objects which were probably reproductive symbols (the double-axe, the pillar, and the cross); and the employment of priestesses instead of priests to administer the rites of the cult. By far the most important act of worship was sacrifice. At the great religious festivals hundreds of animals and large quantities of grain and fruit were brought as grateful offerings to the goddess and her son.

For many years after the discovery of the Minoan-Mycenaean civilization its system of writing remained a complete enigma. At length, however, Sir Arthur Evans succeeded in showing that these Aegean people produced not only one system of writing but three—a hieroglyphic script and two linear scripts, which were used in successive periods. One script, used during the Mycenaean stage, was actually a form of Greek. The other continues to belong to the realm of mystery.[1] No literary texts of the Minoan-Mycenaean civilization have yet been unearthed. It is impossible therefore to tell whether any literature or philosophy had been written. The problem of scientific achievements is easier to solve, since we have material remains for our guidance. Archaeological discoveries on the island of Crete indicate that the ancient inhabitants were gifted inventors and engineers. They built excellent roads of concrete about eleven feet wide. Nearly all the basic principles of modern sanitary engineering were known to the designers of the palace of Knossos, with the result that the royal family of Crete in the seventeenth century B.C. enjoyed comforts and conveniences that were not available to the wealthiest rulers of Western countries in the seventeenth century A.D.

Minoan-Mycenaean writing and scientific achievements

If there was any one achievement of these Aegean people that appears more than others to emphasize the vitality and freedom of their culture, it was their art. With the exception of the Greek, no other art of the ancient world was quite its equal. Its distinguishing features were delicacy, spontaneity, and naturalism. It served not to glorify the ambitions of an arrogant ruling class or to inculcate the doctrines of a religion, but to express the delight of the ordinary man in the world of beauty around him. As a result, it was remarkably free from the retarding influence of ancient tradition. It was unique, moreover, in the universality of its application, for it extended not merely to paintings and statues but even to the humblest objects of ordinary use.

Minoan-Mycenaean art

Of the major arts, architecture was the least developed. The great palaces were not remarkably beautiful buildings but rambling structures designed primarily for capaciousness and comfort. As more and more functions were absorbed by the state, the palaces were enlarged to accommodate them. New quarters were annexed to those already built or piled on top of them without regard for order or symmetry. The interiors, however, were decorated with beautiful paintings and furnishings. The architecture of Crete may be said to have resembled the modern international style in its subordination

Architecture

---

[1] Although his findings are widely disputed, one scholar, Cyrus H. Gordon, maintains that it derives from a Semitic script.

Central Staircase of the Palace of Minos.

of form to utility and in its emphasis upon a pleasing and livable interior as more important than external beauty.

Painting

Painting was the art supreme of the Aegean world. Nearly all of it consisted of murals done in fresco, although painted reliefs were occasionally to be found. The murals in the palaces of Crete were by all odds the best that have survived from ancient times. They revealed almost perfectly the remarkable gifts of the Minoan artist—his instinct for the dramatic, his sense of rhythm, his feeling for nature in her most characteristic moods.

Sculpture, pottery, and engraving

Sculpture and the ceramic and gem-carving arts were also developed to a high stage of perfection. The sculpture of the Cretans differed from that of any other people in the ancient Near Orient. It never relied upon size as a device to convey the idea of power. The Cretans produced no colossi like those of Egypt or reliefs like those of Babylonia depicting a king of gigantic proportions smiting his puny enemies. Instead, they preferred sculpture in miniature. Nearly all of the statues of human beings or of deities that the archaeologists have found are smaller than life-size.

The more barbarous character of Mycenaean culture

The point must be emphasized that the Minoan achievements in the arts, government, and social life were not equaled in the Mycenaean stage. Compared with the Cretans, the Mycenaeans were barbarians who failed to appreciate the subtle refinements of Minoan culture.

Much has been written about the significance of the Minoan-Mycenaean civilization and its relation to the surrounding cultures. By some historians it is regarded as a mere offshoot of the civilization of Egypt. A number of facts can be adduced to support this view. Both civilizations were ethnically similar. Their governments were alike in their theocratic character. Both societies contained elements of matriarchy and economic collectivism. But that is about as

106

far as the comparison can be carried. The differences were just as marked. The Aegean people built no great pyramids or magnificent temples. Only in painting did their art resemble that of Egypt very closely. The systems of writing of the two civilizations appear to have been of entirely independent origin, as is evidenced by the fact that a knowledge of Egyptian helps very little in deciphering Cretan. Whereas the Egyptian religion was an elaborate ethical system based upon the worship of a sun god of righteousness and justice, the religion of the Aegean venerated a goddess of nature with no evidence of a concept of ethical purpose. Finally, the two peoples differed in their basic philosophies of life. The Egyptians believed in the sacrifice of personal interests to the glory and eternity of the state and looked to rewards in an after-existence as a just compensation for good deeds on earth. The people of the Aegean were individualists, intent upon living their own lives of pleasurable activity and concerned with the hereafter merely as an extension of their pleasant and satisfying earthly careers.

The influence of the Minoan-Mycenaean civilization is not easy to estimate. The Philistines, who came from some part of the Aegean world, introduced certain aspects of the culture into Palestine and Syria. There is reason to believe that various elements of Phoenician art and the Samson legends of the Old Testament were really acquired from the Philistines. It is probable also that the religious and aesthetic traditions of the Cretans and perhaps something of their spirit of freedom influenced the Greeks. But a considerable part of the Minoan-Mycenaean civilization was lost or destroyed following the downfall of Knossos. The conquerors were barbarians who were unable to appreciate much of the culture of the people they conquered and consequently allowed it to perish.

Despite its limited influence the Minoan-Mycenaean civilization, especially in its Minoan form, is not without importance for the student of history; for it was one of the few in ancient times which assured to most of its citizens a reasonable share of happiness and prosperity, free from the tyranny of a despotic state and a crafty priesthood. The apparent absence of slavery, brutal punishments, forced labor, and conscription, together with the substantial equality of classes and the dignified status accorded to women, all point to a social regime in striking contrast with those of the Asiatic empires. If additional evidence of this contrast is needed, it can be found in the art of the various nations. The Cretan sculptor or painter gloried not in portraying the slaughter of armies or the sacking of cities but in picturing flowery landscapes, joyous festivals, thrilling exhibitions of athletic prowess, and similar scenes of a free and peaceful existence. Last of all, the Minoan-Mycenaean civilization is significant for its worldly and progressive outlook. This is exemplified in the devotion of the people to comfort and opulence, in their love of amusement, in their individualism, zest for life, and courage for experimentation.

THE MINOAN-MYCENAEAN CIVILIZATION

Relation of the Minoan-Mycenaean to other civilizations

A Minoan Vase. From the Palace of Phaistos, Crete, it was decorated with stalks of grass or cereal.

Gold Pendant from Crete, Seventeenth Century B.C.

107

Throne Room in the Palace of Minos. The throne and bench are original; the fresco has been restored in accordance with fragments found on the site which are now in the Candia Museum on the island of Crete. A remarkable grace characterizes the lilies and the body and head of the mythical animal.

3. THE LYDIANS AND THE PHOENICIANS

The kingdom of Lydia

When the Hittite empire fell in the eighth century B.C., its successor in its main areas of power was the kingdom of Lydia. The Lydians established their rule in what is now the territory of the Turkish Republic in Anatolia. They quickly secured control of the Greek cities on the coast of Asia Minor and of the entire plateau west of the Halys River. But their power was short-lived. In 550 B.C. their fabulous king, Croesus, fancied he saw a good opportunity to add to his domain the territory of the Medes east of the Halys. The Median king had just been deposed by Cyrus the Persian. Thinking this meant an easy triumph for his own armies, Croesus set out to capture the territory beyond the river. After an indecisive battle with Cyrus, he returned to his own capital (Sardis) for reinforcements. Here Cyrus caught him unprepared in a surprise attack and captured and burned the city. The Lydians never recovered from the blow, and soon afterward all of their territory, including the Greek cities on the coast, passed under the dominion of Cyrus the Great.

The Lydians were a people of Indo-European speech, who were probably a mixture of native peoples of Asia Minor with migrant stocks from eastern Europe. Benefiting from the advantages of favorable location and abundance of resources, they enjoyed one of the highest standards of living of ancient times. They were famous for the splendor of their armored chariots and the quantities of gold and articles of luxury possessed by the citizens. The wealth of their kings was legendary, as attested by the simile "rich as Croesus." The chief sources of this prosperity were gold from the streams, wool from the thousands of sheep on the hills, and the profits of the extensive commerce which passed overland from the Tigris-Euphrates valley to the Aegean Sea. But with all their wealth and opportunities for leisure, they succeeded in making only one original contribution to civilization. This was the coinage of money from electrum or "white gold," a natural mixture of gold and silver found in the sands of one of their rivers. Hitherto all systems of money had consisted of weighed rings or bars of metal. The new coins, of varying sizes, were stamped with a definite value more or less arbitrarily given by the ruler who issued them.

In contrast with the Lydians, who gained their ascendancy as a result of the downfall of the Hittites, were the Phoenicians, who benefited from the break-up of Aegean supremacy. But the Phoenicians were neither conquerors nor the builders of an empire. They exerted their influence through the arts of peace, especially through commerce. During most of their history their political system was a loose confederation of city-states, which frequently bought their security by paying tribute to foreign powers. The territory they occupied was the narrow strip between the Lebanon Mountains and the Mediterranean Sea and the islands off the coast. With good harbors and a central location, it was admirably situated for trade. The great centers of commerce included Tyre, Sidon, and Beirut. Under the leadership of the first, Phoenicia reached the zenith of her cultural brilliance, from the tenth to the eighth century B.C. During the sixth century she passed under the domination of the Chaldeans and then of the Persians. In 332 B.C. Tyre was destroyed by Alexander the Great after a siege of seven months.

The Phoenicians were a people of Semitic language, closely related to the Canaanites. They displayed very little creative genius, but were remarkable adapters of the achievements of others. They produced no original art worthy of the name, and they made but slight contributions to literature. Their religion, like that of the Canaanites, was characterized by human sacrifice to the god Moloch and by licentious fertility rites. They excelled, however, in specialized manufactures, in geography and navigation. They founded colonies at Carthage and Utica in North Africa, at Palermo on the island of Sicily, on the Balearic Islands, and at Cadiz and Malaga in Spain. They were renowned throughout the ancient world for their glass and metal industries and for their purple dye obtained from a mollusk in the adjacent seas. They developed the art of navigation to such a stage that they could sail by the stars at

The Lydian people and their culture

The Phoenician cities and confederation

Achievements of the Phoenicians

109

night. To less venturesome peoples, the North Star was known for some time as the Phoenicians' star. A company of Phoenicians is believed to have circumnavigated Africa. Phoenician ships and sailors were recruited by all the great powers. The most lasting achievement of the Phoenicians, however, was the completion and diffusion of an alphabet based upon principles discovered by the Egyptians. The Phoenician contribution was the adoption of a system of signs representing the sounds of the human voice, and the elimination of all pictographic and syllabic characters. The Egyptians, as we have seen, had accomplished the first of these steps but not the second.

4. LESSONS FROM THE HISTORY OF THE NEAR EASTERN STATES

Like most other periods in world history, the period of the states we have studied thus far was an era of contention and strife. Nearly all of the great empires, and the majority of the smaller states as well, devoted their energies most of the time to policies of expansion and aggression. The only notable exceptions were the Minoan and Egyptian, but even the Egyptians, in the later period of their history, yielded to no one in their addiction to imperialism. The causes were largely geographic. Each nation grew accustomed to the pursuit of its own interests in some fertile river valley or on some easily defended plateau. Isolation bred fear of foreigners and an incapacity to think of one's own people as members of a common humanity. The feelings of insecurity that resulted seemed to justify aggressive foreign policies and the annexation of neighboring states to serve as buffers against a hostile world.

Defects of the Near Orient empires

It seems possible to trace nearly all of the woes of the Near Eastern nations to wars of aggression and imperialist greed. Arnold J. Toynbee has shown this in devastating fashion in the case of the Assyrians. He contends that it was no less true of such later peoples as the Spartans, the Carthaginians, the Macedonians, and the Ottoman Turks. Each made militarism and conquest its gods and wrought such destruction upon itself that when it made its last heroic stand against its enemies, it was a mere "corpse in armor." Not death by foreign conquest but national suicide was the fate which befell it.[2] The way of the warrior brought race intolerance, a love of ease and luxury, crime and racketeering, and crushing burdens of taxation. Expansion of empire promoted a fictitious prosperity, at least for the upper classes, and aroused enough envy among poorer nations to make them willing conspirators against a rich neighbor who could easily be portrayed as an oppressor. The use of hungry and discontented allies against powerful rivals is not new in history.

Results of Near Orient imperialism

[2] D. C. Somervell (ed.), A. J. Toynbee's *A Study of History*, I, 338–43.

SELECTED READINGS

· *Items so designated are available in paperbound editions.*

· Blegen, C. W., *Troy*, London and New York, 1963 (Cambridge University Press).

Burn, A. R., *Minoans, Philistines and Greeks*, New York, 1930.

Ceram, C. W., *The Secret of the Hittites*, New York, 1956. The best of recent works.

· Chadwick, John, *The Decipherment of Linear B*, New York, 1958 (Vintage).

· Gordon, Cyrus H., *The Ancient Near East*, New York, 1965 (Norton Library).

· ———, *The Common Background of Greek and Hebrew Civilizations*, New York, 1965 (Norton Library).

· Gurney, O. R., *The Hittites*, Baltimore, 1962 (Penguin).

· Harden, Donald, *The Phoenicians*, New York, 1962 (Praeger).

· Hutchinson, R. W., *Prehistoric Crete*, Baltimore, 1962 (Penguin).

· Lloyd, Seton, *Early Anatolia*, Baltimore, 1956 (Penguin).

· MacDonald, William A., *Progress into the Past: The Rediscovery of Mycenaean Civilization*, New York, 1967.

Moscati, Sabatino, *The World of the Phoenicians*, New York, 1968.

· Nilsson, M. P., *The Mycenaean Origin of Greek Mythology*, New York, 1963 (Norton Library).

Palmer, L. R., *Mycenaeans and Minoans*, New York, 1962. Must be read with care. Author is not entirely impartial.

· Pendlebury, J. D. S., *The Archaeology of Crete*, New York, 1965 (Norton Library).

Wace, A. J. B., *Mycenae*, Princeton, 1949.

Willetts, R. F., *Aristocratic Society in Ancient Crete*, London, 1955.

SOURCE MATERIALS

Evans, Sir Arthur, *Scripta Minoa; the Written Documents of Minoan Crete*.

Hertzler, J. O., *The Social Thought of the Ancient Civilizations*, New York, 1961, pp. 135–44.

Ventris, M., and Chadwick, J., *Documents in Mycenaean Greek*, Cambridge, 1956.

CHAPTER 6

Ancient Indian Civilization

Hinduism does not distinguish ideas of God as true and false, adopting one particular idea as the standard for the whole human race. It accepts the obvious fact that mankind seeks its goal of God at various levels and in various directions, and feels sympathy with every stage of the search.

S. Radhakrishnan, *The Hindu View of Life*

The subcontinent of India has an area slightly more than half that of the United States and is inhabited by almost three times as many people. Not only is India a vast and densely populated region but in addition it includes many different levels of culture, different religions, languages, and economic conditions, and its history is extremely complex. Five or six separate families of languages are represented among its people. The population contains admixtures of all of the three great races of mankind—black, yellow, and white —in various combinations and proportions. One of the most ancient peoples, a Negrito strain related to the Pygmies of Africa, has almost disappeared from India but is still found in the Andaman Islands to the east. In striking contrast to this type are the fair-skinned Mediterraneans of the north and northwest, descendants of the Indo-Aryans who invaded the country some 3500 years ago. The most widespread group in southern India is that known as Dravidian, but because the term is applied to all whose language belongs to the Dravidian family it no longer denotes a single ethnic stock. Another type, perhaps more ancient than the Dravidians, is called Australoid, because of its relationship with primitive peoples extending over parts of southeastern Asia and as far east as Australia. The Mongolian element is confined chiefly to the border region of the north and northeast. Alpine types are found along the western coast, sometimes with a slight Nordic admixture (evidenced by gray or blue eyes). Thus the common practice of referring to the natives of

The peoples of India

113

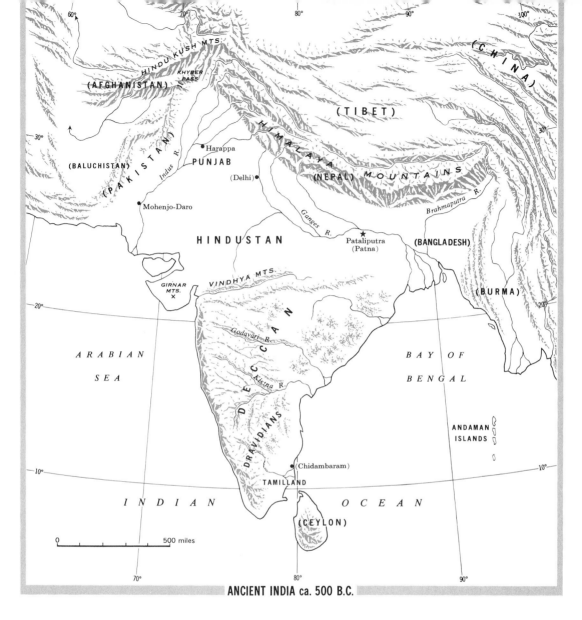

ANCIENT INDIA ca. 500 B.C.

India as "colored" or "brown-skinned" is misleading. Their skins are indeed of various shades, but since early times white stocks have been conspicuously present, especially in northern India. Even today some of the most typical examples of the tall variety of the Mediterranean white race can be seen in the Punjab and the northwest frontier. Yet they exist in close proximity to people who reveal Alpine, Australoid, Mongoloid, or Negrito features. Over the course of centuries, and in spite of the inexorable segregation of the caste system in historic times, India has been a human melting pot.

Geographically India falls into two main divisions. The southern triangle or peninsular portion, known as the Deccan, lies entirely within the tropics. The northern or continental half, also triangular in shape, is in the same latitudes as Mexico and the southern United States and has temperatures ranging from tropical heat to the intense cold of the northern mountain peaks. The northern Deccan is semi-mountainous and heavily forested, and shelters some of the primitive hill tribes whose ancestors were crowded into the wilderness by the pressure of expansion from more civilized communities. The greater part of the peninsula, however, is a gently sloping plateau, traversed by rivers, and containing rich agricultural lands. The northern half of India, called Hindustan, is bounded on the north by the lofty Himalayan range and is separated from the Deccan by the low-lying Vindhya Mountains. Most of Hindustan is a level plain comprising an area about as large as France, Germany, and Italy combined, drained by the great river systems of the Indus and the Ganges. The rivers of Hindustan take their rise in the Himalayas or beyond and are fed by snows and glaciers. The Indus and the Brahmaputra each originate in Tibet and flow in opposite directions around the mountain ranges until they turn south into India, bringing with them virgin soil from the highlands which is deposited on the plain. The gently flowing Ganges, less subject to floods than the Indus, is the most beneficent of all. Referred to as "Mother Ganges," it has long been the sacred river of the Hindus. It is no wonder that its central valley, where every inch of soil is productive and no stone even the size of a pebble can be found, is one of the

The Sprinagar Valley. Low-lying areas are regularly inundated by the flood waters of the Jkelum River, a tributary of the Indus River in northwestern India. The floodwaters leave rich soil in their wake.

most densely populated spots in the world. The mouths of the Ganges (in Bengal) are surrounded by forbidding jungle, and a desert separates the lower Indus valley from the Ganges and its tributaries; but the Indo-Gangetic region as a whole is lavishly endowed by nature. Here the most influential centers of Indian civilization have been located.

India a geographic unit

All India enjoys the advantage of the monsoon rains, and the greater part of the country is suitable for cultivation. Moreover, there is no impenetrable barrier between Hindustan and the Deccan and there has always been communication between the two sections. In spite of its size and contrasting terrain, India is a natural geographic unit. That its peoples have been united politically only during relatively brief periods of their history is attributable to many factors, including disturbances from without, but it cannot be ascribed to geographic necessity.

I. THE VEDIC AGE IN INDIA

The earliest civilization of India

Remains of Neolithic and of early metal-age cultures have been discovered both in Hindustan and the Deccan. The first highly advanced civilization began its history as early as 3000 B.C. and reached its peak between 2500 and 2000 B.C. It covered a large area extending 1000 miles through the Indus valley and along the coast of the Arabian Sea both to the east and west of the mouth of the Indus. It was essentially an urban civilization, with a cosmopolitan society and extensive trade with the outside world. Among a number of metropolitan centers thus far uncovered, the two principal sites are Mohenjo-Daro, about 300 miles from the seacoast, and Harappa, about 400 miles farther up the river. Both were durably

Excavations at Harappa have provided the means of reconstructing the urban civilization of the Indus Valley between 3000 B.C. and 2000 B.C. Note the extensive use of brick in the buildings of the period.

Skeletons at Mohenjo-Daro. Although the downfall of this culture is a mystery, barbarian conquest was an important factor.

constructed of brick and laid out in accordance with ambitious and intelligent planning. Private houses were solidly built and equipped with bathrooms which drained into sewer pipes running underneath the principal streets and discharging into the river. Evidences of intellectual achievement are scanty, although proofs are available that standards of weight and measurement and a system of writing had been developed. The writing was evidently syllabic and designed to be read in alternate lines from right to left and left to right, but it has not yet been deciphered. A group of Scandinavian scholars who are studying it believe that the language of the Indus valley inscriptions can be classified as Proto-Dravidian. Several of the arts reflected a high degree of skill, especially the fabrication of small objects for personal adornment. Some examples of sculpture, also, indicate a talent for grace and naturalness. The religion of this early civilization centered upon the worship of fertility deities, notably a mother goddess. The principal rite was animal sacrifice.

Archaeological evidence supports the conclusion that the Indus valley civilization was one of the earliest in the world and that it was comparable in level of achievement to those of contemporary Egypt and Mesopotamia. Whether it was indigenous to India or was introduced by settlers from the west is still a matter of speculation. It long maintained intercourse with other civilized regions, especially Mesopotamia, where Indus-type stone seals and other objects belonging to the period about 2350 B.C. have been discovered. For reasons unknown the Indus valley civilization disappeared from the scene of history about 1500 B.C. It may have succumbed to barbarian conquest, although floods and other natural disasters probably contributed to its decline. Whatever the causes, the civilization went down to so complete an oblivion that no one was aware of its existence until evidences were unearthed by archaeologists about fifty years ago. Shortly before the downfall of the Indus valley cities, India was invaded by seminomadic tribes who were destined to be the founders of a more enduring civilization. These

Bull Seal. Impression of stone seal from Mohenjo-Daro, 2500 B.C., probably used as a signature. The animal figure (of a Brahmani bull or zebu) is assumed to have had religious significance.

117

were the so-called Aryans,[1] or Indo-Aryans, who came in by way of Afghanistan through the passes of the Hindu Kush Mountains. For many centuries the Aryan influence was confined to northern India, and here it developed the distinctive Hindu pattern of society, culture, and religion. Though the Aryan (Indo-European) languages never became dominant in the south, they are the most widely spoken group of languages in India today.

For some 1000 years following the Indo-Aryan invasions the political history of India is largely unknown. There is no reason to assume a wholesale displacement of population. As the invading tribes extended their sway over northern India they intermingled with the inhabitants of the conquered regions. The process of assimilation between conquerors and conquered affected the culture of the invaders to a degree that cannot be clearly determined but which undoubtedly was profound, especially in the development of religion and social structure. The absence of reliable historical records for such a long period of time, among people who achieved a variegated, colorful, and highly intellectual civilization, is extraordinary. The scarcity of historical information is not entirely accidental, although it is partly accounted for by the fact that the Indo-Aryans had no system of writing until about 1000 years after their settlement in India. A more potent cause was the character of their civilization itself and especially of their philosophy, which stressed the importance of timeless qualities and the relative insignificance of temporal events and conditions. When they looked back to the past, they were inclined to give free scope to their imagination and to reckon in terms of vast eras and aeons, symmetrical but fantastic, extending to millions or even billions of years. The failure to produce factual chronicles does not mean that no changes or exciting events occurred. On the contrary, the available evidence suggests the normal amount of conflict, turmoil, and upheaval.

The sources of information for early Indo-Aryan civilization are almost exclusively in literary tradition. The oldest literary monument is the collection of religious poems and hymns called the *Vedas*. No one knows when they were composed. The oldest portions may have originated as early as 3000 B.C., and they were passed on orally without any written aids whatsoever until several centuries after the collection was complete. The *Vedas* reflect the culture of the primitive Aryan communities in the upper Indus valley and the "Middle Land" between the two rivers, or roughly the period from 2000 to 800 B.C., which is accordingly called the Vedic age. The latter portion of the *Vedas*, however, shows that profound changes had taken place during these centuries. The second major literary

Scantiness of the early records

Dancing Girl. Bronze statuette of a girl dancer, from Mohen-jo-Daro, a striking example of the art of the ancient Indus civilization. Bracelets and bangles have retained their popularity among the women of India to the present day.

Vedas and epics

---

[1] "Aryan" was the name by which these invaders identified themselves. The theory of a distinctive Aryan race, expounded from time to time by various propagandists, has been exploded. In current usage the term "Aryan" is properly applied only to a family of related languages (the Indo-European group).

Dyers' troughs or drains, uncovered at Mohenjo-Daro.

landmark consists of two long epic poems, the *Ramayana* and the *Mahabharata.* Like the *Vedas,* and in spite of their tremendous bulk, the epics were preserved by memory and oral repetition for many generations, but they reflect a different set of conditions, customs, and beliefs from those most typical of the *Vedas.* The epics reveal that by the close of the Vedic age Indo-Aryan culture had been transformed into a complex and stratified social and religious system. It had become Hinduism.

In the early Vedic period the Indo-Aryan tribes had a simple, largely pastoral economy. They cultivated barley and probably other grains, using a wooden plow drawn by bullocks. They ate the flesh of sheep, goats, and oxen, usually at the time of sacrificing these animals to the gods, but their favorite foods were dairy products—milk, cream, and ghee (melted butter). Cattle were the most prized possessions and served as a medium of exchange. Apparently they were not yet worshiped nor was their slaughter forbidden. Domesticated animals also included the horse, used to pull the war chariot and also for chariot racing. All the common handicrafts, including metal work, were practiced. Music, both vocal and instrumental—with flutes, drums, cymbals, and stringed lutes or harps—was a popular source of entertainment, as was dancing. Gambling with dice was a national pastime and seems to have come close to being a national obsession.

In its typical features this early Indian society was vigorous and uninhibited, its members delighting in song and dance, in feasting, carousing, and feats of strength. Warfare was frequent, and many stories have been preserved of the incredible powers of strong-armed heroes. The social unit was the patriarchal family, which does not necessarily imply that the father exercised tyrannical power over his dependents. His functions were religious as well as economic. The wife assisted her husband in sacrifices at the domestic hearth, and women apparently enjoyed almost equal freedom with men. Polygamy was permissible, but such later Hindu institutions as

Unicorn Seal. The "unicorn" (perhaps actually the profile of an ox) is the animal most frequently depicted on the Indus civilization seals. The object under the animal's head may represent a brazier or incense holder. The inscription has not been deciphered. This specimen was found in the Deccan, some 600 miles from the Indus Valley.

119

the immolation of a widow upon her husband's funeral pyre (suttee) and child marriage were completely unknown.

As might be expected, political and legal institutions were rudimentary among the primitive Aryans. Each tribe had its king (raja), whose chief function was to lead his warriors in battle. Associated with the king in ruling was an assembly. Its composition and duties are not at all clear, but its existence suggests a limitation upon the royal authority. Some of the tribes were organized as aristocratic republics rather than hereditary monarchies, with government resting with the heads of the clans or an elected raja. In the early days the raja's powers could hardly have been awe-inspiring in any case. He had no populous cities from which to extract riches, only country villages; and the villages managed their own internal affairs, paying part of their produce to the raja for "protection." The handling of crime and punishment followed patterns similar to those of many other primitive societies. The injured party or his family was expected to take the initiative in prosecuting an offender. Compensation for injuries was usually a payment in money or commodities to the plaintiff or, in the case of murder, to the victim's family. Theft was the most frequent complaint, especially cattle stealing, even though this crime was looked upon as highly reprehensible. An insolvent debtor—usually one who had gambled too recklessly—might be enslaved to his creditor.

Weights. The Indus civilization's flourishing commerce required a system of weights and measures. These stone blocks served as units of weight on the scales used by merchants.

The most significant achievement of the Vedic age was the composition of the poetry and prose which give the period its name. Ultimately there were four *Vedas*, each containing a large collection of prayers, chants, or hymns, supplemented by prose commentary. The literal meaning of *Veda* is "knowledge" or "wisdom," and the entire collection was believed to have been imparted to ancient seers by the gods rather than invented by men. The *Vedas* constitute the canonical books of the Indo-Aryan—and of the later Hindu—religion; they were considered divinely inspired and uniquely sacred, as were the Hebrew and Christian Scriptures by the members of those faiths. However, because the early Aryans were illiterate, their sacred books were said to have been "heard" rather than "revealed." The *Vedas* cover an amazing variety and range of subjects. Some portions are litanies intended to be chanted by priests during a sacrifice. Others are catalogues of spells and charms, including alleged remedies for fever and snake bite, love formulas, and recipes for exterminating one's enemies. Still others incorporate customs and folklore or display a profound insight into philosophical or religious truth. Although much of the content of the *Vedas* is repetitious and monotonous, in vividness and imagination the best verses deserve to rank with the *Iliad* of Homer.

The religion of the early Aryans as illustrated in the *Vedas* was a comprehensive polytheism, with little ethical significance. Their gods—*deva*, or "shining ones"—were the forces of nature or person-

Political institutions

The Vedas as literature

ifications of these forces. No images or temples were erected, and
worship consisted chiefly in performing sacrifices to the gods. Grain
and milk were sacrificed, animal flesh was burned upon the altars
(the worshipers themselves eating the flesh), but the choicest offering was *soma*, an alcoholic beverage fermented from the juice of a
mountain plant. The gods were looked upon in much the same way
as the Olympian deities were regarded by the Greeks. They were
conceived as splendid and powerful creatures, with human attributes but immortal as long as they drank the *soma* juice, and, on
the whole, benevolent. It was assumed that they would reward men
out of gratitude for the homage and gifts presented to them. Gradually, however, the insidious notion took root that if the holy rites
were conducted with unfailing accuracy they would compel the
god to obedience, whether he was willing or not. It is easy to see
how such an interpretation would enhance the prestige and authority of the priests who controlled the wonder-working formulas.

The roster of gods was a large one and tended to increase. While
several deities can be identified with those of other Indo-European
peoples, they did not have as clear-cut personalities as the Greek or
Norse gods. The Indian mind ran toward specialization and abstraction, tending to invent a new god or a new variant of an old god for
every conceivable occasion. Dyaus, lord of the bright sky, was
equivalent to the Greek Zeus (though less important). Varuna represented the sky or heaven in its capacity to encompass all things
and hold the universe together. He was called Asura, a term which
suggests close kinship with the supreme Persian deity, Ahura-
Mazda. At least five different divinities were identified with the sun.
One of them, Mitra, shared a common origin with the Persian
Mithras, but this deity did not assume the prominence in India that
Mithras attained in Persia and the West. Surya was the sun's golden
disk, Pushan embodied its power to assist vegetation and animal
growth, and Vishnu personified the swift-moving orb that traverses
the sky in three strides.

The most popular deity of all in Vedic times was Indra, whose
original significance is uncertain. He was alleged to have benefited
mankind by slaying a malignant serpent, the demon of drought, thus
releasing the pent-up waters to refresh the earth. Also, it was said,
he discovered the light, made a path for the sun, and created lightning. He was chiefly honored as a mighty warrior and god of battle,
the slayer of demons and the "black-skinned" enemies of the
Aryans. Indra was supposed to be particularly fond of *soma*, which
fired his blood for combat, and he was reputed to be able to drink
three lakes of this potent fluid at one draft while devouring the flesh
of 300 buffaloes. *Soma*, the sacred liquor, was also deified, as was the
sacrificial fire, Agni. Agni was conceived both as a god and as the
mouth of the gods or as the servant who carried their savory food
offerings up to the heavens for them.

Although religion in the Vedic age was hardly spiritual, it contained traces of such a quality. Some hymns to Varuna are remarkable for their devoutness and ethical content. Varuna is described as the great regulator of the universe, who keeps the rivers in their courses and the sun and planets in their proper orbits. He is also pictured as the upholder of rules and ordinances for both gods and men, capable of binding sinners with fetters. To him were addressed prayers for forgiveness of sin. Offenses likely to incur divine wrath included not only infractions of religious taboos but also violations of the moral code, such as adultery, witchcraft, gambling, and drunkenness. However, despite intimations of a belief in life after death, by far the greater emphasis was placed upon the enjoyment of life here and now.

**Spiritual and
ethical elements**

Associated with each of the *Vedas* is a prose manual called a *Brahmana* because it was for the instruction and assistance of the Brahmans (priests) who officiated at the sacrifices. While the Vedic hymns are generally unaffected and artless, the *Brahmanas* betray a shrewd calculation on the part of the custodians of the sacred traditions and also illustrate the tendency of such traditions to degenerate into empty mechanical formulas. A modern Indian scholar describes the *Brahmanas* as "an arid desert of puerile speculations on ritual ceremonies," and even as "filthy and repulsive," with a morality "no higher than that of primitive medicine-men." [2] The greed and arrogance of the Brahmans is illustrated by such assertions as that judgment should always be awarded to a Brahman in every dispute with a layman and that murder is not actually murder unless the victim is a Brahman.

The Brahmanas

In view of the decadent tendencies evident in the *Brahmanas* it is all the more notable that the concluding portion of Vedic literature is of an elevated philosophical character, giving proof both of intellectual maturity and of ethical and spiritual insight. Evidently, side by side with the naïve popular cults and with the mechanical rituals of priestcraft had grown up a tradition of skepticism and bold speculation, which attempted to delve beneath the surface of sense experience and formulate answers to eternally recurring questions. This concluding portion, called *Vedanta* ("end of the *Vedas*"), comprises the famous *Upanishads,* of which there are some 200. The *Upanishads* (the word means a "sitting down near" or session with a teacher) are treatises or rambling discourses in prose and poetry, dealing with the nature of being, man, and the universe. Their content varies in subject matter and in quality of thought, ranging from the trivial and absurd to the sublime. Scholars and philosophers from the Occident as well as from the Orient have long been attracted by the subtle probing, the sweeping imagination, and the idealistic concepts evident in the *Upanishads,* the best of which are equal to the

The Upanishads

[2] B. K. Ghosh, in *The History and Culture of the Indian People*, Vol. II, *The Vedic Age*, pp. 225, 418.

finest products of Greek philosophical genius. Although part of the *Vedas*, the *Upanishads* largely ignore the popular mythology of the Vedic hymns and also constitute a challenge to the presumptuousness of the Brahmans and their version of religion as consisting in adherence to ritual and ceremony.

While the *Upanishads* do not fall into a single pattern of thought, their most essential philosophical teachings are fairly consistent. The key concepts, which may be described as idealistic, monistic, and pantheistic, are: (1) the supreme reality of the World Soul or Absolute Being; (2) the unreality of the material world; (3) transmigration, or the rebirth of individual souls; and (4) the attainment of serenity through escape from the cycle of recurring births by union with Absolute Being. Evil and suffering are explained on the ground that they are incidental to matter and material creatures. But matter is held to be an illusion (*maya*); the only true reality is the soul or spirit. If the soul could manage to disentangle itself from matter (which actually is only an appearance anyway), it would be free from discord and suffering. Not only does life in the flesh entail sorrow and pain, but, according to this philosophy, death fails to provide relief because the soul will be born again into another body. In developing the theory of an endless chain of births, the philosophers of the *Upanishads* insisted that the process was not purely accidental and uncontrollable. They taught that a person's conduct in life determined the type of body and condition which he would experience in his next incarnation. He might go down in the scale— even to the animal or insect level—or he might go up—to the state of a noble, king, or saint. This is the *karma* doctrine, which holds that actions, thoughts, and motives bear fruit. It resembles the Christian teaching, "Whatsoever a man soweth, that shall he also reap"—except that the retribution or reward for actions is held over to another earthly existence. However, if it is assumed that all physical existence is unsatisfactory and illusory, obviously there is not much to be gained from moving a few rungs up the ladder of human wretchedness. Hence the *Upanishads* taught that preferable even to the faithful performance of *dharma* (moral uprightness and the conscientious discharge of one's duties) was a deliberate break with the habits and engagements which lead to the renewal of births. Separation from the chain of births could be achieved only by following a standard of conduct higher than that of righteousness in the ordinary sense of the term. Evil action would produce evil fruit or *karma*, and righteous action would produce good *karma*; but still more desirable was conduct which, being "neither black nor white," could lead to the extinction of *karma* altogether. In other words, only when a person acts with complete disinterestedness, detaching himself entirely from the idea of reward for his merit, do the fetters which bind him to the world of sense begin to loosen and ultimately dissolve. When this happens, the liberated soul attains blessedness or *nirvana*, which does not mean either annihilation or entrance into a heaven, but a union with *Brahma*, the undefinable Universal Soul or eternal Absolute Being.

The philosophy of the *Upanishads* is pessimistic regarding the world and man's present state, because it depreciates everything material and holds that the natural physical life is a burden. However, it is optimistic as to ultimate ends and as to the possibility of human emancipation. It teaches that there is in every man an indestructible fragment of reality. The basic precept is that *atman* (the individual soul) is actually a part of *Brahma* (the Universal Soul or rational principle which pervades the universe); and that although the soul has been separated from its source it can be reunited with it—not through a miracle but through the individual's own efforts. Moreover, the state of *nirvana*, while a remote goal for the majority, is declared to be attainable during the mortal existence of a sufficiently dedicated person.

2. THE EPIC AGE: THE EMERGENCE OF HINDUISM

Long before the *Vedas* were completed, the two Indian epics were in process of development. The epics were not cast into their final form until sometime between 400 B.C. and 200 A.D., but they refer to events of a much earlier date, and the Epic age overlaps with the Vedic. The epics were composed in Sanskrit, a dialect which is derived from but not identical with that of the *Vedas*, and which came to be regarded as the "classical" form of the Indo-Aryan speech, somewhat as Latin is regarded as classical by the Indo-European peoples of Europe. Furthermore, in spite of the lack of precise dividing dates, it is clear that the epics represent a later stage of social and cultural evolution than do the *Vedas*.

The Indian epics are comparable to the epic poems of the ancient Greeks in that they celebrate the deeds of legendary national heroes, but they are much more encyclopedic and diffuse than the Homeric poems. The *Mahabharata*, the longer of the two Indian epics, is more than seven times the length of the *Iliad* and *Odyssey* combined. While the epics treat of bloody conflicts and amazing exploits, they also incorporate quantities of religious lore, and through the centuries they, rather than the *Vedas*, have served as a Bible for the common people. This is partly because the Brahmans imposed restrictions upon the study of the sacred Vedic texts, whereas anyone could listen to a recitation of the epics.

The *Ramayana* has as its central theme the story of Prince Rama, who, with his beautiful wife Sita, was exiled through the jealous intrigue of a wicked stepmother. It relates how Sita was carried off to Ceylon by the demon king of that country and finally recovered by Rama with the help of a monkey general. The narrative is highly artificial as well as fantastic, and easily lends itself to allegorical

Ravana, Rama, and Lakshmana. An Indian painting of the eighteenth century depicting an incident from the *Ramayana*. Rama, the epic hero, and his brother Lakshmana are fighting against Ravana, the demon king of Ceylon, who carried off Rama's faithful wife Sita.

interpretation. The poem indicates some familiarity with both southern India and Ceylon and provides evidence that Aryan influence, if not extensive conquests, had penetrated into the Deccan. The story was reworked many times in later Indian literature and embellished with symbolism. Rama and Sita came to be idealized as the perfect types of manly courage and feminine purity and devotion, respectively, and Rama was traditionally regarded as an incarnation of the god Vishnu. It is possible that the poem may be, in part, an allegory of the progress of agriculture, in which Rama represents the plow and Sita the furrow. (In the epic, after returning to her husband's kingdom she is swallowed up by the earth.)

The *Mahabharata* is just as enigmatic as the *Ramayana*, though livelier in its story and richer in the variety and scope of its subject matter. "If it is not in the *Mahabharata*, it is not in India," has become a proverb. A narrative core, which gives the poem its name, is the account of a great battle between two related but feuding families, the Pandavas and the Kauravas, of Bharata descent. The "Great Bharata War" probably commemorates a historic battle fought near the modern city of Delhi about 1400 B.C., but the epic version is a tissue of myth and fable. Some scholars believe that the Pandavas (who on the whole are the heroes of the story) were not really kinsmen of the Kauravas but a different tribe altogether, perhaps of Mongolian race. The five Pandava brothers are described as having one wife in common, an obvious reference to the institution of polyandry, which was foreign to the Aryan communities but which is still practiced by the Tibetans. As a chronicle of battle the poetic version is gory enough but full of odd contradictions. Acts of ruth-

The Mahabharata

125

lessness and chicanery are recorded along with examples of exaggerated chivalry and scrupulousness. The god Krishna (supposedly one of the incarnations of Vishnu) takes part in the encounter with rare impartiality—serving as charioteer for one of the Pandava princes but sending his own forces to fight on the other side. The battle is described as raging furiously for eighteen days, by which time practically all the antagonists on both sides have been killed. Finally the five royal Pandava brothers, victorious but the sole survivors of their line, renounce the world and, with their wife and dog, set off for the Himalayas in search of Paradise. Some of the contradictions and inconsistencies in the account can be explained by the fact that the poem was several centuries in the making. Ethical sensibilities and the warriors' code of conduct changed considerably during this period until rough-and-ready practices which were once considered normal came to be looked upon with disapproval.

The Bhagavad-Gita

Interpolated in the story of the great war is a philosophical dialogue which contrasts startlingly with the rapid pace and bloody tone of the main narrative. This passage, which like the rest of the *Mahabharata* is of unknown authorship, is called the *Bhagavad-Gita* or "the Lord's Song." In form, it is a discourse between the warrior Arjuna and his charioteer Krishna (who represents the god Vishnu), precipitated by Arjuna's reluctance to begin the slaughter of his relatives when the lines of battle are drawn up. In substance, it is a dramatic and colorful exposition of some of the most fertile ideas of the *Upanishads*, with greater emotional impact because it speaks not in abstractions but in terms of love for a personal god. At the outset of the dialogue Arjuna expresses his aversion to combat, saying flatly that he will not engage in it: "Better I deem it . . . to face them weaponless, and bare my breast to shaft and spear, than answer blow with blow." Krishna assures him that he must fight, not because there is any virtue in it but because as a member of the

Cotton tapestry. Embroidered with colored silks and silver (eighteenth century), it illustrates scenes from the Makabharata.

warrior caste fighting is his duty (*dharma*). Similarly, Arjuna is reminded that both death and birth are only incidents and that the soul is indestructible: "Life is not slain." Soon, however, the conversation proceeds to a penetrating discussion of the value of different types of action, suggestive of Christian arguments over the respective merits of "faith" and "works." Krishna outlines four levels of conduct or four paths to virtue. At the lowest level are good works, prescribed by reason. Better than works of diligence is knowledge: "The right act is less than the right-thinking mind." Still higher is worship or pure devotion, meditation which is above the bonds of sense and "troubled no longer by the priestly lore." But on the very highest level is placed the renunciation of self. The ideal worshiper, while not neglecting his duty, will play his part "with unyoked soul," "with spirit unattached." He acts "unmoved by passion and unbound by deeds, setting result aside"—that is, with no thought of reward either material or spiritual. Although in the dialogue the warrior is enjoined to fulfill his warlike function—with complete indifference to victory or defeat—the *Bhagavad-Gita* verses have been interpreted by some Hindus, including Mahatma Gandhi, as a text for pacifism.

Aside from their narrative and philosophical interest, the epics reveal that during the 1000 or 1500 years since the settlement of the Indo-Aryans in India extensive changes had taken place among the people, especially in religion and the organization of society. The carefree, boisterous optimism of the early Vedic period was giving way to attitudes of pessimism, discouragement, and resignation; society, instead of being flexible and largely uninhibited, was tending toward a rigid stratification of functions and privileges. The causes of such marked change are not entirely clear. But whatever the reasons, before the close of the Epic age Indian society had assumed many of the characteristics which have distinguished it down to modern times. Together they make up the culture complex which is Hinduism.

Significance of the epics

Popular religion had changed from a simple polytheism to an intricate network of beliefs and rituals with a tremendous hierarchy of gods. The catalogue and ranking of deities and the forms of worship varied from one locality to another and among different strata of the population. With a few exceptions, the more prominent of the early Aryan deities faded into the background as new gods were added to the pantheon with the absorption of local pre-Aryan cults. Eventually the number of divine and semidivine beings accorded recognition ran into the thousands, or possibly millions. Thus, while philosophy was tending toward monotheism, the popular faiths were moving in the opposite direction. Three gods, however, came to be considered as paramount, although without agreement as to their qualities and import. Vishnu, the old solar deity, believed to have had many incarnations, was worshiped under several names. He was still conceived as a benevolent and cheerful

The growth of Hinduism

Shiva. The dance of Shiva portrayed in this eleventh century bronze is symbolic of the destructive forces in the world.

god, "the Preserver," representing the creative or formative principle in the universe. Because he was supposed to disapprove of bloodshed, Vishnu received no animal sacrifice but was offered garlands of flowers. Quite different was Shiva, "the Destroyer," (perhaps identical with one of the Indus valley deities), who, in spite of his frightening aspects, has proved to be a more widely favored object of worship than Vishnu. Typically Shiva was pictured as five-faced and four-armed. He was regarded as beneficent in some aspects because destructive force—symbolized by the dance of Shiva—is a necessary agency in the evolution of the world and living forms, but his power could be prostrating. While some devotees of Shiva were ascetics and mystics, among other groups his worship called for bloody sacrifice, and was also associated with a fertility cult employing orgiastic rites. The third and least influential of the major deities was Brahma, a personification of the Absolute Being or World Soul of the philosophers. Representing an abstract principle, Brahma did not seize upon the popular imagination as did Vishnu and Shiva. He was visualized as a tiny figure who could sit on a lotus leaf. This god, however, has stimulated mystic contemplation. The avowed end of the famous *yoga* discipline is to attain a union of the soul with Brahma.

In many respects Hinduism differs from the pattern of religion familiar to Western peoples. It has no creed, no set of dogmas, no single congregation of the faithful, no established church. It assumes that divine truth wears many faces and that the paths to salvation are myriad. Hinduism is actually a social and religious complex, presenting a wide range of variations from region to region and from one social level to another, but given coherence by the authority accorded to the Brahmans or priests. Throughout India the Brahmans established themselves as ministrants of the rites and recipients of reverence and material compensation. They did not enforce any orthodox creed or crusade against heretics, but they insisted successfully that only they could mediate between gods and men. The chief points of emphasis in Hinduism as a social discipline came to be: (1) respect for and support of the Brahmans; (2) noninjury to animal life, especially cattle (although there are many exceptions to this rule); (3) the inferior status of women; and (4) acceptance of the regulations of caste.

The institution of caste

The chief distinguishing characteristic of Hindu religious and social life is the institution of caste, the most rigorous and refined instrument of segregation ever invented. Caste is much more complex than the typical division of a nation into social or economic classes, even when these classes are hereditary. Aside from heredity, membership in a caste is not based upon any single principle nor does it follow a logical pattern. The best definition of caste is a simple one: "A group of families internally united by peculiar rules for the observance of ceremonial purity, especially in the matters of diet and marriage." Typically, a person must marry within his or her caste and should not accept food from a member of a lower caste. Caste is the antithesis of democracy. It is a vast hierarchy, exalting the Brahmans at the top and degrading the "untouchables" or outcastes at the bottom of the social pyramid.

According to orthodox Hindu tradition, caste has always existed; it is part of the order of nature. The word used to denote it (*jat*) literally means "species." Historical evidence, however, shows that The development of the caste system caste developed gradually over a long period of time. Caste was unknown to the Indo-Aryan society of the early Vedic age, but by the time of the epics it was already regarded as an ancient institution. Thus the system has probably been operating in India for the past 3000 years, and its origins are lost in obscurity. Its starting point, undoubtedly, was the racial pride of the Aryan conquerors, who were determined to prevent contamination by intermarriage with the supposedly inferior "black-skinned" peoples whom they were fighting and reducing to subjection. In this case the distinction was based on color (*varna*); but as time went on various other criteria entered into the drawing of caste lines, including occupations, religious deviation, migrations from one section of India to another, and later invasions by non-Hindu peoples who could not be expelled but who might be prevented from destroying the Hindu system by assigning them a place within it. While the origins of caste are obscure and its causes multiple, the development and final acceptance of the institution was probably influenced by the exertions of the Brahmans in their struggle for a position of dominance over all other groups, a struggle in which they did not scruple to use religious weapons to discomfit their competitors. The keenest rivalry was between the Brahmans and the warrior nobles (including rajas). The nobles had the advantage of being recognized wielders of authority backed by force; but the Brahmans had the advantage of education, mastery of the sacred *Vedas*, and wonder-working powers in the eyes of the people. Socially the Brahmans and nobles were on a par. There are records of Brahman kings and of kings or nobles who became skilled in the *Vedas*. But eventually the Brahmans won recognition for their claim to the highest rank of all, and the nobles were forced to accept classification as the second caste (*kshatriya*). As the price of their pre-eminence, the Brahmans were expected to devote themselves more unreservedly to their religious and educational functions, adopting a modest and mildly ascetic manner of life and leaving political dominion to the *kshatriyas*. However, as tutors and advisers to kings, the Brahmans managed to retain considerable political influence.

Once the principle of caste was accepted by the leading groups in society, it was not difficult to impose it upon the others. Originating in northern India, the institution was extended among the Dravid- The major castes ians and other peoples of the Deccan as Aryan influence permeated that region. Many occupational groups or guilds became castes, but division does not always follow vocational lines. Brahmans may,

Dravidian Temple of Nataraja at Chidambaram. The gorgeously sculptured spire is a gem of Dravidian art; the temple is believed to be the oldest in South India.

without incurring disapproval, engage in a variety of occupations, including comparatively humble ones. At the same time, members of the higher castes avoid tasks which are considered defiling, such as the disposal of corpses, butchering animals, or preparing hides. It is impossible to enumerate precisely the castes of India because the number is enormous and fluctuates from time to time. Theoretically, there are four great castes with subdivisions: *brahmans* (priests), *kshatriyas* (warriors), *vaisyas* (farmers, herdsmen, and artisans), and *sudras* (laborers, servants, and slaves). Actually, except for the first, these categories have little significance. Probably they once represented the general classes of Aryan society before caste had taken hold, but they are much too broad to define caste as it has existed in historic times. The effective divisions are more minute. There are some 1800 subdivisions of Brahmans alone, and the total number of castes and subcastes in India has been reckoned at more than 3000.

Undeniably caste has had a stultifying effect upon Indian society. The rules of caste observance are arbitrary, tedious, and time-consuming, especially in the everyday matters of social intercourse and eating. The fear of pollution becomes an obsession. Not only are there varying degrees of uncleanness in food (depending on the ingredients and the method of cooking as well as who has prepared it), but absolute prohibitions on certain foods restrict the diet unduly, impairing the health of the population. Whether or not a

Effects of the caste system

130

consequence of caste, the position of women in the patriarchal society of India became degraded as the caste system solidified. A man might in some cases marry beneath his caste; for a woman to do so was considered shameful. Caste duty for a woman lay in absolute obedience to her father and then to her husband. The custom of child marriage was introduced, defended with the argument that it saved a girl from the monstrous crime of falling in love with any other man than her future husband. Although child marriages made it inevitable that there would be a large number of widows, a widow was shamed by the belief that some sin of hers had caused her husband's death. She was forbidden to remarry and could best redeem her reputation by committing suicide in flames on her husband's pyre. The most inhumane feature of caste was the treatment accorded the lowest groups in the scale, especially the "Untouchables," who were considered to be outside the border of even the lowest caste, and therefore hardly human beings at all. In southern India the greatest humiliation of the "Untouchables" took place. Their shadow, it was thought, would pollute a well. They were required to live in segregated quarters and to warn people of their approach by uttering cries.

The fact that the caste system has endured in India for tens of centuries and is still operative (though with important changes) is a testimony to the toughness of social institutions, once they have become established. At the same time it should be pointed out that the role of caste in India was not wholly negative. On the positive side it gave the Indian people a sense of identity when confronted with alien cultures or conquerors. It also offered the individual a feeling of security within his group and fostered various forms of mutual assistance. In spite of inter-caste rivalries, the separate castes learned to cooperate with one another, notably in the constitution and administration of local village councils. Eventually caste came to be looked upon as a normal and necessary arrangement, especially as it was hedged about by religious sanctions. Particularly effectual were the twin beliefs: *karma* and the transmigration or rebirth of souls. These concepts, which were given an idealistic intepretation by the philosophers of the *Upanishads*, served in the popular imagination to explain and justify caste. If a person was born into a high caste he was thought to be receiving his reward for meritorious behavior in a previous existence. He had produced good *karma*, which carried him upward on the ladder. Similarly, a member of the despised castes was supposed to have incurred his lot because of misdeeds in a previous incarnation. Unfair as the distinctions of caste seemed to be, they were accepted as a just and precise recognition of the individual's deserts. The person who suffered abuse was told to blame only himself and to strive for perfection within the prescribed limits of his present caste in order that his condition would be improved the next time his soul returned to earth. Since it was possible to go either up or down in the succession of births, patience, diligence, and conformity became supreme virtues. Devotion to duty and the certainty of retribution—*dharma* and *karma*—were the cement which held the caste structure together.

3. REFORM MOVEMENTS: THE RISE OF BUDDHISM

In the sixth century B.C. the stratification of society and the hardening of religious ritual provoked a simmering discontent that found an outlet in several protest movements, led by members of the nobility. Because these protests were directed against the extravagant claims of the Brahmans, they assumed at the outset a heretical or even antireligious form. Most of them proved to be only temporary, but two resulted in philosophical and religious schools of enduring influence—Jainism and Buddhism. There were many parallels between these two movements. They originated in the same section of India, north of the Ganges in eastern Hindustan, and the leader of each was a member of the noble or *kshatriya* caste. Each repudiated the authority of priests and *Vedas*, rejecting all the paraphernalia of religion and replacing it by a system of philosophy. At the same time each was ethical and reformist, attempting to provide moral and personal satisfaction to its adherents. Each drew heavily upon the background of Hindu philosophic tradition and formulated goals which, though original in form, were not alien to the spirit of this tradition. And, ironically, each finally turned into a religion, Jainism taking its place within Hinduism, and Buddhism becoming a separate faith. Although Buddhism carried within itself many elements of Hindu thought, it ultimately obtained its widest following in Asian lands outside India and practically disappeared in the country of its birth. However, Buddhism flourished in India for 1000 years after the life of its founder; it helped to liberalize Hinduism and to keep it from becoming an agency of unlimited exploitation in the hands of the Brahmans. Buddhism also contributed heavily to Indian architecture and sculpture, and the Buddhist sacred texts were the first works committed to writing in India.

Jainism is associated with a figure known as Mahavira ("Great Hero"), who, although probably not its founder, gave it a distinctive form. Mahavira expounded a complex metaphysics which embraced the notion that not only living creatures but almost every object possesses a soul. Employing the familiar concepts of transmigration and *karma*, he held that the soul when attached to matter is in bondage and that it will never be content until freed from and entirely independent of the physical body. The purport of his message was to point out the way to the soul's liberation. Insisting that prayers and worship were of no avail, he prescribed a course of mental and moral discipline, the highest stage of which was withdrawal into a state of meditation with complete denial of the claims

Jain Temples on Girnar Mountain. These exhibit the lavish sculpture characteristic of Indian architecture.

of the flesh. The exalting of extreme asceticism remained one of the chief characteristics of Jainism, and particular honor was reserved for the zealot who was able to carry self-denial to the point of starving himself to death, as a number of Jain saints are reputed to have done. Another cardinal emphasis among the Jains (derived from their animistic belief in a multiplicity of souls) is the doctrine of *ahimsa,* or the necessity of refraining from injury to any living creature. This doctrine has led to commendable efforts to prevent cruelty to animals, although it has sometimes been carried to extremes in attempting to protect even pests and vermin. Surrounded by the atmosphere of Hinduism, the Jains relinquished their early antireligious tenets, instituting prayers to various deities, including the deified Mahavira. The Jain sect, which numbers slightly more than a million members, is monastic in organization. The monks are bound by five vows, while the laity, who are considered part of the order although not of the same degree of holiness as the monks, may subscribe to "small vows." Through plying the trade of moneylending the Jains became a wealthy order, in spite of their rigorous asceticism.

Much more significant than Jainism was the contemporary movement destined to be known as Buddhism because its founder, Gautama, was accorded the title of Buddha, "the Enlightened One." Gautama (*ca.* 563–483 B.C.) was the son of the head of a small state located on the slopes of the Himalayas in what is now Nepal. This tribal state, like many others of that time, elected its ruler; hence Gautama, although of noble blood, was not a hereditary prince as later tradition claimed. Little is known about the events of his life, but legends have supplied innumerable details, most of them miraculous. There is factual evidence to support the conclusion that he was one of those rare personalities who deliberately relinquished a safe and comfortable existence in order to devote himself to the quest of

Gautama: the founder of Buddhism

133

Gautama Buddha in the state of nirvana. Fragment from Early Khmer Period.

higher values and the service of his fellow men. Tradition has it that at the age of twenty-nine he left his sumptuous abode in the middle of the night after a fond glance at his young wife and infant son, cut off his hair, and sent back his jewels and fine clothes to his father. Then came years of wandering and disappointment in which he found no answer to the problem that vexed him—the cause and cure of human suffering. After studying philosophy with the Brahmans he concluded that this was a vain pursuit. Next, it is said, he spent six years practicing an extreme asceticism, until his body had almost wasted away. This course he also abandoned as leading only to despair. The climax of his life came when, discouraged and weary, he sat down under a large Bo tree to meditate. Suddenly he had an overwhelming experience, a revelation or a flash of insight in which he seemed to penetrate the mystery of evil and suffering. Henceforth he was free from doubts, but, instead of retiring to enjoy his state of Enlightenment, he determined to teach others how they might also secure it. For the next forty years until his death at the age of eighty, he wandered through the Ganges valley, relying upon charity for his livelihood and instructing the disciples who gathered about him.

The substance of Gautama Buddha's teachings has been better preserved than the facts of his life. Some scholars consider him the most intellectual of all the founders of the world's great religions. He had no intention of establishing a religion, and his ideas, although conditioned by his Hindu religious background, were not sectarian. His doctrines embodied a philosophy or metaphysics, a psychology, and an ethics, of which the last is most important. The basis of his philosophy was materialism. In direct opposition to the absolute idealism of the *Upanishads* and in contrast to Mahavira's teaching, he held that nothing exists except matter and denied the actuality of the soul. Because matter is in a state of flux, constantly changing its form, he said that all things are impermanent. Hence, there is no Absolute Being or fixed universal principle other than the law of change—growth and decay. Buddha's psychological principles followed logically from his materialist metaphysics. If there is no soul, no permanent entity, there can be no distinct individual personality or being. Not only the soul but the *self* is an illusion, he affirmed. What seems to be an individual personality is only a bundle of attributes (such as sense experience and consciousness) held together temporarily as the spokes of a wheel are fastened around the hub.

Gautama's negative and deflating intellectual doctrines were intended to be encouraging rather than discouraging, as shown in the development of his system of ethics. The source of human anguish is, as he saw it, the individual's attempt to attain the unattainable. Desire or craving is the root of all evil. It can never be satisfied because the desired objects and emotional states are transitory; but the

Gautama's doctrine
of selflessness

134

abandonment of desire can bring satisfaction and peace (the state of *nirvana*). The most persistent and futile craving, underlying a multitude of vain desires, is the ego impulse—the struggle to enhance and perpetuate the self. Since, according to Gautama, the self is only an illusion, the egoist is doomed to chase a will-o'-the-wisp. Thus it follows that selflessness is more realistic as well as more satisfying than selfishness. Oddly enough, Gautama, while denying the existence of the soul, retained the doctrine of *karma*, insisting that a person's actions would affect the condition of another person yet unborn—just as an expiring lamp can light the flame of another lamp. The ultimate goal which he projected was, like that of the Vedic philosophers, the complete extinction of *karma* through the cultivation of selflessness, so that the cycle of births, travail, and tragedy would be no more.

In his ethical teachings Gautama's emphasis was positive rather than negative. He proclaimed the ideal of universal love, to be exemplified by service and helpfulness. Rather than a saintly hermit, he was apparently a gifted teacher, with a stock of homely illustrations and parables. He gave sensible advice in regard to domestic and marital relations, occupations, business matters, and so on. As a rule of personal conduct he advocated "the Middle Path," by which he meant the avoidance of extremes—renouncing both indulgence and injurious asceticism, rejecting prayers and ritual and also the idea of escape into a heaven of bliss. Gautama repeatedly declared that dogmas are much less important than behavior and inner attitudes. And he was firmly opposed to forcing ideas upon anyone, believing that discussion and the power of example are the only valid means of establishing truth. Although he was an ethical rather than a social reformer and made no direct attack upon the caste system, caste distinctions were dissolved among his own group of disciples. He admonished his followers to develop their faculties to the full and to exert themselves for the benefit of others. His last words are said to have been, "Work out your emancipation with diligence."

The Buddhist movement in Gautama's lifetime had few of the characteristics of a religion. In the course of a century or two, however, it developed its own rites, mystic symbols, and other supernatural elements. The Buddhists in India gradually became an order of monks and nuns. Candidates for admission to the order were required to undergo a long period of training. After completing the training, the novitiate shaved his head, put on the yellow robes, and took the monastic vows of poverty and chastity. In contrast to Christian monks, he did not take a vow of obedience, because membership was considered a matter of free choice. The monks customarily remained in a monastery during the three months of the rainy season, which Gautama had devoted to instructing his disciples; for the rest of the year they lived as wandering mendicants, dependent upon the alms which they received in their beggars'

Gautama's ethical teachings

Gautama: monasticism

bowls as they passed from village to village. Lay men or women who accepted the Buddhist teachings and contributed to the support of the monks were considered adherents of the faith and entitled to its benefits.

Various sects of Buddhism arose as the movement spread. The two principal schools, representing a cleavage which apparently began soon after Gautama's death, are the *Hinayana* ("Lesser Vehicle") and the *Mahayana* ("Great Vehicle"). The term *Hinayana* was at first applied reproachfully, because the members of this group were bent upon their own self-perfection, claiming that it was possible for the diligent individual to attain *nirvana* in three lifetimes. The *Mahayana* school was characterized by the doctrine of the buddha-elect—a person who had won Enlightenment but chose deliberately to remain in the world of sorrow in order to work for the liberation of all mankind. In spite of its noble beginning, however, the *Mahayana* tradition became more corrupted than the *Hinayana* as time went on. The *Hinayana* school of Buddhism is represented in its purest form in Ceylon, where it was established as early as the third century B.C., and it is also the prevailing religion of Burma and Thailand. In these countries, Gautama is still theoretically regarded as a man, but in actual practice he is worshiped as a deity, and offerings of flowers or incense are made to his image. The intellectual vigor and the moral challenge of Gautama's teachings have been greatly obscured, and elements of primitive religions have retained their hold on the people. However, the Buddha's emphasis upon kindliness, patience, and the avoidance of injury to living creatures is still prominent. *Mahayana* Buddhism was eventually developed in many different forms in Nepal, Tibet, and eastern Asia. It came to include the worship not only of Buddha but of his several supposed reincarnations, and it also transformed the concept of *nirvana* into a conventional paradise of bliss.

During the period so far discussed, covering more than 1000 years, the physical and external aspects of Indian civilization were still elementary. Writing was unknown until the eighth, or perhaps the seventh, century B.C., and even then it was used only for business purposes. The people lived in villages or small towns rather than cities, architecture was very simple, and political units were small. There was none of the magnificence which characterized ancient Egypt, Mesopotamia, or the extinct Indus valley civilization. To a remarkable degree the achievements of the ancient Indians were in the fields of the imagination and intellect, expressed in song and poetry, in the epics, and in philosophical and religious speculation. Their intellectual achievements also included considerable scientific progress. Medicine was highly developed as early as the Vedic age. Not only were many specific remedies listed, but dissection was practiced and delicate operations were performed. The knowledge of human anatomy was extensive, and a beginning had

Defeat of Porus by the Macedonians, 327 B.C. Impressed by Porus's valor, Alexander the Great allowed the defeated Indian roja to retain his kingdom and appointed him a Macedonian satrap.

been made in the study of embryology. Medical science and the surgeon's vocation were held in high respect, until the caste system introduced a fear of pollution through bodily contact with unclean persons. Many fanciful elements, however, were intermingled with medical lore. An appreciable knowledge of astronomy was acquired in spite of its perversion into astrology. The suggestion that the earth revolves on its axis and that the sun only appears to rise and set was put forward in the *Vedas*, apparently without being taken very seriously. The most brilliant scientific attainments were those in mathematics. The ancient Indians were able to handle extremely large numbers in their calculations and knew how to extract square and cube roots. Besides using the decimal system they invented the all-important principle of the zero, which was eventually adopted by the rest of the world. In geometry their progress was not equal to that of the Greeks, but they surpassed the Greeks in the development of algebra.

During the fourth and third centuries B.C., partly in response to stimulation from without, political developments in India led temporarily in the direction of greater efficiency and unification. As a result of the conquests of the Persian king, Darius I, about 500 B.C., the Indus valley had become a province (satrapy) of the Persian empire, furnishing mercenary soldiers and an annual tribute in gold. After Alexander the Great, the famous Macedonian conqueror, overthrew the Persian empire, he conducted his troops eastward through the passes of the Hindu Kush Mountains into the upper

Conquest of the Indus valley by Alexander the Great

Indus valley (327–326 B.C.). He spent less than two years in India but traversed most of the Punjab, fought and negotiated with local rajas, and installed Macedonian officials in the region. Although Alexander's invasion provides the first verifiable date in Indian history, it made so little impression upon the Hindus that their contemporary records do not even mention his name. However, the invasion promoted cultural exchange between the Hindus and the Greek-speaking world, and, more immediately, it paved the way for the erection of a powerful state in India.

In the revolts and confusion that followed the death of Alexander in 323 B.C., an Indian adventurer named Chandragupta Maurya seized the opportunity to found a dynasty. Chandragupta had profited from observing Greek military tactics and led in the movement to expel the Macedonian officials from India. Then he turned his army against the Magadha kingdom, which was the strongest state in Hindustan at this time. He defeated and killed the Magadhan king and established himself as ruler in the capital city of Pataliputra (now Patna) on the Ganges. When Seleucus (Alexander's successor in Syria and Persia) tried to recover the lost Indian territory, Chandragupta defeated him soundly and forced him to cede Baluchistan and part of Afghanistan. Chandragupta extended his power over most of northern India and founded the first empire in Indian history. Although his dynasty, known as the Maurya, lasted less than a century and a half, its record is a distinguished one.

Chandragupta was a much more imposing figure than the rajas of the Vedic age. His government was efficient but very harsh. Social and economic activities were carefully regulated, an elaborate tax system had been devised, and the death penalty was meted out freely, sometimes through the administering of poison. The king kept a large standing army, with divisions of infantry, cavalry, chariots, and elephants. In spite of his far-reaching authority, and his maintenance of secret police or spies, he seems to have lived in dread of assassination and took the precaution to change his sleeping quarters every night. On the credit side was his construction and improvement of public irrigation works and the building of roads. The Royal Road, from the capital to the western frontier, was 1200 miles long.

The greatest member of the Maurya Dynasty, and one of the most remarkable rulers in the annals of any civilization, was Chandragupta's grandson, King Asoka, the royal patron of Buddhism, whose beneficent reign lasted some forty years (*ca.* 273–232 B.C.). Merely as a conqueror Asoka could lay claim to fame, because he held under Mauryan rule not only Hindustan and the region northwest of the Indus but most of the Deccan as well, thus bringing the greater part of India into one administration. His conquests, however, were the aspect of his reign that he considered least important. In fact, he fought only one major war—by which he was enabled to

The rise of the Maurya Dynasty

The reign of Chandragupta

King Asoka: Buddhist conqueror

gain control of the Deccan—and he felt remorseful ever after for the bloodshed which accompanied this campaign. Attracted to the Buddhist teachings, he at first became a lay adherent and later took the formal vows and joined the order but without relinquishing his position as king. He attempted, rather, to exemplify the precepts of Buddhism in his personal life and to apply them to the administration of the empire. Thus, without being a theocrat or divine-right ruler, he provides an almost unique example of the injection of religious idealism into statecraft.

It is impossible to know how completely Asoka's benign purposes were carried out. He was particularly active in establishing rest houses for travelers, in having trees planted, wells dug, and watering places built along the roads for the refreshment of man and beast, and in improving facilities for the treatment of the sick. He sent commissioners throughout the kingdom to inquire into the needs of the people, teach them religion, and report on their spiritual progress. In deference to the Buddhist injunction against taking life, Asoka gave up hunting (replacing this sport by "pious tours" or pilgrimages) and gradually reduced the meat consumption in the royal household until—according to his announcement—only a vegetable diet was permitted. He reformed the harsh system of punishments which his grandfather had used, but he did not entirely abolish the death penalty. There is no evidence of any trend toward democracy in Asoka's government. He adhered to the tradition of autocratic rule, but exercised it with conscience and benevolence. Although he was earnest in his support of Buddhism, Asoka opposed fanaticism. He made religious toleration a state policy and urged that the Brahmans of all the Hindu sects be treated with respect. He stated that he cared less about what his subjects believed than he did about their actions and attitudes. To commemorate his authority he

Asokan Bull Capital. From Rampurva, Bihar (northeastern India), third century B.C. Emperor Asoka erected huge stone pillars and utilized some already standing as impressive memorials to his own authority and to the law of Buddha. The bell-shaped capital shows the influence of contemporary Persian architecture.

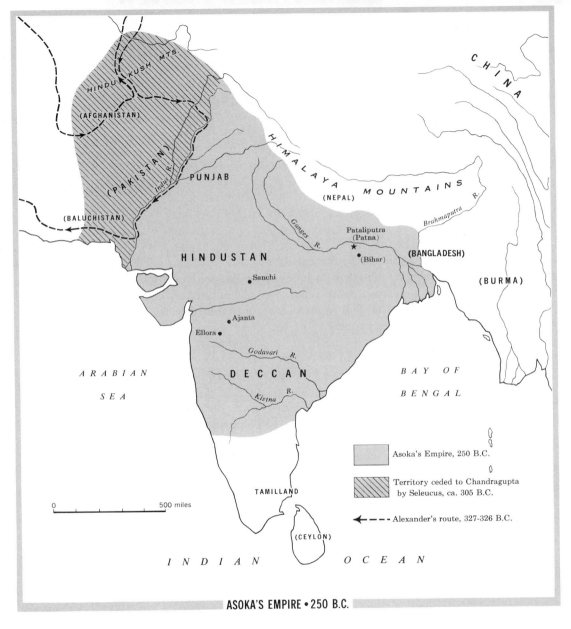

ASOKA'S EMPIRE • 250 B.C.

had erected in various parts of his empire gigantic sandstone pillars, each cut from a single block of stone and standing forty or fifty feet high. The capitals of animal figures and the beautifully polished surface of these columns—some of which are still preserved—testify to the engineering and artistic skill of the royal workmen.

Asoka's patronage during his long reign contributed markedly to the growth of the Buddhist religion. He sent missionaries of the faith to Ceylon, Burma, Kashmir, Nepal, and apparently even west to Macedonia, Syria, and Egypt. The king's own son was the missionary to Ceylon. Buddhist monks held a general council in 250 B.C. at Asoka's capital, Pataliputra, where they agreed upon the basic

Asoka's patronage of Buddhism

Laughing Boy. Terracotta head of a laughing boy, from Pataliputra (Patna). An example of the realistic sculpture of the Maurya period.

texts that should be regarded as authentic. This "Council of Patna" established the canonical books of Buddhism, especially for the *Hinayana* school. The Buddhist scriptures are the oldest written literature of India—that is, they were the first to be committed to writing. However, although the texts were settled upon in 250 B.C., they were still memorized and transmitted only by word of mouth. Except for the excerpts in Asoka's rock carvings, the texts were not actually written out in full until about 80 B.C. in Ceylon.

Asoka's extraordinary administrative system did not long survive him. His successors seem to have been mediocrities who lacked both his reforming zeal and his organizing ability. In 184 B.C. the last Maurya ruler was assassinated by the army commander, an ambitious Brahman who seated his own family on the throne. The efficiency of Asoka's government was not duplicated until about 500 years after the end of his dynasty.

End of the Maurya Dynasty

SELECTED READINGS

· *Items so designated are available in paperbound editions.*

· Basham, A. L., *The Wonder that Was India: A Survey of the Culture of the Indian Sub-Continent Before the Coming of the Muslims*, New York, 1955 (Evergreen) Illustrated.

· Brown, W. N., *The United States and India, Pakistan, Bangladesh*, Cambridge, Mass., 1972 (Harvard). An excellent general introduction.

Cambridge History of India, Vol. I.

Cambridge History of India, Supplementary Volume: Wheeler, Mortimer, *The Indus Civilization*, 3rd ed., 1968.

Conze, Edward, *Buddhist Thought in India*, London, 1962.

READINGS
- Coomaraswamy, A. K., *History of Indian and Indonesian Art*, 1927 (Dover).
- Dasgupta, S. N., *Indian Idealism*, London, 1933 (Cambridge).

Eliot, Charles, *Hinduism and Buddhism: An Historical Sketch*, 3 vols., New York, 1954. A standard work.

Fairservis, W. A., Jr., *The Roots of Ancient India: The Archaeology of Early Indian Civilization*, New York, 1971. An interesting and provocative account.

Hutton, J. S., *Caste in India*, 3rd ed., Oxford, 1961.
- Jacobson, N. P., *Buddhism: The Religion of Analysis*, Carbondale, Ill., 1970 (Southern Illinois University). A modern philosophical interpretation.

Kabir, Humayun, *The Indian Heritage*, New York, 1955.

Keith, Arthur, *The Religion and Philosophy of the Veda and Upanishads*, 2 vols., Cambridge, Mass., 1925.

Kosambi, D. D., *Ancient India: A History of Its Culture and Civilization*, New York, 1966. Stimulating and unconventional.

Kramrisch, Stella, *The Art of India: Traditions of Indian Sculpture, Painting, and Architecture*, New York, 1954. Admirable photographs, with brief introduction.

Lee, S. E., *A History of Far Eastern Art*, New York, 1965.

Majumdar, R. C., ed., *The History and Culture of the Indian People*, Vol. I, London, 1951; Vol. II, 2nd ed., Bombay, 1953.

Moreland, W. H., and Chatterjee, A. C., *A Short History of India*, 4th ed., London, 1957.

Naidis, Mark, *India: A Short Introductory History*, New York, 1966.
- Piggott, Stuart, *Prehistoric India*, Baltimore, 1950. (Penguin)
- Prabhavananda, Swami, and Manchester, F., *The Upanishads, Breath of the Eternal*, New York, 1957 (Mentor).
- Rawlinson, H. G., *India, a Short Cultural History*, rev. ed., New York, 1952 (Praeger). An excellent interpretive study.

Rowland, Benjamin, *The Art and Architecture of India: Buddhist, Hindu, Jain*, Baltimore, 1953. Informative and discriminating.
- Schweitzer, Albert, *Indian Thought and Its Development*, tr. Mrs. Charles Russell, Boston, 1957 (Beacon). Brief but insightful.

Smith, V. A., *Asoka*, Oxford, 1920.

Spear, Percival, ed., *The Oxford History of India*, 3rd ed., New York, 1958. A thorough revision of a standard older history.
- Wheeler, Mortimer, *Civilizations of the Indus Valley and Beyond*, London, 1966 (Thames and Hudson).
- ———, *Early India and Pakistan to Ashoka*, New York, 1959.

SOURCE MATERIALS

- Arnold, Edwin, tr., *The Song Celestial—The Bhagavad-Gita* (Theosophical Publishing House).
- de Bary, W. T., ed., *Sources of Indian Tradition*, "Brahmanism"; "Jainism and Buddhism"; "Hinduism." (Columbia).
- Edgerton, Franklin, tr., *The Bhagavad Gita*, (Torchbooks). Translation and interpretation.

Goddard, Dwight, ed., *A Buddhist Bible*.
- Hamilton, C. H., ed., *Buddhism, a Religion of Infinite Compassion* (Library of Liberal Arts).

Lin Yutang, ed., *The Wisdom of China and India*, Hymns from the *Rigveda*, Selections from the *Upanishads*.
- Mueller, Max, tr., *The Upanishads*, 2 vols. (Dover).
- Narayan, R. K., *Gods, Demons and Others* (Compass). Fine translation of ancient Indian stories.

The *Ramayana* and the *Mahabharata*, Everyman's Library edition.

Sastri, S. R., tr., *The Bhagavadgita*. An accurate translation with explanatory and critical comment.

CHAPTER 7

Ancient Chinese Civilization

There have been many kings, emperors, and great men in history who enjoyed fame and honor while they lived and came to nothing at their death, while Confucius, who was but a common scholar clad in a plain gown, became the acknowledged Master of scholars for over ten generations. All people in China who discuss the six arts, from the emperors, kings, and princes down, regard the Master as the final authority. He may be called the Supreme Sage.
—*Historical Records* of Ssu-ma Ch'ien (145-*ca.* 85 B.C.)

The beginning of a high civilization in China did not occur until about a thousand years after the flowering of the Indus-valley civilization in India. However, when once established the Far Eastern culture continued—not without changes and interruptions but with its essential features intact—into the twentieth century of our own era. The civilization of China, although it took form much later than that of Egypt, Mesopotamia, or the Indus valley, is one of the oldest in existence. The reasons for the long survival are partly geographic and partly historical. During most of her history China did not have aggressive organized states on her borders. More important, perhaps, the pacifist influence of her great philosophers and ethical teachers kept her imperialism within bounds. The Chinese people considered other peoples as inferiors but still members of one great family and seldom provoked either the enmity or the envy of surrounding countries. They did their share of conquering, but the lands they annexed were almost exclusively undeveloped territories. They rarely attempted to impose their will upon conquered peoples by force, but considered it their mission to assimilate them and make them the beneficiaries of their superior ethical system.

Reasons for long survival of Chinese civilization

143

The loess highlands of northern China.

1. THE FORMATIVE STAGE

In our study of preliterate cultures we have learned already that China was the home of one of the earliest human species, the so-called Peking man. His skeletal remains were found between 1926 and 1930 in a cave about forty miles southwest of Peking (Pei-ping). Anthropologists estimate that his species lived at least 500,000 years ago, and that he was probably a contemporary of Java man, one of the oldest human types. Peking man's culture was, of course, extremely primitive, but there is evidence that he used crude stone tools, had a knowledge of fire, and buried his dead. Whether the members of his species were the ancestors of the historic Chinese people is a debated question. An eminent German anthropologist, Franz Weidenreich, maintains that the descent was direct. He bases his conclusion upon peculiarities in the skulls, jaws, and incisor teeth of the ancient specimens which have their counterparts among modern Mongolian peoples.

Although the discovery of Peking man proves the existence of human beings with an Old Stone Age culture in China at least 500,000 years ago, there are many gaps in the record subsequent to that time. Evidence is still scanty for the Late or Upper Paleolithic period (as it is reckoned in Europe), when the advance of the Arctic ice sheet brought a bitter climate to northern China. There is ample archaeological evidence of human habitation of northern China during the Neolithic period, when the climate became warmer. Remains have been found of two varieties of Neolithic culture in this region, distinguished by their pottery—one unpainted and including delicate specimens with a glossy black surface, the other painted and also of excellent workmanship. The painted pottery

Peking man

Archaeological evidence of Neolithic culture

culture, centered in the southeastern portion of the great highland plain that surrounds the Yellow River valley, flourished as early as the fifth millenium B.C.

A contemporary Chinese scholar contends that this semi-arid highland, rather than the flooded plain of the lower river valley, was the cradle of Chinese civilization. In respect to its origins, therefore, the Far Eastern civilization shows a significant contrast with those of Egypt and Mesopotamia, which arose in river deltas. Of course agriculture was as important to the Chinese as to the inhabitants of the Nile and Tigris-Euphrates valleys, but the Chinese apparently began as dry-land farmers and may have lacked irrigation facilities until the sixth century B.C., some 4000 years later. The highlands bordering the middle reaches of the Yellow River are covered with a type of soil known as loess, composed of fine particles of loam and dust borne by northwest winds from the central plateaus of Asia and deposited in the valley and along the northeastern coast. This soil, which from its color has given rise to such geographical names as Yellow River and Yellow Sea, is pliable enough to be easily worked with primitive digging sticks, and also has the advantage of being free from a heavy growth of forest or grasses. In choosing farm sites close to the river or its tributaries but on high ground, the early inhabitants avoided the danger of floods. But they had to depend on plants capable of surviving with a minimum of rainfall. The principal crops of northern China in the Neolithic age were several varieties of millet, hemp, and the mulberry (for raising silkworms). Surprisingly, rice, too, was grown in the marsh areas of the northern plain, probably introduced from the Yangtze region to the south, where it was indigenous.[1]

The loess highlands, cradle of Chinese civilization

By about 1500 B.C. the east central portion of the Yellow River valley was occupied by people of Mongolian stock who had passed beyond the Neolithic into the Bronze Age, had learned how to build fortified cities, and possessed the essential attributes of civilization, including writing. The era of this Bronze Age people corresponds to the period of the Shang Dynasty in Chinese history. It was long believed by scholars that the Shang Dynasty was almost purely legendary. Excavations of the 1930's, however, have proved that it was very real and have recovered many impressive examples of its workmanship. Dates have not yet been precisely established, but the civilization was flourishing by 1400 B.C. A study of the objects which have been unearthed and especially the all-important deciphering of inscriptions have made it possible to construct a fairly complete picture of this formative period of Chinese history.

The Bronze Age and the beginning of the Shang Dynasty

Racially the Shang people present no significant contrast to the earlier inhabitants of the region they conquered nor to the Chinese of later times. Their culture, too, was a continuation and improve-

[1] Ping-ti Ho, "The Loess and the Origin of Chinese Agriculture," *American Historical Review*, LXXV: 1 (October 1969), pp. 1–36.

ment of that of the Neolithic farming communities. Presumably the Shang Dynasty was inaugurated by the conquest of a military chieftain, with no extensive displacement of population. The Shang kingdom occupied only a small part of China. The area under effective control may have been no more than 40,000 square miles, or about the size of the state of Ohio. The Shang people carried on trade with other communities—also agricultural but more primitive than their own—in the Yangtze valley to the south, and they had to defend themselves against barbarian and nomadic tribes from the north and west. The principal royal residence and seat of government was the city which they called by the name of Shang, situated at the northern tip of Honan province, about 80 miles north of the Yellow River (the site of modern Anyang).

Agriculture was the chief source of livelihood of the Shang people, although their tools for cultivating the soil were still quite primitive. Grains were the principal crop, and now wheat and barley were grown in addition to millet. Hunting and herding contributed to the food supply. Many animals had been domesticated, including not only the dog, pig, goat, sheep, ox, horse, and chicken, but also the water buffalo, monkey, and probably the elephant. Dog flesh as well as pork was a popular item of diet. But in spite of the importance of animal husbandry, Shang society was by no means nomadic; and if it had ever passed through such a stage the evidence has disappeared, even from folk traditions and literature. Though developing in close proximity to the wandering herdsmen of Mongolia, the Chinese were primarily a nation of farmers.

The houses the Shang people constructed show an intelligent adaptation to the environment. The Neolithic inhabitants of the region commonly lived in pits hollowed out of the loess. In Shang times rural villagers apparently also occupied pit dwellings, but the city residents built more comfortable houses above ground. For a foundation the firmly packed earth served admirably. Upon the rectangular foundation was erected a gabled-roof structure, with wooden poles holding up the central ridge of the roof and shorter posts supporting each of the two sides at the eaves. Thatching was used for the roof and packed earth for the outside walls of the house. This type of dwelling, which by coincidence is closer in design to the European style of home than to the tents of Mongolia or the mud-brick houses of Egypt and Mesopotamia, has been employed by the Chinese throughout their history.

The specimens of Shang craftsmanship that archaeologists have recovered reveal a high degree of skill and versatility. In spite of familiarity with metal, Shang artisans still made many objects of stone—knives, axes, and even dishes—as well as of bone, shell, and horn. Bone implements inlaid with turquoise and exquisitely carved pieces of ivory were produced in abundance. Cowrie shells were used for jewelry and probably also served as money. The bow and

Bronze Tripod Cup. Shang Dynasty (1523–1027 B.C.). Used in sacrificial ceremonies.

arrow was the most formidable weapon for the hunt or for combat. Bamboo arrows were feathered and tipped with bronze or bone points. The bow was of the composite or reflex type, formed of two separate arcs of wood held together with horn, and said to be almost twice as powerful as the famous English long bow. Two-horse chariots, of elaborate workmanship and with spoked wheels, were probably the exclusive property of the aristocracy. Armor was made of leather, sometimes reinforced with wooden slats. Evidently the people were fond of music. For musical instruments they employed drums, stones emitting a bell-like tone when struck, and a small pipe of hollow bone with five finger-holes—more like an ocarina than a flute.

The artistry of the Shang people is illustrated most strikingly by their sculpture and engraving. The examples of sculpture thus far discovered are generally of small dimensions. A marble ox head, however, greater than life-size and fitted with a pin as if it had been fastened to a body, suggests that some large statuary was produced. Shang metal work was truly remarkable, especially the superb bronze castings of intricate design. Bronze articles included weapons and chariot and harness fittings, but most impressive were the objects intended for religious and ceremonial functions—tripods, libation bowls, drinking cups, and grotesquely figured masks. The technique employed in their making was superlative. A leading American specialist in early Chinese culture asserts that it was more flawless than the technique employed for bronze sculpture at the height of the Italian Renaissance.

As has already been mentioned, this early civilization possessed a system of writing. The writing brush and an ink made of soot had been invented. Writing materials included silk cloth and wood, and it is quite possible that books were compiled with pages which were narrow strips of bamboo joined together by a thong. Fortunately, a great many specimens of writing have been preserved inscribed on pieces of animal bone, horn, and tortoise shells. These served in a process of divination by the king and priests; hence they are referred to as "oracle bones." After a question had been directed to the spirits, a flat piece of split cattle bone or a tortoise shell was heated until it cracked; then the shape of the crack was studied to ascertain the answer from the spirit world. The majority of the oracle bones contain no writing; but for some unknown reason, in about 10 per cent of the cases the question was engraved upon the object after the divination rite had been performed. Although the inscriptions are brief, a careful study of them has thrown light upon many aspects of Shang society and activities.

The Shang writing was not primitive but in an advanced pictographic stage. While the Shang symbols are the earliest examples found in the Far East, they presuppose a long period of evolution from more rudimentary forms. Each character represented an entire

Art of the Shang people

Oracle bone, dating from 1300 B.C., records the appearance of a new star. Note the pictographic characters.

147

Bronze Ritual Vessel. Shang Dynasty.

word, as it does in the classical Chinese. In some cases, only the shape of the sign has changed. For example, the Shang character for *sun* was round—obviously a picture of the sun—while now it is square. Practically all the principles which the Chinese literary language employs in the process of character formation were already in use. The Shang characters were not only pictographs but sometimes ideographs, in which the meaning was conveyed by combining different symbols or concepts (the sun and moon joined together represent *bright* or *brightness;* the sun rising behind a tree stands for *east*). The phonetic principle was also applied. A character having one meaning might be used to indicate a word of different meaning but pronounced the same way. To avoid confusion, the phonetic symbol was combined with a conceptual symbol in the same character. Not surprisingly, fewer characters were employed in Shang times than later, although it is probable that the list compiled from the oracle bones is only partial. About 2500 characters have been distinguished in the Shang records; the written language eventually came to include more than twenty times that number.

Political and social
institutions of the
Shang period

Little definite information is available as to the political and social institutions of the Shang period. Governmental power was vested hereditarily in a royal family, but on the death of the king the crown passed to his younger brother in preference to the king's own sons. In addition to military activities, the king probably supervised public works and was important as the chief religious functionary. He was assisted by an educated class of priests, who served as astrologers, performed the divination rites, and supervised the calendar. Because the calendar was a lunar one, it frequently had to be adjusted to bring it into harmony with the solar year. There is some evidence from the oracle bones that the Shang priests had made considerable achievements in mathematics and astronomy. As early as the fourteenth century B.C. they recorded eclipses and perhaps had already conceived the decimal system.

The family was the basic social institution. The king, or a great aristocrat, might have several wives, but monogamy seems to have been the more usual practice even in the royal family, as it almost certainly was among the people generally. The position of women, at least within the upper classes, was good. Slavery existed and there were gradations in the ranks of society, but there is no evidence of a feudal system during this period.

The family

Ample testimony exists for the religious practices of the Shang people. They worshiped many natural objects and forces—the earth, rivers, the winds, even the directions (East, West, and South). To these gods they performed sacrifices, not out of doors but in temples. Burnt offerings of animal flesh were common, and a kind of wine or beer made from millet was also considered acceptable. Although the Shang were in some ways highly civilized, there is gruesome evidence that they practiced human sacrifice on a large scale. Apparently the victims were usually captives who had been taken in battle, and sometimes raiding expeditions were sent out for the express purpose of securing a batch of foreign tribesmen to be offered in sacrifice. The principal deity seems to have been a god concerned primarily with rainfall, the crops, and war. His name, Shang Ti, has persisted into later times. There is no evidence that Shang religion was essentially spiritual or ethical; it was directed toward the procuring of human prosperity, as among the Sumerians and Babylonians. The king was not a divinity like the Egyptian pharaoh, but he became an object of worship after his death, and sacrifices were performed to the departed spirits of both kings and queens. The royal tombs were sumptuous affairs. A large pit was excavated, provided with stairways, and a wooden tomb chamber was constructed at the bottom. The royal corpse was surrounded with magnificent furnishings, including figured bronzes and pottery, marble statuary, and richly adorned implements and jewels. After the funeral ceremonies the entire excavation was filled with firmly tamped earth.

Religion of the Shang period

Bronze Ritual Vessel with Removable Top. Shang Dynasty.

It is noteworthy that the typical Chinese institution of ancestor worship was already in existence, at least in the circle of the court. Ancestral spirits were believed to possess the power of helping or hurting their descendants, and yet they depended upon their living representatives for nourishment in the form of food offerings. It was also customary, even among people of humble circumstance, to bury valuable objects with the deceased. Divination by means of the oracle bones—the practice which bequeathed so many valuable inscriptions—was a by-product of the cult of ancestor worship and the belief in the potency of departed spirits.

Ancestor worship

The Shang society represents the earliest genuine civilization of Eastern Asia for which historical records are available. In addition, it laid the foundation and provided materials for the distinctive Chinese culture pattern, as illustrated by methods of agriculture, handicrafts, artistic and architectural forms, emphasis upon the family as the basic social unit, religious concepts, and a system of writing. About 1027 B.C. the city of Shang was taken and the dynasty overthrown by semibarbarous invaders from the west. However, these barbarians assimilated, continued, and finally surpassed the culture of the Shang people whom they had conquered, and gave their own name (Chou) to the longest dynasty of China's history.

Significance of the Shang period

2. THE CHOU DYNASTY, THE CLASSICAL AGE OF CHINA (*ca.* 1027–249 B.C.)

While the civilization of the Vedic Age in India was still in its early stages, in the Yellow River valley of China the Shang Dynasty was succeeded by the Chou. However, the seizure of power by the Chou warriors did not bring such a pronounced change in the character of society and culture as did the Indo-Aryan invasion of India. The Chou people, located to the west of the Shang frontier, had had considerable contact with the Shang state previous to their conquest of it. Women from the Shang royal family had been given as wives to some of the Chou rulers—probably in the vain hope that marriage alliances would lessen the danger of attack from that quarter. Although the Chou people of the eleventh century B.C. were hardly more than barbarians, they were not distinct in race from the Shang, and their leaders had sufficient appreciation of Shang culture to wish to continue it. Even when the capital city was taken and the government overthrown, a Shang prince was allowed to continue to administer lands in the center of the state, with the "assistance" of younger sons of the Chou royal house. After this prince became involved in an unsuccessful rebellion of the recently conquered people, he was executed, and a large number of Shang subjects were removed from the scene of the rebellion to a region south of the Yellow River. But even then the Shang royal line was not entirely extinguished—probably as much from fear of provoking the powerful Shang ancestral spirits as from a desire to placate the conquered subjects.

Origin of the Chou Dynasty

The new dynasty exerted zealous efforts to convince the people that it was a legitimate succession rather than a usurpation. Its spokesmen advanced the claim that the last Shang ruler had been incompetent and debauched, and that the divine powers had used the Chou as an instrument for his removal. The "Mandate of Heaven," they alleged, had been transferred from the Shang house to the Chou. There is no evidence that the Shang king was guilty of the faults ascribed to him, but the charge, even if a fabrication,

Efforts of the Chou rulers to establish legitimacy

(MANCHURIA)

(MONGOLIA)

40°

(Peking)

SEA OF
JAPAN

(JAPAN)

SHANTUNG
PENIN.

YELLOW
SEA

Anyang
Yellow (Hwang) R.
Wei R. (Sian) (Loyang)
(HONAN
PROVINCE)

Han R.

C H I N A
(SZECHWAN
PROVINCE)

Yangtze R.

(Shanghai)

EAST CHINA
SEA

30°

Yangtze R.

Hsi R.

(TAIWAN)

20°

500 miles

SOUTH CHINA
SEA

130°

ANCIENT CHINA DURING THE CHOU DYNASTY • 1027-249 B.C.

shows the desire of the conquerors to fit their authority into accepted conventions rather than to break with the past. And the concept of governmental power as a commission from Heaven rather
than an absolute and inalienable right—although possibly invented
by the Chou for propaganda purposes—was to become a persistent
element in Chinese political history.

The Chou form of government was a monarchy, although not
identical with that of the Shang. The throne was hereditary by
primogeniture, as in most European monarchies, whereas under the
Shang it had passed from older brother to younger brother. The
early Chou rulers maintained their capital near modern Sian (Shensi
province) in the Wei valley, where their power had already been

**The Chou
government**

151

established. In addition to the Shang territory they added other conquests, especially southward in the middle Yangtze valley. The king exercised direct rule over the region surrounding his capital but administered the outlying areas indirectly, through appointed officials who were given almost complete jurisdiction within their own districts. The Chou administrative system was roughly similar to that which developed in Europe in the age of feudalism some 2000 years later. The district governors, originally members of the royal family or generals of proved competence, were the king's vassals, but they were also great territorial lords, exercising wide military and judicial powers, and they gradually transformed their position from that of appointive official to hereditary ruler. Chou feudalism—like the later European variety—contained elements of danger for the central government, although for two or three centuries the Chou court was strong enough to remove overly ambitious officials and keep its own authority paramount.

By the eighth century B.C. the vigor of the ruling house had declined to the point where it was no longer able to protect the western frontier effectively against the attacks of barbarians. The fortunes of the dynasty seemed to reach their lowest point in 771 B.C., when a worthless king almost duplicated the villainies that had been unjustifiably attributed to the last of the Shang rulers. King Yu, particularly through his extravagant efforts to amuse his favorite concubine, angered the nobles beyond endurance. When he lit the beacon fires to summon aid in the face of a combined attack by barbarian tribes and one of the outraged nobles, his men refused to answer the summons. King Yu was killed and his palace looted. The dynasty might have been ended then and there, but the nobles of the realm found it expedient to install the king's son as nominal head, keeping in their own hands the actual authority over their respective dominions. This event marks the close of the "Western Chou" period. The royal seat of government was now moved about 100 miles farther east into safer territory (near the modern city of Honan), and the ensuing period (771–ca. 250 B.C.) is known accordingly as the "Eastern Chou."

Bronze Ceremonial Vessel.
Chou Dynasty (1027–249 B.C.).

During the 500 years of the Eastern Chou Dynasty, China suffered from political disunity and internal strife. The king actually ruled over a domain much smaller than that of some of the great hereditary princes. For the kingdom as a whole his powers, while theoretically supreme (he was officially styled "Son of Heaven"), were limited to religious and ceremonial functions and to adjudicating disputes concerning precedence and the rights of succession in the various states. In spite of these conditions, however, it is not quite accurate to describe the Eastern Chou era as an age of feudalism. It is true that hereditary nobles enjoyed social prominence, wealth, and power, and acquired different degrees of rank, roughly equivalent to the European titles of duke, marquis, count, viscount,

Conditions under
the "Eastern
Chou" Dynasty

and baron. They became lords and vassals, held fiefs for which they owed military service, and were supported by the labor of the peasants on their lands. These warrior aristocrats not only raised armies and collected revenues from their dominions but also administered justice. Custom supplied the greater part of law, but severe penalties, including fines, mutilation, and death, were inflicted upon offenders. Nevertheless, a number of factors prevented the complete ascendancy of a feudal regime. In the first place, a large proportion of the nobility failed to acquire estates of their own and remained jealous of the great territorial lords. The lesser aristocracy, generally well educated and frequently unemployed, constituted a sort of middle class that could not fit comfortably into a feudalized society. More important still, towns were growing and trade increasing throughout the Chou period, and the merchants (including part of the aristocracy) attained economic importance. Moreover, rulers of the larger states successfully pushed forward a program of centralization within their own dominions. They introduced regular systems of taxation, based upon agriculture. To offset the entrenched position of the nobles they developed their own administrative bureaucracies and staffed them with trained officials, recruited largely from the ranks of the lesser aristocracy. In spite of the disorganized condition of China as a whole, the period provided valuable experience in the art of government which could eventually be drawn upon in the task of reuniting the country.

Although China was divided during the Eastern Chou period into many principalities with shifting boundaries and frequent wars, a few of the larger states held the balance of power, especially four which were located on the outer frontiers to the north, west, and south. Usually one state at a time was recognized as paramount and its ruler, designated as "First Noble," took the lead in organizing the defense of the kingdom as a whole and even in collecting the revenues. The boundaries of Chinese civilization were extended by the aggressive initiative of the rulers of the frontier states. The Shantung peninsula, the seacoast as far south as modern Shanghai and Hangchow, and the rich Yangtze valley were all brought under Chinese jurisdiction. Thus the total area was much larger than the old Shang kingdom and included more than half of the eighteen provinces which have constituted the state of China during the greater portion of its history. The southern part of Manchuria was also occupied, and walls of earth—the first stages of the famous Great Wall of China—were constructed both south and north of the Yellow River for protection against the nomads of Mongolia.

Expansion of the frontiers

Beginning about the middle of the fifth century B.C., internal conditions became extremely chaotic, inaugurating a bloody period known as that of "the Warring States." The relatively restrained competition which the feudal principalities had carried on with one another gave way to a struggle for supremacy in which proprieties and recognized codes were disregarded. The rulers of several of the states even assumed the title of "king" (*wang*), previously reserved for the prince of Chou. In the fourth and third centuries B.C. the state of Ch'in, seated in the Wei valley on the western frontier, gained ascendancy over the others. Not only were the Ch'in rulers aggressive, but within their own dominions they had developed the most effectively centralized government in China. After annexing the fertile plain lying south of the Wei valley (in modern Szechwan province), they constructed a splendid irrigation system which has lasted until the present day. Probably the Ch'in people had also mingled with and absorbed some of the barbarian tribesmen, but they were no less Chinese in culture than their rivals. In spite of alliances formed against them by other feudal princes, the Ch'in forces, employing ruthlessness, massacre, and treachery, annexed one region after another. Finally, in 256 B.C., they seized the tiny remaining portion of the royal domain and ended the Chou Dynasty. Within thirty-five years the Ch'in prince had brought all the Chinese territories under his control and, to indicate the extent of his triumph, assumed the imposing title of "First Emperor" (Shih Huang Ti). Although the Ch'in Dynasty hardly outlasted its founder, it did China the valuable service of abolishing the remnants of feudalism. The highly centralized government which the Ch'in emperor established did not prove to be permanent, but the feudal system never reappeared.

**Cultural progress
under the Chou**

During the 800 or 900 years of the Chou Dynasty, in spite of internal conflicts, cultural progress was almost continuous. The period is regarded as the classical age of Chinese civilization, and its contributions were fundamental to the whole subsequent history of the Far East. As has already been indicated, the culture of the Chou was based upon foundations that had been laid by their predecessors.

Ceremonial Bronze Basin. Chou Dynasty. The inscription on this bronze piece, known as the *San P'an*, records the settlement of a territorial dispute between the feudal states of San and Nieh in Western Shensi Province.

Handicraft techniques improved under the Chou and the smelting of iron was introduced, although iron did not entirely displace bronze. While the great majority of the population lived in rural villages, there were some large towns and the merchant class assumed importance. Trade was by no means exclusively local. With the introduction of the donkey, and especially the camel (probably not before the third century B.C.), it became possible to develop caravan trade routes across Central Asia for the transportation of grain, salt, silk, and other commodities. Coined copper money came into use before the close of the fifth century B.C. The manufacture of silk, already an old industry, was increased, and the fibers of several domestic plants were also employed in making textiles.

From time immemorial the all-important Chinese enterprise has been farming. It was extended under the Chou by reclamation measures—the building of irrigation canals and reservoirs and the draining of swamps—and also by acquisition of the moist and fertile rice-producing lands of the Yangtze valley. The soybean—valuable not only as a food but for restoring fertility to the soil—was added to the list of crops. The methods of cultivation developed during the Shang and Chou periods have remained essentially unchanged ever since.

The persistence of unvarying techniques over a long period of 3000 years is attributable not to the inability of the Chinese to progress but to the fact that these techniques were admirably adapted to the terrain and to the objectives of Chinese society. While they were primitive in some ways, they embodied a great deal of experience and foresight. China has been said to possess a "vegetable civilization," because its people, while not socially or intellectually stagnant, adapted themselves so completely to the potentialities of their environment. The typical Chinese farming village—with fields of various sizes, often tiny but all carefully tended—appears almost as if it were part of the natural landscape instead of being an effort on man's part to manipulate nature for his own benefit. Although China is a large country, the relative scarcity of arable land made it difficult for food production to keep pace with an expanding population. Much of the country is hilly or mountainous, and the north and west portions are subject to drought which cannot be entirely overcome by irrigation. Consequently, attention was lavished upon every suitable plot that could be found. The bulk of labor was done by hand, with simple tools but in such a way as to produce the greatest possible yield. Wastes which had fertilizing value were collected and returned to the soil, as were ashes and even powdered sun-dried bricks when no longer serviceable for building purposes. Crops were rotated to avoid soil exhaustion, and hillsides were terraced to conserve moisture and prevent erosion.

Although draft animals had been known from early times and the ox-drawn plow was introduced about the sixth century B.C., their use

Large Bronze Bell. This bell, with bosses or nipples, decorative panels, and inscriptions, is typical of the Middle Chou style (ninth century B.C.). It was hung from the ring at the base of the shaft and was sounded by striking with a wooden mallet. The bell has a scooped mouth instead of being even at the bottom. (In the picture it is resting on a cushion.)

was restricted because of the cheapness and—on small plots—greater efficiency of human labor. Besides, hayfields or grazing lands to provide animal fodder represented a curtailment of the area devoted to producing foodstuffs for human beings. The Chinese have subsisted largely on a vegetable diet, not because they had religious scruples against eating flesh as did the Hindus, but for practical reasons of economy. Instead of raising crops to feed cattle and then eating the cattle, they preferred to consume the crops directly themselves. For meats they chose animals that could be reared inexpensively—chickens, ducks, and especially pigs, which were also useful scavengers, and fish, with which even temporary ponds could be profitably stocked. Chinese methods of agriculture thus were intensive rather than extensive. As compared with modern Western countries, particularly the United States and Canada, the yield was low in proportion to the number of men employed and the hours of labor, but high in terms of acreage. While Chinese farming demanded exacting and arduous toil on the part of the cultivators, it made possible the growth of a large population.

Society during the Chou period had a decidedly aristocratic character. There was a tremendous gulf between the great landowners and the peasants who comprised the vast majority of the people. But while class lines were rigidly drawn, Chinese society was never stratified by a caste system like that of India. There were only two clearly distinguished classes, the commoners or serfs and the nobles; and as civilization became more complex the nobility included con-

Left: *Drum Stand of Lacquered Wood*. Late Chou Dynasty. Right: *Ceremonial bronze tripod*. Late Chou Dynasty, fourth century B.C. Probably from the Li-Yu treasure.

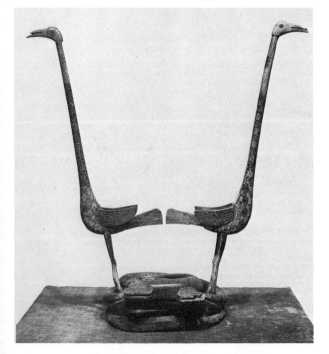

trasting interests and conditions rather than remaining a solidly united order. Because the numbers of the aristocracy tended to increase, many of them consequently possessed little or no landed property. They were forced to seek administrative employment with a powerful noble, to engage in trade, or even to undertake menial occupations, thereby undermining the fiction of the inherent superiority of the hereditary aristocracy. Unfortunately, very little is known about the condition of the lower classes. Evidently before the close of the Chou period a considerable number of peasants had become landowners. Others, however, were actually slaves, and most of the commoners were serfs, attached to the soil without having legal title to it and compelled to give the lord a large share of the produce.

While the family is always a basic social institution, it has been so to an almost unique degree in China. Here the family was a tightly organized unit, bent upon preserving the welfare of its members against any outside agency, official or unofficial, and was probably the only safeguard of any consequence against the unlimited exploitation of the lower classes. Typically the Chinese family was large because it embraced several generations. When a son married he customarily brought his bride home to live under the paternal roof or in a closely neighboring house. Theoretically the family also included the departed ancestral spirits, thus extending vertically into time as well as horizontally among contemporary relatives. Authority was vested in the father (or grandfather), and the utmost emphasis was placed upon respect for elders, so that even grown men were bound by their parents' wishes. Such a custom led to extreme conservatism and sometimes inflicted hardships upon youth, but it had the advantage of developing qualities of patience, loyalty, and consideration for the helpless aged.

The family as a social institution

Women became definitely subordinate to men in the patriarchal family and in Chinese society at large, although their position was not utterly intolerable. Allegedly, in early Chou times the young men and maidens of the peasant class were allowed to choose their mates freely after a Spring Festival characterized by complete license. However that may be, among the aristocracy neither men nor women had freedom of choice in marriage unless they defied convention and parental authority. Marriages were arranged by the parents of the respective parties, usually with the assistance of a matchmaker or go-between. After the bride was brought to her husband's home she was considered as on probation for a three-month period, after which if she had proved satisfactory she was allowed to participate in the ancestral sacrifice and became an accepted member of the family. In regard to the laxity of conduct permitted and the right of divorce, the woman was also at a disadvantage. Only the husband could have recourse to divorce, and he could obtain it on any one of a number of grounds, including that

Subordination of women

his wife talked too much. Actually, however, divorces were rare, especially among people of humble circumstance. Undoubtedly the practices of polygamy and concubinage, permitting a man to have more than one consort, added to the hardships and humiliation of women. But these practices were confined to the wealthy classes and were by no means universal among them. In spite of the inferior position of woman in Chinese society, she had definite rights and privileges and on the whole was much better off than in the caste-ridden society of India. It is strange that, in a predominantly agrarian economy such as China's, labor in the fields was not regarded as woman's normal work, although among poor families she often had to assist. The wife's own family did not renounce all interest in her when she left their home for her husband's and might interfere in case she was abused. Children were taught to love and venerate both parents, and as a woman grew older she shared in the honors accorded to age. The domineering position which a grandmother or mother-in-law sometimes assumed became proverbial.

The family as a religious and political institution

The Chinese family was not only an economic and sociological unit but a religious and political one as well. Some scholars maintain that during the Chou period the servile peasants were not permitted the dignity of having surnames, and that they had no share in the cult of ancestor worship. However, that condition could not endure in view of the tremendous emphasis placed upon family relationships among the dominant classes, in public administration, and in the literature of the age. Throughout the greater part of Chinese history, religion for the ordinary person consisted largely in caring for his family graves and making prayers and offerings to the spirits of his ancestors. As a political unit the family enforced discipline and considered misconduct on the part of one of its members as a collective disgrace. Very commonly the inflicting of punishment for minor offenses was left to the head of a family rather than to a public official. The strong solidarity and sense of collective responsibility of the family had disadvantages as well as advantages. Because the family was answerable for the behavior of its members, one of them might be punished for the misconduct of another if the true offender was not apprehended by the authorities, or a whole family might be wiped out for a crime committed by one person. On the whole, however, the family gave the individual a greater feeling of security and support than has been typical in most societies.

Religion in the Chou period

Religion was fundamentally the same as it had been in Shang times. Many deities were worshiped, ranging from local spirits and nature gods with limited powers to such majestic divinities as Earth and Heaven. The practice of human sacrifice gradually disappeared and came to be strongly condemned, but animals, agricultural produce, and liquor were offered upon the altars. Evidence of a "chariot sacrifice" was uncovered by archaeologists north of the Yellow River when they excavated a deep pit about 30 feet square.

In this instance seventy-two horses harnessed to twelve chariots, and eight dogs with bells fastened to their necks, had apparently been placed in the pit and buried alive. While worship did not necessarily include prayer, prayers were sometimes written out and burned with the sacrificial offering. A prominent deity from Chou times on was the one called T'ien, translated as "Heaven." Although of separate origin, this divinity was similar to and became practically identical with the earlier Shang Ti. T'ien was not conceived of primarily as a personal god but as representing the supreme spiritual powers collectively, the universal moral law, or an underlying impersonal cosmic force. It was by the "Mandate of Heaven" (*T'ien-ming*) that the king was supposed to rule, and he was referred to as "Son of Heaven," without, however, implying that he was divine. The worship of the earth as an agricultural deity came to be supplemented by the veneration of a specific locality with which the fortunes of the worshipers were associated. Every village had its sacred mound of earth; the lord of large territories had a mound to represent his domain; and the mound of the king was believed to have significance for the whole land of China. The most important rituals took place either at these mounds or in ancestral temples.

Among the Chinese at this time, as among the Hindus, there was no clear-cut religious system, no fixed creed, and no church. In contrast to Hindu society, however, the Chinese priests did not become a sacrosanct class in a position to dominate other groups. The priests, like those of the ancient Greeks, were merely assistants in the ritual. The indispensable religious functionaries were the heads of families, including, of course, the king, whose ancestral spirits were particularly formidable, and who propitiated the great deities of the rivers, earth, and sky. For most of the people religion was either a family affair, consisting of social functions invested with sentiment and emphasizing filial piety, or a matter of state, maintained by the proper authorities to ensure the general welfare. Sacrifices to the greatest gods were ordinarily performed only by the highest officials, to lesser deities by lower officials, and so on down to the ordinary folk who sacrificed to their own ancestors in the form of wooden tablets. They believed that the spirits of these ancestors could bring prosperity to the family and that dire consequences would follow any neglect of the rites. Aside from traditional ceremonies, everyday life was complicated by a medley of folklore and superstition hardly classifiable as religion but exerting a potent influence. This included the belief in witchcraft, in good and evil omens, in divination and spirit messages conveyed through mediums, and in the necessity of avoiding offense to numerous malignant beings. "Hungry ghosts," whose sacrifices had been neglected or cut off through the extinction of a family, were considered especially dangerous. In spite of the strong faith that the soul outlived the body, the notion of rewards and punishments in an afterlife was almost entirely lacking. The worst fate that could happen to a disembodied spirit, it was thought, was for it to be deprived of the nourishment supplied by sacrificial offerings.

By far the most significant contributions of the Chou period were in the fields of literature and philosophy. The Shang system of writing, already highly advanced, was continued with slight modifications. Evidently the Chinese now considered written records as indispensable to the conduct of both public and private affairs. They sometimes recorded important transactions in lengthy inscriptions on bronze vessels, but they more frequently wrote with the brush upon wood or cloth of silk. Books composed of thin strips of bamboo were produced in abundance. Although only a minority of the population was literate, it must have been a large minority and included the feudal nobility as well as the merchants. In contrast to the Feudal Age of Western Europe when writing was confined almost entirely to the clergy, the Chou aristocrats were versed in literature and kept full records of their properties, their dependents, and sometimes of their personal activities. Not only the king but the head of every feudal state maintained archives to preserve the luster of family traditions and to aid in settling disputes with rival princes. The Chinese, even in ancient times, were at the opposite pole from the Hindus in their attitude toward the importance of chronology and the recording of factual events (although this does not mean that Chinese documents were entirely accurate or free from fanciful elements). A young nobleman or prince, in the process of his education, was reminded by his tutors that later generations would study the annals of his administration and that he should, accordingly, choose his actions with care. Princes were regularly given instruction in history "to stimulate them to good conduct and warn them against evil"—apparently with no better results than have attended most modern efforts in this direction.

Of the tremendous output of Chou literature, only a few authentic portions have survived (aside from the imperishable bronze inscriptions). Some of them, however, are from a date earlier than 600 B.C. Probably the most ancient work is the *Book of Changes*. It contains a collection of hexagrams formed of straight and broken lines arranged in different combinations, with accompanying text. The figures, like the earlier Shang oracle bones, were used for divination. Thus the book was originally hardly more than a sorcerer's manual, but it came to be venerated as a work of mystic and occult wisdom.[2] Very different is the *Document Classic* (less accurately called "*Book of History*"), which is a collection of official documents, proclamations, and speeches purporting to be from the early

---

[2] For a contrary view see H. Wilhelm, *Change; Eight Lectures on the I Ching*, trans. C. F. Baynes, New York, 1960. Wilhelm interprets the classic as an affirmation of man's ability to control his own destiny.

Chou period. The *Book of Etiquette*, dealing with ceremonial behavior, formal occasions, and preparation for adult responsibilities, was intended to assist in the education of the lesser aristocracy. Most interesting of all is the *Book of Poetry*, an anthology of about 300 poems covering a wide range of subjects and moods. Some of the poems are religious, in the nature of prayers or hymns to accompany the rites of sacrifice; others celebrate the exploits of heroes; still others are lyrical in quality, voicing the laments of a discharged official, a soldier's homesickness, delight in the beauties of nature, and the frustration or rapture of young lovers. Neither in quantity nor in profundity do these odes approach the *Vedas* of India, but they are graceful in expression and show vividly the practical down-to-earth temperament of the Chinese and their lively interest in and optimistic attitude toward the business of living—at least among the aristocracy. While the poems on the whole are neither philosophical nor spiritual, a few suggest the reforming fervor of the Hebrew prophets.

In view of the extent and the variety of writing during the Chou period, the literary collections which have survived are rather disappointing. But this deficiency is amply compensated for by achievements in the realm of philosophy, which reached a brilliant climax between the sixth and third centuries B.C. For some unexplained reason—perhaps by mere coincidence—philosophical activity of a high order was carried on at about the same time in three widely separated regions of the ancient world. While the Greeks were inquiring into the nature of the physical universe, and Indian thinkers were pondering the relationship of the soul to Absolute Being, Chinese sages were attempting to discover the basis of human society and the underlying principles of good government. The Chinese thinkers were not much interested in either physical science or metaphysics; the philosophy they propounded was social, political, and ethical. Exhortatory and reformist in tone, it undoubtedly reflected the influence of the recurrent strife and political disorders of a period when feudal ideas and institutions were becoming increasingly irrelevant but had not yet been clearly repudiated. Against the background of upheaval which marked the late Chou era, philosophers sought to formulate principles for the stabilizing of society and the betterment of the individual. The leaders in this intellectual activity were largely from the lesser aristocracy, men of energy and ambition who could not find employment suitable to their talents and who were distressed by the turbulent state of public affairs. They were a scholarly group, fond of disputation, but also maintaining an interest in the practice of government and sometimes holding administrative posts or coaching pupils who aspired to such posts. It was a time of lively interchange of ideas, and a great variety of opinions was put forward. Out of this intellectual ferment and debate—one of the most productive in the annals of human thought

Philosophy

161

—four main philosophic schools emerged, the most important being the Confucianist and the Taoist.

Confucius (*ca.* 551–479 B.C.), who has proved to be one of the most influential men in all history, was largely a failure from the standpoint of what he hoped to accomplish. He spent his life advocating reforms that were not adopted; yet he left an indelible stamp upon the thought and political institutions of China and other lands that came under Chinese influence. He was a native of the state of Lu (in modern Shantung province) and was reputed to have been the child of an aged father, a gentleman soldier named K'ung (Confucius is the Latinized form of the name K'ung Fu-tzu, or "Master K'ung"). Probably his family was of the lesser aristocracy, respectable but poor. In any event, he showed a sincere interest in the common people and did not choose his disciples on the basis of birth or rank. When he was only about twenty-one he began to teach informally a group of young friends who were attracted by his alert mind and by his precocious knowledge of traditional forms and usages. Although his reputation spread rapidly, little is known concerning the incidents of his career. Possibly as a mature man he held office for a short time under the Duke of Lu. For more than ten years, until old age overtook him, he wandered from state to state, refusing to be employed as a time-serving flatterer but continually hoping that some ruler would give him a chance to apply his ideals and thus set in motion a tide of reform that might sweep the entire country. Although revered by his small band of disciples, some of whom became officeholders, Confucius received no offer of appointment that he could accept in good conscience. Finally he returned to his native country where he died, discouraged, at the age of seventy-two.

Frustrated as a statesman, Confucius made his real contribution as a teacher. The memoranda of his conversations with his disciples (the *Analects*)—which are considered on the whole authentic, even though not written down in the master's lifetime—convey the impression of a lively and untrammeled mind which challenged those with whom it came in contact. Like his contemporary Gautama Buddha, and like his near-contemporary Socrates, Confucius earnestly believed that knowledge was the key to happiness and successful conduct. He also believed that almost anyone was capable of acquiring knowledge, but only through unrelenting effort. He insisted that his student-disciples should think for themselves, saying that if he had demonstrated one corner of a subject it was up to them to work out the other three corners, and constantly pricking their complacency. He recognized the difficulties in the thorough assimilation of ideas and was never satisfied with quick agreement. While no ascetic, he frowned on indulgence and urged his associates to strive continually for improvement. Though he had moments of petulance and harshness, the nobility of his character is unmistak-

Confucius

Confucius in Royal Dress. A traditional representation in bronze.

Confucius as a teacher

able, and he refused to let his disappointments make him cynical.
His regret, he said, was not that he was misunderstood but that he
did not understand others sufficiently.

The doctrines of Confucius centered upon the good life and the
good community. He respected religious ceremonies as part of established custom, but he refused to speculate on religious or supernatural questions, saying, in substance: "We do not know life; how
can we understand death? We do not fully understand our obligations to the living; what can we know of our obligations to the
dead?" He was optimistic regarding the material world and regarding human nature, which he thought was essentially good; but he
believed that the individual's worth would not be realized unless he
was properly guided in the development of his faculties. For this
reason he stressed propriety and the observance of ceremonial
forms—which he thought were helpful in the acquisition of self-
discipline—although he was really more concerned with sincerity
and intelligence than with appearances. Impressed as he was by the
evils of feudal contention, Confucius advocated the restoration of
central authority in the kingdom, combined, however, with a logical
distribution of power. He visualized the ideal state as a benevolent
paternalism, with the ruler not only commanding but also setting an
example of conduct for the people to follow. He did not endorse a
totalitarian system, nor mere passivity on the part of the people. He
intended the ruler to be guided in his administration by the judgment of his officials, chosen on the basis of merit from the class of
scholars. The health of the entire state would depend upon the welfare of each village, and harmony would be achieved by the combined efforts of the common people from below and of the officials
from above.

Confucius' teachings therefore embodied a political philosophy,
which regarded the state as a natural institution but modifiable by
man, and devoted to promoting the general well-being and the fullest growth of individual personalities. The state existed for man, not
man for the state. On the ethical side he emphasized fellow feeling
or reciprocity, the cultivation of sympathy and cooperation, which
must begin in the family and then extend by degrees into the larger
areas of association. He stressed the importance of the five cardinal
human relationships which were already traditional among the Chinese: (1) ruler and subject, (2) father and son, (3) elder brother
and younger brother, (4) husband and wife, and (5) friend and
friend. These could be expanded indefinitely and were not bounded
even by Chinese lines. The logic of this train of thought was summarized in the famous saying, "All men are brothers." But Confucius argued that a person must be a worthy member of his own
community before he could think in terms of world citizenship.
Laying no claim to originality, Confucius urged a return to an ideal
order which he attributed to the ancients but which actually had

never existed. Unknowingly, he was supplying guiding principles which could be utilized in the future.

Mencius and
Hsün-tzu

Aside from its founder, the ablest exponent of the Confucianist school was Mencius (Meng-tzu), who lived about a century later (*ca.* 373–288 B.C.) Like his master, Mencius affirmed the inherent goodness of human nature and the necessity of exemplary leadership to develop it. He looked upon government primarily as a moral enterprise, and he was more emphatic than Confucius in insisting that the material condition of the people should ·be improved. He wanted the government to take the initiative in lessening inequalities and in raising the living standards of the common folk. Perhaps because political confusion had increased since Confucius' day, he was outspoken in criticizing contemporary rulers. He taught that only a benevolent government, resting upon the tacit consent of the people, can possess the "Mandate of Heaven," and he defended the people's right to depose a corrupt or despotic sovereign. Hsün-tzu (*ca.* 300–237 B.C.) is usually classified as a Confucianist, although his precepts diverged radically from those of Mencius. While both Confucius and Mencius had started with the assumption that man has a natural propensity for good, Hsün-tzu regarded human nature as basically evil. However, like the earlier Confucianists he believed that man can be improved by proper education and rigorous discipline. He laid great stress upon observance of ritual, formal training in the classics, and a strictly hierarchical ordering of society. In spite of his gloomy view of the natural man, he was far from a complete pessimist. He recommended vigorous action by the state to institute reforms and, like Mencius, favored the regulation of economic activities.

Lao-tzu and
Taoism

The Taoist philosophical school was in many ways the opposite of the Confucianist. Its traditional founder was Lao-tzu ("Old Sage"), a shadowy figure of the sixth century B.C. Little is known about the facts of his life, and some scholars doubt that he was an actual historical person. According to tradition he served as an official at the Chou capital in charge of the archives until, becoming weary of the world, he set out for the western mountains in quest of peace and, at the request of a guard at the mountain pass, set down his words of wisdom in a little book before he disappeared. But the real authorship of the *Tao Teh Ching* (Classic of Nature and Virtue), from which the principles of Taoism are derived, is undetermined, and it may not have been written earlier than the third century B.C. The book is not only brief but enigmatical, paradoxical, and perhaps ironical. With its terse and cryptic style it seems almost like an intentional antidote to the Confucian glorification of scholarship, exhortation, and patient explanation. On the whole the Taoist book exalts nature (sometimes in the sense of impersonal cosmic force, "the Boundless" or Absolute) and deprecates human efforts. Its spirit is romantic, mystical, anti-intellectual. It not only lauds the perfection of nature but idealizes the primitive, suggesting that people would be better off without the arts of civilization, living in blissful ignorance and keeping records by means of knotted cords rather than writing. Wealth creates avarice and laws produce criminals, it asserts. It is useless to try to improve society by preachment, ritual, or elaborate regulations; the more virtue is talked about the less it is practiced. "Those who teach don't know anything; those who know don't teach." A person learns more by staying home than by traveling; the wise man sits and meditates instead of bustling about trying to reform the world.

As a political philosophy, Taoism advocates laissez faire. Unlike Confucius, Lao-tzu believed that governmental interference was the source of iniquity and that, if people were left to follow their intuition, they would live in harmony with nature and with one another. Nevertheless, Lao-tzu's ideal was not pure anarchism. Like Confucius he assumed the necessity of a wise and benevolent (although largely passive) ruler, and agreed that the only legitimate purpose of government was to promote human happiness. Perhaps his thought also reflects a rural protest against both the self-important aristocracy and the artificial society of the rapidly growing towns. In Lao-tzu's teachings there are strains of pacifism and the doctrine of non-retaliation for injury ("The virtuous man is for patching up; the vicious man is for fixing guilt"); of the efficacy of love in human relations ("Heaven arms with love those it would not see destroyed"); and of equalitarianism ("It is the way of Heaven to take away from those that have too much and give to those that have not enough"). The Taoist school produced several able thinkers in late Chou times and played a part in the shaping of Chinese philosophical traditions. However, in contrast to Confucianism, the Taoist doctrines were eventually transformed into a religious system, with a priesthood, temples, ritual, and emotional elements. But the Taoism which became one of the prominent religions of China had little connection with the principles expounded in the *Tao Teh Ching*.

A third school of political and ethical philosophy was associated with Mo Ti (or Mo-tzu), whose career is placed in the middle of the fifth century B.C. A man of decided originality, Mo Ti may have been of peasant stock; his sympathies lay with the downtrodden, and he regarded luxury and extravagance with aversion. The distinguishing feature of his thought is that he combined the doctrine of utilitarianism—insisting that everything should be judged by its usefulness—with a sweeping idealism that drew inspiration from religious faith. He condemned elaborate ceremonies dear to Confucianists, including the traditional three-year period of mourning, on the ground that they entailed needless expense. Sports, amusements, and even music met his disapproval because they were unproductive, absorbing energies which might be employed in useful labor. The

Taoist political and ethical philosophy

Mo Ti

pressing need, as he saw it, was to increase the supply of food and basic commodities to improve the health, longevity, and numbers of the population; and such a program called for hard work on the part of both common people and officials. His strong denunciation of offensive warfare was also rooted in utilitarianism.

Mo Ti's ethics were by far the boldest of any of the Chinese philosophers. In place of the Confucian system of an expanding series of loyalties beginning with the family and radiating outward, he proclaimed the universal and impartial love of all mankind and declared that there can be no satisfactory community until the distinction between "self" and "other" is completely transcended. Applying his utilitarian yardstick, he reasoned that, by cultivating sympathy and mutual helpfulness with everyone, the individual was ensuring his own welfare as well as contributing to the security of others. But while his doctrine of universal and impartial affection linked altruism to self-interest, it called for a rare degree of discipline and high-mindedness, and its similarity to the ethics of Christianity has often been remarked. Mo Ti believed that the state, like other human institutions, was created by divine ordinance and that it was the duty of the ruler to carry out the will of Heaven, which he interpreted to mean promoting the common welfare. Although the Mohist school, as it is called, was prominent for a while and attracted many adherents, it practically disappeared after the downfall of the Chou Dynasty—partly because of the enmity of the Confucianists—and the teachings of the utilitarian philosopher were almost entirely forgotten until modern times.

Altruism and utilitarianism

A fourth philosophical school, known as the "Legalist," stood far removed both from the bold idealism of Mo Ti and the optimistic humanism of Confucius. Formulated during the hectic period which witnessed the final collapse of the Chou Dynasty and the triumph of the Ch'in, it reflects Hsün-tzu's harsh view of human nature and his emphasis upon coercive discipline. At the same time the Legalists were indebted to Taoism in their contempt for scholarship, the intelligentsia, and conventional ethics; and in their preference for a simple agrarian society over a mobile, sophisticated, and economically diversified one. But, unlike the Taoists, they did not exalt nature or any supernatural agency, and they completely rejected laissez faire. Rather than mystics they were hardheaded realists, or even cynics. Asserting that man is by nature hopelessly selfish and incorrigible, they prescribed complete and unquestioning submission to the ruler. People's behavior, they argued, could be controlled only by carefully defined rewards and punishments, by a code of laws which was fundamentally punitive and which derived not from custom or natural instinct but from the will of the sovereign. Of all the schools of Chinese political thought, the Legalist was the most uncompromisingly authoritarian. Although its principles were systematically applied only during the short-lived Ch'in Dynasty, they

The Legalist school

exerted a continuing influence upon later dynasties also—tempered somewhat by the opposing Confucian tradition—and they find perhaps more than an echo in the present Chinese totalitarian regime.

Although the later centuries of the Chou Dynasty were marked by strife and unrest and encumbered by the remnants of decaying feudal institutions, the material basis for a productive society had been laid and intellectual progress had reached a high point. An abundant and many-sided literature was in existence. Philosophers had come to grips in mature fashion with fundamental problems of individual and group behavior. Scholarship was an honorable profession, and scholars were considered indispensable to the business of government. There was a growing tradition—not yet very effective—that government entailed moral responsibilities as well as privileges, that those who exercised authority did so on sufferance and only so long as they conformed to the "Decree of Heaven." Moreover, the Chinese had come to think of themselves as composing a unique society, not merely a political affiliation but the "Middle Kingdom"—the heart of civilization as contrasted with outlying "barbarian" areas. They had already mingled with and partially absorbed many non-Chinese tribes, and it is significant that the distinction between their civilization and the "barbarian" regions was not based upon race or nationality. The attitude of superiority which they adopted sometimes made them arrogant, but it gave them a toughness in resisting the shock of invasion and other adversities.

SELECTED READINGS

· *Items so designated are available in paperbound editions.*

Bishop, C. W., *Origin of the Far Eastern Civilizations*, Washington, 1942.

Chang Kwang-chih, *The Archaeology of Ancient China*, New Haven, 1968.

Ch'en, K. K. S., *Buddhism in China; a Historical Survey*, Princeton, 1964. A solid and lucid study.

· Creel, H. G., *The Birth of China*, New York, 1937 (Ungar). A fascinating account of archaeological exploration of Shang civilization, and an excellent introduction to the basic culture pattern of ancient China.

· ———, *Chinese Thought from Confucius to Mao Tse-tung*, Chicago, 1953 (Mentor).

· ———, *Confucius and the Chinese Way*, New York, 1960 (Torchbooks).

———, *The Origins of Statecraft in China*, Vol. I: *The Western Chou Empire*, Chicago, 1970. A valuable contribution.

Fairbank, J. K., Reischauer, E. O., and Craig, A. M., *East Asia: Tradition and Transformation*, Boston, 1973. A shortened edition of a major text.

· Fitzgerald, C. P., *China, a Short Cultural History*, 3rd ed., New York, 1961 (Praeger). Frequently unconventional in viewpoint.

· Fung Yu-lan, *A Short History of Chinese Philosophy*, ed. Derk Bodde, New York, 1948 (Macmillan).

· Goodrich, L. C., *A Short History of the Chinese People*, 3rd ed., New York, 1959 (Torchbooks). Brief but informative; fulfills the promise of its title.

READINGS Harrison. J. A., *The Chinese Empire: A Short History of China from Neolithic Times to the End of the Eighteenth Century*, New York, 1972. A good synthesis.

King, F. H., *Farmers of Forty Centuries, or Permanent Agriculture in China, Korea and Japan*, Emmaus, Penn., 1948. A classic description.

Latourette, K. S., *The Chinese, Their History and Culture*, 4th ed., 2 vols. in one, New York, 1964. A solid contribution, comprehensive in scope.

Li Chi, *The Beginnings of Chinese Civilization: Three Lectures Illustrated with Finds at Anyang*, Seattle, 1957.

· Li, Dun J., *The Ageless Chinese, a History*, 2nd ed., New York, 1971 (Scribner's).

· Moore, C. A., ed., *The Chinese Mind: Essentials of Chinese Philosophy and Culture*, Honolulu, 1967 (East-West Center).

Needham, Joseph, *Science and Civilization in China*, New York, 1954, Vol. I; 1956, Vol. II; 1959, Vol. III; 1962–1971, Vol. IV. A far-ranging and challenging study.

Treistman, Judith, *The Prehistory of China: An Archaeological Exploration*, Garden City, N. Y., 1972.

Tuan Yi-fu, *China*, Chicago, 1970. An excellent cultural geography.

· Watson, Burton, *Early Chinese Literature*, New York, 1962 (Columbia).

Wheatley, Paul, *The Pivot of the Four Quarters: A Preliminary Enquiry into the Origins of the Character of the Ancient Chinese City*, Chicago, 1971.

· Wilhelm, Hellmut, *Change: Eight Lectures on the I Ching*, tr. C. F. Baynes, New York, 1960 (Princeton, 1973).

SOURCE MATERIALS

· de Bary, W. T., ed., *Sources of Chinese Tradition*, "The Classical Period" (Columbia).

Chai Ch'u, and Chai, Winberg, *A Treasury of Chinese Literature*.

Chan Wing-tsit, ed. and tr., *A Source Book in Chinese Philosophy*. Traces the history of Chinese philosophy from Confucianism to Communism.

· Giles, H. A., ed., *Gems of Chinese Literature* (Dover).

· Legge, James, tr., *The I Ching (The Book of Changes)* (Dover).

· ———, *The Works of Mencius* (Dover).

Lin Yutang, ed., *The Wisdom of China and India*, "Laotse, the Book of Tao."

Mei, Y. P., tr., *The Ethical and Political Works of Motse*.

Soothill, W. E., tr., *The Analects of Confucius*.

Waley, Arthur, ed. and tr., *The Book of Songs; The Way and Its Power* (Evergreen); *Three Ways of Thought in Ancient China* (Anchor).

· Watson, Burton, tr., *Mo Tzu: Basic Writings* (Columbia).

PART **II**

The World in the
Classical Era

After 600 B.C. the chief centers of civilization in the ancient world were no longer confined to North Africa and Asia. By that time new cultures were already growing to maturity in Greece and Italy. Both had started their evolution considerably earlier, but the civilization of Greece did not begin to ripen until about 600 B.C., while the Romans showed little promise of original achievement before 500. About 300 B.C. Greek civilization, properly speaking, came to an end and was superseded by a new culture representing a fusion of elements derived from Greece and from the Near Orient. This was the Hellenistic civilization, which lasted until about the beginning of the Christian era and included not only the Greek peninsula but Egypt and most of Asia west of the Indus River. The outstanding characteristic that served to distinguish these three civilizations from their predecessors was secularism. No longer did religion absorb the interests of man to the extent that it did in ancient Egypt or in the nations of Mesopotamia. The state was now above the church, or perhaps we should say it included the church, and the authority of the priests to determine the direction of cultural evolution was greatly reduced. Somewhat similar developments were taking place in the Far East. In India, Hinduism and the dominance of the Brahman caste were challenged by the ethical and non-theological system of Guatama Buddha. Buddhism also spread to China and Japan and became a major stimulus of cultural vitality in all three countries.

	POLITICS	ARTS AND LETTERS
	Mycenaean stage, *ca.* 1500–1100	*Vedas* in India, 1200–800
	Dark Ages of Greek history, 1100–800	
800 B.C.	Beginning of city-states in Greece, *ca.* 800	*Iliad* and *Odyssey*, *ca.* 800
	Rome founded, *ca.* 750	*Upanishads*, 800–600
	Feudalism in China, *ca.* 800–250	
	Age of the Tyrants in Greece, 650–500	
	Reforms of Solon, 594–560	Doric architecture, 650–500
	Reforms of Cleisthenes, 508–502	Aeschylus, 525–456
500 B.C.	Overthrow of monarchy in Rome and establishment of republic, *ca.* 500	Phidias, 500?–432?
		Ionic architecture, *ca.* 500–400
	Patrician-plebeian struggle in Rome, 500–287	
	Greco-Persian War, 493–479	Sophocles, 496–406
	Delian League, 479–404	Herodotus, 484–425
	Perfection of Athenian democracy, 461–429	Euripides, 480–406
	Law of the Twelve Tables (Rome), *ca.* 450	Thucydides, 471?–400?
	Peloponnesian War, 431–404	Parthenon, *ca.* 460
400 B.C.	Decline of democracy in Greece, 400	Aristophanes, 448?–380?
	Theban supremacy in Greece, 371–362	Corinthian architecture, *ca.* 400–300
	Macedonian conquest of Greece, 338–337	Praxiteles, 370?–310?
	Conquests of Alexander the Great, 336–323	
	Division of Alexander's empire, 323	
300 B.C.		Classical age of Hindu culture, *ca.* 300–800 A.D.
	Hortensian Law (Rome), 287	
	Punic Wars, 264–146	
	Reign of Emperor Asoka in India, *ca.* 273–232	
	Ch'in Dynasty in China, 221–207	
	Building of Great Wall in China, *ca.* 220	
	Han Dynasty in China, 206 B.C.–220 A.D.	
200 B.C.		
	Revolt of the Gracchi, 133–121	
100 B.C.	Beginning of Japanese state, *ca.* 100	
		Vergil, 70–19
		Horace, 65–8
	Dictatorship of Julius Caesar, 46–44	
	Principate of Augustus Caesar, 27 B.C.–14 A.D.	
		Tacitus, 55?–117? A.D.
		Colosseum, *ca.* 80 A.D.
100 A.D.	Barbarian invasions of Rome, *ca.* 100–476 A.D.	
	Completion of Roman law by the great jurists, *ca.* 200 A.D.	
300 A.D.	Diocletian, 284–305 A.D.	
	Constantine I, 306–337 A.D.	
		Beginning of temple architecture in India, 400 A.D.
	Theodosius I, 379–395 A.D.	Adoption of Chinese system of writing in Japan, *ca.* 405 A.D.
476 A.D.	Deposition of last of Roman emperors, 476 A.D.	
	Taika Reform Edict, creating imperial government in Japan based on Chinese model, 645 A.D.	

PHILOSOPHY AND SCIENCE	ECONOMICS	RELIGION	
	Rise of caste system in India, 1000–500	Development of worldly, non-ethical religion of the Greeks, 1200–800	**800 B.C.**
	Economic Revolution and colonization in Greece, 750–600		
	Rise of middle class in Greece, 750–600		
Thales of Miletus, 640?–546			
Pythagoras, 582?–507?		Gautama Buddha, *ca.* 563–483	
Confucius, 551?–479?			
Lao-tzu, *ca.* 550	Use of iron in China, *ca.* 500	Orphic and Eleusinian mystery cults, 500–100	**500 B.C.**
Protagoras, 490?–420?			
Socrates, 469–399			
Hippocrates, 460–377?			
Democritus, 470?–362?			
Sophists, *ca.* 450–400			
Plato, 427–347	Development of coinage in China, *ca.* 400		**400 B.C.**
Aristotle, 384–322			
Epicurus, 342–270			
Zeno (the Stoic), 320?–250?	Growth of advertising and insurance, 300 B.C.–100 A.D.		
Euclid, 323?–285			
Aristarchus, 310–230	Hellenistic world trade, 300 B.C.–100 A.D.		**300 B.C.**
	International money economy, 300 B.C.–100 A.D.		
	Growth of serfdom in Hellenistic empires, 300 B.C.–100 A.D.		
Archimedes, 287?–212	Growth of metropolitan cities, 300 B.C.–100 A.D.		
Eratosthenes, 276?–195?	Growth of slavery in Rome, 250–100	Oriental mystery cults in Rome, 250–50	
	Rise of middle class in Rome, 250–100		
Herophilus, 220?–150?	Decline of small farmer in Rome, 250–100		
Polybius, 205?–118			
	Depressions and unemployment in Hellenistic world, 200 B.C.–100 A.D		**200 B.C.**
Skeptics, 200–100	Decline of slavery in Hellenistic world 200 B.C.–100 A.D.	Development of mysticism and otherworldliness, 200	
Introduction of Stoicism into Rome, *ca.* 140	Use of iron in sub-Saharan Africa, 200 B.C.		
Cicero, 106–43			**100 B.C.**
Lucretius, 98–55			
Seneca, 34 B.C.–65 A.D.	Decline of slavery in Rome, 27 B.C.–476 A.D.	Spread of Mithraism in Rome, 27 B.C.–270 A.D.	
		First persecution of Christians in Rome, *ca.* 65 A.D.	
Marcus Aurelius, 121–180 A.D.	Manufacture of paper in China, *ca.* 100 A.D.		**100 A.D.**
Galen, 130–200? A.D.	Expansion of Bantu people in Africa, 200–900 A.D.	Rapid development of Buddhism in China, 200–500 A.D.	
Neo-Platonism, 250–600 A.D.	Growth of serfdom and extralegal feudalism in Rome, 300–500 A.D.	Beginning of toleration of Christians in Rome, 311 A.D.	
	Use of camel for transport in Africa, 300 A.D.		**300 A.D.**
	West African Kingdom of Ghana, *ca.* 450 A.D.	Christianity made official religion of Roman Empire, 380 A.D.	
	Manufacture of glass and invention of gunpowder and magnetic compass in China, *ca.* 500 A.D.		**476 A.D.**
		Spread of Buddhism to Japan, *ca.* 552 A.D.	

CHAPTER 8

The Hellenic Civilization

There Lawfulness dwells and her sisters,
Safe foundation of cities,
Justice and Peace, who was bred with her,
Dispensers of wealth to men
Golden daughters of wise-counselling Right.
—Pindar, on the city of Corinth, *Olympian Ode XIII*

Now, what is characteristic of any nature is that which is best
for it and gives most joy. Such to man is the life according to reason, since it is this that makes him man.
—Aristotle, *Nichomachean Ethics*

Among all the peoples of the ancient world, the one whose culture
most clearly exemplified the spirit of Western man was the Hellenic
or Greek. No other of these nations had so strong a devotion to
liberty, at least for itself, or so firm a belief in the nobility of
human achievement. The Greeks glorified man as the most important creature in the universe and refused to submit to the dictation
of priests or despots or even to humble themselves before their gods.
Their attitude was essentially secular and rationalistic; they exalted
the spirit of free inquiry and made knowledge supreme over faith. It
was largely for these reasons that they advanced their culture to the
highest stage which the ancient world was destined to reach. But the
Greeks did not begin without foundations. It is necessary to remember that the groundwork for many of their achievements had already been laid by certain of the Oriental peoples. The rudiments of
their philosophy and science had been prepared by the Egyptians.
The Greek alphabet was derived from Phoenicia. And probably to a
larger extent than we shall ever realize the Hellenic appreciation of
beauty and freedom was a product of Minoan-Mycenaean influence.

*The character
of Hellenic
civilization*

1. EARLY STAGES

The early history of Greece is divided into two basic periods, the
Mycenaean from about 1500 to 1100 B.C. and the Dark Ages from
about 1100 to 800 B.C. In the sixteenth century a Greek people

175

THE HELLENIC
CIVILIZATION

The Mycenaean
period

Mycenaean
culture

The beginning
of the Dark Ages

known subsequently as Achaeans burst the confines of their original home and expanded southward. In time they conquered Mycenae and made it their principal stronghold. They were henceforth called in Greek history Mycenaeans, although they had other important centers at Athens, Thebes, Pylos, and elsewhere. In 1400 B.C. they conquered Knossos. The Mycenaeans were a semibarbarous people whose social and political systems resembled those of the Orient. The great lords or kings who ruled in the fortified strongholds seemed to wield a monopoly over production, trade, and artistic activity. The chief function of their subjects was to work and strive for the king's enrichment. These officials resided in magnificent palaces surrounded by objects of gold, bronze, and ivory, skillfully fashioned by talented workmen. To obtain these riches traders and colonizers roamed the whole world of the Aegean and penetrated as far as Italy and Central Europe.

The arts of the Mycenaeans never equaled the delicacy and grace of the painting and sculpture of the Minoans. Much of it was copied boldly from the Orient, and for the most part it remained stilted and lifeless. They did, nevertheless, produce some excellent pottery and exquisitely inlaid daggers. Their massive palaces and tombs indicate that they understood stresses and how to counteract them. The Mycenaeans had a system of writing, which has been definitely established as an early form of Greek. But they seem to have used it almost exclusively for keeping the fiscal records of their all-encompassing governments. No trace of anything resembling literature, history, or philosophy has thus far been found.

The fall of the Mycenaean civilization was a major catastrophe for the Greek world. It ushered in a period now called by historians the Dark Ages, which lasted from about 1100 to 800 B.C. Written records disappeared, except where accidentally preserved, and culture reverted to simpler forms than had been known for centuries. Whether the collapse came as a result of foreign invasion or of internal revolt against oppression has not been determined. Perhaps it

Ruins of the Palace of Nestor at Pylos. See the opposite page for an artist's conception of the original.

A Reconstruction of the Palace of Nestor. Shown here is the central court and the hearth.

was a combination of both. According to tradition, about 1200 B.C. the cities were attacked by an invading horde of more primitive Greeks known as Dorians. They were illiterate, and though they possessed weapons of iron, their knowledge of the arts and crafts was no more than rudimentary. They burned the palace at Mycenae and sacked a number of the others. Some historians maintain that the destruction of despotic Mycenae was a necessary prelude to the emergence of the freer and more enlightened Hellenic outlook.

The culture of many of the Greeks had always been rudimentary. That of the Mycenaeans rapidly deteriorated following the destruction of Mycenae. We can therefore conclude that cultural achievement in most of Greece remained at a low ebb throughout the period from 1100 to 800 B.C. Toward the end some decorated pottery and skillfully designed metal objects began to appear on the islands of the Aegean Sea, but essentially the period was a long night. Aside from the development of writing at the very end, intellectual accomplishment was limited to folk songs, ballads, and short epics sung and embellished by bards as they wandered from one village to another. A large part of this material was finally woven into a great epic cycle by one or more poets in the ninth century B.C. Though not all the poems of this cycle have come down to us, the two most important, the *Iliad* and the *Odyssey*, the so-called Homeric epics, provide us with a rich store of information about many of the customs and institutions of the Dark Ages.

The primitive culture of the Dark Ages

The political institutions of the Dark Ages were exceedingly primitive. Each little community of villages was independent of external control, but political authority was so tenuous that it would not be too much to say that the state scarcely existed at all. The *basileus* or ruler was not much more than a tribal leader. He could not make or enforce laws or administer justice. He received no

Government in the Dark Ages

177

*Mycenean Stirrup Jar, Twelfth
Century* B.C.

The rudimentary
pattern of social
and economic life

Religious con-
ceptions in the
Dark Ages

178

remuneration of any kind, and had to cultivate his farm for a living
the same as any other citizen. Practically his only functions were
military and priestly. He commanded the army in time of war and
offered sacrifices to keep the gods on the good side of the community. Although each little community had its council of nobles and
assembly of warriors, neither of these bodies had any definite membership or status as an organ of government. The duties of the
former were to advise and assist the ruler and prevent him from
usurping despotic powers. The functions of the latter were to ratify
declarations of war and assent to the conclusion of peace. Almost
without exception custom took the place of law, and the administration of justice was private. Even willful murder was punishable only
by the family of the victim. While it is true that disputes were
sometimes submitted to the ruler for settlement, he acted in such
cases merely as an arbitrator, not as a judge. As a matter of fact, the
political consciousness of the Greeks of this time was so poorly developed that they had no conception of government as an indispensable agency for the preservation of social order. When
Odysseus, ruler of Ithaca, was absent for twenty years, no regent
was appointed in his place, and no session of the council or assembly
was held. No one seemed to think that the complete suspension of
government, even for so long a time, was a matter of critical importance.

The pattern of social and economic life was amazingly simple.
Though the general tone of the society portrayed in the epics is
aristocratic, there was actually no rigid stratification of classes.
Manual labor was not looked upon as degrading, and there were apparently no idle rich. That there were dependent laborers of some
kind who worked on the lands of the nobles and served them as
faithful warriors seems clear from the Homeric epics, but they appear
to have been serfs rather than slaves. The slaves were chiefly
women, employed as servants, wool processors, or concubines.
Many were war captives, but they do not appear to have been badly
treated. Agriculture and herding were the basic occupations of free
men. Except for a few skilled crafts like those of wagonmaker,
swordsmith, goldsmith, and potter, there was no specialization of
labor. For the most part every household made its own tools, wove
its own clothing, and raised its own food. So far were the Greeks of
this time from being a trading people that they had no word in their
language for "merchant," and barter was the only method of exchange that was practiced.

To the Greeks of the Dark Ages religion meant chiefly a system
for: (1) explaining the physical world in such a way as to remove
its awesome mysteries and give man a feeling of intimate relationship with it; (2) accounting for the tempestuous passions that seized
man's nature and made him lose that self-control which the Greeks
considered essential for success as a warrior; and (3) obtaining such
tangible benefits as good fortune, long life, skill in craftsmanship,

and abundant harvests. The Greeks did not expect that their religion would save them from sin or endow them with spiritual blessings. As they conceived it, piety was neither a matter of conduct nor of faith. Their religion, accordingly, had no commandments, dogmas, or sacraments. Every man was at liberty to believe what he pleased and to conduct his own life as he chose without fear of the wrath of the gods.

As is commonly known, the deities of the early Greek religion were merely human beings writ large. It was really necessary that this should be so if the Greek was to feel at home in the world over which they ruled. Remote, omnipotent beings like the gods of most Oriental religions would have inspired fear rather than a sense of security. What the Greek wanted was not necessarily gods of great power, but deities he could bargain with on equal terms. Consequently he endowed his gods with attributes similar to his own— with human bodies and human weaknesses and wants. He imagined the great company of divinities as frequently quarreling with one another, needing food and sleep, mingling freely with men, and even procreating children occasionally by mortal women. They differed from men only in the fact that they subsisted on ambrosia and nectar, which made them immortal. They dwelt not in the sky or in the stars but on the summit of Mount Olympus, a peak in northern Greece with an altitude of about 10,000 feet.

The deities of the early Greek religion

The religion was thoroughly polytheistic, and no one deity was elevated very high above any of the others. Zeus, the sky god and wielder of the thunderbolt, who was sometimes referred to as the father of the gods and of men, frequently received less attention than did Poseidon, the sea god, Aphrodite, goddess of love, or Athena, variously considered goddess of wisdom and war and patroness of handicrafts. Since the Greeks had no Satan, their religion cannot be described as dualistic. Nearly all of the deities were capable of malevolence as well as good, for they sometimes deceived men and caused them to commit wrongs. The nearest approach to a god of evil was Hades, who presided over the nether world. Although he is referred to in the Homeric poems as "implacable and unyielding" and the most hateful of gods to mortals, he was never assumed to have played an active role in affairs on earth. He was not considered as the source of pestilence, earthquake, or famine. He did not tempt men or work to defeat the benevolent designs of other gods. In short, he was really not regarded as anything more than the guardian of the realm of the dead.

Poseidon

The Greeks of the Dark Ages were almost completely indifferent to what happened to them after death. They did assume, however, that the shades or ghosts of men survived for a time after the death of their bodies. All, with a few exceptions, went to the same abode —to the murky realm of Hades situated beneath the earth. This was neither a paradise nor a hell: no one was rewarded for his good deeds, and no one was punished for his sins. Each of the shades ap-

Battle between the Gods and the Giants. This frieze dates from before 525 B.C. and is from the sanctuary of Apollo at Delphi.

peared to continue the same kind of life its human embodiment had lived on earth. The Homeric poems make casual mention of two other realms, the Elysian Plain and the realm of Tartarus, which seem at first glance to contradict the idea of no rewards and punishments in the hereafter. But the few individuals who enjoyed the ease and comfort of the Elysian Plain had done nothing to deserve such blessings; they were simply persons whom the gods had chosen to favor. The realm of Tartarus was not really an abode of the dead but a place of imprisonment for rebellious deities.

The external and mechanical character of worship

Worship in early Greek religion consisted primarily of sacrifice. The offerings were made, however, not as an atonement for sin, but chiefly in order to please the gods and induce them to grant favors. In other words, religious practice was external and mechanical and not far removed from magic. Reverence, humility, and purity of heart were not essentials in it. The worshiper had only to carry out his part of the bargain by making the proper sacrifice, and the gods would fulfill theirs. For a religion such as this no elaborate institutions were required. Even a professional priesthood was unnecessary. Since there were no mysteries and no sacraments, one man could perform the simple rites about as well as another. The Greek temple was not a church or place of religious assemblage, and no ceremonies were performed within it. Instead it was a shrine which the god might visit occasionally and use as a temporary house.

Conceptions of virtue and evil

As intimated already, the morality of the Greeks in the Dark Ages had only the vaguest connection with their religion. While it is true that the gods were generally disposed to support the right, they did not consider it their duty to combat evil and make righteousness prevail. In meting out rewards to men, they appear to have been influenced more by their own whims and by gratitude for sacrifices offered than by any consideration for moral character.

The only crime they punished was perjury, and that none too consistently. Nearly all the virtues extolled in the epics were those which would make the individual a better soldier—bravery, self-control, patriotism, wisdom (in the sense of cunning), love of one's friends, and hatred of one's enemies. There was no conception of sin in the Christian sense of wrongful acts to be repented of or atoned for.

At the end of the Dark Ages the Greek was already well started along the road of social ideals that he was destined to follow in later centuries. He was an optimist, convinced that life was worth living for its own sake, and he could see no reason for looking forward to death as a glad release. He was an egoist, striving for the fulfillment of self. As a consequence, he rejected mortification of the flesh and all forms of denial which would imply the frustration of life. He could see no merit in humility or in turning the other cheek. He was a humanist, who worshiped the finite and the natural rather than the otherworldly or sublime. For this reason he refused to invest his gods with awe-inspiring qualities, or to invent any conception of man as a depraved and sinful creature. Finally, he was devoted to liberty in an even more extreme form than most of his descendants in the classical period were willing to accept.

2. THE EVOLUTION OF THE CITY-STATES

About 800 B.C. the village communities which had been founded mainly upon tribal or clan organization, began to give way to larger political units. As the need for defense increased, an acropolis or citadel was built on a high location, and a city grew up around it as the seat of government for a whole community. Thus emerged the city-state, the most famous unit of political society developed by the Greeks. Examples were to be found in almost every section of the Hellenic world. Athens, Thebes, and Megara on the mainland; Sparta and Corinth on the Peloponnesus; Miletus on the shore of Asia Minor; and Mitylene and Samos on the islands of the Aegean Sea were among the best known. They varied enormously in both area and population. Sparta with more than 3000 square miles and Athens with 1060 had by far the greatest extent; the others averaged less than a hundred. At the peak of their power Athens and Sparta, each with a population of about 400,000, had approximately three times the numerical strength of most of their neighboring states.

The origin and
nature of the
city-states

More important is the fact that the Greek city-states varied widely in cultural evolution. From 800 to 500 B.C., commonly called the Archaic period, the Peloponnesian cities of Corinth and Argos were leaders in the development of literature and the arts. In the seventh century Sparta outshone many of her rivals. Preeminent above all were the Ionian cities on the coast of Asia Minor and the islands of the Aegean Sea. Foremost among them was Miletus,

181

where, as we shall see, a brilliant flowering of philosophy and science occurred as early as the sixth century. Athens lagged behind until at least 100 years later.

The evolution of the city-states

With a few exceptions the Greek city-states went through a similar political evolution. They began their histories as monarchies. During the eighth century they were changed into oligarchies. About a hundred years later, on the average, the oligarchies were overthrown by dictators, or "tyrants," as the Greeks called them, meaning usurpers who ruled without legal right whether oppressively or not. Finally, in the sixth and fifth centuries, democracies were set up, or in some cases "timocracies," that is, governments based upon a property qualification for the exercise of political rights, or in which love of honor and glory was the ruling principle.

The causes of the political cycle; the growth of colonization

On the whole, it is not difficult to determine the causes of this political evolution. The first change came about as a result of the concentration of landed wealth. As the owners of great estates waxed in economic power, they determined to wrest political authority from the ruler, now commonly called king, and vest it in the council, which they generally controlled. In the end they abolished the kingship entirely. Then followed a period of sweeping economic changes and political turmoil.

The results of Greek expansion

These developments affected not only Greece itself but many other parts of the Mediterranean world. For they were accompanied and followed by a vast overseas expansion. The chief causes were an increasing scarcity of agricultural land, internal strife, and a general temper of restlessness and discontent. The Greeks rapidly learned of numerous areas, thinly populated, with climate and soil similar to those of the homelands. The parent states most active in the expansion movement were Corinth, Chalcis, and Miletus. Their citizens founded colonies along the Aegean shores and even in Italy and Sicily. Of the latter the best known were Tarentum and Syracuse. They also established trading centers on the coast of Egypt and as far east as Babylon. The results of this expansionist movement can only be described as momentous. Commerce and industry grew to be leading pursuits, the urban population increased, and wealth assumed new forms. The rising middle class now joined with dispossessed farmers in an attack upon the landholding oligarchy. The natural fruit of the bitter class conflicts that ensued was dictatorship. By encouraging extravagant hopes and promising relief from chaos, ambitious demagogues attracted enough popular support to enable them to ride into power in defiance of constitutions and laws. Ultimately, however, dissatisfaction with tyrannical rule and the increasing economic power and political consciousness of the common citizens led to the establishment of democracies or liberal oligarchies.

Unfortunately space does not permit an analysis of the political history of each of the Greek city-states. Except in the more backward sections of Thessaly and the Peloponnesus, it is safe to conclude that the internal development of all of them paralleled the account given above, although minor variations due to local conditions doubtless occurred. The two most important of the Hellenic states, Sparta and Athens, deserve more detailed study.

3. THE ARMED CAMP OF SPARTA

The history of Sparta [1] was the great exception to the political evolution of the city-states. Despite the fact that her citizens sprang from the same origins as most of the other Greeks, she failed to make any progress in the direction of democratic rule. Instead, her government gradually degenerated into a form more closely resembling a modern élite dictatorship. Culturally, also, the nation stagnated after the seventh century. The causes were due partly to isolation. Hemmed in by mountains on the northeast and west and lacking good harbors, the Spartan people had little opportunity to profit from the advances made in the outside world. Besides, no middle class arose to aid the masses in the struggle for freedom.

The peculiar development of Sparta

The major explanation is to be found, however, in militarism. The Spartans had come into the eastern Peloponnesus as an invading army. At first they attempted to amalgamate with the Mycenaeans they found there. But conflicts arose, and the Spartans resorted to conquest. Though by the end of the ninth century they had gained dominion over all of Laconia, they were not satisfied. West of the Taygetus Mountains lay the fertile plain of Messenia. The Spartans determined to conquer it. The venture was successful, and the Messenian territory was annexed to Laconia. About 640 B.C. the Messenians enlisted the aid of Argos and launched a revolt. The war that followed was desperately fought, Laconia itself was invaded, and apparently it was only the death of the Argive commander and the patriotic pleas of the fire-eating poet Tyrtaeus that saved the day for the Spartans. This time the victors took no chances. They confiscated the lands of the Messenians, murdered or expelled their leaders, and forced the masses into serfdom. The Spartans' appetite for conquest was not unlimited, however. Following the Messenian wars they devoted themselves to keeping what they had already gained.

The Spartan desire for conquest

There was scarcely a feature of the life of the Spartans that was not the result of their wars with the Messenians. In subduing and despoiling their enemies they unwittingly enslaved themselves; for they lived through the remaining centuries of their history in deadly fear of insurrections. It was this fear which explains their

The results of Spartan militarism

[1] Sparta was the leading city of a district called Laconia or Lacedaemonia; sometimes the *state* was referred to by one or the other of these names. The people, also, were frequently called Laconians or Lacedaemonians.

183

conservatism, their stubborn resistance to change, lest any innovation result in a fatal weakening of the system. Their provincialism can also be attributed to the same cause. Frightened by the prospect that dangerous ideas might be brought into their country, they discouraged travel and prohibited trade with the outside world. The necessity of maintaining the absolute supremacy of the citizen class over an enormous population of serfs required an iron discipline and a strict subordination of the individual; hence the Spartan collectivism, which extended into every branch of the social and economic life. Finally, much of the cultural backwardness of Sparta grew out of the atmosphere of coarseness and hate which inevitably resulted from the bitter struggle to conquer the Messenians and hold them under stern repression.

The Spartan
government

The Spartan constitution, which tradition ascribed to an ancient lawgiver, Lycurgus, provided for a government preserving the forms of the old system of the Dark Ages. Instead of one king, however, there were two, representing separate families of exalted rank. The Spartan sovereigns enjoyed but few powers and those chiefly of a military and priestly character. A second and more authoritative branch of the government was the council, composed of the two kings and twenty-eight nobles sixty years of age and over. This body supervised the work of administration, prepared measures for submission to the assembly, and served as the highest court for criminal trials. The third organ of government, the assembly, approved or rejected the proposals of the council and elected all public officials except the kings. But the highest authority under the Spartan constitution was vested in a board of five men known as the ephorate. The ephors virtually were the government. They presided over the council and the assembly, controlled the educational system and the distribution of property, censored the lives of the citizens, and exercised a veto power over all legislation. They had power also to determine the fate of newborn infants, to conduct prosecutions before the council, and even to depose the kings if the religious omens appeared unfavorable. The Spartan government was thus very decidedly an oligarchy. In spite of the fact that the ephors were chosen for one-year terms by the assembly, they were indefinitely reeligible, and their authority was so vast that there was hardly any ramification of the system they could not control. Moreover, it should be borne in mind that the assembly itself was not a democratic body. Not even the whole citizen class, which was a small minority of the total population, was entitled to membership in it, but only those males of full political status who had incomes sufficient to qualify them for enrollment in the heavy infantry.

The population of Sparta was divided into three main classes. The ruling element was made up of the Spartiates, or descendants of the original conquerors. Though never exceeding one-twentieth of the total population, the Spartiates alone had political privileges. Next in order of rank were the perioeci, or "dwellers around." The origin of this class is uncertain, but it was probably composed of peoples that had at one time been allies of the Spartans or had submitted voluntarily to Spartan domination. In return for service as a buffer population between the ruling class and the serfs, the perioeci were allowed to carry on trade and to engage in manufacturing. At the bottom of the scale were the helots, or serfs, bound to the soil and despised and persecuted by their masters.

Among these classes only the perioeci enjoyed any appreciable measure of comfort and freedom. While it is true that the economic condition of the helots cannot be described in terms of absolute misery, since they were permitted to keep for themselves a good share of what they produced on the estates of their masters, they were personally subjected to such shameful treatment that they were constantly wretched and rebellious. On occasions they were compelled to give exhibitions of drunkenness and lascivious dances as an example to the Spartan youth of the effects of such practices. At the beginning of each year, if we can believe the testimony of Aristotle, the ephors declared war upon the helots, presumably for the purpose of giving a gloss of legality to the murder of any by the secret police upon suspicion of disloyalty.

Those who were born into the Spartiate class were doomed to a respectable slavery for the major part of their lives. Forced to submit to the severest discipline and to sacrifice individual interests, they were little more than cogs in a vast machine. Their education was limited almost entirely to military training, supplemented by exposure and merciless floggings to harden them for the duties of war. Between the ages of twenty and sixty they gave all their time to service to the state. Although marriage was practically compulsory, no family life was permitted. Husbands carried off their wives on the wedding night by a show of force. But they did not live with them. Instead, they were supposed to contrive means of escaping at night to visit them secretly. According to Plutarch, it thus sometimes happened that men "had children by their wives before ever they saw their faces by daylight." [2] No jealousy between marital partners was allowed. The production of vigorous offspring was all-important. Whether they were born within the limits of strict monogamy was a secondary consideration. In any case, children were the property not of their parents but of the state. It may be doubted that the Spartiates resented these hardships and deprivations. Pride in their status as the ruling class probably compensated in their minds for harsh discipline and denial of privileges.

The economic organization of Sparta was designed almost solely for the ends of military efficiency and the supremacy of the citizen class. The best land was owned by the state and was originally

[2] Plutarch, "Lycurgus," *Lives of Illustrious Men*, I, 81.

divided into equal plots which were assigned to the Spartiate class as inalienable estates. Later these holdings as well as the inferior lands were permitted to be sold and exchanged, with the result that some of the citizens became richer than others. The helots, who did all the work of cultivating the soil, also belonged to the state and were assigned to their masters along with the land. Their masters were forbidden to emancipate them or to sell them outside of the country. The labor of the helots provided for the support of the whole citizen class, whose members were not allowed to be associated with any economic enterprise other than agriculture. Trade and industry were reserved exclusively for the perioeci.

The Spartan economic system is frequently described by modern historians as communistic. It is true that some of the means of production (the helots and the land) were collectively owned, in theory at least, and that the Spartiate males contributed from their incomes to provide for a common mess in the clubs to which they belonged. But with these rather doubtful exceptions the system was as far removed from communism as it was from anarchy. Essentials of the communist ideal include the doctrines that all the instruments of production shall be owned by the community, that no one shall live by exploiting the labor of others, and that all shall work for the benefit of the community and share the wealth in proportion to need. In Sparta commerce and industry were in private hands; the helots were forced to contribute a portion of what they produced to provide for the subsistence of their masters; and political privileges were restricted to an hereditary aristocracy, most of whose members performed no socially useful labor whatever. With its militarism, its secret police, its minority rule, and its closed economy, the Spartan system would seem to have resembled fascism more nearly than true communism. But even with respect to fascism the resemblance was not complete. The Spartan system was not revolutionary, as fascism usually is in the beginning, but was always rather strongly conservative.

4. THE ATHENIAN TRIUMPH AND TRAGEDY

Athens began her history under conditions quite different from those which prevailed in Sparta. The district of Attica had not been the scene of an armed invasion or of bitter conflict between opposing peoples. As a result, no military caste imposed its rule upon a vanquished nation. Furthermore, the wealth of Attica consisted of mineral deposits and splendid harbors in addition to agricultural resources. Athens, consequently, never remained a predominantly agrarian state but rapidly developed a prosperous trade and a culture essentially urban.

Until the middle of the eighth century B.C. Athens, like the other Greek states, had a monarchical form of government. During the century that followed, the council of nobles, or Council of the Areopagus, as it came to be called, gradually divested the king of his powers. The transition to rule by the few was both the cause and the result of an increasing concentration of wealth. The introduction of vine and olive culture about this time led to the growth of agriculture as a great capitalistic enterprise. Since vineyards and olive orchards require considerable time to become profitable, only those farmers with abundant resources were able to survive in the business. Their poorer and less thrifty neighbors sank rapidly into debt, especially since grain was now coming to be imported at ruinous prices. The small farmer had no alternative but to mortgage his land, and then his family and himself, in the vain hope that some day a way of escape would be found. Ultimately many of his class became serfs when the mortgages could not be paid.

Bitter cries of distress now arose and threats of revolution were heard. The middle classes in the towns espoused the cause of the peasant in demanding liberalization of the government. Finally, in 594 B.C., all parties agreed upon the appointment of Solon as a magistrate with absolute power to carry out reforms. The measures Solon enacted provided for both political and economic adjustments. The former included: (1) the establishment of a new council, the Council of Four Hundred, and the admission of the middle classes to membership in it; (2) the enfranchisement of the lower classes by making them eligible for service in the assembly; and (3) the organization of a supreme court, open to all citizens and elected by universal manhood suffrage, with power to hear appeals from the decisions of the magistrates. The economic reforms benefited the poor farmers by canceling existing mortgages, prohibiting enslavement for debt in the future, and limiting the amount of land any one individual could own. Nor did Solon neglect the middle classes. He introduced a new system of coinage designed to give Athens an advantage in foreign trade, imposed heavy penalties for idleness, ordered every man to teach his son a trade, and offered full privileges of citizenship to alien craftsmen who would become permanent residents of the country.

Significant though these reforms were, they did not allay the discontent. The nobles were disgruntled because some of their privileges had been taken away. The middle and lower classes were dissatisfied because they were still excluded from the offices of magistracy, and because the Council of the Areopagus was left with its powers intact. Worse still was the fact that Solon, like many rulers in all times, attempted to divert the people from their domestic troubles by persuading them to embark upon military adventures abroad. An old quarrel with Megara was revived, and Athens committed her fate to the uncertainties of war. The chaos and disillusionment that followed paved the way in 560 B.C. for the triumph of the first of the Athenian tyrants. Although he proved to be a benevo-

From monarchy to oligarchy in Athens

Threats of revolution and the reforms of Solon

The rise of dictatorship

187

The reforms of
Cleisthenes

lent despot, one of his two sons who succeeded him was a ruthless and spiteful oppressor.

In 510 B.C. tyranny was overthrown by a group of nobles with aid from Sparta. Factional conflict raged anew until Cleisthenes, an intelligent aristocrat, enlisted the support of the masses to eliminate his rivals from the scene. Having promised concessions to the people as a reward for their help, he proceeded to reform the government in so sweeping a fashion that he has since been known as the father of Athenian democracy. He greatly enlarged the citizen population by granting full rights to all free men who resided in the country at that time. He established a new council and made it the chief organ of government with power to prepare measures for submission to the assembly and with supreme control over executive and administrative functions. Members of this body were to be chosen by lot. Any male citizen over thirty years of age was eligible. Cleisthenes also expanded the authority of the assembly, giving it power to debate and pass or reject the measures submitted by the Council, to declare war, to appropriate money, and to audit the accounts of retiring magistrates. Lastly, Cleisthenes is believed to have instituted the device of ostracism, whereby any citizen who might be dangerous to the state could be sent into honorable exile for a ten-year period. The device was quite obviously intended to eliminate men who were suspected of cherishing dictatorial ambitions. Too often its effect was to eliminate exceptional men and to allow mediocrity to flourish.

The perfection
of Athenian
democracy

The Athenian democracy attained its full perfection in the Age of Pericles (461–429 B.C.). It was during this period that the assembly acquired the authority to initiate legislation in addition to its power to ratify or reject proposals of the council. It was during this time also that the famous Board of Ten Generals rose to a position roughly comparable to that of the British cabinet. The Generals were chosen by the assembly for one-year terms and were eligible for reelection indefinitely. Pericles held the position of Chief Strategus or President of the Board of Generals for more than thirty years. The Generals were not simply commanders of the army but the chief legislative and executive officials in the state. Though wielding enormous power, they could not become tyrants, for their policies were subject to review by the assembly, and they could easily be recalled at the end of their one-year terms or indicted for malfeasance at any time. Finally, it was in the Age of Pericles that the Athenian system of courts was developed to completion. No longer was there merely a supreme court to hear appeals from the decisions of magistrates, but an array of popular courts with authority to try all kinds of cases. At the beginning of each year a list of 6000 citizens was chosen by lot from the various sections of the country. From this list separate juries, varying in size from 201 to 1001, were made up for particular trials. Each of these juries constituted a court with power to decide by majority vote every question involved in the case. Although one of the magistrates presided, he had none of the prerogatives of a judge; the jury itself was the judge, and from its decision there was no appeal. It would be difficult to imagine a system more thoroughly democratic.

The Athenian democracy differed from the modern form in various ways. First of all, it did not extend to the whole population, but only to the citizen class. While it is true that in the time of Cleisthenes (508–502 B.C.) the citizens probably included a majority of the inhabitants because of his enfranchisement of resident aliens, in the Age of Pericles they were distinctly a minority. It may be well to observe, however, that within its limits Athenian democracy was more thoroughly applied than is the modern form. The choice by lot of nearly all magistrates except the Ten Generals, the restriction of all terms of public officials to one year, and the uncompromising adherence to the principle of majority rule even in judicial trials were examples of a serene confidence in the political capacity of the average man which few modern nations would be willing to accept. The democracy of Athens differed from the contemporary ideal also in the fact that it was direct, not representative. The Athenians were not interested in being governed by men of reputation and ability; what vitally concerned them was the assurance to every citizen of an actual voice in the control of all public affairs. Nevertheless, their democracy did not last much longer than a hundred years.

In the century of her greatest expansion and creativity, Athens fought two major wars. The first, the war with Persia, was an outgrowth of the expansion of that empire into the eastern Mediterranean area. The Athenians resented the conquest of their Ionian kinsmen in Asia Minor and aided them in their struggle for freedom. The Persians retaliated by sending a powerful army and fleet to attack the Greeks. Although all Greece was in danger of conquest, Athens bore the chief burden of repelling the invader. The war, which began in 493 B.C. and lasted with interludes of peace for about fourteen years, is commonly regarded as one of the most significant in the history of the world. The decisive victory of the Greeks put an end to the menace of Persian conquest and forestalled at least for a time the submergence of Hellenic ideals of freedom in Near Eastern despotism. The war also had the effect of strengthening democracy in Athens and making that state the leading power in Greece.

The other of the great struggles, the Peloponnesian War with Sparta, had results of a quite different character. Instead of being another milestone in the Athenian march to power, it ended in tragedy. The causes of this war are of particular interest to the student of the downfall of civilizations. First and most important was the growth of Athenian imperialism. In the last year of the war with Persia, Athens had joined with a number of other Greek states in the formation of an offensive and defensive alliance known as the Delian League. When peace was concluded the league was not dissolved, for many of the Greeks feared that the Persians might come back. As time went on, Athens gradually transformed the league into a naval empire for the advancement of her own interests. She used some of the funds in the common treasury for her own purposes. She tried to reduce all the other members to a condition of vassalage, and when one of them rebelled, she overwhelmed it by force, seized its navy, and imposed tribute upon it as if it were a conquered state. Such high-handed methods aroused the suspicions of the Spartans, who feared that an Athenian hegemony would soon be extended over all of Greece.

Other causes of the Peloponnesian War

A second major cause was to be found in the social and cultural differences between Athens and Sparta. Athens was democratic, progressive, urban, imperialistic, and intellectually and artistically advanced. Sparta was aristocratic, conservative, agrarian, provincial, and culturally backward. Where such sharply contrasting systems exist side by side, conflicts are almost bound to occur. The attitude of the Athenians and Spartans had been hostile for some time. The former looked upon the latter as uncouth barbarians. The Spartans accused the Athenians of attempting to gain control over the northern Peloponnesian states and of encouraging the helots to rebel. Economic factors also played a large part in bringing the conflict to a head. Athens was ambitious to dominate the Corinthian Gulf, the principal avenue of trade with Sicily and southern Italy. This made her the deadly enemy of Corinth, the chief ally of Sparta.

The defeat of Athens

The war, which broke out in 431 B.C. and lasted until 404, was a record of frightful calamities for Athens. Her trade was destroyed, her democracy overthrown, and her population decimated by a terrible pestilence. Quite as bad was the moral degradation which followed in the wake of the military reverses. Treason, corruption, and brutality were among the hastening ills of the last few years of the conflict. On one occasion the Athenians even slaughtered the whole male population of the state of Melos, and enslaved the women and children, for no other crime than refusing to abandon neutrality. Ultimately, deserted by all her allies except Samos and with her food supply cut off, Athens was left with no alternative but to surrender or starve. The terms imposed upon her were drastic enough: destruction of her fortifications, surrender of all foreign possessions and practically her entire navy, and submission to Sparta as a subject state. Though Athens recovered her leadership for a time in the fourth century, her period of glory was approaching its end.

5. POLITICAL DEBACLE—THE LAST DAYS

Not only did the Peloponnesian War put an end, temporarily, to the supremacy of Athens; it annihilated freedom throughout the Greek world and sealed the doom of the Hellenic political genius. Following the war Sparta asserted her power over all of Hellas. Oli-

GREECE AT THE END OF THE AGE OF PERICLES

Map legend:
- Sparta and allies
- Athens and allies
- Neutral Greek states

0 — 100 miles

garchies supported by Spartan troops replaced democracies wherever they existed. Confiscation of property and assassination were
the methods regularly employed to combat opposition. Although in
Athens the tyrants were overthrown after a time and free government restored, Sparta was able to dominate the remainder of Greece
for more than thirty years. In 371 B.C., however, Epaminondas of
Thebes defeated the Spartan army at Leuctra and thereby inaugurated a period of Theban supremacy. Unfortunately Thebes
showed little more wisdom and tolerance in governing than Sparta,
and nine years later a combination was formed to free the Greek
cities from their new oppressor. Failing to break up the alliance, the
Thebans gave battle on the field of Mantinea. Both sides claimed the
victory, but Epaminondas was slain, and the power of his empire
soon afterward collapsed.

The long succession of wars had now brought the Greek states to
the point of exhaustion. Though the glory of their culture was yet
undimmed, politically they were prostrate and helpless. Their fate

191

The Macedonian conquest

was soon decided for them by the rise of Philip of Macedon. Except for a thin veneer of Hellenic culture, the Macedonians were barbarians; but Philip, before becoming their king, had learned how to lead an army while a hostage at Thebes. Perceiving the weakness of the states to the south, he determined to conquer them. A series of early successes led to a decisive victory in 338 B.C. and soon afterward to dominion over all of Greece except Sparta. Two years later Philip was murdered as the sequel to a family brawl.

Alexander the Great

Rule over Hellas now passed into the hands of his son Alexander, a youth of twenty years. After putting to death all possible aspirants to the throne and quelling some feeble revolts of the Greeks, Alexander conceived the grandiose scheme of conquering Persia. One victory followed another until in the short space of twelve years the whole ancient Near Orient from the Indus River to the Nile had been annexed to Greece as the personal domain of one man. Alexander did not live to enjoy it long. In 323 B.C. he fell ill of Babylonian swamp fever and died at the age of thirty-two.

The significance of Alexander's career

It is difficult to gauge the significance of Alexander's career. Historians have differed widely in their interpretations. Some have seen him as one of the supreme galvanizing forces in history. Others would limit his genius to military strategy and organization and deny that he made a single major contribution of benefit to humanity.[3] There can be no doubt that he was a master of the art of war (he never lost a battle), and that he was intelligent and endowed with charm and physical courage. Unquestionably, also, he was a man of vibrant energy and overpowering ambitions. Just what these ambitions were is not certain. Evidence eludes us that he aspired to conquer the world or to advance the Hellenic ideals of freedom and justice. It seems doubtful that he had much interest in lofty ideals or in using military force to extend them. As the British historian A. R. Burn has said: "His abiding ideal was the glory of Alexander."[4] Nevertheless, he did introduce Macedonian standards of administrative efficiency into the government of the Near East. Aside from this, the primary significance of the great conqueror seems to lie in the fact that he carried the Hellenic drive into Asia farther and faster than would otherwise have occurred. He undoubtedly caused the Greek influence to be more widely felt. At the same time he appears to have placed too great a strain upon Hellenism with the result of encouraging a sweeping tide of Oriental influences into the West. Within a short period Hellenic and Oriental cultures interpenetrated to such an extent as to produce a new civilization. This was the Hellenistic civilization to be discussed in the chapter that follows.

[3] Compare W. W. Tarn, *Alexander the Great*, and A. R. Burn, *Alexander the Great and the Hellenistic World*.
[4] *Alexander the Great and the Hellenistic World*, p. 23.

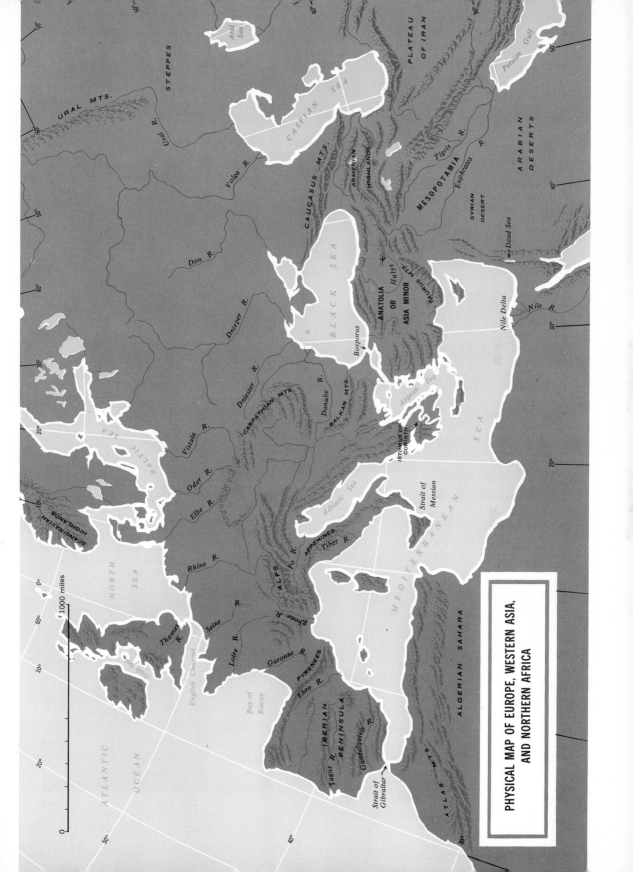

PHYSICAL MAP OF EUROPE, WESTERN ASIA, AND NORTHERN AFRICA

Geometric Horse, VIII cent. B.C. Greek art of this early period was angular, formal, and conventionalized.

Geometric Jar, VIII cent. B.C. Another example of the stylized decorative patterns of early Greek art.

Sphinx, *ca.* 540–530 B.C. Though doubtless of Oriental derivation, Greek sphinxes had a softer and more human aspect than the Oriental.

Statue of an Amazon, one of the fabled tribe of women warriors, V cent. B.C. (Roman copy)

Departure of a Warrior. Gravestone, *ca.* 530 B.C., a period when naturalism was the dominant note of Greek art.

Athena, *ca.* 460 B.C. The young, graceful patron-goddess of Athens is about to send forth an owl as a sign of victory.

Jar, 500–490 B.C. The figures depicted in a fine black glaze on the natural red clay show athletes in the Panathenaic games.

Chorus of Satyrs, *ca.* 420 B.C. The background is black with the figures in red clay. The satyrs, dressed in fleecy white, with flowing tails, are the chorus of a play.

Toilet Box, 465–460 B.C., showing the Judgment of Paris, an early incident in the Trojan War.

Marble Stele with Law against Tyranny, 338 B.C. Sculptured relief shows a woman (Democracy) crowning an aged man (the people of Athens). The law provides that if anyone establishes a dictatorship in Athens, a person who kills him shall be held guiltless.

6. HELLENIC THOUGHT AND CULTURE

From what has been said in preceding chapters it should be clear that the popular notion that all philosophy originated with the Greeks is fallacious. Centuries earlier the Egyptians had given much thought to the nature of the universe and to the social and ethical problems of man. The achievement of the Greeks was rather the development of philosophy in a more inclusive meaning than it had ever possessed before. They attempted to find answers to every conceivable question about the nature of the universe, the problem of truth, and the meaning and purpose of life. The magnitude of their accomplishment is attested by the fact that philosophy ever since has been largely a debate over the validity of their several conclusions.

The antecedents of Greek philosophy

Greek philosophy had its origins in the sixth century B.C. in the work of the so-called Milesian school, whose members were natives of the great commercial city of Miletus on the shore of Asia Minor. Their philosophy was fundamentally scientific and materialistic. The problem which chiefly engaged their attention was to discover the nature of the physical world. They believed that all things could be reduced to some primary substance or original matter which was the source of worlds, stars, animals, plants, and men, and to which all would ultimately return. Thales, the founder of the school, perceiving that all things contained moisture, taught that the primary substance is water. Anaximander insisted that it could not be any particular thing such as water or fire but some substance "ungendered and imperishable" which "contains and directs all things."

The philosophy of the Milesian school

193

He called this substance the Infinte or the Boundless. A third member of the school, Anaximenes, declared that the original material of the universe is air. Air when rarefied becomes fire; when condensed it turns successively to wind, vapor, water, earth, and stone.

Although seemingly naïve in its conclusions the philosophy of the Milesian school was of real significance. It broke through the mythological beliefs of the Greeks about the origin of the world and substituted a purely rational explanation. It revived and expanded the Egyptian ideas of the eternity of the universe and the indestructibility of matter. It suggested very clearly, especially in the teachings of Anaximander, the concept of evolution in the sense of rhythmic change, of continuing creation and decay.

Before the end of the sixth century Greek philosophy developed a metaphysical turn; it ceased to be occupied solely with problems of the physical world and shifted its attention to abstruse questions about the nature of being, the meaning of truth, and the position of the divine in the scheme of things. First to exemplify the new tendency were the Pythagoreans, who interpreted philosophy largely in terms of religion. Little is known about them except that their leader, Pythagoras, migrated from the island of Samos to southern Italy and founded a religious community at Croton. He and his followers apparently taught that the speculative life is the highest good, but that in order to pursue it, man must purify himself from the evil desires of the flesh. They held that the essence of things is not a material substance but an abstract principle, number. Their chief significance lies in the sharp distinctions they drew between spirit and matter, harmony and discord, good and evil. Perhaps it is accurate to regard them as the real founders of dualism in Greek thought.

A consequence of the work of the Pythagoreans was to intensify the debate over the nature of the universe. Some of their contemporaries, notably Parmenides, argued that stability or permanence is the real nature of things; change and diversity are simply illusions of the senses. Directly opposed to this conception was the position taken by Heracleitus, who argued that permanence is an illusion, that change alone is real. The universe, he maintained, is in a condition of constant flux; therefore "it is impossible to step twice into the same stream." Creation and destruction, life and death, are but the obverse and reverse sides of the same picture. In affirming such views Heracleitus was really contending that the things we see and hear and feel are all that there is to reality. Evolution or constant change is the law of the universe. The tree or the stone that is here today is gone tomorrow; no underlying substance exists immutable through all eternity.

Renewal of the
debate over the
nature of the
universe

The eventual answer to the question of the underlying character of the universe was provided by the atomists. The philosopher chiefly responsible for the development of the atomic theory was

Democritus, who lived in Abdera on the Thracian coast in the second half of the fifth century. As their name implies, the atomists held that the ultimate constituents of the universe are atoms, infinite in number, indestructible, and indivisible. Although these differ in size and shape, they are exactly alike in composition. Because of the motion inherent in them, they are eternally uniting, separating, and reuniting in different arrangements. Every individual object or organism in the universe is thus the product of a fortuitous concourse of atoms. The only difference between a man and a tree is the difference in the number and arrangement of their atoms. Here was a philosophy which represented the final fruition of the materialistic tendencies of early Greek thought. Democritus denied the immortality of the soul and the existence of any spiritual world. Strange as it may appear to some people, he was a moral idealist, affirming that "Good means not merely not to do wrong, but rather not to desire to do wrong." [5]

Solution of the problem by the atomists

About the middle of the fifth century B.C. an intellectual revolution began in Greece. It accompanied the high point of democracy in Athens. The rise of the common man, the growth of individualism, and the demand for the solution of practical problems produced a reaction against the old ways of thinking. As a result philosophers abandoned the study of the physical universe and turned to consideration of subjects more intimately related to man himself. The first exponents of the new intellectual trend were the Sophists. Originally the term meant "those who are wise," but later it came to be used in the derogatory sense of men who employ specious reasoning. Since most of our knowledge of the Sophists was derived, until comparatively recently, from Plato, one of their severest critics, they were commonly considered to have been the enemies of all that was best in Hellenic culture. Modern research has exposed the fallacy of so extreme a conclusion. Some members of the group, however, did lack a sense of social responsibility and were quite unscrupulous in "making the worse appear the better cause." It is said that a few of them charged the equivalent of $10,000 to educate a single individual.

The intellectual revolution begun by the Sophists

The greatest of the Sophists was undoubtedly Protagoras, a native of Abdera who did most of his teaching in Athens. His famous dictum, "Man is the measure of all things," comprehends the essence of the Sophist philosophy. By this he meant that goodness, truth, justice, and beauty are relative to the needs and interests of man himself. There are no absolute truths or eternal standards of right and justice. Since sense perception is the exclusive source of knowledge, there can be only particular truths valid for a given time and place. Morality likewise varies from one people to another. The Spartans encourage adultery in certain cases on the part of wives as well as

The doctrines of Protagoras

[5] Quoted by Frank Thilly, *History of Philosophy*, p. 40.

husbands; the Athenians seclude their women and refuse even to allow them a normal social life. Which of these standards is right? Neither is right in any absolute sense, for there are no absolute canons of right and wrong eternally decreed in the heavens to fit all cases; yet both are right in the relative sense that the judgment of man alone determines what is good.

Some of the later Sophists went far beyond the teachings of their great master. The individualism which was necessarily implicit in

The extremist
doctrines of the
later Sophists

the teachings of Protagoras was twisted by Thrasymachus into the doctrine that all laws and customs are merely expressions of the will of the strongest and shrewdest for their own advantage, and that therefore the wise man is the "perfectly unjust man" who is above the law and concerned with the gratification of his own desires.

Yet there was much that was admirable in the teachings of all the Sophists, even of those who were the most extreme. Without exception they condemned slavery and the racial exclusiveness of the

The valuable
contributions
of the Sophists

Greeks. They were champions of liberty, the rights of the common man, and the practical and progressive point of view. They perceived the folly of war and ridiculed the silly chauvinism of many of the Athenians. Perhaps their most important work was the extension of philosophy to include not only physics and metaphysics, but ethics and politics as well. As Cicero expressed it, they "brought philosophy down from heaven to the dwellings of men."

It was inevitable that the relativism, skepticism, and individualism of the Sophists should have aroused strenuous opposition. In the judgment of the more conservative Greeks these doctrines appeared

The reaction
against Sophism

to lead straight to atheism and anarchy. If there is no final truth, and if goodness and justice are merely relative to the whims of the individual, then neither religion, morality, the state, nor society itself can long be maintained. The result of this conviction was the growth of a new philosophic movement grounded upon the theory that truth is real and that absolute standards do exist. The leaders of this movement were perhaps the three most famous individuals in the history of thought—Socrates, Plato, and Aristotle.

Socrates was born in Athens in 469 B.C. of humble parentage; his father was a sculptor, his mother a midwife. How he obtained an

The career of
Socrates

education no one knows, but he was certainly familiar with the teachings of earlier Greek thinkers, presumably from extensive reading. The impression that he was a mere gabbler in the market place is quite unfounded. He became a philosopher on his own account chiefly to combat the doctrines of the Sophists. In 399 B.C. he was condemned to death on a charge of "corrupting the youth and introducing new gods." The real reason for the unjust sentence was the tragic outcome for Athens of the Peloponnesian War. Overwhelmed by resentment and despair, the people turned against Socrates because of his associations with aristocrats, including the traitor Alcibiades, and because of his criticism of popular belief.

There is evidence that he disparaged democracy and contended that no government was worthy of the name except intellectual aristocracy.

For the reason that Socrates wrote nothing himself, historians have been faced with a problem in determining the scope of his teachings. He is generally regarded as primarily a teacher of ethics with no interest in abstract philosophy or any desire to found a new school of thought. Certain admissions made by Plato, however, indicate that a large part of the famous doctrine of Ideas was really of Socratic origin. At any rate we can be reasonably sure that Socrates believed in a stable and universally valid knowledge, which man could possess if he would only pursue the right method. This method would consist in the exchange and analysis of opinions, in the setting up and testing of provisional definitions, until finally an essence of truth recognizable by all could be distilled from them. Socrates argued that in similar fashion man could discover enduring principles of right and justice independent of the selfish desires of human beings. He believed, moreover, that the discovery of such rational principles of conduct would prove an infallible guide to virtuous living, for he denied that anyone who truly knows the good can ever choose the evil.

The philosophy of Socrates

By far the most distinguished of Socrates' pupils was Plato, who was born in Athens in 427 B.C., the son of noble parents. His real name was Aristocles, "Plato" being a nickname supposedly given to him by one of his teachers because of his broad frame. When he was twenty years old he joined the Socratic circle, remaining a member until the tragic death of his teacher. He seems to have drawn inspiration from other sources also, notably from the teachings of Parmenides and the Pythagoreans. Unlike his great master he was a prolific writer, though some of the works attributed to him are of doubtful authorship. The most noted of his writings are such dialogues as the *Apology*, the *Protagoras*, the *Phaedrus*, the *Timaeus*, and the *Republic*. He was engaged in the completion of another great work, the *Laws*, when death overtook him in his eighty-first year.

Plato

Plato's objectives in developing his philosophy were similar to those of Socrates although somewhat broader: (1) to combat the theory of reality as a disordered flux and to substitute an interpretation of the universe as essentially spiritual and purposeful; (2) to refute the Sophist doctrines of relativism and skepticism; and (3) to provide a secure foundation for ethics. In order to realize these objectives he developed his celebrated doctrine of Ideas. He admitted that relativity and constant change are characteristics of the world of physical things, of the world we perceive with our senses. But he denied that this world is the complete universe. There is a higher, spiritual realm composed of eternal forms or Ideas which only the mind can conceive. These are not, however, mere abstractions in-

Plato's philosophy of Ideas

197

vented by the mind of man, but spiritual things. Each is the pattern of some particular class of objects or relation between objects on earth. Thus there are Ideas of man, tree, shape, size, color, proportion, beauty, and justice. Highest of them all is the Idea of the Good, which is the active cause and guiding purpose of the whole universe. The things we perceive with our senses are merely imperfect copies of the supreme realities, Ideas.

Plato's ethical and religious philosophy was closely related to his doctrine of Ideas. Like Socrates he believed that true virtue has its basis in knowledge. But the knowledge derived from the senses is limited and variable; hence true virtue must consist in rational apprehension of the eternal Ideas of goodness and justice. By relegating the physical to an inferior place, he gave to his ethics a mildly ascetic tinge. He regarded the body as a hindrance to the mind and taught that only the rational part of man's nature is noble and good. In contrast with some of his later followers, he did not demand that appetites and emotions should be denied altogether, but urged that they should be strictly subordinated to the reason. Plato never made his conception of God entirely clear. Sometimes he referred to the Idea of the Good as if it were a divine power of subordinate rank, at other times as if it were the supreme creator and ruler of the universe. Probably the latter is what he really meant. At any rate it is certain that he conceived of the universe as spiritual in nature and governed by intelligent purpose. He rejected both materialism and mechanism. As for the soul, he regarded it not only as immortal but as preexisting through all eternity.

As a political philosopher Plato was motivated by the ideal of constructing a state which would be free from turbulence and self-seeking on the part of individuals and classes. Neither democracy nor liberty but harmony and efficiency were the ends he desired to achieve. Accordingly, he proposed in his *Republic* a famous plan for society which would have divided the population into three principal classes corresponding to the functions of the soul. The lowest class, representing the appetitive function, would include the farmers, artisans, and merchants. The second class, representing the spirited element or will, would consist of the soldiers. The highest class, representing the function of reason, would be composed of the intellectual aristocracy. Each of these classes would perform those tasks for which it was best fitted. The function of the lowest class would be the production and distribution of goods for the benefit of the whole community; that of the soldiers, defense; the aristocracy, by reason of special aptitude for philosophy, would enjoy a monopoly of political power. The division of the people into these several ranks would not be made on the basis of birth or wealth, but through a sifting process that would take into account the ability of each individual to profit from education. Thus the farmers, artisans, and merchants would be those who had shown the least intellectual

Plato's ethical and religious philosophy

Plato as a political philosopher

capacity, whereas the philosopher-kings would be those who had shown the greatest.

The last of the great champions of the Socratic tradition was Aristotle, a native of Stagira, born in 384 B.C. At the age of seventeen he entered Plato's Academy,[6] continuing as student and teacher there for twenty years. In 343 he was invited by King Philip of Macedon to serve as tutor to the young Alexander. Perhaps history affords few more conspicuous examples of wasted talent, except for the fact that the young prince acquired an enthusiasm for science and for some other elements of Hellenic culture. Seven years later Aristotle returned to Athens, where he conducted a school of his own, known as the Lyceum, until his death in 322 B.C. Aristotle wrote even more voluminously than Plato and on a greater variety of subjects. His principal works include treatises on logic, metaphysics, rhetoric, ethics, natural sciences, and politics. A considerable number of the writings credited to him have never been found.

Aristotle

Though Aristotle was as much interested as Plato and Socrates in absolute knowledge and eternal standards, his philosophy differed from theirs in several outstanding respects. To begin with, he had a higher regard for the concrete and the practical. In contrast with Plato, the aesthete, and Socrates, who declared he could learn nothing from trees and stones, Aristotle was a scientist with a compelling interest in biology, medicine, and astronomy. Moreover, he was less inclined than his predecessors to a spiritual outlook. And lastly, he did not share their strong aristocratic sympathies.

Aristotle compared with Plato and Socrates

Aristotle agreed with Plato that universals, Ideas (or forms as he called them), are real, and that knowledge derived from the senses is limited and inaccurate. But he refused to go along with his master in ascribing an independent existence to universals and in reducing material things to pale reflections of their spiritual patterns. On the contrary, he asserted that form and matter are of equal importance; both are eternal, and neither can exist inseparable from the other. It is the union of the two which gives to the universe its essential character. Forms are the causes of all things; they are the purposive forces that shape the world of matter into the infinitely varied objects and organisms around us. All evolution, both cosmic and organic, results from the interaction of form and matter upon each other. Thus the presence of the form *man* in the human embryo molds and directs the development of the latter until it ultimately evolves as a human being. Aristotle's philosophy may be regarded as halfway between the spiritualism and transcendentalism of Plato, on the one hand, and the mechanistic materialism of the atomists on the other. His conception of the universe was *teleological*—that is, governed by purpose; but he refused to regard the spiritual as completely overshadowing its material embodiment.

Aristotle's conception of the universe

[6] So called from the grove of Academus, where Plato and his disciples met to discuss philosophic problems.

That Aristotle should have conceived of God primarily as a First Cause is no more than we should expect from the dominance of the scientific attitude in his philosophy. Unlike Plato's Idea of the Good, Aristotle's God did not fulfill an ethical purpose. His character was that of a Prime Mover, the original source of the purposive motion contained in the forms. In no sense was he a personal God, for his nature was pure intelligence, devoid of all feelings, will, or desire. Aristotle seems to have left no place in his religious scheme for individual immortality: all the functions of the soul, except the creative reason which is not individual at all, are dependent upon the body and perish with it.

Aristotle's ethical
philosophy of the
golden mean

Aristotle's ethical philosophy was less ascetic than Plato's. He did not regard the body as the prison of the soul, nor did he believe that physical appetites are necessarily evil in themselves. He taught that the highest good for man consists in self-realization, that is, in the exercise of that part of man's nature which most truly distinguishes him as a human being. Self-realization would therefore be identical with the life of reason. But the life of reason is dependent upon the proper combination of physical and mental conditions. The body must be kept in good health and the emotions under adequate control. The solution is to be found in the *golden mean*, in preserving a balance between excessive indulgence on the one hand and ascetic denial on the other. This was simply a reaffirmation of the characteristic Hellenic ideal of *sophrosyne*, "nothing too much."

Although Aristotle included in his *Politics* much descriptive and analytical material on the structure and functions of government, he dealt primarily with the broader aspects of political theory. He considered the state as the supreme institution for the promotion of the good life among men, and he was therefore vitally interested in its origin and development and in the best forms it could be made to assume. Declaring that man is by nature a political animal, he denied that the state is an artificial product of the ambitions of the few or of the desires of the many. On the contrary, he asserted that it is rooted in the instincts of man himself, and that civilized life outside of its limits is impossible. He considered the best state to be neither a monarchy, an aristocracy, nor a democracy, but a *polity*—which he defined as a commonwealth intermediate between oligarchy and democracy. Essentially it would be a state under the control of the middle class, but Aristotle intended to make sure that the members of that class would be fairly numerous, for he advocated measures to prevent the concentration of wealth. He defended the institution of private property, but he opposed the heaping up of riches beyond what is necessary for intelligent living. He recommended that the government should provide the poor with money to buy small farms or to "make a beginning in trade and husbandry" and thus promote their prosperity and self-respect.[7]

[7] *Politics*, Maurice Francis Egan (ed.), pp. 158–59.

Contrary to a popular belief, the period of Hellenic civilization, strictly speaking, was not a great age of science. The vast majority of the scientific achievements commonly thought of as Greek were made during the Hellenistic period, when the culture was no longer predominantly Hellenic but a mixture of Hellenic and Oriental.[8] The interests of the Greeks in the Periclean age and in the century that followed were chiefly speculative and artistic; they were not deeply concerned with material comforts or with mastery of the physical universe. Consequently, with the exception of some important developments in mathematics, biology, and medicine, scientific progress was relatively slight.

The founder of Greek mathematics was apparently Thales of Miletus, who is supposed to have originated several theorems which were later included in the geometry of Euclid. Perhaps more significant was the work of the Pythagoreans, who developed an elaborate theory of numbers, classifying them into various categories, such as odd, even, prime, composite, perfect, and so forth. They are also supposed to have discovered the theory of proportion and to have proved for the first time that the sum of the three angles of any triangle is equal to two right angles. But the most famous of their achievements was the discovery of the theorem attributed to Pythagoras himself: the square of the hypotenuse of any right-angled triangle is equal to the sum of the squares on the other two sides. The Greek who first developed geometry as a science is now considered to have been Hippocrates of Chios, not to be confused with the physician, Hippocrates of Cos.[9]

The first of the Greeks to manifest an interest in biology was the philosopher Anaximander, who developed a crude theory of organic evolution based upon the principle of survival through progressive adaptations to the environment. The earliest ancestral animals, he asserted, lived in the sea, which originally covered the whole face of the earth. As the waters receded, some organisms were able to adjust themselves to their new environment and became land animals. The final product of this evolutionary process was man himself. The real founder of the science of biology, however, was Aristotle. Devoting many years of his life to painstaking study of the structure, habits, and growth of animals, he revealed many facts which were not destined to be discovered anew until the seventeenth century or later. The metamorphoses of various insects, the reproductive habits of the eel, the embryological development of the dog-fish—these are only samples of the amazing extent of his knowledge. Unfortunately he committed some errors. He denied the sexuality of plants, and although he subscribed to the general theory of evolution, he believed in the spontaneous generation of certain species of worms and insects.

[8] See the chapter on The Hellenistic Civilization.
[9] George Sarton, *An Introduction to the History of Science,* I, 92.

Greek Surgical Instruments. A bas-relief from the temple of Asklepio in Athens. The open case in the middle contains operating knives. On the two sides are retractors and cupping glasses for bleeding the patient.

Greek medicine also had its origin with the philosophers. A pioneer was Empedocles, exponent of the theory of the four elements (earth, air, fire, and water). He discovered that blood flows to and from the heart, and that the pores of the skin supplement the work of the respiratory passages in breathing. More important was the work of Hippocrates of Cos in the fifth and fourth centuries. By general consensus he is still regarded as the father of medicine. He dinned into the ears of his pupils the doctrine that "Every disease has a natural cause, and without natural causes, nothing ever happens." In addition, by his methods of careful study and comparison of symptoms he laid the foundations for clinical medicine. He discovered the phenomenon of crisis in disease and improved the practice of surgery. Though he had a wide knowledge of drugs, his chief reliances in treatment were diet and rest. The main fact to his discredit was his development of the theory of the four humors—the notion that illness is due to excessive amounts of yellow bile, black bile, blood, and phlegm in the system. The practice of bleeding the patient was the regrettable outgrowth of this theory.

Homer

Generally the most common medium of literary expression in the formative age of a people is the epic of heroic deeds. It is a form well adapted to the pioneering days of battle and lusty adventure when men have not yet had time to be awed by the mystery of things. The most famous of the Greek epics, the *Iliad* and the *Odyssey*, were put into written form at the end of the Dark Ages and commonly attributed to Homer. The first, which deals with the Trojan War, has its theme in the wrath of Achilles; the second describes the wanderings and return of Odysseus. Both have supreme literary merit in their carefully woven plots, in the realism of their character portrayals, and in their mastery of the full range of emotional intensity. They exerted an almost incalculable influence upon later writers. Their style and language inspired the fervid emotional poetry of the sixth century, and they were an unfailing source of plots and themes for the great tragedians of the Golden Age of the fifth and fourth centuries.

The three centuries which followed the Dark Ages were distinguished, as we have already seen, by tremendous social changes. The rural pattern of life gave way to an urban society of steadily increasing complexity. The founding of colonies and the growth of commerce provided new interests and new habits of living. Individuals hitherto submerged rose to a consciousness of their power and importance. It was inevitable that these changes should be reflected in new forms of literature, especially of a more personal type. The first to be developed was the elegy, which was probably intended to be declaimed rather than sung to the accompaniment of music. Elegies varied in theme from individual reactions toward love to the idealism of patriots and reformers. Generally, however, they were devoted to melancholy reflection on the disillusionments of life or to bitter lament over loss of prestige. Outstanding among the authors of elegiac verse was Solon the legislator.

In the sixth century and the early part of the fifth, the elegy was gradually displaced by the lyric, which derives its name from the fact that it was sung to the music of the lyre. The new type of poetry was particularly well adapted to the expression of passionate feelings, the violent loves and hates engendered by the strife of classes. It was employed for other purposes also. Both Alcaeus and Sappho used it to describe the poignant beauty of love, the delicate grace of spring, and the starlit splendor of a summer night. Meanwhile other poets developed the choral lyric, intended to express the feelings of the community rather than the sentiments of any one individual. Greatest of all the writers of this group was Pindar of Thebes, who wrote during the first half of the fifth century. The lyrics of Pindar took the form of odes celebrating the victories of athletes and the glories of Hellenic civilization. They are significant also for their religious and moral conceptions. Pindar had accepted the idea that Zeus is a god of righteousness, and that he will punish the wicked with the "direst doom" and reward the good with a life "that knows no tears."

The supreme literary achievement of the Greeks was the tragic drama. Like so many of their other great works, it had its roots in religion. At the festivals dedicated to the worship of Dionysus, the god of spring and of wine, a chorus of men dressed as satyrs, or goatmen, sang and danced around an altar, enacting the various parts of

Development
of the elegy

Lyric poetry

The origins of
tragic drama

Interior of a Greek Cup. Depicted here is Achilles bandaging the wound of Patrokolus. Ca. 500 B.C.

a dithyramb or choral lyric that related the story of the god's career. In time a leader came to be separated from the chorus to recite
the main parts of the story. The true drama was born about the beginning of the fifth century when Aeschylus introduced a second
"actor" and relegated the chorus to the background. The name
"tragedy," which came to be applied to this drama, was probably
derived from the Greek word *tragos* meaning "goat."

Greek tragedy stands out in marked contrast to the tragedies of
Shakespeare, Eugene O'Neill, or Arthur Miller. There was, first of
all, little action presented on the stage; the main business of the
actors was to recite the incidents of a plot which was already familiar to the audience, for the story was drawn from popular legends.
Secondly, Greek tragedy devoted little attention to the study of
complicated individual personality. There was no unfoldment of
personal character as shaped by the vicissitudes of a long career.
Those involved in the plot were scarcely individuals at all, but
types. On the stage they wore masks to disguise any characteristics
which might serve to distinguish them too sharply from the rest of
humanity. In addition, Greek tragedies differed from the modern
variety in having as their theme the conflict between man and the
universe, not the clash of individual personalities, or the conflict of
man with himself. The tragic fate that befell the main characters in
these plays was external to man himself. It was brought on by the
fact that someone had committed a crime against society, or against
the gods, thereby offending the moral scheme of the universe.
Punishment must follow in order to balance the scale of justice.
Finally, the purpose of Greek tragedies was not merely to depict
suffering and to interpret human actions, but to purify the emotions
of the audience by representing the triumph of justice.

As already indicated, the first of the tragic dramatists was Aeschylus (525–456 B.C.). Though he is supposed to have written about
eighty plays, only seven have survived in complete form, among
them *The Persians, Seven against Thebes, Prometheus Bound,* and a
trilogy known as *Oresteia.* Guilt and punishment is the recurrent
theme of nearly all of them. The second of the dramatists, Sophocles (496–406), is often considered the greatest. His style was more
polished and his philosophy more profound than that of his predecessor. He was the author of over a hundred plays. More than any
other writer in Greek history, he personified the Hellenic ideal of
"nothing too much." His attitude was distinguished by love of
harmony and peace, intelligent respect for democracy, and profound
sympathy for human weakness. The most famous of his plays now
extant are *Oedipus Rex, Antigone,* and *Electra.*

The work of the last of the tragedians, Euripides (480–406), reflects a far different spirit. He was a skeptic, an individualist, a humanist, who took delight in ridiculing the ancient myths and the
"sacred cows" of his time. An embittered pessimist who suffered
from the barbs of his conservative critics, he loved to humble the

204

Greek Theater in Epidauros. The construction, to take advantage of the slope of the hill, and the arrangement of the stage are of particular interest. Greek dramas were invariably presented in the open air.

proud in his plays and to exalt the lowly. He was the first to give the ordinary man, even the beggar and the peasant, a place in the drama. Euripides is also noted for his sympathy for the slave, for his condemnation of war, and for his protests against the exclusion of women from social and intellectual life. Because of his humanism, his tendency to portray men as they actually were (or even a little worse), and his introduction of the love *motif* into drama, he is often considered a modernist. It must be remembered, however, that in other respects his plays were perfectly consistent with the Hellenic model. They did not exhibit the evolution of individual character or the conflict of egos to any more notable extent than did the works of Sophocles or Aeschylus. Nevertheless, he has been called the most tragic of the Greek dramatists because he dealt with situations having analogues in real life. Among the best-known tragedies of Euripides are *Alcestis*, *Medea*, and *The Trojan Women*.

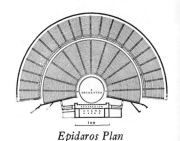

Epidaros Plan

Hellenic comedy was definitely inferior to tragedy. In common with tragedy it appears to have grown out of the Dionysiac festivals, but it did not attain full development until late in the fifth century B.C. Its only outstanding representative was Aristophanes (448?–380?), a somewhat coarse and belligerent aristocrat who lived in Athens. Most of his plays were written to satirize the political and intellectual ideals of the radical democracy of his time. In *The Knights* he pilloried the incompetent and greedy politicians for their reckless adventures in imperialism. In *The Frogs* he lampooned

205

Euripides for the innovations the latter had made in the drama. *The Clouds* he reserved for ridicule of the Sophists, ignorantly or maliciously classifying Socrates as one of them. While he was undoubtedly a clever poet with a mastery of subtle humor and imaginative skill, his ideas were founded largely upon prejudice. He is deserving of much credit, however, for his sharp criticisms of the stupid policies of the war-hawks of Athens during the struggle with Sparta. Though written as a farce, his *Lysistrata* cleverly pointed a way—however infeasible—to the termination of any war.

No account of Greek literature would be complete without some mention of the two great historians of the Golden Age. Herodotus, the "father of history" (484–425), was a native of Halicarnassus in Asia Minor. He traveled extensively through the Persian empire, Egypt, Greece, and Italy, collecting a multitude of interesting data about various peoples. His famous account of the great war between the Greeks and the Persians included so much background that the work seems almost a history of the world. He regarded that war as an epic struggle between East and West, with Zeus giving victory to the Greeks against a mighty host of barbarians.

If Herodotus deserves to be called the father of history, much more does his younger contemporary, Thucydides, deserve to be considered the founder of scientific history. Influenced by the skepticism and practicality of the Sophists, Thucydides chose to work on the basis of carefully sifted evidence, rejecting opinion, legends, and hearsay. The subject of his *History* was the war between Sparta and Athens, which he described scientifically and dispassionately, emphasizing the complexity of causes which led to the fateful clash. His aim was to present an accurate record which could be studied with profit by statesmen and generals of all time, and it must be said that he was in full measure successful. If there were any defects in his historical method, they consisted in overemphasizing political factors to the neglect of the social and economic and in failing to consider the importance of emotions in history. He also had a prejudice against the democratic factions in Athens after the death of Pericles.

The Greek
historians:
Herodotus

Marble Statue of the Apollo Type. Probably end of seventh century B.C. At this time Greek sculpture was still under Egyptian influence.

7. THE MEANING OF GREEK ART

Art even more than literature probably reflected the true character of Hellenic civilization. The Greek was essentially a materialist who conceived of his world in physical terms. Plato and the followers of the mystic religions were, of course, exceptions, but few other Greeks had much interest in a universe of spiritual realities. It would be natural therefore to find that the material emblems of architecture and sculpture should exemplify best the ideals the Greek held before him.

What did Greek art express? Above all, it symbolized humanism—the glorification of man as the most important creature in the uni-

Young Men Playing a Ball Game. This relief, ca. 510 B.C., depicts what may have been a forerunner of modern field hockey.

verse. Though much of the sculpture depicted gods, this did not detract in the slightest from its humanistic quality. The Greek deities existed for the benefit of man; in glorifying them he thus glorified himself. Both architecture and sculpture embodied the ideals of balance, harmony, order, and moderation. Anarchy and excess were abhorrent to the mind of the Greek, but so was absolute repression. Consequently, his art exhibited qualities of simplicity and dignified restraint—free from decorative extravagance, on the one hand, and from restrictive conventions on the other. Moreover, Greek art was an expression of the national life. Its purpose was not merely aesthetic but political: to symbolize the pride of the people in their city and to enhance their consciousness of unity. The Parthenon at Athens, for example, was the temple of Athena, the protecting goddess who presided over the corporate life of the state. In providing her with a beautiful shrine which she might frequently visit, the Athenians were giving evidence of their love for their city and their hope for its continuing welfare.

See color plates at pages 193, 224

The ideals embodied in Greek art

The art of the Hellenes differed from that of nearly every people since their time in an interesting variety of ways. Like most of the tragedies of Aeschylus and Sophocles, it was universal. It included few portraits of personalities either in sculpture or in painting.[10] The human beings depicted were generally types, not individuals. Again, Greek art differed from that of most later peoples in its ethical purpose. It was not art for the sake of mere decoration or for the expression of the artist's individual philosophy, but a medium for the ennoblement of man. This does not mean that it was didactic in the sense that its merit was determined by the moral lesson it taught, but rather that it was supposed to exemplify qualities of living essen-

Greek art compared with that of later peoples

[10] Most of the portraits in sculpture commonly considered Greek really belong to the Hellenistic Age, although a few were produced at the end of the fourth century B.C.

tially artistic in themselves. The Athenian, at least, drew no sharp distinction between the ethical and aesthetic spheres; the beautiful and the good were really identical. True morality, therefore, consisted in rational living, in the avoidance of grossness, disgusting excesses, and other forms of conduct aesthetically offensive. Finally, Greek art may be contrasted with most later forms in the fact that it was not "naturalistic." Although the utmost attention was given to the depiction of beautiful bodies, this had nothing to do with fidelity to nature. The Greek was not interested in interpreting nature for its own sake, but in expressing *human* ideals.

The history of Greek art divides itself naturally into three great periods. The first, which can be called the archaic period, covered the seventh and sixth centuries. During the greater part of this age sculpture was dominated by Egyptian influence, as can be seen in the frontality and rigidity of the statues, with their square shoulders and one foot slightly advanced. Toward the end, however, these conventions were thrown aside. The chief architectural styles also had their origin in this period, and several crude temples were built. The second period, which occupied the fifth century, witnessed the full perfection of both architecture and sculpture. The art of this time was completely idealistic. During the fourth century, the last period of Hellenic art, architecture lost some of its balance and simplicity and sculpture assumed new characteristics. It came to reflect more clearly the reactions of the individual artist, to incorporate traces of realism, and to lose some of its quality as an expression of civic pride.

For all its artistic excellence, Greek temple architecture was one of the simplest of structural forms. Its essential elements were really only five in number: (1) the cella or nucleus of the building, which was a rectangular chamber to house the statue of the god; (2) the columns, which formed the porch and surrounded the cella; (3) the entablature or lintel, which rested upon the columns and supported the roof; (4) the gabled roof itself; and (5) the pediment or triangular section under the gable of the roof. Two different architectural styles were developed, representing modifications of certain of these elements. The more common was the Doric, which made use of a rather heavy, sharply fluted column surmounted by a plain capital. The other, the Ionic, had more slender and more graceful columns with flat flutings, a triple base, and a scroll or volute capital. The so-called Corinthian style, which was chiefly Hellenistic, differed from the Ionic primarily in being more ornate. The three styles differed also in their treatment of the entablature or lintel. In the Ionic style it was left almost plain. In the Doric and Corinthian styles it bore sculptured reliefs. The Parthenon, the best example of Greek architecture, was essentially a Doric building, but it reflected some of the grace and subtlety of Ionic influence.

According to the prevailing opinion among his contemporaries, Greek sculpture attained its acme of development in the work of

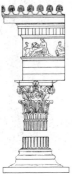

Corinthian

Ionic

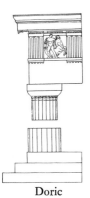

Doric

Details of the Three Famous Orders of Greek Architecture

The Parthenon. The largest and most famous of Athenian temples, the Parthenon is considered the classic example of Doric architecture. Its columns were made more graceful by tapering them in a slight curve toward the top. Its friezes and pediments were decorated with lifelike sculptures of prancing horses (see below), fighting giants, and benign and confident deities.

Phidias (500?–432?). His masterpieces were the statue of Athena in the Parthenon and the statue of Zeus in the Temple of Olympian Zeus. In addition, he designed and supervised the execution of the Parthenon reliefs. The main qualities of his work are grandeur of conception, patriotism, proportion, dignity, and restraint. Nearly all of his figures are idealized representations of deities and mythological creatures in human form. The second most renowned fifth-century sculptor was Myron, noted for his statue of the discus thrower and for his glorification of other athletic types. The names of three great sculptors in the fourth century have come down to us. The most gifted of them was Praxiteles, renowned for his portrayal of humanized deities with slender, graceful bodies and countenances of philosophic repose. The best known of his works is the statue of Hermes with the infant Dionysus. His older contemporary, Scopas, gained distinction as an emotional sculptor. One of his most successful creations was the statue of a religious ecstatic, a worshiper of Dionysus, in a condition of mystic frenzy. At the end of the century Lysippus introduced even stronger qualities of realism and individualism into sculpture. He was the first great master of the realistic portrait as a study of personal character.

Parthenon Frieze

8. ATHENIAN LIFE IN THE GOLDEN AGE

The population of Athens in the fifth and fourth centuries was divided into three distinct groups: the citizens, the metics, and the slaves. The citizens, who numbered at the most about 160,000, included only those born of citizen parents, except for the few who were occasionally enfranchised by special law. The metics, who probably did not exceed a total of 100,000, were resident aliens, chiefly non-Athenian Greeks, although some were Phoenicians and Jews. Save for the fact that they had no political privileges and generally were not permitted to own land, the metics had equal opportunities with citizens. They could engage in any occupation they desired and participate in any social or intellectual activities. Contrary to a popular tradition, the slaves in Athens were never a majority of the population. Their maximum number does not seem to have exceeded 140,000. Urban slaves, at least, were very well treated and were sometimes rewarded for faithful service by being set free. They could work for wages and own property, and some of them held responsible positions as minor public officials and as managers of banks. The treatment of slaves who worked in the mines, however, was often cruel.

Life in Athens stands out in rather sharp contrast to that in most other civilizations. One of its leading features was the amazing degree of social and economic equality that prevailed among all the inhabitants. Although there were many who were poor, there were few who were very rich. Nearly everyone, whether citizen, metic, or slave, ate the same kind of food, wore the same kind of clothing, and participated in the same kind of amusement. This substantial equality was enforced in part by the system of *liturgies*, which were services to the state rendered by wealthy men, chiefly in the form of contributions to support the drama, equip the navy, or provide for the poor.

The amazing degree of social and economic equality

A second outstanding characteristic of Athenian life was its poverty in comforts and luxuries. Part of this was a result of the low

Porch of the Maidens of the So-Called Erechtheum, a Temple of Athena on the Acropolis

Left: *The Discobolus or Discus Thrower of Myron.* The statue reflects the glorification of the human body characteristic of Athens in the Golden Age. Now in the Vatican Museum. Right: *Hermes with the Infant Dionysus, by Praxiteles, Fourth Century* B.C. Original in the Olympia Museum, Greece.

income of the mass of the people. Teachers, sculptors, masons, carpenters, and common laborers all received the same standard wage of one drachma per day. Part of it may have been a consequence also of the mild climate, which made possible a life of simplicity. But whatever the cause, the fact remains that, in comparison with modern standards, the Athenians endured an exceedingly impoverished existence. They knew nothing of such common commodities as watches, soap, newspapers, cotton cloth, sugar, tea, or coffee. Their beds had no springs, their houses had no drains, and their food consisted chiefly of barley cakes, onions, and fish, washed down with diluted wine. From the standpoint of clothing they were no better off. A rectangular piece of cloth wrapped around the body and fastened with pins at the shoulders and with a rope around the waist served as the main garment. A larger piece was draped around the body as an extra garment for outdoor wear. No one wore either stockings or socks, and few had any footgear except sandals.

But lack of comforts and luxuries was a matter of little consequence to the Athenian citizen. He was totally unable to regard these as the most important things in life. His aim was to live as interestingly and contentedly as possible without spending all his days in grinding toil for the sake of a little more comfort for his family. Nor was he interested in piling up riches as a source of power or prestige. What each citizen really wanted was a small farm or business that would provide him with a reasonable income and at the same time allow him an abundance of leisure for politics, for gossip in the market place, and for intellectual or artistic activities if he had the talent to enjoy them.

It is frequently supposed that the Athenian was too lazy or too snobbish to work hard for luxury and security. But this was not quite the case. True, there were some occupations in which he would not engage because he considered them degrading or destructive of moral freedom. He would not break his back digging silver or copper out of a mine; such work was fit only for slaves of the lowest intellectual level. On the other hand, there is plenty of evidence to show that the great majority of Athenian citizens did not look with disdain upon manual labor. Most of them worked on their farms or in their shops as independent craftsmen. Hundreds of others earned their living as hired laborers employed either by the state or by their fellow Athenians. Cases are on record of citizens, metics, and slaves working side by side, all for the same wage, in the construction of public buildings; and in at least one instance the foreman of a crew was a slave.[11]

In spite of expansion of trade and increase in population, the economic organization of Athenian society remained comparatively simple. Agriculture and commerce were by far the most important enterprises. Even in Pericles' day the majority of the citizens still lived in the country. Industry was not highly developed. Very few examples of large-scale production are on record, and those chiefly in the manufacture of pottery and implements of war. The largest establishment that ever existed was apparently a shield factory owned by a metic and employing 120 slaves. No other was more than half as large. The enterprises which absorbed the most labor were the mines, but they were owned by the state and were leased in sections to petty contractors to be worked by slaves. The bulk of industry was carried on in small shops owned by individual craftsmen who produced their wares directly to the order of the consumer.

Religion underwent some notable changes in the Golden Age of the fifth and fourth centuries. The primitive polytheism and anthropomorphism of the Homeric myths were largely supplanted, among intellectuals at least, by a belief in one God as the creator and sustainer of the moral law. Such a doctrine was taught by many of the philosophers, by the poet Pindar, and by the

[11] A. E. Zimmern, *The Greek Commonwealth*, p. 258.

dramatists Aeschylus and Sophocles. Other significant consequences flowed from the mystery cults. These new forms of religion first became popular in the sixth century because of the craving for an emotional faith to make up for the disappointments of life. The more important of them was the Orphic cult, which revolved around the myth of the death and resurrection of Dionysus. The other, the Eleusinian cult, had as its central theme the abduction of Persephone by Hades, god of the nether world, and her ultimate redemption by Demeter, the great Earth Mother. Both of these cults had as their original purpose the promotion of the lifegiving powers of nature, but in time they came to be fraught with a much deeper significance. They expressed to their followers the ideas of vicarious atonement, salvation in an afterlife, and ecstatic union with the divine. Although entirely inconsistent with the spirit of the ancient religion, they made a powerful appeal to certain classes and were largely responsible for the spread of the belief in personal immortality. The more thoughtful Greeks, however, seem to have persisted in their adherence to the worldly, optimistic, and mechanical faith of their ancestors and to have shown little concern about a conviction of sin or a desire for salvation in a life to come.

It remains to consider briefly the position of the family in Athens in the fifth and fourth centuries. Though marriage was still an important institution for the procreation of children who would become citizens of the state, there is reason to believe that family life had declined. Men of the more prosperous classes, at least, now spent the greater part of their time away from their families. Wives were relegated to an inferior position and required to remain secluded in their homes. Their place as social and intellectual companions for their husbands was taken by alien women, the famous *hetaerae*, many of whom were highly cultured natives of the Ionian cities. Marriage itself assumed the character of a political and economic arrangement devoid of romantic elements. Men married wives so as to ensure that at least some of their children would be legitimate and in order to obtain property in the form of a dowry. It was important also, of course, to have someone to care for the household. But husbands did not consider their wives as their equals and did not appear in public with them or encourage their participation in any form of social or intellectual activity.

The family in Athens in the Golden Age

9. THE GREEK ACHIEVEMENT AND ITS SIGNIFICANCE FOR US

No historian would deny that the achievement of the Greeks was one of the most remarkable in the history of the world. With no great expanse of fertile soil or abundance of mineral resources, they succeeded in developing a higher and more varied civilization than any of the most richly favored nations of Africa and Western Asia. With only a limited cultural inheritance from the past to build upon as a foundation, they produced intellectual and artistic achievements which have served ever since as the chief inspiration to man in his quest for wisdom and beauty. It seems reasonable to conclude also that they achieved a more normal and more rational mode of living than most other peoples who strutted and fretted their hour upon this planet. The absence of violent revolution, except in the earlier period, and during the Peloponnesian War, the infrequency of brutal crimes, and the contentment with simple amusements and modest wealth all point to a comparatively happy and satisfied existence. Moreover, the sane moral attitude of the Greek helped to keep him almost entirely free from the nervous instability and emotional conflicts which wreak so much havoc in modern society. Suicide, for example, was exceedingly rare in Greece.[12]

It is necessary to be on our guard, however, against uncritical judgments that are sometimes expressed in reference to the achievement of the Greeks. We must not assume that all of the natives of Hellas were as cultured, wise, and free as the citizens of Athens and of the Ionian states across the Aegean. The Spartans, the Arcadians, the Thessalians, and probably the majority of the Boeotians remained untutored and benighted from the beginning to the end of their history. Further, the Athenian civilization itself was not without its defects. It permitted some exploitation of the weak, especially of the ignorant slaves who toiled in the mines. It was based upon a principle of racial exclusiveness which reckoned every man a foreigner whose parents were not both Athenians, and consequently denied political rights to the majority of the inhabitants. Its statecraft was not sufficiently enlightened to avoid the pitfalls of imperialism and even of aggressive war. Finally, the attitude of its citizens was not always tolerant and just. Socrates was put to death for his opinions, and two other philosophers, Anaxagoras and Protagoras, were forced to leave the country. The former was condemned to death by the assembly, and the books of the latter were ordered to be burned. It must be conceded, however, that the record of the Athenians for tolerance was better than that of most other nations, both ancient and modern. There was probably more freedom of expression in Athens during the war with Sparta than there was in the United States during World War I.

Nor is it true that the Hellenic influence has really been as great as is commonly supposed. No intelligent student could accept the sentimental verdict of Shelley: "We are all Greeks; our laws, our literature, our religion, our arts have their roots in Greece." Our laws do not really have their roots in Greece but chiefly in Hellenistic and Roman sources. Much of our poetry is undoubtedly Greek

---

[12] For a discussion of this point see E. A. Westermarck, *The Origin and Development of Moral Ideas*, pp. 247 ff.

in inspiration, but such is not the case with most of our prose literature. Our religion is no more than partly Greek; except as it was influenced by Plato, Aristotle, and the Romans, it reflects primarily the spirit of Western Asia. Even our arts take their form and meaning from Rome almost as much as from Greece. Actually, modern civilization has been the result of the convergence of several influences coming from a variety of sources. The influence from Greece has been partly overshadowed by heritages from Western Asia and from the Romans and the Germans. Philosophy appears to have been the only important segment of Greek civilization that has been incorporated into modern culture virtually intact.

In spite of all this, the Hellenic adventure was of profound significance for the history of the world. For the Greeks were the founders of nearly all those ideals we commonly think of as peculiar to the West. The civilizations of ancient Western Asia, with the exception, to a certain extent, of the Hebrew and Egyptian, were dominated by absolutism, supernaturalism, ecclesiasticism, the denial of both body and mind, and the subjection of the individual to the group. Their political regime was the reign of force as expressed in an absolute monarch supported by a powerful priesthood. Their religion in many cases was the worship of omnipotent gods who demanded that man should humble and despise himself for the purpose of their greater glory. Culture in these mighty empires served mainly as an instrument to magnify the power of the state and to enhance the prestige of rulers and priests.

By contrast, the civilization of Greece, notably in its Athenian form, was founded upon ideals of freedom, optimism, secularism, rationalism, the glorification of both body and mind, and a high regard for the dignity and worth of the individual man. Insofar as the individual was subjected at all, his subjection was to the rule of the majority. This, of course, was not always good, especially in times

The influence of the Greeks on the West

Contrast of Greek and Oriental ideals

The Acropolis Today. Occupying the commanding position is the Parthenon. To the left is the Erechtheum with its Porch of the Maidens facing the Parthenon.

of crisis, when the majority might be swayed by prejudice. Religion was worldly and practical, serving the interests of human beings. Worship of the gods was a means for the ennoblement of man. As opposed to the ecclesiasticism of the Orient, the Greeks had no organized priesthood at all. They kept their priests in the background and refused under any circumstances to allow them to define dogma or to govern the realm of intellect. In addition, they excluded them from control over the sphere of morality. The culture of the Greeks was the first to be based upon the primacy of intellect— upon the supremacy of the spirit of free inquiry. There was no subject they feared to investigate, or any question they regarded as excluded from the province of reason. To an extent never before realized, mind was supreme over faith, logic and science over superstition.[13]

The tragedy of
Hellenic history

The supreme tragedy of the Greeks was, of course, their failure to solve the problem of political conflict. To a large degree, this conflict was the product of social and cultural dissimilarities. Because of different geographic and economic conditions the Greek city-states developed at an uneven pace. Some went forward rapidly to high levels of cultural superiority, while others lagged behind and made little or no intellectual progress. The consequences were discord and suspicion, which gave rise eventually to hatred and fear. Though some of the more advanced thinkers made efforts to propagate the notion that the Hellenes were one people who should reserve their contempt for non-Hellenes, or "barbarians," the conception never became part of a national ethos. Athenians hated Spartans, and *vice versa*, just as vehemently as they hated Lydians or Persians. Not even the danger of Asian conquest was sufficient to dispel the distrust and antagonism of Greeks for one another. The war that finally broke out between Athenians and Spartans sealed the doom of Hellenic civilization just as effectively as could ever have resulted from foreign conquest. For a time it appeared as if a new world, largely devoid of ethnic distinctions, might emerge from the ruins of the Greek city-states as a result of the conquests of Alexander the Great. Alexander dreamed of such a world, in which there would be neither Athenian nor Spartan, Greek nor Egyptian, but unfortunately neither he nor his generals knew any means of achieving it except to impose it by force. The parallels between the last phases of Hellenic history and the developments in our own time are at least interesting, if not conclusive.

SELECTED READINGS

· *Items so designated are available in paperbound editions.*

· Agard, Walter, *What Democracy Meant to the Greeks*, Chapel Hill, 1942 (University of Wisconsin).

[13] For further discussion of the contrast between Hellas and the Orient see the admirable study by Edith Hamilton, *The Greek Way*.

Andrewes, Antony, *The Greeks*, New York, 1967.

· Barker, Ernest, *Greek Political Theory: Plato and His Predecessors*, New York, 1919, 2 vols. (Barnes & Noble). One of the best of the commentaries.

· Boardman, John, *Greek Art*, New York, 1964 (Praeger).

· ———, *The Greeks Overseas*, Baltimore, 1964 (Penguin).

· Burn, A. R., *Pericles and Athens*, New York, 1962 (Collier).

· Clagett, Marshall, *Greek Science in Antiquity*, New York, 1963 (Collier).

· Dickinson, G. L., *The Greek View of Life*, New York, 1927 (Ann Arbor, Collier). An excellent interpretation.

· Dodds, E. R., *The Greeks and the Irrational*, Berkeley, 1963 (Univ. of California).

· Ehrenberg, Victor, *The Greek State*, New York, 1960 (Norton Library).

· Farrington, Benjamin, *Greek Science*, Baltimore, 1961 (Penguin).

· Finley, M. I., *The Ancient Greeks: An Introduction to Their Life and Thought*, New York, 1963 (Compass).

· Forrest, W. G., *A History of Sparta, 950–152 B.C.*, London, 1968 (Norton Library).

· Freeman, Kathleen, *The Greek City-States*, New York, 1963 (Norton Library).

· Glotz, Gustave, *Ancient Greece at Work*, London, 1927 (Norton Library).

· Hamilton, Edith, *The Greek Way*, New York, 1930 (Norton Library). Thoughtful and stimulating.

· Kitto, H. D. F., *The Greeks*, Baltimore, 1957 (Penguin). Probably the best one-volume survey in English.

· Larsen, J. A. O., *Representative Government in Greek and Roman History*, Berkeley, 1955 (University of California).

· MacKendrick, Paul, *The Greek Stones Speak*, New York, 1962 (Mentor).

· Marrou, H. I., *A History of Education in Antiquity*, New York, 1964 (Mentor).

· Mitchell, H., *Sparta*, New York, 1952 (Cambridge).

· Nilsson, M. P., *A History of Greek Religion*, New York, 1964 (Norton Library). Interesting and authoritative.

Richter, G. M. A., *Greek Art*, New York, 1963.

Ridder, A. H. P. de, and Deonna, Waldemar, *Art in Greece*, New York, 1927. An excellent one-volume account.

· Rose, H. J., *A Handbook of Greek Literature*, New York, 1960 (Dutton).

· ———, *A Handbook of Greek Mythology*, New York, 1959 (Dutton).

· Snell, Bruno, *The Discovery of the Mind*, New York, 1960 (Torchbook).

Starr, C. G., *The Origins of Greek Civilization*, New York, 1961.

· Webster, T. B. L., *From Mycenae to Homer*, New York, 1964 (Norton Library).

· Zimmern, A. E., *The Greek Commonwealth*, New York, 1911 (Galaxy). Good, though perhaps a bit too laudatory of the Athenians.

SOURCE MATERIALS

Most Greek authors have been translated in the appropriate volumes of the Loeb Classical Library, Harvard University Press.

In addition the following may be helpful:

· Barnstone, Willis (trans.), *Greek Lyric Poetry*, New York, 1962 (Bantam).

· Kagan, Donald, *Sources in Greek Political Thought*, Glencoe, Ill., 1965 (Free Press).

· Kirk, G. S., and Raven, J. E., *The Presocratic Philosophers*, Cambridge, 1957 (Cambridge University Press).

CHAPTER 9

The Hellenistic Civilization

Beauty and virtue and the like are to be honored, if they give pleasure, but if they do not give pleasure, we must bid them farewell.

——Epicurus, "On the End of Life"

I agree that Alexander was carried away so far as to copy oriental luxury. I hold that no mighty deeds, not even conquering the whole world, is of any good unless the man has learned mastery of himself.

—Arrian, *Anabasis of Alexander*

The death of Alexander the Great in 323 B.C. constituted a watershed in the development of world history. Hellenic civilization as it had existed in its prime now came to an end. Of course, the old institutions and ways of life did not suddenly disappear, but Alexander's career had cut so deeply into the old order that it was inconceivable that it could be restored intact. The fusion of cultures and intermingling of peoples resulting from Alexander's conquests accomplished the overthrow of many of the ideals of the Greeks in their Golden Age of the fifth and fourth centuries. Gradually a new pattern of civilization emerged, based upon a mixture of Greek and Oriental elements. To this new civilization, which lasted until about the beginning of the Christian era, the name Hellenistic is the one most commonly applied.

A new stage in world history

Though the break between the Hellenic and Hellenistic eras was as sharp as that between any two other civilizations, it would be a mistake to deny all continuity. The language of the new cultured classes was predominantly Greek, and even the hordes of people whose heritage was non-Greek considered it desirable to have some Hellenic culture. Hellenic achievements in science provided a foundation for the great scientific revolution of the Hellenistic Age. Greek emphasis upon logic was likewise carried over into Hellenistic philosophy, though the objectives of the latter were in many cases quite different. In the spheres of the political, social, and eco-

Comparison of the Hellenistic Age with the Golden Age of Greece

219

nomic the resemblances were few indeed. The classical ideal of democracy was now superseded by despotism perhaps as rigorous as any that Egypt or Persia had ever produced. The Greek city-state survived in some parts of Greece itself, but elsewhere it was replaced by the big monarchy, and in the minds of some leaders by notions of a world state. The Hellenic devotion to simplicity and the golden mean gave way to extravagance in the arts and to a love of luxury and riotous excess. Golden Age intensity of living was superseded by a craving for novelty and breadth of experience. In the economic realm the Athenian system of small-scale production was supplanted largely by the growth of big business and vigorous competition for profits. In view of these changes it seems valid to conclude that the Hellenistic Age was sufficiently distinct from the Golden Age of Greece to justify its being considered the era of a new civilization.

I. POLITICAL HISTORY AND INSTITUTIONS

The Hellenistic states

When Alexander died in 323 B.C., he left no legitimate heir to succeed him. His nearest male relative was a feeble-minded half-brother. Tradition relates that when his friends requested him on his deathbed to designate a successor, he replied vaguely, "To the best man." After his death his highest-ranking generals proceeded to divide the empire among them. Some of the younger commanders contested this arrangement, and a series of wars followed which culminated in the decisive battle of Ipsus in 301 B.C. The result of this battle was a new division among the victors. Seleucus took possession of Persia, Mesopotamia, and Syria; Lysimachus assumed control over Asia Minor and Thrace; Cassander established himself in Madeconia; and Ptolemy added Phoenicia and Palestine to his original domain of Egypt. Twenty years later these four states were reduced to three when Seleucus defeated and killed Lysimachus in battle and appropriated his kingdom. In the meantime most of the Greek states had revolted against the attempts of the Macedonian king to extend his power over them. By banding together in defensive leagues several of them succeeded in maintaining their inde-

Scythian Pectoral Found at Ordzhonikidze in Southern Russia. The Scythians were supposedly a warlike people living on the fringes of Greece. However, the pectoral shows pastoral activities. The heavy gold jewelry exhibits a great skill and workmanship.

pendence for nearly a century. Finally, between 146 and 30 B.C. nearly all of the Hellenistic territory passed under Roman rule.

The dominant form of government in the Hellenistic Age was the despotism of kings who represented themselves as at least semidivine. Alexander himself was recognized as a son of God in Egypt and was worshiped as a god in Greece. His most powerful successors, the Seleucid kings in western Asia and the Ptolemies in Egypt, made systematic attempts to deify themselves. A Seleucid monarch, Antiochus IV, adopted the title "Epiphanes" or "God Manifest." The later members of the dynasty of the Ptolemies signed their decrees "Theos" (God) and revived the practice of sister marriage which had been followed by the Pharaohs as a means of preserving the divine blood of the royal family from contamination. Only in the kingdom of Macedonia was despotism tempered by a modicum of respect for the liberties of the citizens.

Two other political institutions developed as by-products of Hellenistic civilization: the Achaean and Aetolian Leagues. We have already seen that most of the Greek states rebelled against Macedonian rule following the division of Alexander's empire. The better to preserve their independence, several of these states formed alliances among themselves, which were gradually expanded to become confederate leagues. The organization of these leagues was essentially the same in all cases. Each had a federal council composed of representatives of the member cities with power to enact laws on subjects of general concern. An assembly which all of the citizens in the federated states could attend decided questions of war and peace and elected officials. Executive and military authority was vested in the hands of a general, elected for one year and eligible for reelection only in alternate years. Although these leagues are frequently described as federal states, they were scarcely more than confederacies. The central authority, like the government of the American States under the Articles of Confederation, was dependent upon the local governments for contributions of revenue and troops. Furthermore, the powers delegated to the central government were limited primarily to matters of war and peace, coinage, and weights and measures. The chief significance of these leagues is to be found in the fact that they embodied the principle of representative government and constituted the nearest approach ever made in Greece to voluntary national union.

2. SIGNIFICANT ECONOMIC AND SOCIAL DEVELOPMENTS

The history of the Hellenistic civilization was marked by economic developments second only in magnitude to the Commercial and Industrial Revolutions of the modern era. Several important causes can be distinguished: (1) the opening up of a vast area of

Alexander the Great. Shown here is a tetradrachma struck in Thrace at the order of King Lysimachus, ca. 300 B.C.

The Achaean and Aetolian Leagues

221

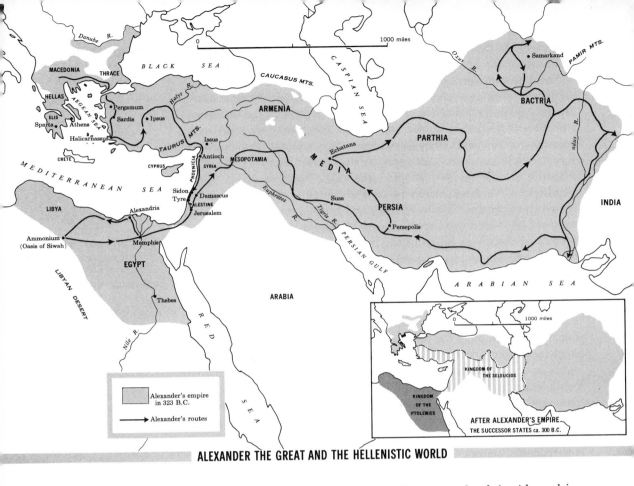

ALEXANDER THE GREAT AND THE HELLENISTIC WORLD

Inset map labels: KINGDOM OF THE SELEUCIDS, KINGDOM OF THE PTOLEMIES, AFTER ALEXANDER'S EMPIRE, THE SUCCESSOR STATES ca. 300 B.C.

Legend: Alexander's empire in 323 B.C. / Alexander's routes

trade from the Indus River to the Nile as a result of the Alexandrian conquests; (2) the rise in prices as a consequence of the release of the enormous Persian hoard of gold and silver into the channels of circulation, resulting in an increase in investment and speculation; and (3) the promotion of trade and industry by governments as a means of augmenting the revenues of the state. The net result was the growth of a system of large-scale production, trade, and finance, with the state as the principal capitalist and entrepreneur.

Agriculture was as profoundly affected by the new developments as any other branch of the economic life. The most striking phenomena were the concentration of holdings of land and the degradation of the agricultural population. One of the first things the successors of Alexander did was to confiscate the estates of the chief landowners and add them to the royal domain. The lands thus acquired were either granted to the favorites of the king or leased to tenants under an arrangement calculated to ensure an abundant income for the crown. The tenants were generally forbidden to leave the lands they cultivated until after the harvest and were not allowed to dispose of their grain until after the king had had a chance to sell the share he received as rent at the highest price the market

Margin notes: The economic revolution and its causes

The concentration of land ownership

222

would bring. When some of the tenants went on srike or attempted to run away, they were all bound to the soil as hereditary serfs. Many of the small independent farmers also became serfs when they got into debt as a result of inability to compete with large-scale production.

In an effort to make all of the resources of the state contribute to the profit of the government, the rulers of Egypt and the Seleucid empire promoted and regulated industry and trade. The Ptolemies established factories and shops in nearly every village and town to be owned and operated by the government for its own financial benefit. In addition, they assumed control over all of the enterprises that were privately owned, fixing the prices the owners could charge and manipulating markets to the advantage of the crown. A similar plan of regimentation for industry, although not on quite so ambitious a scale, was enforced by the Seleucid rulers of western Asia. Trade was left by both of these governments very largely in private hands, but it was heavily taxed and regulated in such a way as to make sure that an ample share of the profits went to the king. Every facility was provided by the government for the encouragement of new trading ventures. Harbors were improved, warships were sent out to police the seas, and roads and canals were built. Moreover, the Ptolemies employed famous geographers to discover new routes to distant lands and thereby gain access to valuable markets. As a result of such methods Egypt developed a flourishing commerce in the widest variety of products. Into the port of Alexandria came spices from Arabia, copper from Cyprus, gold from Abyssinia and India, tin from Britain, elephants and ivory from Nubia, silver from the northern Aegean and Spain, fine carpets from Asia Minor, and even silk from China. Profits for the government and for some of the merchants were often as high as 20 or 30 per cent.

State regimentation of industry and trade

Further evidence of the significant economic development of the Hellenistic Age is to be found in the growth of finance. An international money economy, based upon gold and silver coins, now became general throughout the Near East. Banks, usually owned by the government, developed as the chief institutions of credit for business ventures of every description. Speculation, cornering of markets, intense competition, the growth of large business houses, and the development of insurance and advertising were other significant phenomena of this remarkable age.

The growth of finance

According to the available evidence, the Hellenistic Age, during the first two centuries at least, was a period of prosperity. Although serious crises frequently followed the collapse of speculative booms, they appear to have been of short duration. But the prosperity that existed seems to have been limited chiefly to the rulers, the upper classes, and the merchants. It certainly did not extend to the peasants or even to the workers in the towns. The daily wages of both

The disparity between rich and poor

223

Hellenistic Coins. Obverse and reverse sides of the silver tetradrachma of Macedon, 336–323 B.C. Objects of common use from this period often show as much beauty of design as formal works of art.

skilled and unskilled workers in Athens in the third century had dropped to less than half of what they had been in the Age of Pericles. The cost of living, on the other hand, had risen considerably. To make matters worse, unemployment in the large cities was so serious a problem that the government had to provide free grain for many of the inhabitants. Slavery declined in the Hellenistic world, partly because of the influence of the Stoic philosophy, but mainly for the reason that wages were now so low that it was cheaper to hire a free laborer than to purchase and maintain a slave.

An interesting result of social and economic conditions in the Hellenistic Age was the growth of metropolitan cities. Despite the fact that a majority of the people still lived in the country, there was an increasing tendency for men to become dissatisfied with the dullness of rural living and to flock into the cities, where life, if not easier, was at least more exciting. But the chief reasons are to be found in the expansion of industry and commerce, in the enlargement of governmental functions, and in the desire of former independent farmers to escape the hardships of serfdom. Cities multiplied and grew in the Hellenistic empires almost as rapidly as in nineteenth- and twentieth-century America. Antioch in Syria quadrupled its population during a single century. Seleucia on the Tigris grew from nothing to a metropolis of several hundred thousand in less than two centuries. The largest and most famous of all the Hellenistic cities was Alexandria in Egypt, with over 500,000 inhabitants and possibly as many as 1,000,000. No other city in ancient times, not even Rome, surpassed it in size or in magnificence. Its streets were well paved and laid out in regular order. It had splendid public buildings and parks, a museum, and a library of 750,000 volumes. It was the most brilliant center of Hellenistic cultural achievement, especially in the field of scientific research. The masses of its people, however, were a disorganized mob without any share in the brilliant and luxurious life around them, although it was paid for in part out of the fruits of their labor.

The growth of metropolitan cities

224

Bronze Mirror Case, V cent. B.C. Greek articles of everyday use were commonly finished with the same delicacy and precision as major works of art.

Diadoumenos, after Polykleitos, V cent. B.C. An idealized statue of a Greek athlete tying the "diadem," or band of victory, around his head.

Bracelet Pendant, IV–III cent. B.C. This tiny figure of the god Pan is a masterpiece of detail and expression.

Woman Arranging Her Hair, 400–300 B.C. Sculptors of antiquity took pride in these statuettes of ordinary people in ordinary activities, which were usually made of terra cotta painted soft blue, pink, or yellow.

Head of an Athlete, *ca.* 440–420 B.C. The sculptor aimed to express manly beauty in perfect harmony with physical and intellectual excellence.

Comic Actor, 200–100 B.C. Hellenistic realism often included portrayal of ugly and even deformed individuals.

Sleeping Eros, 250–150 B.C. Along with a penchant for realism, Hellenistic sculptors were fond of portraying serenity or repose.

Statuette of Hermarchos, III cent. B.C. An example of the realism of Hellenistic sculpture.

GREECE AND HER COLONIES IN 550 B.C.

Hellenistic philosophy exhibited two trends that ran almost parallel throughout the civilization. The major trend, exemplified by Stoicism and Epicureanism, showed a fundamental regard for reason as the key to the solution of man's problems. This trend was a manifestation of Greek influence, though philosophy and science, as combined in Aristotle, had now come to a parting of the ways. The minor trend, exemplified by the Skeptics, Cynics, and various Asian cults, tended to reject reason, to deny the possibility of attaining truth, and in some cases to turn toward mysticism and a reliance upon faith. Despite the differences in their teachings, the philosophers of the Hellenistic Age were generally agreed upon one thing: the necessity of finding some way of salvation for man from the hardships and evils of his existence.

Trends in philosophy

The first of the Hellenistic philosophers were the Cynics, who had their origin about 350 B.C. Their foremost leader was Diogenes, who won fame by his perpetual quest for an "honest" man. Essentially this meant the adoption of the "natural" life and the repudiation of everything conventional and artificial. The Cynics adopted as their principal goal the cultivation of "self-sufficiency": every man should cultivate within himself the ability to satisfy his own needs. Obviously the Cynics bore some resemblance to other movements that have cropped up through the ages—the hippie movement of our own day, for example. There were notable differences, however. The Cynics spurned music and art as manifestations of artificiality, and they were not representative of a youth generation. But all such movements seem to reflect a sense of frustration and hopeless conflict in society.

The Cynics

Epicureanism and Stoicism both originated about 300 B.C. The founders were, respectively, Epicurus (342–270) and Zeno (fl. after 300), who were residents of Athens; the former was born on the island of Samos, and the latter was a native of Cyprus, probably of Phoenician descent. Epicureanism and Stoicism had several features in common. Both were individualistic, concerned not with the welfare of society primarily, but with the good of the individual. Both were materialistic, denying categorically the existence of any spiritual substances; even divine beings and the soul were declared to be formed of matter. In Stoicism and Epicureanism alike there were definite elements of universalism, since both implied that men are the same the world over and recognized no distinctions between Greeks and "barbarians."

Epicureanism and Stoicism

But in many ways the two systems were quite different. Zeno and his principal disciples taught that the cosmos is an ordered whole in which all contradictions are resolved for ultimate good. Evil is, therefore, relative; the particular misfortunes which befall human

225

beings are but necessary incidents to the final perfection of the universe. Everything that happens is rigidly determined in accordance with rational purpose. Man is not master of his fate; his destiny is a link in an unbroken chain. He is free only in the sense that he can accept his fate or rebel against it. But whether he accepts or rebels, he cannot overcome it. The supreme duty of man is to submit to the order of the universe in the knowledge that that order is good; in other words, to resign himself as graciously as possible to his fate. Through such an act of resignation he will attain to the highest happiness, which consists in tranquillity of mind. The individual who is most truly happy is therefore the man who by the assertion of his rational nature has accomplished a perfect adjustment of his life to the cosmic purpose and has purged his soul of all bitterness and whining protest against evil turns of fortune.

The ethical and
social teachings of
the Stoics

The Stoics developed an ethical and social theory that accorded well with their general philosophy. Believing that the highest good consists in serenity of mind, they naturally emphasized duty and self-discipline as cardinal virtues. Recognizing the prevalence of particular evil, they taught that men should be tolerant and forgiving in their attitudes toward one another. Unlike the Cynics, they did not recommend that man should withdraw from society but urged participation in public affairs as a duty for the citizen of rational mind. They condemned slavery and war, but it was far from their purpose to preach any crusade against these evils. They were disposed to think that the results that would flow from violent measures of social change would be worse than the diseases they were supposed to cure. Besides, what difference did it make if the body were in bondage so long as the mind was free? Despite its negative character, the Stoic philosophy was the noblest product of the Hellenistic Age. Its equalitarianism, pacifism, and humanitarianism were important factors in mitigating the harshness not only of that time but of later centuries as well.

Whereas the Stoics went back to Heracleitus for much of their conception of the universe, the Epicureans derived their metaphysics chiefly from Democritus. Epicurus taught that the basic ingredients of all things are minute, indivisible atoms, and that change and growth are the results of the combination and separation of these particles. Nevertheless, while accepting the materialism of the atomists, Epicurus rejected their absolute mechanism. He denied that an automatic, mechanical motion of the atoms can be the cause of all things in the universe. Though he taught that the atoms move downward in perpendicular lines because of their weight, he insisted upon endowing them with a spontaneous ability to swerve from the perpendicular and thereby to combine with one another. The chief reason for this peculiar modification of the atomic theory was to make possible a belief in human freedom. If the atoms were capable only of mechanical motion, then man, who is made up of atoms, would be reduced to the status of an automaton, and fatalism would be the law of the universe. In this repudiation of the mechanistic interpretation of life, Epicurus was probably closer to the Hellenic spirit than either Democritus or the Stoics.

The ethical philosophy of the Epicureans was based upon the doctrine that the highest good for man is pleasure. But they did not include all forms of indulgence in the category of genuine pleasure. The so-called pleasures of the debauched man should be avoided, since every excess of carnality must be balanced by its portion of pain. On the other hand, a moderate satisfaction of bodily appetites is permissible and may be regarded as a good in itself. Better than this is mental pleasure, sober contemplation of the reasons for the choice of some things and the avoidance of others, and mature reflection upon satisfactions previously enjoyed. The highest of all pleasures, however, consists in serenity of soul, in the complete absence of both mental and physical pain. This end can be best achieved through the elimination of fear, especially fear of the supernatural, since that is the sovereign source of mental pain. Man must recognize from the study of philosophy that the soul is material and therefore cannot survive the body, that the universe operates of itself, and that the gods do not intervene in human affairs. The gods live remote from the world and are too intent upon their own happiness to bother about what takes place on earth. Since they do not reward or punish men either in this life or in a life to come, there is no reason why they should be feared. The Epicureans thus came by a different route to the same general conclusion as the Stoics—the supreme good is tranquillity of mind.

The Epicurean pursuit of tranquillity of mind through overcoming fear of the supernatural

The ethics of the Epicureans as well as their political theory rested squarely upon a utilitarian basis. In contrast with the Stoics, they did not insist upon virtue as an end in itself but taught that the only reason why man should be good is to increase his own happiness. In like manner, they denied that there is any such thing as absolute justice; laws and institutions are just only in so far as they contribute to the welfare of the individual. Certain rules have been found necessary in every complex society for the maintenance of security and order. Men obey these rules solely because it is to their advantage to do so. Generally speaking, Epicurus held no high regard for either political or social life. He considered the state as a mere convenience and taught that the wise men should take no active part in public life. Unlike the Cynics, he did not propose that man should abandon civilization and return to nature; yet his conception of the happiest life was essentially passive and defeatist. The wise man will recognize that he cannot eradicate the evils in the world no matter how strenuous and intelligent his efforts; he will therefore withdraw to "cultivate his garden," study philosophy, and enjoy the fellowship of a few congenial friends.

The ethical and political theories of the Epicureans

A more radically defeatist philosophy was that propounded by the Skeptics. Skepticism reached the zenith of its popularity about 200 B.C. under the influence of Carneades. The chief source of its inspiration was the Sophist teaching that all knowledge is derived from sense perception and therefore must be limited and relative. From this was deduced the conclusion that we cannot prove anything. Since the impressions of our senses deceive us, no truth can be certain. All we can say is that things *appear* to be such and such; we do not know what they really *are*. We have no definite knowledge of the supernatural, of the meaning of life, or even of right and wrong. It follows that the sensible course to pursue is suspension of judgment; this alone can lead to happiness. If man will abandon the fruitless quest for absolute truth and cease worrying about good and evil, he will attain that equanimity of mind which is the highest satisfaction that life affords. The Skeptics were even less concerned than the Epicureans with political and social problems. Their ideal was the typically Hellenistic one of escape for the individual from a world he could neither understand nor reform.

The nonrational trend in Hellenistic thought reached its farthest extreme in the philosophies of Philo Judaeus and the Neo-Pythagoreans in the last century B.C. and the first century A.D. The proponents of the two systems were in general agreement as to their basic teachings, especially in their predominantly religious viewpoint. They believed in a transcendent God so far removed from the world as to be utterly unknowable to mortal minds. They conceived the universe as being sharply divided between spirit and matter. They considered everything physical and material as evil; man's soul is imprisoned in his body, from which an escape can be effected only through rigorous denial and mortification of the flesh. Their attitude was mystical and nonintellectual: truth comes neither from science nor from reason but from revelation. Philo maintained that the books of the Old Testament were of absolute divine authority and contained all truth; the ultimate aim in life is to accomplish a mystic union with God, to lose one's self in the divine. Both Philo and the Neo-Pythagoreans influenced the development of Christian theology—Philo, in particular, with his dualism of matter and spirit and his doctrine of the Logos, or highest intermediary between God and the universe.

Hellenistic literature is significant mainly for the light it throws upon the character of the civilization. Most of the writings showed little originality or depth of thought. But they poured forth from the hands of the copyists in a profusion that is almost incredible when we consider that the art of printing by movable type was unknown. The names of at least 1100 authors have been discovered already, and more are being added from year to year. Much of what they wrote was trash, comparable to some of the cheap novels of our own day. Nevertheless, there were several works of more than mediocre quality and a few which met the highest standards ever set by the Greeks.

The leading types of Hellenistic poetry were the drama, the pastoral, and the mime. Drama was almost exclusively comedy, represented mainly by the plays of Menander. His plays were entirely different from the comedy of Aristophanes. They were distinguished by naturalism rather than by satire, by preoccupation with the seamy side of life rather than with political or intellectual issues. Their dominant theme was romantic love, with its pains and pleasures, its intrigues and seductions, and its culmination in happy marriage. The greatest author of pastorals and mimes was Theocritus of Syracuse, who wrote in the first half of the third century B.C. His pastorals, as the name implies, celebrate the charm of life in the country and idealize the simple pleasures of rustic folk. The mimes, on the other hand, portray in colorful dialogue the squabbles, ambitions, and varied activities of the bourgeoisie in the great metropolitan cities.

The field of prose literature was dominated by the historians, the biographers, and the authors of utopias. By far the ablest of the writers of history was Polybius of Megalopolis, who lived during the second century B.C. From the standpoint of his scientific approach and his zeal for truth, he probably deserves to be ranked second only to Thucydides among all the historians in ancient times; but he excelled Thucydides in his grasp of the importance of social and economic forces. Although most of the biographies were of a light and gossipy character, their tremendous popularity bears eloquent testimony to the literary tastes of the time. Even more significant was the popularity of the utopias, or descriptive accounts of ideal states. Virtually all of them depicted a life of social and economic equality, free from greed, oppression, and strife, on an imaginary island or in some distant, unfamiliar region. Generally in these paradises money was considered to be unknown, trade was prohibited, all property was held in common, and all men were required to work with their hands in producing the necessaries of life. We are probably justified in assuming that the profusion of this utopian literature was a direct result of the evils and injustices of Hellenistic society and a consciousness of the need for reform.

Hellenistic art did not preserve all of the characteristic qualities of the art of the Greeks. In place of the humanism, balance, and restraint which had distinguished the architecture and sculpture of the Golden Age, qualities of exaggerated realism, sensationalism, and voluptuousness now became dominant. The simple and dignified Doric and Ionic temples gave way to luxurious palaces, costly mansions, and elaborate public buildings and monuments symbolical of power and wealth. A typical example was the great lighthouse of Alexandria, which rose to a height of nearly 400 feet, with three diminishing stories and eight columns to support the light at the top. Sculpture likewise exhibited tendencies in the direction of extravagance and sentimentality. Many of the statues and figures in relief were huge and some of them almost grotesque. Violent emotionalism and exaggerated realism were features common to the majority. But by no means all of Hellenistic sculpture was over-wrought and

Hellenistic poetry

Historians, biographers, and authors of utopias

Hellenistic art

See color plates at page 224

229

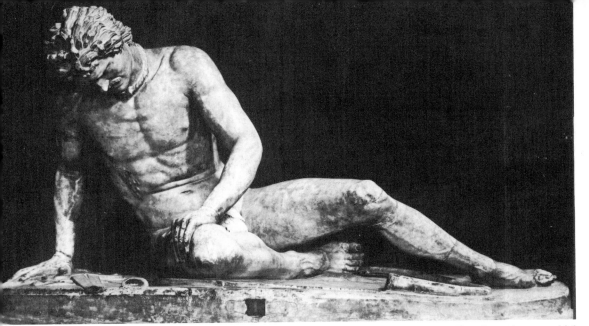

The Dying Gaul. A good example of Hellenistic realism in sculpture, which often reflected a preoccupation with the morbid and sensational. Every detail of the warrior's agony is dramatically portrayed. Now in the Capitoline Museum, Rome.

grotesque. Some of it was distinguished by a calmness and poise and compassion for human suffering reminiscent of the best work of the great fourth-century artists. Statutes which exemplify these superior qualities include the *Aphrodite of Melos* (*Venus de Milo*) and the *Winged Victory of Samothrace.*

4.   THE FIRST GREAT AGE OF SCIENCE

Factors responsible for the remarkable progress of science

The most brilliant age in the history of science prior to the seventeenth century A.D. was the period of the Hellenistic civilization. Indeed, many of the achievements of the modern age would scarcely have been possible without the discoveries of the scientists of Alexandria, Syracuse, Pergamum, and other great cities of the Hellenistic world. The reasons for the phenomenal development of science in the centuries after the downfall of Alexander's empire are not difficult to discover. Alexander himself had given some financial encouragement to the progress of research. More important was the stimulus provided for intellectual inquiry by the fusion of Chaldean and Egyption science with the learning of the Greeks. Possibly a third factor was the new interest in luxury and comfort and the demand for practical knowledge which would enable man to solve the problems of a disordered and unsatisfying existence.

The most popular sciences

The sciences which received major attention in the Hellenistic Age were astronomy, mathematics, geography, medicine, and physics. Chemistry, aside from metallurgy, was practically unknown. Except for the work of Theophrastus, who was the first to recognize the sexuality of plants, biology was also largely neglected. Neither chemistry nor biology bore any definite relationship to trade or to the forms of industry then in existence, and apparently they were not regarded as having much practical value.

The most renowned of the earlier astronomers of this time was Aristarchus of Samos (310–230 B.C.), who is sometimes called the "Hellenistic Copernicus." His chief title to fame comes from his deduction that the earth and the other planets revolve around the sun. Unfortunately this deduction was not accepted by his successors. It conflicted with the teachings of Aristotle and with the anthropocentric ideas of the Greeks. Besides, it was not in harmony with the beliefs of the Jews and other Orientals who made up so large a percentage of the Hellenistic population. The only other astronomer of much importance in the Hellenistic Age was Hipparchus, who did his most valuable work in Alexandria in the latter half of the second century B.C. His chief contributions were the invention of the astrolabe and the approximately correct calculation of the diameter of the moon and its distance from the earth. His fame was eventually overshadowed, however, by the reputation of Ptolemy of Alexandria, the last of the Hellenistic astronomers. Although Ptolemy made few original discoveries, he systematized the work of others. His principal writing, the *Almagest*, based upon the geocentric theory, was handed down to medieval Europe as the classic summary of ancient astronomy.

The Winged Victory of Samothrace. In this figure and in the *Venus de Milo,* Hellenistic sculptors preserved some of the calmness and devotion to grace and proportion characteristic of Hellenic art in the Golden Age. Now in the Louvre.

Closely allied with astronomy were two other sciences, mathematics and geography. The Hellenistic mathematician of greatest renown was, of course, Euclid (*ca.* 323–*ca.* 285 B.C.), erroneously considered the founder of geometry. Until the middle of the nineteenth century his *Elements of Geometry* remained the accepted basis for the study of that branch of mathematics. Much of the material in this work was not original but was a synthesis of the discoveries of others. The most original of the Hellenistic mathematicians was probably Hipparchus, who laid the foundations of both plane and spherical trigonometry. Hellenistic geography owed most of its development to Eratosthenes (*ca.* 276–*ca.* 195 B.C.), astronomer, poet, philologist, and librarian of Alexandria. By means of sun dials placed some hundreds of miles apart, he calculated the circumference of the earth with an error of less than 200 miles. He produced the most accurate map that had yet been devised, with the surface of the earth divided into degrees of latitude and longitude. He propounded the theory that all of the oceans are really one, and he was the first to suggest the possibility of reaching India by sailing west. One of his successors divided the earth into the five climatic zones which are still recognized, and explained the ebb and flow of the tides as due to the influence of the moon.

Perhaps none of the Hellenistic advances in science surpassed in importance the progress in medicine. Especially significant was the work of Herophilus of Chalcedon, who conducted his researches in Alexandria about the beginning of the second century. Without question he was the greatest anatomist of antiquity and, according to Galen, the first to practice human dissection. Among his most important achievements were a detailed description of the brain, with an attempt to distinguish between the functions of its various parts; the discovery of the significance of the pulse and its use in diagnosing illness; and the discovery that the arteries contain blood alone, not a mixture of blood and air as Aristotle had taught, and that their function is to carry blood from the heart to all parts of the body. The value of this last discovery in laying the basis for a knowledge of the circulation of the blood can hardly be overestimated.

The ablest of the colleagues of Herophilus was Erasistratus, who flourished in Alexandria about the middle of the third century. He is considered the founder of physiology as a separate science. Not only did he practice dissection, but he is believed to have gained a great deal of his knowledge of bodily functions from vivisection. He discovered the valves of the heart, distinguished between motor and sensory nerves, and taught that the ultimate branches of the arteries and veins are connected. He was the first to reject absolutely the humoral theory of disease and to condemn excessive blood-letting as a method of cure. Unfortunately this theory was revived by Galen, the great encyclopedist of medicine who lived in the Roman Empire in the second century A.D.

Prior to the third century B.C. physics had been a branch of philosophy. It was made a separate experimental science by Archimedes of Syracuse (*ca.* 287–212 B.C.). Archimedes discovered the law of floating bodies, or specific gravity, and formulated with scientific exactness the principles of the lever, the pulley, and the screw. Among his memorable inventions were the compound pulley, the tubular screw for pumping water, the screw propeller for ships, and the burning lens. Although he has been called the "technical Yankee of antiquity," there is evidence that he set no high value upon his ingenious mechanical contraptions and preferred to devote his time to pure scientific research.

Certain other individuals in the Hellenistic Age were quite willing to give all their attention to applied science. Preeminent among them was Hero or Heron of Alexandria, who lived in the last century B.C. The record of inventions credited to him almost passes belief. The list includes a fire engine, a siphon, a jet engine, a hydraulic organ, a slot machine, and a catapult operated by compressed air. How many of these inventions were really his own is impossible to say, but there appears to be no question that such contrivances were actually in existence in his time or soon thereafter. Nevertheless, the total progress in applied science was comparatively slight, probably for the reason that human labor continued to be so abundant and cheap that it was not worthwhile to substitute the work of machines.

5. RELIGION IN THE HELLENISTIC AGE

If there was one aspect of the Hellenistic civilization which served more than others to accent the contrast with Hellenic culture, it was the new trend in religion. The civic religion of the Greeks as it was in the age of the city-states had now almost entirely disappeared. For the majority of the intellectuals its place was taken by the philosophies of Stoicism, Epicureanism, and Skepticism. Some who were less philosophically inclined turned to the worship of Fortune or became followers of dogmatic atheism.

Among the masses a tendency to embrace emotional religions was even more clearly manifest. The Orphic and Eleusinian mystery cults attracted more votaries than ever before. The worship of the Egyptian mother-goddess, Isis, threatened for a time to become dominant throughout the Near Orient. The astral religion of the Chaldeans likewise spread rapidly, with the result that its chief product, astrology, was received with fanatical enthusiasm throughout the Hellenistic world. But the most powerful influence of all came from the offshoots of Zoroastrianism, especially from Mithraism and Gnosticism. While all of the cults of Oriental origin resembled each other in their promises of salvation in a life to come, Mithraism and Gnosticism had a more ethically significant mythology, a deeper contempt for this world, and a more clearly defined

233

doctrine of redemption through a personal savior. These were the ideas which satisfied the emotional cravings of the common people, convinced as they were of the worthlessness of this life and ready to be lured by extravagant promises of better things in a world to come. If we can judge by conditions in our own time, some of the doctrines of these cults must have exerted their influence upon members of the upper classes also. Even the most casual observer of modern society knows that pessimism, mysticism, and otherworldliness are not confined to the downtrodden. In some cases the keenest disgust with this life and the deepest mystical yearnings are to be found among those whose pockets bulge with plenty.

The influence of
the Jews

A factor by no means unimportant in the religious developments of the Hellenistic Age was the dispersion of the Jews. As a result of Alexander's conquest of Palestine in 332 B.C. and the Roman conquest about three centuries later, thousands of Jews migrated to various sections of the Mediterranean world. It has been estimated that 1,000,000 of them lived in Egypt in the first century A.D. and 200,000 in Asia Minor. They mingled freely with other peoples, adopting the Greek language and no small amount of the Hellenic culture which still survived from earlier days. At the same time they played a major part in the diffusion of Oriental beliefs. Their religion had already taken on a spiritual and messianic character as a result of Persian influence. Their leading philosopher of this time, Philo Judaeus of Alexandria, developed a body of doctrine representing the farthest extreme which mysticism had yet attained. Many of the Hellenistic Jews eventually became converts to Christianity and were largely instrumental in the spread of that religion outside of Palestine. A notable example, of course, was Saul of Tarsus, known in Christian history as the Apostle Paul.

6.   A FORETASTE OF MODERNITY?

Hellenistic
civilization com-
pared with that
of the modern
age

With the possible exception of the Roman, no great culture of ancient times appears to suggest the spirit of the modern age quite so emphatically as does the Hellenistic civilization. Here as in the world of the twentieth century were to be found a considerable variety of forms of government, the growth of militarism, a decline of respect for democracy, and a trend in the direction of authoritarian rule. Many of the characteristic economic and social developments of the Hellenistic Age are equally suggestive of contemporary experience: the growth of big business, the expansion of trade, the zeal for exploration and discovery, the interest in mechanical inventions, the devotion to comfort and the craze for material prosperity, the growth of metropolitan cities with congested slums, and the widening gulf between rich and poor. In the realms of intellect and art the Hellenistic civilization also bore a distinctly modern flavor. This was exemplified by the exaggerated emphasis upon sci-

Statue of an Old Market Woman. In the Hellenistic Age the idealism and restraint of Hellenic art were succeeded by a tendency to portray the humble aspects of life and to express compassion for human suffering. Original in the Metropolitan Museum of Art, New York.

ence, the narrow specialization of learning, the penchant for realism and naturalism, the vast production of mediocre literature, and the popularity of mysticism side by side with extreme skepticism and dogmatic unbelief.

Because of these resemblances there has been a tendency among certain writers to regard our own civilization as decadent. But this is based partly upon the false assumption that the Hellenistic culture was merely a degenerate phase of Greek civilization. Instead, it was a new social and cultural organism born of a fusion of Greek and Near Eastern elements. Moreover, the differences between the Hellenistic civilization and that of the contemporary world are perhaps just as important as the resemblances. The Hellenistic political outlook was essentially cosmopolitan; nothing comparable to the national patriotism of modern times really prevailed. Despite the remarkable expansion of trade in the Hellenistic Age, no industrial revolution ever took place, for reasons which have already been noted. Finally, Hellenistic science was somewhat more limited than that of the present day. Modern pure science is to a very large extent a species of philosophy—an adventure of the mind in the realm of the unknown. Notwithstanding frequent assertions to the contrary, much of it is gloriously impractical and will probably remain so.

Basic differences

235

SELECTED READINGS

· *Items so designated are available in paperbound editions.*

Bamm, Peter, *Alexander the Great: Power as Destiny*, New York, 1968.

· Burn, A. R., *Alexander the Great and the Hellenistic World*, New York, 1962 (Collier).

· Bury, J. B., and others, *The Hellenistic Age*, New York, 1923.

Cary, Max, *The Legacy of Alexander: A History of the Greek World from 323 to 146 B.C.*, New York, 1932.

· Clagett, Marshall, *Greek Science in Antiquity*, New York, 1963 (Collier).

Festugière, A. J., *Epicurus and His Gods*, Cambridge, Mass., 1956.

· Finley, M. I., *The Ancient Greeks: An Introduction to Their Life and Thought*, New York, 1963 (Compass).

· Grant, F. C., *Hellenistic Religions*, New York, 1963 (Library of Liberal Arts).

· Hadas, Moses, *Hellenistic Culture*, New York, 1959 (Norton Library).

· Hamilton, Edith, *The Echo of Greece*, New York, 1964 (Norton Library).

· Larsen, J. A. O., *Representative Government in Greek and Roman History*, Berkeley, 1955 (University of California).

Starr, C. G., *A History of the Ancient World*, New York, 1964.

· Tarn, W. W., *Alexander the Great*, Boston, 1956 (Beacon).

· ———, *Hellenistic Civilization*, New York, 1952 (Meridian).

Vermeule, Emily, *Greece in the Bronze Age*, Chicago, 1964.

· Wilcken, Ulrich, *Alexander the Great*, New York, 1967 (Norton Library).

SOURCE MATERIALS

Greek source materials for the Hellenistic period are available in the appropriate volumes of the Loeb Classical Library, Harvard University Press.

CHAPTER 10

Roman Civilization

Like Hercules, citizens, they said just now
He had sought the laurel at the cost of death:
Returning from Spain, seeking his household gods,
    Caesar has conquered.

After sacrifice to the just gods, let his
wife come forth, happy for her matchless husband,
And the sister of our famous leader, and,
    Wearing the bands of

Suppliants, mothers of young men and maidens
Who are now safe . . .
                —Horace, *Odes,* III.xiv

Long before the glory of Greece had begun to fade, another civilization, derived in large measure from that of the Greeks, had started its growth on the banks of the Tiber in Italy. In fact, by the time the Greeks had entered their Golden Age, Rome was already a dominant power on the Italian peninsula. For more than six centuries thereafter her might increased, and she still maintained her supremacy over the civilized world when the glory of Greece was no more than a memory.

The rise of Rome

But the Romans never equaled the Greeks in intellectual or artistic accomplishments. The reasons may have been partly geographic. Except for some excellent marble and small quantities of copper, gold, and iron, Italy has no mineral resources. Her extensive coast line is broken by only two good harbors, Tarentum and Naples. On the other hand, the amount of her fertile land is much larger than that of Greece. As a consequence, the Romans were destined to remain a predominantly agrarian people through the greater part of their history. They never enjoyed the intellectual stimulus which comes from extensive trading with other nations. In addition, the topography of Italy is such that the peninsula was more easily accessible to invasion than was Greece. The Alps opposed no effectual barrier to the influx of peoples from central Europe, and the

Why Roman civilization was generally inferior to that of the Greeks

237

low-lying coast in many places invited conquest by sea. As a result, domination of the country by force was more common than peaceful intermingling of immigrants with original settlers. The Romans became absorbed in military pursuits almost from the moment of their settlement on Italian soil, for they were forced to defend their own conquests against other invaders.

I. FROM THE BEGINNING TO THE OVERTHROW OF THE MONARCHY

The earliest inhabitants of Italy

Archaeological evidence indicates that Italy was inhabited at least as far back as the Upper Paleolithic Age. At this time the territory was occupied by a people closely related to the Cro-Magnon race of southern France. In the Neolithic period people of Mediterranean stock entered the land, some coming in from northern Africa and others from Spain and Gaul. The beginning of the Bronze Age witnessed several new incursions. From north of the Alps came the first of the immigrants of the Indo-European language group. They were herdsmen and farmers, who brought the horse and the wheeled cart into Italy. Their culture was based upon the use of bronze, although after 1000 B.C. they appear to have acquired a knowledge of iron. These Indo-Europeans seem to have been the ancestors of most of the so-called Italic peoples, including the Romans. Racially they were probably related to the Hellenic invaders of Greece.

The Etruscans and the Greeks

Probably during the eighth century B.C. two other nations of immigrants occupied different portions of the Italian peninsula: the Etruscans and the Greeks. Where the Etruscans came from is a question which has never been satisfactorily answered. Most authorities believe that they were natives of some part of the Near Orient, probably Asia Minor. Although their writing has never been completely deciphered, enough materials survive to indicate the nature of their culture. They had an alphabet based upon the Greek, a high degree of skill in the metallurgical arts, a flourishing trade with the East, and a religion based upon the worship of gods in hu-

An Etruscan Sarcophagus. The Etruscans often depicted social events, sports, funeral banquets, and processions, either in painting or relief, on their tombs. Seen here are preparations for a funeral.

Sarcophagus. This Etruscan work of the fourth century B.C., located in the Museum of Fine Arts, Boston, depicts a husband and wife.

man form. They bequeathed to the Romans a knowledge of the arch and the vault, the practice of divination, and the cruel amusement of gladiatorial combats. The Etruscans established a great empire in the sixth century that included Latium, the Po valley, and Campania. The Greeks located mainly along the southern and southwestern shores of Italy and on the island of Sicily. Their most important settlements were Tarentum, Syracuse, and Naples, each of which was an entirely independent city-state. From the Greeks the Romans derived their alphabet, a number of their religious concepts, and much of their art and mythology.

The actual founders of Rome were Italic peoples who lived in the district of Latium south of the Tiber River. Though the exact year of the founding of the city is unknown, recent archaeological research places the event quite near the traditional date of 753 B.C. Latium included a number of towns, but Rome, by reason of its strategic location, soon came to exercise an effective suzerainty over several of the most important of them. One conquest followed another until, by the end of the sixth century B.C., the territory dominated by the Roman state was probably coextensive with the whole Latin plain from the slopes of the Apennines to the Mediterranean Sea.

The founding of Rome

The political evolution of Rome in this early period resembled in some ways the governmental development of the Greek communities in the formative stage of their history. But it was far from being the same. The Romans appear from the first to have had a much stronger interest in authority and stability than in liberty or democracy. Their state was essentially an application of the idea of the patriarchal family to the whole community, with the king exercising a jurisdiction over his subjects comparable to that of the head of the family over the members of his household. But just as the authority of the father was limited by custom and by the requirement

Etruscan Bust of Jove

239

The government
of Rome under
the monarchy;
the powers of the
king

that he respect the wishes of his adult sons, the sovereignty of the king was limited by the ancient constitution, which he was powerless to change without the consent of the chief men of the realm. His prerogatives were not primarily legislative but executive and judicial. He punished men for infractions of order, usually by infliction of the death penalty or by flogging. He judged all civil and criminal cases, but he had no authority to pardon without the consent of the assembly. Although his accession to office had to be confirmed by the people, he could not be deposed, and there was no one who could really challenge the exercise of his regal powers.

In addition to the kingship the Roman government of this time included an assembly and a Senate. The former was composed of all the male citizens of military age. As one of the chief sources of sovereign power, according to the theory, this body had an absolute veto on any proposal for a change in the law which the king might make. Besides, it determined whether pardons should be granted and whether aggressive war should be declared. But it was essentially a ratifying body with no right to initiate legislation or recommend changes of policy. Its members could not even speak except when invited to do so by the king. The Senate, or council of elders, comprised in its membership the heads of the various clans which formed the community. Even more than the common citizens, the rulers of the clans embodied the sovereign power of the state. The king was only one of their number to whom they had delegated the active exercise of their authority. When the royal office became vacant, the powers of the king immediately reverted to the Senate until the succession of a new monarch had been confirmed by the people. In ordinary times the chief function of the Senate was to examine proposals of the king which had been ratified by the assembly and to veto them if they violated rights established by ancient custom. It was thus almost impossible for fundamental changes to be made in the law even when the majority of the citizens were ready to sanction them. This extremely conservative attitude of the ruling classes persisted until the end of Roman history.

Toward the end of the sixth century B.C. senatorial jealousy of the kings increased to such a point that the monarchy was overthrown and an oligarchic republic set up. While the real nature of this revolution was doubtless a movement of the aristocracy to gain supreme power for itself, factors of nationalism may also have played some part in it. Tradition relates that the last of the Roman kings was an Etruscan, whose family, the Tarquins, had usurped the royal office some years before. The Romans of later centuries described in lurid fashion the wicked deeds of these rulers and implied that the overthrow of the monarchy was due primarily to a revolt against alien oppressors. In any event the Etruscan empire was already in a state of decay. Its collapse made easier the establishment of Roman dominance in Italy.

The history of the Roman Republic for more than two centuries after its establishment was one of almost constant warfare. The causes which led to the series of conflicts are not easy to untangle. It is possible that the overthrow of the Tarquins resulted in acts of reprisal by their kinsmen in neighboring countries. It is conceivable also that other nations on the borders took advantage of the confusion accompanying the revolution to slice off portions of Roman territory. But doubtless the compelling reason was desire for more land. The Romans were already a proud and aggressive people with a rapidly growing population. As the number of the inhabitants increased, the need for outlets into new territory became ever more urgent. Their final conquests included the Greek cities in the southernmost portion of Italy. Not only did these add to the Roman domain, but they also brought the Romans into fruitful contact with Greek culture. The Romans were then frequently confronted with revolts of peoples previously conquered. The suppression of these revolts awakened the suspicions of surrounding states and sharpened the appetite of the victors for further triumphs. New wars followed each other in what seemed an unending succession, until by 265 B.C. Rome had conquered the entire Italian peninsula, with the exception of the Po valley.

The origins of Roman imperialism

This long series of military conflicts had profound social and economic effects upon the subsequent history of Rome. It affected adversely the interests of the poorer citizens and furthered the concentration of land in the possession of wealthy proprietors. Long service in the army forced the ordinary farmers to neglect the cultivation of the soil, with the result that they fell into debt and frequently lost their farms. Many took refuge in the city, until they were settled later as tenants on great estates in the conquered territories. The wars had the effect also of confirming the agrarian character of the Roman nation. The repeated acquisition of new lands made it possible to absorb the entire population into agricultural pursuits. As a consequence there was no need for the development of industry and commerce as means of earning a livelihood. Lastly, as in the case of Sparta, the Roman wars of conquest enslaved the nation to the military ideal.

Effects of the early military conflicts

During this same period of the early Republic, Rome underwent some significant political changes. These were not products so much of the revolution of the sixth century as of the developments of later years. The revolution which overthrew the monarchy was about as conservative as it is possible for a revolution to be. Its chief effect was to substitute two elected consuls for the king and to exalt the position of the Senate by vesting it with control over the public funds and with a veto on all actions of the assembly. The consuls themselves were usually senators and acted as the agents of their

Political changes following the overthrow of the monarchy

class. They did not rule jointly, but each was supposed to possess the full executive and judicial authority which had previously been wielded by the king. If a conflict arose between them, the Senate might be called upon to decide; or, in time of grave emergency, a dictator might be appointed for a term not greater than six months. In other respects the government remained the same as in the days of the monarchy.

Not long after the establishment of the Republic a struggle began by the common citizens for a larger share of political power. Before the end of the monarchy the Roman population had come to be divided into two great classes—the patricians and the plebeians. The former were the aristocracy, wealthy landowners, who were apparently the descendants of the old clan leaders. They monopolized the seats in the Senate and the offices of magistracy. The plebeians were the common people—small farmers, craftsmen, and tradesmen. Many were clients or dependents of the patricians, obliged to fight for them, to render them political support, and to cultivate their estates in return for protection. The grievances of the plebeians were numerous. Compelled to pay heavy taxes and forced to serve in the army in time of war, they were nevertheless excluded from all part in the government except membership in the assembly. Moreover, they felt themselves the victims of discriminatory decisions in judicial trials. They did not even know what legal rights they were supposed to enjoy, for the laws were unwritten, and no one but the consuls had the power to interpret them. In suits for debt the creditor was frequently allowed to sell the debtor into slavery. It was in order to obtain a redress of these grievances that the plebeians rebelled soon after the beginning of the fifth century B.C.

The plebeians gained their first victory about 470 B.C., when they forced the patricians to agree to the election of a number of tribunes with power to protect the citizens by means of a veto over unlawful acts of the magistrates. This victory was followed by a successful demand for codification of the laws about 450 B.C. The result was the publication of the famous Law of the Twelve Tables, so called because it was written on tablets of wood. Although the Twelve Tables came to be revered by the Romans of later times as a kind of charter of the people's liberties, they were really nothing of the sort. For the most part they merely perpetuated ancient custom without even abolishing enslavement for debt. They did, however, enable the people to know where they stood in relation to the law, and they permitted an appeal to the assembly against a magistrate's sentence of capital punishment. About a generation later the plebeians won eligibility to positions as lesser magistrates, and about 366 B.C. the first plebeian consul was elected. Since ancient custom provided that, upon completing their term of office, consuls should automatically enter the Senate, the patrician monopoly of seats in

The struggle between patricians and plebeians

The victories of the plebeians

that body was broken. The final plebeian victory came in 287 B.C. with the passage of the Hortensian Law (named for the dictator Quintus Hortensius), which provided that measures enacted by the assembly should become binding upon the state whether the Senate approved them or not.

The significance of these changes must not be misinterpreted. They did not constitute a revolution to gain more liberty for the individual but merely to curb the power of the magistrates and to win for the common man a larger share in government. The state as a whole remained as despótic as ever, for its authority over the citizens was not even challenged. As Theodor Mommsen says, the Romans from the time of the Tarquins to that of the Gracchi "never really abandoned the principle that the people were not to govern but to be governed."[1] Because of this attitude the grant of full legislative powers to the assembly seems to have meant little more than a formality; the Senate continued to rule as before. Nor did the admission of plebeians to membership in the Senate have any effect in liberalizing that body. So high was its prestige and so deep was the veneration of the Roman for authority, that the new members were soon swallowed up in the conservatism of the old. Moreover, the fact that the magistrates received no salaries prevented most of the poorer citizens from seeking public office.

Intellectually and socially the Romans appear to have made but slow advancement as yet. The times were still harsh and crude. Though writing had been adopted as early as the sixth century, little use was made of it except for the copying of laws, treaties, and funerary inscriptions and orations. Inasmuch as education was limited to instruction imparted by the father in manly sports, practical arts, and soldierly virtues, probably the great majority of the people were still illiterate. War and agriculture continued as the chief occupations for the bulk of the citizens. A few craftsmen were to be found in the cities, and a minor development of trade had occurred, evidenced by the founding of a maritime colony at Ostia on the coast in the fourth century. But the comparative insignificance of Roman commerce at this time is pretty clearly revealed by the fact that the country had no standard system of coinage until 269 B.C.

The period of the early Republic was the period when the Roman religion assumed the character it was destined to retain through the greater part of the nation's history. In several ways this religion re- sembled the religion of the Greeks, partly for the reason that the Etruscan religion was deeply indebted to the Greek, and the Romans, in turn, were influenced by the Etruscans. Both the Greek and Roman religions were worldly and practical with neither spiritual nor ethical content. The relation of man to the gods was external and mechanical, partaking of the nature of a bargain or contract

---

[1] *The History of Rome*, I. 313.

between two parties for their mutual advantage. The deities in both religions performed similar functions: Jupiter corresponded roughly to Zeus as god of the sky, Minerva to Athena as goddess of wisdom and patroness of craftsmen, Venus to Aphrodite as goddess of love, Neptune to Poseidon as god of the sea, and so on. The Roman religion no more than the Greek had any dogmas or sacraments or belief in rewards and punishments in an afterlife.

Contrasts with Greek religion

But there were significant differences also. The Roman religion was distinctly more political and less humanistic in purpose. It served not to glorify man or to make him feel at home in his world but to protect the state from its enemies and to augment its power and prosperity. The gods were less anthropomorphic; indeed, it was only as a result of Greek and Etruscan influences that they were made personal deities at all, having previously been worshiped as *numina* or animistic spirits. The Romans never conceived of their deities as quarreling among themselves or mingling with human beings after the fashion of the Homeric divinities. Finally, the Roman religion contained a much stronger element of priestliness than the Greek. The priests, or pontiffs as they were called, formed an organized class, a branch of the government itself. They not only supervised the offering of sacrifices, but they were guardians of an elaborate body of sacred traditions and laws which they alone could interpret. It must be understood, however, that these pontiffs were not priests in the sense of intermediaries between the individual Roman and his gods; they heard no confessions, forgave no sins, and administered no sacraments.

Morality in the early Republic

The morality of the Romans in this as in later periods had almost no connection with religion. The Roman did not ask his gods to make him good, but to bestow upon the community and upon his family material blessings. Morality was a matter of patriotism and of respect for authority and tradition. The chief virtues were bravery, honor, self-discipline, reverence for the gods and for one's ancestors, and duty to country and family. Loyalty to the state took precedence over everything else. For the good of the state the citizen must be ready to sacrifice not only his own life but, if necessary, the lives of his family and friends. The courage of certain consuls who dutifully put their sons to death for breaches of military discipline was a subject of profound admiration. Few peoples in European history with the exception of the Spartans and perhaps the modern Germans have ever taken the problems of national interest so seriously or subordinated the individual so completely to the good of the state.

3. THE FATEFUL WARS WITH CARTHAGE

By 265 B.C., as we have already learned, Rome had conquered and annexed the whole of Italy, except for the Po valley. Proud and confident of her strength, she was almost certain to strike out into new fields of empire. The prosperous island of Sicily was not yet within her grasp, nor could she regard with indifference the situation in other parts of the Mediterranean world. She was now prone to interpret almost any change in the *status quo* as a threat to her own power and security. It was for such reasons that Rome after 264 B.C. became involved in a series of wars with other great nations which decidedly altered the course of her history.

THE FATEFUL WARS WITH CARTHAGE

The beginning of imperialism on a major scale

The first and most important of these wars was the struggle with Carthage, a great maritime empire that stretched along the northern coast of Africa from Numidia to the Strait of Gibraltar. Carthage had originally been founded about 800 B.C. as a Phoenician colony. In the sixth century it severed its ties with the homeland and gradually developed into a rich and powerful nation. The prosperity of its upper classes was founded upon commerce and upon exploitation of the silver and tin resources of Spain and Britain and the tropical products of north central Africa. Conditions within the country were far from ideal. The Carthaginians appear to have had no conception of free and orderly government. Bribery and oppression were methods regularly employed by the plutocracy to maintain its dominant position. The form of government itself can best be described as an oligarchy. At the head of the system were two magistrates, or *suffetes*, who exercised powers approximating those of the Roman consuls. The real governors, however, were thirty merchant princes who constituted an inner council of the Senate. These men controlled elections and dominated every other branch of the government. The remaining 270 members of the Senate appear to have been summoned to meet only on special occasions. In spite of these political deficiencies and a gloomy and cruel religion, Carthage had a civilization superior in luxury and scientific attainment to that of Rome when the struggle between the two countries began.

Carthage

The initial clash with Carthage began in 264 B.C.[2] The primary cause was Roman jealousy over Carthaginian expansion in Sicily. Carthage already controlled the western portion of the island and was threatening the Greek cities of Syracuse and Messana on the eastern coast. If these cities should be captured, all chances of Roman occupation of Sicily would be cut off. Faced with this danger, Rome declared war upon Carthage with the hope of forcing her back into her African domain. Twenty-three years of fighting finally brought victory to the Roman generals. Carthage was compelled to surrender her possessions in Sicily and to pay an indemnity of 3200 talents, or about 2½ million dollars at present silver prices.

Causes of the First Punic War

But the Romans were unable to stand the strain of this triumph. They had had to put forth such heroic efforts to win that when victory was finally secured it made them more arrogant and greedy than ever. As a result, the struggle with Carthage was renewed on

The Second Punic War

[2] The wars with Carthage are known as the Punic Wars. The Romans called the Carthaginians *Poeni*, i.e., Phoenicians, whence is derived the adjective "Punic."

A Roman Battle Sarcophagus Depicts the Horrors of War

two different occasions thereafter. In 218 B.C. the Romans interpreted the Carthaginian attempt to rebuild an empire in Spain as a threat to their interests and responded with a declaration of war. This struggle raged through a period of sixteen years. Italy was ravaged by the armies of Hannibal, the famous Carthaginian commander, whose tactics have been copied by military experts to the present day. Rome escaped defeat by the narrowest of margins. Only the durability of her system of alliances in Italy saved the day. As long as these alliances held, Hannibal dared not besiege the city of Rome itself for fear of being attacked from the rear. In the end Carthage was more completely humbled than before. She was compelled to abandon all her possessions except the capital city and its surrounding territory in Africa, and to pay an indemnity of 10,000 talents.

The Third Punic War and the destruction of Carthage

Roman vindictiveness and avarice reached their zenith about the middle of the second century B.C. By this time Carthage had recovered a modicum of her former prosperity—enough to excite the envy and fear of her conquerors. Nothing would now satisfy the senatorial magnates but the complete destruction of Carthage and the expropriation of her land. In 149 B.C. the Senate dispatched an ultimatum demanding that the Carthaginians abandon their city and settle at least ten miles from the coast. Since this demand was tantamount to a death sentence for a nation dependent upon commerce, it was refused—as the Romans probably hoped it would be. The result was the Third Punic War, which was fought between 149 and 146 B.C. Seldom has the world witnessed a more desperate and more barbarous struggle. The final assault upon the city was carried into the houses of the natives themselves, and a frightful butchery took place. When the resistance of the Carthaginians was finally broken, the few citizens who were left to surrender were sold into slavery, and their once magnificent city was razed to the ground. The land was organized into a Roman province with the best areas parceled out as senatorial estates.

The wars with Carthage had momentous effects upon Rome. First, they brought her into conflict with eastern Mediterranean powers and thereby paved the way for world dominion. During the Second Punic War, Philip V of Macedon had entered into an alliance with Carthage and had plotted with the king of Syria to divide Egypt between them. In order to punish Philip and to forestall the execution of his plans, Rome sent an army into the East. The result was the conquest of Greece and Asia Minor and the establishment of a protectorate over Egypt. Thus before the end of the second century B.C. virtually the entire Mediterranean area had been brought under Roman dominion. The conquest of the Hellenistic East led to the introduction of semi-Oriental ideas and customs into Rome. Despite formidable resistance, these ideas and customs exerted considerable influence in changing some aspects of social and cultural life.

Results of the
wars with
Carthage:
(1) conquest of
the Hellenistic
East

By far the most important effect of the Punic Wars was a great social and economic revolution that swept over Rome in the third and second centuries B.C. The incidents of this revolution may be enumerated as follows: (1) a marked increase in slavery due to the capture and sale of prisoners of war; (2) the decline of the small farmer as a result of the establishment of the plantation system in conquered areas and the influx of cheap grain from the provinces; (3) the growth of a helpless city mob composed of impoverished farmers and workers displaced by slave labor; (4) the appearance of a middle class comprising merchants, moneylenders, and "publicans" or men who held government contracts to operate mines, build roads, or collect taxes; and (5) an increase in luxury and vulgar display, particularly among the *parvenus* who fattened on the profits of war.

As a consequence of this social and economic revolution, Rome was changed from a republic of yeoman farmers into a nation with a complex society and new habits of luxury and indulgence. Though property had never been evenly distributed, the gulf which separated rich and poor now yawned more widely than before. The old-fashioned ideals of discipline and devotion to the service of the state were sadly weakened, and men began to make pleasure and wealth their gods. A few members of the senatorial aristocracy exerted efforts to check the evil tendencies and to restore the homely virtues of the past. The eminent leader of this movement was Cato the Elder, who inveighed against the new rich for their soft living and strove to set an example to his countrymen by performing hard labor on his farm and dwelling in a house with a dirt floor and no plaster on the walls. But his efforts had little effect, perhaps because of his own inconsistencies. He fought everything new, the good as well as the evil. He staunchly defended slavery and condemned the humane philosophy of Stoicism. The rich continued to indulge their expensive tastes and to rival each other in vulgar consumption of wealth. At the same time public morality decayed. Tax gatherers plundered the provinces and used their illicit gains to purchase the votes of the poor. The anarchic masses in the city came to expect that politicians would feed them and provide for their amusement with ever more brutal shows. The total effect was so serious that some authorities date the beginning of Rome's decline from this period.[3]

4. THE REVOLUTION OF THE LATE REPUBLIC

The new period of turbulence

The period from the end of the Punic Wars in 146 B.C. to about 30 B.C. was one of the most turbulent in the history of Rome. It was between these years that the nation reaped the full harvest of the seeds of violence sown during the wars of conquest. Bitter class conflicts, assassinations, desperate struggles between rival dictators, wars, and insurrections were the all too common occurrences of this time. Even the slaves contributed their part to the general disorder: first, in 104 B.C. when they ravaged Sicily; and again in 73 B.C. when 70,000 of them under the leadership of Spartacus held the consuls at bay for more than a year. Spartacus was finally slain in battle and 6000 of his followers were captured and crucified.

The revolt of the Gracchi: the land program of Tiberius

The first stage in the conflict between classes of citizens began with the revolt of the Gracchi. The Gracchi were leaders of the liberal, pro-Hellenic elements in Rome and had the support of the middle classes and a number of influential senators as well. Though of aristocratic lineage themselves, they earnestly strove for a program of reforms to alleviate the country's ills. They considered these to be a result of the decline of the free peasantry, and proposed the simple remedy of dividing state lands among the landless. The first of the brothers to take up the cause of reform was Tiberius. Elected tribune in 133 B.C., he proposed a law that restricted the current renters or holders of state lands to a maximum of 620 acres. The excess was to be confiscated by the government and given to the poor in small plots. Conservative aristocrats bitterly opposed this proposal and brought about its veto by Tiberius' colleague in the tribunate, Octavius. Tiberius removed Octavius from office, and when his own term expired, determined to stand for re-election. Both of these moves were unconstitutional and gave the conservative senators an excuse for violence. Armed with clubs and legs of chairs, they went on a rampage during the elections and murdered Tiberius and 300 of his followers.

Nine years later Gaius Gracchus, the younger brother of Tiberius, renewed the struggle for reform. Though Tiberius' land law had finally been enacted by the Senate, Gaius believed that the crusade must go further. Elected tribune in 123 B.C., and reelected in

[3] See D. C. Somervell (ed.), A. J. Toynbee's *A Study of History*, I, 258.

122, he procured the enactment of various laws for the benefit of the less privileged. The first provided for stabilizing the price of grain in Rome. For this purpose great public granaries were built along the Tiber River. A second law proposed to extend the franchise to Roman allies, giving them the rights of Latin citizens. Still a third gave the middle class the right to make up the juries that tried governors accused of exploiting the provinces. These and similar measures provoked so much anger and contention among the classes that civil war broke out. Gaius was proclaimed an enemy of the state, and the Senate authorized the consuls to take all necessary steps for the defense of the Republic. In the ensuing conflict Gaius and 3000 of his followers were killed.

The Gracchan revolt had a broad significance. It demonstrated, first of all, that the Roman Republic had outgrown its constitution. The assembly had gained, over the years, *de facto* powers almost equal to those of the Senate. Instead of working out a peaceful accommodation to these changes, both sides resorted to violence. By so doing they set a precedent for the unbridled use of force by any politician ambitious for supreme power and thereby paved the way for the destruction of the Republic. The Romans had shown a remarkable capacity for organizing an empire and for adapting the Greek idea of a city-state to a large territory, but the narrow conservatism of their upper classes was a fatal hindrance to the health of the state. They appeared to regard all change as evil. They failed to understand the reasons for internal discord and seemed to think that repression was its only remedy.

From 146 B.C. to the downfall of the Republic, Rome engaged in a series of wars. The victorious commanders in these wars frequently made themselves rulers of the state. The first of these conquering heroes to make capital out of his military reputation was Marius, who was elevated to the consulship by the masses in 107 B.C. and reelected six times thereafter. Unfortunately Marius was no statesman and accomplished nothing for his followers beyond demonstrating the ease with which a military leader with an army at his back could override opposition. Following his death in 86 B.C. the aristocrats took a turn at government by force. Their champion was Sulla, another victorious commander. Appointed dictator in 82 B.C. for an unlimited term, Sulla proceeded to exterminate his opponents and to restore to the Senate its original powers. Even the senatorial veto over acts of the assembly was revived, and the authority of the tribunes was sharply curtailed. After three years of rule Sulla decided to exchange the pomp of power for the pleasures of the senses and retired to a life of luxury and ease on his Campanian estate.

It was not to be expected that the "reforms" of Sulla would stand unchallenged after he had relinquished his office, for the effect of his decrees was to give control to a bigoted and selfish aristocracy. Several new leaders now emerged to espouse the cause of the people. The most famous of them were Pompey (106–48 B.C.) and

249

Pompey

Caesar's
triumph and
downfall

Julius Caesar

Julius Caesar (100–44 B.C.). For a time they pooled their energies and resources in a plot to gain control of the government, but later they became rivals and sought to outdo each other in bids for popular support. Pompey won fame as the conqueror of Syria and Palestine, while Caesar devoted his talents to a series of brilliant forays against the Gauls, adding to the Roman state the territory of modern Belgium and France. In 52 B.C., after a series of mob disorders in Rome, the Senate turned to Pompey and caused his election as sole consul. Caesar was eventually branded an enemy of the state, and Pompey conspired with the senatorial faction to deprive him of political power. The result was a deadly war between the two men. In 49 B.C. Caesar began a march on Rome. Pompey fled to the East in the hope of gathering a large enough army to regain control of Italy. In 48 B.C. the forces of the two rivals met at Pharsalus in Thessaly. Pompey was defeated and soon afterward was murdered by agents of the king of Egypt.

After dallying for a season at the court of Cleopatra in Egypt, Caesar returned to Rome. There was now no one who dared to challenge his power. With the aid of his veterans he cowed the Senate into granting his every desire. In 46 B.C. he became dictator for ten years, and two years later for life. In addition, he assumed nearly every other magisterial title that would augment his power. He was consul, censor, and supreme pontiff. He obtained from the Senate full authority to make war and peace and to control the revenues of the state. For all practical purposes he was above the law, and the other agents of the government were merely his servants. It seems unquestionable that he had little respect for the constitution, and there were rumors that he intended to make himself king. At any rate, it was on such a charge that he was assassinated in 44 B.C. by a group of conspirators, under the leadership of Brutus and Cassius, representing the old aristocracy.[4]

Through the centuries ever since, students of history have been blinded by hero worship in estimating Caesar's political career. It is undoubtedly erroneous to acclaim him as the savior of his country or to praise him as the greatest statesman of all time. For he treated the Republic with contempt and made the problem of governing more difficult for those who came after him. What Rome needed at this time was not the rule of force, however efficiently it might be exercised, but an enlightened attempt to correct the inequities of her political and economic regime. Though it is true that Caesar carried out numerous reforms, not all of them were really fundamental. With the aid of a Greek astronomer he revised the official calendar so as to bring it into harmony with the Egyptian solar calendar of 365 days, with an extra day added every fourth year. He

[4] During the last few months of his life Caesar became more ill-tempered and domineering than ever. Perhaps this change was due to the fact that he was really a sick man, his old affliction of epilepsy having returned. W. E. Heitland, *The Roman Republic*, III, 355.

investigated extravagance in the distribution of public grain and reduced the number of recipients by more than 50 per cent. He made plans for codification of the law and increased the penalty for criminal offenses. By conferring citizenship upon thousands of Spaniards and Gauls he took an important step toward eliminating the distinction between Italians and provincials. He settled a great many of his veterans and a considerable proportion of the urban poor on unused lands not only in Italy but throughout the empire, and he ordered the proprietors of large estates to employ at least one free citizen to every two slaves. It seems fair to say that his greatest fault lay in his exercise of dictatorial power. By ignoring the Senate entirely he destroyed the main foundation on which the Republic rested.

5. ROME BECOMES SOPHISTICATED

During the last two centuries of republican history Rome came under the influence of Hellenistic civilization. The result was a modest flowering of intellectual activity and a further impetus to social change beyond what the Punic Wars had produced. The fact must be noted, however, that several of the components of the Hellenistic pattern of culture were never adopted by the Romans at all. The science of the Hellenistic Age, for example, was largely ignored, and the same was true of some of its art.

One of the most notable effects of Hellenistic influence was the adoption of Epicureanism and Stoicism by numerous Romans of the upper classes. The most renowned of the Roman exponents of the Epicurean philosophy was Lucretius (98–55 B.C.), author of a didactic poem entitled *On the Nature of Things*. In writing this work Lucretius was moved to explain the universe in such a way as to liberate man from all fear of the supernatural, which he regarded as the chief obstacle to peace of soul. Worlds and all things in them, he taught, are the results of fortuitous combinations of atoms. Though he admitted the existence of the gods, he conceived of them as living in eternal peace, neither creating nor governing the universe. Everything is a product of mechanical evolution, including man himself and his habits, institutions, and beliefs. Since mind is indissolubly linked with matter, death means utter extinction; consequently, no part of the human personality can survive to be rewarded or punished in an afterlife. Lucretius' conception of the good life was perhaps even more negative than that of Epicurus: what man needs, he asserted, is not enjoyment but "peace and a pure heart."

Stoicism was introduced into Rome about 140 B.C. Although it soon came to include among its coverts numerous influential leaders of public life, its most distinguished representative was Cicero (106–43 B.C.), the famous orator and statesman. Although Cicero adopted doctrines from a number of philosophers, including both Plato and Aristotle, the fact remains that he derived more of his

251

ideas from the Stoics than from any other source. Certainly his chief ethical writings reflect substantially the doctrines of Zeno and his school. The basis of Cicero's ethical philosophy was the premise that virtue is sufficient for happiness, and that tranquillity of mind is the highest good. He conceived of the ideal man as one who has been guided by reason to an indifference toward sorrow and pain. In political philosophy Cicero went considerably beyond the earlier Stoics. He was one of the first to deny that the state is superior to the individual and taught that government had its origin in a compact among men for their mutual protection. In his *Republic* he set forth the idea of a higher law of eternal justice which is superior to the statutes and decrees of governments. This law is not made by man but is a product of the natural order of things and is discoverable by reason. It is the source of those rights to which all men are entitled as human beings and which governments must not assail. As we shall see presently, this doctrine influenced considerably the development of the Roman law by the great jurists of the second and third centuries A.D. By reason of his contributions to political thought, and by virtue of his urbanity and tolerance, Cicero deserves to be ranked as one of the greatest men Rome produced. He typified the genius of the nation at its best. It was his misfortune that, as a defender of the old Republic, he came to be associated in the public mind with the leaders of the aristocracy who had assassinated Julius Caesar. In 43 B.C. he was proscribed by Mark Antony, Caesar's friend, and hunted down and killed.

Roman literary
progress

Hellenistic influence was in large measure responsible for Roman literary progress in the last two centuries of the Republic. It now became the fashion among the upper classes to learn the Greek language and to strive to reproduce in Latin some of the more popular forms of Hellenistic literature. Noteworthy results were some excellent comedy, lyric poetry, and above all, the letters, essays, and orations of Cicero, which are generally regarded as the finest examples of Latin prose.

Social conditions
in the late Re-
public

The conquest of the Hellenistic world accelerated the process of social change which the Punic Wars had begun. The effects were most clearly evident in the growth of luxury, in a widened cleavage between classes, and in a further increase in slavery. The Italian people, numbering about 2,000,000 at the end of the Republic, had come to be divided into four main castes: the aristocracy, the equestrians, the common citizens, and the slaves.[5] The aristocracy included the senatorial class with a total membership of 300 citizens and their families. The majority of them inherited their status, although occasionally a plebeian would gain admission to the Senate through serving a term as consul or quaestor. Most of the aristocrats

[5] In addition, of course, there were numerous aliens, who really did not constitute a separate class. Many were on about the same level as the common citizens. Others were slaves.

gained their living as office holders and as owners of great landed estates. The equestrian order was made up of government contractors, bankers, and the wealthier merchants. Originally this class had been composed of those citizens with incomes sufficient to enable them to serve in the cavalry at their own expense, but the term *equites* had now come to be applied to all outside of the senatorial class who possessed property in substantial amount. The equestrians were the chief offenders in the indulgence of vulgar tastes and in the exploitation of the poor and the provincials. As bankers they regularly charged interest rates of 12 per cent and three or four times that much when they could get it. By far the largest number of the citizens were mere commoners or plebeians. Some of these were independent farmers, a few were industrial workers, but the majority were members of the city mob. When Julius Caesar became dictator, 320,000 citizens were actually being supported by the state.

The Roman slaves were scarcely considered people at all but instruments of production like cattle or horses to be worked for the profit of their masters. Notwithstanding the fact that some of them were refined and intelligent foreigners, they had none of the privileges granted to slaves in Athens. The policy of many of their owners was to get as much work out of them as possible during the years of their prime and then to turn them loose to be fed by the state when they became old and useless. Of course, there were exceptions, especially as a result of the civilizing effects of Stoicism. Cicero, for example, reported himself very fond of his slaves. It is, nevertheless, a sad commentary on Roman civilization that nearly all of the productive labor in the country was done by slaves. They produced practically all of the nation's food supply, for the amount contributed by the few surviving independent farmers was quite insignificant. At least 80 per cent of the workers employed in shops were slaves or former slaves. But many of the members of the

ROME BECOMES SOPHISTICATED

The status of the slaves

Atrium of an Upper-class House in Pompeii, seen from the Interior. Around the atrium or central court were grouped suites of living rooms. The marble columns and decorated walls still give an idea of the luxury and refinement enjoyed by the privileged minority.

servile population were engaged in nonproductive activities. A lucrative form of investment for the business classes was ownership of slaves trained as gladiators, who could be rented to the government or to aspiring politicians for the amusement of the people. The growth of luxury also required the employment of thousands of slaves in domestic service. The man of great wealth must have his doorkeepers, his litter-bearers, his couriers (for the government of the Republic had no postal service), his valets, and his pedagogues or tutors for his children. In some great mansions there were special servants with no other duties than to rub the master down after his bath or to care for his sandals.

The religious beliefs of the Romans were altered in various ways in the last two centuries of the Republic—again mainly because of the extension of Roman power over most of the Hellenistic states. There was, first of all, a tendency of the upper classes to abandon the traditional religion for the philosophies of Stoicism and Epicureanism. But many of the common people also found worship of the ancient gods no longer satisfying. It was too formal and mechanical and demanded too much in the way of duty and self-sacrifice to meet the needs of the masses, whose lives were now empty and meaningless. Furthermore, Italy had attracted a stream of immigrants from the East, most of whom had a religious background totally different from that of the Romans. The result was the rapid spread of Oriental mystery cults, which satisfied the craving for a more emotional religion and offered the reward of a blessed immortality to the wretched and downtrodden of earth. From Egypt came the cult of Isis and Osiris (or Sarapis, as the god was now more commonly called), while from Phrygia was introduced the worship of the Great Mother, with her eunuch priests and wild, symbolic orgies. So strong was the appeal of these cults that the decrees of the Senate against them proved almost impossible to enforce. In the last century B.C. the Persian cult of Mithraism, which came to surpass all the others in popularity, gained a foothold in Italy.

Changes in religion

6. THE PRINCIPATE OR EARLY EMPIRE (27 B.C.–284 A.D.)

Shortly before his death in 44 B.C., Julius Caesar had adopted as his sole heir his grandnephew Octavian (63 B.C.–14 A.D.), then a young man of eighteen quietly pursuing his studies in Illyria across the Adriatic Sea. Upon learning of his uncle's death, Octavian hastened to Rome to take over control of the government. He soon found that he must share his ambition with two of Caesar's powerful friends, Mark Antony and Lepidus. The following year the three men formed an alliance for the purpose of crushing the power of the aristocratic clique responsible for Caesar's murder. The methods employed were not to the new leaders' credit. Prominent members of the aristocracy were hunted down and slain and their

The triumph of Octavian or Augustus Caesar

property confiscated. The most noted of the victims was Cicero, brutally slain by Mark Antony's soldiers though he had taken no part in the conspiracy against Caesar's life. The real murderers, Brutus and Cassius, escaped and organized an army of 80,000 republicans, but were finally defeated by Octavian and his colleagues in 42 B.C. About eight years later a quarrel developed among the members of the alliance themselves, inspired primarily by Antony's jealousy of Octavian. The ultimate outcome in 31 B.C. was the triumphant emergence of Caesar's heir as the most powerful man in the Roman state.

The victory of Octavian ushered in a new period in Roman history, the most glorious and the most prosperous that the nation experienced. Although problems of peace and order were still far from being completely solved, the deadly civil strife was ended, and the people now had their first decent opportunity to show what their talents could achieve. Unlike his great uncle, Octavian seems to have entertained no monarchical ambitions. He was determined, at any rate, to preserve the forms if not the substance of constitutional government. He accepted the titles of Augustus and Imperator conferred upon him by the Senate and the army.[6] He held the authority of proconsul and tribune permanently; but he refused to make himself dictator or even consul for life, despite the pleas of the populace that he do so. In his view the Senate and the people were the supreme sovereigns, as they had been under the early Republic. The title by which he preferred to have his authority designated was Princeps, or First Citizen of the State. For this reason the period of his rule and that of his successors is properly called the Principate, or early Empire, to distinguish it from the period of the Republic (sixth century B.C. to 27 B.C.) and from the period of the late Empire (284 A.D. to 476 A.D.)

Octavian, or Augustus as he was now more commonly called, ruled over Italy and the provinces for forty-four years (31 B.C.–14 A.D.). At the beginning of the period he governed by military power and by common consent, but in 27 B.C. the Senate bestowed upon him the series of offices and titles described above. His work as a statesman at least equaled in importance that of his more famous predecessor. Among the reforms of Augustus were the establishment of a new coinage system, the creation of a centralized system of courts under his own supervision, and the bestowal of a large measure of local self-government upon cities and provinces. For the nation as a whole he laid the foundations for an elaborate postal service. He insisted upon experience and intelligence as qualifications for appointment to administrative office. By virtue of his proconsular authority he assumed direct control over the provincial governors and punished them severely for graft and extortion. He

See color plates between pages 256 and 257

The revival of constitutional government

The reforms of Augustus

---

[6] The title Augustus signified "consecrated" and implied the idea that its bearer was specially favored by the gods. Imperator meant "victorious general."

Augustus

The Pax Romana

abolished the old system of farming out the collection of taxes in the provinces, which had led to such flagrant abuses, and appointed his own personal representatives as collectors at regular salaries. But he did not stop with political reforms. He procured the enactment of laws designed to check the more glaring social and moral evils of the time. By his own example of temperate living he sought to discourage luxurious habits and to set the precedent for a return to the ancient virtues.

After the death of Augustus in 14 A.D. Rome had few enlightened and capable rulers. Several of his successors were brutal tyrants who squandered the resources of the state and kept the country in an uproar by their deeds of bloody violence. As early as 68 A.D. the army began to take a hand in the selection of the Princeps, with the result that on several occasions thereafter the head of the government was little more than a military dictator. Between 235 and 284 A.D. sheer anarchy prevailed: of the twenty-six men who were elevated to power in that time only one escaped violent death. As a matter of fact, in the 270 years which followed the demise of Augustus, Rome had scarcely more than four or five rulers of whom much good could be said. The list would include Nerva (96–98 A.D.), Trajan (98–117), Antoninus Pius (138–161), and Marcus Aurelius (161–180).

These rulers and their great predecessor, Augustus, succeeded in maintaining, for about two centuries, the celebrated *Pax Romana*. On three occasions Augustus himself ceremonially closed the doors of the temple of Janus to symbolize the reign of absolute peace in the Empire. Yet the *Pax Romana* was primarily a peace of subjugation. Augustus added more territory to the empire than did any other Roman ruler. His stepsons pushed the frontiers into central and eastern Europe, conquering the territories known today as Switzerland, Austria, and Bulgaria. They attempted the subjugation of the territory occupied by modern Germany, but met with only minimal success. The *Pax Romana* rested upon an efficient navy and a vast imperial army. Though comparatively small, the navy performed its functions so well that the Romans maintained their control over the Mediterranean Sea for 200 years without fighting a battle. The army, numbering about 300,000 men, was much less successful. It was badly defeated in Germany and eventually lost nearly all of the territory it had conquered there. To prevent revolts, more than twenty of its twenty-eight legions were pinned down in Spain, Syria, and Egypt and on the Rhine and the Danube. Feeding and supplying these hordes of armed men put a constant strain on the resources of the state. Even a sales tax had to be adopted to supplement the usual sources of revenue.

How can this comparative failure of the political genius of the Romans in the very best period of their history be accounted for? The assertion is frequently made that it was due to the absence of any definite rule of hereditary succession to the office of Princeps.

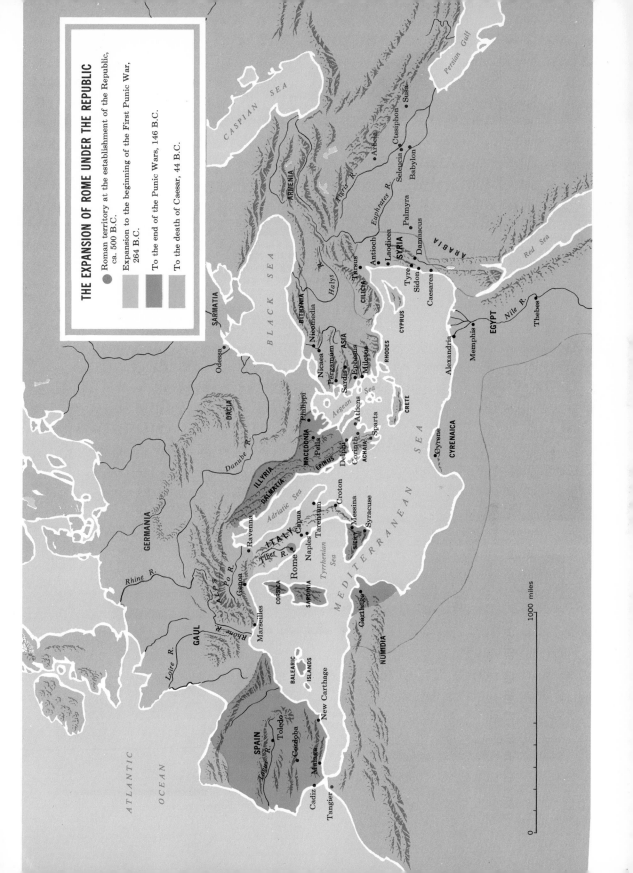

THE EXPANSION OF ROME UNDER THE REPUBLIC

- Roman territory at the establishment of the Republic, ca. 500 B.C.
- Expansion to the beginning of the First Punic War, 264 B.C.
- To the end of the Punic Wars, 146 B.C.
- To the death of Caesar, 44 B.C.

1000 miles

ATLANTIC

OCEAN

SPAIN
Tagus R.
Toledo
Cordoba
Malaga
Cadiz
Tangier
New Carthage

GAUL
Loire R.
Rhône R.
Marseilles
Rhine R.
Genoa
ALPS
Po R.

BALEARIC
ISLANDS

CORSICA
SARDINIA

NUMIDIA
Carthage

GERMANIA

Danube R.

DACIA

ILLYRIA
DALMATIA
Adriatic Sea
Ravenna
ITALY
Tiber R.
Rome
Capua
Naples
Tarentum
Croton
Messina
Syracuse
SICILY
Tyrrhenian
Sea

MEDITERRANEAN
SEA

SARMATIA

Odessa

BLACK SEA

BITHYNIA
Nicomedia
Nicaea
Pergamum
Sardis
ASIA
Ephesus
Miletus
RHODES

Halys R.

MACEDONIA
Philippi
Pella
EPIRUS
Delphi
Corinth
Athens
ACHAEA
Sparta
Aegean Sea

CRETE

CYRENE
CYRENAICA

ARMENIA

Tigris R.

CILICIA
Tarsus
Antioch
Laodicea
SYRIA
Tyre
Sidon
Caesarea
Palmyra
Damascus

CYPRUS

Euphrates R.
Seleucia
Ctesiphon
Babylon
Arbela
Susa

ARABIA

CASPIAN SEA

Persian Gulf

Red Sea

EGYPT
Alexandria
Memphis
Nile R.
Thebes

Unidentified Man, I cent. B.C. The Romans excelled in portraits of sharp individuality.

Augustus, Reigned 31 B.C.–14 A.D. This portrait suggests the contradictory nature of the genius who gave Rome peace after years of strife.

Constantine, Reigned 306–337 A.D. The head is from a statue sixteen feet in height.

Mummy Portrait, II cent. A.D. A Roman woman buried in Egypt.

Mosaic, I cent. A.D. A floor design composed of small pieces of colored marble fitted together to form a picture.

Wall Painting of a Satyr Mask, I cent. B.C. The belief in satyrs, thought to inhabit forests and pastures, was taken over from the Greeks.

Architectural Wall Painting from a Pompeiian Villa, I cent. B.C., suggesting the Greek origin of Roman forms of architecture.

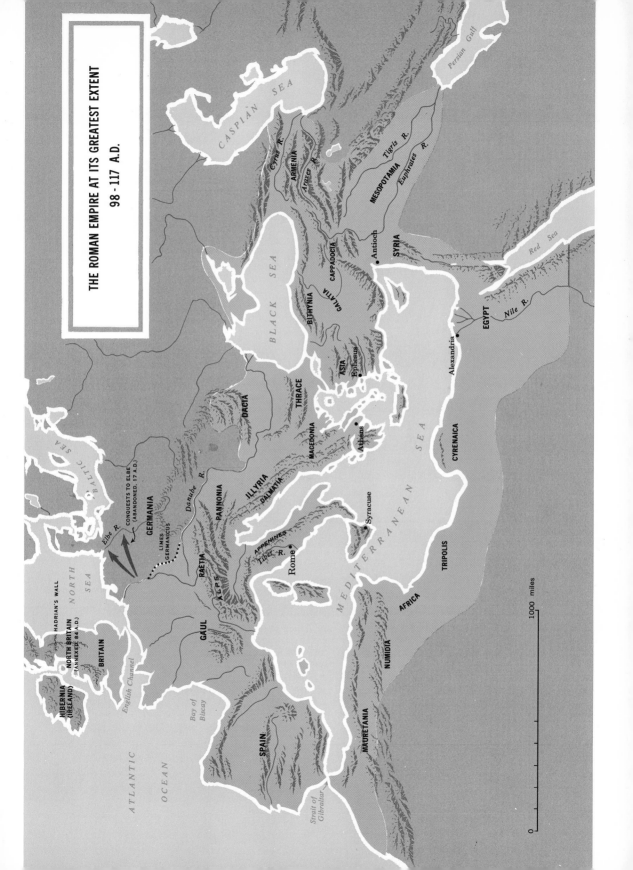

THE ROMAN EMPIRE AT ITS GREATEST EXTENT
98 - 117 A.D.

CASPIAN SEA

Cyrus R.
ARMENIA
Araxes R.
MESOPOTAMIA
Tigris R.
Euphrates R.

Antioch
SYRIA
CAPPADOCIA
GALATIA
BITHYNIA

BLACK SEA

Red Sea

Persian Gulf

ASIA
Ephesus
THRACE

EGYPT
Nile R.

Alexandria

MACEDONIA
Athens

CYRENAICA

DACIA

Danube R.
PANNONIA
ILLYRIA
DALMATIA

Syracuse

MEDITERRANEAN SEA

TRIPOLIS

Elbe R.
CONQUESTS TO ELBE
(ABANDONED, 17 A.D.)
GERMANIA
LIMES GERMANICUS
RAETIA
ALPS
APPENNINES
Tiber R.
Rome

AFRICA

BALTIC SEA

NORTH SEA

HADRIAN'S WALL
NORTH BRITAIN
(ANNEXED 84 A.D.)
BRITAIN

English Channel

GAUL

NUMIDIA

MAURETANIA

HIBERNIA
(IRELAND)

Bay of Biscay

SPAIN

Strait of Gibraltar

ATLANTIC OCEAN

1000 miles

0

Saint John Writing His Gospel. From an Anglo-Frankish illuminated manuscript, *ca.* 850, produced in a Carolingian monastery. The unknown artist knew nothing of perspective, but excelled in coloring and conveying a sense of vitality and energy. (Morgan Library)

Gold Cup, Byzantine, VI–IX cent. The figure is a personification of Constantinople, a queen or goddess holding the scepter and orb of imperial rule. (MMA)

Merovingian Fibula or Brooch, VII cent. A fabulous gold-plated animal set with garnets and colored paste reveals the lively imagination of the early Middle Ages. (MMA)

Enthroned Madonna and Child, Byzantine School, XIII cent. The painters of Siena followed the opulent and brilliant style of Byzantine art. Their madonnas were not earthly mothers, but celestial queens reigning in dignified splendor. (National Gallery)

But this answer rests upon a misconception of the nature of the Roman constitution at this time. The government Augustus established was not intended to be a monarchy. Although the Princeps was virtually an autocrat, the authority he possessed was supposed to be derived exclusively from the Senate and the people of Rome; he could have no inherent right to rule by virtue of royal descent. The explanation must therefore be sought in other factors. The Romans were now reaping the whirlwind which had been sown in the civil strife of the late Republic. They had grown accustomed to violence as the way out when problems did not admit of an easy solution. Furthermore, the long wars of conquest and the suppression of barbarian revolts had cheapened human life in the estimation of the people themselves and had fostered the growth of crime. As a consequence it was practically inevitable that men of vicious character should push their way into the highest political office.

7. CULTURE AND LIFE IN THE PERIOD OF THE PRINCIPATE

From the standpoint of variety of intellectual and artistic interests the period of the Principate outshone all other ages in the history of Rome. Most of the progress took place, however, in the years from 27 B.C. to 200 A.D. It was between these years that Roman philosophy attained its characteristic form. This period witnessed also the feeble awakening of an interest in science, the growth of a distinctive art, and the production of the best literary works. After 200 A.D. economic and political decay stifled all further cultural growth.

Cultural progress under the Principate

Trajan Addressing His Troops. This relief on the Column of Trajan dates to the first century A.D.

Stoicism was now the prevailing philosophy of the Romans. Much of the influence of Epicureanism lingered and found occasional expression in the writings of the poets, but as a system it had ceased to be popular. The reasons for the triumph of Stoicism are not hard to discover. With its emphasis upon duty, self-discipline, and subjection to the natural order of things, it accorded well with the ancient virtues of the Romans and with their habits of conservatism. Moreover, its insistence upon civic obligations and its doctrine of cosmopolitanism appealed to the Roman political-mindedness and pride in world empire. Epicureanism, on the other hand, was a little too negative and individualistic to agree with the social consciousness of Roman tradition. It seemed not only to repudiate the idea of any purpose in the universe, but even to deny the value of human effort. Since the Romans were men of action rather than speculative thinkers, the Epicurean ideal of the solitary philosopher immersed in the problem of his own salvation could have no permanent attraction for them. It is necessary to observe, however, that the Stoicism developed in the days of the Principate was somewhat different from that of Zeno and his school. The old physical theories borrowed from Heracleitus were now discarded, and in their place was substituted a broader interest in politics and ethics. There was a tendency also for Roman Stoicism to assume a more distinctly religious flavor than that which had characterized the original philosophy.

Three eminent apostles of Stoicism lived and taught in Rome in the two centuries that followed the rule of Augustus: Seneca (4 B.C.–65 A.D.), millionaire adviser for a time to Nero; Epictetus, the slave (60?–120 A.D.); and the Emperor Marcus Aurelius (121–180 A.D.). All of them agreed that inner serenity is the ultimate goal to be sought, that true happiness can be found only in surrender to the benevolent order of the universe. They preached the ideal of virtue for virtue's sake, deplored the sinfulness of man's nature, and urged obedience to conscience as the voice of duty. Seneca and Epictetus adulterated their philosophy with such deep mystical yearnings as to make it almost a religion. They worshiped the cosmos as divine, governed by an all-powerful Providence who ordains all that happens for ultimate good. The last of the Roman Stoics, Marcus Aurelius, was more fatalistic and less hopeful. Although he did not reject the conception of an ordered and rational universe, he shared neither the faith nor the dogmatism of the earlier Stoics. He was confident of no blessed immortality to balance the sufferings of one's earthly career. Living in a melancholy time, he was inclined to think of man as a creature buffeted by evil fortune for which no distant perfection of the whole could fully atone. He urged, nevertheless, that men should continue to live nobly, that they should neither abandon themselves to gross indulgence nor break down in angry protest, but that they should derive what contentment they could from dignified resignation to suffering and tranquil submission to death.

Marcus Aurelius. The mounted figure of the great emperor-philosopher is one of the few equestrian statues surviving from the ancient world. It was originally entirely gilded. Now on the Piazza del Campidoglio, Rome.

The literary achievements of the Romans bore a definite relation to their philosophy. This was especially true of the works of the most distinguished writers of the Augustan Age. Horace (65–8 B.C.), for example, in his famous *Odes* drew copiously from the teachings of both Epicureans and Stoics. He confined his attention, however, to their doctrines of a way of life, for like most of the Romans he had little curiosity about the nature of the world. He developed a philosophy which combined the Epicurean justification of pleasure with the Stoic bravery in the face of trouble. While he never reduced pleasure to the mere absence of pain, he was sophisticated enough to know that the highest enjoyment is possible only through the exercise of rational control.

Roman literature: Horace

Vergil (70–19 B.C.) likewise reflects a measure of the philosophical temper of his age. Though his *Eclogues* convey something of the Epicurean ideal of quiet pleasure, Vergil was much more of a Stoic. His utopian vision of an age of peace and abundance, his brooding sense of the tragedy of human fate, and his idealization of a life in harmony with nature indicate an intellectual heritage similar to that of Seneca and Epictetus. Vergil's most noted work, the *Aeneid*, like several of the *Odes* of Horace, was a purposeful glorification of Roman imperialism. The *Aeneid* in fact was an epic of empire recounting the toils and triumphs of the founding of the state, its glorious traditions, and its magnificent destiny. The only other major writers of the Augustan Age were Ovid (43 B.C.?–17 A.D.) and Livy (59 B.C.–17 A.D.). The former, the greatest of Roman elegiac poets, was the chief representative of the cynical and individualist tendencies of his day. His writings, although brilliant and witty, often reflected the dissolute tastes of the time, and their popularity gives evidence of the failure of the efforts of Augustus to regenerate Roman society. The chief claim of Livy to fame rests upon his skill as a prose stylist. As a historian he was woefully deficient. His main work, a history of Rome, is replete with dramatic and picturesque

Vergil, Ovid, and Livy

259

narrative, designed to appeal to the patriotic emotions rather than to present the impartial truth.

The literature of the period which followed the death of Augustus also exemplified conflicting social and intellectual tendencies. The novels of Petronius and Apuleius and the epigrams of Martial are specimens of individualist writing generally descriptive of the meaner aspects of life. The attitude of the authors is unmoral; their purpose is not to instruct or uplift but chiefly to tell an entertaining story or turn a witty phrase. An entirely different viewpoint is presented in the works of the other most important writers of this age: Juvenal, the satirist (60?–140 A.D.), and Tacitus, the historian (55?–117? A.D.). Juvenal wrote under the influence of the Stoics but with little intelligence and narrow vision. Laboring under the delusion that the troubles of the nation were due to moral degeneracy, he lashed the vices of his countrymen with the fury of an evangelist. A somewhat similar attitude characterized the writing of his younger contemporary, Tacitus. The best-known of Roman historians, Tacitus described the events of his age not entirely with a view to scientific analysis but largely for the purpose of moral indictment. His description of the customs of the ancient Germans in his *Germania* served to heighten the contrast between the manly virtues of an unspoiled race and the effeminate vices of the decadent Romans. Whatever his failings as a historian, he was a master of ironic wit and brilliant aphorism. Referring to the boasted *Pax Romana*, he makes a barbarian chieftain say: "They create a wilderness and call it peace." [7]

The period of the Principate was the period when Roman art first assumed its distinctive character as an expression of the national life. Before this time what passed for an art of Rome was really an importation from the Hellenistic East. Conquering armies brought back to Italy wagonloads of statues, reliefs, and marble columns as part of the plunder from Greece and Asia Minor. These became the

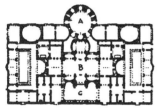

Floor Plan of the Baths of Caracalla

Petronius, Apuleius, Martial, Juvenal, and Tacitus

Achievements in art

[7] Tacitus, *Agricola*, p. 30.

The Baths of Caracalla, Rome. The gigantic scale is typical of late Empire buildings. Elaborate and luxurious public baths like these were often presented to the public by the emperor or rich citizens. The floor plan above indicates the separate chambers for hot tub baths.

property of wealthy publicans and bankers and were used to embellish their sumptuous mansions. As the demand increased, hundreds of copies were made, with the result that Rome came to have by the end of the Republic a profusion of objects of art which had no more cultural significance than the Rembrandts or Botticellis in the home of some modern broker. The aura of national glory which surrounded the early Principate stimulated the growth of an art more nearly indigenous. Augustus himself boasted that he found Rome a city of brick and left it a city of marble. Nevertheless, much of the old Hellenistic influence remained until the talent of the Romans themselves was exhausted.

The arts most truly expressive of the Roman character were architecture and sculpture. Both were monumental, designed to symbolize power and grandeur rather than freedom of mind or contentment with life. Architecture contained as its leading elements the round arch, the vault, and the dome, although at times the Corinthian column was employed, especially in the construction of temples. The materials most commonly used were brick, squared stone blocks, and concrete, the last generally concealed with a marble facing. As a further adornment of public buildings, sculptured entablatures and façades, built up of tiers of colonnades or arcades, were frequently added. Roman architecture was devoted primarily to utilitarian purposes. The foremost examples were government buildings, amphitheaters, baths, race courses, and private houses. Nearly all were of massive proportions and solid construction. Among the largest and most noted were the Pantheon, with its dome having a diameter of 142 feet, and the Colosseum, which could accommodate 65,000 spectators at the gladiatorial combats. Roman sculpture included as its main forms triumphal arches and columns, narrative reliefs, altars, and portrait busts and statues. Its distinguishing characteristics were individuality and naturalism. Even more than architecture it served to express the vanity and love of power of the Roman aristocracy, although some of it was marked by unusual qualities of harmony and grace.[8]

As scientists the Romans accomplished comparatively little in this period or in any other. Scarcely an original discovery of fundamental importance was made by a man of Latin nationality. This fact seems strange when we consider that the Romans had the advantage of Hellenistic science as a foundation upon which to build. But they neglected their opportunity almost completely. Why should this have been so? It was due, first of all, to the circumstance that the Romans were absorbed in problems of government and military conquest. Forced to specialize in law, politics, and military strategy, they had very little time for investigation of nature. A reason of

CULTURE AND LIFE IN
THE PERIOD OF THE
PRINCIPATE

Architecture
and sculpture

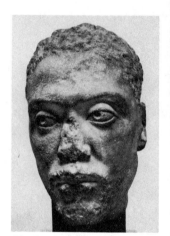

Head of a Young Man, ca. 140 A.D.

Why the Romans
accomplished
little as scientists

[8] A great many of the best examples of both architecture and sculpture were produced not by Romans at all but by Greeks resident in Italy.

The Pantheon in Rome. Built by the emperor Hadrian and dedicated to the deities of the seven planets.

more vital importance was the fact that the Romans were too practical-minded. They had none of that divine fire which impels man to lose himself in the quest for unlimited knowledge. They had no vigorous intellectual curiosity about the world in which they lived. In short, they were not philosophers.

Mainly because of this lack of talent for pure science, the achievements of the Romans were limited almost entirely to engineering and the organization of public services. They built marvelous roads, bridges, and aqueducts. They provided the city of Rome with a water supply of 300,000,000 gallons daily. They established the first hospitals in the Western world and the first system of state medicine for the benefit of the poor. But their own writers on scientific subjects were hopelessly devoid of critical intelligence. The most renowned and the most typical of them was Pliny the Elder (23-79 A.D.), who completed about 77 A.D. a voluminous encyclopedia of "science" which he called *Natural History*. The subjects discussed varied from cosmology to economics. Despite the wealth of material

Lack of scientific originality

262

it contains, the work is of limited value. Pliny was totally unable to distinguish between fact and fable. In his estimation, the weirdest tales of wonders and portents were to be accepted as of equal value with the most solidly established facts. The other best-known author of an encyclopedia of science was Seneca (4 B.C.?–65 A.D.), the Stoic philosopher, who took his own life at Nero's command in 65 A.D. Seneca was less credulous than Pliny but no more original. Besides, he maintained that the purpose of all scientific study should be to divulge the moral secrets of nature. If there was any Latin who could be considered an original scientist, the title would have to be given to Celsus, who flourished during the reign of Tiberius. Celsus wrote a comprehensive treatise on medicine, including an excellent manual of surgery, but there is a strong suspicion that the entire work was compiled, if not actually translated, from the Greek. Among the operations he described were tonsillectomy, operations for cataracts and goiter, and plastic surgery.

No account of the scientific aspects of Roman civilization would be complete without some mention of the work of Hellenistic scientists who lived in Italy or in the provinces during the period of the Principate. Nearly all of them were physicians. The most distinguished, although apparently not the most original, was Galen of Pergamum, who was active in Rome at various times during the latter half of the second century. While his fame rests primarily upon his medical encyclopedia, systematizing the learning of others, he is

Hellenistic scientists in Italy

Roman Aqueduct at Segovia, Spain. Aqueducts conveyed water from mountains to the larger cities.

The Colosseum. The Colosseum was built by the Roman emperors as a place of entertainment and public exhibition. It was the scene of gladiatorial combats and of the throwing of Christians to the lions.

deserving of more credit for his own experiments which brought him close to a discovery of the circulation of the blood. He not only taught but proved that the arteries carry blood, and that severance of even a small one is sufficient to drain away all of the blood of the body in little more than half an hour. But Galen was not the only Hellenistic physician who made important contributions in this time. At least one other is entitled to more recognition than is commonly given to him: Rufus of Ephesus, who wrote the first accurate description of the liver and of the rhythm of the pulse, and was the first to recommend boiling of suspicious water before drinking it.

Roman society exhibited the same general tendencies under the Principate as in the last days of the Republic. A few significant differences, however, can be noted. Owing in part to the influence of the Stoic philosophy and in part to the abundance of free labor, slavery began to decline. Despite the efforts of Augustus to limit the manumission of slaves, the number of freedmen steadily increased. They crowded into every field of employment, including the civil service. Many succeeded in becoming proprietors of small shops, and some even became rich. Related to these developments was the growth of the institution of clientage. Members of the citizen class who had lost their property or who had been driven out of business by the competition of enterprising freedmen now frequently became "clients" or dependents of wealthy aristocrats. In return for pittances of food and money these "shabby genteel" served the great magnates by applauding their speeches and fawning before them when they appeared in public. Custom made it practically obligatory for every man of great wealth to maintain a retinue of these miserable flatterers.

Although the evidence has frequently been exaggerated, the period of the Principate was apparently marked by changing morals. According to the records there were 32,000 prostitutes in Rome during the reign of Trajan, and, if we can judge from the testimony of some of the most noted writers, homosexuality was exceedingly common and even fashionable. While political corruption had been subjected to more stringent control, crimes of violence appear to have increased. But the most serious moral indictment which can be brought against the age would seem to have been a further growth of the passion for cruelty. The great games and spectacles became bloodier and more disgusting than ever. The Romans could no longer obtain a sufficient thrill from mere exhibitions of athletic prowess; pugilists were now required to have their hands wrapped with thongs of leather loaded with iron or lead. The most popular amusement of all was watching the gladiatorial combats in the Colosseum or in other amphitheaters capable of accommodating thousands of spectators. Fights between gladiators were nothing new, but they were now presented on a much more elaborate scale. Not only the ignorant rabble attended them, but wealthy aristocrats also, and frequently the head of the government himself. The gladiators fought to the accompaniment of savage cries and curses from the audience. When one went down with a disabling wound, it was the privilege of the crowd to decide whether his life should be spared or whether the weapon of his opponent should be plunged into his heart. One contest after another was staged in the course of a single exhibition. Should the arena become too sodden with blood, it was covered over with a fresh layer of sand, and the revolting performance went on. Most of the gladiators were condemned criminals or slaves, but some were volunteers even from the respectable classes. The Princeps Commodus, the worthless son of Marcus Aurelius, entered the arena several times for the sake of the plaudits of the mob.

Signs of moral change

Notwithstanding its low moral tone, the age of the Principate was characterized by an even deeper interest in salvationist religions than that which had prevailed under the Republic. Mithraism now gained adherents by the thousands, absorbing most of the followers of the cults of the Great Mother and of Isis and Sarapis. About 40 A.D. the first Christians appeared in Rome. The new sect grew rapidly and eventually succeeded in displacing Mithraism as the most popular of the mystery cults. For some time the Roman gov-

The spread of Mithraism and Christianity

265

The Maison Carrée at Nîmes, France. The most perfect example of Roman temple extant. Reflecting possible Etruscan influence, it was built on a high base or podium with great steps leading to the entrance. It dates from the beginning of the Christian era.

ernment was no more hostile toward Christianity than it was toward the other mystery religions. While some members of the sect were put to death by Nero in response to the demand for a scapegoat for the disastrous fire of 64 A.D., there was no systematic persecution of Christians as such until the reign of Decius nearly 200 years later. Even then the persecution was inspired by political and social considerations more than by religious motives. Because of their otherworldliness and their refusal to take the customary oaths in the courts or participate in the civic religion, the Christians were regarded as disloyal citizens and dangerous characters. Moreover, their ideals of meekness and nonresistance, their preaching against the rich, and their practice of holding what appeared to be secret meetings made the Romans suspect them as enemies of the established order. In the end, persecution defeated its own purpose. It intensified the zeal of those who survived, with the result that the new faith spread more rapidly than ever.

The establishment of stable government by Augustus ushered in a period of prosperity for Italy which lasted for more than two centuries. Trade was now extended to all parts of the known world, even to Arabia, India, and China. Manufacturing reached more than insignificant proportions, especially in the production of pottery, textiles, and articles of metal and glass. As a result of the development of rotation of crops and the technique of soil fertilization, agriculture flourished as never before. In spite of all this, the economic order was far from healthy. The prosperity was not evenly distributed but was confined primarily to the upper classes. Since the stigma attached to manual labor persisted as strong as ever, production was bound to decline as the supply of slaves diminished. Perhaps worse was the fact that Italy had a decidedly unfavorable balance of trade. The meager industrial development was by no means sufficient to provide enough articles of export to meet the demand for luxuries imported from the provinces and from the outside world. As a consequence, Italy was gradually drained of her supply of precious metals. By the third century signs of economic collapse were already abundant.

8. ROMAN LAW

There is general agreement that the most important legacy which the Romans left to succeeding cultures was their system of law. This system was the result of a gradual evolution which may be considered to have begun with the publication of the Twelve Tables about 450 B.C. In the later centuries of the Republic the law of the Twelve Tables was modified and practically superseded by the growth of new precedents and principles. These emanated from different sources: from changes in custom, from the teachings of the Stoics, from the decisions of judges, but expecially from the edicts of the praetors. The Roman praetors were magistrates who had authority to define and interpret the law in a particular suit and issue instructions to the jury for the decision of the case. The jury merely decided questions of fact; all issues of law were settled by the praetor, and generally his interpretations became precedents for

A Street in Ostia. This town was the seaport of ancient Rome. The round arches and masonry columns form the balcony of a rich man's house.

267

the decision of similar cases in the future. Thus a system of judicial practice was built up in somewhat the same fashion as the English common law.

It was under the Principate, however, that the Roman law attained its highest stage of development. This later progress was the result in part of the extension of the law over a wider field of jurisdiction, over the lives and properties of aliens in strange environments as well as over the citizens of Italy. But the major reason was the fact that Augustus and his successors gave to certain eminent jurists the right to deliver opinions, or *responsa* as they were called, on the legal issues of cases under trial in the courts. The most prominent of the men thus designated from time to time were Gaius, Ulpian, Papinian, and Paulus. Although most of them held high judicial office, they had gained their reputations primarily as lawyers and writers on legal subjects. The responses of these jurists came to embody a science and philosophy of law and were accepted as the basis of Roman jurisprudence. It was typical of the Roman respect for authority that the ideas of these men should have been adopted so readily even when they upset, as they occasionally did, time-honored beliefs.

Roman law under the Principate; the great jurists

The Roman law as it was developed under the influence of the jurists comprised three great branches or divisions: the *jus civile*, the *jus gentium*, and the *jus naturale*. The *jus civile*, or civil law, was essentially the law of Rome and her citizens. As such it existed in both written and unwritten forms. It included the statutes of the Senate, the decrees of the Princeps, the edicts of the praetors, and also certain ancient customs operating with the force of law. The *jus gentium*, or law of peoples, was the law that was held to be common to all men regardless of nationality. It was the law which authorized the institutions of slavery and private ownership of property and defined the principles of purchase and sale, partnership, and contract. It was not superior to the civil law but supplemented it as especially applicable to the alien inhabitants of the empire.

The three divisions of Roman law

The most interesting and in many ways the most important branch of the Roman law was the *jus naturale*, or natural law. This was not a product of judicial practice, but of philosophy. The Stoics had developed the idea of a rational order of nature which is the embodiment of justice and right. They had affirmed that all men are by nature equal, and that they are entitled to certain basic rights which governments have no authority to transgress. The father of the law of nature as a legal principle, however, was not one of the Hellenistic Stoics, but Cicero. "True law," he declared, "is right reason consonant with nature, diffused among all men, constant, eternal. To make enactments infringing this law, religion forbids, neither may it be repealed even in part, nor have we power through Senate or people to free ourselves from it." [9] This law is prior to

The jus naturale

[9] *The Republic*, III, 22.

the state itself, and any ruler who defies it automatically becomes a tyrant. With the exception of Gaius, who identified the *jus naturale* with the *jus gentium*, all of the great jurists subscribed to conceptions of the law of nature very similar to those of the philosophers. Although the jurists did not regard this law as an automatic limitation upon the *jus civile*, they thought of it nevertheless as a great ideal to which the statutes and decrees of men ought to conform. This development of the concept of abstract justice as a legal principle was one of the noblest achievements of the Roman civilization.

9.   THE LATE EMPIRE (284–476 A.D.)

The last period of Roman history, from 284 to 476 A.D., is properly called the period of the late Empire. With the accession of Diocletian in 284, the government of Rome finally became an undisguised autocracy. It is true, of course, that constitutional government had been little more than a fiction for some time, but now all pretense of maintaining the Republic was thrown aside. Both in theory and in practice the change was complete. No longer was the doctrine advanced that the ruler was the mere agent of the Senate and the people; he was now held to be absolutely sovereign on the assumption that the people had surrendered all power to him. Diocletian adopted the regalia and ceremony of an Oriental despot. In place of the simple military garb of the Princeps he substituted a purple robe of silk interwoven with gold. He required all his subjects who were admitted to an audience with him to prostrate themselves before him. Needless to say, the Senate was now completely excluded from participation in the government. It was not formally abolished, but it was reduced to the status of a municipal council and a social club for the plutocracy. The chief reason for these political changes is undoubtedly to be found in the economic decline of the third century. The people had lost confidence in themselves, as they frequently do under such circumstances, and were ready to sacrifice all of their rights for the faint hope of security.

The triumph of absolute autocracy

Diocletian's successors continued his system of absolutism. The most famous of them were Constantine I (306–337), Julian (361–363), and Theodosius I (379–395). Constantine is best known for his establishment of a new capital, called Constantinople, on the site of ancient Byzantium, and for his policy of religious toleration toward Christians. Contrary to a common belief, he did not make Christianity the official religion of the Empire; his various edicts issued in 313 simply gave Christianity equal status with the pagan cults, thereby terminating the policy of persecution. Later in his reign he bestowed upon the Christian clergy special privileges and caused his sons to be brought up in the new faith, but he continued to maintain the imperial cult. Although he was acclaimed by historians of the Church as Constantine the Great, his practice of favoring Christianity was dictated primarily by political motives. A

Diocletian's successors

generation after Constantine's death the Emperor Julian attempted to stimulate a pagan reaction. He was a devoted admirer of Hellenic culture and thought of Christianity as an alien and enemy religion. His attempt to accomplish a pagan revival ended in failure, partly because Christianity was too firmly entrenched, and partly because his reign was too short. The last of the noted pagan emperors, he has been branded by Christian historians as Julian the Apostate. The other most prominent of the rulers of Rome in its dying stage was Theodosius I, who, in spite of his butchery of thousands of innocent citizens on imaginary charges of conspiracy, is also known as "the Great." The chief importance of his reign comes from his decree of 380 commanding all of his subjects to become orthodox Christians. A few years later he classified participation in any of the pagan cults as an act of treason.

From the standpoint of cultural achievement the period of the Empire is of little significance. With the establishment of a despotic state and the degradation of intellect by mystical and otherworldly religions, creative talent was destroyed. The few literary works produced were characterized by an overemphasis upon form and a neglect of content. A barren and artificial rhetoric took the place of the study of the classics in the schools, and science died out completely. Aside from the teachings of the Christian Fathers, which will be discussed later, the prevailing philosophy of the age was Neo-Platonism. This philosophy, purporting to be a continuation of the system of Plato, was really an outgrowth of the doctrines of the Neo-Pythagoreans and of Philo Judaeus.[10] The first of its basic teachings was emanationism: everything that exists proceeds from God in a continuing stream of emanations. The initial stage in the process is the emanation of the world-soul. From this come the divine Ideas or spiritual patterns, and then the souls of particular things. The final emanation is matter. But matter has no form or quality of its own; it is simply the privation of spirit, the residue which is left after the spiritual rays from God have burned themselves out. It follows that matter is to be despised as the symbol of evil and darkness. The second major doctrine was mysticism. The soul of man was originally a part of God, but it has become separated from him through its union with matter. The highest goal of life should be mystic reunion with the divine, which can be accomplished through contemplation and through emancipation of the soul from bondage to matter. Man should be ashamed of the fact that he possesses a physical body and should seek to subjugate it in every way possible. Asceticism was therefore the third main teaching of this philosophy.

The real founder of Neo-Platonism was Plotinus, who was born in Egypt about 204 A.D. In the later years of his life he taught in Rome and won many followers among the upper classes. His princi-

Gold Medallion of Constantine I

Neo-Platonism

[10] See pp. 228–29

pal successors diluted the philosophy with more and more bizarre superstitions. In spite of its anti-intellectual viewpoint and its utter indifference to the state, Neo-Platonism became so popular in Rome in the third and fourth centuries A.D. that it almost completely supplanted Stoicism. No fact could have expressed more eloquently the extent of the social and intellectual decline that the Roman nation had experienced.

Plotinus

10. DECAY AND DECLINE

In 476 A.D. the last of the emperors in the West, the insignificant Romulus Augustulus, was deposed, and a barbarian chieftain assumed the title of King of Rome. Though this event is commonly taken to have marked the end of Roman history, it was really only the final incident in a long process of disintegration. The fall of Rome did not occur with dramatic suddenness, but extended over a period of approximately two centuries. A large part of the civilization was already dead before the Empire collapsed. Indeed, for all practical purposes the pagan culture of Rome from the middle of the third century on could be considered as belonging to a dark age.

The decline and fall of Rome

More has been written on the fall of Rome than on the death of any other civilization. The theories offered to account for the tragedy have been many and various. Moralist historians have found the explanation in the evidences of lechery unearthed at Pompeii or revealed in the satires of Juvenal and Martial. They overlook the fact, however, that nearly all of this evidence comes from the early Principate, and that in the centuries preceding the collapse of the Empire, morality became more austere through the influence of ascetic religions. Historians of a sociological bent have attributed the downfall to a declining birth rate. But there is little to indicate that Rome could have been saved by greater numbers. The Athenian civilization reached the height of its glory during the very centuries when growth of population was most strictly limited.

Alleged causes of the decline

If there was one primary factor which operated more than others to accomplish the downfall of Roman civilization, it was probably imperialism. Nearly all of the troubles that beset the country were traceable in some measure to the conquest of a great empire. It was this which was largely responsible for the creation of the city mob, for the growth of slavery, for the strife between classes and the widespread political corruption. It was also imperialism that was partly responsible for the barbarian invasions, for the exhaustion of the resources of the state to maintain a huge military machine, and for the influx of alien ideas which the Romans could not readily assimilate. The idea that Rome became a civilized nation as a result of her conquests is undoubtedly a fallacy. Instead, her repeated victories caused her ruling population to become greedy and domineering. It is true that she appropriated much of the Hellenistic culture after her conquest of the Near East; but the really valuable elements

Actual causes: (1) imperialism

271

The Arch of Titus

of this culture would eventually have been acquired anyway through the normal expansion of trade, while the evil consequences of domination of vast areas by force would have been avoided.

Another important cause, closely related to imperialism, deserves analysis: namely, the revolution in economic and social conditions that swept over Italy in the third and fourth centuries A.D. This revolution, which differed radically from the one that had occupied the third and second centuries B.C., had the following features: (1) the disappearance of money from circulation and the return to a natural economy; (2) the decline of industry and commerce; (3) the growth of serfdom and the rise of an extralegal feudalism; (4) the extension of government control over a large portion of the economic sphere; and (5) the transition from a regime of individual initiative to a regime of hereditary status. The primary cause of this revolution seems to have been the unfavorable balance of trade that Italy suffered in her commerce with the provinces. In order to check the withdrawal of precious metals from the country, the government, instead of encouraging manufactures for export, resorted to the hazardous expedient of debasing the coinage. Nero began the practice, and his successors continued it until the proportion of baser metal in the Roman coins had increased to 98.5 per cent. The inevitable result was disappearance of money from circulation. Commerce could no longer be carried on, salaries had to be paid in food and clothing, and taxes collected in produce. The scarcity of money in turn led to a decline in production, until the government intervened with a series of decrees binding peasants to the soil and compelling every townsman to follow the occupation of his father. The great landlords, now that they had control over a body of serfs,

(2) revolution in economic and social conditions

272

entrenched themselves on their estates, defied the central government, and ruled as feudal magnates. So close were the peasants to the margin of starvation that some of them sold their newborn children or gave them up for adoption in order to escape from the burden of supporting them.

No one can present an exhaustive list of causes of Rome's decline. Among others of at least minor significance were the following: (1) the unjust policy of taxation, which rested most heavily on the business and farming classes and resulted in the discouragement of productive enterprise; (2) the social stigma attached to work, resulting in the deliberate choice by thousands of the debasing relationship of clientage in preference to useful labor; (3) exhaustion of the soil, resulting in part from unscientific farming and in part from the attempt of too many people to make a living from the land; and (4) the disastrous plagues of Asiatic origin which broke out in 166 and 252 A.D., resulting in depopulating whole sections of Italy and thereby opening the way for barbarian incursions. To the last of these causes should be appended the fact that as lands along the low-lying coast were withdrawn from cultivation because of the competition of grain from the provinces, malaria spread. The effect of this disease in undermining the vigor of the Italian population is impossible to estimate, but it must have been considerable.

11. THE ROMAN HERITAGE

It is tempting to believe that the modern world owes a vast debt to the Romans: first of all, because Rome is nearer to us in time than any of the other civilizations of antiquity; and secondly, because Rome seems to bear such a close kinship to the modern temper. The resemblances between Roman history and the history of Great Britain or the United States in the nineteenth and twentieth centuries have often been noted. The Roman economic evolution progressed all the way from a simple agrarianism to a complex urban system with problems of unemployment, monopoly, gross disparities of wealth, and financial crises. The Roman Empire, in common with the British and the American, was founded upon conquest and upon visions of Manifest Destiny. It must not be forgotten, however, that the heritage of Rome was an ancient heritage and that consequently, the similarities between the Roman and modern civilizations are not so important as they seem. As we have noted already, the Romans disdained industrial activities, and they were incredibly naïve in matters of science. Neither did they have any idea of the modern national state; the provinces were mere appendages, not integral parts of a body politic. It was largely for this reason that the Romans never developed an adequate system of representative government. Finally, the Roman conception of religion was vastly different from our own. Their system of worship, like that of the Greeks, was external and mechanical, not inward or spiritual in any

The Forum, the Civic Center of Ancient Rome. In addition to public squares, the Forum included triumphal arches, magnificent temples, and government buildings. In the foreground is the Temple of Saturn. Behind it is the Temple of Antoninus and Faustina. The three columns at the extreme right are what is left of the Temple of Castor and Pollux, and in the farthest background is the arch of Titus.

sense. What Christians consider the highest ideal of piety—an emotional attitude of love for the divine—the Romans regarded as gross superstition.

Nevertheless, the civilization of Rome was not without a definite influence upon later cultures. The form, if not the spirit, of Roman architecture was preserved in the ecclesiastical architecture of the Middle Ages and survives to this day in the design of most of our government buildings. The sculpture of the Augustan Age also lives on in the equestrian statues, the memorial arches and columns, and in the portraits in stone of statesmen and generals that adorn our boulevards and parks. Although subjected to new interpretations, the law of the great jurists became an important part of the Code of Justinian and was thus handed down to the later Middle Ages. Modern lawyers and especially American judges frequently cite maxims originally invented by Gaius or Ulpian. Further, the legal systems of nearly all Continental European countries today incorporate much of the Roman law. This law was one of the grandest of the Romans' achievements and reflected their genius for governing a vast and diverse empire. It should not be forgotten either that Roman literary achievements furnished much of the inspiration for the revival of learning that spread over Europe in the twelfth century and reached its zenith in the Renaissance. Nor should the debt of the Western world to Rome for the transmission of Greek culture be overlooked. Perhaps not so well known is the fact that the organization of the Catholic Church, to say nothing of part of its ritual, was adapted from the structure of the Roman state and the complex of the Roman religion. For example, the Pope still bears the title of Supreme Pontiff (*Pontifex Maximus*), which was used to designate the authority of the emperor as head of the civic religion. But the most important element in the Roman influence has probably been the idea of the absolute authority of the state. In the judgment of nearly all Romans, with the exception of philosophers such as Cicero and Seneca, the state was legally omnipotent. However much the Roman may have detested tyranny, it was really only *personal* tyranny that he feared; the despotism of the Senate as the organ of popular sovereignty was perfectly proper. This conception survives to our own day in the popular conviction that the state can do no wrong, and especially in the doctrines of absolutist political philosophers that the individual has no rights except those which the state confers upon him.

One other political conception, emanating from the Romans, has had lasting significance. This is the conception of a world empire established and maintained by a single people by virtue of its martial prowess and its superior civilization. The Romans brought to a temporary end the regime of local independence that had prevailed during most of previous history except during the brief rule of the Hellenistic empires. Under the *Pax Romana* none of the smaller states was really master of its own fate. All were mere appendages of Rome, in theory if not in actuality. They had not chosen this fate for themselves but had been obliged to accept it because of the overwhelming power of their mighty neighbor. As a consequence, the Mediterranean Sea, which washed the shores of most of what was then the civilized Western world, had become a Roman lake. This same *Pax Romana* provided much of the inspiration for the *Pax Britannica* of the nineteenth century. Controlling a population amounting to one-fourth of the world's total and maintaining a navy equal in strength to the combined navies of any two other powers, Great Britain molded the destinies of most of the Western world. In this way she succeeded in preventing major wars and in acquiring cultural and economic supremacy. At the end of the nineteenth century many Americans also fell under the spell of the *Pax Romana*. Politicians and propagandists such as Albert J. Beveridge, William Allen White, and Theodore Roosevelt proclaimed it the mission of the American people to become the "master organizers" of the world, to enforce peace, and to advance the cause of human welfare. They insisted that their country had been given a divine appointment as "trustee of the civilization of the world." [11]

The Roman conception of a world empire

[11] For an extended discussion of this subject see E. M. Burns, *The American Idea of Mission*, pp. 206–10.

SELECTED READINGS

· Items so designated are available in paperbound editions.

POLITICAL HISTORY

· Adcock, F. E., *Roman Political Ideas and Practice*, Ann Arbor, 1964 (University of Michigan).

  Bloch, Raymond, *The Origins of Rome*, New York, 1960.

  Boak, A. E. R., *A History of Rome to 565 A.D.*, New York, 1929. Clear and concise.

· Cowell, F. R., *Cicero and the Roman Republic*, New York, 1948 (Penguin). A good account of the fall of the Republic.

· Haywood, R. M., *The Myth of Rome's Fall*, New York, 1962 (Apollo).

· Katz, Solomon, *The Decline of Rome*, Ithaca, 1955 (Cornell).

· Mommsen, Theodor, *The History of Rome*, Chicago, 1957 (Meridian, Wisdom Library). A reprint of a great masterpiece.

· Scullard, H. S., *From the Gracchi to Nero*, New York, 1959 (Barnes & Noble).

· Starr, C. G., *The Emergence of Rome*, Ithaca, 1953 (Cornell).

· Syme, Ronald, *The Roman Revolution*, New York, 1939 (Oxford, 1960).

· Warmington, B. H., *Carthage*, Baltimore, 1965 (Penguin).

CULTURAL AND SOCIAL HISTORY

  Arnold, E. V., *Roman Stoicism*, New York, 1911.

  Badian, Ernst, *Roman Imperialism in the Late Republic*, Oxford, 1967.

  Bailey, Cyril, ed., *The Legacy of Rome*, New York, 1924.

  Balston, J. P. V. D., *Life and Leisure in Ancient Rome*, New York, 1969.

· Carceopino, Jerome, *Daily Life in Ancient Rome*, New Haven, 1960 (Yale University Press).

· Clagett, Marshall, *Greek Science in Antiquity*, New York, 1963 (Collier). Includes developments in late antiquity.

· Dill, Samuel, *Roman Society from Nero to Marcus Aurelius*, New York, 1905 (Meridian). Old but still highly regarded.

· Duff, J. W., *A Literary History of Rome in the Golden Age*, New York, 1964 (Barnes & Noble).

· ———, *A Literary History of Rome in the Silver Age*, New York, 1960 (Barnes & Noble, 1964).

  Earl, Donald, *The Moral and Political Tradition of Rome*, Ithaca, 1967.

· Fowler, W. W., *Social Life at Rome in the Age of Cicero*, New York, 1915 (St. Martin's Library).

  ———, *The Religious Experience of the Roman People*, London, 1911.

  Frank, Tenney, *Economic History of Rome*, Baltimore, 1927. Perhaps the best economic history.

· Hamilton, Edith, *The Roman Way*, New York, 1932 (Norton Library).

· Laistner, M. L. W., *The Greater Roman Historians*, Berkeley, 1947 (University of California, 1963).

· Lot, Ferdinand, *The End of the Ancient World*, New York, 1931 (Torchbook).

· Mattingly, Harold, *Christianity in the Roman Empire*, New York, 1967 (Norton Library).

· ———, *The Man in the Roman Street*, New York, 1947 (Norton Library).

  Rostovtzev, M. I., *Social and Economic History of the Roman Empire*, New York, 1957, 2 vols. Has become almost a classic.

276 Scullard, H. H., *The Etruscan Cities and Rome*, Ithaca, 1967.

· Starr, C. G., *Civilization and the Caesars*, New York, 1954 (Norton Library).
Westermann, W. L., *The Slave Systems of Greek and Roman Antiquity*, Philadelphia, 1955.
· Wheeler, Mortimer, *The Art of Rome*, New York, 1964 (Praeger).
White, Lynn T., Jr., ed., *Transformation of the Roman World*, Berkeley, 1966.

SOURCE MATERIALS

Translations of Roman authors are available in the appropriate volumes of the Loeb Classical Library.

See also:

Lewis, Naphtali, and Reinhold, M., *Roman Civilization*, New York, 1955, 2 vols.

CHAPTER **11**

The Far East and Africa in Transition

(*ca.* 200 B.C.-900 A.D.)

> If brave and ambitious men have sincere understanding and aware-
> ness; if they fear and heed the warnings of disaster and use tran-
> scendent vision and profound judgment; if they . . . rid them-
> selves of the blind notion that the mandate of Heaven can be
> pursued like a deer in chase and realize that the sacred vessel of
> rule must be given from on high; . . . then will fortune and bless-
> ing flow to their sons and grandsons, and the rewards of Heaven
> will be with them to the end of their days.
> —Pan Piao, *History of the Former Han Dynasty*

During the period when the Greco-Roman classical civilization was
being extended throughout the Mediterranean world under the auspices of the Roman Empire, a high stage of cultural development had
been reached in both India and China. The disturbances that characterized the downfall of the Roman Empire in the West had their parallels in Asia too. However, the invasions and political upheavals in
the Far East did not produce the same drastic changes as those in the
West. The structure of society continued without serious modification in India and China, and the cultures of these two countries attained a brilliant peak while Europe was experiencing its Dark Ages.
In India a combination of commerical prosperity—which encouraged the growth of large cities—and the religious enthusiasm
accompanying the spread of Buddhism stimulated an outpouring of
artistic talent. During this period Indian influence extended far beyond the borders of the country. Buddhism was planted in Central
Asia and from there carried to China, Korea, and Japan. Indian
colonization led to the introduction of both Buddhism and Hinduism, together with their art and literature, in Southeast Asia and the
Malay Archipelago (which is still called Indonesia). China, while
importing a major religion from India, showed much greater success

*Contrasts of
East and West*

279

in achieving political unification and an effective administrative system. So great was the prestige of imperial China that its culture was studied and eagerly assimilated by the Japanese in the sixth and succeeding centuries A.D. At the same time the West received some impact from the civilizations of Asia by way of the Hellenistic and imperial Roman commercial centers and, later, through the initiative of the Arabs.

I. THE FLOWERING OF HINDU CIVILIZATION

The Maurya Dynasty, under the energetic and devout King Asoka, had projected a common rule over the greater part of India. Upon the overthrow of this dynasty early in the second century B.C., the empire quickly fell apart, leaving India in a condition of political discord. For the next several hundred years the most powerful kingdoms were centered not in the Indo-Gangetic plain but in the Deccan, where a succession of dynasties contended with one another, and some of them emerged as major states with extensive territories and resources. It is clear that by this time the arts of civilization were well advanced in southern India, even though the most distinctive historic influences—Vedic literature and philosophy, the traditional religious and social concepts of Hinduism, and the creative force of Buddhism—had originated in the north. Moreover, the invasions which began to trouble northern India did not penetrate into the Deccan. The states of the Deccan carried on commercial intercourse with neighboring and even distant areas but were not seriously threatened with hostile assaults from foreign powers. On the contrary, their merchants and missionaries were ensuring the cultural ascendancy of India over Southeast Asia.

After a period of domination by nomadic tribes from Turkestan, the political initiative in India was recovered by a native house which established a highly effective rule and was even more remarkable for its advancement of culture. The Gupta Dynasty, as it was called, governed most of northern India during the fourth and fifth centuries A.D. The dynasty's founder, Chandragupta I, was probably not descended from the Chandragupta who had instituted the Maurya Dynasty after the death of Alexander the Great, but the Guptas ruled from the same capital—Pataliputra (Patna) on the Ganges—and also revived some of the principles of the renowned King Asoka. The climax of the Gupta period came in the reign of Vikramaditya ("Sun of Power"), 375–413 A.D., which inaugurated a golden age not unworthy of comparison with Athens' Golden Age in the days of Pericles. Valuable information on conditions in northern India at this time has been preserved in the brief account written by a Chinese pilgrim, Fa Hsien, who spent six years in the realm of Vikramaditya. Buddhism had already spread into China, and the monk Fa Hsien undertook his hazardous journey to acquire sacred texts and first-hand knowledge of the religion in the land of its birth. His comments, however, were not restricted to religious matters, and because he was an intelligent and civilized foreigner, his observations may be taken as objective and generally reliable. The travels of Fa Hsien in themselves represent no mean undertaking. He made his way on foot across Sinkiang and the mountain passes, taking six years to reach India (399–405 A.D.). Here he taught himself the Sanskrit language, procured texts, drawings, and relics at the Gupta capital, and then returned to his native land by sea, spending two years in Ceylon en route and also visiting Java on the voyage. Altogether, during the fifteen years of his pilgrimage he traversed a distance of some 8000 miles.

According to Fa Hsien's testimony, Buddhism was flourishing in India, especially in the Gupta empire, but all the Hindu cults were tolerated and the rivalry among the different religions was not embittered by persecution. Evidently the impact of Buddhism and the traditions of Asoka had stimulated the growth of humane sentiments, given practical expression in public hospitals, rest houses, and other charitable institutions receiving state support. Fa Hsien asserted that the Indians scrupulously refrained from the use of liquor and were vegetarians to such an extent that they slaughtered no living creatures—undoubtedly a pious exaggeration. Apparently, also, the caste system had not become utterly rigid, probably because Buddhism was still vigorous and also because segregation was impracticable in the cosmopolitan society of the thriving commercial centers. Fa Hsien, who had no reason to bestow unmerited praise (he does not even mention the name of the great king Vikramaditya), described the government as just and beneficent. The roads, he indicated, were well maintained, brigandage was rare, taxes were relatively light, and capital punishment was unknown. He testified to a generally high level of prosperity, social contentment, and intellectual vitality at a time when the nations of Western Europe were sinking into a state of semibarbarism.

Another invasion of India destroyed the Gupta power and brought a period of confusion lasting for more than a century. Almost simultaneously with the formal demise of the Roman Empire in the West, a group of nomads called "White Huns" defeated the Gupta forces and made themselves masters of northern India (480 A.D.). By the early sixth century the White Huns had staked out an empire extending from Bengal in the east into Afghanistan and Central Asia. However, it was much more barbaric than its predecessors, and disrupted the splendid administrative system of the Guptas. The Huns in India were gradually absorbed by the native population, but on the northwestern borders a promising artistic movement was blighted before the Hunnish power disintegrated in accordance with the usual cycle of hastily

Culture and society under the Guptas

The overthrow of Gupta rule by Hun invaders

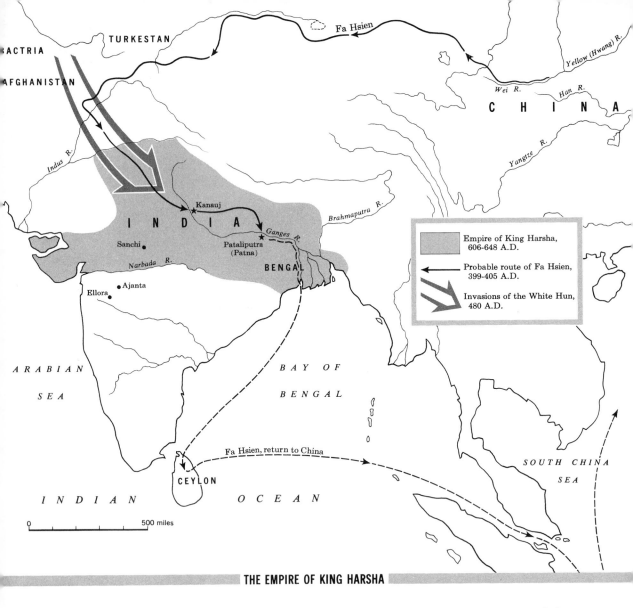

constructed nomadic states. After the Hunnish menace receded, an able government was re-established by one of the most famous rulers in Indian history, King Harsha (606–648 A.D.).

Although Harsha's state was not literally a continuation of the Gupta, it was so similar in important features that the term "Gupta" is often used to designate the civilization of northern India from the fourth to the seventh century, a period of cultural maturity despite the devastating interlude of the Hunnish invasion. King Harsha was a mighty conqueror who, with a huge army efficiently organized in divisions of infantry, cavalry, and elephants, reunited most of northern India. He was also a capable administrator, an intelligent and prudent statesman, and a generous patron of art, literature, and reli-

The reign of King Harsha (606–648 A.D.)

282

gion. His capital, Kanauj, extending four miles along the river in the central Ganges valley, was a splendid city, adorned with hundreds of temples and imposing public buildings, and enlivened with festive pageantry. As in the reign of Vikramaditya, the account of a Chinese Buddhist pilgrim throws revealing light upon Harsha's administration.

According to the narrative of this pilgrim (Hsün-tsang or Yuan Chwang) and other contemporary records, Harsha's administration was in the Gupta tradition but slightly less gentle. The state revenue was derived chiefly from taxes on the royal domains, which amounted to one-sixth of the produce of the villages and could hardly be regarded as oppressive. Harsha allotted only one-fourth of his income to administrative expenses, devoting the remainder to the rewarding of public servants, to charity, and to the promotion of education, religion, and the arts. In contrast to the mild punishments employed by the earlier Gupta regime, King Harsha inflicted such severe penalties as mutilation and death through starvation. Nevertheless, crimes of violence seem to have become more numerous. Religious toleration was still the official policy. Although Harsha is supposed to have been converted to the *Mahayana* school of Buddhism, he continued to worship the Sun and Shiva, and no attempt was made to enforce a religious orthodoxy. Despite this policy, the Brahmans were beginning to recover their ascendancy, and it was only a question of time before Buddhism, with its universalist and caste-dissolving tendencies, would be crowded out or absorbed by the cults so deeply rooted in Indian local tradition, literature, and social institutions. During the upheaval which followed the death of Harsha, this trend became more pronounced.

During the first seven or eight centuries of the Christian era, in spite of invasions and disunity, political vigor and artistic and intellectual creativity in India reached their height. This period, in which Hindu civilization attained its full maturity, ranks as a major era in the history of the world's cultures. What the Periclean Age and the Augustan Age were for the classical civilizations of the West the reigns of Vikramaditya and Harsha were for India and, to a considerable extent, for other portions of Southern Asia. Undoubtedly the development of industry and commerce helps explain the generally prosperous state of Indian society and the cultural advances. At this time, and later also, India was the center of an intercontinental market, and her merchants took the initiative in navigation on the high seas. During the first two centuries A.D. there was extensive intercourse between India and the Near East, especially with the city of Alexandria. Many products were also being exported from India to the Roman West, including jewels, ivory, tortoise shells, pepper, cinnamon and other spices, fine muslin cloth, and silks of both Indian and Chinese manufacture. In exchange the Indians imported linen, glass, copper, wines, and other items, but the

Harsha's administrative policies

The climax of Hindu culture

trade balance was so decidedly in India's favor that the Roman emperors became alarmed at the drainage of gold to the East and tried to curtail the use of silk for wearing apparel. Some of this trade was overland, but Indian merchants had from early days sailed across the Arabian Sea and up the Red Sea to Egypt. Not until the first century A.D. did Western traders discover the monsoon winds which enabled them to sail east to the Indian coast during the summer and then return when the wind direction changed in October. Traffic between the Near Eastern ports and southern India was probably even greater than with northern India. Pearls and beryls from the Deccan were especially prized, and Roman coins, testifying to a once flourishing trade, have been discovered along both the southwestern and southeastern coasts of the Indian peninsula. Apparently no obstacles were placed by the Indian rulers in the way of foreign intercourse or even against settlement by foreign traders, some of whom took up permanent residence in India. Southern India acquired small colonies of Romans, Jews, Nestorian Christians from Syria and Persia (a Syriac-speaking Christian church still exists in southwestern India), and Arabs.

Influence upon
the West

Through commercial contacts India probably exerted more influence upon the West than has been generally recognized, although much of it came somewhat later and with the Arabs as intermediaries. The Indian numerals ("Arabic"), which were not adopted by Europeans until the late Middle Ages, were perhaps known in Alexandria as early as the second century A.D. In the eighth and ninth centuries important scientific and medical treatises were translated from Sanskrit into Arabic. In addition, it is quite possible that familiarity with Indian philosophy and religion contributed a stimulus to the growth of Christian monasticism. The earliest Christian hermit-ascetics appeared in Egypt, where there was considerable knowledge of Hinduism and Buddhism, both of which religions stressed the concepts of renunciation and mystic exaltation.

Buddhist
patronage of
education

The manifold intellectual activity of this period of Indian history reflected the interests of a cosmopolitan society, the patronage of wealthy rulers, and—most strongly of all—the incentives of religious faith. High levels of scholarship were maintained both by the Brahmans and by Buddhist monks, and large libraries came into being. Particularly noteworthy were the educational foundations, for which the chief credit should be given to the Buddhists. The role of the Buddhist monks in education was comparable to that of the Christian monks of the West during the early Middle Ages, but the scope of their studies was broader because the general level of knowledge was far higher in India than in the West at this time. Some Buddhist monasteries were internationally famous centers of learning, unmatched in Europe until the rise of such universities as Paris, Montpellier, and Oxford in the late Middle Ages. One of the greatest Buddhist universities, at Nalanda in the Ganges valley (in

Ruins at Nalanda. The remains of the ancient university town, early seat of Buddhist learning.

modern Bihar), was functioning as early as the fourth or fifth century A.D. Endowed by the Gupta rulers with a substantial income, it maintained residence halls for students—with free tuition, board, lodging, and medical care for poor boys who were able to pass the entrance examinations—and had a library that occupied three buildings. Pilgrims visiting the university in the seventh century reported that 5000 students were in attendance, including some from Tibet, China, and Korea. Although Nalanda was a Buddhist foundation and provided instruction in eighteen different schools of Buddhism, its faculty also offered courses in Hindu philosophy, grammar, medicine, mathematics, and in both Vedic and contemporary literature.

While the literary output was prolific and uninhibited, it betrayed a veneration for the past in that Sanskrit—the ancient language of the Epic Age—became the universally accepted literary vehicle, in the Deccan as well as in Hindustan. Even the Buddhists felt constrained to translate their sacred texts from *Pali* (the dialect of King Asoka's day) into Sanskrit, and it was the Sanskrit versions which were carried by missionaries into Central Asia, China, Korea, and ultimately Japan. Literature of the Gupta Age, in both prose and poetry, ranged from scientific treatises and biographies to tales for popular entertainment. The latter included long romantic narratives suggestive of—and perhaps the prototype of—the *Arabian Nights;* and also "Beast Fables" comparable to those attributed to Aesop. The most impressive literary medium was the drama, which, as in Europe somewhat later, evolved out of a popular type of religious instruction and entertainment. The Sanskrit drama, in its perfected form, combined song, dance, and gesture with narrative and dialogue, and thus resembled the Western opera or cantata more

Literature: romantic narratives, fables, and drama

285

than the typical stage play. The plots, often diffuse, were usually concerned with romantic love, drew heavily upon legendary themes from the epics, and resorted to miracles whenever necessary to resolve a difficulty in the story. Although they employed pathos, the dramas were never tragedies, always ending happily. They also utilized the peculiarly artificial device of having the principal characters speak in classical Sanskrit while women and lesser figures used the less elegant dialect of ordinary conversation. Although the Sanskrit drama never provided the suspense or realism characteristic of the modern Western theater, it did attain undeniable beauty, both in descriptions of nature and in lyrical passages expressing human emotions of tenderness and anguish.

The most superb expression of the Indian creative faculties during these centuries was in art, especially architecture and sculpture, although some excellent paintings were also produced. By the Gupta era, architecture was nearing a point of perfection, as evidenced by imposing stone structures in all sections of India. As in so many other fields, the Buddhists pioneered in the development of artistic forms. The evolution of the Buddhist monasteries and temples set the pattern for practically the whole of Hindu architecture (and sculpture also). During the early centuries when *Hinayana* Buddhism was dominant, neither temples nor images of Gautama were made. Hence the first typical Buddhist monument was the *stupa,* a simple burial mound in the shape of a dome or hemisphere crowned with an umbrella—the Indian symbol of sovereignty. Inside the brick- or rock-faced mound was buried a sacred relic, usually some object associated with Gautama or with a revered Buddhist saint. The most famous *stupa* is the large one at Sanchi in the very center of India, still in an excellent state of preservation, although it was begun in Asoka's reign and substantially completed during the first century B.C. More impressive than the stone-faced mound (which has a diameter at the base of 120 feet) are the four carved gateways surrounding the *stupa.* These massive fences of stone are supported by pillars 35 feet high and, in spite of their huge proportions, are adorned with intricate carvings, both pictorial and symbolic, with a profusion of delicately formed human and animal figures. After the *stupa,* the next step in the evolution of religious architecture was the assembly hall, where monks and lay disciples gathered to honor the memory of Gautama, the "Master of the Law." These halls were commonly tunneled out of solid rock in a mountain or the side of a cliff. Their general plan was similar to that of the Roman basilica and early Christian church in that it emphasized a central passageway or nave separated from aisles on either side by round columns. Paralleling the evolution of the temple was the development of the Buddhist monastery. Like the assembly hall or temple, the monastery was often carved out of a single mass of rock, with successive stories of cells or cubicles so arranged that the structure as a whole

Buddhist Missionary. Sixth-century carving supposed to represent the first Indian Buddhist missionary to China. Buddhism had probably been introduced into China as early as the first century A.D.

The Great Stupa at Sanchi. Begun by Asoka and completed under the Andhra Dynasty (72–25 B.C.), it was originally a burial mound containing relics of the Buddha. The fully developed stupa, designed with mathematical precision, became an architectural symbol of the cosmos. The tiered mast on top of the structure represents the earth's axis penetrating the dome of heaven.

appeared to be a terraced pyramid. Devotees of the Hindu cults soon began to construct temples in imitation of the Buddhist and eventually even more elaborate.

Although some free-standing temples were erected as early as the first century A.D., for several centuries the Indians seemed to prefer the more arduous method of hewing their edifices out of the solid rock of caves and cliffs. More than 1200 rock-cut temples and monasteries were executed in various sections of India, the larger proportion being along the western coast. The two most remarkable groups of cliff excavations are located at Ajanta and Ellora, about 70 miles apart, in the northern part of what later became Hyderabad. The Ajanta caves were Buddhist sanctuaries, some of them dating from the second century B.C. and some from as late as the fifth century A.D. They include both assembly halls and monasteries, complete with stone beds, tables, water cisterns, and niches for oil reading lamps. The even more splendid caves at Ellora represent about 900 years of architectural and sculptural enterprise, extending from the fourth to the thirteenth century. The Buddhists were the first to utilize the site, but some of the caves were the work of Jains and the largest number were constructed as Hindu temples, of tremendous size and lavish design.

Temples composed of separate stone blocks, in contrast to the cave type, began to be more common in Gupta times and were typical of the most active period of Hindu temple building, between the sixth and the thirteenth centuries. The essential architectural

Rock-cut temples and monasteries

287

Entrance to the Ajanta Caves. The Gupta period (fourth to seventh centuries A.D.) constitutes the Golden Age of Indian art —in sculpture, architecture, and painting —as well as the climax of classical Sanskrit literature.

Eastern Gateway of the Great Stupa at Sanchi. The relief carvings, depicting incidents from the life of the Buddha, are remarkable for their fine detail, vitality, and naturalism.

features of these free-standing Hindu temples are (1) a base consisting of a square or rectangular chamber to house the image of the god, and (2) a lofty tower which rises from the roof of the chamber and dominates the entire edifice. The shape of the tower distinguishes the two main styles of Hindu temples. The "Dravidian" style, found only in the tropics, is identified by a terraced steeple divided into stories like a step pyramid and decidedly reminiscent of the early Buddhist rock-cut monasteries. The "Indo-Aryan" style, prevalent in northern India, has a curvilinear tower with vertical ribs which may possibly be derived from the Buddhist *stupa*.

Sculpture usually develops in close conjunction with architecture, and this was especially true in India, where so many sacred halls and chambers were literally carved out of stone. Decorative engravings, including figures in relief, were typically an integral part of the building itself. Chiseled decorations were very successfully applied to the gateways and pillars surrounding some of the early Buddhist *stupas*. The figures on the gates of the great *stupa* at Sanchi (first century B.C.) are particularly fine examples. Although they were intended to commemorate events of sacred tradition and embody pious symbolism, they are invested with vigor, freshness, and spontaneity, suggesting an uninhibited delight in the natural world rather than a brooding melancholy. Meanwhile a significant school of sculpture was arising in northwestern India and beyond the borders in Afghanistan and Bactria. The initial stimulus undoubtedly was Greek or Hellenistic, but Persian and other influences played a part, and the school developed its own original characteristics with Buddhist concepts predominant. It was in this region that the figure of Gautama was delineated for the first time, and relief sculptures depicted the legendary incidents of his life from infancy to Enlightenment. The large statues of the Buddha clearly revealed Greek influence at the beginning: the head resembled an Apollo or Zeus and the garment was draped like a toga rather than a monk's robe. However, there was a gradual approach toward the conventional form—in cross-legged posture and an attitude of benign repose—which eventually came to represent the Buddha all over the Far East. This Greco-Buddhist school of sculpture continued to flourish in the border regions of Central Asia, acquiring a more and more hearty realism, until it was snuffed out by the Hun invasions in the early sixth century.

During the Gupta Age, Indian sculpture largely emancipated itself from foreign influences and assumed characteristics peculiarly expressive of Indian ideals. The treatment of the human form was handled with a subtle delicacy, conveying a sense both of rhythmic movement and tranquillity. Garments on the figures were shown as almost transparent or suggested only in faint outline so that the effect is that of nudity, although chaste rather than voluptuous. The harmonious proportions and graceful curves of the limbs were derived from a study of plant forms as well as from human anatomy. Thus Gupta art, particularly as exemplified in the statues of Buddha, was idealistic and spiritual rather than realistic.

The richest creations of the Hindu artistic genius are to be found in the relief sculpture and fresco paintings executed in the rock-cut temples upon which so much energy was expended during the period corresponding to the Classical and Medieval ages of the West. The Buddhist caves at Ajanta contain the most important surviving collection of wall paintings. After almost 2000 years they are still magnificent, although exposure to the air since the opening of the caves in the early nineteenth century has darkened the colors. Religious in inspiration, they are at the same time spontaneous and unrestrained, skillfully combining the naturalism of the early Buddhist *stupa* carvings with a poetic mysticism. The paintings proclaim an unabashed delight in physical beauty and seem to suggest the conviction that the physical and spiritual aspects of experience can be brought into perfect accord, just as some of the art of the Italian Renaissance attempted to fuse the pagan ideal of joyous living with the Christian ideal of renunciation. In the Hindu temples, which increased in number from the seventh century on as Buddhism began to decline, decoration was usually in sculpture rather than painting. The relief sculptures in the Hindu cave-temples at Ellora have never been surpassed in India and rank among the supreme masterpieces of the world's art. In these carvings not only the gods but a galaxy of figures and dramatic episodes out of India's historic and legendary past seem to come alive. Many scenes are boldly realistic, but the Hindu tendency toward abstraction is also evident in the practice of depicting gods with several

Yakshi or "Tree Spirit." A female figure derived from an early fertility cult but here symbolizing the transition from the sensuous world of illusion to the world of the spirit.

289

Relief Sculpture in the Hindu Cave Temple at Ellora, Hyderabad (eighth century A.D.). The central figures are the god Shiva and his consort Parvati.

pairs of arms or several faces to signify their separate attributes. The themes portrayed range from voluptuous ecstasy and heroic struggle to attitudes of piety and mystic contemplation.

The spread of Indian culture

While the Indian communities were bringing their civilization to a point of refinement, they were also implanting it among various other peoples of Southeast Asia. Indian navigators and merchants were active in the eastern waters of the Indian Ocean as well as in the Arabian Sea to the west and apparently led the world in maritime enterprise during this period. Some of the Indian states maintained navies and had a Board of Shipping as a governmental department. They not only promoted commerce but chartered companies of merchants, giving them trade monopolies in certain areas and authority to establish colonies. During the early centuries A.D. Indian colonies were planted in the Malay Peninsula, Annam (eastern Indochina), Java, Sumatra, and many other islands of the Malay Archipelago. Between the fifth and tenth centuries an empire ruled by a Buddhist dynasty and possessing formidable naval strength was based on the island of Sumatra. It also controlled western Java, extended into the Malay Peninsula, sent colonists to Borneo and from thence to the Philippine Islands. It dominated the Strait of Malacca and effectively policed the waters of this area against piracy. Although weakened by a long struggle with one of the Hindu mainland states, the empire (known as the Srivijaya) remained intact until the fourteenth century. Indian influence was extensive in the peninsula of Indochina—in the Cham state on the southeastern coast (later absorbed into the Annamese empire), in the Cambodian kingdoms of the lower Mekong valley, and among the Thais (Siamese) to the northwest.

The political vicissitudes of these various Eastern states were too complex to be enumerated here, but the entire region long remained an outpost of Indian culture. Sanskrit literature was introduced,

290

along with Buddhism and the leading cults of Hinduism. Art and architecture, originating in Indian prototypes, were assiduously cultivated and attained considerable individuality. During the eighth and ninth centuries the Srivijaya empire in Sumatra and Java was perhaps the foremost center of Buddhist art. A colossal *stupa* in central Java, dating from the late eighth century, is considered by some the greatest Buddhist monument in the world. Actually, although crowned with a *stupa*, this structure is a whole mountaintop carved into nine stone terraces, with staircases, covered gateways, balustrades, and four galleries containing 1500 sculptured panels. In the ninth century, building on an ambitious scale was in progress in the Cambodian empire established by the Khmers, a native people who wielded dominion over a large part of Indochina between the ninth and the fourteenth centuries, and who responded energetically to the stimulus of Indian cultural contacts. Their capital city, Angkor (recovered from the jungle by French archaeologists in the twentieth century), was of almost incredible magnificence in its heyday. Among several huge temples the most imposing was that of Angkor Wat, about a mile south of the capital, built during the twelfth century and said to be the largest work of its kind in the world, surpassing in mass even Luxor and Karnak of ancient Egypt. Angkor Wat was dedicated to the Hindu god Vishnu and was also designed as a tomb for the emperor, who was deified after his death and identified in some way with Vishnu. The storied carvings, however, honored various Hindu deities, warned sinners of the numerous hells awaiting the wicked, celebrated the king's earthly conquests, and depicted scenes from the classic Sanskrit epics of India. While Hindu influence was ascendant in Cambodia, Buddhism was also a potent

Ruins of Cham Civilization (South Vietnam). The influence of Indian architecture is readily apparent.

Wall Carvings at Angkor Wat. The walls of this twelfth century monument to the God Vishnu are covered with bas reliefs of celestial dancers, parading kings, and marching armies.

force there. Khmer statues of Buddha are distinguished by the "smile of Angkor"—a countenance expressing the height of benevolence and the supreme peace associated with the attainment of an inner state of enlightenment or *nirvana*.

Flourishing culture of "Greater India" During the Middle Ages the whole region surrounding the Bay of Bengal, while comprising separate political units, was dominated by Indian culture, imparted through commerical contacts and manifest in the fields of religion, literature, and art. The creative activity in this "Greater India" was not inferior to that of the motherland. In some ways it was even bolder, more vigorous and experimental, and it continued to flourish after the onslaught of fanatical Moslem conquerors from Afghanistan had brought a decay in India. However, a decline finally overtook the Buddhist and Hindu civilizations of Southeast Asia as the result of exhausting struggles among the competing states, pressure from China to the north, and—more decisive—the impact of Arab and other Moslem adventurers who traded, proselytized, and conquered successfully in this area during the fourteenth, fifteenth, and sixteenth centuries.

2. THE TERRITORIAL, POLITICAL, AND CULTURAL GROWTH OF CHINA

The Ch'in Dynasty, inaugurated after the overthrow of the Chou, lasted only fourteen years (221–207 B.C.), but it was one of the most important in Chinese history because it carried out a drastic reorganization of the government with permanent effects upon the character of the state. The founder of the dynasty, who assumed the title of "First Emperor" (Shih Huang Ti), was a man of iron will and administrative genius. He did away with the rival kingdoms, divided the country into provinces, and instituted an elaborate bureaucracy directly responsible to himself. The centralized administration and effective military organization that had been carefully cultivated in the state of Ch'in was now applied to all of China, thus effecting a momentous break with the past. The feudal institutions of 500 years' standing were almost completely extinguished and the government was brought into direct contact with the people. Determined to eliminate any competition for authority, the emperor's chief minister forbade the philosophic schools to continue their discussions and commanded their writings to be destroyed. His order for the burning of the books was a sweeping one, carrying the death penalty for disobedience, although copies of the forbidden works were locked up in the imperial library. Some Taoist writings were exempted from the proscription because the emperor was attracted by their reputed magic-working formulas. He was particularly anxious to root out the Confucianist and Mohist teachings because they emphasized moral restraints upon the ruler and his dependence upon the advice of learned counselors.

Every aspect of Shih Huang Ti's reign reveals tremendous force of personality and a ruthless determination. He carried out conquests in all directions. In the south he not only annexed regions but built canals, one of which linked the Yangtze to the West River (of

The Ch'in Dynasty (221–207 B.C.)

Shih Huang Ti, "First Emperor"

The Great Wall of China at Nankow Pass. The Wall was erected about 221–207 B.C. for defense against Northern invaders.

Ancient Irrigation Canal. Still in use, this is part of one of the oldest and most elaborate irrigation systems in the world.

which Canton is the principal port). While raising large armies by conscription he disarmed the bulk of the Chinese people as a precautionary measure. With forced labor he executed an ambitious building program that included a network of military roads radiating from his capital. His most impressive engineering project was to complete and join together the series of fortifications in the north, by which he created the Great Wall of China, reaching from the seacoast some 1400 miles inland. At his capital (near Sian, the site of the old Western Chou capital) he had constructed a sumptuous palace measuring 2500 by 500 feet and capable of accommodating 10,000 people. In addition to such undertakings he and his ministers found time to standardize weights, measures, and even the axle length of carts, and—still more important—to unify the style of writing in China, with the result that communication among the various sections was made easy in spite of the diversity of spoken dialects. In his administrative policies the First Emperor probably borrowed some features from the Persian monarchs and from the Indian ruler Chandragupta Maurya. That he made a great impression not only upon the Chinese but upon foreign powers is illustrated by the fact that his country came to be known in other lands as "China"—after the name of his dynasty. This indomitable monarch's chief weakness was his addiction to superstitious fancies. He undertook several journeys in search of the elixir of immortality and died on one of these expeditions. Three years later his dynasty ended in a round of court conspiracies and assassinations, and his great palace was burned to the ground.

Social reforms and totalitarian methods of Shih Huang Ti

The Ch'in emperor had aimed at a social as well as political reconstruction, and although this was a more difficult undertaking it succeeded in part. On the whole his policy was to encourage and promote agriculture above commerce, assisting the farmers and holding the merchant class in check. Officially he abolished serfdom, decreeing that the peasants should be owners of the lands they worked. It is doubtful, however, that their lot was actually much better than before. Not only were there great differences between the small and the large proprietors, but the poor peasants became burdened with debts contracted with the merchants and moneylenders, the very group the government had intended to restrain. The

Ch'in ruler exacted heavy taxes of various sorts, including a poll tax, and conscripted men for military and labor service with a callous disregard for human suffering. Thus, while the state was concerning itself more directly and actively than ever before with the welfare of the whole community, it reduced the dignity and freedom of the individual to a minimum. Large numbers of the population were forcibly moved from one region to another and many were made slaves of the state. People's actions and, as far as possible, their thoughts also were controlled by the government. The Ch'in rule carried into practice the Legalist doctrines of coercion, punishment, and fear, and bore a striking resemblance to the European totalitarian regimes of the twentieth century.

The overthrow of the Ch'in Dynasty was followed soon afterward by the establishment of the Han, founded by a military adventurer who had risen from the ranks. In the course of Chinese history many dynasties came and went—some very brief and some with only a local jurisdiction—but most of them tended to follow a similar course and met with a similar fate. From time to time a new ruling house was inaugurated by force or usurpation, sometimes by an alien or by a leader of lowly birth (the founder of the Han Dynasty was said to have come from a poor peasant family). If he could vindicate his authority and maintain order, he was looked upon as a legitimate ruler entitled to all the imperial dignities, regardless of the previous status of his family. To be accepted, however, the dynasty had to promote general prosperity as well as defend the country and suppress internal strife. The typical dynastic cycle of China illustrates not only the rise and fall of successive ruling families but also the close relationship between the condition of society and the durability of a political regime. Usually during the early years of a dynasty vigorous and efficient rule was accompanied by internal peace, prosperity, and an increase in population. When the imperial court and its officers became venal and corrupt, neglected administrative problems, and demanded exorbitant taxes, domestic upheaval ensued, frequently joined to the threat of attack from without. If the dynasty failed to resolve the crisis, it went down in bloodshed, and a new firm hand seized control, cleared away the debris, and began the process all over again under a new dynastic name. The rise and fall of the Han Dynasty (206 B.C.–220 A.D.) illustrates the general pattern which was typical of China's successive political episodes. At the same time the Han Dynasty marks one of the most splendid periods in Chinese history, characterized by cultural progress and by the development of a form of government so satisfactory that its essential features remained unchanged—except for temporary interruptions—until the present century.

The Han government was a centralized bureaucracy but conducted with some regard for local differences and with deference to

The Han Dynasty (206 B.C.–220 A.D.)

295

Centralized
government

ancient traditions. Certain aspects of feudalism were reintroduced as the first Han emperor granted estates in the form of fiefs to his relatives and other prominent figures. However, the danger of feudal principalities becoming powerful and independent, as had happened in Chou times, was circumvented by a decree requiring the estates of nobles to be divided among the heirs instead of passing intact to the eldest son. Chinese society was still far from being equalitarian, but its aristocratic structure had been severely jolted. The imperial administration cut across class lines, and there was little danger that it would ever again be constituted on feudal principles. The power of the old Chou states was broken beyond recovery. Obviously, the Han rulers were profiting from and continuing the work begun by the hated house of Ch'in, although they softened the harshest features of the Ch'in regime. Whereas the Ch'in emperor had antagonized the class of scholars, the Han ruler sought their favor and support and instructed his officials to recommend to the public service young men of ability irrespective of birth. The Confucianists profited most from the government's policy of toleration toward the philosophical schools. Some of their books had escaped the flames, and the scholars had long memories. Under the patronage of the emperor, Confucianist teachings were reinterpreted, with more emphasis upon the supremacy of the central authority than Confucius had probably intended. Thus, instead of serving as a stumbling block, they assisted in the creation of an efficient imperial government.

The Han rule, while energetic, efficient, and relatively enlightened, was sufficiently severe. As under the Ch'in, ambitious public works of reclamation and canal- and road-building entailed enormous labor, much of which was performed by slaves. Taxes were high, the salt and iron industries were made state monopolies, and the currency was debased to yield a profit to the government at the expense of the people. At the same time, the emperor attempted to regulate prices, not merely for the protection of the poorer consumers but to divert the middleman's profit into the imperial coffers. The government also participated in the rapidly expanding foreign commerce of the empire.

The severity of
Han rule

As under most strong dynasties, efforts were directed to expanding the territorial frontiers. The Huns after many campaigns were forced to acknowledge Han suzerainty and compelled to furnish tribute and military support. Chinese control was established over much of Central Asia, including not only the Tarim basin of Sinkiang but parts of Turkestan beyond the mountains. Southern Manchuria and northern Korea were annexed, and Chinese settlers and culture penetrated this area. The provinces south of the Yangtze were secured and also northeastern Indochina (Tonkin). Both in territorial extent and in power, China under the Han was almost equal to the contemporary Roman Empire. Nor was China isolated

Expansion of the
empire

from other civilized areas. Her trade connections were far-reaching, especially by the caravan routes which traversed Sinkiang and Turkestan. The Chinese had also begun to venture on the high seas, although ocean traffic was conducted chiefly by Indian navigators who sailed to the South China Sea and the Gulf of Tonkin. Chinese merchants exchanged products not only with India and Ceylon, but also with Japan, Persia, Arabia, Syria, and—indirectly—with Rome. The trade balance was generally favorable to China because of the high price commanded by her leading export, silk, frequently paid for in gold or precious stones.

The Han Dynasty reached its climax in the latter half of the second century B.C., under the able leadership of an emperor who ruled for more than fifty years (Han Wu Ti, 140–87 B.C.). At the opening of the first century A.D. a usurper named Wang Mang seized the throne and attempted to carry out radical reforms. If he had succeeded in realizing his program, the character of Chinese society would have been revolutionized. Wang Mang decreed the nationalization of all land so that it could be divided into equal plots and given to the peasant cultivators. He fixed prices and anticipated the agricultural-assistance policies of modern Western nations by having the state enter directly into the commodity market, buying up surpluses and holding them to sell during periods of scarcity. He also arranged government loans at low rates of interest to help struggling farmers. Even more startling was his decision to abolish slavery, although he found it impossible to enforce this measure and substituted in its place a special tax upon slave owners. His humanitarian projects on behalf of the forgotten men of toil earned for Wang the unrelenting antagonism of merchants and wealthy property owners. Revolts broke out against him; he was assassinated and his program scrapped (23 A.D.). The Han family recovered the throne and retained it for two more centuries—a period known as

Crisis and decay of the Han Dynasty

Bronze Rain Drum. Han Dynasty. Note the frogs on the circumference.

the Later or Eastern Han because the capital was moved eastward to the site of Honan. The Later Han period exhibited the typical symptoms of decay at court and within the ruling house, although the administrative system remained intact and China's reputation in foreign parts was upheld by skillful diplomacy and force of arms. The dynasty crumbled as rebellions broke out and power passed into the hands of warlords, one of whom deposed the Han emperor in 220 A.D.

For almost four centuries after the collapse of the Han Dynasty, China was in a state of turbulence and upheaval. The country was divided, warfare was frequent, and it seemed that all the gains of the previous era were in jeopardy. Although the dates are not identical, this period of political disunity in China is comparable to the time of confusion which Europe experienced after the fall of the Roman Empire in the West. As in Europe during the Early Middle Ages, the central government was weak or nonexistent; barbarian invasions affected a wide area; and, just as Christianity became rooted among the Latin and Germanic peoples of the West, a new otherworldly religion—Buddhism—made tremendous headway in China. Aside from these parallels, however, China's period of disunion was very different from the Early Middle Ages in Europe. In China there was no appreciable decline in commerce or in city life, nor was there a serious modification of culture and institutions. The absence of a strong central authority was the only real disadvantage from which the country suffered, and this defect could be remedied by reviving the administrative machinery which had been temporarily disrupted. The Han state had been a practical and effective expression of Chinese experience, utilizing existing social and economic institutions and emphasizing ancient traditions. Consequently, even a long period of semi-anarchy could not destroy China's civilization. This period, dismal as it was, gave evidence of the toughness of Chinese society and culture, embodied in the patriarchal family, the village organization, and the sturdy enterprise of farmers who literally worshiped the soil on which they labored and were determined to make it support them regardless of the political controversies that raged on all sides.

As might be expected, the nomadic peoples on China's northern borders took advantage of her internal weakness to overrun the country. For about 250 years, from the fourth to the late sixth century A.D., practically all northern China including the Wei and Yellow River valleys was ruled by nomad dynasties of Hunnish, Turkish, and related stocks. It was not, however, successfully incorporated into any of the extensive but short-lived empires which arose in Central Asia and often impinged upon India as well as China. The dominance of non-Chinese rulers over the Yellow River valley—the historic center of Chinese culture—did not by any means destroy this culture. On the contrary, the rulers seemed eager to be accepted as custodians and defenders of civilization, and in the Far East civilization was synonymous with Chinese institutions. The nomads who settled south of the Great Wall assimilated the speech and customs of the older inhabitants. One of the few permanent changes in the habits of the Chinese people that can be attributed to their contact with the steppe nomads was in costume. During the fourth and fifth centuries they adopted trousers and boots similar to those worn by the northern horsemen, and this style of dress gradually supplanted the flowing tunic even in south China.

The contrast between China and Western Europe during the medieval era is accentuated by the fact that four centuries of disunity in China were followed by another vigorous and highly successful dynasty, the T'ang (618–907), which re-established the imperial administration, again pushed back the territorial frontiers, and promoted brilliant cultural achievements. Thus, at the very time when feudalism was taking root in Europe and a new type of civilization was in process of formation there, China was resuming the course that had been marked out in Han times. Although it followed so closely upon the period of invasion and division, the T'ang Dynasty in many respects marked the culmination of China's cultural evolution.[1]

Restoration of power and unity under the T'ang Dynasty (618–907)

The T'ang Dynasty was at its height during the first half of the eighth century, covered almost entirely by one distinguished reign, when the area under Chinese control was slightly greater than the Han dominions and greater than it has ever been since under a native Chinese monarch. Wars in Mongolia broke the power of the Turks, who had been dominant there for about 150 years, and some of them became allies of the T'ang emperor. Parts of Manchuria were annexed, all Korea was tributary for a brief span, and control was again asserted over northern Indochina. The most redoubtable advances were in Central Asia. Chinese jurisdiction was recognized as far west as the Caspian Sea and the borders of Afghanistan and India, and some of the Indus valley princes accepted Chinese suzerainty. In carrying out their military exploits the T'ang rulers relied heavily upon the assistance of the non-Chinese peoples with whom their subjects were by this time familiar, either as friends or as foes. Now that the Chinese dragon was in the ascendancy, Mongols, Turks, and Huns were glad to be accepted as allies.

The height of T'ang power

Imposing as was the T'ang hegemony over Central Asia, it could not be maintained indefinitely. When the rapid expansion of Islam and the Saracenic empire began under Arab leadership in the seventh century, it seemed for a while that China, in spite of her remoteness from the West, was the only power to offer effective resistance. The last Sassanid king of Persia, fleeing from the Arabs, sought refuge at the T'ang court, and T'ang forces with the assis-

Decline of the T'ang empire

[1] Actually the brief Sui Dynasty (589–618) had already reunited China and inaugurated the new era of progress.

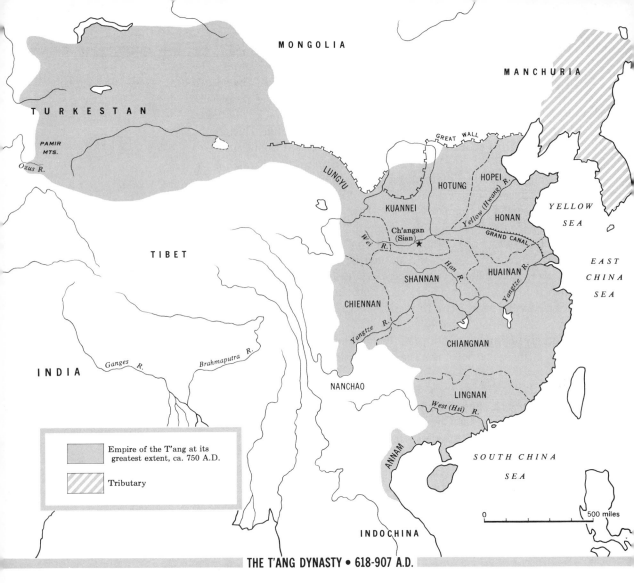

THE T'ANG DYNASTY • 618-907 A.D.

tance of local princes checked the Moslem advance in Turkestan. The check was only temporary, however. When the T'ang administration passed its zenith (about 750), the Arabs gained control of Turkestan—bequeathing the religion of Islam as a permanent heritage—and for a time their influence extended as far east as the border of China's Kansu province. The T'ang rulers also encountered trouble with Tibet, which previously had remained in isolation from the turbulent politics of Central Asia. Early in the seventh century a kingdom was founded in the highland country by a leader who attained sufficient prestige to be given both a Chinese and an Indian princess in marriage. The Tibetans invaded Chinese territory several times, allied themselves alternately with the Turks and with the Arabs, and interrupted trade between China and Persia by blocking the passes through the Pamir Mountains. In 798 the

T'ang court succeeded in obtaining a treaty of alliance with the famous Harun-al-Raschid, caliph of Baghdad, and the Tibetan power subsided in the ninth century. Meanwhile, a division of Turks had reoccupied Mongolia, and in spite of a long struggle the Chinese were unable to hold their northern and western frontiers inviolate. By the end of the ninth century internal rebellions, together with governmental corruption and decadence in the ruling house, had led again to a state of general disorder.

The T'ang administrative machinery, similar to the Han, was centralized under the emperor and staffed by a large bureaucracy. China proper was divided into fifteen provinces, which were subdivided into prefectures, and these again into smaller units or subprefectures, and each of the units was headed by an official appointed from the capital. The Han practice of recruiting talent for the imperial service had now developed into a rudimentary civil-service system in which written examinations were offered periodically throughout the provinces, and officeholders were chosen from among the successful candidates. Appointments were not confined solely to those who had taken the examinations, nor were all successful candidates rewarded with positions; but the system did provide opportunities for public service to young men of ability from every class of the population, in keeping with the policy advocated by Confucius a thousand years earlier.

Development of
the civil service

Since the abolition of feudalism and the establishment of peasant proprietorship by the Ch'in emperor, the character of Chinese society had not greatly changed. Many peasants were tenants rather than independent owners, and slavery had not entirely disappeared, although the precentage of slaves in the population was small. Inequalities in wealth and distinctions of rank were conspicuous. The T'ang emperors supported a titled nobility of several grades, but its prestige was based upon governmental favor rather than upon the possession of landed estates. Instead of hereditary titles carrying administrative power as in a feudal regime, the titles were bestowed upon eminent officials as a reward for their services. Ordinarily the emperor did not rule as a military despot but maintained a clear separation between the civil and military authority. It was only during periods of weakness and disorder that war lords usurped political functions. By T'ang times the Chinese had acquired a conviction that military regimes were incompatible with a normal, civilized state of affairs. By tradition society was believed to be properly composed of five classes ranked in the order of their value to the commonwealth. These were, first, scholars; second, farmers; third, artisans; fourth, merchants; and last, soldiers, lumped together with beggars, thieves, and bandits.[2] The notable aspects of this classification are the high recognition granted to intellectual ability, the

Chinese society
under the T'ang

[2] A famous ancient Chinese proverb is: "Good iron is not used to make a nail; a good man is not used to make a soldier."

deprecation of violence and of nonproductive occupations, and the fact that the categories are based upon individual talents and capacities rather than upon birth. The five-class system was never fully realized or perfectly respected, but it was an ideal which tended to lessen the rigidity of Chinese institutions. On the more practical side, the prominence of scholars in the administration and the system of competitive examinations helped to prevent the dominance of aristocratic families. In addition, the circumstance that the imperial throne did not remain in any one family for more than a few centuries provided an object lesson not to be forgotten.

Agriculture

Continuing the policy of encouraging agriculture, every vigorous dynasty gave attention to irrigation works, usually maintained public granaries to provide food distribution in famine years, and sometimes attempted to relieve the farmers from their heavy burden of debt and taxes. Nevertheless, while China was already one of the world's leading agricultural countries, the poorer peasants undoubtedly suffered from a miserably low standard of living as has been the case throughout history. Furthermore, the farmer bore the chief burden of supporting the state. Theoretically the emperor reserved the right to redistribute holdings, but in practice he was usually content to break the power of overly ambitious wealthy houses that might challenge his own authority. Too often the interest of officials in the peasants centered upon the fact that they constituted the most lucrative and dependable source of taxation, collectible either in produce or labor, the latter including conscription for military service.

Commerce and urban growth

Curiously enough, in spite of the honored position of the farmer and the pro-agrarian policies of the government, the merchant class attained a prominence far superior to that of European merchants during this period, and the steady increase of trade induced the growth of thriving cities. During the eighth century the T'ang capital in the Wei valley (on the site of Sian, but known during this period as Ch'ang-an), the eastern terminus of the trans-Asiatic caravan routes, apparently had a population of close to 2 million, while the population of China as a whole was between 40 and 50 million—about 7 per cent of the present number. Foreign commerce was greater under the T'ang than ever before, and an increasing proportion of it was oceanic, the leading ports of exchange being Canton and other cities along the southeast coast, where merchants of various nationalities from the Near and Middle East were to be found. In addition to silk and spices, porcelain ware was becoming a notable item in China's export trade.

Significant developments in religion took place during the period under consideration. The most important was the introduction of Buddhism, which brought the Chinese for the first time into contact with a complex religion with an elaborate theology, ecclesiastical organization, and emphasis upon personal salvation. For several centuries following the life of Gautama, the Buddhist faith gained such momentum in the regions surrounding India that it was bound to reach China. It was brought in over the northern trade routes as early as the first century A.D. and made rapid headway during the period of disunion that followed the collapse of the Han Dynasty. Buddhism met with a mixed reception in China, arousing both enthusiastic interest and repugnance. Mysticism, asceticism, contempt for the physical world, and the concept of transmigration of souls were quite alien to Chinese tradition; and the monastic life seemed to involve a repudiation of sacred family loyalties. On the other hand, Buddhism offered consolations not found in the native Chinese cults or philosophical disciplines. It was non-aristocratic, open to all classes, and—in contrast to the Confucian emphasis upon the inflexible will of Heaven—its *karma* doctrine affirmed that anyone could improve his chances in a future existence by diligent application. Converts were attracted by the rich symbolism of the new religion, and the voluminous scriptures which the Buddhist missionaries brought with them impressed the Chinese, who venerated scholarship. Buddhism's otherworldly orientation appealed particularly to the downtrodden and oppressed. In spite of violent opposition from some Chinese rulers, Buddhism continued to recruit adherents; congregations of women as well as of men were organized; pilgrims went to India to study and returned with copies of the Buddhist canons. By about 500 A.D. China had practically become a Buddhist country.

It might be supposed that after the restoration of a strong monarchy the interest in this imported salvationist faith would have subsided, but such was not the case. Although a few of the T'ang emperors tried to root out Buddhism (one emperor is reputed to have destroyed 40,000 temples), several of them encouraged it, and it was under the T'ang Dynasty that Chinese Buddhism reached its height as a creative influence. Many varieties of the religion had been brought into China—chiefly of the *Mahayana* school—and others were developed on Chinese soil, appealing to different temperaments and degrees of education. One of the most popular sects, called the "Pure Land" or "Lotus" school, promised an easy salvation in a Western Paradise to all who invoked the name of Amida (or Amitabha). Amida, theoretically an incarnation of Buddha, was actually visualized as a god, alleged to have been born of a lotus in the heavenly Western realm of bliss. Several of the sects, however, encouraged a zeal for scholarship and also stimulated interest in the problems of government and society. The most vigorous philosophical speculation under the T'ang was found in Buddhist circles. But in spite of the great success of Buddhism its triumph was not comparable to the ascendancy of Christianity in Western Europe during this same period. The Chinese Buddhists were not united in a common discipline, had no coercive power, and their organization did

The introduction
of Buddhism

Varieties of
Chinese Buddhism

303

not replace or challenge the authority of the state as did the Christian hierarchy in the West. And the fact that Buddhism was practiced in almost all parts of the country did not mean that other religions had ceased to exist. The idea of an inclusive universal church was foreign to Chinese conceptions.

Paralleling the spread of Buddhism, Taoism, which had originated as a philosophical school, acquired the characteristic features of an otherworldly religion with wide popular appeal. Taoism developed not only a priesthood but an ecclesiastical hierarchy headed by a "Prince Celestial Master," who established pontifical headquarters in south central China. This Taoist hierarchy was given official recognition in the eighth century and was not formally abolished until 1927. The religion, incorporating many primitive beliefs, expounded the Way (*Tao*), which was interpreted to mean the road to individual happiness defined usually in material terms, although it offered elements to attract intellectuals and encouraged acts of charity. Taoism was greatly affected by Buddhism and borrowed ideas from the foreign faith, including the concepts of *karma* and transmigration and the belief in thirty-three heavens and eighteen hells. Its priesthood was modeled after the Buddhist monastic order, except that the Taoists did not practice celibacy; and the later Taoist scriptures show a strong resemblance to Buddhist texts. Inevitably rivalry sprang up between the two competing religions, but neither was able to eliminate the other and both received imperial as well as popular support. Some Taoist apologists claimed that their master, Lao-tzu, had actually been the Buddha or else had instructed him; while Buddhists countered with the assertion that Lao-tzu had rendered homage to Gautama.

In spite of the popularity of Taoism and the temporary ascendancy of Buddhism, Confucianism began to be revived in the later T'ang period and retained its hold upon the allegiance of the Chinese. Although usually described as one of the three great religions of China, Confucianism was not and never became a religion in the strict sense of the term. It was a body of ethical principles, of etiquette and formal ceremony, and also—as a result of the policies of Han and T'ang emperors—a code of government, strengthened by the practice of recruiting officials from scholars versed in the Confucian classics. Veneration for the great teacher finally became part of the state cult and was invested with formal religious observances. The later Han emperors had prescribed sacrifices to Confucius in every large city, and a T'ang ruler of the seventh century ordered temples to be built in his honor in each prefecture and subprefecture. Thus the sage, together with other famous men of antiquity, revered rulers, outstanding generals, etc., was ensured perpetual homage and respect, but he was not worshiped as were the Buddhist and Taoist deities. The Chinese idea of religion, it should be remembered, was different from that of most other peoples. The typical

Taoism as a religion

Confucianism as a state cult

Chinese would be a Confucianist as a matter of course; but he might also be a Taoist, a Buddhist, or a combination of both.

Many economic and cultural·changes took place during the thousand years between the Ch'in Dynasty and the end of the T'ang. Some items were borrowed from Western lands—grapes and alfalfa among the agricultural products, astrological concepts and the seven-day week from the Manicheans. The Chinese began to use coal for fuel and for smelting iron in the fourth century A.D., far in advance of Europeans. Their astrologers had observed sunspots as early as 28 B.C.; a crude seismograph was constructed in 132 A.D. The magnetic compass, apparently developed by the Taoists around 500 A.D., was used chiefly to determine favorable locations for grave sites. The properties of gunpowder had also been discovered. At this time, however, gunpowder was employed not to blow people to bits but in the manufacture of firecrackers to frighten away evil spirits. The highly important invention of paper (made of bark, hemp, and rags) was achieved by the beginning of the second century A.D., and printing from blocks was introduced about 500 years later. By the tenth century the printing of books was common not only in China but in Korea and Japan.

A great deal of the intellectual and artistic progress of this era must be credited to the Buddhists, whose contributions were not confined to religion exclusively. Buddhism enriched Chinese music by the introduction of a liturgy of vocal chants and also with several new musical instruments, including the psaltery, guitar or mandolin and other stringed instruments, the reed organ, clarinet, and a type of flute. It was in the visual arts, however, that the impetus of Buddhism was most notable. The Buddhists of northern India, who had absorbed artistic motifs from the Greeks and Persians, spread them into Central Asia and thence into China. During

Porcelain Ewer or Pitcher, in the Form of a Court Lady.

The Ancestor of all Seismographs. Invented by a Chinese mathematician and geographer in 132 A.D. it was described in a contemporary document as an "earthquake weathercock." These conjectural reconstructions show the interior of the bronze, bell-shaped instrument. (A) The pendulum carries jointed arms radiating in eight directions, each arm ending in a crank connected with a dragon head. (B) When an earth tremor causes the pendulum to swing, one of the dragon heads is raised and releases a ball which drops into the mouth of a toad below. After the swing of the pendulum, a catch mechanism immobilizes the instrument. Thus, by observing which ball has fallen, it is possible to determine the direction of the initial shock wave.

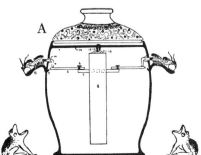

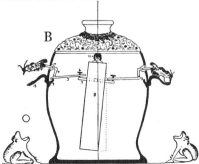

305

Two Carved Wood Bodhisatt-vas. T'ang Dynasty. The Bo-dhisattva, or Buddha-to-be, represented a person eligible for enlightenment but who remained in the world to help others on the upward path. In Mahayana Buddhism a number of Bodhisattvas came to be worshiped as deities.

the period of disunion and the early T'ang Dynasty, Chinese sculpture reached its climax, successfully blending together Indian, Iranian, and Hellenic characteristics into a distinctive Chinese style. Superbly beautiful examples of this sculpture have survived, the best of which were produced in the late sixth and early seventh centuries. The most impressive works of architecture were Buddhist temples or sacred grottoes in northwestern China, carved out of rock caves after the Indian manner. Painting, too, reached a peak of realism and sensitivity which has rarely been surpassed. Skill in this medium was stimulated by the Chinese habit of writing with brush and ink, and pictorial figures or scenes were often combined with masterly specimens of calligraphy executed on scrolls of silk. Some paintings in fresco have been preserved from T'ang times and, like the sculpture, they show Buddhist influence. Outstanding among the minor arts was the production of pottery figurines representing human beings and animals with grace and naturalness, used chiefly as funeral presents to the departed. The manufacture of white porcelain—the beginning of the world-famous "china" ware—apparently began in the sixth or seventh century.

As early as Chou times, the Chinese civilization was highly literary, and by the T'ang period China had probably the most abundant collection of writings of any nation in the world. Philosophical activity did not equal the creative age of Confucius, Mo Ti, and Mencius, but a great variety of literary forms had come into existence, showing maturity of thought, sophistication, and aesthetic sensitivity. Writers of the T'ang period produced histories, essays, dictionaries, short stories and romances for popular entertainers, an embryonic form of the drama, and—outshining all the rest—poetry. Poetry had been developing prolifically during the centuries of disunion and civil strife. The influence of Buddhism and Taoism imparted emotional intensity and a quality of mysticism conducive to lyrical richness. The final result was a flowering in the eighth and ninth centuries which made the T'ang the supreme age of Chinese poetry. The verse forms were usually short, with words carefully chosen to evoke beauty of tone as well as to convey pithy thought and vivid imagery. While sometimes expressing philosophical ideas, they were frequently poignant in mood and romantic in theme, treating especially of nature, love, and friendship. A few of the best examples were tinged with a deep melancholy, expressing compassion for the miserable lot of the poor, distress over abuses in government, revulsion against the senseless brutality of war, and bewilderment at the apparent triumph of evil over good.

3. EARLY CIVILIZATION IN JAPAN

Of the great civilizations of the Far East, Japan's was the latest to develop. In origin it was derived from and was largely an adaptation of cultures from the mainland, especially from China. However, the fact that the Japanese lagged many centuries behind China and India and made their most rapid progress under the stimulus of borrowings from China does not prove that the island dwellers were lacking in ability or originality. Not only did the Japanese display remarkable ingenuity in assimilating foreign elements and in modifying them to meet their particular needs, but during some periods of history they seemed to possess more initiative than any of the other Far Eastern nations. The backwardness of Japan in early times is explained, at least in part, by the geographical circumstance of her isolation from the continent of Asia. Before oceanic commerce was well advanced, the Japanese islands could not be readily affected by political and cultural changes taking place on the mainland. These islands stand in the same relationship to Asia as do the British Isles to Europe. Just as European civilization was slowly extended from the Near Eastern centers westward to Italy and then to the northern countries, reaching Britain last of all, so Far Eastern civilization gradually radiated from the Yellow River valley to the south, west, and northeast, and necessarily reached Japan belatedly. Actually Japan is much more remote from the neighboring continent than is Britain from Continental Europe. At the narrowest point the Strait of Dover is only about 20 miles wide, while more than 100 miles separate the islands of Japan from the closest point on the Korean peninsula.

Japan's geographic setting is in some ways very favorable. Of the approximately 3000 islands composing the group, only about 600 are inhabited, and the bulk of the population is concentrated on the four principal islands. The entire archipelago lies within the temperate zone, and the largest island, Honshu, holding about half of the Japanese people, lies between almost exactly the same latitudes as the state of California. The Black Current drifting northward from tropical seas, moderates the severity of winter; and cyclonic storms, while sometimes destructive, bring fluctuations in temperature that are conducive to physical and mental vigor. Their proximity to the ocean encouraged the Japanese to develop navigation and to become hardy fishermen. With its expanse of seacoast, mountains, volcanoes and snow-capped peaks, the region is scenically one of the most beautiful in the world, a factor which has undoubtedly contributed to the keen aesthetic sensibilities of the Japanese people. At the same time Japan is by no means perfectly endowed by nature and suffers from several disadvantages. Except for having fair deposits of coal, the islands are poor in mineral resources. Even more serious has been the scarcity of good agricultural land, owing to the rocky or mountainous character of much of the country. Although throughout most of their history the Japanese have been a nation of farmers, only about 16 per cent of their soil is cultivable. This sufficed when the population was small and generally stationary; it has posed a tremendous problem in modern times.

The retarded development of civilization in Japan

Geographic advantages and disadvantages

307

EARLY JAPAN

Small as is the land area of Japan (slightly less than that of California) and in spite of its relative isolation, it was inhabited even in
early times by people of various stocks as the result of successive
migrations from the continent. The earliest inhabitants, so far as is
known, were a primitive people who possessed a Neolithic culture,
crude in many respects but distinguished by pottery of striking
design and skillfully fashioned weapons. They are represented today
by the Ainu, a light-colored, flat-faced, and hairy people, who have
largely disappeared except from Hokkaido and the Kurile Islands to
the north. For the most part the Japanese nation is descended from
Mongoloid invaders who crossed over to the islands at various times
during the Neolithic Age and even later, chiefly by way of Korea.

308

From the time of the Ch'in Dynasty on, the settlers in Japan possessed some knowledge of Chinese culture, which had already penetrated into Korea. Bronze mirrors, carved jewels, and swords of Chinese or Mongolian type appear in graves dating from the second and first centuries B.C. By the close of the first century B.C. the Japanese had begun to use iron as well as bronze.

Quite understandably, the leading centers of cultural evolution were in the south and west of Japan—the areas closest to Korea, from which the chief migrations came—and developments in this region gradually spread to the north and east. The real nucleus of the Japanese state was the peninsula of Yamato, on the southeastern side of the great island of Honshu, to which a group of families had migrated from Kyushu (opposite Korea) perhaps as early as the first century A.D. The Japanese communities at this time were very primitive. People wore clothing made from hemp or bark, although silk was not entirely unknown. They carried on trade by barter only and had no system of writing. The chief unit of society was the clan, a group of families claiming to be related by blood. Each clan venerated some particular deity, who was supposed to be the ancestor of the group; but the worship of human ancestors had not yet become an institution. The headship of the clan was vested hereditarily in a specific family, and the clan leader served both as a warrior chieftain and as priest. In primitive Japanese society women seem to have held a position of prominence, perhaps even of superiority. The clan head was sometimes a woman, and evidence points to the conclusion that originally the family was matriarchal, with descent traced through the mother—a remarkable circumstance in view of the rigid subordination of women in later times. The transition to a patriarchal system, however, was effected at an early date. According to Chinese accounts from the third century A.D., polygamy was a common practice, especially among men of the higher classes. Various crafts and skills were organized as occupational groups in the form of guilds with hereditary membership. Each guild was attached to a clan and tended to merge with it eventually, although a few guilds whose members performed distinctive services, such as administering religious rites, retained an independent existence and honorable status. Members of the agricultural and artisans' guilds, on the other hand, were practically serfs. Society was decidedly aristocratic, rank was generally hereditary, and slavery existed, although the number of slaves was relatively small.

Japanese religion, while comparable to that of other primitive peoples, was in some ways unique. It was basically animistic, a type of unreflecting and almost universal nature worship, with no well-defined conception of the nature of divine being. In a general way it was polytheistic, except that the term probably suggests too definite a catalogue of gods or too precise a theology. The Japanese later gave their religion the name of *Shinto* ("the way of the Gods"), simply because they needed to distinguish it from Buddhism when this articulate and mature faith began to compete with the native cult. Although the Japanese recognized some great deities, associated with the sun, moon, earth, crops, and storms, these were not endowed with distinct personalities and were not represented by images. Objects of worship were designated as *kami*, a term meaning "superior" but which was applied to almost anything having mysterious or interesting properties, ranging from heavenly phenomena to irregularly shaped stones and such lowly objects as sand, mud, and vermin. No sharp line was drawn between the natural and the supernatural or between magic and worship. The notion of life after death was extremely shadowy, and religion was largely devoid of ethical content. It involved taboos and scrupulous concern for ceremonial cleanness, with purification rites to remove contamination, but the requirements were not based on considerations of morality or even always of health. Uncleanness, for example, was associated with childbirth, with contact with the dead, and with wounds whether inflicted honorably or not. To placate the gods, respectful gestures, prayers, and sacrifices were employed. Offerings of food and drink gradually tended to be superseded by symbolic objects—of pottery, wood, and eventually paper.

In spite of its diffuse and elementary character, the native Japanese religion was not lacking in attractive elements. It reflected an attitude of cheerfulness and a rare sympathy for and appreciation of nature. The gods were not thought of as cruel and terrifying creatures; even the god of the storm was generally conceived as benign. On the whole, the religion of the Japanese was one "of love and gratitude rather than of fear, and the purpose of their religious rites was to praise and thank as much as to placate and mollify their divinities." [3] It was enlivened also with picturesque legends and poetic phrases that suggest a spontaneous delight in the natural world.

The clan which was dominant on the plain of Yamato, and gradually acquired an ascendancy over adjacent regions, probably came from Kyushu and claimed descent from the Sun Goddess. There was nothing remarkable in such a claim because all important families traced their ancestry to gods or goddesses. However, myths associated with the Sun Goddess assumed greater significance as the Yamato clan extended its political power and attempted to secure fuller recognition of its paramountcy over the other clans, for which purpose it was helpful to foster the legend that the Yamato chief had been divinely appointed to rule over Japan (even though most of it was still unconquered from the aborigines). According to this legend the Sun Goddess had sent down to earth her own grandson,

Attractive elements in native Japanese religion

Founding of the Japanese state

310　　[3] G. B. Sansom, *Japan, a Short Cultural History*, p. 47.

Ninigino-Mikoto. Ninigi, "thrusting apart the many-piled clouds of Heaven, clove his way with an·awful way-cleaving" to land on the western island of Kyushu, carrying with him the three symbols of Japanese royalty—a jewel, a sword, and a mirror. The grandson of this Ninigi, it was related, advanced along the coast of the larger island to Yamato, where he began to rule as Jimmu, the "first emperor." National tradition dates the empire from February 11, 660 B.C. Actually, it was at least 600 or 700 years later that the Yamato state was established, and then it was anything but imperial. The saga of the Sun Goddess and her descendants did not become a distinctive element in the national cult of Japan until the sixth century A.D., and not until the modern era was it deliberately exploited on a national scale for the purpose of instilling a fanatical and unquestioning patriotism among the people.

For many centuries the Japanese maintained contact with and continued to receive cultural impetus from Korea, which means that they were being influenced indirectly by the older and richer civilization of China of the Han and later dynasties. The Japanese even controlled a small section at the southern tip of Korea from about 100 to 560 A.D. and intervened in Korean politics to maintain a balance of power, siding with one and then another of the three kingdoms into which Korea was divided during this time. Of fundamental importance for the later history of Japan was the introduction, by way of Korea, of the Chinese system of writing (about 405 A.D.) and of Buddhism (about 552 A.D.).

While the technique of writing was essential to the advance of civilization, it was unfortunate for the Japanese that they acquired it from China. If they had been able to devise or borrow a phonetic or alphabetic system, the problem of writing their language would have been comparatively simple. The Chinese characters—fundamentally pictographic or ideographic, with very little apparent relationship to the pronunciation of the words for which they stand —had been developed to a state of complexity and utilized in producing masterpieces of Chinese literature; but they were ill suited to represent Japanese. The Japanese language is phonetically quite different from the Chinese, and the attempt to write it with Chinese characters was a feat as difficult as it would be to try to write English in Chinese characters. Nevertheless, the Japanese struggled heroically with the task and eventually developed a script of their own, or, rather, two varieties of script. Although the original Chinese characters were abbreviated considerably and, during the ninth and tenth centuries, given phonetic value by identification with individual Japanese syllables, the resulting product was still cumbersome. Hence, the process of learning to write Japanese was, and still is, a laborious undertaking. The fact that the system of writing is alien to the structure, inflection, and idiosyncrasies of the spoken language has hampered clarity of expression and partially

Japanese tomb culture. Clay grave statues of ordinary people, such as this soldier, surround the tombs of more important men. This reflects the influence of Korean culture. Such statuary began to appear in the third and fourth centuries A.D.

Japanese writing

311

Great Buddha, Todaiji Temple, Nara.
This statue, cast in the middle of the
eighth century A.D., is one of the two
largest bronze figures in the world.
The seated Buddha is 53 feet high.

accounts for the tendency toward ambiguity in many official Japanese documents. To compensate for these disadvantages, however, along with the Chinese-derived script a great many Chinese words were adopted bodily by the Japanese, enriching their language in vocabulary and concepts. In view of the circumstances in which writing was introduced in Japan, a person who wished to become educated was almost bound to learn the Chinese language, especially since it was the vehicle of all literature considered worthy of the name. For several centuries Japanese scholars, officials, and men of letters wrote in classical Chinese, in somewhat the same manner that educated Europeans used Latin during the Middle Ages and later.

In the middle of the sixth century Buddhism began to obtain a foothold in Japan. The first Buddhist missionary is said to have come from Korea; other evangelists of the new faith arrived not only from Korea but from China and even from India. As in the case of China, the *Mahayana* school of Buddhism, with its elaborate theology and emphasis upon the soul's redemption, was most in evidence. And, just as had happened in China, a number of different sects arose in Japan from time to time. The appearance of Buddhism in Japan produced perhaps even greater agitation than had accompanied its introduction into China a few centuries earlier. The Chinese were at least familiar with mystical concepts through Taoism, but the Japanese had had no previous experience either with this type of otherworldly religion or with any analogous philosophy. Part of the appeal of Buddhism to the Japanese lay in its novelty. The Buddhist scriptures raised questions that had apparently never occurred to the Japanese before—as to the soul, the nature of the immaterial world, rewards and punishments after death—and then proceeded to answer them with impressive eloquence. For a while, sharp controversy raged over the acceptability of the foreign faith (the first statue of the Buddha sent from Korea was thrown into a

The establishment of Buddhism in Japan

canal when an epidemic of disease broke out). However, one prominent aristocratic family in Yamato, the Soga, adopted and championed the cause of Buddhism and prevailed upon the imperial clan to favor it, so that before the close of the sixth century the success of the religion was assured. To some extent its success was attributable to political maneuvers and expediency. In patronizing the scholarly faith the Soga family sought to enhance its own prestige and, through the benefit of whatever supernatural power the religion contained, to secure an advantage in the struggle against rival families. Buddhism rapidly acquired a wide following both among the common people and the aristocracy and became so firmly entrenched that it could survive any shift in equilibrium among the contending clans. Probably its popularity is largely explained by its being interpreted as a miraculous protector against disasters both in this world and the next rather than by its philosophical heritage. Nevertheless, the increasing familiarity with Buddhist doctrines stimulated intellectual activity and was conducive to the cultivation of attitudes of sympathy and humaneness.

One of the most significant aspects of the spread of Buddhism in Japan was that it proved to be a highly effective medium for disseminating Chinese culture, especially art, architecture, and literature. Temples and shrines were erected, paintings and images of the Buddha were produced, and libraries of the sacred texts were accumulated. Converts from the aristocratic class frequently went to China to study, returning with a broadened viewpoint and refined tastes. The native Japanese cult, now beginning to be called *Shinto*, was by no means extinguished, but it was influenced considerably by contact with Buddhism. There was very little antagonism between the two religions. Buddhism in Japan became tinged with national traditions, and frequently the same shrine was regarded as sacred to both faiths. The Japanese priests, whether Buddhist or

Buddhism a
medium for
disseminating
Chinese culture

Horyuji Temple, Nara. The Horyuji Temple, founded in 607 A.D. by Prince Shotoku, Regent of the Empress-Regnant Suiko, is a complex of about forty buildings, and includes some of the oldest wooden structures in the world.

Other examples
of Chinese
influence

Japanese Religious Sculpture
(twelfth century or earlier).
Wooden figure of Bishamon,
revered as one of the Four
Guardian Kings of the Buddhist kingdom.

Shinto, did not constitute a hierarchy with coercive powers over the
people any more than did the priests in China, although the Buddhist monasteries gained in economic importance as they were
endowed with lands.

During the most vigorous period of the T'ang Dynasty, the
impact of Chinese civilization upon Japan reached such a climax that
it marks a turning point in the evolution of Japanese institutions. It
is not at all strange that the Japanese turned avidly to China for
tutelage at this time. China under the early T'ang rulers was one of
the most highly civilized states in the world, as well as the most
powerful, and in the Far East had no close rivals for such a distinction. Throughout the seventh and eighth centuries the government
in Yamato sent a succession of official embassies to the T'ang court,
largely for the purpose of recruiting personnel trained in the sciences, arts, and letters. The result was a wholesale copying of Chinese techniques and ideas, affecting almost every aspect of Japanese
life and society. Chinese medical practices, military tactics, and
methods of road building were introduced; also styles of architecture, of household furniture, and even of dress. A system of weights
and measures was adopted, and in the early eighth century coined
money came into use. Many works of art had previously been
imported and copied, but now Japanese painters and sculptors began
to display both technical proficiency and originality. The Chinese
classics, especially the Confucian writings, were studied intently,
since every well-bred person was expected to be familiar with them.
Along with these concrete and visible innovations came an attempt
to fit the social structure into the Chinese pattern. A new emphasis
was placed upon family solidarity and filial devotion, including the
duty of sacrificing to ancestral spirits.[4] Japanese leaders and intellectuals seemed determined to remake their country in the image of
China.

The most comprehensive project involved nothing less than re-
constituting the government according to the T'ang model. It was
announced by a decree known as the Taika Reform Edict, issued in
645 A.D. by the Yamato ruler at the instigation of a clique of scholar-
reformers. This declaration, rather than the mythical events of 660
B.C., represents the founding of the Japanese imperial system. By the
Taika Edict the ruler assumed the role not of a mere clan leader but
of an emperor, with absolute power, although professedly honoring
Confucian principles. All Japan was to be divided into provinces,
prefectures, and subprefectures, which would be administered by a
centrally appointed bureaucracy recruited from the populace. Faithful to the example of China, the reformers instituted a civil service,

[4] Some Japanese scholars deny that the custom of ancestor worship was an
importation; but in any case it was intensified by contacts with the Chinese.
An unfortunate consequence was the increasing subordination of women to
male authority in the patriarchal family and in society at large.

Benten Playing on a Biwa. A Japanese painting on silk, by an artist of the Heian (Fujiwara) Period, 893–1185.

offering examinations to candidates for government posts, whose selection would be based not on familiarity with the problems of Japan but on proficiency in Chinese philosophy and classical literature. To give the new administration an economic foundation and to bring it to bear directly upon the people, the Reform Edict proclaimed that all the land belonged to the emperor, and that it would be divided equitably among the farmers and redistributed every six years. In return, every landholder would be required to pay taxes (in commodities, money, or labor) directly to the state.

Altogether, the reform program of the seventh century was one of the most ambitious that any government has ever attempted. It sought to graft upon a still fairly primitive society an administrative system that was the product of almost a thousand years of evolution among a people with cultural maturity and deeply entrenched traditions. Similarly, it involved an effort on the part of one corner of Japan to impose its regime on the entire area, much of which had hardly advanced beyond the Neolithic stage. In adopting the scheme of a centralized paternalism, one aspect of the Chinese prototype was studiously avoided: namely, the concept that imperial authority is conditional upon the promotion of public welfare and that it may be terminated—by rebellion as a last resort—if it fails in this objective. The Yamato group tried to attach a bureaucracy of scholar-officials to a government that called for perpetual rule by one family, whose head occupied a position of inviolable sanctity. To strengthen the prestige of the emperor, greater emphasis than ever before was placed upon his reputed descent from the Sun Goddess. He was represented as the embodiment of a "lineal succession un-

Consolidation of the Japanese government

315

broken for ages eternal" and as divine in his own person—a significantly different concept from that of the "Mandate of Heaven," the conditional and temporary divinity that hedged the Chinese emperor. In addition to this fundamental contrast between the official Chinese and Japanese theories as to the ultimate basis and limits of political authority, there was a notable divergence in practice also. China knew many different dynasties, most of them begun through rebellion or usurpation; but when a vigorous emperor sat on the throne he usually ruled effectively and sometimes autocratically, as is attested by the records of the first few rulers of every major dynasty. In Japan, on the other hand, while the imperial family was· never dethroned in spite of violent or revolutionary changes within society and in foreign relations, and while the fiction of imperial sanctity was carefully preserved, the actual power for the most part was exercised by some other family, agency, or clique, using the sacred imperial office as a front. Indirect government, sometimes removed by several stages from the nominal sovereign, has been the rule rather than the exception in Japan ever since her attempt to incorporate the Chinese political machinery.

In view of the inherent difficulties, it is not surprising that the reform program of the seventh century was not entirely successful. The new administrative system existed on paper but not as an operating reality. The imperial clan, which had previously enjoyed only a limited and largely ceremonial authority over the others, could not compel absolute obedience from remote areas, and aristocratic traditions were too strong to be broken immediately. The emperor made it a practice to appoint clan heads as officials in their own territories instead of replacing them by loyal servants sent out from the capital. Thus the local magnates acquired new titles and kept much of their former power. Examinations were provided for candidates desiring posts in the government service, but important positions were almost always reserved for members of the aristocracy, while capable men of the lower class found themselves employed as underlings and clerks. The announced policy of land equalization, which was intended to serve as the basis for a uniform tax system, was the most dismal failure of all. It had been inspired by the Chinese ideal of community interest in the land, a sentiment which condemned the appropriation of land for the exclusive benefit of any individual and taught that it should be distributed equally among the cultivators. This was only a theory in China, and in Japan it was thoroughly unrealistic. Later large proprietors managed to evade taxation and so increased the burden upon the poorer farmers that some of them ran away from their homes in sheer desperation. In this manner the amount of taxable land diminished, and the emperors themselves contributed to the process by giving away estates to courtiers or to endow Buddhist monasteries. Furthermore, the decree regarding periodic redistribution of land applied only to the fields that had already been brought under rice cultivation, a relatively small area. As the frontier clans added to their domains either by conquest from the aborigines or by reclaiming waste lands for cultivation, these new territories were regarded as personal holdings not directly subject to imperial assessment. Consequently, economic progress lessened rather than increased the proportion of the land under effective control by the central government. Instead of securing large funds from taxation, the court became more and more dependent for revenue upon estates that were owned outright by the imperial family.

Although the central government failed in its political objectives, it succeeded in promoting cultural progress to an appreciable degree. Before the seventh century there had been no fixed Japanese capital even in Yamato, or in fact no cities at all. Impressed with the splendor of the T'ang capital, the great city of Ch'ang-an, the Japanese determined to build one like it to serve as the imperial headquarters. Their city, begun in 710 and located near the modern town of Nara, followed the Chinese model faithfully in its broad streets and carefully aligned squares of equal size, although it was unwalled and much smaller than Ch'ang-an. Even so, its plan was too large for the population that occupied it. In 794 a more imposing capital was built at Kyoto, which has been an important city ever since. The construction of these cities under imperial patronage, with palaces, temples, and other public buildings, provided a stimulus to all the arts. Scholarship, bent on the production of histories, treatises, and literary criticism, also flourished at the imperial court. If the bureaucracy had little real public responsibility, its members could find satisfaction and enhanced social prestige in polishing their classical Chinese, translating Buddhist sutras, painting, or composing poetry of a rather strained and artificial type. The refinement of ceremony and etiquette also received much attention. Life in court circles tended to become effete and frivolous, but it harbored some artistic and intellectual talent of high caliber. Odd as it may seem, the best Japanese literature of this period was produced by women of the nobility and of the imperial household. Their contributions, outstanding in the tenth and eleventh centuries, were chiefly prose, typically in the form of diaries but including one justly famous romantic novel (*Tale of Genji*). In this instance it was fortunate that women, even of the court, were not held to the same educational standards as men. "While the men of the period were pompously writing bad Chinese, their ladies consoled themselves for their lack of education by writing good Japanese, and created, incidentally, Japan's first great prose literature." [5]

Governmental stimulation of culture

[5] E. O. Reischauer, *Japan, The Story of a Nation*, pp. 34–35.

4. THE FOUNDATION OF CIVILIZATIONS IN AFRICA SOUTH OF THE SAHARA

The retarded development of civilization in Africa

The advance of civilization in sub-Saharan Africa was relatively slow. Africa's lack of early development, like Japan's, may be explained in part by its geographical isolation. The continent possessed few natural harbors, leaching of the soil's nutrients contributed to a general scarcity of good agricultural land, and the vast Sahara inhibited meaningful cultural and profitable commercial exchange. Desert transportation was dangerous and unreliable with horses or oxen.

Before 200 B.C. nearly all Africans south of the Sahara functioned on a nomadic hunting and gathering level. Religion, deeply rooted in superstition, remained basically animistic. Leadership was exercised

Early mechanisms for social control

by priests or family elders. Population density was exceedingly low everywhere, obviating the need to form large, centralized governing units. With an abundance of unoccupied land, Africans found permanent settlements unnecessary, and in the absence of external threats, there was no compulsion to organize military cadres for defense. Government was therefore rudimentary. Many clans engaged in ancestor worship for the purpose of establishing a sense of continuity and exerting a measure of moral control. Intermediaries were chosen from among elders in the group to interpret the will of the ancestors and gods and to lead rituals in their honor.

The Iron Age wrought revolutionary changes in African lifestyles after about 200 B.C. At that time, small bands of Bantu-speaking Negroes living along the modern Nigerian-Cameroon border in West Africa learned how to forge iron ore into spears and hoes. We do not yet know whether they developed the ability to

The Iron Age in Africa. An iron smelter in Tanzania such as those that enabled the Bantu to create iron tools and weapons.

Agriculture. A Ndebele granary in southern Rhodesia. The ability to sustain sedentary village life depended on the community's ability to stockpile foodstuffs.

smelt iron independently or whether the technique was introduced by immigrants from North Africa or from the lands of Kush. In any case, it endowed the Bantu with an immediate technological advantage over others. With their superior iron implements they expanded southward into the Equatorial woodlands of West Central Africa. Then in approximately 1 A.D., in the watershed of the Congo-Zambezi river systems, they encountered high-yield food crops, including the nutritious banana, coco-yam and plantain. These plants had probably spread up the Zambezi River valley from Madagascar island. They were brought to Madagascar by seaborne southeast Asian immigrants of Javanese origin. The Bantu, possessing sturdy iron hoes, were in an excellent position to cultivate these new food crops.

Iron metallurgy, together with superior southeast Asian crops, greatly accelerated the transition from a food-gathering to a food-producing economy. By 200 A.D. agricultural surpluses had triggered a population explosion among the Bantu, propelling them in easterly and westerly directions across the breadth of Equatorial Africa from coast to coast. Small, segmented Neolithic populations were either absorbed or eliminated by the Bantu, who enjoyed greater social cohesion and practiced efficient methods of farming and pastoralism. With plentiful food and meat, they could support many wives and large, extended families. Consequently, their numbers quickly multiplied.

Food-producing economies led to the emergence of village life. Trade became a necessary handmaiden to agriculture as metallurgists bartered their finished tools for iron ore, copper, salt, and other essential commodities. By the close of the tenth century, most Africans were using iron implements; and from the Cameroons to the South African veld they spoke Bantu-related languages. Bantu peoples had thus initiated an agricultural revolution and accelerated the development of new mechanisms for social organization and control in East, Central, and Southern Africa. In effect, they laid

319

the necessary foundations for the civilizations which emerged in the millennium after 900 A.D.

Iron technology brought forth similar changes in West Africa, even though the Bantu diaspora did not extend there. For centuries, Nubians from the upper Nile and Saharan Berbers, bearing iron tools and weapons, had infiltrated Negro cultures of the West African grasslands. Marrying local women, they quickly lost their ethnic identity. An excellent environment for fishing and cereal cultivation in the Niger River area and Chad basin had already stimulated a dramatic growth of the indigenous population.

Before the introduction of the camel, Carthaginians and later Romans had conducted a miniscule Saharan trade by horse-drawn chariot. But few if any of them ever established direct commercial connections with West Africans. Their small purchases of gold, ivory, slaves, and pepper were made through the middlemen of Garamante in the Fezzan oases of central Sahara. The clever Garamantes received glass beads, fine cloth, and dates which they passed on to the West African producers. By 300 A.D. camels had come into wide use in the Sahara as transport vehicles. Camels possessed an exceptional capacity for carrying heavy loads over long distances and maneuvering effectively under sandy conditions. They became, in effect, ships of the desert and greatly facilitated the movement of peoples and goods between North and West Africa. An ensuing revival and expansion of trans-Saharan trade led to the eventual flowering of market centers and coherent civilizations in the grassland expanse between southern Mauretania and Lake Chad.

Roman departure from North Africa in the fourth century A.D. seems to have coincided with the organization by desert Berbers of the first West African kingdom, called Ghana, or Awkar. This Negro-Berber state, located in the southeastern corner of modern Mauretania, thrived on its middleman position between the gold miners of the southern forests and the Berber traders of North Africa. By the eighth century the "Ghana," or king, of Awkar was a Negro, and his people were known in North Africa and the Middle East as the world's major gold exporters.

Trans-Saharan traffic remained small and informally organized until the mid-seventh century when Moslem Arabs overran the strategic Fezzan oases. By 740 A.D. desert Berbers had begun to embrace Islam and to withdraw more deeply into the Sahara where they set up new trade centers. At Sijilmasa they exchanged Ghanaian gold with the Arabs for Saharan salt. The salt was resold in the south to perspiring miners while the Arabs carried their gold into North Africa and Europe.

The Arab presence in North Africa encouraged Berbers to probe more deeply into West Africa in search of gold or to seek refuge from Islamic persecution. Zaghawa Berbers established communities of highly cultured farmers and fishermen around Lake Chad. In 846 A.D. they founded a ruling dynasty, based on concepts of divine

Introduction of the camel in the trans-Saharan trade

Foundation of Ghana, West Africa's first kingdom

The Arab invasion of North Africa

kingship. Like the Berbers in Ghana, they readily married into local families and were ethnically absorbed within a few generations.

READINGS

Small chieftaincies were gradually coalescing into larger governing units from the upper Senegal eastward to the shores of Lake Chad. By about 800 A.D. trade routes had reached the upper Niger River, where caravan paths from Morocco, Algeria, Tunis, Tripoli, and Egypt converged at the emporium of Gao. West Africa's rolling grasslands had become famous in Arab commercial circles as the Bilad-as-Sudan or "Land of the Blacks."

The West African Sudan: Land of the Blacks

Similar commercial and political trends were discernible along the coast of East Africa. The rise of Persian sea power in the late seventh century resulted in the eclipse of Ethiopian trade in the Red Sea and western Indian Ocean. Arabs from the Persian Shiraz swarmed along the Banadir coast of modern Somalia, where they established permanent trading settlements. Within a few generations they turned their sailing boats, or dhows, southward along the coast of modern Kenya and Tanzania. There they encountered Bantu-speaking people who, centuries before, had reached the coast from the Equatorial savanna. By 900 A.D. the Bantu were beginning to marry into Arab Shirazi and Indian families, who had only recently converted to Islam. Together they founded dynasties and organized a formal seaborne trade propelled by monsoon winds. As of old, turtle shells, ivory, rhinoceros horns, and small numbers of slaves were exported to Arabian ports and northwestern India. But by 900 A.D. increasing quantities of Central African copper had begun to arrive on the Mozambique coast. Growing Asian demands for copper led to trading operations through the Zambezi valley to reach the mines of Katanga. Indian Ocean trade, like that of the Sahara, acted as a powerful catalyst for the centralization of authority among groups engaged in mining and marketing activities.

Indo-Shirazi penetration along the East African coast

The catalytic effect of Indian Ocean trade

Meanwhile, along the upper reaches of the Nile, a number of Christian Nubian kingdoms appeared. The Nubians, though influenced by Byzantine Greece, developed their own language, laid out beautiful cities, constructed impressive brick monasteries and cathedrals, and adorned them with paintings. They also enjoyed a highly sophisticated tradition of ceramic art, with pottery of outstanding design. Their civilization reached its zenith during the ninth and tenth centuries. Powerful Nubian armies were strong enough to resist Moslem intrusions for nearly four centuries afterward.

The flowering of Nubian civilization

SELECTED READINGS

- · *Items so designated are available in paperbound editions.*
- · Binyon, Laurence, *Painting in the Far East*, 3rd ed., 1923 (Dover).
- · ———, *The Spirit of Man in Asian Art*, 1935 ed. (Dover).
- · Nakamura Hajime, *Ways of Thinking of Eastern Peoples: India, China, Tibet, Japan*, ed. P. P. Wiener, Honolulu, 1964 (East-West Center).

READINGS INDIA—*See also Readings for Chapter 6*

Devahuti, D., *Harsha: A Political Study*, Oxford, 1970.

Panikkar, K. M., *India and the Indian Ocean*, New York, 1945.

Sen, Gertrude E., *The Pageant of India's History*, Vol. I, New York, 1948.

van Leur, J. C., *Indonesian Trade and Society*, New York, 1955.

CHINA—*See also Readings for Chapter 7*

Bagchi, P. C., *India and China, a Thousand Years of Cultural Relations*, rev. ed., New York, 1951.

Balazs, Etienne, *Chinese Civilization and Bureaucracy*, New Haven, 1964. An important interpretation of Chinese society.

Carter, T. F., and Goodrich, L. C., *The Invention of Printing in China and Its Spread Westward*, 2nd ed., New York, 1955.

Eberhard, W., *History of China*, Berkeley, 1950 (E. W. Dickes, tr.). Particularly full on the period of disunion.

Eliot, Charles, *Hinduism and Buddhism: An Historical Sketch*, Vol. III, New York, 1954. Buddhism in China.

· Lattimore, Owen, *The Inner Asian Frontiers of China*, 2nd ed., New York, 1951 (Beacon).

Munsterberg, Hugo, *Short History of Chinese Art*, New York, 1949.

Shryock, J. K., *The Origin and Development of the State Cult of Confucius*, New York, 1932.

Sickman, L., and Soper, A., *The Art and Architecture of China*, Baltimore, 1956. Reliable; richly illustrated.

Sullivan, Michael, *An Introduction to Chinese Art*, Berkeley, 1961.

Sun, E. Z., and De Francis, John, *Chinese Social History*, Washington, 1956. Translations of articles by modern Chinese scholars.

· Wittfogel, K. A., *Oriental Despotism: A Comparative Study of Total Power*, New Haven, 1957 (Yale). Attempts to explain the despotic character of the Chinese imperial government by the necessities of a "hydraulic society," in which flood control and efficient irrigation systems were imperative.

Wright, Arthur F., *Buddhism in Chinese History*, Stanford, 1959. Brief but good.

Zurcher, E., *The Buddhist Conquest of China: The Spread and Adaptation of Buddhism in Early Medieval China*, 2 vols., Leiden, 1959. An illuminating study of the interaction between Chinese culture and Buddhism to the early fifth century A.D.

JAPAN

Anesaki, Masaharu, *Art, Life and Nature in Japan*, Boston, 1933.

——, *History of Japanese Religion*, London, 1930.

Brower, R. H., and Miner, E., *Japanese Court Poetry*, Stanford, 1961. Covers the period from the sixth to the fourteenth centuries.

Eliot, Charles, *Japanese Buddhism*, New York, 1959. A standard text, reprinted from the 1935 edition.

· Fenollosa, E. F., *Epochs of Chinese and Japanese Art*, 1927 ed., 2 vols. (Dover).

· Hall, J. W., *Japan: From Prehistory to Modern Times*, New York, 1971 (Delta).

Langer, P. F., *Japan, Yesterday and Today*, New York, 1966. An excellent summary.

· Moore, C. A., ed., *The Japanese Mind: Essentials of Japanese Philosophy and Culture*, Honolulu, 1967 (East-West Center). A symposium.

· Morris, Ivan, *The World of the Shining Prince*, Baltimore, 1969 (Penguin).

322

- Munsterberg, Hugo, *The Arts of Japan: An Illustrated History*, Rutland, **READINGS** Vt., 1957 (Tuttle).
- Reischauer, E. O., *Japan: The Story of a Nation*, New York, 1970 (Knopf). Lucid and well organized.

  Sansom, George B., *A History of Japan to 1334*, Stanford, 1958. An outstanding work by an eminent British scholar.

  ———, *Japan: A Short Cultural History*, rev. ed., New York, 1962.

  Swann, Peter C., *An Introduction to the Arts of Japan*, New York, 1958.
- Warner, Langdon, *The Enduring Art of Japan*, Cambridge, Mass., 1952 (Evergreen).

  Whitney, J. H., and Beardsley, R. K., *Twelve Doors to Japan*, New York, 1965.

AFRICA

- Bovill, E. W., *The Golden Trade of the Moors* (Oxford).
- Oliver, Roland, ed., *The Dawn of African History*, New York, 1968.
- Posnansky, Merrick, ed., *Prelude to East African History*, London, 1966.

SOURCE MATERIALS

Aston, W. G., tr., *Nihongi: Chronicles of Japan from the Earliest Times to* A.D. *697*, 2 vols.

Ayscough, Florence, *Tu Fu, the Autobiography of a Chinese Poet*.

Beal, Samuel, tr., *Buddhist Records of the Western World*, 2 vols.

Bynner, Witter, and Kiang Kanghu, trs., *The Jade Mountain, a Chinese Anthology*.

- de Bary, W. T., ed., *Sources of Chinese Tradition*, "The Imperial Age: Ch'in and Han"; "Neo-Taoism and Buddhism," New York, 1960 (Columbia).
- ———, ed., *Sources of Indian Tradition*, "Hinduism," New York, 1958 (Columbia).
- ———, ed., *Sources of Japanese Tradition*, "Ancient Japan"; "The Heian Period," New York, 1964 (Columbia).
- Fage, J. D., and Oliver, R. A., eds., *Papers in African Prehistory*, New York, 1970 (Cambridge).
- Keene, Donald, ed., *Anthology of Japanese Literature, from the earliest era to the mid-nineteenth century*, New York, 1956 (Evergreen).

  Morris, Ivan, tr., *As I Crossed the Bridge of Dreams: Recollections of a Woman in Eleventh-Century Japan*.

  Sanskrit Dramas: *Sakuntala, The Little Clay Cart*.
- Thompson, L., and Ferguson, J., eds., *Africa in Classical Antiquity*, New York, 1969 (Africana).

  Waley, Arthur, tr., *Ballads and Stories from Tun-Huang, an Anthology* (T'ang era); *The Tale of Genji; Translations from the Chinese*, New York, 1960.

  Watson, Burton, tr., *Records of the Grand Historian of China, Translated from the Shih Chi of Ssu-ma Ch'ien*, 2 vols., New York, 1961.
- Whitehouse, W., and Yanagisawa, E., trs., *The Tale of Lady Ochikubo* (Anchor).

PART **III**

The Early Middle Ages

During the period from 284 to 476 A.D. Roman civilization was strongly influenced by a revival of Oriental ideals of despotism, otherworldliness, pessimism, and fatalism. In the midst of economic distress and cultural decay men lost interest in earthly achievement and began to yearn for spiritual blessings in a life after death. This change in attitude was due primarily to the spread of Near Eastern religions, especially Christianity. When the Roman Empire finally collapsed, the victory of Orientalism was almost complete. The result was the evolution of new civilizations, compounded in part of elements taken from Greece and from Rome but with religion as a dominant factor behind most of their achievements. Altogether three new cultures finally emerged: the civilization of western Europe in the early Middle Ages, the Byzantine civilization, and the Saracenic civilization. The periods covered by the history of all three overlapped. The civilization of western Europe in the early Middle Ages extended from about 400 to 1000. Although Constantine established his capital on the site of ancient Byzantium in the fourth century A.D., Byzantine civilization did not begin its independent evolution until after 500. It survived until the capture of Constantinople by the Turks in 1453. The Saracenic civilization flourished from the seventh century to the end of the thirteenth. India and China bloomed in their fullest splendor between 600 and 900 and were by no means stagnant during the remainder of the period.

325

A Chronological Table

	WESTERN EUROPE	**BYZANTINE EMPIRE**
	Germanic migrations and invasions, 100 B.C.–600 A.D. Rise of the Papacy, 50–300 Growth of the colonate, *ca.* 200–500	
300		Rise of monasticism, *ca.* 300 Council of Nicaea, 325 Constantinople established as capital, 330
	Invasions of England by Angles and Saxons, 400–600 Decline of industry and commerce, 400–800 Capture of Rome by Visigoths, 410 St. Augustine's *City of God*, 413–426 Merovingian dynasty in France, 481–751 Ostrogothic rule in Italy, 493–552 Boethius' *Consolation of Philosophy*, 523 Origin of Seven Liberal Arts, *ca.* 550	Monophysite movement, 450–565
500		Justinian's empire, 527–565 Revision and codification of Roman law, 527–535 Construction of church of Santa Sophia, 532–537 Byzantine conquest of Italy, 535–552
	Lombard invasion of Italy, 568	
		Iconoclastic movement, 725–850
800	Battle of Tours, 732 Carolingian dynasty, 751–887 Development of feudalism, 800–1300 Charlemagne's empire, 800–814 Unification of England under Saxon Kings, 802–1066 Treaty of Verdun, 843 Holy Roman Empire, 962– Founding of national monarchy in France, 987	
		Separation of Eastern and Western churches, 1054 Battle of Manzikert, 1071
1100	The Crusades, 1096–1204	
		Capture of Constantinople by Crusaders of Fourth Crusade, 1204
1453		Capture of Constantinople by Ottoman Turks, 1453

THE SARACENS

Mohammed, 570?–632

The Hegira, 622
Capture of Mecca, 630
Conquest of Persia, Egypt, Palestine, Syria,
 North Africa, Spain, 632–732
Division of Islam into sects—Sunnites,
 Shiites, and Sufis, *ca.* 640

Development of steel manufacturing, textile manufacturing, leather tooling, and
 paper making, *ca.* 800–1400

Hindu-Arabic system of numerals, *ca.* 1000
Saracenic world trade, *ca.* 1000–1500

Cultivation of cotton, sugar, oranges, lemons, bananas, coffee, *ca.* 1100
Transmission of complete works of Aristotle to Europe, *ca.* 1150

Transmission of compass and astrolabe to
 Europe, *ca.* 1400

300

500

800

1100

1453

CHAPTER 12

The Civilization of the
Early Middle Ages

Think not that I am come to destroy the law, or the prophets:
I am not come to destroy, but to fulfill.
—Jesus of Nazareth, The Sermon on the Mount, *Matthew* v.17

Although checked for the time, this pernicious superstition
[Christianity] broke out again . . . throughout the City, in which
the atrocities and shame from all parts of the world center and
flourish. Therefore those who confessed were first seized, then on
their information a great multitude were convicted, not so much
of the crime of incendiarism, as of hatred of the human race.
—Tacitus on Nero's persecution of Christians

Sometime during the Renaissance the practice arose of dividing the
history of the world into three great epochs: ancient, medieval, and
modern. This classification has come to be accepted with almost
dogmatic finality. It ties in with the average man's belief that this
planet of ours has witnessed only two great periods of progress: the
time of the Greeks and the Romans and the age of modern invention. Between these two periods were the Middle Ages, popularly
regarded as an interlude of abysmal ignorance and superstition when
man lived enveloped in a cowl, oblivious of the wonders of knowledge, and concerned only with escape from the miseries of this
world and the torments of hell. The very word "medieval" has an
odious meaning in the average mind of today. It has come to be a
synonym for reactionary or unprogressive. Thus when a modern
reformer wishes to cast reproach upon the ideas of his conservative
opponent, all he has to do is to brand them as "medieval."

The reason for such erroneous judgments lies in the conventional
notion that the entire medieval period from the fall of Rome to the
beginning of the Renaissance was a cultural unit, that the ideals and

*Misinterpreta-
tion of the word
"medieval"*

329

institutions of the sixth century, for example, were the same as those of the thirteenth. Nothing could be farther from the truth. The medieval period, in western Europe, really encompassed two civilizations, as different from each other as Greece from Rome or the Renaissance from the nineteenth and twentieth centuries. The first of these civilizations, beginning about 400 A.D., when the process of Roman decay was nearly complete, and extending until 1000, was that of the early Middle Ages. It was this period alone which was really distinguished by most of those attributes commonly referred to as "medieval." The culture of the early Middle Ages undoubtedly represented in certain respects a reversion to barbarism. Intellect did not merely stagnate but sank to very low depths of ignorance and credulity. Economic activity declined to primitive levels of barter and ruralism, while morbid asceticism and contempt for this world superseded more normal social attitudes. With the Carolingian Renaissance of the ninth century, however, a brief intellectual revival occurred in Europe. In the eleventh, twelfth, and thirteenth centuries the human spirit soared to much greater heights. The result was another of the world's great cultures, distinguished alike by intellectual progress and a high degree of prosperity and freedom. Indeed, this later medieval civilization, which endured until the end of the thirteenth century, was more nearly similar to the modern age than most people realize.

Only the period from 400 to 1000 A.D. really dark

I. THE CHRISTIAN FOUNDATION OF EARLY MEDIEVAL CULTURE

Three main factors combined to produce the civilization of early medieval Europe: the Christian religion, the influence of the Germanic barbarians, and the heritage from the classical cultures. The effect of the third was probably less than that of the others. Outside the realm of philosophy the influence of the Greek and Hellenistic civilizations was comparatively slight. While the Roman heritage was still powerful, the men of the early Middle Ages rejected some portions of it as inconsistent with Christianity and barbarized much of the remainder.

Factors influencing early medieval culture

The most important foundation of the new culture was the Christian religion, whose founder, Jesus of Nazareth, was born in a small town of Judea some time near the beginning of the Christian era. Judea was then under Roman rule, though the Jews themselves recognized only their own king, Herod I, as their rightful sovereign. The atmosphere of the country was charged with religious emotionalism and political discontent. Some of the people, notably the Pharisees, looked forward to the coming of a political messiah, a son of David, who would rescue the country from foreign rule. Others, for example, the Essenes, thought in terms of spiritual deliverance through asceticism, repentance, and mystical union with God. It

The career of Jesus of Nazareth

330

was this latter sect, together with others of a similar character, which prepared the way for the ministry of Jesus. When he was about twenty-eight years old, he was acclaimed by an ascetic evangelist, John the Baptist, as one "mightier than I, whose shoes I am not worthy to bear." [1] Thenceforth for about three years the career of Jesus, according to the New Testament accounts, was a continuous course of preaching and teaching and of healing the sick, "casting out devils," restoring sight to the blind, and raising the dead. He not only denounced shame, greed, and licentious living but set the example himself by a life of humility and self-denial. Though the conception he held of himself is somewhat obscure, he apparently believed· that he had a mission to oppose Roman rule and to save mankind from error and sin. His preaching and other activities eventually aroused the antagonism of some of the chief priests and conservative rabbis. They disliked his caustic references to the legalism of the Pharisees, his contempt for form and ceremony, and his scorn for pomp and luxury. They feared also that his active leadership would cause trouble with the Romans. Accordingly, they brought him into the highest court in Jerusalem, where he was solemnly condemned for blasphemy and for setting himself up as "King of the Jews" and turned over to Pontius Pilate, the Roman governor, for execution of the sentence. After hours of agony he died on the cross between two thieves on the hill of Golgotha outside Jerusalem.

The crucifixion of Jesus marked a great climax in Christian history. At first his death was viewed by his followers as the end of their hopes. Their despair soon vanished, however, for rumors began to spread that the Master was alive, and that he had been seen

The crucifixion

[1] Matthew 3:11.

Nazareth. A modern view of the small town in Judea where Jesus spent his early life, where he worked for a time as a carpenter and began his career of preaching.

by certain of his faithful disciples. The remainder of his followers
were quickly convinced that he had risen from the dead, and that he
was truly a divine being. With their courage restored, they organized their little band and began preaching and testifying in the name
of their martyred leader. Thus another of the world's great religions
was launched on a career that would ultimately shake the foundations of no less an empire than mighty Rome.

There has never been perfect agreement among Christians as to
the precise teachings of Jesus of Nazareth. The only dependable

*The teachings
of Jesus*

records are the four Gospels, but the oldest of these was not written
until at least a generation after Jesus' death. According to the beliefs
of his orthodox followers, the founder of Christianity revealed himself as the Christ, the divine Son of God, who was sent on this earth
to suffer and die for the sins of mankind. They were convinced that
after three days in the tomb, he had risen from the dead and
ascended into heaven, whence he would come again to judge the
world. The Gospels at least make it clear that he included the following among his basic teachings: (1) the fatherhood of God and
the brotherhood of man; (2) the Golden Rule; (3) forgiveness and
love of one's enemies; (4) repayment of evil with good; (5) self-
denial; (6) condemnation of hypocrisy and greed; (7) opposition to
ceremonialism as the essence of religion; (8) the imminent approach
of the end of the world; and (9) the resurrection of the dead and
the establishment of the kingdom of Heaven.

Christianity was broadened and invested with a more elaborate
theology by some of the successors of Jesus. Chief among them was

*The influence
of Paul*

the Apostle Paul, originally known as Saul of Tarsus. Although of
Jewish nationality, Paul was not a native of Palestine but a Jew of
the Diaspora,[2] born in the city of Tarsus in southeastern Asia
Minor. Here he came into contact with the Stoic philosophy, but he
was possibly more deeply influenced by Gnosticism. Eventually
converted to Christianity, he devoted his limitless energy to propagating that faith throughout the Near East. It would be almost
impossible to overestimate the significance of his work. Denying
that Jesus was sent merely as the redeemer of the Jews, he proclaimed Christianity to be a universal religion. But this was not all.
He gave major emphasis to the idea of Jesus as the Christ, as the
God-man who existed from the foundation of the world and whose
death on the cross was an atonement for the sins of mankind. Not
only did he reject the works of the Law (i.e., Jewish ritualism) as of
primary importance in religion, but he declared them to be utterly
worthless in procuring salvation. Man is a sinner by nature, and he
can therefore be saved only by faith and by the grace of God
"through the redemption that is in Christ Jesus." It follows, according to Paul, that man's fate in the life to come is almost entirely de-

[2] See pp. 78–79

pendent upon the will of God; for "Hath not the potter power over the clay, of the same lump to make one vessel unto honour, and another unto dishonour?"[3] He has mercy "on whom he will have mercy, and whom he will he hardeneth."[4]

By the beginning of the Middle Ages the triumph of Christianity over its rivals was almost complete. The Emperor Galerius' edict of toleration in 311 was already an admission that the religion was too strong to be stamped out by persecution. By a series of decrees between 380 and 392 Christianity was recognized as the only lawful faith of the Roman Empire. How is this triumph to be explained? Perhaps as much as anything else it was a result of the composite character of Christianity. Here was a religion which ultimately came to embody elements from a wide variety of sources. A large number of them were taken from Judaism: the name of the deity, the cosmogony, the world history, the Ten Commandments, and such doctrines as original sin and the providence of God. In addition, several of the ethical doctrines were really of Jewish origin. Although many of these elements were modified by Jesus and his followers, there can be no doubt that the Hebrew contributions to Christianity were of great importance.

But obviously Christianity derived much from other than Jewish sources. Some idea of the debt it owed to religions of Persian origin has been indicated in a preceding chapter.[5] Zoroastrianism had already made the ancient world familiar with such concepts as otherworldliness and an eternal conflict between good and evil. Suggested also was the belief in secret revelation and the notion of a primal man or God-man becoming incarnate in human form. Supplementing these influences was that of the philosophy of Stoicism, which had familiarized the educated classes with ideals of cosmopolitanism and the brotherhood of man. In short, mystery religions and Hellenistic philosophy had already brought into existence a large deposit of doctrines and practices upon which Christianity could draw, at the same time preserving its distinctive character. The early Church was an organism that fed upon the whole pagan world, selecting and incorporating a wide variety of ideas and practices which were not inconsistent with its own nature. The appeal of Christianity was therefore more nearly universal than that of any other of the ancient religions.

A Carved Tablet, ca. 400 A.D., Depicting Christ's Tomb and Ascension into Heaven

The other main reasons for the triumph of Christianity can be summarized briefly. It admitted women to full rights of participation in worship, whereas Mithraism, the strongest of its early competitors, excluded them. It enjoyed the advantage for about fifty years of systematic persecution by the Roman government, a factor which enormously strengthened the cohesiveness of the

[3] Romans 9:21.
[4] Romans 9:18.
[5] See pp. 73–78

movement, since those who remained in the faith had to be ready to die for their convictions. While most of the other religions revolved around imaginary figures, the creatures of grotesque legends, Christianity possessed as its founder a historic individual of clearly defined personality. Lastly, the triumph of Christianity is partly explained by the fact that it made a stronger appeal to the poor and oppressed than did any of the other mystery religions. Although it included the ideal of the equality of all men in the sight of God, its founder and some of his followers had condemned the rich and exalted the lowly. It propagated a new and exceedingly democratic morality, with meekness, self-effacement, and love of one's enemies as primary virtues. Perhaps these were the qualities most likely to find ready acceptance among the helpless masses who had long since abandoned hope of bettering their material condition.

The division of Christians into rival sects: Arians, Athanasians, and Nestorians

Hardly had Christianity emerged victorious over its rivals than disaffection developed within its own ranks. This was due partly to the heterogeneous elements out of which the religion had been formed, and partly also to the compromising attitudes displayed by the leaders as the success of the movement increased. A more fundamental reason seems to have been the conflict between the intellectual and emotional tendencies within the religion. Representing the former were the Arians and the Nestorians. Both of these sects agreed in their refusal to accept what has since become the orthodox doctrine of the Trinity. Under the influence of Greek philosophy they rejected the idea that the Christ could be the equal of God. The Arians maintained that the Son was created by the Father and therefore was not co-eternal with him or formed of the same substance. Their chief opponents were the Athanasians, who held that Father, Son, and Holy Ghost were all absolutely equal and composed of identical substance. The Nestorians broke away from the rest of the Church with the contention that Mary should be called the mother of Christ but not the mother of God, implying of course that they considered the Christ something less than divine.

Gnostics and Manicheans

The most important of the sects that emphasized the emotional character of Christianity were the Gnostics and the Manicheans. Both were extreme ascetics and mystics. Believing that genuine religious truth was a product of revelation exclusively, they were inclined to be strongly suspicious of any attempt to rationalize the Christian faith. They were opposed also to the tendency toward worldliness which was making itself evident among many of the clergy. The Gnostics and the Manicheans were not originally sects of Christianity at all, but eventually many of them went over to that faith. Those who became Christians retained their old doctrines of exaggerated spiritualism and contempt for matter as evil. Naturally, along with these went an abiding distrust of every variety of human knowledge. The doctrines of all these sects, with the exception of the Athanasian, were eventually condemned by Church councils as heresies.

Notwithstanding the condemnation of many beliefs as heresies, the body of Christian doctrine was never very firmly fixed during the early Middle Ages. Of course, all Christians believed in a God who was the creator and governor of the universe, in salvation from sin, and in rewards and punishments after death. But as regards many other questions of dogma there was confusion and uncertainty. Even the concept of the Trinity continued to be an issue of debate for several centuries. Many of the Eastern Christians never accepted the extreme Athanasian view of the relation of the Father and the Son adopted by the Council of Nicaea (325). Further, there was no clearly formulated theory at this time of the number and the precise nature of the sacraments, nor was the doctrine of the powers of the priesthood definitely established. The theory of the Mass was not formally defined until 1215. In general, there were two main points of disagreement affecting all of these issues. Some very devout believers clung to an ideal of Christianity similar to that of the Apostolic age, when the Church was a community of mystics, each of them guided by the Inner Light in matters of faith and conduct. Others envisaged the Christian Church as an organized society prescribing its own rules for the government of its members in accordance with the practical requirements of the time.

The growth of Christian organization was one of the outstanding developments of the whole medieval era. Even during the first few centuries of that period the Church and its related institutions evolved into an elaborate structure which ultimately became the principal framework of society itself. As the Roman Empire in the West decayed, the Church took over many of its functions and helped to preserve order amid the deepening chaos. That anything at all was saved out of the wreckage was due in large part to the stabilizing influence of the organized Church. It aided in civilizing the barbarians, in promoting ideals of social justice, and in preserving and transmitting the antique learning.

The organization of the Church was at first quite simple. The early Christian congregations met in the homes of their members and listened to the spiritual testimony of various of the brethren who were believed to have been in direct communication with the Holy Ghost. No distinction between laymen and clergy was recognized. Each independent church had a number of officers, generally known as bishops and elders, whose functions were to preside at the services, discipline members, and dispense charity. Gradually, under the influence of the pagan mystery religions, the ritual of Christianity increased to such a stage of complexity that a professional priesthood·seemed to become necessary. The need for defense against persecution and the desire to attain uniformity of belief also favored the development of ecclesiastical organization. The consequence was that about the beginning of the second century one bishop in each important city came to be recognized as supreme over all the clergy in that vicinity. The sphere of his jurisdiction corresponded

The persistence of doctrinal disputes

The importance of Christian organization

The evolution of Church organization

A Fourth Century A.D. Sarcophagus Depicting Stories and Lessons from the Bible

to the *civitas*, the smallest administrative unit of the Roman state. As the number of congregations multiplied, and as the influence of the Church increased due to the adoption of Christianity as the official religion of Rome, distinctions of rank among the bishops themselves began to appear. Those who had their headquarters in the larger cities came to be called metropolitans, with authority over the clergy of an entire province. In the fourth century the still higher dignity of patriarch was established to designate those bishops who ruled over the oldest and largest of Christian communities—such cities as Rome, Constantinople, Antioch, and Alexandria, with their surrounding districts. Thus the Christian clergy by 400 A.D. had come to embrace a definite hierarchy of patriarchs, metropolitans, bishops, and priests.

The climax of all this development was the growth of the primacy of the bishop of Rome, or in other words the rise of the papacy. For several reasons the bishop of Rome enjoyed a preeminence over the other patriarchs of the Church. The city in which he ruled was venerated by the faithful as a scene of the missionary activities of the Apostles Peter and Paul. The tradition was widely accepted that Peter had founded the bishopric of Rome, and that therefore all of his successors were heirs of his authority and prestige. This tradition was supplemented by the theory that Peter had been commissioned by the Christ as his vicar on earth and had been given the keys of the Kingdom of Heaven with power to punish men for their sins and even to absolve them from guilt.[6] This theory, known as the doctrine of the Petrine Succession, has been used by Popes ever since as a basis for their claims to authority over the

336   [6] See Matthew 16:18–19.

Church. The bishops of Rome had an advantage also in the fact that after the transfer of the imperial capital to Constantinople there was seldom any emperor with effective sovereignty in the West. Finally, in 455 the Emperor Valentinian III issued a decree commanding all Western bishops to submit to the jurisdiction of the Pope. It must not be supposed, however, that the Church was yet under a monarchical form of government. The patriarchs in the East regarded the extreme assertions of the papal claims as a brazen effrontery, and even many bishops in the West continued to ignore them for some time.

The organization of the Church was by no means confined to an ecclesiastical hierarchy. In any study of Christian institutions a prominent place must be given to monasticism. Since monasticism was originally an outgrowth of asceticism, it becomes necessary, first of all, to examine the relationship between that ideal and the Christian religion. Original Christianity was only mildly ascetic. Neither Jesus nor his immediate followers practiced any extremes of self-torture. To be sure, Jesus did not marry; he declared that he had no place to lay his head; and he was supposed to have fasted for forty days in the wilderness; but these examples could scarcely have encouraged the pathological excesses of mortification of the flesh indulged in by the hermits of the third and fourth centuries. We must therefore look for additional causes of the growth of this later asceticism. Perhaps the following may be considered fundamental:

Reasons for the popularity of asceticism

(1) The choice of morbid self-torture as a substitute for martyrdom. With the abandonment of persecution by the Romans all chances of winning a crown of glory in heaven by undergoing death for the faith were eliminated. But the desire to give evidence of one's religious ardor by self-abasement and suffering was still present and demanded an outlet.

(2) The desire of some Christians who were sincerely devoted to the faith to set an example of exalted piety and unselfishness as an inspiration to their weaker brethren. Even though most men should fail to attain the ideal, the general level of morality and piety would be raised.

(3) The influence of other Near Eastern religions, especially Gnosticism and Manicheism, with their exaggerated spiritualism, contempt for this world, and degradation of the body.

The earliest Christian ascetics were hermits, who withdrew from the world to live in seclusion in some wilderness or desert. This form of asceticism seems to have originated in Egypt in the third century. From there it spread into other provinces of the eastern section of the Empire and continued to be popular for more than 100 years. It developed into a kind of religious mania characterized by morbid excesses. We read of hermits or anchorites grazing in the fields after the manner of animals, rolling naked in thorn bushes, or living in swamps infested with snakes. The famous St. Simeon

The asceticism of Christian hermits

Stylites passed a whole summer "as a rooted vegetable in a garden" and then began the construction of his celebrated pillar. He built it to a height of sixty feet and spent the remaining thirty years of his life on the top. Such absurdities as these, while certainly not typical of the attitude of the majority of Christians at this time, were probably the natural fruit of too strong an emphasis upon the spiritual way of life.

The rise of monasticism

In time the force of the anchorite hysteria subsided. Certain of the more practical Christian ascetics came to the conclusion that the solitary life of the hermit was not good for the soul, since it sometimes drove men insane. The result of this conclusion was the origin of monasticism. The most prominent early leader of monasticism was St. Basil, a bishop of Cappadocia, who was the first to issue a set of rules for the government of a monastic order. Disapproving of extreme self-torture, St. Basil required his monks to discipline themselves by useful labor. They were not to engage in prolonged fasting or in degrading laceration of the flesh, but they were compelled to submit to obligations of poverty and humility and to spend many hours of the day in silent religious meditation. The Basilian type of monasticism came to be adopted universally in the eastern areas of Christendom. Many of its units are still to be seen perched on lofty crags to which access can be gained only by climbing long rope ladders or being hauled up in a basket. There was no important monasticism in the West until the sixth century, when St. Benedict drafted his famous rule which ultimately became the guide for nearly all the monks of Latin Christendom. The Benedictine rule imposed obligations similar to those of the rule of St. Basil— poverty, obedience, labor, and religious devotion. Yet there was an

A Monastery of the Basilian Order on Mt. Athos. The asceticism of the Basilian monks caused them to build their monasteries in almost inaccessible places on lofty crags or on the steep sides of rugged mountains.

absence of severe austerities. The monks were allowed a sufficiency of simple food, good clothing, and enough sleep. They were permitted to have wine but no meat. They were allowed no recreation and few baths, unless they were sick. They were subject to the absolute authority of the abbot, who could flog them for disobedience. The original Benedictine monastery was established at Monte Cassino, halfway between Rome and Naples. Eventually it came to possess one of the finest libraries in medieval Europe. It was destroyed by Allied bombing during World War II, but has since been rebuilt.

The influence of monasticism upon the society of the early Middle Ages would be difficult to exaggerate. The monks were generally the best farmers in Europe; they reclaimed waste lands, drained swamps, and made numerous discoveries relating to the improvement of the soil. They preserved some of the building skill of the Romans and achieved noteworthy progress in many of the industrial arts, especially in wood carving, metal-working, weaving, glass-making, and brewing. It was monks, furthermore, who wrote most of the books, copied the ancient manuscripts, and maintained the majority of the schools and libraries and nearly all of the hospitals that existed during the early Middle Ages. The growth of monasticism also profoundly affected the history of the Church. It led to a division in the ranks of the clergy. Living according to a definite rule or *regula*, the monks came to be called the *regular* clergy; while the priests, bishops, and archbishops, who carried on their activities in the midst of the affairs of the world (*saeculum*), were henceforth known as the *secular* clergy. Between the two groups intense rivalry developed, with the monks sometimes organizing reform movements against the worldiness of the priests. The Benedictine monks enjoyed the special favor of the Popes, and it was partly on account of an alliance between the papacy and monasticism that the former was able to extend its power over the Church.

The results of monasticism

2. THE GERMANIC FOUNDATIONS OF THE NEW CULTURE

The second most important of the factors which combined to produce the civilization of early medieval Europe was the influence of the Germanic barbarians. They were not the only northern peoples who helped to mold the pattern of early medieval society; the contributions of the Celts in Brittany and Ireland and of the Slavs in central and eastern Europe were by no means insignificant. Nevertheless, the Germanic influence appears to have been the most extensive. Where the Germans came from originally is a problem upon which scholars disagree, but they seem to have migrated into northern Europe from western Asia. By the beginning of the Christian

The ancient Germans

The Germanic
invasions of the
Roman Empire

era they had come to be divided into several peoples: Scandinavians, Vandals, Goths, Franks, Burgundians, Anglo-Saxons, Dutch, and so on. Both in language and in physical characteristics they bore some affinity to the Greeks and the Romans.

For centuries different nations of Germanic barbarians had been making incursions into Roman territory. At times they came as invading armies, but generally they filtered in slowly, bringing their families and belongings with them and occupying depopulated or abandoned areas. Many were brought in by Roman commanders and rulers. Julius Caesar was impressed by their value as warriors and enrolled thousands of them in his armies. They were to be found in the bodyguard of nearly every Princeps and Emperor. Finally, by the time of Constantine, they formed the bulk of the soldiers in the entire Roman army. Many were also drawn into the civil service and thousands were settled by the government as *coloni* or serfs on the great estates. In view of these conditions it is not surprising that Rome should eventually have been taken over by the Germans. As more and more of them gained a foothold in Italy, others were bound to be tempted by the opportunities for plunder. It must be emphasized that many of the supposed invasions were mere "folk wanderings," and not necessarily motivated by a desire for conquest. Although armed invasions of Italy began as early as the second century B.C., and were repeated several times thereafter, there were no really disastrous incursions until the fourth and fifth centuries A.D. In 378 the Visigoths, angered by the oppression of imperial governors, raised the standard of revolt. They overwhelmed a Roman army at Adrianople and then marched westward into Italy. In 410 under Alaric they captured and plundered Rome, later moving on into southern Gaul. In 455 Rome was sacked by the Vandals, who had migrated from their original home between the Oder and Vistula rivers and established a kingdom in the province of Carthage. Other Germanic peoples also made their way into Italy, and before the end of the fifth century the Roman Empire in the West had passed completely under the domination of the barbarians.

Ancient German
society

For our knowledge of ancient Germanic society we are dependent primarily upon the *Germania* of Tacitus, written in 98 A.D. The literature and the laws of the Germans themselves also contain much information, but these were not put into written form until after Roman and Christian influences had begun to exert their effect. When Tacitus wrote, the Germanic barbarians had attained a cultural level about equal to that of the early Greeks. They were illiterate and ignorant of any knowledge of the arts. Their houses were built of rough timber plastered over with mud. While they had achieved some development of agriculture, they preferred the risks of plundering expeditions to the prosaic labor of tilling the soil. Nearly all of the work was done by the women and old men and other dependents. When not fighting or hunting, the warriors spent most of their time sleeping and carousing. Gambling and drunken-

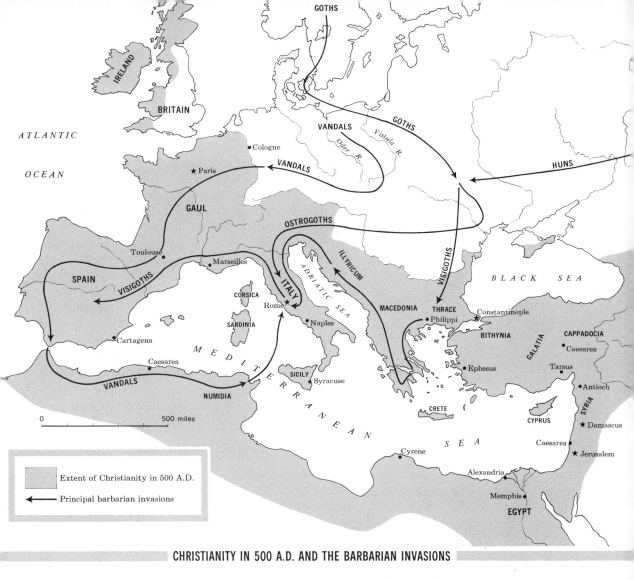

CHRISTIANITY IN 500 A.D. AND THE BARBARIAN INVASIONS

ness were glaring vices, but, if we can believe the testimony of
Tacitus, sex morality was singularly pure. Monogamous marriage
prevailed, except in those cases where a chief might be permitted to
take more than one wife for political reasons. Adultery was rare and
was severely punished; divorce was almost unknown. In some tribes
even widows were forbidden to remarry.

The economic and political institutions of the Germans were such
as befitted a people who were just emerging into a settled existence.
The tiny proportion of trade carried on rested solely upon a basis of
barter, while cattle were still the main article of wealth. Whether
the agricultural land was individually or collectively owned is still a
debated question, but there seems little doubt that the forests and
pastures were held and used in common. Possibly the community
controlled the distribution of new lands as they were acquired,
allotting the arable portions as individual farms. There is evidence

Economic and
political institu-
tions

341

that a class of wealthy proprietors had grown up as an aristocracy in certain of the tribes. Although Tacitus states that the Germans had slaves, it seems probable that most of their dependents were serfs, since they had houses of their own and paid their masters only a portion of what they produced. Their servitude in some cases was a result of capture in war but in others of indebtedness and especially reckless gambling, in which men staked their own liberty when everything else had been lost. The state scarcely existed at all. Law was a product of custom, and the administration of justice remained largely in private hands. While the Germans had their tribal courts, the function of these bodies was chiefly to mediate between plaintiff and defendant. Judicial procedure consisted mainly of oaths and ordeals, both of which were considered as appeals to the judgment of the gods. The most important of the remaining political institutions was the primary assembly of the warriors. But this body had no lawmaking powers beyond those involved in the interpretation of custom. Its main function was to decide questions of war and peace and whether the tribe should migrate to some new locality. Originally the German tribes had no kings. They had chiefs elected by the freemen, but these were little more than ceremonial officials. In time of war a military leader was elected and endowed with considerable power, but as soon as the campaign was over his authority lapsed. Nevertheless, as wars increased in frequency and duration, some of the military leaders actually became kings. The formality of election, however, was generally retained.

The influence of the Germans upon the Middle Ages, while not so important as is sometimes imagined, was extensive enough to deserve consideration. Above all, they were largely responsible for several of the elements of feudalism: (1) the conception of law as an outgrowth of custom and not as the expression of the will of a sovereign; (2) the idea of law as a personal possession of the individual which he could take with him wherever he went, in contrast to the Roman conception of law as limited to a definite territory; (3) the notion of a contractual relationship between rulers and subjects, involving reciprocal obligations of protection and obedience; (4) the theory of an honorable relationship between lord and vassal, growing out of the Germanic institution of the *comitatus* or military band, in which the warriors were bound by pledges of honor and loyalty to fight for and serve their leader; (5) trial by ordeal as a prevailing mode of procedure in the feudal courts; and (6) the idea of elective kingship.

The Germanic influence

3. POLITICAL AND ECONOMIC DEVELOPMENTS IN THE EARLY MIDDLE AGES

Between 500 and 700 A.D. most of western Europe languished in a kind of backward age. The barbarian kings who usurped the authority of the Roman Emperors proved themselves wholly incapable of maintaining the administrative organization that passed into their hands. They appeared to have no conception of efficient government for the public welfare and regarded their kingdoms as private estates to be exploited for their own benefit. They allowed the Roman tax system to break down and delegated much of their political authority to the nobility and the Church. Although many of the old Roman towns survived, they declined in importance, and the ancient urban culture largely disappeared. The characteristic institutions were now the monastery, the peasant village, and the great villa or semifeudal estate cultivated by tenant farmers. No longer was the economy international as it had been in the heyday of Rome. Except for the exchange of a few luxury items, it sank rapidly into localism or rural self-sufficiency.

The only barbarian ruler who did anything in Italy to check the progress of deterioration was Theodoric the Ostrogoth, who conquered the peninsula in 493. Until nearly the end of his reign of thirty-three years, he gave Italy a more enlightened rule than it had known under many of the Caesars. He fostered agriculture and commerce, repaired public buildings and roads, patronized learning, and enforced religious toleration. But in his last years he became querulous and suspicious, accusing some of his faithful subordinates of plotting with the Roman aristocracy to overthrow him. Several were put to death, including the philosopher Boethius. After the death of Theodoric decay set in once more, hastened this time by new wars of conquest. When Justinian became Emperor at Constantinople in 527 he determined to reconquer Italy and the provinces in the West. Not until 552 was the project completed. The devastation of the long war was so great that Italy was opened for invasion by the Lombards in 568. The Lombards succeeded in holding most of the peninsula under the rule of semi-independent dukes until the conquest of Charlemagne in the late eighth century.

Deterioration continued apace in Spain. The Spanish Church was corrupt, and the barbarian (Visigothic) kings were ignorant and predatory. By allowing their power to slip into the hands of an oppressive nobility they made their country an easy prey for Moslem conquest in the eighth century. Deterioration was also evident in France. In 481 a youth by the name of Clovis became king of an important tribe of the Salian Franks, who dwelt on the left bank of the Rhine. The Merovingian dynasty,[7] which he founded, occupied the throne of the Frankish state until 751. Eventually, however, the royal line began to degenerate. A series of short-lived weaklings, the so-called do-nothing kings, inherited the crown of their lusty forebears. Absorbed in the pursuit of pleasure, these worthless youths delegated most of their authority to their chief subordinates, the mayors of the palace. Nothing more natural could have happened

---

[7] So called from Merovech, the half-mythical founder of the family to which Clovis belonged.

Charlemagne, Painting by Dürer

than the eventual displacement of the Merovingian kings by these very officials to whom they had entrusted their powers. The most capable and aggressive of the mayors of the palace was Charles Martel ("the Hammer"), who may be considered a second founder of the Frankish state. He won fame in 733 by defeating the Moors at Poitiers, a town a little more than 100 miles from Paris. Although his opponents were merely a marauding band, the Battle of Poitiers is nevertheless important as the high-water mark of Moorish invasion of France. Yet, even after his victory, Charles was content with the substance of power and did not bother to assume the royal title. It was left for his son, Pepin the Short, to have himself elected king of the Franks in 751 and thereby to put an end to Merovingian rule. the new dynasty became known as the Carolingian from the name of its most famous member, Carolus Magnus or Charlemagne (742–814).

In the minds of most students of history Charlemagne stands out as one of the two or three most important individuals in the whole medieval period. By some of his contemporaries he was acclaimed as a new Augustus who would bring peace and prosperity to western Europe. There can be no question that he established more efficient government, and that he did much to combat the centrifugal tendencies which had gathered momentum during the reigns of the later Merovingians. Not only did he abolish the office of mayor of the palace, but he eliminated the tribal dukes and bestowed all the powers of local government upon his own appointees, the counts. He modified the old system of private administration of justice by authorizing the counts to summon accused persons to court and by vesting the magistrates with more control over judicial procedure. He revived the Roman institution of the sworn inquest, in which a number of persons were summoned by agents of the king and bound by oath to tell what they knew of any crimes committed in their locality. This institution survived the downfall of the Carolingian state and was carried by the Normans to England, where it eventually became an important factor in the origin of the grand-jury system. Although much of the remainder of the political structure Charlemagne established perished with the end of his dynasty, the precedent that he set for strong government undoubtedly influenced many of the French kings in the later Middle Ages and the German emperors as well. There was scarcely a people of western Europe against whom he did not fight, except the English. Since most of his campaigns were successful, he annexed to the Frankish domain the greater part of central Europe and northern and central Italy. But some of these conquests were made possible only by a fearful sacrifice of blood and a resort to measures of the harshest cruelty. The campaign against the Saxons met with such stubborn opposition that Charlemagne finally ordered the beheading of 4500 of them. It is typical of the spirit of the times that all of this was done under the pretext of inducing the pagans to adopt Christianity.

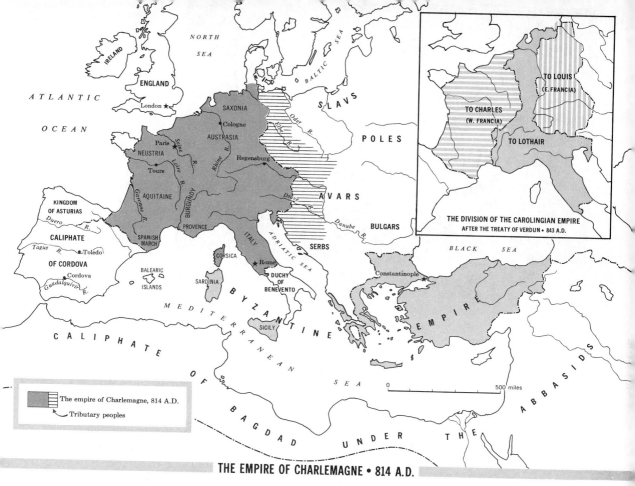

THE EMPIRE OF CHARLEMAGNE • 814 A.D.

In the inset:

THE DIVISION OF THE CAROLINGIAN EMPIRE
AFTER THE TREATY OF VERDUN • 843 A.D.

TO LOUIS (E. FRANCIA)
TO CHARLES (W. FRANCIA)
TO LOTHAIR

Legend:
The empire of Charlemagne, 814 A.D.
Tributary peoples

In fact, it was Charlemagne's constant intervention in religious
affairs which led to the climax of his whole career—his coronation
as Roman Emperor by Pope Leo III. Leo had been in trouble for
some time. Accused of being a tyrant and a rake, he so aroused the
indignation of the people of Rome that in 799 they gave him a
severe beating and forced him to flee from the city. Struggling over
the mountains to Germany, he implored the aid of Charlemagne.
The great king sent him back to Italy and was instrumental in restoring him to the papal throne. On Christmas Day, 800, as Charles
knelt in prayer in St. Peter's Church, the grateful Pope placed a
crown on his head while the assembled multitude hailed him as
"Augustus, crowned of God, great and pacific Emperor of the
Romans." The significance of this event is rather hard to appraise. It
seems doubtful that Charles was under any illusions as to the nature
of the act. For all practical purposes it was merely the recognition
of an accomplished fact. By his conquests Charles had made himself
ruler of nearly all of western and central Europe. In 794 he established a permanent capital at Aachen that was called "New Rome."
He never acknowledged any sovereignty of the Pope over him. In
his view ecclesiastical affairs were as much a part of his domain as

Charlemagne becomes em-peror

345

Charlemagne Weeping for His Knights. A panel commissioned by Frederick Barbarosa for the shrine of Charlemagne at Aachen.

were secular matters. Though he did not attempt to prescribe Church doctrine, he displayed an interest in maintaining uniformity of both discipline and theology. He summoned a number of Church synods during his reign and presided over one of them. In the eyes of the Pope the coronation had a quite different significance. He regarded all kings as his stewards exercising their authority for the benefit of the Church. True, Charles was now an emperor, but it was the Pope who had given him this dignity; and what the Pope could grant he could also take away. This conflict of views foreshadowed the great struggle of the eleventh, twelfth, and thirteenth centuries—a struggle over who should be supreme in western Europe, the Emperor or the Pope.

At the beginning of the early Middle Ages a large part of what is now England was still under Roman rule. But in the fifth century the Romans were forced to withdraw on account of increasing trouble with Germanic invasions into Italy. Soon afterward England was overrun by hordes of Saxons, Angles, and Jutes from the Continent. They brought with them the customs and institutions of their homeland, which were similar to those of the other Germanic barbarians. Driving the original Celtic natives into the mountains of Wales and Cornwall, they quickly established their own kingdoms. At one time there were seven, mutually suspicious and hostile. In the ninth century tribes of Danes took advantage of the strife among the Saxon kingdoms and attempted their conquest. Efforts to defeat the new enemy brought the seven kingdoms into a strong confederation under the leadership of Wessex and its celebrated ruler, Alfred the Great (849–899). King Alfred reorganized the army, infused new vigor into local government, and revised and broadened the laws. In addition, he founded schools and fostered an interest in literature and other elements of a national culture.

The Saxon kingdoms in England

346

King Alfred's successors were men of weaker fiber. One of them, Ethelred the Unready, surrendered his kingdom to the powerful Danish King Canute. For eighteen years England was ruled as part of a North Sea empire which also included Norway and Denmark. But in 1035 Canute died, and the Saxon dynasty regained control of England. It was not for long. Ethelred's son, Edward the Confessor, was more interested in cultivating a reputation for piety than he was in statecraft, and allowed affairs of his country to be regulated by the Duchy of Normandy, across the Channel. Upon Edward's death the Duke of Normandy, subsequently known as William the Conqueror (1027–1087), laid claim to the crown of England. Landing an army in Sussex in 1066, he caught the English monarch, Harold, unprepared and defeated him in the Battle of Hastings. Harold fell mortally wounded, and his forces disintegrated. Apparently regarding discretion as the better part of valor, the surviving magnates offered the crown to Duke William. The Battle of Hastings is considered a turning point in English history, for it ended the period of Anglo-Saxon supremacy and prepared the way for the ultimate establishment of a nation state under William the Norman's successors.

Most of the records of economic life in the early Middle Ages present a mournful picture of return to primitive conditions and, in some cases, actual misery. The decline of Italy in the second half of the fifth century was especially swift. The forces that were set in motion by the economic revolution of the preceding 200 years had now attained their full momentum. Commerce and industry were rapidly becoming extinct, lands that were formerly productive were

Duke William of Normandy Crossing the Channel to Conquer England, from the Bayeux Tapestry. The Bayeux Tapestry depicts, in needlework on linen, 72 scenes of the Norman Conquest. It was probably completed under the direction of Bishop Odo of Bayeux, the Conqueror's half-brother.

growing up in briars and brambles, and the population was declining so noticeably that a law was enacted forbidding any woman under forty years of age to enter a convent. While the proprietors of the great landed estates extended their control over agriculture and over many of the functions of government as well, larger and larger numbers of the masses of the people became serfs. During the reign of Theodoric this process of economic decline was arrested in some measure as a result of the benefits he extended to agriculture and commerce and his reduction of taxes. But Theodoric was unable to eliminate serfdom or to reverse the concentration of landed wealth, for he felt that he needed the support of the aristocracy. After his death the forces of decay again became operative; yet had it not been for Justinian's war of reconquest, Italy might still have preserved a degree of the prosperity she had gained under the Ostrogothic king. The long military conflict brought the country to the verge of stark barbarism. Pestilence and famine completed the havoc wrought by the contending armies. Fields were left untilled, and most of the activities in the towns were suspended. Wolves penetrated into the heart of the country and fattened on the corpses that remained unburied. So great was the widespread hunger that cannibalism appeared in some areas. Only in the larger cities were the normal functions of civilization continued to any appreciable extent.

Economic change in what is now France followed a pattern very similar to that in Italy, but it proceeded at a slower rate. In Roman times southern Gaul had had a flourishing commerce and considerable industry. By the end of the ninth century, however, stagnation was almost complete. The streets of the city of Marseilles were grown over with grass and weeds, and the port itself was deserted for over 200 years. In some other Mediterranean towns and in the interior of the country, trade on a petty scale continued to be carried on, mostly by Jews and Syrians and later by Lombards; but even the activities of these men became steadily more difficult as brigandage increased, the roads deteriorated, and money disappeared from general circulation. The economic history of France was also characterized by the growth of an irregular feudalism similar to that which had sprung up in Italy. Several of the causes were closely related to the policies of the Merovingian and Carolingian kings. Nearly all of these rulers compensated their officials by grants of land. Both Pepin the Short and Charlemagne adhered to the example of Charles Martel in expropriating lands of the Church and turning them over to their chief followers as rewards for military services. More serious was the practice of granting *immunities*, or exemptions from the jurisdiction of the king's agents. Their legal effect was to make the holder subject to the exclusive jurisdiction of the king; but as the king was far away and generally preoccupied with other matters, the nobles took advantage of the opportunity to increase their own independence. Wars, brigandage, and oppression also contributed to the growth of a largely feudal structure of society by forcing

*Economic
conditions
in France;
the foundations
of feudalism*

the weaker citizens to seek the protection of their more powerful neighbors. The result was a tendency toward a division of the population into two distinct classes: a landed aristocracy and serfs.

4. INTELLECTUAL ATTAINMENTS OF THE EARLY MIDDLE AGES

Generally speaking, the intellectual culture of early medieval Europe was not of a high order. Superstition and credulity frequently characterized the work even of many of the outstanding writers. A fondness for compilation rather than for original achievement was also a distinguishing feature of much of the intellectual endeavor. Few men any longer had much interest in philosophy or science, except insofar as these subjects could be made to serve religious purposes. Such an attitude often led to mystical interpretations of knowledge and to the acceptance of fables as fact when they appeared to be freighted with symbolical significance for the sphere of religion. In spite of all this, the mind of the times was not hopelessly submerged in darkness. The light of antique learning was never entirely extinguished; even some of the most pious of Church Fathers recognized the value of classical literature. Moreover, there were a few men in the period who, if not creative geniuses, at least had abilities of scholarship which would not have been rated inferior in the best days of Greece.

Nearly all of the philosophers of the early Middle Ages may be classified as either Christians or pagans, although a few seem to have been nominal adherents of the Church who wrote in the spirit of pagan thought. The Christian philosophers tended to divide into two different schools: (1) those who emphasized the primacy of authority; and (2) those who believed that the doctrines of the faith should be illumined by the light of reason and brought into harmony with the finest products of pagan thinking. The authoritarian tradition in Christian philosophy stemmed originally from Tertullian, a priest of Carthage who lived about the beginning of the third century. For him, Christianity was a system of sacred law to be accepted entirely upon faith. The wisdom of men was mere foolishness with God, and the more a tenet of the faith contradicted reason the greater was the merit in accepting it. Even today theologians can be found who insist upon this absolute supremacy of authority over intellect, of faith over the powers of reason.

While few of the Christian Fathers went as far as Tertullian in despising intellectual effort, there were several who adhered to his general principle that the dogmas of the faith were not to be tested by reason. The most influential was Pope Gregory I (540–604), known in Church history as Gregory the Great. The scion of a rich senatorial family, Gregory scorned the seductions of wealth and power in order that he might dedicate his life to the Church. He turned his father's palace into a convent and gave all of the re-

349

mainder of the wealth he had inherited to the poor. In his work as a theologian he laid great stress upon the idea of penance as essential to the remission of sins and strengthened the notion of purgatory as a place where even the righteous must suffer for minor offenses in order to be purified for admission to heaven.

The most eminent of the Christian philosophers who may be described as representatives of a rationalist tradition were Clement of Alexandria and Origen. Both lived in the third century and were deeply influenced by Neo-Platonism and Gnosticism. Far from despising all human knowledge, they taught that the best of the Greek thinkers had really anticipated the teachings of Jesus, and that Christianity is improved by being brought into harmony with pagan learning. While Clement and Origen would not qualify as rationalists in the modern sense, inasmuch as they took a great many of their beliefs on faith, they nevertheless recognized the importance of reason as a fundamental basis of knowledge, whether religious or secular. They denied the omnipotence of God and taught that God's power is limited by His goodness and wisdom. They rejected the fatalism of many of their opponents and insisted that man by his own free will molds his course of action while on earth. Both Clement and Origen condemned the extreme asceticism of some of their more zealous brethren; in particular, they deplored the tendency of such men as Tertullian to speak of marriage as simply a legalized form of carnality. Finally, they maintained that the purpose of all future punishment is purification and not revenge. Consequently, punishment in hell cannot be eternal, for even the blackest of sinners must eventually be redeemed. If it were not so, God would not be a God of goodness and mercy.

The most erudite and perhaps the most original of all the early Christian philosophers was St. Augustine. Insofar as it is possible to classify him at all, he occupied an intermediate position between Clement and Origen, on the one hand, and Tertullian and Gregory on the other. Though contending that truths of revelation were above natural reason, he perceived the need for an intellectual understanding of what he believed. Born in 354, the son of a pagan father and a Christian mother, Augustine was torn by conflicting impulses throughout the greater part of his life. As a young man he was addicted to sensual pleasures, from which he tried vainly to escape, though he admits in his *Confessions* that his efforts were not wholly sincere. Even after his engagement to marry he could not resist the temptation to take a new mistress. Meanwhile, when he was about eighteen years old, he was attracted to philosophy by reading Cicero's *Hortensius*. He passed from one system of thought to another, unable to find spiritual satisfaction in any. For a brief period he considered the possibilities of Christianity, but it impressed him as too crude and superstitious. Then for nine years he was a Manichean, but ultimately he became convinced that that faith was decadent. Next he was attracted to Neo-Platonism, and then finally returned to Christianity. Though already in his thirty-third year when he was baptized, Augustine advanced rapidly in ecclesiastical positions. In 395 he became Bishop of Hippo in northern Africa, an office he held until his death in 430.

Augustine believed that the supremely important knowledge is knowledge of God and His plan of redemption for mankind. Though most of this knowledge must be derived from the revelation contained in the Scriptures, it is nevertheless the duty of man to understand as much of it as possible in order to strengthen his belief. On the basis of this conclusion St. Augustine developed his conception of human history as the unfoldment of the will of God. Everything that has happened or ever will happen represents but an episode in the fulfillment of the divine plan. The whole race of human beings comprises two great divisions: those whom God has predestined to eternal salvation constitute the City of God; all others belong to the Earthly City. The end of the drama of history will come with the Day of Judgment, when the blessed few who compose the City of God will put on the garment of immortality, while the vast multitude in the earthly kingdom will be cast into the fires of hell. This, according to St. Augustine, is the whole meaning of human existence.

The philosophy of St. Augustine

St. Augustine's theology was an integral part of his philosophy. Believing as he did in a deity who controls the operation of the universe down to the smallest detail, he naturally emphasized the omnipotence of God and set limits to the freedom of the will. Since man is sinful by nature, the will has to struggle against an inclination to commit evil. Although man has the power to choose between good and bad, it is God who provides the motive or "inspiration" for the choice. God created the world in the knowledge that some men would respond to the divine "invitation" to lead holy lives, and that others would resist or refuse to cooperate. In this way God *predestined* a portion of the human race to be saved and left the remainder to perish; in other words, He fixed for all time the number of inhabitants of the heavenly city. It was not that He elected some for salvation and denied to all others the opportunity to be saved. Rather, He knew that some would not *wish* to be saved. The influence of St. Augustine was enormous. In spite of the fact that his teachings were modified considerably by the theologians of the later Middle Ages, he is revered to this day as one of the most important Fathers of the Roman Catholic religion. Lutheran and other Protestant Reformers also held him in the highest esteem, although the interpretations they gave to his teachings frequently differed from those of the Catholics.

St. Augustine theology

Practically the only pagan school of philosophy in early medieval Europe was that of the Neo-Platonists, whose doctrines were discussed in a preceding chapter. There was one other individual thinker, however, who cannot be positively classified as either a pagan or a Christian. It is quite probable that he was a Christian,

The Neo-Platonists and Boethius

though he makes no reference to the Church or to the name of Christ in his chief work. The name of this man was Boethius. Born about 480 of aristocratic parentage, Boethius eventually became principal adviser to Theodoric, the Ostrogothic king. Later he fell out with that monarch, was accused of treason, and thrown into prison. In 524 he was put to death. The chief philosophical work of Boethius, which he wrote while languishing in prison, is entitled *The Consolation of Philosophy*. Its dominant theme is the relation of man to the universe. The author considers such problems as fate, the divine government of the world, and individual suffering. After carefully weighing the various conceptions of fortune, he comes to the conclusion that true happiness is synonymous with philosophic understanding that the universe is really good, and that evil is only apparent. Although he seems to assume the immortality of the soul, he refers to no definitely Christian belief as a source of consolation. His attitude is essentially that of the Stoics, colored by a trace of Neo-Platonist mysticism. Few treatises on philosophy were more popular in medieval Europe than Boethius' *Consolation of Philosophy*. Not only was it ultimately translated into nearly every vernacular language, but numerous imitations of it also were written.

Literature in the early Middle Ages

The history of literature in the early Middle Ages was marked, first of all, by a decline of interest in the classical writings and later by the growth of a crude originality that ultimately paved the way for the development of new literary traditions. By the fifth century the taste for good Latin literature had already begun to decline. Some of the Christian Fathers who had been educated in pagan schools were inclined to apologize for their attachment to the ancient writings; others expressly denounced them; but the attitude that generally prevailed was that of St. Augustine. The great bishop of Hippo declared that men should continue to study the pagan classics, not for their aesthetic value or their human appeal, but "with a view to making the wit more keen and better suited to penetrate the mystery of the Divine Word." [8] Toward the close of the period the vernacular languages, which had been slowly evolving from a fusion of barbarian dialects, with some admixture of Latin elements, began to be employed for crude poetic expression. The consequence was a new and vigorous literary growth which attained its full momentum about the thirteenth century.

Beowulf and other examples of vernacular literature

The best-known example of this literature in the vernacular is the Anglo-Saxon epic poem *Beowulf*. First put into written form about the eighth century, this poem incorporates ancient legends of the Germanic peoples of northwestern Europe. It is a story of fighting and seafaring and of heroic adventure against deadly dragons and the forces of nature. The background of the epic is heathen, but the author of the work introduced into it some qualities of Christian

[8] Quoted by Thompson and Johnson, *An Introduction to Medieval Europe*, p. 221.

idealism. *Beowulf* is important, not only as one of the earliest specimens of Anglo-Saxon or Old English poetry, but also for the picture it gives of the society of the English and their ancestors in the early Middle Ages. No account of the vernacular literature of this time would be complete without some mention of the achievements of the Irish. Ireland in the late sixth and early seventh centuries experienced a brilliant renaissance which made that country one of the brightest spots in the early Middle Ages. Irish monks and bards wrote stories of fantastic adventure on land and sea and hundreds of poems of remarkable sensitivity to natural beauty. The Irish monasteries of this time were renowned centers of learning and art. Their inmates excelled in illuminating manuscripts and in composing both religious and secular verse. As missionaries, under the leadership of St. Columban, they conveyed their influence to Scotland and to many parts of the Continent.

Aside from theological works, the leading productions of authors who wrote in Latin during the early Middle Ages were the histories of Gregory of Tours and Bede. Bishop Gregory of Tours, a near-contemporary of Clovis, wrote with a view to defense of the faith. In his *History of the Franks* he condoned the murders of Clovis on the ground that they were committed in the service of the Church. Although his work contains interesting information about the events of his time, he tended to give a supernatural interpretation to every occurrence. By far the best of the historical writings of the early medieval period was the Venerable Bede's *Ecclesiastical History of the English Nation*. Bede, an English monk, lived between 673 and 735. Apparently more interested in scholarship than in pious meditation, he pursued his studies so assiduously that he gained a reputation as one of the most learned men of his time. In collecting material for his history he devoted careful attention to sources. He did not hesitate to reject the statements of some of the most respectable authorities when he found them to be in error; and when the evidence was a matter of mere oral tradition, he was honest enough to say so.

No account of intellectual attainments in the early Middle Ages would be complete without some reference to developments in education. After the reign of Theodoric, the old Roman system of state schools rapidly disappeared. Throughout the remainder of western Europe the monasteries had a practical monopoly of education. The man who did most to establish the monasteries as institutions of learning was Cassiodorus, formerly chief secretary to Theodoric. Following his retirement from official service, Cassiodorus founded a monastery on his ancestral estate in Apulia and set the monks to work copying manuscripts. The precedent he established was gradually adopted in nearly all the Benedictine institutions. Cassiodorus also insisted that his monks should be trained as scholars, and for this purpose he prepared a curriculum based upon seven subjects, which

The historians

Developments in education; the Seven Liberal Arts

353

came to be called the Seven Liberal Arts. These subjects were divided, apparently by Boethius, into the *trivium* and the *quadrivium*. The former included grammar, rhetoric, and logic, which were supposed to be the keys to knowledge; the *quadrivium* embraced subjects of more definite content—arithmetic, geometry, astronomy, and music.

The textbooks used in the monastic schools were for the most part elementary. In some of the best schools, however, translations of Aristotle's logical works were studied. But nowhere was attention given to laboratory science, and history was largely neglected. Learning was largely memorization, with limited opportunity for criticism or refutation. No professional training of any kind was provided, except for careers in the Church. Learning was, of course, a privilege for the few; the masses as a rule received no education, save what they acquired incidentally, and even most members of the secular aristocracy were illiterate. Yet, with all of its shortcomings, this system of education did help to save European culture from complete eclipse. And it is worth remembering that the best of the monastic and cathedral schools—notably those at Yarrow and York in England—provided the main impetus for the first of the revivals of learning which occurred in the later Middle Ages.

SELECTED READINGS

· *Items so designated are available in paperbound editions.*

· Artz, F. B., *The Mind of the Middle Ages*, New York, 1954.

· Bark, W. C., *Origins of the Medieval World*, Stanford, 1958 (Doubleday).

· Bury, J. B., *The Invasion of Europe by the Barbarians*, London, 1928 (Norton Library).

· Chadwick, Henry, *The Early Church*, Baltimore, 1967 (Penguin).

· Chambers, Mortimer, *The Fall of Rome: Can It Be Explained?* New York, 1963 (European Problem Series, Holt, Rinehart & Winston).

Deanesley, Margaret, *A History of Early Medieval Europe*, New York, 1960.

· Dill, Samuel, *Roman Society in the Last Century of the Western Empire*, London, 1921 (Meridian). Valuable for excerpts from the writers of the fifth century.

· ———, *The Wandering Saints of the Middle Ages*, New York, 1959 (Norton Library).

· Ganshof, Francois Louis, *Frankish Institutions under Charlemagne*, Providence, 1968 (Norton Library).

Hearnshaw, F. J. C., *The Social and Political Ideas of Some Great Medieval Thinkers*, New York, 1923.

Laistner, M. L. W., *Thought and Letters in Western Europe, A.D. 500–900*, rev. ed., New York, 1957.

Latouche, Robert, *The Birth of Western Economy*, New York, 1960.

Latourette, K. S., *A History of Christianity*, New York, 1953.

· Lot, Ferdinand, *The End of the Ancient World and the Beginning of the Middle Ages*, New York, 1931 (Torchbook). An excellent account of the decline of Rome and the transition to the Middle Ages.

- Lyon, Bryce, *The Origins of the Middle Ages*, New York, 1971 (Norton).
- Moss, H. St. L. B., *The Birth of the Middle Ages, 395–814*, New York, 1935 (Galaxy). Clear and concise.

  Patch, R. R., *The Tradition of Boethius*, New York, 1935.
- Rand, E. K., *Founders of the Middle Ages*, Cambridge, Mass., 1928 (Dover). A very good presentation of the contributions of individuals.
- Rops, Daniel, *Jesus and His Times*, New York, 1954 (Doubleday).

  Russell, J. B., *A History of Medieval Christianity*, New York, 1968.
- Taylor, H. O., *The Classical Heritage of the Middle Ages*, New York, 1925 (Torchbook).

  ———, *The Medieval Mind*, New York, 1927, 2 vols.
- Wallace-Hadrill, J. M., *The Barbarian West*, New York, 1962 (Torchbook).

SOURCE MATERIALS

- Boethius, *The Consolation of Philosophy*, New York, 1962 (Library of Liberal Arts, Ungar).
- Brentano, Robert, *The Early Middle Ages, 500–1000*, 1964, Glencoe, Ill. (Free Press).

COLUMBIA RECORDS OF CIVILIZATIONS

- Gregory of Tours, *History of the Franks*, New York, 1965 (Norton).

  King, J. E., ed., *The Historical Works of Bede*, 2 vols., Harvard.

  St. Augustine, *The City of God*, especially Books IV, VII, X, XII, XIV, XV, XVII.

  ———, *Confessions.*

  ———, *Enchiridion*, especially Chs. XXVI, XXVII, XXX–XXXIII, XLI, L, LI, XCVIII, XCIX.

  Shotwell, J. T., and Loomis, L. R., eds., *The See of Peter*, New York, 1927.

CHAPTER **13**

The Byzantine and Saracenic
Civilizations

What is there greater, what more sacred than imperial majesty?
Who so arrogant as to scorn the judgment of the Prince, when
lawgivers themselves have precisely and clearly laid down that
imperial decisions have the force of law?

—Justinian

Muhammad is the messenger of Allah. And those with him are
hard against the disbelievers and merciful among themselves.
Allah hath promised, unto such of them as believe and do good
works, forgiveness and immense reward.

—*The Koran,* Sùrah XLVIII

The so-called medieval period of history does not concern Europe
alone. In addition to the cultures of the European Middle Ages,
medieval history includes two other civilizations, the Byzantine and
the Saracenic or Islamic. Although each occupied territory on the
European continent, the larger portions of their empires were located
in Africa and in Asia. Of greater significance is the fact that the features of both civilizations were largely those of the Near East.
While the Saracens were Moslems and the Byzantine people Christians, religion was a dominant factor in the lives of both. The two
states were so closely linked with the religious organizations that
their governments appeared more theocratic than many of those in
the West. Moreover, both civilizations were characterized by attitudes of pessimism and fatalism and by a tendency for the mystical
point of view to gain supremacy over the rational. It should be noted,
however, that the Saracens especially made distinctive contributions to philosophy and science, while the Byzantine Empire was
exceedingly important for its art and for its work in preserving
innumerable achievements of the Greeks and Romans.

The semi-Ori-
ental character
of the Byzan-
tine and Sara-
cenic civilizations

357

1. THE BYZANTINE EMPIRE AND ITS CULTURE

The founding of
the Byzantine
Empire

In the fourth century the Emperor Constantine established a new capital for the Roman Empire on the site of the old Greek colony of Byzantium. When the western division of the Empire collapsed, Byzantium (or Constantinople, as the city was now more commonly called) survived as the capital of a powerful state which included the Near Eastern provinces of the Caesars. Gradually this state came to be known as the Byzantine Empire, although the existence of a Byzantine civilization was not clearly recognized before the sixth century. Even after that there were many who believed that Rome had merely shifted its center of gravity to the East.

Byzantine culture
more distinctly
Near Eastern
than that of
Latin Europe

Although Byzantine history covered a period similar to that of the Middle Ages, the cultural pattern was far different from the one which prevailed in western Europe. Byzantine civilization had a more pronounced Near Eastern character. Indeed, most of the territories of the Empire actually lay outside of Europe. The most important among them were Syria, Asia Minor, Palestine, and Egypt. Furthermore, Greek and Hellenistic elements entered into the formation of Byzantine culture to a greater extent than was ever true in western Europe. The language of the eastern state was predominantly Greek, while the traditions in literature, art, and science were largely Hellenistic. Lastly, the Christianity of the Byzantine Empire differed from that of Latin Europe in being more mystical, abstract, and pessimistic, and more completely subject to political control. Notwithstanding all these differences, Byzantine civilization was distinctly superior to that of western Europe.

Nationalities in
the Byzantine
Empire

The population of the territories under Byzantine rule comprised a great number of nationalities. The majority of the inhabitants were Greeks and Hellenized Orientals—Syrians, Jews, Armenians, Egyptians, and Persians. In addition, the European sections of the Empire included numerous barbarians, especially Slavs and Mongols. There were some Germans also, but the emperors at Constantinople were generally able to divert the German invasions to the west. The encroachments of the Slavs and the Mongols, on the other hand, proved to be much more difficult to deal with. The original home of the Slavs, a round-headed people of Alpine stock, was apparently the region northeast of the Carpathian Mountains, principally in what is now southwestern Russia. A peaceful agricultural folk, they seldom resorted to armed invasion but gradually expanded into thinly settled territories whenever the opportunity arose. Not only did they move into the vast empty spaces of central Russia, but they occupied many of the regions vacated by the Germans and then slowly filtered through the frontiers of the Eastern Empire. By the seventh century they were the most numerous people in the entire Balkan peninsula, as well as in the whole region of Europe east of the Germans. The Mongolian inhabitants of the Empire came into

Europe from the steppes of what is now Asiatic Russia. They were herdsmen, with the furious energy and warlike habits characteristic of that mode of existence. After entering the valley of the Danube, many of them forced their way into Byzantine territory. It was a fusion of some of these Mongolian peoples with Slavs which gave rise to such modern nations as the Bulgarians and the Serbs.

Byzantine political history

The early history of the Byzantine Empire was marked by struggles to repel the Germanic barbarians. The confidence inspired by the success of these struggles encouraged the Emperor Justinian to begin the reconquest of Italy and North Africa, but most of Italy was soon afterward abandoned to the Lombards, and Norh Africa to the Moslems. In the early seventh century Byzantium became involved in a great war with Persia, which eventually exhausted both empires and laid their territories open to Saracenic conquest. By 750 the Byzantine state had lost all of its possessions outside of Europe with the exception of Asia Minor. After the tide of Saracenic advance had spent its force, Byzantium enjoyed a brief recovery and even regained the province of Syria, the island of Crete, and some portions of the Italian coast, as well as certain territories on the Balkan peninsula which had been lost to the barbarians. In the eleventh century, however, the Empire was attacked by the Seljuk Turks, who rapidly overran the eastern provinces and in 1071 annihilated a Byzantine army of 100,000 men at Manzikert. The Emperor Romanus Diogenes was taken prisoner and held for a ransom of one million pieces of gold. Soon afterward the government sent an appeal for aid to the West. The result was the Crusades, launched originally against the Moslems but eventually turned into plundering attacks upon Byzantine territory. In 1204 the Crusaders captured Constantinople and treated that city "with more barbarity than the barbarian Alaric had treated Rome eight hundred years before."[1] But even these disasters did not prove fatal. During the late thirteenth and early fourteenth centuries the Empire once again recovered some measure of its former strength and prosperity. Its history was finally brought to an end with the capture of Constantinople by the Ottoman Turks in 1453.

Factors in the stability of the Byzantine Empire

During this long period of approximately 1000 years the stability of Byzantine rule was frequently menaced not only by foreign aggression but also by palace intrigues, mutinies in the army, and violent struggles between political factions. How then can it be explained that the Empire survived so long, especially in view of the rapid decay of the West during the early centuries of this period? Geographic and economic factors were probably the major causes. The location of Constantinople made it almost impregnable. Surrounded on three sides by water and on the fourth by a thick, high wall, the city was able to resist capture practically as long as any

[1] J. B. Bury, *History of the Later Roman Empire* (1931 ed.), I, 3.

will to defend it remained. Furthermore, the Near East suffered no decay of industry and commerce like that which had occurred in Italy during the last centuries of the empire in the West. Last of all, the Byzantine government had a well-filled treasury which could be drawn upon for purposes of defense. The annual revenues of the state have been estimated as high as $167 million (1972 dollars).

The government of the Byzantine Empire was similar to that of Rome after the time of Diocletian, except that it was even more despotic and theocratic. The emperor was an absolute sovereign with unlimited power over every department of national life. His subjects not only fell prostrate before him, but in petitioning his grace they customarily referred to themselves as his slaves. Moreover, the spiritual dignity of the emperor was in no sense inferior to his temporal power. He was the vicar of God with a religious authority supposed to be equal to that of the Apostles. Although some of the emperors were able and hard-working officials, most of the actual functions of the government were performed by an extensive bureaucracy, many of whose members were highly trained. A great army of clerks, inspectors, and spies maintained the closest scrutiny over the life and possessions of every inhabitant.

The economic system was as strictly regulated as in Hellenistic Egypt. In fact, the Byzantine Empire has been described as a "paradise of monopoly, of privilege, and of paternalism." [2] The state exercised a thorough control over virtually every activity. The wage of every workman and the price of every product were fixed by government decree. In many cases it was not even possible for the individual to choose his own occupation, since the system of guilds which had been established in the late Roman Empire was still maintained. Each worker inherited his status as a member of one guild or another, and the walls which surrounded these organizations were hermetically sealed. Nor did the manufacturer enjoy much greater freedom. He could not choose for himself what quantity or quality of raw materials he would purchase, nor was he permitted to buy them directly. He could not determine how much he would produce or under what conditions he would sell his product. A number of large industrial enterprises were owned and operated by the state. Chief among them were the murex or purple fisheries, the mines, the armament factories, and the establishments for the weaving of cloth. An attempt was made at one time to extend monopolistic control over the silk industry, but the government factories were unable to supply the demand, and permission had to be given to private manufacturers to resume production.

The agricultural regime developed under the late Roman Empire was also perpetuated and extended in the Byzantine territories. Most of the land was divided into great estates operated by feudal magnates. Except in the hilly and mountainous regions, there were

The government of the Byzantine Empire

State control of the economic system

[2] J. W. Thompson, *Economic and Social History of the Middle Ages*, p. 336.

few independent farmers left. In the richest areas the agricultural population was made up almost entirely of tenant farmers and serfs. The number of the latter was increased in the fifth century, when the Emperor Anastasius issued a decree forbidding all peasants who had lived on a particular farm for thirty years ever to remove therefrom. The purpose of the decree was to ensure a minimum of agricultural production, but its natural effect was to bind the peasants to the soil and make them actual serfs of their landlords. Another of the significant agricultural developments in the Byzantine Empire was the concentration of landed wealth in the hands of the Church. The monasteries, especially, came to be included among the richest proprietors in the country. With the increasing difficulty of making a living from the soil and the growing popularity of asceticism, more and more farmers sought refuge in the cloister and made gifts of their lands to the institutions which admitted them. The estates acquired by the Church were cultivated, not by the monks or the priests, but by serfs. During the seventh and eighth centuries many of the serfs gained their freedom and became owners of the lands they cultivated. But by the eleventh century the great estates had reappeared, and the independent peasantry virtually ceased to exist.

The agricultural regime

No subject appears to have absorbed the interest of the Byzantine people more completely than religion. They fought over religious questions as vehemently as citizens of the modern world quarrel over issues of government control versus private ownership or democracy versus totalitarianism. They took great delight in theological subtleties which would impress most people in our time as barren and trivial. Gregory of Nyssa, one of their own Church Fathers, thus described Constantinople in the fourth century: "Everything is full of those who are speaking of unintelligible things. I wish to know the price of bread; one answers: 'The Father is greater than the Son'; I inquire whether my bath is ready; one says, 'The Son has been made out of nothing.' " [3]

The absorbing interest in religion

The most crucial of the religious issues, however, were those which grew out of the Monophysite and Iconoclastic movements, although neither of these movements was exclusively religious in character. The Monophysites derived their name from their contention that the Christ was composed of only one nature, and that that nature was divine. This doctrine, which was probably a reflection of the Neo-Platonist contempt for everything physical or material, flatly contradicted the official theology of Christianity. Having begun as early as the fifth century, the Monophysite movement reached its height during the reign of Justinian (527–565). Its strength lay chiefly in Syria and in Egypt, where it served as an expression of nationalist resentment against subjection to Constantinople. In dealing with the sect Justinian was caught between two fires. Not only was he ambitious to unite his subjects in allegiance to

Religious controversies; the Monophysite movement

[3] A. A. Vasiliev, *History of the Byzantine Empire*, I, 99 f.

a single faith, but he was anxious to win the support of Rome. On the other hand, he was reluctant to take any steps for the suppression of the Monophysites, partly because of their strength and also because his wife, the popular actress Theodora, was a member of the sect. It was her will that finally prevailed. During the seventh century the Monophysites broke away from the Eastern Church. The sect survives to this day as an important branch of Christendom in Egypt, Syria, and Armenia. They are now commonly called Coptic Christians.

The Iconoclastic movement was launched about 725 by a decree of the Emperor Leo III forbidding the use of images in the Church. In the Eastern Church any image of God, the Christ, or a saint was called an icon. Those who condemned the use of icons in worship were known as Iconoclasts, or image-breakers. The Iconoclastic movement was a product of several factors. First of all, it had a certain affinity with the Monophysite movement in its opposition to anything sensuous or material in religion. Secondly, it was a protest against paganism and worldliness in the Church. But perhaps more than anything else it represented a revolt of certain of the emperors against the increasing power of the ecclesiastical system. The monasteries in particular were absorbing so large a proportion of the national wealth and enticing so many men away from service in the army and from useful occupations that they were undermining the economic vitality of the Empire. Since the monks derived a large part of their income from the manufacture and sale of icons, it was logical that the reforming emperors should center their attacks upon the use of images in the Church. Naturally they had the support of many of their pious subjects, who resented what they considered a corruption of their religion by idolatrous practices.

The Iconoclasts

Although the struggle against the worship of images was continued until well into the ninth century, it really accomplished no more than the elimination of sculptured representations; the flat or painted icons were eventually restored. Nevertheless, the Iconoclastic controversy had more than a trivial significance. It may be said to have represented an important stage in the irrepressible conflict between Roman and Near Eastern traditions, which occupied so large a place in Byzantine history. Those who upheld the use of images generally believed in an ecclesiastical religion in which symbols and ceremony were regarded as indispensable aids to worship. Most of their opponents were mystics and ascetics who condemned any form of institutionalism or veneration of material objects and advocated a return to the spiritualism of primitive Christianity. Many of the ideals of the Iconoclasts were similar to those of the Protestant Reformers of the sixteenth century, and the movement itself may be said to have foreshadowed the great revolt of Luther and Calvin against what were considered pagan elements in the Roman Catholic religion. Finally, the Iconoclastic controversy was a potent cause of the separation of the Greek and Roman branches of the Church in

Significance of the Iconoclastic controversy

362

1054. Even though the attack upon the use of images was not entirely successful, it went far enough to arouse much antagonism between Eastern and Western Christians. The Pope excommunicated the Iconoclasts and turned from the Byzantine emperors to the Frankish kings for support. From this point on the East and the West drew farther apart.

Social conditions in the Byzantine Empire presented a marked contrast with western Europe during the early Middle Ages. Whereas large sections of Italy and France sank to almost primitive levels in the ninth and tenth centuries, Byzantine society continued to maintain its essentially urban and luxurious character. Approximately a million people lived in the city of Constantinople alone, to say nothing of the thousands who dwelt in Nicaea, Edessa, Thessalonica, and other great urban centers. Merchants, bankers, and manufacturers ranked with the great landlords as members of the aristocracy, for there was no tendency in Byzantium as there had been in Rome to despise the man who derived his income from industry or trade. The rich lived in elegance and ease, cultivating the indulgence of opulent tastes as a fine art. A large part of the industrial activity of the nation was absorbed in the production of articles of luxury to meet the demand of the wealthier classes. Magnificent garments of wool and silk interwoven with gold and silver thread, gorgeously colored tapestries of brocaded or damasked stuffs, exquisite glass and porcelain ware, illuminated gospels, and rare and costly jeweled ornaments composed only a small part of the sumptuous output of factories and shops, both public and private.

A Silver Byzantine Plate Portraying David and Goliath

The life of the lower classes was poor and mean by comparison. And yet the common man in the Byzantine Empire was probably better off than the average citizen in most other parts of the Christian world at that time. The extensive industrial and commercial development and the high degree of economic stability provided opportunities for employment for thousands of urban workers. Even the lot of the serf who was attached to the estate of some one of the great secular proprietors was probably superior to that of the peasants in western Europe, since the landlord's powers of exploitation were at least regulated by law.

A Byzantine Plate of Gold and Enamel Portraying the Christ

The tone of morality in the Empire exhibited sharp contrasts. The Byzantine people, in spite of their Greek antecedents, apparently had no aptitude for the typical Hellenic virtues of balance and restraint. In place of the golden mean they seemed always to prefer the extremes. Consequently, the most extravagant self-indulgence was frequently to be found side by side with the humblest self-denial or laceration of the flesh. The contradictory qualities of sensuality and piety, charity and heartless cruelty, were commonly evident in the same stratum of society or even in the same individuals. For example, the great reform Emperor, Leo III, tried to improve the lot of the peasants, but he also introduced mutilation as a punishment for crime. Life at the imperial court and among some

Extremes of asceticism and sensual indulgence

363

members of the higher clergy appears to have been characterized by indolence, luxurious vice, and intrigue. As a consequence, the very word "Byzantine" has come to be suggestive of elegant sensuality and refinements of cruelty.

Revision and
codification of
the Roman law

In the intellectual realm the Byzantine people won little distinction for originality. Comparatively few discoveries or contributions in any of the fields of knowledge can actually be credited to them. Probably their most noteworthy achievement was the revision and codification of the ancient Roman law. After the time of the great jurists (second and third centuries A.D.) the creative genius of the Roman lawyers subsided, and nothing new was added to the philosophy or the science of law. The volume of statutory enactments, however, continued to grow. By the sixth century Roman law had come to contain numerous contradictory and obsolete provisions. Moreover, conditions had changed so radically that many of the old legal principles could no longer be applied, particularly on account of the establishment of an Oriental despotism and the adoption of Christianity as the official religion. When Justinian came to the throne in 527, he immediately decided upon a revision and codification of the existing law to bring it into harmony with the new conditions and to establish it as an authoritative basis of his rule. To carry out the actual work he appointed a commission of lawyers under the supervision of his minister, Tribonian. Within two years the commission published the first result of its labors. This was the Code, a systematic revision of all of the statutory laws which had been issued from the reign of Hadrian to the reign of Justinian. The Code was later supplemented by the Novels, which contained the legislation of Justinian and his immediate successors. By 532 the commission had completed the Digest, representing a summary of all of the writings of the great jurists. The final product of the work of revision was the Institutes, a textbook of the legal principles which were reflected in both the Digest and the Code. The combination of all four of these results of the program of revision constitutes the *Corpus Juris Civilis*, or the body of the civil law.

The Institutes
and the Digest

From the historical standpoint the two most important sections of the *Corpus Juris* were unquestionably the Institutes and the Digest. It was these which contained the philosophy of law and of government which had come to prevail in Justinian's time. There is a popular but inaccurate belief that this philosophy was the same as that of Ulpian, Papinian, and the other great jurists of 300 years before. While it is true that most of the old theory was preserved, a few fundamental changes were introduced. First, the *jus civile* was more completely denationalized than it had ever been during Roman times and was now made applicable to citizens of a great many divergent nationalities. The *jus naturale* was now declared to be divine and consequently superior to all of the enactments of men—a conception which was destined to become exceedingly popular in later medieval philosophy. There was a tendency also for Justinian's jurists to speak of the emperor as the sole legislator, on the assumption that the people had surrendered all of their power to him. In other words, the classical Roman law was being revised to make it fit the needs of an Oriental monarch whose sovereignty was limited only by the law of God.

The supreme artistic achievement of the Byzantine civilization was its architecture. Its finest example was the Church of Santa Sophia (Holy Wisdom), built at enormous cost by the Emperor Justinian. Although designed by architects of Hellenic descent, it was vastly different from any Greek temple. Its purpose was not to express man's pride in himself or his satisfaction with this life, but to symbolize the inward and spiritual character of the Christian religion. It was for this reason that the architects gave little attention to the external appearance of the building. Nothing but plain brick covered with plaster was used for the exterior walls; there were no marble facings, graceful columns, or sculptured entablatures. The interior, however, was decorated with richly colored mosaics, gold leaf, colored marble columns, and bits of tinted glass set on edge to refract the rays of sunlight after the fashion of sparkling gems. It was for this reason also that the building was constructed in such a way that no light appeared to come from the outside at all but to be manufactured within.

The structural design of Santa Sophia was something altogether new in the history of architecture. Its central feature was the application of the principle of the dome to a building of square shape. The church was designed, first of all, in the form of a cross, and then over the central square was to be erected a magnificent dome, which would dominate the entire structure. The main problem was how to fit the round circumference of the dome to the square area it

The Church of
Santa Sophia

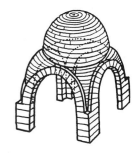

Plan of Santa Sophia Dome

The Church of Santa Sophia in Constantinople. Built by Justinian in the sixth century A.D., it is an outstanding example of Byzantine architectural design. As the diagram shows, the central dome rests upon four massive arches. Its tremendous downward thrust necessitates buttressing with enormous masonry piles and half-domes. The minarets were added later by the Moslems.

was supposed to cover. The solution consisted in having four great arches spring from pillars at the four corners of the central square. The rim of the dome was then made to rest on the keystones of the arches, with the curved triangular spaces between the arches filled in with masonry. The result was an architectural framework of marvelous strength, which at the same time made possible a style of imposing grandeur and even some delicacy of treatment. The great dome of Santa Sophia has a diameter of 107 feet and rises to a height of nearly 180 feet from the floor. So many windows are placed around its rim that the dome appears to have no support at all but to be suspended in mid-air.

Other Byzantine arts

The other arts of Byzantium included ivory-carving, the making of embossed glassware and brocaded textiles, the illumination of manuscripts, the goldsmith's and jeweler's arts, and considerable painting. The last, however, was not so highly developed as some of the others. In place of painting, the Byzantine artist generally preferred mosaics. These were designs produced by fitting together small pieces of colored glass or stone to form a geometric pattern, symbolical figures of plants and animals, or even an elaborate scene of theological significance. Representations of saints and of the Christ were commonly distorted to create the impression of extreme piety.

See color plates at page 257

The Byzantine influence in eastern Europe

The importance of the Byzantine civilization is usually underestimated. It was undoubtedly the most powerful factor in determining the course of development of eastern Europe. To a large extent the civilization of imperial Russia was founded upon the institutions and achievements of Byzantium. The Russian Orthodox Church was an offshoot of the so-called Greek Orthodox or Eastern church, which broke away from Rome in 1054. The Tsar as the head of the religion as well as the state occupied a position analogous to that of the emperor at Constantinople. The architecture of the Russians, their calendar, and a large part of their alphabet were also of Byzantine origin. Perhaps even the despotism of the Soviet regime can be traced in some measure to the long-standing tradition of absolute rule in Russia, which ultimately goes back to Byzantine influence.

The Byzantine influence in the West

But the influence of the Byzantine civilization was not limited to eastern Europe. It would be hard to overestimate the debt of the West to scholars in Constantinople and the surrounding territory who copied and preserved manuscripts, prepared anthologies of Greek literature, and wrote encyclopedias embodying the learning of the ancient world. Moreover, Byzantine scholars exerted a notable influence upon the Italian Renaissance. The extensive trade between Venice and Constantinople in the late Middle Ages fostered cultural relations between East and West. Consequently, long before the fifteenth century when eminent Greek scholars arrived in Italy, a foundation for the revival of interest in the Greek classics had already been laid. Likewise, Byzantine art exerted its effect upon the art of western Europe. Several of the most famous churches in Italy,

A Byzantine Mosaic Depicting Jesus Entering Jerusalem

for example St. Mark's in Venice, were built in close imitation of the Byzantine style. Byzantine painting also influenced the painting of the Renaissance, especially of the Venetian school. Finally, it was the *Corpus Juris* of Justinian which really made possible the transmission of the Roman law to the late Middle Ages and to the modern world.

2. ISLAM AND THE SARACENIC CIVILIZATION

The history of the Saracenic or Arabian civilization began a little later than the history of Byzantium and ended a short time earlier. The dates were roughly 630 A.D. to 1300. In many ways the Saracenic civilization was one of the most important in the Western world—not only because it was the orbit of a new religion, which has attracted converts by the hundreds of millions, but mainly because its impact upon Christian Europe was responsible for social and intellectual changes that can only be described as revolutionary. The term "Saracen" originally meant an Arab, but later it came to be applied to any member of the Islamic faith, regardless of his nationality. Some of the Saracens were Jews, some were Persians, some were Syrians. Nevertheless, the founders of the civilization were Arabs, and it therefore becomes necessary to examine the culture of that people on the eve of their expansion beyond the borders of their homeland.

Importance of the Saracenic civilization

Toward the end of the sixth century the people of Arabia had come to be divided into two main groups: the urban Arabs and the Bedouins. The former, who dwelt in such cities as Mecca and Yathrib, were traders and petty craftsmen. Many were literate, and some were comparatively wealthy. The Bedouins were mostly nomads, subsisting on dates and the flesh and milk of their animals. Ignorant and superstitious, they practiced infanticide and occasional human sacrifice. They were frequently involved in bloody warfare over possession of wells and oases. Neither Bedouins nor urban

Conditions in Arabia before Mohammed

367

St. Mark's Church, Venice. The most splendid example of Byzantine architecture in Italy.

Arabs had any organized government. The clan and the tribe took the place of the state. When a member of one clan committed a crime against a member of another, the issue was settled by means of the blood feud, which sometimes raged until scores had been killed on each side. The religion was generally polytheistic, although some of the better educated townsmen had adopted a belief in Allah as the only God. From time immemorial Mecca had been a sacred city. Here was the shrine known as the Kaaba, containing a sacred black stone which was supposed to have been miraculously sent down from heaven. The men who controlled this shrine formed the tribe of the Kuraish, the nearest approach to an Arabian aristocracy that ever existed before the migrations.

The Islamic religion as a driving force in the civilization

Whether the Saracenic civilization would ever have originated without the development of the Islamic religion is a question almost impossible to answer. It is commonly assumed that a new religion was necessary to unite the people and to imbue them with ardor in a common cause. Yet other nations had expanded before this and had accomplished great things without the influence of any particularly inspiring system of belief. Nevertheless, in the case of the Arabs it was a new religion which undoubtedly provided much of the driving force behind the development of their civilization. The origin and nature of that religion must therefore be given attention.

The founder of the new faith was born in Mecca about the year 570. The child of parents who belonged to one of the poorest clans of the Kuraish tribe, he was given the common Arabic name of Muhammad or Mohammed. Little is known about his early life. He was left an orphan while still very young and was reared by his grandfather and his uncle. When he was about twenty-five years old, he entered the employment of a rich widow and accompanied her caravans, perhaps as far north as Syria. Soon afterward he became her husband, thereby acquiring leisure and security to devote all of his time to religious interests.

Exactly what influences led Mohammed to become the founder of a new religion, no one knows. He was apparently of a highly emotional nature. At times he seems to have believed that he heard voices from heaven. Quite early in his life he became acquainted with numerous Jews and Christians who lived in the cities of northern Arabia, and he appears to have been deeply impressed by their religious beliefs. In addition, he seems to have developed the idea that social and moral conditions in his country were badly in need of reform. He began to denounce the plutocrats of Mecca for their greed and to reproach his people for their bloody feuds and their practice of infanticide. Gradually he came to conceive of himself as the appointed instrument of God to rescue the Arabian people from the path of destruction.

Mohammed's preaching was not at first particularly successful. After almost nine years of communicating the revelations of Allah to all who would listen, he had managed to win very few converts outside of his immediate family. The wealthy Kuraish were naturally against him, and even the common people of Mecca were generally indifferent. In 619 he decided to seek a more promising field for the propagation of his teachings. He had learned that the city of Yathrib on the caravan route to the north had been torn for some time by factional strife, and that there might be some chance for a neutral leader to step in and assume control. In 622, he and the

The Interior of St. Mark's Cathedral in Venice

The Kaaba. It contains the black stone which was supposed to have been miraculously sent down from heaven, and rests in the courtyard of the great mosque in Mecca.

remainder of his followers decided to abandon the sacred city of Mecca and to risk their future in the new location. This migration to Yathrib is known to Mohammedans as the Hegira, from the Arabic word meaning "flight," and is considered by them so important that they regard it as the beginning of their era and date all their records from it.

Mohammed changed the name of Yathrib to Medina (the "city of the Prophet"), and quickly succeeded in establishing himself as ruler of the city. But to obtain means of support for his followers was a somewhat more difficult matter. Besides, the Jews in Medina rejected his leadership. Under these circumstances Mohammed began to enlist the support of the Bedouins for a holy war against his enemies. In a single year approximately 600 Jews were massacred, and then the followers of the Prophet launched their plundering attacks upon the caravans of the merchants of Mecca. When the latter took up arms to resist, they were badly defeated in battle. In 630 Mohammed entered Mecca in triumph. He murdered a few of his leading opponents and smashed the idols in the temple, but the Kaaba itself was preserved, and Mecca was established as a sacred city of the Islamic faith. Two years later Mohammed died, but he lived to see the religion he had founded a militant and successful enterprise.

The doctrines of the Islamic religion as developed by the Prophet are really quite simple. They revolve around a belief in one God, who is called by the old Arabic name Allah, and in Mohammed as His Prophet. This God desires that men shall be kind to their neighbors, lenient toward debtors, honest, and forgiving; and that they shall refrain from infanticide, eating swine's flesh, drinking intoxicating beverages, and waging the blood feud. The religion also enjoins the faithful observance of certain obligations. Chief among

The conquest of Mecca

The doctrines of the Islamic religion

these are the giving of alms to the poor, fasting during the day throughout the sacred month of Ramadan, praying five times a day, and making a pilgrimage, if possible, at least once in a lifetime to Mecca. Almost as much emphasis is placed upon purity of heart and practical benevolence as in Christianity or Judaism. Several passages in the Koran, which constitutes the Islamic Scriptures, provide ample warrant for such a conclusion. One of them declares that "There is no piety in turning your faces toward the east or the west, but he is pious who believeth in God, and the last day, and the angels, and the Scriptures, and the prophets; who for the love of God disburseth his wealth to his kindred, and to the orphans, and the needy, and the wayfarer and those who ask, and for ransoming." [4] Another affirms that the highest merit is "to free the captive; or to feed, in a day of famine, the orphan who is of kin, or the poor man who lieth on the ground." [5] There are no sacraments in the system of worship taught by Mohammed, and there are no priests. The religion itself is officially known as "Islam," a word meaning "to submit, or to surrender oneself absolutely to God." The official designation of a believer is a "Moslem," which is the participle of the same verb of which "Islam" is the infinitive.

The sources of the religion of Islam are somewhat in doubt. Judaism was unquestionably one of them. Mohammed taught that the Arabs were descendants of Ishmael, Abraham's oldest son. Moreover, a good many of the teachings of the Koran are quite similar to doctrines in the Old Testament: strict monotheism, the sanction of polygamy, and the prohibition of usury and the eating of pork. Christianity was also an exceedingly important source. Mohammed considered the New Testament as well as the Old to be a divinely inspired book, and he regarded Jesus as one of the greatest of a long line of prophets. Besides, the Islamic doctrines of the resurrection of the body, the last judgment, rewards and punishments after death, and the belief in angels were more probably derived from Christianity than from any other system of belief. On the other hand, it is necessary to remember that the Christianity with which Mohammed was acquainted was far from the orthodox variety. Nearly all of the Christians who lived in Syria as well as those in Arabia itself were Ebionites or Nestorians. It is perhaps for this reason that Mohammed always thought of Jesus as human, the son of Joseph and Mary, and not as a god.

It was not long after the origin of Islam that its followers split into a number of sects not entirely dissimilar to some of the offshoots of Christianity. The three most important of the Islamic sects were the Sunnites, the Shiites, and the Sufis. The first two had a political as well as a religious character. The Sunnites maintained that the head of the Islamic state and successor to the Prophet should be elected by representatives of the whole body of believers, in accord-

The probable
sources of Islam

The principal
Islamic sects

[4] Sura 2:V. 172.
[5] Sura 90:V. 12.

ance with the ancient Arabian custom of election of tribal chiefs. In matters of religion they contended that the *sunna*, or traditions which had grown up outside of the Koran, should be accepted as a valid source of belief. The Shiites were opposed to the elevation of anyone to the highest political and religious office who was not related to the Prophet himself, either by blood or by marriage. In general, they represented the absolutist ideal in Islam as distinct from the democratic ideal of the Sunnites. What is more, the Shiites were against the acceptance of anything but the Koran as a source of religious belief. The Sufis adhered to a mystical and ascetic ideal. Denying absolutely the validity of rational judgment, they maintained that the only truth of any worth is that which proceeds from divine revelation. They believed that it is possible for man to partake of this divine revelation through torturing his body and thereby releasing the soul for a mystic union with God. Many of the fakirs and dervishes in India, Pakistan, and Iran today are members of the Sufi sect.

The political history of the Saracenic civilization is closely interwoven with the growth of the religion. As we have already seen, Mohammed became the founder not merely of a religion but also of an Arabic state with its capital at Medina. Following his death in 632 his companions chose as his successor Abu-Bekr, one of the earliest converts to the faith and the father-in-law of Mohammed. The new ruler was given the title of *caliph*, that is, successor to the Prophet. After Abu-Bekr's death two other caliphs were chosen in succession from among the earlier disciples of Mohammed. In 656, however, a long struggle began for possession of the supreme power in Islam. First the Shiites succeeded in deposing a member of the Ommiad family and in electing Ali, the husband of Mohammed's daughter Fatima, as caliph. Five years later Ali was murdered, and the Ommiads came back into power. Soon afterward they transferred the capital to Damascus and established their family as a reigning dynasty with a luxurious court in imitation of the Byzantine model. In 750 the Shiites revolted again, this time under the leadership of a member of the Abbasid family, who was a distant relative of the Prophet. The Abbasids seized the throne and moved the capital to the city of Baghdad on the Tigris River, where they ruled as Oriental despots for more than three centuries. A few of them were enlightened patrons of learning, especially Harun-al-Raschid (786–809) and Al-Mamun (813–33).

In the meantime, a great wave of Saracenic expansion had swept over Asia, Africa, and Europe. When Mohammed died in 632, the authority of his little state probably did not extend over more than one-third of the Arabian peninsula. A hundred years later at least one-third of the civilized world was under Moslem domination. The Saracenic empire extended from the borders of India to the Strait of Gibraltar and the Pyrenees Mountains. One after another, with

Political history
of the Islamic
state: the caliphs

The Saracenic
conquests

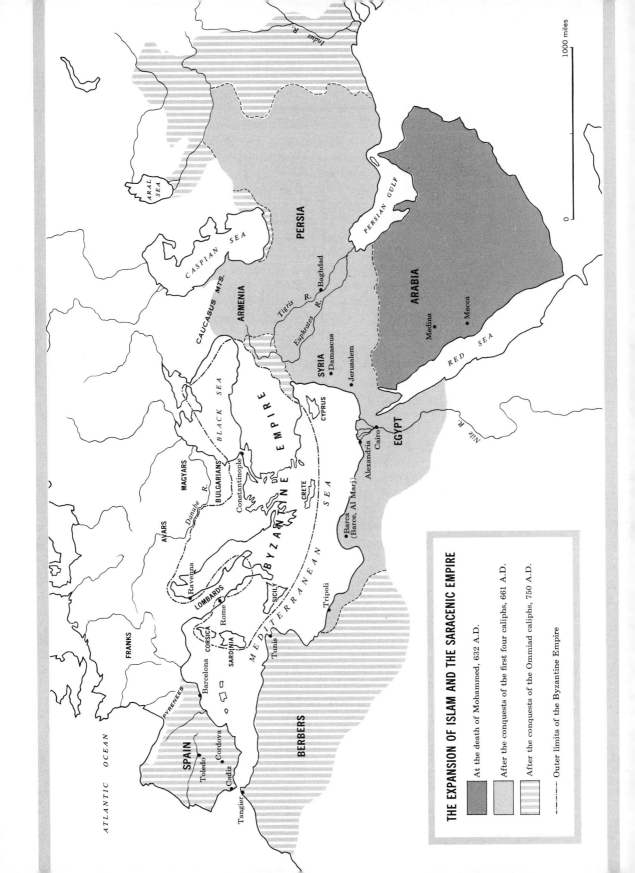

THE EXPANSION OF ISLAM AND THE SARACENIC EMPIRE

At the death of Mohammed, 632 A.D.

After the conquests of the first four caliphs, 661 A.D.

After the conquests of the Ommiad caliphs, 750 A.D.

Outer limits of the Byzantine Empire

1000 miles

ATLANTIC OCEAN

SPAIN
Toledo
Cordova
Cadiz
Tangier
Barcelona
PYRENEES

FRANKS

AVARS
MAGYARS
BULGARIANS
Danube R.
Constantinople
BYZANTINE EMPIRE
Ravenna
LOMBARDS
Rome
CORSICA
SARDINIA
Tunis
SICILY
MEDITERRANEAN SEA
CRETE
Tripoli
Barca (Barce, Al Marj)
CYPRUS

BERBERS

BLACK SEA
CAUCASUS MTS.
CASPIAN SEA
ARAL SEA
ARMENIA
PERSIA
Tigris R.
Euphrates R.
Baghdad

Indus R.

SYRIA
Damascus
Jerusalem
Alexandria
Cairo
EGYPT
Nile R.

ARABIA
Medina
Mecca
RED SEA
PERSIAN GULF

startling rapidity, Persia, Syria, Egypt, North Africa, and Spain had been conquered. How can this prodigious expansion be explained? Contrary to common belief, it was not the result primarily of religious ardor. The Saracens were not engaged in a great crusade to impose their beliefs upon the rest of the world. Naturally there were outbreaks of fanaticism from time to time, but as a rule the Moslems of this period did not really care very much whether the nations they conquered accepted their religion or not. Subject peoples were usually quite leniently treated. As long as they refrained from the possession of arms and paid the tribute levied upon them, they were permitted to retain their own beliefs and customs. Jews and Christians lived unmolested in the Saracenic empire for centuries, and some rose to positions of prominence in political and intellectual circles.

In truth, economic and political factors were much more important than religion in causing the Saracenic expansion. First of all, it must be borne in mind that the majority of the Arabs were a prolific race of nomads. Since the men were polygamists, the occasional practice of infanticide was far from sufficient to prevent a rapid increase in population. Arabia, moreover, was suffering from a serious drought, which extended over a number of years shortly after the beginning of the seventh century. Oases that had formerly provided good crops of dates and good pasturage for flocks and herds were gradually being absorbed by the surrounding desert. Discontent among the famished tribes increased to such a point that they would probably have seized upon almost any excuse to plunder neighboring countries. The initial attacks upon Byzantine territory appear to have grown out of a revolt of Arab mercenaries in Syria. The leaders of the rebellion appealed to the followers of the Prophet in Medina, who already had some reputation for military prowess as a result of their conquest of Mecca. The outcome of this appeal was a great wave of military invasion which soon made the Arabs masters not merely of Syria, but also of Persia, Palestine, and Egypt. Finally, it should be noted that the conquests of the Moslems were facilitated by the fact that the Byzantine and Persian empires had fought each other to the point of exhaustion in the previous century, and their governments were now attempting to replenish their treasuries by heavier taxation. As a consequence, many of the inhabitants of these empires were disposed to welcome the Arabs as deliverers.

The decline of the Saracenic empire was almost as swift as its rise. The Arabs themselves lacked political experience; besides, the empire they conquered was too vast in extent and too heterogeneous in population ever to be welded into a strong and cohesive political unit. But a more decisive reason for its downfall was sectarian and factional strife. Sunnites and Shiites were never able to reconcile their differences, and widening cleavages between the mystics and rationalists also helped weaken the religion, which was the basis of the state. In

929 members of the Ommiad family succeeded in establishing an independent caliphate at Cordova in Spain. Soon afterward descendants of Ali and Fatima proclaimed themselves independent rulers of Morocco and Egypt. Meanwhile, the caliphs at Baghdad were gradually succumbing to the debilitating effects of Oriental customs. Aping the practices of Eastern monarchs, they retired more and more into the seclusion of the palace and soon became the puppets of their Persian viziers and later of their Turkish mercenary troops. In 1057 they surrendered all of their temporal power to the Sultan of the Seljuk Turks, who two years before had taken possession of Baghdad. For all practical purposes this marked the extinction of the Saracenic empire, although much of the territory continued to be ruled by peoples who had adopted the Islamic faith—the Seljuk Turks until the middle of the twelfth century and the Ottoman Turks from the fifteenth century to 1918.

The intellectual achievements of the Saracens were far superior to any in Christian Europe before the twelfth century. In conquering Persia and Syria the Saracens came into possession of a brilliant intellectual heritage. In both of these countries traditions of Greek learning had survived. Numerous physicians of Greek nationality had been attracted to the court of the Persian kings, while in Syria there were excellent schools of philosophy and rhetoric and several libraries filled with copies of writings of the Hellenic philosophers, scientists, and poets. Of course, it would be foolish to suppose that very many of the Arabs themselves were able to appreciate this cultural heritage; their function was rather to provide the encouragement and the facilities for others to make use of it.

Saracenic philosophy was essentially a compound of Aristotelianism and Neo-Platonism. Its basic teachings may be set forth as follows: Reason is superior to faith as a source of knowledge; the doctrines of religion are not to be discarded entirely, but should be interpreted by the enlightened mind in a figurative or allegorical sense; when thus interpreted they can be made to yield a pure philosophical knowledge which is not in conflict with reason but supplementary to it. The universe never had a beginning in time but is created eternally; it is a series of emanations from God. Everything that happens is predetermined by God; every event is a link in an unbroken chain of cause and effect; both miracles and divine providence are therefore impossible. Although God is the First Cause of all things, He is not omnipotent; His power is limited by justice and goodness. There is no immortality for the individual soul, for no spiritual substance can exist apart from its material embodiment; only the soul of the universe goes on forever, since its primal substance is eternal.

The development of Saracenic philosophy was limited to two brief periods of brilliance: the ninth and tenth centuries in the Baghdad caliphate and the twelfth century in Spain. Among the phi-

Periods of
development

Astronomy,
mathematics,
physics, and
chemistry

losophers in the East three great names stand out—Al Kindi, Al Farabi, and Avicenna. The first of them died about 870, and the last was born in 980. All seem to have been of Turkish or Persian nationality. In the eleventh century Saracenic philosophy in the East degenerated into religious fundamentalism and mysticism. Like the Sufis, from whom they derived a great many of their doctrines, the Eastern philosophers denied the competence of reason and urged a reliance upon faith and revelation. After their time philosophy died out in the Baghdad caliphate. The most renowned of the philosophers in the West, and probably the greatest of all the Saracenic thinkers, was Averroës of Cordova (1126–98). His influence upon the Christian Scholastics of the thirteenth century was especially profound.

In no subject were the Saracens farther advanced than in science. In fact, their achievements in this field were the best the world had seen since the end of the Hellenistic civilization. The Saracens were brilliant astronomers, mathematicians, physicists, chemists, and physicians. Despite their reverence for Aristotle, they did not hesitate to criticize his notion of a universe of concentric spheres with the earth at the center, and they admitted the possibility that the earth rotates on its axis and revolves around the sun. Their celebrated poet, Omar Khayyàm, developed one of the most accurate calendars ever devised. The Saracens were also capable mathematicians and developed algebra and trigonometry considerably beyond the stage these had reached in Hellenistic times. Although they did not invent the celebrated "Arabic" system of numerals, they were nevertheless responsible for adapting it from the Indian system and making it available to the West. Saracenic physicists founded the science of optics and drew a number of significant conclusions regarding the theory of magnifying lenses and the velocity, transmission, and refraction of light. As is commonly known, the chemistry of the Moslems was an outgrowth of alchemy, the famous pseudoscience that was based upon the principle that all metals were the same in essence, and that baser metals could therefore be transmuted into gold if only the right instrument, the philosopher's stone, could be found. But the efforts of scientists in this field were by no means confined to this fruitless quest. Some even denied the whole theory of transmutation of metals. As a result of innumerable experiments by chemists and alchemists alike, various new substances and compounds were discovered; among them carbonate of soda, alum, borax, bichloride of mercury, nitrate of silver, saltpeter, and nitric and sulphuric acids. In addition, Saracenic scientists were the first to describe the chemical processes of distillation, filtration, and sublimation.

The accomplishments in medicine were just as remarkable. Saracenic physicians appropriated the knowledge contained in the medical writings of the Hellenistic Age, but some of them were not content with that. Avicenna (980–1037) discovered the contagious nature of tuberculosis, described pleurisy and several varieties of nervous ailments, and pointed out that disease can be spread through contamination of water and soil. His chief medical writing, the *Canon*, was venerated in Europe as an authoritative work until late in the seventeenth century. Avicenna's older contemporary, Rhazes (850–923), was the greatest clinical physician of the medieval world. His supreme achievement was the discovery of the true nature of smallpox. Other Saracenic physicians discovered the value of cauterization and of styptic agents, diagnosed cancer of the stomach, prescribed antidotes for cases of poisoning, and made notable progress in treating diseases of the eyes. In addition, they recognized the highly infectious character of the plague, pointing out that it could be transmitted by garments, by eating utensils and drinking cups, as well as by personal contact. Finally, the Saracens excelled all other medieval peoples in the organization of hospitals and in the control of medical practice. Authentic records indicate that there were at least thirty-four great hospitals located in the principal cities of Persia, Syria, and Egypt. They appear to have been organized in a strikingly modern fashion. Each had its wards for particular cases, its dispensary, and its library. The chief physicians and surgeons lectured to the students and graduates, examined them, and issued diplomas or licenses to practice. Even the owners of leeches, who in most cases were also barbers, had to submit them for inspection at regular intervals.

So far as literature was concerned, the Saracens derived their inspiration almost entirely from Persia. If they knew anything about the classic poetry of the Greeks, they evidently found it of little interest. As a result, their own writings are colorful, imaginative, sensuous, and romantic; but with a few exceptions they make no very strong appeal to the intellect. The best-known example of their poetry is the *Rubáiyát* by Omar Khayyàm (*ca.* 1048–*ca.* 1124). The *Rubáiyát*, as it is preserved for us in the translation by Edward Fitzgerald, appears to reflect the qualities of an effete Persian culture much more than the ideals of the Arabs themselves. Its philosophy of mechanism, skepticism, and hedonism is quite similar to that of the Book of Ecclesiastes in the Old Testament. The most notable example of Saracenic literature in prose is the so-called *Arabian Nights*, or *Book of the 1001 Nights*, written mainly during the eighth and ninth centuries. The material of the collection includes fables, anecdotes, household tales, and stories of erotic adventures derived from the literatures of various nations from China to Egypt. The chief significance of the collection of tales is to be found in the picture they present of the sophisticated life of the Moslems in the best days of the Baghdad caliphate.

Since the Arabs themselves had scarcely any more of an artistic background than the Hebrews, it was necessary that the art of the Saracenic civilization should be an eclectic product. Its primary sources were Byzantium and Persia. From the former came many of

Saracenic contributions to medicine

Saracenic literature

377

the structural features of the architecture, especially the dome, the column, and the arch. Persian influence was probably responsible for the intricate, nonnaturalistic designs which were used as decorative motifs in practically all of the arts. From both Persia and Byzantium came the tendency to subordinate form to rich and sensuous color. Architecture is generally considered the most important of the Saracenic arts; the development of both painting and sculpture was inhibited by religious prejudice against representation of the human form. By no means all of the examples of this architecture were mosques or churches; many were palaces, schools, libraries, private mansions, and hospitals. Indeed, Saracenic architecture had a much more decidedly secular character than any in medieval Europe. Among its principal elements were bulbous domes, minarets, horseshoe arches, and twisted columns, together with the use of tracery in stone, alternating stripes of black and white, mosaics, and Arabic script as decorative devices. As in the Byzantine style, comparatively little attention was given to exterior ornamentation. The so-called minor arts of the Saracens included the weaving of gorgeous pile carpets and rugs, magnificent leather tooling, and the making of brocaded silks and tapestries, inlaid metal work, enameled glassware, and painted pottery. Most of the products of these arts were embellished with complicated patterns of interlacing geometric designs, plants and fruits and flowers, Arabic script, and fantastic animal figures. The richness and variety of these works of art, produced in defiance of a religion which often displayed a puritanical trend, afford most convincing proof of the vitality of Saracenic civilization.

The economic development of the Saracenic civilization remains to this day one of the marvels of history. In areas which had produced practically nothing for centuries, the Saracens literally made the desert to blossom as the rose. Where only squalid villages encumbered the landscape, they built magnificent cities. The products of their industries were known from China to France and from the interior of Africa to the shores of the Baltic. As the builders of a vast commercial empire, they excelled the Carthaginians. The reasons for this astounding economic development do not lend themselves to easy explanation. Perhaps it was the result in some measure of the long experience with trade which many of the Arabs had had in their homeland. When a wider field opened up, they made the most of their skill. The diffusion of the Arabic language over a vast expanse of territory also helped to extend the avenues of trade. In addition, the great variety of resources in the various sections of the empire served to stimulate exchange of the products of one region for those of another. The principal reason, however, was probably the advantageous location of the Saracenic empire at the crossroads of the world. It lay athwart the major trade routes between Africa, Europe, India, and China.

The Court of the Lions in the Alhambra, Granada, Spain. The palace-fortress of the Alhambra is one of the finest monuments to Saracenic architectural style. Notable are the graceful columns, the horseshoe arches, and the delicate tracery in stone that surmounts the arches.

Commerce and manufacturing were the main foundations of the national wealth. Both were developed in extraordinary degree. The Saracens made use of a great many of the instruments of commerce familiar to the modern world: checks, receipts, bills of lading, letters of credit, trade associations, joint-stock companies, and various others. Saracenic merchants penetrated into southern Russia and even into the equatorial regions of Africa. Caravans of thousands of camels traveled overland to the gates of India and China. Saracenic ships furrowed new paths across the Indian Ocean, the Persian Gulf, and the Caspian Sea. Except for the Aegean Sea and the route from Venice to Constantinople, the Saracens dominated the Mediterranean almost as if it were a private lake. But so vast an expansion of commerce would scarcely have been possible without a corresponding development of industry. It was the ability of the people of one region to turn their natural resources into finished products for sale to other regions which provided a basis for a large part of the trade. Nearly every one of the great cities specialized in some particular variety of manufactures. Mosul was a center of the manufacture of cotton cloth; Baghdad specialized in glassware, jewelry, pottery, and silks; Damascus was famous for its fine steel and for its "damask," or woven-figure silk; Morocco was noted for the manufacture of leather; and Toledo for its excellent swords. The products of these cities, of course, did not exhaust the list of Saracenic manufactures. Drugs, perfumes, carpets, tapestries, brocades, woolens, satins, metal products and a host of others were turned out by the craftsmen of many cities. From the Chinese the Saracens learned the art of paper-making, and the products of that industry were in great demand, not

Commerce and industry

379

only within the empire itself but in Europe as well. The men engaged in the various industries were organized into guilds, over which the government exercised only a general supervision for the prevention of fraudulent practices. For the most part, the guilds themselves regulated the conduct of business by their own members. Control by the state over economic affairs was much less rigid than in the Byzantine Empire.

Agriculture

The Saracens developed farming to as high a level as did any other people of the medieval world. They repaired and extended the irrigation systems originally built by the Egyptians, the Sumerians, and the Babylonians. They terraced the slopes of the mountains in Spain in order to plant them with vineyards, and here as elsewhere they converted many barren wastes into highly productive lands by means of irrigation. Experts attached to the imperial palaces and the mansions of the rich devoted much attention to ornamental gardening, to the cultivation of shrubs and flowers of rare beauty and delightful fragrance. The variety of products of the Saracenic farms and orchards almost passes belief. Cotton, sugar, flax, rice, wheat, spinach, asparagus, apricots, peaches, lemons, and olives were cultivated as standard crops almost everywhere, while bananas, coffee, and oranges were grown in the warmer regions. Some of the farms were great estates, worked in part by serfs and slaves and in part by free peasants as tenants, but the major portion of the land was divided into small holdings cultivated by the owners themselves.

The intellectual and artistic influence of the Saracenic civilization

The influence of the Saracenic civilization upon medieval Europe and upon the Renaissance was almost incalculable, and some of that influence has, of course, persisted until the present time. The philosophy of the Saracens was almost as important as Christianity in providing a basis for the Scholastic thought of the thirteenth century; for it was the Saracens who made available to the West most of the works of Aristotle and indicated more thoroughly than ever before the use to which those writings could be put as a support for religious doctrine. The scientific achievements of the Saracens furnished even more enduring contributions. Though the activity of the Saracens in literature was not as extensive as in science, their literary influence has been important. The songs of the troubadours and some other examples of the love poetry of medieval France were partly inspired by Saracenic writings. Some of the stories in the *Book of the 1001 Nights* found their way into Boccaccio's *Decameron* and Chaucer's *Canterbury Tales*. The art of the Saracens has likewise had an influence of deep significance. A considerable number of the elements in the design of Gothic cathedrals were apparently derived from the mosques and palaces of the Saracens. A partial list would include the cusped arches, the traceried windows, the pointed arch, the use of script and arabesques as decorative devices, and possibly ribbed vaulting. The architecture

Interior of the Great Mosque at Córdoba, Spain. This splendid specimen of Moorish architecture gives an excellent view of the cusped arches and alternating stripes of black and white so commonly used by Saracenic architects.

of late medieval castles was even more closely copied from the design of Saracenic buildings, especially the fortresses of Syria.[6]

Finally, the Saracens exerted a profound influence upon the economic development of late medieval and early modern Europe. The revival of trade which took place in western Europe in the eleventh, twelfth, and thirteenth centuries would scarcely have been possible without the development of Saracenic industry and agriculture to stimulate the demand for new products in the West. From the Saracens, western Europeans acquired a knowledge of the compass, the astrolabe, the art of making paper, and possibly the production of silk, although knowledge of the last may have been obtained somewhat earlier from the Byzantine Empire. Furthermore, it seems probable that the development by the Saracens of the joint-stock company, checks, letters of credit, and other aids to business transactions had much to do with the beginning of the Commercial Revolution in Europe about 1300. Perhaps the extent of Saracenic economic influence is most clearly revealed in the enormous number of words now in common usage which were originally of Arabic or Persian origin. Among them are "traffic," "tariff," "risk," "check," "magazine," "alcohol," "cipher," "zero," "algebra," "muslin," and "bazaar."[7]

Economic contributions

[6] For a more complete discussion of the influence of Saracenic literature and art, see Arnold and Guillaume, (eds.), *The Legacy of Islam.*

[7] It must not be supposed, of course, that Saracenic influence upon medieval Europe was entirely one-sided. There was also a reverse influence of substantial proportions.

381

International
significance of
the Saracenic
civilization

The Saracenic civilization has significance also for the modern world from the standpoint of international relations. The Saracenic empire was itself an international state. Though loosely organized, it united peoples as diverse as Persians, Arabs, Turks, and Berbers. Its binding cement was a great religion. The spread of this empire and religion constituted the first threat from the Orient that the Western world had faced since the destruction of Carthage. The long conflict between East and West, which extended at least from the Battle of Tours to the end of the Crusades, was commonly represented as a struggle of ideals. The rise and expansion of the Saracens anticipated in several respects the dynamism of such twentieth-century movements as Nazism and communism. There was one outstanding difference, however. Despite their fanaticism at times, the Saracens devoted only part of their energies to military objectives. They adopted the cultures of the peoples they conquered, built a civilization that surpassed in magnificence any that then existed, and left a splendid legacy of original discoveries and achievements.

SELECTED READINGS

· *Items so designated are available in paperbound editions.*

BYZANTINE CIVILIZATION

Baynes, N. H., *The Byzantine Empire*, London, 1925. Compact and interestingly written.

· ———, and Moss, H. St. L. B., eds., *Byzantium*, New York, 1948 (Oxford).

Diehl, Charles, *History of the Byzantine Empire*, New Brunswick, N. J., 1956. Perhaps the definitive work.

Kaegi, Walter E., *Byzantium and the Decline of Rome*, Princeton, 1968.

Ostrogorsky, George, *History of the Byzantine State*, New Brunswick, N. J., 1957.

· Runciman, Steven, *Byzantine Civilization*, New York, 1933 (Meridian). Complete and thorough; easily readable.

· Vasiliev, A. A., *History of the Byzantine Empire, 324–1453*, Madison, Wisc., 1928–1929, 2 vols. (University of Wisconsin).

Vryonis, Speros, *Byzantium and Europe*, New York, 1967.

SARACENIC CIVILIZATION

Arnold, Thomas, and Guillaume, Alfred, eds., *The Legacy of Islam*, New York, 1931. Excellent as a study of Saracenic influence.

De Boer, T. J., *History of Philosophy in Islam*, London, 1903. The best account; concise and clear.

· Gibb, H. A. R., *Mohammedanism: An Historical Survey*, New York, 1953 (Oxford).

· Hitti, P. K., *The Arabs, A Short History*, Princeton, 1946 (Gateway, new ed.).

382 · Lewis, Bernard, *The Arabs in History*, New York, 1960 (Torchbook).

Margoliouth, D. S., *Mohammed and the Rise of Islam*, New York, 1927. Complete and interesting.

· Pirenne, Henri, *Mohammed and Charlemagne*, New York, 1939 (Meridian).

Saunders, J. J., *A History of Medieval Islam*, New York, 1965.

· von Grunebaum, G. E., *Medieval Islam*, 2d ed., New York, 1961 (Phoenix).

SOURCE MATERIALS

Dewing, H. B., tr., *Procopius: History of the Wars*, Harvard, 1915. 7 vols.
Lane-Poole, Stanley, ed., *Speeches and Table Talk of the Prophet Mohammed*, London, 1882.

Sanders, T. C., tr., *The Institutes of Justinian*, New York, 1924.

· *The Koran* (Penguin).

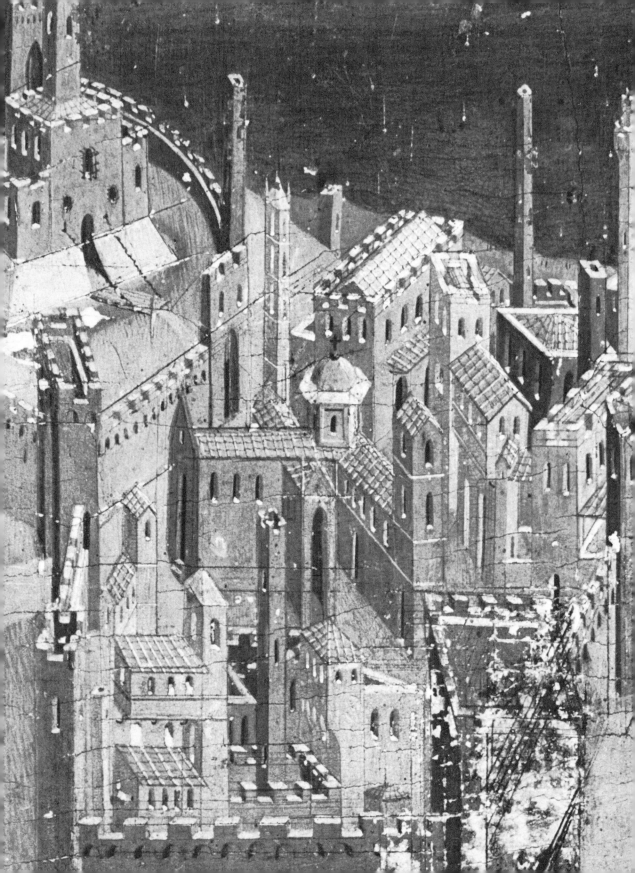

PART IV

The Later Middle Ages
and the Transition
to the Modern World

Soon after 1000 A.D. there began in Europe several movements of intellectual awakening which culminated finally in a brilliant flowering of culture in the twelfth and thirteenth centuries. In fact, so remarkable was the progress in western Europe from the eleventh century to the end of the thirteenth that the achievements of that period can justifiably be called a new civilization. While some of these achievements were discarded during the subsequent period of the Renaissance, quite a few were preserved and have exerted their influence to the present day. Indeed, the civilization of the later Middle Ages and that of the Renaissance had more in common than is usually suspected. Both were distinguished by humanism, by a new interest in man as the most important creature in the universe. In the later Middle Ages and the Renaissance alike there was a tendency to glorify the life of adventure and of conquest in place of the early Christian ideals of humility and self-effacement. It should be noted, however, that before the end of the Renaissance a religious revolution known as the Reformation began, which in some respects attempted to turn the clock back to the very beginning of the Middle Ages. The great nations of southern and eastern Asia continued their cultural evolution along lines already established. Both India and China were invaded, however, by Mongols from the West and North who introduced alien elements originally derived from Moslem sources. Japan adopted political feudalism and more and more aspects of Chinese culture. The spread of the religion of Islam in Africa promoted political and cultural progress in several regions of that vast continent.

A Chronological Table

	EUROPE AS A WHOLE	SOUTHERN EUROPE	NORTHERN EUROPE
1000	Cluny movement, 950–1100 Romanesque architecture, 1000–1150 Scholasticism, 1050–1300 Revival of trade with the East, 1050–1150 Struggle between secular and spiritual powers, 1050–1350 Separation between Eastern and Western churches, 1054 Establishment of the College of Cardinals, 1059 The Crusades, 1096–1204		
1100	Rise of merchant and craft guilds, 1100–1300 Growth of cities, 1100–1300 Development of the sacramental system of the Church, 1100–1300 First universities, *ca.* 1150 Gothic architecture, 1150–1300	St. Francis of Assisi, 1182–	Norman Conquest of England, 1066 Romances of chivalry, 1100–1300 Holy Roman (Hohenstaufen) Empire, 1152–1254
1200	Orders of friars, 1200– Fourth Lateran Council, 1215	1226 Dante, 1265–1321	Roger Bacon, 1214?–1294 Magna Charta, 1215 St. Thomas Aquinas, 1225–1274 Origin of Parliament in England, 1265–1295 Hanseatic League, 1300–1500
1300	Feudalism declines, 1300–1500 Rise of capitalism, 1300–1500 Growth of banking and development of money economy, 1300–1600 Black Death, 1347–1349	Boccaccio, 1313–1375 Savonarola, 1452–1498 Leonardo da Vinci, 1452–1519 Machiavelli, 1469–1527 Michelangelo, 1475–1564 Unification of Spain, 1492 Cervantes, 1547–1616 Galileo, 1564–1642	Establishment of Estates-General in France, 1302 Hundred Years' War, 1337–1453 Christian Renaissance, 1400–1500 War of the Roses in England, 1455–1485. Erasmus, 1466?–1536 Copernicus, 1473–1543 Tudor dynasty in England, 1485–1603
1500			Montaigne, 1533–1592 Sir Francis Bacon, 1561–1626 Shakespeare, 1564–1616 Sir William Harvey, 1578–1657

AFRICA	**INDIA AND THE FAR EAST**	
	Sung Dynasty in China, 960–1279	
Expansion of Islam, 1000–1500		
	Moslem invasions of India, 1000–1500	**1000**
Consolidation of states, 1000–1500		
Bantu, Arab, and Indian cultures blend in Swahili civilization along eastern coast, *ca.* 1100–1500		**1100**
	Neo-Confucianism, 1130–1200	
	Highest development of landscape painting in China, 1141–1279	
	Explosive powder used in weapons in China, *ca.* 1150	
Decline of Kingdom of Ghana, *ca.* 1224	Genghis Khan, 1162?–1227	
	Establishment of Shogunate in Japan, 1192	
	Zen Buddhism in Japan, *ca.* 1200	
	Inoculation for smallpox in China, *ca.* 1200	**1200**
	Turkish Sultanate at Delhi, 1206–1526	
	Development of Chinese drama, *ca.* 1235	
	Marco Polo in China, 1275–1292	
Mali empire in middle Niger region, *ca.* 1300–1500	Mongol (Yüan) Dynasty in China, 1279–1368	
	Rise of *daimyo* in Japan, 1300–1500	**1300**
University of Timbuktu, *ca.* 1330		
	Ming Dynasty, 1368–1644	
	Sack of Delhi by Timur, 1398	
Expansion of Songbay, *ca.* 1493–1582		
	Founding of Sikh religious sect in India, *ca.* 1500	**1500**
Decline of Songbay after defeat by Moroccans, 1591	Introduction of Christianity into Japan, 1549–1551	

CHAPTER 14

The Later Middle Ages (1050-1350): Political and Economic Institutions

> The count asked if he was willing to become completely his man, and the other replied "I am willing," and with clasped hands, surrounded by the hands of the count, they were bound together by a kiss. Secondly, he who had done homage gave his fealty to the representative of the count in these words, "I promise on my faith that I will in future be faithful to count William and will observe my homage to him completely against all persons in good faith and without deceit," and thirdly, he took his oath to this upon the relics of the saints.
>
> —Description of Ceremony of Homage and Fealty at court of Count of Flanders, twelfth century

Long before the famous Renaissance of the fourteenth and succeeding centuries, western Europe began slowly to emerge from the backwardness of earlier times. The start of this gradual awakening can be dated as far back as 1050 A.D. During the three centuries that followed, the people of Latin Christendom cast off at least some of their winter garments of repentance and otherworldliness and put on the less restrictive attire of the man who is determined to live in this world and mold his environment to his own advantage. The causes of this change in attitude were many and various: among them were the influence of contact with the Saracenic and Byzantine civilizations, the increase in economic security, and the influence of monastic education. In addition, the revival of trade in the eleventh and twelfth centuries and the growth of cities led to an increase in prosperity and sophistication which greatly stimulated the progress of enlightenment. The results of these several causes were reflected in a brilliant intellectual and artistic civilization which reached the zenith of its development in the thirteenth century. Probably the most distinctive element in the social and political structure of this civilization was the feudal regime.

The cultural revival of the later Middle Ages

389

We must not overlook the fact, however, that from the twelfth century on the role of the commercial and industrial classes in the cities was an exceedingly important one.

I. THE ORIGINS OF THE FEUDAL REGIME

The meaning of feudalism

Feudalism may be defined as a structure of society in which the powers of government are exercised by private barons over persons economically dependent upon them. It is a system of overlordship and vassalage in which the right to govern is conceived as a property right belonging to anyone who is the holder of a fief. The relationship between the overlord and his vassals is a contractual relationship involving reciprocal obligations. In return for the protection and economic assistance they receive, the vassals are bound to obey their lord or suzerain, to serve him faithfully, and generally to compensate him by dues or taxes for the services he renders in their interest. Defined in this fashion, feudalism was not limited to the later Middle Ages. Examples of it had existed in several other periods of world history—in many parts of the Roman Empire, for instance, and throughout the early Middle Ages. Late medieval feudalism, however, differed from the earlier specimens in being a legally recognized framework of society. Men did not apologize for it as a crude substitute for centralized government but glorified it as an ideal system, much as we idealize democracy and the national state at the present time.

Roman origins of feudalism

How did late medieval feudalism originate? To some extent it was the outgrowth of ancient Roman institutions. One of these was *clientage*. From very early times Roman citizens who had fallen upon evil days had sought the protection of wealthy patrons, becoming their clients or personal dependents. During the confusion that accompanied the decline of the Empire, clientage was greatly extended. A second of these Roman institutions was the *colonate*. In a desperate attempt to check the decline of agricultural production during the economic revolution of the third and fourth centuries, the government of the Empire bound many of the agricultural laborers and tenants to the soil as *coloni* or serfs, and in effect placed them under the control of the proprietors of large estates. The *colonate* had much to do with the growth of an extralegal feudalism in late Roman history, for it increased the wealth and importance of the great landed proprietors. As time went on, the tendency of these men was to ignore or defy the central government and to arrogate to themselves the powers of sovereign rulers over their estates. They levied taxes upon their dependents, made laws for the regulation of their affairs, and administered what passed for justice.

Feudalism was also derived in part from significant economic and political developments of the early Middle Ages. One of these was the growth of the institution of *beneficium*. *Beneficium* consisted in the grant of a *benefice*, or the right to use land in return

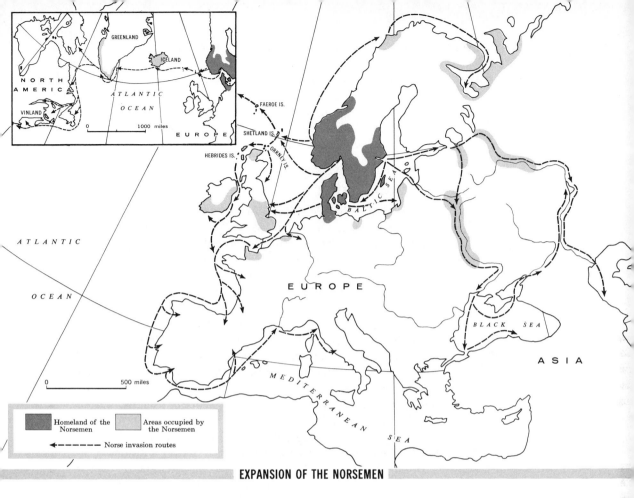

Homeland of the
Norsemen

Areas occupied by
the Norsemen

←------- Norse invasion routes

EXPANSION OF THE NORSEMEN

for rent or services. In the seventh century the Merovingian kings adopted the practice of rewarding their counts and dukes with benefices, thereby cementing a bond between public office and land-holding. Not long afterward Charles Martel and the Carolingian kings resorted to the granting of benefices to local nobles in return for furnishing mounted troops to fight against the Moors. The result was to increase the dependence of the central government upon the principal landowners throughout the country. The bestowal of *immunities* by the Frankish kings upon some of the holders of benefices also accelerated the growth of a feudal regime. Immunities were exemptions of the lands of a secular or ecclesiastical noble from the jurisdiction of the king's agents. The natural outcome was the exercise of public authority by the noble himself as a virtually independent sovereign, subject only to the nominal overlordship of the king. These developments were accentuated by the chaos that accompanied the breakup of Charlemagne's empire following his death in 814. Yet another important development in the early Middle Ages which hastened the growth of a feudal organization of society was the invasions of the Norsemen, the Magyars, and the Moslems. In the eighth and ninth centuries these peoples began mak-

Other origins of
feudalism

391

ing swift incursions into the settled portions of western Europe, plundering the richer areas and occasionally massacring the inhabitants. The attacks of the Norsemen in particular were widely feared. As a consequence, many small farmers who had hitherto maintained their independence now sought the protection of their more powerful neighbors, who frequently had armed retainers and strongholds in which men could take refuge.

2. FEUDALISM AS A POLITICAL, SOCIAL, AND ECONOMIC STRUCTURE

Feudalism as a system of government

As a system of government, feudalism embodied a number of basic conceptions. First of all, as we have seen, it included the notion that the right to govern was a privilege belonging to any man who was the holder of a fief; but it was a privilege entailing very definite obligations, the violation of which might be followed by loss of the fief. Secondly, it included the notion that all government rests upon contract. Rulers must agree to govern justly in accordance with the laws, both human and divine. Subjects must pledge themselves to obey so long as their rulers govern justly. If either party violates the contract, the other is absolved from his obligations and has the right to take action for redress. In the third place, feudalism was based upon the ideal of limited sovereignty, upon opposition to absolute authority no matter by whom it might be exercised. Feudal government was supposed to be a government of laws and not of men. No ruler, regardless of his rank, had any right to impose his personal will upon his subjects in accordance with the dictates of his own whims. Indeed, under feudal theory, no ruler had the right to make law at all; law was the product of custom or of the will of God. The authority of the king or the baron was limited to the issuance of what might be called administrative decrees to put the law into effect. Whether the ideals of feudalism were carried out less successfully in practice than the ideals of political systems generally is a very hard question to answer. Yet organized revolts against political oppression were not of frequent occurrence in the later Middle Ages, notwithstanding the fact that the existence of the *right* to revolt against a ruler who had made himself a tyrant was commonly taught.

Fiefs, vassals, and overlords

Not only in theory but also in practice the feudal regime was a system of overlordship and vassalage, based upon the granting and holding of fiefs. In the main, a fief was a benefice that had become hereditary. It was not always an area of land, however; it might be an office or position, or the right to collect tolls at a bridge, or even the right to coin money or to establish markets and enjoy the profits therefrom. The man who granted the fief was a lord or suzerain, irrespective of his rank; the man who received the fief to hold and transmit to his descendants was a vassal, whether he was a knight, count, or duke. As a rule, the king was the highest suzerain.

Immediately below him were the great nobles, who were variously known as dukes, counts, earls, or margraves. These nobles in turn had acquired vassals of their own through dividing their fiefs and granting them to lesser nobles, who were commonly called viscounts or barons. At the bottom of the scale were the knights, whose fiefs could not be divided. Thus, according to the general pattern, every lord except the king was the vassal of some other lord, and every vassal except the knight was a lord over other vassals. But this apparently logical and orderly arrangement was broken by numerous irregularities. There were vassals who held fiefs from a number of different lords, not all of them of the same rank. There were lords some of whose vassals held fiefs from the same overlord as they themselves did. And in some cases there were kings who actually held fiefs from certain of their counts or dukes and were therefore to some extent vassals of their own vassals.

Moreover, the fact must be borne in mind that feudalism was not the same in all countries of western Europe. Many of its features commonly assumed to have been universal were found only in France, where the system was most fully developed, or in one or two other countries at the most. For example, the rule of primogeniture, under which the fief descended intact to the oldest son, was not in force in Germany; nor were social distinctions so sharply defined there as in France. Further, not all of the lands and not all of the inhabitants of any European country were included under the feudal regime. Most of the farmers in the hilly and mountainous regions of France, Italy, and Germany did not hold their lands as fiefs but owned them outright, as their ancestors had for centuries.

Each member of the feudal nobility was involved in an elaborate network of rights and obligations which varied with his status as a suzerain or a vassal. The most important rights of the suzerain were the right to serve as legal guardian in case any of the fiefs he had granted should be inherited by a minor; the right of escheat, or the right to take back the fief of a vassal who had died without heirs; and the right of forfeiture, or the right to confiscate a vassal's fief for violation of contract. The last of these rights could be exercised, however, only after the vassal had been condemned by a court composed of his own equals. The suzerain himself merely presided over this court. Aside from this privilege of being judged only by his equals, the noble in his capacity as a vassal had only one other important right. That was the right to repudiate his lord for acts of injustice or failure to provide adequate protection. The obligations of the vassal were more numerous than his rights. He was required to render military service for a number of days each year, attend the lord's court, ransom his lord if he were captured, and pay a heavy tax if he inherited or sold a fief.

Feudal society was, of course, highly aristocratic. It was a regime of status, not of individual initiative. In almost all cases the members

Feudalism not the same in all countries

Feudal rights and obligations

393

A regime of
status, with a
few exceptions

of the various ranks of the nobility owed their positions to heredity, although occasionally noble rank would be conferred upon a commoner for his services to the king. Seldom was it possible for a man to win advancement under the system by his own efforts or intelligence. Nevertheless, an important exception was to be found in the case of the *ministeriales* in Germany and in the Low Counties. The *ministeriales*, as their name implies, formed a class of administrative officials under feudal rule. They had charge of castles, toll gates, bridges, market places, and so on. Some of the most capable rose to be bailiffs or administrators of towns or districts, serving under a great prince or bishop or even under the emperor himself. Their position was of such high advantage that ultimately they invaded the ranks of the lesser nobility and came to form a subordinate class of knights.

The life of the
feudal nobles

The life of the feudal nobility was scarcely the idyllic existence frequently described in romantic novels. While there was undoubtedly plenty of excitement, there was also much hardship, and death took its toll at an early age. From a study of medieval skeletons a modern scientist has estimated that the peak of the mortality rate in feudal times came at the age of forty-two,[1] whereas at the present time it occurs at about seventy-five. Moreover, conditions of living even for the richest nobles were comparatively poor. Until almost the end of the eleventh century the feudal castle was nothing but a crude blockhouse of timber. Even the great stone castles of later date were far from being models of comfort and convenience. Rooms were dark and damp, and the bare stone walls were cold and cheerless. Until after the revival of trade with the Orient, which led to the introduction of carpets and rugs, floors were generally covered with rushes or straw, a new layer being put down from time to time as the old became vile from the filth of hunting dogs. The food of the noble and his family, though plentiful and substantial, was neither particularly varied nor appetizing. Meat and fish, cheese, cabbages, turnips, carrots, onions, beans, and peas were the staples of their diet. The only fruits obtainable in abundance were apples and pears. Coffee and tea were unknown, and so were spices until after trade with the Orient had continued for some time. Sugar was eventually introduced, but for a long time it remained so rare and costly that it was often sold as a drug.

*See color
plates at page
448*

Feudal warfare

Although the nobles did not work for a living, their days were not spent in idleness. The conventions of their society dictated an active life of war, high adventure, and sport. Not only did they wage war on flimsy pretexts for the conquest of neighboring fiefs, but they fought for the sheer love of fighting as an exciting adventure. So much violence resulted that the Church intervened with the Peace of God in the tenth century and supplemented this with the Truce

[1] J. W. Thompson, *An Economic and Social History of the Middle Ages*, p. 718.

The World of Sports in the Later Middle Ages. Among the activities shown are fishing, bird netting, archery, and boar sticking. From *A Book of Rural Profits* by Petrus Crescentius.

of God in the eleventh. The Peace of God pronounced the solemn anathemas of the Church against any who did violence to places of worship, robbed the poor, or injured members of the clergy. Later the same protection was extended to merchants. The Truce of God prohibited fighting entirely from "vespers on Wednesday to sunrise on Monday" and also from Christmas to Epiphany (January 6) and throughout the greater part of the spring, late summer, and early fall. The purpose of the last regulation was obviously to protect the peasants during the seasons of planting and harvesting. The penalty against any noble who violated this truce was excommunication. Perhaps if rules such as these could really have been maintained, human beings would eventually have abandoned war as senseless and unprofitable. But the Church itself, in launching the Crusades, was largely responsible for making the rules a dead letter. The holy wars against the infidel were fought with a great deal more barbarity than had ever resulted from the petty squabbles among feudal nobles.

Feudalism flourished throughout the Middle Ages, but until after 1000 its customs were crude and barbaric. In the earlier period gluttony was a common vice, and the quantities of wine and beer consumed at a medieval castle brawl would stagger the imagination of a modern toper. At dinner everyone carved his meat with his own dagger and ate it with his fingers. Bones and scraps were thrown on the floor for the omnipresent dogs to fight over. Women were treated with indifference and sometimes with contempt and brutality, for this was a world dominated by men. During the eleventh century, however, the manners of the aristocratic classes were softened and improved considerably by the growth of what is known as chivalry. Chivalry was the social and moral code of feudalism, the embodiment of its highest ideals and the expression of its virtues. The origins of this code were mainly Germanic and Christian, but Saracenic influence also played some part in its development. Chivalry set forth the ideal of a knight who is not only

Early and later feudalism; chivalry

395

Tournament with Lances. Engraving by Lucas Cranach. Tournaments, imitating the conditions of medieval warfare but with blunted spears and lances, were among the principal recreational pursuits of the feudal aristocracy.

brave and loyal but generous, truthful, reverent, kind to the poor and defenseless, and disdainful of unfair advantage or sordid gain. Above all, perhaps, the perfect knight must be the perfect lover. The chivalric ideal made the lofty love of ladies a veritable cult with an elaborate ceremonial which the hot-blooded young noble had to be careful to follow. As a result, women in the later Middle Ages were elevated to a much higher status than they had enjoyed in early medieval Europe. Chivalry also imposed upon the knight the obligation of fighting in defense of noble causes. It was especially his duty to serve as the champion of the Church and to further its interest with sword and spear.

The basic economic unit that served as an adjunct to the feudal regime was the manorial estate, although manorialism itself had a political as well as an economic aspect. The manor, or manorial estate, was generally the fief of an individual knight. Lords of higher rank held many manors, the number frequently running into the hundreds or thousands. No one knows even the average size of these economic units, but the smallest appear to have included at least 300 or 400 acres. Each manorial estate comprised one or more villages, the lands cultivated by the peasants, the common forest and pasture lands, the land belonging to the parish church, and the lord's demesne, which included the best farm land on the manor. With minor

The manorial estate; systems of agriculture

exceptions, all of the arable land was divided into three main blocks: the spring planting ground, the autumn planting ground, and the fallow. These were rotated from year to year, so that the spring planting ground one year would become the autumn planting ground the next, and so on. Such was the famous *three-field system*, which seems to have originated in western Europe toward the end of the eighth century. Manorial agriculture was also conducted largely under the *open-field system*. The holding allotted to each peasant was not a compact area of the manor, but consisted of a number of strips located in each of the three main blocks of arable land. These strips, averaging about an acre in size, were generally separated only by a narrow band of unplowed turf. The main object of the system was apparently to give to each serf his fair share of the three different kinds of land. In cultivating these strips the peasants worked cooperatively, chiefly because their holdings were scattered, and it was therefore logical for a number of men to combine their efforts in farming all the strips in a particular area. Besides, no one peasant had enough oxen to draw the crude wooden plows through the stubborn soil.

Except for the noble and his family, the parish priest, and possibly a few administrative officials, the entire population of the manor consisted of persons of servile status. These might be embraced in as many as four different classes: villeins; serfs; crofters and cotters; and slaves. Though villeins and serfs eventually came to be almost indistinguishable, there were at one time several important differences between them. Villeins were originally small farmers who had surrendered their lands as individuals to some powerful neighbor. The ancestors of the serfs had frequently been subjected *en masse*, whole villages of them at once. The villeins were perpetual tenants, not bound in person to the soil, whereas the serfs were bought and sold with the land to which they were attached. Another difference was that the villein was liable to obligations only within the definite terms of his customary contract, while the labor of the serf could be exploited virtually as his owner saw fit. Finally, the villein could be taxed only within limits fixed by custom, but the serf was taxable at the lord's mercy. By the thirteenth century, however, most of these differences had disappeared. And it is a notable fact that the villeins were not degraded to the level of serfs; instead, the serfs rose to the level of villeins. Neither serfs nor villeins were included in the personal relations of feudalism. They had numerous obligations of a servile character, but they shared none of the political or social privileges of the lords and vassals.

The servile classes; villeins and serfs

Although the other dependent classes on the manor were much less numerous than the villeins and serfs, a word or two must be said about them. The crofters and cotters were wretchedly poor men who had no definite status under the feudal regime at all. Unlike even the meanest of the serfs, they had no strips of land which they could cultivate for their living. They occupied small cottages or

Crofters, cotters, and slaves

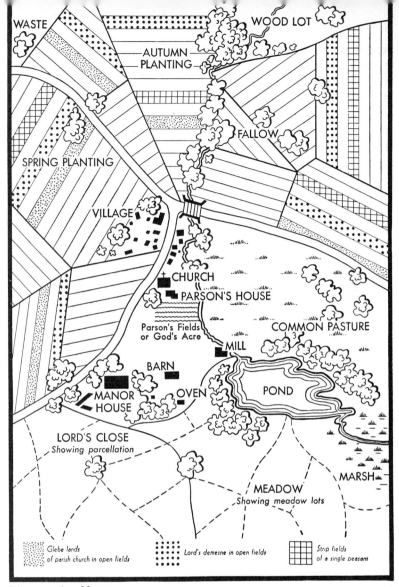

Diagram of a Manor

shanties and hired themselves out to the richer villeins or did odd jobs for the lord of the manor. A few slaves continued to be held throughout the later Middle Ages, but in steadily diminishing numbers. They did not fit in well with the manorial type of economy, for the manor was not a plantation but an aggregate of petty farms cultivated under perpetual lease. The few slaves who were to be found were employed mainly as household servants. After the year 1000 slavery as an institution became practically extinct in western Europe.

Like all other members of the subject classes under feudalism, the villeins and serfs were liable for numerous obligations. Although these appear at first glance to have been exceedingly oppressive, it is necessary to remember that they took the place of both rent and taxes. The most important of these obligations were the following: the *capitatio*, the *cens*, the *taille*, the *banalités* and the *corvée*. The *capitatio* was a head tax imposed only upon serfs. The *cens* was a species of rent paid only by villeins and freemen. The *taille* was a percentage of nearly everything produced on the lands of both villeins and serfs. The *banalités* were fees paid to the lord for the use of the village mill, winepress, brewery, bake-oven, and sometimes even for the use of the village well. The final form of peasant obligations, the *corvée* consisted of forced labor which the villeins and serfs were required to perform in cultivating the lord's demesne and in building and repairing roads, bridges, and dams.

By no stretch of the imagination could the lot of the medieval peasant be considered an enviable one. During the planting and harvesting seasons, at least, he toiled from sunrise to sunset, and the rewards of his labor were few. His home was generally a miserable hovel constructed of wattle plastered over with mud. A hole in the thatched roof served as the only outlet for smoke. The floor was the bare earth, which was often cold and damp from the infalling rain and snow. For a bed the peasant had a box filled with straw, and his easy chair was a three-legged stool. His food was coarse and monotonous—black or brown bread, a few vegetables from his garden in the summer and fall, cheese and porridge, and salt meats and fish, which were often badly cured and half putrid. When crops were bad, he suffered from famine, and death from starvation was by no means unknown. He was, of course, invariably illiterate and was commonly the victim of superstitious fears and sometimes of the dishonesty of unscrupulous stewards. Perhaps the most lamentable aspect of the peasant's life was the fact that he was a despised and degraded creature. Spokesmen for the nobles and townsmen alike seldom referred to him except in the most scornful and odious terms.

Obligations of the villeins and serfs

The lot of the medieval peasant

Scene in a Medieval Village. Among the activities shown are plowing, grinding grain, and slaughtering a boar for meat. In the lower right two friars are dispensing bread and soup to the poor.

The medieval
peasant and the
modern worker

Yet the medieval peasant enjoyed some advantages which undoubtedly helped to redress the balance of his miseries. Many of the fears and uncertainties that plague the lowly in modern times meant nothing to him. He was in very little danger of loss of employment or of insecurity in old age. It was an established principle of feudal law that the peasant could not be deprived of his land. If the land was sold, the serf went with it and retained the right to cultivate his holdings as before. When he became too old or too feeble to work, it was the duty of the lord to care for him through the remainder of his days. Although he worked hard during the busiest seasons, he had at least as many holidays as are allowed to the laborer today. In some parts of Europe these amounted to about sixty out of the year, not counting Sundays. Moreover, it was customary for the lord of the manor to feast his peasants after the spring planting was completed and after the harvest was gathered, as well as during the principal religious holidays. Last of all, the peasant was under no obligation to render military service. His crops might be trampled and his cattle driven off by the armies of warring nobles, but at least he could not be compelled to sacrifice his life for the benefit of some ruler with questionable motives.

The decline of
feudalism: economic causes

No sooner had feudalism reached the height of its development than it began to show signs of decay. The decline was already noticeable in France and Italy by the end of the twelfth century. The system continued longer in Germany and England, but by 1500 it was almost extinct in all countries of western Europe. Many relics of it, of course, survived until much later—some till the middle of the nineteenth century in central and eastern Europe. The causes of the decline of the feudal regime are not far to seek. Many of them were closely associated with the revolutionary economic changes of the eleventh and succeeding centuries. The revival of trade with the Near East and the growth of cities led to an increased demand for products of the farms. Prices rose, and as a consequence some peasants were able to buy their freedom. Moreover, the expansion of commerce and industry created new opportunities for employment and tempted many serfs to flee to the towns. Once they had made good their escape, it was almost impossible to bring them back. Still another economic cause was the opening up of new lands to agricultural production, mainly on account of the higher prices for products of the soil. In order to get peasants to clear forests and drain swamps, it was frequently necessary to promise them their freedom. The Black Death, which swept over Europe in the fourteenth century, while not exactly an economic factor, had results similar to those of the causes already mentioned. It produced a scarcity of labor and thereby enabled the serfs who survived to enforce their demands for freedom. With the peasant a free man, the manorial system was practically impossible to operate.

The political causes of the downfall of feudalism were also of major significance. One was the establishment of professional armies and the inducements offered to the peasants to become mercenary soldiers. Another was the adoption of new methods of warfare (especially firearms) which rendered the knights somewhat less indispensable as a military class. A third was the condition of chaos produced by the Hundred Years' War and the peasant insurrections resulting therefrom. A fourth was the influence of the Crusades in eliminating powerful nobles, in promoting the adoption of direct taxation, and in compelling the sale of privileges to communities of serfs as a means of raising money to equip armies. But probably the most important political cause was the rise of strong national monarchies, especially in France and England. By various means the ambitious kings of these countries in the later Middle Ages gradually deprived the nobles of all of their political authority.

3. THE RISE OF NATIONAL MONARCHIES

Soon after the death of Charlemagne in 814 the strong government which he had built up in western Europe collapsed. In 843, by the Treaty of Verdun, his grandsons agreed to divide the Carolingian Empire into three separate parts. The two largest portions became the kingdoms of East Francia and West Francia, corresponding roughly to the modern states of Germany and France. A wide belt of land between the two was formed into a middle kingdom including the territories of modern Belgium, Holland, Alsace, and Lorraine. Such was the beginning of some of the most important political divisions in the map of Europe today.

Meanwhile all three of these kingdoms passed rapidly under feudal domination. The real rulers were not the descendants of the great Carolingian king, but a host of petty princes, counts, and dukes. The kings themselves sank to the level of mere feudal overlords, dependent upon the local nobles for their soldiers and their revenues. While as kings their moral preponderance was still very great, their actual authority over the people was practically nonexistent. By the end of the tenth century, however, signs of change in this condition began to appear in France. In 987 the last of the weak Carolingian monarchs was displaced by the Count of Paris, Hugh Capet. The direct descendants of this man were to occupy the throne of France for more than 300 years. Although neither Hugh nor any of his immediate successors exercised the degree of sovereignty commonly associated with the royal office, several of the later Capetians were powerful rulers. A number of factors aided these kings in establishing their dominant position. First of all, they were fortunate enough for hundreds of years to have sons to succeed them, and often an only son. Consequently there were no deadly quarrels over the right of succession, nor was there any necessity of dividing the royal property among disgruntled relatives who might be able to defend a claim to the throne. In the second place, most of these kings lived to an advanced age, with the result that their sons were already mature men when they came to the throne. There were therefore no regencies to haggle the royal power away during the minority of a prince. Another factor was the growth of trade, which afforded the kings new sources of revenue and enabled them to find powerful allies among the bourgeoisie for their struggle against the nobles. Finally, considerable credit must be given to the shrewdness and vigor of several of the kings themselves.

France developed into a national monarchy between the beginning of the eleventh century and the middle of the fifteenth. This development was enhanced by a number of outstanding royal personalities. Foremost among them were Philip Augustus (1180–1223), Louis IX (1226–1270), and Philip IV (1285–1314), or Philip the Fair. These kings instituted numerous changes that undermined feudalism and paved the way for royal autocracy. By one device or another they appropriated the domains of powerful nobles. They commuted feudal dues into money payments, employed mercenary soldiers, and sold charters to cities. They established their own systems of coinage for the whole realm and limited the right of the feudal courts to hear appeals in cases involving treason and breaches of the peace. They issued ordinances and proclaimed them as law, without the consent of their vassals. The culmination of these usurpations of authority by the kings was the creation of the Estates General by Philip IV in 1302. He included in it not only the clergy and the higher nobility but also representatives of the towns. Its main purpose was to approve new forms of taxation. Originally it was not a legislative body but a council of advisers to the king. As time went on, however, it came to be regarded as a true legislative assembly, and was so regarded by the leaders of the great Revolution of 1789 in their eagerness to find precedents for limitations upon the power of the king. Of greater significance, undoubtedly, was its inclusion of commoners in the government.

Monarchical power in France underwent still further consolidation as a result of the Hundred Years' War (1337–1453). This war grew out of a number of causes. The primary one was probably the long-standing conflict between the French and English kings over territory in France. At the beginning of the fourteenth century, English monarchs still held portions of two provinces in southwestern France as vassals of the French crown. The French monarchs resented the presence of a foreign power on their soil. Moreover, they feared that the English interest in the woolen trade of Flanders might lead to an alliance with the Flemish burghers against the king of France.

The Hundred Years' War actually covered more than a century, although the fighting was by no means continuous. At first the English armies were generally victorious. They were better organized, better disciplined, and better equipped. Besides, England did not suffer from the extremes of internal discord which plagued the French. By 1420 the Duke of Burgundy had deserted the French cause, and all of the

Founders of the French monarchy

A Coin Depicting Philip Augustus

The course and climax of the conflict

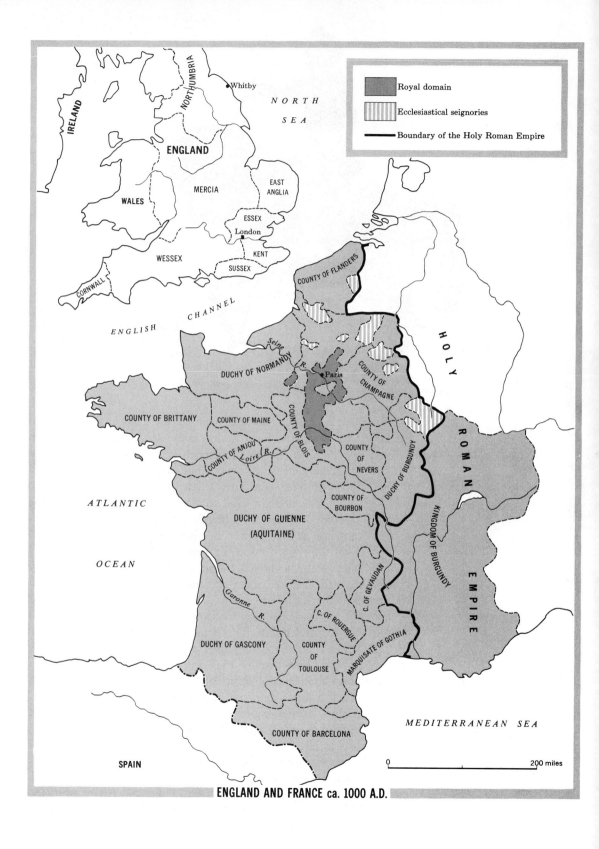

ENGLAND AND FRANCE ca. 1000 A.D.

IRELAND

NORTHUMBRIA
Whitby

NORTH SEA

ENGLAND

WALES

MERCIA

EAST ANGLIA

ESSEX
London

WESSEX

KENT

SUSSEX

CORNWALL

CHANNEL

ENGLISH CHANNEL

Royal domain

Ecclesiastical seignories

Boundary of the Holy Roman Empire

COUNTY OF FLANDERS

Seine R.

DUCHY OF NORMANDY

Paris

COUNTY OF CHAMPAGNE

HOLY ROMAN EMPIRE

COUNTY OF BRITTANY

COUNTY OF MAINE

COUNTY OF BLOIS

COUNTY OF ANJOU

Loire R.

COUNTY OF NEVERS

DUCHY OF BURGUNDY

ATLANTIC OCEAN

DUCHY OF GUIENNE (AQUITAINE)

COUNTY OF BOURBON

KINGDOM OF BURGUNDY

Garonne R.

C. OF ROUERGUE

C. OF GEVAUDAN

DUCHY OF GASCONY

COUNTY OF TOULOUSE

MARQUISATE OF GOTHIA

MEDITERRANEAN SEA

COUNTY OF BARCELONA

SPAIN

0   200 miles

Statue of Joan of Arc, Orléans. A modern idealization of the French heroine of the 15th century.

northern half of France had been occupied by English soldiers. Soon afterward occurred the most dramatic incident of the war, which **Jeanne d'Arc** infused new confidence into the French armies and paved the way for their ultimate victory. A devout but simple peasant girl, Jeanne d'Arc or Joan of Arc, came forward with the declaration that she had been commissioned by God to "drive the English out of the whole kingdom of France." Though she was completely uneducated, "knowing neither A nor B," her piety and sincerity made such a strong impression upon the French soldiers that they firmly believed they were being led by an angel from heaven. In a few months she had liberated most of central France and had brought the dauphin Charles VII to Reims, where he was crowned King of France. But in May 1430, she was captured by the Burgundians and turned over to the English. The latter regarded her as a witch and set up a special court of the clergy to try her for heresy. Found guilty, she was given over to the secular government on May 30, 1431, and burned in the public square of Rouen.

As is often true of martyrs, Jeanne d'Arc was more powerful dead than alive. Her memory lingers in France to this day as the **Effects of the** spiritual embodiment of a patriotic cause. The years that followed **Hundred Years'** her death witnessed a series of uninterrupted triumphs for the **War** French armies. In 1453 the capture of Bordeaux, the last of the English strongholds, brought the war to an end. Only the port of Calais remained of the once extensive English holdings in France. But the **404** Hundred Years' War did more than expel the English from French territory. It added the capstone to the consolidation of royal power in the kingdom of France. The attempts of both the Estates General and the great nobles to control the government had proved abortive. In spite of the confusion and sufferings of the greater part of the war, France had emerged with enough of a national consciousness to enable her kings to centralize their power in accordance with a pattern of absolute monarchy. The completion of this process marked the final transition from feudalism to something resembling a modern state.

The development of a national monarchy in England goes back to the reign of William the Conqueror. His conquest of the island in 1066 resulted in the establishment of a stronger monarchy than had previously existed under the Saxon rulers. The enlargement of power thus effected was not necessarily deliberate. King William made few sweeping changes. For the most part he preserved Anglo-Saxon laws and institutions. He brought over certain elements of feudalism from the Continent, but he took care to prevent too great a degree of decentralization. By the Salisbury Oath he required his vassals to swear allegiance to him directly instead of to their immediate overlords. He prohibited private warfare and retained the right to coin money as a royal prerogative. When he granted lands to his followers, he rarely gave any of them large estates composed of compact territory. He transformed the old advisory council of the Anglo-Saxon kings into a royal court, composed primarily of his own retainers and administrative subordinates. By the end of his reign the constitution of England had been markedly changed, but the alterations had been so gradual that few were aware of their significance.

Foundations of national monarchy in England

William the Conqueror's immediate successors continued their father's policies, but after the death of Henry I in 1135 a violent quarrel broke out between rival claimants for the throne, and the country was plunged into anarchy. When Henry II (1133–1189) became king in 1154, he found the treasury depleted and the barons entrenched in power. His first objectives, therefore, were to increase the royal revenues and to reduce the power of the nobles. In pursuance of the former, he made a regular practice of commuting the feudal obligation of military service to a money payment, and levied the first English taxes on personal property and on incomes. In his war against the nobles he demolished hundreds of castles that had been built without authorization and curtailed the jurisdiction of the feudal courts. But he apparently realized that the power of the barons could not be permanently restricted without thoroughgoing changes in the law and in judicial procedure. Accordingly, he gathered around him a staff of eminent lawyers to advise him regarding the laws that ought to be in force. In addition, he followed a practice already established of appointing itinerant judges to administer justice in the various parts of the realm. These judges, traveling from one region to another, applied a

The reforms of Henry II

uniform law throughout the kingdom. The precedents laid down by their decisions gradually supplanted local customs and came to be recognized as the Common Law of England. Henry also issued writs commanding the sheriffs to bring before the judges as they went from shire to shire groups of men who were familiar with local conditions. Under oath these men were required to report every case of murder, arson, robbery, or similar crime they knew to have occurred since the judges' last visit. This was the origin of the grand jury. Another of Henry's reforms made it possible for either party to a civil dispute to purchase a writ which would order the sheriff to bring both plaintiff and defendant, together with twelve citizens who knew the facts, before the judge. The twelve were then asked under oath if the plaintiff's statements were true, and the judge rendered his decision in accordance with the answer. Out of this practice grew the institution of the trial jury.

Henry's quarrel with Thomas à Becket

There was one branch of the administration of justice which Henry failed to bring under royal control, though he made strenuous efforts to do so. This was the judging and punishing of members of the clergy. Priests and other members of the ecclesiastical hierarchy were not tried in ordinary courts but in Church courts under the rules of the canon law. Punishment was notoriously lax. A priest, for instance, convicted of murder, was deprived of his clerical status but was rarely given any further penalty. Not only this, but decisions handed down in any English courts on ecclesiastical matters could be appealed to the papal court in Rome. In an effort to eradicate these practices Henry issued the Constitutions of Clarendon in 1164. The Constitutions provided that any clergyman accused of crime must be taken into a royal court first. If the royal court found that a crime had been committed, the defendant would be sent to a Church court for trial. If found guilty he would be sent back to the royal court to be sentenced. From such judgments no appeal could be taken to Rome without the king's consent. In attempting to enforce the constitutions, Henry ran afoul of the Archbishop of Canterbury. The latter, Thomas à Becket, was as devoted to the interests of the Church as Henry was to the strengthening of the monarchy. The quarrel reached a tragic climax when the Archbishop was murdered by a band of Henry's knights after the king, in an outburst of anger, had rebuked his followers for doing nothing to rid him of "a turbulent priest." The crime so shocked the English public that the whole program of bringing the ecclesiastical courts under royal control was largely abandoned. The Archbishop was revered as a martyr and eventually canonized by the Pope.

During the reigns of Henry's sons, Richard I and John, feudalism enjoyed a partial recovery. For all but six months of his ten-year reign Richard was absent from England waging the Third Crusade or defending his possessions on the Continent. Moreover, the heavy taxation which had to be imposed to defray his military expenses angered many of the barons. The feudal revolt reached its height during the reign of King John, who was perhaps not much worse a tyrant than some of his predecessors. But John had the misfortune to have two powerful enemies in King Philip Augustus of France and Pope Innocent III; and when he lost most of his possessions in France to Philip and suffered a humiliating defeat at the hands of the Pope, it was inevitable that the barons would take advantage of the opportunity to regain their power. In 1215 they compelled John to sign the famous Magna Carta, a document which remains to this day an important part of the British Constitution. The popular interpretation placed upon Magna Carta is really erroneous. It was not intended to be a Bill of Rights or a charter of liberties for the common man. On the contrary, it was a feudal document, a written feudal contract in which the king as an overlord pledged himself to respect the traditional rights of his vassals. It was chiefly important at the time as an expression of the principle of limited government, of the idea that the king is bound by the law.

The opposition of the barons continued during the reign of John's son, Henry III (1216–1272). They now drew considerable support from the middle class and found a new leader in Simon de Montfort. Civil war broke out, in which the king was taken prisoner. In 1265 Simon de Montfort, wishing to secure popular support for his plans to limit the powers of the crown, called together an assembly or parliament which included not only the higher nobles and churchmen but also two knights from each shire and two citizens from each of the more important towns. Thirty years later this device of a parliament composed of members of the three great classes became a regular agency of the government when Edward I (1272–1307) convoked the so-called Model Parliament in 1295. Edward's purpose in summoning this parliament was not to inaugurate democratic reform but merely to broaden the political structure and thereby make the king less dependent upon the nobles. Nevertheless, a precedent was established that representatives of the commons should always meet with the two higher classes to advise the king. By the end of the reign of Edward III (1327–1377) Parliament had divided for all practical purposes into two houses, and they had increased their control over taxation and were assuming lawmaking authority. The subsequent evolution of the English Parliament into the sovereign power in the country will be discussed in later chapters. The last feudal levy was written in 1381.

During the fourteenth century England was profoundly affected by economic changes which had begun somewhat earlier on the Continent. The development of commerce and industry, the growth of cities, the greater use of money, the scarcity of labor—all of these seriously weakened the manorial system and consequently undermined feudal power. In addition, the Hundred Years' War in-

Revolt of the barons against King John

King John. An effigy in Worchester Cathedral.

Origin of the English Parliament

The extinction of feudalism in England

creased the military and financial powers of the kings and tended to make them more independent of baronial support. Feudalism in England was finally extinguished in a great struggle among rival factions for control of the crown. This struggle, known as the War of the Roses, lasted from 1455 to 1485. The death of a great many of the nobles in this war and the disgust of the people with continual disorder enabled the new king, Henry Tudor, or Henry VII (1485–1509), to establish a more highly consolidated rule than the country had known up to this time.

Although the feudal regime became extinct in Germany by the fifteenth century and in Italy somewhat earlier, in neither of these countries was a national monarchy set up until long after the close of the Middle Ages. The power of the dukes in Germany and the power of the Pope always proved too strong to overcome. Some of the German emperors might have succeeded in building up centralized rule if they had been content to remain in their own country, but they persisted in interfering in Italy, thereby antagonizing the Popes and encouraging revolts at home.

The failure of Germany and Italy to form national states

When the eastern branch of the Carolingian dynasty died out in 911, the Germans returned to their ancient practice of electing a king. The most noted of the rulers thus chosen was Otto the Great, who became king in 936. From the beginning of his reign Otto apparently entertained ambitions of becoming something more than a mere king of Germany. He had himself crowned at Aachen, probably to convey the idea that he was the rightful successor of Charlemagne. Soon afterward he intervened in Italian affairs and assumed the title of King of the Lombards. From this it was only a step to becoming involved with the papacy. In 961 Otto responded to an appeal from Pope John XII for protection against his enemies, and in January of the following year he was rewarded by being crowned Roman Emperor.

The empire of Otto the Great

In the twelfth century the crown of Otto the Great came into possession of the Hohenstaufen family, whose most powerful representatives were Frederick Barbarossa (1152–1190) and Frederick II (1220–1250). Both of these rulers were outspoken in asserting their claims to imperial dignity. Frederick Barbarossa called the empire of Germany and Italy the Holy Roman Empire on the theory that it was a universal empire established directly by God and coordinate in rank with the Church. Frederick II, who was king of Sicily and southern Italy as well as Holy Roman Emperor, was much more interested in his southern kingdom than he was in Germany. Nevertheless, he believed just as firmly as did his grandfather Barbarossa in a universal empire as the highest secular power in western Europe. But he considered that the only possible way to make the claims of the Emperor a reality was to build a strong state in Sicily and southern Italy and then extend its power northward. He swept away the vestiges of feudalism almost at a single stroke. Like William the Conqueror, he required all nobles, regardless

The Holy Roman Empire of Frederick Barbarossa and Frederick II

THE HOLY ROMAN EMPIRE ca. 1200 A.D.

of rank, to swear allegiance to him directly. He established a professional army, introduced direct taxation, and abolished trial by ordeal and by combat. He appointed traveling judges to promote the development of a uniform law and judicial procedure. He decreed it to be an act of sacrilege even to discuss the Emperor's statutes or judgments. He set up rigid control over commerce and industry and founded government monopolies of the grain trade, the exchange of money, and the manufacture of textiles and other commodities. He even anticipated modern dictators in a campaign for racial purity, declaring that "When the men of Sicily ally themselves with the daughters of foreigners, the purity of the race becomes besmirched." He seemed to forget the fact that the

409

The Emperor Frederick Barbarossa (Frederick I) and His Two Sons. A miniature dating from about 1180.

blood of most of his people was already mixed with Saracenic, Greek, Italian, and Norman infusions, and that he himself was half German and half Norman.

The succession of the Hapsburgs to the throne

Frederick II was no more successful than any of his predecessors in increasing the power of the Holy Roman Empire. His great mistake was his failure to enlist the support of the middle class in the cities, as the Capetian monarchs in France had done. Without this it was impossibe to break through the wall of papal opposition. After Frederick died the Popes proceeded to eliminate the remaining contenders of the Hohenstaufen line. In 1273 Rudolf of Hapsburg was elected to the imperial throne, but the Holy Roman Empire over which he and his descendants ruled was seldom very powerful. When finally abolished in 1806 by Napoleon, it was little more than a political fiction.

4. URBAN LIFE IN THE LATER MIDDLE AGES

Importance of the cities

By no means all of the inhabitants of western Europe in the later Middle Ages lived in castles, manor houses, or peasant villages. Thousands of others dwelt in cities and towns; and from the eleventh century on, at least, the activities of the urban classes were just as important as the fighting and love-making of nobles or the toiling and roistering of peasants. Indeed, the cities were the real centers of most of the intellectual and artistic progress of the later Middle Ages.

Origins of the medieval cities

The oldest of the medieval cities in western Europe were undoubtedly those which had survived from Roman times. But outside of Italy these were few indeed. Others came into being through a variety of causes. By far the greatest number originated as a result of the revival of trade which began in the eleventh century. The leaders in this revival were the Italian towns of Venice, Genoa, and Pisa. Their merchants rapidly built up a flourishing commerce with the Byzantine Empire and with the great Saracenic cities of Baghdad, Damascus, and Cairo. The products brought in by these merchants stimulated a brisk demand not only in Italy but also in Germany, France, and England. As a result, new markets were opened up, and many people turned to manufacturing to imitate products imported from the Near East. Cities and towns multiplied so rapidly that in some regions half the population had been drawn from agriculture into commercial and industrial pursuits by the fourteenth centuıy.

As one would expect, the largest cities during the late Middle Ages were located in southern Europe. Palermo on the island of Sicily, with possibly 300,000 inhabitants, surpassed all the others in size and probably in magnificence also. The metropolis of northern Europe was Paris, with a population of about 240,000 in the thirteenth century. The only other cities with a population of 100,000 or over were Venice, Florence, and Milan. Although England doubled the number of her inhabitants between the eleventh century and the fourteenth, only about 45,000 of them lived in London in the thirteenth century. By the end of the Middle Ages nearly all of the cities of western Europe had gained some degree of exemption from feudal control. Their citizens had complete freedom to dispose of their property as they saw fit, to marry whom they pleased, and to go and come as they liked. All feudal dues were either abolished or commuted to monetary payments; provision was made for cases involving townsmen to be tried in the municipal courts. Some of the largest and wealthiest towns were almost entirely free, having organized governments with elected officials to administer their affairs. This was especially true in northern Italy, Provence, northern France, and Germany. The great cities of Ghent, Bruges, and Ypres, grown rich from trade and woolen manufactures, virtually dominated all of Flanders. The freedom of the medieval cities was secured in a variety of ways—frequently by purchase, occasionally by violence, and sometimes by taking advantage of the weakness of the nobles or their preoccupation with quarrels of their own. The governments of these cities were generally dominated by an oligarchy

The cities and their governments

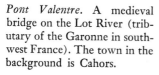
Pont Valentre. A medieval bridge on the Lot River (tributary of the Garonne in southwest France). The town in the background is Cahors.

A Section of the Medieval Town of Nordlingen, Germany. The need for protection against invaders led to congested housing conditions inside the walls.

of merchants, but in some cases forms of democracy prevailed. Annual elections of magistrates were relatively common; universal suffrage was occasionally employed; in a few towns the rich were disfranchised entirely, and the government was controlled by the masses.

Social problems in
the cities

Most of the medieval cities grew so rapidly that it would have been almost impossible to provide optimum standards of healthfulness and comfort for the inhabitants even if there had been sufficient knowledge and inclination to do so. Overcrowding was so bad that sometimes as many as sixteen people lived in three rooms. Part of this congestion was due to the need of the cities for protection against nobles and brigands. To fulfill this need, fortified walls had to be built around each city with gates that could be securely barred to shut out marauders. Naturally, it was too much trouble to tear down these walls and build new ones with every substantial increase in the population, although eventually this had to be done several times in a great many of the principal towns. Land values within these walls rose to fantastic heights and brought into existence a wealthy rent-collecting class. Because of the high cost of land, houses were built with upper stories that projected over the street, and even space on the walls was utilized for cottages and gardens. Streets were narrow and crooked and generally remained unpaved for centuries. The practice of paving began in Italy in the eleventh century and then gradually spread northward, but no thoroughfare in Paris had a hard surface until 1184 when Philip Augustus paved a single roadway in front of the Louvre. With space in the cities so limited, the streets served as the common playgrounds for boys and young men. Many were the protests voiced by their elders and by the clergy against wrestling, bowling, and pitching of quoits in the

412

streets. "Football was constantly denounced, with good reason, as it was not an orderly game with a fixed number of players . . . but a wild struggle between opposing parties to force the ball through the streets from one end of the town to the other, frequently resulting in broken legs." [2]

Prominent among the economic institutions in the medieval cities were the guilds. Of the two, the merchant and the craft guilds, the merchant organizations were the older, having developed as far back as the eleventh century. At first these included both traders and artisans, and then as industry became more specialized, the original guilds were split into separate organizations of craftsmen and merchants. The main functions of the merchant guild were to maintain a monopoly of the local market for its own members and to preserve a stable, noncompetitive economic system. To accomplish these ends the guild severely restricted trading by foreign merchants in the city, guaranteed to every member the right to participate in every purchase of goods made by any other member, required all of its members to charge uniform prices for the goods they sold, drastically punished cornering of the market, and prohibited many forms of advertising. It should be borne in mind that the merchant guilds were involved primarily in local trade. They had little or nothing to do with international commerce. This was conducted by large commercial firms, chiefly in Italy and Flanders. Their methods were not dissimilar to those of modern capitalism. Vigorous competition, adjustment of prices to market conditions, and use of the credit facilities of banks were typical examples.

The merchant guilds

A Medieval Tailor

Each of the craft guilds had three different classes of members—the master craftsmen, the journeymen, and the apprentices. Only the first two had any voice in the management of guild affairs, and toward the close of the Middle Ages even the journeymen lost most of their privileges. The master craftsmen were always the aristocrats of medieval industry; they owned their shops, employed other workers, and were responsible for the training of apprentices. The

The craft guilds

[2] L. F. Salzman, *English Life in the Middle Ages*, pp. 82–83.

The Walls of Avila, Central Spain. Medieval cities were generally surrounded by fortified walls. The apse of the cathedral built into the massive walls is the supposed birthplace of St. Theresa (1515–1582).

A Medieval Baker

A Medieval Shoemaker

whole craft guild system operated largely for their benefit. The journeymen (from the French *journée* meaning "day" or "day's work") were craftsmen who worked in the masters' shops for wages. In some parts of Germany it was customary for the young journeyman to spend a year wandering about the country picking up casual employment, the so-called *Wanderjahr*, before settling down in any particular place. But in most other sections of Europe he seems to have lived with the master's family. The industrious and intelligent journeyman could eventually become a master craftsman by accumulating enough money to set up his own shop and by passing an examination, which sometimes included the submission of a masterpiece. As in many specialized trades today, entrance into the medieval craft could be accomplished only through serving an apprenticeship, varying in length from two to seven years. The apprentice was entirely under the control of the master craftsman, who was commonly held responsible for the boy's education in elementary subjects and for the development of his character as well as for teaching him his trade. Usually the apprentice received no compensation except his food, lodging, and clothing. When the period of training was over, he became a journeyman. During the waning of the Middle Ages the craft guilds grew more and more exclusive. Terms of apprenticeship were lengthened, and it was made increasingly difficult for journeymen ever to become masters.

The functions of the craft guilds were similar to those of the related organizations of merchants, except for the additional responsibility of maintaining standards of quality. The craftsmen were just as ambitious as the merchants to preserve monopolies in their particular fields and to prevent any real competition among those producing the same article. Consequently, they required uniformity of prices and wages, prohibited working after hours, and set up elaborate regulations governing methods of production and the quality of materials used. They even went to the extreme of discouraging new inventions and discoveries unless they were made available to all and everyone adopted them. As a rule, no one was permitted to practice his trade in a town without first becoming a member of the guild. But in spite of all these regulations there were evidently a good many "chiselers." We read of millers who stole part of their customers' grain, of upholsterers who stuffed their mattresses with thistledown, and of metal-workers who substituted iron for copper and covered it over with gilt.

The medieval craft guilds bore no actual relationship to the labor unions of today, despite a superficial resemblance to those modern unions which are organized on the basis of separate crafts, such as the associations of carpenters, plumbers, and electricians. But the differences are more fundamental. Unlike the modern labor union, the craft guilds were not strictly confined to the working class; the master craftsmen were capitalists, owners of the means of production, and employers as well as workers. Furthermore, they included not only men who worked with their hands but some who would now be classified as professional men entirely outside the ranks of labor. For example, there were guilds of notaries, physicians, and pharmacists. Finally, the craft guild had a much greater breadth of purpose. It was really a miniature industrial system in itself, combining the functions of the modern corporation, the trade association, and the labor union.

Both the craft and merchant guilds performed other functions besides those directly related to production and trade. They served the purposes of religious associations, benevolent societies, and social clubs. Each guild had its patron saint and chapel, and its members celebrated together the chief religious holidays and Church festivals. With the gradual secularization of the drama, the miracle and mystery plays were transferred from the church to the market place, and the guilds assumed charge of presenting them. In addition, each organization ministered to the needs of its members who were sick or in distress of any kind. Money was appropriated to provide for the care of widows and orphans. A member who was no longer able to work or who had been thrown into jail by his enemies could look to his colleagues for assistance. Even an unfortunate brother's debts might be assumed by the guild if his financial plight was serious.

The economic theory upon which the guild system rested was vastly different from that which prevails in capitalist society. It reflected, first of all, some of the ascetic flavor of Christianity. In the eyes of the Church the vitally important aim in life should be the salvation of one's soul. Everything else should be kept in a subordinate place. It was not proper that men should expend their energies in the pursuit of luxury, or even that they should strive to become too comfortable. Moreover, the religion had been founded upon the idea that riches are a hindrance to the welfare of the soul. St. Ambrose, one of the most influential of the Christian Fathers, had even referred to private property as "a damnable usurpation." However, the economic theory of the later Middle Ages was influenced not only by Christianity but by Aristotle's doctrines of the golden mean and the just price and by his condemnation of usury. This theory included the following basic assumptions:

(1) The purpose of economic activity is to provide goods and services for the community and to enable each member of society to live in security and freedom from want. Its purpose is not to furnish opportunities for the few to get rich at the expense of the many.

(2) Every commodity has its "just price," which is equal to its cost of production, plus expenses and a reasonable profit. The contract price and the true economic value of the product must be equivalent. Generally speaking, the just price was simply the price for which goods could be sold without fraud.

(3) No man is entitled to a larger share of this world's goods than

A Medieval Weaver

The economic theory of the guild system

Basic doctrines

415

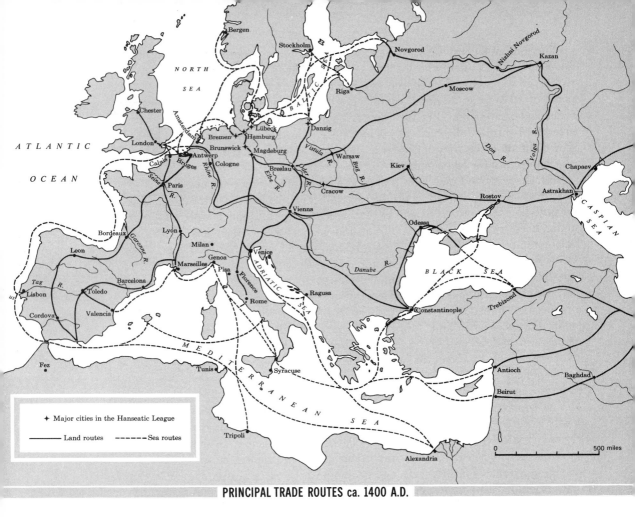

PRINCIPAL TRADE ROUTES ca. 1400 A.D.

Map legend:
✦ Major cities in the Hanseatic League
—— Land routes   - - - Sea routes

is necessary for his reasonable needs. Any surplus that may come into his possession is not rightfully his but belongs to society. St. Thomas Aquinas, the greatest of all the medieval philosophers, taught that if a rich man refuses to share his wealth with the poor, it is entirely justifiable that his surplus should be taken from him.

(4) No man has a right to financial reward unless he engages in socially useful labor or incurs some actual risk in an economic venture. The taking of interest on loans where no genuine risk is involved constitutes the sin of usury.

It would be foolish, of course, to suppose that these lofty ideals were ever carried out to perfection. As we have seen, manifestations of greed were not lacking among many members of the guilds. But more than this, the noncapitalistic guild system did not extend into every sphere of medieval economic activity. For example, long-distance trade, as we have seen, was carried on by great mercantile establishments in Flanders and in the cities of Italy. In other cases it was in the hands of *associations* of merchants. Characteristic of the latter were the Teutonic Hanse, or associations of German merchants engaged in exchanging the furs, fish, amber, leather, salt, and

Exceptions to the ideal

416

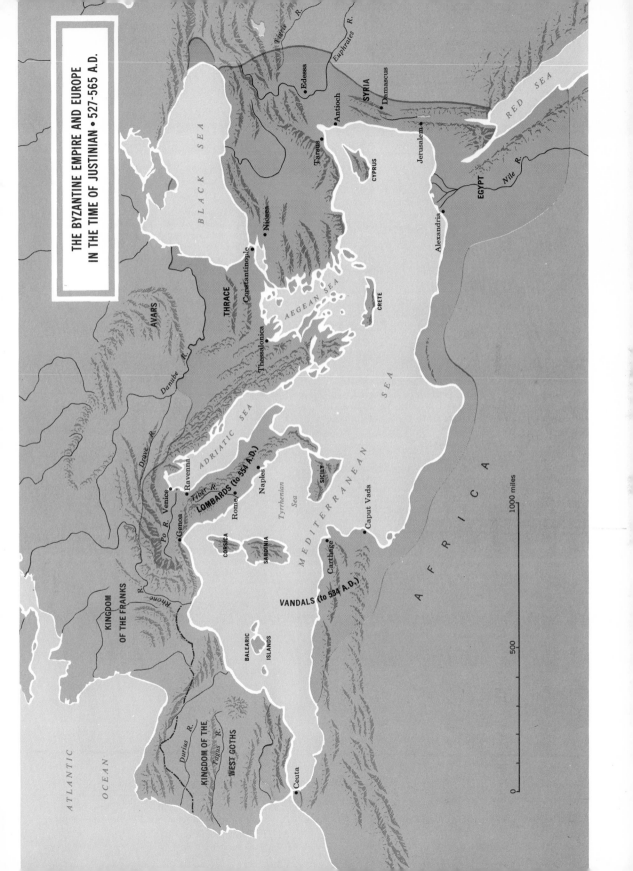

THE BYZANTINE EMPIRE AND EUROPE
IN THE TIME OF JUSTINIAN · 527-565 A.D.

ATLANTIC

OCEAN

KINGDOM
OF THE FRANKS

KINGDOM OF THE

WEST GOTHS

Durius R.

Tagus R.

Rhone R.

Ceuta

BALEARIC
ISLANDS

CORSICA

SARDINIA

VANDALS (to 534 A.D.)

Carthage

A F R I C A

Caput Vada

MEDITERRANEAN

SEA

Genoa

Venice

Po R.

Ravenna

Tiber R.

LOMBARDS (to 554 A.D.)

Rome

Naples

Tyrrhenian
Sea

SICILY

ADRIATIC SEA

Drave R.

Danube R.

AVARS

THRACE

Thessalonica

Constantinople

Nicaea

AEGEAN SEA

CRETE

BLACK SEA

Tarsus

Antioch

Edessa

SYRIA

Damascus

CYPRUS

Jerusalem

Alexandria

EGYPT

Nile R.

Euphrates R.

Tigris R.

RED SEA

0   500   1000 miles

The Young King, Louis IX, XIII cent. Though Louis was widely revered as a saint, the artist has endowed him with distinctively human features. (Morgan Library)

Aquamanile, German, XII–XIII cent. Aquamaniles were water jugs used for handwashing during church ritual, or at meal times. (MMA)

Ivory Plaque, German, X cent. The plaque shows Otto the Great presenting a church to Christ while St. Peter watches, a reference to Otto's building an empire by cooperating with the Church. (MMA)

Kings in Battle, French, *ca.* 1250. A scene depicting, with the trappings of knighthood, Joshua's fight against the five kings of Canaan. In the center Joshua raises his hand, commanding the sun and moon to stand still to enable him to complete his victory. (Morgan Library)

Chalice, German, XIII cent. A beautifully embellished wine cup used in the sacrament of the Eucharist. (MMA)

grain from the Baltic region for the wines, spices, textiles, fruits, and other products of the west and the south. By the fourteenth century these associations had developed into the powerful Hanseatic League with a membership of about eighty towns under the leadership of Lübeck, Hamburg, and Bremen. The Hanse was essentially a profit-making organization, and the activities of its members foreshadowed the growth of a capitalist economy in northern Europe.

SELECTED READINGS

· *Items so designated are available in paperbound editions.*

Barraclough, Geoffrey, ed., *Medieval Germany*, New York, 1961, 2 vols.

· ———, *Origins of Modern Germany*, New York, 1946 (Capricorn).

· Bloch, Marc, *Feudal Society*, Chicago, 1961 (Phoenix, 2 vols.).

· Boissonnade, Prosper, *Life and Work in Medieval Europe*, New York, 1927 (Torchbook). Interesting and dependable.

· Brooke, Christopher, *From Alfred to Henry III, 1871–1272*, London, 1961 (Norton Library History of England).

· Bryce, James, *The Holy Roman Empire*, New York, 1919 (Schocken).

Buchan, Alice, *Joan of Arc and the Recovery of France*, New York, 1948.

Clough, S. B., and Cole, C. W., *Economic History of Europe*, Boston, 1947. Contains excellent chapters on medieval economy.

· Fawtier, Robert, *The Capetian Kings of France*, New York, 1960 (St. Martin's Library).

· Ganshof, F. L., *Feudalism*, New York, 1952 (Torchbook). A high-level and somewhat technical account. Valuable for a clear understanding of feudal theory and institutions.

· Haskins, Charles H., *The Normans in European History*, Boston, 1915 (Norton Library).

· Hollister, C. W., *Medieval Europe: A Short History*, New York, 1964 (Wiley). Concise, authoritative, and delightfully written.

· Holmes, *The Later Middle Ages*, 1272–1485 (Norton Library, History of England).

Kantorowicz, Ernst, *Frederick II*, New York, 1957.

· Labarge, M. W., *A Baronial Household of the Thirteenth Century*, New York, 1965 (Barnes & Noble).

Loyn, H. R., *Anglo-Saxon England and the Norman Conquest*, New York, 1963.

Luchaire, A., *Social France in the Time of Philip Augustus*, New York, 1912.

· Mundy, J. H., and Riesenberg, Peter, *The Medieval Town*, Princeton, 1958 (Anvil). A valuable supplement to Pirenne.

· Myers, A. R., *England in the Late Middle Ages*, London, 1952 (Penguin).

· Painter, Sidney, *The Rise of Feudal Monarchies*, Ithaca, 1951 (Cornell).

· ———, *Medieval Society*, 1951 (Cornell). A brief but scholarly survey.

· Pirenne, Henri, *Economic and Social History of Medieval Europe*, New York, 1956 (Harvest). Stimulating and authoritative.

· ———, *Medieval Cities*, Princeton, 1925 (Anchor). The most highly regarded book on the subject.

· Power, Eileen, *Medieval People*, London, 1924 (Anchor).

· Runciman, Steven, *A History of the Crusades, The First Crusade and the Foundation of the Kingdom of Jerusalem*, New York, 1951, Vol. 1 (Torchbook).

· Sayles, G. O., *The Medieval Foundations of England*, London, 1952 (Perpetua).

READINGS   · Stephenson, Carl, *Medieval Feudalism*, New York, 1935 (Cornell).

· Tawney, R. H., *Religion and the Rise of Capitalism*, New York, 1947 (Mentor). Interesting for the light it throws on medieval economic theory under the influence of the Church.

Ziegler, Philip, *The Black Death*, New York, 1969.

SOURCE MATERIALS

Coulton, G. G., *Life in the Middle Ages*, New York, 1955, 4 vols.

· ——, *The Medieval Village, Manor, and Monastery*, New York, 1960 (Torchbook).

· Dante, *De Monarchia (On World Government)*, 2d rev. ed., New York, 1957 (Library of Liberal Arts).

John of Salisbury, *Policraticus*, New York, 1909, 2 vols.

· Johnes, Thomas, *Froissart's Chronicles of England, France, Spain and the Adjoining Countries*, Vol. I, 240–41; Vol. II, 94–95, New York, 1961 (Dutton).

· Lopez, Robert S., and Raymond, Irving W., *Medieval Trade in the Mediterranean World*, New York, 1955 (Norton).

McKechnie, W. S., *Magna Carta*, 2d rev. ed., New York, 1914.

Marsiglio of Padua, *Defensor Pacis (Defender of the Peace)*, especially Book I, Chs. IV, XII, XV.

· Otto of Freising, *The Deeds of Frederick Barbarossa*, New York, 1953 (Norton).

· *Portable Medieval Reader* (Viking).

CHAPTER 15

The Later Middle Ages (1050-1350): Religious and Intellectual Developments

> Now in those things which we hold about God there is truth in two ways. For certain things that are true about God wholly surpass the capability of human reason, for instance that God is three and one; while there are certain things to which even natural religion can attain, for instance that God is, that God is one, and others like these, which even the philosophers proved demonstratively of God, being guided by the light of natural reason.
> —St. Thomas Aquinas, *Summa Contra Gentiles*, Book I

It has already been mentioned more than once that the civilization of western Europe between 1050 and 1350 was vastly different from that which had existed at the beginning of the medieval period. Nowhere was the contrast more striking than in the spheres of religion and the intellect. The religious and intellectual attitudes of the early Middle Ages were products of a time of transition and of considerable chaos. The Roman political and social structure had disintegrated, and no new regime had yet emerged to take its place. As a consequence, the thinking of this time was directed toward pessimism and otherworldly concerns. But after the tenth century these attitudes gradually gave way to more optimistic sentiments and to an increasing interest in worldly affairs. The original causes were directly related to the progress of monastic education, to the rise of more stable government, and to an increase in economic security. Later such factors as the influence of the Saracenic and Byzantine civilizations and the growth of cities brought the culture of the later Middle Ages to a magnificent climax of intellectual achievement in the twelfth and thirteenth centuries. At the same time religion took on a less otherworldly aspect and evolved into an institution more deeply concerned with the affairs of this life.

The change in religious and intellectual attitudes

419

During the later Middle Ages, Christianity underwent so many significant developments from its early medieval character that it seemed in some respects to be almost a new religion. To be sure, such cardinal features as faith in one God, the belief in the Trinity, and the hope for salvation in a world to come continued to be accepted in their original form, but other elements in the religion of St. Augustine and Gregory the Great were modified or eliminated and different ones substituted for them. The transformation began about 1050 and reached its zenith in the thirteenth century under the influence of such leaders as St. Thomas Aquinas, St. Francis, and Innocent III.

Late medieval Christianity

Perhaps the most important developments were in matters of doctrine and religious attitudes. The religion of the early Middle Ages had been pessimistic, fatalistic, and, theoretically at least, opposed to everything worldly as a compromise with the devil. Man was considered to be inherently wicked and incapable of any good works except as the beneficiary of God's grace. God Himself was omnipotent, selecting for reasons of His own those human beings who would enter His paradise, and leaving the rest to follow the path to destruction. By the thirteenth century quite different religious conceptions had come to prevail. Life in this world was now held to be exceedingly important, not only as a preparation for eternity but for its own sake as well. No longer was human nature regarded as totally evil. Man could therefore cooperate with God in achieving the salvation of his soul. Instead of emphasizing the omnipotence of God, philosophers and theologians now stressed the divine justice and mercy.

New doctrines and new attitudes

The most inclusive statements of late medieval theology were contained in the *Summa theologica* of St. Thomas Aquinas and in the pronouncements issued by Church councils, especially the Fourth Lateran Council of 1215. New elements in this theology included the theory of the priesthood and the theory of the sacraments. There had, of course, been priests and sacraments in the Church long before the eleventh century, but neither the exact functions of the priests nor the precise nature of the sacraments had ever been clearly formulated. The theory now came to be held that the priest, by virtue of his ordination by a bishop and the latter's confirmation by the Pope, was the inheritor of a portion of the authority conferred by the Christ upon the Apostle Peter. In effect, this meant that the priest had the power to cooperate with God in performing certain miracles and in releasing sinners from the temporal consequences of their wickedness.

The new theology: (1) the theory of the priesthood

By the end of the twelfth century the number of sacraments had come to be accepted as seven. The seven were and still are: baptism; confirmation; penance; the Eucharist, or Lord's Supper; marriage; ordination; and extreme unction, or the last rites administered to the dying. The Roman Church defines a sacrament as an instrumentality whereby divine grace is communicated to men. The sacramental theory as it came to be accepted during the last centuries of the Middle Ages included a number of separate doctrines. First, there was the doctrine that the sacraments were indispensable means of procuring God's grace, that no individual could be saved without them. Second, there was the principle that the sacraments were automatic in their effects. In other words, it was held that the efficacy of the sacraments did not depend upon the character of the priest who administered them. The priest might be a very unworthy man, but the sacraments in his hands would remain as unpolluted as if they were administered by a saint. Finally, at the Fourth Lateran Council, the doctrine of transubstantiation was made an integral part of the sacramental theory. This doctrine means that the priest, at a given moment in the Eucharistic ceremony, actually cooperates with God in the performance of a miracle whereby the bread and wine of the sacrament are changed or transubstantiated into the body and blood of Christ. The change, of course, is considered a change in essence only; the "accidents" of taste and appearance remain the same.

(2) the theory of the sacraments

The adoption of these two fundamental theories, the theory of the priesthood and the theory of the sacraments, had potent effects in exalting the power of the clergy and in strengthening the formal and mechanical elements in the Latin Church. However, medieval Catholicism was revitalized and made into a civilizing influence by two other developments that marked the later Middle Ages. One was the adoption of a rationalist philosophy by the leading theologians, and the other was the growth of a humanizing attitude. The influence of rationalist philosophy will be discussed farther on in this chapter. The humanizing element in religion expressed itself in a variety of ways—in the revolt against the selfish asceticism of monks and hermits, in the naturalism of St. Francis, and perhaps most of all in the veneration of saints and the Virgin Mary. All through the later medieval period, the veneration or "invocation" of saints was a popular practice, especially among the common people. For the average person God and Christ were remote and sublime beings who could hardly be bothered with the petty problems of men. But the saints were human; one could ask them for favors which one would hesitate to request of God. For example, a woman could implore the aid of St. Agnes in helping her find a husband. Even more popular than the invocation of saints was reverence for the Virgin Mary, which came to be almost a religion in itself during the twelfth and thirteenth centuries. Devotion to Mary as the beautiful and compassionate Mother undoubtedly served as one of the strongest expressions of the humanizing tendency in medieval religion. For she was venerated not only as the ideal woman but also as Our Lady of Sorrows. The grief that she experienced over the tragic death of her Son was believed to endow her with a special

Mechanical religion modified by rationalism and a humanizing attitude

Changes in the
organization of
the Church

sympathy for the sorrows of mankind. Though revered as the Queen of Heaven, she was, above all, the goddess of this life.

Significant developments in ecclesiastical organization and the adoption of new forms of religious discipline also occurred during the later Middle Ages. In 1059 the College of Cardinals was established as a papal electoral college. Originally the members of this body were the deacons, priests, and bishops of certain churches in the city of Rome. Later high ranking clergy from nearly all countries of the Western world were appointed to membership, although the College included a majority of Italians until 1946. At present there are 134 members, and a two-thirds vote is necessary to elect the Pope, who is invariably a cardinal himself. Prior to 1059 Popes were chosen in a variety of ways. In the early days they had been elected by the clergy of the diocese of Rome, but later they were often appointed by powerful nobles and frequently by the German emperors. The vesting of the sole right of election in the College of Cardinals was part of a great reform movement to free the Church from political control. The other main development in religious organization was the growth of the papal monarchy. The first of the Popes to achieve much success in extending his supremacy over the whole ecclesiastical hierarchy was Nicholas I (858–867). Intervening in disputes between bishops and archbishops, he forced all of them to submit to his own direct authority. Nicholas was followed, however, by a series of weak successors, and the papal monarchy was not revived until the reign of Gregory VII (1073–1085). It reached the highest stage of its medieval developments during the pontificate of Innocent III (1198–1216).

New methods of
discipline

During the later centuries of the Middle Ages the Church made systematic attempts to extend its moral authority over all of its lay members, whether of high or of low degree. The chief methods adopted were excommunication and the requirement of oral confession. Excommunication was not used to any extent before the eleventh century. Its effect was to expel an individual from the Church and to deprive him of all the privileges of a Christian. His body could not be buried in consecrated ground, and his soul was temporarily consigned to hell. All other Christians were forbidden to associate with him, under penalty of sharing his fate. Sometimes a decree of excommunication against a king or a powerful noble was fortified by placing an *interdict* upon the area over which he ruled. The interdict, by withholding most of the benefits of religion from a ruler's subjects, was intended to kindle their resentment against him and force him to submit to the Church. Both excommunication and the interdict proved to be powerful weapons until about the end of the thirteenth century; after that their effectiveness waned. By a decree of the Fourth Lateran Council in 1215 the Church adopted the requirement that every individual must make an oral confession of his sins to a priest at least once a year, and then undergo the punishment imposed before becoming eligible to partake of the Eucharist. The result of this decree was to give the priest the authority of a moral guardian over every individual in his parish.

As the Church became more successful, it tended to become more worldly. Long before the great Reformation of the sixteenth century, medieval Catholicism went through a series of reformations calculated to restore the institutions of the Church to some earlier state of purity or to make them more useful to society. The first of these reform movements was the Cluny movement or the Cluniac revival, which derived its name from the French monastery of Cluny founded in 910. The original purpose of the Cluny movement was simply to reform monasticism. The Benedictine monasteries, which were practically the only ones in existence by the tenth century in western Europe, had grown corrupt and were rapidly passing under the control of feudal nobles. Consequently the Cluniac leaders took as their objectives the enforcement of the rules of piety and chastity upon the monks and the liberation of the monasteries themselves from feudal domination. But by the eleventh century the movement had gained a much broader significance. In fact, its purposes were now so different from the original ones that it is often referred to as the New Cluny movement. No longer were the reformers content merely to purify monasticism and free it from the clutches of the lay feudality; their primary aims were now to eliminate corruption and worldliness from the entire Church, to abolish feudal control over the secular clergy as well as over monks, and to establish the absolute supremacy of the Pope in ecclesiastical matters. They centered their attacks, first of all, upon *simony*, which was interpreted to include the buying and selling of Church offices, any form of appointment to Church offices contrary to the canon law, and the investing of bishops and abbots with the symbols of their spiritual power by secular authorities. In addition, the reformers demanded celibacy for all grades of the clergy. Nearly all of these elements in their program were directed toward making the Church entirely independent of the great nobles, especially by depriving them of their power to dictate the appointment of bishops, abbots, and priests. The movement aroused bitter opposition, for it struck at the very basis of the feudal relationship which had been established between secular rulers and the clergy. But most of the program was eventually put into effect, due in large part to the fanatical zeal of such leaders as Hildebrand, the "holy Satan" who in 1073 became Pope Gregory VII.

By the middle of the eleventh century the Cluniac monks had begun to sink into the same morass of worldliness as their older Benedictine brothers whom they had set out to reform. The result was the launching of new movements to set an even stronger example of purity and austerity for the regular clergy. In 1084 the Carthusian order was established with a set of rules more rigorous than any hitherto adopted in the West. The Carthusian monks were required to live in cells, to fast three days each week on bread and water, to

Medieval reform movements: (1) the Cluniac revival

(2) the Carthusian and Cistercian movements

423

wear hair shirts, and to spend all their time in prayer, meditation, and manual labor. A few years later the Cistercian order was founded at Citeaux in Burgundy and soon proved to be one of the most popular of them all. By the middle of the twelfth century more than 300 Cistercian monasteries were receiving converts from all over western Europe. Although not so strict in their requirements of individual asceticism as the Carthusians, the founders of the Cistercian order saw to it that the rules would be puritanical enough to constitute an emphatic protest against the luxury and idleness of the Cluniac monks. Only a vegetarian diet was allowed, and manual labor was strictly enforced.

Undoubtedly the most significant reform movement of the later Middle Ages was the rise of the friars in the thirteenth century. Though the friars are often regarded as simply another species of monks, they were really quite different. Originally they were not members of the clergy at all but laymen. Instead of shutting themselves up in monasteries, they devoted all of their time to social welfare work and to preaching and teaching. The growth of the new orders was symptomatic of an attempt to bring religion into harmony with the needs of a world which had completely outgrown the so-called Dark Ages. Men were now coming to realize that the main business of religion was not to enable a few self-serving monks to save their own souls at the expense of society, but to help make this world a happier place in which to live and to rescue the great mass of mankind from ignorance and sin.

The founder of the original order of friars was St. Francis of Assisi (1182–1226). The son of a rich merchant, the young Francis became dissatisfied with the values of his social class and determined to become a servant of the poor. Giving away all of his property and donning the rags of a beggar, he set out on his great mission of preaching salvation in the darkest corners of the Italian cities and ministering to the needs of helpless outcasts. The philosophy of St. Francis was different from that of many other Christian leaders. The major portion of it was founded almost literally upon the gospel of Jesus. St. Francis followed Jesus in his selflessness, in his devotion to poverty as an ideal, in his indifference to doctrine, and in his contempt for form and ceremony. In addition he had a profound love not merely for man but for every creature around him, and even for the objects of inanimate nature. He found God revealed in the sun, the wind, the flowers, and everything that existed for the use or delight of man. His disciples related how he would never put out a fire, but "treated it reverently," and how "he directed the brother who cut and fetched the fire wood never to cut a whole tree, so that some part of it might remain untouched for the love of Him who was willing to work out our salvation upon the wood of the cross." [1] Finally, it should be made clear that St. Francis was not an ascetic in the

(3) the rise of the orders of friars: the Franciscan order

St. Francis of Assisi

[1] Quoted by H. O. Taylor, *The Medieval Mind*, I, 454–55.

Illuminated Manuscript from *Les Belles Heures de Jean, Duc de Berry*, a book of hours. Monks reading prayers at the bier of their deceased brother, St. Anthony. Illuminated manuscripts have value not merely as works of art but for their portrayals of medieval life and culture.

Tandē fratus ātbonus p̄ mlta ⁊ inuinerabilia
demonium temptaměta q̄ passus e̅ dn̄i inta
lxxxmuicā ducēt qua sc̄ ⁊ pleuit a.xr̄.sue uter ā
no usq̄; ad.c.v. quicuit i̅ pace āno dn̄i. iij. rl.°

accurate meaning of that term. Although he denied himself comforts and pleasures, he did not despise the body or practice laceration of the flesh to achieve the salvation of his soul. His abandonment of earthly possessions was done primarily to conquer pride and bring himself down to the level of the people whom he wished to help.

The second of the orders of friars was the Dominican order, founded about 1215 by St. Dominic, a Castilian noble who lived in southern France. The Dominicans adopted as their principal task the combating of heresy. Believing that an effective means to this end was education, they prepared themselves by diligent study to refute the arguments of pagans and skeptics. Many members of the order gained teaching positions in the universities and contributed much to the development of philosophy and theology. Unfortunately, they were carried away at times by a zeal for persecuting; they were active leaders of the medieval, or Papal Inquisition. By the fourteenth century both the Dominican and Franciscan orders had departed widely from the teachings of their founders, but they continued to exert a strong influence upon late medieval civilization. The majority of the philosophers and scientists of the thirteenth and fourteenth centuries were either Dominicans or Franciscans.

The Dominican order

2. THE STRUGGLE BETWEEN THE SECULAR AND SPIRITUAL AUTHORITIES

As it happened, the growth of the Church in the later Middle Ages was accompanied by the rise of ambitious political leaders. A

425

conflict between secular and spiritual authorities was practically un-avoidable, since the jurisdictions claimed by each frequently over-lapped. The struggle began about 1050 and continued with varying intensity until well into the fourteenth century.

The two great opponents in the early stages of the struggle were Pope Gregory VII and the German emperor, Henry IV. The quarrel between these powerful rivals was related to the New Cluny movement, of which Gregory had been the leader for some time before he became Pope. As noted previously, one of the fundamental aims of this movement was to free the Church from secular control. During a period of many years the practice had been established that a bishop, abbot, or priest who held his position as a fief should be invested with the symbols of his office by the king or noble who granted the fief. This practice, known as lay investiture, was a thorn in the side of such zealous reformers as Gregory; they feared that as long as the clergy owed allegiance in any degree to secular over-lords, papal supremacy would be impossible. But this was not the only issue involved; there was also the question of the Pope's right to exercise temporal authority. Just how much temporal jurisdiction Gregory intended to claim is not clear. Sometimes it appears from his decrees that he regarded himself as the supreme ruler of the world and thought of all princes and kings as his vassals. But leading scholars of medieval political theory have denied that this was the case. They contend that Gregory's conception of his authority was merely that of *pastor of the Christian flock*, and that he never claimed an unlimited right to create and depose secular rulers or annul their decrees. He would intervene only to protect the inter-ests of the Church and the religious rights of Christians.[2] Naturally, this was a rather extensive authority, but it would still fall short of the right to rule as an autocrat over the whole world.

The overlapping
of jurisdiction

The quarrel between Henry and Gregory was one of the most bitter in the Middle Ages. When Henry refused to obey decrees of the Pope prohibiting lay investiture, Gregory threatened to excom-municate him. The king retaliated by denouncing the Pope as a false monk and ordering him to descend from the throne "to be damned throughout the ages." Whereupon Gregory not only excommuni-cated Henry but declared his throne vacant and released all his sub-jects from allegiance to him. Faced with revolt by his vassals, Henry had no alternative but to make peace with the Pope. He journeyed over the Alps in the depth of winter to Canossa in northern Italy and implored the Pope's forgiveness. Later on, he had his revenge when he led an army into Italy, set up an anti-pope, and compelled Gregory to flee from Rome. The great apostle of reform died in exile in 1085.

The struggle
between Gregory
VII and Henry IV

Before the struggle ended in the fourteenth century, nearly all of the monarchs of western Europe had been involved. Among them

[2] Cf. C. H. McIlwain, *The Growth of Political Thought in the West*, pp. 208 ff.

Shrine of the Three Kings, Cologne Cathedral. Richly decorated shrines are one of the principal forms of interior ornamentation in Gothic cathedrals. The cathedral of Cologne (Köln) in western Germany contains the Shrine of the Three Kings, or the Three Wise Men of the East, who are supposed to have brought gifts to the infant Jesus. According to legend, the bones of the Three Kings were brought from Italy in the twelfth century by Frederick Barbarossa and buried in Cologne.

were the Holy Roman Emperors, Frederick Barbarossa and Frederick II; the French kings, Philip Augustus and Philip the Fair; and the English king, John. The leading contenders on the papal side were Innocent III, Innocent IV, and Boniface VIII. The issues included the right of the Holy Roman Emperors to rule over Italy, the freedom of Italian towns from German domination, and the right of kings to tax the property of the Church. Furthermore, the Popes were now extending their claims to temporal authority a degree or two beyond what had been asserted by Gregory VII. Innocent III declared that "it is the business of the pope to look after the interests of the Roman empire, since the empire derives its origin, and its final authority from the papacy."[3] Innocent IV appears to have gone a step further and to have claimed jurisdiction over all temporal affairs and over all human beings, whether Christians or not. Nevertheless, it must be borne in mind that none of these Popes was really demanding absolute power. What they were insisting upon was not legislative but a judicial authority, an authority to judge and punish rulers for their sins. The fundamental issue was whether rulers were directly responsible to God for their official acts or indirectly through the Pope.

Issues of the struggle

The conflict between Popes and secular authorities had momentous results not only for medieval Europe but for subsequent ages as well. For a time the Popes were almost uniformly successful. With the aid of the Lombard cities and the rebellious dukes in Germany, they checked the ambitions of the Holy Roman Emperors and finally broke the power of the Empire entirely. By means of interdicts Innocent III compelled Philip Augustus to take back the wife he had repudiated and forced King John to recognize England and Ireland as fiefs of

Results of the conflict

[3] O. J. Thatcher and E. H. McNeal, *A Source Book for Medieval History*, p. 220.

the papacy. At the beginning of the fourteenth century, however, Boniface VIII went down to humiliating defeat at the hands of King Philip the Fair of France. As the outcome of a quarrel over Philip's attempt to tax the property of the Church, Boniface was taken prisoner by the king's soldiers, and a month later he died. The Archbishop of Bordeaux was chosen to succeed him, and the papal capital was transferred to Avignon in France, where it remained for seventy years. There were also other results. Many pious Christians now came to believe that the Popes were carrying their ambitions for political power too far and were forgetting their spiritual functions. As a consequence, the papacy lost prestige, and the way was opened for repudiation of its leadership even in religious affairs. In like manner, papal meddling in the internal politics of different countries tended to strengthen the growth of national feeling, particularly in England and France. Finally, the struggle led to a quickening of intellectual activity. As each side attempted to justify its position, interest was awakened in ancient writings, an incentive was provided for the study of Roman law, and many valuable contributions were made to political theory.

3. THE CRUSADES

The Crusades an
expression of me-
dieval imperialism

It is probably not inaccurate to regard the Crusades as the chief expression of medieval expansionism. Unfortunately it appears to be true that nearly every civilization sooner or later develops imperialist tendencies. Certain ones, of course, have been much worse offenders than others, but expansionism in some degree has been characteristic of nearly all of them. It seems to be the natural fruit of the increasing complexity of economic life and of the growth of pride in the real or fancied superiority of a system.

Religious causes
of the Crusades:
(1) mass pilgrim-
ages

Although the Crusades were by no means exclusively a religious movement, there can be no denying the importance of the religious factor in producing them. The century in which they were launched was an age when religion occupied a predominant place in men's thinking. The medieval Christian had a deep conviction of sin. He feared its consequences in the form of eternal damnation and was anxious to avert them by acts of penance. For hundreds of years the most popular type of penance had been the making of pilgrimages to sacred places. A trip to the Holy Land, if at all possible, had been the cherished ambition of every Christian. By the eleventh century the religious revivalism generated by the Cluniac reform movement, combined with the opening up of trade with the Near East, had made pilgrimages to Palestine especially appealing. Hundreds of people now joined the roving bands that trailed across central and eastern Europe on their way to the Levant. In 1065 the Bishop of Bamberg led a horde of 7000 Germans to visit the holy places in and around Jerusalem. Of course, not everyone who joined these mass migrations was inspired by religious ardor. Pilgrimages afforded an opportunity for adventure and sometimes even for profit. Besides, what better chance was there to escape the responsibilities of life for a season and have a good time in the bargain? Every pilgrim who returned brought back stories of the wonderful sights he had seen and thereby aroused the desire of others to follow his example. Without these mass pilgrimages, interest in conquest of the Holy Land would probably never have developed.

Other religious causes must also be mentioned. For a time during the late eleventh century, prospects for papal supremacy did not look bright. Gregory VII had been driven from the throne and had died in exile. His successor was an aged friend who went to his own grave after a year of failure. The cardinals then chose a younger and more vigorous man, who adopted the name of Urban II. Urban had been a French noble who had renounced the world to become a monk at Cluny. Subsequently he became the talented assistant of Gregory VII. Elected Pope himself in 1088, he turned his attention to the glorious dream of uniting all classes of Christians in support of the Church. Perhaps he might even force a reunion of the Eastern and Western branches of Christendom. At any rate, a war against the infidel to rescue the Holy Places from desecration would enable Latin Christians to forget their differences and to rally behind the Pope. The papacy had already inspired or given its blessing to wars on behalf of religion. Predecessors of Urban II had blessed the Norman conquest of England, the campaigns of Robert Guiscard against heretical Greeks in Italy, the wars of Teutons against Slavs on Germany's northern and eastern borders, and the crusades of Christians against Moors in Spain. To merge these efforts in a grand enterprise against the whole unbelieving world must have seemed like a logical climax to what had already occurred.

(2) religious wars as means of promoting unity

For more than a century religious leaders in Europe had been disturbed by the prevalence of fighting among the feudal nobles. Despite the Peace of God and the Truce of God, the warfare of barons and knights continued to be a menace to the security of the Church. The rights of clergy, peasants, and other noncombatants were often trampled upon, merchants were robbed, and religious edifices pillaged and burned. Against these depredations the penalty of excommunication was of little avail. Small wonder, therefore, that Popes should have turned to the idea of protecting the Church and its members by diverting the military ardor of the nobles into a holy war against the heathen. Still another religious cause was surplus idealism left over from the New Cluny movement. Movements of this kind, which strike deeply into the emotional nature of man, generally stir up more enthusiasm than is necessary for their immediate objectives. Some of this surplus must then find new outlets, just as in later years the fanaticism engendered by the Crusades themselves burst forth into persecution of the Jews.

(3) other religious causes

To discover some of the most important economic causes of the Crusades, one has only to read the speech of Pope Urban II at the

THE MAJOR CRUSADES ca. 1096 A.D.

Legend:
- Population predominantly Christian
- Population predominantly Moslem
- → First Crusade
- +++→ Second Crusade
- – –→ Third Crusade
- ·····→ Fourth Crusade

Political boundaries shown are those of the time of the First Crusade

0   500 miles

Council of Clermont inviting the nobles of France to take up arms for the conquest of Palestine. He urged them to let nothing detain them, "since this land which you inhabit, shut in on all sides by the sea and surrounded by mountain peaks, is too narrow for your large population; nor does it abound in wealth; and it furnishes scarcely enough food for its cultivators. . . . Enter upon the road to the Holy Sepulchre; wrest that land from the wicked race and subject it to yourselves. That land which, as the Scripture says, 'floweth with milk and honey,' was given by God into the possession of the children of Israel. Jerusalem is the navel of the world; the land is fruitful above others, like another paradise of delights." [4] There is evidence also that a good many nobles, because of extravagance or poor

Economic causes

[4] O. J. Thatcher and E. H. McNeal, *A Source Book for Medieval History*, pp. 519–20.

430

French Knights about to Depart on a Crusade. Their chief weapons are the long bow and the spear.

management of their estates had fallen into debt. Further, the rule of primogeniture in France and in England created the problem of what to do with the younger sons. New fiefs were hard to obtain, and positions in the Church were becoming scarce. As a result, these surplus offspring of the nobles tended to form a rebellious and disorderly class, alert for any opportunity to despoil a weak neighbor of his property. Confronted by such problems as these, the nobles of western Europe needed no second invitation to respond to Pope Urban's plea.

But the catalyst or immediate cause of the Crusades was the advance of the Seljuk Turks in the Near East. In about 1050 these people had come down into western Asia and had gained control over the Baghdad caliphate. Soon afterward they conquered Syria, Palestine, and Egypt. In 1071 they slaughtered a Byzantine army at Manzikert and then swept through Asia Minor and captured Nicaea, within a few miles of Constantinople. After the death of the great Sultan, Malik Shah, in 1092 the Seljuk empire began to disintegrate. The time now seemed ripe for the Byzantine Emperor, Alexius Comnenus, to attempt the reconquest of his lost possessions. Realizing the difficulty of this task, since his own government was exhausted from previous struggles, he sent an appeal in 1095 to the Pope, probably for aid in recruiting mercenary soldiers. Urban II, the reigning pontiff, took full advantage of this opportunity. He summoned a council of French nobles and clergy at Clermont and exhorted them in a fiery speech to make war upon the accursed race of Turks. He employed every artful device of eloquence to arouse the fury and cupidity of his hearers, emphasizing especially the horrible atrocities which he declared the Turks were committing upon Christians. When he had finished, it is reported that all who were present cried out with one accord, "It is the will of God," and rushed forward to take the crusader's oath.

The first of the organized Crusades was not actually started until late in 1096. The majority of those who participated in it were

The immediate cause of the Crusades

431

Frenchmen and Normans. Altogether, between 1096 and 1244, three other major Crusades and a number of minor ones were launched. Only the first achieved much success in destroying Turkish control over Christian territory. By 1098 most of Syria had been captured, and a year later Jerusalem was taken. But these gains were only temporary. In 1187 Jerusalem was recaptured by the Moslems under Saladin, Sultan of Egypt. Before the end of the thirteenth century every one of the petty states established by the crusaders in the Near East had been wiped out.

The ultimate failure of the Crusades resulted from several causes. To begin with, the expeditions were frequently badly managed; there was seldom any unified command, and rival leaders quarreled among themselves. In some of the later expeditions the original purpose of conquering the Holy Land from the Turks was lost sight of altogether. The Fourth Crusade, for example, turned out to be a gigantic plundering foray against Constantinople. There was also another cause which cannot be overlooked: the conflicting ambitions of the East and the West. According to the evidence, the Byzantine Emperor, Alexius Comnenus, in appealing to the Pope for aid, professed a desire to protect the Christian churches of the Orient. But this was not his primary objective. He had come to the conclusion that the time was ripe for a major offensive against the Turks. He was not interested simply or even primarily in driving them out of the Holy Land but in reconquering all of the Asiatic provinces of his empire. By contrast, Pope Urban II had the grandiose dream of a holy war of all of Latin Christendom to expel the infidel from Palestine. His underlying purpose was not to rescue the Byzantine Empire but to strengthen Latin Christianity, to exalt the papacy, and perhaps to restore the union of the Eastern and Western churches.

In line with a common tendency to overestimate the importance of wars, the Crusades were at one time considered as the primary cause of nearly all of European progress in the later Middle Ages. It was assumed that they led to the growth of cities, to the overthrow of feudalism, and to the introduction of Saracenic philosophy and science into Latin Europe. For several reasons most historians now regard this assumption as being of limited validity. First, the progress of civilization in the later Middle Ages was already well under way before the Crusades began. Second, the educated classes in Europe did not generally take part in the military expeditions; as a result, the soldiers who actually went were totally devoid of the intellectual background necessary for an appreciation of Saracenic learning. Third, very few of the armies ever reached the real centers of Saracenic civilization, which were not Jerusalem or Antioch, but Baghdad, Damascus, Toledo, and Cordova. European intellectual progress in the twelfth and thirteenth centuries was due far more to the revival of trade with the Near East and to the work of scholars and translators in Spain and Sicily than to any influence of holy wars against the Turks. Nor were the Crusades primarily responsi-

Krak des Chevaliers, Northern Syria. This Castle of the Knights is considered the most magnificent of all the Crusader fortresses and one of the best-preserved relics of the Middle Ages.

ble for the political and economic changes at the end of the Middle Ages. The decline of feudalism, for instance, occurred chiefly because of the Black Death, the growth of an urban economy, and the rise of national monarchies; and these in turn were only in minor degree the results of the Crusades.

What effects, then, is it possible to ascribe to the great holy wars against Islam? To some extent they hastened the emancipation of the common people. Nobles who were hard pressed for money sold privileges to townsmen and to communities of serfs somewhat earlier than they would otherwise have done. Further, many peasants took advantage of the absence of the nobles to break away from bondage to the soil. Among other economic effects were an increased demand for products of the East, the growth of banking, and the elimination of Constantinople as the middleman in the trade between East and West. Venice, Genoa, and Pisa now gained a virtual monopoly of commerce in the Mediterranean area. In addition, the Crusades had some influence in strengthening the monarchies of France and England by eliminating powerful nobles and providing a pretext for direct taxation; but the political consequences were relatively slight. In the domain of religion, where we would normally expect the most profound results, few positive effects can be discovered. It is impossible to prove that the Popes enjoyed any increase in power or repute as a result of having launched the Crusades. On the contrary, as the true character of the expeditions became more and more transparent, the papacy seems rather to have suffered a loss of prestige. There was, however, an increase in religious fanaticism, which expressed itself particularly in savage persecution of the Jews. These unfortunate people suffered

The actual results of the Crusades

433

nearly everywhere. They were cruelly beaten, sometimes killed in mob attacks, and expelled from several countries. Naturally, the fury against them was partly economic in origin, since they were the chief moneylenders of the time; nevertheless, it is a significant fact that hostility to Jews had one of its chief sources in the holy wars against Islam. Finally, it is doubtless true that the Crusades had some effect in widening geographic knowledge and in encouraging travel and exploration, but these developments were more the result of the gradual expansion of trade.

4.   THE LATE MEDIEVAL MIND

The revival of learning in western Europe

Intellectual progress in the later Middle Ages received its original stimulus from the so-called Carolingian Renaissance of the ninth century. This was a movement initiated by Charlemagne when he brought to his court at Aachen the most distinguished scholars he could find. In doing this the emperor was prompted partly by his own interest in learning but also by his desire to find uniform standards of orthodoxy which could be imposed upon all of his subjects. Fortunately he seems to have allowed the scholars he imported a generous freedom to pursue their own inclinations. The result was a brilliant though superficial revival of learning which continued for some years after the death of its sponsor. After the Carolingian Renaissance intellectual progress in western Europe was interrupted for some time on account of the Norse and Saracenic invasions. A brief revival in Germany in the tenth century was followed by a more virile growth of classical studies in Italy and France after the year 1000. But the climax of intellectual achievement in the later Middle Ages was not reached until the twelfth and thirteenth centuries.

Philosophy: Scholasticism

The outstanding intellectual achievement of the late Middle Ages was the famous system of dialectics known as Scholasticism. This system is usually defined as the attempt to harmonize reason and faith or to make philosophy serve the interest of theology. But no such definition is sufficient to convey an adequate conception of the Scholastic mind. The great thinkers of the Middle Ages did not limit their interests to problems of religion. On the contrary, they were just as anxious as philosophers in any period to answer the great questions of life, whether they pertained to religion, politics, economics, or metaphysics. Perhaps the best way to explain the true nature of Scholasticism is to define it in terms of its characteristics. In the first place, it was rationalistic, not empirical; in other words, it was based primarily upon logic rather than upon science or experience. The Scholastic philosophers, like the Greek thinkers of the Socratic school, did not believe that the highest truth could be derived from sense perception. They admitted that the senses could provide man with a knowledge of the appearances of things, but they maintained that reality or the essential nature of the universe is discoverable mainly by reason. In the second place, Scholastic philosophy was authoritarian. Even reason was not considered a sufficient instrument for the discovery of all knowledge, but the deductions of logic needed to be buttressed by the authority of the Scriptures, of the Church Fathers, and especially of Plato and Aristotle. Third, Scholastic philosophy had a predominantly ethical approach. Its cardinal aim was to discover how man could improve this life and insure salvation in the life to come. Fourth, Scholastic thought, unlike modern philosophy, was not mainly concerned with causes and underlying relationships. Its purpose was rather to discover the attributes of things; the universe was assumed to be static, and therefore it was only necessary to explain the meaning of things and what they were good for, not to account for their origin and evolution.

The primary development of the Scholastic philosophy began with the teachings of Peter Abelard (1079–1142), one of the most interesting figures in the history of thought. This handsome and talented Frenchman was educated in the best schools of Paris and gained a wide reputation for dialectical skill before he was out of his twenties. For a number of years he taught in Paris, drawing great crowds to his lectures on philosophy and theology. Despite the fact that he was a monk, his habits of life were far from ascetic. He was proud, belligerent, and egotistical—boastful of his intellectual triumphs and even of his prowess in love. He avowed that he possessed such advantages of comeliness and youth that "he feared no repulse from whatever woman he might deign to honor with his love." His tragic affair with Heloïse, which he poignantly describes in his autobiography, *The Story of My Misfortunes*, contributed to his downfall. But he had already incurred the enmity of some powerful theologians who regarded him as a heretic. As a philosopher Abelard had accomplishments to his credit for which he had a right to be proud. He was probably the most critical of all the medieval thinkers. In his most famous philosophical work, *Sic et Non (Yes and No)*, he exposed many of the shabby arguments based on authority that were commonly accepted in his time. The preface to this work contains a statement which expresses clearly his conviction about the vital importance of critical reasoning: "For the first key to wisdom is called interrogation, diligent and unceasing. . . . By doubting we are led to inquiry; and from inquiry we perceive the truth."

The heyday of Scholasticism came in the thirteenth century, as a result of the labors of numerous intellectuals in various fields of learning. Two of the greatest were Albertus Magnus and his renowned pupil, St. Thomas Aquinas. These men had the advantage of being able to study most of the works of Aristotle, recently translated from copies in the possession of the Saracens. Albertus Magnus, the only scholar ever to be honored with the title of Great, was born in Germany in 1193. During a long and active career he

Peter Abelard

The heyday of Scholasticism; Albertus Magnus

435

St. Thomas Aquinas (1225–1274).

served as a teacher, especially at Cologne and at the University of Paris. A profound admirer of Aristotle, he strove to emulate the example of that ancient master by taking the whole field of knowledge as his province. His writings included more than twenty volumes on subjects ranging from botany and physiology to the soul and the creation of the universe. He was often skeptical of ancient authorities, and he attempted to found his conclusions upon reason and experience. In referring to hoary myths, such as the one about ostriches eating iron, he would frequently say: "but this is not proved by experience." He defined natural science "as not simply receiving what one is told, but the investigation of causes in natural phenomena." [5]

Thomas Aquinas, the most noted of all the Scholastic philosophers, was born in southern Italy in 1225. Following the example of the great Albert, he entered the Dominican order and devoted his life to teaching. He was a professor at the University of Paris by the time he was thirty-one. His most famous work was his *Summa theologica*, but he wrote on many other subjects as well, including politics and economics. The fundamental aims of St. Thomas were, first, to demonstrate the rationality of the universe, and second, to establish the primacy of reason. He believed that the universe is an ordered whole governed by intelligent purpose. All things were created in order to make possible the fulfillment of the great Christian plan for the promotion of justice and peace on earth and the salvation of mankind in a world to come. The philosophy of St. Thomas implied a serene confidence in the ability of man to know and understand his world. He regarded the intellectual faculties of man and also his senses as God-given. The great *Summaries* he wrote were attempts to build up out of logic and the wisdom of the past comprehensive systems of knowledge which would leave no mysteries unsolved. Though he leaned heavily upon the authority of Aristotle and the Church Fathers he regarded reason as the primary key to truth. Even his attitude toward religion was essentially intellectual rather than emotional; piety to him was a matter of knowledge more than of faith. He admitted that a few doctrines of Christianity, such as the belief in the Trinity and the creation of the world in time, could not be proved by the intellect; but he denied that they were contrary to reason, for God Himself is a rational being. The influence of St. Thomas was not only of cardinal importance in his own time, but it survives to this day. In the late nineteenth century Pope Leo XIII exhorted the bishops of the Church "to restore the golden wisdom of St. Thomas and to spread it far and wide for the defense of the faith, for the good of society, and for the advantage of all the sciences." He recommended St. Thomas as a master and guide for everyone interested in scholarly studies.

[5] Lynn Thorndike, *A History of Magic and Experimental Science*, II, ch. 59.

By the end of the thirteenth century Scholasticism had begun to decline. Its decay was due partly to the teachings of the last of the Scholastics, John Duns Scotus. A member of the Franciscan order, Duns Scotus was inclined to emphasize the emotional and practical side of religion in place of the intellectual. He conceived of piety as an act of will rather than an act of intellect. Less confident of the powers of reason than St. Thomas, he excluded a large number of the doctrines of religion from the sphere of philosophy altogether. From this it was only a step to denial that any religious beliefs were capable of rational demonstration; all would have to be accepted on faith or rejected entirely. When this step was finally taken by Duns Scotus' successors, the overthrow of Scholasticism was speedily accomplished.

The decay of Scholasticism

The other main reason for the decline of Scholasticism was the growing popularity of nominalism. Although nominalism is often considered a form of Scholasticism, actually the nominalists were fundamentally opposed to nearly everything the Scholastics taught. They denied that concepts or class names have any reality, insisting that they are nothing but abstractions invented by the mind to express the qualities common to a number of objects or organisms. Only individual things are real. Far from accepting the Scholastic confidence in reason, the nominalists contended that all knowledge has its source in experience. Anything beyond the realm of concrete experience must be taken on faith, if it is to be accepted at all; the truths of religion cannot be demonstrated by logic. Although some of the earlier nominalists inclined toward religious skepticism, the majority became mystics. Nominalism flourished in the fourteenth century and for some time was the most popular philosophy in western Europe. Nominalism is especially important for having laid the foundations for the scientific progress of the Renaissance and for the mystical religious movements which helped to bring on the Protestant Revolution.

The growth of nominalism

A good many medieval philosophers devoted earnest attention to questions of political authority; a few, in fact, were primarily concerned with such questions. The political theorists of the later Middle Ages were in substantial agreement on a large part of their philosophy. Practically all of them had abandoned the idea of the Church Fathers that the state was established by God as a remedy for sin, and that men must therefore render faithful obedience even to the tyrant. It was now commonly held that the state is a product of man's social nature, and that when justice is the guiding principle of the ruler, government is a positive good, not a necessary evil. In the second place, it was generally agreed by the philosophers of the later Middle Ages that all of western Europe should constitute a single commonwealth under one supreme ruler. There might be many subordinate kings or princes in the different parts of the continent, but one supreme overlord, either the Pope or the Holy Roman Em-

The political theory of the later Middle Age

437

Opposition to
absolutism

peror, should have the highest jurisdiction. The most noted of those who defended the supremacy of the Emperor was Dante in his *De Monarchia*. On the papal side were the Englishman John of Salisbury (*ca.* 1115–1180) and Thomas Aquinas. Virtually without exception the political theorists of the later Middle Ages believed in limited government. They had no use for absolutism in any form. John of Salisbury even went so far as to defend the right of the subjects of a tyrant to put him to death. Practically all of late medieval theory was based upon the assumption that the authority of every ruler, whether pope, emperor, or king, was essentially judicial in character. His function was merely to apply the law, not to make or alter it in accordance with his will. Indeed, the medievalists did not conceive of law as the command of a sovereign at all, but as the product of custom or of the divine order of nature. On the other hand, the medieval political theorists were not democrats, for not one of them believed in the doctrine of majority rule. The man who came closest to an exposition of the democratic ideal was Marsiglio of Padua in the fourteenth century. He advocated that the people should have the right to elect the monarch and even to depose him if necessary. He believed also in a representative body with power to make laws. But Marsiglio was no champion of unlimited popular sovereignty. In fact, he defined democracy as a degraded form of government. His idea of representative government was representation of the citizens according to quality rather than mere numbers, and the law-making powers of his representative body would be confined to the enactment of statutes regulating the structure of the government.

Progress in
science

The record of scientific achievements in the later Middle Ages can scarcely be considered an imposing one. Yet it was probably about all we should expect in view of the absorption of interest in other fields. The names of only a few individual scientists need to be mentioned. One of the most original was Adelard of Bath, who lived in the early years of the twelfth century. Not only did he condemn reliance upon authority, but he devoted many years of his life to direct investigation of nature. He discovered some important facts about the causes of earthquakes, the functions of different parts of the brain, and the processes of breathing and digestion. He was probably the first scientist since the Hellenistic Age to affirm the indestructibility of matter.

Frederick II as
a scientist

The toughest-minded of all the medieval scientists was the notorious Holy Roman Emperor, Frederick II, whose reign occupied the first part of the thirteenth century. Frederick was skeptical of almost everything. He denied the immortality of the soul, and he was accused of having written a brochure entitled *Jesus, Moses and Mohammed: The Three Great Impostors*. But he was not satisfied merely to scoff. He performed various experiments of his own to gratify his boundless curiosity, testing the artificial incubation of eggs, for example, and sealing the eyes of vultures to determine whether they found their food by sight or by smell. His most important scientific contributions were made, however, as a patron of learning. An ardent admirer of Saracenic culture, he brought distinguished scholars to Palermo to translate the writings of the Saracens into Latin. He subsidized leading scientists, especially Leonard of Pisa, the most brilliant mathematician of the thirteenth century. In addition, Frederick instituted measures for the improvement of medical practice. He legalized the practice of dissection, established a system of examining and licensing physicians, and founded the University of Naples with one of the best medical schools in Europe.

By far the best known of medieval scientists was Roger Bacon (*ca.* 1214–1294), possibly because he predicted certain modern inventions such as horseless carriages and flying machines. In reality, Bacon was less critical than Frederick II; he believed that all knowledge must enhance the glory of theology, the queen of the sciences. Moreover, Adelard of Bath preceded him by more than a century in advocating and using the experimental method. Nevertheless, Bacon, by virtue of his strong insistence upon accurate investigation, deserves a high place among medieval scientists. He denied that either reason or authority could furnish valid knowledge unless supported by experimental research. Besides, he himself did some practical work of great value. His writings on optics remained authoritative for several centuries. He discovered much about magnifying lenses, and it seems more than probable that he invented the simple microscope. He demonstrated that light travels faster than sound, and he was apparently the first scientist to perceive the inaccuracy of the Julian calendar and to advocate its revision.

Much of the advancement in philosophy and science in the later Middle Ages would have been quite impossible without the educational progress which marked the centuries from the ninth to the fourteenth. The Carolingian Renaissance resulted in the establishment of better schools and libraries in several of the

Roger Bacon

Alchemists in Their Laboratory. Note the great variety of instruments used and the spectacles worn by the experimenter.

The transfer of
education from
the monasteries
to the cathedral
schools

*See color map
at page 416*

monasteries of western Europe. Many of these institutions, how-ever, were destroyed during the chaos of the ninth century. As a consequence of the religious reform movements of the eleventh cen-tury, the monasteries tended to neglect education, with the result that the monastic schools that had survived were gradually over-shadowed by the cathedral schools. Some of the latter developed into what would now be considered the equivalent of colleges, providing excellent instruction in the so-called liberal arts. This was notably true of the cathedral schools located at Canterbury, Char-tres, and Paris. But by far the most important educational develop-ment of the Middle Ages was the rise of the universities.

The term university (from the Latin, *universitas*) originally meant a corporation or guild. In fact, many of the medieval univer-sities were very much like craft guilds, organized for the purpose of training and licensing teachers. Gradually the word came to have the meaning of an educational institution with a school of liberal arts and one or more faculties in the professional subjects of law, medicine, and theology. No one knows which of the universities was the oldest. It may have been Salerno, which was a center of medical study as far back as the tenth century. The universities of Bologna and Paris are also very ancient, the former having been established about 1150 and the latter before the end of the twelfth century. The next oldest included such famous institutions as the universities of Oxford, Cambridge, Montpellier, Salamanca, and Naples. There were no universities in Germany until the fourteenth century, when schools of this type were organized at Prague, Vienna, Heidelberg, and Cologne. By the end of the Middle Ages some eighty universities had been established in western Europe.

Practically every university in medieval Europe was patterned after one or the other of two different models. Throughout Italy, Spain, and southern France the standard was generally the Univer-sity of Bologna, in which the students themselves constituted the guild or corporation. They hired the teachers, paid their salaries, and fined or discharged them for neglect of duty or inefficient in-struction. Nearly all of these southern institutions were secular in character, specializing in law or medicine. The universities of north-ern Europe were modeled after the one at Paris, which was not a guild of students but of teachers. It included the four faculties of arts, theology, law, and medicine, each headed by an elected dean. In the great majority of the northern universities arts and theology were the leading branches of study. Before the end of the thirteenth century separate colleges came to be established within the Univer-sity of Paris. The original college was nothing more than an endowed home for poor students, but the discovery was soon made that discipline could best be preserved by having all of the students live in colleges. Eventually the colleges became centers of instruc-tion as well as residences. While on the Continent of Europe most

A Noted Teacher, Henricus de Alemania, Lecturing in a Medieval University.
Some interesting comparisons and contrasts may be observed between his students and those in a modern classroom.

of these colleges have ceased to exist, in England the universities of Oxford and Cambridge still retain the pattern of federal organization copied from Paris. The colleges of which they are composed are practically independent educational units.

Though modern universities have borrowed much of their organization from their medieval prototypes, the course of study has been radically changed. No curriculum in the Middle Ages included much history or natural science, nor any great amount of mathematics. The student in the Middle Ages was required, first of all, to spend four or five years in studying the *trivium*—grammar, rhetoric, and logic, or dialectic. If he passed his examinations he received the preliminary degree of bachelor of arts, which conferred no particular distinction. To assure himself a place in professional life he must devote some additional years to the pursuit of an advanced degree, such as master of arts, doctor of laws, or doctor of medicine. For the master's degree three or four years had to be given to study of the *quadrivium*—arithmetic, geometry, astronomy, and music. These subjects were not quite what their names imply now. Their content was highly philosophical; arithmetic, for example, included primarily a study of the theory of numbers, while music was concerned largely with the properties of sound. The requirements for the doctor's degree were generally more severe and included more specialized training. By the end of the Middle Ages the course for the doctorate of theology at Paris had been extended to fourteen years, and the degree could not be conferred unless the candidate was at least thirty-five years of age. Both the master's and

The course of study

doctor's degrees were teaching degrees; even the title of doctor of medicine meant a teacher of medicine, not a practicing physician.

The life of medieval students differed in many ways from that of their modern descendants. The student body in any one university was not a homogeneous group but was composed of diverse nationalities. The young Frenchman or German who wanted to study law would almost certainly go to Bologna or Padua, just as the young Italian with an interest in theology would probably enroll at Paris. The entire university was usually an independent community, and the students were consequently exempt from the jurisdiction of political authorities. A relic of this ancient autonomy is to be found in the fact that some of the German universities still have their own jails. The learning process consisted primarily in taking down copious notes on wax tablets from the master's lecture and then analyzing and discussing them afterwards. The young man's education was supposed to be acquired through logic and memory rather than from extensive reading or research. In other respects, however, student life in the Middle Ages was not so far different from what it is now. If the medieval student knew nothing of intercollegiate sports, he at least had his violent fights with the hoodlums of the town to absorb his surplus energy. In the medieval universities as in those of today there were the sharply contrasting types of sincere, intelligent scholars and frank and frivolous loafers. We hear much about radicalism and activism in modern colleges, but these tendencies were certainly not absent in the universities of the Middle Ages. Many of these institutions were roundly denounced as breeding places of heresy, paganism, and worldliness. It was said that young men "seek theology at Paris, law at Bologna, and medicine at Montpellier, but nowhere a life that is pleasing to God." The students at Paris even had to be admonished to stop playing dice on the altar of Notre Dame after one of their holiday celebrations.

No one who has more than a casual acquaintance with the literature of the later Middle Ages could ever imagine the whole medieval period to have been an era of darkness and otherworldliness. For much of this literature expresses a zest for living as spontaneous, joyous, and free as any attitude revealed in the writings of the Renaissance of the fourteenth and succeeding centuries. Indeed, the spirit of late medieval literature was even closer to that of the modern age than most people realize. Probably the actual amount of religious literature in the later Middle Ages did not bear a much larger ratio to the total quantity of writings produced than would be true at the present time.

Late medieval writings can be classified, first of all, as either Latin or vernacular literature. The revival of classical studies in the cathedral schools and in the earliest universities led to the production of some excellent Latin poetry. The best examples of this were the secular lyrics, especially those written by a group of poets known as the Goliards or *Goliardi*. The Goliards derived their name from the fact that they commonly referred to themselves as disciples of Golias. Who Golias was, no one knows, but one scholar thinks that he was probably the devil.[6] Such a choice of a master would undoubtedly have been appropriate enough, for most of the Goliard poets were regarded by the Church as lewd fellows of the baser sort for whom nothing was too sacred to be ridiculed. They wrote parodies of the creeds, travesties of the mass, and even burlesques of the Gospels. Their lyrics were purely pagan in spirit, celebrating the beauties of the changing seasons, the carefree life of the open road, the pleasures of drinking and gambling, and especially the joys of love. The authors of these rollicking and satirical songs were mostly wandering students, although some appear to have been men more advanced in years. The names of nearly all of them are unknown. Their poetry is particularly significant as the first emphatic protest against the ascetic ideal of Christianity. The following stanzas taken from *The Confession of Golias* may be considered typical of what they wrote:

Latin literature: the poetry of the Goliards

> Prelate, most discreet of priests,
> Grant me absolution!
> Dear's the death whereof I die,
> Sweet my dissolution;
> For my heart is wounded by
>
> Beauty's soft suffusion;
> All the girls I come not nigh
> Mine are in illusion.
> 'Tis most arduous to make
>
> Nature's self-surrender;
> Seeing girls, to blush and be
> Purity's defender!
> We young men our longings ne'er
> Shall to stern law render,
> Or preserve our fancies from
> Bodies smooth and tender.[7]

By no means all of medieval literature was written in Latin. As the Middle Ages waned, the vernacular languages of French, German, Spanish, English, and Italian became increasingly popular as media of literary expression. Until the beginning of the twelfth century nearly all of the literature in the vernacular languages assumed the form of the heroic epic. Among the leading examples were the French *Song of Roland*, the German *Song of the Nibelungs*, the eddas and sagas of the Norsemen, and the Spanish *Poem of My Cid*. These epics picture a virile but unpolished feudal

The growth of vernacular literature

---

[6] C. H. Haskins, *The Renaissance of the Twelfth Century*, p. 177.
[7] J. A. Symonds, *Wine, Women and Song*, p. 66.

society in its earlier stage of evolution, when valorous deeds in battle on behalf of one's suzerain represented the fulfillment of the highest knightly ideal. Heroism, honor, and loyalty were practically the exclusive themes. The tone of the epics was almost entirely masculine. If women were mentioned at all, it was generally in a condescending fashion. The hero must show the utmost devotion to his superior, but it was not considered inappropriate that he should beat his wife.

During the twelfth and thirteenth centuries feudal society in western Europe attained the full flower of its growth. As a result of the progress of learning and of contact with the higher civilization of the Saracens, the feudal aristocracy adopted new attitudes and interests. Chivalry, with its glorification of woman and its emphasis upon kindness and refinement of manners, tended to displace the older conception of a feudal ideal limited to the virtues of the battlefield. The first literary works to reflect and in part to inspire this change in ideals were the songs of the troubadours. The original home of the troubadours was southern France, especially the region known as Provence. Here was one of the most highly civilized areas of feudal Europe. It received the full impact of Saracenic influence from Spain, and it seems to have preserved an extensive inheritance from ancient Rome. Whatever the reasons, there can be no doubt that the troubadours of Provence initiated a movement of profound importance in late medieval literature. The central theme of their songs was romantic love. Woman was idealized now as never before. The virtues of her who had once been condemned by monks and Church Fathers as the very incarnation of evil were extolled to the skies. But the love of the troubadours for the ladies of the feudal courts was not supposed to be sensual; it was a rarefied, almost mystical emotion which could be satisfied by a smile or some trifling memento from the haughty goddesses who were the objects of the singers' affection. The fact must be emphasized also that romantic love was not the only topic in which the troubadours were interested. Many wrote acrid satires against the rapacity and hypocrisy of the clergy, and one even addressed a powerful "poem of blame" to God. The literary tradition originated by the troubadours was continued by the *trouvères* in northern France and by the *minnesingers* in Germany.

The most important of all the writings which expressed the ideals of the feudal aristocracy were the romances of the Arthurian cycle. The material of these romances consisted of legends woven about the career of a Celtic chieftain by the name of Arthur, who had been the hero of the struggle against the Anglo-Saxon invaders of Britain. In the twelfth century certain Norman and French writers, especially Marie de France and Chrétien de Troyes, became interested in these legends as a background for the chivalric ideal. The result was the composition of a number of romances of love and ad-

The literature of chivalry: (1) the songs of the troubadours

(2) the romances of the Arthurian cycle

444

venture, famous alike for their colorful narrative and their poetic beauty. Later the best known of these romances were adapted and completed by German poets. Wolfram von Eschenbach developed what is usually considered the most perfect version of the Parzival legend, while Gottfried von Strassburg gave to the story of Tristan and Isolde its classic medieval form. Although these romances differed in form and in substance, they may yet be said to have had features in common. All of them glorified adventure for its own sake, and taught that experience of the deepest and most varied kind is the only sure road to wisdom. All of them strove to inculcate gentleness, protection of the weak, and rescue of those in distress as knightly obligations, in addition to honor, truthfulness, and bravery. The redeeming power of love was another universal element, although not all of the authors agreed as to the form which this love should assume. Some maintained that it ought to be the faithful affection between husband and wife, but others insisted that it must be love unsustained by wedlock. In the minds of the latter group true love was possible only between knight and mistress, never between husband and wife. Finally, in the best of these romances an element of tragedy was nearly always present. Indeed, such a work as Gottfried von Strassburg's *Tristan* might almost be regarded as the prototype of modern tragic literature. He was certainly one of the first to develop the idea of individual suffering as a literary theme and to point out the indistinct dividing line which separates pleasure from pain. For him, to love is to yearn, and suffering and death are integral chapters of the book of life.

By the thirteenth century the merchants and craftsmen of the towns had risen to a position of power and influence equal if not superior to that of the feudal nobles. We can therefore logically expect that some literature would be written to appeal to burgher tastes. Among the foremost examples of such writings were the romance of *Aucassin and Nicolette* and the short stories in verse known as the *fabliaux*. The romance of *Aucassin and Nicolette* resembles in some ways the romances of chivalry. The hero Aucassin is a young noble, and the main theme of the romance is the imperious demands of love; but the plot is frequently turned into channels distinctly at variance with the chivalric ideal. Aucassin has fallen desperately in love, not with the high-born wife of some noble, but with Nicolette, a Saracen slave girl. Warned that he will suffer in hell if he does not give up his beloved, the hero replies that he does not mind, for in hell he will enjoy the company of all who have really lived. The story is also quite different from the romances of chivalry in its occasional expression of sympathy for the peasant. But the writings which undoubtedly made the strongest appeal to the urban classes were the *fabliaux*. These were stories written not to edify or instruct but chiefly to amuse. Often richly spiced with indecency, they reveal a contempt for the trappings of

Literature of the urban classes

445

chivalry, with its romanticized love and idiotic pursuit of adventure. Most of them are also strongly anti-clerical and indicate no high regard for the religious spirit. Nearly always it is monks and priests who are made the butts of the jokes. The *fabliaux* are significant as expressions of the growing worldliness of the urban classes and as forerunners of the robust realism which was later to appear in the works of such writers as Chaucer and Boccaccio.

The Romance of the Rose

The supreme achievements of medieval literary talent were two great masterpieces written in the thirteenth and fourteenth centuries. The first was the *Romance of the Rose* of William of Lorris and John of Meun, and the second was Dante's *Divine Comedy*. Each in its own way is a kind of summary of late medieval civilization. The *Romance of the Rose* consists of two parts: the first 4000 lines were begun by William of Lorris about 1230; the other part, nearly three times as long, was finished by John of Meun about 1265. The two parts are entirely different, the first being an allegory dealing with the cult of chivalric love, while the second is a eulogy of reason. John of Meun was quite skeptical of the value of the feudal aristocracy to medieval society; he hated superstition; and he satirized the monastic orders, the papacy, and many other established institutions of his time. He embodied the mocking, realistic attitude of the bourgeoisie, as his predecessor, William of Lorris, symbolized the romantic, mystical spirit of chivalry. The work of the two men taken together furnishes a kind of guidebook to the later Middle Ages.

The Divine Comedy

Without doubt the most profound of the medieval summaries was the *Divine Comedy* of Dante Alighieri (1265–1321). Not a great deal is known about the life of Dante except that he was the son of a Florentine lawyer and was active during the early part of his career in the political affairs of his city. Despite his absorption in politics he managed to acquire a full mastery of the philosophic and literary knowledge of his time. In 1302 the party to which he belonged was ousted from power in Florence, and he was compelled to live the remainder of his years outside of his native city. Most of his writings were apparently produced during this period of exile. Dante called his chief work simply the *Comedy*, but his admirers during the Italian Renaissance always spoke of it as the *Divine Comedy*, and that is the title which has come down to us. In form the work may be considered a drama of the struggles, temptations, and ultimate redemption of the soul. But of course it is much more than this; for it embraces a complete summation of medieval culture, a magnificent synthesis of the Scholastic philosophy, the science, the religion, and the economic and ethical ideals of the later Middle Ages. Its dominant theme is the salvation of mankind through reason and divine grace, but it includes many other ideas as well. The universe is conceived as a finite world of which the earth is the center and in which everything exists for the benefit of man. All natural phe-

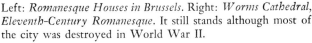
Left: *Romanesque Houses in Brussels*. Right: *Worms Cathedral, Eleventh-Century Romanesque*. It still stands although most of the city was destroyed in World War II.

nomena have their meaning in relation to the divine scheme for peace and justice on earth and salvation in the life beyond. Human beings possess free will to choose the good and avoid the evil. The worst of the sins which man can commit is treason or betrayal of trust; the least serious are those which proceed from weakness of the flesh. Dante took earnest pleasure in the classical authors, almost worshiping Aristotle, Seneca, and Vergil. He chose Vergil rather than some Christian theologian to personify philosophy. By reason of his imaginative power and the warmth and vigor of his style, he deserves to be ranked as one of the greatest poets of all time, but he is especially important to the historian because of the well-rounded picture he presents of the late medieval mind.

5. ART AND MUSIC IN THE LATER MIDDLE AGES

The later Middle Ages produced two great styles of architecture, the Romanesque and the Gothic. The Romanesque was mainly a product of the monastic revival and attained its full development in the century and a half following the year 1000. Fundamentally it was an ecclesiastical architecture, symbolizing the pride of the monastic orders at the height of their power. Naturally, since the Cluniac revival affected the entire Church, the Romanesque style was not confined to monasteries. Nevertheless, it is significant that some of the most impressive Romanesque buildings were houses of the Cluniac order. The essential features of this building style were

Architecture: the Romanesque style

447

the round arch, massive walls, enormous piers, small windows, gloomy interiors, and the predominance of horizontal lines. The plainness of interiors was sometimes relieved by mosaics or by frescoing in bright colors, but the style of construction was not such as to encourage elaborate ornamentation. Moreover, the strong religious spirit in which this architecture was conceived did not generally foster an appeal to the senses. Some of the architects of southern Europe, however, succeeded in breaking away from this somber monastic tradition and often decorated their churches with an elaborate symbolic sculpture.

In the late twelfth and thirteenth centuries the Romanesque architecture was superseded in popularity by the Gothic. The increase in wealth, the advancement of learning, the growth of secular interests, and the pride of the cities in their newly acquired freedom and prosperity led to a demand for a more elaborate architectural style to express the ideals of the new age. Besides, the monastic revival had now spent its force. Gothic architecture was almost exclusively urban. Its monuments were not monasteries situated on lonely crags but cathedrals, bishops' churches, located in the largest cities and towns. It must be understood, though, that the medieval cathedral was not simply a church but a center of the community life. It generally housed a school and a library and was sometimes used as a town hall. It was often large enough to accommodate the whole population of the town. The people of the entire community participated in erecting it, and they rightfully regarded it as civic property. Indeed, many of the Gothic cathedrals were the outcome of town rivalry. For example, the people of Siena became dissatisfied with their modest church after the cathedral at Florence was completed and determined to build a new one on a much more pretentious scale. Frequently the citizens' ambitions got far out of bounds, with the result that many of the buildings were left unfinished. The architects of the Cathedral of Chartres, for instance, planned for several more lofty towers than were ever completed.

Gothic architecture was one of the most intricate of building styles. Its basic elements were the pointed arch, groined and ribbed vaulting, and the flying buttress. These devices made possible a much lighter and loftier construction than could ever have been achieved with the round arch and the engaged pier of the Romanesque. In fact, the Gothic cathedral could be described as a skeletal framework of stone enclosed by enormous windows. Other features included lofty spires, rose windows, delicate tracery in stone, elaborately carved façades, multiple columns, and the use of gargoyles, or representations of mythical monsters, as decorative devices. Ornamentation in the best of the cathedrals was generally concentrated on the exterior. Except for the stained glass windows and the intricate carving on woodwork and altars, interiors were kept rather simple and occasionally almost severe. But the inside of

Quarter Barrel Vaults, Typical of Romanesque Architecture. St. Etienne, Nivers.

See color plates at pages 417, 448

Building Operations. From a French picture Bible, *ca.*
1250. Note the treadmill, with wheel, ropes, and pulley,
by means of which a basket of stones is brought to the
construction level. (Morgan Library)

Above: Siege of a City. From the *Universal Chronicle* by
Jean de Courcy, Flemish, *ca.* 1470. The cannon meant the
end of feudal knights and medieval towered fortresses.
(Morgan Library) Below: A Scholar at Work. From the
Flemish manuscript *The Golden Legend*, 1445–1460.
(Morgan Library)

Stained Glass, German, *ca.* 1300.
Some stained-glass windows were
purely decorative; others told a
story. (MMA)

THE RISE OF THE MEDIEVAL UNIVERSITY

△ Founded in the 12th century
■ Founded in the 13th century
● Founded in the 14th century
△ Founded in the 15th century

Boundaries ca. 1500 A.D.

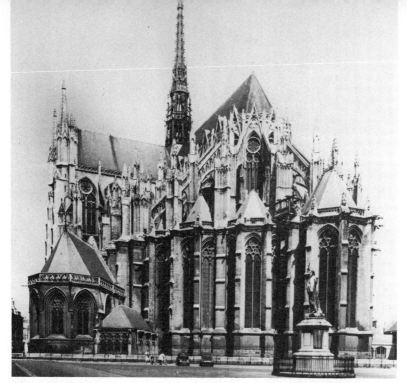

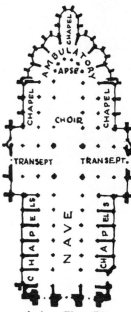

Amiens, Floor Plan

Amiens Cathedral. The floor plan to the right shows features which were typical of thirteenth century Gothic—the side aisles continue around the elongated choir and apse, forming the ambulatory, off which radiate the chapels. The transepts are fully developed with side aisles.

Amiens, Cross Section. Note the pointed Gothic arch which allows for a higher nave vaulting. Note also the typical flying buttresses which take the thrust of the nave vaulting clear of the main structure to the great masonry buttress piers.

the Gothic cathedral was never somber or gloomy. The stained glass windows served not to exclude the light but to glorify it, to catch the rays of sunlight and suffuse them with a richness and warmth of color which nature herself could hardly duplicate even in her gayest moods.

The significance of Gothic architecture is frequently misunderstood. As a matter of fact, its very name, implying that the art was of barbarian origin, was originally a term of reproach given to it by the men of the Renaissance, who wanted to express their contempt for everything medieval. Many people still think of the Gothic cathedral as a product of an ascetic and otherworldly civilization. Nothing could be more inaccurate. Insofar as Gothic architecture was spiritual at all, it was the symbol of a religion which had come to recognize the importance of this life. But as we have already seen, the cathedral was more than a church. It was in large part an expression of the new secular spirit which had grown out of the rise of cities and the progress of enlightenment. Many of the scenes depicted on the stained glass windows—a medieval bakeshop in operation, for instance—had no direct religious significance whatever. The definite appeal to the senses revealed in the sparkling radiance of colored glass and in the naturalistic sculpture of saints

449

The High Chapel of La Sainte-Chapelle, Paris. High Gothic is here carried to its logical extreme. Slender columns, tracery, and stained-glass windows take the place of walls.

and the Virgin gives positive proof that man's interest in his human self and in the world of natural beauty was no longer considered a sin. Last of all, Gothic architecture was an expression of the medieval intellectual genius. Each cathedral, with its detailed mass of carvings of plant and animal life and symbolic figures, was a kind of encyclopedia of medieval knowledge—a culture epic in stone.

Music in the later Middle Ages

Music in the later Middle Ages was the product of an evolution extending far back into the early history of medieval Europe. The beginning of this evolution was the development of the so-called plain chant, a vast body of melodies that is virtually an anthology of folk, cultic, and composed music of many centuries. Its collection and organization took a long time, though it is ascribed by tradition to Pope Gregory the Great—hence its name: Gregorian chant. The Gregorian chant is a single, unaccompanied line of music of great melodic and rhythmic subtlety, much of which is lost on us, accustomed as we are to a harmonic background. By the tenth century we encounter the first written monuments of music for more than one line, which consisted of another line running parallel with the first at the distance of a fourth or fifth. The next step in evolution was the introduction of the principle of contrary motion; the second part asserted its independence by not running parallel with the first but following its own bent. It is significant, however, that the modern concept of *harmony*, that is, a vertical organization of sounds (melody with accompaniment) was lacking. The new line of music (called "voice" or "part") was set *against* the existing one, dot against dot, *punctus contra punctum* ("dot" standing for "note") —hence the term counterpoint. Thus the development was linear, each melodic line was largely independent. This type of music is called polyphonic in contrast to homophonic, the harmonically ordered style. The twelfth and thirteenth centuries produced great schools of musical composition that demonstrated considerable skill in weaving together two, three, and even four independent voice-parts. A particular manifestation of music in the later Middle Ages was the art of the troubadours, *trouvères*, and minnesingers. With them a new and altogether Western conception enters music: individual invention. Troubadour comes from the French verb *trouver*, to find (invent); this kind of musician does not use inherited, traditional tunes but "finds" his own. Among the kings and knights of France of the north and of Provence, there were many fine creative artists. The German minnesingers (from the Middle High German word *minne*, "love") patterned themselves after the composing French aristocracy. Secular music was kept under wraps by the Church, but it was nevertheless well developed and by 1300 we come across reliable descriptions of its nature. Music also formed part of the liberal arts as taught at the university, but its study was purely mathematical and philosophical.

SELECTED READINGS

· *Items so designated are available in paperbound editions.*

· Adams, Henry, *Mont-Saint-Michel and Chartres*, New York, 1913 (Mentor). Stimulating and provocative.

Artz, F. B., *The Mind of the Middle Ages*, New York, 1954. Brief but scholarly and interesting.

· Bainton, R. H., *The Medieval Church*, Princeton, 1964 (Anvil).

· Brundage, J. A., *The Crusades: Motives and Achievements*, New York, 1964 (Heath).

· Cheyney, E. P., *The Dawn of a New Era, 1250–1453*, New York, 1936 (Torchbook). Written in a clear and interesting style.

· Copleston, F. C., *Medieval Philosophy*, New York, 1961 (Torchbook).

Crombie, A. C., *From Augustine to Galileo*, Cambridge, 1961.

Crump, C. G., and Jacob, E. F., *The Legacy of the Middle Ages*, New York, 1926. Especially good on medieval arts and crafts.

Easton, Stewart C., *Roger Bacon and His Search for a Universal Science*, New York, 1952.

Evans, Joan, *Art in Medieval France*, London, 1948.

Gardner, Helen, *Art through the Ages*, New York, 1948. Comprehensive and valuable.

Gilson, E. H., *The Philosophy of St. Thomas Aquinas*, Cambridge, Mass., 1924.

· ———, *Dante the Philosopher*, London, 1948 (Torchbook).

451

READINGS Haskins, C. H., *Studies in Medieval Culture*, New York, 1929.

· ———, *The Renaissance of the Twelfth Century*, Cambridge, Mass., 1928 (Meridian). Excellent.

Hearnshaw, F. J. C., *The Social and Political Ideas of Some Great Medieval Thinkers*, New York, 1923.

· Heer, Friedrich, *The Medieval World*, New York, 1964 (Mentor).

· Huizinga, J., *The Waning of the Middle Ages*, New York, 1954 (Anchor). A provocative interpretation.

Jones, Charles W., ed., *Medieval Literature in Translation*, New York, 1950.

Lang, Paul, *Music in Western Civilization*, New York, 1941.

Latourette, K. S., *A History of Christianity*, New York, 1953.

Leff, Gordon, *Heresy in the Later Middle Ages*, New York, 1967, 2 vols.

· ———, *Medieval Thought*, Baltimore, 1958 (Penguin).

Luscombe, D. E., *The School of Peter Abelard*, New York, 1969.

Mazzeo, J. A., *The Medieval Cultural Tradition in Dante's Comedy*, Ithaca, N.Y., 1960.

· McGiffert, A. C., *History of Christian Thought*, New York, 1932, Vol. II (Scribner Library).

McIlwain, C. H., *The Growth of Political Thought in the West*, New York, 1932. Perhaps the best interpretation.

Morey, C. R., *Medieval Art*, New York, 1942.

· Panofsky, Erwin, *Gothic Architecture and Scholasticism*, Cleveland, 1957 (Meridian).

Rashdall, Hastings, *The Universities of Europe in the Middle Ages*, New York, 1936, 2 vols. The standard work.

Reese, Gustave, *Music in the Middle Ages*, New York, 1940.

Setton, K. M., ed., *A History of the Crusades*, Philadelphia, 1955. Vol. 1.

· Southern, R. W., *The Making of the Middle Ages*, New Haven, 1953 (Yale University Press).

Taylor, H. O., *The Medieval Mind*, New York, 1927, 2 vols. Good for interpretation.

Vossler, Karl, *Medieval Culture: An Introduction to Dante and His Times*, New York, 1929, 2 vols. Profound and very valuable for the student with a good background of medieval knowledge.

· Waddell, Helen, *The Wandering Scholars*, London, 1927 (Anchor). A vivid and sympathetic account.

· ———, *Peter Abelard*, New York, 1933 (Compass). Valuable not only as biography but for its grasp of the spirit of medieval culture.

SOURCE MATERIALS

Abelard, Peter, *The Story of My Misfortunes*.

Baumer, F. L. V., *Main Currents of Western Thought*, New York, 1952.

Coulton, G. G., *A Medieval Garner*, London, 1910.

Jones, C. W., ed., *Medieval Literature in Translation*, New York, 1950.

Krey, A. C., *The First Crusade; The Accounts of Eyewitnesses and Participants*.

· Marzialis, F. T., tr., *Memoirs of the Crusades*, for *Villehardouin's Chronicle of the Fourth Crusade* and *Joinville's Chronicle of the Crusade of St. Louis* (Dutton).

Pegis, A. C., ed., *Basic Writings of St. Thomas Aquinas*, 2 vols.

· Polo, Marco, *Travels* (Dell and others).

· Poole, R. L., *Illustrations of the History of Medieval Thought and Learning* (Dover).

Robinson, Paschal, tr., *The Writings of St. Francis of Assisi*.

Thatcher, O. J., and McNeal, E. H., *A Source Book for Medieval History*, pp. 513-21, Speech of Urban at Council of Clermont.

CHAPTER 16

India, the Far East, and Africa in the
Later Middle Ages

Seldom [have] two civilizations, so vast and so strongly developed, yet so radically dissimilar as the Muhammadan and Hindu, [met and mingled] together. The very contrasts which existed between them, the wide divergences in their culture and their religions, make the history of their impact peculiarly instructive and lend an added interest to the art and above all to the architecture which their united genius called into being.
—Sir John Marshall, in *Cambridge History of India*, Vol. III

The centuries which are known in the West as the Middle Ages did not have quite the same importance for the civilizations of the Eastern lands as they did for the evolution of European civilization. The cultures of India and China were already highly advanced, while the Western Europeans were only beginning to develop a stabilized society and to utilize their intellectual resources to a significant degree. In contrast to Western Europe, which during the late medieval centuries was relatively free from external disturbances, both India and China experienced fresh invasions more sweeping in character than any they had known since the beginnings of their recorded history. They were able to survive the shock of these invasions with the essential features of their cultures intact, although permanent modifications took place in Indian society. Japan was unique among the principal Asiatic states in the fact that she was not subjected to foreign conquest. The tensions and conflicts within her own society, however, were tremendous, and they gradually produced a type of social and political organization which was remarkably similar to the feudal system of Western Europe.

Contrasts with the European Middle Ages

I. THE ESTABLISHMENT OF MOSLEM KINGDOMS IN INDIA (*ca.* 1000–1500)

About the same time that the nations of Western Europe were initiating the economic and intellectual progress which distinguished

453

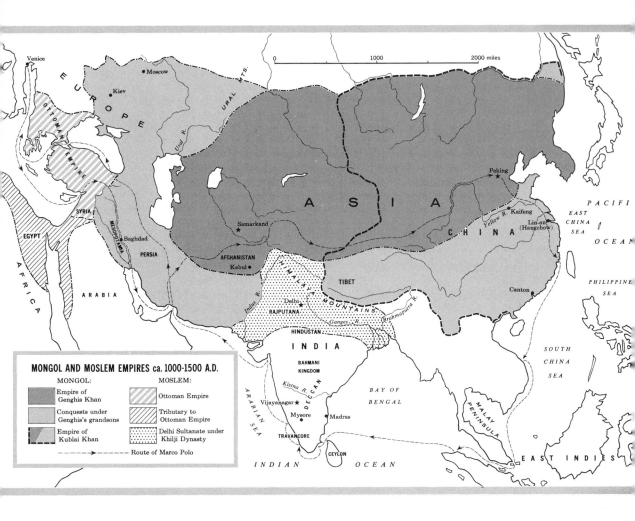

MONGOL AND MOSLEM EMPIRES ca. 1000-1500 A.D.

MONGOL:

- Empire of Genghis Khan
- Conquests under Genghis's grandsons
- Empire of Kublai Khan
- --------> Route of Marco Polo

MOSLEM:

- Ottoman Empire
- Tributary to Ottoman Empire
- Delhi Sultanate under Khilji Dynasty

The Moslem invaders of India

the later Middle Ages and which made possible the brilliant culture of the Renaissance, the peoples of India were harried by a series of marauding raids that devastated their society and sorely impaired their creative talents. The invaders of this period were devotees of Islam. They implanted the Moslem religion in India so firmly that it has ever since been the faith of a substantial minority of the population. But while the expansion of Islam in Africa, Spain, and the Middle East was associated with the quickening of cultural activities and with the attainment of relatively harmonious relations between the conquerors and their subject peoples, the Moslem conquests in India led to wanton destruction and created a deep and abiding cleavage between the opposing religious groups.

The first of the Moslem conquerors of India were Turks from Afghanistan. They did not come in numberless hordes, nor were they unresisted by native troops. The fact that they were able to sweep across the country and work such havoc is a commentary on the fateful political division of India and the lack of solidarity among her people. Ever since the decay of Harsha's empire in the seventh century, Hindustan had been disunited and subject to contention among various states. The strongest of the Hindu states were those inhabited by a group known as Rajputs. The origin of the Rajputs (the word means literally "sons of kings") is not known. It is probable that they were not Indians to begin with but the descendants of Huns and other invaders of the fifth and sixth centuries who had become assimilated into Hindu society. Generally they were regarded as belonging to the *kshatriya* (warrior) caste, and they prided themselves on their military traditions. The rulers and nobility of the Rajput kingdoms had developed a code of chivalrous conduct somewhat like the cult of chivalry of the medieval European knights. They were redoubtable horsemen, proud of their skill with the sword, and hypersensitive to insult. The Rajputs were the fiercest and bravest fighters in India, but they were unable to stem the Moslem advance.

Undoubtedly the helplessness of the Indian people during this time of invasion was intensified by the caste system, which was now exacting a heavy penalty. Each stratum of the population was hedged in by its own prescribed activities and loyalties—military defense was considered to be the function of the *kshatriyas* alone. The lower classes were impoverished and dispirited, and there was little incentive for concerted action in the common interest. By contrast, the Moslem invaders were a fresh and energetic people, excited by the prospect of rich spoils and inspired by an activist creed that promised certain recompense for service in a holy war against idolators. The Hindus were not prepared to cope with such fanatical zeal as their adversaries displayed. Nevertheless, the Rajputs gave a good account of themselves in combat; and some of them, when they saw that opposition was useless, removed with their retainers into the heart of the Indian desert to rebuild their shattered communities in the region which came to be called Rajputana.

After its initial impact the Moslem conquest of northern India entered a new phase, characterized by the establishment of governmental centers and permanent residences on Indian soil. The most important kingdom founded by the Turks, with Delhi as its capital, gradually acquired control over all of Hindustan and even penetrated into the Deccan. Between the thirteenth and the sixteenth centuries, five successive dynasties of Turks or Afghans ruled from Delhi. The fortunes of the kingdom and the character of the rulers during these 300 years cannot be detailed here, but they varied tremendously. In one instance the sultan was a woman named Raziya, who demonstrated great energy and ability but was murdered with her husband—an Ethiopian—by jealous nobles (in 1240). Intrigues and assassinations were frequent because of the absence of an established rule of succession to the throne. By com-

The conquests of the Turks and Afghans

Factors aiding the conquerors

Extension of the Moslem conquests

455

Kutb Minar, near Delhi. This magnificent "pillar of victory," 238 feet high, was erected in the early thirteenth century by Kutb-ud-din, the founder of a Moslem sultanate at Delhi.

parison with the Hindu caste-bound society, the Islamic community was democratic, and even an upstart who seized the throne by violence might be accepted as a legitimate sovereign if he proved capable. It was not uncommon for a slave who had been trained for administrative work to be entrusted with large responsibilities both civil and military and finally to usurp authority when a favorable opportunity arose. In fact, one line of Delhi rulers is known as the "Slave Kings" (1206–1290) because its founder had been a slave and viceroy of an early sultan.

Characteristics of Moslem rule

In spite of the fact that high positions were open to men of low birth, the administration was thoroughly autocratic in operation, and it derived its character from the personality, the ambitions, or the whims of the ruler. Cruelty, depravity, enlightened statesmanship, and humanitarian sensibilities were all exemplified in erratic sequence. For example, the founder of the Khilji Dynasty (1290–1318) was a benevolent and mild-tempered old gentleman who hated to shed the blood even of criminals. The nephew who assassinated and succeeded him was a monster of treachery and cruelty, and so extortionate that he reduced his Hindu subjects to poverty. The next sultan, although scholarly and abstinent by habit, was in some ways even worse than his predecessor. He compelled the entire population of Delhi to move to another site 600 miles distant, leaving the great city desolate. He disrupted commerce by debasing the currency, exacted such heavy taxes that whole villages were abandoned, hunted down men like wild beasts for sport, and dreamed of conquering Persia and China. But this dismal tyrant's successor (promoted to the throne by the army chiefs) during a long and peaceful reign of thirty-seven years adhered to principles of justice and benevolence considerably above the general standard of fourteenth-century states the world over. He reduced taxes, provided poor relief, granted loans to the peasants, and promoted prosperity by reclaiming waste lands and by building extensive irrigation works.

The five-century period of the Turkish invasions and the Delhi Sultanate witnessed many changes in India but few original or constructive cultural developments. The central fact, of course, was the introduction of the Moslem religion and its gradual accommodation to the conditions of the country. At the outset, reconciliation between Islam and Hinduism seemed impossible. Islam was strictly monotheistic, possessed a clear-cut and simple but dogmatic creed, regarded graven images as sinful, and emphasized the equality of believers. Hinduism was polytheistic (although tending toward monotheism or pantheism in its philosophy), taught that there are many equally valid approaches to an understanding of the divine being, delighted in symbols, pictorial forms and architectural profusion, and carried the concept of human inequality to absurd extremes. The Hindus were noncredal and disposed to tolerance; the Moslems considered it their sacred duty to spread the one true faith of Allah and his Prophet. Nevertheless, the two peoples gradually drew closer together. The Moslem sovereigns did not exterminate the Hindus whom they had subjected. They followed the shrewder policy of laying discriminatory assessments upon the "unbelievers"—a poll tax and a tax on Hindu religious festivals and pilgrimages. Naturally, a good many Hindus became converts to Islam, and those who did so were accepted on an equal basis by the dominant Moslem faction. Moreover, intermarriage took place between Hindus and Moslems in spite of religious scruples on both sides. As already indicated, some of the sultans and their officials were intelligent and progressive in outlook. The best of them tried to improve economic conditions; some were patrons of literature and the arts, encouraged scholarship, and erected splendid monuments.

It is apparent, however, that the general effects of the Turkish conquests were depressing. They were accompanied by orgies of slaughter and spoliation. They threw a pall over the creative spirit of the Hindus, bringing a marked decline in a tradition of intellectual and artistic enterprise that had once been vigorous, and they almost completely wiped out the remnants of Buddhism. Mosques of excellent workmanship were constructed—often from the stones of demolished Hindu temples—and not all the existing Indian temples were destroyed; but the building of new Hindu religious edifices was prohibited under severe penalties. It is doubtful whether the equalitarian aspects of the teachings of Islam produced any ameliorative effects upon the Indian population. The immediate result, at least, was to create new divisions in an already too sharply divided society. One social effect of the Moslem impact was the subjection

Mongol invaders:
Genghis Khan

*The Great Mongol Conqueror
Genghis Khan, Grandfather of
the Founder of the Mongol
(Yüan) Dynasty in China.*

The Bahmani
kingdom

458

of women to a greater degree than ever before. The custom of *purdah* (the veiling and seclusion of women) dates from this era.

After the Turkish sultans had established themselves as sovereigns in Hindustan, they found their position threatened not only by potential Hindu rebellion and by intrigues among their own viceroys but also by new invasions from Central Asia, that inexhaustible reservoir of nomadic peoples. At this time the chief source of disturbance was the expansion of the Mongols, whose force was felt throughout the breadth of Asia and even in Europe. Early in the thirteenth century the famous Mongol chieftain and empire builder Genghis Khan made a brief foray into the Indus valley. His raid was only an incident, but the danger of a Mongol attack upon India persisted. Gradually groups of Mongols settled in northern India and adopted agricultural or industrial pursuits, most of them embracing the Moslem religion. So numerous were they in Delhi in the late thirteenth century that a section of the city was called "Mongoltown." Mongols were employed by the sultan as mercenary troops, in which capacity they were sometimes victimized by his suspicion of their loyalty, and tens of thousands of them were massacred.

Near the end of the fourteenth century northern India was visited by the most devastating raid in all its history, led by Timur the Lame (Tamerlane). Timur, of Turkish descent, had started his career as the chieftain of a small tribal state in Turkestan. After misfortunes and amazing adventures he had welded together a powerful force of cavalry and embarked on a sensational career of conquest. Although he never assumed the title of Khan, he won recognition as overlord from most of the Mongols who had previously followed Genghis Khan. He overran Afghanistan, Persia, and Mesopotamia; then he invaded India with the avowed intention of converting infidels to Islam and procuring booty. He and his troops spent less than a year in India (1398–1399) but left a ruin behind them. The city of Delhi, sacked in a three-day orgy, was turned into a ghost town, so destitute that—to quote a contemporary—"for two whole months not a bird moved a wing in the city." Any place that offered resistance was destroyed and its inhabitants slaughtered or enslaved. Lord Timur carried off with him inestimable quantities of gold and precious stuffs, slaves for all his soldiers, and thousands of skilled craftsmen, including stonemasons to build a great mosque at his capital city of Samarkand in Turkestan. The Delhi Sultanate never fully recovered from the blow dealt to it and to its helpless Hindu subjects by Timur, the "Earth Shaker."

Throughout this period India embraced a number of states, both Moslem and Hindu, which were not included in the Delhi Sultanate. In the fourteenth century two large kingdoms came into existence in the Deccan. Ruled by Moslems, the Bahmani kingdom at its height included about half the Deccan, stretching from sea to sea, and was divided into four provinces. Some of the Bahmani sultans were well educated and intelligent men, who built lavishly, encouraged trade, and maintained a cosmopolitan atmosphere at their court. In the late fifteenth century the administration deteriorated and the kingdom was broken up into five separate states.

Even more splendid than the Bahmani kingdom was the Hindu empire of Vijayanagar, which at one time dominated the whole southern end of the peninsula as far north as the Kistna River (including, roughly, Madras, Travancore, and Mysore). The capital city, also named Vijayanagar ("City of Victory"), was strongly fortified, heavily populated, and probably—on the testimony of Italian, Portuguese, and Afghan visitors—one of the greatest cities in the world during the fifteenth century. The commerce of the kingdom was eagerly sought. Several kinds of precious stones, particularly large diamonds, were prominent among its exports. The court was sumptuous and the palaces magnificent. Architecture flourished on a grand scale and with an imaginative boldness reminiscent of the classical Sanskrit age. The foundations which underlay the brilliant culture of this last great Hindu empire, however, were not sound. In spite of an orderly government and in the midst of great wealth, the common people suffered from extreme privation and were fleeced by avaricious officials. Luxurious and profligate courts, the encouragement of prostitution in the temples, and the compulsory burning of widows (requiring the mass immolation of thousands of women on the death of a king) were hardly evidences of a healthy society. Unfortunately, a haughty and embittered rivalry between the Hindu and the Bahmani kingdoms weakened both states. In 1565 the almost impregnable city of Vijayanagar was taken and wantonly destroyed by troops from a league of neighboring Moslem powers, and the southern Hindu empire sank into a permanent decline.

2. CHINA UNDER THE SUNG, MONGOL, AND MING DYNASTIES (960–1644)

For about fifty years following the collapse of the great T'ang Dynasty in the early tenth century, China was a divided country with power in the hands of military dictators. After this chaotic but relatively brief interregnum (known to Chinese tradition as the "Five Dynasties"), unity and a strong central government were reestablished by an able general who assumed the imperial title and founded the Sung Dynasty. This dynasty, like its predecessor, the T'ang, endured for about three centuries (960–1279). Although the first Sung had been an army officer, he revived the ancient administrative system and restored the power of the civilian bureaucracy. In contrast to the T'ang, the Sung rulers did not adopt a policy of imperialism, and even relinquished control over portions of the empire. Territories in the north and the northwest were lost to seminomadic peoples who, while founding independent kingdoms,

459

assimilated many aspects of Chinese culture. One of these northern groups, the Khitan, established a kingdom in southern Manchuria, annexed territory south of the Great Wall in the Peking area, and collected tribute from the Sung emperors. Although the Khitan were entirely separate from the Chinese in origin, a corruption of their name—"Cathay"—came to be a Western designation for China, a circumstance which indicates that the Khitan did not long retain their distinctive traits after coming into close contact with China's mature civilization.

Early in the twelfth century the Khitan state (Liao) was overthrown by a people of similar stock, the Juchên, who not only occupied Manchuria and Mongolia but also conquered the greater part of northern China. Thus, beginning about 1141, the Sung actually controlled only the Yangtze valley and regions to the south. They established their capital at Hangchow (then known as Lin-an), a magnificent port but far distant from the traditional centers of imperial administration. The later, or southern, Sung period was characterized by a less vigorous administration and by the familiar but depressing symptoms of dynastic decay. These disadvantages, however, were to some extent counterbalanced by the fact that southern China felt the influence of Chinese culture more fully than it had before. The peoples of the south and southwest not only became more completely incorporated into Chinese society but also began to contribute leadership to the state. The center of population was shifting to the south, and there was evidence also that originality and initiative were abundant in this area. During the Southern Sung period (1141–1279) northern China continued to be ruled by the Juchên from the old Sung capital at Kaifeng on the Yellow River. While the loss of so much territory to alien conquerors was humiliating to the Sung emperors, it produced no appreciable permanent changes in the north. The Juchên adapted themselves to Chinese ways as readily as had the Khitan. Both Buddhism and Confucianism obtained a strong hold upon them, and the rulers, following the established convention, adopted a Chinese dynastic title (*Chin* or *Kin*, meaning "Gold").

Peace, internal stability, and prolific cultural activity were characteristic of the Sung period, especially during the first century and a half. As earlier, a flourishing commerce contributed to an increase in wealth and promoted a knowledge of foreign lands. Overland trade declined, partly because the caravan routes were no longer controlled by the Chinese, but business was brisk in port cities of the southeastern coast. Foreign merchants, among whom the Arabs still predominated, were granted the right of residence in the trading centers, subject to the jurisdiction of an Inspector of Foreign Trade. At the same time the Chinese themselves were beginning to participate more extensively in oceanic commerce. The early Sung emperors undertook ambitious public works, including irrigation

**The Southern
Sung period**

*Heavy Porcelaneous vase with
simple design.* Sung Dynasty
(960–1279).

460

projects. Apparently society as a whole attained a fair level of prosperity, as evidenced by an increase in population.

The late eleventh century was significant for a reform movement launched by a scholar-official, Wang An-shih (1021–1086), who held the position of chief minister for a number of years. His proposals were the subject of acrimonious controversy and never were carried out in entirety, but they represented a realistic attempt to improve the administration, and they focused attention upon the plight of the common man. Wang promoted the establishment of public schools endowed with state lands, and he advocated revision of the civil-service examinations to encourage a knowledge of practical problems instead of proficiency in classical literary forms. His most determined efforts were directed toward a program of relief for the poor farmers by direct government assistance, by revision of the inequitable tax system and the abolition of forced labor, and by a redistribution of land. He wanted the government to control commerce, fix prices, buy up farm surpluses, and make loans to farmers at a low rate of interest on the security of their growing crops. Wang An-shih's proposals for agrarian relief anticipated some of the measures inaugurated by governments in recent times, and his over-all program approximated a kind of state socialism. Although he insisted that he was merely adapting genuine Confucian principles to the needs of the time, his opponents branded him as a dangerous innovator. The contest between the Innovators (Wang's disciples) and the Conservatives continued into the next century, with the emperors favoring sometimes one and sometimes the other group; but the conservative faction ultimately prevailed. Wang's radical proposals, however, have been studied with interest by modern reformers in China and elsewhere.

An invasion by the Mongols brought about the final collapse of the Sung Dynasty and subjected all China, for the first time in its history, to the rule of a foreign conqueror. The Mongol Asiatic empire, like so many of its predecessors, was established with almost incredible swiftness in a series of military campaigns, but it was for a brief period one of the largest ever known. In the early thirteenth century the great Mongol conqueror Genghis Khan overthrew the kingdoms adjacent to China on the north and then swept westward across all Asia. After making a brief foray into India he subdued Persia and Mesopotamia and occupied large stretches of Russian territory north and west of the Caspian Sea. Although the invasion of China was probably inevitable, the Sung emperor contributed to his own downfall by playing a double game with the Mongols. So eager was he to get rid of the Juchên rulers in north China that he sent troops to help the Mongols against them; then he rashly attacked the Mongol forces and exposed his own dominions to the fury of the ruthless and swift-riding horsemen. The conquest of southern China was completed by Genghis Khan's grandson, Kublai Khan, after

The reforms of Wang An-shih (1021–1086)

The Mongol invaders of China: Genghis Khan and Kublai Khan

461

many years of hard fighting, during which the Mongols not only had to occupy the coastal cities but also had to accustom themselves to naval warfare. In 1279 the last Chinese army was defeated (the commanding general is said to have jumped into the sea with the infant Sung prince in his arms), and Kublai became the master of China.

The huge Asiatic empire of the Mongols, which reached from the China Sea to Eastern Europe, was too large to be administered effectively as a unit and did not long remain intact. Religious differences contributed to its dissolution. Before the end of the thirteenth century most of the western princes (khans) had become Moslems and repudiated the authority of Kublai's family, who favored a Tibetan form of Buddhism. Kublai's descendants, however, from their imperial capital of Peking, governed China for the better part of a century (1279–1368).

The accession of the Mongol (or Yüan) Dynasty seemed to threaten a serious interruption in the normal course of Chinese civilization. Fortunately the damage inflicted was only temporary, and there was actually some progress during this period of foreign domination. The Mongols were notoriously cruel conquerors, leaving ruined cities and mutilated corpses as monuments to the folly of those who resisted them. The bitterly contested occupation of southern China was accompanied by a decimation of the native population in some areas. Nevertheless, the Mongol rulers were wise enough to recognize the desirability of preserving such a great state as China and the advantage to be gained from taxing its people instead of exterminating them. The nomad warriors could not resist the influence of Chinese culture, and the traditional Chinese administrative system was not completely uprooted. The civil service examinations were suspended for a time and Chinese were excluded from most governmental posts, although the Mongol emperors employed foreigners of various nationalities in high positions at court. In the fourteenth century, when the dynasty showed signs of weakening and native unrest became ominous, the emperor reinstituted the examination system and admitted Chinese to office, chiefly at the lower level.

The Mongol rulers were no more intolerant in religious matters than their predecessors. While they patronized Buddhism, they did not seriously interfere with the other native cults and they authorized the construction of Confucian colleges and temples. They also permitted the introduction of Western religions, although Islam was the only one of these to retain a permanent place. Following the precedent of earlier dynasties, the Mongol emperors endowed charitable and educational institutions and maintained public granaries to provide relief in time of famine. They also gave attention to irrigation projects and the improvement of communications. A notable

The Imperial Post Road. This road, through a valley west of Chunking, is part of the old Imperial Post Road connecting Peking with the Tibetan capital, Lhasa.

undertaking was the reconstruction of the Grand Canal linking the capital city of Peking to the Yangtze valley by an inland waterway.

During the Mongol period China was by no means isolated from other regions. The area under the jurisdiction of Peking was considerably larger than the empire of the Sung, and the emperors attempted to increase it still further by schemes of conquest of dubious value. Kublai Khan made two attempts to invade Japan (in 1274 and 1281), employing both Chinese and Korean vessels, but a typhoon wrecked many of his ships and the Japanese annihilated the landing party. Fortunately, peaceful intercourse was continued with other nations, near and far. Overland commerce was facilitated by imperial highways which the Mongols built deep into Central Asia and even to Persia. That travel was comparatively safe is indicated by the large number of foreign visitors in China during this period and also by the fact that Chinese journeyed far from home—to Russia, Persia, the Near East, and occasionally Europe. Russians, Arabs, and Jews entered China for purposes of trade, as did Genoese and Venetians. The renowned Marco Polo was only one of many European visitors. He lived in China for seventeen years (1275–1292), was received at court, and visited various parts of the country. The glowing report with which he astonished his countrymen upon re-

Extension of
foreign contacts

463

turning home (he described Hangchow, the Southern Sung capital, as "the finest and noblest city in the world") was less a tribute to the Mongol Dynasty than to the maturity of Chinese civilization, and was also an unintentional commentary upon the relatively primitive conditions still prevalent in Western Europe.

In the fourteenth century, Mongol power was undermined by the decadence of the ruling house and by the growing discontent of the Chinese people, who never forgot that they had been subjugated by a barbarian conqueror. Rebellion was brought to a successful conclusion under the leadership of a dynamic, if somewhat grotesque, soldier of fortune, who captured Peking in 1368 and drove the last Mongol emperor into the wastes of Mongolia. This rebel leader was a man of low birth who had been orphaned at an early age and had exchanged the life of a Buddhist monk for that of a bandit. Nevertheless, he was accepted as having won the Mandate of Heaven and became the first emperor of the Ming ("Brilliant" or "Glorious") Dynasty, which lasted from 1368 to 1644. The dynasty proved to be extremely successful and gave renewed proof of the potency of Chinese institutions, although it added little that was new. The government adhered to the Sung patterns, or in some ways more closely to the T'ang, particularly in its emphasis upon the forceful expansion of territorial boundaries. Ming China was a large state, with its authority extending into Manchuria, Mongolia, Indochina, Burma, and the southwestern region facing Tibet. While the great Mongol empire of the thirteenth century had fallen to pieces, it gave promise of being resurrected by Timur (Tamerlane), the master of Turkestan and scourge of India. Although the Ming court regarded Timur's emissaries as tribute bearers, the "Earth Shaker" was actually setting forth on an expedition to conquer China when he died prematurely in 1405. In spite of this stroke of fortune, the Ming emperors made little effort to recover either Turkestan or Sinkiang.

A noteworthy aspect of the early Ming period was the development and rapid expansion of Chinese navigation. The mariner's compass had been in use perhaps since the eleventh century, and some large ships had been constructed; but now maritime enterprise was given tremendous impetus. Chinese sailing vessels, equipped with as many as four decks and comfortable living quarters, undertook voyages to the East Indies, the Malay Peninsula, Ceylon, India, and Arabia, returning with merchandise, tribute, and valuable geographical information. They may have ventured westward around Africa's Cape of Good Hope. In its heyday the Ming navy was more than equal to that of any contemporary European state. Overseas expeditions were discontinued, however, about 1424. Henceforth the government restricted Chinese shipping to coastal waters and discouraged foreign travel on the part of its subjects. The result was not only a loss of revenue from commerce but also an unfortunate isolation of China at the very time when the Western

The overthrow of the Mongols and establishment of the Ming Dynasty

Maritime achievements under the Ming Dynasty

Fall of the Ming Dynasty. The death of the last of the Ming emperors at the hands of the invading Manchus when they captured Peking in 1644.

peoples were beginning to emerge from their provincialism. Instead of retaining the initiative on the high seas, the later Ming rulers proved inefficient in defending their own coasts against Japanese pirates and other marauding groups.

A decline in the vitality of the administration was apparent long before the Ming Dynasty came to a close. Officials became lazy and corrupt; power passed into the hands of court favorites and eunuchs; and exorbitant taxes oppressed the peasants to the point of ruin. While the costs of government mounted dizzily—in 1639 military expenditures alone were ten times greater than the entire revenue of the first Ming emperor—territories were being lost through incompetence and rebellion. Although the dynasty finally succumbed to another foreign invasion, internal dissension was the real cause of its collapse.

In turning from the political to the cultural developments that took place in China during the Sung, Mongol, and Ming dynasties, we may note that a renewal of interest in philosophical speculation occurred, reaching a climax in the latter half of the twelfth century. This revival represented a return to the fountainhead of Chinese thought—the sages of antiquity, particularly Confucius—but it introduced several new ideas and was not a mere repetition of ancient formulas. The most noted Chinese thinker of this period was Chu Hsi (1130–1200), who held a position at the Sung court and was an opponent of the so-called Innovators (disciples of Wang An-shih). Although Chu Hsi claimed to be interpreting Confucius' teachings in accordance with their original and uncorrupted meaning, he and his associates actually founded a Neo-Confucian school, with a metaphysics which incorporated elements of Taoism and Buddhism. They stressed the concept of the "Supreme Ultimate" or Absolute, a Final Cause which underlies the whole material universe and is

Decline of the Ming Dynasty

Cultural developments under the Sung and Ming: Neo-Confucianism

465

Fantastic Ceramic Figure of a Deity. Ming Dynasty.

Sung printed book. A page from the *Fa-yuan chu-lin* ("Forest of Pearls in the Garden of the Law"). The book was compiled by the Buddhist monk and scholar Tao-Shih in 688. It was printed in 1124, fully three centuries earlier than the Gutenberg Bible.

antecedent to every rational or moral principle. Nevertheless, Chu Hsi, like his ancient master Confucius, was chiefly interested in human nature and its proper development in an ethical and social order. He reaffirmed Mencius' faith in man's natural capacity for good and upheld the traditional ethical system exemplified by the family and embodied in a paternalistic state administered by a bureaucracy of scholar-officials. The teachings of Chu Hsi, although stoutly contested by rival scholars in his day, eventually came to be regarded as the definitive commentary on the doctrines of the ancient sage. Venerated as orthodoxy, they discouraged creative thought among later scholars and administrators.

A prodigious output of literature has been characteristic of Chinese civilization during almost every period except the most ancient. Printing was very common from Sung times on. Books were printed from wooden blocks, from metal plates, and from movable type made of earthenware, tin, and wood. Poetry seldom equaled the best of the T'ang age in beauty or spontaneity, but lengthy histories, encyclopedias, dictionaries, geographies, and scientific treatises were produced. The most original literary developments were in the fields of the drama and the novel. The Chinese drama attained the level of a major art form during the Mongol Dynasty, partly because the suspension of the civil-service examinations, by cutting off opportunities for official careers, prompted men of talent to turn their attention to a medium of popular entertainment which they had previously considered unworthy of notice. The dramas of the Mongol period, of which more than a hundred have survived, combined lively action with vivid portrayal of character, and they were written in the common idiom of the people rather than in the classical language of scholars. The Chinese theater, like the English theater of Shakespeare's day, was largely devoid of scenery and properties, although the performers made use of elaborate costumes and heavy make-up. Ordinarily all the parts were filled by male actors. The plays were in verse, but, in contrast to the Elizabethan and modern Western drama, the speeches were sung rather than recited and the orchestra (placed directly on the stage) contributed an essential element to the production.

The Chinese novel, originating apparently in the tales of public story-tellers, developed contemporaneously with the drama but matured a little later. Its growth was aided indirectly by the sterility of the academic atmosphere that pervaded the court and the bureaucracy of the Ming Dynasty. In the fifteenth century, veneration for Confucian orthodoxy, especially as embodied in the teachings of Chu Hsi, had become such a fetish among the official coterie of scholars that one of them declared: "The truth has been made manifest. . . . No more writing is needed."[1] Some men of letters sought a creative outlet by composing narratives in the plain lan-

466

[1] L. C. Goodrich, *A Short History of the Chinese People*, p. 196.

Wooden Statue of Kuan-yin, "Goddess of Mercy." This popular deity, usually represented in female form, was actually derived from a legendary Indian bodhisattva. (In Mahayana Buddhism a bodhisattva was one who had attained enlightenment but chose to remain in the world to help others.)

guage of the people. In their hands the novel became a highly successful literary medium, skillfully contrived but purveying robust adventure, humor, warm feeling, and salty realism. Frequently historical themes were chosen for subject matter, but the tales also provided commentary—sometimes satirical—upon contemporary society and government.

A large proportion of the Chinese works of art still extant was produced during the period which is being reviewed here. Sculpture had declined in quality since T'ang times, but painting reached its highest peak of excellence under the Sung. The most beautiful and typical Sung paintings are landscapes, frequently executed in only one color but conveying the impression of an intimate understanding of nature in her various moods. Through economy of line, omission of nonessentials, and painstaking treatment of significant detail, the artists sought to bring to light the reality which lies hidden behind the world of appearances. Their dreamy creations were obviously influenced by the mystical teachings of Buddhism and Taoism. Landscape painting was at its ripest during the Southern Sung period, when the leading artists took full advantage of the natural beauty of the Hangchow region. They sometimes painted panoramic scenes on long strips of silk. These were fastened to rollers and could be viewed leisurely by simply holding the rollers in one's hands and winding the painted scroll from one roller to the other.

Architecture attained particular pre-eminence under the Ming, a dynasty which delighted in glorifying and embellishing the visible

Porcelain Vase. Ming Dynasty.

467

Spring Morning at the Palace of Han. Sung Dynasty. Chinese painting emphasized landscapes rather than people and the representation of poetic or philosophic ideas rather than facts.

Architecture

aspects of Chinese culture. Ming architecture was by no means new in conception, but it was prolific and has left many impressive monuments. The popularity of elaborate gardens, summer residences, game preserves, and hunting lodges among the aristocracy provided opportunities for the designing of graceful pavilions and arched bridges. Fully developed by this period was the pagoda style of temple, distinguished by curving roofs which were usually of tile and frequently in brilliant colors.

China has only rarely been isolated from other parts of the world, and many of her cultural changes were the result of foreign contacts. The Chinese were indebted to the Arabs for contributions in the field of mathematics and probably also in medicine, although the Chinese had themselves accumulated a considerable store of medical

Sage under a Pine Tree. Sung Dynasty. The gnarled and twisted tree exemplifies the Chinese interest in nature in both her pleasant and perverse moods.

"War Spirit." A Ming Dynasty painting (1368–1644).

data. Inoculation against smallpox seems to have been practiced before the end of the Sung Dynasty. Eyeglasses came into use (from Italy) during the Ming period. New crops of Western origin began to be cultivated in China. Sorghum, introduced in the thirteenth century, and maize in the sixteenth have been raised extensively in northern China ever since. Cotton production, which also began in the thirteenth century, was greatly expanded under the Ming. One innovation which may have been of domestic rather than foreign inspiration was in the technique of warfare. The explosive properties of gunpowder had long been known, but not until the eleventh century were they utilized for the manufacture of lethal weapons. The Mongols, in the thirteenth and fourteenth centuries, employed bombs that perhaps were propelled by primitive cannons. Although these early artillery pieces were crude, they foreshadowed the increasingly destructive character of modern warfare.

Achievements in agriculture and in the applied sciences

3. THE RISE OF FEUDALISM AND MILITARY DICTATORS IN JAPAN (*ca.* 900–1600)

Even though Chinese culture had been incorporated into the foundations of Japanese civilization and exerted a lasting influence, social and political trends in Japan during the medieval era were very different from those in the great mainland state. While China was frequently harassed by nomadic invaders and was temporarily subjugated by a foreign dynasty, her society and culture departed little from the ancient pattern. By contrast, Japan, enjoying the natural protection of her insular position, was not seriously affected by disturbances from without; yet her institutions were profoundly altered as the result of conflicts taking place within her own society. A theoretical unity and an arbitrary and artificial scheme of government had been imposed upon Japan by the reform of the mid-seventh century, which attempted to introduce the Chinese imperial

Contrasts between Japan and China

469

A Feudal Stronghold. Hirosaki Castle, in northern Japan, was the residence of one of the "outer *daimyo*" during the Tokugawa Shogunate. The castle grounds are now a popular resort for cherry blossom viewing.

system in its entirety. How completely the attempt had failed is illustrated by the events of the next thousand years. Only belatedly, and after indecisive and exhausting strife, was the basis discovered for a stable and unified society. And when stability was achieved, it was through improvised institutions which were inadequate to solve the problems certain to arise in the wake of economic and cultural change.

The political history of Japan during this period is characterized mainly by two factors: (1) the persistence of an indirect method of government, with the actual power shifting from one family to another but exercised in the name of an inviolate emperor, whose effective authority rarely extended beyond the environs of Kyoto; (2) the feudalization of society and the growth of extralegal military units which imposed their will upon territories under their control. To the end of the sixteenth century the technique of government was variable and uncertain, although the trend from civilian to military authority was unmistakable. At the opening of the seventeenth century a centralized administration was finally established which ended a long period of civil wars, enforced a coherent national policy, and endured almost unshaken until the middle of the nineteenth century. Even when it was overthrown, the habits which it had instilled in the Japanese people could not easily be uprooted.

In the ninth century the Fujiwara family, through intermarriage with the imperial family and through possession of the office of regent, had acquired a dominant position in the government, reducing

Character of Japanese political history

470

the emperor to a figurehead. The Fujiwara retained their ascendancy until the twelfth century, but their rule over the outlying sections became more and more nominal as new lands were brought into production by reclamation or by conquest of the aborigines, and as aggressive landowners succeeded in withdrawing their estates from the jurisdiction of the imperial tax collectors. The men who possessed estates in these frontier regions were not hampered by the elaborate rules of etiquette or by the mania for classical Chinese studies that absorbed the energies of the courtiers at Kyoto. They formulated their own standards of conduct, largely dictated by the desire to preserve and extend their holdings, and quarreled with one another over conflicting claims. Naturally, many small farmers relinquished their property to powerful neighbors in return for protection and sank to a position of serfdom. Gradually a manorial economy came into existence, showing some points of similarity to the manorial regime in Western Europe during the later Middle Ages.

By a remarkable coincidence of history Japanese society took on aspects of feudalism at the very time when feudal institutions were evolving in Western Europe. Of course it would be a mistake to assume that Japanese and Western feudalism were identical, but the parallels between them are striking. In Japan and Western Europe alike, leadership was passing to a class of mounted warriors who owned land, dominated the peasantry, and exercised governmental power as a private right. In Japan the rising class of warrior-landlords was derived partly from clan chieftains, partly from adventurers who had established title purely by the sword, and partly from imperial officials who had converted an administrative office into a family possession. The members of the landed class established hereditary claims to their holdings and entered into binding agreements with one another, creating a series of dependent relationships equivalent to a system of lords and vassals. As in the case of European feudalism, the system was extended partly through the voluntary surrender of property by small landowners who sought a noble's protection, and partly through the granting of benefices or fiefs by great lords to lesser men in order to secure their services as vassals. Another parallel to the growth of European feudalism is seen in the fact that property belonging to religious foundations was frequently converted into fiefs. Some Buddhist monasteries and temples became formidable military units, but Japanese religious orders never attained an independence like that of the higher clergy in medieval Europe. They remained generally subservient to the aristocracy.

The Japanese warriors, who corresponded in status and in profession to the medieval knights, were known as *samurai*, or *bushi*. The *samurai* developed a fraternal spirit and a code of conduct to which they jealously clung as their special prerogative and which they called "the way of the horse and the bow." (The term *bushido*, not

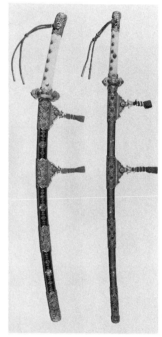

Swords of the Feudal Nobility. This type of curved sword, of fine steel, was worn suspended from the girdle by great *daimyo* or court nobles during Japan's early feudal age (twelfth to fourteenth centuries). Note the jeweled hilts, the ornately decorated scabbards, and the loops for hanging the swords.

used before the eighteenth century, denoted a romantic and artificial version of the old feudal code.) Like the European code of chivalry it stressed valor, loyalty, and the necessity of preferring death to dishonor. The *samurai* was bound above all else to protect, defend, or avenge his lord, to this end sacrificing his own life and, if need be, the lives of his family—a remarkable ideal in view of the sacredness of family ties in Japan. So sensitive was the *samurai* to any taint of dishonor that he was expected to commit suicide (by a ritual of falling on one's sword, known as *hara-kiri*) if there was no other way to wipe out the stain on his reputation.

In the twelfth century, feudal warfare culminated in a struggle between two powerful families, the Taira and the Minamoto. With the victory of the Minamoto, their leader reorganized the government on a basis which frankly recognized the paramount role of the landowning warrior-nobility. To avoid appearing as a usurper, the head of the Minamoto family assumed only a military title, becoming known as *Shogun*, and pretended to be acting as the agent of the emperor. In reality, for the next six and one-half centuries (1192–1867) Japan had a dual government: the civil authority at Kyoto headed by the emperor and embracing various ranks of court nobility whose functions were ornamental rather than essential, and the Bakufu ("Tent Government") headed by the Shogun and commanding the services of the powerful military leaders who owned most of the land. The creation of the Shogunate, as this military-feudal government came to be called, indicates how thoroughly feudalism had permeated Japanese society. The real governors of the country now were not the imperial bureaucracy but the vassals of the Shogun.

Although the Shogunate proved to be a durable institution, it did not remain perpetually in the hands of any one family. On the death of the first Shogun his widow's relatives seized control, with her connivance. This extremely capable woman became known as the "Nun Shogun," because she wielded political influence even after she had nominally retired into holy orders, and with her help the Hojo family came into power. For more than a century the Hojo appointed puppet Shoguns over whom they maintained a regency. Thus, by the early thirteenth century the government of Japan was a confusing series of subterfuges. The central authority (so far as any existed) was exercised by a regent in the name of a puppet general (the Shogun) who, in turn, was theoretically an underling of an emperor, who was himself controlled by a regent (or, in some cases, by an elder member of the imperial family living in retirement). Because the Hojo family had no inherent claim to superiority over other great feudal houses, its ascendancy created jealous dissatisfaction and led inevitably to further conflict. A remarkable incident occurred in 1333 when the Emperor Daigo II attempted to cut through the sham governmental fabric and assert his right to rule as

The Golden Pavilion (Kiukakuji). Residence built by Yoshimitsu, third Ashikaga Shogun in 1397.

well as reign. He mustered sufficient military forces to capture and burn the Shogun's headquarters at Kamakura and ended the Hojo regency. The sequel to this bold stroke, however, was simply a half-century of civil war, with two rival emperors, each bidding for support. The schism in the imperial household was healed and order temporarily restored with the triumph of another great military family, the Ashikaga, who again reduced the emperor to a position of impotence.

The Ashikaga Shoguns (1392–1568) made the serious mistake of taking up residence in Kyoto, where they were exposed to the softening influence of court society and, by relaxing their vigilance, lost effective control over the turbulent lords of outlying districts. Feudal rivalry became increasingly unrestrained until, beginning in the late fifteenth century, Japan experienced 100 years of almost continual warfare. Robbery and pillage were rampant; almost all vestiges of a central government disappeared; even the private estates which the emperor had owned in various parts of the country were absorbed into the feudal domains. The imperial family as well as the Kyoto courtiers were subjected to humiliation by swaggering soldiers. Reduced to poverty, one emperor eked out a living by selling his autograph. In 1500 an imperial corpse lay unburied for six weeks because there was no money in the treasury. The Ashikaga Shogun was almost as impotent as the emperor and quite unable to stop the brigandage and slaughter carried on wantonly by feudal re-

The period of feudal warfare

473

The ascendancy
of the great lords

The daimyo

Economic prog-
ress during
the feudal age

tainers and robber monks. Conditions in Japan seemed to be fast approaching anarchy when, at the close of the sixteenth century, the Shogunate was drastically and effectively reorganized by the Tokugawa family.

In spite of all the confusion and turmoil, however, there were constructive forces at work. The character of Japanese feudalism was changing in a significant direction. Large territorial units were taking shape under fairly competent administrative systems. This trend was the result partly of natural evolution and partly of the policy of the Shoguns. At the outset the Shogun had attempted to control the various fiefs by sending out officials responsible to him and appointed from the military capital at Kamakura; but these officials acquired hereditary status and merged into the hierarchy. The Constable in particular—an officer who was given administrative authority over a province—gradually became a great baron or magnate, absorbing into his own dominion the estates within his jurisdiction. The great lords grew in prestige and material resources at the expense of the lesser fiefholders. During the almost constant warfare of the fifteenth and sixteenth centuries, peasants were pressed into military service, and consequently the importance of the knights began to decline. The appearance of mass armies composed of commoners was comparable to the trend in European countries during this same period; but, while the European armies were recruited chiefly by the kings of national states, the Japanese forces were under the control of feudal lords.

Leadership was passing from the knightly (*samurai*) class as a whole to the great lords, who were known as *daimyo* ("Great Names"). The *daimyo* incorporated many small estates into their own possessions and employed the *samurai* as managers and as subordinate military commanders. The families which attained the status of *daimyo* came to be referred to as clans, but they were actually very different from the clans of early Japanese society. Their territories were feudal provinces, and the people under their rule were bound by vassalage or servitude rather than by blood relationship. The ascendancy of the *daimyo*, while it by no means eliminated feudal dissension, greatly reduced the number of rival units and also ensured a considerable measure of stability within each unit.

Economically and culturally, Japan's feudal age was a period, not of retrogression or stagnation, but of progress. That this was so may seem strange in view of the roughness of the times and the instability of political institutions, but the evidence is undeniable. The Japanese maintained commerical contacts with other Far Eastern countries and continued to receive stimulating influences from China. Foreign trade, increasing steadily from the twelfth century, led to the substitution of money for rice or cloth as a medium of exchange and promoted diversified economic activity. By the fifteenth century the Japanese were exporting not only raw materials, such as lumber, gold, and pearls, but also manufactured goods. Japanese folding fans and screens were in great demand in China, and steel swords were exported by the thousands to a large Far Eastern market. The curved swords forged by Japanese craftsmen in the thirteenth century are said to have been unsurpassed even by the famous blades of Toledo and Damascus. Society during Japan's feudal period was far from being purely agrarian. Commercial and industrial centers came into being, and a few developed into populous cities. Groups of merchants organized guilds for mutual protection and to promote the marketing of their wares. Moreover, in contrast to most of Western Europe, the feudal classes participated in capitalistic enterprises. In addition to professional merchants, monastic orders, *samurai*, great nobles, and occasionally even the Shogun invested in trade.

As in earlier times, various schools of Buddhism contributed to cultural development, largely because they continued to serve as channels for intellectual and aesthetic currents from China. One of the most prominent sects, the Zen (from the Chinese *Ch'an*), was introduced at the close of the twelfth century and spread rapidly among the *samurai*. Zen Buddhism taught that Enlightenment would come to the individual not through study or any intellectual process but by a sudden flash of insight experienced when one was in tune with nature. Because it stressed physical discipline, self-control, and the practice of meditation in place of formal scholarship, the sect appealed to the warrior class, who felt that Zen teachings gave supernatural sanction to the attitudes which they had already come to regard as essential to their station. Though its doctrines were fundamentally anti-intellectual, its monks fostered both learning and art and injected several refinements into Japanese upper-class society. Among these were an unrivaled type of landscape architecture, the art of flower arrangement, and a delicate social ritual known as the tea ceremony—all of which were Chinese importations but elaborated with great sensitivity in Japan.

The samurai and Zen Buddhism

Religious developments in Japan during the medieval period were in many ways distinctive. New sects sprang up and caught the imagination of the common people. Some of them proposed the elimination of ceremony and the abolition of distinctions between clergy and laity. Others encouraged a fierce intolerance and a worship of national greatness. That the Japanese lower classes were aroused and encouraged by the new teachings is certain. During the tumultuous fifteenth and sixteenth centuries uprisings against the feudal nobles were instigated by religious congregations, and in a few instances the revolts were successful. These manifestations of popular intransigence, though, had little or no permanent effect upon Japanese society, which remained predominantly aristocratic in structure and tone.

The growth of religious sects

475

Many other cultural changes resulted from the growth of a productive and diversified economy and from the mutual stimulation among competing religious sects. While sacred writings were being collected and translated in the monasteries, and while courtiers continued to write in the polished but lifeless classical manner, literature was enriched by the addition of tales of daring and high adventure conceived for the entertainment and edification of men of arms. These stories of knightly prowess, composed in a flowing poetical prose and sometimes sung to the accompaniment of a lute, are comparable to the heroic epics of medieval European chivalry. No counterpart of the European poems of romantic love, however, arose in feudal Japan, where woman's role (with a few notable exceptions) was definitely subordinate. All the arts were influenced by Chinese models, but the Japanese had long since demonstrated their originality in adapting styles to their own tastes. Particularly impressive were the paintings executed by monks of the Zen sect in the fifteenth and sixteenth centuries. These were chiefly landscapes and similar in style to those of the Chinese artists of the Ming Dynasty, but they possessed an individuality and freshness of their own.

The exacting aesthetic standards of the aristocratic patrons of the Zen sect are also evident in a specialized form of dramatic art, the *No*, which emerged during this period. The *No* "lyric-drama" or "dance-drama" was not a foreign importation but almost purely a native product. Its origins can be traced to ancient folk dances and also to ritualistic dances associated with both Shintoist and Buddhist modes of worship. In its perfected form, it became a unique vehicle

Costume for the No *Dance-Drama* (seventeenth century). Lavish and colorful pictorial decoration was characteristic of the costumes worn by *No* actors.

The No drama is characterized by rhythmical recitation of texts, traditional music, and symbolic movement of players.

of artistic expression and entertainment, which heightened the appeal of rhythm and graceful postures by relating them to dramatic incidents. The themes of the dance-dramas were traditional narratives, but they were presented with great restraint and by suggestive symbolism rather than by literal re-enactment, somewhat in the manner of a series of tableaus. The performers wore masks as well as rich costumes and chanted their lines to the accompaniment of drums and flutes. The *No* drama achieved great popularity among the *samurai* class and was at its height from the fourteenth to the sixteenth centuries. In spite of its extremely stylized character, it has never entirely disappeared from the artistic heritage of Japan.

4. THE EMERGENCE OF CIVILIZATIONS IN SUB-SAHARAN AFRICA

The period 1000 to 1500 A.D. represented a time of state formation in black Africa. Chieftaincies in many areas were consolidated under divine kings. Numerous kingdoms evolved into expansive territorial empires, embracing a rich diversity of cultures, languages, and religious systems. The process of empire-building was most pronounced in the savanna, or Sudanic zone of West Africa.

Trans-Saharan trade expanded at a rapid rate after the eighth century, due in large measure to the initiative of Arabs and Berbers. Concurrently, growing demands from European and North African merchants for gold motivated West Africans to organize themselves on a larger, more efficient scale in order to meet these demands. Ghana's armies, under a black Soninke dynasty, captured the prosperous Berber trading center of Audoghast in the tenth century. Successive Ghanaian monarchs grew immensely rich by tightly controlling the flow of gold across their territory. A production tax was placed on gold exports and nuggets of a certain size were hoarded in order to keep the mineral rare. Ghana's hegemony extended to the upper Niger and Senegal rivers and to the burgeoning commercial centers of Timbuktu, Jenné, and Gao.

Ghana was not a Moslem empire, but her principal customers and those who controlled the strategic desert oases had become Moslems by the tenth century. Rulers in neighboring Takrur accepted Islam about 1000 A.D. and thus became West Africa's first kingdom to do so. Ghana itself had become dangerously dependent on Moslem financial advisers and merchants. Its pagan king was eventually forced to divide the capital city of Kumbi-Saleh into two parts, one for Moslems, the other for pagans.

Islam, the handmaiden of West African commerce, could not be contained. By 1054, large bands of nomadic Moslem Berbers had declared a holy war, or *jihad*, and succeeded in recapturing the vital Audoghast markets. Ghana, on the Saharan fringe, had already been weakened by environmental deterioration brought on by over-

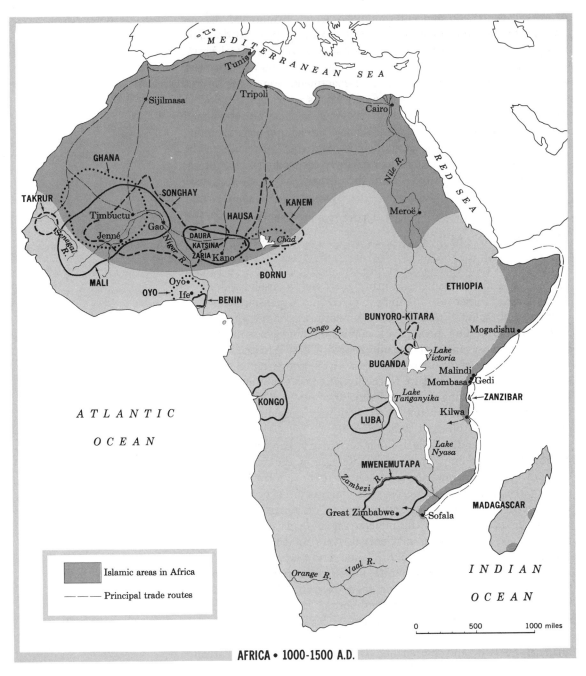

ATLANTIC

OCEAN

INDIAN

OCEAN

Islamic areas in Africa

Principal trade routes

0   500   1000 miles

AFRICA • 1000-1500 A.D.

grazing of pastures and failure to rotate crops. Its capitulation to these puritanical Berber Moslems, called Almoravids, seemed almost inevitable. But the Almoravids brought insecurity to Ghanaian market places and fear along the caravan routes. This condition upset the delicate trade balance between the forest gold miners, the Ghanaian middlemen, and the North African caravan operators.

478

Indeed, Ghana emerged from the Almoravid movement in such a weakened condition that peripheral chieftaincies were able to secede. One of these vassal chieftaincies sacked the Ghanaian capital in 1224 and enslaved the ruling family. A decade later the victor himself succumbed to the superior magic of a Ghanaian royal hostage, named Sunjata.

Ghana was finished, but a new territorial empire called Mali was forged by the magician Sunjata, who is still regarded in Western Sudanic folk traditions as a god-hero and founding father. By gaining control of the gold-producing regions, Sunjata could attract the caravan traffic formerly monopolized by Ghana. The oral record also reveals that Sunjata expanded agriculture by introducing the cultivation and weaving of cotton.

Under Mansa Musa (1312–1337) Mali's authority reached into the middle Niger city-states of Timbuktu, Jenné, and Gao. He put Mali on the European world maps by performing a stunning gold-laden pilgrimmage to Mecca, Islam's spiritual capital in the Middle East. Upon returning, Mansa Musa fostered the growth of Islam by constructing magnificent mosques in the major urban centers. With his seemingly inexhaustible supply of gold he commissioned Spanish and Middle Eastern scholars and architects to transform Malian cities into great seats of Islamic learning. Leading intellectuals were sent to Morocco and Egypt for higher studies, and at Timbuktu foundations were laid for a university at the famed Sankoré mosque. For decades after Musa, Mali enjoyed a reputation in the Moslem world for high standards of public morality and scholarship as well as for law, order, and security. People and goods flowed freely, enabling the cosmopolitan cities of Timbuktu, Jenné, and Gao to flower into major market centers. Through the leadership of Sunjata

The rise of Mali

Mansa Musa

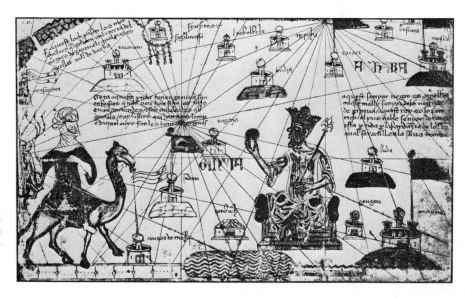

Atlas, a map drawn
Mansa Musa of Mal
waiting to receive a
Moslem trader. De
tail of the Catalan
on the island of
Majorca in 1375.

Sunni Ali and the
formation of
Songhay

Askia Muhammad
Touré and the
growth of Islamic
institutions

and Mansa Musa Islam became more deeply implanted among the elite and spread widely in the important towns.

While Mansa Musa made great advances in establishing an efficient administrative bureaucracy, he neglected to develop a formula for succession. Court intrigue and factional disputes followed the death of each Mansa. Inevitably, central authority weakened. Gao seceded in 1375 and under Sunni Ali (1464–1492) it blossomed into an expansive territorial empire called Songhay.

As in Moslem India, it was not uncommon for slaves in Africa to assume considerable administrative and military responsibilities and on occasion to usurp authority. This happened in Songhay in 1493 when a high-ranking Moslem slave, named Muhammad Touré, staged a brilliant palace coup. Lacking traditional legitimacy rooted in a pagan past, he promoted Islamic practices and found Islam an invaluable instrument for political and cultural control. Using the praise-title of "Askia," Muhammad Touré (1493–1528) extended Songhay's frontiers deep into the strategic Saharan oases, across the middle Niger to include Mali, and eastward to the emporiums of Hausaland. He then created a labyrinthine bureaucracy with ministries for the army, navy, fisheries, forests, and taxation. Songhay itself was decentralized into provinces, each ruled by a Governor chosen from among the Askia's family or royal followers. Muhammad Touré also established vast plantations, worked by slaves under conditions sometimes approaching those in the southern United States before the Civil War.

To facilitate commerce, Muhammad Touré introduced a unified system of weights and measures and appointed market inspectors to protect consumers. The Sankoré mosque at Timbuktu was transformed into an institution comparable to the great European uni-

Gobirau Mosque, Katsina (northern Nigeria). This mosque was built in the fifteenth century, when the Hausa kingdoms shared strong cultural and economic ties with Songhay. It is constructed of mud mixed with a vegetable matter (katse) and oxen blood.

versities of the later Middle Ages, with schools of theology, jurisprudence, mathematics, and medicine. On his pilgrimmage to Mecca in 1497 he befriended world-famous Moslem scholars. A few of them returned with him to Songhay as advisers on government and religion. And like the earlier Mali empire, Songhay established diplomatic relations with Morocco and Egypt, its major trading partners.

Islamic institutions of law, education, and taxation were deeply rooted in the major urban areas by the close of Askia Muhammad's rule in 1528. However, Islam was but a thin veneer elsewhere. Fully 95 per cent of the population, consisting of rural peasants and petty chiefs, continued to follow traditional animistic beliefs and life styles. Nevertheless, in spite of serious internal divisions between Islam and the traditional ways, Songhay continued to prosper, reaching its zenith under Askia Daud (1549–1582). Stretching from the snow-capped Atlas mountains of North Africa to the tropical Cameroon forests and embracing thousands of different cultures, it was clearly one of the world's most expansive empires.

Songhay had overextended itself; and although its armies numbered more than 35,000, it could not keep the outlying regions in subjection. Its vital eastern markets were lost when several Hausa city-states reasserted their independence. In the northwest, Morocco, after defeating the Portuguese, sought direct control over Songhay's mines. Crack Songhay cavalry and archers were no match for Moroccan cannons and imported European arquebusses. After Songhay's defeat by the Moroccans in 1591, the empire—and indeed western Sudanic civilization—rapidly disintegrated. The Moroccans and their Portuguese mercenaries, unable to locate the gold mines or to maintain security on the roads and in the markets, abandoned Songhay altogether in 1612. Political anarchy filled the vacuum, the great cities declined, and trade and Moslem scholarship drifted eastward to the city-states of Hausaland in what is today northern Nigeria and the Niger Republic.

By the twelfth century, uncoordinated self-governing villages in Hausaland had coalesced into centralized kingdoms under semi-divine dynasties. These kingdoms, though politically autonomous, shared a common Hausa language and cultural heritage. Daura, the founding kingdom, exercised a vague spiritual suzerainty over the others.

Islam had begun to penetrate Hausa aristocratic and trading circles in the fourteenth century. After 1452, the rural areas experienced a steady influx of red-skinned Fulani herdsmen, who for centuries had been migrating eastward from the Senegal river. The Fulani, who were fervent Moslems, brought religious books and established new centers of Islamic learning. At this time, Hausaland was experiencing a commercial revolution with the opening of the kola trade with farmers of the southern forests. In Kano, Katsina, and Zaria, huge markets emerged as traders from disintegrating Songhay shifted their operations to the more secure walled towns of Hausaland.

481

The Griot, Africa's historian, Daura Emirate. The Praise Singer is the traditional oral historian of African societies. African history has been passed from generation to generation by griots.

Kanem-Bornu

Hausaland was exceptionally secure, thanks to the military protection offered by the, wealthy and powerful kingdom of Kanem-Bornu, lying eastward near Lake Chad. Kanem-Bornu's geographical position placed it at the gateway to the West African Sudan. Its stable dynasty gained power in 846 A.D. and embraced Islam in 1087. Under Mai Idris Alooma (1580–1617) Kanem-Bornu reached its peak. Alooma established diplomatic relations with Turkey, which had recently captured Tunis in North Africa from Spain. With Turkish advisers, Alooma bureaucratized his government and set it on firm Islamic foundations. A high court of law was organized and staffed by judges who dispensed only Moslem law. The army was equipped with Turkish muskets. The thirteenth-century hostel in Cairo for Bornuese pilgrims and scholars was greatly expanded. Hausaland, sandwiched between Songhay and Bornu, was commercially exploited by both neighbors, but it received considerable cultural enrichment from pilgrims passing through en route to Mecca.

The rise of forest civilizations

After Songhay's collapse in 1591, trade shifted not only to Hausaland but also towards the southern forests. Between 1000 and 1500 A.D. the forest people of modern Nigeria experienced new infusions of grasslanders from the Sudanic zone. Leading lineages were transformed into ruling dynasties. They in turn fused scattered villages under priests and elders into small city-states. Ile Ife exercised the same kind of spiritual hegemony for the Yoruba settlers that Daura held for the Hausa in the north. Yoruba warriors from Ile Ife fanned out and established subordinate dynasties at Oyo, Benin, and elsewhere. Under Eware the Great (1440–1473) Benin city expanded into a territorial forest empire. Benin and Ife became centers of high civilization. Their craft guilds produced naturalistic busts and plaques cast in bronze through the lost wax process. Eware encouraged ivory and wood carving and created a national orchestra. All these secular innovations were aimed at glorifying the ruling

482

families. Art was no longer simply for life's adornment. It now upheld authority and graced the hallways of the sprawling Yoruba palaces.

In the hinterlands of modern Ghana, a similar though unrelated political process had begun not long before 1400. Mande traders from old Mali and Songhay pushed southward in a quest for more gold. Stronger demands from North Africa and Europe encouraged them to establish small centers of exchange at the forest's edge. These burgeoning communities represented a curious blend of pagan and Islamic, of forest and Sudanic cultures. The forest people, called the Akan, reacted to this commercial challenge by forging mini-kingdoms at the crossroads of trading activity. Thus, the southward movement of trade stimulated the rise of forest-based states, which in the sixteenth century reached their zenith as new commercial opportunities emanated from Europeans on the coast.

In chapter eleven it was shown that after the ninth century A.D. the East African coast from Somalia southward received new arrivals. Some were Bantu from the interior, others were Shirazi Arabs from the Somali coast and Persian Gulf, and a few were from northwestern India. The non-African immigrants were sea-oriented merchants in search of African minerals, ivory, and slaves. The Bantu, with inland connections, were in an excellent position to supply their needs. By the twelfth century the Shirazi had founded a series of coastal Moslem city-states, extending southward to modern Mozambique. They married into local Bantu ruling families and initiated Islamic dynasties. Sofala and Kilwa became leading Afro-Asian towns and served as major outlets for gold and copper from the Rhodesian and Katangan plateaus of the interior. Between the twelfth and fifteenth centuries a distinctive Swahili coastal civilization emerged. Swahili civilization grew out of the convergence of Bantu, Arab, and Indian cultures and languages. Swahili mosques, though reminiscent of those gracing the southern Arabian shores, were unique in form and construction. The Swahili language, written in Arabic characters, was soft and melodic.

The Akan forest states

The emergence of Swahili civilization

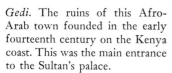
Gedi. The ruins of this Afro-Arab town founded in the early fourteenth century on the Kenya coast. This was the main entrance to the Sultan's palace.

Great Zimbabwe. This 34-foot-high conical tower was probably a shrine in the heart of the Mwenemutapa Empire (Fifteenth century). The tower and adjacent wall were constructed by placing stone upon stone without mortar.

The Swahili city-states, like their Hausa counterparts, were Moslem, cosmopolitan, culturally homogeneous, yet politically independent of one another. They thrived on their middleman position between producers and consumers. Although Kilwa held commercial sway over Sofala intermittently from 1131 to 1333, it did not exhibit any expansionist tendencies. Rather, the various towns, like Mogadishu and Barawa (in modern Somalia), Gedi, Pate, Malindi, and Mombasa (Kenya), Zanzibar and Kilwa (Tanzania), and Sofala (Mozambique) engaged in vigorous competition with one another. Some towns even minted their own coins and maintained huge treasuries.

Middleman position of the Swahili city-states

Indian Ocean trade, like that of the trans-Sahara, encouraged African rulers to centralize their societies in order to better meet foreign demands. Indeed, coastal requests for Katangan copper and Rhodesian gold led to a transition in leadership from ritual-bearing priests to secular kings commanding enormous military and economic power. Katanga in the thirteenth century was the first state to consolidate. Within two hundred years Katangans had carried their ideas of divine kingship to other societies in the Zambezi valley. On the cool Rhodesian plateau a powerful Katangan kingdom arose, with its ruler assuming the praise name of "Mwenemutapa." His capital at Great Zimbabwe was fortified with massive elliptical walls of cut stone laid in place without mortar.

The Mwenemutapa empire and Great Zimbabwe

Unrelated to these developments was the migration of Nilotic pastoralists into the fertile lands northwest of Lake Victoria in modern Uganda. Between the fourteenth and sixteenth centuries these immigrants, imbued with notions of divine kingship, married Bantu cultivators and established powerful kingdoms. These highly centralized polities, such as Bunyoro, Buganda, and Ankole, were non-Islamic, purely African creations.

Non-Islamic African kingdoms

484

· *Items so designated are available in paperbound editions.*

INDIA—*See also Readings for Chapters 6 and 11*

Cambridge History of India, Vol. III.

Ikram, Mohamad, *Muslim Civilization in India,* ed. A. T. Embree, New York, 1964. Scholarly and readable.

Phillips, C. H., *India,* London, 1949. A useful survey, although devoting little space to the period before the coming of Europeans.

Sharma, S. R., *The Crescent in India,* Bombay, 1954.

CHINA—*See also Readings for Chapters 7 and 11*

Bruce, J. P., *Chu Hsi and His Masters,* London, 1923.

· Chang, Carsun, *The Development of Neo-Confucian Thought,* New York, 1957 (College and University Press Services).

Eliot, Charles, *Hinduism and Buddhism: An Historical Sketch,* New York, 1954, Vol. III.

Fairbank, J. K., ed., *Chinese Thought and Institutions,* Chicago, 1957.

Fitzgerald, C. P., *The Southern Expansion of the Chinese People,* New York, 1972.

· Gernet, Jacques, *Daily Life in China (On the Eve of the Mongol Invasion 1250–1276),* Stanford, 1970 (Stanford).

Hucker, C. O., *The Traditional Chinese State in Ming Times (1368–1644),* Tucson, 1961. Brief but informative on political structure and operation.

· Hudson, G. F., *Europe and China: A Survey of Their Relations from the Earliest Times to 1800,* London, 1930 (Beacon). Interestingly presented.

Kracke, E. A., Jr., *Civil Service in Early Sung China, 960–1067,* Cambridge, Mass., 1959. A careful study.

Lin Yutang, *Imperial Peking: Seven Centuries of China,* New York, 1961. A richly illustrated popular account of the great capital under successive dynasties.

Liu, James T.C., *Reform in Sung China: Wang An-shih (1021–1086) and His New Policies,* Cambridge, Mass., 1959. A good, brief interpretive study.

Parsons, J. B., *The Peasant Rebellions of the Late Ming Dynasty,* Tucson, 1970.

· Prawdin, Michael, (E. and C. Paul, trs.), *The Mongol Empire: Its Rise and Legacy,* London, 1940 (Free Press).

Sowerby, A. deC., *Nature in Chinese Art,* New York, 1940.

Waley, Arthur, *An Introduction to the Study of Chinese Painting,* New York, 1958.

Williamson, H. R., *Wang An Shih, a Chinese Statesman and Educationalist of the Sung Dynasty,* 2 vols., London, 1935–1937.

Wright, Arthur F., ed., *Studies in Chinese Thought,* Chicago, 1953.

———, ed., *The Confucian Persuasion,* Stanford, 1960.

JAPAN—*See also Readings for Chapter 11*

· Duus, Peter, *Feudalism in Japan,* New York, 1969 (Knopf). A concise account of political developments from the sixth through the nineteenth century.

Sansom, George B., *A History of Japan, 1334–1615,* Stanford, 1961. A major contribution.

———, *The Western World and Japan,* New York, 1950.

READINGS

Suzuki, D. T., *Zen and Japanese Culture*, New York, 1959.
· Waley, Arthur, No *Plays of Japan*, New York, 1922 (Evergreen).

AFRICA

Ade Ajayi, J. F., and Espie, I., eds., *A Thousand Years of West African History*, Ibadan, 1967.

Boahen, Adu, *Topics in West African History*, London, 1968.

Davidson, Basil, *et al.*, *The Growth of African Civilization: A History of West Africa 1000–1800*, London, 1966.

Gray, Richard, and Birmingham, David, eds., *Pre-Colonial African Trade*, New York, 1970.

Hull, Richard W., *Munyakare: African Civilization Before the Batuuree*, New York, 1972.

Maquet, Jacques, *Civilizations of Black Africa*, New York, 1972.

Ogot, B. A., and Kieran, J. A., eds., *Zamani: A Survey of East African History*, Nairobi, 1968.

Oliver, Roland, ed., *The Middle Age of African History*, New York, 1967.

Ranger, T. O., ed., *Aspects of Central African History*, London, 1969.

SOURCE MATERIALS

Asakawa, Kanichi, ed., *The Documents of Iriki, Illustrative of the Development of the Feudal Institutions of Japan.*

Boxer, C. R., ed., *South China in the Sixteenth Century* (narratives of Portuguese and Spanish visitors, 1550–1575).

Chinese Novels and Short Stories: Buck, Pearl, tr., *All Men Are Brothers*; Howell, E. B., tr., *Inconstancy of Madam Chuang and Other Stories*; Waley, Arthur, tr., *The Monkey.*

· de Bary, W. T., ed., *Sources of Chinese Tradition*, "The Confucian Revival." (Columbia).

· ——, ed., *Sources of Indian Tradition*, "Islam in Medieval India." (Columbia).

· ——, ed., *Sources of Japanese Tradition*, "Medieval Japan." (Columbia).

Gallagher, L. J., tr., *China in the Sixteenth Century: The Journals of Matthew Ricci. 1583–1610* (a Jesuit missionary).

Hodgkin, Thomas, ed., *Nigerian Perspectives.*

· Hsiung, S. I., tr., *The Romance of the Western Chamber* (Columbia).

· Keene, Donald, ed., *Twenty Plays of the No Theatre* (Columbia).

McCullough, H. C., *The Taiheiki: A Chronicle of Medieval Japan.*

McEwan, P. J. M., ed., *Africa from Early Times to 1800.*

Oliver, R., and Mathew, G., eds., *History of East Africa*, Vol. I.

Reischauer, E. O., and Yamagiwa, J. K., *Translations from Early Japanese Literature* (eleventh to thirteenth centuries).

Shinoda, M., *The Founding of the Kamakura Shogunate 1180–1185, with Selected Translations from the Azuma Kagami.* Translation of part of the chief source for the institution and early history of the Shogunate.

Waley, Arthur, tr., *The Travels of an Alchemist, the Journeys of the Taoist Ch'ang Ch'un.*

Yule, Henry, tr., *The Book of Ser Marco Polo.*

CHAPTER 17

The Civilization of the Renaissance:

In Italy

Wherefore it may be surely said that those who are the possessors
of such rare and numerous gifts as were seen in Raphael of Urbino, are not merely men, but, if it not be a sin to say it, mortal
gods . . .

—Giorgio Vasari, *Lives of the Painters*

Soon after 1300 the majority of the characteristic institutions and
ideals of the Middle Ages had begun to decay. Chivalry, feudalism,
the Holy Roman Empire, the universal authority of the papacy, the
guild system of trade and industry were all gradually being weakened and would eventually disappear. The great age of the Gothic
cathedrals was practically over, the Scholastic philosophy was beginning to be ridiculed and despised, and the supremacy of the religious and ethical interpretations of life was being slowly but effectively undermined. In place of all these there gradually emerged
new institutions and ways of thinking of sufficient importance to
stamp the centuries that followed with the character of a different
civilization. The traditional name applied to this civilization, which
extended from 1300 to approximately 1650, is the Renaissance.

The term Renaissance leaves much to be desired from the standpoint of historical accuracy. Literally it means rebirth, and it is
commonly taken to imply that in the fourteenth century, or
Trecento,[1] there was a sudden revival of interest in the classical
learning of Greece and Rome. But this implication is far from
strictly true. Interest in the classics was by no means rare in the

The transition from the Middle Ages to the Renaissance

Meaning of the term Renaissance

---

[1] So called from the Italian word for three hundred, *trecento*, used to designate the century which followed 1300. Quattrocento, from the word four
hundred, is applied to the period of the fifteenth century and Cinquecento to
the sixteenth.

later Middle Ages. Such writers as John of Salisbury, Dante, and the Goliard poets were just as enthusiastic admirers of Greek and Latin literature as any who lived in the fourteenth century. Indeed, the so-called Renaissance was in considerable measure simply the culmination of a series of revivals which began as far back as the tenth century. All of these movements were characterized by a reverence for the ancient authors. Even in the cathedral and monastic schools Cicero, Vergil, Seneca, and, later on, Aristotle frequently received as much worshipful adoration as was given to any of the saints.

The Renaissance was a great deal more than a mere revival of pagan learning. It embraced, first of all, an impressive record of new achievements in art, literature, science, philosophy, education, and religion. Although the foundation of many of these was classical, they soon expanded beyond the measure of Greek and Roman influence. Indeed, many of the achievements in painting, science, politics, and religion bore little relation to the classical heritage. Secondly, the Renaissance incorporated a number of dominant ideals and attitudes that gave it the impress of a unique society. Notable among these in general were optimism, secularism, and individualism; but the most significant of them all was humanism. In its broadest meaning humanism may be defined as emphasis on the human values implicit in the writings of the ancient Greeks and Romans. It was a term derived from Cicero, who used it in the sense of devotion to the liberal arts, or the subjects most compatible with the dignity of man. The humanists rejected the Scholastic philosophy with its preoccupation with theology and logic. They strove for a smooth and elegant style that would appeal more to the aesthetic than to the rational side of man's nature. Though the viewpoint of many of them was pagan, this was not always the case. A large number took Christianity for granted, and some extolled it as the noblest of moral philosophies.

Not only culturally but socially, economically, and politically the Renaissance constituted a new society which differed in many ways from the social pattern of the Middle Ages. To begin with, it was nonecclesiastical. Its great accomplishments were chiefly the work of laymen, not of monks or priests. Such arenas of achievement as the universities, hitherto dominated by the clergy, now went into temporary decline. Gothic and Romanesque architectures, preeminently associated with the medieval church, were superseded by a new style based upon classical models. Latin as a medium of literary expression survived, of course, for it was Roman in origin. But gradually literature in the vernacular acquired a status at least equal to that in Latin. Renaissance society took on an urban rather than a predominantly rural character. The centers of both social and economic life were no longer castles of the feudal nobility or manorial estates but rich cities such as Florence, Milan, Venice, and Rome. Politically, also, the changes were momentous. The decentralized

The Renaissance more than a revival of pagan learning

The Renaissance a new society

feudal regime gave way to consolidated government in either large or small units. The rule of dukes and counts was succeeded by that of monarchs, or in some cases by that of oligarchs whose power sprang from their wealth as bankers or merchants. As a noted authority points out, "the fifteenth and sixteenth centuries were the age of kings." [2]

I. THE CAUSES OF THE RENAISSANCE

To determine the causes of a movement as complex as the Renaissance is not an easy task. In large measure it was a result of the disintegration of a medieval society that was no longer in harmony with changed economic and cultural conditions. The growth of commerce and the rise of national monarchies made the decentralized feudal regime obsolete. The self-sufficient manorial system decayed with the development of trade between distant regions and the appearance of new employment opportunities for villeins and serfs. As cities multiplied the nobles suffered a loss of power to the emerging middle class. Culturally, also, there was radical change. Medieval Scholasticism failed to satisfy the growing interest in natural science. Gothic architecture, which had reached its zenith of harmony and restraint in the thirteenth century, became exaggerated and flamboyant. Asceticism as an ideal was losing its appeal as men uncovered a greater variety of worldly satisfactions. Nearly everywhere, especially in southern Europe, there was a demand for a broader expanse of knowledge, a new style of living, and a greater recognition of the status of the individual. One factor, it may be said, was primarily responsible for nearly all these changes. That factor was the growth of cities, with their stimulating influence and the tendency of their populations to be impatient with old ways of living. But the cities themselves were chiefly the product of the revival of commerce. As far back as the eleventh century a flourishing trade had begun with the Saracenic and Byzantine empires. Material commodities were not the only things exchanged. There was a prosperous commerce also in ideas, manuscripts, and artistic influences. By the fourteenth century the Italian cities engaged in this trade had reached such a state of affluence that they were well adapted to becoming the centers of a cultural revival.

Soon after the Renaissance got under way, its progress was accelerated by the influence of secular and ecclesiastical patrons of learning. Outstanding among the former were the Medici family in Florence and the Sforza family in Milan. Most of these patrons were wealthy merchants who had become despots of the city republics in which they lived. The ecclesiastical patrons included such Popes as Nicholas V, Pius II, Julius II, and Leo X. The

The main causes

Influence of patrons of learning

[2] Denys Hay, *The Italian Renaissance in Its Historical Background*, p. 15.

489

attitude of these men was singularly at variance with what is normally expected of occupants of the fisherman's throne. They displayed no interest in theology or in the conversion of the ungodly. They kept on the payroll of the Church men who openly attacked fundamental Christian doctrines. Nicholas V, for example, employed as a papal secretary the celebrated Lorenzo Valla, who exposed an important document of the Church as a forgery and preached a philosophy of carnal pleasure. Whatever the incongruity of their attitude, the work of these Popes was of inestimable value to cultural progress, for they bestowed their patronage upon some of the most brilliant artists and literary men of the Italian Renaissance.

Before leaving this subject of factors responsible for the Renaissance, it will be desirable to dispose of two alleged causes commonly believed to have been of decisive importance. One of these is the Crusades, and the other is the invention of printing. In a preceding chapter we observed that the intellectual influence of the Crusades was slight. The introduction of Saracenic learning into Europe came about as a result of the work of scholars in the libraries of Toledo and Cordova and as a consequence of the trade revival between the Italian cities and the Near East. Only to the extent that the Crusades weakened feudalism, diminished the prestige of the papacy, and helped to give the Italian cities a monopoly of Mediterranean trade may they be considered as in any way responsible for the beginning of Renaissance civilization. And even these results can be ascribed in large part to other factors.

Alleged causes of the Renaissance: The Crusades

Although the invention of printing was an achievement of the utmost importance, it was perhaps even less than the Crusades a direct cause of the Renaissance. For one thing, it came too late. So far as the evidence shows, no printing press was in operation much before the middle of the fifteenth century. The earliest work known to have been printed from movable type actually dates from 1454.[3] By this time the Renaissance in Italy was already well under way, having started about a century and a half before. Furthermore, many of the early humanists were decidedly hostile toward the new invention. They regarded it as a barbarous German contraption and refused to allow their works to be printed lest they obtain too wide a circulation and be misunderstood by the common people. It should also be noted that the earliest publishing firms were far more interested in turning out religious books and popular stories than in printing the writings of the new learning. The conclusion seems amply justified that the invention of printing served chiefly to accelerate the Renaissance in its later stages, particularly in northern

Printing in the Sixteenth Century

[3] This was an indulgence issued from the press of Johann Gutenberg at Mainz, who is commonly credited with the invention of printing, though it is somewhat doubtful that he did more than perfect the technique developed by others, perhaps as early as 1445.

Europe. Most of the great benefits of the invention came after the Renaissance had ended.

2. THE RENAISSANCE IN ITALY

Reference has already been made to the fact that the Renaissance had its beginning in Italy. Why should this have been so? For one reason, Italy had a stronger classical tradition than any other country of western Europe. All through the medieval period the Italians had managed to preserve the belief that they were descendants of the ancient Romans. They looked back upon their ancestry with pride, ignoring of course the infiltrations of Lombard, Byzantine, Saracenic, and Norman blood that had been poured into the people from time to time. In some of the Italian cities traces of the old Roman system of education still survived in the municipal schools. It is likewise true that Italy had a more thoroughly secular culture than most other regions of Latin Christendom. The Italian universities were founded primarily for the study of law or medicine rather than theology, and, with the exception of the University of Rome, few of them had any ecclesiastical connections whatever. In addition to all this, Italy received the full impact of cultural influences from the Byzantine and Saracenic civilizations. Finally, and perhaps most important of all, the Italian cities were the main beneficiaries of the revival of trade with the East. For years the seaport towns of Venice, Naples, Genoa, and Pisa enjoyed a virtual monopoly of the Mediterranean trade, while the merchants of Florence, Bologna, Piacenza, and other cities of the Lombard plain served as the chief middlemen in the commerce between northern and southern Europe. The economic prosperity thus acquired was the principal foundation of the intellectual and artistic progress.

Why the Renaissance began in Italy

1. THE POLITICAL BACKGROUND It is generally assumed that orderly and efficient government is a necessary condition for the development of a superior culture; but such was not the case with the civilization we are now considering. The Renaissance was born in the midst of political turmoil. Italy was not a unified state when the Renaissance began, and throughout the period the country remained in a turbulent condition. The reasons for this chaos were several. The first was the failure of universal government. In common with the rest of central Europe, Italy was supposed to be part of the Holy Roman Empire. But after the death of Conrad IV in 1254 the imperial throne was vacant for nineteen years. When successors were finally chosen, they proved to be too weak to wield any effective authority beyond their own family domains. The Pope also lost his power as a political ruler over the Italian peninsula. As a result of a quarrel between Pope Boniface VIII and King Philip IV of France the papacy was transferred to Avignon, France, where it remained under greater or less subjection to the French king for

The political crisis in Italy

491

Gattamelata. This statue of the famous condottiere by Donatello stands outside St. Anthony's basilica in Padua.

Francesco Sforza

seventy years. By the time a Pope was finally crowned again in Rome in 1378, the political authority of the universal Church had been eroded. The dozen or more petty states into which Italy was divided had grown accustomed to managing their own affairs. Politically, the Pope was little more than another Italian prince with an uncertain authority limited to a belt of land stretching across the peninsula.

The remainder of the Italian states rapidly solidified their rule as a means of preserving their power. But stability was not easily accomplished. Interstate rivalries, internal revolts, wars of conquest, and threats of invasion combined to continue the enveloping chaos. At the beginning of the Renaissance most of the Italian states were nominally republics. As conflicts increased and ambitions grew, many of them evolved into tyrannies or oligarchies. As early as 1311 the government of Milan became a dictatorship under the head of the Visconti family. In 1450 the Visconti were succeeded by Francesco Sforza, notorious as a *condottiere*, or leader of a band of mercenary soldiers. The new despotism was no less tyrannical than the old and was tolerated by its subjects chiefly because of its success in maintaining order and prosperity.

Despotism in Venice differed from that in Milan in being collective rather than individual. Although a *doge* was the nominal head of the state, he was hemmed in by so many restrictions that he was little more than a figurehead. The real power rested with the heads of the chief business houses, who constituted a tight little oligarchy. They wielded effective authority through the Council of Ten, which took swift and merciless action against suspected enemies of the government. Politically as well as culturally, the most progressive of the Italian states was Florence. But even the Florentines were by no means entirely free from oligarchic evils. Though a constitution adopted in 1282 vested the government in an elected council whose members served short terms, restrictions on the suffrage ensured control of this body by the dominant business interests. Defeat in war and failure to maintain unbroken prosperity discredited this oligarchy, and in 1434 it was replaced by the rule of Cosimo de' Medici. Although Cosimo held no official title, he was accepted by the people as a virtual dictator, mainly because he ruled with an eye to their welfare. He and his descendants, the most famous of whom was his grandson Lorenzo the Magnificent, controlled the political life of Florence for sixty years. To the heads of the Medici family must be given a large measure of credit for the fact that Florence remained for so long the most brilliant center of the Italian Renaissance.

In the view of a number of historians the origins of the modern state system can be traced to Renaissance Italy. The rulers of such states as Milan, Florence, and Venice repudiated the conception of the state as existing for religious purposes and gave it a secular character. They emphasized civic responsibility, loyalty, and concern for the public welfare. They developed a strong notion of the end of the state as the advancement of its own interests. They invented procedures of diplomacy, including a system of permanent ambassadors in foreign capitals. They fostered alliances and toyed with the idea of a balance of power to keep the peace. The balance never really worked, however. Ambitious politicians in some of the states, notably Milan, disturbed it by soliciting help for their schemes from powerful nations outside the peninsula. A tragic consequence was the invasion of Italy by the French in 1494, followed soon afterward by a Spanish invasion from the Kingdom of Aragon. Henceforth the peninsula was at the mercy of competing armies of major European powers.

Perhaps the most "modern" of the activities of the Italian Renaissance states were their ventures in "imperialism." Before the end of the fourteenth century Milan reached out and annexed nearly the whole of the Lombard plain. Needing an agricultural province as a source of food supply and coveting control of mainland trade routes, Venice conquered nearly all of northeastern Italy, including the cities of Padua and Verona. Nor did the republic of Florence lag behind in the development of expansionist ambitions. Before the end of the fourteenth century practically all of the territory of Tuscany had been taken, and in 1406 the great mercantile city of Pisa succumbed to Florentine domination. The papacy also took part in the general movement of territorial aggrandizement. Under such worldly and aggressive Popes as Alexander VI (1492–1503) and Julius II (1503–1513) the dominion of the Papal States was ex-

Venice and Florence

Lorenzo de' Medici by Raphael

Possible origins of the modern state system

Expansionism

THE STATES OF ITALY DURING THE RENAISSANCE ca. 1494

tended over most of central Italy. By the early 1500's nearly the whole peninsula had been brought under the five most powerful states: Milan, Venice, Florence, the Kingdom of Naples, and the States of the Church.

II. THE LITERARY AND ARTISTIC CULTURE No wide gulf separated Italian Renaissance literature from the literature of the later Middle Ages. The majority of the literary achievements between 1300 and 1550 were already foreshadowed in one or another of the different trends initiated in the twelfth and thirteenth centuries. The

494

so-called father of Italian Renaissance literature, Francesco Petrarca or Petrarch (1304–1374), was himself very close to the medieval temper. He employed the same Tuscan dialect that Dante had chosen as the basis of an Italian literary language. Moreover, he believed firmly in Christianity as the way of salvation for man, and he was addicted at times to a monkish asceticism. His best-known writings, the sonnets he addressed to his beloved Laura, partook of the same flavor as the chivalrous love poetry of the thirteenth-century troubadours.

The second of the great figures in the Italian literary Renaissance, Giovanni Boccaccio (1313–1375), was scarcely more of an original genius. Like Petrarch, Boccaccio was a Florentine, the illegitimate son of a prosperous merchant. His father having planned for him a business career, he was sent to Naples to serve an apprenticeship in a branch of the great Florentine banking house of the Bardi. But the young Boccaccio soon displayed more ardor in worshiping in the temple of the Muses than in computing the interest on loans. It was perhaps natural that this should be so, for Naples was a center of gracious living under languorous skies and of strong poetic traditions emanating from the lands of the Saracens and the troubadours. It was an environment especially fitted to stimulate the poetic fancies of youth. Boccaccio was also inspired by a passionate love for the beautiful wife of a Neapolitan citizen. Nearly all of his earlier works were poems and romances dealing with the triumphs and tortures of this love. Gradually his skill in the story-telling art attained perfection, and he eventually found prose a more suitable medium for his purposes. By far the most notable of Boccaccio's writings was his *Decameron*, which he wrote after his return to Florence about 1348. The *Decameron* consists of 100 stories which the author puts into the mouths of seven young women and three young men. The stories do not form a novel revolving about a continuous theme but are united by the artificial plot of having been told by a group of people who are concerned merely with passing the time during their sojourn at a villa outside of Florence to escape the ravages of the Black Death. Though some of the tales were probably invented by Boccaccio, most of them were drawn from the *fabliaux*, from the *Book of the 1001 Nights*, and from other medieval sources. In general, they differ from their medieval prototypes in being slightly more ribald, egoistic, and anticlerical and more deeply concerned with a frank justification of the carnal life. Yet the *Decameron* certainly does not represent, as many people think, the first emphatic protest against the ascetic and impersonal ideals of the early Middle Ages. Its real significance lies in the fact that it set the pattern for Italian prose and exerted considerable influence upon Renaissance writers in other countries.

The character of
literature in the
Quattrocento

The death of Boccaccio in 1375 marks the end of the first period of the Italian Renaissance in literature, the Trecento. The age which followed, known as the Quattrocento, was characterized by a more zealous devotion to the Latin language and a broader conception of humanistic studies. The Italian of Dante and Boccaccio was regarded now by many writers as an inferior language unsuited to the perfection of an elegant style and the expression of noble ideas. No longer were the humanities thought of as synonymous with rhetoric, oratory, grammar, ethics, and poetry, but were held to include history, philosophy, and religion as well. In fine, they embraced every subject considered by the ancients as a proper medium for the study of man. As a third difference, the men of the Quattrocento turned away from the asceticism of Petrarch. They taught that nature had endowed man for action, for usefulness to his family and society, not for religious seclusion. Passion, ambition, and the quest for glory are noble impulses and ought to be encouraged. They refused to condemn the striving for material possessions, for they argued that the history of man's progress is inseparable from his success in gaining mastery over the earth and its resources. A few of the writers of the Quattrocento were completely pagan or atheistic, but most of them were neither religious nor antireligious. They took Christianity for granted and were concerned primarily with worldly interests.

The passion for
Greek studies

The Quattrocento was also the period when the passion for Greek studies was at its zenith. Prior to this time the Italian humanists had achieved but indifferent success in their attempts to learn the Greek language and to discover the treasures of Hellenic culture. But in 1393 a famous scholar of Constantinople, Manuel Chrysaloras, arrived in Venice on a mission from the Byzantine emperor to implore the aid of the West in a war against the Turks. Almost immediately acclaimed by the Italians as an apostle of the glorious Hellenic past, he was eventually persuaded to accept a professorship of the Greek classics at the University of Florence. About the beginning of the fifteenth century several other Byzantine scholars, notably Platonist philosophers, migrated to Italy. The influence of these men in providing information about the achievements of the ancient Greeks seems to have been considerable. At any rate, it was not long until Italian scholars began to make trips to Constantinople and other Byzantine cities in search of manuscripts. Between 1413 and 1423 a certain Giovanni Aurispa, for example, brought back nearly 250 manuscript books, including works of Sophocles, Euripides, and Thucydides. It was in this way that many of the Hellenic classics, particularly the writings of the dramatists, historians, and earlier philosophers, were first made available to the modern world.

The last great age in the development of Italian Renaissance literature was the Cinquecento, the period from 1500 to about 1550.

Vespers of the Holy Ghost, with a View of Paris, Jean Fouquet. From the *Book of Hours* of Etienne Chevalier, 1461. Demons in the sky are sent flying by the divine light from Heaven. The cathedral is Notre Dame. (Robert Lehman)

A Sixteenth-Century Map of the World by Paolo dal Toscanelli, Adviser to Columbus. The European continent is in the upper left. (Scala)

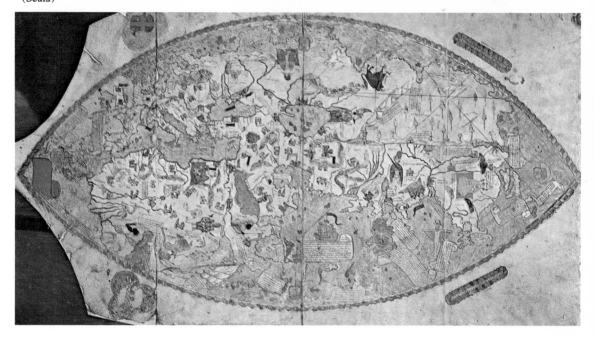

St. Lawrence Enthroned, Fra Lippo Lippi (1406–1469). One of the first of the psychological painters, Fra Lippo Lippi exhibited in this work his gift for portraying pensive melancholy. (MMA)

The Flight into Egypt, Giotto (1276–1337). Giotto is regarded as the founder of the modern tradition in painting. A fresco in the Arena Chapel, Padua. (MMA)

The Birth of Venus, Sandro Botticelli (1444–1510). Botticelli was a mystic as well as a lover of beauty whose works suggest a longing for the glories of the classical world. (Scala)

Mona Lisa, Leonardo da Vinci (1452–1519). Unlike most other Renaissance painters who sought to convey an understandable message, Leonardo created questions to which he gave no answer. Nowhere is this more evident than in the enigmatic countenance of Mona Lisa. (Louvre)

The Virgin of the Rocks, Leonardo da Vinci. This painting reveals not only Leonardo's interest in human character, but also his absorption in the phenomena of nature. (Louvre)

The Last Supper, Leonardo da Vinci. This great fresco depicts the varying reactions of Jesus' disciples when He announces that one of them will betray Him. (Santa Maria della Grazie, Milan)

Above: *The Madonna of the Chair*, Raphael (1483–1520). Raphael's art was distinguished by warmth and serenity, and by an uncritical acceptance of the traditions and conventions of his time. (Pitti Palace, Florence) Right: "Christ and Madonna." From *The Last Judgment*, Michelangelo (1475–1564). This painting above the altar in the Sistine Chapel, Rome, shows Christ as judge condemning sinners to perdition. Even the Madonna at His side seems to shrink from His wrath. (Sistine Chapel)

Charles V, Titian (1488–1576). (Alte Pinakothek)

Pope Paul III and His Nephews, Titian (1477–1576). This painting, with its rich harmony of color, is unusual in being both a group portrait and a study of action. (National Museum, Naples)

Italian was now raised to a full equality with Greek and Latin, classical and modern influences were more perfectly blended, and a deeper originality of both form and content was achieved. But the literary capital of the Renaissance was no longer Florence. In 1494 that city came under the rule of the fanatical reformer Savonarola; and, while the Medici were restored to power about eighteen years later, the brilliant Tuscan metropolis soon afterward fell a victim of factional disputes and foreign invasion. During the first half of the sixteenth century the city of Rome gradually rose to a position of cultural leadership, mainly because of the patronage of the Church, especially during the reign of Pope Leo X (Giovanni de' Medici), the son of Lorenzo the Magnificent. When he was only fourteen years old, his father's influence had been sufficient to procure his appointment as a cardinal. Elevated to St. Peter's throne in 1513, he is reported to have said, "Let us enjoy the papacy since God has given it to us." There can be little doubt that he did enjoy it, for he was a magnificent spendthrift, lavishing rewards upon artists and writers and financing the construction of beautiful churches.

The chief forms of literature developed in the Cinquecento were epic and pastoral poetry, drama, and history. The most eminent of the writers of epics was Ludovico Ariosto (1474–1533), author of a lengthy poem entitled *Orlando Furioso*. Although woven largely of materials taken from the romances of adventure and the legends of the Arthurian cycle, this work differed radically from any of the medieval epics. It incorporated much that was derived from classical sources; it lacked the impersonal quality of the medieval romances; and it was totally devoid of idealism. Ariosto wrote to make men laugh and to charm them with felicitous descriptions of the quiet splendor of nature and the passionate beauty of love. His work represents the disillusionment of the late Rennaissance, the loss of hope and faith, and the tendency to seek consolation in the pursuit of aesthetic pleasure. The development of pastoral poetry at this time probably reflects a similar attitude of disenchantment and loss of confidence. As the name implies, the pastoral romance glorifies the simple life amid rustic surroundings and expresses the yearning for a golden age of unspoiled pleasures and freedom from the worries and frustrations of artificial urban society. The chief author of this type of literature in the Italian Renaissance was Jacopo Sannazaro (1458–1530), who gave to his main work the title of *Arcadia*.

In the field of the drama the Italians never achieved more than moderate success. Their failure as writers of tragedy was particularly noticeable, despite the fact that they had considerable knowledge of classical models from which to profit. The Italian was apparently too much of an individualist to be influenced profoundly by the Greek conception of a tragic conflict between man and society and too much of an optimist to brood over personal suffering. His mind was fixed upon the compensations of life rather than upon its grim and terrifying aspects. His real talents lay in naturalistic description, in the development of light and joyous themes, and in the expression of personal egotism. It was natural, therefore, that the best of his dramas should have been comedies, especially satirical comedies, rather than tragedies. The first and the greatest of the Italian comedians was a man who is far better known as a political philosopher—Niccolò Machiavelli (1469–1527). The finest product of his dramatic skill was a work entitled *Mandragola*, which has been called "the ripest and most powerful play in the Italian language."[4] Sparkling with salacious wit and based upon incidents typical of life in the author's native city of Florence, it is a lurid satire of Renaissance society. In this as in his other writings, Machiavelli reveals his cynical views of human nature. He appears to believe that all human beings are knaves and fools at heart, with their meanness and stupidity only partly concealed by a thin veneer of refinement and learning.

The historians of the High Renaissance in Italy displayed a critical spirit and a degree of objectivity which had not been seen since the end of the ancient world. First among them in order of time although not in order of greatness was Machiavelli. In his main historical work, an account of the evolution of the Florentine republic to the death of Lorenzo de' Medici, he rigidly excluded all theological interpretations and sought to discover the natural laws which govern the life of a people. More scientific in his methods of analysis was Machiavelli's younger contemporary, Francesco Guicciardini (1483–1540). Having served many years as an ambassador of Florence and as a governor of papal territories, Guicciardini enjoyed a unique advantage in acquiring familiarity with the cynical and tortuous political life of his day. His special gifts as a historian were a capacity for minute and realistic analysis and an uncanny ability in disclosing the springs of human action. His masterpiece was his *History of Italy*, a detailed and dispassionate account of the varying fortunes of that country from 1492 to 1534. No study of Renaissance historians would be complete without some mention of Lorenzo Valla (1406–1457), who may properly be regarded as the father of historical criticism. By careful scrutiny of their literary style he challenged the authenticity of a number of accepted documents. He proved the famous "Donation of Constantine" to be a forgery, thereby demolishing one of the principal bases of papal supremacy, since this document purported to have been a grant by the Emperor Constantine of the highest spiritual and temporal power in the West to the Pope. In addition, Valla denied that the so-called Apostles' Creed had ever been written by the Apostles, and he pointed out numerous corruptions in the Vulgate edition of the New Testament as compared with the earlier Greek texts. His critical methods served later on to stimulate a much broader attack by

History

498

[4] J. A. Symonds, "Machiavelli," *Encyclopedia Britannica* (14th ed.), XIV, 577.

the northern humanists upon the doctrines and practices of the organized Church.

Despite the wealth of brilliant accomplishments in literature, the proudest achievements of the Italian Renaissance were made in the realm of art. Of all the arts, painting was undoubtedly supreme. The evolution of Italian painting followed a course of development which roughly paralleled the history of literature. During the initial period of the Trecento, however, there was only one artist of distinction worthy to be compared to Petrarch and Boccaccio in literature. His name was Giotto (1276–1337). With him, painting definitely took on the status of an independent art, although his master Cimabue had already made some beginnings in this direction. Giotto was preeminently a naturalist. So skillful was he in depicting the semblance of life that, according to the story, one of his drawings of a fly so completely deceived Cimabue that he attempted to brush the creature away with his hand. Giotto also displayed more than ordinary talent in the portrayal of action, especially in such frescoes as *Saint Francis Preaching to the Birds, The Massacre of the Innocents*, and his scenes from the life of Christ.

It was not till the Quattrocento, however, that Italian Renaissance painting really attained its majority. By this time the increase in wealth and the partial triumph of the secular spirit had freed the domain of art to a large extent from the service of religion. The Church was no longer the only patron of artists. While subject matter from Biblical history was still commonly employed, it was frequently infused with nonreligious themes. The painting of portraits for the purpose of revealing the hidden mysteries of the soul now became popular. Paintings intended to appeal primarily to the intellect were paralleled by others whose only purpose was to delight the eye with gorgeous color and beauty of form. The Quattrocento was characterized also by the introduction of painting in oil, probably from Flanders. The use of the new technique doubtless had much to do with the artistic advance of this period. Since oil does not dry so quickly as water, the painter could now work more leisurely, taking his time with the more difficult parts of the picture and making corrections if necessary as he went along.

The majority of the painters of the Quattrocento were Florentines. First among them was a precocious youth known as Masaccio (1401–1428). Although he died at the age of twenty-seven, Masaccio inspired the work of Italian painters for a hundred years. He is commonly considered the first of the realists in Renaissance art. Besides, he introduced a tactile quality into his work which profoundly influenced many of his successors. The greatest of his paintings, *The Expulsion of Adam and Eve from the Garden* and *The Tribute Money*, dealt not with specific themes but with the simple emotions common to mankind in all ages. Masaccio was also the first to achieve any notable success in imparting unity of action to

Italian painting in the Trecento: Giotto the naturalist

See color plates between pages 496 and 497

The Expulsion of Adam and Eve from the Garden. Masaccio's painting departed from the tradition of Giotto by introducing emotion and psychological study.

499

Botticelli

See color plates
between pages
496 and 497

Leonardo da
Vinci

See color plates
between pages
496 and 497

Leonardo's artis-
tic approach

groups of figures and in giving the effect of thickness to objects by the use of light and shade.

The best known of the painters who followed directly the paths marked out by Masaccio was Sandro Botticelli (1444–1510), who specialized in depicting both religious and classical themes. He excelled in representing human emotions, but always with an eye for harmony and rhythm. In spite of his sensitive feeling for nature which led him to paint with such delicate skill the subtle loveliness of youth, the summer sky, and the tender bloom of spring, Botticelli was really more deeply interested in the spiritual beauty of the soul. Like others of his time, he was strongly influenced by Neo-Platonism and dreamed of the reconciliation of pagan and Christian thought. As a consequence many of the countenances he painted reveal a pensive sadness, a mystic yearning for the divine. By no means all of his work had a religious import. His *Allegory of Spring* and *Birth of Venus* are based entirely upon classical mythology and suggest little more than an absorbing pleasure in the unfolding of life and a romantic longing for the glories of ancient Greece and Rome.

Perhaps the greatest of the Florentine painters was Leonardo da Vinci (1452–1519), one of the most talented and versatile geniuses who ever lived. Not only was he a gifted painter but a sculptor, musician, and architect of outstanding ability and a brilliant engineer and philosopher. The son of an illicit union of a prominent lawyer and a woman of humble station, he was placed by his father at an early age under the instruction of Verrocchio, a sculptor and painter of some renown and the most celebrated teacher of art in Florence. By the time he was twenty-five Leonardo was already sufficiently distinguished as a painter to win the favor of Lorenzo the Magnificent. But after five or six years he appears to have become dissatisfied with the intellectual and artistic views of the Medici and gladly accepted an offer of regular employment at the court of the Sforza in Milan. It was under the patronage of the Sforza that he produced some of the finest achievements of his life. His work, which embraces the late years of the fifteenth century and the first two decades of the sixteenth, marks the beginning of the so-called High Renaissance in Italy.

As a painter Leonardo da Vinci was impatient with the established tradition of striving to imitate classical models. He believed that all art should have as its basis a scientific study of nature. But he had no intention of confining his interests to the mere surface appearances of things. He was convinced that the secrets of nature are deeply hidden, and that the artist must examine the structure of a plant or probe into the emotions of a human soul as painstakingly as the anatomist would dissect a body. He appears especially to have been fascinated by the grotesque and unusual in nature. Yawning fissures in the earth, jagged pinnacles of rocks, rare plants and animals, embryos, and fossils—these were the phenomena he loved to ponder, evidently in the belief that this mysterious universe yields more of its secrets in the fantastic and unaccustomed than in the things that are commonplace and obvious. For the same reason he devoted much time to the study of exceptional human types, often wandering the streets for hours in quest of some face that would reveal the beauty or terror, the sincerity or hypocrisy, of the personality behind it. As a result of this deliberate selection of subjects, the paintings of Leonardo have a quality of realism decidedly at variance with the ordinary type. He did not generally portray the aspects of nature as they appear to the casual observer but strove to present them as symbols of his own philosophic reflections. He was one of the most profoundly intellectual of painters.

It is generally agreed that Leonardo da Vinci's masterpieces are his *Virgin of the Rocks*, his *Last Supper*, and his *Mona Lisa*. The first represents not only his marvelous technical skill but also his passion for science and his belief in the universe as a well-ordered place. The figures are arranged in geometric composition with every rock and plant depicted in accurate detail. The *Last Supper*, painted on the walls of the rectory of Santa Maria delle Grazie in Milan, is a study of psychological reactions. A serene Christ, resigned to his terrible fate, has just announced to his disciples that one of them will betray him. The purpose of the artist is to portray the mingled emotions of surprise, horror, and guilt revealed in the faces of the disciples as they gradually perceive the meaning of their master's statement. The third of Leonardo's major triumphs, the *Mona Lisa*, reflects a similar interest in the varied moods of the human soul. Although it is true that the *Mona Lisa* (or *Monna Lisa*, i.e., "my Lady Lisa") is a portrait of an actual woman, the wife of Francesco del Giocondo, a Neapolitan, it is more than a mere photographic likeness. The distinguished art critic and historian Bernard Berenson has said of it, "Who like Leonardo has depicted . . . the inexhaustible fascination of the woman in her years of mastery? . . . Leonardo is the one artist of whom it may be said with perfect literalness: 'Nothing that he touched but turned into a thing of eternal beauty.' "[5]

The late Quattrocento, or the beginning of the High Renaissance, was marked by the rise of another celebrated school of Italian painting, the so-called Venetian school. Its chief representatives included Giorgione (1478–1510), Titian (*ca.* 1488–1576), and Tintoretto (1518–1594). Of the three, Titian was perhaps the greatest. The work of all these men reflected the luxurious life and the pleasure-loving interests of the thriving commercial city of Venice. The Venetian painters had none of the preoccupation with philosophical and psychological themes that had characterized the Florentine

Bust of a Warrior by Leonardo da Vinci

See color plates at page 497

The Venetian painters

school. Their aim was to appeal to the senses rather than to the mind. They delighted in painting idyllic landscapes and gorgeous symphonies of color. For their subject matter they chose not merely the opulent beauty of Venetian sunsets and the shimmering silver of lagoons in the moonlight but also the man-made splendor of sparkling jewels, richly colored satins and velvets, and gorgeous palaces. Their portraits were invariably likenesses of the rich and the powerful. In the subordination of form and meaning to color and elegance there were mirrored not only the sumptuous tastes of a wealthy bourgeoisie but also definite traces of Oriental influence which had filtered through from Byzantium during the late Middle Ages.

The painters of the late Renaissance: Raphael

The remaining great painters of the High Renaissance all lived their active careers in the Cinquecento. It was in this period that the evolution of art reached its peak, and the first signs of decay began to appear. Rome was now almost the only artistic center of importance on the mainland of the Italian peninsula, although the traditions of the Florentine school still exerted a potent influence. Among the eminent painters of this period at least two must be given more than passing attention. One of the most noted was Raphael (1483–1520), a native of Urbino, and perhaps the most popular artist of the entire Renaissance. The lasting appeal of his style is due primarily to his intense humanism. He developed a conception of a spiritualized and ennobled humanity. He portrayed the members of the human species, not as dubious, tormented creatures, but as temperate, wise, and dignified beings. Although he was influenced by Leonardo da Vinci and copied many features of his work, he cultivated to a much greater extent than Leonardo a symbolical or allegorical approach. His *Disputá* symbolized the dialectical relationship between the church in heaven and the church on earth. In a worldly setting against a brilliant sky, doctors and theologians ve-

See color plates at page 497

Michelangelo, *The Creation of Adam*. One of a series of frescoes on the ceiling of the Sistine Chapel in Rome. Suggesting philosophical inquiries into the meaning of life and the universe, it represents Renaissance realism at its height.

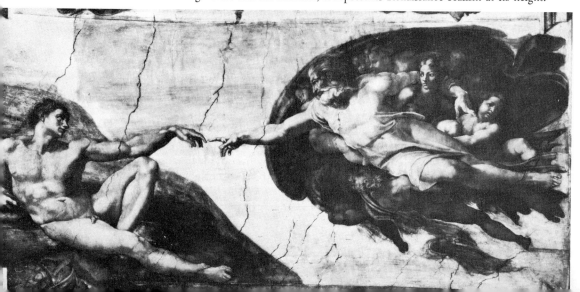

hemently debate the meaning of the Eucharist, while in the clouds above saints and the Trinity repose in the possession of a holy mystery. The *School of Athens* is an allegorical representation of the conflict between the Platonist and Aristotelian philosophies. Plato is shown pointing upward to emphasize the spiritual basis of his world of Ideas, while Aristotle gestures toward the earth to exemplify his belief that concepts or ideas are inseparably linked with their material embodiments. Raphael is noted also for his portraits and Madonnas. To the latter, especially, he gave a softness and warmth that seemed to endow them with a sweetness and piety quite different from the enigmatic and analytical portraits of Leonardo da Vinci.

Another towering giant of the Cinquecento in painting was Michelangelo (1475–1564). Beset by the hardships of poverty, harassed by grasping relatives, and torn by the emotional conflicts of his own tempestuous nature, Michelangelo appears as one of the most tragic figures in the history of art. His dark presentiments were often reflected in his work, with the result that some of his paintings are overwrought and almost morbidly pessimistic. Nevertheless, the sense of tragedy he implanted in the scenes he portrayed was not really personal but universal. After the manner of the Greek dramatists he conceived of the tragic fate of mortals as something external to man himself, a product of the cosmic order of things. If there was any one theme that dominated all of his work, it was humanism in its most intense and eloquent form. He considered the pathos and nobility of man as the only legitimate subjects of art. Rocks and trees and flowers meant nothing to him, not even as background. Michelangelo's grandest achievement as a painter was the series of frescoes he produced on the ceiling of the Sistine Chapel and on the wall above the altar. The sheer physical labor required to complete the task was prodigious. For four and a half years he toiled on a lofty scaffold, most of the time face upward, covering the 6000 square feet of ceiling with nearly 400 figures, many of them as much as ten feet in stature. The series embraces a number of scenes in the mighty epic of the human race according to Christian legend. Among them are *God Dividing the Light from the Darkness, God Creating the Earth, The Creation of Adam, The Fall of Man, The Deluge,* and so on. The culminating scene is *The Last Judgment,* which Michelangelo finished some thirty years later on the wall back of the altar. Sometimes referred to as the most famous painting in the world, this scene depicts a Herculean Christ damning the great mass of mankind to perdition. Although the subject matter is Christian, the spirit is pagan, as indicated by the naked and muscular figures and the suggestion of a ruthless deity who punishes men beyond their deserts. Nowhere else is Michelangelo's conception of universal tragedy more strongly expressed than in this work of his lonely old age.

Michelangelo

See color plates at page 497

Italian Renais-
sance sculpture:
Donatello

Medieval sculpture, as we have already seen, was not an independent art but a mere adjunct of architecture. During the Italian Renaissance a gradual evolution began which ultimately had the effect
of freeing sculpture from its bondage to architecture and establishing its status as a separate art frequently devoted to secular purposes.

The first great master of Renaissance sculpture was Donatello
(1386?–1466). He emancipated his art from Gothic mannerisms
and introduced a more vigorous note of individualism than did
any of his predecessors. His statue of David standing triumphant
over the body of the slain Goliath established a precedent of naturalism and of glorification of the nude which sculptors for many years
afterward were destined to follow. Donatello also produced the first
monumental equestrian statue in bronze since the time of the Romans, a commanding figure of the *condottiere*, Gattamelata.

One of the greatest sculptors of the Italian Renaissance, and probably of all time, was Michelangelo. Sculpture, in fact, was the artistic field of Michelangelo's personal preference. Despite his success as
a painter he considered himself unfitted for that work. Whether he
was ever particularly happy as a sculptor might be open to debate,
for he smashed some of the works upon which he had spent months
of labor and invested others with the same quality of pessimism that
characterized much of his painting. The dominant purpose which
motivated all of his sculpture was the expression of thought in stone.
His art was above mere naturalism, for he subordinated nature to
the force and sweep of his ideas. Other features of his work included the use of distortion for powerful effect, preoccupation with
themes of disillusionment and tragedy, and a tendency to express his
philosophical ideas in allegorical form. Most of his great masterpieces were done for the embellishment of tombs, a fact significantly in harmony with his absorbing interest in death, especially in
his later career. For the tomb of Pope Julius II, which was never
finished, he carved his famous figures of the *Bound Slave* and *Moses*.
The first, which is probably in some degree autobiographical, represents tremendous power and talent restrained by the bonds of fate.
The statue of Moses is perhaps the leading example of Michelangelo's sculpture showing his use of anatomical distortion to heighten
the effect of emotional intensity. Its purpose was evidently to express the towering rage of the prophet on account of the disloyalty
of the children of Israel to the faith of their fathers.

David by Donatello

Some other examples of Michelangelo's work as a plastic artist
create an even more striking impression. On the tombs of the
Medici in Florence he produced a number of allegorical figures representing such abstractions as sorrow and despair. Two of them are
known by the traditional titles of *Dawn* and *Sunset*. The first is that
of a female figure, turning and raising her head like someone called
from a dreamless sleep to awake and suffer. *Sunset* is the figure of a
powerful man who appears to sink under the load of human misery
around him. Whether these allegorical figures were intended to

Michelangelo's
allegorical
sculpture

symbolize the disasters that had overtaken the republic of Florence or merely to express the artist's own sense of the repletion of disappointment and defeat in the world is unknown. As Michelangelo's life drew toward its close, he tended to introduce into his sculpture a more exaggerated and spectacular emotional quality. This was especially true of the *Pietà* intended for his own tomb. The *Pietà* is a statue of the Virgin Mary grieving over the body of the dead Christ. The figure standing behind the Virgin is possibly intended to represent Michelangelo himself, contemplating the stark tragedy which seemed to epitomize the reality of life. It is perhaps fitting that this profound but overwrought interpretation of human existence should have brought the Renaissance epoch in sculpture to a close.

To a much greater extent than either sculpture or painting, Renaissance architecture had its roots in the past. The new building style was eclectic, a compound of elements derived from the Middle Ages and from pagan antiquity. It was not the Hellenic or the Gothic, however, but the Roman and the Romanesque which provided the inspiration for the architecture of the Italian Renaissance. Neither the Greek nor the Gothic had ever found a congenial soil in Italy. The Romanesque, by contrast, was able to flourish there, since it was more in keeping with Italian traditions, while the persistence of a strong admiration for Latin culture made possible a revival of the Roman style. Accordingly, the great architects of the Renaissance generally adopted their building plans from the Romanesque churches and monasteries and copied their decorative devices from the ruins of ancient Rome. The result was an architecture based upon the cruciform floor plan of transept and nave and embodying the decorative features of the column and arch, or the column and lintel, the colonnade, and frequently the dome. Horizontal lines predominated; and, though many of the buildings were churches, the

Gattamelata by Donatello (see also p. 348)

Pietà by Michelangelo. This portrayal of tragedy was made by the sculptor for his own tomb. Note the distortion for effect exemplified by the elongated body and left arm of the Christ. The figure in the rear is Nicodemus, but was probably intended to stand as a symbol of Michelangelo himself. Original in the Cathedral of Florence.

The Villa Rotunda of Palladio. A Renaissance building near Vicenza combining the Roman features of a square floor plan and a central dome with the Greek features of Ionic columns and colonnades.

ideals they expressed were the purely secular ones of joy in this life and pride in human achievement. Renaissance architecture emphasized harmony and proportion to a much greater extent than did the Romanesque style. Under the influence of Neo-Platonism, Italian architects concluded that perfect proportions in man reflect the harmony of the universe, and that, therefore, the parts of a building should be related to each other and to the whole in the same way as the parts of the human body. A fine example of Renaissance architecture is St. Peter's Church in Rome, built under the patronage of Popes Julius II and Leo X and designed by some of the most celebrated architects of the time, including Donato Bramante and Michelangelo. Profusely decorated with costly paintings and sculpture, it remains to this day the most magnificent church in the world.

III. PHILOSOPHY AND SCIENCE   The popular impression that the Renaissance represented in every way a marked improvement over the Middle Ages is not strictly true. It was certainly not more than half true in the realm of philosophy. The early humanists scorned logic and even the rationalism of Scholastic philosophy. Such disciplines they regarded as formal and mechanical hindrances to a fine literary style and to the enhancement of the nobility of man. Instead of Aristotle they chose Cicero as their idol and centered their interest almost exclusively upon moral philosophy. During the Quattrocento many became Platonists after the founding of the Platonic Academy by Cosimo de' Medici in Florence. Outstanding among the philosophers of the Academy were Marsilio Ficino (1433–1499) and Pico della Mirandola (1463–1494). Both were deeply pious and sought to reconcile Christianity with philosophy and even to show the basic harmony of all religions and philosophies. They rejected some of the cardinal tenets of humanism—the indissoluble unity of mind and body and the high valuation of material goods—and preached an asceticism that harked back to the Middle Ages. They adulterated their Platonism with some elements taken from Neo-Platonism and even from astrology and other occult pseudosciences.

Italian Renaissance philosophy: the Platonists

506

But not all the Italian humanists were ecstatic worshipers of Plato. In their zeal for a revival of pagan culture some sought to reawaken an interest in Aristotle for his own sake and not as a bulwark of Christianity. Others became Stoics, Epicureans, or Skeptics. The most original philosophers of the Italian Renaissance were Lorenzo Valla, Leonardo da Vinci, and Niccolò Machiavelli. The fearless and sensational ventures of Lorenzo Valla into the field of historical criticism have already been noted. He was equally unconventional as a philosopher. Defending the principles of Epicurus, he avowed the highest good to be tranquil pleasure, condemned asceticism as utterly vain and worthless, and insisted that it is irrational to die for one's country. Although Leonardo da Vinci wrote nothing that could be called a philosophical treatise, he may yet be considered a philosopher in the broad meaning of the word. He was one of the first to condemn unequivocally reliance upon authority as a source of truth, and he urged the use of the inductive method. It may be worthwhile also to take note of his strictures on war, which he called "that most bestial madness." He wrote that "It is an infinitely atrocious thing to take away the life of a man," and he even refused to divulge the secret of one of his inventions for fear it might be used by unscrupulous rulers to increase the barbarity of war.[6]

Niccolò Machiavelli is by far the most famous—and also the most infamous—political philosopher of the Italian Renaissance. No man did more than he to overturn the basic political conceptions of the Middle Ages, the ideas of universalism, limited government, and the ethical basis of politics. He was the first to conceive of the state in its modern form as a completely sovereign and independent unit. In

Machiavelli's political philosophy

[6] Edward MacCurdy (ed.), *The Notebooks of Leonardo da Vinci*, I, 24.

St. Peter's, Rome. Built to a square cross plan originally conceived by Bramante and revised by Michelangelo. Substantially completed by 1603, the church rises to a total height of 450 feet.

Left: *The Tempietto*. Designed in 1500 by Bramante, its Roman lines represent a turning point in Italian Renaissance architecture. Right: *The Strozzi Palace in Florence*. The heavy rustication of the walls with windows set into wide arches is a typical feature of Italian Renaissance palaces.

his *Discourses on Livy* he praised the ancient Roman republic as a model for all time. He lauded constitutionalism, equality, liberty in the sense of freedom from outside interference, and subordination of religion to the interests of the state. But Machiavelli also wrote *The Prince*. More than the *Discourses* it reflects the unhappy condition of Italy in his time. At the end of the fifteenth century Italy had become the cockpit of international struggles. Both France and Spain had invaded the peninsula and were competing with each other for the allegiance of the Italian states. The latter, in many cases, were torn by internal dissension which made them an easy prey for foreign conquerors. In 1498 Machiavelli entered the service of the republic of Florence as Second Chancellor and Secretary. His duties largely involved diplomatic missions to other states. While in Rome he became fascinated with the achievements of Cesare Borgia, son of Pope Alexander VI, in cementing a solidified state out of scattered elements. He noted with approval Cesare's combination of ruthlessness with shrewdness and his complete subordination of morality to political ends. In 1512 the Medici overturned the government of Florence, and Machiavelli was deprived of his position. Disappointed and embittered, he spent the remainder of his life in exile, devoting his time primarily to writing. In his books, especially in *The Prince*, he described the policies and practices of government, not in accordance with some lofty ideal, but as they actually were. The supreme obligation of the ruler, he avowed, was to maintain the power and safety of the country over which he ruled. No consideration of justice or mercy or the sanctity of treaties should be allowed to stand in his way. Cynical in his views of human nature, Machiavelli maintained that all men are prompted exclusively by motives of self-interest, particularly by desires for personal power and material prosperity. The head of the state should therefore take nothing for granted as to the loyalty or affection of his subjects. Machiavelli was the first important realist in political theory since the time of Polybius. The one ideal he kept before him in his later years was the unification of Italy. But this he believed had no chance of accomplishment except by the methods of the hard-core realist.

Not only did the narrow attitude of the early humanists in Italy retard the progress of philosophy; it also hindered for some time the advancement of science. The early humanists, as we have seen, were not critical minded. They accepted revered authorities of classical antiquity much too readily. Moreover, their interests were in art and literature, not in science. Part of this emphasis may undoubtedly be attributed to the fact that the leaders of the Renaissance for some time had only a limited knowledge of Greek achievements. The early pagan revival was predominantly a revival of Latin antiquity. And it will be recalled that the contributions of the Romans to science were few and mediocre. But in spite of the unfavorable influence of early humanism, Italy became by the fifteenth century the most important center of scientific discovery in Renaissance Europe. Much of the work was done, however, by non-Italians. Men from all over the Continent came to study in Italy and to profit from the researches of her eminent scholars. They laid the foundations for nearly every major discovery of the fifteenth and sixteenth centuries. Such was notably the case in the fields of astronomy, mathematics, physics, and medicine.

Science in the Italian Renaissance

Niccolò Machiavelli

The achievement *par excellence* in astronomy was the revival and demonstration of the heliocentric theory. Contrary to popular opinion, this was the work not of any one man but of several. It will be remembered that the idea of the sun as the center of our universe had originally been set forth by the Hellenistic astronomer Aristarchus in the third century B.C. But then, some 400 years later, the theory of Aristarchus had been superseded by the geocentric explanation of Ptolemy. For more than twelve centuries thereafter the Ptolemaic theory was the universally accepted conclusion as to the nature of the physical universe. The Romans seem never to have questioned it, and it was adopted as a cardinal dogma by the Saracenic and Scholastic philosophers. It was first openly challenged about the middle of the fifteenth century by Nicholas of Cusa, who argued that the earth is not the center of the universe. Soon after-

The revival of the heliocentric theory

ward Leonardo da Vinci taught that the earth rotates on its axis and denied that the apparent revolutions of the sun actually occur. In 1496 the now famous Pole, Nicholas Copernicus (1473–1543), came down into Italy to complete his education in civil and canon law. For ten years he studied in the universities of Bologna, Padua, and Ferrara, adding to his course in the law such subjects as mathematics and medicine. He also acquired an interest in astronomy and studied and worked for some years with the leading professors of that science. But he made no significant discoveries of his own. In the main, he was content to rely upon the observations of others, especially the ancients. His approach was not really scientific. It contained elements of the mystical and such Neo-Platonic assumptions as the notion that the sphere is the perfect shape and the idea that motion is more nearly divine than rest. He accepted most of Ptolemy's premises but denied that they pointed to Ptolemy's conclusion of a geocentric universe. On account of timidity he refrained from publishing his book, *On the Revolutions of the Heavenly Spheres*, until 1543. The proof sheets were brought to him on his deathbed.

The most important astronomical evidence for the heliocentric theory was furnished by the greatest of Italian scientists, Galileo Galilei (1564–1642). With a telescope which he had perfected to a magnifying power of thirty times, he discovered the satellites of Jupiter, the rings of Saturn, and spots on the sun.[7] He was able also to determine that the Milky Way is a collection of celestial bodies independent of our solar system and to form some idea of the enormous distances of the fixed stars. Though there were many who held out against them, these discoveries of Galileo gradually convinced the majority of scientists that the main conclusion of Copernicus was true. The final triumph of this idea is commonly called the Copernican Revolution. Few more significant events have occurred in the intellectual history of the world; for it overturned the medieval world-view and paved the way for modern conceptions of mechanism, skepticism, and the infinity of time and space. Some thinkers believe that it contributed also to the degradation of man, since it swept man out of his majestic position at the center of the universe and reduced him to a mere particle of dust in an endless cosmic machine.

In the front rank among the physicists of the Renaissance were Leonardo da Vinci and Galileo. If Leonardo da Vinci had failed completely as a painter, his contributions to science would entitle him to considerable fame. Not the least of these were his achievements in physics. Though he actually made few complete discoveries, his conclusion that "every weight tends to fall toward the center by

"A Perfect Description of the Celestial Orbes." A diagram by Copernicus showing the relationship of stars, the planets, and the sun.

Leonardo da Vinci and Galileo as physicists

---

[7] Galileo was not the original inventor of the telescope. That honor is usually accorded to Johannes Lippershey, an obscure optician who lived in the Low Countries about the beginning of the seventeenth century. Galileo learned of Lippershey's invention and improved upon it in a single night.

the shortest way" contained the kernel of the law of gravitation.[8] In addition, he worked out the principles of an astonishing variety of inventions, including a diving boat, a steam engine, an armored fighting car, and a marble saw. Galileo is especially noted as a physicist for his law of falling bodies. Skeptical of the traditional theory that bodies fall with a speed directly proportional to their weight, he taught that bodies dropped from various heights would fall at a rate of speed which increases with the square of the time involved. Rejecting the Scholastic notions of absolute gravity and absolute levity, he taught that these are purely relative terms, that all bodies have weight, even those which like the air are invisible, and that in a vacuum all objects would fall with equal velocity. Galileo seems to have had a broader conception of a universal force of gravitation than Leonardo da Vinci, for he perceived that the power which holds the moon in the vicinity of the earth and causes the satellites of Jupiter to circulate around that planet is essentially the same as the force which enables the earth to draw bodies to its surface. He never formulated this principle as a law, however, nor did he realize all of its implications, as did Newton some fifty years later. Galileo's reputation as a scientist is somewhat exaggerated. He was inclined toward intellectual arrogance and not always willing to recognize the merit in his opponents' arguments.

Galileo

The record of Italian achievements in the various sciences related to medicine is also an impressive one. A number of Italian physicians contributed valuable information pertaining to the circulation of the blood. One of them described the valves of the heart, the pulmonary artery, and the aorta, while another located the valves in the veins. Equally significant was the work of certain foreigners who lived and taught in Italy. Andreas Vesalius (1514–1564), a native of Brussels, issued the first careful description of the human body based upon actual investigation. As a result of his extensive dissections he was able to correct many ancient errors. He is commonly considered the father of the modern science of anatomy. Nevertheless, there is danger in giving him too much credit. He was almost as conservative as Copernicus. Whereas the Polish astronomer could not refrain from worshiping Ptolemy, Vesalius revered Galen and deviated from him with great reluctance. Fortunately, Galen was a better physician than Ptolemy was an astronomer. Two other physicians of foreign nationality who were heavily indebted to Italian progress in medicine were the Spaniard Michael Servetus (1511–1553) and the Englishman William Harvey (1578–1657). Servetus discovered the lesser or pulmonary circulation of the blood. In his work entitled *Errors concerning the Trinity* (his major interest was theology, but he practiced medicine for a living), he described how the blood leaves the right chambers of the heart, is carried to the lungs to be purified,

Progress in anatomy and medicine

[8] Edward MacCurdy (ed.), *The Notebooks of Leonardo da Vinci*, I, 18.

511

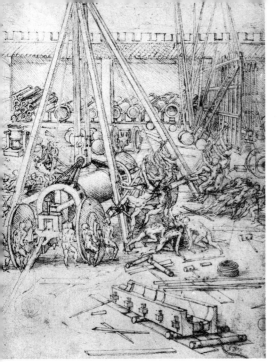

Notebook Sketches by Leonardo da Vinci. Left: A cannon foundry. Right: A mechanical mace. As the vehicle is drawn by horses, the steel balls rotate.

Studies of the Shoulder by Leonardo da Vinci

then returns to the heart and is conveyed from that organ to all parts of the body. But he had no idea of the return of the blood to the heart through the veins. It was left for William Harvey, who had studied under Italian physicians at Padua, to complete the discovery. This he did after his return to England about 1610. In his *Dissertation upon the Movement of the Heart* he described how an artery bound by a ligature would fill with blood in the section nearer the heart, while the portion away from the heart would empty, and how exactly the opposite results would occur when a ligature was placed on a vein. By such experiments he reached the conclusion that the blood is in constant process of circulation from the heart to all parts of the body and back again.

3. THE WANING OF THE ITALIAN RENAISSANCE

About 1550 the Renaissance in Italy came to an end after two and a half centuries of glorious history. The causes of its sudden demise are by no means perfectly clear. Possibly at the head of the list should be placed the French invasion of 1494 and the chaos that quickly ensued. The French monarch, Charles VIII, ruled over the richest and most powerful kingdom in Europe. Italy, weak and divided, seemed an easy prey for his grandiose ambitions. Accordingly, in 1494, he led an army of 30,000 well-trained troops across the Alps. The Medici of Florence fled before him, leaving their city to immediate capture. Halting only long enough to establish a puppet government, the French resumed their advance and conquered Naples. By so doing they aroused the suspicions of the rulers of

Invasion and conquest

512

The Harvesters, Peter Breughel the Elder (1520–1569). Breughel chose to depict the life of humble people. (MMA)

The Virgin and Chancellor Rolin, Jan van Eyck (1390–1444). The early Flemish painters loved to present scenes of piety in the sumptuous surroundings of wealthy burghers. (Louvre)

Erasmus, Hans Holbein the Younger (1497–1543). This portrait is generally regarded as the best representation of the character and personality of the Prince of the Humanists. (Louvre)

St. Andrew and St. Francis, EL Greco (1541–1614). (The Prado)

Burial of the Count of Orgaz, El Greco (1541–1614). El Greco's masterpiece immortalizes the character of the people among whom he dwelt. The elongated figures, gaunt faces, and bold and dramatic colors are typical of his work. (Iglesia S. Tomé, Toledo, Spain)

Spain, who feared an attack on their own possession of Sicily. An alliance of Spain, the Papal States, the Holy Roman Empire, and Venice finally forced Charles to abandon his project. Upon his death in 1498 his successor, Louis XII, repeated the invasion of Italy. Alliances and counteralliances succeeded one another in bewildering confusion. Louis himself formed a combination with Ferdinand of Spain, Pope Julius II, and the Holy Roman Emperor to despoil Venice of her rich lands in the Po valley, but it foundered on the rocks of distrust and perfidy. In 1511 the Pope, fearful of French domination, organized a new "Holy League" with Venice and Spain, which was joined later by Henry VIII of England and the Emperor Maximilian. The French were defeated on two fronts and left Italy in 1512 to the miseries of her own weakness and internal squabbles. In 1530 the peninsula was conquered by the Emperor Charles V after a series of struggles involving pillage and wholesale destruction.

Charles made a practice of restoring favorite princes to the nominal headship of Italian states in order to win their support in his unending struggle with France. They continued to preside over their courts, to patronize the arts, and to adorn their cities with luxurious buildings. But the great days of Italy were over. To the political disorders was added a waning of prosperity. It apparently brought no severe hardship until after 1600, but the shift of trade routes from the Mediterranean to the Atlantic region, following the discovery of America, was bound ultimately to have its effect. Italian cities

The Entrance of Charles VIII into Florence. Painting by Francesco Granacci.

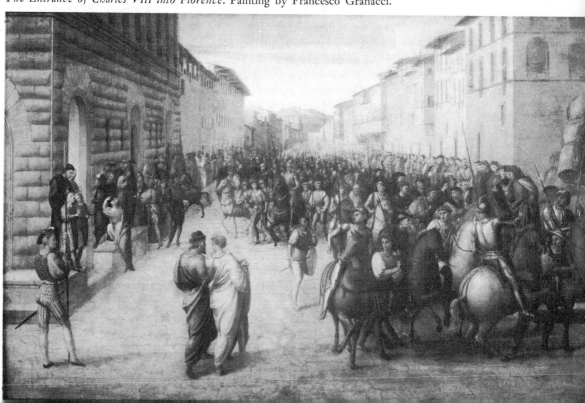

gradually lost their supremacy as the centers of world trade. The prosperity they had enjoyed from a monopoly of trade with the Near East had been one of the chief nourishing influences in the development of their brilliant culture. A source of strength and of great expectations for the future was now being drained away. Yet another cause of cultural decline would seem to have been the Catholic Reformation. During the first half of the sixteenth century the Roman Church was engulfed by waves of intolerance, dogmatism, and asceticism. The objects were partly to combat increasing worldliness and sensuality and partly to strengthen the Church in its campaigns against heresy. In 1542 the Inquisition was established in Rome and soon afterward an Index of Prohibited Books was issued. The arts were censored, publication was controlled, and heretics were burned at the stake. Such procedures could hardly be other than inimical to the free spirit of Renaissance culture.

A glaring symptom of the flimsy foundations of much of Renaissance civilization may be found in the Savonarola affair. Underneath the proud structure of Italian art and learning were smoldering embers of ignorance and superstition ready to be kindled into flame by the first bigot or fanatic who happened along. Girolamo Savonarola was born in Ferrara in 1452, the son of a shiftless and spendthrift father. Though he lived in a gay and worldly city, his early education, directed by his mother and grandfather, seems to have been chiefly religious. At the age of nineteen he fell passionately in love with the daughter of an aristocratic neighbor. The young lady spurned him contemptuously, and soon afterward he decided to renounce the world and fled to a Dominican monastery in Bologna. In 1482 he was transferred to Florence, where Lorenzo the Magnificent was then at the height of his power. The longer Savonarola remained in Florence, the more he was dismayed by the frivolity and paganism he saw all around him. Within two or three years he began preaching in the cloister garden and in the churches of the city, burning into the hearts of his hearers the terrible wrath that would overtake them if they did not flee from their sins. His fiery eloquence and gaunt and unearthly appearance attracted hordes of frightened people. By 1494 his power over the mob had reached such proportions that he became virtual dictator of Florence. For four long years the gay Tuscan metropolis was then subjected to a puritanical rule surpassing in austerity anything that Italy had witnessed since the days of Gregory the Great. Half the year was devoted to Lenten abstinence, and even marriage was discouraged. Citizens were commanded to surrender their articles of luxury and their books and paintings alleged to be immoral; all of these works of the devil were cast into the flames in the public square in the celebrated "burning of the vanities." Though he claimed the gift of prophecy and the ability to work miracles, he finally ran into trouble when he agreed under pressure to go through an ordeal by fire to prove the truth of his doctrines. In

The Savonarola affair

The Burning of Savonarola. In this view of Florence, the Palazzo Vecchio is in the right center and a portion of the cathedral is at the extreme left.

April 1498, an immense throng gathered in the Piazza della Signoria to witness the grisly spectacle. A sudden rainstorm, however, caused the authorities to postpone the ordeal on the ground that God had interposed against it. Deprived of its cruel diversion, the mob turned in rage against Savonarola and forced his arrest and imprisonment. Pope Alexander VI, whose sins he had condemned, took advantage of the opportunity to demand that he be destroyed as a heretic. After a month of excruciating tortures resulting in forced confessions, he was sentenced to death. He was burned in front of the Medici palace and his remains thrown into the Arno River. His career may be regarded not only as a symptom of the weakness of Renaissance society, but as a forerunner of the fanatical zeal of the Reformation.

SELECTED READINGS

· *Items so designated are available in paperbound editions.*

GENERAL

· Allen, J. W., *Political Thought in the Sixteenth Century*, London, 1951 (Barnes & Noble). The standard work on the subject.
· Becker, Marvin B., *Florence in Transition*, Baltimore, 1967–1968, 2 vols.
· Berenson, Bernard, *The Italian Painters of the Renaissance*, New York, 1957 (Meridian). Accurate and interesting.
· Butterfield, Herbert, *The Origins of Modern Science*, New York, 1951 (Collier).
  Cronin, Vincent, *The Florentine Renaissance*, New York, 1967.
· Ferguson, W. K., *The Renaissance*, New York, 1940 (Torchbook). A splendid introduction.

READINGS Gilbert, Felix, *Machiavelli and Guicciardini: Politics and History in Sixeenth-century Florence,* Princeton, 1965.

· Gilmore, M., *The World of Humanism,* New York, 1952 (Torchbook). An excellent general account.

Gould, Cecil, *An Introduction to Italian Renaissance Painting,* London, 1957. Discerning and authoritative.

· Hall, A. R., *The Scientific Revolution, 1450–1650,* Boston, 1956 (Beacon).

Hay, Denys, *The Italian Renaissance in Its Historical Background,* New York, 1961.

· ———, *The Renaissance Debate,* New York, 1965 (European Problem Series).

· Huizinga, J., *The Waning of the Middle Ages,* London, 1924 (Anchor). A good analysis of the decline of feudalism.

· Kristeller, Paul, *Renaissance Thought,* New York, 1961–65, 2 vols. (Torchbook).

Lang, Paul, *Music in Western Civilization,* New York, 1941. The best survey yet published.

Lopez, Robert S., *The Three Ages of the Italian Renaissance,* Charlottesville, Va., 1970.

· Mattingly, Garrett, *Renaissance Diplomacy,* Baltimore, 1964 (Penguin).

Owen, John, *The Skeptics of the Italian Renaissance,* London, 1893.

· Pater, Walter, *The Renaissance,* New York (Mentor, 1959, Meridian, 1961). Interesting interpretations.

Ridolfi, R., *The Life of Girolamo Savonarola,* New York, 1959.

———, *The Life of Niccolò Machiavelli,* Chicago, 1963. Presents Machiavelli in a new and more favorable light.

· Roeder, R., *The Man of the Renaissance,* New York, 1933 (Meridian).

Schevill, Ferdinand, *The First Century of Italian Humanism,* New York, 1928. Scholarly and stimulating.

· Smith, Preserved, *A History of Modern Culture,* New York, 1930, Vol. I (Collier). Thorough and scholarly.

· Taylor, H. O., *Thought and Expression in the Sixteenth Century,* London, 1920. Reliable and suggestive. Also available in paperback under the title, *The Humanism of Italy* (Collier, 2 vols.).

Thorndike, Lynn, *Science and Thought in the Fifteenth Century,* New York, 1929.

· Vallentin, Antonina, *Leonardo da Vinci,* New York, 1938 (Grosset and Dunlap).

Wilkins, Ernest H., *A History of Italian Literature,* Cambridge, Mass., 1954. One of the best accounts of Italian writing since Dante.

· Woodward, G. W. O., *A Short History of Sixteenth-century England,* New York, 1963 (Mentor).

SOURCE MATERIALS

Baumer, F. L. V., *Main Currents of Western Thought,* New York, 1952.

Galileo Galilei, *The Sidereal Messenger.*

MacCurdy, Edward, ed., *The Notebooks of Leonardo da Vinci,* 2 vols. New York, 1955.

· Machiavelli, Niccolo, *The Prince,* especially Chs. 15–21, 26 (Modern Library College Edition).

· ———, *Discourses on Livy,* especially Book I, Chs. 3, 4, 6, 9, 11, 12, 25, 32, 33, 34, 47, 53, 55, 58, 59; Book II, Chs. 2, 5, 13, 19, 22 (Modern Library College Editions).

Robinson, J. H., and Rolfe, H. W., *Petrarch, the First Modern Scholar and Man of Letters.*

Willis, Robert, tr., *The Works of William Harvey, M. D.*

CHAPTER 18

The Expansion of the Renaissance

Art and sciences are not cast in a mould, but are formed and perfected by degrees, by often handling and polishing, as bears leisurely lick their cubs into form.
                                    —Michel de Montaigne, *Works*, II.xii

If a rock falls on your head, that is clearly painful; but shame,
disgrace, and curses hurt only so far as they are felt. What isn't
noticed isn't troublesome. So long as you applaud yourself what
harm are the hisses of the world? And folly is the only key to
this happiness.
                                    —Erasmus, *The Praise of Folly*, II, *The Powers
                                    and Pleasures of Folly*

That a movement as vigorous as the Italian Renaissance should have
spread into other countries was a result no less than inevitable. For
years there had been a continuous procession of northern European
students coming down into Italy to bask in the genial intellectual
climate of Florence, Milan, and Rome. Moreover, the economic and
social changes in northern and western Europe had roughly paralleled those of Italy for some time. Everywhere feudalism was being
supplanted by a capitalist economy, and a new individualism was
superseding the corporate structure of society sanctified by the
Church in the Middle Ages. Common economic and social interests
fostered the growth of a similar culture. But it must not be supposed
that the Renaissance in northern and western Europe was exactly
the same as that in the south. The Italian and the Teuton differed
markedly in temperament and in historical background. More
deeply affected by Saracenic and Byzantine influences, the Italian
was disposed to find in art and literature the most suitable media of
self-expression. Besides, he was the heir of classical traditions, which
also enhanced his aesthetic interests. The northern European tended
to view the problems of life from a moral or religious angle. As a
result of these differences the northern European Renaissance was

*The spread of
the Renaissance*

517

less distinctly an artistic movement than the Renaissance in the
south. Though painting flourished in the Low Countries, elsewhere
it had no more than a limited scope, and sculpture was largely neglected. The main efforts of the northern peoples were concentrated
in literature and philosophy, often with some religious or practical
purpose. It may be added that there was less paganism in the northern Renaissance than there was in the Renaissance in Italy. Perhaps
this condition reflected the fact that theological studies predominated in the curricula of the northern universities as late as 1550.

The political history of the countries of northern and western Europe during the age of the Renaissance was characterized by
developments somewhat similar to those which had occurred in
Italy. There was the same transition from a weak and decentralized
feudal regime to the concentrated rule of despotic princes. There
was also the destruction of the political power of the guilds and the
absorption of their prerogatives of sovereignty by the state. The
chief difference was to be found in the fact that many of the states
outside of Italy were beginning to take on the character of national
units. Each of them occupied a territory of considerable size and
embraced a population knit together by bonds of language and a
vague consciousness of unity as a people. But for the most part these
great political organisms were the creations of ambitious monarchs,
who broke the power of local nobles and welded their petty principalities into huge dynastic empires. In England this process was
abetted by the so-called Wars of the Roses, a series of bloody struggles beginning about 1455 between rival factions of barons. So many
were the nobles killed in these wars and so profound was the disgust
with the long period of disorder that the Tudor dynasty, founded
by Henry VII in 1485, was soon able to crush completely the rem-

*The political
background of
the Renaissance
outside of Italy;
conditions in
England*

Portrait of Henry VIII by Hans
Holbein the Younger. In the
Palazzo Corsini, Rome.

Louis XI as Founder of the Order of St. Michael. A French miniature ca. 1470.

nants of feudal power. The most noted members of this dynasty, Henry VIII and Queen Elizabeth I, were the real founders of despotic government in England—with the support of the middle classes, who desired more protection for their commercial interests than the feudal regime could give.

In the case of France it was also a war which led to the establishment of a consolidated state—but an international war rather than an internal squabble. The struggle which enabled the French kings to stamp out feudal sovereignty was the Hundred Years' War (1337–1453), fought primarily to expel the English from France and to break their commercial alliance with the Flemish cities. As a result of this conflict a national consciousness was aroused in the French people, the nobles who had followed their own selfish ambitions were discredited, and the monarchy was extolled for having saved the country from ruin. Within thirty years the shrewd but unscrupulous Louis XI (1461–1483) extended the royal domain over all of France with the exception of Flanders and Brittany. His policies paved the way for the absolute rule of the Bourbons. Still another important country of western Europe began its emergence as a nation-state toward the end of the fifteenth century. This country was Spain, united partly as a result of the marriage of Ferdinand of Aragon and Isabella of Castile in 1469 and partly through the exigencies of the long war against the Moors. Under Philip II (1556–1598) Spain rose to a place in the very front rank of European powers. Aside from Italy, the only major country of western Europe which was not united into a consolidated state during the age of the Renaissance was Germany. Though it is true that political authority in some of the individual German kingdoms was solidified, the country as a whole remained a part of the Holy Roman Empire, now headed by the Hapsburg monarchs of Austria. The sovereignty

Conditions in France, Spain, and Germany

Philip II of Spain

519

of the Holy Roman Emperors was a mere fiction, mainly because during the Middle Ages they had wasted their energies in a vain attempt to extend their control over Italy, thereby enabling the German dukes to entrench themselves in power.

1. THE INTELLECTUAL AND ARTISTIC RENAISSANCE IN GERMANY

The limited scope of the German Renaissance

One of the first countries to receive the full impact of the Italian humanist movement was Germany. This was a natural development, not only because of the proximity of the two countries, but also because of the large-scale migration of German students to the Italian universities. But the influence of this humanism was short-lived and its fruits rather scanty and mediocre. What the results might have been if Germany had not been hurled so soon into the maelstrom of religious contention cannot be determined. The fact remains, however, that the Protestant Revolution stirred up passions of hate and intolerance which could not be other than inimical to the humanist ideal. A premium was now set upon bigotry and faith, while anything resembling the worship of man or reverence for pagan antiquity was almost certain to be regarded as a work of the devil.

German humanism: the Letters of Obscure Men

To fix a date for the beginning of the German Renaissance is practically impossible. In such prosperous cities of the south as Augsburg, Nuremberg, Munich, and Vienna there was a lively humanist movement, imported from Italy, as early as 1450. By the beginning of the sixteenth century it had taken firm root in university circles, particularly in the cities of Heidelberg, Erfurt, and Cologne. Its most notable representatives were Ulrich von Hutten (1488–1523) and Crotus Rubianus (1480–1539). Both were less interested in the literary aspects of humanism than in its possibilities as an expression of religious and political protest. Von Hutten, especially, made use of his gifts as a writer to satirize the worldliness and greed of the clergy and to indite fiery defenses of the German people against their enemies. He was himself an embittered rebel against almost every institution of the established order. The chief title of von Hutten and Rubianus to fame is their authorship of the *Letters of Obscure Men*, one of the wittiest satires in the history of literature. The circumstances under which it was written are so strikingly like those which frequently occur in the evolution of nations that they deserve to be recounted here. A learned humanist at the University of Heidelberg by the name of Johann Reuchlin had developed a passionate enthusiasm for the study of Hebrew writings. Because he criticized some of the theologians' interpretations of the Old Testament, he was savagely attacked by Christian fanatics and was finally haled before the Inquisitor-General for the Catholic Church in Germany. Numerous pamphlets were published on both sides of the controversy, and the issue was soon sharply drawn between freedom and tolerance, on the one hand, and authoritarianism and bigotry on the other. When it became apparent that rational argument was accomplishing nothing, the friends of Reuchlin decided to make use of ridicule. Rubianus and von Hutten published a series of letters purporting to have been written by some of Reuchlin's opponents, with such ridiculous signatures as Ziegenmelker (Goat-milker), Honiglecker (Honey-licker), and Mistlader (Dungloader). Heinrich Shafmaul (Sheep's mouth), the supposed writer of one of the letters, professed to be worried lest he had sinned grievously by eating an egg which contained a chick on Friday. The author of another of the letters boasted of his brilliant "discovery" that Julius Caesar could not have written the *Commentaries on the Gallic Wars* because he was too busy with his military exploits ever to have learned the Latin language. How much effect these letters had in undermining the influence of the Catholic hierarchy in Germany is impossible to say, but it must have been considerable, for they enjoyed a wide circulation.

The German Renaissance in art was limited entirely to painting and engraving, represented chiefly by the work of Albrecht Dürer (1471–1528) and Hans Holbein (1497–1543). Both of these artists were profoundly influenced by Italian traditions, though much of

Melancholy. A Famous Engraving from a Series by Albrecht Dürer. In the National Gallery, Washington, D.C.

German paint-
ing: Dürer and
Holbein

the Germanic spirit of somber realism is also expressed in their
work. Dürer's best-known paintings are his *Adoration of the Magi*,
the *Four Apostles*, and *The Crucified Christ*. The last is a study in
tragic gloom. It shows the body of the pale Galilean stretched on
the cross against a bleak and sinister sky. The glimmer of light on
the horizon merely adds to the somber effect of the scene. Some of
Dürer's best-known engravings exhibit similar qualities. His *Melancholy* represents a female figure, with wings too small to lift her
body, meditating hopelessly on the problems of life, which appear
to defy all solution. A compass is in her hand, and various other implements upon which man has relied for the control of his environment lie strewn about the floor. Hans Holbein the elder, the other
great artist of the German Renaissance, derives his renown primarily from his portraits and drawings. His portraits of Erasmus
and of Henry VIII are among the most famous in the world.
An impressive example of his drawings is the one known as
Christ in the Tomb. It depicts the body of the Son of God, with
staring eyes and mouth half open, as neglected in death as the corpse
of an ordinary criminal. The artist's purpose was probably to express the utter degradation which the Savior had suffered for the
redemption of man. In his later career Holbein also drew many religious pictures satirizing the abuses in the Catholic Church which
were believed to be the chief justification for the Protestant Revolution. He was one of the few prominent artists to devote his talents
to the Protestant cause.

German science:
Kepler and
Paracelsus

The only German during the age of the Renaissance to make any
significant contribution to science was Johann Kepler (1571–1630).
His interest aroused by the work of Copernicus, he improved the
theory of the distinguished Pole by proving that the planets move in
elliptical, rather than circular, orbits around the sun. Thus he may
be said to have destroyed the last important vestige of the Ptolemaic
astronomy, which had assumed the planets to be imbedded in perfect crystalline spheres. In addition, the laws of planetary motion
which Kepler formulated were of tremendous value in suggesting to
Newton his principle of universal gravitation. There was another
scientist of German nationality whose work can be appropriately
discussed in this connection, though he was actually born in the
vicinity of Zürich, about the end of the fifteenth century. The name
of this man was Theophrastus von Hohenheim, but he chose to call
himself Paracelsus to indicate his own belief in his superiority to
Celsus, the great Roman physician. Although Paracelsus is often
referred to as a quack and an impostor, there is really comparatively
little evidence that this was the case. He was at least sufficiently
skillful as a practitioner of healing to be appointed professor of
medicine at the University of Basel and town physician in 1527.
Moreover, it is his special merit that he went straight to the book of

experience for his knowledge of diseases and their cures. Instead of following the teachings of ancient authorities, he traveled widely, studying cases of illness in different environments and experimenting with innumerable drugs. He denied that the quest for the philosopher's stone should be the function of the chemist and insisted upon the close interrelation of chemistry and medicine. Perhaps his most important specific contribution was his discovery of the relation between cretinism in children and the presence of goiter in their parents.

2. RENAISSANCE CULTURE IN THE LOW COUNTRIES

Despite the fact that the Low Countries did not win independence of foreign domination until the seventeenth century,[1] they were nevertheless one of the most splendid centers of Renaissance culture on the Continent of Europe outside of Italy. The explanation is to be found primarily in the wealth of the Dutch and Flemish cities and in the important trade connections with southern Europe. As early as 1450 there were significant attainments in art in the Low Countries, including the development of painting in oil. Here also some of the first books were printed. While it is true that the Renaissance in the Low Countries was no broader in scope than in several other areas of northern Europe, its achievements were generally of surpassing brilliance.

The history of Renaissance literature and philosophy in the Low Countries begins and ends with Desiderius Erasmus, universally acclaimed as the Prince of the Humanists. The son of a priest and a servant girl, Erasmus was born near Rotterdam, probably in the year 1466. For his early education he had the benefit of the excellent training given in the school of the Brethren of the Common Life at Deventer.[2] Later, after his father and mother were both dead, his guardians placed him in an Augustinian monastery. Here the young Erasmus found little religion or formal instruction of any kind but plenty of freedom to read what he liked. He devoured all the classics he could get his hands on and the writings of many of the Church Fathers. When he was about thirty years of age, he obtained permission to leave the monastery and enroll in the University of Paris, where he completed the requirements for the degree of bachelor of divinity. But Erasmus never entered into the active duties of a priest, choosing rather to make his living by teaching and writing. By extensive reading of the classics he achieved a style of Latin expression so remarkable for its wit and urbanity that everything he wrote was widely read. But Erasmus' love of the classics was not born of pedantic interest. He admired the ancient authors because

Erasmus. A woodcut by Hans Holbein the Younger.

---

[1] They were ruled by the Duchy of Burgundy until 1506 when they were inherited by Charles, the young king of Spain, whose grandfather had married the sole heiress of the Burgundian duke.

[2] See The Renaissance in Religion, §7 in this chapter.

they gave voice to the very ideals of naturalism, tolerance, and humanitarianism which held so exalted a place in his own mind. He was wont to believe that such pagans as Cicero and Socrates were far more deserving of the title of Saint than many a Christian canonized by the Pope. In 1536 Erasmus died in Basel at the end of a long and unfaltering career in defense of scholarship, high standards of literary taste, and the life of reason. He has rightfully been called the most civilized man of his age.

The liberal philosophy of Erasmus

As a philosopher of humanism Erasmus was the incarnation of the finest ideals of the northern Renaissance. Convinced of the inherent goodness of man, he believed that all misery and injustice would eventually disappear if only the pure sunlight of reason could be allowed to penetrate the noisome caverns of ignorance, superstition, and hate. With nothing of the fanatic about him, he stood for liberality of mind, for reasonableness and conciliation, rather than for fierce intolerance of evil. He shrank from the violence and passion of war, whether between systems, classes, or nations. Much of his teaching and writing was dedicated to the cause of religious reform. The ceremonial, dogmatic, and superstitious extravagances in sixteenth-century Catholic life repelled him. But it was alien to his temper to lead any crusade against them. He sought rather by gentle irony, and occasionally by stinging satire, to expose irrationalism in all of its forms and to propagate a humanist religion of simple piety and noble conduct based upon what he called the "philosophy of Christ." Although his criticism of the Catholic faith had considerable effect in hastening the Protestant Revolution, he recoiled in disgust from the bigotry of the Lutherans. Neither did he have much sympathy for the scientific revival of his time. Like most of the humanists he believed that an emphasis upon science would serve to promote a crude materialism and to detract men's interests from the ennobling influences of literature and philosophy. The chief writings of Erasmus were his *Praise of Folly*, in which he satirized pedantry, the dogmatism of theologians, and the ignorance and credulity of the masses, and his *Familiar Colloquies* and *The Handbook of the Christian Knight*, in which he condemned ecclesiastical Christianity and argued for a return to the simple teachings of Jesus, "who commanded us nothing save love for one another." In a less noted work entitled *The Complaint of Peace*, he expressed his abhorrence of war and his contempt for despotic princes.

A Peasant. Drawing by Peter Breughel the Elder.

The artistic Renaissance in the Low Countries was confined almost entirely to painting; and in this field the outstanding achievements were those of the Flemish school. Flemish painting derived no small measure of its excellence from the fact that it was an indigenous art. Here there were no classical influences, no ancient statues to imitate, and no living traditions from the Byzantine or Saracenic cultures. Until comparatively late, even the Italian influence was of little consequence. The painting of Flanders was rather the spontaneous product of a virile and prosperous urban society

The Massacre of the Innocents. This painting by Peter Breughel the Elder pictures the slaughter of women and children by Spanish soldiers. Seldom has great art been used more effectively as a weapon of political protest.

dominated by aspiring merchants interested in art as a symbol of luxurious tastes. The work of nearly all the leading painters—the van Eycks, Hans Memling, and Roger van der Weyden—betrayed this flair for depicting the solid and respectable virtues of their patrons. It was distinguished also by powerful realism, by a relentless attention to the details of ordinary life, by brilliant coloring, and by a deep and uncritical piety. Hubert and Jan van Eyck are noted for their *Adoration of the Lamb,* an altarpiece produced for a church in Ghent soon after the beginning of the fifteenth century. Described by some critics as the noblest achievement of the Flemish school, it portrays a depth of religious feeling and a background of ordinary experience unmatched in Italian art. It was the first great work of the Renaissance to be done by the new method of painting in oil, a process believed to have been invented by the van Eycks. The other two Flemish painters of the fifteenth century, Hans Memling and Roger van der Weyden, are noted, respectively, for naturalism and for the expression of emotional intensity. About 100 years later came the work of Peter Breughel the elder, the most independent and the most socially conscious of the northern artists. Spurning the religious and bourgeois traditions of his predecessors, Breughel chose to depict the life of the common man. He loved to portray the boisterous pleasures of peasant folk at their wedding feasts and village fairs or to illustrate proverbs with scenes from the lives of humble people close to the earth. While he was enough of a realist never to idealize the characters in his paintings, his attitude toward them was definitely sympathetic. He employed his talents for the purpose also of condemning the tyranny of the Spanish regime in the Low Countries.

3. THE FRENCH RENAISSANCE

French
achievements in
art and science

Despite the strong aesthetic interests of the French people, as evidenced by their perfection of Gothic architecture during the Middle Ages, the achievements of their artists in the age of the Renaissance were of comparatively little importance. There was some minor progress in sculpture and a modest advancement in architecture. It was during this time that the Louvre was built, on the site of an earlier structure bearing the same name, while numerous châteaux erected throughout the country represented a more or less successful attempt to combine the grace and elegance of the Italian style with the solidity of the medieval castle. Nor was science entirely neglected, although the major accomplishments were few. They included the contributions of François Viète (1540–1603) to mathematics and of Ambroise Paré (1517?–1590) to surgery. The former invented modern algebraic symbols and elaborated the theory of equations. Paré improved upon the method of treating gunshot wounds by substituting bandages and unguents for applications of boiling oil. He was also responsible for introducing the ligature of arteries as a means of controlling the flow of blood in major

The Château of Chenonceaux in Central France as It Appears Today. Built during the sixteenth century, it represents a transitional type of architecture between Gothic and Renaissance.

amputations. He has rightfully been called the father of modern surgery.

But the outstanding achievements of the French Renaissance were in literature and philosophy, illustrated especially by the writings of François Rabelais (1490?–1553) and Michel de Montaigne (1533–1592). Like Erasmus, Rabelais was educated as a monk, but soon after taking holy orders he left the monastery to study medicine at the University of Montpellier. He finished the course for tne bachelor's degree in the short space of six weeks and obtained his doctorate about five years later, in the meantime having served for a period as public physician in Lyon in addition to lecturing and editing medical writings. He seems from the start to have interspersed his professional activities with literary endeavors of one sort or another. He wrote almanacs for the common people, satires against quacks and astrologers, and burlesques of popular superstitions. In 1532 Rabelais published his first edition of *Gargantua,* which he later revised and combined with another book bearing the title of *Pantagruel.* Gargantua and Pantagruel were originally the names of legendary medieval giants noted for their prodigious strength and their gross appetites. Rabelais' account of their adventures served as a vehicle for his robust, sprawling wit and for the expression of his philosophy of exuberant naturalism. In language far from delicate he satirized the practices of the Church, ridiculed Scholasticism, scoffed at superstitions, and pilloried every form of bigotry and repression. No man of the Renaissance was a more uncompromising individualist or exhibited more zeal in glorifying the human and the natural. For him every instinct of man was healthy, provided it was not directed toward tyranny over others. In common with Erasmus he believed in the inherent goodness of man, but unlike the great Prince of the Humanists he was a thoroughgoing pagan, rejecting not only Christian dogma but Christian morality as well. Any degree of restraint, intellectual or moral, was repugnant to Rabelais. His celebrated description of the abbey of Theleme, built by Gargantua, was intended to show the contrast between his conception of freedom and the Christian ascetic ideal. At Theleme there were no clocks summoning to duties and no vows of celibacy or perpetual membership. The inmates could leave when they liked; but while they remained they dwelt together "according to their own free will and pleasure. They rose out of their beds when they thought good; they did eat, drink, labour, sleep, when they had a mind to it, and were disposed for it. None did awake them, none did offer to constrain them . . . for so Gargantua had established it. In all their Rule and strictest tie of their order there was but this one clause to be observed, *Do what thou wilt."* [3]

A man of far different temperament and background was Michel de Montaigne (1533–1592). His father was a Catholic, his mother a

Achievements in literature and philosophy; Rabelais

Rabelais

[3] Urquhart and Motteux (trans.), *Works of Rabelais,* First Book, p. 165.

Montaigne

Jewess who had become a Protestant. Almost from the day of his birth their son was subjected to an elaborate system of training. Every morning he was awakened by soft music, and he was attended throughout the day by servants who were forbidden to speak any language but Latin. When he was six years old he was ready for the College of Guienne at Bordeaux and at the age of thirteen began the study of law. After practicing law for a time and serving in various public offices, he retired at thirty-seven to his ancestral estate to devote the remainder of his life to study, contemplation, and writing. Always in delicate health, he found it necessary now more than ever to conserve his strength. Besides, he was repelled by the bitterness and strife he saw all around him and was for that reason all the more anxious to find a refuge in a world of intellectual seclusion.

Montaigne's ideas are contained in his famous *Essays,* written during his years of retirement. The essence of his philosophy is skepticism in regard to all dogma and final truth. He knew too much about the diversity of beliefs among men, the welter of strange customs revealed by geographic discoveries, and the disturbing conclusions of the new science ever to accept the idea that any one sect had exclusive possession of "the Truth delivered once for all to the saints." It seemed to him that religion and morality were as much the product of custom as styles of dress or habits of eating. He taught that God is unknowable, and that it is as foolish to "weep that we shall not exist a hundred years hence as it would be to weep that we had not lived a hundred years ago." Man should be encouraged to despise death and to live nobly and delicately in this life rather than to yearn piously for an afterlife that is doubtful at best. Montaigne was just as skeptical in regard to assumptions of final truth in philosophy or science. The conclusions of reason, he taught, are sometimes fallacious, and the senses often deceive us. The sooner men come to realize that there is no certainty anywhere the better chance they will have to escape the tyranny which flows from superstition and bigotry. The road to salvation lies in doubt, not in faith.

A second element in Montaigne's philosophy was cynicism. He could see no real difference between the morals of Christians and those of infidels. All sects, he pointed out, fight each other with equal ferocity, except that "there is no hatred so absolute as that which is Christian." Neither could he see any value in crusades or revolutions for the purpose of overthrowing one system and establishing another. All human institutions in his judgment were about equally futile, and he therefore considered it fatuous that man should take them so seriously as to wade through slaughter in order to substitute one for its opposite. No ideal, he maintained, is worth burning your neighbor for. In his attitude toward questions of ethics Montaigne was not so ribald a champion of carnality as

Montaigne's
cynicism

Rabelais, yet he had no sympathy for asceticism. He believed it ridiculous that men should attempt to deny their physical natures and pretend that everything connected with sense is unworthy. "Sit we upon the highest throne in the world," he declared, "yet we do but sit upon our own behind." The philosophy of Montaigne, tinctured as it was with escapism and disenchantment, marked a fitting close of the Renaissance in France. But in spite of his negative attitude he did more good in the world than most of his contemporaries who founded new faiths or invented new excuses for absolute monarchs to enslave their subjects. Not only did his ridicule help to quench the flames of the cruel hysteria against witches, but the influence of his skeptical teachings had no small effect in combating fanaticism generally and in paving the way for a more generous tolerance in the future.

4.   THE SPANISH RENAISSANCE

During the sixteenth and early seventeenth centuries Spain was at the height of her glory. Her conquests in the Western Hemisphere brought wealth to her nobles and merchants and gave her a proud position in the front rank of European states. Notwithstanding these facts the Spanish nation was not one of the leaders in Renaissance culture. Apparently her citizens were too deeply absorbed in plundering the conquered territories to devote much attention to intellectual or artistic pursuits. Moreover, the long war with the Moors had engendered a spirit of bigotry, the position of the Church was too strong, and the expulsion of the Jews at the end of the fifteenth century had deprived the country of talent it could ill afford to lose. For these reasons the Spanish Renaissance was limited to a few achievements in painting and literature, albeit some of these rank in brilliance with the best that other countries produced.

Reasons for the backwardness of Spain in the Renaissance

Spanish painting bore the deep impression of the bitter struggle between Christian and Moor. As a result it expressed an intense preoccupation with religion and with themes of anguish and tragedy. Its background was medieval; upon it were engrafted influences from Flanders and from Italy. The first of the eminent Spanish painters was Luis de Morales (1517–1586), frequently called "The Divine." His Madonnas, Crucifixions, and Mater Dolorosas typified that earnest devotion to Catholic orthodoxy regarded by many Spaniards of this time as a duty both religious and patriotic. But the most talented artist of the Spanish Renaissance was not a native of Spain at all, but an immigrant from the island of Crete. His real name was Domenico Theotocopuli, but he is commonly called El Greco (1541?–1614?). After studying for some time under Titian in Venice, El Greco settled in Toledo about 1575, to live there until his death. A stern individualist in temperament, he seems to have

The character of Spanish painting; El Greco

Cervantes

imbibed little of the warmth of color and serene joy in satin splendor of the Venetian school. Instead, nearly all of his art is characterized by fevered emotionalism, stark tragedy, or enraptured flights into the supernatural and mystical. His figures are often those of gaunt, half-crazed fanatics; his colors sometimes are cold and severe. His scenes of suffering and death seem deliberately contrived to produce an impression of horror. Among his famous works are *The Burial of the Count of Orgaz, Pentecost*, and *The Apocalyptic Vision*. Better than any other artist, El Greco expresses the fiery religious zeal of the Spanish people during the heyday of the Jesuits and the Inquisition.

Literature in the Spanish Renaissance displayed tendencies not dissimilar to those in painting. This was notably true of drama, which frequently took the form of allegorical plays depicting the mystery of transubstantiation or appealing to some passion of religious fervor. Others of the dramatic productions dwelt upon themes of political pride or sang the praises of the bourgeoisie and expressed contempt for the dying world of feudalism. The colossus among the Spanish dramatists was Lope de Vega (1562–1635), the most prolific author of plays the literary world has seen. He is supposed to have written no fewer than 1500 comedies and more than 400 religious allegories. Of the total about 500 survive to this day. His secular dramas fall mainly into two classes: (1) the "cloak and sword plays," which depict the violent intrigues and exaggerated ideals of honor among the upper classes; and (2) the plays of national greatness, which celebrate the glories of Spain in her prime and represent the king as the protector of the people against a vicious and degenerate nobility.

Few would deny that the most gifted writer of the Spanish Renaissance was Miguel de Cervantes (1547–1616). His great masterpiece, *Don Quixote*, has even been described as "incomparably the best novel ever written." Composed in the best tradition of Spanish satirical prose, it recounts the adventures of a Spanish gentleman (Don Quixote) who has been slightly unbalanced by constant reading of chivalric romances. His mind filled with all kinds of fantastic adventures, he finally sets out at the age of fifty upon the slippery road of knight-errantry. He imagines windmills to be glowering giants and flocks of sheep to be armies of infidels, whom it is his duty to rout with his spear. In his disordered fancy he mistakes inns for castles and the serving-wenches within them for courtly ladies on fire with love of him. Set off in bold contrast to the ridiculous knight-errant is the figure of his faithful squire, Sancho Panza. The latter represents the ideal of the practical man, with his feet on the ground and content with the substantial pleasures of eating, drinking, and sleeping. The book as a whole is a pungent satire on feudalism, especially on the pretensions of the nobles as the champions of honor and right. Its enormous popularity was convincing proof that medieval civilization was approaching extinction even in Spain.

In common with Spain, England also enjoyed a golden age in the sixteenth and early seventeenth centuries. Though her vast colonial empire had not yet been established, she was nevertheless reaping big profits from the production of wool and from her trade with the Continent. Her government, recently consolidated under the rule of the Tudors, was making the prosperity of the middle class the object of its special solicitude. Through the elimination of foreign traders, the granting of favors to English shipping, and the negotiation of reciprocal commercial treaties, the English merchant classes were given exceptional advantages over their rivals in other countries. The growth of a national consciousness, the awakening of pride in the power of the state, and the spread of humanism from Italy, France, and the Low Countries also contributed toward the flowering of a brilliant culture in England. Nevertheless, the English Renaissance was confined primarily to philosophy and literature. The arts did not flourish; perhaps because of the Calvinist influence, which began to make itself felt in Britain by the middle of the sixteenth century.

The economic and political foundations of the Renaissance in England

The earliest philosophers of the English Renaissance may best be described simply as humanists. Although they were not unmindful of the value of classical studies, they were interested chiefly in the more practical aspects of humanism. Most of them desired a simpler and more rational Christianity and looked forward to an educational system freed from the dominance of medieval logic. Others were concerned primarily with individual freedom and the correction of social abuses. The greatest of these early thinkers was Sir Thomas More (1478–1535), esteemed by contemporary humanists as "excellent above all his nation." Following a successful career as a lawyer and as Speaker of the House of Commons, More was appointed in 1529 Lord Chancellor of England. He was not long in this position, however, before he incurred the enmity of his royal master, Henry VIII. More was loyal to Catholic universalism and did not sympathize with the king's design to establish a national church under subjection to the state. When, in 1534, he refused to take the Oath of Supremacy acknowledging the king as the head of the Church of England, he was thrown into the Tower. A year later he was tried before a packed jury, convicted, and beheaded. More's philosophy is contained in his *Utopia*, which he published in 1516. Purporting to describe an ideal society on an imaginary island, the book is really an indictment of the glaring abuses of the time—of poverty undeserved and wealth unearned, of drastic punishments, religious persecution, and the senseless slaughter of war. The inhabitants of Utopia hold all their goods in common, work only six hours a day so that all may have leisure for intellectual pursuits, and practice the natural virtues of wisdom, moderation, fortitude, and justice. Iron is the precious metal "because it is useful," war and

Sir Thomas More. Painting by Holbein.

The early English humanists; Thomas More

531

The Title Page of Sir Francis Bacon's *Novum Organum*, Printed in 1620

monasticism are abolished, and tolerance is granted to all creeds that recognize the existence of God and the immortality of the soul. Despite criticism of the *Utopia* as deficient in wit and originality, the conclusion seems justified that the author's ideals of humanity and tolerance were considerably in advance of those of most other men of his time.

The thinker who has gone down in history as the greatest of all English Renaissance philosophers is Sir Francis Bacon. Born in 1561, the son of a high government official, Bacon was nurtured in the lap of luxury until the age of seventeen when the death of his father compelled him to work for a living. Thereafter the dominating ambition of his life was to obtain some profitable position with the government which would enable him to pursue his intellectual interests. Probably it was this mania for security which accounts for the shady morality of his public career. When occasion arose, he did not shrink from concealing his true beliefs, from disloyalty to his friends, or from sharing in graft. In 1618 he was appointed Lord Chancellor, but after a scant three years in this office he was impeached for accepting bribes. Despite his protestations that the taking of money from litigants had never influenced his decisions, he was convicted and sentenced to pay a fine of $200,000 and to undergo imprisonment in the Tower "at the king's pleasure." King James I remitted the fine and limited the term of imprisonment to four days. Bacon devoted the remaining five years of his life to writ-

Sir Francis Bacon

ing, especially to the completion of the third and enlarged edition of his essays. Among his most valuable works are the *Novum Organum* and *The Advancement of Learning.*

Bacon's monumental contribution to philosophy was the glorification of the inductive method. He was by no means the discoverer of that method, but he trumpeted it forth as the indispensable ground of accurate knowledge. He believed that all seekers of truth in the past had stumbled in darkness because they were slaves of preconceived ideas or prisoners in the dungeons of Scholastic logic. He argued that in order to overcome these obstacles the philosopher should turn to the direct observation of nature, to the accumulation of facts about things and the discovery of the laws that govern them. Induction alone, he believed, was the magic key that would unlock the secrets of truth. Authority, tradition, and syllogistic logic should be as sedulously avoided as the plague. Admirable as these teachings are, they were honored by Bacon himself almost as much in the breach as in the observance. He believed in astrology, divination, and witchcraft. Moreover, the distinction he drew between ordinary knowledge and the truths of religion was hardly in keeping with his staunch defense of induction. "The senses," he wrote, "are like the sun, which displays the face of the earth, but shuts up that of the heavens." For our voyage to the realm of celestial truth, we must "quit the small vessel of human reason and put ourselves on board the ship of the Church, which alone possesses the divine needle for justly shaping the course. The stars of philosophy will be of no further service to us. As we are obliged to obey the divine law, though our will murmur against it, so we are obliged to believe in the word of God, though our reason is shocked at it. The more absurd and incredible any divine mystery is, the greater honor we do God in believing it." It was not such a far cry after all from Roger Bacon in the thirteenth century to Francis Bacon in the seventeenth.

In literature, also, the English followed much more closely in the footsteps of their medieval forerunners than did the Renaissance writers in any other country with the exception of Italy. Indeed, it is difficult to say just when the English Renaissance in literature began. Chaucer's great work, the *Canterbury Tales,* written toward the end of the fourteenth century, is commonly considered medieval; yet it breathed a spirit of earthiness and of lusty contempt for the mystical quite as pronounced as anything to be found in the writings of Shakespeare. If there were any essential differences between the English literature of the Renaissance and that produced during the late Middle Ages, they would consist in a bolder individualism, a stronger sense of national pride, and a deeper interest in themes of philosophic import. The first great poet in England after the time of Chaucer was Edmund Spenser(1552?–1599). His immortal creation, *The Faërie Queene,* is a colorful epic of England's

The Elizabethan dramatists; Marlowe

greatness in the days of Queen Elizabeth. Though written as a moral allegory to express the author's desire for a return to the virtues of chivalry, it celebrates also the joy in conquest and much of the gorgeous sensuousness typical of Renaissance humanism.

But the most splendid achievements of the English in the Elizabethan Age were in the realm of drama. Not since the days of the Greeks had the writing of tragedies and comedies attained such heights as were reached in England during the sixteenth and early seventeenth centuries. Especially after 1580 a galaxy of playwrights appeared whose work outshone that of all their predecessors in 2000 years. Included in this galaxy were such luminaries as Christopher Marlowe (1564–1593), Beaumont and Fletcher (1584–1616; 1579–1625), Ben Jonson (1573?–1637), and Shakespeare (1564–1616), of whom the first and the last are chiefly significant to the historian. Better than anyone else in his time, Christopher Marlowe embodies the insatiable egoism of the Renaissance— the everlasting craving for the fullness of life, for unlimited knowledge and experience. His brief but stormy career was a succession of scandalous escapades and fiery revolts against the restraints of convention until it was terminated by his death in a tavern brawl before he was thirty years old. The best known of his plays, entitled *Doctor Faustus*, is based upon the legend of Faust, in which the hero sells his soul to the devil in return for the power to feel every possible sensation, experience every possible triumph, and know all the mysteries of the universe.

Mr. WILLIAM
SHAKESPEARES
COMEDIES,
HISTORIES, &
TRAGEDIES.

Published according to the True Originall Copies.

William Shakespeare. Portrait made for the First Folio edition of his works, 1623.

William Shakespeare, the most talented genius in the history of drama since Euripides, was born into the family of a petty trades-man in the provincial market town of Stratford-on-Avon. His life is enshrouded in more mists of obscurity than the careers of most other great men. It is known that he left his native village when he was about twenty years old, and that ultimately he drifted to Lon-don to find employment in the theater. Tradition relates that for a time he earned his living by holding the horses of the more prosper-ous patrons of the drama. How he eventually became an actor and still later a writer of plays is unknown, but there is evidence that by the time he was twenty-eight he had already acquired a reputation as an author sufficient to excite the jealousy of his rivals. Before he retired to his native Stratford about 1610 to spend the rest of his days in ease, he had written or collaborated in writing nearly forty plays, to say nothing of 150 sonnets and two narrative poems.

In paying homage to the universality of Shakespeare's genius, we must not lose sight of the fact that he was also a child of the Renais-sance. His work bore the deep impression of most of the virtues and defects of Renaissance humanism. Almost as much as Boccaccio or Rabelais, he personified that intense love of things human and earthly which had characterized most of the great writers since the close of the Middle Ages. Moreover, like the majority of the human-ists, he showed a limited concern with the problems of politics and the values of science. Virtually the only political theory that inter-ested him greatly was whether a nation had a better chance of pros-pering under a good king who was weak or under a bad king who was strong. Though his knowledge of the sciences of his time was extensive, he regarded them as consisting primarily of alchemy, astrology, and medicine.[4] But the force and range of Shakespeare's intellect were far from bounded by the narrow horizons of the age in which he lived. While few of the works of his contemporaries are now widely read, the plays of Shakespeare still hold their rank as a kind of secular Bible wherever the English language is spoken. The reason lies not only in the author's unrivaled gift of expression, but especially in his scintillating wit and his profound analysis of human character assailed by the storms of passion and tried by the whims of fate.

Shakespeare's dramas fall rather naturally into three main groups. Those written during his earlier years conformed to the traditions of existing plays and generally reflected his own confidence in per-sonal success. They include such comedies as *A Midsummer Night's Dream* and *The Merchant of Venice*, a number of historical plays, and the lyrical tragedy, *Romeo and Juliet*. Shortly before 1600 Shakespeare seems to have experienced a change of mood. The re-

The life and writings of William Shakespeare

The character of Shakespeare's work

The main groups of Shakespeare's plays

[4] In psychology, however, he gives evidence of having been ahead of his time, especially in his treatment of mental illness. Perhaps this was natural in view of his profound interest in human emotions, in man's conflict with himself and with the universe of which he is a part.

strained optimism of his earlier plays was supplanted by some deep disillusion which led him to distrust human nature and to indict the whole scheme of the universe. The result was a group of dramas characterized by bitterness, overwhelming pathos, and a troubled searching into the mysteries of things. The series begins with the tragedy of intellectual idealism represented by *Hamlet*, goes on to the cynicism of *Measure for Measure* and *All's Well That Ends Well*, and culminates in the cosmic tragedies of *Macbeth* and *King Lear*. Perhaps the famous speech of Gloucester in the last of these plays may be taken to illustrate the depths of the author's pessimism at this time:

> As flies to wanton boys are we to the gods;
> They kill us for their sport.[5]

The final group of dramas includes those written during the closing years of Shakespeare's life, probably after his retirement. Among them are *The Winter's Tale* and *The Tempest*. All of them may be described as idyllic romances. Trouble and grief are now assumed to be only the shadows in a beautiful picture. Despite individual tragedy, the divine plan of the universe is somehow benevolent and just.

6. RENAISSANCE DEVELOPMENTS IN MUSIC

The evolution of music as an independent art

Music in western Europe in the fifteenth and sixteenth centuries reached such a high point of development that it constitutes, together with painting and sculpture, one of the most brilliant aspects of Renaissance activity. While the visual arts were stimulated by the study of ancient models, music flowed naturally from an independent evolution which had long been in progress in medieval Christendom. As earlier, leadership was supplied by men trained in the service of the Church, but the value of secular music was now appreciated, and its principles were combined with those of sacred music to bring a decided gain in color and emotional appeal. The distinction between sacred and profane became less sharp; most composers did not restrict their activities to either field. Music was no longer regarded merely as a diversion or an adjunct to worship but as an independent art.

Leadership provided by Italy and France

Different sections of Europe vied with one another for musical leadership. As with the other arts, advance was related to the increasingly generous patronage made possible by the expansion of commerce, and was centered in the prosperous towns. During the fourteenth century a pre- or early Renaissance musical movement called Ars Nova (new art) flourished in Italy and France. Its outstanding composers were Francesco Landini (*ca.* 1325-1397) and Guillaume de Machaut (1300-1377). The madrigals, ballads, and

[5] *King Lear*, Act IV, scene 1.

Left: *Musical Instruments in the Sixteenth Century*. Right: *A Print Showing Palestrina Presenting His First Printed Work to Pope Julius III*

other songs composed by the Ars Nova musicians testify to a rich secular art, but the greatest achievement of the period was a highly complicated yet delicate contrapuntal style adapted for motet and chanson. With Machaut we reach the first integral polyphonic setting of the Ordinary of the Mass.

The fifteenth century was ushered in by a synthesis of English, French, Flemish, and Italian elements that took place in the Duchy of Burgundy. It produced a remarkable school of music inspired by the cathedral of Cambrai and the ducal court at Dijon. This music was gentle, melodious, and euphonious, but in the second half of the century it hardened a little as the northern Flemish element gained in importance. As the sixteenth century opened we find these Franco-Flemish composers in every important court and cathedral choir all over Europe, gradually establishing regional-national schools, usually in attractive combinations of Flemish with German, Spanish, and Italian musical cultures. The various genres thus created show a close affinity with Renaissance art and poetry. In the second half of the sixteenth century the leaders of the nationalized Franco-Flemish style were the Italian Palestrina (*ca.* 1525–1594), who, by virtue of his position as papal composer and his devotion to a subtle and crystal-clear vocal style, became the venerated symbol of church music; the Flemish Roland de Lassus (1532–1594), the most versatile composer of the age; and Tomas

Synthesis of national elements

537

Luis de Victoria (*ca.* 1540–1611), the glowing mystic of Spanish music. Music also flourished in England, for the Tudor monarchs were not behind the Medici or the Bavarian dukes in patronizing the arts; several of them were accomplished musicians. It was inevitable that the reigning Franco-Flemish style should reach England, where it was superimposed upon an ancient and rich musical culture. The Italian madrigal, imported toward the end of the sixteenth century, found a remarkable second flourishing in England, but songs and instrumental music of an original cast anticipated future developments on the Continent. In William Byrd (1543–1623) English music produced a master fully the equal of the great Flemish, Roman, and Spanish composers of the Renaissance. The general level of music proficiency seems to have been higher in Queen Elizabeth's day than in ours: the singing of part-songs was a popular pastime in homes and at informal social gatherings, and the ability to read a part at sight was expected of well-bred persons.

In conclusion, it may be observed that while counterpoint had matured, our modern harmonic system had been born, and thus a

The greatness of the Renaissance achievement way was opened for fresh experimentation. At the same time one should realize that the music of the Renaissance constitutes not merely a stage in evolution but a magnificent achievement in itself, with masters who rank among the great of all time. The composers Palestrina and Lassus are as truly representative of the artistic triumph of the Renaissance as are the painters Raphael and Michelangelo. Their heritage, long neglected except at a few ecclesiastical centers, has within recent years begun to be appreciated, and is now gaining in popularity as interested groups of musicians devote themselves to its revival.

7. THE RENAISSANCE IN RELIGION

No account of the age of the Renaissance would be complete without some attention to the Renaissance in religion, or the Christian Renaissance as it is commonly called. This was a movement

The Christian Renaissance almost entirely independent of the Protestant Revolution, which will be discussed in the next chapter. The leaders of the Christian Renaissance were generally humanists, not Protestants. Few of them ever deserted the Catholic faith; their aim was to purify that faith from within, not to overthrow it. Most of them found the bigotry of early Protestantism as repugnant to their religious ideals as any of the abuses in the Catholic Church. The original impetus for the Christian Renaissance appears to have come from the Brethren of the Common Life, a group of pious laymen who maintained schools in the Low Countries and in western Germany. Their aim was to propagate a simple religion of practical piety, as free as possible from dogmatism and ritual. The most noted of their early followers was Thomas a Kempis (1380–1471) who wrote or edited about

1425 a book entitled *The Imitation of Christ*. Though profoundly mystical in tone, the book nevertheless repudiated the extreme otherworldliness of medieval mystics and urged a life of simple devotion to the teachings of Jesus. For over a century the *Imitation* was more widely read in Europe than any other book with the exception of the Bible.

By 1500 the Christian Renaissance had become definitely associated with northern humanism. Writers and philosophers in every country lent their support to the movement. Prominent among them were Sebastian Brant in Germany, Sir Thomas More in England, Erasmus in the Low Countries, and figures of lesser renown in France and Spain. The religious teachings of these men were thoroughly in keeping with the humanist ideal as it was understood in northern Europe. Believing that religion should function for the good of man and not for the benefit of an organized church or even for the glory of an ineffable God, they interpreted Christianity primarily in ethical terms. Many of the theological and supernatural elements in it they regarded as superfluous, if not positively harmful. They likewise had little use for ceremonies of any kind, and they ridiculed the superstitions connected with the veneration of relics and the sale of indulgences. While they recognized the necessity of a limited amount of ecclesiastical organization, they denied the absolute authority of the Pope and refused to admit that priests were really essential as intermediaries between man and God. In fine, what most of these Christian humanists really desired was the superiority of reason over faith, the primacy of conduct over dogma, and the supremacy of the individual over the organized system. They believed that this simple and rational religion could best be achieved, not through violent revolt against the Catholic Church, but through the gradual conquest of ignorance and the elimination of abuses.

The ideals of the Christian Renaissance

The decline of Renaissance culture in the countries of northern and western Europe came much less abruptly than in Italy. Indeed, the change in some respects was so gradual that there was simply a fusion of the old with the new. The achievements in science, for example, were merely extended, although with a definite shift of emphasis as time went on from the mathematical and physical branches to the biological. The Renaissance art of northern Europe, moreover, gradually evolved into the baroque, which dominated the seventeenth and early eighteenth centuries. On the other hand, humanism, in its Renaissance meaning of the worship of man and indifference to everything else, practically died out after the sixteenth century. In philosophy there has since been a tendency to exalt the universe and to relegate man to a place of insignificance as the helpless victim of an all-powerful destiny. When the end of the northern Renaissance did finally come, it probably resulted chiefly from the heritage of bitterness and unreason left by the Protestant Revolution. But that is a subject which can be discussed more appropriately in the chapter that follows.

The decline of the Renaissance outside of Italy

SELECTED READINGS

·Items so designated are available in paperbound editions.

· Beard, M. R., *A History of the Business Man*, New York, 1938 (Ann Arbor). Interesting sketches of Renaissance capitalists.

Benesch, Otto, *The Art of the Renaissance in Northern Europe*, Cambridge, Mass., 1945.

· Bush, D., *The Renaissance and English Humanism*, Toronto, 1939 (University of Toronto Press). A brief but excellent introduction.

Curtis, Mark H., *Oxford and Cambridge in Transition, 1558–1642*, Oxford, 1959.

Elton, G. R., *England Under the Tudors*, London, 1955.

· Gilmore, M., *The World of Humanism*, New York, 1952 (Torchbook). An excellent general account.

· Hay, Denys, *The Renaissance Debate*, New York, 1965 (European Problem Series).

· Huizinga, Johan, *The Waning of the Middle Ages*, London, 1924 (Anchor).

Hyma, Albert, *The Christian Renaissance*, New York, 1924. The most authoritative work on this subject.

———, *Erasmus and the Humanists*, New York, 1930.

Lang, Paul, *Music in Western Civilization*, New York, 1941. The best survey yet published.

McGinn, D. F., *Shakespeare and the Drama of His Age*, New Brunswick, N.J., 1938.

Oxford History of Music, Vols. I–II.

Panofsky, E., *Early Netherlandish Painting; Its Origins and Character*, Cambridge, Mass., 1954. Valuable for an understanding of Flemish painters.

Reese, Gustave, *Music in the Renaissance*, rev. ed., New York, 1959.

· Smith, Preserved, *A History of Modern Culture*, New York, 1930, Vol. I (Collier). Thorough and scholarly.

· ———, *Erasmus, A Study of His Life, Ideals and Place in History*, New York, 1923 (Dover).

· Taylor, H. O., *Thought and Expression in the Sixteenth Century*, London, 1920. Also available in paperback under the title *Humanism of Italy* (Collier, 2 vols.). Reliable and suggestive.

Thorndike, Lynn, *A History of Magic and Experimental Science in the Fourteenth and Fifteenth Centuries*, New York, 1934, 2 vols. Detailed and authoritative.

———, *Science and Thought in the Fifteenth Century*, New York, 1929.

SOURCE MATERIALS

· Bacon, Sir Francis, *The Great Instauration*, Preface (Washington Square Press and others).

Erasmus, Desiderius, *The Complaint of Peace.*

———, *The Handbook of a Christian Knight.*

· ———, *The Praise of Folly* (Ann Arbor, Bantam).

· Montaigne, Michel de, *Essays* (Penguin).

· More, Sir Thomas, *Utopia*, especially Book II (Penguin and others).

· Rabelais, François, *Gargantua and Pantagruel*, especially Book I (Penguin).

CHAPTER **19**

The Age of the Reformation
(1517-*ca.*1600)

For the word of God cannot be received and honored by any
works, but by faith alone.
> —Martin Luther, *On Christian Liberty*

In conformity to the clear doctrine of the Scripture, we assert
that by an eternal and immutable counsel, God has once for all
determined both whom he would admit to salvation and whom
he would condemn to destruction. . . . In the elect, we consider
calling as an evidence of election, and justification as another
token of its manifestation, till they arrive in glory, which constitutes its completion.
> —John Calvin, *Institutes* III.xxi

Preceding chapters have described the unfolding of a marvelous culture which marked the transition from the Middle Ages to the modern world. It became apparent that this culture, known as the
Renaissance, was almost as peculiarly an echo of the past as a herald
of the future. Much of its literature, art, and philosophy, and all of
its superstitions, had roots that were deeply buried in classical
antiquity or in the fabulous centuries of the Middle Ages. Even its
humanism breathed veneration for the past. Only in science and
politics and in the vigorous assertion of the right of the individual to
pursue his own quest for freedom and dignity was there much that
was really new. But the Renaissance in its later stages was accompanied by the growth of another movement, the Reformation, which
somewhat more accurately foreshadowed the modern age. This
movement included two principal phases: the Protestant Revolution, which broke out in 1517 and resulted in the secession of most
of northern Europe from the Roman faith; and the Catholic Reformation, which reached its height about 1560. Although the latter is
not called a revolution, it really was such in nearly every sense of

*The later
stages of the
Renaissance
accompanied by
a religious
revolution*

541

the term; for it effected a profound alteration of some of the notable features of late medieval Catholicism.

In a number of ways the Renaissance and the Reformation were closely related. Both were products of that powerful current of individualism which wrought such havoc to the established order in the fourteenth and fifteenth centuries. Each had a similar background of economic causes in the growth of capitalism and in the rise of a bourgeois society. Both partook of the character of a return to original sources: in the one case, to the literary and artistic achievements of the Greeks and Romans; in the other, to the Scriptures and the doctrines of the Church Fathers. But in spite of these important resemblances, it is misleading to think of the Reformation as merely the religious aspect of the Renaissance. The guiding principles of the two movements had comparatively little in common. The essence of the Renaissance was devotion to the human and the natural, with religion relegated to a subordinate place. The spirit of the Reformation was otherworldliness and contempt for the things of this life as inferior to the spiritual. In the mind of the humanist, man's nature was generally considered good; in the view of the Reformer it was unspeakably corrupt and depraved. The leaders of the Renaissance believed in urbanity and tolerance; the followers of Luther and Calvin emphasized faith and conformity. While both the Renaissance and the Reformation aimed at a recovery of the past, they were really oriented in different directions. The past the humanists strove to revive was Greek and Roman antiquity, though a few were concerned with the original Gospels as sources of an unspoiled religion. The Reformers, by contrast, were interested chiefly in a return to the teachings of St. Paul and St. Augustine. It goes without saying that the Renaissance, being an aristocratic movement, had less influence on the common man than did the Reformation.

The Reforma-
tion not really
a part of the
Renaissance

For reasons such as these it seems justifiable to conclude that the Reformation was not really a part of the Renaissance movement. In actual fact, it represented a much sharper break with the civilization of the later Middle Ages than ever did the movement led by the humanists. The radical Reformers would have nothing to do with the basic theories and practices of thirteenth-century Christianity. Even the simple religion of love and selflessness for the betterment of man, as taught by St. Francis of Assisi, appeared to repel them almost as much as the mysteries of the sacramental theory or the bombastic claims of Innocent III to spiritual and temporal power. In the main, the religious results of this clash with medieval Christianity have endured to this day. Moreover, the Reformation was intimately bound up with certain political trends which have persisted throughout the modern era. National consciousness, as we shall see, was one of the principal causes of the Protestant Revolution. While it is true that several of the humanists wrote under the influence of national pride, perhaps the majority were swayed by altogether different considerations. Many were scornful of politics, being interested solely in man as an individual; others, the great Erasmus among them, were thoroughly international in their outlook. But the Protestant Reformers could scarcely have gained much of a hearing if they had not associated their cause with the powerful groundswell of national resentment in northern Europe against an ecclesiastical system that had come to be recognized as largely Italian in character. For this reason as well as for the reasons mentioned previously, it would seem not unwarranted to regard the Reformation as a gateway to the modern world. And when we speak of the Renaissance in religion, we should think, not of the Reformation, but of the so-called Christian Renaissance, initiated by the Brethren of the Common Life and carried to its highest fulfillment in the teachings of Sir Thomas More and Erasmus. The common assumption that Luther hatched the egg which Erasmus had laid is true only in a very limited sense. The bird which Luther hatched belonged to a much tougher and wilder breed than any that could have descended from the Prince of the Humanists.

I. THE PROTESTANT REVOLUTION

The Protestant Revolution sprang from a multiplicity of causes, most of them closely related to the political and economic conditions of the age. Nothing could be more inaccurate than to think of the revolt against Rome as exclusively a religious movement, though doubtless religious ideas occupied a large place in the mind of sixteenth-century man. But without the basic political changes in northern Europe and the growth of new economic interests, Roman Catholicism would probably have undergone no more than a gradual evolution, perhaps in line with the teachings of the Christian Renaissance. Nevertheless, since religious causes were the most obvious ones, it will be appropriate to consider them first.

The multiplicity of causes of the Protestant Revolution

To the majority of Luther's early followers the movement he launched was chiefly a rebellion against abuses in the Catholic Church. That such abuses existed no careful historian would deny, regardless of his religious affiliations. For example, numerous of the Roman clergy at this time were ignorant. Some, having obtained their positions through irregular means, were unable to understand the Latin of the Mass they were required to celebrate. Further, a considerable number of the clergy led scandalous lives. While some of the Popes and bishops were living in princely magnificence, the lowly priests occasionally sought to eke out the incomes from their parishes by keeping taverns, gaming houses, or other establishments for profit. Not only did some monks habitually ignore their vows of chastity, but a few indifferent members of the secular clergy surmounted the hardships of the rule of celibacy by keeping mistresses. Pope Innocent VIII, who reigned about twenty-five years before the beginning of the Protestant Revolution, was known to have had

Religious causes: abuses in the Catholic Church

Leo X. From an Italian miniature.

eight illegitimate children, several of them born before his election to the papacy. There were numerous evils also in connection with the sale of religious offices and dispensations. As in the case of most civil positions, offices in the Church during the Renaissance period were commonly sold to the highest bidder. It is estimated that Pope Leo X enjoyed an income of more than a million dollars a year from the sale of more than 2000 ecclesiastical offices. This abuse was rendered more serious by the fact that the men who bought these positions were under a strong temptation to make up for their investment by levying high fees for their services. The sale of dispensations was a second malodorous form of ecclesiastical graft. A dispensation may be defined as an exemption from a law of the Church or from some vow previously taken. On the eve of the Reformation the dispensations most commonly sold were exemptions from fasting and from the marriage laws of the Church. By way of illustration, first cousins would be permitted to marry for the payment of a fee of one ducat.

The sale of indulgences

But the abuses which seemed to arouse the most ardent pressure for reform were the sale of indulgences and the superstitious veneration of relics. An indulgence is a remission of all or of part of the temporal punishment due to sin—that is, of the punishment in this life and in purgatory; it is not supposed to have anything to do with punishment in hell. The theory upon which the indulgence rests is the famous doctrine of the Treasure of Merit developed by Scholastic theologians in the thirteenth century. According to this doctrine, Jesus and the saints, by reason of their "superfluous" virtues on earth, accumulated an excess of merit in heaven. This excess constitutes a treasure of grace upon which the Pope can draw for the benefit of ordinary mortals. Originally indulgences were not issued for payments of money, but only for works of charity, fasting, going on crusades, and the like. It was the Renaissance Popes, with their insatiable greed for revenue, who first embarked upon the sale of indulgences as a profitable business. The methods they employed were far from scrupulous. The traffic in "pardons" was often turned over to bankers on a commission basis. As an example, the Fuggers in Augsburg had charge of the sale of indulgences for Leo X, with permission to pocket one-third of the proceeds. Naturally, but one motive dominated the business—to raise as much money as possible.

Abuses connected with the veneration of sacred relics

For centuries before the Reformation the veneration of sacred relics had been an important element in Catholic worship. It was believed that objects used by the Christ, the Virgin, or the saints possessed a miraculous healing and protective virtue for anyone who touched them or came into their presence. It was inevitable that this belief should open the way for innumerable frauds. Superstitious peasants could be easily convinced that almost any ancient splinter of wood was a fragment of the true cross. And there was evidently no dearth of relic-mongers quick to take advantage of such credulity. The results were fantastic. According to Erasmus, the churches

An Interior with a Woman Drinking, with Two Men and a Maidservant, Pieter de Hooch (1629–1677?). The subjects and setting contrast strongly with those of the Italian artists. (National Gallery, London) Below: *Crucifixion*, Matthias Grünewald (?–1528). This work is the central panel of the Isenheim Altarpiece, in the Unterlinden Museen, Colmar. (Scala)

THE RELIGIOUS SITUATION IN EUROPE
AT THE HEIGHT OF THE REFORMATION

PRINCIPAL CHRISTIAN CHURCHES IN 1560:

Anglicans

Lutherans

Calvinists and
Zwinglians

Roman
Catholics

MINORITIES:

L Lutherans   RC Roman Catholics
CZ Calvinists,   WM Waldensians,
   Zwinglians   Moravians
ASA Anabaptists, Socinians, Antitrinitarians
------ Approximate extent of the revolt
         from the Roman Church

of Europe contained enough wood of the true cross to build a ship. No fewer than five shinbones of the ass on which Jesus rode to Jerusalem were on exhibition in different places, to say nothing of twelve heads of John the Baptist. Martin Luther declared in a pamphlet lampooning his enemy, the Archbishop of Mainz, that the latter claimed to possess "a whole pound of the wind that blew for Elijah in the cave on Mount Horeb and two feathers and an egg of the Holy Ghost."[1]

Modern historians agree, however, that abuses in the Catholic Church were not the primary religious cause of the Protestant Revolution. It was medieval Catholicism itself, not the abuses therein, to which the Reformers objected. Moreover, just before the revolt broke out, conditions had begun to improve. Many pious Catholics themselves had started an agitation for reform, which in time would probably have eliminated most of the glaring evils in the system. But as so often happens in the case of revolutions, the improvement had come too late. Other forces more irresistible in character had been gradually gathering momentum. Conspicuous among these was the growing reaction against late medieval theology, with its elaborate sacramental theory, its belief in the necessity of good works to supplement faith, and its doctrine of divine authority in the hands of the priests.

Abuses not the primary causes of the Protestant Revolution

From preceding chapters the reader will recall that two different systems of theology had developed within the medieval Church.[2] The first was formulated mainly by followers of St. Augustine in the early Middle Ages, on the basis of teachings in the Pauline Epistles. It was predicated on the assumption of an omnipotent God, who sees the whole drama of the universe in the twinkling of an eye. Not even a sparrow falls to the ground except in accordance with the divine decree. Human nature is hopelessly depraved, and it is therefore as impossible for man to perform good works as for thistles to bring forth figs. Man is absolutely dependent upon God, not only for grace to keep him from sin but also for his fate after death. Only those mortals can be saved whom God for reasons of His own has predestined to inherit eternal life. Such in its barest outlines was the system of doctrine commonly known as Augustinianism. It was a theology well suited to the age of chaos which followed the breakup of the classical world. Men in this time were prone to fatalism and otherworldliness, for they seemed to be at the mercy of forces beyond their control. But the system never wholly died out. It was preserved intact for centuries in certain areas, especially in parts of Germany, where the progress of late medieval civilization was comparatively slow. To Luther and many of his followers it seemed the most logical interpretation of Christian belief.

The clash between two different systems of theology: the Augustinian system

[1] Preserved Smith, *The Age of the Reformation*, pp. 495–96.
[2] See the chapters on The Early Middle Ages and The Later Middle Ages: Religious and Intellectual Developments.

The late medi-
eval theology of
Peter Lombard
and St. Thomas
Aquinas

With the growth of a more abundant life in the cities of southern and western Europe, it was natural that the pessimistic philosophy of Augustinianism should have been replaced by a system which would restore to man some measure of pride in his own estate. The change was accelerated also by the growth of a dominant Church organization. The theology of Augustinianism, by placing man's fate entirely in the hands of God, had seemed to imply that the functions of an organized Church were practically unnecessary. Certainly no sinner could rely upon the ministrations of priests to improve his chances of salvation, since those who were to be saved had already been "elected" by God from all eternity. The new system of belief was finally crystallized in the writings of Peter Lombard and St. Thomas Aquinas in the twelfth and thirteenth centuries. Its cardinal premise was the idea that man had been endowed by God with freedom of will, with power to choose the good and avoid the evil. However, man could not make this choice entirely unaided, for without the support of heavenly grace he would be likely to fall into sin. It was therefore necessary for him to receive the sacraments, the indispensable means for communicating the grace of God to man. Of the seven sacraments of the Church, the three most important for the layman were baptism, penance, and the Eucharist. The first wiped out the stain of previous sin; the second absolved the contrite sinner from guilt; the third was especially significant for its effect in renewing the saving grace of Christ's sacrifice on the cross. Except in emergencies, none of the sacraments could be administered by persons outside the ranks of the priesthood. The members of the clergy, having inherited the power of the keys from the Apostle Peter, alone had the authority to cooperate with God in forgiving sins and in performing the miracle of the Eucharist, whereby the bread and wine were transubstantiated into the body and blood of the Savior.

The Protestant
Revolution a re-
bellion against
the late medi-
eval system of
theology

The Protestant Revolution was in large measure a rebellion against the second of these systems of theology. Although the doctrines of Peter Lombard and St. Thomas Aquinas had virtually become part of the theology of the Church, they had never been universally accepted. To Christians who had been brought up under Augustinian influence, they seemed to detract from the sovereignty of God and to contradict the plain teachings of Paul that man's will is in bondage and his nature unspeakably vile. Worse still, in the opinion of these critics, was the fact that the new theology greatly strengthened the authority of the priesthood. In sum, what the Reformers wanted was a return to a more primitive Christianity than that which had prevailed since the thirteenth century. Any doctrine or practice not expressly sanctioned in the Scriptures, especially in the Pauline Epistles, or not recognized by the Fathers of the Church, they were strongly inclined to reject. It was for this reason that they condemned not only the theory of the priesthood and the sacramental system of the Church, but also such medieval additions to the faith as the worship of the Virgin, the belief in purgatory, the invocation of saints, the veneration of relics, and the rule of celibacy for the clergy. Motives of rationalism or skepticism had comparatively little to do with it. While it is true that Luther ridiculed the worship of relics as a form of superstition, in the main the early Protestants were even more suspicious of reason than the Catholics. Their religious ideal rested upon the Augustinian dogmas of original sin, the total depravity of man, predestination, and the bondage of the will—which were certainly more difficult to justify on a rational basis than the liberalized teachings of St. Thomas.

A few remaining religious causes deserve at least passing mention. One was the decline of respect for the papacy in consequence of the so-called "Babylonian Captivity" of the papacy. The "Babylonian Captivity" grew out of a quarrel between King Philip IV of France and Pope Boniface VIII at the beginning of the fourteenth century. The soldiers of the king arrested the Pope, and soon afterward Boniface died from the effects of the humiliation. A short time later King Philip's own candidate was elected to St. Peter's throne, and the papal capital was transferred to Avignon in the Rhone valley, where it remained for nearly seventy years. Surrounded by French influences, the Popes who reigned at Avignon were unable to escape the charge of subservience to French interests. In the minds of many Christians the papacy had ceased to be an international institution and had been degraded into the mere plaything of a secular power. In 1378 the head of the Church suffered an even greater loss of prestige. An effort to restore the papacy to its original capital led to the election of two Popes, one at Avignon and one at Rome, each loudly proclaiming himself the rightful successor of the Apostle Peter. The resulting division of the Church into two factions, supporting respectively the claims of the French and Italian Popes, is known as the Great Schism. Though finally healed by the Council of Constance in 1417, its effect in weakening the position of the papacy could hardly be overestimated.

Influence of the "Babylonian Captivity" of the papacy and the Great Schism

Still another factor of some importance in hastening the Protestant Revolution was the influence of the mystics and early reformers. For more than two centuries before the time of Luther, mysticism had become one of the most popular forms of religious expression in northern Europe. And it is not without significance that the vast majority of the mystics were Germans or natives of the Low Countries. Though none of the mystics preached open rebellion against the Catholic system, they were vehemently opposed to the ritualistic route to salvation sponsored by the medieval Church. Their version of religion was one in which the individual would attain the highest heaven through extinction of selfish desires and absolute surrender of the soul to God. No sacraments or priestly miracles would be necessary. Faith and a deep

Influence of the mystics and early reformers

St. John Lateran, the Pope's Cathedral in Rome. The "Mother Church" of Catholic Christendom, it derives its name from Plautius Lateranus, a rich nobleman whose property in this area was confiscated by Nero.

emotional piety would accomplish more wonders in reconciling sinful man to God than all the Masses in the calendar of the Church. Along with the mystics a number of pre-Reformation reformers exerted considerable influence in preparing the ground for the Protestant Revolt. At the end of the fourteenth century an Oxford professor by the name of John Wyclif launched an attack upon the Catholic system which anticipated much of the thunder of Luther and Calvin. He denounced the immorality of the clergy, condemned indulgences and the temporal power of the Church, recommended marriage of the clergy, insisted upon the supreme authority of the Scriptures as the source of belief, and denied transubstantiation. Most of Wyclif's teachings were ultimately carried to central Europe by Czech students from Oxford. They were actively propagated in Bohemia by John Huss, who was burned at the stake in 1415. Luther acknowledged his deep indebtedness to the Bohemian martyr.

As a political movement the Protestant Revolt was mainly the result of two developments: first, the growth of a national consciousness in northern Europe; and second, the rise of absolute monarchs. Ever since the late Middle Ages there had been a growing spirit of independence among many of the peoples outside of Italy. They had come to regard their own national life as unique and to resent interference from any external source. Although they were not nationalists in the modern sense, they tended to view the Pope as a foreigner who had no right to meddle with local affairs in England, France, or Germany. This feeling was manifested in England as early as the middle of the fourteenth century, when the famous Statutes of Provisors and Praemunire were passed. The first prohibited appointments by the Pope to Church offices in England; the

The political causes of the Protestant Revolution: the growth of national consciousness

second forbade the appeal of cases from the English courts to Rome. A law more extreme than either of these was issued by the king of France in 1438. The French law practically abolished all papal authority in the country, including the appointive authority and the right to raise revenue. To the civil magistrates was given the power to regulate religious affairs within their own districts. In Germany, despite the fact that there was no solid political unity, national feeling was by no means absent. It expressed itself in violent attacks upon the clergy by the Imperial Diet and in numerous decrees by the rulers of separate states prohibiting ecclesiastical appointments and the sale of indulgences without their consent.

The growth of a national consciousness in all of these countries went hand in hand with the rise of absolute monarchs. Indeed, it would be difficult to say how much of the sense of nationality was spontaneous and how much of it was stimulated by ambitious princes intent upon increasing their power. At any rate it is certain that the claims of rulers to absolute authority were bound to result in defiance of Rome. No despot could be expected to tolerate long the exclusion of religion from his sphere of control. He could not *be* a despot so long as there was a double jurisdiction within his realm. The appetite of princes for control over the Church was whetted originally by the revival of the Roman law, with its doctrine that the people had delegated *all* of their power to the secular ruler. From this doctrine it was a comparatively easy step to the idea that all of the Pope's authority could be properly assumed by the head of the state. But whatever the reasons for its growth, there can be no doubt that the ambition of secular princes to establish churches under their own control was a primary cause of the mounting antagonism against Rome.

Historians disagree as to the importance of economic causation of the Protestant Revolution. Those who conceive of the movement as primarily a religious one think of the sixteenth century as a period of profound and agonized concern over spiritual problems. Such a condition may well have characterized the mass of the people. But it does not alter the fact that in the sixteenth century, as in all ages, there were ruling groups greedy for wealth and quite willing to use and even to cultivate mass ideologies for their own advantage. Prominent among the economic objectives of such groups were acquisition of the wealth of the Church and elimination of papal taxation. In the course of its history from the beginning of the Middle Ages, the Church had grown into a vast economic empire. It was by far the largest landowner in western Europe, to say nothing of its enormous movable wealth in the form of rich furnishings, jewels, precious metals, and the like. Some of these possessions had been acquired by the Church through grants by kings and nobles, but most of them came from the gifts and bequests of pious citizens. Religious restrictions on taxation were also a galling grievance to

The rise of absolute monarchs

Economic causes: the desire to confiscate the wealth of the Catholic Church

549

secular rulers. Kings, panting for big armies and navies, had an urgent need for more revenue. But Catholic law prohibited the taxing of Church property. The exemption of episcopal and monastic property from taxation meant a heavier burden on the possessions of individual owners, especially on the property of merchants and bankers. Moreover, the lesser nobles in Germany were being threatened with extinction on account of the collapse of the manorial economy. Many of them looked with covetous eyes upon the lands of the Church. If only some excuse could be found for expropriating these, their difficult situation might be relieved.

Resentment against papal taxation

Papal taxation, by the eve of the Protestant Revolution, had assumed a baffling variety of irritating forms. The most nearly universal, if not the most burdensome, was the so-called *Peter's pence,* an annual levy on every household in Christendom.[3] It must be understood that this tax was in addition to the *tithe,* which was supposed to be one-tenth of every Christian's income paid for the support of the parish church. Then there were the innumerable fees paid into the papal treasury for indulgences, dispensations, appeals of judicial decisions, and so on. In a very real sense the moneys collected for the sale of Church offices and the *annates,* or commissions levied on the first year's income of every bishop and priest, were also forms of papal taxation, since the officials who paid them eventually reimbursed themselves through increased collections from the people. But the main objection to these taxes was not that they were so numerous and burdensome. The real basis of grievance against the papal levies was their effect in draining the northern countries of so much of their wealth for the enrichment of Italy. Economically the situation was almost exactly the same as if the nations of northern Europe had been conquered by a foreign prince and tribute imposed upon them. Some Germans and Englishmen were scandalized also by the fact that most of the money collected was not being spent for religious purposes, but was being squandered by worldly Popes to maintain luxurious courts. The reason for the resentment, however, was probably as much financial as moral.

Conflicts between middle-class ambitions and the ascetic ideals of the Church

A third important economic cause of the Protestant Revolution was the conflict between the ambitions of the new middle class and the ascetic ideals of medieval Christianity. It was shown in a preceding chapter that the Catholic philosophers of the later Middle Ages had developed an elaborate theory designed for the guidance of the Christian in matters of production and trade.[4] This theory was founded upon the assumption that business for the sake of profit is

---

[3] Peter's pence derived its name from the fact that it was a tax of one penny. But the English penny at the end of the Middle Ages was the equivalent in purchasing power of slightly more than one dollar of our money. H. E. Barnes, *An Economic History of the Western World,* p. 121.

[4] See the chapter on The Later Middle Ages: Political and Economic institutions.

essentially immoral. No one has a right to any more than a reasonable wage for the service he renders to society. All wealth acquired in excess of this amount should be given to the Church to be distributed for the benefit of the needy. The merchant or craftsman who strives to get rich at the expense of the people is really no better than a common thief. To gain an advantage over a rival in business by cornering the market or beating down wages is contrary to all law and morality. Equally sinful is the damnable practice of usury—the charging of interest on loans where no actual risk is involved. This is sheer robbery, for it deprives the person who uses the money of earnings that are justly his; it is contrary to nature, for it enables the man who lends the money to live without labor.

While it is far from true that these doctrines were universally honored even by the Church itself, they nevertheless remained an integral part of the Catholic ideal, at least to the end of the Middle Ages. Even to this day they have not been entirely abandoned, as our study of liberal Catholicism in the nineteenth and twentieth centuries will show.[5] However, the age of the Renaissance was accompanied by the growth of an economic pattern distinctly incompatible with most of these doctrines. A ruthless, dynamic capitalism, based upon the principle of "dog eat dog," was beginning to supplant the old static economy of the medieval guilds. No longer were merchants and manufacturers content with a mere "wage" for the services they rendered to society. They demanded profits, and they could not see that it was any business of the Church to decide what a man's earnings should be. Wages were fit only for hirelings, who had neither the wit nor the industry to go after the big rewards. In addition to all this, the growth of banking meant an even more violent conflict with the ascetic ideal of the Church. As long as the business of moneylending was in the hands of Jews and Moslems, it mattered little that usury should be branded as a sin. But now that Christians were piling up riches by financing the exploits of kings and merchants, the shoe was on another foot. The new crop of bankers resented being told that their lucrative trade in cash was contrary to the laws of God. This seemed to them an attempt of spokesmen for an outmoded past to dictate the standards for a new age of progress. But how was it that Italy did not break with the Catholic Church in view of the extensive development of banking and commerce in such cities as Florence, Genoa, Milan, and Venice? Perhaps one explanation is to be found in the fact that such business activities had taken earlier and deeper roots in Italy than in most parts of Germany. They had been established for so long a time that any possible conflict between them and religious ideals had been largely ignored. Besides, the religion of many Italians, espe-

Effects of the rise of competitive capitalism

---

[5] See the paragraph on Christian Socialism in the chapter on Critics and Apologists of Industrialization.

cially during the Renaissance period, tended to approximate that of the ancient Romans; it was external and mechanical rather than profoundly spiritual. To many northern Europeans, by contrast, religion had a deeper significance. It was a system of dogmas and commandments to be observed literally under pain of the awful judgment of a wrathful God. They were, therefore, more likely to be disturbed by inconsistencies between worldly practices and the doctrines of the faith.

The full story of why the Protestant Revolution began in Germany is so complex that only a few of the possible reasons can be suggested as topics for the student to ponder. Was Germany relatively more backward than most other areas of western Europe? Had the Renaissance touched her so lightly that medieval religiosity remained quite pervasive? Or did economic factors operate more strongly in Germany than elsewhere? The Church in Germany held an enormous proportion of the best agricultural lands, and evidence exists that the country was seething with discontent on account of a too rapid transition from a feudal society to an economy of profits and wages. It seems to be true, finally, that Germany was the victim of Catholic abuses to a greater extent than most other countries. How crucial was the shock resulting from these is impossible to say, but at least they provided the immediate impetus for the outbreak of the Lutheran revolt. Unlike England and France, Germany had no powerful king to defend her interests against the papacy. The country was weak and divided. At least partly for this reason, Pope Leo X selected German territory as the most likely field for the sale of indulgences.

Why the Protestant Revolution began in Germany

I. THE LUTHERAN REVOLT IN GERMANY By the dawn of the sixteenth century Germany was ripe for religious revolution. All that was necessary was to find a leader who could unite the dissatisfied elements and give a suitable theological gloss to their grievances. Such a leader was not long in appearing. His name was Martin Luther, and he was born in Thuringia in 1483. His parents were originally peasants, but his father had left the soil soon after his marriage to work in the mines of Mansfeld. Here he managed to become moderately prosperous and served in the village council. Nevertheless, young Martin's early environment was far from ideal. He was whipped at home for trivial offenses until he bled, and his mind was filled with hideous terrors of demons and witches. Some of these superstitions clung to him until the end of his life. His parents intended that he should become a lawyer, and with this end in view they placed him at the age of eighteen in the University of Erfurt. During his first four years at the university, Luther worked hard, gaining more than an ordinary reputation as a scholar. But in 1505, while returning from a visit to his home, he was overtaken by a violent storm and felled to the ground by a bolt of lightning. In terror lest an angry God strike him dead, he vowed to St. Anne to become

Martin Luther by Lucas Cranach the Elder, 1520

a monk. Soon afterward he entered the Augustinian monastery at Erfurt.

Here he gave himself up to earnest reflection on the state of his soul. Obsessed with the idea that his sins were innumerable, he strove desperately to attain a goal of spiritual peace. He engaged in long vigils and went for days on end without a morsel of food. But the more he fasted and tortured himself, the more his anguish and depression increased. Told that the way of salvation lies in love of God, he was ready to give up in despair. How could he love a Being who is not even just, who saves only those whom it pleases Him to save? "Love Him?" he said to himself, "I do not love Him. I hate Him." But in time, as he pondered the Scriptures, especially the story of the Crucifixion, he gained a new insight into the mysteries of the Christian theology. He was profoundly impressed by the humiliation of the Savior's death on the cross. For the benefit of sinful humanity, the Christ, the God-man, had shared the fate of common criminals. Why had He done so except out of love for His creatures? The God of the storm whose chief attribute appeared to be anger had revealed Himself as a Father who pities His children. Here was a miracle which no human reason could understand. It must be taken on faith; and by faith alone, Luther concluded, can man be justified in the sight of God. This doctrine of justification by faith alone, as opposed to salvation by "good works," quickly became the central doctrine of the Lutheran theology.

But long before Luther had completed his theological system, he was called to lecture on Aristotle and the Bible at the University of Wittenberg, which had recently been founded by Frederick the Wise of Saxony. While serving in this capacity, he was confronted by an event which furnished the spark for the Protestant Revolution. In 1517 an unprincipled Dominican friar by the name of Tetzel appeared in Germany as a hawker of indulgences. Determined to raise as much money as possible for Pope Leo X and the Archbishop

The doctrine of justification by faith alone

Luther's revolt against the sale of indulgences

Luther Preaching. With one hand he points to popes, monks, and cardinals going down hell's mouth. Hell is a beast with a snout, tusk, and eye. With the other hand, Luther points to the crucifix. The Lord's Supper is being administered, both the bread and the wine, to the laity. The chalice on the table emphasizes the evangelical practice of giving the cup to the laity.

of Mainz who had employed him, Tetzel deliberately represented the indulgences as tickets of admission to heaven. Though forbidden to enter Saxony, he came to the borders of that state, and many natives of Wittenberg rushed out to buy salvation at so attractive a price. Luther was appalled by such brazen deception of ignorant people. Accordingly, he drew up a set of ninety-five theses or statements attacking the sale of indulgences, and posted them, after the manner of the time, on the door of the castle church on October 31, 1517. Later he had them printed and sent to his friends in a number of cities. Soon it became evident that the Ninety-five Theses had voiced the sentiments of a nation. All over Germany, Luther was hailed as a leader whom God had raised to break the power of an arrogant and hypocritical clergy. A violent reaction against the sale of indulgences was soon in full swing. Tetzel was mobbed and driven from the country. The revolt against Rome had begun.

The condemnation and excommunication of Luther

With the revenue from indulgences cut off, it was inevitable that the Pope should take action. Early in 1518 he commanded the general of the Augustinian order to make the rebellious friar recant. Luther not only refused but published a sermon stating his views more strongly than ever. Forced by his critics to answer questions on many points other than indulgences, he gradually came to realize that his own religion was utterly irreconcilable with that of the Roman Church. There was no alternative except to break with the Catholic faith entirely. In 1520 his teachings were formally condemned in a bull promulgated by Leo X, and he was ordered to recant within sixty days or be dealt with as a heretic. Luther replied by publicly burning the Pope's proclamation. For this he was excommunicated and ordered to be turned over to the secular arm for punishment. Germany at this time was still under the technical rule of the Holy Roman Empire. Charles V, who had recently been elevated to the throne of this ramshackle state, was anxious to be rid of the insolent rebel at once, but he dared not act without the approval of the Imperial Diet. Accordingly, in 1521, Luther was summoned to appear before a meeting of this body at Worms. Since many of the princes and electors who composed the Diet were themselves hostile toward the Church, nothing in particular was done, despite Luther's stubborn refusal to retract any of the things he had said. Finally, after a number of the members had gone home, the Emperor forced through an edict branding the obstreperous friar as an outlaw. But Luther had already been hidden away in the castle of his friend, the Elector of Saxony. Here he remained until all danger of arrest by the Emperor's soldiers had passed. Charles soon afterward withdrew to conduct his war with France, and the Edict of Worms was never enforced.

Thenceforth until his death in 1546 Luther was occupied with his work of building an independent German church. Despite the fundamental conflict between his own beliefs and Catholic theology, he nevertheless retained a good many of the elements of the Roman system. With the passing of the years he became more conservative than many of his own followers and compared some of them to Judas betraying his Master. Though he had originally denounced transubstantiation, he eventually came around to adopting a doctrine which bore at least a superficial resemblance to the Catholic theory. He denied, however, that any change in the substance of the bread and wine occurs as the result of a priestly miracle. The function of the clergyman is simply to *reveal* the presence of God in the bread and wine. Still, the changes he made were drastic enough to preserve the revolutionary character of the new religion. He substituted German for Latin in the services of the church. He rejected the entire ecclesiastical system of Pope, archbishops, bishops, and priests as custodians of the keys to the kingdom of heaven. By abolishing monasticism and insisting upon the right of priests to marry, he went far toward destroying the barrier which had separated clergy from laity and given the former their special status as representatives of God on earth. He recognized only baptism and the Eucharist as sacraments, and he denied that even these had any supernatural effect in bringing down grace from heaven. Since he continued to emphasize faith rather than good works as the road to salvation, he naturally discarded such formalized practices as fasts, pilgrimages, the veneration of relics, and the invocation of saints. On the other hand, the doctrines of predestination and the supreme authority of the Scriptures were given in the new religion a higher place than they had ever enjoyed in the old. Last of all, Luther abandoned the Catholic idea that the Church should be supreme over the state. Instead of having bishops subject to the Pope as the Vicar of Christ, he organized his church under superintendents who were essentially agents of the government.

Of course, Luther was not alone responsible for the success of the Protestant Revolution. The overthrow of Catholicism in Germany was also abetted by the outbreak of social revolt. In 1522–1523 there occurred a ferocious rebellion of the knights. These petty nobles were being impoverished by competition from the great estates and by the change to a capitalist economy. They saw as the chief cause of their misery the concentration of landed wealth in the hands of the great princes of the Church. Obsessed with national sentiments they dreamed of a united Germany free from the domination of powerful landlords and grasping priests. The leaders of the movement were Ulrich von Hutten, who had turned from a humanist into a fierce partisan of Luther, and Franz von Sickingen, a notorious robber baron and soldier of fortune. To these men the gospel of Luther seemed to provide an excellent program for a war on behalf of German liberty. Although their rebellion was speedily crushed by the armies of the archbishops and richer nobles, it apparently had considerable effect

Founding the Lutheran church; Luther's doctrines

The outbreak of social revolution; the revolt of the knights

555

in persuading the pillars of the old regime that too much resistance to the Lutheran movement would scarcely be wise.

The revolt of the knights was followed by a much more violent uprising of the lower classes in 1524–1525. Though most who took part were peasants, a great many poor workmen from the cities were attracted to the movement also. The causes of this second rebellion were somewhat similar to those of the first: the rising cost of living, the concentration of holdings of land, and the religious radicalism inspired by Luther's teachings. But the peasants and urban workers were stirred to action by many other factors as well. The decay of the feudal regime had eliminated the paternal relationship between noble and serf. In its place had grown up a mere cash nexus between employer and worker. The sole obligation now of the upper classes was to pay a wage. When sickness or unemployment struck, the laborer had to make shift with his slender resources as best he could. Furthermore, most of the old privileges which the serf had enjoyed on the manorial estate, of pasturing his flocks on the common lands and gathering wood in the forest, were being rapidly abolished. To make matters worse, landlords were attempting to meet advancing prices by exacting higher rents from the peasants. Finally, the lower classes were angered by the fact that the revival of the Roman law had the effect of bolstering property rights and of strengthening the power of the state to protect the interests of the rich.

Many of the downtrodden folk who participated in the so-called Peasants' Revolt belonged to a religious sect known as the Anabaptists. The name means "re-baptizers," and was derived from the fact that the members of the sect held infant baptism to be ineffectual and insisted that the rite should be administered only when the individual had reached the age of reason. But a belief in adult baptism was not really their principal doctrine. The Anabaptists were extreme individualists in religion. Luther's teaching that every man has a right to follow the dictates of his own conscience they took exactly as it stood. Not only did they reject the Catholic theory of the priesthood, but they denied the necessity of any clergy at all, maintaining that every individual should follow the guidance of the "inner light." They refused to admit that God's revelation to man had ceased with the writing of the last book of the New Testament, but they insisted that He continues to speak directly to certain of His chosen followers. They attached much importance to literal interpretation of the Bible, even of its most occult portions. They believed that the church should be a community of saints and required of their followers abstention from lying, profanity, gluttony, lewdness, and drinking intoxicating liquors. Many of the members looked forward to the early destruction of this world and the establishment of Christ's kingdom of justice and peace, in which they would have a prominent place. But the Anabaptists were not merely a group of religious extremists; they represented as well the most radical social tendencies of their time. Though it is certainly an exaggeration to call them communists, they did denounce the accumulation of wealth and taught that it was the duty of Christians to share their goods with one another. In addition, they declined to recognize any distinctions of rank or class, declaring all men equal in the sight of God. Many also abominated the taking of oaths, condemned military service, and refused to pay taxes to governments that engaged in war. They abstained in general from political life and demanded the complete separation of church and state. Their doctrines represented the extreme manifestation of the revolutionary fervor generated by the Protestant movement.

The Peasants' Revolt of 1524–1525 began in southern Germany and spread rapidly to the north and west until most of the country was involved. At first it had more of the character of a strike than a revolution. The rebels contented themselves with drafting petitions and attempting peaceably to persuade their masters to grant them relief from oppression. But before many months had passed, the movement came under the control of such fanatics as Thomas

The Peasants'
Revolt of
1524–1525

Pages from a Bible Translated by Martin Luther, 1534. Left: **The** title page. Right: An illustration showing several episodes from the story of Jonah in a single composite picture.

The Siege of Münster in 1534

Münzer, who urged the use of fire and sword against the wicked
nobles and clergy. In the spring of 1525 the misguided rustics began
plundering and burning cloisters and castles and even murdering
some of their more hated opponents. The nobles now turned against
them with fiendish fury, slaughtering indiscriminately both those
who resisted and those who were helpless. Strange as it may seem,
the lords were encouraged in this savagery by several of the Reformers, including the great Luther himself. In a pamphlet *Against
the Thievish, Murderous Hordes of Peasants* he urged everyone
who could to hunt the rebels down like mad dogs, to "strike, strangle, stab secretly or in public, and let him remember that nothing
can be more poisonous, harmful, or devilish than a man in rebellion." [6] To Luther's credit, it should perhaps be added that he
feared anarchy more than he did the particular doctrines of the
Anabaptists. He believed that the use of force by anyone except the
lawful authorities would result in the destruction of the social order.

But the brutal suppression of the Peasants' Revolt did not mark
the end of revolutionary activities on the part of the submerged
classes. In 1534 a group of Anabaptists gained control of the episcopal city of Münster in Westphalia. Thousands of their fellow believers from the surrounding country came pouring in, and Münster
became a New Jerusalem where all of the accumulated vagaries of
the lunatic fringe of the movement were put into practice. The
property of unbelievers was confiscated, and polygamy was introduced. A certain John of Leyden assumed the title of king, proclaiming himself the successor of David with a mission to conquer

[6] Quoted by H. S. Lucas, *The Renaissance and the Reformation,* p. 457.

the world and destroy the heathen. But after a little more than a year of this, Münster was recaptured by its bishop, and the leaders of Zion were put to death by horrible tortures. This second disaster proved to be the turning point in the revolt of the have-nots of the sixteenth century. Convinced of the futility of violence, they now abandoned the fanatical dogmas of their fallen leaders and returned to the religious quietism of earlier years. Most of the radical economic teachings were also dropped. Some of the survivors of the persecutions now joined the sect of Mennonites, so called from Menno Simons (1492–1559), whose teachings were partly derived from those of the original Anabaptists. Others fled to England to become the spiritual ancestors of the Quakers.

II. THE ZWINGLIAN AND CALVINIST REVOLTS IN SWITZERLAND The special form of Protestantism developed by Luther did not prove to be particularly popular beyond its native environment. Outside of Germany, Lutheranism became the official religion only in Denmark, Norway, and Sweden. But the force of the Lutheran revolt made itself felt in a number of other lands. Such was especially the case in Switzerland, where national consciousness had been gathering strength for centuries. At the close of the Middle Ages the gallant herdsmen and peasants of the Swiss cantons had challenged the right of the Austrians to rule over them, and finally in 1499 had compelled the Emperor Maximilian to recognize their independence, not only of the house of Hapsburg but of the Holy Roman Empire as well. Having thrown off the yoke of a foreign Emperor, the Swiss were not likely to submit indefinitely to an alien Pope. Moreover, the cities of Zürich, Basel, Berne, and Geneva had grown into flourishing centers of trade. Their populations were dominated by solid burghers who were becoming increasingly contemptuous of the Catholic ideal of glorified poverty. Here also northern humanism had found welcome lodgment in cultivated minds, with the effect of creating a healthy distrust of priestly superstitions. Erasmus had lived for a number of years in Basel. Lastly, Switzerland had been plucked by the indulgence peddlers to an extent only less grievous than that in Germany, while the city of Berne had been the scene of some particularly flagrant monkish frauds.

The father of the Protestant Revolution in Switzerland was Ulrich Zwingli (1484–1531). Only a few weeks younger than Luther, he was the son of a well-to-do magistrate, who was able to provide him with an excellent education. As a student he devoted nearly all of his time to philosophy and literature, with no interest in religion save in the practical reforms of the Christian humanists. Although he took holy orders at the age of twenty-two, his purpose in entering the priesthood was mainly the opportunity it would give him to cultivate his literary tastes. Ultimately, he turned his interest to religion and devoted his energies to reform of the Church. He accepted nearly all of the teachings of Luther except that he regarded

Causes of the Protestant Revolution in Switzerland

Ulrich Zwingli. A sixteenth-century woodcut.

559

the bread and wine as mere symbols of the body and blood, and he reduced the sacrament of Holy Communion to a simple memorial service. So ably did he marshal the anti-Catholic forces that by 1528 nearly all of northern Switzerland had deserted the ancient faith.

From the northern cantons the Protestant Revolution in Switzerland spread to Geneva. This beautiful city, located on a lake of the same name near the French border, had the doubtful advantage of a double government. The people owed allegiance to two feudal suzerains, the local bishop and the Count of Savoy. When these high-born chieftains conspired to make their power more absolute, the citizens rebelled against them. The result was their expulsion from the town about 1530 and the establishment of a free republic. But the movement could hardly have been successful without some aid from the northern cantons. Thus it was not long until Protestant preachers from Zürich and Berne began arriving in Geneva.

The spread of
the Protestant
Revolution to
Geneva

It was soon after these events that John Calvin (1509–1564) arrived in Geneva. Although destined to play so prominent a role in the history of Switzerland, he was not a native of that country but of France. He was born at Noyon in Picardy. His mother died when he was very young, and his father, who did not like children, turned him over to the care of an aristocratic friend. For his higher education he was sent to the University of Paris, where, because of his bilious disposition and fault-finding manner, he was dubbed "the accusative case." Later he shifted at his father's wish to study of law at Orléans. Here he came under the influence of disciples of Luther, evidently to a sufficient extent to cause him to be suspected of heresy. Consequently, in 1534, when the government began an attack on the wavering ones, Calvin fled to Switzerland. He settled for a time in Basel and then moved on to Geneva, which was still in the throes of political revolution. He began preaching and organizing at once, and by 1541 both government and religion had fallen completely under his sway. Until his death from asthma and dyspepsia in 1564 he ruled the city with a rod of iron. History contains few examples of men more dour in temperament and more stubbornly convinced of the rightness of their own ideas.

John Calvin

Under Calvin's rule Geneva was transformed into a religious oligarchy. The supreme authority was vested in the Congregation of the Clergy, who prepared all legislation and submitted it to the Consistory to be ratified. The latter body, composed, in addition to the clergy, of twelve elders representing the people, had as its principal function the supervision of public and private morals. This function was carried out, not merely by the punishment of antisocial conduct but by a persistent snooping into the private life of every individual. The city was divided into districts, and a committee of the Consistory visited each household without warning to conduct an in-

Calvin's rule at
Geneva

quisition into the habits of its members. Even the mildest forms of human folly were strictly prohibited. Dancing, card-playing, attending the theater, working or playing on the Sabbath—all were outlawed as works of the Devil. Innkeepers were forbidden to allow anyone to consume food or drink without first saying grace, or to permit any patron to sit up after nine o'clock unless he was spying on the conduct of others. Needless to say, penalties were severe. Not only murder and treason were classified as capital crimes, but also adultery, witchcraft, blasphemy, and heresy; and the last of these especially was susceptible to a broad interpretation. During the first four years after Calvin became ruler of Geneva, there were no fewer than fifty-eight executions out of a total population of only 16,000.[7] The good accomplished by all of this harshness seems to have been small indeed. There were more cases of vice in Geneva after the Reformation than before.[8]

The essentials of Calvin's theology are contained in his *Institutes of the Christian Religion*, which was published originally in 1536 and revised and enlarged several times thereafter. His ideas resemble those of St. Augustine more than any other theologian. He conceived of the universe as utterly dependent upon the will of an Almighty God, who created all things for His greater glory. Because of Adam's transgression all men are sinners by nature, bound hand and foot to an evil inheritance they cannot escape. Nevertheless, God for reasons of His own has predestined some for eternal salvation and damned all the rest to the torments of hell. Nothing that human beings may do can alter their fate; their souls are stamped with God's blessing or curse before they are born. But this did not mean, in Calvin's opinion, that the Christian could be indifferent to his conduct on earth. If he were among the elect, God would have implanted in him the desire to live right. Abstemious conduct is a sign, though not an infallible one, that he who practices it has been chosen to sit at the throne of glory. Public profession of faith and participation in the sacraments are also presumptive evidences of election to be saved. But most of all, the Calvinists required an active life of piety and good morality as a solemn obligation resting upon members of the Christian Commonwealth. Like the ancient Hebrews, they conceived of themselves as chosen instruments of God with a mission to help in the fulfillment of His purposes on earth. Their duty was not to strive for their soul's salvation but for the glory of God. Thus it will be seen that the Calvinist system did not encourage its followers to sit with folded hands serene in the knowledge that their fate was sealed. No religion has fostered a more abundant zeal in the conquest of nature, in missionary activity,

Calvin's theology

[7] Preserved Smith, *The Age of the Reformation*, p. 171.
[8] *Ibid.*, p. 174.

561

or in the struggle against political tyranny. Doubtless the reason lies in the Calvinist's belief that as the chosen instrument of God he must play a part in the drama of the universe worthy of his exalted status. And with the Lord on his side he was not easily frightened by whatever lions lurked in his path.

The religion of Calvin differed from that of Luther in a number of ways. First, it was more legalistic. Whereas the Wittenberg Reformer had emphasized the guidance of individual conscience, the dictator of Geneva stressed the sovereignty of law. He thought of God as a mighty legislator who had handed down a body of rules in the Scriptures which must be followed to the letter. Secondly, the religion of Calvin was more nearly an Old Testament faith than that of Luther. This can be illustrated in the attitude of the two men toward Sabbath observance. Luther's conception of Sunday was similar to that which prevails in modern Continental Europe. He insisted, of course, that his followers should attend church, but he did not demand that during the remainder of the day they should refrain from all pleasure or work. Calvin, on the other hand, revived the old Jewish Sabbath with its strict taboos against anything faintly resembling worldliness. In the third place, the religion of Geneva was more closely associated with the ideals of the new capitalism. Luther's sympathies lay with the nobles, and on at least one occasion he sharply censured the tycoons of finance for their greed. Calvin sanctified the ventures of the trader and the moneylender and gave an exalted place in his ethical system to the business virtues of thrift and diligence. Finally, Calvinism as compared to Lutheranism represented a more radical phase of the Protestant Revolution. As we have seen, the Wittenberg friar retained a good many features of Roman worship and even some Catholic dogmas. Calvin rejected everything he could think of that smacked of "popery." The organization of his church was constructed in such a way as to exclude all traces of the episcopal system. Congregations were to choose their own elders and preachers, while an association of ministers at the

*The religion of
Calvin com-
pared with
that of Luther*

*The Fury of the Reformation
Brandishing Its Three Main
Villains, Calvin, Luther, and
Beza.* Contemporary antire-
form woodcut.

top would govern the entire church. Ritual, instrumental music, stained glass windows, pictures, and images were ruthlessly eliminated, with the consequence that the religion was reduced to "four bare walls and a sermon." Even the observance of Christmas and Easter was sternly prohibited.

The popularity of Calvinism was not limited to Switzerland. It spread into most countries of western Europe where trade and finance had become leading pursuits. The Huguenots of France, the Puritans of England, the Presbyterians of Scotland, and the members of the Reformed church in Holland were all Calvinists. It was preeminently the religion of the bourgeoisie; though, of course, it drew converts from other strata as well. Its influence in molding the ethics of modern times and in bolstering the revolutionary courage of the middle class was enormous. Members of this faith had much to do with the initial revolts against despotism in England and France, to say nothing of their part in overthrowing Spanish tyranny in the Netherlands.

The spread of Calvinism

III. THE PROTESTANT REVOLUTION IN ENGLAND The original blow against the Roman Church in England was not struck by a religious enthusiast like Luther or Calvin but by the head of the government. This does not mean, however, that the English Reformation was exclusively a political movement. Henry VIII could not have succeeded in establishing an independent English church if such action had not had the endorsement of large numbers of his subjects. And there were plenty of reasons why this endorsement was readily given. Though the English had freed themselves in some measure from papal domination, national pride had reached such a point that any degree of subordination to Rome was resented. Besides, England had been the scene for some time of lively agitation for religious reform. The memory of Wyclif's scathing attacks upon the avarice of the priests, the temporal power of Popes and bishops, and the sacramental system of the Church had lingered since the fourteenth century. The influence of the Christian humanists, notably Sir Thomas More, in condemning the superstitions in Catholic worship, had also been a factor of considerable importance. Finally, soon after the outbreak of the Protestant Revolution in Germany, Lutheran ideas were brought into England by wandering preachers and through the circulation of printed tracts. As a result, the English monarch, in severing the ties with Rome, had no lack of sympathy from some of the most influential of his subjects.

Underlying causes of the Protestant Revolution in England

The clash with the Pope was precipitated by Henry VIII's domestic difficulties. For eighteen years he had been married to Catherine of Aragon and had only a sickly daughter to succeed him. The death of all the sons of this marriage in infancy was a grievous disappointment to the king, who desired a male heir to perpetuate the Tudor dynasty. But this was not all, for Henry later became deeply infatuated with the dark-eyed lady-in-waiting, Anne Boleyn, and determined to make her his queen. He therefore appealed in 1527 to Pope Clement VII for an annulment of the marriage to Catherine. The law of the Church did not sanction divorce, but it did provide that a marriage could be annulled if proof could be presented that conditions existing at the time of the marriage made it unlawful. Queen Catherine had previously been married to Henry's older brother, Arthur, who had died a few months after the ceremony was performed. Recalling this fact, Henry's lawyers found a passage in the Book of Leviticus which pronounced a curse of childlessness upon the man who should marry his deceased brother's wife. The Pope was now in a difficult position. If he rejected the king's appeal, England would probably be lost to the Catholic faith, for Henry was apparently firmly convinced that the Scriptural curse had blighted his chances of perpetuating his dynasty. On the other hand, if the Pope granted the annulment he would provoke the wrath of the Emperor Charles V, who was a nephew of Catherine. Charles had already invaded Italy and was threatening the Pope with a loss of his temporal power. There seemed nothing for Clement to do but to procrastinate. At first he made a pretense of having the question settled in England, and empowered his own legate and Cardinal Wolsey to hold a court of inquiry to determine whether the marriage to Catherine had been legal. After long delay the case was suddenly transferred to Rome. Henry lost patience and resolved to take matters into his own hands. In 1531 he convoked an assembly of the clergy and, by threatening to punish them for violating the Statute of Praemunire in submitting to the papal legate, he induced them to recognize himself as the head of the English church, "as far as the law of Christ allows." Next he persuaded Parliament to enact a series of laws abolishing all payments of revenue to the Pope and proclaiming the Anglican church an independent, national unit, subject to the exclusive authority of the king. By 1534 the last of the bonds uniting the English church to Rome had been cut.

But the enactments put through by Henry VIII did not really make England a Protestant country. Though the abolition of papal authority was followed by the gradual dissolution of the monasteries and confiscation of their wealth, the church remained Catholic in doctrine. The Six Articles, adopted by Parliament at the king's behest in 1539, left no room for doubt as to official orthodoxy. Auricular confession, Masses for the dead, and clerical celibacy were all confirmed; death by burning was made the penalty for denying the Catholic dogma of the Eucharist. Yet the influence of a minority of Protestants at this time cannot be ignored. Their numbers were steadily increasing, and during the reign of Henry's successor, Edward VI (1547–1553), they actually gained the ascendancy. Since the new king was only nine years old when he inherited the crown, it was inevitable that the policies of the government should be dictated by powers behind the throne. The men most active in this work were Thomas Cranmer, Archbishop of Canterbury, and the Dukes of Somerset and Northumberland, who successively dominated the council of regency. All three of these officials had strong Protestant leanings. As a result, the creeds and ceremonies of the Church of England were given some drastic revision. Priests were permitted to marry; English was substituted for Latin in the services; the use of images was abolished; and new articles of belief were drawn up repudiating all sacraments except baptism and the Lord's Supper and affirming the Lutheran dogma of justification by faith. When the youthful Edward died in 1553, it looked as if England had definitely entered the Protestant camp.

Surface appearances, however, are frequently deceiving. They were never more so than in England at the end of Edward's reign. The majority of the people had refused to be weaned away from the usages of their ancient faith, and a reaction had set in against the high-handed methods of the radical Protestants. Moreover, the English during the time of the Tudors had grown accustomed to obeying the will of their sovereign. It was an attitude fostered by national pride and the desire for order and prosperity. The successor of Edward VI was Mary (1553–1558), the forlorn and graceless daughter of Henry VIII and Catherine. It was inevitable that Mary should have been a Catholic, and that she should have abhorred the revolt against Rome, for the origin of the movement was painfully associated with her mother's sufferings. Consequently, it is not strange that upon coming to the throne she should have attempted to turn the clock back. Not only did she restore the celebration of the Mass and the rule of clerical celibacy, but she prevailed upon Parliament to vote the unconditional return of England to papal allegiance. But her policies ended in lamentable failure for several reasons. First of all, she fell into the same error as her predecessors in forcing through changes that were too radical for the temper of the times. The people of England were not ready for a Lutheran or Calvinist revolution, but neither were they in a mood to accept immediate subjection to Rome. Probably a more serious cause of her failure was her marriage to Philip, the ambitious heir to the Spanish throne. Her subjects feared that this union might lead to foreign complications, if not actual domination by Spain. When the queen allowed herself to be drawn into a war with France, in which England was compelled to surrender Calais, her last foothold on the Continent of Europe, the nation was almost ready for rebellion. Death ended Mary's inglorious reign in 1558.

The Catholic reaction under Mary

The question whether England was to be Catholic or Protestant was left to be settled by Mary's successor, her half-sister Elizabeth (1558–1603), daughter of the vivacious Anne Boleyn. Though reared as a Protestant, Elizabeth had no deep religious convictions. Her primary interest was statecraft, and she did not intend that her kingdom should be rent in twain by sectarian strife. Therefore she decided upon a policy of moderation, refusing to ally herself with either the

The Elizabethan compromise

extreme Catholics or the fanatical Protestants. So carefully did she hew to this line that for some years she deceived the Pope into thinking that she might turn Catholic. Nevertheless, she was enough of a nationalist to refuse even to consider a revival of allegiance to Rome. One of the first things she did after becoming queen was to order the passage of a new Act of Supremacy declaring the English sovereign to be the "supreme governor" of the independent Anglican church. The final settlement, completed about 1570, was a typical English compromise. The church was made Protestant, but certain articles of the creed were left vague enough so that a moderate Catholic might accept them without too great a shock to his conscience. Moreover, the episcopal form of organization was retained and much of the Catholic ritual. Long after Elizabeth's death this settlement remained in effect. Indeed, most elements in it have survived to this day. And it is a significant fact that the modern Church of England is broad enough to include within its ranks such diverse factions as the Anglo-Catholics, who differ from their Roman brethren only in rejecting papal supremacy, and the "low-church" Anglicans, who are as radical in their Protestantism as the Lutherans.

2. THE CATHOLIC REFORMATION

As noted at the beginning of this chapter, the Protestant Revolution was only one of the phases of the great movement known as the Reformation. The other was the Catholic Reformation, or the Counter Reformation as it used to be called, on the assumption that the primary purpose of its leaders was to cleanse the Catholic Church in order to check the growth of Protestantism. Modern historians have shown, however, that the begings of the movement for Catholic reform were entirely independent of the Protestant Revolt. In Spain, during the closing years of the fifteenth century, a religious revival inaugurated by Cardinal Ximenes, with the approval of the monarchy, stirred that country to the depths. Schools were established, abuses were eliminated from the monasteries, and priests were goaded into accepting their responsibilities as shepherds of their flocks. Though the movement was launched primarily for the purpose of strengthening the Church in the war against heretics and infidels, it nevertheless had considerable effect in regenerating the spiritual life of the nation. In Italy also, since the beginning of the sixteenth century, a number of earnest clerics had been laboring to make the priests of their Church more worthy of their Christian calling. The task was a difficult one on account of the paganism of the Renaissance and the example of profligacy set by the papal court. In spite of these obstacles the movement did lead to the founding of several religious orders dedicated to high ideals of piety and social service.

The beginnings of Catholic reform

But the fires of Catholic reform burned rather low until after the Protestant Revolution began to make serious inroads upon the ancient faith. Not until it appeared that the whole German nation was likely to be swept into the Lutheran orbit did any of the Popes become seriously concerned about the need for reform. The first of the Holy Fathers to attempt a purification of the Church was Adrian VI of Utrecht, the only non-Italian to be elected to the papal throne in nearly a century and a half, and the last in history. But his reign of only twenty months was too short to enable him to accomplish much, and in 1523 he was succeeded by a Medici (Clement VII), who ruled for eleven years. The campaign against abuses in the Church was not renewed until the reign of Paul III (1534–1549). He and three of his successors, Paul IV (1555–1559), Pius V (1566–1572), and Sixtus V (1585–1590), were the most zealous crusaders for reform who had presided over the See of Peter since the days of Gregory VII. They reorganized the papal finances, filled the Church offices with priests renowned for austerity, and dealt drastically with those clerics who persisted in idleness and vice. It was under these Popes that the Catholic Reformation reached its height. Unfortunately, they were also responsible for reviving the Inquisition, which had fallen into disuse during the Italian Renaissance.

These direct activities of the Popes were supplemented by the decrees of a great Church council convoked in 1545 by Paul III, which met in the city of Trent (modern Trento), at intervals between 1545 and 1563. This council was one of the most important in the history of the Church. The main purpose for which it had been summoned was to redefine the doctrines of the Catholic faith, and several of the steps in this direction were highly significant. Without exception the dogmas challenged by the Protestant Reformers were reaffirmed. Good works were held to be as necessary for salvation as faith. The theory of the sacraments as indispensable means of grace was upheld. Likewise, transubstantiation, the apostolic succession of the priesthood, the belief in purgatory, the invocation of saints, and the rule of celibacy for the clergy were all confirmed as essential elements in the Catholic system. On the much-debated question as to the proper source of Christian belief, the Bible and the traditions of apostolic teaching were held to be of equal authority. Not only was papal supremacy over every bishop and priest expressly maintained, but there was more than a faint suggestion that the authority of the Pope transcended that of the Church council itself. By this admission the government of the Church was reconstituted as monarchical in form. The great movement of the fourteenth and fifteenth centuries which had attempted to establish the superior authority of the general council was ignored entirely.

The Council of Trent did not confine its attention to matters of dogma. It passed important legislation also for the elimination of

The Council of Trent

Reforms of
the Council of
Trent

abuses and for reinforcing the discipline of the Church over its members. The sale of indulgences was flatly prohibited, and even their issuance for considerations other than money was restricted temporarily. Bishops and priests were forbidden to hold more than one benefice, so that none could grow rich from a plurality of incomes. To eliminate the evil of an ignorant priesthood it was provided that a theological seminary must be established in every diocese. Toward the end of its deliberations the Council decided upon a censorship of books to prevent heretical ideas from corrupting the minds of those who still remained in the faith. A commission was appointed to draw up an index or list of writings which ought not to be read. The publication of this list by the Pope in 1564 resulted in the formal establishment of the Index of Prohibited Books as a part of the machinery of the Church. Later a permanent agency known as the Congregation of the Index was set up to revise the list from time to time. Altogether more than forty such revisions have been made. The majority of the books condemned have been theological treatises, and probably the effect in retarding the progress of learning has been slight. Nonetheless, the establishment of the Index must be taken as a symptom of the intolerance which had come to infect both Catholics and Protestants.

The founding of
the Society of
Jesus by Loyola

The Catholic Reformation would never have been as thorough or as successful as it was if it had not been for the activities of the Jesuits, or members of the Society of Jesus. They did most of the rough political work in the Council of Trent, which enabled the Popes to dominate that body in its later and more important sessions. The Jesuits also were largely responsible for winning Poland and southern Germany back into the Catholic fold. The founder of the Society of Jesus was Ignatius of Loyola (1491–1556), a Spanish nobleman from the Basque country. His early career seems not to have been particularly different from that of other Spaniards of his class—a life of philandering and marauding as a soldier of the king. But about the time the Protestant Revolution was getting well under way in Germany, he was painfully wounded in a battle with the French. While waiting for his injuries to heal, he read a pious biography of Jesus and some legends of the saints which profoundly changed his emotional nature. Overwhelmed by a consciousness of his wasted life, he determined to become a soldier of Christ. After a period of morbid self-tortures, in which he saw visions of Satan, Jesus, and the Trinity, he went to the University of Paris to learn more about the faith he intended to serve. Here he gathered around him a small group of devoted disciples, with whose aid in 1534 he founded the Society of Jesus. The members took monastic vows and pledged themselves to go on a pilgrimage to Jerusalem. In 1540 their organization was approved by Pope Paul III. From then on it grew rapidly. When Loyola died it could boast of no fewer than 1500 members.

Ignatius Loyola. Engraving by Lucas Vorstiman, 1621.

The Society of Jesus was by far the most militant of the religious orders fostered by the spiritual zeal of the sixteenth century. It was not merely a monastic society but a company of soldiers sworn to defend the faith. Their weapons were not to be bullets and spears but eloquence, persuasion, instruction in the right doctrines, and if necessary more worldly methods of exerting influence. The organization was patterned after that of a military company, with a general as commander-in-chief and an iron discipline enforced on the members. All individuality was suppressed, and a soldierlike obedience to the general was exacted of the rank and file. Only the highest of the four classes of members had any share in the government of the order. This little group, known as the Professed of the Four Vows, elected the general for life and consulted with him on important matters. They were also bound to implicit obedience.

THE CATHOLIC REFORMATION

Organization of the Society of Jesus

As suggested already, the activities of the Jesuits were numerous and varied. First and foremost, they conceived of themselves as the defenders of true religion. For this object they obtained authority from the Pope to hear confessions and grant absolution. Many of them became priests in order to gain access to the pulpit and expound the truth as the oracles of God. Still others served as agents of the Inquisition in the relentless war against heresy. In all of this work they followed the leadership of Mother Church as their infallible guide. They raised no questions and attempted to solve no mysteries. Loyola taught that if the Church ruled that white was black, it would be the duty of her sons to believe it. But the Jesuits were not satisfied merely to hold the field against the attacks of Protestants and heretics; they were anxious to propagate the faith in the farthest corners of the earth—to make Catholics out of Buddhists, Moslems, the Parsees of India, and even the untutored savages of the newly discovered continents. Long before the Reformation had ended, there were Jesuit missionaries in Africa, in Japan and China, and in North and South America. Yet another important activity of Loyola's soldiers of Christ was education. They founded colleges and seminaries by the hundreds in Europe and America and obtained positions in older institutions as well. Until the Society ran into conflict with several monarchs and was finally suppressed by the Pope in 1773, it had a monopoly of education in Spain and a near-monopoly in France. That the Catholic Church recovered so much of its strength in spite of the Protestant secession was due in large measure to the manifold and aggressive activities of the Jesuits.

Activities of the Jesuits

3. THE REFORMATION HERITAGE

The most obvious result of the Reformation was the division of western Christendom into a multitude of hostile sects. No longer was there one fold and one shepherd for the whole of Latin and Teutonic Europe as had been true in the Middle Ages. Instead, northern

Results of the
Reformation:
the effect in
promoting re-
ligious tolera-
tion

Germany and the Scandinavian countries had become Lutheran;
England had adopted a compromise Protestantism of her own; Calvinism had triumphed in Scotland, Holland, and French Switzerland. In the vast domain once owing allegiance to the Vicar of
Christ only Italy, Austria, France, Spain and Portugal, southern
Germany, Poland, and Ireland were left; and even in several of these
countries aggressive Protestant minorities were a thorn in the side of
the Catholic majority. Strange as it may seem, this splintering of
Christianity into rival factions was, indirectly at least, a source of
some good to man. It worked in the long run to curb ecclesiastical
tyranny and thereby to promote religious freedom. As the sects multiplied in various countries, it gradually became evident that no one
of them could ever become strong enough to enforce its will upon
the rest. Mutual toleration was made necessary in order for any of
them to survive. To be sure, this was an incidental and long-delayed
result, but its importance cannot be denied.

The Reformation also gave an added momentum to individualism
and to the expansion of popular education. By asserting the right of
private judgment and by simplifying ritual and organization, the
leaders of the Protestant Revolution liberated man from some of the
constraints of medieval ecclesiasticism. It would be a mistake, however, to assume that Lutherans, Calvinists, and Anglicans really
believed at this time in genuine religious freedom. They had no
interest whatever in tolerating anyone who disagreed with their
own respective orthodoxies. About all they did was to set a new and
stronger precedent for challenging the authority and beliefs of a
universal church. By so doing they promoted self-assertion in the
religious sphere in somewhat the same degree as it already existed in
the political and economic spheres. In addition, the Reformation had
some effect in promoting the education of the masses. The Renaissance, with its absorbing interest in the classics, had had the unfortunate result of distorting the curricula of the schools into an
exaggerated emphasis upon Greek and Latin and of restricting education to the aristocracy. The Lutherans, Calvinists, and Jesuits
changed all of this. Ambitious to propagate their respective doctrines, they established schools for the masses, where even the son of
the cobbler or peasant might learn to read the Bible and theological
tracts in the vernacular. Practical subjects were often introduced in
place of Greek and Latin, and it is a significant fact that some of
these schools eventually opened their doors to the new science.

A good case can be made for the theory that the Reformation
furthered democracy, in the form, at least, of limited government.
Every one of the sects, whether Protestant or Catholic, raised arguments against the absolute state. Even the Lutherans, despite their
adoption of St. Paul's doctrine that "the powers that be are ordained
of God," nevertheless recognized the right of the German princes
to rebel against the Holy Roman Empire. Luther wrote that disobedience was a greater sin than murder, unchastity, dishonesty, or

EUROPE ca. 1550 A.D.

theft; but what he meant was the disobedience of the common man. He generally held that the authority of kings and princes was absolute and never to be questioned by their subjects. Some observers see in Luther's influence a powerful stimulus to the growth of authoritarian government in Germany. A more critical attitude toward secular rulers was taken by the Calvinists. In France, England, and the Low Countries they not only asserted the right of revolution but actively practiced it. Jesuit philosophers taught that the authority of the secular ruler is derived from the people, and some even affirmed the right of the ordinary citizen to kill a tyrant. Among the leaders of many sects, efforts were made to revive the medieval idea of a higher law of nature, embodying principles of right and justice, which should be recognized as an automatic limitation upon the power of rulers.

571

The St. Bartholomew's Day Massacre. Thousands of Huguenots were killed in the continuing religious strife of the sixteenth century.

Religious wars

The Reformation resulted in a series of religious wars which kept Europe in turmoil for two score years. The first to break out was the Schmalkaldic War (1546–1547), waged by Charles V in an effort to restore the unity of the Holy Roman Empire under the Catholic faith. In a few months he succeeded in cowing the Protestant princes of Germany into submission, but he was unable to force their subjects back into the Roman religion. The strife was ultimately settled by a compromise treaty, the Religious Peace of Augsburg (1555), under which each German prince was to be free to choose either Lutheranism or Catholicism as the faith of his people. The religion of each state was thus made to depend upon the religion of its ruler. A much more sanguinary struggle took place in France between 1562 and 1593. Here the Protestants, or Huguenots

572

as they were called, were decidedly in the minority, but they included some of the ablest and most influential members of the commercial and financial classes. Besides, they composed a political party involved in machinations against the Catholics for control of the government. In 1562 a faction of ultra-Catholics under the leadership of the Duke of Guise forced their way into power and, by their threats of persecution of the Huguenots, plunged the country into civil war. The struggle culminated ten years later in the frightful massacre of St. Bartholomew's Day. The regent, Catherine de' Medici, in a desperate effort to put an end to the strife, plotted with the Guises to murder the Protestant chiefs. The conspiracy unloosed the ugly passions of the Paris mob, with the result that in a single night 2000 Huguenots were slain. The war dragged on until 1593 when Henry IV became a Catholic in order to please the majority of his subjects, but the religious issue did not approach a settlement until 1598 when Henry issued the Edict of Nantes guaranteeing freedom of conscience to Protestants.

To a large extent the Revolt of the Netherlands was also an episode in the religious strife stirred up by the Reformation. Long after the Protestant Revolution began in Germany, the countries now known as Belgium and Holland were still being governed as dominions of the Spanish crown. Though Lutheranism and Calvinism had gained a foothold in the cities, the Protestants of the Netherlands were yet but a fraction of the total population. With the passage of time, however, the numbers of Calvinists increased until they included a majority of the townsmen, at least, in the Dutch provinces of the north. Interference by the Spanish government with their freedom of religion led to a desperate revolt in 1565. Religious causes were, of course, not the only ones. Nationalist feeling was a leading factor also, particularly since the Spanish king, Philip II, persisted in treating the Netherlands as mere subject provinces. In addition, there were serious economic grievances—high taxation and the restriction of commerce for the benefit of Spanish merchants. On the other hand, it was religious hatred that was largely responsible for the bitterness of the struggle. Philip II regarded all Protestants as traitors, and he was determined to root them out of every territory over which he ruled. In 1567 he sent the bigoted Duke of Alva with 10,000 soldiers to quell the revolt in the Netherlands. For six years Alva terrorized the land, putting hundreds of the rebels to death and torturing or imprisoning thousands of others. The Protestants retaliated with almost equal savagery, and the war continued its barbarous course until 1609. It ended in victory for the Protestants, largely through the bravery and self-sacrifice of their original leader, William the Silent. The chief result of the war was the establishment of an independent Dutch Republic comprising the territories now included in Holland. The southern or Belgian prov-

The Revolt of the
Netherlands

573

The Cities of Schmal-kaldic League Sur-rendering to Charles V. Engraving by Hieronymus Cock, 1560.

inces, where the majority of the people were Catholics, returned to Spanish rule.

Bigotry, witchcraft, and persecution

Actual warfare between nations and sects was not the only type of barbarity which the Reformation directly encouraged. For other examples we need only recall the atrocities perpetrated by the Catholic Inquisition, the savage persecution of Anabaptists in Germany, and the fierce intolerance of Calvinists against Catholics. The horrible witchcraft persecution, which will be discussed in the next chapter, was also in some measure the product of the seeds of fanaticism sown by the Reformation. On the whole, the amount of intolerance was now much greater than at any other time in the history of Christianity, not excepting the age of the Crusades. In more than one instance the victims of persecution were distinguished philosophers or scientists, whose talents the world of that day could ill afford to lose. The most eminent of the martyrs to the new learning put to death by the Catholics was Giordano Bruno. Despite his philosophy of mystical pantheism, Bruno set forth in startling fashion a number of the cardinal axioms of modern science. He taught the eternity of the universe, revived the atomic theory of matter, and denied that the heavenly bodies contain any superior element not found in the earth. Partly for these teachings and partly also for his pantheism and for his rejection of miracles, he was haled before the Inquisition and burned at the stake in 1600. One of the victims of Calvinist persecution at Geneva was Michael Servetus, the discoverer of the lesser circulation of the blood. Servetus was convicted of rejecting the doctrines of the Trinity and predestination and of teaching that Palestine is a barren country in defiance of the Old Testament description of it as a land flowing with milk and honey. In 1553 he was condemned to be burned at the stake by slow fire. Some admirers of Calvin have argued that the Genevan Reformer opposed the burning of Servetus: he wanted him beheaded! But even the evidence for this rather doubtful display of mercy is not conclusive.

· *Items so designated are available in paperbound editions.*

· Bainton, R. H., *The Age of the Reformation*, New York, 1956 (Anvil). The best short treatise. Half of it consists of documents.

· ———, *Here I Stand: A Life of Martin Luther*, Nashville, 1950 (Apex).

Bax, E. B., *The Peasants' War in Germany*, New York, 1899. The best account in English but not especially scholarly.

· Beard, C., *The Reformation of the Sixteenth Century in Its Relation to Modern Thought and Knowledge*, New York, 1927 (Ann Arbor).

· Burns, E. M., *The Counter Reformation*, Princeton, 1964 (Anvil).

Bury, J. B., *History of the Freedom of Thought*, New York, 1913.

Cohn, Norman, *The Pursuit of the Millennium*, Oxford, 1970.

· Erikson, E. H., *Young Man Luther*, New York, 1961 (Norton Library).

· Harkness, G. E., *John Calvin: the Man and His Ethics*, New York, 1931 (Apex).

· Huizinga, Johan, *Erasmus and the Age of Reformation*, New York, 1957 (Torchbook).

Janelle, Pierre, *The Catholic Reformation*, Milwaukee, 1949.

Jenkins, B. A., *The World's Debt to Protestantism*, Boston, 1930.

· Jones, R. M., *The Spiritual Reformers of the Sixteenth and Seventeenth Centuries*, New York, 1914 (Beacon).

Kidd, B. J., *The Counter-Reformation, 1550–1600*, New York, 1933. A complete account of the Jesuits, the Inquisition, and the Council of Trent.

Latourette, K. S., *A History of Christianity*, New York, 1953.

Lindsay, T. M., *History of the Reformation*, New York, 1928, 2 vols. Complete and scholarly.

Lucas, H. S., *The Renaissance and the Reformation*, New York, 1934.

· McGiffert, A. C., *Protestant Thought before Kant*, New York, 1911 (Torchbook).

McNeill, J. T., *The History and Character of Calvinism*, New York, 1954.

Marti, O. A., *The Economic Causes of the Reformation in England*, New York, 1930.

Nelson, E. N., *The Idea of Usury*, Princeton, 1949.

Randall, J. H., Jr., *The Making of the Modern Mind*, New York, 1926. Ch. VII.

Schwiebert, E. G., *Luther and His Times*, St. Louis, 1952.

· Smith, Preserved, *The Age of the Reformation*, New York, 1920 (Collier, 2 vols.). The best general survey.

———, *The Life and Letters of Martin Luther*, New York, 1914.

Smithson, Robert, *The Anabaptists*, London, 1935.

· Tawney, R. H., *Religion and the Rise of Capitalism*, New York, 1926 (Mentor). Thoughtful and provocative.

Van Dyke, P., *Ignatius Loyola, The Founder of the Jesuits*, New York, 1926.

· Weber, Max, *The Protestant Ethic and the Spirit of Capitalism*, New York, 1948 (Scribner Library). A stimulating sociological interpretation.

SOURCE MATERIALS

· Calvin, John, *Institutes of the Christian Religion*, especially Book II, Chs. 1–3; Book III, Chs. 19, 21–25; Book IV, Chs. 3, 14, 17, 20 (Wm. B. Eerdmans Publishing Co., 2 vols.).

Catechism of the Council of Trent.

Luther, Martin, *Works* (Jacobs, tr.), "On Trade and Usury," Vol. IV.

· ———, *On Christian Liberty* (Fortress, 1940).

———, *Address to the Christian Nobility of the German Nation.*

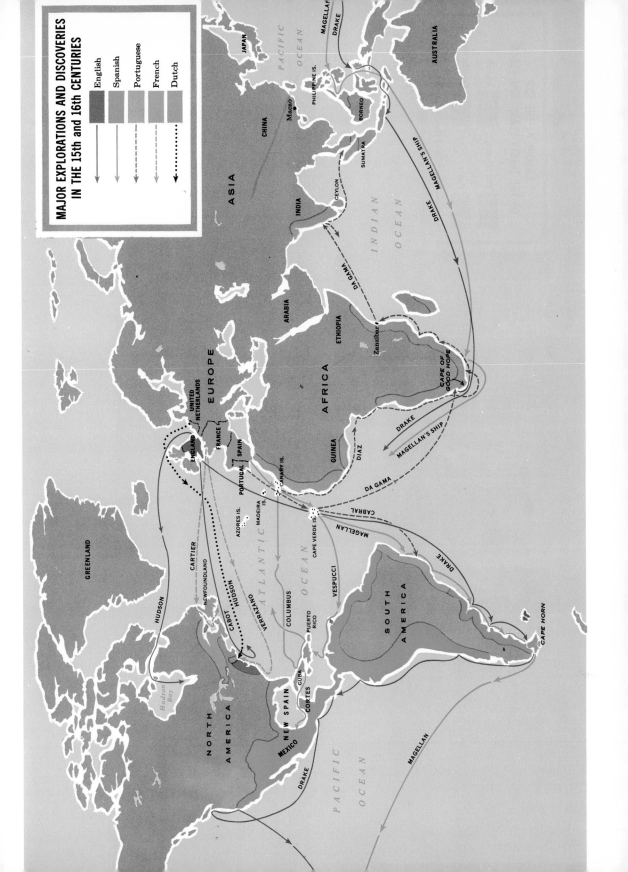

MAJOR EXPLORATIONS AND DISCOVERIES
IN THE 15th and 16th CENTURIES

English
Spanish
Portuguese
French
Dutch

**EUROPE AT THE END
OF THE THIRTY YEARS' WAR · 1648**

Austria

Brandenburg-
Prussia

The Church

Spain

—— Boundary of the Holy Roman Empire

RUSSIA

SWEDEN

BALTIC SEA

Stockholm

DENMARK

Copenhagen

Christiania

Lithuania

POLAND

Kiev

Warsaw

Danzig

E. PRUSSIA

Vistula R.

BRANDENBURG

Berlin

MECKLEN-
BURG

Hamburg

HANOVER

SAXONY

Elbe R.

Vienna

AUSTRIA

HUNGARY

Budapest

Danube R.

BLACK SEA

Constantinople

OTTOMAN EMPIRE

CYPRUS
(To Ottoman Empire)

CRETE
(To Venice)

AEGEAN SEA

NORTH
SEA

UNITED
PROVINCES

Amsterdam

SPANISH
NETH.

HESSE

WÜRTEN-
BERG

BAVARIA

LORRAINE

SWITZ.

Rhine

FRANCHE
COMTÉ

Paris

Seine R.

VENICE

Adriatic Sea

Zara

Ragusa
Cattaro

Florence

PAPAL
STATES

Rome

GENOA

MODENA

PARMA

TUSCANY

MILAN

To Venice

To Venice

SCOTLAND

Edinburgh

IRELAND

Dublin

Liverpool

ENGLAND

London

Bristol

English Channel

Loire R.

FRANCE

Garonne R.

Bordeaux

Marseilles

Rhone R.

AVIGNON

CORSICA
(To Genoa)

SARDINIA
(To Spain)

KINGDOM

OF THE

TWO SICILIES

Naples

MEDITERRANEAN SEA

TUNIS

OTTOMAN EMPIRE

ALGERIA

ATLANTIC
OCEAN

BALEARIC
ISLANDS

PORTUGAL

Lisbon

SPAIN

Madrid

Douro R.

Strait of
Gibraltar

500 miles

Le Mezzetin, Antoine Watteau (1684–1721). Mezzetin was a popular character in Italian comedy who was much liked in France. Watteau enjoyed portraying the make-believe world of the court with its festivals and formalized elegance. (MMA)

The Blue Boy, Thomas Gainsborough (1727–1788). Though the costume suggests the romantic ideal of Prince Charming, the face is a penetrating study of the moodiness and uncertainty of adolescence. (Huntington Library)

Sarah Siddons as the Tragic Muse, Sir Joshua Reynolds (1723–1792). Mrs. Siddons, a famous actress of the XVIII cent., is here portrayed as the Queen of Tragedy, in accordance with Reynolds' habit of depicting wealthy patrons in impressive classical poses. (Huntington Library)

Above: *Landscape with the Burial of Phocion*, Nicolas Poussin (1594–1665). Many consider his paintings of the Roman hills to be models of French classicism. (Louvre) Left: *The Calling of St. Matthew*, Caravaggio (1573–1610). Painted for the altarpiece of the Church of San Luigi dei Francesci, Rome. (Scala)

CHAPTER **20**

The Commercial Revolution
and the New Society (ca. 1300-1700)

Although a Kingdom may be enriched by gifts received, or by
purchases taken from some other Nations, yet these are things
uncertain and of small consideration when they happen. The ordinary means therefore to encrease our wealth and treasure is by
Forraign Trade, wherein wee must ever observe this rule: to sell
more to strangers yearly than wee consume of theirs in value.
—Thomas Mun, *England's Treasure by Forraign Trade*

The last three chapters described the intellectual and religious transition from the medieval to the modern world. It was observed
that the Renaissance, despite its kinship in many ways with the
Middle Ages, spelled the doom of Scholastic philosophy, undermined the supremacy of Gothic architecture, and overthrew
medieval conceptions of politics and the universe. Likewise, it
was noted that, before the Renaissance had completed its work, a
mighty torrent of religious revolution had swept Christianity from
it medieval foundations and cleared the way for spiritual and moral
attitudes in keeping with the trends of the new age. That both the
Renaissance and the Reformation should have been accompanied by
fundamental economic changes goes without saying. Indeed, the intellectual and religious upheavals would scarcely have been possible
had it not been for drastic alterations in the medieval economic
pattern. This series of changes, marking the transition from the
semistatic, localized, nonprofit economy of the late Middle Ages to
the dynamic, worldwide, capitalistic regime of the fourteenth and
succeeding centuries, is what is known as the Commercial Revolution.

**The meaning of
the Commercial
Revolution**

I. THE CAUSES AND INCIDENTS OF THE COMMERCIAL REVOLUTION

Causes of
the Commercial
Revolution

The causes which led to the beginning of the Commercial Revolution about 1300 are none too clear. This arises from the fact that the initial stage of the movement was more gradual than is commonly supposed. In so far as it is possible to isolate particular causes, the following may be said to have been basic: (1) the capture of a monopoly of Mediterranean trade by the Italian cities; (2) the development of a profitable commerce between the Italian cities and the merchants of the Hanseatic League in northern Europe; (3) the introduction of coins of general circulation, such as the ducat of Venice and the florin of Florence; (4) the accumulation of surplus capital in trading, shipping, and mining ventures; (5) the demand for war materials and the encouragement given by the new monarchs to the development of commerce in order to create more taxable wealth; and (6) the desire for the products of the Far East stimulated by the reports of travelers, especially the fascinating account of the wealth of China published by Marco Polo upon his return from a trip to that country toward the end of the thirteenth century. This combination of factors gave to the men of the early Renaissance new visions of riches and power and furnished them with some of the equipment necessary for an expansion of business. Henceforth they were bound to be dissatisfied with the restricted ideal of the medieval guilds with its ban upon trading for unlimited profit.

See color map
at page 576

The voyages of
overseas discovery

About two centuries after it began, the Commercial Revolution received a powerful stimulus from the voyages of overseas discovery. The reasons why these voyages were undertaken are not hard to perceive. They were due primarily to Spanish and Portuguese ambitions for a share in the trade with the Orient. For some time this trade had been monopolized by the Italian cities, with the consequence that the people of the Iberian peninsula were compelled to pay high prices for the silks, perfumes, spices, and tapestries imported from the East. It was therefore quite natural that attempts should be made by Spanish and Portuguese merchants to discover a new route to the Orient independent of Italian control. A second cause of the voyages of discovery was the missionary fervor of the Spaniards. Their successful crusade against the Moors had generated a surplus of religious zeal, which spilled over into a desire to convert the heathen. To these causes should be added the fact that advances in geographical knowledge and the introduction of the compass and the astrolabe [1] gave mariners more courage to venture into the open

A Moslem Astrolabe, Thirteenth Century

[1] The astrolabe is a device for measuring the altitude or position of heavenly bodies. It was invented by Hellenistic astronomers and perfected by the Saracens. Especially useful in determining locations at sea, it has since been replaced by the sextant.

sea. But the effect of these things must not be exaggerated. The popular idea that all Europeans before Columbus believed that the earth was flat is simply not true. From the twelfth century on it would be almost impossible to find an educated man who did not accept the fact that the earth is a sphere. Furthermore, the compass and the astrolabe were known in Europe long before any mariners ever dreamed of sailing the Atlantic, with the exception of the Norsemen. The compass was brought in by the Saracens in the twelfth century, probably from China. The astrolabe was introduced even earlier.

If we except the Norsemen, who discovered America about 1000 A.D., the pioneers in oceanic navigation were the Portuguese. By the middle of the fifteenth century they had discovered and settled the islands of Madeira and the Azores and had explored the African coast as far south as Guinea. In 1497 their most successful navigator, Vasco da Gama, rounded the tip of Africa and sailed on the next year to India. In the meantime, the Genoese mariner, Christopher Columbus, became convinced of the feasibility of reaching India by sailing west. Rebuffed by the Portuguese, he turned to the Spanish sovereigns, Ferdinand and Isabella, and enlisted their support of his plan. The story of his epochal voyage and its result is a familiar one and need not be recounted here. Though he died ignorant of his real achievement, his discoveries laid the foundations for the Spanish claim to nearly all of the New World. Other discoverers representing the Spanish crown followed Columbus, and soon afterward the conquerors, Cortes and Pizarro. The result was the establishment of a vast colonial empire including what is now the southwestern portion of the United States, Florida, Mexico, and the West Indies, Central America, and all of South America with the exception of Brazil.

The Spaniards and Portuguese

Hernando Cortes

The English and the French were not slow in following the Spanish example. The voyages of John Cabot and his son Sebastian in 1497–1498 provided the basis for the English claim to North America, though there was nothing that could be called a British empire in the New World until after the settlement of Virginia in 1607. Early in the sixteenth century the French explorer Cartier sailed up the St. Lawrence, thereby furnishing his native land with some shadow of a title to eastern Canada. More than a hundred years later the explorations of Joliet, La Salle, and Father Marquette gave the French a foothold in the Mississippi valley and in the region of the Great Lakes. Following their victory in their war for independence the Dutch also took a hand in the struggle for colonial empire. The voyage of Henry Hudson up the river which bears his name enabled them to found New Netherland in 1623, which they were forced to surrender to the English some forty years later. But the most valuable possessions of the Dutch were Malacca, the Spice Islands, and the ports of India and Africa taken from Portugal in the early seventeenth century.

The British, French, and Dutch

579

THE COMMERCIAL
REVOLUTION AND THE
NEW SOCIETY

The expansion
of commerce in-
to a world en-
terprise

The results of these voyages of discovery and the founding of colonial empires were almost incalculable. To begin with, they expanded commerce from its narrow limits of Mediterranean trade into a world enterprise. For the first time in history the ships of the great maritime powers now sailed the seven seas. The tight little monopoly of Oriental trade maintained by the Italian cities was thoroughly punctured. Genoa, Pisa, and Venice sank henceforth into relative obscurity, while the harbors of Lisbon, Bordeaux, Liverpool, Bristol, and Amsterdam were crowded with vessels and the shelves of their merchants piled high with goods. A second result was a tremendous increase in the volume of commerce and in the variety of articles of consumption. To the spices and textiles from the Orient were now added potatoes, tobacco, and maize from North America; molasses and rum from the West Indies; cocoa, chocolate, quinine, and the cochineal dye from South America; and ivory, slaves, and ostrich feathers from Africa. In addition to these commodities hitherto unknown or obtainable only in limited quantities, the supply of certain older products was greatly increased. This was especially true of sugar, coffee, rice, and cotton, which were brought in in such amounts from the Western Hemisphere that they ceased to be articles of luxury.

Another significant result of the discovery and conquest of lands overseas was an expansion of the supply of precious metals. When Columbus discovered America, the quantities of gold and silver in Europe were scarcely sufficient to support a dynamic economy. Indeed, it was nearly fifty years before the full impact of wealth from America made itself felt. For some time gold was the more abundant metal and was relatively cheap in relation to silver. The white metal, which came chiefly from the mines of Germany, was more highly prized than gold. About 1540 this relation was reversed. Massive im-

The increase in
the supply of
precious metals

Aden. A sixteenth-century woodcut of the seaport which was a base for merchants and travelers sailing to India.

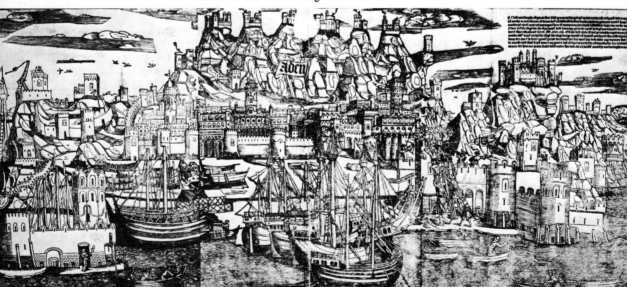

ports of silver from the mines of Mexico, Bolivia, and Peru produced such a depreciation in the value of silver that quantities of gold had to hoarded for critical transactions. Henceforth, for about eighty years, the European economy ran on silver. The result was a tremendous inflation. Prices and wages rose to fantastic heights in what may be considered an artificial prosperity. It did not affect all parts of Europe alike. The German mines were ruined by the flood of silver from the Americas. As a consequence, the position of Germany declined, while England and the Netherlands rose to preeminence. For a brief period Spain shared this preeminence, but she was ill-fitted to continue it. Her industrial development was too feeble to supply the demand for manufactured products from the European settlers in the Western Hemisphere. Accordingly, they turned to the north of Europe for the textiles, cutlery, and similar products they urgently needed. About 1535 Spain suffered a severe crisis which gradually spread to other countries.

The incidents or features of the Commercial Revolution have been partly suggested by the foregoing discussion of causes. The outstanding one was the rise of capitalism. Reduced to its simplest terms, capitalism may be defined as a system of production, distribution, and exchange in which accumulated wealth is invested by private owners for the sake of gain. Its essential features are private enterprise, competition for markets, and business for profit. Generally it involves also the wage system as a method of payment of workers; that is, a mode of payment based not upon the amount of wealth they create, but rather upon their ability to compete with one another for jobs. As indicated already, capitalism is the direct antithesis of the semistatic economy of the medieval guilds, in which production and trade were supposed to be conducted for the benefit of society with only a reasonable charge for the service rendered, instead of unlimited profits. Although capitalism did not come to its full maturity until the nineteenth century, nearly all of its cardinal features were developed during the Commercial Revolution.

Incidents of the Commercial Revolution: (1) the rise of capitalism

A second important incident of the Commercial Revolution was the growth of banking. Because of the strong disapproval of usury, banking had scarcely been a respectable business during the Middle Ages. For centuries the little that was carried on was virtually monopolized by Moslems and Jews. Nevertheless, exceptions did exist. Descendants of the Lombards ignored the prohibitions of the Church. The rise of national monarchies toward the end of the Middle Ages led to borrowing on contract to pay for wars or for the operations of government. Lending money for interest on such contracts was not considered sinful if the king took the guilt upon himself in a special clause of the contract. By the fourteenth century the business of lending money for profit was an established business. The rate on loans to governments was often 15 per cent, and in times of crisis much higher. The real founders of banking were certain of the great commercial houses of the Italian cities. Most of them com-

(2) the growth of banking

Jacob Fugger

bined money lending with the management of manufacturing enterprises in their localities. Notable among them was the Medici firm, with its headquarters in Florence, but with branches throughout Italy and as far north as Bruges. By the fifteenth century the banking business had spread to southern Germany and France. The leading firm in the north was that of the Fuggers of Augsburg, with a capital of $40,000,000. The Fuggers lent money to kings and bishops, served as brokers for the Pope in the sale of indulgences, and provided the funds that enabled Charles V to buy his election to the throne of the Holy Roman Empire. The rise of these private financial houses was followed by the establishment of government banks, intended to serve the monetary needs of the national states. The first in order of time was the Bank of Sweden (1657), but the one which was destined for the role of greatest importance in economic history was the Bank of England, founded in 1694. Although not technically under government control until 1946, it was the bank of issue for the government and the depositary of public funds.

(3) the expansion of credit facilities

The growth of banking was necessarily accompanied by the adoption of various aids to financial transactions on a large scale. Credit facilities were extended in such a way that a merchant in Amsterdam could purchase goods from a merchant in Venice by means of a bill of exchange issued by an Amsterdam bank. The Venetian merchant would obtain his money by depositing the bill of exchange in his local bank. Later the two banks would settle their accounts by comparing balances. Among the other facilities for the expansion of credit were the adoption of a system of payment by check in local transactions and the issuance of bank notes as a substitute for gold and silver. Both of these devices were introduced by the Italians and were gradually adopted in nothern Europe. The system of payment by check was particularly important in increasing the volume of trade, since the credit resources of the banks

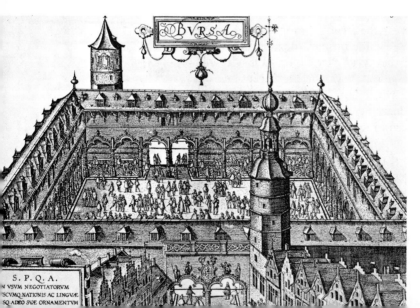

The Antwerp Bourse. Built in the sixteenth century, it was the place of exchange for merchants from all countries.

———————— Major trade routes	- - - - - - Lesser trade routes	═══════ Navigable rivers	

Wine   Herring fisheries   Wool   Linen   Silk   Mining

THE COMMERCIAL REVOLUTION IN CENTRAL AND WESTERN EUROPE ca. 1500

could now be expanded far beyond the actual amounts of cash in their vaults.

The Commercial Revolution was not confined, of course, to the growth of trade and banking. Included in it also were fundamental changes in methods of production. The system of manufacture developed by the craft guilds in the later Middle Ages was rapidly becoming defunct. The guilds themselves, dominated by the master craftsmen, had grown selfish and exclusive. Membership in them was commonly restricted to a few privileged families. Besides, they were so completely choked by tradition that they were unable to

(4) the decline of the craft guilds and the rise of new industries

583

*Printing Plant in the Late
Seventeenth Century*

(5) the domes-
tic, or putting-out
system

Advantages and
disadvantages
of the domestic
system

make adjustments to changing conditions. Moreover, new industries
had sprung up entirely outside the guild system. Characteristic examples were mining and smelting and the woolen industry. The
rapid development of these enterprises was stimulated by technical
advances, such as the invention of the spinning wheel and the stocking frame and the discovery of a new method of making brass,
which saved about half of the fuel previously used. In the mining
and smelting industries a form of organization was adopted similar
to that which has prevailed ever since. The tools and plant facilities
belonged to capitalists, while the workers were mere wage laborers
subject to hazards of accident, unemployment, and occupational
disease.

But the most typical form of industrial production in the Commercial Revolution was the domestic system, developed first of all in
the woolen industry. The domestic system derives its name from the
fact that the work was done in the homes of individual artisans instead of in the shop of a master craftsman. Since the various jobs in
the manufacture of a product were given out on contract, the system is also known as the putting-out system. Notwithstanding the
petty scale of production, the organization was basically capitalistic.
The raw material was purchased by an entrepreneur (known as a
clothier in the woolen industry) and assigned to individual workers,
each of whom would complete his allotted task for a stipulated payment. In the case of the woolen industry the yarn would be given
out first of all to the spinners, then to the weavers, fullers, and dyers
in succession. When the cloth was finally finished, it would be taken
by the clothier and sold in the open market for the highest price it
would bring. The domestic system was, of course, not restricted to
the manufacture of woolen cloth. As time went on, it was extended
into many other fields of production. It tied in well with the new
glorification of riches and with the conception of a dynamic economy. The capitalist could now thumb his nose at the old restrictions
on profits. No association of his rivals could judge the quality of his
product or the wages he paid to his workers. Perhaps best of all he
could expand his business as he saw fit and introduce new techniques
that would reduce costs or increase the volume of production.

Undoubtedly the domestic system had advantages for the workers
themselves, especially as compared to its successor, the factory system. Though wages were low, there was no regular schedule of
hours, and it was generally possible for the laborer to supplement his
family income by cultivating a small plot of land and raising a few
vegetables, at least. Furthermore, conditions of work in the homes
were more healthful than in factories, and the artisan had his family
to assist him with the simpler tasks. Freedom from the supervision
of a foreman and from the fear of discharge for petty reasons must
also be accounted definite advantages. On the other hand, it must
not be forgotten that the workers were too widely scattered to organize effectively for common action. As a consequence they had

Merchants' Houses in Amsterdam, 17th Century. Several of the principal streets of Amsterdam are canals.

no means of protecting themselves from dishonest employers, who cheated them out of part of their wages or forced them to accept payment in goods. It is also true that toward the end of the Commercial Revolution the workers became more and more dependent upon the capitalists, who now furnished not only the raw materials but the tools and equipment as well. In some cases the laborers were herded into large central shops and compelled to work under a fixed routine. The difference between this and the high-pressure methods of the factory system was only a matter of degree.

That the Commercial Revolution would involve extensive changes in business organization was practically assured from the start. The prevailing unit of production and trade in the Middle Ages was the shop or store owned by an individual or a family. The partnership was also quite common, in spite of its grave disadvantage of unlimited liability of each of its members for the debts of the entire firm. Obviously no one of these units was well adapted to business involving heavy risks and a huge investment of capital. The first result of the attempt to devise a more suitable business organization was the formation of *regulated companies*. The regulated company was an association of merchants banded together for a common venture. The members did not pool their resources but agreed merely to cooperate for their mutual advantage and to abide by certain definite regulations. Usually the purpose of the combination was to maintain a monopoly of trade in some part of the world. Assessments were often paid by the members for the upkeep of docks and warehouses and especially for protection against "interlopers," as those traders were called who attempted to break into the monopoly. A leading example of this type of organization was

(6) changes in business organization; the growth of regulated companies

585

an English company known as the Merchant Adventurers, established for the purpose of trade with the Netherlands and Germany.

In the seventeenth century the regulated company was largely superseded by a new type of organization at once more compact and broader in scope. This was the *joint-stock company*, formed through the issuance of shares of capital to a considerable number of investors. Those who purchased the shares might or might not take part in the work of the company, but whether they did or not they were joint owners of the business and therefore entitled to share in its profits in accordance with the amount they had invested. The joint-stock company had numerous advantages over the partnership and the regulated company. First, it was a permanent unit, not subject to reorganization every time one of its members died or withdrew. And second, it made possible a much larger accumulation of capital, through a wide distribution of shares. In short, it possessed nearly every advantage of the modern corporation except that it was not a person in the eyes of the law with the rights and privileges guaranteed to individuals. While most of the early joint-stock companies were founded for commercial ventures, some were organized later in industry. A number of the outstanding trading combinations were also *chartered companies*. This means that they held charters from the government granting a monopoly of the trade in a certain locality and conferring extensive authority over the inhabitants. Through a charter of this kind the British East India Company ruled over India as if it were a private estate until 1784, and even in a sense until 1858. Other famous chartered companies were the Dutch East India Company, the Hudson's Bay Company, the Plymouth Company, and the London Company. The last of these founded the colony of Virginia and governed it for a time as company property.

The remaining feature of the Commercial Revolution which needs to be considered was the growth of a more efficient money economy. Money, of course, had been in use ever since the revival of trade in the eleventh century. Nevertheless, there were few coins with a value that was recognized other than locally. By 1300 the ducat of Venice and the florin of Florence, each with a value of about $4.00, had come to be accepted in Italy and also in the international markets of northern Europe. But no country could be said to have had a uniform monetary system. Nearly everywhere there was great confusion. Coins issued by kings circulated side by side with the money of local nobles and even with Saracenic currency. Moreover, the types of currency were modified frequently, and the coins themselves were often debased. A common method by which kings expanded their own personal revenues was to increase the proportion of cheaper metals in the coins they minted. But the growth of trade and industry in the Commercial Revolution accentuated the need for more stable and uniform monetary systems. The problem was solved by the adoption of a standard system of money by every

The Spanish Milled Dollar or "Piece of Eight." It was one of the first coins to have its circumference scored or "milled." It was cut into halves and quarters to make change.

important state to be used for all transactions within its borders. Much time elapsed, however, before the reform was complete. England began the construction of a uniform coinage during the reign of Queen Elizabeth, but the task was not finished until late in the seventeenth century. The French did not succeed in reducing their money to its modern standard of simplicity and convenience until the time of Napoleon. In spite of these long delays it appears safe to conclude that national currencies were really an achievement of the Commercial Revolution.

2. MERCANTILISM IN THEORY AND PRACTICE

The Commercial Revolution in its later stages was accompanied by the adoption of a new set of doctrines and practices known as mercantilism. In its broadest meaning, mercantilism may be defined as a system of government intervention to promote national prosperity and increase the power of the state. Though frequently considered as a program of economic policy exclusively, its objectives were quite largely political. The purpose of the intervention in economic affairs was not merely to expand the volume of manufacturing and trade, but also to bring more money into the treasury of the king, which would enable him to build fleets, equip armies, and make his government feared and respected throughout the world. Because of this close association with the ambitions of princes to increase their own power and the power of the states over which they ruled, mercantilism has sometimes been called *statism*. Certainly the system would never have come into existence had it not been for the growth of absolute monarchy in place of the weak, decentralized structure of feudalism. But kings alone did not create it. Naturally

The meaning of
mercantilism

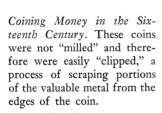

Coining Money in the Sixteenth Century. These coins were not "milled" and therefore were easily "clipped," a process of scraping portions of the valuable metal from the edges of the coin.

the new magnates of business lent support, since they would obviously derive great advantages from active encouragement of trade by the state. The heyday of mercantilism was the period between 1600 and 1700, but many of its features survived until the end of the eighteenth century.

If there was any one principle which held the central place in mercantilist theory, it was the doctrine of bullionism. This doctrine means that the prosperity of a nation is determined by the quantity of precious metals within its borders. The greater the amount of gold and silver a country contains, the more money the government can collect in taxes, and the richer and more powerful the state will become. The growth of such an idea was fostered by knowledge of the prosperity and power of Spain, which seemed to be the direct results of the flood of precious metals pouring in from her American colonies. But what of those countries that owned no bullion-producing colonies? How were *they* to achieve riches and power? For these questions the mercantilists had a ready answer. A nation without access to gold and silver directly should attempt to increase its trade with the rest of the world. If its government took steps to ensure that the value of exports would always exceed the value of imports, more gold and silver would come into the country than would have to be shipped out. This was called maintaining a "favorable balance of trade." To preserve this balance, three main devices would be necessary: first, high tariffs to reduce the general level of imports and to shut out some products entirely; second, bounties on exports; and third, extensive encouragement of manufactures in order that the nation might have as many goods to sell abroad as possible.

The theory of mercantilism also included certain elements of economic nationalism, paternalism, and imperialism. By the first is meant the ideal of a self-sufficient nation. The policy of fostering new industries was not intended merely as a device for increasing exports, but also as a means of making the nation independent of foreign supplies. In similar fashion, the mercantilists argued that the government should exercise the functions of a watchful guardian over the lives of its citizens. Generous relief should be provided for the poor, including free medical attention if they were unable to pay for it. These things were to be done, however, not with any view to charity or justice, but mainly in order that the state might rest upon a secure economic foundation and have the support of a numerous and healthy citizenry in case of war. Finally, the mercantilists advocated the acquisition of colonies. Again, the primary purpose was not to benefit individual citizens of the mother country, but to make the nation strong and independent. The types of possessions most ardently desired were those that would enlarge the nation's hoard of bullion. If these could not be obtained, then colonies providing tropical products, naval stores, or any other commodities which the mother country could not produce would be ac-

Other elements
of mercantilism:
economic na-
tionalism, pa-
ternalism, and
imperialism

ceptable. The theory which underlay this imperialism was the notion that colonies existed for the benefit of the state that owned them. For this reason they were not allowed to engage in manufacturing or shipping. Their function was to produce raw materials and to consume as large a proportion of manufactured products as possible. In this way they would infuse lifeblood into the industries of the mother country and thus give her an advantage in the struggle for world trade.

The majority of those who wrote on mercantilist theory were not professional economists but philosophers and men of action in the world of business. Among the political philosophers were such advocates of absolute monarchy as the Frenchman Jean Bodin (1530–1596) and the Englishman Thomas Hobbes (1588–1679), who were naturally disposed to favor any policy that would increase the wealth and power of the ruler. While most of the apologists for mercantilism were interested in it mainly as a device for promoting a favorable balance of trade, others conceived it as a species of paternalism for increasing prosperity within the country. For example, the Englishman Edward Chamberlayne advocated a policy somewhat similar to contemporary ideas of government spending. He recommended that the state should appropriate a huge fund for the relief of the poor and for the construction of public works as a means of stimulating business.

The defenders
of mercantilism

Attempts to put various mercantilist doctrines into practice characterized the history of many of the nations of western Europe in the sixteenth and seventeenth centuries. The theories, however, were not universally applied. Spain, of course, had the initial advantage by reason of the flow of bullion from her American empire. And while the Spaniards did not need to resort to artificial devices in order to bring money into their country, their government nevertheless maintained a rigid control over commerce and industry. The policies of other nations were designed to make up for the lack of bullion-producing colonies by capturing a larger share of export trade. This naturally involved a program of bounties, tariffs, and extensive regulation of manufacturing and shipping. Mercantilist policies were largely adopted in England during the reign of Queen Elizabeth I and were continued by the Stuart monarchs and by Oliver Cromwell. Most of these rulers engaged in a furious scramble for colonies, bestowed monopolistic privileges upon trading companies, and sought in a wide variety of ways to control the economic activities of the citizens. The most interesting examples of mercantilist legislation in England were, first, the Elizabethan laws designed to eliminate idleness and stimulate production and, second, the Navigation Acts. By a series of laws enacted toward the end of the sixteenth century, Queen Elizabeth gave to the justices of the peace the authority to fix prices, regulate hours of labor, and compel every able-bodied citizen to work at some useful trade. The first of the Navigation Acts was passed in 1651 under Oliver Cromwell.

Mercantilism in
practice: in
Spain and in
England

589

With the aim of destroying Dutch predominance in the carrying trade, it required that all colonial exports to the mother country should be carried in English ships. A second Navigation Act was passed in 1660, which provided not merely that colonial exports should be shipped in British vessels but prohibited the sending of certain "enumerated articles," especially tobacco and sugar, directly to Continental European ports. They were to be sent first of all to England, whence, after the payment of customs duties, they could be reshipped elsewhere. Both of these laws were based upon the principle that colonies should serve for the enrichment of the mother country.

The Germanic states during the Commercial Revolution were too completely occupied with internal problems to take an active part in the struggle for colonies and overseas trade. As a consequence, German mercantilism was concerned primarily with increasing the strength of the state from within. It partook of the dual character of economic nationalism and a program for a planned society. But, of course, the planning was done chiefly for the benefit of the government and only incidentally for that of the people as a whole. Because of their dominant purpose of increasing the revenues of the state, the German mercantilists are known as cameralists (from *Kammer*, a name given to the royal treasury). Most of them were lawyers and professors of finance. Cameralist ideas were put into practice by the Hohenzollern kings of Prussia, notably by Frederick William I (1713–1740) and Frederick the Great (1740–1786). The policies of these monarchs embraced a many-sided scheme of intervention and control in the economic sphere for the purpose of increasing taxable wealth and bolstering the power of the state. Marshes were drained, canals dug, new industries established with the aid of the government, and farmers instructed as to what crops they should plant. In order that the nation might become self-sufficient as soon as possible, exports of raw materials and imports of manufactured products were prohibited. The bulk of the revenues gained from these various policies went for military purposes. The standing army of Prussia was increased by Frederick the Great to 160,000 men.

The most thorough, if not the most deliberate, application of mercantilism was probably to be found in France during the reign of Louis XIV (1643–1715). This was due partly to the fact that the French state was the complete incarnation of absolutism and partly to the policies of Jean Baptiste Colbert (1619–1683), chief minister under *le grand monarque* from 1661 until his death. Colbert was no theorist but a practical politician, ambitious for personal power and intent upon magnifying the opportunities for wealth of the middle class, to which he belonged. He accepted mercantilism, not as an end in itself, but simply as a convenient means for increasing the wealth and power of the state and thereby gaining the approval of his sovereign. He firmly believed that France must acquire as large

Mercantilism in Germany: the cameralists

Jean Baptiste Colbert

an amount of the precious metals as possible. To this end he prohibited the export of money, levied high tariffs on foreign manufactures, and gave liberal bounties to encourage French shipping. It was largely for this purpose also that he fostered imperialism, hoping to increase the favorable balance of trade through the sale of manufactured goods to the colonies. Accordingly, he purchased islands in the West Indies, encouraged settlements in Canada and Louisiana, and established trading posts in India and in Africa. Furthermore, he was as devoted to the idéal of self-sufficiency as any of the cameralists in Prussia. He gave subsidies to new enterprises, established a number of state-owned industries, and even had the government purchase goods which were not really needed in order to keep struggling companies on their feet. But he was determined to keep the manufacturing industry under strict control, so as to make sure that companies would buy their raw materials only from French or colonial sources and produce the commodities necessary for national greatness. Consequently he clamped upon industry an elaborate set of regulations prescribing nearly every detail of the manufacturing process. Finally, it should be mentioned that Colbert took a number of steps to augment the political strength of the nation directly. He provided France with a navy of nearly 300 ships, drafting citizens from the maritime provinces and even criminals to man them. He sought to promote a rapid growth of population by discouraging young people from becoming monks or nuns and by exempting families with ten or more children from taxation.

3. THE RESULTS OF THE COMMERCIAL REVOLUTION

It goes without saying that the Commercial Revolution was one of the most significant developments in the history of the Western world. The whole pattern of modern economic life would have been impossible without it, for it changed the basis of commerce from the local and regional plane of the Middle Ages to the worldwide scale it has occupied ever since. Moreover, it exalted the power of money, inaugurated business for profit, sanctified the accumulation of wealth, and established competitive enterprise as the foundation of production and trade. In a word, the Commercial Revolution was responsible for a large number of the elements that go to make up the capitalist regime.

The foundation for modern capitalism

But these were not the only results. The Commercial Revolution brought into being wide fluctuations of economic activity. What we now call booms and recessions alternated with startling rapidity. The inflow of precious metals, combined with a "population explosion" which doubled the inhabitants of Europe between 1450 and 1650, led to rising prices and an unprecedented demand for goods. Businessmen were tempted to expand their enterprises too rapidly;

Booms and recessions

591

bankers extended credit so liberally that their principal borrowers, especially nobles, often defaulted on loans. Spain and Italy were among the first to suffer setbacks. In both, failure of wages to keep pace with rising prices brought incredible hardships to the lower classes. Impoverishment was rife in the cities, and banditry flourished in the rural areas. In Spain some ruined aristocrats were not too proud to join the throngs of vagrants who wandered from city to city. At the end of the fifteenth century the great Florentine bank of the Medici, with its branches in Venice, Rome, and Naples, closed its doors. The middle of the century that followed saw numerous bankruptcies in Spain and the decline of the Fuggers in Germany. Meanwhile, England, Holland, and to some extent France, waxed prosperous. This prosperity was especially characteristic of the "age of silver," which lasted from about 1540 to 1620. In the seventeenth century decline set in once more after inflation had spent its force, and as a consequence of religious and international wars and civil strife.

The alternation of booms and recessions was followed by orgies of speculation. These reached their climax early in the eighteenth century. The most notorious were the South Sea Bubble and the Mississippi Bubble. The former was the result of inflation of the stock of the South Sea Company in England. The promoters of this company agreed to take over a large part of the national debt and in return received from the English government an exclusive right to trade with South America and the Pacific islands. The prospects for profit seemed almost unlimited. The stock of the company rose rapidly in value until it was selling for more than ten times its original price. The higher it rose, the more gullible the public became. But gradually suspicion developed that the possibilities of the enterprise had been overrated. Buoyant hopes gave way to fears, and investors made frantic attempts to dispose of their shares for whatever they would bring. A crash was the inevitable result.

During the very same years when the South Sea Bubble was being inflated in England, the French were going through a similar wave of speculative madness. In 1715 a Scotsman by the name of John Law, who had been compelled to flee from British soil for killing his rival in a love intrigue, settled in Paris, after various successful gambling adventures in other cities. He persuaded the regent of France to adopt his scheme for paying off the national debt through the issuance of paper money and to grant him the privilege of organizing the Mississippi Company for the colonization and exploitation of Louisiana. As the government loans were redeemed, the persons who received the money were encouraged to buy stock in the company. Soon the shares began to soar, ultimately reaching a price forty times their original value. Nearly everyone who could scrape together a few livres of surplus cash rushed forward to participate in the scramble for riches. Stories were told of butchers and tailors who were supposed to have become millionaires by buying a few shares and holding them for a rise in price. But as the realization grew that the company would never be able to pay more than a nominal dividend on the stock at its inflated value, the more cautious investors began selling their holdings. The alarm spread, and soon everyone was as anxious to sell as he had been to buy. In 1720 the Mississippi Bubble burst in a wild panic. Thousands of people who had sold good property to buy the shares at fantastic prices were ruined. The collapse of the South Sea and Mississippi companies gave a temporary chill to the public ardor for gambling. It was not long, however, until the greed for speculative profits revived, and the stock-jobbing orgies that followed in the wake of the Commercial Revolution were repeated many times over during the nineteenth and twentieth centuries.

Among other results of the Commercial Revolution were the rise of the bourgeoisie to economic power, the beginning of Europeanization of the world, and the revival of slavery. Each of these requires brief comment. By the end of the seventeenth century the bourgeoisie had become an influential class in nearly every country of western Europe. Its ranks included the merchants, the bankers, the shipowners, the principal investors, and the industrial entrepreneurs. Their rise to power was mainly the result of increasing wealth and their tendency to ally themselves with the king against the remnants of the feudal aristocracy. But as yet their power was purely economic. Not until the nineteenth century did middle-class supremacy in politics become a reality. By the Europeanization of the world is meant the transplanting of European manners and culture in other continents. As a result of the work of traders, missionaries, and colonists, North and South America were rapidly stamped with the character of appendages of Europe. No more than a beginning was made in the transformation of Asia, but enough was done to foreshadow the trend of later times when even Japanese and Chinese would adopt Western locomotives and shell-rimmed spectacles. The most regrettable result of the Commercial Revolution was the revival of slavery. As we learned in our study of the Middle Ages, slavery practically disappeared from European civilization about the year 1000. But the development of mining and plantation farming in the English, Spanish, and Portuguese colonies led to a tremendous demand for unskilled labor. At first an attempt was made to enslave the American Indians, but they usually proved too hard to manage. The problem was solved in the sixteenth century by the importation of African Negroes. For the next 200 years and more, Negro slavery was an integral part of the European colonial system, especially in those regions producing tropical products.

Europeanization of the world and the revival of slavery

Finally, the Commercial Revolution was exceedingly important in preparing the way for the Industrial Revolution. This was true for a number of reasons. First, the Commercial Revolution created a class

THE COMMERCIAL
REVOLUTION AND THE
NEW SOCIETY

Effects of the
Commercial
Revolution in
preparing
the way for the
Industrial
Revolution

of capitalists who were constantly seeking new opportunities to invest their surplus profits. Second, the mercantilist policy, with its emphasis upon protection for infant industries and production of goods for export, gave a powerful stimulus to the growth of manufactures. Third, the founding of colonial empires flooded Europe with new raw materials and greatly increased the supply of certain products which had hitherto been luxuries. Most of these required fabrication before they were available for consumption. As a consequence, new industries sprang up wholly independent of any guild regulations that still survived. The outstanding example was the manufacture of cotton textiles, which, significantly enough, was one of the first of the industries to become mechanized. Last of all, the Commercial Revolution was marked by a trend toward the adoption of factory methods in certain lines of production, together with technological improvements, such as the invention of the spinning wheel and the stocking frame, and the discovery of more efficient processes of refining ores. The connection between these developments and the mechanical progress of the Industrial Revolution is not hard to perceive.

4. REVOLUTIONARY DEVELOPMENTS IN AGRICULTURE

To a large extent the sweeping changes that occurred in agriculture between the fourteenth century and the eighteenth may be regarded as effects of the Commercial Revolution. For example, the rise in prices and the increase in urban population eventually made agriculture a profitable business and thus tended to promote its absorption into the capitalist system. In addition, the development of the woolen industry in England caused many landowners of that country to substitute the pasturing of flocks for ordinary farming as their principal source of income. But there were also other causes not directly connected with the Commercial Revolution at all. One was the influence of the Crusades and the Hundred Years' War in weakening the power of the nobles and in undermining the structure of the old society. Another was the reduction of the supply of agricultural labor on account of the Black Death and the influx of peasants into the cities and towns to take advantage of the new opportunities for a living resulting from the revival of trade with the Near East. A third was the opening up of new farms to cultivation under a system of free labor and individual enterprise. The combined effect of these factors was the destruction of the manorial system and the establishment of agriculture on something like its modern foundations. The transformation was most complete in England, but there were similar developments in other countries also.

An important development of the agricultural revolution was the enclosure movement, which was of notable importance in

England. This movement had two main aspects: first, the enclosing of the common wood and pasture lands of the manor, thereby abolishing the communal rights which the peasants had enjoyed of pasturing their flocks and gathering wood on the untilled portions of the lord's estate; and second, the eviction of large numbers of peasants from their leaseholds or other rights of tenantry on the arable lands. Both of these forms of enclosure resulted in much hardship for the rural population. For centuries the peasant's rights in the common pasture and woodlot had formed an essential element in his scheme of subsistence, and it was difficult for him to get along without them. But the fate of those peasants who were dispossessed entirely of their rights of tenantry was much more serious. In most cases they were forced to become landless wage earners or to make their way in the world as helpless beggars. The chief reason for the enclosures was the desire of the former feudal proprietors to convert as large an area of their estates as possible into pasturage for sheep, on account of the high price which could now be obtained for wool. Usually they began by fencing in the common lands as their own property. This was frequently followed by the conversion of many of the grain fields into pastures also, resulting in the eviction especially of those peasants whose leaseholds were none too secure. Enclosures began in the fifteenth century and were continued beyond the period of the Commercial Revolution. Even as late as 1819 hundreds of acts were still being passed by the British Parliament authorizing the eviction of tenants and the closing in of great estates. In the eighteenth and nineteenth centuries the process was accelerated by the ambition of capitalists to push their way into the aristocracy by becoming gentleman farmers. The enclosure movement completed the transformation of English agriculture into a capitalistic enterprise.

The final stage in the agricultural upheaval which accompanied or followed the Commercial Revolution was the introduction of new crops and improvements in mechanical equipment. Neither of these developments was conspicuous until the beginning of the eighteenth century. It was about this time that Lord Townshend in England discovered the value of raising clover as a means of preventing exhaustion of the soil. Not only is the effect of clover in reducing fertility much less than that of the cereal grains, but it actually helps to improve the quality of the soil by gathering nitrogen and making the ground more porous. The planting of this crop from time to time made unnecessary the old system of allowing one-third of the land to lie fallow each year. Further, the clover itself provided an excellent winter feed for animals, thereby aiding the production of more and better livestock. Only a small number of mechanical improvements were introduced into farming at this time, but they were of more than trivial significance. First came the adoption of the metal plowshare, which made possible a deeper and wider fur-

The enclosure movement

A Ball and Chain Pump. Men walking in the treadmill to the left powered this mid-sixteenth-century irrigation device.

595

row than could ever be accomplished with the primitive wooden plows handed down from the Middle Ages. For a time farmers were reluctant to use the new device in the belief that iron would poison the soil, but this superstition was eventually abandoned. The other most important mechanical improvement of this period was the drill for planting grain. The adoption of this invention eliminated the old wasteful method of sowing grain broadcast by hand, most of it remaining on top of the ground to be eaten by crows. Significant as these inventions were, however, the real mechanization of agriculture did not come until well along in the nineteenth century.

5. THE NEW SOCIETY

Significant social changes: (1) a more rapid growth of population

Profound changes in the texture of society inevitably accompany economic or intellectual revolutions. The society which was brought into being by the Renaissance, the Reformation, and the Commercial Revolution, though retaining characteristics of the Middle Ages, was really quite different in its underlying features. For one thing, the population of Europe was now considerably larger. The number of inhabitants of both Italy and England increased by approximately one-third during the single century from 1500 to 1600. In the same period the estimated population of Germany grew from 12,000,000 to 20,000,000. In 1378 London had a population of about 46,000; by 1605 the total had grown to about 225,000.[2] The reasons for these increases are closely related to the religious and economic developments of the time. Un-

[2] J. W. Thompson, *Economic and Social History of Europe in the Later Middle Ages*, p. 461; Preserved Smith, *The Age of the Reformation*, pp. 453–458.

Interior of a French Peasant's Cottage, Seventeenth Century. Virtually all activities centered about the hearth, the only source of heat for the entire dwelling.

doubtedly in nothern countries the overthrow of clerical celibacy and the encouragement of marriage were factors partly responsible. But far more important was the increase in means of subsistence brought about by the Commercial Revolution. Not only were new products, such as potatoes, maize, and chocolate, added to the food supply, but older commodities, especially sugar and rice, were now made available to Europeans in much larger quantities. In addition, the growth of new opportunities for making a living in industry and commerce enabled most countries to support a larger population than would ever have been possible under the predominantly agrarian economy of the Middle Ages. It is significant that the bulk of the increases occurred in the cities and towns.

A development of even greater consequence than the growth in population was the increasing equality and fluidity of classes. The Renaissance, the Reformation, and the accompanying Commercial Revolution were all, in some degree, leveling movements. It is an impressive fact that the majority of the men who rose to positions of leadership in Renaissance culture were not scions of the nobility. A few, Shakespeare among them, sprang from humble families and at least three men were of illegitimate birth—Boccaccio, Leonardo da Vinci, and Erasmus. The influence of the Renaissance in promoting social equality is illustrated also by the rise of the professions to a higher dignity than they had ever enjoyed in the Middle Ages. The artist, the writer, the lawyer, the university professor, and the physician emerged into a position of importance roughly comparable to that which they hold in modern society. This is confirmed by the incomes which many are known to have received. Michelangelo enjoyed a pension of thousands of dollars a year from the Pope. Raphael left an estate which even by modern standards would be considered princely.[3] Erasmus was able to live in luxury from the gifts and favors received from his patrons. Although few historians would now subscribe to Nietzsche's dictum that the Reformation was simply a revolt of the ignorant masses against their betters, the influence of that movement in weakening the old aristocracy cannot be ignored. By sanctifying the accumulation of wealth it did much to enthrone the middle class. As for the third of the great leveling movements, the Commercial Revolution, we need only recall its effects in providing the opportunities for any lucky or ambitious burgher to pile up a fortune and thereby to climb some of the higher rungs of the social ladder.

The condition of the lower classes did not improve at a rate commensurate with that of the bourgeoisie. Some historians deny that there was any improvement at all, but this view is open to debate. It is true that real wages remained very low: English masons and carpenters were paid the modern equivalent of not more than a dollar a day about 1550. Attempts were even made to prohibit by law any

(2) an increasing equality and fluidity of classes

(3) the modest gains of the lower classes

[3] Preserved Smith, *The Age of the Reformation*, p. 472.

The Peasants Revolt in Germany. This drawing shows the plunder of the monastery of Weissenau in 1525.

rise in the level of wages, as in the English Statute of Laborers of 1351. It is also true that there were numerous strikes and insurrections of the lower classes. The most serious were the Great Revolt in England in 1381 and the so-called Peasants' Revolt in Germany in 1524–1525. In both, large numbers of workers from the towns took part along with the peasants. But there were also uprisings of the urban proletariat alone. An example is furnished by the revolt of the workers of Florence between 1379 and 1382 against the denial of their right to form unions and to participate in the government of the city. This revolt, like the others, was put down with merciless severity. Desperate though these uprisings were, we cannot be sure that they indicate a condition of absolute wretchedness among the lower classes. It must be understood that in a time of transition the spirit of revolution is in the air. Indeed, the fact that revolts occurred may perhaps be taken as a sign that the lot of the workers was not always deplorable. Men do not generally rebel unless their economic condition has improved sufficiently to give them some confidence of success. Finally, it is almost impossible to believe that none of the working classes would share in the increasing prosperity of the age. It is probably never strictly true that all of the poor grow poorer while the rich grow richer.

Notwithstanding the cultural and economic progress of the period under review, social and moral conditions do not appear to have sustained much improvement. For one thing, the new egoism that characterized the middle and upper classes stood as a barrier to more generous treatment of the least fortunate human beings. Hearing a disturbance outside his quarters, the Emperor Charles V, in 1552, was reported to have asked who were causing the commotion. When told that they were poor soldiers, he said, "Let them die," and compared them to caterpillars, locusts, and June bugs that eat the sprouts and other good things of the earth. As a rule, the most pitiable fate was reserved for slaves and demented persons. For the sake of big profits Negroes were hunted like beasts on the coast of Africa and shipped to the American colonies. It may be of interest to note that the Englishman who originated this body-snatching business, Captain John Hawkins, called the ship in which he transported the victims the *Jesus*. In view of the fact that insanity was regarded as a form of demonic possession, it is not strange that the sufferers from this disease should have been cruelly treated. They were generally confined in filthy barracks and flogged unmercifully to drive the demons out of their bodies. A favorite diversion of some of our ancestors was to organize parties to visit the madhouses and tease the insane.

The immediate effect of the Reformation in improving conditions of morality appears to have been almost negligible. Perhaps this is explainable in part by the return to the legalism of the Old Testament. But probably the chief cause was the fierce antagonism between sects. A condition of war is never favorable to the growth of a high morality. Whatever the reasons, the licentiousness and brutality continued unchecked. Even some of the clergy who were closely identified with the work of religious reform could scarcely be said to have been armored with the breastplate of righteousness. An acquaintance of Luther's seems to have experienced no difficulty in getting a new pastorate after he had been dismissed from an earlier one on charges of seduction. Several of the Protestant Reformers considered polygamy less sinful than divorce, on the ground that the former was recognized in the Old Testament while the latter was prohibited in the New. So doubtful was the quality of moral standards among the Catholic clergy that the Reformers of that

Social and moral conditions

The effect of the Reformation upon moral standards

599

faith found it necessary to introduce the closed confessional box for the protection of female penitents. Formerly women as well as men had been required to kneel at the knees of the priest while confessing their sins. The effects of the Reformation upon the virtues of truthfulness and tolerance were woeful indeed. Catholic and Protestant Reformers alike were so obsessed with the righteousness of their own particular cause that they did not hesitate to make use of almost any extreme of falsehood, slander, or repression that seemed to guarantee victory for their side. For example, Luther expressly justified lying in the interests of religion, and the Jesuits achieved a reputation for tortuous reasoning and devious plotting for the advantage of the Church. No one seemed to have the slightest doubt that in the sphere of religion the end justified the means.

The widespread adoption of the tobacco and coffee habits in the seventeenth century ultimately had interesting social and perhaps physiological effects. Although the tobacco plant was brought into Europe by the Spaniards about fifty years after the discovery of America, another half century passed before many Europeans adopted the practice of smoking. At first the plant was believed to possess miraculous healing powers and was referred to as "divine tobacco" and "our holy herb nicotian."[4] The habit of smoking was popularized by English explorers, especially by Sir Walter Raleigh, who had learned it from the Indians of Virginia. It spread rapidly through all classes of European society despite the condemnation of the clergy and the "counterblaste" of King James I against it. The enormous popularity of coffee drinking in the seventeenth century had even more important social effects. Coffee houses or "cafes" sprang up all over Europe and rapidly evolved into leading institutions. They provided not merely an escape for the majority of men from a cribbed and monotonous home life, but they took others away from the sordid excesses of the tavern and the gambling-hell. In addition, they fostered a sharpening of wits and promoted more polished manners, especially inasmuch as they became favorite rendezvous for the literary lions of the time. If we can believe the testimony of English historians, there was scarcely a social or political enterprise which did not have its intimate connections with the establishments where coffee was sold. Some, indeed, were the rallying places of rival factions, which may in time have evolved into political parties. In London, according to Macaulay,

> There were coffee houses where the first medical men might
> be consulted. . . . There were Puritan coffee houses where no
> oath was heard and where lank-haired men discussed election
> and reprobation through their noses; Jew coffee houses where
> dark-eyed money-changers from Venice and Amsterdam

Effects of the coffee and tobacco habits

[4] The word "nicotian" or "nicotine" is derived from Jean Nicot, the French ambassador to Portugal who introduced the tobacco plant into France.

greeted each other; and Popish coffee houses where, as good Protestants believed, Jesuits planned, over their cups, another great fire, and cast silver bullets to shoot the king.[5]

Despite its remarkable attainments in intellect and the arts, the period was by no means free from superstitions. Even at the peak of the Renaissance numerous quaint and pernicious delusions continued to be accepted as valid truths. The illiterate masses clung to their beliefs in goblins, satyrs, and wizards and to their fear of the devil, whose malevolence was assumed to be the cause of diseases, famine, storms, and insanity. But superstition was not harbored in the minds of the ignorant alone. The famous astronomer, Johann Kepler, believed in astrology and depended upon the writing of almanacs, with predictions of the future according to signs and wonders in the heavens, as his chief source of income. Not only did Sir Francis Bacon accept the current superstition of astrology, but he also contributed his endorsement of the witchcraft delusion. Eventually the enlightenment of the Renaissance might have eliminated most of the harmful superstitions if a reaction had not set in during the Reformation. The emphasis of the Reformers upon faith, their contempt for reason and science, and their incessant harping on the wiles of the devil fostered an attitude of mind decidedly favorable to prejudice and error. Besides, the furor of hate stirred up by religious controversy made it almost impossible for the average man to view his social and individual problems in a calm and intelligent spirit.

The persistence
of superstitions

The worst of all the superstitions that flourished in this period was unquestionably the witchcraft delusion. Belief in witchcraft was by no means unknown in the Middle Ages or even in the early Renaissance, but it never reached the proportions of a dangerous madness until after the beginning of the Protestant Revolution. And it is a significant fact that the persecutions attained their most virulent form in the very countries where religious conflict raged the fiercest, that is, in Germany and France. The witchcraft superstition was a direct outgrowth of the belief in Satan which obsessed the minds of so many of the Reformers. Luther maintained that he often talked with the Evil One and sometimes put him to rout after a session of argument by calling him unprintable names.[6] Calvin insisted that the Pope never acted except on the advice of his patron the devil. In general, the tendency of each camp of theologians was to ascribe all the victories of their opponents to the uncanny powers of the Prince of Darkness. With such superstitions prevailing among religious leaders, it is not strange that the mass of their followers should have harbored bizarre and hideous notions. The belief grew that the devil was really more powerful than God, and that no man's life or soul was safe from destruction. It was assumed that Satan not

The witch-
craft delusion

[5] Thomas Babington Macaulay, *History of England,* I, 335.
[6] Preserved Smith, *The Age of the Reformation,* p. 653.

only tempted mortals to sin, but actually forced them to sin by sending his minions in human form to seduce men and women in their sleep. This was the height of his malevolence, for it jeopardized chances of salvation.

According to the definition of the theologians, witchcraft consisted in selling one's soul to the devil in return for supernatural powers. It was believed that a woman who had concluded such a bargain was thereby enabled to work all manner of spiteful magic against her neighbors—to cause their cattle to sicken and die, their crops to fail, or their children to fall into the fire. But the most valuable gifts bestowed by Satan were the power to blind husbands to their wives' misconduct or to cause women to give birth to idiots or deformed infants. It is commonly assumed that the so-called witches were toothless old hags whose cranky habits and venomous tongues had made them objects of suspicion and dread to all who knew them. Undoubtedly a great many of the victims of the Salem trials in Massachusetts in 1692 did belong to this class. However, the writers on the Continent of Europe generally imagined the witch to be a "fair and wicked young woman," and a large percentage of those put to death in Germany and France were adolescent girls and matrons not yet thirty.[7]

The earliest persecutions for witchcraft were those resulting from the crusades launched against heretics by the Papal Inquisition in the thirteenth century. With the growth of intolerance of heresy it was probably inevitable that members of sects like the Albigenses should be accused of trafficking with the devil. But the amount of persecution in this period was comparatively small. A second campaign against witches was initiated by Pope Innocent VIII in 1484, who instructed his inquisitors to use torture in procuring convictions. But, as we have already seen, it was not until after the beginning of the Protestant Revolution that witchcraft persecution became a mad hysteria. Luther himself provided some of the impetus by recommending that witches should be put to death with fewer considerations of mercy than were shown to ordinary criminals. Other Reformers quickly followed Luther's example. Under Calvin's administration in Geneva thirty-four women were burned or quartered for the alleged crime in 1545.[8] From this time on the persecutions spread like a pestilence. Women, young girls, and even mere children were tortured by driving needles under their nails, roasting their feet in the fire, or crushing their legs under heavy weights until the marrow spurted from their bones, in order to force them to confess filthy orgies with demons. To what extent the persecutions were due to sheer sadism or to the greed of magistrates, who were sometimes permitted to confiscate the property of those convicted, is impossible to say. Certainly there were few people who

Hanging Witches. A woodcut from the late sixteenth century.

[7] Preserved Smith, *A History of Modern Culture*, I, 436–37.
[8] Preserved Smith, *The Age of the Reformation*, p. 656.

did not believe that the burning of witches was justifiable. One of the most zealous defenders of the trials was the political philosopher, Jean Bodin. As late as the eighteenth century John Wesley declared that to give up the belief in witchcraft was to give up the Bible.

The witchcraft persecutions reached their peak during the later years of the sixteenth century. The number of victims will never be known, but it was certainly not fewer than 30,000. We read of cities in Germany in which as many as 900 were put to death in a single year, and of whole villages in which practically no women were left alive.

The peak of the witchcraft persecutions

After 1600 the mania gradually subsided on the Continent of Europe, though it continued for some years longer in England. The reasons for the decline are not far to seek. In some measure it was the consequence of a recovery of sanity by the people themselves, particularly as the fogs of suspicion and hate produced by religious warfare gradually lifted. But the principal causes were the revival of reason and the influence of scientists and skeptical philosophers. At the very zenith of the witch-burning frenzy certain lawyers began to have doubts as to the value of the evidence admitted at the trials. In 1584 an English jurist by the name of Reginald Scott published a book condemning the belief in witchcraft as irrational and asserting that most of the lurid crimes confessed by accused women were mere figments of disordered minds. Such eminent scientists as Pierre Gassendi (1592–1655) and William Harvey also denounced the persecutions. But the most effective protest of all came from the pen of Montaigne. This distinguished French skeptic directed the shafts of his most powerful ridicule against the preposterous nonsense of the sorcery trials and the cruelty of men like Bodin who would have witches killed on mere suspicion.

The end of the witchcraft persecutions

From what has been said in preceding paragraphs the conclusion must not be drawn that the period of the Renaissance, the Reformation, and the Commercial Revolution was an age of universal depravity. Of course, there were numerous individuals as urbane and tolerant as any who lived in less boisterous times. It must be remembered also that this was the age of Sir Thomas More and Erasmus, who were at least as civilized as the majority of men historians have chosen to honor. The enormous popularity of Castiglione's *Book of the Courtier* may likewise be taken to indicate that the period was not hopelessly barbarous. This treatise, which ran through more than 100 editions, set forth the ideal of a knight who was not merely brave in battle and accomplished in the social graces, but courteous, unaffected, and just. In spite of all this, the dolorous fact remains that for large numbers of men ethics had lost their true meaning. The cardinal aims were now gratification of self and victory in the struggle to make the whole world conform to one's own set of dogmas. Perhaps these were inevitable accompaniments of the chaotic transition from the impersonal society of the Middle Ages.

The age not one of universal depravity

· *Items so designated are available in paperbound editions.*

· Burckhardt, Jacob, *The Civilization of the Renaissance in Italy*, London, 1890 (Mentor, Torchbook, 2 vols.) No longer considered authoritative.

· de Roover, Raymond, *The Rise and Decline of the Medici Bank, 1397–1494*, Cambridge, 1964 (Norton Library).

· Ford, Franklin, *Robe and Sword*, Cambridge, 1953 (Torchbook).

· Haring, C. H., *The Spanish Empire in America*, New York, 1947 (Harbinger). One of the best studies of the subject.

Heaton, Herbert, *Economic History of Europe*, New York, 1936.

Heckscher, E. E., *Mercantilism*, New York, 1935, 2 vols.

Kimble, G. H. T., *Geography in the Middle Ages*, London, 1938. A graphic account of geographic notions before the time of Columbus.

Morison, S. E., *Admiral of the Ocean Sea; A Life of Christopher Columbus*, Boston, 1942, 2 vols.

· Nowell, C. E., *The Great Discoveries and the First Colonial Empires*, Ithaca, N.Y., 1954 (Cornell). Brief but good.

Ogg, F. A., and Sharp, W. R., *Economic Development of Modern Europe*, New York, 1929.

Packard, L. B., *The Commercial Revolution*, New York, 1927.

Parr, C. M., *So Noble a Captain: The Life and Times of Ferdinand Magellan*, New York, 1953. Scholarly.

· Penrose, Boies, *Travel and Discovery in the Renaissance (1420–1620)*, Cambridge, Mass., 1952 (Atheneum).

Randall, J. H., Jr., *The Making of the Modern Mind*, New York, 1926, Chs. VI–X.

Rees, William, *Industry before the Industrial Revolution*, Cardiff, 1968, 2 vols.

Sée, Henri, *Modern Capitalism: Its Origin and Evolution*, London, 1928.

· Smith, Preserved, *The Age of the Reformation*, New York, 1920 (Collier, 2 vols.).

· ———, *A History of Modern Culture*, New York, 1930, Vol. I (Collier).

Sombart, Werner, *The Quintessence of Capitalism*, London, 1915. A suggestive interpretation.

· Sykes, P., *A History of Exploration from the Earliest Times to the Present*, London, 1934 (Torchbook). Comprehensive.

· Tawney, R. H., *Religion and the Rise of Capitalism*, New York, 1926 (Mentor).

Wrong, G. M., *The Rise and Fall of New France*, New York, 1928, 2 vols. A thorough account.

SOURCE MATERIALS

· More, Sir Thomas, *Utopia*, Part I, pp. 175–78, the Enclosure Movement (Penguin and others).

· Mun, Thomas, *England's Treasure by Foreign Trade*, Chs. I–IV, XX, XXI.

Richter, J. P., *The Literary Works of Leonardo da Vinci*, Vol. II, pp. 304–5, Leonardo da Vinci on Witchcraft, New York, 1939, 2 vols.

PART V

The Early Modern World
1400-1789

The period from 1400 to 1700 in Europe was the heyday of the Commercial Revolution, which overthrew the static economy of the medieval guilds and introduced a dynamic regime of business for profit. The entire era was marked by the growth of absolute governments, headed in some instances by kings who equated themselves with the state and professed to rule by divine right. States increased in size and in power and gradually absorbed the feudal duchies and principalities. Finally, during the years from 1600 to 1789, there occurred an intellectual revolution, culminating in the enthronement of reason and in the development of the concept of a mechanistic universe governed by inflexible laws. In Asia as in Europe, a rise in the level of civilization was accompanied by the establishment of autocratic centralized governments. The Mogul rulers of India and the Manchu Dynasty in China brought a large measure of stability and prosperity to those countries, but extravagance and a series of disastrous wars led the Mogul Dynasty to an early decline. In Japan, although feudalism remained intact, the rise of the Tokugawa Shoguns in 1603 provided the substance if not the form of absolute government. In contrast with Western European varieties, both Chinese and Japanese despotism survived into the twentieth century. Meanwhile, the maritime supremacy and commercial initiative of Western Europeans enabled them to exploit the riches of Africa. The widespread trade in African slaves, while swelling the coffers of European merchants, not only intensified conflict among and within African states but also hastened the decline of brilliant civilizations on that continent.

607

A Chronological Table

	WESTERN EUROPE	EASTERN AND CENTRAL EUROPE
1400	The domestic system, 1400–1750	Copernicus, 1473–1543
1500	Tudor Dynasty in England, 1485–1603	Catholic Reformation, 1500–1563
	Joint stock companies, 1550 Sir Francis Bacon, 1561–1626 Shakespeare, 1564–1616 Beginning of international law: Hugo Grotius, 1583–1645 Spanish Armada, 1588 Bourbon dynasty in France, 1589–1792 Edict of Nantes, 1598	Beginning of Protestant Revolution, 1517
1600	Mercantilism, 1600–1789 Classicism in literature and the arts, 1600–1750 Thirty Years' War, 1618–1648 Colbert, 1619–1683 Deism, 1630–1800 Rationalism in philosophy, 1630–1700 Puritan Revolution in England, 1640–1649 Beginning of modern state system, 1648 Commonwealth and Protectorate in England, 1649–1659	Classicism in literature and the arts, 1600–1750 Cameralism, 1600–1800 Thirty Years' War, 1618–1648
1650	Restoration of Stuart dynasty, 1660–1688	
	The Enlightenment, 1680–1800	Peter the Great, 1682–1725
	Revocation of Edict of Nantes, 1685	J. S. Bach, 1685–1750
	Newton's law of gravitation, 1687 Glorious Revolution in England, 1688–1689 John Locke, *Two Treatises of Civil Government*, 1690	
1700	Agricultural Revolution, 1700–1800	Agricultural Revolution, 1700–1800 Age of Enlightened Despots, 1740–1796 Frederick the Great, 1740–1786
	Physiocrats, 1750–1800	
	Seven Years' War, 1756–1763 Rousseau, *The Social Contract*, 1762 Beginning of factory system, *ca.* 1770	Mozart, 1756–1791 Catherine the Great, 1762–1796
1775	Joseph Priestley discovers oxygen, 1774	
	Adam Smith, *Wealth of Nations*, 1776 Romanticism, 1780–1830	Romanticism, 1780–1830 Kant, *The Critique of Pure Reason*, 1781
1789	Lavoisier discovers indestructibility of matter, 1789	
	Edward Jenner develops vaccination for smallpox, 1796	Goethe, *Faust*, 1790–1808

AFRICA AND THE AMERICAS

INDIA AND THE FAR EAST

Height of West African forest civilizations, 1400–1472		**1400**
Voyages of discovery and exploration, 1450–1600		**1500**
European maritime activity along African coasts, 1500–1800		
Growth of African slave trade, 1500–1800		
Portuguese dominance of East Coast city-states, 1505–1650	Arrival of Portuguese traders in China and Japan, 1537–1542	
Conquest of Mexico, 1522	Jesuit missionaries active in China and Japan, 1550–1650	
Conquest of Peru, 1537	Akbar the Great Mogul, 1556–1605	**1600**
Founding of Jamestown, 1607		
Landing of Pilgrims, 1620		
	British East India Co. chartered, 1600	
	Tokugawa Shogunate, 1603–1867	
	Taj Mahal, 1632–1647	
	Japanese isolation, 1637–1854	
Downfall of Kingdoms of Kongo and Ngola, 1665–1671	Manchu Dynasty in China, 1644–1912	**1650**
	Maratha Confederacy in India, 1650–1760	
Rise of Asante empire, founded on Gold Coast trade, 1700–1750		**1700**
Benjamin Franklin, 1706–1790	Decline of Mogul Empire in India, 1700–1800	
Asiento monopoly acquired by Britain, 1713		
French and Indian War, 1754–1763		
American War for Independence, 1775–1783		**1775**
Declaration of Independence, 1776		
U.S. Constitution goes into effect, 1789		**1789**
Bill of Rights, 1791		

CHAPTER 21

The Age of Absolutism (1485-1789)

There are four essential characteristics or qualities of royal authority.
First, royal authority is sacred.
Second, it is paternal.
Third, it is absolute.
Fourth, it is subject to reason.
—Jacques Bossuet, *Politics Drawn from the Very Words of Holy Scripture*

It becomes necessary now to go back and attempt to analyze the major political developments which accompanied the birth of modern civilization. During the fourteenth and fifteenth centuries the decentralized feudal regime of the Middle Ages broke down and was gradually replaced by dynastic states with governments of absolute power. For this there were numerous causes, some of which have already been discussed.[1] The position of the nobles was weakened by the growth of an urban economy, by the decay of the manorial system, and by the effects of the Crusades, the Black Death, and the Hundred Years' War. But these factors would not necessarily have laid the foundations for absolute monarchy. They might just as conceivably have resulted in chaos or in the democratic rule of the masses. We must therefore look for other causes to account for the rise of despotic governments. Apparently the most significant of these causes were the wars of the sixteenth and seventeenth centuries. These wars were themselves a product of a variety of factors. With the decay of feudalism, great struggles occurred between the forces of centralization and the forces of localism or decentralization. Ambitious kings sought to eliminate powerful princes and dukes who in some cases were their overlords. Struggles for empire also resulted from the geographic expansion incident to the Commercial Revolution. From the

The rise of the new absolutism

---

[1] See especially the paragraphs on the decline of feudalism in the chapter on The Later Middle Ages: Political and Economic Institutions.

611

colonies and into the royal coffers flowed wealth which was used in many cases to build navies and to hire professional soldiers. To organize and equip armies and fleets, large bureaucracies of civil servants became necessary. These also aided in the consolidation of monarchical power. Finally, the Protestant Revolution contributed not a little to the growth of royal omnipotence. It broke the unity of the Christian Church, abolished papal overlordship over secular rulers, fostered nationalism, revived the doctrine of the Apostle Paul that "the powers that be are ordained of God," and encouraged the kings of northern Europe to extend their authority over religious as well as over civil affairs.

1. THE GROWTH AND DECAY OF ABSOLUTE GOVERNMENT IN ENGLAND

The real founders of despotic government in England were the Tudors. The first of the kings of this line, Henry VII, came to the throne in 1485 at the end of the Wars of the Roses, in which rival factions of nobles had fought each other to the point of exhaustion. So great was the disgust on account of the turmoil of these wars that many of the citizens welcomed the establishment of absolute monarchy as an alternative to anarchy. The middle class, especially, desired the protection of consolidated government. This factor more than anything else accounts for the remarkable success of the Tudors in regulating the consciences of their subjects and in binding the nation to their will. It should be added that the most celebrated members of the dynasty, Henry VIII (1509–1547) and Elizabeth I (1558–1603), gained some of their power through shrewdly maintaining a semblance of popular government. When they desired to enact measures of doubtful popularity, they regularly went through the formality of obtaining parliamentary approval. Or when they wanted more money, they manipulated procedure in such a way as to make the appropriations appear to be voluntary grants by the representatives of the people. But the legislative branch of the government under these sovereigns was little more than a rubber stamp. They convoked Parliament irregularly and limited its sessions to very brief periods;[2] they interfered with elections and packed the two houses with their own favorites; and they cajoled, flattered, or bullied the members as the case might require in order to obtain their support.

In 1603 Elizabeth I, the last of the Tudors, died, leaving no direct descendants. Her nearest relative was her cousin, King James VI of Scotland, who now became the sovereign of both England and Scotland under the name of James I. His accession marks the beginning of the troubled history of the Stuarts, the last of

Absolutism in England founded by the Tudor monarchs

The establishment of divine-right monarchy by James I

[2] During Elizabeth's reign it was in session on the average only three or four weeks out of the year.

Queen Elizabeth I (1558–1603). In this regal portrait the queen is shown armed with the two symbols of power and justice, the scepter and the orb. A touch of cynicism seems to be revealed in her face.

the absolute dynasties in England. A curious mixture of stubbornness, vanity, and erudition, King James was appropriately called by Henry IV of France "the wisest fool in Christendom." Though he loved to have his courtiers flatter him as the English Solomon, he did not even have sense enough to emulate his Tudor predecessors in being satisfied with the substance of absolute power; he insisted upon the theory as well. From France he appropriated the doctrine of the divine right of kings, contending that "as it is atheism and blashemy to dispute what God can do, so it is presumption and high contempt in a subject to dispute what a king can do." In his speech to Parliament in 1609, he declared that "Kings are justly called gods, for they exercise a manner of resemblance of Divine power upon earth." [3]

That such ridiculous pretensions to divine authority would arouse opposition among the English people was a result which even James himself should have been able to foresee. Despite the clever machinations of the Tudor sovereigns and the desire of the middle class for stable government, England still had traditions of liberty which could not be ignored. The feudal ideal of limited government expressed in Magna Carta had never been entirely destroyed. Moreover, the policies of the new king were of such a character as to antagonize even some of his most conservative subjects. He insisted upon supplementing his income by modes of taxation which had never been sanctioned by Parliament; and when the leaders of that body remonstrated, he angrily tore up their protests and dissolved

The high-handed policies of James I

[3] Quoted by R. G. Gettell, *History of Political Thought*, p. 201.

the two houses. He interfered with the freedom of business by granting monopolies and extravagant privileges to favored companies. He conducted foreign relations in disregard for the economic interests of some of the most powerful citizens. Ever since the days of Hawkins and Drake, English merchants had been ambitious to destroy the commercial empire of Spain. They openly desired a renewal of the war, begun during Elizabeth's reign, for that purpose. But James made peace with Spain and entered into negotiations for marriage alliances favorable to Catholic sovereigns.

It was not marriage alliances alone that involved King James in religious troubles. The Elizabethan Compromise, which brought the Reformation in England to a close, had not been satisfactory to the more radical Protestants. They believed that it did not depart widely enough from the forms and doctrines of the Roman Church. During the reign of Queen Mary many of them had been in exile in France and had come under the influence of Calvinism. When Elizabeth's compromise policy took shape, they denounced it as representing too great a concession to Catholicism. Gradually they came to be called Puritans from their desire to "purify" the Anglican church of all traces of "Popish" ritual and observances. In addition, they preached an ascetic morality and condemned the episcopal system of church government. However, they did not form a united group. One faction believed that it could transform the Anglican church by working within that organization. The other preferred to withdraw from the Anglican fold and establish separate congregations where they could worship as they pleased. The members of this latter group came to be designated Separatists. They achieved fame in American history as the so-called Pilgrims, who founded Plymouth Colony.

Any brand or faction of Puritans was anathema to King James. Though not much interested in theology, he distrusted any religion that did not fit in with his own ideas of relations between church and state. In his estimation the Puritans, by repudiating the episcopal system of church government, were threatening to pull down one of the chief pillars of monarchy itself. Refusal to submit to the authority of bishops appointed by the king was identical in his mind with disloyalty to the sovereign. For this reason he regarded the Puritans as the equivalent of traitors and threatened to "harry them out of the land." He showed little more wisdom or discretion in his dealings with the Catholics. For the most part, he favored them, though he could not resist the temptation to levy fines upon them from time to time for violating the severe code which came down from the Reformation. In 1605 a group of fanatical adherents of the Roman faith organized the Gunpowder Plot. They planned to blow up the Parliament building while the king and the legislators were assembled in it, and in the resulting confusion, seize control of the government. The plot was discovered, and Parliament enacted even

Religious dissension during the reign of James I

Relations with Puritans and Catholics

614

more stringent laws against the Catholics. James, however, allowed the measures to go unenforced. Needless to say, his persistent leniency antagonized his Protestant subjects and made him more unpopular than ever.

From 1611 to 1621 King James ruled virtually without Parliament. But this did not mean that his troubles were over. In 1613 the rights of the people found a new champion when Sir Edward Coke was appointed Chief Justice. Coke was no democrat, but he did have a profound reverence for the common law and for the basic liberties inferred from Magna Carta. Moreover, he was a staunch defender of the privileged position of lawyers and judges. When the king insisted that he also had the faculty of reason and could interpret the law as well as the judges, Coke reminded him that he was not learned in the law, and that causes which concerned the lives and fortunes of his subjects were not be be decided by natural reason but only on the basis of long study and experience. Furthermore, the Chief Justice developed a rudimentary concept of judicial review. In the celebrated Dr. Bonham's case, he held that "when an act of Parliament is against common right and reason, or repugnant, or impossible to be performed, the common law will control it, and adjudge such act to be void." [4] There is evidence that this opinion was highly regarded in colonial America, and that it was one of the factors which later gave rise to the idea that the Supreme Court of the United States has the authority to nullify laws of Congress which conflict with the Constitution.

The first of the Stuart kings died in 1625 and was succeeded by his son as Charles I (1625–1649). The new monarch was more regal in appearance than his father, but he held the same inflated notions of royal power. As a consequence he was soon in hot water with the Puritans and the leaders of the parliamentary opposition. As in the case of his father, the conflict was precipitated by questions of taxation. Soon after his accession to the throne Charles became involved in a war with France. His need for revenue was desperate. When Parliament refused to make more than the customary grants, he resorted to forced loans from his subjects, punishing those who failed to comply by quartering soldiers upon them or throwing them into prison without a trial. The upshot of this tyranny was the famous Petition of Right, which Charles was compelled by the leaders of Parliament to agree to in 1628. This document declared all taxes not voted by Parliament illegal. It condemned also the quartering of soldiers in private houses and prohibited arbitrary imprisonment and the establishment of martial law in time of peace.

But acceptance of the Petition of Right did not end the conflict. Charles soon resumed his old tricks of raising money by various irregular means. He revived obsolete feudal laws and collected fines

The revolt of the judiciary

Charles I and the Petition of Right

4 Quoted by George H. Sabine, *A History of Political Theory*, p. 452.

from all who violated them. He compelled rich burghers to apply
for knighthood and then charged them high fees for their titles. He
sold monopolies at exorbitant rates and admonished his judges to increase the fines in criminal cases. But the most unpopular of all his
expedients for raising revenue was his collection of ship money.
Under an ancient custom the English seaboard towns had been required to contribute ships for the royal navy. Since the needs of the
fleet were now provided for in other ways, Charles maintained that
the towns should contribute money; and he proceeded to apply the
new tax not merely to the coastal cities but to the inland counties as
well. The levies of ship money were particularly irritating to the
middle class and served to crystallize the opposition of that group to
monarchical tyranny. Many refused to pay, and the king's attorney-
general finally decided to prosecute. A wealthy squire by the name
of John Hampden was haled into court in a test case. When convicted by a vote of seven to five, he acquired a sort of martyrdom.
For years he was venerated by the middle class as a symbol of resistance to royal autocracy.

Like his blundering father before him, Charles also aroused the
antagonism of the Calvinists. He appointed as Archbishop of Canterbury a clergyman by the name of William Laud, whose sympathies were decidedly high-Anglican. He outraged the Sabbatarian-
ism of the Puritans by authorizing public games on Sunday. Worse
still, he attempted to impose the episcopal system of church
government upon the Scottish Presbyterians, who were even more
radical Calvinists than the Puritans. The result was an armed rebellion by his northern subjects.

In order to get money to punish the Scots for their resistance,
Charles was finally compelled in 1640 to summon Parliament, after
more than eleven years of autocratic rule. Knowing full well that
the king was helpless without money, the leaders of the House of
Commons determined to take the government of the country into
their own hands. They abolished ship money and the special tribunals which had been used as agencies of tyranny. They impeached
and sent to the Tower the king's chief subordinates, Archbishop
Laud and the Earl of Strafford. They enacted a law forbidding the
monarch to dissolve Parliament and requiring sessions at least every
three years. Charles replied to these invasions of his prerogative by a
show of force. He marched with his guard into the House of Commons and attempted to arrest five of its leaders. All of them escaped, but the issue was now sharply drawn between king and Parliament, and an open conflict could no longer be avoided. Both sides
collected troops and prepared for an appeal to the sword.

These events ushered in a period of civil strife, which lasted from
1642 to 1649. It was a struggle at once political, economic, and religious. Arrayed on the side of the king were most of the chief nobles
and landowners, the Catholics, and the staunch Anglicans. The followers of Parliament included, in general, the small landholders,

tradesmen, and manufacturers. The majority were Puritans and Presbyterians. The members of the king's party were commonly known by the aristocratic name of Cavaliers. Their opponents, who cut their hair short in contempt for the fashionable custom of wearing curls, were called in derision Roundheads. At first the party of the royalists, having obvious advantages of military experience, won most of the victories. In 1644, however, the parliamentary army was reorganized, and soon afterward the fortunes of battle shifted. The Cavalier forces were badly beaten, and in 1646 the king was compelled to surrender. The struggle would now have ended had not a quarrel developed within the parliamentary party. The majority of its members, who were now Presbyterians, were ready to restore Charles to the throne as a limited monarch under an arrangement whereby the Presbyterian faith would be imposed upon England as the state religion. But a radical minority of Puritans, made up principally of Separatists but now more commonly known as Independents, distrusted Charles and insisted upon religious toleration for themselves and all other Protestants. Their leader was Oliver Cromwell (1599–1658), who had risen to command of the Roundhead army. Taking advantage of the dissension within the ranks of his opponents, Charles renewed the war in 1648 but after a brief campaign was forced to concede that his cause was hopeless.

The second defeat of the king gave an indisputable mastery of the situation to the Independents. Cromwell and his friends now resolved to put an end to "that man of blood," the Stuart monarch, and remodel the political system in accordance with their own desires. They conducted a purge of the legislative body by military force, ejecting 143 Presbyterians from the House of Commons; and then with the "Rump Parliament" that remained—numbering about sixty members—they proceeded to eliminate the monarchy. An act was passed redefining treason so as to apply to the offenses of the king. Next a special High Court of Justice was established, and Charles was brought to trial before it. His conviction was a mere matter of form. On January 30, 1649, he was beheaded in front of his palace of Whitehall. A short time later the House of Lords was abolished, and England became an oligarchic republic. The first stage in the so-called Puritan Revolution was now completed.

The work of organizing the new state, which was given the name of the Commonwealth, was entirely in the hands of the Independents. Since the Rump Parliament continued as the legislative body, the really fundamental change was in the nature of the executive. In place of the king there was set up a Council of State composed of forty-one members. Cromwell, with the army at his back, soon came to dominate both of these bodies. However, as time went on he became exasperated by the attempts of the legislators to perpetuate themselves in power and to profit from confiscation of the wealth of their opponents. Accordingly, in 1653, he marched a

Cavaliers and Roundheads

The defeat and execution of the king

Oliver Cromwell

The Trial of Charles I, King of Great Britain and Ireland, 1625–1649. His armies defeated by the forces of Cromwell and himself a prisoner, Charles was tried by a special court in Westminster Hall and convicted of treason "by levying war against the parliament and kingdom of England." Soon afterward he was beheaded. His dignity in his last hours fitted Shakespeare's lines: "Nothing in his Life became him, like the leaving it."

detachment of troops into the Rump and ordered the members to disperse, informing them that the Lord Jehovah had no further use for their services. This action was followed by the establishment of a virtual dictatorship under a constitution drafted by officers of the army. Called the Instrument of Government, it was the nearest approach to a written constitution Britain has ever had. Extensive powers were given to Cromwell as Lord Protector for life, and his office was made hereditary. At first a Parliament exercised limited authority in making laws and levying taxes, but in 1655 its members were abruptly dismissed by the Lord Protector. Thereafter the government was but a thinly disguised autocracy. Cromwell now wielded a sovereignty even more despotic than any the Stuart monarchs would have dared to claim. In declaring his authority to be from God he even revived what practically amounted to the divine right of kings.

That Cromwell's regime would have its difficulties was certainly to be expected, since it rested upon the support of only a small minority of the British nation. He was opposed not only by royalists and Anglicans but by various dissenters more radical than he. Like all upheavals of a similar character, the Puritan Revolution tended to move farther and farther in an extremist direction. Many of the Puritans became Levellers, who derived their name from their advocacy of equal political rights and privileges for all classes. Expressly disclaiming any intention of equalizing property, they confined their radicalism to the political sphere. They insisted that sovereignty inheres in the people and that government should rest upon the consent of the governed. Long in advance of any other party, they demanded a written constitution, universal manhood suffrage, and the supremacy of Parliament. The Levellers were especially powerful in the army and through it exerted some influence upon the government. Still farther to the left were the Diggers, so called from their attempt to seize and cultivate unenclosed common land and distribute the produce to the poor. Though in common with the Levellers the Diggers appealed to the law of nature as a source of rights, they were more interested in economic than in political equality. They espoused a kind of primitive communism based upon the idea that the land is the "common treasury" of all. Every ablebodied man would be required to work at productive labor, and all persons would be permitted to draw from the common fund of wealth produced in proportion to their needs. The church would be transformed into an educational institution and the clergy would become schoolmasters, giving instruction every seventh day in public affairs, history, and the arts and sciences. "To know the secrets of nature is to know the works of God" was one of the Digger mottoes.

In September 1658, the stout-hearted Protector died. He was succeeded by his well-meaning but irresolute son Richard, who managed to hold office only until May of the following year. Perhaps even a man of much sterner fiber would also have failed eventually, for the country had grown tired of the austerities of Calvinist rule. Neither the Commonwealth nor the Protectorate had ever had the support of a majority of the English nation. Royalists regarded the Independents as usurpers. Republicans hated the disguised monarchy which Oliver Cromwell had set up. Catholics and Anglicans resented the branding of their acts of worship as criminal offenses. Even some members of the middle class gradually came to suspect that Cromwell's war with Spain had done more harm than good by endangering English commerce with the West Indies. For these and similar reasons there was general rejoicing when in 1660 a newly elected Parliament proclaimed Prince Charles king and invited him to return to England and occupy the throne of his father. The new king had gained a reputation for joyous living and easy morality, and his accession was hailed as a welcome relief from the somber rule of soldiers and zealots. Besides, he pledged himself not to reign as a despot, but to respect Parliament and to observe Magna Carta and the Petition of Right; for he admitted that he was not anxious to "resume his travels." England now entered upon a period known as the Restoration, covered by the reigns of Charles II (1660–1685) and his brother James II (1685–1688). Despite its

Charles II

auspicious beginning, many of the old problems had not really been solved but were simply concealed by the fond belief that the nation had regained its former stability.

Toward the end of the seventeenth century England went through a second political upheaval, the so-called Glorious Revolution of 1688–1689. Several of the causes were grounded in the policies of Charles II. That amiable sovereign was extravagant and lazy but determined on occasion to let the country know whose word was law. His strongly pro-Catholic attitude aroused the fears of patriotic Englishmen that their nation might once again be brought into subservience to Rome. Worse still, he showed a disposition, in spite of earlier pledges, to defy the authority of Parliament. In 1672 he suspended the laws against Catholics and other Dissenters and nine years later resolved to dispense with the legislative branch entirely. The policies of Charles II were continued in more insolent form by his brother, who succeeded him in 1685. King James II was an avowed Catholic and seemed bent upon making that faith the established religion of England. He openly violated an act of Parliament requiring that all holders of public office should adhere to the Anglican church, and proceeded to fill important positions in the army and the civil service with his Romanist followers. He continued his brother's practice of exempting Catholics from the disabilities imposed upon them by Parliament, even going so far as to demand that the Anglican bishops should read his decrees for this purpose in their churches. As long as his opponents could expect that James II would be succeeded by one of his two Protestant daughters, they were inclined to tolerate his arbitrary rule, lest the country be plunged again into civil war. But when the king acquired a son by his second wife, who was a Catholic, the die of revolution was cast. It was feared that the young prince would be infected with his father's doctrines, and that, as a consequence, England would be fettered with the shackles of despotic and papist rule for an indefinite time to come. To forestall such a result it seemed necessary to depose the king.

The "Glorious Revolution" of 1688–1689 was an entirely bloodless affair. A group of politicians from both the upper and middle classes secretly invited Prince William of Orange and his wife Mary, the elder daughter of James II, to become joint rulers of England.[5] William crossed over from Holland with an army and occupied London without firing a shot. Deserted even by those whom he had counted as loyal supporters, King James took refuge in France. The English throne was now declared vacant by Parliament and the crown presented to the new sovereigns. But their enthronement did not complete the revolution. Throughout the year 1689 Parliament

The failure of the Puritan Revolution paves the way for the Glorious Revolution of 1688–1689

Results of the Glorious Revolution

---

[5] There is evidence that William himself was a party to the secrets of the dissatisfied Englishmen, and he may even have inspired the invitation. Threatened with war by the king of France, he could make very good use of the resources and military power of England.

passed numerous laws designed to safeguard the rights of Englishmen and to protect its own power from monarchical invasion. First
came an act requiring that appropriations should be made for one
year only. Next the Toleration Act was passed, granting religious
liberty to all Christians except Catholics and Unitarians. Finally, on
the sixteenth of December the famous Bill of Rights was enacted
into law. It provided for trial by jury and affirmed the right of Englishmen to petition the government for a redress of grievances. It
condemned excessive bail, cruel punishments, and exorbitant fines.
And it forbade the king to suspend laws or to levy taxes without the
consent of Parliament. More sweeping in its provisions than the
Petition of Right of 1628, it was backed by a Parliament that now
had the power to see that it was obeyed.

The significance of the revolution of 1688–1689 would be almost
impossible to exaggerate. Since it marked the final triumph of Parliament over the king, it therefore spelled the doom of absolute
monarchy in England. Never again was any crowned head in Britain
able to defy the legislative branch of the government as the Stuart
monarchs had done. The revolution also dealt the *coup de grâce* to
the theory of the divine right of kings. It would have been impossible for William and Mary to have denied the fact that they received
their crowns from Parliament. And the authority of Parliament to
determine who should be king was made more emphatic by the passage of the Act of Settlement in 1701. This law provided that upon
the death of the heiress-presumptive Anne, younger sister of Mary,
the crown should go to the Electress Sophia of Hanover or to the
eldest of her heirs who might be Protestant.[6] There were some
forty men or women with a better claim to the throne than Sophia,
but all were eliminated arbitrarily by Parliament on the ground of
their being Catholics. Finally, the Glorious Revolution contributed
much to the American and French revolutions at the end of the
eighteenth century. The example of the English in overthrowing
absolute rule was a powerful inspiration to the opponents of despotism elsewhere. It was the British revolutionary ideal of limited government which furnished the substance of the political theory of
Voltaire, Jefferson, and Paine. And a considerable portion of the
English Bill of Rights was incorporated in the French Declaration of
the Rights of Man in 1789 and in the first ten amendments to the
American Constitution.

*Significance
of the
Glorious
Revolution*

2. ABSOLUTE MONARCHY IN FRANCE AND SPAIN

The development of absolutism in France followed a course quite
similar in some respects to that in England. Although France remained Catholic, her rulers had to contend with a Calvinist (Hugue-

[6] In this way the House of Hanover, the ruling dynasty until 1901, came to
the English throne. The first Hanoverian king was Sophia's son, George I
(1714–1727).

not) opposition almost as formidable as that of the Puritans in England. They also had a prosperous middle class to which they could look for support, on occasions, against the nobility. Both nations had their staunch defenders of absolutism among lawyers and political philosophers. But there was one notable difference. England enjoyed an advantage of geographic isolation that sheltered her from foreign danger. Her soil had not been invaded since the Norman Conquest in 1066. As a consequence her people felt secure, and her rulers found it difficult to justify a huge professional army. They did, of course, maintain large fleets of war vessels, but a "bluewater" navy could not be used in the same manner as an army stationed in inland garrisons to overawe subjects or to stifle incipient revolutions. France, on the other hand, like most Continental nations, faced almost constant threats of invasion. Her northeastern and eastern frontiers were poorly protected by geographic barriers and had been penetrated several times. As a result, it was easy for the French kings to argue the need for massive armies of professional soldiers. And such troops could readily be utilized to nip domestic disturbances in the bud. It would doubtless be a mistake to give all of the credit to this difference in geographic position for the longer persistence of absolute government in France, but it was certainly a major factor.

The growth of royal despotism in France was the product of a gradual evolution. Some of its antecedents went back to the reigns of Philip Augustus, Louis IX, and Philip IV in the thirteenth and fourteenth centuries. These kings solidified royal power by hiring mercenary soldiers, subsituting national taxation for feudal dues, arrogating to themselves the power to administer justice, and restricting the authority of the Pope to regulate ecclesiastical affairs in their kingdom. The Hundred Years' War (1337–1453) produced an even further accretion of power for the kings of France. They were now able to introduce new forms of taxation, to maintain a huge standing army, and to abolish the sovereignty of the feudal nobles. The members of this latter class were gradually reduced to the level of courtiers, dependent mainly upon the monarch for their titles and prestige.

The trend toward absolutism was interrupted during the sixteenth century when France was involved in a war with Spain and torn by a bloody struggle between Catholics and Huguenots at home. Ambitious nobles took advantage of the confusion to assert their power and contested the succession to the throne. Peace was restored to the distracted kingdom in 1593 by Henry of Navarre (1589–1610), who four years before had proclaimed himself king as Henry IV. He was the founder of the Bourbon dynasty. Though at one time a leader of the Huguenot faction, Henry perceived that the nation would never accept him unless he renounced the Calvinist religion. Flippantly remarking that Paris was worth a Mass, he formally

Contrasting conditions in England and France

The origins of absolutism in France

Henry IV and the Duke of Sully

adopted the Catholic faith. In 1598 he issued the Edict of Nantes, guaranteeing freedom of conscience and political rights to all Protestants. With the grounds for religious controversy thus removed, Henry could turn his attention to rebuilding his kingdom. In this work, he had the able assistance of his chief minister, the Duke of Sully. Grim, energetic, and penurious, Sully was a worthy forerunner of Colbert in the seventeenth century. For years the king and his faithful servant labored to repair the shattered fortunes of France. Sully devoted his efforts primarily to fiscal reform, so as to eliminate corruption and waste and bring more revenue into the royal treasury. He endeavored also to promote the prosperity of agriculture by draining swamps, improving devastated lands, subsidizing stock-raising, and opening up foreign markets for the products of the soil. The king gave most of his attention to fostering industry and commerce. He introduced the manufacture of silk into France, encouraged other industries by subsidies and monopolies, and made favorable commercial treaties with England and Spain. But Henry did not stop with economic reforms. He was deeply concerned with crushing the renascent power of the nobility, and so successful were his efforts in this direction that he restored the monarchy to the dominant position it had held at the end of the Hundred Years' War. He was active also in sponsoring the development of a colonial empire in America. During his reign the French acquired a foothold in Canada and began their exploration in the region of the Great Lakes and the Mississippi Valley. His rule was intelligent and benevolent but none the less despotic.

The reign of Henry IV was brought to an end by the dagger of a crazed fanatic in 1610. Since the new king, Louis XIII, was only

The Assassination of Henry IV. This contemporary engraving shows the manner in which Rivaillic, a Catholic monk, climbed upon the wheel of Henry's carriage in order to stab the French ruler.

Cardinal Richelieu

nine years old, the country was ruled by his mother, Marie de Médicis, as regent. In 1624 Louis XIII, no longer under the regency, entrusted the management of his kingdom to a brilliant but domineering cleric, Cardinal Richelieu, whom he made his chief minister. Richelieu dedicated himself to two objectives: (1) to destroy all limitations upon the authority of the king; and (2) to make France the chief power in Europe. In the pursuit of these aims he allowed nothing to stand in his way. He ruthlessly suppressed the nobility, destroying its most dangerous members and rendering the others harmless by attaching them as pensioners to the royal court. Though he fostered education and patronized literature, he neglected the interests of commerce and allowed graft and extravagance to flourish in the government. His main constructive achievements were the creation of a postal service and the establishment of a system under which *intendants*, or agents of the king, took charge of local government. Both were conceived as devices for consolidating the nation under the control of the crown, thereby eradicating surviving traces of feudal authority.

Richelieu's foreign policy

Richelieu's ambitions were not limited to domestic affairs. To make France the most powerful nation in Europe was alleged to require an aggressive diplomacy and eventual participation in war. France was still surrounded by what Henry IV had referred to as a "Hapsburg ring." On her southern border was Spain, ruled since 1516 by a branch of the Hapsburg family. To the north, less than 100 miles from Paris, were the Spanish Netherlands. Other centers of Hapsburg power included Alsace, the Franche-Comté, Savoy, Genoa, and Milan, and still farther to the east the great Austrian Empire itself. Cardinal Richelieu eagerly awaited an opportunity to break this ring. As we shall see, he finally found it in the Thirty Years' War. Though engaged in suppressing Protestants at home, he did not hesitate to ally himself with Gustavus Adolphus, king of

The Inauguration of the Invalides. A detail from the painting by Martin the Younger shows Louis XIV arriving at the site of the home for war heroes.

Sweden and leader of a coalition of Protestant states. Long before his death in 1642 the great cardinal-statesman had forged to the front as the most powerful individual in Europe.

Absolute monarchy in France attained its zenith during the reigns of the last three Bourbon kings before the Revolution. The first of the monarchs of this series was Louis XIV (1643–1715), who epitomized the ideal of absolutism more completely than any other sovereign of his age. Proud, extravagant, and domineering, Louis entertained the most exalted notions of his position as king. Not only did he believe that he was commissioned by God to reign, but he regarded the welfare of the state as intimately bound up with his own personality. The famous phrase imputed to him, *l'état c'est moi* (I am the state), may not represent his exact words, but it expresses very clearly the conception he held of his own authority. He chose the sun as his official emblem to indicate his belief that the nation derived its glory and sustenance from him as the planets do theirs from the actual sun. He gave personal supervision to every department and regarded his ministers as mere clerks with no duty but to obey his orders. In general, he followed the policies of Henry IV and Richelieu in consolidating national power at the expense of local officials and in trying to reduce the nobles to mere parasites of the court. But any possible good he may have done was completely overshadowed by his extravagant wars and his reactionary policy in religion. In 1685 he revoked the Edict of Nantes, which had granted freedom of conscience to the Huguenots. As a result, large numbers of his most intelligent and prosperous subjects fled from the country.

Until the beginning of the Revolution in 1789 the form of the French government remained essentially as Louis XIV had left it. His successors, Louis XV (1715–1774) and Louis XVI (1774–1792), also professed to rule by divine right. But neither of these kings had the desire to emulate the Grand Monarch in his enthusiasm for work and his meticulous attention to the business of state. Louis XV was lazy and incompetent and allowed himself to be dominated by a succession of mistresses. Problems of government bored him incredibly, and when obliged to preside at the council table he "opened his mouth, said little, and thought not at all." His grandson, who succeeded him, the ill-fated Louis XVI, was weak in character and mentally dull. Indifferent to politics, he amused himself by shooting deer from the palace window and playing at his hobbies of lock-making and masonry. On the day in 1789 when mobs stormed the Bastille, he wrote in his diary "Nothing." Yet both of these monarchs maintained a government which, if not more despotic, was at least more arbitrary than had ever been the case before. They permitted their ministers to imprison without a trial persons suspected of disloyalty; they suppressed the courts for refusing to approve their decrees; and they brought the country to

Louis XIV, the supreme incarnation of absolute rule

Louis XIV by Rigaud

Louis XV and Louis XVI

Versailles. This seventeenth-century painting shows the château which was the focus of social life during the reign of Louis XIV.

the verge of bankruptcy by their costly wars and by their reckless extravagance for the benefit of mistresses and worthless favorites. If they had deliberately planned to make revolution inevitable, they could scarcely have succeeded better.

The rise of absolutism in Spain

The growth of absolute monarchy in Spain was swifter and less interrupted than was true of its development in France. As late as the thirteenth century what is now Spain was divided into five parts. Four Christian kingdoms—Aragon, Castile, León, and Navarre—maintained a precarious existence in the north, while the southern half of the country was in the possession of the Moors. In the fifteenth century *de facto* unification was accomplished by the marriage of Ferdinand of Aragon and Isabella of Castile. Though ruling nominally as independent monarchs, for all practical purposes they were sovereigns of a united Spain. Like their predecessors, they continued the crusade against the Moors, completing as their major achievement the conquest of Granada, last stronghold of Moorish power on the Iberian peninsula. The surviving Moors were expelled from the country, along with the Jews, for in the desperate struggle to drive out an alien invader all forms of non-Christian belief had come to be regarded as treason.

The empire of Charles V

Queen Isabella died in 1504, and King Ferdinand in 1516. Their entire kingdom was inherited by their daughter Joanna, who had married into the Hapsburg family. Her son succeeded to the throne of Spain as Charles I in 1516. Three years later he was elected Holy Roman Emperor as Charles V, thereby uniting Spain with Central Europe and southern Italy. Charles was interested not merely in the destinies of Spain but in the welfare of the Church and in the politics of Europe as a whole. He dreamed that he might be the instrument of restoring the religious unity of Christendom, broken by the Protestant Revolution and of making the empire over which he presided a worthy successor of Imperial Rome. Though successful in holding his disjointed domain together and in fighting off attempts of the French to conquer his Italian possessions and of the Turks to overrun Europe, he failed in the achievement of his larger objectives. At the age of fifty-six, overcome with a sense of discouragement and futility, he abdicated and retired into a monastery. The German princes chose his brother, Ferdinand I, to succeed him as Holy Roman Emperor. His Spanish and Italian possessions, including the colonies overseas, passed to his son, who became king as Philip II.

Philip II came to the throne of Spain at the height of its glory. But he also witnessed, and to a considerable extent was responsible for, the beginning of its decline. His policies were mainly an intensification of those of his predecessors. He was narrow, despotic, and cruel. Determined to enforce a strict conformity in matters of religion upon all of his subjects, he is reputed to have boasted that he would gather faggots to burn his own son if the latter were guilty of heresy. Reference has already been made to the horrors of the Spanish Inquisition and of the war for suppression of the revolt in the Netherlands. Philip was equally shortsighted in his colonial policy. Natives were butchered or virtually enslaved. Their territories were greedily despoiled of their gold and silver, which were dragged off to Spain in the mistaken belief that this was the surest means of increasing the nation's wealth. No thought was given to the development of new industries in either the colonies or the mother country. Instead, the gold and silver were largely squandered in furthering Philip's military and political ambitions. It can be said, however, in the king's defense that he was following the accepted theories of the time. Doubtless most other monarchs with a like opportunity would have imitated his example. Philip II's crowning stupidity was probably his war against England. Angered by the

Philip II of Spain. This painting by Coello shows the famous protruding chin and lower lip which were characteristic features of the Hapsburg family.

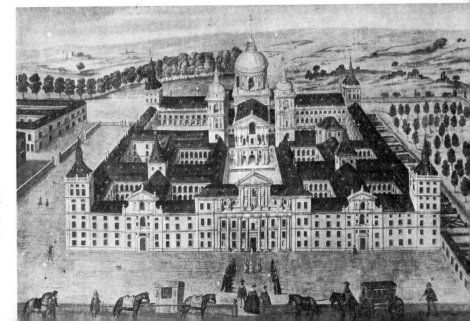

The Escorial. Built in the sixteenth century by Philip II of Spain, it originally served as his retreat.

attacks of English privateers upon Spanish commerce, and frustrated in his schemes to bring England back into the Catholic faith, he sent a great fleet in 1588, the "Invincible Armada," to destroy Queen Elizabeth's navy. But Philip had little knowledge of either the new techniques of naval warfare or of the robust patriotism of the English. A combination of fighting seamanship and disastrous storms sent most of his 132 ships to the bottom of the Channel. Spain never recovered from the blow. Though a brilliant afterglow, exemplified in the work of the Renaissance artists and dramatists, continued for some years, the greatness of Spain as a nation was approaching its end.

The destruction of the Armada

3.   ABSOLUTISM IN CENTRAL EUROPE

The chief countries of Central Europe where despotism flourished on its most grandiose scale were Prussia and Austria. The founder of absolute rule in Prussia was the Great Elector, Frederick William, a contemporary of Louis XIV. Not only was he the first member of the Hohenzollern family to acquire full sovereignty over Prussia, but he brought all of his dominions under centralized rule, abolishing their local Diets and merging their petty armies into a national military force. The work of the Great Elector was continued and extended by his grandson, known as Frederick William I (1713–1740), since he now had the title of *King* of Prussia. This miserly monarch ruled over his people like a Hebrew patriarch, regulating their private conduct and attending personally to the correction of their short-comings. His consuming passion was the army, which he more than doubled in size and drilled to a machine-like efficiency. He even sold the furniture in the palace to hire recruits for his famous regiment of Potsdam Giants. Those whom money could not buy he is alleged to have kidnaped. He traded musicians and prize stallions for soldiers who were well over six feet in height.

The beginning of absolute monarchy in Prussia

The most noted of the Prussian despots was Frederick II (1740–1786), commonly known as Frederick the Great. An earnest disciple of the reformist doctrines of the new rationalist philosophy, Frederick was the leading figure among the "enlightened despots" of the eighteenth century. Declaring himself not the master but merely the "first servant of the state," he wrote essays to prove that Machiavelli was wrong and rose at five in the morning to begin a Spartan routine of personal management of public affairs. He made Prussia in many ways the best-governed state in Europe, abolishing torture of accused criminals and bribery of judges, establishing elementary schools, and promoting the prosperity of industry and agriculture. He fostered scientific forestry and imported crop rotation, iron plows, and clover from England. He opened up new lands in Silesia and brought in hundreds of thousands of immigrants to cultivate them. When wars ruined their farms, he supplied the

Frederick William I

The Spanish Armada. This contemporary engraving shows the defeat of the Spanish by the English in the Channel.

peasants with new livestock and tools. As an admirer of Voltaire, whom he entertained for some time at his court, he tolerated all sorts of religious beliefs. He declared that he would build a mosque in Berlin if enough Moslems wished to locate there. Yet he was perversely anti-Semitic. He levied special taxes on the Jews and made efforts to close the professions and the civil service to them. Moreover, such benevolence as he showed in internal affairs was not carried over into foreign relations. Frederick robbed Austria of Silesia, conspired with Catherine of Russia to dismember Poland, and contributed at least his full share to the bloody wars of the eighteenth century.

The full bloom of absolutism in Austria came during the reigns of Maria Theresa (1740–1780) and Joseph II (1780–1790). Under the rule of the beautiful but high-strung empress a national army was established, the powers of the Church were curtailed in the interest of consolidated government, and elementary and higher education was greatly expanded. Unlike the despots of most other countries, Maria Theresa was sincerely devoted to Christian morality. Though she participated in the dismemberment of Poland to make up for the loss of Silesia, she did so with grave misgivings—an attitude which prompted the scornful remark of Frederick the Great: "She weeps, but she takes her share." The reforms of Maria Theresa were extended, at least on paper by her son Joseph II. Inspired by the teachings of French philosophers, Joseph determined to remake his empire in accordance with the highest ideals of justice and reason. Not only did he plan to reduce the powers of the Church by confiscating its lands and abolishing monasteries, but he aspired to humble the nobles and improve the condition of the masses. He decreed that the serfs should become free men and promised to relieve them of the feudal obligations owed to their masters. He aimed

Absolutism in Austria

629

to make education universal and to force the nobles to pay their proper share of taxes. But most of his magnificent plans ended in failure. He antagonized not merely the nobles and clergy but also the proud Hungarians, who were deprived of all rights of self-government. He alienated the sympathies of the peasants by making them liable to compulsory military service. He was scarcely any more willing than Louis XIV or Frederick the Great to sacrifice personal power and national glory even for the sake of his lofty ideals.

4. ABSOLUTISM IN RUSSIA

Russia at the beginning of the early modern age was a composite of European and Oriental characteristics. Much of her territory had been colonized by the Norsemen in the early Middle Ages. Her religion, her calendar, her system of writing had been derived from Byzantium. Even her feudal regime, with its boyars, or magnates, and serfs, was not greatly dissimilar to that of western Europe. On the other hand, much of Russia's culture, and many of her customs, were distinctly not European. Her arts were limited almost entirely to icon painting and an onion-domed religious architecture. There was no literature in the Russian language, arithmetic was barely known, Arabic numerals were not used, and bankers and merchants made their calculations with the abacus. Nor were manners and customs comparable to those of the West. Women of the upper classes were veiled and secluded. Flowing beards and skirted garments were universal for men. Knives and forks were considered superfluous. Seasons of wild revelry alternated with periods of repentance and morbid atonement. Geographically, also, Russia had an Asiatic orientation. The Russian heartland looked out upon Siberia, Persia, and China, with Europe in the rear. It would be a mistake, however, to suppose that Russia was totally cut off from Europe. As early as the fourteenth century, German merchants of the Hanse conducted some trade in Russian furs and amber. In the 1550's English merchants discovered the White Sea and made Archangel a port of entry through which military supplies could be exchanged for a few Russian goods and even products from Persia and China. But with Archangel frozen most of the year, the volume of this trade was undoubtedly small.

Russia at the beginning of the modern age

As late as the thirteenth century Russia was a collection of small principalities. They were besieged from the west by Swedes, Lithuanians, Poles, and the Teutonic Knights, or members of the Teutonic Order. The Teutonic Order was one of several religious and military organizations that sprang from the Crusades. Established originally for charitable purposes, it developed into a military club whose members adopted as their mission the conquest of lands on Germany's eastern frontier. Their operations set a precedent for the famous *Drang nach Osten* (Drive to the East) which later occu-

Foreign invaders; the Mongols

pied such a prominent place in German history. From the east Russia was threatened by the Mongols (Tartars) or the Golden Horde, who had established a great empire in central Asia, eventually including both northern India and China. In 1237 the Mongols began an invasion which led to their conquest of nearly all of Russia. Mongol rule was in several ways a disaster. It marked the development of a stronger Asiatic orientation. Henceforth Russia turned more and more away from Europe and looked beyond the Urals as the arena of her future development. Her citizens intermarried with Mongols and adopted many elements of their way of life.

Eventually, Mongol power declined, in accordance with the common fate of vast empires. In 1380 a Russian army defeated the Tartars and thus initiated a movement to drive them back into Asia. The state which assumed the leadership of this movement was the Grand Duchy of Moscow. Under strong rulers it had been increasing its power for some time. Located near the sources of the great rivers flowing both north and south, it had geographic advantages surpassing those of the other states. Moreover, it had recently been made the headquarters of the Russian church. The first of the princes of Moscow to put himself forward as Tsar (Caesar) of Russia was Ivan the Great (1462–1505). Taking as his bride the niece of the last of the Byzantine Emperors, who had perished in the capture of Constantinople in 1453, he proclaimed himself his successor by the grace of God. He adopted as his insignia the Byzantine double-headed eagle and imported Italian architects to build him an enormous palace, the Kremlin, in imitation of the one in Constantinople. Avowing his intention to recover the ancient lands that had been lost to foreign invaders, he forced the Prince of Lithuania to acknowledge him as sovereign of "all the Russias" and pushed the Tartars out of northern Russia and beyond the Urals.

The rise of Moscow; Ivan the Great

The first of the Tsars to attempt the Europeanization of Russia was Peter the Great (1682–1725). He stands out as the most powerful and probably the most intelligent autocrat yet to occupy the Russian throne. With a reckless disregard for ancient customs, Peter endeavored to force his subjects to change their ways of living. He forbade the Oriental seclusion of women and commanded both sexes to adopt European styles of dress. He made the use of tobacco compulsory among the members of his court. He summoned the great nobles before him and clipped their flowing beards with his own hand. In order to make sure of his own absolute power he abolished all traces of local self-government and established a system of national police. For the same reason he annihilated the authority of the patriarch of the Orthodox church and placed all religious affairs under a Holy Synod subject to his own control. Profoundly interested in Western science and technology, he made journeys to Holland and England to learn about shipbuilding and industry. He imitated the mercantilist policies of Western nations by improving

Peter the Great. An eighteenth-century mosaic.

631

agriculture and fostering manufactures and commerce. In order to get "windows to the west" he conquered territory along the Baltic shore and transferred his capital from Moscow to St. Petersburg, his new city at the mouth of the Neva. But the good that he did was greatly outweighed by his extravagant wars and his fiendish cruelty. He put thousands to death for alleged conspiracies against him. He murdered his own son and heir because the latter boasted that when *he* became Tsar he would return Russia to the ways of her fathers. To raise money for his expensive wars he debased the currency, sold valuable concessions to foreigners, established government monopolies on the production of salt, oil, caviar, and coffins, and imposed taxes on almost everything, from baths to beehives.

The significance of Peter the Great

The significance of Peter the Great is not easy to evaluate. He did not singlehandedly transform Russia into a Western nation. Western influences had been seeping into the country as a consequence of trade contacts for many years. But Peter accelerated the process and gave it a more radical direction. Evidence abounds that he really did aim to remake the nation and to give it at least a veneer of civilization. He sent many of his countrymen abroad to study. He simplified the ancient alphabet and established the first newspaper to be published in Russia. He ordered the publication of a book on polite behavior, teaching his subjects not to spit on the floor or to scratch themselves or gnaw bones at dinner. He encouraged exports, built a fleet on the Baltic, and fostered new industries such as textiles and mining. Though a reaction set in after Peter's death against many of his innovations, some of them survived for at least two centuries. The church, for example, continued as essentially an arm of the state, governed by a Procurator of the Holy Synod appointed by the Tsar himself. Serfdom not only survived but continued in the extended forms required or authorized by Peter. No longer were serfs bound to the soil; they could be bought and sold at any time, even for work in factories and mines. Finally, the absolutism devel-

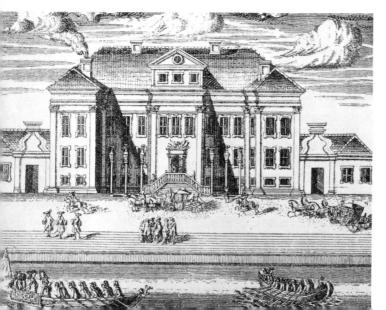

The Winter Palace. This contemporary engraving shows the palace built by Peter the Great in the town that bore his name, St. Petersburg.

oped by Peter showed few signs of abating until the twentieth century. It was an absolutism based upon force, with a secret police, an extensive bureaucracy, and a subordinated church as instruments for imposing the autocrat's will.

The other most noted of the Russian monarchs in the age of absolutism was Catherine the Great (1762–1796), who before her marriage was a German princess. Frequently classified as one of the "enlightened despots," Catherine corresponded with French philosophers, founded hospitals and orphanages, and expressed the hope that someday the serfs might be liberated. Ambitious to gain for herself a place in the Enlightenment, she purchased Diderot's library and rose at five in the morning to dabble in scholarship. She wrote plays, published a digest of Blackstone's *Commentaries on the Laws of England,* and even began a history of Russia. Her accomplishments as a reformer, however, had only a limited scope. She took steps toward a codification of the Russian laws, restricted the use of torture, and remodeled and consolidated local government. Any plans she may have had, however, for improving the lot of the peasants were abruptly canceled after a violent serf rebellion in 1773–1774. Landlords and priests were murdered and the ruling classes terrified as the revolt swept through the Urals and the valley of the Volga. Catherine responded with stern repression. The captured leader of the peasants was drawn and quartered, and as a guaranty against future outbreaks, the nobles were given increased powers over their serfs. They were permitted to deal with them virtually as if they were chattel slaves. Catherine's chief significance lies in the fact that she continued the work of Peter the Great in introducing Russia to Western ideas and in making the country a formidable power in European affairs. She managed to extend the boundaries of her country to include not only eastern Poland but lands on the Black Sea.

Catherine the Great

5. THE WARS OF THE DESPOTS

Between 1485 and 1789 the years of peace in Europe were actually outnumbered by the years of war. The earlier conflicts were largely religious in character and have already been dealt with in the chapter on the Reformation. The majority of the wars after 1600 partook of the nature of struggles for supremacy among the powerful despots of the principal countries. But religion was also a factor in some of them, and so was the greed of the commercial classes. In general, nationalistic motives were much less important than in the wars of the nineteenth and twentieth centuries. Peoples and territories were so many pawns to be moved back and forth in the game of dynastic aggrandizement.

The major warfare of the seventeenth century revolved around a titanic duel between Hapsburgs and Bourbons. Originally the rulers of Austria, the Hapsburgs had gradually extended their power over

633

Underlying causes of conflict

Hungary and Bohemia as well. In addition, the head of the family enjoyed what was left of the distinction of being Holy Roman Emperor. Since the time of Charles V (1519–1556) branches of the Hapsburgs had ruled over Spain, the Netherlands, the Franche-Comté, Alsace, Savoy, Genoa, Milan, and the Kingdom of the Two Sicilies.[7] For many years this expansion of Hapsburg power had been a source of profound disturbance to the rulers of France. They regarded their country as encircled and longed to break through the enclosing ring. But tensions were building up in other parts of Europe also. The princes of Germany looked with alarm upon the growing power of the Holy Roman Emperor and sought opportunities to restrict him in ways that would increase their own stature. The kings of Denmark and Sweden were also developing expansionist ambitions, which could hardly be realized except at the expense of the Hapsburg Empire. Finally, the seeds of religious conflict, sown by the Reformation, were about ready to germinate in a new crop of hostilities. In 1608–1609 two opposing alliances had been formed, based upon principles of religious antagonism. The existence of these mutually hostile leagues added to the tension in central Europe and contributed toward making an eventual explosion almost a certainty. The conflict that followed, known as the Thirty Years' War (1618–1648), was one of the most tragic in history.

The immediate cause of the Thirty Years' War was an attempt of the Holy Roman Emperor, Matthias, to consolidate his power in Bohemia. Though the Hapsburgs had been overlords of Bohemia for a century, the Czech inhabitants of the country had retained their own king. When the Bohemian throne became vacant in 1618, Matthias conspired to obtain the position for one of his kinsmen, Duke Ferdinand of Styria. By exerting pressure he induced the Bohemian Diet to elect Ferdinand king. The Czech leaders resented this since both nationalist and Protestant traditions were strong in the country. The upshot was the invasion of the Emperor's headquarters in Prague by Czech noblemen and the proclamation of Bohemia as an independent state with Frederick, the Calvinist Elector Palatine, as king. The war now began in earnest. The success of the Hapsburgs in suppressing the Bohemian revolt and in punishing Frederick by seizing his lands in the valley of the Rhine galvanized the Protestant rulers of northern Europe into action. Not only the German princes but King Christian IV of Denmark and Gustavus Adolphus of Sweden joined the crusade against Austrian aggression —with the additional purpose, of course, of expanding their own dominions. In 1630 the French intervened with donations of arms

Gustavus Adolphus

[7] Charles V was the grandson of Ferdinand and Isabella of Spain and became king of that country as Charles I in 1516. Three years later he was made Holy Roman Emperor. He was also the grandson of Maximilian I of Austria and therefore a Hapsburg. When Charles abdicated as Emperor in 1556, his realm was divided. The Spanish and Italian dominions and the colonies in America went to his son Philip II and his central European possessions to his brother, Ferdinand I.

and money to the Protestant allies, and after 1632, when Gustavus Adolphus was killed in battle, France bore the brunt of the struggle. The war was no longer a religious conflict, but essentially a contest between the Bourbon and Hapsburg houses for mastery of the Continent of Europe. The immediate objectives of Cardinal Richelieu, who was directing affairs for Louis XIII, were to wrest the province of Alsace from the Holy Roman Empire and to weaken the hold of the Spanish Hapsburgs on the Netherlands and on Italy. For a time the French armies suffered reverses, but the organizing genius of Richelieu and of Cardinal Mazarin, who succeeded him in 1643, ultimately brought victory to France and her allies. Peace was restored to a distracted Europe by the Treaty of Westphalia in 1648.

Most of the results of the Thirty Years' War were unmitigated evils. By the Treaty of Westphalia France was confirmed in the possession of Alsace and other smaller territories. Sweden received territory in Germany; the independence of Holland and Switzerland was formally acknowledged; and the Holy Roman Empire was reduced to a mere fiction, since each of the German princes was now recognized as a sovereign ruler with power to make war and peace and to govern his state as he chose. But most of these changes merely laid the foundations for bitter international squabbles in the future. In addition, the war wrought terrible havoc in central Europe. Probably few military conflicts since the dawn of history had caused so much misery to the civilian population. It is estimated that fully one-third of the people in Germany and Bohemia lost their lives as a consequence of famine and disease and the marauding attacks of brutal soldiers. The armies of both sides pillaged, tortured, burned, and killed in such manner as to convert whole regions into veritable desert. In Saxony one-third of the land went out of cultivation, and packs of wolves roamed through areas where thriving villages once had stood. In the midst of such misery, education and intellectual achievement of every description were bound to decline, with the result that civilization in Germany was retarded by at least a century.

Results of the Thirty Years' War

In 1700 the French king saw what appeared to be a new opportunity for expanding Bourbon power. In that year Charles II, king of Spain, died with neither children nor brothers to succeed him, and willed his dominion to the grandson of Louis XIV. The Austrians denounced this settlement, and formed a new alliance with England, Holland, and Brandenburg. The War of the Spanish Succession, which broke out in 1702 when Louis attempted to enforce the claim of his grandson, was the last important stage in the struggle between Bourbons and Hapsburgs.[8] By the Peace of Utrecht (1713–1714) the grandson of Louis XIV was permitted to occupy the

Final stage: the War of the Spanish Succession

[8] The War of the Austrian Succession (1740–1748), in which France fought on the side of Prussia against Great Britain and Austria, also involved a struggle between Bourbons and Hapsburgs. But the results for France were indecisive: the war was mainly a duel between Prussia and Austria.

Spanish throne, on condition that France and Spain should never be united. Nova Scotia and Newfoundland were transferred to England from France, and Gibraltar from Spain. The Belgian Netherlands, Naples, and Milan were given to the Austrian Hapsburgs.

Significance of the War of the Spanish Succession

It would be difficult to exaggerate the significance of the War of the Spanish Succession. Since it involved most of the nations of Europe and also the lands overseas, it was the first of what can be called "world wars." It was fought, however, not by mass armies but chiefly by professional soldiers. It was the prototype, therefore, of most of the wars of the eighteenth century. These were wars among kings, in which the masses of the people were little involved. Among large-scale conflicts the War of the Spanish Succession was the first in which religion played almost no part. Secular rivalries over commerce and sea power were the major bones of contention. The war disposed of the claims of the smaller states to equal rank with their larger neighbors. Brandenburg and Savoy were the only important exceptions. The first came to be called Prussia and the second, Sardinia. Aside from Sardinia, the rest of the Italian states dwindled into insignificance. Austria henceforth was overshadowed by Prussia. Holland suffered such a strain from the war that she ceased to be a prime factor in the competition for world power. With a Bourbon king on the throne, Spain was reduced to subservience to France. Her Bourbon dynasty continued to rule, with brief interruptions, until the overthrow of Alphonso XIII in 1931. The War of the Spanish Succession left France and Great Britain as the two major powers in Europe. Of these, the latter was the principal victor. Not only did she acquire valuable possessions, but she muscled her way into the Spanish commercial empire. By an agreement known as the Asiento she gained the privilege of providing Spanish America with African slaves. This privilege opened the way to the smuggling of all kinds of goods into the Spanish colonies, and contributed toward making Great Britain the richest nation on earth.

The Seven Years' War

The most important of the wars of the despots in the eighteenth century was the Seven Years' War (1756–1763), known in American history as the French and Indian War. The causes of this struggle were closely related to some of the earlier conflicts already discussed. A chief factor in several of these wars had been commercial rivalry between England and France. Each had been striving for supremacy in the development of overseas trade and colonial empires. The Seven Years' War was simply the climax of a struggle which had been going on for nearly a century. Hostilities began, appropriately enough, in America as the result of a dispute over possession of the Ohio valley. Soon the whole question of British or French domination of the North American continent was involved. Eventually, nearly every major country of Europe was drawn in on one side or the other. Louis XV of France enlisted the aid of his kinsman, the Bourbon king of Spain. A struggle begun in 1740 between Frederick

636

the Great and Maria Theresa over possession of Silesia was quickly merged with the larger contest. The Seven Years' War thus reached the proportions of what virtually amounted to a world conflict, with France, Spain, Austria, and Russia arrayed against Great Britain and Prussia in Europe, and with English and French colonial forces striving for mastery not only in America but also in India.

The outcome of the Seven Years' War was exceedingly significant for the later history of Europe. Frederick the Great won a decisive victory over the Austrians and forced Maria Theresa to surrender all claims to Silesia. The acquisition of this territory increased the area of Prussia by more than a third, thereby raising the Hohenzollern kingdom to the status of a first-rank power. In the struggle for colonial supremacy the British emerged with a sensational triumph. Of her once magnificent empire in America, France lost all but two tiny islands off the coast of Newfoundland, Guadeloupe and a few other possessions in the West Indies, and a portion of Guiana in South America.[9] She was allowed to retain her trading privileges in India, but she was forbidden to build any forts or maintain any troops in that country. France was now crippled beyond much hope of a quick recovery. Her treasury was depleted, her trade almost ruined, and her chances of dominance on the Continent of Europe badly shattered. These disasters, brought on by the stupid policies of her rulers, had much to do with preparing the ground for the great revolution of 1789. By contrast, Britain was now riding the crest of the wave—in a literal as well as a figurative sense, for her triumph in the Seven Years' War was a milestone in her struggle for supremacy on the seas. The wealth from her expanded trade enriched her merchants, thereby enhancing their prestige in political and social affairs. But perhaps most important of all, her victory in the struggle for colonies gave her an abundance of raw materials which enabled her to take the lead in the Industrial Revolution.

Results of the Seven Years' War

6. THE POLITICAL THEORY OF ABSOLUTISM

The autocratic behavior of the despots in the sixteenth, seventeenth, and eighteenth centuries was not all of their own making. As indicated at the beginning of this chapter, they were encouraged by various economic and political factors for which they were not solely responsible. To these causes must be added another: the influence of political theory. Several of the Stuart and Bourbon kings, for example, derived justification for their policies from philosophers who expressed the prevailing ideas of their time in systematic and forceful writings. These ideas were, of course, not those of the

The influence of political philosophers in buttressing absolute rule

[9] All of the territory given up by the French was acquired by Great Britain, with the exception of Louisiana, which France turned over to Spain as a reward for her part in the war.

Jean Bodin

common people, but they did reflect the desires of those whom John Adams used to call "the rich, the well-born, and the able."

One of the first of the philosophers to lend encouragement to the absolutist ambitions of monarchs was Jean Bodin (1530–1596), whose zeal in the persecution of witches had earned for him the title of "Satan's Attorney-General." Bodin was not quite so extreme as some of his colleagues in exalting monarchical power. He agreed with the medieval philosophers that rulers were bound by the law of God, and he even acknowledged that the prince had a moral duty to respect the treaties he had signed. But Bodin had no use for parliaments of any description. He emphatically denied the right of a legislative body to impose any limits upon royal power. And while he admitted that princes who violated the divine law or the law of nature were tyrants, he refused to concede that their subjects would have any right of rebellion against them. The authority of the prince is from God, and the supreme obligation of the people is passive obedience. Revolution must be avoided at all costs, for it destroys that stability which is a necessary condition for progress. The main contribution of Bodin, if such it can be called, was his doctrine of sovereignty, which he defined as "supreme power over citizens and subjects, unrestrained by the laws." By this he meant that the prince, who is the only sovereign, is not bound by man-made laws. There is no *legal* restriction upon his authority whatever—nothing except obedience to the natural or moral law ordained by God.

The most noted of all the apostles of absolute government was the Englishman Thomas Hobbes (1588–1679). Writing during the Puritan Revolution and in close association with the royalists, Hobbes was disgusted with the turn which events had taken in his native country and longed for a revival of the monarchy. However, his materialism and his doctrine of the secular origin of the kingship made him none too popular with the Stuarts. For the title of his chief work Hobbes chose the name *Leviathan*, to indicate his conception of the state as an all-powerful monster.[10] All associations within the state, he declared, are mere "worms in the entrails of Leviathan." The essence of Hobbes' political philosophy is directly related to his theory of the origin of government. He taught that in the beginning all men lived in a state of nature, subject to no law but brutal self-interest. Far from being a paradise of innocence and bliss, the state of nature was a condition of universal misery. Every man's hand was against his neighbor. Life for the individual was "solitary, poor, nasty, brutish, and short." [11] In order to escape from this war of each against all, men eventually united with one another to form a civil society. They drew up a contract surrendering all of their rights to a sovereign, who would be strong enough to

The Title Page of *Leviathan*

[10] In the Book of Job, Leviathan is the monster that ruled over the primeval chaos. Job 41:1.

[11] *Leviathan* (Routledge ed.), p. 81.

protect his subjects from violence. Thus the sovereign, while not a party to the contract, was made the recipient of absolute authority. The people gave up *everything* for the one great blessing of security. In contrast with Bodin, Hobbes did not recognize any law of nature or of God as a limitation upon the authority of the prince. Absolute government, he maintained, had been established by the people themselves, and therefore they would have no ground for complaint if their ruler became a tyrant. On the basis of pure deduction, without any appeal to religion or history, Hobbes arrived at the conclusion that the king is entitled to rule despotically—not because he has been appointed by God, but because the people have *given* him absolute power.

In a sense the great Dutchman, Hugo Grotius (1583–1645), may also be considered an exponent of absolutism; though with him the question of power within the state was more or less incidental to the larger question of relations among the states. Living during the period of religious strife in France, the revolt of the Netherlands, and the Thirty Years' War, Grotius was impressed by the need for a body of rules that would reduce the dealings of governments with one another to a pattern of reason and order. He wrote his famous *Law of War and Peace* to prove that the principles of elemental justice and morality ought to prevail among nations. Some of these principles he derived from the Roman *jus gentium* and some from the medieval law of nature. So well did he present his case that he has been regarded ever since as one of the chief founders of international law. Grotius' revulsion against turbulence also inspired him to advocate despotic government. He did not see how order could be preserved within the state unless the ruler possessed unlimited authority. He maintained that in the beginning the people had either surrendered to a ruler voluntarily or had been compelled to submit to superior force; but in either case, having once established a government, they were bound to obey it unquestioningly forever.

Hugo Grotius

The theories just discussed were not simply those of a few ivory-tower philosophers, but rather the widely accepted ideas of an age when order and security were considered more important than liberty. They reflected the desire of the commercial classes, especially, for the utmost degree of stability and protection in the interest of business. Mercantilism and the policies of the despots went hand in hand with the new theories of absolute rule. The dictum, "I am the state," attributed to Louis XIV, was not just the brazen boast of a tyrant, but came close to expressing the prevailing conception of government—in Continental Europe at least. Those who had a stake in society really believed that the king *was* the state. They could hardly conceive of a government able to protect and assist their economic activities except in terms of centralized and despotic authority. Their attitude was not so far different from

The significance of philosophers' attempts to justify absolutism

639

that of some people today who believe that a dictatorship of one form or another is our only means for security and plenty.

7. SIGNIFICANCE OF THE AGE OF ABSOLUTISM

The age of absolutism was important not merely for the establishment of absolute monarchies. It bears even greater significance for its effects upon international relations. It was during this period that the modern state system came into existence. During the era of approximately 1000 years after the fall of Rome, states, in the sense in which we now understand the term, scarcely existed in Europe west of the Byzantine Empire. True, there were kings in England and France, but until almost the end of the Middle Ages, their relations with their subjects were essentially those of lords with their vassals. They had *dominium* but not sovereignty. In other words, they had the highest proprietary rights over the lands which constituted their fiefs; they did not necessarily possess supreme political authority over all the persons who lived on their lands. Only through extension of the taxing power, the judicial power, and the establishment of professional armies did such rulers as Philip Augustus of France, Henry II of England, and Frederick II of the Holy Roman Empire take steps toward becoming sovereigns in the modern sense. Even so, their domains continued their essentially feudal character for several more centuries. In yet another respect these rulers were not sovereign: they were not free from external control. In theory, they were subject to the Holy Roman Emperor, who was supposed to have a universal secular authority over Western Christendom. More important, they were responsible for their personal conduct and even for their relations with their subjects to the spiritual authority of the Pope. For example, Pope Innocent III compelled King Philip Augustus of France, by means of an interdict on his kingdom, to take back the wife he had repudiated. The same Pope forced King John of England to acknowledge England and Ireland as fiefs of the papacy.

By some historians the beginnings of the modern state system are considered to date from the invasion of Italy in 1494 by King Charles VIII of France. Involved in this war for conquest of foreign territory were considerations of dynastic prestige, the balance of power, elaborate diplomacy, and alliances and counteralliances. It was in no sense a religious or ideological war but a struggle for power and territorial aggrandizement. Other historians conceive of the Reformation as the primary cause of the modern state system. The Protestant Revolution broke the unity of Western Christendom. It facilitated the determination of kings and princes to make their own power complete by repudiating the authority of a universal Church. As early as 1555 the Peace of Augsburg gave to each German prince the right to decide whether Lutheranism or Catholicism should be the faith of his people. It was probably the Treaty of

Beginnings of the modern state system

Causes of the rise of the state system

0   500 miles

NORTH SEA

SCOTLAND △ ADAM SMITH, 1723
△ Edinburgh
HUME, 1711
BURNS, 1759
GOLDSMITH, 1728
ENGLAND
IRELAND
• Dublin
PRIESTLEY, 1733
SWIFT, 1667
Liverpool
NEWTON, 1642
RICHARDSON, 1689
PAINE, 1737
DRYDEN, 1631
S. JOHNSON, 1709
WREN, 1632
GAINSBOROUGH, 1727
LOCKE, 1632
FIELDING, 1707
△ London
HOBBES, 1588

BACON, 1561
DEFOE, 1659
GIBBON, 1737
MILTON, 1608
POPE, 1688

DENMARK
• Copenhagen
KANT, 1724
Königsberg •

BALTIC SEA

Hamburg •
Elbe R.
Berlin •
POLAND
Vistula R.

NETHERLANDS
VERMEER, 1632
Delft • Leiden
REMBRANDT, 1606
HANDEL, 1685
Göttingen △
BACH, 1685
• Erfurt
Oder R.

HOLY ROMAN
RUBENS, 1577
VAN DYCK, 1599
GOETHE, 1749
• Prague

WATTEAU, 1684
Frankfurt • Nuremberg
• Mannheim
Danube R. Vienna △

Seine R.
Rhine R.
EMPIRE
KEPLER, 1571 • Munich
Salzburg
MOZART, 1756
HAYDN, 1732
AUSTRIA
HUNGARY

VOLTAIRE, 1694
LAVOISIER, 1743
• Paris
DESCARTES, 1596
DIDEROT, 1713
• Dijon
SWITZ.
ROUSSEAU, 1712
Geneva

ATLANTIC OCEAN

Loire R.
FRANCE
PASCAL, 1623
Rhone R.

MONTESQUIEU, 1689
Bordeaux •
Garonne R.
• Toulouse
Marseilles •

Verona •
Turin •
• Genoa
• Bologna
• Florence
GALILEO, 1564
ITALY
ADRIATIC SEA

OTTOMAN EMPIRE

Rome △
BERNINI, 1598
Naples •

CORSICA
SARDINIA
SICILY

Barcelona •

PORTUGAL
Tagus R.
• Madrid
SPAIN
△ Lisbon

VELAZQUEZ, 1599
Seville •

BALEARIC ISLANDS

MEDITERRANEAN SEA

THE INTELLECTUAL REVOLUTION
OF THE SEVENTEENTH AND EIGHTEENTH CENTURIES

● Birthplaces of scientists, artists, and writers
△ Scientific academies
—·—· Boundaries ca. 1740 A.D.

Left: *The Last Judgment*, Peter Paul Rubens (1577–1640). Vivid colors, voluptuous figures, and classical themes are typical of Rubens' work. (Alte Pinakothek, Munich) Above: *England and Scotland Crowning Charles I*, Rubens. This scene was part of a series painted in Whitehall Palace, London, to glorify the Stuart family. (Minneapolis Institute of Art)

Above: *The Marchessa Durazzo*, Anthony Van Dyck (1599–1641). This portrait of a Genoese noblewoman suggests the Italian Renaissance sophistication admired by the Flemish burghers. (MMA) Right: *Pope Innocent X*, Velásquez. (Doria-Pamphili Collection)

Westphalia, however, that played the dominant role in making the modern state system a political reality. This treaty, which ended the Thirty Years' War in 1648, transferred territories from one rule to another with no regard for the nationality of their inhabitants. It recognized the independence of Holland and Switzerland and reduced the Holy Roman Empire to a fiction. Each of the German princes was acknowledged as a sovereign ruler with power to make war and peace and to govern his domain as he chose. Finally, the treaty introduced the principle that *all* states, regardless of their size or power, were equal under international law and endowed with full and complete control over their territories and inhabitants.

Whatever its origins, the modern state system may be considered to embody the following elements: (1) the equality and independence of all states; (2) the right of each state to pursue a foreign policy of its own making, to form alliances and counteralliances, and to wage war for its own advantage; (3) the use of diplomacy as a substitute for war, often involving intrigue, espionage, and treachery to the extent necessary for political advantage; (4) the balance of power as a device for preventing war or for assuring the support of allies if war becomes necessary. Most of these elements of the state system have continued to the present day. Even the establishment of the League of Nations and the United Nations brought no substantial change, for both were founded upon the principle of the sovereign equality of independent states. Some observers believe that there will be no genuine prospect of world peace until the system of sovereign independent states is recognized as obsolete and is replaced by a world community of nations organized on a federal basis.

Elements of the modern state system

SELECTED READINGS

· *Items so designated are available in paperbound editions.*

HISTORICAL AND BIOGRAPHICAL

Adams, G. B., *Constitutional History of England*, New York, 1921. A standard work, still highly regarded.

· Aylmer, G. E., *A Short History of Seventeenth-Century England*, New York, 1963 (Mentor).

· Beloff, Max, *The Age of Absolutism*, New York, 1962 (Torchbook).

Bruun, Geoffrey, *The Enlightened Despots*, New York, 1929. The best short treatise.

Carston, F. L., *The Origins of Prussia*, London, 1954.

Coles, Paul, *The Ottoman Impact on Europe*, New York, 1968.

· Elliott, J. H., *Imperial Spain, 1469–1716*, New York, 1964 (Mentor).

· Elton, G. R., *The Tudor Revolution in Government*, New York, 1959 (Cambridge University Press). A thoughtful interpretation.

· Ford, Franklin L., *Strasbourg in Transition, 1648–1789*, Cambridge, (Norton Library).

· Gardiner, S. R., *Oliver Cromwell*, New York, 1901 (Collier).

Gipson, L. H., *The Great War for the Empire*, New York, 1954.

READINGS
- Harris, R. W., *A Short History of Eighteenth-Century England*, New York, 1963 (Mentor).
- Hill, Cristopher, *The Century of Revolution, 1603–1714*, London, 1963 (Norton Library).

Holborn, Hajo, *A History of Modern Germany: 1648–1840*, New York, 1964.
- Keir, D. L., *The Constitutional History of Modern Britain, Since 1485*, Princeton, 1960 (Norton Library). An excellent introductory survey.
- Neale, J. E., *Queen Elizabeth*, New York, 1931 (Anchor).

Nowak, Frank, *Medieval Slavdom and the Rise of Russia*, New York, 1930.

Ogg, David, *Louis XIV*, New York, 1951. A good brief account.

Packard, L. B., *The Age of Louis XIV*, New York, 1929. An excellent short treatise.
- Pares, Sir Bernard, *A History of Russia*, New York, 1965 (Vintage).

Petrie, C., *Earlier Diplomatic History, 1492–1713*, New York, 1949. Valuable for origins of the state system.
- Pollard, A. F., *Henry VIII*, New York, 1951 (Torchbook).

Riasanovsky, N. V., *A History of Russia*, New York, 1963.

Schenk, W., *The Concern for Social Justice in the Puritan Revolution*, New York, 1948. Valuable and interesting.

Scherger, G. L., *The Evolution of Modern Liberty*, New York, 1904.
- Sumner, B. H., *Peter the Great and the Emergence of Russia*, London, 1950 (Collier).
- Trevelyan, G. M., *England under the Stuarts*, New York, 1904 (Barnes & Noble). Thoughtful and very readable.
- ———, *The English Revolution 1688–1689*, London, 1938 (Galaxy). Emphasizes results.

Trevor-Davies, R., *The Golden Century of Spain*, London, 1937. A good brief account.
- Wedgwood, C. V., *The Thirty Years' War*, London, 1938 (Anchor). A complete and well-reasoned account.
- ———, *Richelieu and the French Monarchy*, New York, 1950.
- Wolf, John B., *The Emergence of the Great Powers, 1685–1715*, New York, 1951 (Torchbook).
- ———, *Louis XIV*, New York, 1968 (Norton).

POLITICAL THEORY
- Allen, J. W., *History of Political Thought in the Sixteenth Century*, New York, 1928 (Barnes & Noble). The standard work, still unsurpassed.
- Figgis, J. N., *The Divine Right of Kings*, Cambridge, 1922 (Torchbook).
- Friedrich, C. J., *The Age of the Baroque, 1610–1660*, New York, 1952 (Torchbook). Emphasizes political theory.

Sabine, G. H., *A History of Political Theory*, New York, 1961. Especially good on sixteenth and seventeenth centuries.

SOURCE MATERIALS

Bodin, Jean, *Six Books Concerning the State*, especially Book I, Chs. I, VI, VIII, X, Cambridge, 1962.
- Grotius, Hugo, *The Law of War and Peace*, especially Prolegomena and Book I, Ch. I, New York, 1963 (Library of Liberal Arts).
- Hobbes, Thomas, *Leviathan*, Part I, Chs. XIII–XV; Part II, Chs. XIII, XVIII, XIX, XXI, XXVI, New York (Library of Liberal Arts and others).

Webster, Hutton, *Historical Selections*, pp. 640–42, "The Bill of Rights."

CHAPTER **22**

The Intellectual Revolution
of the Seventeenth and
Eighteenth Centuries

> I wish we could derive the rest of the phenomena of nature . . .
> from mechanical principles, for I am induced by many reasons
> to suspect that they may all depend upon certain forces by which
> the particles of bodies, by some causes hitherto unknown, are
> either mutually impelled towards one another, and cohere in reg-
> ular figures, or are repelled and recede from one another. These
> forces being unknown, philosophers have hitherto attempted the
> search of Nature in vain; but I hope the principles here laid down
> will afford some light either to this or some truer method of
> philosophy.
> —Sir Isaac Newton, Preface to the First Edition,
> *Mathematical Principles* (*Principia Mathematica*)

By one of the ironies of history, the period when arrogant despots
bestrode the nations of the European continent was a period of
stupendous intellectual achievement. To one who understands the
underlying forces at work in this and in preceding ages, however,
the cultural progress of the seventeenth and eighteenth centuries is
not particularly mysterious. The absolute monarchs, of course, had
nothing to do with it. Though a few, like Frederick the Great, dabbled in philosophy and science, not one of them could accurately be
described as a patron of learning. The intellectual advance of their
time was due rather to factors growing out of the principal economic and cultural movements in European history after the end of
the Middle Ages. Characteristic examples were the influence of the
Renaissance, the increasing prosperity of the middle and lower
classes, and the widened intellectual horizons produced by the new
knowledge of distant lands and strange peoples.

*Causes of intel-
lectual advance
in the 17th and
18th centuries*

Character of
the Intellectual
Revolution

*See color map
at page 640*

The achievements in philosophy and science in the seventeenth and eighteenth centuries, together with the new attitudes resulting therefrom, constitute what is commonly known as the Intellectual Revolution. But to speak of this revolution as if it were an event without precedent in the records of man leads to an erroneous conception. On several occasions before this, developments had occurred which went quite as far in upsetting old habits of thinking as did any of the discoveries of the seventeenth and eighteenth centuries. Illustrations may be found in the radicalism and individualism of the Sophists in fifth-century Athens and in the disturbing effects of the revival of paganism and worldliness in the later Middle Ages. Nevertheless, the Intellectual Revolution of the seventeenth and eighteenth centuries was somewhat broader in scope than any of these earlier upheavals, and its results were perhaps more significant for our own generation.

I. PHILOSOPHY IN THE SEVENTEENTH CENTURY

The rationalism
and dualism of
René Descartes

Perhaps without straining the imagination too much, we can say that the Intellectual Revolution had a triple paternity. Its fathers were René Descartes, Sir Isaac Newton, and John Locke. More will be said later about Newton and Locke. For the present we need to examine the teachings of the renowned Frenchman who initiated the dominant philosophic trend of the seventeenth century. René Descartes (1596–1650), soldier of fortune, mathematician, and physicist, was an unswerving advocate of rationalism in philosophy. He was, of course, not the first exponent of reason as the pathway to knowledge; but his rationalism differed from that of most earlier thinkers—the medieval Scholastics, for instance—in his rigid exclusion of authority. He scorned reliance upon books, no matter how venerable the reputation of their authors. Convinced that both traditional opinion and the ordinary experiences of mankind are untrustworthy guides, he determined to adopt a new method entirely unprejudiced by either. This method was the mathematical instrument of pure deduction. It would consist in starting with simple, self-evident truths or axioms, as in geometry, and then reasoning from these to particular conclusions. Descartes believed that he had found such an axiom in his famous principle: "I think, therefore I am." From this he maintained that it is possible to deduce a sound body of universal knowledge—to prove, for example, that God exists, that man is a thinking animal, and that mind is distinct from matter. These "truths," he declared, are just as infallible as the truths of geometry, for they are products of the same unerring method.

But Descartes is important not only as the father of the new rationalism. He was also partly responsible for introducing the conception of a mechanistic universe. He taught that the whole world of matter, organic and inorganic alike, could be defined in terms of extension and motion. "Give me extension and motion," he once boldly declared, "and I will construct the universe." Every individual thing—a solar system, a star, the earth itself—is a self-operating machine propelled by a force arising from the original motion given to the universe by God. Descartes did not even exclude the bodies of animals and of men from this general mechanistic pattern. The whole world of physical nature is one. The behavior of animals and the emotional reactions of men flow automatically from internal or external stimuli. He insisted, however, that man is distinct from all other creatures in the possession of a reasoning faculty. Mind is not a form of matter, but an entirely separate substance implanted in the body of man by God. Along with this dualism of mind and matter, Descartes also believed in *innate* ideas. He taught that self-evident truths having no relation to sensory experience must be inherent in the mind itself. Man does not learn them through the use of his senses, but perceives them instinctively because they have been part of his mental equipment from birth.

Of the several teachings of Descartes the new rationalism and mechanism were by far the most influential. In fact, these two doctrines were almost sufficient in themselves to have produced a revolution, for they involved the rejection of nearly all the theological bias of the past. No longer need the philosopher pay homage to revelation as a source of truth; reason was now held to be the solitary fount of knowledge, while the whole idea of spiritual meaning in the universe was cast aside like a worn-out garment. Descartes' principles of rationalism and mechanism were adopted in some form or other by the majority of the philosophers of the seventeenth century. The most noted of his intellectual successors were the Dutch Jew Benedict Spinoza and the Englishman Thomas Hobbes, whom we have already encountered as a political theorist. Benedict (or Baruch) Spinoza was born in Amsterdam in 1632 and died an outcast from his native community forty-five years later. His parents were members of a group of Jewish immigrants who had fled from persecution in Portugal and Spain and had taken refuge in the Netherlands. At an early age Spinoza came under the influence of a disciple of Descartes and as a result grew critical of some of the dogmas of the Hebrew faith. For this he was expelled from the synagogue, cursed by the chief priests and elders, and banished from the community of his people. From 1656 till his death he lived in various cities of Holland, eking out a meager existence by grinding lenses. During these years he developed his philosophy, incorporating the rationalism and mechanism but not the dualism of Descartes. Spinoza maintained that there is only one essential substance in the universe, of which mind and matter are but different aspects. This single substance is God, who is identical with nature itself. Such a conception of the universe was, of course, pure pantheism; but it

An Illustration from Descartes' *De Homine*, Showing the Relationship between Perception and Motion of the Hand

Descartes' intellectual successors: Benedict Spinoza

was grounded upon reason rather than upon faith, and it was intended to express the scientific notions of the unity of nature and the continuity of cause and effect. It is not without significance that one of the greatest of modern scientists, Albert Einstein, declared that his idea of God was the same as that of Spinoza.

Much more than Descartes, Spinoza was interested in ethical questions. Having come to the conclusion early in life that the things men prize most highly—wealth, pleasure, power, and fame—are empty and vain, he set out to inquire whether there was any perfect good which would give lasting and unmitigated happiness to all who attained it. By a process of geometric reasoning he attempted to prove that this perfect good consists in "love of God"—that is, in worship of the order and harmony of nature. If men will but realize that the universe is a beautiful machine, whose operation cannot be interrupted for the benefit of particular persons, they will gain that serenity of mind for which philosophers have yearned through the ages. We can only be delivered from impossible hopes and cringing fears by acknowledging to ourselves that the order of nature is unalterably fixed, and that man cannot change his fate. In other words, we gain true freedom by realizing that we are not free. But with all his determinism, Spinoza was an earnest apostle of tolerance, justice, and rational living. He wrote in defense of religious liberty and, in the face of cruel mistreatment, set a noble example in his personal life of kindliness, humanity, and freedom from vengeful passions.

Spinoza's ethical philosophy

The third of the great rationalists of the seventeenth century was Thomas Hobbes. Born before either Descartes or Spinoza, he outlived both. Hobbes agreed with his two contemporaries in the belief that geometry furnished the only proper method of discovering philosophic truth. But he denied the doctrine of innate ideas, maintaining that the *origin* of all knowledge is in sense perception. He likewise refused to accept either the dualism of Descartes or the pantheism of Spinoza. According to Hobbes, absolutely nothing exists except matter. Mind is simply motion in the brain or perhaps a subtle form of matter, but in no sense a distinct substance. God, also, if we can believe that He exists, must be assumed to have a physical body. There is nothing spiritual anywhere in the universe of which the mind can conceive. This was the most thoroughgoing materialism to make its appearance since the days of Lucretius. Naturally it was combined with mechanism, as materialism usually is. Hobbes contended that not only the universe but man himself can be explained mechanically. All that man does is determined by appetites or aversions, and these in turn are either inherited or acquired through experience. In similar fashion, Hobbes maintained that there are no absolute standards of good and evil. Good is merely that which gives pleasure; evil, that which brings pain. Thus did Hobbes combine with materialism and mechanism a thoroughgoing philosophy of hedonism.

Thomas Hobbes

2. THE ENLIGHTENMENT

The climax of the Intellectual Revolution in philosophy was a movement known as the Enlightenment. Beginning in England about 1680, it quickly spread into most of the countries of northern Europe and was not without influence in America. The supreme manifestation of the Enlightenment, however, was in France, and the period of its real importance was the eighteenth century. Few other movements in history have had such profound effects in molding men's thoughts or in shaping the course of their actions. The philosophy of the Enlightenment was built around a number of significant concepts, chief among which were the following:

The chief philosophical concepts of the Enlightenment

(1) Reason is the only infallible guide to wisdom. All knowledge has its roots in sense perception, but the impressions of our senses are but the raw material of truth, which has to be refined in the crucible of reason before it can have value in explaining the world or in pointing the way to the improvement of life.

(2) The universe is a machine governed by inflexible laws which man cannot override. The order of nature is absolutely uniform and not subject in any way to miracles or to any other form of divine interference.

(3) The future is bright with promise if men will abandon old superstitions and prejudices and live in accordance with the dictates of reason. The leaders of the Enlightenment believed in the possibility of a "heavenly city" delivered from ignorance, intolerance, and oppression. It would be purged also of artificiality and enslavement to outworn conventions. Religion, government, and economic institutions would be reduced to their simplest and most natural forms in order to lessen the possibility of tyranny and greed.[1]

Sir Isaac Newton

(4) There is no such thing as original sin. Men are not inherently depraved but are driven to acts of cruelty and meanness by scheming priests and war-making despots. The infinite perfectibility of human nature, and therefore of society itself, would become easily realized if men were free to follow the guidance of reason and their own instincts.

The inspiration for the Enlightenment came partly from the rationalism of Descartes, Spinoza, and Hobbes, but the real founders of the movement were Sir Isaac Newton (1642–1727) and John Locke (1632–1704). Although Newton was not a philosopher in the ordinary sense, his work has the deepest significance for the history of thought. His majestic achievement was to bring the whole world of nature under a precise mechanical interpretation. His celebrated principle that "every particle of matter in the universe attracts every other particle with a force varying inversely as the square of the distance between them and directly proportional to

The founders of the Enlightenment: (1) Sir Isaac Newton

[1] The political and economic doctrines of the Enlightenment will be treated more fully in the following chapter on The French Revolution.

the product of their masses" was held to be valid not only on this earth but throughout the endless expanse of solar systems. From this it was an easy step to the conclusion that every event in nature is governed by universal laws, which can be formulated as precisely as mathematical principles. The discovery of these laws is the chief business of science, and the duty of man is to allow them to operate unhindered. Gone was the medieval conception of a universe guided by benevolent purpose; men now dwelt in a world in which the procession of events was as automatic as the ticking of a watch. Newton's philosophy did not rule out the idea of a God, but it deprived Him of His power to guide the stars in their courses or to command the sun to stand still.

The influence of John Locke was quite different from that of Newton, but it was no less important. Locke was the father of a new theory of knowledge, which served as the keynote of the philosophy of the Enlightenment. Rejecting Descartes' doctrine of innate ideas, he maintained that all of man's knowledge originates from sense perception. This theory had already been asserted by Hobbes; but Locke systematized and enlarged it. He insisted that the human mind at birth is a blank tablet, a "white paper," upon which absolutely nothing is inscribed. It does not even contain the idea of a God or any notions of right and wrong. Not until the newborn child begins to have experiences, to perceive the external world with its senses, is anything registered in its mind. But the simple ideas which result directly from sense perception are merely the foundations of knowledge; no human being could live intelligently on the basis of them alone. These simple ideas must be integrated and fused into *complex ideas*. This is the function of the reason or understanding, which has the power to combine, coordinate, and organize the impressions received from the senses and thus to build a usable body of general truth. Sensation and reason are both indispensable—the one for furnishing the mind with the raw materials of knowledge and the other for working them into meaningful form. It was this modification of rationalism which became a leading element in the philosophy of the Enlightenment. Locke is significant also for his defense of religious toleration and for his liberal political theory, which will be discussed in the chapter on the French Revolution.

The Enlightenment blossomed forth in its fullest glory in France during the eighteenth century under the leadership of Voltaire and other like-minded critics of the established order. Voltaire, or François Marie Arouet as he was originally named, epitomized the Enlightenment in somewhat the same way as Luther did the Reformation or Leonardo da Vinci the Italian Renaissance. A son of the bourgeoisie, Voltaire was born in 1694 and, despite his delicate physique, lived to within eleven years of the outbreak of the French Revolution. He developed a taste for satiric writing early in his life and got himself into numerous scrapes by his ridicule of noblemen

(2) John Locke

Voltaire, the
supreme incar-
nation of the
Enlightenment

648

An Illustration from *Candide* by Voltaire

and pompous officials. As a consequence of one of his lampoons he was sent to the Bastille and afterwards exiled to England. Here he remained for three years, acquiring a deep admiration for British institutions, and composing his first philosophic work, which he entitled *Letters on the English*. In this work he popularized the ideas of Newton and Locke, whom he had come to regard as two of the greatest geniuses who ever lived. Most of his later writings—the *Philosophical Dictionary*, *Candide*, his histories, and many of his poems and essays—were also concerned with exposition of the doctrine that the world is governed by natural laws, and that reason and concrete experience are the only dependable guides for man to follow. Voltaire had contempt for the smug optimism which taught that the ills of each make up the good of all, and that everything is for the best in the best of all possible worlds. He saw, on the contrary, universal misery, hatred, strife, and oppression. Only in his utopia of El Dorado, which he placed somewhere in South America, were freedom and peace conceivable. Here there were no monks, no priests, no lawsuits, and no prisons. The inhabitants dwelt together without malice or greed, worshiping God in accordance with the dictates of reason, and solving their problems by logic and science. But this idyllic life was made possible only by the fact that the land was cut off by impassable mountains from the "regimented assassins of Europe."

Voltaire is best known as a champion of individual freedom. He regarded all restrictions upon liberty of speech and opinion as barbarous. In a letter to one of his opponents he wrote what has often been quoted as the highest criterion of intellectual tolerance: "I do not agree with a word that you say, but I will defend to the death your right to say it." [2] But if there was any one form of repression that Voltaire abhorred more than others, it was the tyranny of organized religion. He blasted with fire and brimstone

Voltaire
as a champion
of individual
liberty

[2] E. B. Hall, *Voltaire in His Letters*, p. 65.

against the monstrous cruelty of the Church in torturing and burning intelligent men who dared to question its dogmas. With reference to the whole system of persecuting and privileged orthodoxy, he adopted as his slogan, "Crush the infamous thing." He was almost as unsparing in his attacks upon political tyranny, especially when it resulted in the slaughter of thousands to glut the ambitions of despots. "It is forbidden to kill," he sarcastically asserted: "therefore all murderers are punished unless they kill in large numbers and to the sound of trumpets." [3]

Other philoso-
phers of the
Enlightenment:
the Encyclo-
pedists

Among the other philosophers of the Enlightenment in France were Denis Diderot and Jean d'Alembert, both of whom lived in the latter part of the eighteenth century. Diderot and d'Alembert were the chief members of a group known as the Encyclopedists, so-called from their contributions to the *Encyclopedia*, which was intended to be a complete summation of the philosophic and scientific knowledge of the age. In general, both of them agreed with the rationalism and liberalism of Voltaire. Diderot, for example, maintained that "men will never be free till the last king is strangled with the entrails of the last priest." D'Alembert, while accepting the rationalist and individualist tendencies of the Enlightenment, differed from most of his associates in advocating a diffusion of the new doctrines among all the people. The general attitude of his contempo-

[3] *Philosophical Dictionary*, article on "War."

A Gathering of the Philosophes. The seated figures are Voltaire with his left hand raised, then moving to his left, Diderot, Père Adam, Condorcet, d'Alembert, Abbé Maury, and Laharpe.

raries, notably Voltaire, was to despise the common man, to regard him as a mere clodhopper beyond redemption from ignorance and grossness. But for d'Alembert the only assurance of progress lay in universal enlightenment. Accordingly, he maintained that the truths of reason and science should be taught to the masses in the hope that eventually the whole world might be freed from darkness and tyranny.

Although the Enlightenment was of much less importance in Germany than in France or England, it did give birth to some progressive ideas. The most widely recognized of its German leaders was Gotthold Lessing (1729–1781), primarily a dramatist and critic but also a philosopher of humane and far-sighted views. The essence of his philosophy is tolerance, founded upon a sincere conviction that no one religion has a monopoly of truth. In his play, *Nathan the Wise*, he expounded the idea that nobility of character has no particular relation to theological creeds. He maintained that, historically, men of charitable spirit were as often found among Jews and Moslems as among Christians. Largely for this reason he condemned adherence to any one system of dogma and taught that the development of each of the world's great religions (Christianity included) was simply a step in the spiritual evolution of mankind. One of Lessing's friends and disciples turned out to be the foremost Jewish philosopher of the Enlightenment. His name was Moses Mendelssohn (1729–1786), and he was a sickly product of the ghetto in the German town of Dessau. Agreeing with Lessing that religions should be judged by their effects upon the conduct of their followers, Mendelssohn urged his Jewish brethren to give up their notion of themselves as the Chosen People of God. They should look upon Judaism merely as one of a number of good religions. He recommended also that Jews should renounce their clannishness, that they should cease to long for a return to Zion, and that they should adapt themselves to the civic requirements of the countries in which they lived. His teachings, along with those of Moses Maimonides, the great rationalist Jew of the twelfth century, were among the principal sources of what has since come to be known as Reform Judaism.

The Enlightenment in Germany

Two other philosophers are commonly given a place in the Enlightenment—the Scotsman David Hume (1711–1776) and the Frenchman Rousseau (1712–1778).[4] Neither, however, was in full agreement with the majority of his contemporaries. Hume is noted above all for his skepticism. He taught that the mind is a mere bundle of impressions, derived exclusively from the senses and tied together by habits of association. That is, we learn from experience to associate warmth with fire and nourishment with bread. If we had never actually experienced the sensation of warmth, no reasoning faculty in our minds would enable us to draw the conclusion

David Hume, the foremost skeptic of the Enlightenment

[4] By birth Rousseau was French Swiss, a native of Geneva, but he lived the greater part of his life in France.

that fire produces heat. But constant repetition of the fact that when we see a flame we generally experience warmth leads to the habit of associating the two in our minds. Impressions and associations are all that there is to knowing. Since every idea in the mind is nothing but a copy of a sense impression, it follows that we can know nothing of final causes, the nature of substance, or the origin of the universe. We cannot be sure of any of the conclusions of reason except those which, like the principles of mathematics, can be verified by actual experience. All others are likely to be the products of feelings and desires, of animal urges and fears. In thus denying the competence of reason, Hume placed himself almost entirely outside the main intellectual trend of the Enlightenment. As a matter of fact, he helped to prepare its death.

In similar measure Jean Jacques Rousseau repudiated many of the basic assumptions which had stemmed from Newton and Locke. A

Rousseau's antirationalism

hopeless misfit wallowing in the mire of his emotions, Rousseau would have been a marvel indeed if he had championed the rationalist doctrines of the Enlightenment. Whole segments of his personality appear to have been out of joint. He failed in nearly every occupation he undertook. He preached lofty ideals of educational reform, but abandoned his own children to a foundling asylum. He quarreled wih everybody and reveled in morbid self-disclosures. Undoubtedly it was these qualities of temperament which were largely responsible for his revolt against the coldly intellectual doctrines of his contemporaries. He maintained that to worship reason as the infallible guide to conduct and truth is to lean upon a broken reed. Reason, of course, has its uses, but it is not the whole answer. In the really vital problems of life it is much safer to rely upon feelings, to follow our instincts and emotions. These are the ways of nature and are therefore more conducive to happiness than the artificial lucubrations of the intellect. The "thinking man is a depraved animal." [5] Yet notwithstanding his contempt for reason, Rousseau was in other ways thoroughly in agreement with the viewpoint of the Enlightenment. He extolled the life of the "noble savage" even more fervently than did any of his associates. In his prize-winning essay, the *Discourse on the Arts and Sciences*, he contrasted the freedom and innocence of primitive men with the tyranny and wickedness of civilized society, even insisting that the progress of learning is destructive of human happiness. He shared the impatience of the Enlightenment with every sort of restriction upon individual freedom, though he was much more concerned about the liberty and equality of the masses than were the other reformers of his time. He regarded the origin of private property as the primary source of misery in human society.

It would be almost impossible to fix limits to the influence of Rousseau. As the first significant writer to uphold the validity of

[5] *A Discourse on the Origin of Inequality* (Everyman Library ed.), p. 181.

conclusions dictated by emotion and sentiment he is commonly considered the father of romanticism. For fifty years after his time Europe was bathed in literary tears, and it was difficult to find a philosopher who would boldly assert the inerrancy of reason. His slogan, "Back to nature," furnished the foundation for a veritable cult dedicated to the pursuit of the simple life. The new fashion spread even to the simpering courtiers at Versailles. The queen herself designed a dainty rural village in a corner of the palace grounds and diverted herself by playing milkmaid. But Rousseau's influence was not limited to the founding of romanticism and the encouragement of sentimental devotion to nature. His dogmas of equality and popular sovereignty, though frequently misinterpreted, became the rallying cries of revolutionaries and of thousands of more moderate opponents of the existing regime. And, as the chapter on the French Revolution will show, it was Rousseau's political philosophy that provided the real inspiration for the modern ideal of majority rule.

Rousseau Playing a Hurdy-Gurdy

The most typical religious philosophy of the Enlightenment was deism. The originator of this philosophy appears to have been an Englishman by the name of Lord Herbert of Cherbury (1583–1648). In the eighteenth century deistic doctrines were propagated by such men as Voltaire, Diderot, and Rousseau in France; Alexander Pope, Lord Bolingbroke, and Lord Shaftesbury in England; and Thomas Paine, Benjamin Franklin, and Thomas Jefferson in America. Not satisfied with condemning the irrational elements in religion, the deists went on to denounce every form of organized faith. Christianity was spared no more than the others. Institutionalized religions were branded as instruments of exploitation, devised by wily scoundrels to enable them to prey upon the ignorant masses. As Voltaire expressed it, "the first divine was the first rogue who met the first fool." [6] But the aims of the deists were not all destructive. They were interested not merely in demolishing Christianity but in constructing a simpler and more natural religion to replace it. The fundamental tenets of this new religion were about as follows: (1) there is one God who created the universe and ordained the natural laws that control it; (2) God does not intervene in the affairs of men in this world: He is not a capricious deity, like the God of the Christians and Jews, making "one vessel unto honour and another unto dishonour" in accordance with His peculiar whims; (3) prayer, sacraments, and ritual are mere useless mumbo jumbo; God cannot be wheedled or bribed into setting aside natural law for the benefit of particular persons; (4) man is endowed with freedom of will to choose the good and avoid the evil; there is no predestination of some to be saved and others to be damned, but rewards and punishments in the life hereafter are determined solely by the individual's conduct on earth.

The religious doctrines of the Enlightenment: deism

[6] *Philosophical Dictionary*, article on "Religion."

The influence
of the
Enlightenment

Naïve though many of its assumptions were, the influence of the Enlightenment was tremendous. No other movement, with the possible exception of humanism, had done more to dispel the accumulated fogs of superstition and illogical restraint that still enveloped the Western world. The rationalism of the Enlightenment helped to break the shackles of political tyranny and to weaken the power of conscienceless priests. Its ideal of religious freedom was a leading factor in the ultimate separation of church and state and in the liberation of the Jews from ancient restrictions. The humanitarianism implied in the opposition to oppression carried over into agitation for penal reform and for the abolition of slavery. The desire for a natural order of society contributed to a demand for the overthrow of relics of feudalism and for the destruction of monopoly and unearned privilege. If there was any evil result of the Enlightenment, it probably consisted in an exaggerated development of individualism. Liberty of the individual against political and religious tyranny was sometimes easily translated into the right of the strong to satisfy economic greed at the expense of the weak.

3. REVOLUTIONARY SCIENTIFIC DISCOVERIES

Achievements
in the physical
sciences:
(1) physics

The major scientific interests of the Intellectual Revolution followed very largely the paths marked out during the late Renaissance. Accordingly, primary attention was given to the physical sciences. Unquestionably the most illustrious physicist of the Intellectual Revolution was Sir Isaac Newton. His conclusions molded men's thinking in philosophy for a hundred years. His influence upon science was even more lasting; the Newtonian physics stood virtually unchallenged until the twentieth century. It was in 1687 that Newton published his renowned law of universal gravitation. Based in part upon the work of Galileo, this law provided a single unifying principle for the entire world of matter. Besides, it re-

The Manuscript of Newton's *Philosophie Naturalis Principia Mathematica*. The first edition was published in 1687.

An Early Eighteenth-Century Laboratory as Seen in Diderot's *Encyclopedia*

moved all doubt as to the validity of the Copernican hypothesis. But Newton's researches in physics were not confined to the problem of gravitation. He devised a series of tables, of great value to navigation, by which the changing positions of the moon among the stars could be accurately predicted. He invented the sextant for measuring these positions and thereby determining latitude and longitude. Some of his other achievements proved of substantial value in paving the way for later discoveries regarding the nature of light. He shares with Galileo the honor of being the father of modern physics.

Some preliminary progress was made during the Intellectual Revolution in connection with the understanding of electrical phenomena. At the beginning of the seventeenth century the Englishman William Gilbert (1540–1603), discovered the properties of lodestones and introduced the word "electricity" into the language.[7] Other scientists quickly became interested, and sensational results were anticipated from experiments with the marvelous "fluid." A learned Jesuit even suggested that two persons might communicate at a distance by means of magnetized needles which would point simultaneously to identical letters of the alphabet. Late in the eighteenth century Alessandro Volta (1745–1827) constructed the first battery. Still another important achievement in electrical physics was the invention in 1746 of the Leyden jar for the storage of electric energy. It was mainly as a result of this invention that Benjamin Franklin was able to show that lightning and electricity are identical. In his celebrated kite experiment in 1752 he succeeded in charging a Leyden jar from a thunderstorm.

(2) progress in the understanding of electrical phenomena

[7] "Electric" comes from the Greek word for amber. Gilbert and others had observed that amber rubbed on fur will attract paper, hair, straw, and various other things. Preserved Smith, *A History of Modern Culture*, I, 63–64.

Almost as spectacular as the progress in physics was the development of chemistry. If any one scientist can be called the founder of modern chemistry, the title must be given to Robert Boyle (1627–1691). The son of an Irish nobleman, Boyle achieved distinction in 1661 with the publication of his *Sceptical Chymist, or Chymico-Physical Doubts and Paradoxes.* In this work he rejected the theories of the alchemists and thereby contributed toward the establishment of chemistry as a pure science. In addition, he distinguished between a mixture and a compound, learned a great deal about the nature of phosphorus, produced alcohol from wood, suggested the idea of chemical elements, and reviewed the atomic theory. No scientist before his time had foreshadowed so much of the knowledge of modern chemistry.

Despite the work of Boyle, little further development of chemistry occurred for almost 100 years. The reason lay partly in the wide

The discovery of hydrogen and oxygen

acceptance of errors concerning such matters as heat, flame, air, and the phenomenon of combustion. The most common of these errors was the so-called phlogiston theory. Phlogiston was the fire substance. When an object burned, phlogiston was supposed to be given off. The remaining ash was said to be the true material. In the second half of the eighteenth century important discoveries were made which ultimately overthrew this theory and cleared the way for a true understanding of some of the most familiar chemical reactions. In 1766 Henry Cavendish, one of the richest men in England, reported the discovery of a new kind of gas obtained by treating iron, zinc, and other metals with sulphuric acid. He showed that this gas, now known as hydrogen, would not of itself support combustion, and yet would be rapidly consumed by a fire with access to the air. In 1774 oxygen was discovered by Joseph Priestley, who had managed for some years to squeeze enough time out of his profession of Unitarian minister to perform some extensive experiments in natural science. He found that a candle would burn with extraordinary vigor when placed in the new gas—a fact which indicated clearly that combustion was not caused by any mysterious principle in the flame itself. A few years after this discovery Cavendish demonstrated that air and water, long supposed to be elements, are a mixture and a compound, respectively, the first being composed principally of oxygen and nitrogen and the second of oxygen and hydrogen.

Lavoisier

The final blow to the phlogiston theory was administered by Antoine Lavoisier (1743–1794), one of the greatest of all scientists of the Intellectual Revolution. By some he has been called "the Newton of Chemistry." Lavoisier proved that both combustion and respiration involve oxidation, the one being rapid and the other slow. He provided the names for oxygen and hydrogen, demonstrated that the diamond is a form of carbon, and argued that life itself is essentially a chemical process. But undoubtedly his greatest accomplishment was his discovery of the law of the conservation of mass. He found evidence that "although matter may alter its state in a series of chemical actions, it does not change in amount; the quantity of matter is the same at the end as at the beginning of every operation, and can be traced by its weight." This "law" has, of course, been modified by later discoveries regarding the structure of the atom and the conversion of some forms of matter into energy. It is hardly too much to say that as a result of Lavoisier's genius chemistry became a true science. To the lasting shame of the French Revolutionists, he was put to death on the guillotine at the age of fifty-one, a victim of the Reign of Terror.

Although it was the physical sciences that received the major attention in the Intellectual Revolution, the biological sciences were by no means neglected. One of the greatest of the early biologists was Robert Hooke (1635–1703), the first man to see and describe the cellular structure of plants. This achievement was soon followed by the work of Marcello Malpighi (1628–1694) in demonstrating the sexuality of plants and in comparing the function of vegetable leaves with that of the lungs of animals. About the same time a Dutch businessman and amateur scientist, Anthony van Leeuwenhoek (1632–1723), discovered protozoa and bacteria and wrote the first description of human spermatozoa. The seventeenth century also witnessed some progress in embryology. About 1670 the Dutch physician, Jan Swammerdam (1637–1680), carefully described the life history of certain insects from the caterpillar stage to maturity and compared the change of tadpole into frog with the development of the human embryo.

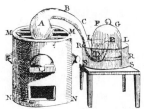

Lavoisier's Apparatus for the Decomposition of Air

The biological scientists: Hooke, Malpighi, Leeuwenhoek, and Swammerdam

In many ways the end of the seventeenth century appeared to mark a decline of originality in the sciences that deal with living things. During the next 100 years biologists were inclined more and more to center their efforts upon description and classification of knowledge already in existence. The most brilliant classifier of biological knowledge was the Swedish scientist, Carl von Linné (1707–1778), more commonly known by his Latinized name of Linnaeus. In his *System of Nature* and in his *Botanical Philosophy* Linnaeus divided all natural objects into three kingdoms: stone, animal, and vegetable. Each of these kingdoms he subdivided into classes, genera, and species. He invented the system of biological nomenclature still in use, by which every plant and animal is designated by two scientific names, the first denoting the genus and the second the species. Thus he called man *Homo sapiens*. Though some people condemned Linnaeus for presuming to rename the animals that Adam had named, his classification was nevertheless widely adopted even in his own time. Despite certain defects which have had to be corrected, it still has its value.

Linnaeus

The second great genius of descriptive biology in the eighteenth century was the Frenchman Georges Buffon (1707–1788). His *Natural History* in forty-four volumes, though intended as a summation of practically all science, dealt mainly with man and other

Buffon

vertebrates. While much of the material in this work was taken from the writings of other scientists and from the accounts of travelers, the author did have a unique ability in reducing a vast body of knowledge to orderly arrangement and in enlivening it with his own interpretations. The chief importance of Buffon to us lies in his recognition of the close relationship between man and the higher animals. Though he could never quite bring himself to accept the full implications of the evolutionary theory, he was nonetheless strongly impressed by the striking resemblances among all of the higher species. He admitted the possibility that the entire range of organic forms had descended from a single species.

The paucity of
medical
achievements in
the 17th century

The development of physiology and medicine progressed rather slowly during the seventeenth century. Among the several reasons, one was the inadequate preparation of physicians, many of whom had begun their professional careers with little more training than a kind of apprenticeship under an older practitioner. Another was the common disrepute in which surgery was held as a mere trade, like that of barber or blacksmith.[8] Perhaps the most serious of all was the prejudice against dissection of human bodies as a basis of anatomical study. As late as 1750 medical schools which engaged in this practice were in danger of destruction by irate mobs. Despite these obstacles some progress was still possible. About 1670 Malpighi and Leeuwenhoek confirmed the famous discovery of Sir William Harvey by observing the actual flow of blood through the network of capillaries connecting the arteries and veins. At approximately the same time an eminent physician of London, Thomas Sydenham, proposed a new theory of fever as nature's attempt to expel diseased material from the system. The substance of this theory is still quite generally accepted; in fact, new evidence has been discovered which strongly confirms it.

Medical
progress in the
18th century

Medical progress during the eighteenth century was somewhat more rapid. Among the noteworthy achievements were the discovery of blood pressure, the founding of histology or microscopic anatomy, the development of the autopsy as an aid to the study of disease, and the recognition of scarlet fever as a malady distinct from smallpox and measles. But the chief milestones of medical advancement in this period were the adoption of inoculation and the development of vaccination for smallpox. Knowledge of inoculation came originally from the Near East, where it had long been employed by the Saracens. Information concerning its use was relayed to England in 1717 through the letters of Lady Montagu, wife of the British ambassador to Turkey. The first systematic application of the practice in the Western world, however, was due to the efforts of the great Puritan leaders, Cotton and Increase Mather, who implored the physicians of Boston to inoculate their patients in

[8] As a matter of fact, surgery in northern Europe was very commonly left in the hands of barbers. Surgeons in England are still referred to as "Mr."

the hope of curbing an epidemic of smallpox which had broken out in 1721. By the middle of the century inoculation was quite generally employed by physicians in Europe and in America. In 1796 the milder method of vaccination was discovered by Edward Jenner. It was now revealed that direct inoculation of human beings with the deadly virus of smallpox was unnecessary: a vaccine manufactured in the body of an animal would be just as effective and much less likely to have disastrous results. Vast possibilities were thus opened up for the elimination of contagious diseases.

4.   CLASSICISM IN ART AND LITERATURE

In so far as there was any one purpose dominating the art and literature of the seventeenth and eighteenth centuries, it was the desire to preserve or recapture the spirit of ancient Greece and Rome. The artists and writers of the Intellectual Revolution strove to imitate classical models. They chose classical titles and themes for many of their works and embellished them wherever possible with allusions to antique mythology. Deploring the destruction of ancient civilization by "Christian barbarians," they were unable to see much value in the cultural achievements of later centuries. In particular, they despised the Middle Ages as a long night of barbaric darkness. Doubtless most of them would have agreed with the dictum of Rousseau that the Gothic cathedrals were "a disgrace to those who had the patience to build them." In all of these attitudes the men of the Intellectual Revolution were following in the footsteps of the humanists. Devotion to the achievements of classical antiquity was at least one important element of Renaissance culture that had not

The nature of the new classicism

Below: *The Petit Trianon.* Designed by J. A. Gabriel and completed in 1768, it was Louis XV's gift to Madame Pompadour. It was later given by Louis XVI to Marie Antoinette. Right: *St. Paul's Cathedral, London.* Designed by Christopher Wren and completed in 1710, its dome measures 112 feet in diameter. The stone cross at its top is 366 feet above the ground.

St. Peter's, Rome. A contemporary print showing the colonnades designed by Bernini.

yet died out. Nevertheless, it must not be forgotten that the classicism of the seventeenth and eighteenth centuries was by no means exactly the same as that of the humanists. As a rule, it was more sentimental, grandiose, and extravagant. Besides, it was less sincere, since it was frequently employed for the glorification of cynical monarchs and their corrupt and frivolous dependents. Finally, classicism was now perhaps even less a universal theme than it had been during the age of the Renaissance. A number of the great artists and writers of the seventeenth and eighteenth centuries sought to escape from its influence entirely.

Classicism
in architecture:
the baroque
style

The leading arts to be developed during the age of the Intellectual Revolution were architecture and painting. Sculpture ceased to be an independent art, as it had been in the Renaissance, and was relegated to its earlier function of a mere aid to the adornment of buildings. The prevailing style of architecture in the seventeenth century was the so-called baroque. Originating in Italy, it spread to France, England, and Spain and was eventually adopted for churches, palaces, opera houses, museums, and government buildings in practically every Western country. In European capitals to this day it meets the eye in every direction. Among its celebrated monuments still standing are the Luxembourg palace and the main palaces at Versailles in France, St. Paul's Cathedral in London, the government buildings in Vienna and Brussels, and the palaces of the Tsars at Peterhof near Leningrad in Russia. The most noted of the baroque architects were Giovanni Lorenzo Bernini (1598–1680), who designed the colonnade and square in front of St. Peter's Church in Rome, and Sir Christopher Wren (1632–1723), whose masterpiece was St. Paul's Cathedral. The baroque style was supposed to be founded upon the architecture of ancient Rome, but it was much more lavish than anything the Romans produced. Its principal features were hugeness, artificiality, extravagance of ornamentation, and the extensive use of such "classical" elements as the column, the dome, and sculptured representations of mythological scenes. So much detail was added to the surface of the buildings that they often give the impression of having been carved, like the altars in medieval churches. A similar passion for splendor and magnificence was reflected in the enrichment of interiors with gilt and silver, flashing mirrors, and colored marble. Originally, baroque architecture was a style inspired by the Catholic Reformation. It represented an attempt by the Church to strengthen its hold upon Catholics through manifestations of grandeur and magnificence. Later it was used by rulers of the chief dynastic states to symbolize their power and opulence.

During the eighteenth century the heavy and pompous architectural style of the age of Louis XIV gave way to still other adaptations of the classical. The first to be developed was the rococo architecture in France, so called from the fantastic scrolls and shell-like designs that were commonly employed for ornamentation. The rococo differed from the baroque not only in being lighter but also in the impression of grace and sumptuous refinement it was intended to create. In place of a struggle for dynastic power and for colonial empire, it was now the indolent ease and elegant manners of the court of Louis XV which set the standard for French society. A

The rococo and Georgian styles

St. Nicholas' Cathedral, Prague. This photo shows the interior of the baroque masterpiece.

Venus and Adonis by Peter Paul Rubens. Rubens often painted classical themes, which he conceived on a grand scale and executed with sweeping vigor.

Rubens' Portrait of His Son Nicolaus

more delicate and effeminate architecture seemed to be necessary to accompany this change. Well-known examples of the rococo style are the Petit Trianon at Versailles and the palace of Sans Souci at Potsdam, built by Frederick the Great. About the middle of the eighteenth century a reaction set in against both the rococo and the baroque, and efforts were made to produce a truer and less flamboyant imitation of the classical. Perhaps the best results were achieved in England and in the American colonies with the development of the so-called Georgian style, named from the era when the four Georges reigned successively as kings of England (1714–1830) and known on this side of the ocean as colonial architecture. Though the Georgian retained certain elements of the baroque—the columns, the dormer windows, and often the cupola or dome—it at least had the classical merit of simplicity.

To a certain extent the evolution of painting during the seventeenth and eighteenth centuries paralleled that of architecture. The greatest of the painters who may be considered to have expressed the baroque tradition were the Flemings, Peter Paul Rubens (1577–1640) and Anthony Van Dyck (1599–1641), and the Spaniard, Diego Velásquez (1599–1660). Rubens was not merely the outstanding genius among these three, but he was the greatest of all the Flemish painters. In such famous works as *The Fates Spinning* and *Venus and Adonis* he combined classical themes with the sumptuous color and richness so pleasing to the affluent burghers and nobles of his day. The pink and rounded flesh of his full-blown nudes is thoroughly in keeping with the robust vitality of the age. Both Rubens and his gifted pupil, Anthony Van Dyck, are noted for their portraits of rulers and nobles. These were done in highly aristocratic fashion with full attention to the gorgeous details of elegant apparel and opulent furnishings in the background. Van Dyck's best-known portraits are those of the English kings, James I and Charles I, and their families. Velásquez, the third great artist of the baroque tradition, was the court painter to Philip IV of Spain. Much of his work consisted of paintings of royal faces, suffused in soft and silvery light but empty of meaning or emotional expression.

All of the painters mentioned thus far were exponents in some degree of the classical influence. But there were others in both the seventeenth and eighteenth centuries who refused to be bound by the prevailing artistic conventions. Foremost among them was Rembrandt van Rijn (1606–1669), now universally acclaimed as one of the greatest painters of all time. The son of a well-to-do miller of Leyden, Rembrandt was allowed to begin his artistic education at an early age. Under a series of native masters he learned the technique of subtle coloring and skillful depiction of the unusual in nature. Famous by the time he was twenty-five, he fell upon evil days later in his life, mainly as a consequence of bad investments and the failure of critics to appreciate his more recondite works. In 1656 he was stripped by his creditors of all he possessed, even to his table linen, and driven from his house. Apparently these reverses served mainly to broaden and deepen his philosophy, for in this very same year he

See color plates at page 641

Self-Portrait by Rembrandt

The painters who defied classical conventions: (1) Rembrandt

The Return of the Prodigal Son by Rembrandt. The painting now hangs in the Hermitage Museum in Leningrad.

See color
plates at page
672

(2) Hals and
Goya

See color
plates at page
769

Classicism in
literature: the
French poets
and dramatists

produced some of his greatest achievements. As a painter Rembrandt surpassed all the other members of the Dutch school and deserves to be ranked with the great masters of the High Renaissance in Italy. No artist had a keener understanding of the problems and trials of human nature or a stronger perception of the mysteries of this life. His portraits, including those of himself, are imbued with an introspective quality and with a suggestion that the half is not being told. The subjects he delighted to paint were not the incidents of classical mythology but solemn rabbis, tattered beggars, and scenes from the Old and New Testaments, rich in drama and in human interest. Some of his best-known works include *The Good Samaritan, The Woman Taken in Adultery, The Marriage of Samson,* and *The Night Watch.*

Two other noted artists of the period of the Intellectual Revolution also departed widely from the classical tradition. The first was the Dutchman Frans Hals (1580–1666) and the second was the Spaniard Francisco Goya (1746–1828). Like his great contemporary Rembrandt, Hals insisted upon choosing the subjects he liked, regardless of whether they conformed to the notions of genteel critics. Most of his works are realistic portraits. He loved to depict the imbecilic grin in the face of the tavern drunkard, the naïve enthusiasm of itinerant singers and players, or the bewildered misery of some beaten and hopeless derelict. Goya was not merely a rebel against accepted artistic standards but a political and social revolutionary as well. He detested the aristocracy, despised the Church, and ridiculed the hypocrisy of respectable society. But he reserved his deepest contempt for absolute monarchy. His *Charles IV on Horseback* has been called "the most impudent portrait of royalty ever painted." Goya also made use of his talents to indict the cruelty of war, especially during the period when Europe was ravaged by Napoleon's armies.

The history of literature in the seventeenth and eighteenth centuries exhibited tendencies quite similar to those of art. The most popular literary ideal was classicism, which generally meant not only a studied imitation of classical forms but also an earnest devotion to reason as a way of life, on the assumption that the Greeks and Romans had been rationalists above everything else. Although classicism was not confined to any one country, its principal center was France. Here lived during the reign of Louis XIV a distinguished company of poets and dramatists, who gave more genuine luster to their country than had ever been won by the Grand Monarch in his boldest exploits of diplomacy and war. The most noted member of this company was Jean-Baptiste Poquelin (1622–1673), who is much better known by his adopted name of Molière. Much of the work of these writers was marked by qualities similar to those of the baroque in art: it was decorative, turgid, affected, artificial, and in general expressive of a tendency to subordinate content to form. The writings of Molière, however, stand out as a brilliant exception.

Less respectful of ancient formalism than any of his associates, Molière was the most original of French comedians. Few keener critics of human nature have ever lived. "The business of comedy," he once declared, "is to represent in general all the defects of men and especially of the men of our time." The mortal weakness he delighted most to ridicule was pretentiousness. But with all of his penchant for satire, Molière had a measure of pity for the evil fortunes of men. In a number of his plays sympathy and even melancholy go hand in hand with clever wit and pungent scorn. His genius was probably broader in scope than that of any other dramatist since Shakespeare.

England also had a luxuriant growth of literary effort in the classical style. The first great master of this style as applied to English literature was the renowned Puritan poet, John Milton (1608–1674). The leading philosopher of the Puritan Revolution, Milton wrote the official defense of the beheading of Charles I and later held the position of Secretary for Foreign Tongues under Cromwell's Commonwealth. Nearly all of his writings were phrased in the rich and stately expression of the classical tradition, while many of the lesser ones revolved about themes from Greek mythology. But Milton was as much a Puritan as he was a classicist. He could never quite get away from the idea that the essence of beauty is morality. Moreover, he was deeply interested in theological problems. His greatest work, *Paradise Lost*, is a synthesis of the religious beliefs of his age, a majestic epic of the Protestant faith. In spite of the fact that Milton was a Puritan, his views in this work departed widely from Calvinist dogma. Its principal themes are the moral responsibility of the individual and the importance of knowledge as an instrument of virtue. Paradise is lost repeatedly in human life to the extent that man allows passion to triumph over reason in determining the course of his actions. Milton also threw Calvinist doctrine to the winds in his *Areopagitica*, perhaps the most eloquent defense of freedom of speech in the English language.

Classicism in English literature reached its zenith in the eighteenth century in the poetry of Alexander Pope (1688–1744) and in the writings of a score of masters of prose. Pope was the great exponent in verse of the mechanistic and deistic doctrines of the Enlightenment. In such works as his *Essay on Man* and his *Essay on Criticism* he set forth the view that nature is governed by inflexible laws, and that man must study and follow nature if he would bring any semblance of order into human affairs. The chief masters of prose who wrote under classicist influence were the journalist and writer of popular fiction Daniel Defoe (1660?–1731); the satirist Jonathan Swift (1667–1745); and the historian Edward Gibbon (1737–1794), author of *The Decline and Fall of the Roman Empire*.

The age of classicism in English prose was also the period that witnessed the origin of the modern novel. To some extent the new literary form was anticipated by Daniel Defoe's *Robinson Crusoe*,

John Milton

Alexander Pope and the masters of English prose

665

a story based upon the fictional adventures of a shipwrecked sailor who had spent five years on a desolate island off the coast of Chile. But the true modern novel, with its more or less elaborate plot of human behavior and its psychological analysis of life and love, springs from the work of Henry Fielding (1707–1754). His *History of Tom Jones* has been acclaimed by some critics as the greatest novel in the English language. Rich in humor and in colorful description of manners and customs, it provided the inspiration for innumerable others, not only in England but on the Continent of Europe as well.

Earlier in this chapter we learned that the rationalistic and mechanistic philosophy of the Enlightenment was followed by a romantic revolt, expressed first of all in the teachings of Rousseau. We have now to observe that an almost identical development took place in literature. Beginning about 1750 a reaction set in against the intellectualism and high-flown formalism involved in the classical tradition. A group of writers now demanded a return to simplicity and naturalism with less attention to man as a rational creature and more to his instincts and feelings. No longer was it considered disgraceful for the poet to show sympathy or pity or to display any other of his deepest emotions; the heart should rule the head, at least in all cases where problems vital to man's happiness were concerned. No longer was nature regarded as a cold, automatic machine but worshiped as the embodiment of beauty, sublimity, and charm, or tenderly revered as a source of protection and solace. God now ceased to be a mere First Cause and came to be identified with the universe itself or mystically adored as the soul of nature. Still another element in the romantic ideal was glorification of the common man, often accompanied by a generous compassion for the weak and oppressed. Although some of this regard for the lowly had been implied in the humanitarianism of the Enlightenment, most of the leaders of that movement had little respect for the masses. Now under the influence of romanticism the humble herdsman and peasant were given a recognition in literature long overdue.

Though literary romanticism had its roots in France in such sentimental works as *Émile* and *The New Héloïse* of Rousseau, the movement attained its most vigorous development in Great Britain and Germany. Among the eighteenth-century romantic poets in Britain were Thomas Gray (1716–1771), author of the *Elegy Written in a Country Churchyard;* and, to a certain extent, Oliver Goldsmith (1728–1774), who celebrated the rustic innocence of Auburn, "loveliest village of the plain." The most original of them all, however, was the Scotsman Robert Burns (1759–1796). In his homely dialect verse the romantic feeling for nature and sympathy for the common man received their finest expression. No writer has inspired more tenderness for the humblest things of this earth or filled the world with a deeper respect for those who toil for their bread. Moreover, Burns was unique among poets of his age in com-

The beginning of romanticism in literature

Goethe

The early romantic poets in Britain: Gray, Goldsmith, and Burns

bining an extraordinary pathos with a delicate touch of humor. He had the rare gift of being passionately earnest without being solemn. In the very last years of the eighteenth century two other romantic poets began their literary activities on British soil. Their names were William Wordsworth and Samuel Taylor Coleridge. But since most of the work of these men was done in the nineteenth century, they can be discussed more appropriately in a later chapter.

The romantic movement in German literature developed primarily under the brilliant guidance of Friedrich Schiller (1759–1805) and Johann Wolfgang von Goethe (1749–1832). Schiller grew up during the period of the *Sturm und Drang* (Storm and Stress), when writers all over Germany were denouncing restraints and conventions and attempting to free the culture of their country from foreign domination. As a consequence his romanticism generally embraced as its important elements the idealization of heroic deeds and the glorification of struggles for freedom. While a strong quality of individualism pervades a number of his plays, Schiller's conception of liberty seems to have been closely akin to nationalism. This is revealed quite clearly in his *William Tell*, a drama of the struggle of the Swiss against Austrian tyranny. This natonalistic aspect of Schiller's work was probably the one which had the major influence upon later German writers.

The greatest name in the history of German literature is unquestionably that of Schiller's older contemporary, Johann Wolfgang von Goethe. The two men were associated for a number of years at the court of the Duke of Weimar. Born in Frankfurt, the son of a family of ample means, Goethe was educated for the law but soon found the limits of knowledge in that profession unsatisfying. His indefatigable spirit drove him to the study of medicine, and then of the fine arts and the natural sciences. His first important literary production was *The Sorrows of Young Werther*, a romantic novel about a love-sick youth who takes his own life with the pistol of his rival and friend. Written in dashing sentimental style, it attained an enormous popularity not only in Germany but also in England and France. Though the author apparently intended that it should express the idea that weakness of character is the greatest of sins, it came to be taken as a symbol of profound dissatisfaction with the world and as a basis of fiery revolt. In 1790 Goethe published the first part of his drama *Faust*, which he finally completed in 1831, a year before his death. Universally acknowledged as his grandest achievement, *Faust* not only epitomizes the personal philosophy of the author but expresses the spirit of the modern age as few other writings have done. Part I reflects some of the quality of rebellion in the *Sturm und Drang*, but in Part II the conviction grows that freedom from restraint is not enough; the individual must go on in an endless quest for mastery of all knowledge and for enrichment of life through unlimited experience. Considered as a whole, the drama is a symbol of perpetual unrest, of that ceaseless yearning for the

An Illustration from *The Sorrows of Young Werther* by Goethe

Goethe

667

fullness of life which has come to be one of the most distinctive traits of modern civilization.

5 · MUSIC IN THE SEVENTEENTH AND EIGHTEENTH CENTURIES

The birth of opera and the concerto

As was observed in a preceding chapter,[9] the sixteenth century marked the culmination of a long era of music illustrated by choral works of polyphonic structure. The seventeenth opens with a general rebellion against polyphony, a rebellion so powerful and pervasive that the Palestrinian style became completely archaic within twenty-five years of the death of its creator. The new ideal, a primary voice *accompanied* by one or several instruments, which swept Italy in an incredibly short time, became known as *monody*. One of the main reasons for this radical change was the Italians' powerful dramatic instinct; they realized that the feelings of an individual cannot be expressed by a many-voiced chorus. The same trends that created modern theater and the dramatic architecture of the Jesuits invaded music and led to the creation of opera, which reached its first magnificent manifestation in *Orfeo* (1607) by Claudio Monteverdi (1567–1643), the dominating musical personality in the first half of the new century. Within a generation operas were performed in most important cities in Italy, and by 1736 Venice boasted an opera house for every parish. Now the already respectable instrumental music of the Renaissance began to make rapid gains and a fine literature arose for beautifully constructed instruments—organ, harpsichord, and the various string and wind instruments. In the last third of the century instrumental music created the concerto, along with opera one of the greatest original stylistic accomplishments of the Italian baroque. Both opera and concerto spread beyond the Alps and conquered every country, producing national offshoots. Though the seventeenth century was preoccupied with experiments, it created an impressive synthesis upon which the first half of the eighteenth century could build the final great edifices of the late baroque.

Johann Sebastian Bach

The origin of the modern novel

The late baroque culminated in two towering figures: Johann Sebastian Bach (1685–1750) and George Frederick Handel (1685–1759). Though both were born in Saxony, Bach became the epitome of German musical genius, while Handel, who lived for almost half a century in London and became a British subject, embodied an English national style. Bach combined an unbounded imagination and a capacious intellect with heroic powers of discipline and an unquenchable zeal for work. By lifelong study he made himself the master of most existing types and styles of music, from little

[9] See §6 in the chapter on The Expansion of the Renaissance.

dance pieces for the clavichord to gigantic choral works. Being a church musician, Bach's duty was to provide new music for the elaborate Sunday and holy day services. Therefore the bulk of his work is made up of cantatas (over 200 preserved), oratorios, Passions, and Masses. His settings of the Gospel according to St. John and St. Matthew represent the unsurpassable peak of this genre. Fundamentally, though, Bach was an instrumental composer, the creator of tremendous works for the organ and harpsichord. Then there are his spacious concertos, sonatas for various combinations of instruments, and suites for orchestra. Bach was still steeped in an almost medieval German Protestant mysticism that no longer fitted the age of the Enlightenment. Thus it happened that soon after his death he was overshadowed by a musical world devoted to more mundane aims. But when the nineteenth century rediscovered him his influence became paramount; to this day composers have been known to "return" to Bach for inspiration and guidance.

Handel was the absolute antithesis of his great fellow-Saxon. After four years spent in Italy he completely absorbed Italian techniques and modes of composition, subsequently settling in England where for years he ran an opera company that produced nothing but Italian operas, mostly his own. Though many of these are masterpieces that we are just beginning to appreciate, the fact remains that Italian opera did not suit the taste of the large English middle class public, and after decades spent in composing and producing dozens of operas, Handel finally realized that he must turn to something more acceptable to the English mind. This he found in the "oratorio," a rather loose definition for the English music drama intended for an ideal theater. With the exception of *Messiah*, the most famous of the oratorios, these works were not religious music,

George Frederick
Handel

"The Charming Brute."
A contemporary caricature of Handel, engraved by Joseph Groupy, 1754.

669

although the themes came from the Old Testament. Undoubtedly one reason for Handel's success in his adopted country was the fact that his virile and heroic oratorios symbolized the English people, their pride in their institutions and their attainment of national greatness. Handel lived in circumstances wholly different from those permitted to Bach and most other Continental composers. He was not a salaried artisan but a free citizen, an English squire who ran his own business and left behind a respectable estate.

The birth of
classicism in
music

After a transition era in music led by J.S. Bach's gifted sons we reach the period dominated by the Viennese School, so called because its leading masters were active in or near the Austrian capital. By about 1770 a remarkable stylistic synthesis reconciled baroque weightiness, rococo charm, and pre-romantic excitement. This peace between warring extremes created an island in the romantic stream, an art that truly deserves the term applied to it: classicism. Vienna now assimilated every musical thought, from Naples to Hamburg. Christoph Willibald Gluck (1714–1787) reformed the declining "serious" opera into a noble drama that recalls the tone of classical antiquity. But the mischievous, Italian comic opera, the *opera buffa*, was victorious in the end and forced a fusion with the serious opera which reached its unsurpassable height in the operas of Wolfgang Amadeus Mozart (1756–1791), while chamber and orchestral music reached a new formal and expressive level under the leadership of Joseph Haydn (1732–1809).

Mozart; his early
life

The eighteenth century was full of music, but its social organization was as cruel to the creative artist as is our own free society. If the artist was not employed by a court, noble house, church, or municipality, if he was not an internationally acclaimed virtuoso or a renowned teacher, he was ground up in the effort to make a living. Mozart was among the first to shed the security of the "musical

Left: *Mozart and His Sister at the Piano.* In this painting of somewhat dubious authenticity, their father is seen holding the violin while their mother's portrait hangs above the piano. Right: *A Portion of the Original Score for Mozart's Quartet in C Major, K 465*

lackey" and try the free artistic economy of the metropolis. While a child prodigy he was adored and admired, but when he left the employ of the Archbishop of Salzburg to take up the career of a free lance artist in Vienna, a shadow fell over him that he was not able to elude. The remaining ten years of his life were spent in bountiful productivity. Yet he had to live from hand to mouth—the world was not yet ready for the independent artist.

When appraising the music of the classical era we must realize that in spite of the magnificent sonatas and symphonies, the stylistic core of the era was still in dramatic music. This classical music, with its clear, absolute forms, emphasized on the stage everything that is permanent and finite. Mozart used these forms to shape the characters, fates, and conflicts of human beings in a way that they too became permanent and finite. Drama and melody, characterization and absolute form evolve simultaneously on Mozart's stage. Each great opera—*The Marriage of Figaro, Don Giovanni, The Magic Flute*—provides a center around which cluster piano sonatas, quartets, quintets, concertos, and symphonies. The nineteenth century's likening of Mozart to Apollo was neither an accident nor a mistake, but men failed to understand that hidden behind the Appollonian poise and smile were deep wounds.

Mozart's operas

Haydn was carved from harder timber than Mozart; his peasant background made him tenacious and stubborn. If Mozart embodied the aristocratic spirit, Haydn did that of the liberated plebeian. It was because of their diametrically opposed personalities that the two musicians got along so well; they complemented each other, learned from each other, and fulfilled the hopes and aspirations of the second half of the eighteenth century. Haydn had a sharp intellect and he acquired his extensive knowledge of music through incessant study and experimentation. His art conveys the impressions of the village and the countryside, but also the elegance of the princely household that employed him for many years, as well as the solemnity of the cathedral. Haydn's compositions are so numerous that a complete edition of them has never been made. They include many operas and Masses, oratorios, concertos, over eighty string quartets, and more than 100 symphonies. It was Haydn who firmly established the technical and stylistic principles of symphonic construction, creating, with Mozart, the pattern of the symphony orchestra which remained the basis for all future developments.

Joseph Haydn

6. SOCIAL IDEALS AND REALITIES DURING THE AGE OF THE ENLIGHTENMENT

A movement as profoundly disturbing to Western society as the Intellectual Revolution was bound to have its effects upon social customs and individual habits. These effects were especially discernible during the bloom of the Enlightenment in the eighteenth century. Of course, not all of the social progress of this time can be traced to intellectual influences; much of it derived from the bulging prosperity induced by the expansion of trade in the Commercial Revolution. Nevertheless, the progress of philosophy and science had more than incidental effects in clearing away the cobwebs of ancient prejudice and in building a more liberal and humane society.

Social idealism: (1) the reform of criminal codes

Mention has already been made of the influence of the Enlightenment in promoting the cause of social reform. A characteristic expression of this influence was agitation for revision of drastic criminal codes and for more liberal treatment of prisoners. In regard to both, the need for reform was urgent. Penalties even for minor offenses were exceedingly severe in practically all countries, death being the punishment for stealing a horse or a sheep or for the theft of as little as five shillings in money. During the first half of the eighteenth century no fewer than sixty crimes were added to the capital list in England. The treatment accorded to bankrupts and debtors was also a standing disgrace. Beaten and starved by cruel jailers, they died by the thousands in filthy prisons. Conditions such as these eventually challenged the sympathies of several reformers. Foremost among them was Cesare Beccaria, a jurist of Milan, who had been deeply influenced by the writings of French rationalist philosophers. In 1764 he published his famed treatise on *Crimes and Punishments*, in which he condemned the common theory that penalties should be made as horrible as possible in order to deter potential offenders. Insisting that the purpose of criminal codes should be the prevention of crime and the reform of the wayward rather than vengeance, he urged the abolition of torture as unworthy of civilized nations. He likewise condemned capital punishment as contrary to the natural rights of man, since it cannot be revoked in case of error. Beccaria's book created a veritable sensation. It was translated into a dozen languages, and it stimulated efforts to improve conditions in many lands. By the end of the eighteenth century considerable progress had been made in reducing the severity of penalties, in relieving debtors from punishment, and in providing work and better food for prisoners.

(2) opposition to slavery and war

The humanitarian spirit of the Enlightenment found an outlet also in other directions. Several of the scientists and philosophers, notably Buffon and Rousseau, denounced the evils of slavery. Many more condemned the slave trade. The efforts of intellectuals in this regard were warmly seconded by the leaders of certain religious groups, especially by prominent Quakers in America. Even John Wesley, conservative as he was on many social issues, branded slavery as an abomination. Pacifism was another ideal of many of the new liberal thinkers. Voltaire's strictures on war were by no means the only example of such sentiments. Even the sentimental Rousseau could perceive the illogic in Grotius' attempt to draw a distinction been just and unjust wars. From the pens of other *philosophes* emanated various ingenious plans of insuring perpetual peace, in-

The Night Watch, Rembrandt. (The Rijksmuseum)

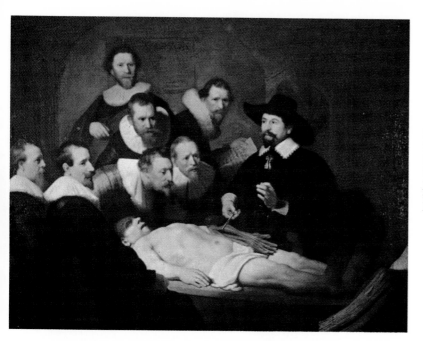

The Anatomy Lesson, Rembrandt van Rijn (1606–1669). Rembrandt scorned the classical themes of most of his contemporaries and turned to character analysis and the portrayal of life. (Mauritshuis, The Hague)

The Stonemason's Yard,
Canaletto (1697–1768). A
quiet scene of everyday life,
in strong contrast to the portrait below. (National Gallery, London)

Madame de Pompadour,
François Boucher (1703–
1770). This portrait idealizes
the favorite mistress of Louis
XV. (The Wallace Collec-
tion, London)

cluding a scheme for a league of nations with power to take concerted action against aggressors.[10]

Perhaps it was natural that humanitarian agitation for reform should be accompanied by an increase of sympathy for the lower classes. This was especially true during the final stage of the Enlightenment. With the progress of reason and the increasing emphasis upon the natural rights of man, the strong reaction against the evils of slavery and war was eventually translated into a protest against every form of suffering and oppression. Thus the hardships of the poor came in for a larger share of attention than they had received since the time of the Sophists. Besides, the middle class, in the pursuit of its ambition to dethrone the aristocracy, needed the support of the peasants and urban workers. Out of such factors there developed a tendency on the part of leading thinkers to espouse the cause of the common man. In some quarters, it became popular to despise aristocratic lineage or royal birth. Thomas Paine echoed the sentiments of many when he declared that a single honest plowman was worth more than all the crowned ruffians who ever lived. The great Scottish economist, Adam Smith, deplored the habit of feeling more pity for a royal scoundrel like Charles I than for the thousands of common citizens slaughtered in the civil war. Several of the French philosophers of the Enlightenment went considerably farther in professions of sympathy for the masses. Gabriel de Mably (1709–1785), the Marquis de Condorcet (1743–1794), and Rousseau advocated an absolute equality of freedom and privileges for every man. Mably and Condorcet, at least, perceived that this could not be attained except by a redistribution of wealth.

(3) increase of sympathy for the lower classes

[10] This was the famous scheme of the Abbé de Saint-Pierre (1658–1743).

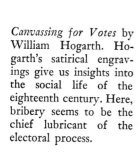

Canvassing for Votes by William Hogarth. Hogarth's satirical engravings give us insights into the social life of the eighteenth century. Here, bribery seems to be the chief lubricant of the electoral process.

Morality as
exemplified in
the customs
and practices of
the upper
classes

While they did not propose socialism, they nevertheless argued that landed property should be held in substantially equal amounts, so that exploitation of the poor by the rich would be practically impossible.

The moral ideals of the Enlightenment were reflected not only in the books of the philosophers; they were also revealed in the principal customs and social practices of the time. The eighteenth century, in particular, was an age of pampered elegance and gracious living decidedly at variance with the ascetic taboos of the church. The houses of the nobles were resplendently furnished with shining mirrors, crystal chandeliers, and graceful sofas and chairs richly upholstered in brocaded silk. Men of the upper classes arrayed themselves in powdered wigs, velvet coats with lace at the cuffs, silk stockings, and knee breeches of delicate hue. Not since the days of the Renaissance had fashion played so dominant a part in the lives of both sexes. Habits of personal behavior were also characterized by similar qualities of elegance and artificiality. Form was everything; motive, nothing. The ladies and gentlemen of the best society addressed even those whom they cordially hated with the most fulsome compliments and groveled disgustingly in the presence of higher rank.

Manners as a
substitute for
morals

Among the upper classes, manners very largely took the place of morals. The ladies and gentlemen who danced the stately minuet and deported themselves with such charming grace quite commonly ridiculed married love as a relic of a benighted past. Adultery became fashionable and almost a virtue. A husband sometimes lived on friendly terms with his wife's lovers, for no one in this cultivated society would be so uncouth as to display any sentiment of jealousy. Prostitution had not only its apologists but also its defenders, and brothels were quite commonly permitted to remain open on Sundays, though theaters had to be closed. A prevailing attitude toward relations between the sexes appears to have been that of Buffon, who declared that "there is nothing good in love but the physical."

The more violent and brutish aspects of 18th-century society

Eighteenth-century society also had its more violent and brutish aspects, which were largely survivals from the turbulent days of the Renaissance. Despite the severity of penal laws, vicious crimes were still very common. In many large cities bands of hooligans roamed the streets at night, while footpads infested the highways in the open country. In London such hoodlums were known as Mohawks, and their favorite diversions, aside from robbery, were beating constables, "turning women upside down," and gouging out the eyes of any who tried to restrain them. Drunkenness continued in much the same measure as before, though the consumption of hard liquor by the poorer classes appears to have increased. About this time gin became popular, especially in England, as the poor man's drink. Gambling and cruel games and sports likewise survived unabated. Yet another of the prevailing vices of this period was dueling, although it was confined primarily to the upper and middle classes. The gentleman of spirit was still supposed to avenge any real or imaginary insult by challenging the offender to a mortal combat with sword or pistol. Even so prominent a statesman as William Pitt the younger felt obliged to meet an opponent on the so-called field of honor.

It is necessary to observe, however, that the picture of social conditions in the eighteenth century was not altogether dark. For one thing, there was a definite improvement in the standard of living, certainly for the middle classes and probably even for some of the poor. This is evidenced by the increasing per capita consumption of sugar, chocolate, coffee, and tea, which were not merely substituted for other foods and beverages but were additions to the average diet. The growing demand for linen and cotton cloth, and for such articles of luxury as mahogany furniture designed by such masters as Chippendale, Hepplewhite, and Sheraton, may be taken as a further indication of rising prosperity. Such evidences applied, however, only to a small proportion of the population, chiefly to the nobles and to the merchants, bankers, and lawyers in the larger cities. The life of the peasants, with a few exceptions, was still one of privation. In England large tenant farmers enjoyed some luxuries, but the condition of the small, independent yeomen was far from prosperous. Because of instability of prices, increasing taxes, and the costs of new farming methods, many were forced down into the ranks of agricultural wage earners. In France the peasants constituted about 80 per cent of the population, but less than one-twentieth of them owned their land. The remainder were serfs, tenant farmers, and *métayers*, who were required to surrender half of the produce of the lands they occupied to the lord. Most wretched of all were the peasants of eastern Europe. In East Prussia peasants often had to work from three to six days a week for their lord, and some had only late evening or night hours to cultivate their own lands. In Russia landlords had the power of life and death over their serfs, and could sell them apart from the land and even apart from their families.

Evidences of improvement in standards of living

The other of the more favorable aspects of social life during the age of the Enlightenment was a sharp reduction of the death rate. This came about as the result of several causes. Probably the most important was the effective control of smallpox as a consequence of inoculation and vaccination. A second factor was the establishment of maternity hospitals, which, in combination with improved obstetrical methods, reduced the mortality among infants in the second half of the century by more than 50 per cent and among mothers by an even larger proportion. Finally, advancement in sanitation, together with the adoption of more hygienic habits by people of all classes, contributed not a little to the conquest of various diseases and to lengthening the span of life.

Improvements in health and sanitation

· *Items so designated are available in paperbound editions.*

PHILOSOPHY

· Artz, F. B., *The Enlightenment in France*, Kent, Ohio, 1968 (Kent State).
· ———, *From the Renaissance to Romanticism: 1300–1820*, Chicago, 1962
· Becker, C. L., *The Heavenly City of the Eighteenth Century Philosophers*, New Haven, 1932 (Yale University Press).

Brandes, Georg, *Voltaire*, New York, 1930, 2 vols. A brilliant evaluation by a distinguished critic.

Chapman, J. W., *Rousseau—Totalitarian or Liberal?* New York, 1956.

· Church, W. F., *The Influence of the Enlightenment on the French Revolution*, New York, 1964 (Heath).
· Crocker, Lester G., *The Age of Enlightenment*, New York, 1970 (Torchbook).
· Gay, Peter, *The Enlightenment: The Rise of Modern Paganism*, New York, 1970 (Vintage).

Green, F. C., *Jean-Jacques Rousseau: A Critical Study of His Life and Writings*, New York, 1955.

· Hazard, Paul, *European Thought in the Eighteenth Century*, New York, 1954 (Meridian).

Hertzberg, Arthur, *The French Enlightenment and the Jews*, New York, 1968.

Kropotkin, Peter, *Ethics: Origin and Development*, New York, 1924. Stimulating and suggestive.

Lecky, W. E. H., *History of the Rise and Influence of the Spirit of Rationalism in Europe*, New York, 1914, 2 vols. A classic.

· Lovejoy, Arthur, *Essays in the History of Ideas*, Baltimore, 1948 (Capricorn). Includes good chapters on the Intellectual Revolution.
· McGiffert, A. C., *Protestant Thought before Kant*, New York, 1915 (Torchbook). An excellent survey.
· Manuel, Frank E., *The Age of Reason*, Ithaca, 1951 (Cornell).
· Martin, Kingsley, *The Rise of French Liberal Thought*, New York, 1954, 2d. rev. edn. A brilliant but somewhat biased account. Also available in paperback under the title, *French Liberal Thought in the Eighteenth Century: A Study of Political Ideas from Bayle to Condorcet*. (Torchbook).

Morais, H. M., *Deism in Eighteenth Century America*, New York, 1934.

Morley, John, *Rousseau*, New York, 1891, 2 vols.

———, *Voltaire*, New York, 1871.

Mowat, R. B., *The Age of Reason*, New York, 1934. A good general account.

· Muller, H. J., *Religion and Freedom in the Modern World*, Chicago, 1963 (Phoenix).
· Plumb, J. H., *et al.*, James L. Clifford, ed., *Man versus Society in Eighteenth Century Britain*, New York, 1968.

Randall, J. H., Jr., *The Making of the Modern Mind*, New York, 1926. Chs. XI, XII, XVI.

· Rossi, Paoli, *Francis Bacon: From Magic to Science*. Trans. by Saca Rabinovitch, Chicago, 1968 (University of Chicago).

Rowe, Constance, *Voltaire and the State*, New York, 1955.

· Rudé, George, *The Crowd in History: A Study of Popular Disturbances in France and England, 1730–1848*, New York, 1964 (Wiley).

Schapiro, J. S., *Condorcet and the Rise of Liberalism in France*, New York, 1934.

· Smith, Preserved, *A History of Modern Culture*, New York, 1934, Vol. II (Collier).

- Snyder, L. L., *The Age of Reason*, Princeton, 1953 (Anvil). Includes a good interpretive essay as well as selections from original sources.
- Stephen, Leslie, *History of English Thought in the Eighteenth Century*, New York, 1927 (Harbinger, 2 vols.).

  Vaughan, C. E., *The Romantic Revolt*, New York, 1930.

SCIENCE

- Butterfield, Herbert, *The Origins of Modern Science*, New York, 1951 (Collier).
- Hall, A. R., *The Scientific Revolution, 1500–1800*, Boston, 1956 (Beacon).
- Hogben, Lancelot, *Mathematics for the Million*, New York, 1937. (Pocket Book).

  Nordenskiöld, Erik, *The History of Biology*, New York, 1928.

  Singer, Charles, *A Short History of Medicine*, New York, 1928.
- Smith, Preserved, *History of Modern Culture*, New York, 1934, Vol. II (Collier).

  Taylor, Frank, *Galileo and the Freedom of Thought*, London, 1938.

LITERATURE, ART, AND MUSIC

  Bukofzer, Manfred F., *Music in the Baroque Era*, New York, 1947.

  Davenport, Marcia, *Mozart*, New York, 1932.
- Guérard, A. L., *France in the Classical Age: Life and Death of an Ideal*, New York, 1928 (Torchbook).

  Lang, Paul, *Music in Western Civilization*, New York, 1941.

  ———, *George Friedrich Handel*, New York, 1966.

  Machlis, Joseph, *The Enjoyment of Music*, 3rd ed., New York, 1970. Excellent.

  Robertson, J. G., *A History of German Literature*, New York, 1930.
- Schweitzer, Albert, *J. S. Bach*, London, 1923, 2 vols. (Bruce Humphries, 2 vols.).
- Stephen, Leslie, *English Literature and Society in the Eighteenth Century*, New York, 1907 (Barnes & Noble).

  Vaughan, C. E., *The Romantic Revolt*, New York, 1930.

  Wright, C. H. C., *French Classicism*, Cambridge, Mass., 1920.

SOURCE MATERIALS

  Baumer, F. L. V., *Main Currents of European Thought*, New York, 1952.
- Milton, John, *Areopagitica; The Tenure of Kings and Magistrates*. (Appleton-Century-Crofts, Inc.).

  Newton, Sir Isaac, *Principia, Third Book*. Rules of Reasoning in Philosophy.

  Spinoza, Benedict, *A Theological-Political Treatise*.

  Voltaire, *Philosophical Dictionary; Candide; Essay on Toleration*.
- Redman, B. R., ed., *The Portable Voltaire*, New York, 1949 (Viking).

CHAPTER 23

India, the Far East, and Africa during the Early Modern Era (*ca.* 1500-1800)

Fuji-ichi was a clever man, and his substantial fortune was amassed in his own lifetime. . . . He noted down the market ratio of copper and gold; he inquired about the current quotations of the rice brokers; he sought information from druggists' and haberdashers' assistants on the state of the market at Nagasaki; for the latest news on the prices of ginned cotton, salt, and saké, he noted the various days on which the Kyoto dealers received dispatches from the Edo branch shops. Every day a thousand things were entered in his book, and people came to Fuji-ichi if they were ever in doubt. He became a valuable asset to the citizens of Kyoto.
—I. Saikaku, *The Tycoon of All Tenants* (1688)

Between the sixteenth and the nineteenth centuries a reinvigorated Indian empire headed by a new dynasty attained the rank of a major power; China, under the last of a long series of imperial dynasties, waxed even stronger, becoming the largest and most populous country in the world; and Japan adapted her feudal institutions to the requirements of a despotic government. In both India and China, and to a lesser degree in Japan, splendor and magnificence reflected the tastes of wealthy societies and mighty rulers, as was also true in much of Europe during this same period. In the long run, however, the great Asian states found themselves at a disadvantage because they played a passive rather than an active role in the Commercial Revolution. As Western European nations turned to empire-building and expanded their naval forces, they established direct contacts with the coastal regions of Asia, took over the bulk of the trade between East and West, and frequently threatened the independence of non-European peoples. For several centuries the principal Eastern states were strong enough to protect themselves against the threat of aggression from the West. Faced with rigid trade restrictions in China and almost totally excluded

Impact of the West upon the East

679

from Japan, the seafaring Europeans turned to other quarters. In the 1570's the Spanish occupied the Philippines, subduing the native tribes and the communities of Chinese colonists in the Islands. A few years later the Dutch, through their East India Company, laid the foundations of a rich empire in Indonesia, dislodging the Portuguese who had preceded them by almost a century. The British and French somewhat belatedly turned their attention to the mainland of India, where they secured valuable trading posts in the course of the seventeenth century.

1. INDIA UNDER THE MOGUL DYNASTY

Babur "the Tiger"

In the sixteenth century a new invasion of India by Moslem forces from the north produced very different results from those that had accompanied the Turkish inroads and the institution of the Delhi Sultanate. It led to the establishment of the dynasty known as the Mogul—a Persian variant of the word "Mongol"—which created an efficient and, on the whole, successful pattern of government and, most significant, demonstrated the possibility of an

The Court of the Emperor Barbur "the Tiger," Founder of the Mogul Dynasty.

integration of the Indian people regardless of religious profession. Actually, the ruling family and the administrative officers were far from pure-blooded Mongols. Babur ("the Tiger"), the founder of the dynasty, was descended on his father's side from Timur (of Turkish stock) and on his mother's side from the Mongol conqueror Genghis Khan. His own descendants were of mixed parentage, including Turkish, Persian, and Indian strains. Babur, like many another conqueror, began his career as the head of a small state in Turkestan. By advancing into Afghanistan he secured control of the frontier mountain passes commanding the route to the Punjab. Within the space of five years (ended by his death in 1530) he conquered the greater part of Hindustan, while retaining his territories in Afghanistan and southern Turkestan. His conquest was facilitated by the fact that he possessed artillery and match-fired muskets of European manufacture, although these guns were very primitive. The empire which Babur had begun to mark out was fully established and also given its most distinctive character by his grandson, Akbar.

Akbar, deservedly termed "the Great Mogul," was truly remarkable both as a personality and as a sovereign. He is generally considered India's greatest ruler, although he evidently fell short of the noble idealism exemplified by Asoka some 1800 years earlier. Perhaps the scarcity of records for Asoka's reign makes a comparison unfair. At any rate, enough data are available for Akbar's period to show that he was unquestionably one of the world's outstanding political figures in the sixteenth century. His reign was a long one—from 1556 to 1605 (the dates almost coincide with the reign of Elizabeth I of England). Much of it was devoted to schemes of conquest, unsuccessfully in the Deccan but resulting in the extension of Mogul authority over all northern India and the neighboring portion of Afghanistan. Far more important was Akbar's determination to conciliate and secure the support of the Hindu population, a decision to which he adhered inflexibly throughout his reign. For his large harem (said to number over 5000) he chose wives of several different nationalities, partly with an eye toward political expediency. By contracting marriage alliances with the proud Rajput clans, whose spirit had never been broken by the Turks, he hoped to win their allegiance. (Akbar's favorite wife and the mother of his successor to the throne was a Rajput princess.) Early in his reign he took the important step of abolishing the special taxes on non-Moslems, and he appointed Hindus—especially Rajputs—to civil and military office. A Hindu raja served in the highly responsible post of minister of finance. Akbar abandoned entirely all attempts to win converts to Islam by coercion and introduced a policy of religious toleration, although he tried to discourage those Hindu practices which he considered reprehensible, such as animal sacrifice, child marriage, and suttee.

Akbar, the Great Mogul

Akbar's
administrative
methods

Akbar's administration was bureaucratic and relatively efficient. At the head of each of the provinces and districts into which he divided the state he placed a military governor who was paid a generous salary but was required to maintain a prescribed number of troops and was held to a strict accountability for his actions. Thus the government was not feudal in basis, although there was a nobility of various grades (including some Hindus and Indian Moslems as well as Moguls). While Akbar was unable to keep an adequate check on every part of his large dominions, he made a sincere effort to enforce justice among his mixed population, and he severely punished officials whose corruption was detected. The criminal code was a savage one, but not more barbarous than in most European countries of that day. Civil law was based largely upon Islamic tradition and the Koran. Akbar's chief source of revenue was a land tax, assessed upon the fields actually under cultivation and amounting to one-third of the annual value of the crop, based on the average yield over a ten-year period. Undoubtedly the rate of assessment was exorbitant, imposing a heavy burden upon the cultivators; but it was applied uniformly, receipts were issued to the taxpayers, and there were safeguards against the cupidity of local officials.

Prosperity for the
rich, hardships for
the poor

The latter part of Akbar's long reign was generally peaceful, and, in spite of the invasions and the murderous strife of preceding centuries, a high level of prosperity seems to have been reached in India. Akbar maintained a sound currency, typified by gold coins of extraordinary fineness. Commerce throve, cities expanded, and a substantial middle class of traders and skilled artisans flourished. Common laborers, however, were far from prosperous, and many were slaves. The country villagers also, who made up the majority of the population, apparently subsisted on a very low standard of living. Great wealth and lavish display were confined to large landowners and officials and were most conspicuous in the court of the emperor. It is estimated that Akbar's total revenue from all sources was equal to more than $200,000,000 a year.

Abkar's
personality and
his cultural
interests

Akbar's unusual personality and rare combination of interests left their mark upon all aspects of his reign. Endowed with a superb physique, he loved feats of strength and dangerous exploits, sometimes risking his life in the most reckless fashion by attacking a lion singlehanded or by riding wild elephants. In a fit of temper he could be pitilessly cruel, but he was generally fair in judgment and frequently generous to a defeated opponent. This high-strung emperor was endowed with lively intellectual curiosity and a capacious mind. He is credited with several inventions, chiefly in connection with the improvement of artillery. Although he stubbornly refused to learn to read or write, he was fond of literature and metaphysical speculation and collected a huge library. A gifted musician, he not only acquired skill as a performer (especially on a

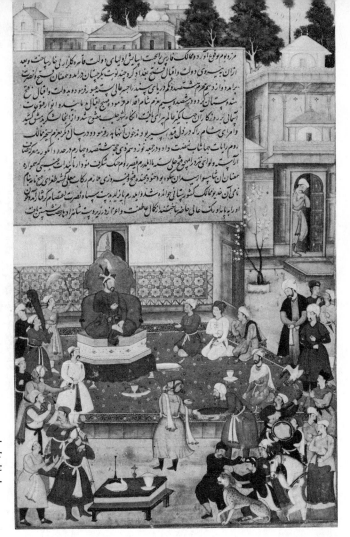

Turkish Prisoners Before Timur. Indian painting from the period of Akbar (1556-1605). The use of Arabic script as a decorative device reflects the Moslem influence.

type of kettle drum) but also became versed in the highly intricate theory of Hindu vocalization. The promotion of art and architecture was another of his ardent pursuits.

The Mogul rulers did not lack heirs, but each reign usually ended with princes revolting against their father and joining in fratricidal strife with one another. Nevertheless, the administrative system and policies of Akbar were retained substantially for half a century after his death. The most renowned of his successors was Shah Jahan, whose reign extended from 1627 to 1658. Shah Jahan devoted much of his resources to peaceful pursuits, especially the erection of costly buildings to gratify a sumptuous but exquisite taste. He established his chief royal residence at Delhi, where he laid out a new city and named it after himself. Both Delhi and Agra in the seventeenth century were among the world's greatest cities in respect to number of inhabitants and impressive public

Shah Jahan

683

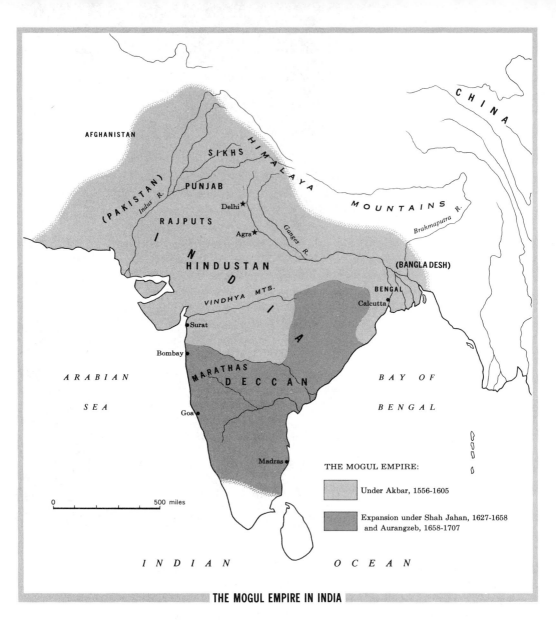

THE MOGUL EMPIRE:

Under Akbar, 1556-1605

Expansion under Shah Jahan, 1627-1658
and Aurangzeb, 1658-1707

THE MOGUL EMPIRE IN INDIA

buildings. Agra, with a population of 600,000, was divided into
separate sections for the different types of merchants and artisans
and contained seventy great mosques and 800 public baths. The
new Delhi was protected by walls rising 60 feet above the river.
Here was constructed a huge royal palace that beggars description.
It housed the famous Peacock Throne, inlaid with precious metals
and jewels, the value of which has been estimated as in excess of
$5,000,000. Shah Jahan's most celebrated monument is the Taj
Mahal, located at Agra and designed as a mausoleum and memorial
to his favorite wife (who died while bearing her fourteenth child
to the emperor). The Taj engaged the labor of 20,000 workmen

and was some fifteen years in construction. The design of the building is of dubious architectural integrity; its charm lies largely in its setting, amid shaded walks, lakes, and gardens.

Before the Moguls had completed their cycle of power, they were confronted with a hostile Hindu confederacy known as the Marathas, located in the hilly region of the western Deccan. The Maratha tribesmen, reputedly of the lowest (*sudra*) caste, were a sturdy people who, under the leadership of their wily and resourceful king Sivaji, became a scourge to the Moguls' supremacy. Masters of guerilla tactics, the Marathas could not be crushed, even though their strongholds were taken and the "Mountain Rat" was himself held captive for a time. The confederacy became a state within the state, collecting taxes and governing a large section of the Deccan, apparently with greater satisfaction to the inhabitants than under the Mogul administration.

The Maratha Confederacy

Another Hindu element which acquired an undying hatred for the Moguls was the Sikhs of the Punjab. In origin the Sikhs were a religious group with progressive and idealistic convictions. The sect had been founded in the fifteenth century by Nanak, a philanthropic and spiritually minded preacher who sought to establish a common bond between Hindus and Moslems. The essence of his teaching was the brotherhood of man, the oneness of God, and the duty of acts of charity:

The Sikhs

> Make love thy mosque; sincerity thy prayer-carpet; justice thy Koran;
> Modesty thy circumcision; courtesy thy Kaaba; truth thy Guru; charity thy creed and prayer;
> The will of God thy rosary, and God will preserve thine honor, O Nanak.[1]

[1] Quoted in H. G. Rawlinson, *India, A Short Cultural History*, p. 378.

The Taj Mahal at Agra. Built by Shah Jahan in memory of Mumtaz Mahal, it is considered one of the finest examples of Indian Moslem architecture.

Top: *Mumtaz Mahal ("Ornament of the Palace")*. Favorite wife of Shah Jahan, who died in childbirth in 1631 at the age of 39. Bottom: *Shah Jahan (1627–1658)*. The Mogul Emperor was famous for his luxurious court and his magnificent buildings.

Thus Nanak's religion was a blend of Islamic and Hindu doctrines but rejected formal scriptures and mechanical rites. Because he utterly repudiated caste he gained many adherents from among the depressed classes of Hindus. Akbar had treated the Sikhs kindly and made a grant of land to their Guru (spiritual teacher), but the hostility of later Moguls goaded them to fury. The sect which had begun as a peaceful reformist movement was gradually transformed into a military order. Its members were initiated by a rite called "Baptism of the Sword," and many of them adopted the surname Singh, meaning "Lion." While they retained an antipathy toward caste and subscribed to a strict code of personal discipline, they lost much of the generous idealism of their early leaders. Appearing sometimes as no better than brigands, they showed particular relish for slaughtering Moslems. Thus at the opening of the eighteenth century the Mogul power was menaced not only by the usual court intrigues but also by the spirited defiance of powerful Hindu groups—Rajputs, Marathas, and Sikhs.

The long and calamitous reign of Shah Jahan's son Aurangzeb (1658–1707) pushed the empire to its farthest territorial limits but drained it of much of its strength. A man of tremendous energy, sobriety, and fanatical piety, Aurangzeb sacrificed almost every principle of prudent statesmanship in a futile attempt to establish religious conformity and orthodoxy. He demolished Hindu temples and revived the hated poll tax on non-Moslems which Akbar had wisely rescinded. He waged wars not only against Hindu princes but also against heretical Moslem states in the Deccan. Although he devoted some 25 years to military campaigns and won many victories, he created enemies faster than he could subdue them and he left the Marathas—whom he had tried to destroy—more firmly united than ever.

One further catastrophe robbed the Mogul Dynasty of most of its remaining vitality, although the Moguls were accorded the formal dignity of ruling sovereigns until long after the British had entrenched themselves in India. In 1739 a usurper to the throne of Persia, Nadir Shah, invaded India and sacked Delhi with terrific carnage. He carried off an enormous quantity of booty, including the Peacock Throne, and left much of the city in ruins.

The Mogul period in India was one of considerable activity in intellectual and artistic fields. The emperors were generally cosmopolitan in outlook and welcomed both commercial and cultural intercourse with foreign states. A fusion of Indian, Turkish, Arabic, and Persian elements took place as manifested in literature, the arts, and the general tone of society. As might be expected, architecture illustrates most perfectly the interaction of Hindu and Islamic motifs. Moslem builders introduced the minaret or spire, the pointed arch, and the bulbous dome; Hindu and Jain traditions emphasized horizontal lines and elaborate ornamentation. Because

Indian stonemasons and architects were frequently employed even on Moslem religious edifices, there was bound to be a fruitful interchange of ideas, and this culminated in the sixteenth and seventeenth centuries in the production of a distinctive Indo-Moslem architectural style. Some of Akbar's constructions at Agra, of durable red sandstone, are still standing; and so is most of an entire city which he conceived and had completed at a site a few miles west of Agra and then abandoned only five years later. But Akbar's forts and government halls lacked the choice materials, the refinement, and the sensuous beauty of the buildings executed for Shah Jahan a half-century later. In place of sandstone, these employed the finest marbles, agate, turquoise, and other semi-precious stones, and were frequently decorated with inlays of gold and silver. Shah Jahan's dazzling structures, contrasting markedly with the robustness of Akbar's work, betray an excessive elegance bordering on decadence.

The Islamic taboos against pictorial representation were almost totally disregarded by the Mogul rulers, who were enthusiastic collectors and connoisseurs of painting. Reflecting the influence of contemporary Persian art, the most typical examples of painting were miniatures, including landscapes and especially portraits, executed with realism and meticulous detail. Calligraphy also enjoyed the status of a fine art, and many manuscripts were illuminated with pictures as in medieval Europe. Texts from the Koran were employed as decorative devices on screens and the façades of buildings, in keeping with a general practice in Moslem countries.

Painting and
calligraphy

Probably the most significant expression of Indian creative talent during the Mogul period was literature, which was stimulated by royal patronage and also by the fact that several languages could be drawn upon. Both Turkish and Persian were spoken in court cir-

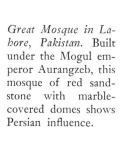

Great Mosque in Lahore, Pakistan. Built under the Mogul emperor Aurangzeb, this mosque of red sandstone with marble-covered domes shows Persian influence.

cles; familiarity with Arabic, the language of the Koran, was a necessity for educated Moslems; and a knowledge of the native dialects of northern India was essential for administrators. A permanent result of the intermingling between Turko-Persian and Indian cultures was the rise of a variety of speech known as Urdu ("the camp language"). While Urdu in its vocabulary includes many Persian and Arabic words and is written in Arabic script, its grammatical structure is basically the same as that of Hindi, the most prevalent Aryan vernacular of northern India. Both Urdu and Hindi came to be standard mediums of communication throughout northern India. (Urdu is now confined chiefly to Pakistan.)

While the Mogul rulers fostered a cosmopolitan atmosphere at court, attracting thither many Persian scholars and poets, the literary works of most enduring value were produced by Hindus, especially during the tolerant regime of Akbar. This emperor showed great interest in India's literary treasures as well as in her art and music, and he had Persian translations made from the *Vedas* and the Epics. Tulsi Das, one of India's greatest poets, lived during Akbar's reign. His principal work was an idealized and highly spiritual version of the ancient epic, the *Ramayana*. This poem, which combines fine craftsmanship with a warm and fervent moral earnestness, was written in the vernacular tongue rather than in Sanskrit, although its author was a Brahman.

The reigns of Akbar's later successors, so disastrous to the political fortunes of the Mogul state, were also marked by social unrest and cultural decline. The fanatical Aurangzeb frowned upon art as idolatrous and discouraged literature on the ground that it exalted human vanity. He banished music from his court and, in his extreme mania for orthodoxy, even replaced the Persian solar calendar with the clumsier lunar calendar because the latter had been used by Mohammed. Mogul culture at its best, however, had always been largely a phenomenon of the court and nobility, with few roots among the mass of the populace. Consequently its decline, which was rapid in the eighteenth century, had little effect upon the great body of Hindu society. In many parts of India skillful craftsmanship and exacting artistic standards were carried on much as they had been before the Moslem invasions. Particularly notable was the so-called Rajput school of painting, which was fostered at the courts of native princes in Rajputana and which was more vigorous and less sensuous than the Mogul school.

One aspect of the Mogul period which was bound to have tremendous consequences for the future was the coming of Europeans to India. Although the trading settlements which they established at various points on the coast were small and seemingly insignificant, they denoted the awakening of Europeans to the commercial possibilities of the Far East. The maritime enterprise so highly developed by the Indian states in earlier times had fallen into decay;

and even the Mogul empire, for all its splendor, did not long maintain an effective navy. The rise of powerful Western European states ended the control of Eastern waters by Arab navigators and brought direct pressure to bear on Indian territory.

In the early sixteenth century the Portuguese acquired and fortified several ports on the Indian coast and in Ceylon. Although they lost most of these to more powerful European rivals, they managed to retain Goa, Damão, and Diu until forcibly dispossessed by the Government of independent India in December 1961. More significant for the future was the activity of the British East India Company, which was chartered in 1600 and a few years later acquired a port at Surat, north of Bombay on the western coast. This was the fruit of patient negotiation carried on with officials of the Mogul emperor, for whose power the British agents necessarily felt a healthy respect. The Moguls were reluctant to offend the Portuguese as long as the latter commanded the sea routes which Moslem pilgrims used in traveling to Mecca; consequently, only minor concessions were granted to the English in the beginning. William Hawkins, a swashbuckling adventurer, and the more sedate Sir Thomas Roe served successively as English representatives at the court of the Mogul Jahangir, and each wrote a lively account of this eccentric and self-indulgent emperor, who showered hospitality upon his foreign visitors but shrewdly avoided committing himself to a formal treaty. Sir Thomas Roe, while resolutely upholding the dignity of his station before the Mogul courtiers, at the same time warned his own countrymen not to repeat the Portuguese policy of seizing territory and attempting to found colonies in India. The English, he urged, should seek profit "at sea and in quiet trade," remembering that "war and traffic are incompatible." This advice was little heeded in the subsequent history of the East India Company. Before the close of the seventeenth century the company had secured three locations, of strategic as well as commercial importance, in widely separated regions of India: the island of Bombay off the western coast (given by Portugal in 1661 when the English king, Charles II, married a Portuguese princess), Madras on the southeastern coast, and Fort William (Calcutta) at the mouth of the Ganges.

2. CHINA UNDER THE MANCHU (CH'ING) DYNASTY

With the disintegration of the Ming Dynasty it was China's fate to succumb, for the second time in her history, to conquest by a foreign invader. By the early seventeenth century a strong military organization had been formed in the Amur River region by the Manchus, kinsmen of the Juchên who had divided China with the

Sung emperors 500 years before. Taking advantage of China's weakness and factional strife, the Manchu forces pushed southward through Manchuria and occupied Peking in 1644. A few years previously their chieftain had exchanged his tribal title of khan for that of emperor and assumed a Chinese dynastic name—Ch'ing, meaning "Clear" or "Pure." While the Manchu (or Ch'ing) Dynasty, which lasted until the Revolution of 1911, is dated from 1644, it was not firmly established until considerably later. Northern China was occupied with little opposition, but many campaigns were required to subdue the stubbornly resisting southern Chinese. Near the end of the seventeenth century a rebellion led by Chinese generals was so nearly successful that it threatened to detach southern China from Manchu rule entirely, but it was finally crushed in 1681 by the young Manchu emperor, K'ang Hsi. Not until 1683 was the last anti-Manchu regime overthrown in Formosa, which was then incorporated into the Chinese empire. K'ang Hsi took steps to make revolt more difficult in the future. He strengthened the control of the central government at Peking over the provinces and distributed the authority in each province among several officials so that each could exercise a check upon the others. Instead of uprooting Chinese political institutions, he adapted them to the requirements of a uniform and centralized administrative system and laid the foundations for a long period of internal peace.

From the material standpoint the Manchu Dynasty, which proved to be the last of China's imperial ruling houses, was one of the most successful of all. The state was larger than at any other time in its history except for the brief period in the thirteenth century when China was part of the pan-Asian Mongol empire. It included Manchuria, Mongolia, Sinkiang, and Formosa, while Tibet was a protectorate, and Korea, Burma, Nepal, and parts of Indochina were tributary dependencies. The government was also remarkably efficient during the first century and a half of the dynasty's history, partly because most of this period was covered by the reigns of two very able and long-lived emperors. K'ang Hsi, who while still a youth had broken the rebellion in south China, reigned for sixty-one years (1661–1722). He was therefore a contemporary of King Louis XIV of France, but he was far more of a statesman than the celebrated "Sun King." Under K'ang Hsi's grandson, Ch'ien Lung, who ruled for another sixty years (1736–1796), the dynasty reached the climax of its prestige and effectiveness. Thus, while Europe was in a condition of turbulence and shaken by the wars of rival despots, China enjoyed the advantages of unity and peace under a government which was stable if not entirely benevolent. That Chinese society was generally prosperous is indicated by a phenomenally rapid growth in population under the Manchus. It is no exaggeration to say that in the eighteenth century China was one of the best governed and most highly civilized

Ch'ien Lung (1736–1796). The great Manchu Emperor under whom the Ch'ing Dynasty reached its climax. (Painting on silk by a nineteenth-century artist.)

states in the world, besides being the largest in territory and in the number of its inhabitants.

Obviously, the Manchu Dynasty was by no means a repetition of the Mongol, even though it was founded by northern invaders of nomadic origin. From the outset the Manchu emperors attempted to identify themselves with the culture and institutions of their Chinese subjects and to rule in accordance with accepted traditions. As a safeguard against rebellion they stationed garrisons in various parts of the country, composed of Chinese and Mongol troops as well as Manchu. They required Chinese men to braid their hair in a queue after the Manchu fashion and to adopt the Manchu style of dress as a token of submission. At the same time they preserved the ancient administrative framework, continued the civil-service examinations, and exalted the state cult of Confucius by requiring temples to be maintained in every district and by elevating the spirit of the ancient sage to the highest rank of official deities. In appointments to office the Manchus showed partiality to their own national group, but nothing like the extreme discrimination which had characterized the Mongol rule. More than 80 per cent of the lower governmental offices were filled by Chinese. The top administrative posts were divided about equally between Manchus and Chinese, with half of the Chinese quota going to northerners and half to southerners. Unfortunately, this seemingly equitable arrangement was somewhat unfair to southern China because this region was the more heavily populated.

The substantial material progress that took place during the Manchu period was not an unmixed benefit to the entire nation. Nothing equivalent to an industrial revolution occurred, but there were sufficient social and economic changes to create serious problems for the future. While Chinese society remained basically unaltered in organization and structure between the tenth and the nineteenth centuries, it experienced a great increase in numbers. From time to time the imperial government had taken a census of the population, and the returns—though probably incomplete and inaccurate—indicate an upward trend, especially during the period of Manchu rule. By the early twelfth century, under the Sung, the number of Chinese people had grown to about 100 million. Following the Mongol conquest there was an appreciable decline, but this was only temporary. During the first two centuries of the Manchu Dynasty the population seems to have increased about threefold. It is estimated that by the middle of the nineteenth century the Empire included approximately 300 million Chinese, besides 10 million Manchus. The causes of this rapid growth are not entirely clear, but it is certain that before the end of the Manchu Dynasty, China was feeling acute distress from the pressure of population upon food supply. The lack of sufficient arable land to support such large numbers led to the clearing and cropping of areas in the

Manchu administrative policies

Problems of population growth

Father Adam Schall with His Astronomical Instruments. Director of the Imperial Board of Astronomy, he wears the "mandarin square" of a Manchu civilian official.

Father Matteo Ricci of Macerata, the First Jesuit Missionary to Work in China and His Chief Convert, Hsii Kuangch'i Pao-lu of Shanghai.

upper river valleys which had hitherto been left to nature. Soil erosion subsequently increased the danger of floods and droughts, thus aggravating China's agrarian problem in the modern era.

Although the Chinese were basically one people in their fundamental institutions and cultural heritage, significant sectional differences, which augured trouble for the Manchu regime, had developed between the northern and the southern portions of the country. The sectional contrasts were largely the result of geographic and climatic differences between north and south, but they were intensified by historic factors. The Yangtze valley and the southeastern coastal region were by far the most productive agricultural areas and also contained the largest cities, which had long been centers of international commerce. The inhabitants of these areas were characterized by a breadth and diversity of interests and frequently by an independence of spirit which stemmed not so much from an extreme individualism as from a strong sense of family solidarity. Southern Chinese resented the fact that they paid the greater share of taxation, and yet the government seemed to spend most of its money for the benefit of the Peking region. They also felt that they were discriminated against in the competitive examinations, so that the leadership which they might have supplied was denied adequate recognition. In spite of their efforts toward conciliation, the Manchu emperors were never able to repose complete confidence in the loyalty of the southern Chinese, and the revolution which finally overthrew the dynasty had its origin in the south.

Not the least among the problems with which the Manchu regime ultimately had to contend was that caused by the penetration of Europeans into the Far East, although as long as the dynasty remained vigorous it experienced little difficulty in holding the foreigners within bounds. The overseas expansion of the Western nations during the Commercial Revolution affected China as well as India and other Eastern lands. By the early sixteenth century the Portuguese had occupied Malacca, and one of their trading vessels reached Canton in 1516. The Chinese authorities, long accustomed to peaceful commercial intercourse with Arabs and other foreigners, at first had been disposed to grant the normal privileges to the newcomers. Portuguese adventurers, however, pillaged Chinese ships engaged in trade with the Indies and raided coastal cities, looting and massacring the inhabitants. Such actions convinced the Chinese that Europeans were no better than pirates; nor was their opinion favorably revised with the arrival, a little later, of the Dutch and the English. The wanton depredations perpetrated by these early Western seafarers were responsible for the unflattering name which the Chinese came to apply to Europeans—"Ocean Devils." The government finally determined to exclude Europeans from the coastal cities but allowed the Portuguese to maintain a trading center and settlement at Macao in the far south. Established in 1557, this post has been retained by the Portuguese to the present day. As a security measure, the local officials constructed a wall blocking off the Portuguese settlement on the island of Macao and imposed rigid restrictions upon the activities of the foreigners. The trade was too profitable for the Chinese to want to abolish it altogether, and the Portuguese were soon extended the privilege of docking at Canton at prescribed times and under strict supervision.

Thus, before the Manchu conquest of China, precedents had already been set for dealing with Western traders. When the Manchus attacked the Ming empire, the Portuguese assisted the Ming court, supplying artillery and some military personnel. This intervention was a portent of things to come, suggesting the ominous possibilities of European interference in Chinese affairs; but its immediate effect was to implant in the Manchu rulers a prejudice against the meddling "Ocean Devils" at the very time when the new regime was being inaugurated. Nevertheless, as the Manchu emperors succeeded in strengthening their position, they were willing to allow European trade to continue, though restricting it chiefly to Canton. Meanwhile, the suspicion attaching to Europeans had been partially dispelled through contacts with Christian missionaries, especially the Jesuits, who had been active in the Far East since the sixteenth century. Many of these Catholic missionaries impressed the Chinese with their breadth of scholarship, their respect for Chinese culture, and their sincere interest in the people among whom they had come to work. Consequently they were permitted to win converts to Christianity and were welcomed into intellectual circles. The early Manchu emperors were generally cordial to Christian missionaries, particularly the French Jesuits, whom they employed at court in such various capacities as instructors in science, mathematics, and cartography.

While the maritime expansion of Western nations was bringing Portuguese, Spanish, French, and others into the Far East, China came into more direct contact with another European power as Russia extended the frontier of her empire overland toward the Pacific. By the latter seventeenth century the Russians were encroaching on the Manchurian border. The success of the Manchus in meeting this threat from the north illustrates the strength of the state at this time, in decided contrast to the weakness which it exhibited before the great Western powers a century and a half later. In 1689 a treaty negotiated with Russian officials defined the boundary between the two countries, provided for a limited commercial intercourse, and arranged for the reciprocal extradition of criminals. This treaty (and subsequent ones negotiated during the

693

Cultural
conservatism

Vitality
in philosophy

Originality in
the novel

eighteenth century) in no way impaired the sovereignty or prestige of China. Her day of humiliation under the impact of Western imperialism was yet to come.

In cultural fields the Manchu period was one of abundant productivity but little originality. It is probably correct to say that the over-all trend was toward sterility or even decadence. Chinese culture was still of high level and even brilliant, but it was largely an echo of the genius of earlier centuries. This does not mean that the Chinese had deteriorated in vitality or innate capacity. The decline was partly due to the rigidity of their social institutions and to the fact that they had developed an extreme veneration for ancient authorities, which fostered an attitude of stiff conservatism. More directly it was the result of the government's policy of encouraging docility among the people and frowning upon all innovation. Under the Manchu emperors more than under any native Chinese dynasty the accumulated dogmas of orthodox Confucianism (the Neo-Confucianism of Chu Hsi) were upheld inflexibly and perpetuated in the civil-service examinations through which officials were recruited. Inevitably, as the bureaucracy grew ever more conventional and inelastic in its thinking, it was ill-prepared to cope with new problems as they arose. The exalting of orthodoxy above every other virtue led slowly but surely to a state of intellectual stagnation.

Examples can be found, however, of vigorous and independent thinkers among the Chinese of this period, even in the field of philosophy. Valuable contributions were made by a school of critical scholars who pioneered in the objective and scientific study of ancient classics. The prime objective of this school was to purge Chinese philosophy of the Buddhist and Taoist influences which had encrusted it during the Sung period. Hence, in spite of their perceptiveness and their defiance of conventions, the "Han Learning" scholars were attempting to rehabilitate the distant past rather than to deal directly with the needs of the present. While they were unable to dislodge the narrow conservatism that prevailed in high quarters, the movement was not devoid of results. That such was the case is indicated by the decline of Buddhism as an intellectual force in China even though it remained a popular religion.

If freshness and originality were lacking in most fields of expression, a notable exception was provided by the novel, which continued to be a successful literary medium and reached an even higher state of excellence than it had under the Ming. The best Chinese novels of this period readily bear comparison with significant prose works of other nations, Eastern or Western. As under the Ming, the novel was sometimes a vehicle for satire or trenchant criticism of governmental policies. One early nineteenth-century novel embodied an attack upon the subjection of women and advocated sweeping social and educational reforms.

During the early Manchu period Chinese culture—retrogressive as it may have been—created a more distinct impression upon the civilized nations of the West than had ever been true before. In the eighteenth century especially, Chinese-style gardens, pagodas, and pavilions became fashionable among the wealthy classes of Western Europe. Other items borrowed from China included sedan chairs, lacquer, and incense, while the craze for Chinese porcelain reached such proportions that it had the unfortunate effect of lowering the quality of the product. In addition, largely through translations and commentaries prepared by the Jesuits, European intellectuals were introduced to Chinese thought and literature. European acquaintance with these subjects was, of course, limited and superficial, but it was sufficient to arouse curiosity and admiration. Spokesmen of the Enlightenment upheld the somewhat mythical "Chinese sage" as an example of how man could be guided by reason, and fragments of Confucian texts were cited in support of deism.

The Manchu rulers had demonstrated their ability to adapt themselves to the institutions and traditions of their subjects. At the same time, they proved their inability to escape the enfeebling influences that tended to undermine every successful Chinese dynasty. By the nineteenth century their leadership had degenerated seriously, control was slipping into the hands of palace eunuchs, and the court was becoming the scene of soft living and intrigue. As the rulers grew less effectual, they were inclined to compensate for their own deficiencies by appearing more stern and arrogant than their predecessors. Occasionally they instigated persecution of the Christians, and they displayed a haughty and overbearing attitude toward the few European delegations which sought an audience with the emperor. Meanwhile, domestic discontent was manifest in rebellions—both incipient and overt—in various parts of China. Secret societies, hostile to the Manchu government, were organized. The dynasty was probably doomed even before friction with the Western powers later in the nineteenth century created new and distressing problems.

Chinese Porcelain. Decorated with "famille verte," a vivid green enamel typical of the K'ang Hsi period (1661–1722).

3. JAPAN UNDER THE TOKUGAWA SHOGUNATE

The most turbulent period of Japanese feudalism was ended rather abruptly at the close of the sixteenth century when a series of military campaigns forced the *daimyo* (great lords) to acknowledge the authority of a single ruler. The rise of the *daimyo*[2] had led to the establishment of fairly effective government within their individual domains, some of which were large enough to include several of the ancient provinces. Hence, when the great lords were brought under a common central authority, the way was open for

[2] See p. 521.

a genuine unification of the country, and Japan entered upon an era of comparative peace and stability which brought her to the threshold of modern times. Hideyoshi, a man of low birth who had worked his way up to a high military command under one of the leading *daimyo*, almost succeeded in unifying Japan, but he diverted his energies to the ambitious project of conquering China. Although he invaded Korea, he met with stiff opposition from Korean and Chinese forces, and he lacked sufficient naval support to control the supply lines between Japan and the mainland. He died in 1598 with his dream unfulfilled. Hideyoshi's work in Japan, however, was ably completed by his former vassal Ieyasu, who smashed the remnants of opposition and transferred the fruits of victory to his own family, the Tokugawa. Ieyasu assumed the office of Shogun, but he made it a much more efficient instrument of government than it had ever been before.

Under the Tokugawa Shogunate (1603–1867), Japan's feudal institutions remained intact, but they were systematized and made to serve the interests of a strong central government. Ieyasu founded his capital at Edo (now Tokyo), where he built a great castle surrounded with moats and an elaborate series of outer defenses. The great domains of central and eastern Japan were held by members of the Tokugawa or by men who had helped Ieyasu in his campaigns. These trusted supporters of the regime were known as "hereditary *daimyo*," while the lords who had acknowledged Ieyasu's supremacy only when forced to do so were called "outer *daimyo*." The members of both groups were hereditary vassals of the Shogun and were kept under careful surveillance lest they should try to assert their independence. The Shogun employed a corps of secret police to report any signs of disaffection throughout the country. As a special precaution he required all *daimyo* to maintain residences in Edo and reside there every other year, and also to leave their wives and children as hostages when they returned to their own estates. The system Ieyasu devised was so well organized and thorough that it did not depend on the personal ability of the Shogun for its operation. For the first time Japan had a durable political framework, which remained undisturbed in the hands of the Tokugawa for two and a half centuries. While the Shogunate was essentially a feudal power structure, it developed for administrative purposes a large bureaucracy of carefully recruited and competent officials.

Centralization of authority

It should be noted that the Japanese government was still dual in form. The imperial family and a decorative court nobility continued to reside at Kyoto, while the real power was lodged in the Bakufu, the military hierarchy headed by the Shogun at Edo. The Tokugawa Shoguns cultivated the fiction that they were carrying out the will of a divine emperor. By emphasizing the emperor's sanctity they added an aura of invulnerability to their own posi-

Persistence of dual government

Five-Storied Pagoda at Nikko, in Central Japan. It was built in 1636 and dedicated to Tokugawa Ieyasu, founder of the Tokugawa Shogunate. The structure (about 100 feet high) is ornately carved, painted, and lacquered, but is given a magnificent natural setting by the surrounding forest.

tion, and by keeping him in seclusion they rendered him harmless. The shadow government at Kyoto was now entirely dependent upon the Shogun even for its financial support, but it was carefully and respectfully preserved as a link with Japan's hallowed past.

The most serious problem of the early Tokugawa period concerned relations with Europeans. Before the close of the sixteenth century both the Portuguese and the Spanish were carrying on considerable trade in Japan, and the Dutch and the British secured trading posts early in the following century. Europeans had been accorded a favorable reception by the Japanese, who seemed eager to learn from them. Firearms, acquired from the Portuguese, came into use for the first time in Japan and played a part in the feudal battles of the late sixteenth century. The introduction of gunpowder had the effect temporarily of stimulating the construction of heavy stone castles by the *daimyo*, a practice which was carefully regulated by the Tokugawa after they had seized the Shogunate.

Along with the Western traders came missionaries, who at first encountered little hostility. Vigorous proselyting by Portuguese Jesuits and Spanish Franciscans met with remarkable success in

Relations with Europeans

697

The growth and
suppression of
Christianity

winning converts to the Catholic faith among all classes of the population, including some of the feudal nobles. By the early seventeenth century there were close to 300,000 Christian converts in Japan, chiefly in the south and west where the European trading centers were located. Eventually, however, the Shoguns decided that Christianity should be proscribed, not because they objected to the religion as such but because they were afraid it would divide the country and weaken their authority. They were annoyed by the bickering between rival European groups and also feared that their subjects were being enticed into allegiance to a foreign potentate, the Pope. The first persecutions were mild and were directed against Japanese Christians rather than against the Europeans; but when the missionaries refused to halt their work they were severely dealt with, and many were executed. Finally, in 1637, when a peasant revolt against oppressive taxation developed into a Christian rebellion, the Shogun's forces conducted a real war against the Christian strongholds in southwestern Japan and, in spite of the most heroic resistance, wiped out the Christian communities and exterminated the religion almost completely.

The expulsion of
Europeans and the
adoption of
isolationism

Following this bloody purge, the Shoguns adopted a policy of excluding all Europeans from Japanese settlement. That they were able to enforce it shows how strong their government had become. Reluctant to cut off Western trade entirely, they made a slight exception in the case of the Dutch, who seemed to be the least dangerous politically. The Dutch were permitted to unload one ship each year at the port of Nagasaki in the extreme western corner of Japan, but only under the strictest supervision. Going even farther along the line of reaction, the Shogun next forbade his Japanese subjects to visit foreign lands on pain of forfeiting all their rights and commanded that no ship should be built large enough to travel beyond the coastal waters of the island empire. Although traffic with China was continued, the Shoguns forced upon their country a policy of almost complete isolationism, thus reversing the course which had been followed advantageously during many centuries preceding.

A hierarchical
society; exaltation
of the warrior

The Tokugawa era gave Japan a long period of peace and orderly government and promoted the ideal of a perpetually hierarchical society. Theoretically, the social structure was arranged in accordance with the classes of China, which ranked, in order of importance: (1) scholar-officials, (2) farmers, (3) artisans, (4) merchants, and (5) soldiers, bandits, and beggars. In Japan, however, the realities of a feudalized society produced a peculiar distortion of the ideal arrangement, which was somewhat fanciful even in China. The warrior (*samurai*), who had enjoyed a position of leadership for centuries, was elevated from the lowest category to the highest. In return for the place of honor assigned to him he was expected to exhibit the qualities of the scholar also, and to a considerable extent he did. The *daimyo* and the *samurai* were no longer the uncouth, lawless ruffians of early feudal days but refined aristocrats, who cultivated literature and the arts and took pride in the rigorous discipline to which they were bred. Still, their pre-eminence had been won in the first instance by force, and their position was regarded as a hereditary right, not to be challenged by men of superior ability who had been born to a lower class.

The artificiality and formal rigidity of the Tokugawa regime did not stifle economic progress. By the early eighteenth century Japan's population had reached a total of 30 million; thenceforth it increased but slightly for a century and a half. This slow rate of population growth apparently was more the result of voluntary family planning than of a scarcity of resources, although occasional famines did occur. The country as a whole was prosperous; industry and internal trade continually expanded even though foreign commerce had been curtailed. Communication was relatively easy through all parts of Japan, both by waterways and by improved highways. A brisk exchange of agricultural and manufactured goods promoted the growth of a capitalist economy. Rice merchants occupied a strategic position in the world of finance and their establishments, offering commercial credit and daily price quotations, bore some resemblance to a modern stock exchange. Cities grew in size, especially in the central area of the country. By the late eighteenth century Edo had attained a population of one million and was probably the largest city in the world at that time.

Prosperity and stability

Economic progress, coupled with a rigid and inherently authoritarian political regime, produced severe strains within society. The position of the *samurai* became more and more anomalous. While they possessed a monopoly of the profession of arms, they found little opportunity to practice it because the Shogun discouraged feudal quarrels, and there were no foreign wars. Thus the *samurai* became, by and large, a group of respectable parasites, although many of them displayed both talent and energy. They were often employed in administrative functions by the *daimyo*, and sometimes took over the management of a great domain so completely that the *daimyo* was reduced to little more than a figurehead. On the other hand the merchants, who were ranked at the bottom of the social pyramid, steadily accumulated wealth, formed their own trade associations to replace the older and more restrictive guilds, and exerted a potent influence over the whole national economy. Inevitably they imparted a bourgeois tone to society in the bustling cities.

Japanese Bronze (Eighteenth Century). The figure depicted is Kuan Ti, Chinese "God of War"—actually a deified military hero of the early third century A.D. Regarded as the patron of military officials, he was particularly revered in China during the late Ch'ing (Manchu) period.

Until recently historians commonly assumed that the peasants' lot under the Tokugawa was a miserable one, but research in Japanese sources has discredited this assumption. It is true that peasant labor supported the upper classes of *daimyo* and *samurai* as well as the Shogun and his bureaucracy. It is also true that peasants endured privation and sometimes cruel treatment at the hands of their social

Condition of the peasants

699

superiors, who dismissed them contemptuously as seeds to be pressed or cattle to be driven. The outbreak of riots and actual local rebellions—in a society as disciplined as the Tokugawa—indicates the reality and the depth of popular discontent. But the evidence is undeniable that Japanese farmers and tenants not only contributed to but also shared in the country's rising prosperity. Forbidden to bear arms, they were relieved from the burden of military service, and they benefited from the two and a half centuries of almost uninterrupted peace that followed the accession of Tokugawa Ieyasu.

Japanese agriculture was vastly more progressive than in earlier times. The amount of land under cultivation doubled, new crops were introduced, intensive fertilization and better tools, including a mechanical thresher, came into use, and irrigation was extended through the cooperative efforts of farm villages. A steady expansion in productivity, together with regional specialization keyed to market demands, enabled the majority of peasants to sustain a rising standard of living in spite of tax increases during the eighteenth century. But while agriculture enjoyed a flourishing condition, its rewards were not evenly distributed. A trend away from large family combinations to smaller units that could be run more efficiently widened the spread between prosperous and indigent peasants, and there was an increase in tenantry as opposed to individual farm ownership. At the same time the emergence of a mobile class of wage earners stimulated the growth of village industries—processing silk, cotton, salt, tobacco, saké, and sugar cane—and provided a reserve labor force which eventually contributed to the rapid industrialization of Japan in the post-Tokugawa period.

Expansion of agricultural productivity

During the Tokugawa era Japanese culture, being largely cut off from outside contacts, acquired a distinctive national character. This is not negated by the fact that intellectual circles manifested a heightened interest in Chinese philosophy. A number of Chinese scholars had fled to Japan when the Ming Dynasty was overthrown by the Manchus and, more importantly, the Shoguns encouraged study of the Confucian classics, particularly among the aristocracy, because they thought it would help to inculcate habits of discipline in their subjects. These writings, of course, had long been honored in Japan, but now they were diligently examined for the purpose of developing a native school of philosophers who, through their example and through their position as administrators, could inculcate the principles of virtue—especially obedience—among all classes of the population. The ascendancy of Confucian philosophy among intellectuals had the effect of weakening the influence of Buddhism, even though the Shogun, when engaged in his campaign to exterminate Christianity in Japan, had made it a point to encourage Buddhist forms of worship.

The growing interest in Chinese philosophy

The most significant cultural changes were those related to the growth of large cities, such as Edo, Osaka, and Kyoto, where men of wealth were creating an atmosphere of comfort and gaiety in contrast to the restrained decorum of the feudal nobility. In these populous commercial and industrial centers the trend in art and literature and especially in the field of entertainment was toward a distinctly middle-class culture, which was sometimes gaudy but appealing in its exuberance and spontaneity. In the pleasure quarters of the cities an important figure was the *geisha* girl, who combined the qualities of a modern beauty queen with the talents of a night-club entertainer. Trained in the art of conversation as well as in song and dance, she provided the sparkling companionship which men too often missed in their own homes because of the habits of docility and self-effacement that they instilled into their wives and daughters. Prostitution, also, was prevalent on a large scale in the towns, in spite of attempts by the authorities to curtail the evil. Inherently sordid as was the practice, it took on a specious refinement under the patronage of the well-to-do, and some courtesans acquired an enviable standing in the loose but highly sophisticated society which flouted established conventions. Not only merchants and business men but even *samurai* and *daimyo* were attracted by the gay diversions of city life, and surreptitiously exchanged the boredom of their routine existence for the delights of a "floating world" of pleasure and uninhibited self-expression.

The dissolute society of the Tokugawa cities was by no means utterly degenerate. Some of the best creative talents in Japan catered to bourgeois appetites, just as they did in Italy during the Renaissance. Racy novels, satirizing contemporary figures and piquant with gossip, innuendo, and scandal, came into vogue. Previously art had been chiefly aristocratic and religious, except for

Life and customs
in the large cities

The culture of the
middle and lower
classes

Woman Weaving Cloth.

The Art of Tile Making. A wood-block by Hokusai (1760–1849), an artist famous for landscapes.

the exquisitely designed articles of ordinary household use produced by the various handicrafts. Now a type of folk art was appearing that mirrored society realistically and also was enlivened with humor and caricature. Its chief medium was the wood-block color print, which could be produced cheaply enough to reach a wide public and which has ever since been a popular art form. Another proof of the influence that urban tastes were exerting in the aesthetic sphere is seen in the evolution of the *Kabuki* drama. In contrast to the *No*, the highly stylized and austere dance-drama that had been perfected a few centuries earlier under the patronage of the aristocracy, the *Kabuki* offered entertainment appealing to the middle and lower classes of the towns. Although it owed something to traditional dance forms, the *Kabuki* drama was derived more immediately from the puppet theater and, unlike the *No*, it was almost entirely secular in spirit. As developed in the seventeenth and eighteenth centuries, the *Kabuki* drama attained a high degree of realism, with exciting plots, lively action, and effective stage devices. In the opinion of some theatrical experts, it deserves to rank as the greatest drama any civilization has ever produced.

Various forces at work in Japan tended to undermine the foundations of Tokugawa institutions in spite of their apparent durability. The partial transformation of Japan's economy from an agrarian to a mercantile basis enhanced the importance of men engaged in manufacture, trade, and transport. As a result feudalism was rendered obsolete, and the feudal classes began to feel the pinch of adversity. Although money had been in circulation for many centuries, the incomes of *daimyo* and of their *samurai* retainers were still computed in measures of rice, the chief agricultural staple. The merchants who provisioned such great cities as Edo and Osaka controlled the marketing of a large proportion of the rice crop; hence they were able to foresee fluctuations in price and sometimes even to induce fluctuations for their own benefit. Naturally, the *daimyo* and *samurai* were at a disadvantage in a period of unstable prices, because their incomes were from land rents, and because their necessities were increasingly supplied by articles that had to be purchased in the cities. Often the price of rice was considerably below the general price level, and even when it was high the middleman appropriated most of the profit. The landed aristocrats found their real incomes diminishing while low-born traders and brokers grew richer and richer.

Inevitably, class lines began to break down, just as they did in Western Europe under similar conditions during the period of the Commercial Revolution. Wealthy Japanese merchants purchased *samurai* rank and title, while nobles adopted children of bourgeois families or contracted marriage alliances with this class in an effort

Kabuki Theater. Left: Kabuki actor (Matsumoto Koshiro) portrayed here as a fishmonger by Sharaku, a wood-block artist noted for his caricatures of actors (1794 or 1795). Right: Famous actor Mitsugoro Bando portraying the aged warrior Ikyu in the play "Sukeroku."

Woman Playing the Flute. The flutist is by Harunobu (1724–1770), earliest master of the multi-colored-print technique.

Contributions
of the
Tokugawa
period

to recoup their fortunes. Feeling honor-bound to maintain their accustomed style of living—at least in appearances—the aristocrats borrowed recklessly. As early as 1700 the indebtedness of the *daimyo* class was reputed to have reached a figure one hundred times greater than the total amount of money in Japan. Impoverished *samurai* pawned their ceremonial robes and even the swords which were their badge of rank. While townspeople in large numbers were entering the lower grades of *samurai*, *samurai* and farmers were flocking to the towns, where the more successful ones merged into the bourgeois class.

The unrest generated by economic dislocation was further augmented by cultural trends in the later Tokugawa period. As a national spirit developed, it was accompanied by a renewal of interest in Japan's past. Shintoism, the ancient cult over which the imperial family presided, had been largely eclipsed by Buddhism. Gradually its popularity revived, and several new Shinto sects obtained an enthusiastic following. The study of ancient records (historical and mythological) stimulated reflection on the unique character of Japan—"founded by a heavenly ancestry, country of the gods"—and on the alleged origins of the imperial office. It directed attention to the fact that the Shogunate was a comparatively recent innovation or actually a usurpation, not an authentic part of the ancient political structure. At the same time, familiarity with China's political heritage—fostered by the vogue of Confucian scholarship which the Shoguns themselves had promoted—raised doubts among Japanese intellectuals as to the merits of a dual administrative system and of feudal institutions. Moreover, Western books and ideas were seeping into Japan through the port of Nagasaki where the Dutch were permitted a very limited trade. Even before Japan was "opened" in the nineteenth century, considerable interest had been aroused in Western guns, ships, watches, glassware, and scientific instruments. Thus Japan's insulation from the outside world was beginning to develop cracks at the same time that internal discontent had reached a dangerous point. By the opening of the nineteenth century the Shogun's position was precarious, unlikely to withstand the shock of a severe crisis, especially since other powerful families were eagerly watching for any sign of weakness on the part of the Tokugawa.

In spite of its defects, before its eventual collapse the Tokugawa regime had given the Japanese nation a long period of security and had, perhaps against its own intentions, laid the foundation for Japan's transformation into a modern state. Class structure was not so rigid as to prevent the realization of a fairly homogeneous society, especially as urban centers grew and communication facilities improved. Education advanced significantly; by the end of the Tokugawa period about 45 per cent of the male population was literate (only 15 per cent of the female), a record unmatched in the rest of Asia. Although Japan was still a predominantly agrarian country, capital techniques had been developed and applied to agriculture as well as to commerce and manufacture. Japan had reached the stage of commercial capitalism, which, as illustrated by the history of the Industrial Revolution in England, was a logical precursor of full-scale industrialization.

4. AFRICA UNDER DIVINE RULERS AND RITUAL CHIEFS

The period 1500 to 1800 witnessed the arrival of European traders and adventurers on Africa's sub-Saharan shores. A revolution in maritime and military technology enabled Europeans to navigate beyond sight of land and to conduct an efficient ocean-borne trade with swift, well-armed ships. For West Africans this necessitated a reorientation of trade from their ancient North African markets across the Sahara to Western Europe and the Americas via the Atlantic. A voluminous and highly profitable Atlantic traffic ensued with explosive force and required a concentration of territorial power in the hands of a few rulers. Instability generated by the introduction of arms trafficking and slave raiding forced weaker communities either to coalesce in self defense or to seek the protection of larger, better organized societies in neighboring areas. First coastal kingdoms, then empires, emerged in the tall forests after the 1650s in response to increasing opportunities for trade in guns, gunpowder, and exotic luxury items.

European presence on the coast forces a reorientation of trade

Long-distance trading networks from coast to interior and coastwise by canoe from the Niger Delta to the Ivory Coast antedated European contact. Indeed, small, independent fishing communities had dotted the palm-studded coast at least since 1300. Fisherfolk exchanged ocean salt and dried fish with forest farmers for yams, goats, and cattle. Later, such local industries as fishing, weaving, and brewing were weakened when communities turned to the less expensive though often inferior European substitutes. Ultimately, European traders fostered economic rivalries and precipitated civil wars between African communities to prevent indigenous traders and chiefs from uniting. Such unity could inflate prices and weaken the European trade advantage. Nevertheless, on an individual basis, African traders sometimes proved superior to Europeans in the art of bargaining.

Pre-European trading networks

Between about 1730 and 1800 the less accessible interior states sought to extend their authority to the sea in order to trade directly with the Europeans. Seldom, however, were foreign traders permitted to operate beyond the coast. In Benin, Dahomey, and Oyo they were restricted to designated seaports and could only lease the land upon which they constructed their warehouses, fortresses, and slave markets.

European traders restricted to the coast

Some states, like Oyo, Benin, and Asante, prospered and became territorial empires. Others, particularly Kongo, Ngola, and

705

Mwenemutapa, failed to keep the Europeans at arm's length or to comprehend fully their true motives. Their history was punctured by foreign intrigue, political instability, and eventual collapse. Numerous African governments became so dependent on European trade that a shift in pattern spelled economic doom.

Divine kings and territorial aggrandizement

During this era, kings, claiming divine attributes, aggrandized their authority through military force. Often, neighbors were reduced to tributary status. Royal subordinates, dispatched to the conquered areas, guarded against conspiracies and assimilated the vanquished. Folkways and authority patterns, if strong, were usually left intact, while prisoners of war and dissidents were sold into slavery in order to replenish supplies of gunpowder. Africa's human losses were America's gains in this vicious circle initiated by amoral white traffickers and facilitated by selfish black collaborators.

Aloofness of the divine rulers

Like the divine emperors of Japan, the Obas of Benin, Asantehenes of Asante, Manikongos of Kongo, Alafins of Oyo, and other African monarchs shrouded themselves in mystery and appeared only on ceremonial occasions. Much of their time was devoted to state rituals and sacrifices to ancestral heroes. They evolved rigid codes of court etiquette and communicated with commoners only through intermediaries. Some wore finely crafted, oversized sandals to shield their feet from direct contact with the sacred earth. All of them fostered a hieratic art, aimed as exalting the sanctity of the state. To achieve this, guild artists were supported by the monarchy and forced to remain within the palace confines so that their talents would not pass to others.

Royal Dignitary. Bronze plaque fragment. Bini tribe, Benin.

These kings, their paramount chiefs, and lesser titled hereditary officials devised ingenious systems of checks and balances to prevent a concentration of power in any single office. In the Oyo empire (in western Nigeria) the Alafin served as hereditary secular leader. Yet his power had to be shared with a royally appointed nobility, which organized itself into a kind of electoral college and administrative watchdog called the Oyo *Mesi*. Its leading member, the *Bashorun*, acted as Prime Minister and as spokesman for most of the powerful national cults or religious orders. As a counterforce to the Oyo *Mesi*, the Alafin appointed trusted slaves, called *Ilari*. They were responsible for collecting tribute and overseeing local government. At the same time, every important town was headed by a hereditary mayor or *Oba*. Though the *Oba*'s authority derived from ancestral mandate and tradition, his powers were limited by the Ogboni Society. This organization of influential and prosperous townsfolk linked the masses of peasants, traders, and artisans to royal authority. Everyone in the Oyo empire, from the Alafin down to the poorest peasant, swore allegiance to the Oni of Ifé. Ifé was the founding city-state of the Oyo empire, the fount of Yoruba civilization; and the ancient office of Oni served as the supreme authority over spiritual matters. Power was therefore diffused throughout society. From at least the fifteenth to the late eighteenth century the Yoruba peoples of Oyo were well served by this unwritten constitution.

In the 1790's, the authority and prestige of the Alafin's office, so vital to national solidarity, was severely diminished when its holder challenged the spiritual supremacy of the Oni of Ifé. The time-honored rules of the game eroded further when the *Bashorun*, or Prime Minister, tested his own strength against the Alafin's. Preoccupation with such power struggles weakened central authority and enabled the tributary states to secede. Civil war erupted, and in the mid-nineteenth century the crumbling empire fell prey to European intrigue from the south and Moslem Fulani challenges from the north.

Even though the Oyo empire disintegrated, its artistic and musical traditions continued to thrive. In both Oyo and neighboring Benin, guilds of Yoruba craftsmen turned out a rich variety of sculpture in brass, bronze, ivory, and wood. Metal commemorative busts and plaques, some antedating European contact by centuries, were delicate, strikingly naturalistic, and secular in intent. Companies of professional acrobats, dancers, and musicians travelled about the countryside giving performances which were sometimes critical of government practices, royal behavior, and social convention. In many ways, their programs were like an editorial column of a modern newspaper.

Many forest states could boast of magnificent capital cities, holding sprawling palaces and temples with sunken atriums surrounded by columns. Benin city was one of the world's few urban centers to be laid out on a gridiron pattern, with broad tree-lined avenues intersecting streets at near right angles. Kumasi, the capital of Asante, was described by foreigners as Africa's garden city because of its lush flowering undergrowth set against tidy compounds with multicolored stylized facades.

Belt Mask. Ivory. Bini Tribe, Benin.

It is significant that most West African forest civilizations had emerged, and in some cases reached their zenith, before European involvement. The Obaship in Benin was well established before Portuguese explorers arrived at Benin's major seaport of Gwato in 1472. Likewise, the Manikongo of Kongo ruled over an expansive domain with almost unchallenged authority before Portuguese contact a decade later. And Ifé was already recognized by the Yoruba as their major religious and cultural center.

Many African leaders received the Portuguese initially with great enthusiasm, hoping to taste the fruits of new techniques in agriculture, industry, and warfare. Before 1505 Benin and Kongo dispatched ambassadors and young intellectuals to Lisbon and the Vatican. But when America's vast resources were discovered by European explorers, it became obvious that the wealth could best be exploited by cheap labor in massive quantities. Only nearby Africa seemed to possess that necessary commodity. Thus, after about 1505, traders, missionaries, and other European visitors to

Africa had different intentions from their predecessors. They came not as skilled technicians but as "advisers" who would gradually infiltrate African governments in order to better organize them for the slave trade. Thus, even though the political unification of Portugal and Spain in 1580 sacrificed African involvement to other interests, it in no way spelled an end to the Atlantic trade in humans.

European rivalries
for the African
trade

Portuguese initiative in nautical science had already passed to the English, Dutch, and French—all of whom had begun to establish their own colonies of exploitation and settlement in the New World. Between 1637 and 1642 the Portuguese lost almost all their enclaves in West Africa to the Dutch. The Hollanders, unable to buy enough slaves on the West African coast, soon looked to the Ngoła kingdom farther south. Only there did the Portuguese mount a successful resistance.

Demoralizing
effects of the
slave and arms
trade

In the course of the seventeenth century, royally chartered companies from many European states formed monopoly enterprises and constructed warehouses and strings of stone fortresses along the West African coast. In 1672 the Royal African Company received a charter from the English crown and soon became the most active buyer of West African gold and slaves. Still, fierce competition with

Dutch Ambassador Welcomed by King Alvaro II of the Kongo. Early in the seventeenth century the Dutch began to rival the Portuguese for control of the kingdoms near the mouth of the Congo River.

the Dutch in arms and munitions sales to Africans quickly led to a proliferation of deadly weapons among certain forest societies. To many African chiefs, slave raiding and trading became a painful necessity. If they refused to engage in it, the Europeans would supply arms to rivals who might in turn use them to sell their people into captivity. Dahomey and the Kongo, initially opposed to the slave trade, soon found it necessary either to play the European game or face possible economic and political ruin. Benin was one of the few African states that successfully controlled slave trading. It remained an independent political entity until the British invasion of 1897.

A number of small states were born in the seventeenth century in the Akan forest behind the Gold Coast. They were known to have supplied by that time more than 20 per cent of Europe's gold reserves. Under the stimulus of the Royal African Company, this trade increased and led in the late seventeenth century to the rise of the Asante empire. The Akan peoples of Asante grew extremely powerful and wealthy by taxing trade passing through their territory en route to the coast. Between 1721 and 1750 Asante civilization reached its zenith. Asante artisans crafted earrings, anklets, pendants, and armbands from gold and bronze. On horizontal strip looms they wove polychromed togas of varied designs. Each pattern had a name and conveyed a symbolic meaning.

The Atlantic slave trade received a great boost after 1713 when England secured the Spanish *Asiento,* or license, to supply slaves to Spanish New World possessions. In response, the Yoruba state of Oyo expanded into a territorial empire, serving as middleman in the slave trade between the Hausaland interior and the coast. Other states exhibited a similar pattern. Immediately west of Oyo appeared the highly centralized kingdom of Dahomey. Between 1724 and 1729 Dahomey swept into the coastal Aja states and assimilated them. Unable to foster other sorts of trade with the Europeans, the Dahomeans became both suppliers and brokers in the slave trade. Oyo, fearful of this competition, diverted traffic to its own ports in 1750. To survive the consequent economic dislocation, the Dahomean government developed a state-controlled totalitarian economic and political system unparalleled in the eighteenth century. All state officials were appointed by the king, who ruled as a dictator, and a secret police was established to enforce his will. No system of checks and balances existed; only precedent and ancestral sanction guided his rule. Acting as high priest, the king dominated the major cults. He also controlled the craft guilds which produced pictorial tapestries and graceful statues to glorify royal power. A national military draft of men and women was instituted as well as a census bureau to administer it. Slave-worked plantations were established and placed under the close supervision of a Minister of Agriculture. Dahomey's economy was tightly regulated with central control over taxation and currency. Prices and wages, on the other hand, were set

Asante civilization

Dahomey: example of extreme centralization

709

Kongo and Ngola
become major
sources for slaves
and fail to survive
European
intrusions

by producers' organizations. Culturally, westernization was actively discouraged by recourse to an aggressive policy of conquest and enforced assimilation into the traditional Fon way of life. Dahomey outlived the destructive effects of the slave trade and was able to safeguard its dynamic cultural institutions until French guns disrupted them in 1894.

Kongo and Ngola, in the savanna zone of West Central Africa, did not fare as well. After 1482 the Kongolese monarch, anxious to learn the secrets of European technology, assumed a Christian name and converted to Catholicism. But within two decades, Catholic missionaries had driven a wedge between the king and the nobility, who wished to follow the time-honored indigenous traditions. In 1556 rivalries among Portuguese advisers in the Kongo and Ngola dragged these two kingdoms into a destructive war against each other. Ngola won, but the real beneficiaries were European and mulatto slavers who reaped huge profits selling the war prisoners and refugees. Escalating demands for miners in Portuguese Brazil finally led to the total destruction of Kongo and Ngola (called Angola by the Portuguese) in 1665 and 1671 respectively. Their governments collapsed, although the Kongolese tradition of fine raffia cloth weaving remained vigorous. Slave trading persisted and resulted in a further moral and ethical deterioration among certain segments of the population. Successor African Lunda and Luba kingdoms arose deep in the interior, safely beyond direct Portuguese interference. Some of these highly centralized kingdoms survived into the twentieth century, but only to lose their independence to a new wave of Europeans, in search not of slaves but of copper.

Portuguese involvement on the East African coast was equally destructive, even though it had little to do with the slave trade. In 1498 Vasco Da Gama rounded the Cape and sailed northward along

Islam in East Africa. Mombassa Mosque with minaret. Sixteenth century.

Portuguese in East Africa. Fort Jesus was built in 1593 at Mombassa by the Portuguese. It served as their major foothold in East Africa until 1728, when they were driven out under a combined Afro-Arab siege.

the Swahili coast in search of the East Indies. He was astounded to discover a series of prosperous and highly civilized city-states with strong commercial and cultural links to Arabia, the Persian Gulf, and India. But it was distressing to him that their Sultans were fervent practitioners of Islam. It is no wonder that Da Gama had battles in three of the four city-states he visited. At Malindi his reception was cordial, only because Da Gama had sacked Malindi's commercial rival, Mombasa.

The Portuguese reaction to Swahili civilization

The Portuguese were impressed by the gold and copper flowing out of Central Africa and by the extensive Indian Ocean trading network which carried the ore to distant ports. They hoped to use the Swahili city-states as a springboard to the Indies and as a source of gold for financing commercial operations in India and the Spice Islands. By 1505, after several Portuguese voyages of plunder and bombardment, the city-states were reduced to tributary status.

The Portuguese did not intend to govern the Swahili city-states. Rather, they attempted, with only limited success, to monopolize the Indian Ocean trade through their Viceroy at Goa on the western coast of India. After troubles with Turkish pirates and pillaging Zimba tribesmen, the Portuguese in 1593 constructed a massive stone citadel, called Fort Jesus, at Mombasa, and the malleable Sultan of Malindi was appointed to govern on their behalf. In 1622 the Portuguese were driven out of Ormuz, their strategic stronghold in the Persian Gulf, by a powerful Persian fleet. The fragility of Portuguese rule soon became evident to others. From the 1630's they had to suppress costly revolts in numerous Swahili towns. After Muscat, the gateway to the Persian Gulf, fell in 1650, the Omani Arabs emerged as a formidable naval power. In 1698 they drove the Portuguese out of Mombasa, their major port of call en route to India, and Portuguese supremacy north of Mozambique crumbled like a house of cards. In its wake lay the ruins of a once magnificent Swahili civilization. The Omani came to East Africa as liberators, but stayed on

Stool with Caryatid. Wood. Luba, Congo.

711

African Craftsmen. Dye pits in Kano (in northern Nigeria) were and still are owned by traditional craft guilds.

as conquerors, practicing a kind of benign neglect which led to further cultural and economic deterioration.

Portuguese repelled

The Portuguese also failed in their attempts to control the gold and copper mines of the Rhodesian and Katangan plateaus. After one hundred and eighty years of interference in the political and religious institutions of the Mwenemutapa empire, they were forced to retreat to the Mozambique coast. Their traders and soldiers were simply no match against the more determined and better organized Shona armies. African resistance was clearly stronger than the Portuguese will to conquer. In 1798 the Portuguese attempted to link their colony in Angola with Mozambique in the hope of forging a transcontinental African empire. But malaria and the unwillingness of the Crown to administer such a vast area were responsible for its failure.

Europeans contribute little to the advance of African civilization

Africans gained little from the Europeans in their first three centuries of contact. The exchange of guns, powder, alcoholic beverages, and cheap manufactured textiles for humans, gold, ivory, pepper, and palm oil stimulated the centralization of African authority in some areas and contributed to the growth of empires. But it added little to the advance of African civilizations. Christianity, introduced by force and often for ulterior motives, did not take firm hold. On the other hand, Islam, having suffered a severe setback in the western Sudan after the Moroccan invasion of Songhay in 1591, flourished in the Hausa city-states in northern Nigeria. After 1725 Islamic Sufi orders had begun to declare *jihads*, or holy wars, in the Senegal region and to establish theocratic states based on strict adherence to Islamic practices. Yet Islam remained an unknown factor until the nineteenth century for the vast majority of sub-Saharan Africans.

Unlike Japan, Africa's real economic growth was slowed by the exploitative, nonproductive nature of the European trade. African society, traditionally communalistic and egalitarian, became more class-conscious as relations between master and servant, free and nonfree were formalized in areas exposed to the opportunities and dangers of external trade. Yet, in spite of these disruptive influences, these three centuries witnessed steady artistic advancement. Royal families in the centralized states became wealthy and commissioned artisans to fashion rings, pendants, bracelets, and hairpins from gold, copper, ivory, and exotic woods. Impressive mud or reed palaces were constructed with galleries and courtyards adorned with polychromed woven, batik, or tied-and-dyed tapestries. Basic ideals of beauty were expressed through distinct symbols stamped onto cloth, molded in high relief on the facades of buildings, or shaped into fine wood or metal sculpture. Forms such as the circle, rectangle, oval, and square were brilliantly translated into artistic symbols and given deep philosophical and religious meaning. And complex notions of God and the universe were expressed in the verbal symbolism of proverbs and epic poems or in the intricate designs of royal thrones, scepters, swords, and craftsmen's tools. Over the course of these three centuries, the forest civilizations, with their unlimited supplies of timber, used a wide variety of wood as the primary art medium for sculpturing. They achieved a brilliant artistic synthesis of surrealist and expressionist, abstract and naturalistic elements. The cubist tradition itself was born not in Western Europe in the early twentieth century but among artistic circles in the West African forest societies centuries before. Although Europeans robbed Africans of much of their physical and human resources, they did not succeed in weakening their artistic vitality. Indeed, the trauma of European contact seemed to propel Africans toward even greater cultural achievements.

The failure to win Christian converts

SELECTED READINGS

• *Items so designated are available in paperbound editions.*

CHINA

Harrison, J. A., *The Chinese Empire: A Short History of China from Neolithic Times to the End of the Eighteenth Century*, New York, 1972.

Ho Ping-ti, *Studies on the Population of China, 1368–1953*, Cambridge, Mass., 1959. A masterful survey of population trends and related social and economic problems.

Honour, Hugh, *Chinoiserie: The Vision of Cathay*, New York, 1962. An account of the rise of European interest in the arts and crafts of the Orient.

• Hudson, G. F., *Europe and China: A Survey of Their Relations from the Earliest Times to 1800*, London, 1930 (Beacon).

Latourette, K. S., *The Chinese, Their History and Culture*, 4th ed., 2 vols. in one, New York, 1964. Comprehensive in scope; extensive bibliographies.

READINGS

- Li, Dun J., *The Ageless Chinese, A History*, 2nd ed., New York, 1971 (Scribner's).

  Michael, Franz, *The Origin of Manchu Rule in China*, Baltimore, 1942.

- Moore, C. A., ed., *The Chinese Mind: Essentials of Chinese Philosophy and Culture*, Honolulu, 1967 (East-West Center).

  Needham, Joseph, *Science and Civilization in China*, New York, 1954, Vol. I; 1956, Vol. II; 1959, Vol. III; 1962–1971, Vol. IV.

  Rowbotham, A. H., *Missionary and Mandarin: The Jesuits at the Court of China*, Berkeley, 1942.

  Scott, A. C., *The Classical Theater of China*, New York, 1957.

  Shryock, J. K., *The Origin and Development of the State Cult of Confucius*, New York, 1932.

  Sickman, L., and Soper, A., *The Art and Architecture of China*, Baltimore, 1956. Reliable, richly illustrated.

- Sullivan, Michael, *A Short History of Chinese Art*, rev. ed., Berkeley, 1970 (California).

  Tuan Yi-fu, *China*, Chicago, 1970. An excellent cultural geography.

JAPAN

Bellah, R. N., *Tokugawa Religion: The Values of Pre-Industrial Japan*, Glencoe, Ill., 1957.

Dore, R. P., *Education in Tokugawa, Japan*, Berkeley, 1965.

- Duus, Peter, *Feudalism in Japan*, New York, 1969 (Knopf). A concise account of political developments through the nineteenth century.

Eliot, Charles, *Japanese Buddhism*, New York, 1959. A standard text.

Embree, J. F., *The Japanese Nation*, New York, 1945. A brilliant and well-balanced study by an anthropologist.

- Ernst, Earle, *The Kabuki Theatre*, New York, 1956 (Evergreen).

- Hall, J. W., *Japan: From Prehistory to Modern Times*, New York, 1971 (Delta).

Harootunian, H. D., *Toward Restoration: The Growth of Political Consciousness in Tokugawa Japan*, Berkeley, 1970. A work of thorough scholarship.

- Keene, Donald, *Japanese Literature: An Introduction for Western Readers*, New York, 1955 (Evergreen).

Langer, P. F., *Japan, Yesterday and Today*, New York, 1966. An excellent summary.

- Moore, C. A., ed., *The Japanese Mind: Essentials of Japanese Philosophy and Culture*, Honolulu, 1967 (East-West Center).

- Munsterberg, Hugo, *The Arts of Japan: An Illustrated History*, Rutland, Vt., 1957 (Tuttle).

- Reischauer, E. O., *Japan: The Story of a Nation*, New York, 1970 (Knopf). Lucid and well organized.

Sadler, A. L., *The Maker of Modern Japan: The Life of Tokugawa Ieyasu*, London, 1937.

Sansom, G. B., *Japan, a Short Cultural History*, rev. ed., New York, 1952. A substantial but highly readable work by an eminent British scholar.

——, *The Western World and Japan*, New York, 1950.

Sheldon, C. D., *The Rise of the Merchant Class in Tokugawa Japan, 1600–1868: An Introductory Survey*, Locust Valley, N.Y., 1958.

- Smith, T. C., *The Agrarian Origins of Modern Japan*, Stanford, 1959 (Atheneum).

Swann, Peter C., *An Introduction to the Arts of Japan*, New York, 1958.

- Warner, Langdon, *The Enduring Art of Japan*, Cambridge, Mass., 1952 (Evergreen).

Yukio, Y., *Two Thousand Years of Japanese Art*, New York, 1958.

Curtin, Philip D., ed., *Horizon History of Africa*, New York, 1972.

Davidson, Basil, *The African Genius*, Boston, 1969.

Gailey, H. A., *History of Africa: From Earliest Times to 1800*, New York, 1970.

Hallett, Robin, *Africa to 1875*, Ann Arbor, 1970.

Hull, Richard W., *Munyakare: African Civilization before the Batuuree*, New York, 1972.

SOURCE MATERIALS

· de Bary, W. T., ed., *Sources of Chinese Tradition*, Chaps. XXII, XXIII (Columbia).

· ——, ed., *Sources of Indian Tradition*, "Islam in Medieval India"; "Sikhism" (Columbia).

· ——, ed., *Sources of Japanese Tradition*, "The Tokugawa Period" (Columbia).

Gallagher, L. J., tr., *China in the Sixteenth Century. The Journals of Matthew Ricci: 1583–1610.*

· Hibbett, Howard, *The Floating World in Japanese Fiction* (Evergreen).

· Keene, Donald, ed., *Anthology of Japanese Literature* (Evergreen).

Markham, C. R., ed., *The Hawkins' Voyages.*

Morse, H. B., ed., *The Chronicles of the East India Company Trading to China*, 5 vols.

Oliver, Roland, ed., *The Middle Age of African History*, New York, 1967.

Smith, V. A., ed., *F. Bernier: Travels in the Mogul Empire* A.D. *1656–1668.*

Vansina, Jan, *Kingdoms of the Savanna*, Madison, Wis., 1966.

Wang, C. C., tr., *Dream of the Red Chamber* (Chinese novel).

PART VI

The Later Modern World
(1789-1914)

The period 1789–1914 marked a climax in the world's history. Accumulated tendencies of the past four centuries reached their peak and wrought miracles of change unheard of since the time of the Greeks. The French Revolution gathered together a number of these tendencies and made them vital forces in the world for more than 100 years. This was notably true of nationalism, individualism, equalitarianism, and opposition to absolute monarchy. Advances in medical science and improvements in food supply made possible a doubling of the population of the globe in little more than a century. The Commercial Revolution and the Industrial Revolutions affected the course of history more deeply than all the "decisive battles" since the days of the Pharaohs. The individualism of the Renaissance and the rationalism of the Enlightenment prepared the way for the liberalism and democracy of the nineteenth and twentieth centuries. So great was the appeal of these forces that they were not confined to Europe and the Americas but spread ultimately to the Far East. Thus the great lords of Japan, in adopting a constitution in 1889, saw fit to establish the forms of cabinet government, while the leader of the Chinese Revolution of 1911 made "democracy" one of his shibboleths. But the most powerful current reaching its climax between 1800 and 1914 was undoubtedly nationalism. New states multiplied especially in Europe and in Latin America. Asia lagged behind the West, but it was only a matter of time until the peoples of the Middle and Far East would strike out boldly for control of their own destinies. The peoples of Africa were less fortunate. Although the notorious slave trade was gradually ended, the political and technological advantages accruing to the leading Western nations were utilized by them to strengthen their hold on the resources of disunited Africa.

717

A Chronological Table

THE AMERICAS	INDIA, THE MIDDLE AND FAR EAST
Great Awakening, 1740–1810	Manchu Dynasty in China, 1644–1912

1775

American Revolution, 1775–1783
Declaration of Independence, 1776

Adoption of the Constitution of the U.S., 1787
John Fitch's steamboat, 1787

The Bill of Rights, 1791
Thomas Paine, *The Rights of Man*, 1791
Invention of cotton gin, increasing de-demand for slaves, 1795

1800

Jeffersonian Revolution, 1800–1801

Latin American wars for independence, 1808–1826
Abolition of slave trade by United States, 1808

Independence of Argentina, 1816

Independence of Brazil, 1822
Independence of Mexico, 1822
Monroe Doctrine, 1823

1825

Jacksonian Revolution, 1828–1837

Mechanization of agriculture, 1835–

Anglo-Chinese War (Opium War), 1839–1842

Use of ether as an anesthetic, 1842
Telegraph, 1844

1850

Taiping Rebellion, 1851–1864

Opening of Japan, 1854
Great Mutiny in India, 1857–1858
British Crown assumes rule in India, 1858

First oil well, 1859

EUROPE	AFRICA

EUROPE

Physiocrats, 1750–1800
Development of steam engine, 1769
Beethoven, 1770–1827
William Wordsworth, 1770–1850
Beginning of factory system, *ca.* 1770
Adam Smith, *The Wealth of Nations*, 1776
Classical economics, 1776–1880
Immanuel Kant, *Critique of Pure Reason*, 1781
French Declaration of Rights of Man, 1789
French Revolution, 1789–1799
Utilitarianism, 1790–1870
Edward Jenner develops vaccination for smallpox, 1796
Franz Schubert, 1797–1828
Coup d'état of Napoleon, 1799
Romanticism in literature and arts, 1800–1900
Victor Hugo, 1802–1885
First Empire in France, 1804–1814
Abolition of legal slave trade, 1805–1808
Revival of atomic theory, 1810
Charles Dickens, 1812–1870
Richard Wagner, 1813–1883
Congress of Vienna, 1814–1815
Battle of Waterloo, 1815
Carlsbad Decrees, 1819
Feodor Dostoievski, 1821–1881
First railroad, 1825
Henrik Ibsen, 1828–1906
Leo Tolstoi, 1828–1910
Independence of Greece, 1829

July Revolution in France, 1830
Realism in literature and arts, 1830–1914
Independence of Belgium, 1831
First Reform Act, 1832
Unification of Germany, 1833–1871
Chartist Movement, 1838–1848
Tchaikovsky, 1840–1893
Émile Zola, 1840–1902
Law of conservation of energy, 1847
February Revolution in France, 1848
Communist Manifesto, 1848
Second Republic in France, 1848–1852
Unification of Italy, 1848–1870
Law of dissipation of energy, 1851
Second Empire in France, 1852–1870

Bessemer process, 1856
Charles Darwin, *Origin of Species*, 1859
J. S. Mill, *On Liberty*, 1859

AFRICA

British occupation of Cape Colony, 1795

House-Canoe system in Niger Delta, ca. 1800
Expansion of East African trade, 1800–1875
Sultan Sayyid, Zanzibar, 1805–1856

Sierra Leone founded, 1808

Liberia founded, 1821

British consulates in coastal states, 1830–1860

Exploration of interior of continent, 1830–1875
Decline of slave trade, 1840–1863

1775

1800

1825

1850

	THE AMERICAS	INDIA, THE MIDDLE AND FAR EAST

THE AMERICAS

INDIA, THE MIDDLE AND FAR EAST

Civil War, 1861–1865
Empire of Maximilian in Mexico, 1862–1867

Sun Yat-sen, 1866–1925
Meiji Restoration, 1867
End of Shogunate in Japan, 1867
Mahatma Gandhi, 1869–1948
End of feudalism in Japan, 1871

1875

Telephone, 1876

Pragmatism, 1880–1930

Organization of Indian National Congress, 1885
Adoption of Constitution in Japan, 1889
Jawaharlal Nehru, 1889–1964
Sino-Japanese War, 1894–1895

Republic of Brazil, 1889
Beginning of finance capitalism, 1890
Populism, 1890–1897

William James, *The Will to Believe*, 1897
Spanish-American War, 1898

Open-door policy in China, 1899

Boxer Rebellion, 1900

1900

Progressive movement, 1901–1916
First airplane flight, 1903

Russo-Japanese War, 1904–1905

Model T Ford, 1908

Young Turk Revolution, 1908

Madero Revolution in Mexico, 1911

Revolution in China, 1911

EUROPE	AFRICA

Emancipation of serfs in Russia, 1861
Antiseptic surgery, 1865

Second Reform Act, 1867
Franco-Prussian War, 1870–1871
Impressionism, 1870–1890   Opening of Suez Canal, 1869
Paris Commune, 1871
German Empire, 1871–1918
Development of dynamo, 1873
Germ theory of disease, 1875
Third Republic in France, 1875–1940
Internal-combustion engine, 1876
Herbert Spencer, *Data of Ethics*, 1879   Destruction of Zulu empire, 1879

Triple Alliance, 1882–1914
Third Reform Act, 1884
Berlin-to-Baghdad Railway, 1890–1907
Post-impressionism, 1890
Dreyfus affair, 1894–1905
Discovery of X-ray, 1895
Diesel engine, 1897

Wireless telegraph, 1899

　　　　　　　　　　　　　　Boer War, 1899–1902

Hugo DeVries, mutation theory, 1901
Cubism, 1903–
Entente Cordiale, 1904
Russo-Japanese War, 1904–1905
Founding of psychoanalysis, *ca.* 1905
Russian Revolution of 1905
Einstein theories, 1905–1910
Triple Entente, 1907
Young Turk Revolution, 1908
Bosnian crisis, 1908
Discovery of protons and electrons, *ca.*
　1910
Balkan wars, 1912–1913

CHAPTER 24

The French Revolution (1789-1799)

Today the third estate is everything, the nobility but a word. . . .
—Abbé Sieyès, *What Is the Third Estate?*

France, when she let loose the reins of regal authority, doubled the licence of a ferocious dissoluteness in manners, and of an insolent irreligion in opinions and practices; and has extended through all ranks of life, as if she were communicating some privilege, or laying open some secluded benefit, all the unhappy corruptions that usually were the disease of wealth and power.
—Edmund Burke, *Reflections on the Revolution in France*

Profound changes were wrought in the political history of the Western world in the latter part of the eighteenth century. This period witnessed the death throes of that peculiar system of government and society which had grown up during the age of the despots. In England this system had already been largely overthrown by 1689, but in other nations of Europe it lingered on, growing more and more ossified and corrupt with the passing of the years. It flourished in every major country of Europe under the combined influence of militarism and the ambitions of monarchs to consolidate their power at the expense of the nobles. But scarcely anywhere did it exist in so deplorable a form as in France during the reigns of the last three Bourbon kings. Louis XIV was the supreme incarnation of absolute rule. His successors, Louis XV and Louis XVI, dragged the government to very low depths of extravagance and irresponsibility. Moreover, their subjects were sufficiently enlightened to be keenly aware of their disadvantages. Yet the French Revolution was not an isolated event. In many ways it was simply the French aspect of a great Western revolution which had begun in the American Colonies in the 1770's, had spread to Ireland in 1782–1783, to the Low Countries, and to Hungary and Poland. The French outbreak was the climax of this widespread Western revolution. Moreover, it was the broadest and most significant. It involved not merely the king and the nobility but the

The era of revolution

723

middle class, the peasants, and even the "little people" of the cities and towns.

I. THE CAUSES OF THE FRENCH REVOLUTION

For convenience we can divide the causes of the French Revolution into three main classes: political, economic, and intellectual. Naturally, this division is somewhat arbitrary, for none of these classes was entirely distinct. The intellectual causes, for example, and to some extent the political also, were largely economic in origin. Nevertheless, for purposes of simplification it will be best to keep them separate. One of the major political causes has already been mentioned. This was the despotic rule of the Bourbon kings. For nearly 200 years government in France had been largely a one-man institution. During the fourteenth, fifteeth, and sixteeth centuries a kind of parliament known as the Estates General, composed of representatives of the clergy, the nobility, and the common people, had met at irregular intervals. But after 1614 it was no longer summoned. Henceforth the king was the sole repository of sovereign power. In a very real sense the king was the state. He could do almost anything his imperious will might dictate, without fear of impeachment or legislative restrictions of any kind. No questions of constitutionality or the natural rights of his subjects need trouble him. He could throw men into prison without a trial by means of royal orders, or *lettres de cachet*. He could prevent any criticism of his policies by clamping a rigid censorship on the press or by restricting freedom of speech. It must be conceded, however, that the tyranny of the French kings has often been exaggerated. In actual practice there was comparatively little interference with what men wrote or said, particularly during the reigns of Louis XV and Louis XVI. No action of these monarchs inhibited the mordant wit of Voltaire or suppressed the radical books of Rousseau.[1] On the contrary, the attacks by these and other philosophers increased in virulence the nearer the Revolution approached. The explanation, of course, is not to be found in any liberalism of Louis XV and his dull-witted grandson but rather in their indifference to politics.

A second political cause of the French Revolution was the illogical and unsystematic character of the government. Confusion reigned in nearly every department. The political structure was the product of a long and irregular growth extending back into the Middle Ages. New agencies had been established from time to time to meet some particular condition, with a total disregard for those already in existence. As a result there was much overlapping of functions, and numerous useless officials drew salaries from the pub-

Louis XV

Louis XVI

---

[1] Voltaire was imprisoned for a time and afterwards exiled to England for one of his vitriolic lampoons, but this was early in his career. Most of his trenchant criticisms of the government and the Church were written *after his return* from England.

lic purse. Conflicts of jurisdiction between rival departments frequently delayed action on vital problems for months at a stretch. Almost everywhere inefficiency, waste, and graft were the ruling qualities of the system. Even in financial matters there was no more regularity than in other branches of public policy. The collection of public revenues was exceedingly haphazard. Instead of appointing official collectors, the king employed the old Roman system of farming out the collection of taxes to private corporations and individuals, permitting them to retain as profit all that they could gouge from the people in excess of a stipulated amount. Similar disorganized conditions prevailed in the realm of law and judicial procedure. Nearly every province of France had its special code based upon local custom. As a consequence an act punishable as a crime in southern France, where the Roman influence was strongest, might be no concern of the law in a central or northern province.

Probably the most decisive of the political causes was the disastrous wars into which France was plunged during the eighteenth century. Revolutions are not made by sporadic attacks upon a system still in its prime, no matter how oppressive some of its policies may be. Before a great political and social upheaval (which is the way we must define a true revolution) can occur, it seems to be necessary that there shall be a near collapse of the existing order. Something must happen to produce a condition of chaos, to reveal the incompetence and corruption of the government, and to create such disgust and hardship that many of those who formerly supported the old regime shall now turn against it. Nothing could be better calculated to achieve these ends than conflict with foreign powers resulting in humiliating defeat or at least in serious reverses. As a matter of fact, it is almost impossible to conceive of any of the great revolutions of modern times except as a consequence of long and disastrous wars.[2] The first of the wars that prepared the ground for the French Revolution was the Seven Years' War (1756–1763), fought during the reign of Louis XV. In this struggle France was pitted against England and Prussia and, in spite of aid from Austria and also for a time from Russia, went down to overwhelming defeat. As a result, the French were compelled to surrender nearly all of their colonial possessions. It was natural and, on the whole quite justifiable, that the blame for this catastrophe should be placed on the incompetence of the government. The effects of this blow were made worse when Louis XVI decided in 1778 to intervene in the American War for Independence. Though France was now on the winning side, the cost of maintaining fleets and armies in the Western Hemisphere for more than three years virtually bankrupted the government. As we shall see, it was this condition of financial helplessness in the face of an impossible burden of

The costly wars of the French kings

---

[2] A distinction, of course, must be drawn between true revolutions and those of the "palace" variety, so common in Africa, Southeast Asia, and in Latin America, which are really very little more than substitutes for elections.

The French
Revolution not
the result of
misery and
poverty among
the people

The real eco-
nomic causes:
(1) the rise of
the middle class

debt which led directly to the quarrel between the king and the middle class and the consequent outbreak of revolution.

In turning to the economic causes of the French Revolution, we must note first of all that universal wretchedness among the mass of the people was not one of them. The popular notion that the Revolution occurred because the majority of the people were starving for want of bread, and because the queen said, "Let them eat cake," is far from historically accurate. Despite the loss of her colonial empire, France on the eve of the Revolution was still a rich and prosperous nation. Some conditions were critical, however. The government was so close to bankruptcy that it could pay its debts only by borrowing money at ruinous rates of interest. Though some industries were prospering, others were scraping the bottom of the barrel to make ends meet. As for the bulk of the rural population, it is the opinion of some modern scholars that the French peasants in the eighteenth century were better off than the rural folk in any other country of Europe except England.[3] Only about one-twentieth of the French population still languished in serfdom, and the proportion was gradually diminishing. What the downtrodden classes did in 1789 was not to initiate the Revolution, but to provide an army of followers after it had been started by others. The fact cannot be emphasized too strongly that the French Revolution was launched as a middle-class movement. Its original objectives were primarily for the benefit of the bourgeoisie. Since the leaders of this class needed the support of a larger percentage of the people, they naturally took some notice of the grievances of the peasants, and eventually of the proletarians.

What then were the real economic causes? Perhaps we should place at the head of the list the rise of the middle class to a position of extraordinary affluence and prestige. The emergence of a new economic group with a sense of grievances and a consciousness of its own strength and importance seems to be a necessary condition to the outbreak of any revolution. This class is never composed of miserable dregs of humanity—wretched, starving, and hopeless. On the contrary, its ranks must be permeated by a sense of confidence inspired by previous success and strengthened by the belief that additional effort will being greater gains in the future. During the years preceding the Revolution the French bourgeoisie had grown to be the dominant economic class. It controlled the resources of trade, manufacturing, and finance. Moreover, its members appear to have been growing richer year by year. In 1789 the foreign commerce of France reached the unprecedented total of 1,153,000,000 francs.[4] But the chief effect of this rising prosperity was to sharpen bourgeois discontent. No matter how much money a merchant,

[3] L. R. Gottschalk, *The Era of the French Revolution*, pp. 30–31.
[4] *Ibid.*, p. 44.

manufacturer, banker, or lawyer might acquire, he was still excluded from political privileges. He had almost no influence at the court; he could not share in the highest honors; and, except in the choice of a few petty local officers, he could not even vote. Besides, he was looked down upon as an inferior by the idle and frivolous nobility. As the middle class rose in affluence and in consciousness of its own importance, its members were bound to resent such attempts at social discrimination. But above all it was the demand of the commercial, financial, and industrial leaders for political power commensurate with their economic position that made the bourgeoisie a revolutionary class.

A demand for political power was not the only consequence of the growing prosperity of the middle class; there was also an increasing clamor for the abandonment of mercantilist policies. In earlier times mercantilism had been welcomed by merchants and manufacturers because of its effects in procuring new markets and fostering trade. But those times were at the beginning of the Commercial Revolution when business was still in its swaddling clothes. As commerce and industry flourished through succeeding centuries, the bourgeoisie became increasingly confident of its ability to stand on its own feet. The result was a growing tendency to look upon the regulations of mercantilism as oppressive restrictions. Merchants disliked the special monopolies granted to favored companies and the interference with their freedom to buy in foreign markets. Manufacturers chafed under the laws controlling wages, fixing prices, and restricting the purchase of raw materials outside of France and her colonies. These were only a few of the more annoying regulations enforced by a government operating under the twin objectives of paternalism and economic self-sufficiency. Perhaps it is not strange that the middle class should have come to think of pure economic liberty as a paradise, worthy to be gained at terrific cost. At any rate, it can scarcely be doubted that the desire of businessmen to be rid of mercantilism was one of the principal causes of the French Revolution.

A third factor, mainly economic in character, which contributed much to the outbreak of the French Revolution was the system of privilege entrenched in the society of the *ancien régime*. Prior to the Revolution the population of France was divided into three great classes or estates: the first was composed of the clergy; the second, of the nobles; and the third, of the common people. The first estate really included two different ranks: (1) the higher clergy, made up of cardinals, archbishops, bishops, and abbots; and (2) the lower clergy or parish priests. Though all of these servants of the Church were supposed to be members of a privileged group, in actual fact a wide gulf separated the two ranks. The lower clergy were frequently as poor as their humblest parishioners and were generally disposed to sympathize with the common man. By

(2) opposition to mercantilism

(3) the survival of privilege: the first estate

727

contrast, the higher clergy lived on the fattest fruits of the land and moved in the gay and sophisticated circle of the king and his court. Including no more than 1 per cent of the total population, they nevertheless owned about 20 per cent of all the land, to say nothing of vast wealth in the form of castles, paintings, gold, and jewels. Several of the bishops and archbishops had incomes running into hundreds of thousands of francs. Naturally, most of these gilded prelates gave little attention to religious affairs. Some of them dabbled in politics, aiding the king in maintaining his absolute rule. Others gambled or devoted their energies to more scandalous vices. Though it cannot be assumed that all of them were depraved and neglectful of their professional duties, a sufficient number were corrupt, domineering, and vicious to convince many people that the Church was rotten to the core and that its leaders were guilty of robbing the people and wasting the nation's resources.

The second estate, comprising the secular nobility, was also divided into two subordinate castes. At the top were the *nobles of the* *sword*, whose titles went all the way back to the feudal suzerains of the Middle Ages. Beneath them were the *nobles of the robe*, whose immediate ancestors had acquired some judicial office conferring a title of nobility; the "robe" was the magistrate's or judge's gown. Though commonly despised by their brethren of more ancient lineage, the nobles of the robe were by far the most intelligent and progressive members of the upper classes. Several of their number became ardent reformers, while a few played prominent roles in the Revolution itself. Their ranks included such famous critics of the established order as Montesquieu, Mirabeau, and Lafayette. It was the nobles of the sword who really constituted the privileged class in the second estate. Together with the higher clergy they monopolized the leading positions in the government, usually delegating the actual work to subordinates. While they owned vast estates, they customarily resided at Versailles and depended upon stewards or bailiffs to extort enough from the peasants to provide for their luxurious needs. Few, indeed, of these high-born wastrels performed any useful function. They acted as if they believed that their only responsibilities to society were to flatter the king, to cultivate the graces of courtly life, and occasionally to patronize the decadent classical art. In a very real sense, most of them were worthless parasites consuming the wealth which others labored hard to produce.

Among the most valuable privileges of clerics and nobles were those relating to taxation. And the inequitable system of taxation may well be considered a fourth economic cause of the French Revolution. Taxes in France, long before 1789, had come to consist of two main types. First, there were the direct taxes, which included the *taille*, or tax on real and personal property; the poll tax; and the tax on incomes, originally at the rate of 5 per cent, but in the eighteenth century more commonly 10 or 11 per cent. The indirect taxes, or taxes added to the price of commodities and paid

The second estate

(4) the inequitable system of taxation

Le Hameau. This rustic villa was constructed in the English style on the grounds of the Petit Trianon at Versailles. Here Marie Antoinette and ladies of the court mimicked peasant life.

by the ultimate consumer, embraced mainly the tariffs on articles imported from foreign countries and the tolls levied on goods shipped from one province of France to another. In addition, the *gabelle,* or tax on salt, may also be considered a form of indirect tax. For some time the production of salt had been a state monopoly in France, and every individual inhabitant was required to buy at least seven pounds a year from the government works. To the cost of production was added a heavy tax, with the result that the price to the consumer was often as much as fifty or sixty times the actual value of the salt. While exceedingly burdensome, the indirect taxes were not as a rule unfairly distributed. It was difficult, of course, for anyone, regardless of his social status, to avoid paying them. The case of most of the direct taxes, however, was far otherwise. The clergy, by virtue of the medieval rule that the property of the Church could not be taxed by the state, escaped payment of both the *taille* and the income tax. The nobles, especially those of higher rank, made use of their influence with the king to obtain exemption from practically all direct levies. As a result, the main task of providing funds for the government fell upon the common people, or members of the third estate. And since few of the artisans and laborers had much that could be taxed, the chief burden had to be borne by the peasants and the bourgeoisie.

A final economic cause of the Revolution was the survival of relics of feudalism in France as late as 1789. While the feudal system itself had long since become extinct, vestiges of it remained and served as convenient instruments for maintaining the power of the king and the privileged position of the nobles. In some backward

729

(5) the survival
of relics of
feudalism

areas of the country serfdom still lingered, but the prevalence of this institution must not be exaggerated. The highest estimate ever given of the number of peasants who were serfs is 1,500,000, out of a total rural population of at least 15,000,000. The vast majority of the peasants were free men. A considerable proportion owned the lands they cultivated. Others were tenants or hired laborers, but the largest percentage appear to have been sharecroppers, farming the lands of the nobles for a portion of the harvest, generally ranging from a third to a half. However, even those peasants who were entirely free were still required to perform obligations which had come down from the later Middle Ages. One of the most odious of these was the payment of an annual rental to the lord who had formerly controlled the land. Another was the donation to the local noble of a share of the price received whenever a tract of land was sold. In addition, the peasants were still required to contribute the *banalités*, or fees supposedly for the use of various facilities owned by the noble. During the Middle Ages *banalités* had been paid for the use of the lord's flour mill, his wine press, and his bake oven. In spite of the fact that by the eighteenth century many of the peasants owned such equipment themselves and no longer benefited by the services provided by the noble, the *banalités* were still collected in the original amounts.

Probably the most exasperating of all the relics of feudalism were the *corvée* and the hunting privileges of the nobility. The *corvée*, formerly a requirement of labor on the lord's demesne and in the building of roads and bridges on the manorial estate, was now an obligation to the government. For several weeks each year the peasant was forced to put his own work aside and devote his labor to maintaining the public highways. No other class of the population was required to perform this service. Even greater inconvenience was suffered by the rural citizens as a result of the hunting privileges of the nobles. From time immemorial the right to indulge in the diversions of the chase had been regarded as a distinctive badge of aristocracy. The man of gentle birth must have unlimited freedom to pursue this exciting pastime wherever he wished. Naturally, nothing so trivial as the property rights of the peasants should be allowed to stand in the way. In some parts of France the peasants were forbidden to weed or mow in breeding time lest they disturb the nests of the partridges. Rabbits, crows, and foxes could not be killed regardless of how much damage they did to the crops or to domestic fowl and young animals. Furthermore, the peasant was supposed to resign himself to having his fields trampled at any time by the horses of some thoughtless crew of noble hunters.

The corvée
and the hunting
privileges of
the nobility

Every great social upheaval of modern times has developed out of a background of intellectual causes. Before a movement can reach the proportions of an actual revolution, it is necessary that it be supported by a body of ideas, providing not only a program of action

but a glorious vision of the new order that is finally to be achieved.
To a large extent these ideas are the product of political and economic ambitions, but in time they take on the significance of independent factors. Eventually the fulfillment of the ideas is accepted as an end in itself and draws the allegiance of men like the gospel of a new religion. The intellectual causes of the French Revolution were mainly an outgrowth of the Enlightenment. This movement produced two interesting political theories, which have exerted influence ever since. The first was the *liberal* theory of such writers as Locke and Montesquieu; and the second was the *democratic* theory of Rousseau. While the two were fundamentally opposed, they nevertheless had elements in common. Both were predicated upon the assumption that the state is a necessary evil and that government rests upon a contractual basis. Each had its doctrine of popular sovereignty, although with contrasting interpretations. And, finally, both upheld in some measure the fundamental rights of the individual.

The father of the liberal theory of the seventeenth and eighteenth centuries was John Locke (1632–1704). Locke's political philosophy is contained chiefly in his *Second Treatise of Civil Government*, published in 1690. In this he developed a theory of limited government which was used to justify the new system of parliamentary rule set up in England as a result of the Glorious Revolution. He maintained that originally all men had lived in a state of nature in which absolute freedom and equality prevailed, and there was no government of any kind. The only law was the law of nature, which each individual enforced for himself in order to protect his natural rights to life, liberty, and property. It was not long, however, until men began to perceive that the inconveniences of the state of nature greatly outweighed its advantages. With every individual attempting to enforce his own rights, confusion and insecurity were the unavoidable results. Accordingly, the people agreed among themselves to establish a civil society, to set up a government, and to surrender certain powers to it. But they did not make that government absolute. The only power they conferred upon it was the executive power of the law of nature. Since the state is nothing but the joint power of all the members of society, its authority "can be no more than those persons had in a state of nature before they entered into society, and gave it up to the community."[5] All powers not expressly surrendered are reserved to the people themselves. If the government exceeds or abuses the authority explicitly granted in the political contract, it becomes tyrannical; and the people then have the right to dissolve it or to rebel against it and overthrow it.

Locke condemned absolutism in every form. He denounced despotic monarchy, but he was no less severe in his strictures against the absolute sovereignty of parliaments. Though he defended the

---

[5] *Second Treatise of Civil Government* (Everyman Library ed.), p. 184.

supremacy of the law-making branch, with the executive primarily an agent of the legislature, he nevertheless refused to concede to the representatives of the people an unlimited power. Arguing that government was instituted among men for the preservation of property (which he generally defined in the inclusive sense of life, liberty, and estate),[6] he denied the authority of any political agency to invade the natural rights of a single individual. The law of nature, which embodies these rights, is an automatic limitation upon every branch of the government. Regardless of how large a majority of the people's representatives should demand the restriction of freedom of speech or the confiscation and redistribution of property, no such action could legally be taken. If taken illegally it would justify effective measures of resistance on the part of the majority of citizens. Locke was much more concerned with protecting individual liberty than he was with promoting stability or social progress. If forced to make a choice, he would have preferred the evils of anarchy to those of despotism in any form.

Locke's
influence

The influence of few political philosophers in the history of the world has exceeded that of Locke. Not only were his doctrines of natural rights, limited government, and the right of resistance against tyranny an important source of French Revolutionary theory, but they found ready acceptance in American thought as well. They furnished most of the theoretical foundation for the colonial revolt against British oppression. They were reflected so clearly in the Declaration of Independence that whole passages of that document might almost have been copied from the *Second Treatise of Civil Government*. Lockian principles also influenced the drafting of the Constitution and especially the arguments advanced by Hamilton, Madison, and Jay in the *Federalist* urging its ratification. Later, when the new government enacted the Alien and Sedition laws, it was mainly on the basis of Lockian theory that Madison and Jefferson in the Virginia and Kentucky Resolutions appealed to the several States to resist the usurpation of power.

The liberal political theory of Voltaire

In France the foremost exponents of the liberal political theory were Voltaire (1694–1778) and Baron de Montesquieu (1689–1755). As was indicated earlier, Voltaire considered orthodox Christianity to be the worst of the enemies of mankind, but he reserved plenty of contempt for tyrannical government. During his exile in England he had studied the writings of Locke and had been deeply impressed by their vigorous assertions of individual freedom. Returning to France while still a comparatively young man, he devoted a large part of the remainder of his life to the fight for intellectual, religious, and political liberty. In common with Locke he conceived of government as a necessary evil, with powers which ought to be limited to the enforcement of natural rights. He main-

732   [6] *Ibid.*, p. 159.

tained that all men are endowed by nature with equal rights to liberty, property, and the protection of the laws. But Voltaire was no democrat. He was inclined to think of the ideal form of government as either an enlightened monarchy or a republic dominated by the middle class. To the end of his life he continued to be more than a little afraid of the masses. He was even fearful that his attacks upon organized religion might serve to incite the multitude to deeds of violence. It is related that after he had been robbed by some peasants, he attended church for a season in order to persuade the country bumpkins that he still believed in God.

A more systematic political thinker than Voltaire was his older contemporary, Baron de Montesquieu. Though, like Voltaire, a student of Locke and an ardent admirer of British institutions, Montesquieu was a unique figure among the political philosophers of the eighteenth century. In his celebrated *Spirit of Laws* he brought new methods and new conceptions into the theory of the state. Instead of attempting to found a science of government by pure deduction, he followed the Aristotelian method of studying actual political systems as they were supposed to have operated in the past. He denied that there is any one perfect form of government suitable for all peoples under all conditions. He maintained, on the contrary, that political institutions in order to be successful must harmonize with the physical conditions and the level of social advancement of the nations they are intended to serve. Thus he declared that despotism is best suited to countries of vast domain; limited monarchy to those of moderate size; and republican government to those of small extent. For his own country, France, he was disposed to think that a limited monarchy would be the most appropriate form, since he regarded the nation as too large to be made into a republic unless on some kind of federal plan.

Montesquieu

Montesquieu is especially famous for his theory of the separation of powers. He avowed that it is a natural tendency of man to abuse any extent of power entrusted to him, and that consequently every government, regardless of its form, is liable to degenerate into despotism. To prevent such a result he argued that the authority of government should be broken up into its three natural divisions of legislative, executive, and judicial. Whenever any two or more of these are allowed to remain united in the same hands, liberty, he declared, is at an end. The only effective way to avoid tyranny is to enable each branch of the government to act as a check upon the other two. For example, the executive should have the power by means of the veto to curb the encroachments of the lawmaking branch. The legislature, in turn, should have the authority of impeachment in order to restrain the executive. And, finally, there should be an independent judiciary vested with power to protect individual rights against arbitrary acts of either the legislature or the executive. This favorite scheme of Montesquieu was not intended,

The separation of powers and checks and balances

733

of course, to facilitate democracy. In fact, its purpose was largely the opposite: to prevent the absolute supremacy of the majority, expressed as it normally would be through the people's representatives in the legislature. It was a typical illustration of that strong dislike which the bourgeoisie had come to have for despotic government in any form, whether of the few or of the many. Montesquieu's principle of the separation of powers was none the less influential. It was incorporated in the first of the governments set up during the French Revolution, and it found its way with very few changes indeed into the Constitution of the United States.[7]

The second of the great political ideals which occupied an important place in the intellectual background of the French Revolution was the ideal of democracy. In contrast with liberalism, democracy, in its original meaning, was much less concerned with the defense of individual rights than with the enforcement of popular rule. What the majority of the citizens wills is the supreme law of the land, for the voice of the people is the voice of God. It is generally assumed that under democracy the minority will continue to enjoy full liberty of expression, but this assumption does not necessarily hold. The only sovereign right of the minority is the right to become the majority. As long as a particular group remains a minority, its members cannot claim any rights of individual action beyond the control of the state. Exponents of democracy today commonly maintain their devotion to freedom of speech and freedom of the press as rights which the government cannot legally infringe. But this attitude springs from the fact that the current ideal is generally combined with liberalism. Indeed, democracy and liberalism have now come to be used as if they were identical in meaning. Originally, however, they were entirely separate ideals. Historic democracy also included a belief in the natural equality of all men, opposition to hereditary privilege, and an abiding faith in the wisdom and virtue of the masses.

The founder of democracy as described above was Jean Jacques Rousseau (1712–1778). Since Rousseau was also the father of romanticism, we can expect that sentiment should have deeply colored his political judgments. Consistency, moreover, was not always his crowning virtue. The most significant of his writings on political theory were his *Social Contract* and his *Discourse on the Origin of Inequality*. In both of these he upheld the popular thesis that men had originally lived in a state of nature. But in contrast with Locke he regarded this state of nature as a veritable paradise. No one suffered inconvenience from maintaining his own rights against others. Indeed, there were very few chances of conflict of any sort; for private property did not exist for a long time, and every man was the equal of his neighbor. Eventually, however,

The democratic political theory

Rousseau, the founder of democracy

---

[7] For the influence of Montesquieu upon the founders of the American government, see E. M. Burns, *James Madison: Philosopher of the Constitution*, pp. 180–83.

evils arose, due primarily to the fact that some men staked off plots of land and said to themselves, "This is mine." It was in such manner that various degrees of inequality developed; and, as a consequence, "cheating trickery," "insolent pomp," and "insatiable ambition" soon came to dominate the relations among men.[8] The only hope of security was now for men to establish a civil society and to surrender all of their rights to the community. This they did by means of a social contract, in which each individual agreed with the whole body of individuals to submit to the will of the majority. Thus the state was brought into existence.

Rousseau developed an altogether different conception of sovereignty from that of the liberals. Whereas Locke and his followers had taught that only a portion of sovereign power is surrendered to the state, the rest being retained by the people themselves, Rousseau contended that sovereignty is indivisible, and that all of it became vested in the community when civil society was formed. He insisted further that each individual in becoming a party to the social contract gave up all of his rights to the people collectively and agreed to submit absolutely to the general will. It follows that the sovereign power of the state is subject to no limitations whatever. The general will, expressed through the vote of the majority, is the court of final appeal. What the majority decides is always right in the political sense and is absolutely binding upon every citizen. The state, which in actual practice means the majority, is legally omnipotent. But this does not really imply, according to Rousseau, that the liberty of the individual is entirely destroyed. On the contrary, subjection to the state has the effect of enhancing *genuine* liberty. Individuals in surrendering their rights to the community merely exchange the animal liberty of the state of nature for the true freedom of reasoning creatures in obedience to law. Compelling an individual to abide by the general will is therefore merely "forcing him to be free." It must be understood, also, that when Rousseau referred to the state he did not mean the government. He regarded the state as the politically organized community, which has the sovereign function of expressing the general will. The authority of the state cannot be represented, but must be expressed directly through the enactment of fundamental laws by the people themselves. The government, on the other hand, is simply the executive agent of the state. Its function is not to formulate the general will but merely to carry it out. Moreover, the community can set the government up or pull it down "whenever it likes." [9]

The influence of Rousseau's political theory would be hard to exaggerate. His dogmas of equality and the supremacy of the majority were the chief inspiration for the second stage of the French

Rousseau's conception of sovereignty

---

[8] *Discourse on the Origin of Inequality* (Everyman Library ed.), p. 207.
[9] *The Social Contract* (Everyman Library ed.), p. 88.

Revolution. Doctrinaire radicals like Robespierre were among his most fervent disciples. But Rousseau's influence was not confined to his own country. Some of his theories made their way to America and found an echo in certain of the principles of Jacksonian Democracy–although, of course, it is extremely improbable that many of Jackson's followers had ever heard of Rousseau. The German Romantic Idealists, who, in the early nineteenth century, glorified the state as "God in history," would also appear to have been indebted to the philosophy of *The Social Contract*. From Rousseau's doctrines that the state is legally omnipotent, and that true liberty consists in submission to the general will, it was not a very difficult step to exalting the state as an object of worship and reducing the individual to a mere cog in the political machine.[10] Even though Rousseau suggested that the majority would be limited by moral restraints and insisted upon the right of the people to "pull down" their government, these limitations were not enough to counteract the effect of his stress upon absolute sovereignty.

As a final intellectual cause of the French Revolution, the influence of the new economic theory must be given at least passing attention. In the second half of the eighteenth century a number of brilliant writers began attacking the traditional assumptions in regard to public control over production and trade. Their special target of criticism was mercantilist policy. To a large extent the new economics was founded upon the basic conceptions of the Enlightenment, particularly the idea of a mechanistic universe governed by inflexible laws. The notion now came to prevail that the sphere of the production and distribution of wealth was subject to laws just as irresistible as those of physics and astronomy. The new economic theory may also be regarded as the counterpart of political liberalism. The cardinal aims of the two were quite similar: to reduce the powers of government to the lowest minimum consistent with safety and to preserve for the individual the largest possible measure of freedom in the pursuit of his own devices.

The greatest of all the economists of the age of the Enlightenment and one of the most brilliant of all time was Adam Smith (1723–1790). A native of Scotland, Smith began his career as a lecturer on English literature at the University of Edinburgh. From this he was soon advanced to a professorship of logic at Glasgow College. He first won fame in 1759 with the publication of his *Theory of Moral Sentiments*. In 1776 he published his *Inquiry into the Nature and Causes of the Wealth of Nations*, generally considered the foundation of modern economic theory. In this work he maintained that labor, rather than agriculture or the bounty of nature, is the real source of wealth. While in general he accepted the principle of *laissez faire*, avowing that the prosperity of all can best be promoted

The influence of Rousseau

The influence of the new economic theory

The economics of Adam Smith

---

[10] For a discussion of the political theory of the Romantic Idealists see §3 in the chapter on The Age of Romanticism and Reaction.

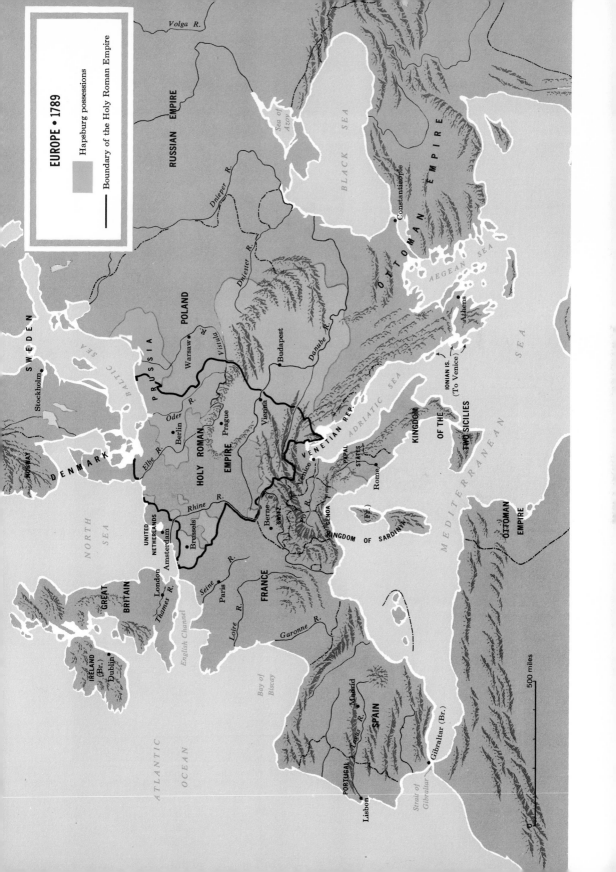

EUROPE • 1789

Hapsburg possessions

Boundary of the Holy Roman Empire

Volga R.

RUSSIAN EMPIRE

BLACK SEA

Sea of Azov

Dnieper R.

Dniester R.

OTTOMAN EMPIRE

Constantinople

AEGEAN SEA

SWEDEN

BALTIC SEA

Stockholm

POLAND

PRUSSIA

Warsaw

Vistula R.

Budapest

Danube R.

ADRIATIC SEA

Athens

IONIAN IS. ("To Venice")

NORWAY

DENMARK

Oder R.

Berlin

Elbe R.

Prague

Vienna

HOLY ROMAN EMPIRE

VENETIAN REP.

Venice

PAPAL STATES

KINGDOM OF THE TWO SICILIES

Rome

OTTOMAN EMPIRE

MEDITERRANEAN SEA

NORTH SEA

UNITED NETHERLANDS

Amsterdam

Brussels

Rhine R.

Berne

SWITZ.

Po R.

GENOA

KINGDOM OF SARDINIA (Fr.)

GREAT BRITAIN

London

Thames R.

English Channel

Seine R.

Paris

FRANCE

Loire R.

Garonne R.

IRELAND (Br.)

Dublin

Bay of Biscay

ATLANTIC OCEAN

PORTUGAL

Lisbon

Tagus R.

Madrid

SPAIN

Strait of Gibraltar

Gibraltar (Br.)

500 miles

Madame Recamier, Jacques Louis David (1748–1825). David was the exponent of a new classicism during and after the French Revolution. The couch, the lamp, and the costume are copied from Rome and Pompeii. (Louvre)

Napoleon's Coronation, David. (Versailles Museum)

by allowing each individual to pursue his own interest, he nevertheless recognized that certain forms of governmental interference would be desirable. The state should intervene for the prevention of injustice and oppression, for the advancement of education and the protection of public health, and for the maintenance of necessary enterprises which would never be established by private capital. Notwithstanding these rather broad limitations upon the principle of laissez faire, Smith's *Wealth of Nations* was adopted as Holy Writ by the economic individualists of the eighteenth and nineteenth centuries. Its influence in causing the French Revolution was indirect but none the less profound. It furnished the final answer to mercantilist argument and thereby strengthened the ambition of the bourgeoisie to have done with a political system which continued to block the path to economic freedom.

2. THE DESTRUCTION OF THE ANCIEN RÉGIME

Early in the year 1789 the volcano of discontent in France burst forth into revolution. The immediate causes were a series of economic troubles for which no one seemed to be able to find an acceptable remedy. As a consequence of bad harvests bread prices almost doubled. In December 1788, 80,000 workers were reported unemployed in Paris. Most serious of all was the near bankruptcy of the French government. To meet the mounting deficit, the king's finance ministers proposed new taxes, notably a stamp duty and a direct tax on the annual production of the soil. Meanwhile, such earlier impositions as the *taille* and the *gabelle* would continue in effect. Additional taxation might well have provided the government with the revenue it so desperately needed had there not been confusion and discord in the administration of fiscal policies. Every proposed reform threatened the interests of some powerful group. Conditions moved rapidly from bad to worse as the government continued its makeshift policy of borrowing and spending. Prices rose so rapidly that the cost of bread alone consumed more than 50 per cent of the poor man's income. In 1787 the king summoned an Assembly of Notables in the hope that the chief magnates of the realm might consent to bearing a larger share of the fiscal burden. Factional discord soon split the Assembly. The nobles of the sword and the higher clergy staunchly supported the monarchy and demanded retention of their privileges. The judicial oligarchy, or nobles of the robe, took a broader view. Inspired by the philosophy of the Enlightenment and the American Revolution, they argued not merely in favor of fiscal revision but of governmental reform. Specifically, they demanded convocation of the Estates General to deal with the national crisis.

Although the Estates General had not met for 175 years, the belief prevailed widely that it alone could save the country in a dire

The immediate causes of the French Revolution

737

FRANCE IN 1789 • THE "GOVERNMENTS"

emergency. As its name implies, the Estates General was supposed to represent the three great estates or classes of the nation. During the period when it was convoked more or less regularly, the representatives of each estate had met and voted as a body. Generally this meant that the first and second estates combined against the third. By the late eighteenth century the third estate had attained such importance that it was not willing to tolerate such an arrangement. Consequently its leaders demanded that the three orders should sit together and vote as individuals. Leaving this issue unresolved, King Louis XVI, in the summer of 1788, yielded to popular clamor and summoned the Estates General to meet in May of the following year. After weeks of wrangling, the third estate, on June 17, boldly proclaimed itself the National Assembly and invited the representatives of the privileged orders to join in its work. Many of them actually did so. Within two days a

738

majority of the clergy went over and a sprinkling of the nobles also. But then the king intervened. When the rebellious deputies assembled at their hall on the morning of June 20, they found its doors guarded by troops. There were now no alternatives but to submit or to defy the sovereign power of the monarch himself. Confident of the support of a majority of the people, the commoners and their allies withdrew to a near-by hall, variously used as a riding academy and a tennis court. Here under the leadership of Mirabeau and the Abbé Sieyès they bound themselves by a solemn oath not to separate until they had drafted a constitution for France. This Oath of the Tennis Court, on June 20, 1789, was the real beginning of the French Revolution. By claiming the authority to remake the government in the name of the people, the Estates General was not merely protesting against the arbitrary rule of Louis XVI but asserting its right to act as the highest sovereign power in the nation. On June 27 the king virtually conceded this right by ordering the remaining delegates of the privileged classes to meet with the third estate as members of a National Assembly.

The course of the French Revolution was marked by three great stages, the first of which extended from June 1789 to August 1792. During most of this period the destinies of France were in the hands of the National Assembly, dominated by the leaders of the third

The Opening of the Estates General in Versailles, May 5, 1789

The Tennis Court Oath by David. In the hall where royalty played a game known as *jeu de paume* (similar to tennis) leaders of the Revolution swore to draft a constitution. In the center of this painting with his arm extended is Jean Bailly, president of the National Assembly. Seated at the table below him is Abbé Sieyès. Somewhat to the right of Sieyès with both hands on his chest is Robespierre. Mirabeau, with hat in his left hand and wearing a black coat, stands somewhat farther to the right.

estate. In the main, this stage was a moderate, middle-class stage. The masses had not yet gained any degree of political power, nor were they in a position to seize control of the economic system. Aside from the destruction of the Bastille on July 14, 1789, and the murder of a few members of the royal guard, there was comparatively little violence in Paris or Versailles. In certain of the country districts, however, a more unruly spirit prevailed. Many of the peasants grew impatient over the delay in granting reforms and determined to deal with the situation directly. Arming themselves with pitchforks and scythes, they set out to destroy what they could of the *ancien régime*. They demolished *châteaux* of hated nobles, plundered monasteries and residences of bishops, and murdered some of the lords who offered resistance. Most of this violence occurred during the summer of 1789 and had much to do with frightening the upper classes into surrendering some of their privileges.

The most significant developments of the first stage of the Revolution were the achievements of the National Assembly between 1789 and 1791. The initial one of these achievements was the destruction of most of the relics of feudalism. This came about largely as a result of the rebellious temper displayed by the peasants. By the beginning of August 1789, such alarming reports of anarchy in the villages had reached the National Assembly that an urgent need for concessions soon came to be recognized by many of the members. On the fourth of August a certain noble proposed in an eloquent speech that all of his brethren should renounce their feudal privileges. His plea stirred the Assembly to a wild enthusiasm, compounded partly of fear and partly of revolutionary zeal. Nobles, churchmen, and burghers vied with each other in suggesting reforms. Before the night had ended, numerous remnants of the hoary structure of vested rights had been swept away. Ecclesiastical tithes and the *corvée* were formally abolished. Serfdom was eliminated. The hunting privileges of the nobles were declared at an end. Exemption from taxation and monopolies of all kinds were sacrificed as contrary to natural equality. While the nobles did not surrender all of their rights, the ultimate effect of these reforms of the "August Days" was to annihilate distinctions of rank and class and to make all Frenchmen citizens of an equal status in the eyes of the law.[11]

Achievements of the first stage: (1) the destruction of feudal privileges

Following the destruction of privilege the Assembly turned its attention to preparing a charter of liberties. The result was the Declaration of the Rights of Man and of the Citizen, issued in September 1789. Modeled in part after the English Bill of Rights and embodying the teachings of liberal political philosophers, the French Declaration was a typical middle-class document. Property was declared to be a natural right as well as liberty, security, and "resistance to oppression." No one was to be deprived of anything he possessed except in case of public necessity, and then only on condition that he should have been "previously and equitably indemnified." Proper consideration was also to be given to personal rights. Freedom of speech, religious toleration, and liberty of the press were held to be inviolable. All citizens were declared to be entitled to equality of treatment in the courts. No one was to be imprisoned or otherwise punished except in accordance with due process of law. Sovereignty was affirmed to reside in the people, and officers of the government were made subject to deposition if they abused the powers conferred upon them. Nothing was said about any right of the common man to an adequate share of the wealth he produced or even to protection by the state in case of inability to earn a living. The authors of the Declaration of Rights were not socialists, nor were they interested particularly in the economic welfare of the masses.

(2) the Declaration of the Rights of Man

ON NE CONNOIT ICI QUE LA DÉNOMINATION DE CITOYEN.

"Only the Title of Citizen Is Employed Here." A placard from the revolutionary period.

The next of the main accomplishments of the National Assembly was the secularization of the Church. Under the *ancien régime* the higher clergy had been a privileged caste, rewarding the king for his favors by a staunch support of absolute rule. As a result, the Church

[11] Along with these reforms in connection with the destruction of monopolies and feudal privileges, the guilds were also abolished and workers were forbidden to form unions.

Assignat

had come to be regarded as an instrument of greed and oppression almost as odious as the monarchy itself. Moreover, the ecclesiastical institutions were the possessors of vast estates, and the new Revolutionary government was desperately in need of funds. Accordingly, in November 1789, the National Assembly resolved to confiscate the lands of the Church and to use them as collateral for the issue of *assignats*, or paper money. In July of the following year the Civil Constitution of the Clergy was enacted, providing that all bishops and priests should be elected by the people and should be subject to the authority of the state. Their salaries were to be paid out of the public treasury, and they were required to swear allegiance to the new legislation. The secularization of the Church also involved a partial separation from Rome. The aim of the Assembly was to make the Catholic Church of France a truly national institution with no more than a nominal subjection to the papacy.

Not until 1791 did the National Assembly manage to complete its primary task of drafting a new constitution for the nation. Too many other problems of more immediate concern had absorbed its attention. Besides, autocratic government was already a thing of the past. The constitution as it finally emerged gave eloquent testimony to the dominant position now held by the bourgeoisie. France was not made a democratic republic, but the government was converted merely into a limited monarchy, with the supreme power virtually a monopoly of the well-to-do. The privilege of voting was restricted to those who paid a direct tax equal to three days' wages, while eligibility for holding office was limited to citizens of comparative wealth. As to the structure of the government, the principle of the separation of powers was to be the basic feature. For this the founders of the new system went back to Montesquieu's idea of independent legislative, executive, and judicial departments. The lawmaking powers were bestowed upon a Legislative Assembly chosen indirectly by the people through a process somewhat similar to that by which the President of the United States was originally supposed to be selected. The king was deprived of the control he had formerly exercised over the army, the Church, and local government. His ministers were forbidden to sit in the Assembly, and he was shorn of all power over the legislative process except a suspensive veto, which in fact could be overridden by the issuance of proclamations. Thus the new system, although far removed from absolute monarchy, was decidedly not a government the masses could claim as their own.

In the summer of 1792 the French Revolution entered a second stage, which lasted for about two years. This stage differed from the first in a number of ways. To begin with, France was now a republic. On the tenth of August the Legislative Assembly voted to suspend the king and ordered the election, by universal manhood suffrage, of a National Convention to draft a new constitution. Soon

The Execution of Louis XVI. The event took place on what is now the Place de la Concorde in Paris, on January 21, 1793.

afterward Louis XVI was brought to trial on charges of plotting with foreign enemies of the Revolution, and on January 21, 1793, he was beheaded. In addition to its republican character, the second stage differed from the first in the fact that it was dominated by the lower classes. No longer was the course of the Revolution dictated by relatively conservative members of the bourgeoisie. Instead, it was extremists representing the proletariat of Paris who were largely responsible for determining the nature of the movement. The liberal philosophy of Voltaire and Montesquieu was now replaced by the radical, equalitarian doctrines of Rousseau. Yet another difference was the more violent and bloody character of the second stage. This was the period not only of the execution of the king but also of the September massacres (1792) and of the Reign of Terror from the summer of 1793 to the summer of 1794.

The second or radical stage of the Revolution

What factors may be taken to explain this spectacular transition from a comparatively moderate, middle-class phase to a stage of radicalism and turmoil? First of all may be mentioned the disappointed hopes of the proletariat. The Revolution in its beginning had held out what appeared to be glorious promises of equality and justice for every citizen. Hope had been built particularly on the Declaration of Rights, in spite of its emphasis upon the sanctity of private property. But now after more than three years of social and political upheaval it was just as hard for the urban worker to earn his bread as it had been before. In actual fact, it was probably

Causes of the transition to a radical stage

743

A Contemporary Engraving of the September Massacres in Paris

harder. In the spring of 1791 the government abolished the public workshops which had provided employment for thousands who had been left jobless by the disruption of business. Moreover, new laws were passed prohibiting the formation of unions, collective bargaining, picketing, and strikes. Another disappointment developed when the common man discovered after the adoption of the Constitution of 1791 that he was not even to be allowed to vote. Ever more clearly the realization dawned that he had simply exchanged one set of masters for another. In such a state of mind he was bound to be attracted by the preaching of extremists, who offered to lead him into the Promised Land of security and plenty. A second cause of the transition to a radical stage was the accumulated momentum of the Revolution itself. Every great movement of this kind generates an atmosphere of discontent, which is breathed more deeply by some men than by others. The result is the emergence of a kind of professional revolutionist, who is eternally dissatisfied no matter how much has been accomplished. He denounces the leaders of the revolution in its preliminary stage even more scathingly than he condemns the adherents of the old order. For him, no price of slaughter and chaos is too great to pay in order to purchase the fulfillment of his own ideals. He will murder his closest associates, the moment they disagree with him, just as readily as he will consign the most hated reactionary to outer darkness. He is the political counterpart of the religious fanatic who believes that sword and faggot are proper instruments for hastening the reign of God's righteousness and peace.

Yet perhaps the most important cause of the triumph of the radicals was the outbreak of war between France and foreign states. In several European countries the progress of the French Revolution was coming to be viewed with increasing alarm by reactionary rulers. The fear was particularly strong in Austria and Prussia, where numerous *émigrés,* or French royalists, had taken refuge and were convincing the monarchs of those countries of the danger that the Revolution might spread. Besides, the French queen, Marie Antoinette, was a member of the Hapsburg family and was making frenzied appeals to the Emperor to come to the aid of her husband. In August 1791, the Austrian and Prussian rulers joined in issuing the Declaration of Pillnitz, in which they boldly avowed that the restoration of order and of the rights of the monarch in France was a matter of "common interest to all sovereigns of Europe." Naturally this pronouncement was keenly resented by the French, since it could hardly be interpreted in any other way than as a threat of intervention. Moreover, there was a tendency on the part of many of the revolutionists to welcome a conflict with a foreign enemy. While the moderate faction expected that military success would solidify the loyalty of the people to the new regime, many of the radicals were clamoring for war in the secret hope that the armies of France would suffer defeat, and that the monarchy would thereby be discredited. A republic could then be set up, and the heroic soldiers of the people would turn defeat into victory and carry the blessings of freedom to all the oppressed of Europe. With such considerations in mind, the Assembly voted for war on April 20, 1792. As the radicals had hoped, the forces of the French met serious reverses. By August the allied armies of Austria and Prussia had crossed the frontier and were threatening the capture of Paris. A fury of rage and despair seized the capital. The belief prevailed that the military disasters had been the result of treasonable dealings with the enemy on the part of the king and his conservative followers. As a consequence, a vigorous demand arose for drastic action against all who were suspected of disloyalty to the Revolution. It was this situation more than anything else which brought the extremists to the fore and enabled them to gain control of the Legislative Assembly and to put an end to the monarchy.

From 1792 to 1795—that is, during the second stage of the Revolution and for more than a year longer—the governing power of France was the National Convention. As originally set up, this body was supposed to draft a new constitution and then surrender its authority to a regular government. In 1793 a new constitution was actually drawn up, the most democratic in history thus far. It provided for universal manhood suffrage and the right of referendum. It declared that society owes a living to the poor, either by finding work for them or giving them the means of subsistence. It made the provision of education an obligation of the state. Never before had the needs of social democracy been so clearly recognized in an instrument of government. But on account of the disordered conditions of the time, the Constitution of 1793 was never put into effect. With the justification that a national

The threat of foreign intervention

The government of France during the second stage: the National Convention

745

emergency existed, the Convention simply prolonged its life from year to year. After the spring of 1793 it delegated its executive functions to a group of nine (later twelve) of its members, known as the Committee of Public Safety. This agency conducted foreign relations, supervised the command of the armies, and enforced the Reign of Terror. The Convention itself was composed of a number of factions representing various shades of radical opinion. The most important were the Girondists and the Jacobins. The Girondists drew their support largely from regions outside of Paris and were inclined to distrust the proletariat. They were republicans but not extreme democrats. Their Jacobin opponents were among the most thoroughgoing radicals of the Revolution.[12] Though most of them sprang from the middle class, they were ardent disciples of Rousseau and militant champions of the urban workers. They accused the Girondists of desiring an "aristocratic republic" and of plotting to destroy the unity of France by putting into effect some kind of federal plan in which the *départements* or provinces would be exalted at the expense of Paris.

Leadership in the National Convention was furnished by some of the most interesting and dramatic personalities of modern history. Famous among those who usually identified themselves with the Girondists were Thomas Paine (1737–1809) and the Marquis de Condorcet (1743–1794). Following his brilliant work as a pamphleteer in the American Revolution, Paine sailed for England, determined to open the eyes of the people of that country "to the madness and stupidity of the government." In 1791 he published his celebrated *Rights of Man*, a blistering attack upon Edmund Burke's *Reflections on the Revolution in France*, issued the previous year. *The Rights of Man* created a sensation, especially after the bungling attempts of the government to suppress it. The author was indicted for treason, but he escaped to France before he could be seized for trial. In 1792 he was elected to the National Convention and immediately began an active career as one of the more moderate leaders of that body. He urged the destruction of the monarchy but opposed the execution of the king on the ground that it would alienate American sympathy. Ultimately he incurred the suspicion of some of the extremists and escaped the guillotine by the sheerest accident.

A man of milder temperament than Paine but of similar philosophic interests was the Marquis de Condorcet. Originally a disciple of Voltaire and Turgot, he eventually went considerably beyond these bourgeois liberals in his demands for reform. He condemned not only the evils of absolutism, mercantilism, slavery, and war, as did many of the enlightened thinkers of his time, but he was one of the first to insist that the elimination of poverty should be a cardinal

Thomas Paine

The moderate leaders in the National Convention: (1) Thomas Paine

(2) Condorcet

[12] The Jacobin Club had not always been radical. During the earlier years of the Revolution it had numbered among its members such well-known moderates as Mirabeau, Sieyès, and Lafayette. In 1791, however, it had come under the domination of extremists led by Maximilien Robespierre.

purpose of statecraft. He thought that this end could be largely attained through the destruction of monopoly and privilege and the abolition of primogeniture and entail. The removal of these obstacles would permit a wide distribution of property, especially land, and thereby enable most individuals to achieve economic independence. He also advocated old-age pensions and cooperative banking to provide cheap credit.[13] At the height of the Terror, Condorcet was outlawed for denouncing the violence of the Jacobins and was compelled to flee for his life. Disguised as a carpenter, he wandered half-starved through the country until one night he aroused suspicion, was apprehended, and thrown into prison. The next morning he was found dead on the floor. Whether he collapsed from suffering and exposure or swallowed poison he was supposed to have carried in a ring is unknown.

Foremost among the leaders of the extremist factions were Marat, Danton, and Robespierre. Jean Paul Marat (1743-1793) was educated as a physician, and, by 1789, had already earned enough distinction in that profession to be awarded an honorary degree by St. Andrews University in Scotland. Almost from the beginning of the Revolution he stood as a champion of the common people. He opposed nearly all of the dogmatic assumptions of his middle-class colleagues in the Assembly, including the idea that France should pattern her government after that of Great Britain, which he recognized to be oligarchic in form. He was soon made a victim of persecution and was forced to find refuge in sewers and dungeons, but this did not stop him from his efforts to rouse the people to a defense of their rights. In 1793 he was stabbed through the heart by Charlotte Corday, a young woman who was fanatically devoted to the Girondists. In contrast with Marat, Georges Jacques Danton (1759-1794) did not come into prominence until the Revolution was three years old, but, like Marat, he directed his activities toward goading the masses into rebellion. Elected a member of the Committee of Public Safety in 1793, he had much to do with organizing the Reign of Terror. As time went on he appears to have wearied of ruthlessness and displayed a tendency to compromise. This gave his opponents in the Convention their opportunity, and in April 1794, he was sent to the guillotine. Upon mounting the scaffold he is reported to have said: "Show my head to the people; they do not see the like every day."

The most famous and perhaps the greatest of all the extremist leaders was Maximilien Robespierre (1758-1794). Born of a family reputed to be of Irish descent, Robespierre was trained for the law and speedily achieved a modest success as an advocate. In 1782 he was appointed a criminal judge, but soon resigned because he could not bear to impose a sentence of death. Of a nervous and timid disposition, he was never able to display much executive ability, but he

The extremist leaders: Marat and Danton

Robespierre

Robespierre

[13] J. S. Schapiro, *Condorcet and the Rise of Liberalism*, pp. 142-55.

made up for this lack of talent by fanatical devotion to principle. He had adopted the belief that the philosophy of Rousseau held the one great hope of salvation for all mankind. To put this philosophy into practice he was ready to employ any means that would bring results, regardless of the cost to himself or to others. This passionate loyalty to a gospel that exalted the masses eventually won him a following. Indeed, he was so lionized by the public that he was allowed to wear the knee breeches, silk stockings, and powdered hair of the old society until the end of his life. In 1791 he was accepted as the oracle of the Jacobin Club, now purged of all but its most radical elements. Later he became president of the National Convention and a member of the Committee of Public Safety. Though he had little or nothing to do with originating the Reign of Terror, he was nevertheless responsible for enlarging its scope. He actually came to justify ruthlessness as a necessary and therefore laudable means to revolutionary progress. In the last six weeks of his virtual dictatorship, no fewer than 1285 heads rolled from the scaffold in Paris. But sooner or later such methods were bound to bring his own doom. On July 28, 1794, he and twenty-one of his lieutenants were beheaded, after no more pretense of a trial than Robespierre himself had allowed to his opponents.

The actual extent of violence during the second stage of the Revolution will probably never be known. Many of the stories of horrible butchery that circulated then and later were highly exaggerated. No streets ran red with blood and no rivers were clogged with corpses. Nevertheless, an appalling amount of bloodshed did actually occur. During the period of the Terror, from September 1793 to July 1794, the most reliable estimates place the number of executions at approximately 20,000 in France as a whole. A law of September 17, 1793, made every person who had been identified in any way with the Bourbon government or with the Girondists an object of suspicion; and no one who was a suspect or who was suspected of being a suspect was entirely safe from persecution. When some time later the Abbé Sieyès was asked what he had done to distinguish himself during the Terror, he responded dryly, "I lived." Yet when all is said, it must be conceded that the slaughter during the French Revolution was much less than that which has accompained most civil and international wars. The 20,000 victims of the Reign of Terror can hardly be compared, for example, to the hundreds of thousands slain during the American War between the States. Napoleon Bonaparte, whom many people worship as a hero, was responsible for at least twenty times as many deaths as all of the members of the Committee of Public Safety. This comparison is not meant to condone the savagery of the Terror, but it may serve to correct a distorted picture.

Despite the violence of the Reign of Terror, the second stage of the French Revolution was marked by some worthy achievements.

Jacobins. Contemporary drawings by Heuriot.

Meeting of a Revolutionary Committee during the Reign of Terror

Such leaders as Robespierre, fanatical though they might have been, were nevertheless sincere humanitarians, and it was not to be expected that they would ignore the opportunity to inaugurate reforms. Among their most significant accomplishments were the abolition of slavery in the colonies; the prohibition of imprisonment for debt; the establishment of the metric system of weights and measures; and the repeal of primogeniture, so that property might not be inherited exclusively by the oldest son but must be divided in substantially equal portions among all of the immediate heirs. The Convention also attempted to supplement the decrees of the National Assembly in abolishing the remnants of feudalism and in providing for greater freedom of economic opportunity. The property of enemies of the Revolution was confiscated for the benefit of the government and the lower classes. Great estates were broken up and offered for sale to poorer citizens on easy terms. The indemnities hitherto promised to the nobles for the loss of their privileges were abruptly canceled. To curb the rise in the cost of living, maximum prices for grain and other necessities were fixed by law, and merchants who profiteered at the expense of the poor were threatened with the guillotine. Still other measures of reform were those in the sphere of religion. At one time during the Terror an effort was made to abolish Christianity and to substitute the worship of Reason in its place. In accordance with this purpose a new calendar was adopted, dating the year from the birth of the republic (September 22, 1792) and dividing the months in such a way as to eliminate the Christian Sunday. When Robespierre came to power, he supplanted this cult of Reason by a deistic religion dedicated to the worship of a Supreme Being and to the belief in the immortality of the soul. Finally, in 1794, the Convention took the more sensible step of mak-

Reforms achieved during the second stage

749

The Death of Marat. Painting by David.

ing religion a private concern of the individual. It was decided that church and state should be entirely separate, and that all beliefs not actually hostile to the government should be tolerated.

In the summer of 1794 the Reign of Terror came to an end, and soon afterward the Revolution passed into its third and final stage. The event which inaugurated the change was the Thermidorian Reaction, so called from the month of Thermidor (heat month—July 19 to August 18) in the new calendar. The execution of Robespierre on July 28, 1794 represented the completion of a cycle. The Revolution had now devoured its own children. One after another the radical giants had fallen—first Marat, then Hébert and Danton, and now finally Robespierre and Saint-Just. The only remaining leaders in the Convention were men of moderate sympathies. As time went on they inclined toward increasing conservatism and toward any kind of political chicanery which would serve to keep them in power. Gradually the Revolution came once more to reflect the interests of the bourgeoisie. Much of the extremist work of the radicals was now undone. The law of maximum prices and the law against "suspects" were both repealed. Political prisoners were freed, the Jacobins were driven into hiding, and the Committee of Public Safety was shorn of its despotic powers. The new situation made possible the return of priests, royalists, and other *émigrés* from abroad to add the weight of their influence to the conservative trend.

In 1795 the National Convention adopted a new constitution, which lent the stamp of official approval to the victory of the pros-

The end of the second stage: the Thermidorian Reaction

perous classes. The new organic law, known as the Constitution of the Year III, granted suffrage to all adult male citizens who could read and write, but they were permitted to vote only for electors, who in turn would choose the members of the Legislative Body; and in order to be an elector, one had to be the proprietor of a farm or other establishment with an annual income equivalent to at least 100 days of labor. It was thus made certain that the authority of the government would actually be derived from citizens of considerable wealth. Since it was not practicable to restore the monarchy, lest the old aristocracy also come back into power, executive authority was vested in a board of five men known as the Directory, chosen by the legislative body. The new constitution included not only a bill of rights but also a declaration of the *duties* of the citizen. Conspicuous among the latter was the obligation to bear in mind that "it is upon the maintenance of property . . . that the whole social order rests."

The third stage of the French Revolution was of little historical importance compared with the other two. In general it was a period of stagnation, wholesale corruption, and cynicism. The burning zeal for reform that had characterized the other two stages now disappeared into thin air. The members of the new government were interested much more in opportunities for personal profit than in the shining ideals of philosophers for remaking the world. Graft was a familiar accompaniment of the levying and collecting of taxes and the disbursement of public funds. Even some members of the Directory coolly demanded bribes as the price of favors which the duties of their office should normally have required them to bestow. This cynical greed in high places was bound to have its effect upon the tone of society. It is therefore not surprising that the age of the Di-

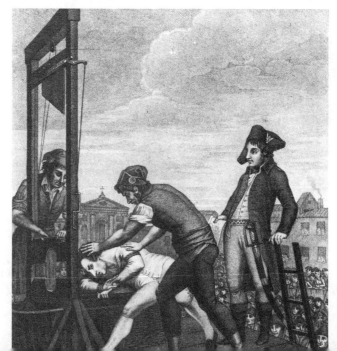

The Death of Robespierre

The end of the
Revolution: the
coup d'état of
Napoleon
Bonaparte

rectory should have been a period of riotous extravagance, dissipation, and frenzied pursuit of wealth. Speculation and gambling tended to crowd legitimate business into a secondary place. While famine stalked the slums of Paris, profiteers accumulated fortunes and flaunted their gains at the expense of the people in senseless display. Thus were the glorious promises of the Revolution trailed in the mud, even by some who had originally sworn to uphold them.

In the fall of 1799 the Revolution in France came to a close. The event that marked its end was the *coup d'état* of Napoleon Bonaparte on the eighteenth Brumaire (November 9). This, however, was merely the final blow. For some time the regime set up by the Constitution of the Year III had been hovering on the verge of collapse. Though for a while it was bolstered up by victories in the war which was still going on against foreign enemies of the Revolution, eventually even this support was torn away. In 1798–1799 the aggressive policy of the Directory had involved France in a struggle with a new combination of powerful foes—Great Britain, Austria, and Russia. The fortunes of battle soon shifted. One after another the satellite states the French had erected on their eastern frontier collapsed. The armies of the republic were driven from Italy. Soon it appeared as if all the gains of previous years were to be blotted out. Meanwhile the Directory had been suffering an even greater loss of prestige from its conduct of internal affairs. Thousands of people were disgusted with the shameful corruption of public officials and their indifference to the needs of the poor. To make matters worse, the government was partly responsible for a serious financial crisis. In order to defray the cost of wars and to make up for the extravagance of incompetent officials, the issuance of *assignats* or paper money was increased. The inevitable results were wild inflation and utter chaos. Within a short time the *assignats* had depreciated until they were actually worth no more

The Eighteenth Brumaire: A Detail of Napoleon. Painting by Bronchot.

than 1 per cent of their face value. By 1797 conditions had grown so hopeless that the only alternative was to repudiate all of the outstanding paper currency. During the period of financial chaos millions of cautious and respectable citizens who had managed to accumulate some property were reduced to the level of proletarians. The effect was naturally to turn them into bitter enemies of the existing government.

Under these deplorable circumstances the accession of Napoleon Bonaparte was rendered comparatively easy. Disgust with the banality and indifference of the Directory, resentment on account of the hardships suffered from the inflation, the sense of being humiliated as a result of defeat in the war—these were the factors which encouraged a widespread conviction that the existing regime was intolerable, and that only the appearance of a "man on horseback" could save the nation from ruin. In other words, Napoleon rose to power under conditions quite similar to those which presided at the birth of more recent dictatorships in Germany and Italy. But, of course, young Bonaparte was a military hero, which Hitler and Mussolini were not. In 1795 he had endeared himself to the friends of law and order by defending the National Convention with a "whiff of grapeshot" against an uprising of Parisian insurgents. Later he had come trailing clouds of glory from his campaigns in Italy and in Egypt. True, his reports of success in the latter country were slightly colored, but they convinced patriotic Frenchmen that here at last was a general in whose skill they could place absolute trust. Besides, no one could doubt the fact that he had driven the Austrians from Italy and had added Savoy and Nice and the Austrian Netherlands to France. It is no wonder that he should have come to be regarded as the man of the hour. His name became a symbol of national greatness and the glorious achievements of the Revolution. And as the revulsion of feeling against the Directory increased, he was hailed more than ever as the incorruptible hero who would deliver the nation from shame and disaster.

The reasons for Napoleon's triumph

3. THE GOOD AND EVIL FRUITS OF THE REVOLUTION

While the coming to power of Napoleon Bonaparte as a military dictator marked the beginning of a new era, it by no means erased the influence of the French Revolution. Indeed, as will subsequently be shown, Napoleon himself preserved quite a few of the Revolutionary achievements and posed as an embattled champion of Equality and Fraternity, if not of Liberty. But even if he had done none of these things, the heritage of the Revolution would most certainly have survived. No movement which had so thoroughly shaken the foundations of society could ever have passed into history without leaving a train of momentous results. Its influence reverberated through most of the years of the nineteenth century

The influence of the French Revolution

"Am I Not Your Brother?"
An antislavery woodcut from
the revolutionary period in
France.

and was felt in a score of nations of the Western world. The new passion for liberty was the activating force behind numerous insurrections and so-called revolutions which punctuated the period between 1800 and 1850. First came the uprising of the Spaniards against Joseph Bonaparte in 1808. This was followed by a veritable epidemic of revolutionary disturbances between 1820 and 1831 in such countries as Greece, Italy, Spain, France, Belgium, and Poland. Finally, the revolutionary movements of 1848 were far from unrelated to the great French upheaval of 1789, since most of them were infused with the same nationalist enthusiasm and with similar ideals of political liberty.

The French Revolution also had other results of more enduring character and of greater benefit to mankind as a whole. It dealt, first of all, a powerful blow to absolute monarchy. Thenceforth few kings dared to claim an unlimited authority. Even though a Bourbon was restored to the throne of France in 1814, he made no pretensions to a divine appointment to rule as he liked. Secondly, the French Revolution was responsible for the destruction of most of the remnants of a decadent feudalism, including serfdom and the feudal privileges of the nobles. The guilds also were abolished, never to be revived. Though a few of the elements of mercantilism still survived, its days as a recognized policy of governments were numbered. Although the separation of church and state, accomplished in 1794, was eventually nullified by Napoleon, it nevertheless furnished a precedent for an ultimate divorce of religion from politics, not only in France but in other countries as well. Among the remaining beneficial results of the Revolution may be mentioned the abolition of slavery in the French colonies, the elimination of imprisonment for debt, the overthrow of the rule of primogeniture, and a wider distribution of land through the breaking up of great estates. Finally, the groundwork of two of Napoleon's most significant achievements, his educational reforms and his codification of the laws, was actually prepared by Revolutionary leaders.

On the other hand, the fact cannot be ignored that the French Revolution bore some bitter fruit. It was largely responsible for the growth of jingoistic nationalism as a dominant ideal. Nationalism, of course, was nothing new. It can be traced almost as far back as the unfoldment of the earliest civilizations. It manifested itself in the Chosen People belief of the Hebrews and in the racial exclusiveness of the Greeks. Nevertheless, nationalism did not really become an all-pervading force until after the French Revolution. It was the pride of the French people in what they had achieved and their determination to protect those achievements that gave rise to a fanatical patriotism exemplified in the stirring battle song, the *Marseillaise*. For the first time in modern history a whole nation was girded for war. In contrast to the relatively small professional armies of former days, the National Convention in 1793 enrolled a force of

The legacy of
evil results

754

nearly 800,000 men, while millions behind the lines devoted their energies to the task of suppressing disaffection at home. Workers, peasants, and bourgeois citizens alike rallied to the slogan of "Liberty, Equality, and Fraternity" as to a holy cause. The cosmopolitanism and pacifism of the philosophers of the Enlightenment were completely forgotten. Later this militant patriotism infected other lands, contributing the weight of its influence to notions of national superiority and to racial hatreds. Finally, the French Revolution resulted in a deplorable cheapening of human life. The butchery of thousands during the Reign of Terror, often for no crime at all but merely as a method of striking fear into the hearts of enemies of the Revolution, tended to create the impression that the life of a man was of very small worth compared to the noble aims of the faction in power. Perhaps this impression helps to explain the comparative indifference with which France accepted, a few years later, the sacrifice of hundreds of thousands of her citizens to satisfy the boundless ambitions of Napoleon.

SELECTED READINGS

· *Items so designated are available in paperbound editions.*

Aldridge, A. D., *Man of Reason: the Life of Thomas Paine*, London, 1960.
• Arendt, Hannah, *On Revolution*, New York, 1963 (Compass).
Barber, E. G., *The Bourgeoisie in Eighteenth-Century France*, Princeton, 1955.
• Brinton, C. C., *A Decade of Revolution, 1789–1799*, New York, 1934 (Torchbook). Stimulating and critical.
——, *The Jacobins: An Essay in the New History*, New York, 1930.
• Cobban, Alfred, *Aspects of the French Revolution*, New York, 1970 (Norton Library).
——, *In Search of Humility; the Role of the Enlightenment in Modern History*, London, 1960.
Cone, Carl B., *The English Jacobins*, New York, 1968.
• Ford, Franklin, *Robe and Sword: The Regrouping of the French Aristocracy after Louis XIV*, Cambridge, Mass., 1953 (Torchbook).
Gershoy, Leo, *The French Revolution, 1789–1799*, New York, 1932. A dependable summary.
•——, *From Despotism to Revolution*, New York, 1944 (Torchbook). Valuable for background of the Revolution.
• Geyl, Pieter, *Napoleon, For and Against*, New Haven, 1949 (Yale University Press).
• Gooch, G. P., *English Democratic Ideas in the Seventeenth Century*, New York, 1962 (Torchbook).
Gooch, R. K., *Parliamentary Government in France, Revolutionary Origins, 1781–1791*, Ithaca, N.Y., 1960.
Gottschalk, L. R., *The Era of the French Revolution*, New York, 1929.
——, *Jean Paul Marat; a Study in Radicalism*, New York, 1927.
Hampson, Norman, *A Social History of the French Revolution*, Toronto, 1963.
Kerr, W. B., *The Reign of Terror, 1793–94*, Toronto, 1927.
• Lefebvre, Georges, *The Coming of the French Revolution*, Princeton, 1947 (Vintage). An excellent study of the causes and early events of the Revolution.

755

READINGS   · Martin, Kingsley, *French Liberal Thought in the Eighteenth Century*, Boston, 1929 (Torchbook).

· Mathiez, Albert, *The French Revolution*, New York, 1928 (Universal Library). A liberal interpretation.

Moore, J. M., *The Roots of French Republicanism*, New York, 1962.

O'Gorman, F., *The Whig Party and the French Revolution*, New York, 1967.

Palmer, R. R., *The Age of the Democratic Revolution: A Political History of Europe and America, 1760–1800*, Princeton, 1964.

· ——, *Twelve Who Ruled*, Princeton, 1941 (Atheneum). Excellent biographical and interpretive studies.

——, *The World of the French Revolution*, New York, 1970.

· Rudé, George, *The Crowd in History: A Study of Popular Disturbances in France and England, 1730–1848*, New York, 1964 (Wiley).

Schapiro, J. S., *Condorcet and the Rise of Liberalism in France*, New York, 1934. A splendid study of revolutionary idealism.

Sée, Henri, *Economic and Social Conditions in France during the Eighteenth Century*, New York, 1927.

Sydenham, M. J., *The Girdondins*, London, 1961. A reinterpretation of the significance of this faction.

Thompson, J. M., *Leaders of the French Revolution*, New York, 1929.

· ——, *Robespierre and the French Revolution*, New York, 1953 (Collier). An excellent short biography.

SOURCE MATERIALS

Higgins, E. L., *The French Revolution as Told by Contemporaries*, Boston, 1938.

Locke, John, *Second Treatise on Civil Government* (Everyman Library ed.), London, 1924.

· Montesquieu, Baron de, *The Spirit of Laws*, especially Books, I, II, III, XI (Hafner Library of World Classics).

Rousseau, J. J., *The Social Contract* (Everyman Library ed.), London, 1913.

Sieyès, Abbé, *What Is the Third Estate?*

Smith, Adam, *The Wealth of Nations*, Introduction and Books I, IV.

Stewart, J. H., *A Documentary Survey of the French Revolution*, New York, 1951.

· Tocqueville, Alexis de, *The Old Regime and the French Revolution*, Garden · City, L. I., 1955 (Anchor).

University of Pennsylvania Translations and Reprints, Vol. I, No. 5, Declaration of the Rights of Man and of the Citizen.

Young, Arthur, *Travels in France during the Years 1787, 1788, 1789*, New York, 1929. A contemporary account of the life of the peasants.

756

CHAPTER 25

Romanticism and Reaction
(1800-1830)

The principle of non-intervention is very popular in England; false in its essence, it may be maintained by an island-state. New France has not failed to appropriate this principle and to proclaim it loudly. It is brigands who object to police, and incendiaries who complain about firemen. We can never admit a claim as subversive as this is of all social order; we recognize, however, that we always have the right to answer any appeal for help addressed to us by a legitimate authority, just as we recognize that we have the right of extinguishing the fire in a neighbor's house in order to prevent its catching our own.

—Prince Metternich, 1830

The century that followed the French Revolution was a period of rapid and tremendous change. By comparison, life in preceding ages seems almost static. Never before in so short a time had there been such radical alteration of modes of living or such wholesale destruction of venerable tradition. As a result of a welter of inventions the speed of living was accelerated to a pace which would have startled Leonardo da Vinci or Sir Isaac Newton. The population of Europe increased from 180 million at the close of the French Revolution to the almost incredible total of 460 million by 1914. Never before in little more than a century had anything like such an increase occurred. As a result life for modern man took on a degree of complexity and variety hitherto unknown. New political and social ideals multiplied in bewildering confusion. The entire age was an age of flux, of conflicting tendencies and sharp disagreements over the problems of society. We must not suppose, however, that the nineteenth century was totally unrelated to preceding periods. Although Napolean declared after his *coup d'état* of 1799 that the great aims of the years of turbulence had been accomplished, such was not really the case. In the minds of a great many people

Character of the new age

757

the objectives of the French Revolution remained as goals worth striving for. Through a period of thirty years and more the Western world was disturbed by what virtually amounted to a civil war between the defenders of those goals and those who would repudiate freedom and equality and force men back under obedience to authority. It was a condition not unlike that which followed the Russian revolution of 1917 when a conflict between Communists and their opponents fanned out into other countries and eventually took on global dimensions.

1. THE SIGNIFICANCE OF NAPOLEON

We have seen that the *coup d'état* of the eighteenth Brumaire dealt what seemed to be a final blow to the French Revolution.

Napoleon not a
true son of the
French Revo-
lution

Therefore, the period of Napoleon's rule, from November 1799 to April 1814 and during the Hundred Days from March until June 1815, may properly be regarded as the initial stage of the nineteenth-century reaction against the liberal ideals which had made the Revolution possible. To be sure, Napoleon professed to be in sympathy with some of these ideals, but he established a form of government scarcely compatible with any of them. His real aim, so far as it concerned the work of the Revolution, was to preserve those achievements which comported with national greatness and with his own ambitions for military glory. In other words, he fostered and strengthened Revolutionary patriotism and continued those accomplishments of his predecessors which could be adapted to the purposes of concentrated government. But liberty in the sense of the inviolability of personal rights meant nothing to him; in fact, he declared that what the French people needed was not liberty but equality. Moreover, he interpreted equality as meaning little more than a fair opportunity for all regardless of birth. That is, he did not propose to restore serfdom or to give back the land to the old nobility, but neither did he plan any restrictions upon the economic activities of the rich.

In order to understand the historical significance of Napoleon, it is necessary to know something of his personal life and of the part

The early ca-
reer of Napo-
leon

he played in the dramatic events preceding his rise to power. Born in 1769 in a little town in Corsica just a year after the island had been ceded to France, Napoleon was the son of a proud but impoverished family that held a title of nobility from the republic of Genoa. In 1779 he entered a school at Brienne in France and five years later was admitted to the military academy in Paris. As a student he appears to have led an unhappy existence, abstaining from all social pleasures, eating dry bread to save expenses, and growing ever more bitter against the French, whom he accused of enslaving his fellow Corsicans. He achieved no distinction in any academic subject except mathematics, but he applied himself so assiduously to military science that he won a commission as a sub-lieutenant of artillery at the age of sixteen. The progress of the Revolution and the outbreak of foreign war brought rapid promotion, since many of the officers appointed under the *ancien régime* fled from the country. By 1793 he had become Colonel Bonaparte and had been entrusted with the difficult task of expelling the British from Toulon. Soon afterward he was rewarded with a promotion to brigadier-general. In 1795 he defended the National Convention against an uprising of reactionaries in Paris and was placed in command the following year of the expedition against the Austrians in Italy. His brilliant success in this campaign elevated him to the status of a national hero. His name was on everybody's lips. Politicians feared him and tumbled over one another to grant his every desire. While the comfortable classes adored him as a bulwark against radicalism, many ordinary folk were deceived by his honeyed pledges of devotion to Revolutionary doctrine. To all whose emotions had been set aflame by the new patriotism he loomed as the symbol of victory and of hope for a glorious future.

Had conditions in France been more stable than they were in 1799, it is probable that Napoleon Bonaparte would have lived out his days as no more than a talented army officer. But we have seen that conditions in this and in preceding years were exceedingly chaotic. Corruption, profiteering, and financial ruin added to the woes of a people already bowed down by the miseries of a long revolution. So profound was the mood of despair that thousands welcomed a new despotism as the only hope of relief. Besides, the government of the Directory was shot through with intrigue. One of its members, the Abbé Sieyès, was actually conspiring to overthrow it and was casting about for a popular hero to assist him. Napoleon had the advantage of being married to the mistress of one of the Directors, but his triumph was due also to certain qualities of his own personality. He was shrewd, egotistical, and unscrupulous. He had the sagacity to perceive that the people were tired of disorder and corruption, and that they longed for the return of stability. Convinced that destiny had touched his brow, he determined to let nothing stand in the way of fulfillment of his lofty ambitions. Moreover, he was endowed with an indefatigable energy. He endeared himself to his soldiers by his ability to withstand hardships and by his infinite capacity for personal attention to every detail necessary to the success of a military campaign. Lastly, Napoleon had a keen instinct for the dramatic, a gift of eloquence, and a magnetic ability to exact from his followers the highest measure of devotion. He knew how to make the most of an inspiring setting and to fill the imaginations of all around him with magnificent visions of glory and power.

The new regime set up by Napoleon after the *coup d'état* of the eighteenth Brumaire was a thinly disguised autocracy. The constitution, drafted by the conspirators themselves, bore some of the hall-

THE SIGNIFICANCE OF NAPOLEON

Napoleon. A famous unfinished painting by David.

Napoleon's triumph

The Empress Josephine

marks of democracy, but the whole system depended in last analysis upon the will of the executive. Yet the framers of the constitution made a pretense of deferring to popular sovereignty, since the principle of universal manhood suffrage was revived. In December 1799, the new instrument of government was submitted to a popular referendum and was approved by a stupendous majority. When the votes were finally counted, it was found (or at least it was claimed) that only 1562 out of more than 3,000,000 had been cast in the negative. However, 4,000,000 eligible voters had abstained. The constitution thus adopted went into effect on January 1, 1800; but since the Revolutionary calendar was still technically in force, it is known as the Constitution of the Year VIII.

Though Napoleon was now an absolute monarch in nearly everything but name, he still was not satisfied. In 1802 he obtained the consent of the people to extend his term of office from ten years to life. All that then remained was to make his position hereditary. In 1804 by another plebiscite he won permission to convert the government into an empire. Soon afterward, in the midst of impressive ceremonies in the Cathedral of Notre Dame, he placed a crown upon his own head and assumed the title of Napoleon I, Emperor of the French. His action in making this change was influenced partly by the growth of opposition. Several attempts had recently been made to take his life, and royalist plots were being hatched against him. Napoleon proceeded against the conspirators with characteristic ruthlessness. Scores were arrested upon mere suspicion, and some of the most prominent were singled out for execution. Having thus disposed of his chief enemies, Napoleon evidently concluded that the best way to guard against future trouble would be to establish a dynasty of his own and thereby cut the ground from under all Bourbon pretenders. Especially if he could obtain for his rule the benediction of the Church, there would be few who would dare to oppose him. For this reason, he brought Pope Pius VII all the way from Rome to officiate at his coronation, though he was careful to produce the impression that His Holiness was acting as the mere agent of God and not as an international sovereign who could create and depose the emperor.

It is unfortunately true that most of the fame of Napoleon Bonaparte rests upon his exploits as a soldier. His work as a statesman was much more important. In the latter capacity he made at least a few notable contributions to civilization. He confirmed the redistribution of land accomplished by the Revolution, thereby permitting the average peasant to remain an independent farmer. He eliminated graft and waste from the government, reformed the system of taxation, and established the Bank of France to promote a more efficient control over fiscal affairs. He drained marshes, enlarged harbors, built bridges, and constructed a network of roads and canals. Most of these achievements were completed mainly for military purposes, but partly also in order to win the support of the commercial classes. In addition, he centralized the government of France, dividing the country into uniform districts or *départements*, each under a prefect taking orders from Paris.[1] Perhaps his accomplishment of greatest significance was his completion of the educational and legal reforms begun during the Revolution. He ordered the establishment of *lycées* or high schools in every important town, and a normal school in Paris for the training of teachers. To supplement these changes, he brought the military and technical schools under control of the state and founded a national university to exercise supervision over the entire system. But he was never willing to allocate more than a small fraction of his budget for educational purposes, with the consequence that only a tiny proportion of the children of France received instruction at the expense of the state. In 1810, with the aid of a staff of jurists, he completed his famous Code Napoléon, a revision and codification of the civil and criminal laws on the basis of plans worked out by the National Convention. Despite its harsh provisions—the death penalty, for example, was retained for theft, parricides were to have their hands cut off before execution, and slavery was reestablished in the colonies—the Code Napoléon was hailed as the work of a second Justinian. With modifications it remained the law of France and Belgium for more than a century, and substantial portions of it were incorporated in the legal systems of Germany, Italy, Switzerland, Japan, and the French colony of Louisiana, where it was to persist even after the purchase of that territory by the United States.

Napoleon's work as a statesman included many other changes in the political system of France. For one thing, he restored the union between the Catholic Church and the state. In 1801 he signed a Concordat with the Pope, which provided that bishops be nominated by the First Consul and that the salaries of the clergy be paid by the government. Even if the Catholic Church did not regain the legal monopoly it had enjoyed under the *ancien régime*, since other religions were also to be tolerated, it was nevertheless placed in a position of decided advantage and was thereby able to increase its power in succeeding years. Not until 1905, when the Concordat of 1801 was finally broken, was Catholicism again reduced to equality with other faiths. Napoleon was responsible also for curtailing the liberties of his subjects almost from the moment he came into power. He abolished trial by jury in certain cases, imposed a strict censorship on the press, and suspended many journals that he suspected of being hostile toward his policies.

Although a detailed account of Napoleon's campaigns must be left to the military historian, the subject cannot be ignored. His ex-

Other results of Napoleon's statecraft

---

[1] The *départments* were originally established by the Revolutionary National Assembly, but not under a centralized arrangement. Their officers were to be elected by the people.

The Battle of Trafalgar. This engraving by Pollard after a painting by Serres depicts one of the decisive events in British history. It was in this battle that Napoleon's naval power was destroyed, along with any hope that he might have had of conquering Britain.

ploits as a military commander had considerable effect in shaping the course of history. To his credit it should perhaps be said that the wars in which he engaged were not all of his own making. Upon his accession to power in 1799 he inherited from the Directory the struggle with the Second Coalition, composed of Great Britain, Austria and Russia.[2] By a series of brilliant forays he eliminated Austria and Prussia from the war and neutralized Italy and the Netherlands. Russia withdrew, while Britain bided her time.

By 1808 the star of Napoleon was at its zenith. He was master of nearly all of the Continent of Europe west of Russia. He had destroyed what was left of the Holy Roman Empire and had brought most of the German states outside of Austria into a Confederation of the Rhine of which he himself was Protector. He had not only extended the boundaries of France, but he had created as his personal domain a new kingdom of Italy including the Po valley and what had once been the republic of Venice. In addition, he had placed relatives and friends on several of the remaining thrones of Europe. His brother Joseph had been made king of Naples, his brother Louis king of Holland, and his brother Jerome king of Westphalia. He had selected his friend, the king of Saxony, to be the ruler of the duchy of Warsaw, a new Poland created mainly out of territories taken from Prussia. Not since the days of Charles V had so much of Europe been dominated by any one man. Yet Napoleon's position was far from secure, for he still had the "contemptible nation of shopkeepers" across the English Channel to deal with.

The beginning of Napoleon's wars: the destruction of the Second Coalition

Napoleon at the zenith of his power

See color map at page 768

[2] The First Coalition was the original combination of European powers formed in opposition to the French Revolution. It was organized in 1793 and was made up of Austria, Prussia, Great Britain, Spain, Holland, and some lesser states.

Having lost to the British in the great naval battle of Trafalgar (October 1805), he determined to wear them down by the indirect method of ruining their commerce. In 1806 and the years following he established his famous Continental System, a scheme by which his various puppet states were obliged to cooperate with France in excluding British goods from the whole of Continental Europe. By depriving the English nation of its markets, Napoleon hoped that he could eventually sap its wealth to such a degree that the people would turn against their government and force it to capitulate. By the Treaty of Tilsit he even managed to bring Russia into the scheme.

The story of Napoleon's career from 1808 to 1815 is a record of the gradual decay of his fortunes. From his overthrow of the Directory in 1799 to the Peace of Tilsit in 1807 he had steadily climbed to an eminence which even an Alexander or a Caesar might well have envied. But soon after the latter event his difficulties began to multiply until finally they overwhelmed him in disaster. The explanation is to be found in several factors. First of all, with the passage of the years, he grew more egotistical, and therefore less inclined to accept advice even from his most capable subordinates. He kept nurturing the idea that he was a man of destiny until it developed into an obsession, a superstitious fatalism that destroyed the resiliency of his mind. Second, his aggressive militarism provoked an inevitable reaction among its victims. The more it became evident that Napoleon's conquests were the sordid fruits of a maniacal ambition for power, the stronger was the determination of the vanquished to regain their freedom. Peoples that had at one time mistakenly welcomed him as an apostle of Revolutionary liberty now turned against him as a hated foreign oppressor. In addition, militarism was producing its effect upon France itself. The bones of hundreds of thousands of the best young men of the nation had been strewn in the dust of battlefields all over Europe. The problem not merely of filling their places in the ranks of the army but also of maintaining the levels of

The causes of Napoleon's downfall

See color plates at page 737

763

agricultural and industrial production was becoming more and more serious. Finally, the Continental System proved to be a boomerang. It actually inflicted more damage upon France and her allies than it did upon England. Napoleon found it impossible to enforce the exclusion of British products from the Continent, since most of the countries he dominated were agricultural nations and insisted upon trading the things they produced for manufactured goods from England. Moreover, the British retaliated with a series of Orders in Council making all vessels trading with France or her allies subject to capture. The effect was to cut Napoleon's empire off from sources of supply in neutral countries.

The Spanish revolt

The first episode of Napoleon's downfall was the Spanish revolt which broke out in the summer of 1808. In May of that year Napoleon had tricked the Spanish king and the crown prince into resigning their claims to the throne and had promoted his brother Joseph from king of Naples to king of Spain. But scarcely had the new monarch been crowned than the people rose in revolt. Though Napoleon sent an army against them, he was never able to crush the rebellion entirely. With encouragement and assistance from the British, the Spaniards kept up a series of guerilla attacks which caused no end of expense and annoyance to the great warlord of France. Further, the courage of Spain in resisting the invader promoted a spirit of defiance elsewhere, with the result that Napoleon could no longer count upon the docility of any of his victims.

The disastrous campaign against Russia

The second stage in the downfall of the Corsican adventurer was the disruption of his alliance with Russia. As a purely agricultural country, Russia had suffered a severe economic crisis when she was no longer able, as a result of the Continental System, to exchange her surplus grain for British manufactures. The consequence was that the Tsar Alexander began to wink at trade with Britain and to ignore or evade the protests from Paris. By 1811 Napoleon decided that he could endure this flouting of the Continental System no longer. Accordingly, he collected an army of 600,000 men and set out in the spring of 1812 to punish the Tsar. The project ended in disaster. The Russians refused to make a stand, thereby leading the French farther and farther into the heart of their country. They finally permitted Napoleon to occupy their ancient capital. But on the very night of his entry, fire of suspicious origin broke out in the city. When the flames subsided, little but the blackened walls of the Kremlin remained to shelter the invading troops. Hoping that the Tsar would eventually surrender, Napoleon lingered amid the ruins for more than a month, finally deciding on October 22 to begin the homeward march. The delay was a fatal blunder. Long before he had reached the border, the terrible Russian winter was upon him. Swollen streams, mountainous drifts of snow, and bottomless mud slowed the retreat almost to a halt. To add to the miseries of bitter cold, disease, and starvation, Cossacks rode out of the blizzard to harry the exhausted troops. Each morning the miserable remnant

The Retreat from Russia. In this painting by Charlet, the horrors of the Russian winter can be seen.

that pushed on left behind circles of corpses around the campfires of the night before. On December 13 a few thousand broken, starved, and half-demented soldiers crossed the frontier into Germany—a miserable fraction of what had once been proudly styled the *Grande Armée.* The lives of nearly 300,000 men had been sacrificed in the Russian adventure.

The disastrous outcome of the Russian campaign destroyed the myth that Napoleon was invincible. Soon the Prussians and the Austrians regained their courage and, with Russian aid, joined in a War of Liberation. Napoleon hastily collected a new army and marched to suppress the revolts. He won a few modest victories in the spring and summer of 1813 but was finally cornered at Leipzig by an allied army of 500,000 men. Here on October 16–19 was fought the celebrated Battle of the Nations, in which Napoleon was decisively beaten. His grand empire now collapsed like a house of cards; his vassal states deserted him; and France itself was invaded. On March 31, 1814, the victorious allies entered Paris. Thirteen days later Napoleon signed the Treaty of Fontainebleau, renouncing all of his claims to the throne of France. In return he was granted a pension of two million francs a year and full sovereignty over the island of Elba, located in the Mediterranean Sea within sight of his native Corsica. The victors then took up with the French Senate the problem of reorganizing the government of France. It was agreed that the Bourbon line should be restored in the person of Louis XVIII, brother of the king who had been sent to the guillotine in 1793. It was carefully stipulated, however, that there was not to be a full restoration of the *ancien régime.* Louis XVIII was made to

The Battle of Leipzig

765

understand that he must not interfere with the political and economic reforms which still survived as fruits of the Revolution. In accordance with this requirement the new sovereign issued a charter confirming the Revolutionary liberties of the citizen and providing for a limited monarchy.

Napoleon's escape from Elba; the Battle of Waterloo

But the restoration of 1814 proved to be short-lived. The exiled emperor was growing impatient with his tiny island kingdom and eagerly awaiting the first opportunity to escape. His chance came in the spring of 1815. The French people were showing signs of disgust with the prosaic rule of Louis XVIII and with the effrontery of returning nobles of the *ancien régime*. Under these circumstances Napoleon slipped away from Elba and landed on the coast of southern France on March 1. Everywhere he was received by peasants and former soldiers in a delirium of joy. Officers sent to arrest him went over to his side with whole regiments of his former comrades in arms. On March 20, after a journey of triumph across the country, Napoleon entered Paris. Louis XVIII, who had sworn that he would die in defense of his throne, was already on his way to Belgium. But Napoleon was not to enjoy his new triumph long. Almost immediately upon learning of the escape from Elba, the allies proclaimed the Corsican an outlaw, and prepared to depose him by force. On June 12, 1815, Napoleon set out from Paris with the largest army he could gather in the

The French Campaign. A painting by Meissonier hanging in the Louvre. After his escape from exile on Elba, Napoleon leads his loyal troops to Paris.

Louis XVIII Leaves the Tuileries. A painting by Gros showing Louis, surrounded by family and those loyal to him, preparing to leave Paris as Napoleon returns to power.

hope of routing the enemy forces before they could invade his country. Six days later at Waterloo in Belgium he suffered a crushing defeat at the hands of the Duke of Wellington in command of an army of British, Dutch, and Germans. With all hope lost, Napoleon returned to Paris, abdicated his throne a second time, and made plans to escape to America. Finding the coast too heavily guarded, he was compelled to take refuge on a British ship. He was subsequently exiled by the British government to the rocky South Atlantic island of St. Helena. There he died, on May 5, 1821, a lonely and embittered man.

In attempting a final estimate of the significance of Napoleon Bonaparte, we must not lose sight of the fact that his name has been richly embellished with legend. The myth-mongering of patriots and hero-worshipers has raised his reputation almost to supernatural proportions. With the single exception of Jesus of Nazareth, he is actually the most written-about figure in history. But whether he deserves so exalted a fame is at least debatable. He was by no means a universal genius with a mastery of all knowledge or a patent on wisdom. Aside from mathematics, he knew little about any of the sciences, and his grasp of economics was too feeble to save him from the colossal errors of the Continental System. Though he was undoubtedly a clever tactician, the blunders of his Russian campaign indicate that even in military affairs he was not infallible. But worse than any other of his shortcomings were his defects of character. He was unscrupulous and unprincipled. Moreover, his boundless egotism made him coldly indifferent to the shedding of blood. His real significance lies in the fact that he helped to preserve some of the major results of the French Revolution. Though he

The significance of Napoleon

767

might easily have done so, he refused to restore the regime of privilege which had flourished in the days of the Bourbons. He confirmed the abolition of serfdom and the repeal of primogeniture, and he allowed the peasants to keep the lands they had acquired through the breakup of the great estates. What is more, he was at least indirectly responsible for spreading Revolutionary ideals into other countries. For example, it was his smashing defeat of Prussia in 1806 which finally persuaded the leading men of that nation of the necessity of adopting the main reforms of the French Revolution as the only means by which their state could rise again to smite the oppressor. The Prussian government in 1807–1808 abolished serfdom and threw open the various occupations and professions to men in all ranks of society. Unfortunately these measures were accompanied by an outburst of extreme nationalism, which found characteristic expression in the adoption of compulsory military service, one of the tyrannical devices employed by Napoleon himself. True, he did not invent it. It had been initiated by the Revolution before him. But he continued it, as he did the whole Revolutionary concept of a nation in arms and of war as a mass endeavor rather than a game of kings and generals.

2. THE NEW EUROPE

Following the overthrow of Napoleon, an overwhelming desire for peace and order seized the minds of the conservative classes in the victorious countries. Nearly everything that had happened since the Corsican had come into power now came to be regarded as a horrible nightmare. In some quarters there was a desire to return to the *status quo* of 1789, to undo the work of the Great Revolution, and to revive the power and the glamour of the *ancien régime*. The government of the Papal States proceeded to abolish street lighting in Rome as a dangerous novelty, while the Elector of Hesse restored pigtails to the freshly-powdered heads of his faithful soldiers. The leading statesmen realized, however, that a complete restoration of the old order would not be possible. For example, it was perfectly evident that the French people would not tolerate a revival of serfdom or the return of confiscated lands to the nobles and clergy. Therefore, while the portly Louis XVIII was put back on the throne, it was understood that he would continue to rule in conformity with the Charter of 1814. Furthermore, some of the victorious powers were not ready to give up the conquests they had made at the expense of France. Hence it was found necessary to modify suggestions frequently made for redrawing the map of Europe in accordance with the form it had had in the days of Louis XVI.

Most of the work of deciding the fate of Europe at the conclusion of the long war which had involved nearly the whole of the Western world was done at the so-called Congress of Vienna. To refer to

The movement to return to the *status quo*

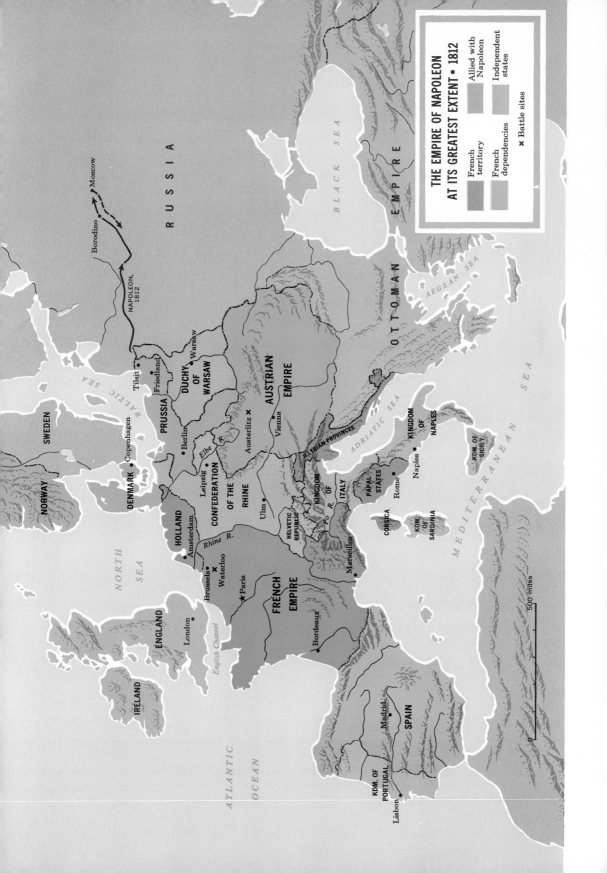

THE EMPIRE OF NAPOLEON
AT ITS GREATEST EXTENT · 1812

French territory

French dependencies

Allied with Napoleon

Independent states

× Battle sites

NORWAY

SWEDEN

DENMARK • Copenhagen

RUSSIA

Moscow •

Borodino •

NAPOLEON, 1812

Tilsit •

Friedland ×

PRUSSIA

• Berlin

DUCHY
OF
WARSAW

Warsaw •

AUSTRIAN
EMPIRE

Leipzig •

Elbe R.

Austerlitz ×

Vienna •

BLACK SEA

OTTOMAN EMPIRE

AEGEAN SEA

NORTH
SEA

BALTIC SEA

HOLLAND

Amsterdam •

CONFEDERATION
OF THE
RHINE

Rhine R.

Ulm •

HELVETIC
REPUBLIC

ILLYRIAN PROVINCES

ADRIATIC SEA

KINGDOM
OF
ITALY

Po R.

PAPAL
STATES

Rome •

KINGDOM
OF
NAPLES

Naples •

KDM. OF
SICILY

MEDITERRANEAN SEA

IRELAND

ENGLAND

London •

English Channel

Brussels •
Waterloo ×

★ Paris

FRENCH
EMPIRE

Bordeaux •

Marseilles •

CORSICA

KDM.
OF
SARDINIA

ATLANTIC
OCEAN

SPAIN

Madrid •

KDM. OF
PORTUGAL

Lisbon •

500 miles

0

Execution of the Rioters, Francisco Goya (1746–1828). Unlike most artists of his time, Goya dealt unflinchingly with suffering, violence, fear, and death. Depicted here is the execution of Spanish rebels by Napoleon's soldiers in 1808. This harshness caused the rebellion to spread over the whole peninsula. (Prado)

The Raft of the Medusa, Théodore Géricault. Agony and suffering is vividly portrayed in Géricault's realistic figures. (Louvre)

this body as a "Congress" is to be guilty of a misnomer, for, as a matter of fact, no plenary session of all the delegates was ever held. As in the drafting of the Versailles Treaty more than a hundred years later, the vital decisions were really made by small committees. Nevertheless, the assemblage at Vienna was staged with such pomp and splendor that even the most neglected member was made to feel that he was participating in events of epochal importance. No fewer than six monarchs attended: the Tsar of Russia, the Emperor of Austria, and the kings of Prussia, Denmark, Bavaria, and Württemberg. Great Britain was represented by Lord Castlereagh and the "Iron Duke" of Wellington. From France came the subtle intriguer Talleyrand, who had served as a bishop under Louis XVI, as foreign minister at the court of Napoleon, and who now stood ready to espouse the cause of reaction.

The dominant roles at the Congress of Vienna were played by Alexander I and Metternich. The dynamic Tsar was one of the most baffling figures in history. Reared at the voluptuous court of Catherine the Great, he imbibed the doctrines of Rousseau from a French Jacobin tutor. In 1801 he succeeded his murdered father as Tsar and for the next two decades disturbed the dreams of his fellow sovereigns by becoming the most liberal monarch in Europe. After the defeat of Napoleon in the Russian campaign, his mind turned more and more into mystical channels. He conceived of a mission to convert the rulers of all countries to the Christian ideals of justice and peace. But the chief effect of his voluble expressions of devotion to "liberty" and "enlightenment" was to frighten conservatives into suspecting a plot to extend his power over all of Europe. He was accused of intriguing with Jacobins everywhere to substitute an all-powerful Russia for an all-powerful France.

The most commanding figure at the Congress was Klemens von Metternich, born in 1773 at Coblenz in the Rhine valley, where his father was Austrian ambassador at the courts of three small German

The Congress of Vienna

Alexander I

Metternich

The Congress of Vienna. The figure to the left of center is Metternich. Seated at the right with his arm on the table is Talleyrand.

states. As a student at the University of Strassburg the young Metternich witnessed some excesses of mob violence connected with the outbreak of the French Revolution, and to these he attributed his life-long hatred of political innovation. After completing his education he entered the field of diplomacy and served for nearly forty years as Minister of Foreign Affairs. He was active in fomenting discord between Napoleon and the Tsar Alexander, after the two became allies in 1807, and he played some part in arranging the marriage of Napoleon to the Austrian archduchess, Marie Louise. In 1813 he was made a hereditary prince of the Austrian Empire. At the Congress of Vienna Metternich distinguished himself for charm of manner and skillful intrigue. His two great obsessions were hatred of political and social change and fear of Russia. Actually the two were related. It was not simply that he feared revolutions as such; he feared even more revolutions inspired by the "Jacobin" Tsar for the sake of establishing Russian supremacy in Europe. For this reason he favored moderate terms for France in her hour of defeat, and was ready at one time to sponsor the restoration of Napoleon as Emperor of the French under the protection and overlordship of the Hapsburg monarchy.

Legitimacy

The basic idea that guided the work of the Congress of Vienna was the principle of *legitimacy*. This principle was invented by Talleyrand as a device for protecting France against drastic punishment by her conquerors, but it was ultimately adopted by Metternich as a convenient expression of the general policy of reaction. Legitimacy meant that the dynasties of Europe that had reigned in pre-Revolutionary days should be restored to their thrones, and that each country should regain essentially the same territories it had held in 1789. In accordance with this principle Louis XVIII was recognized as the "legitimate" sovereign of France, and the restoration of Bourbon rulers in Spain and the Two Sicilies was also confirmed. France was compelled to pay an indemnity of 700,000,000 francs, but her boundaries were to remain essentially the same as in 1789. Other territorial arrangements likewise adhered to the idea of a return to the *status quo*. The Pope was allowed to recover his temporal possessions in Italy; Switzerland was restored as an independent confederation under guaranties of neutrality by the principal powers; while the Polish kingdom set up by Napoleon was abolished and the country again divided among Russia, Austria, and Prussia.

Violations of
legitimacy

But the Congress of Vienna was a bit cynical in applying the principle of legitimacy. Before the lace-cuffed princes had gone very far in restoring the old map of Europe, they diluted the principle of legitimacy with their curious system of compensations. The real purpose of this system was to enable certain of the major powers to gratify their hunger for spoils. For example, Great Britain was permitted to keep the valuable territories she had taken from the Dutch, who had fought for a time on the side of France. Among these rich prizes were South Africa, a portion of Guiana in South America, and the island of Ceylon. Then to compensate the Dutch for the loss of so large a part of their empire, provision was made for transferring the Austrian Netherlands, or Belgium, to Holland. Since this involved a sacrifice on the part of Austria, the Hapsburgs were rewarded with an extensive foothold in Italy. They received the republic of Venice and the duchy of Milan, and members of the family were placed on the thrones of Tuscany, Parma, and Modena. Thus Austria profited by gaining a compact empire occupying a commanding position in central Europe. A similar series of compensations was provided to reward Russia for her part in conquering Napoleon. The Tsar was allowed to retain Finland, which he had seized from Sweden in 1809. Sweden, in turn, was compensated by the acquisition of Norway from Denmark. All of these arrangements were put through with a total disregard for the interests of the peoples concerned.

One of the cardinal purposes of Metternich and his conservative colleagues was to erect the Vienna settlement into a permanent bulwark of the *status quo*. With this end in view they established the Quadruple Alliance of Great Britain, Austria, Prussia, and Russia as an instrument for maintaining the settlement intact. In 1818 France was admitted to the combination, thereby making it a Quintuple Alliance. For some years this aggregate of powers functioned as a kind of League of Nations to enforce the system of Metternich. It is also frequently referred to as the Concert of Europe, for its members were pledged to cooperate in suppressing any disturbances which might arise from the attempts of peoples to throw off their "legitimate" rulers or to change international boundaries. In the minds of liberals and nationalists of this period the Quintuple Alliance was often confused with another combination that also grew out of the settlement at Vienna. This was the so-called Holy Alliance, a product of the sentimental idealism of the Tsar Alexander I. In September 1815, Alexander proposed that the monarchs of Europe should "take as their sole guide . . . the precepts of Justice, Christian Charity, and Peace," and that they should base international relations as well as the treatment of their subjects "upon the sublime truths which the Holy Religion of our Savior teaches. . . ." But none of the Tsar's fellow sovereigns took him seriously. Though most of them signed the agreement he proposed, they were inclined to regard it as so much mystical verbiage. As a matter of fact, the Holy Alliance was never anything more than a series of pious pledges. The real weapon for preserving the triumph of reaction was not the Holy Alliance but the Quintuple Alliance.

The purposes of the Quintuple Alliance were achieved primarily through a series of international congresses which met between 1818 and 1822. It was at the second of these conferences, the Congress of Troppau, that the true character of the Alliance was most clearly revealed. Here the assembled delegates drew up an agreemnt avow-

The system of alliances

NORTH SEA

KINGDOM OF NORWAY AND SWEDEN

Stockholm

SCOTLAND

Edinburgh

IRELAND

GREAT BRITAIN

Dublin

Liverpool

Birmingham

ENGLAND

London

KINGDOM OF DENMARK

Copenhagen

SCHLESWIG

HOLSTEIN

Hamburg

MECK-LENBURG

HANOVER

Berlin

P R U S S I A

BALTIC SEA

RUSSIAN EMPIRE

POLAND

ATLANTIC OCEAN

Amsterdam

KINGDOM OF THE NETHERLANDS

BELGIUM

LUXEMBOURG

Paris

LORRAINE

ALSACE

BADEN

HESSE

SAXONY

REPUBLIC OF CRACOW

KINGDOM OF FRANCE

WÜRTEM-BERG

BAVARIA

Munich

Vienna

AUSTRIAN EMPIRE

HUNGARY

Budapest

MOLDAVIA

Berne

SWISS CONFED.

Bordeaux

Marseilles

KINGDOM OF SARDINIA

LOMBARDY-VENETIA

Milan

PARMA

MODENA

LUCCA

TUSCANY

PAPAL STATES

ADRIATIC SEA

WALLACHIA

OTTOMAN EMPIRE

MONTENEGRO

Constan

KINGDOM OF PORTUGAL

KINGDOM OF SPAIN

Madrid

Barcelona

CORSICA

Rome

Naples

Lisbon

BALEARIC ISLANDS
(To Spain)

M E D I T E R R A N E A N

Palermo

KINGDOM OF THE TWO SICILIES

S E A

MOROCCO

ALGERIA

TUNISIA

0   500 miles

EUROPE AFTER THE CONGRESS OF VIENNA • 1815

The activities
of the Quintu-
ple Alliance

ing the intention of the great powers to intervene by force of arms
to suppress any revolution that might threaten the stability of Europe. In two different instances the policy of intervention was actually carried out. After an uprising in the Kingdom of the Two
Sicilies, in which the Bourbon monarch, Ferdinand I, was compelled
to swear allegiance to a liberal constitution, Metternich convoked
the Congress of Laibach in 1821. King Ferdinand was summoned
before it, commanded to disavow his oath, and persuaded to invite
an Austrian army to march into Naples. As a result, the constitution
was revoked, and Ferdinand was restored to his position as an
autocratic sovereign. In 1822 the Congress of Verona was summoned to deal with an insurrection in Spain, which also had had the
effect of forcing the king to subscribe to a liberal constitution.

772

After considerable wrangling among the powers as to the measures which should be taken to crush the revolt, it was finally decided that the king of France should send an army into Spain to support his Bourbon kinsman. Not only was the revolt speedily crushed, but intervention was followed by the blackest reaction Europe had yet seen. Hundreds of devoted liberals were put to death; even greater numbers were chained in prison. And it is not without interest that some of the ruthless measures of the Spanish king were the result of direct encouragement from the leaders of the Quintuple Alliance.

Although foreign intervention was confined to Spain and the Kingdom of the Two Sicilies, these were by no means the only countries where violent conflicts occurred between liberals and conservatives. The system of Metternich involved a regime of stern repression in domestic affairs by the governments of the great powers as well as the suppression of revolutions in the lesser states. But the more blind and bitter the policy of repression, the greater was the number of uprisings against it. In Great Britain the rule of the Tories for the benefit of the landed aristocracy evoked powerful opposition from intellectual radicals like William Godwin, from the poets Shelley and Byron, and from the new industrial classes. When the protests of these groups were silenced by laws prohibiting public meetings and muzzling the press, some of the more desperate leaders organized the Cato Street Conspiracy in 1820 to murder the whole Tory Cabinet. Discovery of the plot was a foregone conclusion, and five of the conspirators were hanged. In France the modest compromise with progressive ideas which Louis XVIII incorporated in his Charter of 1814 proved to be more than his die-hard followers were willing to stand. As a result, the years between 1815 and 1820 were fraught with savage and sometimes bloody strife between Ultra-Royalists and their liberal and moderate opponents. In 1824 the victory of the forces of reaction was strengthened further when Louis XVIII died and was succeeded by his brother, Charles X, the leader of the Ultra-Royalists.

The clash of liberals and conservatives: (1) in Great Britain and France

Similar struggles occurred in central and eastern Europe with almost identical results. In Germany students in the universities organized secret societies and participated in stormy agitation against conservative regimes. These activities convinced Metternich, who dominated the Germanic Confederation, that all of central Europe was about to be engulfed by a radical revolution. Accordingly, he forced through the federal Diet a program of repressive measures known as the Carlsbad Decrees (1819). By the terms of these it was provided that every university should have a government supervisor; rebellious professors were to be removed from their positions; student societies were ordered to be dissolved; and the press was to be subject to a strict censorship. Vigorous enforcement of the Carlsbad Decrees put the liberal movement in Germany under a cloud, from which it did not emerge until 1848.

(2) in Germany

773

(3) in Russia

Meanwhile, the change in the attitude of Tsar Alexander I had produced some rumblings of discontent in Russia. Time was when Alexander had been one of the most enlightened monarchs of Europe. He had founded schools and universities. He had emancipated a few of the serfs and had considered plans for freeing the remainder. He had even toyed with the idea of granting a written constitution. But after 1818 he turned reactionary. This change of heart of the Tsar was the signal for the growth of an opposition movement among officers of the army and the intellectual classes. When Alexander died in 1825, the leaders of this movement determined to prevent the reaction from going any farther. They organized the Dekabrist revolt (from the Russian word for December) to compel the accession to the throne of the liberal Grand Duke Constantine in place of his hard-shell brother, Nicholas. Unfortunately Constantine would have nothing to do with the rebellion, and Nicholas speedily crushed it. The ensuing reign was one of the worst in Russian history. Not only did Nicholas abolish freedom of the press, but he established a system of secret police and converted the nation into a huge military camp where every move of the citizen could be watched and controlled by the government.

Causes of the decline of the system of Metternich: (1) the withdrawal of Great Britain

In spite of what semed to be enduring victories for the cause of reaction, by 1830 the system of Metternich had begun to break down. The initial step in the process was the withdrawal of Great Britain from the Quintuple Alliance. As early as 1822 the British refused to participate in Metternich's scheme for suppression of the revolution in Spain. Soon afterward they flatly repudiated the entire policy of intervention in the internal affairs of foreign states. It was not that the British of this time were more liberal than their allies on the Continent; it was rather that the Industrial Revolution was forcing Britain to seek new markets for the things she produced. Therefore she was strongly opposed to a foreign policy that would antagonize other nations and cut off her channels of trade. She had developed a lucrative commerce with the states of Central and South America, which had lately thrown off their allegiance to Spain, and she was fearful that the system of Metternich might be used to force these former colonies back under Spanish rule.

(2) the Russo-Turkish War of 1828–1829

About the same time that Great Britain was weakening her ties with the Concert of Europe, Russia began to develop ambitions which also threatened the supremacy of Metternich's system. For some years the Russians had been greedily awaiting the breakup of the Ottoman Empire in the hope that that would pave the way for an easy expansion into the Balkans. The Russian opportunity came after 1821 when the Greeks launched a rebellion against Turkish rule. Since the Tsar, Alexander I, was still bound by loyalty to the doctrine of legitimacy, nothing was done until after his death in 1825. His successor, Nicholas I, entertained no such scruples. Especially when he observed in England and France expressions of the profoundest sympathy for the Greeks in their heroic struggle against an infidel oppressor, he determined to go to their rescue. Accordingly, in 1828, he declared war against Turkey. In a little more than a year a Russian army fought its way almost to the gates of the Turkish capital and forced the Sultan to sign the Treaty of Adrianople. By the terms of this treaty Turkey was compelled to acknowledge the independence of Greece, to grant autonomy to Serbia, and to permit the establishment of a Russian Protectorate over the provinces which later became the kingdom of Rumania. In thus contributing to the dismemberment of the empire of a "legitimate" ruler, Russia, with considerable encouragement from England and France, dealt a powerful blow to the system of political stagnation which Metternich was striving to maintain. For all practical purposes the empire of the Tsars had ceased to be a member of the Quintuple Alliance.

The system of Metternich was weakened still further by the series of revolutions that broke out in western Europe in 1830. The first in the series was the July Revolution in France, which resulted in the overthrow of Charles X, the last of the regular line of Bourbon kings. As was indicated previously, Charles X, who had suc-

(3) the July Revolution in France

The July Revolution of 1830. Charles X was overthrown in favor of Louis Philippe, upon whom hopes of popular sovereignty were based.

ceeded Louis XVIII in 1824, was the perfect embodiment of the spirit of reaction. His stubborn and vindictive attitude inspired relentless hatred, especially among the ranks of the bourgeoisie, who resented his reduction of the interest on government bonds and his attempt to disfranchise three-fourths of the voters. As evidence accumulated that the king was determined to rule in complete defiance of Parliament, barricades were thrown up in the streets. After futile efforts to quell the insurrection with a remnant of loyal troops, Charles abdicated his throne and fled to England. The leaders of the bourgeoisie then chose as his successor Louis Philippe, a member of the Orleanist branch of the Bourbon family and a former Jacobin who had taken an active part in the revolution of 1789. The new government was proclaimed to be a constitutional monarchy founded upon the principle of popular sovereignty; and the white flag of the Bourbons was replaced by the tricolor originally invented by the apostles of Liberty, Equality, and Fraternity.

Soon after the July Revolution in France a revolt broke out in the Belgian Netherlands. It will be recalled that in the Vienna settlement of 1815 the Belgian or Austrian Netherlands had been subjected to the rule of Holland in defiance of the obvious differences of language, nationality, and religion between the Belgians and the Dutch. An additional basis of friction was the divergent economic interests of the two peoples. Whereas the Dutch were engaged primarily in commerce and agriculture, the occupations of the Belgians were largely industrial. These differences, combined with the stupid tyrannies of the Dutch king, incited the Belgians in the fall of 1830 to strike a blow for independence. The revolt was regarded with favor by the new government in France and also by the British, who hoped that it might benefit their trade. Consequently, the following year, an international agreement was signed in London that recognized the independence of Belgium as a constitutional monarchy. The Dutch had no alternative but to acquiesce in an accomplished fact. In 1839 the independence and neutrality of Belgium were guaranteed by all the great powers.

The revolutionary movement of 1830 spread into a number of other countries, but the results were not so successful. The major one of serious dimensions was the insurrection of the Poles in 1831, a desperate attempt of that harassed people to regain independence from Russia. Had the Poles been as fortunate as the Belgians in obtaining aid from foreign nations, they might have won. But the British and the French were now too busy with affairs in western Europe and gave nothing more than verbal support. As a consequence, the Tsar Nicholas I was able to crush the revolt with murderous severity. Hundreds of the rebellious leaders were shot or exiled to the dreary wastes of Siberia, and Poland was governed henceforth as a conquered province.

(4) the revolt
of the Belgians

The unsuccessful
revolt of the Poles

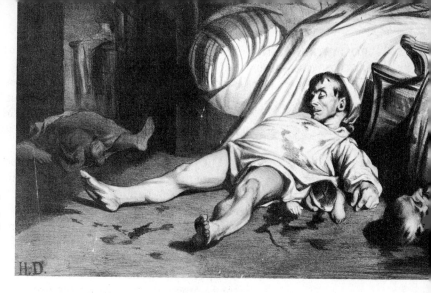

Rue Transnonain. Drawn by Honoré Daumier in 1834. A typically powerful statement on a series of insurrections.

3. EFFORTS TO RESTORE THE STATUS QUO

Just as there was a struggle in the years from 1800 to 1830 between liberals and conservatives in the political sphere, so there was a similar clash in the realm of ideas. And the outcome of this second struggle was not so far different from that of the first. In general, throughout the period, the doctrines of intellectual conservatives enjoyed supremacy. Order was exalted above liberty. The interests of groups, of society, and especially of the state were given pre-eminence over those of the individual. An emphasis upon faith, authority, and tradition superseded the eighteenth-century belief in the primacy of reason and science. A group of French philosophers under the leadership of Joseph de Maistre (1754–1821) sought to inaugurate a Catholic revival in which mystical piety, supernaturalism, and the belief in an infallible Church would serve as the lamps to guide men's feet from the pitfalls of anarchy. Maistre acclaimed obedience as the first political virtue and regarded the executioner as the bulwark of social order.

For this ascendancy of conservative patterns of thought various factors were responsible. Probably the major factor, in the beginning at least, was the strong revulsion of feeling which had set in against the horrors of the French Revolution. All who had been frightened by the violence of that movement were inclined to blame it on the rationalism, materialism, and individualism of the age of the Enlightenment. Hence they were disposed to swing to the opposite extreme of glorifying faith, authority, and tradition. Such in particular was the attitude expressed by Edmund Burke (1729–1797), the renowned British orator and Whig statesman of the late eighteenth century. Although he did not live to see the end of the French Revolution, Burke denounced that movement with all the

777

fiery eloquence he could command. To him the Revolution was an attempt to repudiate the accumulated wisdom of the ages. This world, he averred, cannot be made over in a single night. No one generation has the right to set itself up as the judge of society's future needs. The institutions and traditions which have come down to us from the past have an enduring value. To lay violent hands upon them is to threaten the vital elements of civilization itself.

The body of thought that stands as the most perfect expression of the age of reaction was the German philosophy of Romantic Idealism. This philosophy derives its name from the fact that it was a combination of the romanticist theory of truth with the idealist conception of the universe. The Romantic Idealists deviated sharply from the individualism and humanism of eighteenth-century philosophy. They regarded the individual as totally devoid of significance except insofar as he was a member of some social group. Therefore, they argued, the welfare of the group must come first, and that of the individual will automatically follow. Society and the state are social organisms, products of a *natural* evolution, and not the artificial creations of man himself for his own convenience. No such thing as a state of nature ever existed, nor was political society founded by a social compact. Consequently the individual cannot claim any inviolable sphere of rights beyond the jurisdiction of organized society. His duty is rather to submerge his own interests in those of the group and thereby gain the true liberty which consists in obedience to law and in respect for accumulated tradition.

The philosopher who provided the original inspiration for Romantic Idealism was a methodical little German who lived most of his life in the eighteenth century. His name was Immanuel Kant, and he was born in Königsberg in 1724; there he died in 1804 without once having left his native city, except for a brief period of tutoring in a neighboring village. Devoting most of his life to teaching, he matured his philosophic ideas very slowly. Not until he was fifty-seven years old did he finish his first great work, the *Critique of Pure Reason*. As a philosopher, Kant owed considerable to the great minds of the Enlightenment. They contributed particularly to his political ideas. Unlike most of his followers, he believed in the natural rights of man and even defended the separation of powers as a necessary protection for the liberty of the citizen. But in the field of general philosophy Kant departed widely from the rationalism of the eighteenth century. He divided the entire universe into two worlds: one, the realm of physical nature, or the world of *phenomena;* and the other, the realm of ultimate reality, or the world of *noumena*. The methods of knowing applicable to these realms are entirely different. Sense perception and reason can give us knowledge only of the realm of *phenomena*, of the world of physical things. But in the higher realm of the spiritual, which is the world

Romantic Idealism

Romantic Idealism founded by Immanuel Kant

of ultimate reality, such methods have no value. Since all ordinary knowledge rests in final analysis upon sense perception, we cannot prove by reason or science that God exists, that the human will is free, or that the soul is immortal. Nevertheless, we are justified in assuming that these things are true. In the realm of *noumena*, faith, intuition, and deep conviction are just as valid instruments of knowledge as logic and science in the realm of *phenomena*.

Undoubtedly the most influential philosopher of the Romantic Idealist movement was Georg Wilhelm Hegel (1770–1831). Professor of philosophy for a considerable period at the University of Berlin, Hegel won a great number of adherents, and through them exerted a potent force in shaping intellectual currents for many years. The central doctrine of Hegel's philosophy is the idea of purposive evolution. He regarded the universe as in a condition of flux, with everything tending to pass over into its opposite. In particular, each institution or social or political organism grows to maturity, fulfills its mission, and then gives way to something different. But the old itself is never entirely destroyed; the clash of opposites results eventually in a fusion, in the creation of a new organism made up of elements taken from the two opposites themselves. Then the process is repeated over and over again with each new stage representing an improvement over that which has gone before. But Hegel's conception of evolution was not mechanistic. He believed the whole process to be guided by the universal reason or God. Evolution, he maintained, is the unfoldment of God in history. Further, he argued that the war of opposites would ultimately lead to a beneficent goal. This goal he described as the perfect state, in which the interests of every citizen would be perfectly blended with the interests of society. Actually, Hegel worshiped the state in a much more

Hegel

Hegel Lecturing to His Students at the University of Berlin

ecstatic fashion than did any of the other Romantic Idealists. He held that true liberty consists in subjection to political society, and that the individual has no rights which the state is bound to respect, for without the state the individual would be nothing but an animal. "The State is the Divine Idea as it exists on earth." [3]

The influence
of Romantic
Idealism

Romantic Idealism cast its influence in many directions. In one or another of its forms it was adopted as the principal gospel of nearly all in the conservative camp. Churchmen who had been disturbed by the attacks of deists and skeptics were delighted to find a philosophy that recognized the merits of faith and exalted the world of spirit. People with a stake in the maintenance of order rejoiced in the new worship of tradition and authority and in the implied condemnation of revolution. Especially pleasing to the ruling class were the political teachings of Hegel, who enjoyed such prestige at the Prussian court that his enemies called him "the official philosopher." The doctrines of Hegel and Fichte strengthened the rising tide of nationalism and ultimately contributed their quota to the devastating flood of fascism.[4] But Romantic Idealism also bore certain other fruits not exactly to the liking of its principal exponents. One of their younger contemporaries, Arthur Schopenhauer (1788–1860), developed the notion of a universal force, directing all growth and movement, into a philosophy of stark pessimism. He taught that this force is *will*—a blind, unconscious craving of individuals and species to survive. Since the will to live is present in all animate forms, and since it leads the strong to devour the weak, this world is the worst of all possible worlds. Selfishness, pain, and misery are inseparable from life, and therefore the only road to happiness for man consists in as complete a denial of life as possible after the manner of an Oriental ascetic. Still another of the strange offshoots of Romantic Idealism was the philosophy of history of Karl Marx. For his celebrated doctrine of dialectical materialism, Marx was heavily indebted to Hegel. Both believed in a progressive evolution through a clash of opposing systems, resulting finally in a perfect society. But whereas Hegel assumed that the ultimate goal would be a perfect state, Marx argued that it would be communism. It was the proud boast of the great socialist leader that he turned Hegel right side up.

Utilitarianism,
founded by
Jeremy Bentham

Romantic Idealism was most popular in Germany. In other countries, especially in England and France, where the influence of the Enlightenment had taken deeper root, philosophy was generally more liberal in tone. The leading system of thought in England in the early nineteenth century was Utilitarianism, founded by Jeremy Bentham (1748–1832). Despite a frail and nervous physique, Bentham displayed prodigious intellectual talent throughout the greater part of his long life. He began the study of Latin when he

---

[3] Hegel, *Philosophy of History* (J. Sibree, trans.), p. 87.
[4] Hegelian ideas influenced the growth of fascism not only in Germany but also in Italy. See H. W. Schneider, *Making the Fascist State*, pp. 20–24.

was only three years old and was graduated from Oxford at the age of fifteen. When he was nearly seventy he was still propounding schemes for prison reform and for cutting canals across the Isthmus of Panama and the Isthmus of Suez. His chief philosophical work, the *Principles of Morals and Legislation*, was published in 1789. Bentham's Utilitarianism derives its name from his cardinal teaching that the supreme test to which every belief and institution should be made to conform is the test of utility or usefulness. This test he defined as contributing to the greatest happiness of the greatest number. Any doctrine or practice which fails to meet this requirement should be rejected forthwith, regardless of how much hoary tradition may stand behind it. Despite its social connotations, Bentham's ideal was the acme of individualism. Not only did he maintain that the interest of the community is simply the sum of the interests of the several members who compose it, but he was quite frank in admitting that the motives of individuals are purely selfish. The mainspring of human action is the desire to secure pleasure and to avoid pain. Therefore society should leave to each of its members complete freedom to follow his own enlightened self-interest. Since every individual knows better than anyone else what constitutes his own good, the welfare of society can best be promoted by allowing to each of its members the maximum liberty of action. Bentham was firmly convinced that granting this concession would not mean a reversion to the ways of the jungle. He insisted that every man would be obliged to respect his neighbor's rights through fear of retaliation; that men would obey the laws for the simple reason that the "probable mischiefs of obedience are less than the probable mischiefs of disobedience." [5]

Bentham's most faithful disciple was James Mill (1773–1836), but the greatest of all the Utilitarian philosophers was James Mill's oldest son, John Stuart Mill (1806–1873). Educated exclusively by his father, John Stuart Mill surpassed even Bentham as an intellectual prodigy. He learned the Greek alphabet at the age of three, and by the time he was eight had read all of Herodotus and a considerable portion of Plato in the original. When scarcely thirteen he had completed a rigorous course of training in history, Scholastic logic, and Aristotelian philosophy. His greatest works are his *Logic*, his *Principles of Political Economy*, his essay *On Liberty*, and his *Representative Government*. As a philosopher, John Stuart Mill summed up nearly all of the major tendencies in English thought initiated by Locke, Hume, and Bentham. He was a skeptic in regard to final truth and a champion of the liberal and practical point of view. But he was also an original and independent thinker and made a number of distinct contributions of his own. He founded a new system of logic, based upon experience as the origi-

John Stuart Mill

[5] W. A. Dunning, *History of Political Theories*, III, 216.

nal ground of all knowledge. All of the so-called self-evident truths, even the axioms of mathematics, he argued, are simply inferences derived from the observed facts that nature is uniform and that every effect has a cause. Knowledge comes neither from inborn ideas nor from mystic intuition. Though Mill agreed with the general purport of Bentham's teachings, he rejected the doctrine that the pursuit of pleasure and the avoidance of pain are the sole determinants of human conduct (the "pig philosophy," as Thomas Carlyle once called it). According to Mill the conduct of individuals is often influenced by mere habit and by the desire for unity with their fellow beings. Further, he maintained that pleasures themselves differ in quality, arguing that it is better to be "Socrates dissatisfied than a fool satisfied." In his later years Mill also modified much of Bentham's individualism. While repudiating socialism on the ground that it would involve the destruction of personal liberty, he nevertheless advocated a considerable degree of intervention by the state for the benefit of its less fortunate members. He looked forward to a time "when society will no longer be divided into the idle and the industrious; when the rule that they who do not work shall not eat, will be applied not to paupers only, but impartially to all. . . ." [6]

Positivism

The nearest approach to a liberal and practical philosophy on the Continent of Europe was the Positivism of Auguste Comte (1798–1857). Positivism takes its name from Comte's doctrine that the only knowledge of any value is *positive* knowledge, or knowledge which comes from the sciences. Comte's philosophy may therefore be placed, along with Utilitarianism, in the classification of *empirical* philosophies, which includes those deriving all truth from experience or from observation of the physical world. Comte rejected metaphysics as utterly futile; no man can discover the hidden essences of things—why events happen as they do, or what is the ultimate meaning and goal of existence. All we really know is how things happen, the laws which control their occurrence, and the relations existing between them. If there was any one purpose preeminent over others in Comte's philosophy, it was to devise means for improving relations among men. He did not agree with Bentham that the actions of individuals are motivated exclusively by self-interest. He avowed, on the contrary, that men are influenced by nobler impulses of *altruism*, or feelings for others, as well as by instincts of selfishness. The great object of all social teaching should be to promote the supremacy of altruism (a word invented by Comte) over egoism. Believing that this purpose could be achieved only through an appeal to the emotions of love and self-sacrifice, Comte developed what he called the Religion of Humanity, which was supposed to bring men together in a common devotion to justice, charity, and benevolence. Although this religion included no

[6] J.S. Mill, *Autobiography* (Uniform Library ed.), p. 231.

belief in the supernatural, it was provided with an extensive ritual and even with a Trinity and a priesthood. Ridiculed by its critics as "Catholicism minus Christianity," it nevertheless represented an attempt to build a system of belief dedicated to the aim of social progress.

4· ROMANTICISM IN LITERATURE AND THE ARTS

In the chapter on the Intellectual Revolution it was observed that toward the end of the eighteenth century a romantic revolt set in against the dominant classical tendencies in literature. The essence of romanticism was the glorification of the instincts and emotions as opposed to a worship of the intellect. Included in it also were such elements as a deep veneration for nature, a contempt for formalism, a sentimental love for humble folk, and often a flaming zeal to remake the world. Among the leaders of the new movement in its infancy were Rousseau, Thomas Gray, Oliver Goldsmith, Robert Burns, and Friedrich Schiller. Romanticism flourished after the beginning of the nineteenth century, attaining the zenith of its growth about 1830. No longer was it confined to literature; it was a vital force in painting and to a considerable extent also in music. Though it still had to compete in some fields with classicism, especially in France during the era of Napoleon, it was by far the most vigorous literary and artistic influence in the first three decades of the nineteenth century. Its kinship with the revolt of youth in our own time is fairly obvious.

The nature of the romantic revolt

Romanticism in literature had its deepest and longest roots in England. Its two great prophets at the beginning of the nineteenth century were the poets William Wordsworth (1770–1850) and Samuel Taylor Coleridge (1772–1834). Wordsworth is noted for his mystical adoration of nature, not alone in its surface beauties but especially as the embodiment of a universal spirit which unites all living things in a kinship of divinity. He believed that a sensuous worship of nature would bring man to a deeper awareness of the nobility of life, that it would enable him to hear "the still sad music of humanity" and thereby increase his love and compassion for his fellow creatures. The special gift of Coleridge was an ability to make the weird and fantastic credible. Though he sometimes wandered into the dense jungles of metaphysics, he succeeded in the magic stanzas of *The Ancient Mariner* in producing some of the most colorful imaginative writing in the English language. This work reveals his unusual power of combining tender, almost womanly sentiment with witching descriptions of strange, supernatural terrors, of phantoms and specters that rise out of the murky depths of the emotions to torment man with a sense of his helplessness.

Romanticism in English literature: Wordsworth and Coleridge

Perhaps the most typical of the English romantic poets were John Keats (1795–1821), Percy Bysshe Shelley (1792–1822), and

Lord Byron

George Gordon, Lord Byron (1788–1824). Keats differed from most of his contemporaries in identifying beauty with intellectual passion in somewhat the same way as the Greeks identified the beautiful with the good. The substance of his creed is expressed in the well-known lines from the *Ode on a Grecian Urn:* "Beauty is truth, truth beauty,—that is all ye know on earth, and all ye need to know." His conception was one of ideal beauty, which endures independently of the fading of the flower or the passing of the loveliness of youth. The other two short-lived poets of the English romantic circle were much more interested in political and social questions. In spite of their upper-class origins, both were rebels against stubborn conservatism and employed their talents in passionate appeals for justice and freedom. Shelley was expelled from Oxford on a charge of atheism and then for some years was a disciple of William Godwin, the philosophical anarchist. Though he eventually modified some of his youthful radicalism and allowed his thoughts to wander more and more into vaporous abstractions, he never relinquished his hatred of injustice or his hopes for a golden dawn of happiness and freedom. Lord Byron, who inherited the title of baron at the age of ten, was even more than Shelley a poet of stormy defiance, of romantic daring, and of sardonic laughter at the hypocrisy and arrogance of the human race. Not only in the qualities of his proud personality, but also in the scandals which enveloped his career and in the directness and audacity of his poetic style he typified for the age the spirit of romantic man. His death while aiding the Greeks in their war for independence was a fitting climax to his brief, adventurous life.

Except for the dramas of Schiller and Goethe, discussed in a preceding chapter,[7] romantic literature in Continental countries is scarcely to be compared with that in England. The only other important writer in Germany was Heinrich Heine (1797–1856), born of orthodox Jewish parents but later a convert to Christianity for the sake of expediency. Like Shelley and Byron, Heine was an individualist and a relentless critic of conservatism. He devoted nearly the whole of his active life to what he loved to call "humanity's war of liberation." But he was not merely a witty satirist and pungent critic of smugness and reaction. In his *Book of Songs* he displayed lyric gifts of tenderness and melancholy and a haunting charm of melody which few other poets of his day could surpass. He has been aptly called "a nightingale nesting in the wig of a Voltaire."

Romanticism in France as in England wavered between a mystic irrationalism, on the one hand, and a gallant defense of individual liberty and social reform on the other. The chief exponent of the irrational tendency was François de Chateaubriand (1768–1848). Chateaubriand found in the mysteries of Christianity and in the

784

[7] See p. 667

"holy innocence" of simple folk the sublimest beauty in the universe. He was the prophet of a Catholic revival designed to guide men back to an age of faith and thus save them from the perils of reason. The libertarian and individualist aspect of French romanticism was best exemplified by the work of George Sand (1804–1876) and Victor Hugo (1802–1885). The former, whose real name was Aurore Dupin, wrote novels of country life with an idyllic charm that has endeared them to countless readers. She was one of the first to make peasants and humble laborers the heroes of fiction. Later she became a zealous advocate of republicanism and of the rights of women to a love untrammeled by marital convention. A novelist of much wider influence was Victor Hugo, who for many years was the living voice of French romanticism. Intensely interested in public affairs, he was an eloquent champion of political freedom and of justice for those who were caught in the web of fate. His best-known work is *Les Miserables,* an epic of the redemption of a soul purified by heroism and suffering and a powerful indictment of social cruelty.

Studies for a Sculpture of Victor Hugo by Rodin

In attempting to judge the importance of literary romanticism as a factor of social and intellectual progress, we should note, first of all, its grave limitations. The disdain for reason and scientific analysis by even the most liberal of the romanticists was certainly a handicap to any permanent solution of humanity's problems. Excesses of sentimentality are not easily controlled. To allow free reign to the emotions in one direction is to run the risk of an impairment of judgment in others. Thus we find Victor Hugo hurling bitter invectives against Napoleon III, whom he called "Napoleon the Little," but singing paeans of praise to Napoleon I. It was perhaps for this reason also that the liberalism of so many of the romanticists eventually gave way to nationalism, as in the case of Schiller, or even to hopeless reaction, as in the case of Wordsworth. Yet, notwithstanding these weaknesses, literary romanticism accomplished no small amount of good in combating repression in many of its forms and in proclaiming the nobility of the common man. And probably it is safe to say that it was these elements of strength which really survived to influence the work of such writers as Dickens, George Eliot, and John Ruskin in the middle and later years of the nineteenth century.

The importance of literary romanticism

The growth of a romantic movement in art was scarcely noticeable until after the downfall of Napoleon. This was especially true in France. With the outbreak of the French Revolution a strong reaction set in against the elegant rococo style of the old order. But instead of launching a new tradition, the artists of the Revolution simply went back to what was supposed to be a *pure* classicism, on the assumption that this would be in harmony with the rationalist ideals of the new order. The advent of Napoleon made no perceptible change. The Little Corporal liked to think of himself as a modern Caesar or Alexander the Great. Accordingly, he adopted the

The revival of classicist art

Roman imperial eagle as one of his emblems, invested his son with
the title of King of Rome, and erected arches, columns, and temples
of triumph in the city of Paris. Under such influences it is not surprising that a classicist movement in art of more than ordinary vitality should have crystallized in France in the first two decades of the
nineteenth century. It reached its apex in painting under the leadership of Jacques David (1748–1825) and Jean Auguste Ingres
(1780–1867). The work of both of these men was characterized by
order and restraint, by a strict attention to form, and by a liberal
choice of themes from Greek and Roman mythology.

The eventual
triumph of
romanticism in
painting

Notwithstanding the vigor of the classical revival, the force of the
romantic influence, overflowing from the channels of literature and
philosophy, was not to be denied. After the defeat of Napoleon at
Waterloo the period of the Enlightenment and the Revolution was
definitely accepted as a closed chapter. There seemed to be no
longer any reason for trying to preserve the ideals of a bygone age.
As a consequence, classicism in painting was quickly supplanted by
romanticism. The foremost champion of the new style in France
was Eugène Delacroix (1798–1863), who gloried in portraying
struggles for freedom and other dramatic scenes from history. In

See color
plates at pages
769, 801, 832, 833

place of the restraint and sobriety of classical painting, he substituted an emotionalism in some cases as overwrought as that of
Michelangelo. Inspired also by Rubens and the Venetians, he employed small strokes of pure color that seem to merge into the
actual flesh of his subjects. The work of Delacroix was paralleled
to a certain distance by that of the romantic landscape painters.
Their chief representative was Camille Corot (1796–1875), leader
of the Barbizon school, so called from the village of Barbizon near
Paris. Among others who followed the same tradition was the
Englishman J. M. W. Turner (1775–1851). The romantic landscape
painters were just as addicted to effusive displays of emotionalism
as Delacroix, but it was an emotionalism of a quieter tone. They
were poets of nature who suffused forests and streams and mountains with a gentle haze of tender worship.

Architecture
not greatly
affected
by romanticism

From what we have learned about the influence of romanticism
upon literature and painting, we should normally expect that architecture also would be deeply affected. Such, however, was not the
case. While it is true that, under romantic inspirations, a movement
was started about 1840 to revive the medieval Gothic, the results
were only moderately significant. A large number of churches with
soaring spires and pointed arches were built, and even some government buildings also; but not infrequently what was supposed to be
pure Gothic turned out to be a crude eclecticism made up of elements taken only partly from the Gothic. In general, the classical
influence was still too strong to be overcome, with the result that
throughout the greater part of the nineteenth century variations of
the baroque continued to be the most popular building styles. Not

A Page from the Score of Beethoven's Piano Sonata Opus 109 in E Major
Right: *Ludwig van Beethoven*

until about 1900 was there much evidence of a desire to create a new and original architecture more truly expressive of our own civilization.

In music, as in painting and literature, the first decades of the nineteenth century saw the rise of romanticism. The romanticists regarded music not essentially as objective beauty but mainly as a medium for expressing man's inner moods. It must not merely please but must stir a sympathetic vibration in the listener. Attempts were made to capture in tone the various aspects of nature and, above all, human sentiments and passions. To some extent the composers, like the poets, responded to the exciting political drama about them. It is significant that at first musical romanticism found its congenial expression in lyricism—piano pieces and songs. This represents a rebellion against the logical architecture of the large symphonic forms. Since the redoubtable guardian of the latter, Ludwig van Beethoven (1770–1827), stood there as a formidable sentinel, the spirit of romanticism moved into chamber and orchestral music only gradually.

The beginning of romanticism in music

Ludwig van Beethoven was born in the west German town of Bonn but spent most of his productive years in Vienna, then regarded as the musical capital of Europe. Poverty and a harsh father made his childhood unhappy, and his adult life was a succession of difficulties, largely occasioned by his impractical nature and irascible temper. He was not only coarse in manner, careless in

Ludwig van Beethoven

dress, and blunt to the point of rudeness, but overly sensitive and suspicious, frequently injuring his closest friends because of resentment toward some imaginary slight. In spite of such traits he was able to retain the loyalty of his friends and to fascinate and humble the Viennese aristocracy, both male and female. The crowning source of Beethoven's suffering was his deafness, which began to trouble him before he was thirty and became total in his later years. As a result, he was not only forced to give up playing in public, but was never able to hear many of his greatest works.

The first two decades of Beethoven's life in Vienna saw the composition of dozens of piano sonatas, much chamber music, eight symphonies, overtures, one opera, and one Mass. The most remarkable thing about these works is their uniqueness: each represents a new solution of the problems of the respective genre. In the Fifth Symphony Beethoven reaches the summit of symphonic logic, the Sixth is a glorification of nature, the Seventh a Dionysian revelry, the Eighth a genial conjuring up of the spirit of the eighteenth-century symphony. Then Beethoven embarks on his last artistic journey; the deaf composer takes us into the world of visions, though everything remains ordered by an iron will. Five piano sonatas, five string quartets, the Ninth Symphony and the great Mass called *Missa Solemnis* constitute his final legacy. They fill the listener with awe not so much because of their unusual form or their vast proportions, but because of their tone, a tone altogether new in the history of music. It expresses boundless will and power and ecstasy, the tone of unspeakable solitude breaking into the open. It is this tone and harnessed power that made Beethoven the Titan of music.

Franz Schubert (1797–1828), the Viennese schoolteacher's son, does not fit very well into any scheme or schedule. He was no one's disciple; he just assimilated music that was around him and by his eighteenth year composed masterpieces—surely the embodiment of what is called "God-given" natural talent. But this was a dangerous precocity. Perhaps Schubert felt that he must hasten, for he died in his thirty-first year. After he left the paternal home he lived a romantic bohemian life with a group of like-minded poets, painters, and singers, eternally poor, eternally working, and eternally hoping. In this genial company perhaps three friends shared one hat and five one purse, but the world was wrong in construing from this carefree existence the parochial picture of unfortunate derelicts perishing in the adventure. These people lived a life congenial to them, but it was a life that did not agree with the pattern set by the ruling Biedermeier bourgeoisie. They did not need much, they got together in the evenings to make music, and on nice days went out into the country where Schubert would compose on the back of a country-inn menu half a dozen songs and waltzes in one afternoon. It is thus that Schubert's music came to reflect Vienna's grace and the rhythm of its life. Schubert was the greatest of song composers, but he was also the only one of the age who could be ranked next to **READINGS** Beethoven as an instrumental composer. Though they lived in the same town, Schubert was so overawed by Beethoven that he never dared to address him. Among his eight symphonies, numerous chamber music works, piano sonatas and Masses there are many incomparable masterpieces. Only his operas failed to show the full weight of his genius.

SELECTED READINGS

· *Items so designated are available in paperbound editions.*

THE AGE OF NAPOLEON

· Brinton, Crane, *The Lives of Talleyrand*, New York, 1932 (Norton Library).
· Bruun, Geoffrey, *Europe and the French Imperium*, New York, 1938 (Torchbook).
  Gershoy, Leo, *The French Revolution and Napoleon*, New York, 1933. A brief but excellent account.
· Geyl, Pieter, *Napoleon, For and Against*, New Haven, 1949 (Yale University Press).
  Gottschalk, L. R., *The Era of the French Revolution, 1715-1815*, New York, 1929. Thorough and scholarly.
  Kircheisen, F. M., *Napoleon*, New York, 1932.
  Tarle, Eugene, *Napoleon's Invasion of Russia*, New York, 1942. An exciting account.
  Thompson, J. M., *Napoleon Bonaparte*, New York, 1952. A recent evaluation.

THE AGE OF REACTION

· Artz, F. B., *Reaction and Revolution, 1814-1832*, New York, 1934 (Torchbook).
· Gulick, E. V., *Europe's Classical Balance of Power*, Ithaca, N.Y., 1955 (Norton Library).
· May, A. J., *The Age of Metternich, 1814-1848*, New York, 1933 (Holt, Rinehart & Winston). A good summary.
· Nicholson, Harold, *The Congress of Vienna*, London, 1946 (Compass).

INTELLECTUAL AND ARTISTIC DEVELOPMENTS, 1800-1830

  Artz, F. B., *France under the Bourbon Restoration, 1814-1830*, New York, 1963. Emphasizes social and intellectual developments.
  Bell, Clive, *Landmarks in Nineteenth Century Painting*, New York, 1927.
  Boas, George, *French Philosophies of the Romantic Period*, Baltimore, 1934.
  Brandes, Georg, *Main Currents in Nineteenth Century Literature*, New York, 1901-06.
· Brinton, Crane, *English Political Thought in the Nineteenth Century*, New York, 1962 (Torchbook). A new edition.
  ———, *Political Ideas of the English Romanticists*, London, 1926.
  Davidson, W. L., *Political Thought in England from Bentham to Mill*, New York, 1916.
  Einstein, Alfred, *Music in the Romantic Era*, New York, 1947.
  Lang, Paul, *Music in Western Civilization*, New York, 1941.
  Machlis, Joseph, *The Enjoyment of Music*, 3rd ed., New York, 1970.

789

READINGS   Randall, J. H., Jr., *The Making of the Modern Mind*, New York, 1926. Chs. XVI, XVII.

Wright, C. H. C., *A History of French Literature*, New York, 1925.

SOURCE MATERIALS

Bentham, Jeremy, *A Fragment on Government.*

——, *Principles of Penal Law*, Part II, Book II, Ch. XII.

· Burke, Edmund, *Reflections on the Revolution in France* (Holt, Rinehart & Winston and others).

· de Caulaincourt, A. A. L., *With Napoleon in Russia*, New York, 1935 (Universal Library). An eye-witness account by one of Napoleon's officers.

· Herold, J. C., ed., *The Mind of Napoleon*, New York, 1955 (Collier).

Johnston, R. M., ed., *The Corsican: A Diary of Napoleon in His Own Words.*

· Kant, Immanuel, *Plan for Perpetual Peace* (Library of Liberal Arts).

· Mill, John Stuart, *Autobiography*, New York, 1924 (Library of Liberal Arts and others).

Thompson, J. M., ed., *Napoleon Self-Revealed*, Boston, 1934.

CHAPTER 26

The Early Industrial Revolutions

It may not be true, in spite of *Punch* cartoons, that coal-miners drank champagne in 1871–1873; but certainly many wage-earners were getting more cake as well as tea, cocoa, meat, sugar, rice, and fats. They might return home a little earlier for the evening meal, as trade union pressure was chipping the working .week from sixty (or more) hours down toward fifty-five, with a Saturday half-holiday. If they lived in Britain the public health service was beginning to make their living environment a bit better. . . . Parliament had given them a vote in 1867, and in 1870 it finally insisted that the children it had shut out of the factories must go to school. Things had moved since the Hungry Forties.
—Herbert Heaton, "Economic Change and Growth,"
The New Cambridge Modern History, X

The years from about 1760 to 1860 were marked by economic changes so sweeping in character as to deserve the label Industrial Revolution. Actually they continued beyond this time until well into the twentieth century. Many historians divide the movement into two stages, with the year 1860 marking the approximate boundary between them. The stage from 1860 to 1914 is often referred to as the Second Industrial Revolution. It differed from the first primarily in being based on electricity and the internal combustion engine instead of their more cumbersome predecessors, coal and the steam engine.

The First and Second Revolutions

1. CAUSES AND EARLY BEGINNINGS

The First Industrial Revolution sprang from a multitude of causes. It may be well to consider first the early improvements in technology. The marvelous inventions of the late eighteenth century did not spring full-blown like Athena from the brow of Zeus. On the contrary, there had been a more or less fruitful interest in mechanical innovations for some time. The period of the Commercial Revolution had witnessed the invention of the pendulum clock, the thermometer, the air pump, and the spinning wheel, to say nothing of improvements in the techniques of smelting ores and making brass. About 1580 a mechanical loom was devised, capable of weaving several strands of ribbon at the same time. There were also important technological advances in such industries as glass blowing, clock making, and wood finishing. Several of the early inventions made necessary the use of factory methods. For example, the silk-throwing machine invented in Italy about 1500 had to be housed in a large building and required a considerable corps of workers. In the Temple Mills on the Thames above London, according to a description by Daniel Defoe in 1728, brass was beaten into kettles and pans by enormous hammers operated by water power. These early technological improvements are hardly to be compared in significance with those made after 1760, but they do indicate that the machine age did not burst upon the world out of a clear sky.

Among other causes of paramount importance were several more direct consequences of the Commercial Revolution. That movement brought into existence a class of capitalists who were constantly seeking new opportunities to invest their surplus wealth. At first this wealth could be readily absorbed by trade or by mining, banking, and shipbuilding ventures; but as time went on the opportunities in such fields became limited. As a consequence more and more capital was made available for the development of manufacturing. But a rapid development of manufacturing would scarcely have occurred had there not been a growing demand for industrial products. This demand grew largely from the establishment of colonial empires and from the marked increase in the population of Europe. It will be recalled that one of the primary objects in the acquisition of colonies was to expand the market for manufactured goods from the mother country. At the same time the potential markets at home were being rapidly enlarged by the large increase of population in western European countries. In England the number of inhabitants rose from 4,000,000 in 1600 to 6,000,000 in 1700 and to 9,000,000 by the end of the eighteenth century. The population of France grew from 17,000,000 in 1700 to 26,000,000 about a hundred years later. Finally, the Commercial Revolution gave a stimulus to the growth of manufactures through its basic gospel of mercantilism. The mercantilist policy was designed, as much as for any other purpose, to increase the quantity of manufactured goods available for export and thereby to ensure a favorable balance of trade.

Despite the importance of the causes already mentioned, the Industrial Revolution would undoubtedly have been delayed had there not been a need for fundamental mechanical improvements in certain fields of production. By 1700 the demand for charcoal for smelting iron had so depleted the resources of timber that several of

The Staffordshire Collieries. In the building to the right is a whimsey, or coal-powered steam engine, used to lift loads of coal from mines.

the nations of western Europe were threatened with deforestation. A partial solution was found about 1709 when Abraham Darby discovered that coke could be used for smelting. But in order to obtain sufficient coke it was necessary that coal be mined in much larger quantities than ever before. Since the chief obstacle to the extraction of coal was the accumulation of water in the mines, the need for the new fuel led to a search for some convenient source of power to drive the pumps. Various experiments in connection with this search finally resulted in the invention of the steam engine. An even more crucial need for mechanization existed in the textile industry. With the increasing popularity of cotton clothing in the seventeenth and eighteenth centuries, it was simply impossible to provide enough yarn with the primitive spinning wheels still in use. Even when every available woman and child was pressed into service, the demand could not be met. The result was the development later of the spinning jenny and the water frame, the forerunners of a series of important inventions in the textile industry. As the practicability of these machines was soon demonstrated, mechanization was bound to be extended to other manufactures.

The need for
fundamental
mechanical improvements in
certain
industries

2. WHY INDUSTRIALIZATION BEGAN IN BRITAIN

At first thought it may seem strange that a small island kingdom should not only have become the industrial leader of the world but should have held that leadership for more than a century.

793

See color map
at page 800

Possibly we should place first as a primary cause the fact that Britain had profited most from the Commercial Revolution. Though it is true that about 1750 France had a foreign trade 25 per cent larger than that of Britain, it must be remembered that the French population was at least three times as large as the British. Moreover, France had reached her limit of imperial aggrandizement, while much of the profit of her world trade was being diverted through loans and taxes to the upkeep of a costly army and a frivolous and extravagant court. Britain, on the other hand, was just on the brink of a golden age of power and prosperity. She had already acquired the most valuable colonies in the Western Hemisphere, and she was soon to clinch her imperial and commercial supremacy by defeating the French in the Seven Years' War. In addition, a much larger proportion of Britain's gains from overseas trade was available for productive investment. Her government was comparatively free from corruption and wasteful expenditure. Her military establishment cost less than that of the French, and her revenues were much more efficiently collected. As a result, her merchants and shipowners were left with a larger share of surplus earnings, which they were eager to invest in any conceivable business venture that might be the source of additional profit.

In view of these facts it is not strange that Britain should have emerged as the leading capitalist nation in the early eighteenth century. Nowhere was the joint-stock company more highly developed. Trading in securities was organized as a legitimate business when the London Stock Exchange was chartered in 1698. Britain, moreover, had perhaps the best banking system in Europe. At its apex was the Bank of England, founded in 1694. Though established for the purpose of raising funds for the government, it was organized as a private corporation. Its stock was privately owned, and its management was not subject to any official control by the state. Nevertheless, it always operated in close association with the government, and even in its early days served as an important stabilizing factor in public finance. With the financial stability of the government thus assured, leaders of business enterprise could carry on their activities unhindered by fear of national bankruptcy or ruinous inflation.

Political and social factors were not alone important in accounting for the beginning of the Industrial Revolution in Britain. Although the British government of the eighteenth century was far from democratic, it was at least more liberal than most of the governments on the Continent. The Glorious Revolution of 1688–1689 had done much to establish the conception of limited sovereignty. The doctrine was now widely accepted that the power of the state should extend no farther than the protection of man's natural rights to liberty and to the enjoyment of property. Under

Favorable factors operating in Britain

Britain the leading capitalist nation

Favorable political and social conditions in Britain

the influence of this doctrine Parliament repealed old laws providing for special monopolies and interfering with free competition. Mercantilist principles continued to be applied to trade with the colonies, but in the sphere of domestic business many restrictions were gradually abolished. Furthermore, Britain was already coming to be recognized as a haven for refugees from other countries. More than 40,000 Huguenots settled in her villages and cities after being driven from France in 1685 by the revocation of the Edict of Nantes. Thrifty, energetic, and ambitious, these people instilled new vigor into the British nation. Social conditions also were distinctly favorable to the industrial development of Britain. Her nobility had ceased to be a hereditary caste exclusively and was rapidly becoming an aristocracy of wealth. Almost anyone who had made a fortune could rise to the highest levels of social distinction.

A few other causes must be added to complete the picture. First may be mentioned the fact that the damp climate of the British Isles was singularly favorable for the manufacturing of cotton cloth, since the thread would not become brittle and break easily when woven by machines. And it is sufficient to call to mind that it was the mechanization of the textile industry which ushered in the age of machines. Second, the guild system of production, with its elaborate restrictions, had never become so firmly implanted in Britain as on the Continent. Even the regulations that were established had been thrown off, especially in the northern counties, by the end of the seventeenth century. Lastly, since wealth was more evenly distributed in Britain than in most other nations at that time, her manufacturers could devote their attention to the production of large quantities of cheap and ordinary wares instead of to the making of limited supplies of luxury goods. This factor had considerable influence in promoting the adoption of factory methods in the hope of achieving a larger output. In France, by contrast, the demand was for articles *de luxe* to gratify the tastes of a small class of elegant wastrels. Since quality of workmanship was a primary consideration in this type of goods, there was little incentive to invent machines.

Other favorable factors in Britain

3. THE PROGRESS AND SPREAD OF INDUSTRIALIZATION

The initial stage of the Industrial Revolution, from about 1760 to 1860, witnessed a phenomenal development of the application of machinery to industry that laid the foundations for our modern mechanical civilization. As we have seen, the first of the branches of industry to be mechanized was the manufacture of cotton cloth. The first invention essential to the development of this industry was the spinning jenny invented by James Hargreaves in 1767. The spinning "jenny," so called from the name of the inventor's wife,

The application of machinery to cotton manufactures

The Spinning Jenny Invented by James Hargreaves in 1767

was really a compound spinning wheel, capable of producing sixteen threads at once. Unfortunately the threads it spun were not strong enough to be used for the longitudinal fibers, or warp, of cotton cloth. It was not until the invention of the water frame by Richard Arkwright about two years later that quantity production of both kinds of cotton yarn became possible.

The problems of the cotton industry were still not entirely solved. The invention of spinning machines had more than made up for the deficiency of yarn, but now there was a scarcity of weavers. It soon became obvious that the only remedy for this shortage would be the invention of some kind of automatic machine to take the place of the hand loom. Many declared such a contrivance impossible, but a Kentish clergyman, the Reverend Edmund Cartwright, was not to be discouraged so easily. He reasoned that if automatic machinery could be applied to spinning, it could be just as logically extended to weaving. Knowing little about mechanics himself, he hired a carpenter and a smith to put his ideas into effect. The result was the power loom, which Cartwright patented in 1785. A good many years elapsed, however, before it was sufficiently improved to be more than a modest success. Not until about 1820 did it largely displace more primitive methods of weaving. Meanwhile, the invention of a machine for separating the seeds from the cotton fiber made possible a much more abundant supply of raw cotton at a lower price. This machine was the cotton gin, invented by a Yankee schoolteacher, Eli Whitney, in 1792.

Several of the new inventions in the textile industry contributed to the growth of the factory system. The water frame and the automatic loom were large and heavy machines which could not possibly be set up in the cottages of individual workers. All were eventually designed to be driven by power, and, besides, they cost so much that no one but a wealthy capitalist could afford to buy them. It was therefore inevitable that they should be installed in large buildings, and that the workers employed to operate them should be brought under the supervision of the owner or of a manager acting for him. Such were the essentials of the factory system

The power loom and the cotton gin

Origin of the factory system

796

in its original form. Appropriately enough, the real founder of this system was Richard Arkwright, inventor of the water frame. By indomitable perseverance and shrewd management, Arkwright rose from the status of an obscure barber and wigmaker to that of a captain of industry. Commonly working from five in the morning until nine at night, he struggled against obstacles for years. He was accused, perhaps with some truth, of stealing his ideas for the water frame from others. Altogether he is said to have spent some $60,000 before his plans brought him any profit. He established his first factory, operated by water power, in 1771.

It is difficult to believe that the factory system would ever have assumed much importance had it not been for the perfection of the steam engine. That steam could be employed as a means of power had been known for centuries. Crude steam engines had been devised by Hero of Alexandria in the first century B.C., by Leonardo da Vinci during the Renaissance, and by various individuals in the early modern period. None of these, however, had been put to any practical use. The first man to apply the power of steam to industrial purposes was Thomas Newcomen, who in 1712 devised a crude but effective engine for pumping water from the British coal mines. By the middle of the century nearly 100 of his engines were in use.

Newcomen's steam engine

Though of great value to the coal mining industry, Newcomen's engine suffered from defects which prevented its being widely used for industrial purposes. For one thing, it wasted both fuel and power. It was constructed in such a way that after each stroke of the piston, the steam had to be condensed by spraying cold water into the cylinder. This meant that the cylinder had to be heated again before the next stroke, and this alternate heating and cooling greatly retarded the speed of the engine. In the second place, Newcomen's "Miner's Friend" was adaptable only to the straight-line motion necessary for pumping; the principle of converting the straight-line action of the piston into a rotary motion had not been discovered. Both of these defects were eventually remedied by James Watt, a maker of scientific instruments at the University of Glasgow. In 1763 Watt was asked to repair a model of the Newcomen engine. While engaged in this task he conceived the idea that the machine would be greatly improved if a separate chamber were added to condense the steam, so as to eliminate the necessity of cooling the cylinder. He patented his first engine incorporating this device in 1769. Unfortunately Watt's genius as an inventor was not matched by his business ability. He admitted that he would "rather face a loaded cannon than settle a disputed account or make a bargain." As a consequence he fell into debt in attempting to place his machines on the market. He was rescued by Matthew Boulton, a wealthy hardware manufacturer of Birmingham. The two men formed a partnership, with Boulton providing the capital. By 1800 the firm had sold 289 engines for use in factories and mines.

Newcomen's engine greatly improved by James Watt

James Watts' Steam Engine

The importance of the steam engine

Few single inventions have had greater influence upon the history of modern times than the steam engine. Contrary to popular opinion, it was not the initial cause of the Industrial Revolution; instead, it was partly an effect. Watt's engine, at least, would never have become a reality if there had not been a demand for an effective source of power to operate the heavy machines already invented in the textile industry. On the other hand, the perfection of the steam engine was certainly a cause of the more rapid growth of industrialization. It raised the production of coal and iron to a new importance. It made possible a revolution in transportation. It provided almost unlimited opportunities for accelerating the manufacture of goods, thereby making the industrialized nations the richest and most powerful in the world. Before the development of the steam engine, the resources of power were largely at the mercy of the weather. In time of drought, low water in the streams would probably force the mills to curtail operations or even to shut down entirely. Ships on ocean voyages might be delayed for weeks by lack of wind. Now, however, there was a constant supply of energy, which could be tapped and used when needed. It is therefore not too much to say that the invention of Watt's engine was the real beginning of the age of power.

Early development of the iron industry

One of the industries that owed its rapid development to the improvement of the steam engine was the manufacture of iron and iron products. While many of the new machines, such as the spinning jenny and the water frame, could be constructed of wood, steam engines required a more substantial material. Moreover, the cylinders of these engines needed to be bored as accurately as possible in order to prevent a loss of power. This made necessary a considerable advance in the production of machine tools and in scientific methods of iron manufacture. The pioneer in this work was John Wilkinson, a manufacturer of cannon. In 1774 Wilkinson patented a method of boring cylinders which reduced the percentage of error to a very small amount for that day. Even more important than the achievements of Wilkinson were the accomplishments of another Englishman, who devised the method of puddling, or stirring the molten iron to eliminate a larger percentage of its carbon content. This process made possible the production in quantity of the tougher grade of metal known as wrought iron. A few years later came the invention of the rolling mill for the manufacture of sheet iron. These two achievements revolutionized the industry. Within less than twenty years the production of iron in England quadrupled, and the price dropped to a fraction of what it had been.

The first signs of a definite improvement in methods of travel began to appear about 1780. It was about that time that the construction of turnpikes and canals in England was started in earnest. By 1830 nearly all of the highways had been drained and covered with a surface of broken stone, while the principal streams had been linked together by a network of 2500 miles of canals. The improvement of roads made possible a faster stagecoach service. In 1784 the postmaster general inaugurated a mail service with coaches that ran continuously day and night, covering a distance of 120 miles in twenty-four hours. By the end of the century special stages, known as "flying machines," operated between all of the principal cities, sometimes achieving the sensational speed of nine or ten miles per hour.

But the really significant progress in transportation did not come until after the steam engine had been generally accepted as a dependable source of power. Attempts were first made to adapt the use of steam to stagecoaches, and several of these ancestors of the modern automobile were actually put on the highways. Gradually the opinion grew that it would be more profitable to use the steam engine to draw a train of cars over iron rails. A number of such railroads were already in existence for the purpose of transporting coal, but the cars were drawn by horses. The man primarily responsible for the first steam railway was George Stephenson, a self-made engineer who had not even learned to read until he was seventeen years of age. In 1822 he convinced a group of men who were projecting a coal railroad from Stockton to Darlington of the merits of steam traction, and was appointed engineer for the line with full liberty to carry out his plans. The result was the opening three

THE PROGRESS AND
SPREAD OF
INDUSTRIALIZATION

Early developments in transportation: (1) roads and canals

(2) the first railroads

Puffing Billy. Built by Timothy Hackworth in 1813, it was the first commercially successful railway engine and a predecessor of George Stephenson's famous *Rocket.*

The Crimple Valley Viaduct. Located in York, England, and built during the 1840's, this and others like it were essential to the rapid development of British railroads in the early part of the nineteenth century.

years later of the first railway operated entirely by steam. The locomotives he built for this line attained a speed of fifteen miles an hour, the fastest rate at which human beings had yet traveled.

(3) the beginning of steam navigation

Meanwhile the steam engine was being gradually applied to water transportation. Here it was Americans rather than Englishmen who took the lead. Precisely who should receive credit for inventing the steamboat is a matter of dispute. There is evidence that a number of men had something to do with it. About 1787 an American metal worker, John Fitch, constructed a boat that actually carried passengers on the Delaware for several months. But Fitch was never able to make his craft a financial success. After vainly attempting to persuade governments to adopt his invention, he committed suicide in 1798. Another American, Robert Fulton, is given the credit for having made the steamboat commercially successful. That Fulton was any more ingenious than Fitch is open to doubt, but he was a good enough salesman and promoter to secure the backing of a wealthy capitalist, and he knew how to keep himself in the public eye. In April 1838, the first steamships, the *Sirius* and the *Great Western*, crossed the Atlantic. Two years later Samuel Cunard founded the famous Cunard Line, providing a regular transoceanic service with vessels propelled entirely by steam.

The invention of the telegraph

The one significant improvement in communications, during the first stage of the Industrial Revolution was the invention of the telegraph. As early as 1820 the French physicist Ampère discovered that electromagnetism could be used for sending messages by wire between distant points. About all that remained was to devise effective instruments for transmitting and receiving the messages. Experiments for this purpose were carried on by a number of individ-

**ENGLAND AT THE START OF
THE INDUSTRIAL REVOLUTION**

Population centers
● Principal manufacturing cities
Coal fields
✕✕✕ Iron ore deposits

Glasgow
Edinburgh

SCOTLAND

NORTHUMBERLAND

Newcastle

CUMBERLAND
Gateshead

DURHAM

Middlesbrough

WESTMORELAND

Ouse R.

✕✕✕
✕✕

*NORTH
SEA*

I. OF MAN

*IRISH
SEA*

YORK

York

Leeds

Wakefield

Hull

LANCASTER

Manchester

Liverpool

Rotherham

Grimsby

ANGLESEY

Northwich

CHESTER

DERBY

Trent R.

Lincoln

LINCOLN

Stoke

NOTTINGHAM

Nottingham

STAFFORD

Cardigan Bay

LEICESTER

RUTLAND

Norwich

WALES

SALOP

Walsall

Leicester

Aston Manor

Birmingham

NORTHAMPTON

NORFOLK

Great Yarmouth

WORCESTER

WARWICK

HUNTINGDON

CAMBRIDGE

SUFFOLK

HEREFORD

Avon R.

Northampton

✕✕✕

✕✕

BEDFORD

Ipswich

Gloucester

OXFORD

BUCKING-
HAM

HERTFORD

ESSEX

MONMOUTH

GLOUCESTER

Oxford

London

Swansea

Newport

BERKS

MIDDLESEX

Thames R.

Cardiff

Bristol

WILTS

Reading

Chatham

Bath

Devizes

SURREY

KENT

SOMERSET

HANTS

Taunton

Southampton

SUSSEX

Brighton

Hastings

DEVON

DORSET

Portsmouth

Eastbourne

Bournemouth

I. OF WIGHT

Strait of Dover

CORNWALL

Plymouth

Bristol Channel

ENGLISH CHANNEL

0   50   100 miles

The Massacre of Chios, Eugène Delacroix (1798–1863). During the Greek war for independence, Turks slaughtered more than 20,000 Greeks in 1822, depicted in this famous painting. (Louvre)

Liberty Leading the People, Eugene Delacroix (1798–1863). Delacroix was a colorful painter of dramatic and emotional themes, as exemplified by this imaginary scene from the Revolution of 1830. (Louvre)

uals. Three of them succeeded almost simultaneously. In 1844 a telegraph line efficient enough for commercial purposes was established. This was the line between Baltimore and Washington, which an American, Samuel Morse, succeeded in having built on the strength of improvements in his own invention. Once started, telegraph systems multiplied all over the world. Soon all important cities were linked, and in 1866 the first Atlantic cable was laid under the direction of the American capitalist, Cyrus Field.

The Industrial Revolution also had its agricultural aspects. They were especially noticeable in the first sixty years of the nineteenth century. Among them were the production of better breeds of livestock; the introduction of new crops, such as the sugar beet, which was now being extensively cultivated in Germany and France; and the development of agricultural chemistry by Justus von Liebig, which made possible the production of artificial fertilizers. Agriculture in this period also came under the influence of mechanization. Better plows and harrows were designed, and the threshing machine was quite generally adopted. In 1834 the American farmer, Cyrus McCormick, patented his mechanical reaper and soon afterward began its manufacture in Chicago. By 1860 these machines were being sold at the rate of 20,000 a year. As a result of these various improvements, agriculture all over the world rejoiced in an unprecedented prosperity, which lasted until the great depression of 1873.

Improvements in agriculture

As early as the year 1000 the Saracens were producing excellent steel swords at Damascus. Beginning with the later Middle Ages, Europeans had also known how to manufacture the desirable material. But the methods were slow and difficult and the product expensive. In 1856 Sir Henry Bessemer discovered that the introduction of a jet of air into the molten iron in a blast furnace would eliminate all but the tiniest percentage of carbon and thereby convert the iron into steel. The result was to reduce the price of steel to less than a seventh of its former cost. By 1878 a method was discovered whereby even low-grade iron with a heavy content of phosphorus could also be converted into steel. The consequences of this advance were astounding. Not only was the phosphoric iron of England brought into production, but enormous deposits in Lorraine, in Belgium, and in the United States now became immensely valuable. Between 1880 and 1914 the output of steel in Great Britain rose from 2,000,000 tons to 7,000,000, in Germany from 1,000,000 to 15,000,000, and in the United States from 1,600,000 to 28,000,000. Steel almost entirely supplanted iron for railroad rails, for the framework of large buildings, for bridges, and for other purposes where a cheap metal with a high degree of tensile strength was desired.

The Bessemer Process of Manufacturing Steel. This process involved the introduction of a jet of air into the molten iron to reduce its impure elements and thereby toughen it for the production of steel.

The partial displacement of coal as a basic source of power resulted, first of all, from the invention of the dynamo, a machine for converting mechanical energy into electrical energy. Although the principle of the dynamo was formulated by Michael Faraday in 1831, no machine of this kind capable of practical use was available

801

An Early Dynamo Used for Lighting

The internal-combustion engine

The growth of mass production and the adoption of automatic and highly specialized processes in industry

until 1873. From that time on the harnessing of electrical energy to the mechanism of industry went rapidly ahead. The steam engine came to be relegated gradually to the background, to be used primarily for driving dynamos. The electric energy thus generated is converted by electric motors into mechanical energy. In some areas, especially where coal is scarce, the steam engine for driving dynamos has been superseded by water power. By 1914 electricity provided more than half of the power required by industry in Great Britain and an even larger proportion in Germany.[1] The German A.E.G. (Allgemeine Elektrizitäts Gesellschaft), manufacturing motors, generators, and other electrical equipment, had evolved into the largest industrial unit in Europe.

A second revolutionary development making available new sources of power was the utilization of petroleum products to add to the supply of energy. The existence of petroleum had been known for some time before its value was discovered. Until the middle of the nineteenth century it was regarded as a curiosity. Labeled as Indian Oil or Seneca Oil, it was sold in the United States for its alleged medicinal properties. Even after its value for lubricating purposes was revealed, its use was limited by scarcity. In 1859 Edwin L. Drake solved the problem of an inadequate supply by drilling the first oil well near Titusville, Pennsylvania. New uses for the product were gradually found, although for many years most of it went into the manufacture of kerosene for lamps. In 1876, however, Nikolaus Otto invented the first successful internal-combustion engine. This was the starting point of a series of developments which heralded the dawn of a motorized age.

Among the most typical features of the Second Industrial Revolution were the introduction of automatic machinery, an enormous increase in mass production, and a division of the tasks of labor into minute segments of the manufacturing process. All three of these things date from the years just preceding World War I. A characteristic example of the development of automatic machinery was the invention of the photoelectric cell, or the "electric eye," which could be used to throw switches, to open doors, to sort eggs, to inspect tin cans, to count sheets of paper and measure their thickness, and even to eliminate counterfeit bills. Machines were invented to direct and operate other machines and to complete whole series of manufacturing processes which formerly required much human labor. Not only did automatic machinery result in a marked increase in mass production, but the volume of goods turned out by industry was also greatly expanded by the adoption of the endless conveyor belt. The idea for this was copied originally by Henry Ford about 1908 from the Chicago packers, who used an overhead trolley to move carcasses of beef along a line of butchers. Ford gradually im-

[1] Herbert Heaton, *Economic History of Europe*, p. 518.

proved the device to a point where he could assemble a complete chassis of his famous Model T in an hour and thirty-three minutes. The principle of the conveyor belt and the assembly line, which requires each worker to toil all day at a simple, monotonous task, was subsequently adopted in every automobile factory in the United States and in many other industries as well. It provided the world with a staggering abundance of goods and reduced the prices of some articles which were formerly luxuries for the rich, but no one was then able to foresee how serious might be its effects upon society.

Radical changes in methods of production came not only from the invention of intricate machines but also from a growing domination of industry by science. Actually, the significant discoveries of the Second Industrial Revolution emanated more often from the laboratory of the physicist or chemist than from the brain of the individual inventor. The supremacy of science in the realm of industry was originally foreshadowed in 1856 when William Henry Perkin produced the first aniline or coal-tar dyes. This was the beginning of a marvelous development of synthetic chemistry. From this same coal tar it was discovered that literally hundreds of dyes could be derived, together with an infinite variety of other products, such as aspirin, oil of wintergreen, essence of orange blossoms, saccharine, carbolic acid, and vanilla. As the years passed, many additional subtances were added to the list of synthetic products. Methods were devised for manufacturing nitric acid out of the nitrogen in the air, for making glucose from corn, and for pro-

The growing domination of industry by science

An Early Assembly Line of the Ford Motor Co., 1913. Bodies were slid down the ramp and attached to the chassis as they passed through the line below. Production amounted to 1000 cars a day.

ducing textile fibers from wood and from minerals. Chemists likewise came to the aid of many of the older industries, discovering methods of utilizing hitherto worthless by-products or of increasing the yield from available supplies of raw materials. For example, cotton seeds were turned into celluloid, cosmetics, smokeless powder, and salad oil, while the cracking process of refining gasoline greatly increased the yield from a given quantity of petroleum. Though not recognized at the time, many of these products of industrial chemistry were not biologically degradable. They therefore constituted a problem in helping nature to maintain a balance of forces.

The second stage of the Industrial Revolution saw perhaps an even greater revolution in transportation and communication than did the first. The years after 1860 were marked by feverish activity in railroad building. Before that date there were hardly more than 30,000 miles of railroad in the entire world. By 1890 there were 20,000 miles in Great Britain alone, 26,000 in Germany, and 167,000 in the United States. The service itself was greatly improved by the invention of the air brake in 1868 and by the introduction of the sleeping car, the dining car, and the automatic block-signal system soon afterward. As the years passed, however, the railroads began to suffer under competition from newer forms of transportation, especially from the automobile and the commercial airplane.

The revolution in transportation: the extension and improvement of the railroads

It is impossible to assign credit for invention of the automobile to any one person, though various individuals have claimed it. Both Daimler and Benz made gasoline vehicles in Germany as early as the 1880's, but their original inventions were little more than motorized tricycles. The first man to apply the principle of the internal-combustion engine to a carriage seems to have been the Frenchman Émile Levassor. About 1890 he designed a vehicle with the engine in front and with the power transmitted to the rear wheels by means of a clutch, a shaft, and reduction and differential gears. So far as the evidence shows, this was the first true automobile in history. Obviously, many other inventions were necessary in order to ensure the success of the motorcar as a comfortable and efficient means of travel. Not the least of these were the pneumatic tire developed by J. B. Dunlop in 1888 and the electric self-starter by Charles Kettering about 1910. But the automobile might have remained indefinitely a toy for the rich had it not been for the determination of Henry Ford to produce a car that could be bought by persons of moderate incomes. In 1908 he began the manufacture of his Model T on the basis of the theory that he could make more money by selling a great quantity of cheap cars on a small margin of profit than by turning out an expensive product for the wealthy few. Other companies followed his example, with the result that eventually the automobile industry grew into the largest single branch of manufacturing in the United States.

The automobile

No more than the perfection of the automobile can the invention of the airplane be credited to any one person. The idea that some day man might be able to fly is an old one indeed. Not only was it suggested by Roger Bacon in the thirteenth century, but it was actually embodied in some definite plans for flying machines conceived by the fertile mind of Leonardo da Vinci. Nevertheless, the birth of aviation as a mechanical possibility really dates from the 1890's. It was about that time that Otto Lilienthal, Samuel P. Langley, and others began their experiments with heavier-than-air machines. The work of Langley was carried forward by the Wright brothers, who, in 1903, made the first successful flight in a motor-driven plane. From that point on advancement was rapid. In 1908 the Wright brothers flew nearly 100 miles. The following year Louis Bleriot crossed the English Channel in the monoplane he had recently invented. During World War I each of the belligerent nations made strenuous efforts to utilize the possibilities of the airplane as a weapon of slaughter. As a consequence, improvements in design and in efficiency came thick and fast. However, it should be remembered that, even without the war, progress would still have been rapid; for, once an invention has been successfully launched, improvements follow in a kind of geometric ratio.

The early Industrial Revolution, or the age of coal and iron, resulted in but one important advance in communication. This, as we have seen, was the invention of the telegraph, which was already in extensive use by 1860. The age of electricity and the internal-combustion engine were accompanied by the perfection of a number of devices that went far toward annihilating both time and distance in the dissemination of news and in communicating with far-off places. First came the telephone, for which the credit is commonly given to

Wireless telegraphy, radio, and television

The First Successful Airplane Flight. The Wright brothers' motor-driven craft takes to the air at Kitty Hawk, North Carolina, on December 17, 1903.

Alexander Graham Bell, though only a few hours after Bell had applied for a patent in Washington on February 15, 1876, Elisha Gray appeared with practically the same idea.[2] Next came the invention of the wireless telegraph by Guglielmo Marconi, on the basis of discoveries by Heinrich Hertz and others relative to the transmission of electromagnetic waves through the ether. In 1899 Marconi dispatched a wireless message across the English Channel and two years later across the Atlantic. The invention of wireless telegraphy paved the way for the development of radio, the wireless telephone, and television.

4. THE NEW CAPITALISM

The Second Industrial Revolution was distinguished from the First not merely by technological advances, but even more strikingly by the development of new forms of capitalist organization.

The growth of finance capitalism

The age of coal and iron was also, generally speaking, the age of small enterprise. Until the middle of the nineteenth century, at least, the partnership was still the dominant form of business organization. To be sure, many of these partnerships did business on a considerable scale, but they were hardly to be compared with the giant corporations of later years. Their capital came mainly from profits plowed back into the business, and their owners generally took an active part in the work of management. Many joint-stock companies had also been formed, but, except for their attributes of permanence and limited liability, they differed little from the partnerships. All of these types of business organization, insofar as they were concerned with manufacturing, mining, or transportation, may be designated as forms of *industrial capitalism*. During the Second Revolution, especially after 1890, industrial capitalism was largely superseded by *finance capitalism*, one of the most crucial developments of the modern age. Finance capitalism has four outstanding characteristics: (1) the domination of industry by investment banks and insurance companies; (2) the formation of huge aggregations of capital; (3) the separation of ownership from management; and (4) the growth of holding companies.

One of the earliest examples of the domination of industry by investment bankers was the formation of the United States Steel Corporation in 1901 with the aid of J. P. Morgan and Company.

The domination of industry by investment institutions

Thenceforth financial institutions gained control over an increasing number of corporations. Of course they did not own all of the stock, or any considerable fraction of it. Many corporations had tens of thousands of stockholders. But these people were chiefly absentee owners; they had little to do with influencing corporate policy, and some of their shares did not even carry voting privileges.

[2] Clive Day, *Economic Development in Modern Europe*, p. 26.

Banks and insurance companies wielded control in some cases through ownership of a majority of the *voting stock* and in others through floating loans under terms which provided the lenders with extensive powers or with representation on boards of directors.

Another element in finance capitalism was the separation of ownership from management. The real owners of industrial enterprises were the thousands of men and women who had invested their savings in shares of stock; management was in the hands of a group of officers and directors, chosen by a minority of shareholders who had monopolized the voting stock or collected the proxies of absentee owners. In some cases the officers were little more than salaried employees, owning but a tiny percentage of the company's capital. Indeed, it was not unknown that some of them preferred to invest their surplus earnings in sounder enterprises than the ones over which they presided.

Lastly, finance capitalism included the growth of the holding company as a basic form of capitalist organization. The holding company is a device whereby a number of producing units are united under the control of a company that owns their stock. The holding company does not engage in production but receives its income from management fees and from dividends paid by the producing units. Though sometimes justified on the ground that it promotes integration of industry and facilitates business expansion, it is really a symbol of the triumph of the financier over the old-fashioned type of productive capitalist.

In addition to the foregoing changes in the structure and organization of capitalism, the fundamental character of the system underwent a transformation with the advent of the Second Industrial Revolution. The 100-year period from 1770 to about 1870 was the heyday of the free market economy. Free trade, free competition, and freedom of contract were the golden calves that the business establishments in nearly all countries theoretically worshiped. Monopolies, tariffs, and other special privileges conferred by governments were gradually abolished. Every manufacturer and merchant was supposed to compete on equal terms with his rivals. If success did not crown his efforts, he had nothing but the laws of bankruptcy to save him from disaster. The rule that he who does not work shall not eat was ruthlessly applied to the working classes, not necessarily to those who lived by owning. Strikes and collective bargaining were almost universally condemned. Labor unions were few and weak in opposing the system. Nothing resembling the welfare state was tolerated lest a premium be given to indolence and improvidence. The success of the free market economy depended, in theory at least, upon the use of a uniform monetary standard. In 1821 Great Britain put into operation the gold standard, a device whereby the value of all other commodities was measured in terms of gold. The other leading countries gradually adopted it, and most of them clung to it until the Great Depression of the 1930's. The financial classes preferred it because it placed obstacles in the path of government manipulation of currencies and served as a convenient means of balancing accounts between nations.

Such was the ideal economic system during what is often thought of as a golden age of economic liberalism, when Britain led the world in the development of industry and finance. Some authorities, however, maintain that it never really existed except as a British utopia. Perhaps it was not even that. Instead of a smoothly functioning machine, it was subject to interruptions and frequent breakdowns. Years of prosperity were followed by panics and depressions. Jobless men stood in bread lines or begged handouts from door to door. Little was done by governments to help them, and public welfare was unknown. The prevailing theory held that only a sufficient amount of "bloodletting" could effect a cure. When enough businesses and industries had been put through the wringer, the wheels of industry would start turning again. Prosperity would gradually return, and all would be well, until . . . When the workers became desperate enough, they frequently struck. Owners of the plants appealed to the police to defend their property. The powers of the police were often supplemented by the National Guard or private "detective" agencies. Bitter conflict was generally the rule until late in the nineteenth century. The owning classes were left with fruits of victory until labor came into its own on the eve of World War II.

In addition to the class conflict that punctuated the history of the late nineteenth and early twentieth centuries, the economic history of that time departed widely in other respects from the classical model. There was perhaps never a time when all the features of the system remained unchallenged. Great Britain herself did not adopt free trade until 1846. Prussia established protectionism in 1818 and laid the foundations soon afterward for a customs union, or *Zollverein*, for all of Germany. United States tariff policy became strongly protectionist in 1816. It may be noted also that most of the railroads in Continental Europe were built and operated under government ownership. These modifications, however, were pygmy deviations compared with those that were to follow after 1870. Increasing attention was now given to government subsidy and sponsorship. In France, for example, the tobacco and match industries became government monopolies. In practically all countries except Great Britain tariffs for the protection of domestic manufacturers were boosted sky-high. Labor unions waxed in power, and the right of collective bargaining was increasingly recognized. Most important of all, perhaps, a trend toward the welfare state made definite progress. In the 1880's Bismarck inaugurated his program of social insurance, and other governments, including even that of Great Britain, gradually followed suit. Even in the early 1900's some leaders, notably Louis D. Brandeis,

The ideal and the reality

Wider departures in countries other than Britain

later Associate Justice of the United States Supreme Court, were boldly proclaiming the need of a guaranteed annual income. In many quarters it was coming to be recognized that poverty is not always the fruit of laziness and improvidence, but may often be the product of conditions beyond the individual's control. These it may be the duty of the state to reduce or correct.

Basic organizations of capital rapidly emerged to take advantage of new economic opportunities and to serve in part as a checkmate to the power of labor. By the middle of the nineteenth century partnerships and joint-stock companies were giving way to trusts. These in turn were followed by mergers and cartels. Trusts are combinations of all or nearly all of the producers of certain articles in order to control their price and production. Mergers are combinations of companies producing the same or related articles. They differ from trusts in the fact that their constituent units generally lose their identity and are "merged" into a controlling corporation. Cartels may be defined as loose associations of independent companies for the primary purpose of restricting competition in the sale of their products. They differ from both trusts and mergers in not being corporate entities. They do not generally issue any stock or bonds of their own. The first cartels originated in Germany about 1870, but they did not become extensive until the decade before World War I. They flourished because they enabled German producers to gain great leverage in world trade. They did this by keeping domestic prices high and selling at a loss in foreign markets.

Trusts, mergers, and cartels

During the age of coal and iron, mechanized production was restricted primarily to Great Britain, France, Belgium, and the United States; and Great Britain was far in advance of the others. After 1860 industrialization spread until every one of the major powers had reaped a full harvest of its benefits and evils. The adoption of the new methods was especially conspicuous in Germany. Before 1860 the German states had been predominantly agrarian, with at least 60 per cent of their people obtaining their living from the soil. By 1914 the empire of the Kaisers was the greatest industrial nation in Europe, producing more steel than Great Britain and leading the world in the manufacture of chemicals, aniline dyes, and electrical and scientific equipment. For such remarkable expansion there were several main explanations. In the first place, Germany had no tradition of laissez faire. Her economists had been preaching for years that the state should intervene in every way possible to promote the economic strength of the nation. As a consequence it was easy for the government to bolster up feeble industries, to nationalize the railroads and operate them for the benefit of business, and even to encourage the growth of trusts. As a second reason may be mentioned the German emphasis upon applied science in the schools, resulting in an abundant supply of technicians who could be hired by industrial corporations for a low wage. The famous Krupp

The spread of industrialization: the Industrial Revolution in Germany

Industrialization in Germany. The Krupp munitions works at Essen in 1876.

munitions works at Essen employed a larger staff of trained scientists than any university in the world. Last, but by no means of least importance, was the fact that Germany acquired, as a result of her victory over France in 1870, the rich iron deposits of Lorraine, which ultimately supplied her with three-fourths of the ore for her basic industry of steel manufacture.

Industrialization did not spread into eastern Europe quite so soon as it did into Germany, nor did it proceed as far. Nevertheless, by 1890 a considerable development of the factory system and of mechanized transportation had begun in Russia. The Industrial Revolution in Russia, like that in Germany, was in part the result of governmental encouragement. Through the influence of Count Serge Witte, able but domineering minister under Alexander III and Nicholas II, the government of the Tsars levied prohibitive tariffs and borrowed money from France to subsidize railroads and numerous industrial enterprises. These and other efforts bore some amazing fruit. By 1914 Russia was producing more iron than France, her coal production had more than doubled, and in textiles she ranked fourth in the world. No fewer than 3,000,000 people were engaged directly in manufacturing, while some of her industrial establishments employed as many as 10,000 workers.[3] The Industrial Revolution in Italy and Japan was also advanced largely by state intervention, at least in its earlier stages. In both countries the movement began about 1880 and had completed a cycle of definite progress by the outbreak of World War I. In Italy the government extended the railway system and fostered the growth of silk and cotton manufactures in such measure that Italian exports increased nearly 300 per cent between 1895 and 1914. The achievements of Japan were even

The industrialization of Russia, Italy, and Japan

810   [3] Clive Day, *op. cit.*, p. 388.

more remarkable. By 1914 the little island empire had 6000 miles of railroad, almost entirely owned by the state. Her textile industry almost equaled that of Great Britain, while her foreign commerce had risen in value from virtually nothing to nearly $700,000,000.

5. THE PERSISTENCE OF SOCIAL AND ECONOMIC PROBLEMS

The First Industrial Revolution left numerous economic and social problems in its wake. The Second Revolution continued and accentuated some of these and brought others in its train. In some cases the source of these problems was largely economic, but in a goodly number it was basically social.

Notable among these problems essentially social was an enormous increase in population. Between the French Revolution and World War I the population of nearly every civilized country grew at an unprecedented rate. Some evidences of this phenomenon were noticeable as early as 1800, especially in England, where the increase was about 50 per cent in the second half of the eighteenth century. But in the main the spectacular growth came later. Between the Battle of Waterloo and the outbreak of World War I the population of England and Wales nearly quadrupled. That of Germany rose from about 25,000,000 in 1815 to almost 70,000,000 a hundred years later. The number of inhabitants in France almost doubled between the overthrow of Napoleon and the Franco-Prussian War, and the total of Russians more than doubled in the fifty years preceding 1914. In spite of such adverse factors as famine in Ireland and Russia, emigration to America, and disease resulting from congestion in cities, the population of Europe as a whole mounted from an estimated 190,000,000 in 1800 to 460,000,000 in 1914. During the same period the population of the United States increased from 5,000,000 to almost 100,000,000.

The phenomenal growth of population

811

To discover the reasons for this unprecedented growth in numbers we must look to several factors. First, it was due in some measure to the effects of the Commercial Revolution in improving the vigor of peoples by providing a more abundant and a more varied diet. Second, it was a consequence of the establishment of infant and maternity hospitals and of advancements in medical science and sanitation, which led to the practical elimination of smallpox, scurvy, and cholera, at least from western Europe and America. A third cause was the influence of nationalism, of the growth of racial, pride and patriotic obsession. Peoples with a solid conviction of their own superiority and buoyant with hopes of victory in future struggles are almost certain to reproduce very rapidly. These were the qualities that characterized most of the nations in the nineteenth century. An equally important cause in Europe at least, was the influence of the industrial revolutions in making it possible for limited areas to support large numbers of people. This increase in population came about not only because the mechanization of agriculture increased the yield from the land, but also because the factory system enlarged the opportunities for earning a living away from the soil. Thus it became possible for countries rich in industrial resources to support several times as many people as ever could be done on an agrarian basis.

Closely related to growth of population as an effect of the industrial revolutions was an increasing urbanization of Western society. By 1914 the artificial conditions of city life had come to be the accepted norm for a large percentage of the inhabitants of industrialized nations. Growth in urbanization was particularly striking in such countries as Germany and England. In the former as late as 1840 there were only two cities of 100,000 inhabitants or more; in 1910 there were forty-eight. In England during the last thirty years of the nineteenth century, approximately one-third of the agricultural population withdrew permanently from the land. The English census of 1901 revealed that the number of persons engaged in farming was only about 20 per cent of the number employed in industrial pursuits. In the United States, despite its wealth of agricultural resources, there was a similar movement away from the land, albeit at a slower pace. By 1915 the proportion of Americans living in urban areas had risen to about 40 per cent. The causes of this drift to the cities and towns were the increasing attractions of urban life and the steady decline in need for agricultural labor as a result of mechanized farming. The effects were a mixture of good and evil. Escape from the soil freed large numbers of men and women from the isolation of rural life, from the tyranny of the weather, from the idiocies of primitive folkways, and from a humdrum existence of lonely toil on stubborn acres. But at the same time it transformed many of them into pawns or tools of their employers. It made some of them robots, who performed their tasks automatically with little sense of responsibility or comprehension of their place in the economic

Wentworth Street by Gustav Doré. The artist was much concerned with the overcrowding squalor which resulted from early industrialization in London.

scheme, and with nothing to inspire their efforts but the hope of a living wage. If it rescued them from the hazards of blight and drought, it plunged them into new dangers of loss of employment from overproduction and forced them to live pell-mell like rats in wretched slums.

A third great result of the Second Revolution was the creation of two new classes: an industrial bourgeoisie and a proletariat. The industrial bourgeoisie, composed of the owners of factories, mines, and railroads, cast in its lot with the old middle class of merchants, bankers, and lawyers. Thus strengthened in numbers and in influence, the combined bourgeoisie soon ceased to be merely a middle class and became for all practical purposes the ruling element in society. In some cases this rise to power was accomplished by pushing the old landed aristocracy into the background; in others, by joining with it. But no sooner had the capitalists and entrepreneurs gained the ascendancy than they began to divide among themselves. The great bankers and magnates of industry and commerce came to constitute an upper bourgeoisie with ambitions somewhat distinct from those of the lower bourgeoisie, made up of small merchants, small industrialists, and professional men. The tendency was for the upper bourgeoisie to become more and more deeply absorbed in finance capitalism. Its members were interested in stock-jobbing operations, in launching new ventures for an immediate profit, and in reorganizing businesses already in existence for purposes of monopolistic or speculative control. To the leaders of this class most forms of government intervention, except protective tariffs and suppression of strikes, were anathema; they insisted that free enterprise was absolutely essential to vigorous economic growth. The lower bourgeoisie began to show signs of an interest in economic stability and security.

The emergence of the industrial bourgeoisie

813

In some countries members of this class were to be found advocating measures to curb speculation, to fix prices, and even to provide for state ownership of public utilities.

The rise of
the proletariat

The industrial revolutions also brought into existence a proletariat, which ultimately attained sufficient strength to challenge the supremacy of the bourgeoisie. In a sense the proletariat has existed since the dawn of civilization, for the term includes all persons who are dependent for their living upon a wage. The free workers in ancient Greece and Rome were proletarians, and so were the journeymen and the crofters and cotters in the Middle Ages. But prior to the First Industrial Revolution the wage earners were a small proportion of the working class, since the majority of those who toiled for a living were engaged in agriculture, originally as serfs and later as tenant farmers and sharecroppers. Further, the few proletarians who did exist were scarcely conscious of their identity as a class. The industrial revolutions, by concentrating large numbers of workers in the cities and subjecting them to common abuses, infused into wage earners a degree of solidarity and imbued them with a sense of common grievances. Nevertheless, their power as an economic class was limited for many years by stringent legislation. The right to strike, for instance, was not granted by any Western nation until after 1850. And not until late in the nineteenth century were the organized workers able to exert much influence upon the policies of governments.

The uneven
material benefits
of the industrial
revolutions

That the industrial revolutions bestowed both social and material benefits upon the inhabitants of Western nations is a conclusion which few critics would flatly deny. Without question they supplied modern man with tremendous quantities of goods and with an astounding number of useful appliances. But whether the various classes participated in these benefits in anything like a just ratio is a different question. There seems little doubt that real wages, or wages in terms of purchasing power, rose quite rapidly during the nineteenth century. A leading economist, Sir Josiah Stamp, estimated that the ordinary Englishman in 1913 was four times as well off, in relation to the amount his income would buy, as were his ancestors in 1801. Evidences of improvement in standards of living were indicated by substantial increases in the consumption of quality foods, notably meat and milk. The per capita consumption of meat in Germany, for example, advanced from 38 pounds in 1816 to 115 pounds in 1912.

Early effects
upon living
conditions

On the other hand, it is at least open to doubt that the mechanization of industry contributed as much to the well-being of the laboring classes as is commonly supposed, as during the First Revolution the introduction of machines often meant that able-bodied men were thrown out of employment by the cheap labor of women and children. Moreover, many of the factories and mines were dangerous and unsanitary. As a result, many British factory employees were scarcely much better off than the slaves on American planta-tions. But against these evils must be reckoned the fact that the industrial revolutions did facilitate the organization of workers, thus enabling them to use the power of collective action to improve their condition. Besides, the common people undoubtedly benefited from lower prices made possible by mass production.

6. THE DECLINE OF LAISSEZ FAIRE

Before the Second Industrial Revolution had run its course, it had begun to exert an influence toward economic democracy. That cabinets should be responsible to parliaments, and that every citi-zen should be entitled to vote, seemed to be matters of comparatively small moment so long as workers were at the mercy of a ruthlessly competitive industrial system. As generally defined, economic democracy implies that all men shall have a substantially equal op-portunity to make the most of their latent abilities, and that no one shall suffer needlessly from the misfortunes of life. It is not synony-mous with the old liberal concept of equality before the law, which, as Anatole France scornfully remarked, "forbids the rich man as well as the poor man to sleep under bridges, to beg in the streets, and to steal bread." Economic democracy means that little children shall not be exploited by selfish employers, that old people shall not be thrown on the human scrap heap when no longer able to work, and that the poor and helpless shall not be compelled to bear the whole burden of industrial accidents, unemployment, and disease. In short, it involves a somewhat drastic modification of the ideal of laissez faire, which appeared to be so firmly entrenched during most of the nineteenth century.

The meaning of economic demo-cracy

On the other hand, it should be remembered that the decline of laissez faire was not exclusively the result of the movement for eco-nomic democracy. The original form which modification of laissez faire often took on the Continent of Europe was protectionism, prompted by the desire of the rising industrial bourgeoisie to stave off competition from England. Protectionism was sometimes fol-lowed by outright subsidies, illustrated by the bounties given by the Italian and French governments to the silk industry and to various branches of agriculture. In such nations as Germany, Italy, and Rus-sia the railroads and telegraph and telephone lines were either built by the state, or nationalized afterwards, primarily for purposes of military efficiency. In France the tobacco and match manufacturing industries were taken over by the state as sources of public revenue, and were operated as government monopolies. Even a great deal of the social legislation enacted in Continental countries was inspired by factors of nationalism, militarism, and paternalism. Governments desired to win the loyalty of all classes of their subjects and to make sure of a healthy supply of cannon fodder in time of war.

Reasons for the decline of laissez faire

815

The first of the great powers to enact a comprehensive program of social legislation was Germany, under the guidance of her shrewd but dictatorial Chancellor, Prince von Bismarck. The reasons why Germany should have taken the lead are not difficult to fathom. Unlike Great Britain and France she had never been deeply affected by eighteenth-century liberalism; hence she had no strong traditions of individualism or laissez faire. While her political philosophers were persistently affirming the subjection of the individual to the state, her economists were preaching doctrines of national self-sufficiency and paternalism. Bismarck himself maintained that it was the duty of the state to regulate all functions of society in the national interest and to look after the weaker citizens, "that they may not be run over and trampled under foot on the highway of life." But he had other reasons also for engaging in what appeared to be a defense of the workers' rights. He was anxious to undermine the growing popularity of socialism by stealing a portion of its thunder. In a speech in the Reichstag he frankly avowed his purpose of insuring the workingman against sickness and old age so that "these gentlemen [the Social Democrats] will sound their bird call in vain." In addition, he had military purposes in mind. He was desirous of making the German proletarian a loyal soldier and of safeguarding his health in some measure from the debilitating effects of factory labor. Bismarck's program of social legislation was initiated in 1883–1884 with the adoption of laws insuring workmen against sickness and accidents. These acts were soon followed by others providing for rigid factory inspection, limiting the employment of women and children, fixing maximum hours of labor, establishing public employment agencies, and insuring workers against incapacity on account of old age. By 1890, when Bismarck was forced to retire, Germany had adopted nearly all the elements, with the exception of unemployment insurance, in the pattern of social legislation that later became familiar in the majority of Western nations.

Bismarck

Other countries on the Continent of Europe soon followed the German example. A French law of 1892 not only regulated the employment of women and children but prescribed a maximum day of ten hours for all workers; in 1905 this limit was reduced to nine hours. Other acts of the French parliament ensured free medical attendance for laborers and their families, accorded protection to the activities of labor unions, and compelled employers to compensate workers for injuries. The capstone of this system of legislation was added in 1910 with the passage of a law providing old-age pensions. The series of laws enacted in Italy was much the same, except for the absence of the provision regarding free medical attention. The Italian laws were supplemented, however, by an act of 1912 providing for nationalized life insurance and also by measures encouraging cooperative stores.

Because of her strong individualist traditions, Great Britain lagged behind the other great powers in western Europe. To be sure, there had been some early progress, illustrated by laws prohibiting the employment of women and children in underground labor in the mines. But the British government adopted no extensive measures of social reform until after the rejuvenated Liberal party came into power in 1905. The old generation of Liberals under Gladstone, representing primarily the business classes, had been committed to principles of laissez faire. Their energies had been absorbed very largely in problems of political reform and of home rule for Ireland. But in 1898 Gladstone died, and control over his party passed into younger hands. Several of the new leaders—Herbert Asquith, David Lloyd George, and Winston Churchill—were enthusiastic idealists, resolved to wage "implacable warfare" against misery and squalor. Upon coming to power in 1905 these ardent reformers determined to throw the old-fashioned doctrines of their party to the winds and transform Britannia into a paradise of fair treatment for all. During the years that followed, down to the beginning of World War I, they succeeded in having written into the statutes the most remarkable schedule of reform legislation since the Glorious Revolution. First came the Workmen's Compensation Act of 1906 and the Old Age Pensions law of 1908. Next came the Trade Boards Act of 1909, authorizing special commissions to fix the minimum pay for workers in sweatshops. In 1911 the Liberal cabinet procured the passage of the great National Insurance Act introducing a system of contributory insurance against sickness for all wage earners.

To this list of more conventional social reforms of the Liberal government must be added certain others for which there was almost no precedent. In 1909 the Liberal Parliament enacted a law permitting the clearance of slum areas and authorizing local authorities to provide respectable housing for the poor. This law set a precedent for an enormous amount of public housing construction in later years, especially in the period after 1918. Among the most significant of all the social reforms of the Liberal regime were certain provisions incorporated in the Lloyd George budget of 1909. In this remarkable fiscal program David Lloyd George proposed not only to increase the regular income taxes but to levy in addition a super-tax on the incomes of the rich. He recommended also that the government should confiscate 20 per cent of the unearned increment of land values, and that a heavy tax should be imposed on all undeveloped land appraised in excess of £ 50 per acre. The object of these measures was twofold: to raise revenue for old-age pensions and for various forms of social insurance and to level down great fortunes. It was hoped that the tax on unearned increment and on undeveloped lands would help to break the land monopoly of the richer nobles—of such magnates as the Duke of Westminster, who owned

THE DECLINE OF LAISSEZ FAIRE

Social reform in Britain, 1905–1914

New departures in economic and social reform

817

600 acres in London, and the Marquess of Bute, who owned one-half of the area of Cardiff. Thrown out by the House of Lords, the Lloyd George budget was finally enacted into law after the Liberals were returned to power in the January election of 1910.

SELECTED READINGS

· *Items so designated are available in paperbound editions.*

THE FIRST INDUSTRIAL REVOLUTION

· Ashton, T. S., *The Industrial Revolution, 1760–1830*, New York, 1948 (Galaxy). A clear introductory account of the First Revolution.

Bowen, Frank, *A Century of Atlantic Travel*, Boston, 1930.

Day, Clive, *Economic Development in Modern Europe*, New York, 1933. Interesting and well-written.

Dietz, F. C., *The Industrial Revolution*, New York, 1927. Good on technological progress.

Heaton, Herbert, *Economic History of Europe*, New York, 1936, Chs. 21–30.

· Mantoux, Paul, *The Industrial Revolution in the Eighteenth Century*, New York, 1947 (Torchbook).

· Mumford, Lewis, *Technics and Civilization*, New York, 1934 (Harbinger). Stimulating.

Ogg, F. A., and Sharp, W. R., *Economic Development of Modern Europe*, New York, 1929.

Reid, W. S., *Economic History of Great Britain*, New York, 1956.

· Tawney, R. H., *The Acquisitive Society*, New York, 1920 (Harvest).

Taylor, George, *The Transportation Revolution, 1815–1860*, New York, 1956.

Toynbee, Arnold, *Lectures on the Industrial Revolution of the Eighteenth Century in England*, London, 1937. Valuable for the early history.

THE SECOND INDUSTRIAL REVOLUTION

Barnes, H. E., *An Economic History of the Western World*, New York, 1937.

Bonbright, J. C., and Means, G. C., *The Holding Company, Its Public Significance and Its Regulation*, New York, 1932.

· Briggs, A., *The Age of Improvement*, London, 1960 (Torchbook).

Edwards, G. W., *The Evolution of Finance Capitalism*, New York, 1938.

· Feis, Herbert, *Europe, the World's Banker, 1870–1914*, New Haven, 1930 (Norton Library).

Giedion, S., *Mechanization Takes Command*, New York, 1948.

Hobson, J. A., *The Evolution of Modern Capitalism*, New York, 1926.

Levy, H., *The New Industrial System*, London, 1936.

Polakov, W. N., *The Power Age*, New York, 1930.

· Rostow, W. W., *The Stages of Economic Growth*, New York, 1960 (Cambridge University Press).

CHAPTER 27

Critics and Apologists of Industrialization

> If a man does not keep pace with his companions, perhaps it is because he hears a different drummer. Let him step to the music which he hears, however measured or faraway.
> —Henry Thoreau, *Walden*, XVIII, *Conclusion*

The First Industrial Revolution produced its full complement of economic theory—part of it to justify the new order, part of it for critical analysis, and the remainder as a gospel of social reform. No sooner had the factory system been well established and profits begun to flow into the coffers of the new lords of creation than some of the more articulate rose up to defend their privileges. In doing so they often displayed a coldness toward the plight of the masses and a confidence in their own right to inherit the earth which the nobles of the *ancien régime* might well have envied. Indeed, some of the apologists for the new system evolved into a type of economic Bourbons, learning nothing from the past and closing their eyes to the dangers of the future. This attitude was expressed in the doctrines that private property is sacred, that every man has a right to do what he will with his own, and that poverty is invariably the result of laziness and incompetence. Several of the high priests of the new capitalism went so far as to declare that poverty was a good thing for the masses since it taught them to respect their superiors and to be grateful to Providence for such blessings as they did receive.

Economic Bourbonism

I. THE ECONOMIC LIBERALS

But some of the economic theory in defense of the capitalist ideal was more disinterested. Of this type were the teachings of the classical economists, or economic liberals, as they are often called. The founder of classical economics was Adam Smith, whose work was

819

The economic
liberals

discussed in a preceding chapter. Though Smith wrote before industrial capitalism had reached its full stature, and though some of his teachings did not harmonize well with a strict interpretation of laissez faire, there was nevertheless enough in the general implications of his theory to cause him to be acclaimed the prophet of capitalist ideals. The specific doctrines of classical economics, however, were largely the work of Smith's disciples—including such eminent writers as Thomas R. Malthus, David Ricardo, James Mill, and Nassau Senior. The chief elements in the theory subscribed to by most of these men may be summarized as follows:

(1) Economic individualism. Every individual is entitled to use for his own best interests the property he has inherited or acquired by any legitimate method. Each person must be allowed to do what he likes with his own so long as he does not trespass upon the equal right of others to do the same.

(2) Laissez faire. The functions of the state should be reduced to the lowest minimum consistent with public safety. The government should shrink itself into the role of a modest policeman, preserving order and protecting property, but never in any wise interfering with the operation of economic processes.

(3) Obedience to natural law. There are immutable laws operating in the realm of economics as in every sphere of the universe. Examples are the law of supply and demand, the law of diminishing returns, the law of rent, and so on. These laws must be recognized and respected; failure to do so is disastrous.

(4) Freedom of contract. Every individual should be free to negotiate the best kind of contract he can obtain from any other individual. In particular, the liberty of workers and employers to bargain with each other as to wages and hours should not be hampered by laws or by the collective power of labor unions.

(5) Free competition and free trade. Competition serves to keep prices down, to eliminate inefficient producers, and to ensure the maximum production in accordance with public demand. Therefore no monopolies should be tolerated, nor any price-fixing laws for the benefit of incompetent enterprisers. Further, in order to force each country to engage in the production of those things it is best fitted to produce, all protective tariffs should be abolished. Free international trade will also help to keep prices down.

Several of the disciples of Adam Smith made distinctive contributions of their own. For example, Thomas R. Malthus (1766–1834) introduced the element of pessimism which caused the new economics to be branded as "the dismal science." A clergyman of the Anglican church, rector of a small parish in Surrey, Malthus published his memorable *Essay on Population* in 1798. Issued originally in pamphlet form, the *Essay* grew out of some discussions which the author had with his father concerning the perfectibility of man. The elder Malthus was a disciple of Rousseau, but he was so impressed with his son's arguments against the superficial optimism of

T. R. Malthus

the Frenchman that he urged him to put them in writing. The pamphlet created an immediate sensation and provoked discussion for many years afterward. In 1803 it was expanded into a book on the basis of extended researches which the author undertook to refute his critics. The substance of the Malthusian theory is the contention that nature has set stubborn limits to the progress of mankind in happiness and wealth. Because of the voracity of the sexual appetite there is a natural tendency for population to increase more rapidly than the means of subsistence. To be sure, there are powerful checks, such as war, famine, disease, and vice; but these, when they operate effectively, augment still further the burden of human misery. It follows that poverty and pain are inescapable. Even if laws were to be passed distributing all wealth equally, the condition of the poor would be only temporarily improved; in a very short time they would begin to raise larger families, with the result that the last state of their class would be as bad as the first. In the second edition of his work Malthus advocated postponement of marriage as a means of relief, but he continued to stress the danger that population would outrun any possible increase in the means of subsistence.

The main teachings of Malthus were taken over and elaborated by David Ricardo (1772–1823), an English Jew who embraced Christianity at the age of twenty-one and married a Quaker. By the

The Launderers by Honoré Daumier. In his paintings and drawings Daumier's insight as a social critic equaled his abilities as an artist.

time he was twenty-five he had accumulated a fortune on the Stock Exchange and soon became one of the richest men in Europe. As an economist Ricardo is famous, first of all, for his subsistence theory of wages. According to this theory, wages tend toward a level which is just sufficient to enable the workers "to subsist and perpetuate their race, without either increase or diminution." This he held to be an iron law, from which there is no escape. If wages should rise temporarily above the subsistence standard, the population would increase, and the ensuing competition for jobs would quickly force the rate of pay down to its former level. Ricardo is noted, in the second place, for his teachings in regard to rent. He maintained that rent is determined by the cost of production on the poorest land that must be brought under cultivation, and that consequently as a country fills up with people an ever-increasing proportion of the social income is taken by the landlords. Though a great proprietor himself, he denounced the recipients of rent as the real enemies of both the capitalists and the workers. Finally, Ricardo is important for his labor theory of value, which influenced one of the main doctrines of the Marxian socialists. However, he attached some significance also to the role of capital in determining value—an idea which was abhorrent to Marx.

In his later years Ricardo frequently associated himself with an interesting group of reformers in England known as the philosophical radicals. The foremost economist among them was James Mill (1773–1836), who, as already mentioned, enjoyed some reputation as a Utilitarian philosopher. While the teachings of James Mill would now be considered far from radical, they were nevertheless liberal enough to show that the classical economics was not hopelessly benighted and reactionary. The doctrines he incorporated in his *Elements of Political Economy* included the following: (1) the chief object of practical reformers should be to prevent the population from growing too rapidly, on the assumption that the wealth available for productive purposes does not naturally increase as fast as the number of inhabitants; (2) the value of commodities depends entirely upon the quantity of labor necessary to produce them; and (3) the unearned increment of land, or the increase in the value of land which comes exclusively from social causes, such as the building of a new factory in the vicinity, should be heavily taxed by the state. This last doctrine, based upon Ricardo's theory of rent, was destined for a wide popularity in England. In modified form it became part of the gospel of the Liberal party in the early 1900's, and was a feature of the celebrated Lloyd George budget of 1909.

Probably the ablest of the classical economists who came after Ricardo was Nassau William Senior (1790–1864). The first professor of political economy at Oxford, he was also a distinguished lawyer. Like most of his predecessors, Senior regarded economics as a deductive science. He maintained that its truths could all be derived from a limited number of great abstract principles. His main contribution was his theory that *abstinence* creates a title to wealth. He admitted that labor and natural resources are the primary instruments of value, but he contended that abstinence is a secondary instrument. Therefore he argued that the capitalist who has refrained from enjoying all of his wealth in order to accumulate a surplus for investment has a claim on the profits of production. His abstinence involves sacrifice and pain just as does the work of the laborer. Consequently it is unfair to give the entire reward to the latter. The evil reputation of Senior comes primarily from the fact that he condemned the demands of the trade unions for a reduction of the working day. He had an honest but mistaken conviction that the whole net profit of an industrial enterprise is derived from the last hour of operation. Hence to shorten the working day would eliminate profits and thereby result in closing the factories. For this doctrine he was dubbed by his critics "Last Hour" Senior.

2. DOUBTERS AND REBELS

Most of the leading classical economists or economic liberals were citizens of Great Britain. This was true partly because economic liberalism harmonized well with political liberalism, which was stronger in Britain than in any other European country, and partly because British industrialists were beginning to perceive notable advantages from a policy of free trade with the rest of the world. On the Continent of Europe, however, conditions were entirely different. There the old traditions of strong government still lingered. Moreover, Continental manufacturers were attempting to build up industrial establishments which would be able to compete with the British. To achieve this, it was desirable to have the patronage and protection of the state. Hence we should not be surprised to find that the majority of the opponents of economic liberalism were natives of countries on the Continent. Nevertheless, at least one of its abler critics was an Englishman—the brilliant Utilitarian philosopher, John Stuart Mill (1806–1873). Though Mill as an economist is often considered a member of the classical school, he actually repudiated a number of its most sacred premises. First, he rejected the universality of natural law. He admitted that there are unchangeable laws governing the field of production, but he insisted that the distribution of wealth can be regulated by society for the benefit of the majority of its members. Second, he advocated more radical departures from laissez faire than any recommended by his forerunners. He did not oppose legislation, under certain conditions, for shortening the working day, and he believed that the state might properly take preliminary steps toward the redistribution of wealth by taxing inheritances and by appropriating the unearned increment of land. In the fourth book of his *Principles of Political Economy* he urged the abolition of the wage system and looked forward to a society of producers' cooperatives in which the workers would own

John Stuart Mill

the factories and elect the managers to run them. On the other hand, it should not be forgotten that Mill was too much of an individualist ever to go very far in the direction of socialism. He distrusted the state, and his real reason for advocating producers' cooperatives was not to exalt the power of the proletariat but to give to the individual worker the fruits of his labor.

The most noted of the German economists who wrote in direct opposition to the theories of the classical school was Friedrich List (1789–1846), who derived inspiration for some of his ideas from seven years' residence in America. List condemned the doctrines of laissez faire and freedom of international trade. Contending that the wealth of a nation is determined less by natural resources than by the productive powers of its citizens, he declared that it is the duty of governments to further the arts and sciences and to see to it that every individual makes the most of his talents in cooperating for the general good. He stressed the well-rounded development of the nation as all-important regardless of the effects upon the immediate fortunes of particular citizens. Holding that manufactures are essential to such a development, he demanded protective tariffs until the new industries should be able to compete with those of any other country. He believed that the government should regulate and plan the development of industry so as to balance production and consumption. It is interesting that List was also an imperialist. He demanded a German customs union which would extend "over the whole coast from the mouth of the Rhine to the frontier of Poland including Holland and Denmark." [1] He insisted also that Germany had a mission to lead in world affairs and to civilize barbaric and benighted countries. He was one of the earliest exponents of German expansionism and of Germany's destiny as a world power.

We come next to a group of theorists who were more interested in social justice than in discovering economic laws or in laying the foundations of national prosperity. The earliest exemplars of this more radical attitude were the utopian socialists, who take their name from the fact that they proposed idealistic schemes for co-operative societies, in which all would work at their appropriate tasks and share the results of their common efforts. To a considerable extent the utopian socialists were the heirs of the Enlightenment. Like the philosophers of that movement they believed that all crime and greed were the results of an evil environment. If men could be freed from vicious custom and from a social structure which facilitates enslavement of the weak by the strong, then all might live together in harmony and peace. Accordingly, the utopian socialists recommended the establishment of model communities, largely self-contained, where most of the instruments of production would be collectively owned and where government would be mainly on a

Friedrich List

*The utopian
socialists*

[1] S. S. Lloyd (trans.), *The National System of Political Economy*, p. 143.

New Lanark. In his textile mill and workers' town, Robert Owen proved that productivity could increase with a reduction of working hours from fourteen a day to ten. The factory town was a showplace for visitors from abroad during the early nineteenth century.

voluntary basis. Among the original propagators of such plans was the Frenchman Charles Fourier (1772–1837), but the soundest and most realistic of them all was Robert Owen (1771–1858). A native of Wales, Owen rose from an artisan apprentice to co-proprietor and manager of a great cotton mill at New Lanark in Scotland. Here he built new houses for his workers, reduced their hours of work from fourteen to ten, and established free schools for their children. The severe depression that followed in the wake of the Napoleonic wars convinced him that the economic order was in need of reform. Like many others since his day, he concluded that the profit system was the cause of all the trouble. The existence of profit, he maintained, makes it impossible for the worker to buy all the things he has produced. The result is overproduction, periodic crises, and unemployment. As a solution, Owen proposed the organization of society into cooperative communities, in which the sole reward to each member would be payment in proportion to his actual hours of labor. A number of such communities were set up, the most famous being the ones at Orbiston, Scotland, and New Harmony, Indiana. For a variety of reasons all of them failed within a very short time.

A more influential form of socialism was the so-called "scientific socialism" of Karl Marx (1818–1883). The son of a Jewish lawyer who had turned Christian for professional reasons, Marx was born at Trèves near Coblenz in the Rhineland. His father planned for him a career as a conventional bourgeois lawyer and, with that end in view, sent him to the University of Bonn. But young Marx soon displayed a distaste for the law and abandoned his legal studies for the

Karl Marx

825

Friedrich Engels

pursuit of philosophy and history. After a year at Bonn he went to the University of Berlin, where he fell under the influence of a group of disciples of Hegel who were giving the teachings of their master a slightly radical twist. Though Marx earned the degree of doctor of philosophy at the University of Jena in 1841, his critical views prevented him from realizing his ambition of becoming a university professor. He turned to journalism, editing various radical periodicals and contributing articles to others. In 1848 he was arrested on a charge of high treason for participating in the revolutionary movement in Prussia. Though acquitted by a middle-class jury, he was soon afterward expelled from the country. In the meantime he had formed an intimate friendship with Friedrich Engels (1820–1895), who remained his lifelong disciple and *alter ego*. In 1848 the two men issued the *Communist Manifesto*, the "birth cry of modern socialism." From then until his death in 1883 Marx spent nearly all of his years in London, struggling against poverty, occasionally writing a few articles (some of which he sold to the New York *Tribune* for $5 apiece), but giving most of his time to poring over dusty manuscripts in the British Museum, gathering material for a great work on political economy. In 1867 he published the first volume of this work under the title of *Das Kapital*. Two other volumes were issued after his death from manuscripts revised and edited by some of his disciples.

Not all of the teachings of Karl Marx were entirely original. For some of his ideas he was indebted to Hegel; for others to the French socialist, Louis Blanc (1811–1882), and probably to Ricardo. Nevertheless, it was Marx who first combined these ideas into a comprehensive system and gave them meaning as an explanation of the

The Communist Manifesto. A facsimile of the cover of the 1848 edition.

facts of political economy. Since Marxist theory has been one of the most influential bodies of thought in modern times, it is necessary to understand its doctrines. Fundamental among them are the following:

(1) The economic interpretation of history. All of the great political, social, and intellectual movements of history have been determined by the economic environment out of which they arose. Marx did not insist that the economic motive is the sole explanation of human behavior, but he did maintain that every fundamental historical development, regardless of its character on the surface, has been the result of alterations in methods of producing and exchanging goods. Thus the Protestant Revolution was essentially an economic movement; the disagreements over religious belief were mere "ideological veils," concealing the actual causes.

The economic interpretation of history

(2) Dialectical materialism. Every distinct economic system, based upon a definite pattern of production and exchange, grows to a point of maximum efficiency, then develops contradictions or weaknesses within it which produce its rapid decay. Meanwhile the foundations of an opposing system are being gradually laid, and eventually this new system displaces the old, at the same time absorbing its most valuable elements. This dynamic process of historical evolution will continue by a series of victories of the new over the old, until the perfect goal of communism has been attained. After that there will doubtless still be change, but it will be change within the limits of communism itself.

Dialectical materialism

(3) The class struggle. All history has been made up of struggles between classes. In ancient times there was a struggle between masters and slaves; in the Middle Ages there was a conflict between lords and serfs; now there has been a narrowing down to a struggle between the class of capitalists and the proletariat. The former includes those who derive their chief income from *owning* the means of production and from exploiting the labor of others. The proletariat includes those who are dependent for their living primarily upon a wage, who must sell their labor power in order to exist.

The class struggle

(4) The doctrine of surplus value. All wealth is created by the worker. Capital creates nothing, but is itself created by labor. The value of all commodities is determined by the quantity of labor power necessary to produce them. But the worker does not receive the full value which his labor power creates; he receives a wage, which ordinarily is just enough to enable him to subsist and reproduce his kind. Most of the difference between the value he produces and what he receives is *surplus value*, which goes to the capitalist. In general, it consists of three elements: interest, rent, and profits. Since the capitalist creates none of these things, it follows that he is a robber, who appropriates the fruits of the laborer's toil.

Surplus value

(5) The theory of socialist evolution. After capitalism has received its death blow at the hands of the workers, it will be followed by the stage of socialism. This will have three characteristics: the dictatorship of the proletariat; payment in accordance with

work performed; and ownership and operation by the state of all means of production, distribution, and exchange. But socialism is intended to be merely a transition to something higher. In time it will be succeeded by communism, the perfect goal of historical evolution. Communism will mean, first of all, the classless society. No one will live by owning, but all men solely by working. The state will now disappear; it will be relegated to the museum of antiquities, "along with the bronze ax and the spinning wheel." Nothing will replace it except voluntary associations to operate the means of production and provide for social necessities. But the *essence* of communism is payment in accordance with needs. The wage system will be completely abolished. Each citizen will be expected to work in accordance with his faculties and will be entitled to receive from the total fund of wealth produced an amount in proportion to his needs. This is the acme of justice according to the Marxist conception. Psychologically, Marx was one of the original exponents of "alienation." He conceived of modern man as divorced from the conditions of his natural life, a wanderer in a strange land with no sense of his mission or destiny.

The influence of Karl Marx upon the nineteenth and twentieth centuries can only be compared with that of Voltaire or Rousseau upon the eighteenth. His doctrine of the economic interpretation of history is a popular theory even among historians who are not his followers. He numbers his disciples in every civilized nation of this planet and in a great many underdeveloped countries besides. He is almost a god in Russia, where his dogma of dialectical materialism is accepted not only as a foundation of economics but as a test to which science, philosophy, and art must also conform. In every industrialized nation before World War I there was a socialist political party of considerable importance, the one in Germany having the largest representation in the Reichstag after 1912. Nearly everywhere the growth of socialism was a vital influence in furthering the enactment of social insurance and minimum wage laws and in promoting taxation of incomes and inheritances for the purpose of redistributing wealth. Marx, of course, was not interested in these things as ends in themselves, but the ruling classes were eventually persuaded to adopt them as a convenient tub to be thrown to the socialist whale. Socialists have also quite generally lent their support to the co-operative movement, to government ownership of railroads and public utilities, and to innumerable schemes for protecting workers and consumers against the power of monopoly capitalism.

Toward the end of the nineteenth century the followers of Marx split into two factions. The majority in most countries adhered to the doctrines of a group known as the revisionists, who, as their name implies, believed that the theories of Marx should be *revised* to bring them into line with changing conditions. The other faction was made up of the strict Marxists, who insisted that not one jot or tittle of the master's teachings should be modified. In addition to this cleavage in general attitude there were also specific differences. Whereas the revisionists advocated the attainment of socialism by peaceful and gradual methods, the strict Marxists were revolutionists. The revisionists concentrated their attention upon immediate reforms; the strict Marxists demanded the dictatorship of the proletariat or nothing. The leaders of the majority faction were willing to recognize the interests of separate nations; they were prone to talk about duty to the fatherland, and they frequently supported the demands of their governments for increased armaments and for lengthened terms of military service. The strict Marxists, on the other hand, were uncompromising internationalists; they held to the contention of Marx that the world proletariat is one great brotherhood, and they frowned upon patriotism and nationalism as capitalist devices to throw dust in the eyes of the workers. On the whole, it was the revisionists who gained control of the socialist parties in the majority of Western nations. The Social Democratic party in Germany, the Unified Socialist party in France, and the Socialist party in the United States were all largely dominated by the moderate faction. In Britain leadership of the Labour party was supplied in most cases by the Fabian socialists, so named from their policy of delay in imitation of the tactics of Fabius, a Roman general in the wars against Carthage. Prominent among the Fabians were Beatrice and Sidney Webb, the novelist H. G. Wells, and the dramatist George Bernard Shaw.

3. ANARCHISTS AND SYNDICALISTS

Not all critics of the economic and social regime produced by the First Industrial Revolution were socialists. Quite a few became anarchists. Strictly defined, anarchism means opposition to all government based upon force. The followers of this philosophy have generally conceded that some form of social organization is necessary, but they condemn the coercive state as absolutely incompatible with human liberty. As to the problem of what should be done with the economic system, the anarchists have sharply disagreed. Some have been pure individualists, holding that man's right to acquire and use property should be subject only to the laws of nature. The father of anarchism, William Godwin (1756–1836), believed that if the land were made as free as the air, no further change in the economic structure would be necessary. In the judgment of the French anarchist, Pierre Proudhon (1809–1865), an arrangement whereby society would provide every man with free and unlimited credit would be a sufficient means of ensuring economic justice. Such a plan, he thought, would prevent anyone from monopolizing the resources of the earth and would guarantee to the citizen who was thrifty and industrious the full reward of his labors.

829

But the first of the anarchists to exert much influence were those who combined their hatred of the state with a definite philosophy of collectivism. Foremost among them were the three Russian aristocrats, Mikhail Bakunin (1814–1876), Peter Kropotkin (1842–1921), and Leo Tolstoi (1828–1910). Though often classified as a communistic anarchist, Bakunin was really much closer to socialism. Indeed, for a time he was associated with the followers of Marx in the International Workingmen's Association, organized in London in 1864. His program for a new society included collective ownership of the means of production, abolition of surplus value, and payment in accordance with work performed. In other words, it was much like that of the socialist stage of the Marxists, except, of course, that it did not involve the preservation of the state. Bakunin is also sometimes regarded as the father of terroristic anarchism. He advocated the overthrow of the state and of capitalism by violence. His followers were alleged to have been responsible for assassinating President McKinley, President Carnot of France, and King Humbert I of Italy. But most anarchists of the collectivist school condemned these tactics. For example, Prince Kropotkin denounced the use of individual violence under any conditions. He believed that a final revolutionary effort would be necessary, but he preferred that the state should be weakened by peaceful methods, by gradually convincing people that it is an unnecessary evil, that it breeds wars, and that it exists primarily to enable some men to exploit others. From the standpoint of economic reform, Kropotkin was a communist. He insisted that all property except articles of personal use should be socially owned, and that payment should be on the basis of need.

The most noted of all the collectivistic anarchists and one of the most interesting figures of modern times was Count Leo Tolstoi.

Best known for his novels, which will be discussed in a later connection, Tolstoi was also one of the greatest of Russian philosophers. His ideas were born of strenuous emotional conflict and of an almost despairing search for a way of life that would satisfy his restless intellect. He indulged for a time in fashionable dissipation, attempted to relieve his troubled mind by philanthropic activities, and then finally abandoned it all for the life of a simple peasant. He came to the conclusion that no progress could be made in remedying the ills of society until the upper classes renounced their privileges and adopted the humble existence of men who toil for their bread. Tolstoi based much of his philosophy upon the New Testament, especially upon the Sermon on the Mount. He found in Jesus' teachings of meekness, humility, and nonresistance the essential principles of a just society. Above all, he condemned the use of violence, regardless of the purpose for which it is employed. Violence brutalizes man; it places its user in the hands of his enemies; and, as long as force is available as a weapon, reliance upon civilized methods is almost impossible.

A third of the great radical philosophies produced by the Industrial Revolution was syndicalism, whose chief exponent was Georges Sorel (1847–1922). Syndicalism demands the abolition of both capitalism and the state and the reorganization of society into associations of producers. It resembles anarchism in its opposition to the state; but whereas the anarchist demands the abolition of force, the syndicalist would retain it, even after the state has been destroyed. Syndicalism also resembles socialism in that both would involve collective ownership of the means of production; but instead of making the state the owner and operator of the means of production, the syndicalist would delegate these functions to associations of producers. Thus all the steel mills would be owned and operated by the workers in the steel industry, the coal mines by the workers in the coal industry, and so on. Further, these associations or syndicates would take the place of the state, each one governing its own members in all of their activities as producers. In all other matters the workers would be free from interference. On the other hand, Sorel entertained no illusions as to the capacity of the masses for self-government. He regarded the average man as very much of a sheep, fit only to be a follower. He believed, therefore, that the ruling authority in the syndicates should be exercised quite frankly by the intelligent few.

The least radical among all the critics of capitalist economics were the Christian socialists. The founder of Christian socialism was Robert de Lamennais (1782–1854), a French Catholic priest who sought to revive the Christian religion as an aid to reform and social justice. From France the movement spread to England and was adopted by a number of Protestant intellectuals. In its early days Christian socialism was little more than a demand for application of the teachings of Jesus to the problems created by industry, but in later years it began to assume a more concrete form. In 1891 Leo XIII, "the workingman's Pope," issued his famous encyclical *Rerum novarum*, in which he revived with a modern slant the liberal economic attitude of St. Thomas Aquinas. Though the encyclical expressly recognized private property as a natural right and vigorously repudiated the Marxist doctrine of the class war, at the same time it strongly discountenanced unlimited profits. It appealed to employers to respect the dignity of their workers as men and as Christians and not to treat them as "chattels to make money by, or to look upon them merely as so much muscle or physical power." By way of specific proposals, it recommended factory legislation, the formation of labor unions, an increase in the number of small landowners, and limitation of hours of employment.[2] The issuance of this encyclical gave a mighty impulse to the growth of Christian socialism among liberal Catholics. In European countries before

Georges Sorel

ANARCHISTS AND SYNDICALISTS

Syndicalism

Christian socialism

[2] The substance of Leo's encyclical was reaffirmed in 1931 by Pope Pius XI in a new encyclical, *Quadragesimo Anno*.

World War I, Catholic parties frequently played an active role, sometimes in combination with the moderate Marxists, in furthering the movement for social legislation.

4. EXPRESSIONS OF ANTIMATERIALISM

Most writers in the nineteenth century took it for granted that industrialization was a beneficent thing. Since the Industrial Revolution showed itself capable of producing comforts and luxuries without parallel, it must be a boon to mankind. "Wealth" was commonly given its original meaning of "weal" or "welfare." Even the socialists never questioned its desirability but advocated merely that it be better distributed. They seldom doubted that *their* system would accomplish this goal for the masses.

In defense of wealth

Not everyone agreed that industrial growth and the production and accumulation of goods were unmixed blessings. Tolstoi, we have seen, called upon his followers to renounce material wealth and to cultivate a life close to the soil with freedom from the envy and strife of industrial man. Even earlier suggestions of anti-industrialism were to be found in the writings of Thomas Carlyle (1795–1881). True, he sometimes applauded industry and its marvelous possibilities for the benefit of man. But he deplored the depressions it created and characterized the spectacle of men willing to work and unable to find work as "perhaps the saddest sight" under a regime of unequal justice. Most of all, he deplored the substitution of a "cash nexus" between man and man under the new regime of laissez faire. He called for the revival of chivalry, "a chivalry of labor" that would give to the workingman a status of honor equal to that of his employer. Much of Carlyle's philosophy bore a medieval tinge: his contempt for democrcy and utilitarianism and his worship of a universal spirit that guides all the forces of history. Its real progenitor, however, was the German Idealism of Kant and Hegel. In this he found late in life the spiritual solace to displace the agnosticism and despair of his earlier years.

The Anti-industrialists:
(1) Thomas Carlyle

More staunchly representative of antimaterialism was Carlyle's younger contemporary, John Ruskin (1819–1900). Like his forerunner, Ruskin had a tendency to look back to the Middle Ages. Neither had much use for democracy. But Ruskin's philosophy was more nearly that of the aesthete and active reformer. He was repelled not only by the poverty and degradation of the industrial system but also by its ugliness. More emphatically than Carlyle, he condemned the ferocious capitalist struggle for profits and urged that workers be treated as partners in industry, entitled to a more generous share of what they produced.

(2) John Ruskin

Finally, no account of the nineteenth century revolt against materialism would be complete without some attention to the two extremists William Morris (1834–1896) and Henry David Thoreau

The Last of England, Ford Madox Brown (1821–1893). A haunting scene of a couple emigrating from England by one of the most noted Pre-Raphaelites. (The City Museum and Art Gallery, Birmingham, England)

Valley of Aosta—Snowstorm, Avalanche, and Thunderstorm, Joseph M. W. Turner (1175–1851). Turner's complete absorption in light, color, and atmosphere helped to prepare the way for the French impressionists. (MMA)

Portrait of a Gentleman, Jean Auguste
Ingres (1780–1867). A student of
David, Ingres was a devoted admirer
of classical antiquities. But he was also
influenced by romanticism. (MMA)

A Woman Reading, Camille Corot (1796–1875). Corot
was predominantly a naturalist, a painter of lifelike scenes
of innocence and simplicity. He shared the romanticists'
sentimental worship of woods and fields. (MMA)

The Port of La Rochelle, Corot. (Louvre)

(1817–1862). Both were aesthetes and humanitarians, though neither showed great sympathy for the hurts and ills of mankind. Morris was the prophet of a pre-industrial age, of an England of green fields and neat gardens, of cities "small and white and clean." He detested mechanized production with its stress on quantity and neglect of quality. Even in his socialism, as expressed in *News from Nowhere* and the *Dream of John Ball,* he celebrated the merits of small enterprise and hand work. Yet he abandoned the British Socialism he had been active in founding as anarchist influences within the movement gained strength.

The American essayist and critic Thoreau agreed with Morris in only a few particulars. Both were enemies of industrialism but Thoreau took a more radical stance. He abhorred all work and performed just enough to provide the bare necessities of living. He held to the conviction that the less labor a man did, over and above absolute need, the better it woud be for him and for the community. He thought the order of the week ought to be reversed—one day of work followed by six days of rest. He lived on a diet of potatoes and beans and a few other vegetables in season, and declared that "a man who buys a new suit of clothes every year never knows what it is to have a suit that really fits." Though he was a devoted and keenly observant student of nature, he had no use for science as an organized body of knowledge. In politics he was essentially an anarchist. The state with its taxing and war-making powers is chiefly an instrument of tyranny and exploitation. He did not advocate overthrow of the state by violence, yet he did teach that "that government is best which governs not at all." Finally, he taught a doctrine of individual nullification, that is, a citizen should break any law that commanded him to do injustice toward another individual, no matter how humble. His *Essay on Civil Disobedience* is a masterpiece of protest against the overpowering state.

Henry David Thoreau

SELECTED READINGS

· *Items so designated are available in paperbound editions.*

Bell, John F., *A History of Economic Thought,* New York, 1956.

Cole, G. D. H., *What Marx Really Meant,* New York, 1934.

Ferguson, J. M., *Landmarks of Economic Thought,* New York, 1938. A good summary, clearly written.

Gide, Charles, and Rist, Charles, *A History of Economic Doctrines,* Boston, 1948. A good summary.

Ginzberg, Eli, *The House of Adam Smith,* New York, 1934. Authoritative.

Hook, Sidney, *Towards the Understanding of Karl Marx,* New York, 1933. A stimulating analysis, though difficult in some places.

Laidler, H. W., *History of Socialist Thought,* New York, 1927.

Mitchell, Harvey, and Stearns, Peter N., *Workers and Protest: The European Labor Movement, the Working Classes and the Origins of Social Democracy, 1890–1914,* Itasca, Ill., 1970.

READINGS   Newman, P. C., *The Development of Economic Thought*, New York, 1952. An elementary survey.

Russell, Bertrand, *Proposed Roads to Freedom*, New York, 1919.

• Schumpeter, Joseph, *Capitalism, Socialism, and Democracy*, New York, 1942 (Torchbook). A provocative analysis.

Wagner, D. O., ed., *Social Reformers: Adam Smith to John Dewey*, New York, 1934.

• Wilson, Edmund, *To the Finland Station*, Garden City, N. Y., 1953 (Anchor). An interesting and provocative survey of the history of Marxism.

SOURCE MATERIALS

• Malthus, T. R., *An Essay on Population*, especially Books I and IV (Richard D. Irwin and others).

• Mill, J. S., *Autobiography*, New York, 1924 (Library of Liberal Arts and others).

Owen, Robert, *A New View of Society*, New York.

——, *Report to the County of Lanark*.

• Tolstoi, Count Leo, *The Kingdom of God Is Within You*, New York, 1905 (Noonday Press).

• Tucker, Robert C., ed., *The Marx-Engels Reader*, New York, 1972 (Norton). The essential writings, early and late.

Webster, Hutton, *Historical Selections*, pp. 776–80, Children in Factories.

CHAPTER 28

The Ascendancy of Nationalism
(1830-1914)

Our conscience tells us that we have not fulfilled a single act, not written a single line, not uttered a single word that was not inspired by a warm love for the fatherland. . . . We were guided constantly by the inflexible intention of maintaining intact the national dignity, of preserving pure of all stain . . . that glorious tricolored flag which a generous sovereign has entrusted to our care.
—Count Camillo Benso di Cavour, Speech to the Piedmontese Chamber of Deputies, April 16, 1858

The day of small nations has long passed away. The day of Empires has come.
—Joseph Chamberlain, Speech, Birmingham, May 12, 1904

The history of the world from 1830 to 1914 was marked by a vigorous growth of nationalism and its logical offshoot, an extensive and arrogant imperialism. Nationalism may be defined as a program or ideal based upon a consciousness of nationhood. The feeling or consciousness of nationhood may depend upon a number of factors. A people may consider themselves a nation because of peculiarities of race, language, religion, or culture. In most cases, however, the factors which weld diverse groups together are a common history and common aspirations for the future or a belief in a common destiny. Only such elements as these can explain the fact that Belgium, Switzerland, Canada, and the United States are nations, since in all four there are major differences in language, in religion, or in both—to say nothing of different ethnic backgrounds. Although nationalism was in some respects a beneficent force, particularly in the early days when it often took the form of struggles for liberty, to a large extent it was and still is an evil influence. It is especially evil when it expresses itself in jingoism, in militarism, and in ambitions to conquer and dominate.

The meaning of nationalism

Without question nationalism was one of the most powerful forces that molded the history of the Western world between 1830

835

The evolution of
nationalism

The stages of
nationalism

and 1914. From a vague sentiment during the early centuries of the modern era it grew into a veritable cult. For millions of deluded folk it became a stronger force than religion, surpassing Christianity in its appeal to the emotions and to the spirit of sacrifice in a holy cause. Men died for the honor of the flag as cheerfully as any martyrs had ever laid down their lives for the Cross. Though often co-existent with democracy and liberalism, militant nationalism was more powerful than either, and frequently thwarted or stifled both.

Nurtured by the French Revolutionary ideal of Fraternity, modern nationalism evolved through two stages. From 1800 to about 1848 it was little more than an emotional loyalty to a cultural and linguistic group and a yearning for deliverance from foreign oppression. After 1848 it developed into an aggressive movement for national greatness and for the right of each people united by cultural and ethnic ties to determine its own destinies. Its more extreme manifestations were exemplified by a frenzied worship of political power and a slavish devotion to doctrines of racial superiority and illusions of national honor. In such forms it was virtually synonymous with chauvinism, that species of vainglorious patriotism expressed in the sentiment, "My country, right or wrong."

I. THE RISE OF NATIONALISM IN WESTERN AND CENTRAL EUROPE

The greatest outpouring of national feeling at the beginning of the nineteenth century occurred in France. The Revolution of 1789 initiated the sentiment. Nearly every major event that followed reflected in great measure the power of that feeling. The July Revolution of 1830, for example, though primarily a revolt of the bourgeoisie against the reactionary policies of Charles X, was inspired also by a desire to revive the glory of France when she wielded supremacy over most of Europe. Of even greater importance as a manifestation of nationalism was the February Revolution of 1848. As in 1830, the movement began as a revolt against reactionary policies. King Louis Philippe had grown indifferent to the demands of the masses, and his ministers were cynical and corrupt. Moreover, he turned a deaf ear to zealous patriots who wanted France to go to the relief of northern Italians who longed to throw off Austrian rule and of Poles who hated the tyranny of Russia.

The strength of nationalism showed itself clearly in the election that followed the deposition of Louis Philippe. France had been made a republic with a constitution modeled after that of the United States. This meant a powerful executive with the title of President. December 10, 1848, was set as the date of the Presidential election. Four candidates competed in this election: a moderate republican, a socialist, a Catholic, and a man who had something for everybody—Louis Napoleon Bonaparte. More than 7,000,000 votes were cast; and out of this total nearly 5,500,000 went to Louis Napo-

Louis Philippe

leon. Who was this man, who enjoyed such amazing popularity that he could poll more than twice as many votes as the other three candidates combined? Louis Napoleon Bonaparte (1808–1873) was the nephew of Napoleon I, his father being Louis Bonaparte, who for a brief period was king of Holland. After his uncle's downfall, Louis Napoleon went into exile, spending most of his time in Germany and in Switzerland. Returning to France after the July Revolution of 1830, he was imprisoned a few years later for attempting to provoke a local uprising. But in 1846 he escaped to England, where he was liberally supplied with funds by both British and French reactionaries. By the summer of 1848 the situation in France was such that he knew it was safe to return. In fact, he was welcomed with open arms by men of all classes. Conservatives were looking for a savior to protect their property against the onslaughts of the radicals. Proletarians were beguiled by his glittering schemes for prosperity in his book, *The Extinction of Pauperism*, and by the fact that he had corresponded with Louis Blanc and with Pierre Proudhon, the anarchist. In between these two classes was a great multitude of patriots and hero-worshipers to whom the very name Napoleon was a matchless symbol of glory and greatness. It was chiefly to this multitude that the nephew of the Corsican owed his astounding triumph. As one old peasant expressed it: "How could I help voting for this gentleman—I whose nose was frozen at Moscow?"

With grandiose dreams of emulating his uncle, Louis Napoleon was not long content to be merely *President* of France. Almost from the first he used his position to pave the way for a higher calling. He enlisted the support of the Catholics by permitting them to

Louis Napoleon

Louis Napoleon as dictator and then Emperor

An Episode in the Place du Palais-Royal. The date is February 24, 1848, a year when revolutionary fervor spread throughout Europe.

regain control over the schools and by sending an expedition to Rome to restore the Pope to his temporal power. He threw sops to the workers and to the bourgeoisie in the form of old-age insurance and laws for the encouragement of business. In 1851, alleging the need for extraordinary measures to protect the rights of the masses, he proclaimed a temporary dictatorship and invited the people to grant him the power to draw up a new constitution. In the plebiscite held on December 21, 1851, he was authorized by an overwhelming majority (7,500,000 to 640,000) to proceed as he liked. The new constitution, which he put into effect in January 1852, made the President an actual dictator. His term of office was lengthened to ten years, and he was given the exclusive power to initiate legislation and to make war and peace. Although the legislative branch was preserved in name, it could not initiate or amend bills or even change any specific provisions in the budget. Still the little Caesar was not satisfied; he would be content with nothing less than the imperial dignity which had graced the shoulders of his famous uncle. After exactly one year Louis Napoleon Bonaparte ordered another plebiscite and, with the approval of over 95 per cent of the voters, assumed the title of Napoleon III, Emperor of the French.

The regime of Napoleon III

The Second Empire in France endured from December 1852, to September 1870. Its creator and preserver ruled by methods not dissimilar to those of other Caesars both before and since. He stimulated an imposing prosperity by draining swamps, building roads, improving harbors, subsidizing railroads, and constructing a magnificent system of boulevards in Paris. He cultivated the favor of the lower classes by mouthing Revolutionary phrases and by schemes for social welfare. At the same time he strove to make sure that radicals would not become troublesome. He subjected the press to strict surveillance and controlled elections by paying the expenses of *official* candidates and by requiring all others to take an oath of fidelity to the Emperor. Nor did he neglect opportunities to add luster to his regime by an aggressive foreign policy. He annexed Alge-

The Crimean War. This photograph taken between 1854 and 1855 is by Roger Fenton. (See the illustration on the opposite page.)

Roger Fenton's Photographic Van. Fenton was one of the first noted European photographers and gained fame by covering the events of the Crimean War.

ria in northern Africa and established a protectorate over Indochina. In 1854 he plunged into the Crimean War with Russia under the pretext of protecting Catholic monks in Turkey. Since Napoleon had the aid of Great Britain and Turkey and also for a time of Sardinia, he managed to emerge from this war on the victorious side. Now more than ever he could rejoice in the plaudits of the mob and pose as the arbiter of the destinies of Europe.

By 1860 the glamour of Napoleon's reputation had begun to wear thin. The first great blow to his prestige was a result of the outcome of his Italian adventure. In 1858 he had formed an alliance with the Italian nationalists to help them expel the Austrians; but as soon as he saw that his erstwhile friends were bent upon consolidating the whole Italian peninsula into a nation-state and upon destroying the temporal sovereignty of the Pope, he promptly deserted them. By so doing, he antagonized thousands of his more liberal followers, who reproached him for abandoning a gallant people to Austrian oppression. In 1862 Napoleon intervened in Mexico. He sent an army into that country to establish an empire and then offered the throne to the Archduke Maximilian of Austria. But at the conclusion of the American Civil War the government of the United States compelled the withdrawal of the French troops, and soon afterward Maximilian was captured and shot by the Mexicans. As a consequence of this tragic adventure, opposition to Napoleon's rule markedly increased. After the elections of 1869 he decided that it would be expedient to make some concessions. He granted to the Assembly the right to initiate laws and to criticize and ratify or reject the budget. But in 1870 he resolved to gamble once more on a bold stroke of foreign policy to retrieve his fortunes. Shortly before this the government of Spain had been overturned, and the revolutionists had offered the crown to Prince Leopold of Hohenzollern, a cousin of the King of Prussia. Militarists and fire-eating "patriots" in France professed to see in this a threat to the security of the French

The decline and fall of the Second Empire

839

nation. Napoleon himself probably did not desire a war. He apparently assumed that vigorous diplomatic measures would give France all she needed in the way of a glorious triumph. But he allowed himself to be dominated by a militant clique that surrounded the Empress Eugénie and included several of his ministers. Members of this clique emphasized the rapid growth of the Prussian nation and its commanding position in central Europe. Accordingly, they advocated a preventive war. Now or never was their motto. France must seize the initiative while she still had an equality in numbers and a superiority, they believed, in military power. They maneuvered Napoleon into sending the French ambassador to meet with King William I of Prussia at the spa of Ems and there to demand that the king *never* allow a member of the Hohenzollern family to become a candidate for the Spanish throne. Though annoyed by this demand, King William wanted peace. But even less than Napoleon III was he master in his own house. The real dictator of policy in Prussia was the minister-president, Otto von Bismarck. And Bismarck lusted for war, if for no other reason than to rally the south German states behind the Prussian standard and unite all Germans in one great nation. France was badly defeated in the ensuing war, which lasted only a few weeks. After the battle of Sedan (September 2, 1870) Napoleon himself was taken prisoner, and two days later his government was overthrown by a group of republicans in Paris.

The founding of the Third Republic

Following the collapse of Napoleon's empire a provisional government was organized to rule the country until a new constitution could be drafted. Elections were held in February 1871 for a national constituent assembly, resulting in the choice of some 500 monarchists and only about 200 republicans. The explanation lies in the fact that during the electoral campaign the republicans had urged a renewal of the war, while the monarchists took the attitude that France was already defeated, and that she might as well negotiate with her conquerors for the best terms she could get. It was not that the French people overwhelmingly preferred a monarchy, but rather that they longed for peace. Fortunately the monarchists were hopelessly divided. Angry discord among them postponed for almost four years a definite decision as to the permanent form the French government should take. Finally, in January 1875 the National Assembly adopted the first of a series of constitutional laws recognizing the government as republican in form. This action signified the formal establishment of the Third Republic in France.

The Paris Commune

France in this era was not destined to have a happy future. It was almost torn apart by nationalist discord and social conflict from the beginning. The first episode of this kind was the Commune of Paris in 1871. Though this movement is commonly described as a rebellion of dangerous radicals intent upon the destruction of law and order, it was in reality quite different. Most of its members were not socialists or anarchists. They resembled the Jacobins of the First Revolution and were largely members of the middle class. They did

The Paris Commune. A view of Champs Elysées showing damage resulting from the 1871 uprising. The Arc de Triomphe may be seen in the distance.

not advocate the abolition of private property but rather its wider distribution. The movement was precipitated by the discontent of the Franco-Prussian War—bitterness over the defeat of Napoleon III and exhaustion by the long siege of Paris that followed. Added to these were fears that the central government would be dominated by the rural population to the disadvantage of the urban masses in the capital. After several weeks of frustrating disputation, the Commune turned into a bloody civil war. The Communards killed about sixty hostages, including the Archbishop of Paris. The government numbered its victims by the thousands. The courts-martial which were set up executed twenty-six. Thousands of others were sentenced to imprisonment or banishment in New Caledonia.

The collapse of the Paris Commune did not end the troubles of France that grew out of her defeat in the Franco-Prussian War. Monarchists and clericals charged the Republic with weakness and corruption and longed for a more autocratic government to lead the nation back to the path of glory. Some of them won applause by clamoring for a war of revenge against Germany. By harping on scandals recently exposed in the republican regime, they endeared themselves to the monarchists and also to conservative Catholics, who hated the Republic for its anti-clerical program. In the 1890's the reactionaries adopted anti-Semitism as a spearhead for the advancement of their aims. The fact that certain Jewish bankers had recently been involved in scandalous dealings with politicians lent color to the monarchist charge that the government was shot through with corruption and that money-grabbing Jews were largely to blame. Catholics were persuaded to believe that Jewish politicians had dictated the anticlerical legislation of the republican regime. In the face of such charges it is not strange that anti-Semitism should have flared into a violent outbreak. In 1894 a Jewish captain of

The Execution of a Communard by Government Troops

841

artillery, Alfred Dreyfus, was accused by a clique of monarchist officers of selling military secrets to Germany. Tried by court-martial, he was convicted and sentenced for life to Devil's Island. At first the verdict was accepted as the merited punishment of a traitor; but in 1897 Colonel Picquart, a new head of the Intelligence Division, announced his conclusion that the documents upon which Dreyfus had been convicted were forgeries. A movement was launched for a new trial, which the War Department promptly refused. Soon the whole nation was divided into friends and opponents of the luckless captain. On the side of Dreyfus were the radical republicans, the socialists, people of liberal and humanitarian sympathies, and such prominent literary figures as Émile Zola and Anatole France. The anti-Dreyfusards included the monarchists, the clericals, the Jew-baiters, the militarists, and a considerable number of conservative workingmen and sincere but mistaken patriots. Dreyfus was finally set free by executive order in 1899, and six years later he was cleared of all guilt by the Supreme Court and restored to the army. He was immediately promoted to the rank of major and decorated with the emblem of the Legion of Honor. The outcome of the Dreyfus affair effectively squelched the monarchist movement in France. Thereafter its adherents were gradually reduced to political insignificance—a mere "handful of old nuts rattling in a bag."

As already intimated, the Dreyfus affair was an element in a broader struggle over the issue of church and state, which also had nationalist implications. From the beginning of its history the Third Republic had been tinctured with anticlericalism. Its founders were not necessarily atheists, but they did believe that a powerful church with ambitions to extend its political and social influence was a threat to republican government. The aims of the anticlericals were to curb this influence, to reduce the economic privileges of the

*The roots of
anticlericalism*

*Alfred Dreyfus Leaving the
Courthouse after His Court-
Martial*

Catholic Church, and to break the stranglehold the clergy had gained upon education. Anticlericalism was, in part, a result of the Industrial Revolution, which fostered materialistic interest and intensified the struggle between the bourgeoisie and the die-hard conservatives. It was also a product in some measure of the growth of science and of skeptical and liberal philosophies, which were often employed as primary weapons in fighting religious conservatism. Probably the main cause of its growth was the rise of a militant nationalism. The Catholic Church was not only committed to an internationalist outlook, but as late as the 1860's Popes were still asserting their rights to temporal power and pouring out their anathemas upon rulers who would establish omnipotent states. Wherever nationalism gathered powerful momentum, clericalism was almost certain to be regarded as a primary enemy.

Anticlericalism in France reached the peak of its fury between 1875 and 1914. The great majority of the leaders of the Third Republic were hostile to the Church; and naturally so, for the Catholic hierarchy was aiding the monarchists at every turn. Clericals conspired with monarchists, militarists, and anti-Semites in attempting to discredit the Republic during the Dreyfus affair. But in the end they overreached themselves. The outcome of the Dreyfus affair not only sounded the knell of monarchism but led to a furious attack upon the Church. In 1901 the government passed a series of acts prohibiting the existence of religious orders not authorized by the state, forbidding members of religious orders to teach in either public or private schools, and finally, in 1905, dissolving the union of Church and state. For the first time since 1801 the adherents of all creeds were placed on an equal basis. No longer were the Catholic clergy to receive their salaries from the public purse. Although some of these measures were modified in later years, clericalism remained in the minds of most Frenchmen under a heavy cloud of suspicion.

The results of anticlericalism in France

The February Revolution in France touched off a series of revolts in central Europe, beginning with an uprising in Austria on March 13. Mobs of students and workingmen rioted in Vienna and forced the resignation of that last great pillar of the *ancien régime*, Prince Metternich. Frightened by the refusal of his troops to fire upon the rebels, the Emperor promised a constitution for Germanic Austria, excluding Hungary and the Italian possessions. The constitution as finally adopted provided for a cabinet responsible to parliament and for a liberal franchise, and the assembly which drew it up also abolished the remaining feudal obligations of the peasants. Almost immediately the Hungarians took advantage of the turmoil in Vienna to establish a liberal government, and in April 1849, under the leadership of Louis Kossuth, they proclaimed the independence of the Hungarian Republic. But neither of these revolutions was permanently successful, for the reason that they soon became entangled in the discords of nationalism. The Hungarian liberals were no more

The revolution of 1848 in Austria and Hungary

843

willing than the Austrians to grant the privileges to subject nationalities that they claimed for themselves. As a consequence, the Hapsburgs were able to stir up ill feeling among the Slavs and to use them to good advantage in curbing the ambitions of the dominant nationalities. By the summer of 1849 the Emperor had succeeded in overthrowing the Hungarian Republic and in revoking the Austrian constitution. The discontent, however, continued until a compromise known as the *Ausgleich* was finally worked out between the Austrians and the Hungarians in 1867. The *Ausgleich* established a dual monarchy, with the head of the House of Hapsburg serving as both Emperor of Austria and King of Hungary. Each of the two parts of the empire was made practically autonomous, with its own cabinet and parliament. Three joint ministers, of war, finance, and foreign affairs, looked after the interests of the state as a whole in their respective spheres. Enabling both the Magyars in Hungary and the Germans in Austria to rule as master races, this arrangement survived until the Dual Monarchy was broken into fragments in 1918.

A major drive of nationalists in Germany was unification of their country. Since 1815 the German states, together with Austria, had constituted the thirty-eight members of the German Confederation. Influential liberals among the nationalists hoped to unite all of Germany into a great empire. Many others, however, were more deeply concerned with advancing *German* ideals and *German* culture. They ardently believed in the superiority of the German *Volk*, German law, and the concept of a German Reich. Some were frankly expansionist, proclaiming Germany's right to civilize backward peoples and even to occupy their territories. Most of the dogmas of these men of violence fitted in with the aims of the later militants from Bismarck to Hitler.

The movement for German unification

German nationalism reached its first climax in the Revolution of 1848. Agitation by liberal dissenters forced the German princes to grant or to promise reforms. In May high-minded leaders convoked a great national assembly in Frankfurt to draft a constitution for a united Germany. From the beginning, controversy raged over numerous issues: should the government be a republic or a limited monarchy? If the latter, who should be offered the crown? Should Austria or only the strictly German states be included? Such were the rocks on which the Frankfurt Assembly foundered. Soon afterward it broke up in disgust with nothing to show for its efforts. Most of the reforms which had been secured outside of the Assembly likewise gradually melted away, and thousands of the revolutionaries emigrated from the country and took refuge in the United States.

The Frankfurt Assembly

The unification of Germany was now left to be achieved by the hard realism of Bismarck. Otto von Bismarck (1815–1898) was born into the class of Junkers, or landed aristocrats, who for centuries had furnished the Prussian state with the bulk of its bureaucrats

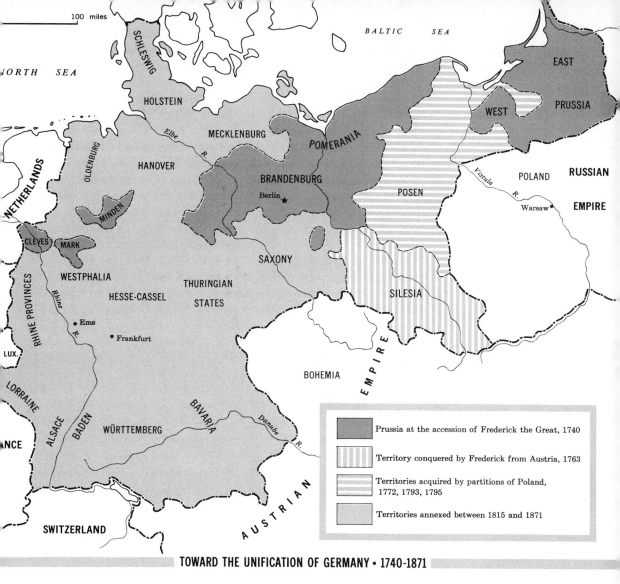

100 miles

BALTIC SEA

NORTH SEA

SCHLESWIG

HOLSTEIN

MECKLENBURG

Elbe R.

POMERANIA

EAST

WEST

PRUSSIA

OLDENBURG

HANOVER

BRANDENBURG

POSEN

POLAND

RUSSIAN

Berlin ★

Vistula R.

Warsaw •

EMPIRE

NETHERLANDS

MINDEN

CLEVES

MARK

WESTPHALIA

SAXONY

SILESIA

HESSE-CASSEL

THURINGIAN
STATES

RHINE PROVINCES

Rhine R.

• Ems R.

LUX.

• Frankfurt

BOHEMIA

E M P I R E

LORRAINE

ALSACE

BADEN

WÜRTTEMBERG

BAVARIA

Danube R.

FRANCE

SWITZERLAND

A U S T R I A N

Prussia at the accession of Frederick the Great, 1740

Territory conquered by Frederick from Austria, 1763

Territories acquired by partitions of Poland, 1772, 1793, 1795

Territories annexed between 1815 and 1871

TOWARD THE UNIFICATION OF GERMANY • 1740-1871

and high army officers. During the revolutionary movement of 1848 he served in the Prussian Parliament as a staunch upholder of divine-right monarchy. He was one of a group of intransigent aristocrats who urged the Prussian king not to accept a "crown of shame" from the Frankfurt Assembly. Later Bismarck was instrumental in organizing the Conservative party, dedicated to protecting the interests of the Junker class, the established church, and the army, and to the building of a powerful Prussia as the nucleus of a German nation. In 1862 he was summoned by King William I to become Minister-President of his beloved Prussia.

Bismarck

In consolidating the German states into a united nation, Bismarck followed a succession of steps of almost diabolical cleverness. First he plotted to eliminate Austria from her commanding position in the Germanic Confederation. As a preliminary means to this end

845

Bismarck's pre-
liminary steps in
consolidating
German unity

he entered into a dispute with Denmark over possession of Schleswig and Holstein. Inhabited largely by Germans, these two provinces had an anomalous status. Since 1815 Holstein had been included in the Germanic Confederation, but both were subject to the personal overlordship of the King of Denmark. When, in 1864, the Danish king attempted to annex them, Bismarck invited Austria to participate in a war against Denmark. A brief struggle followed, at the end of which the Danish ruler was compelled to renounce all his claims to Schleswig and Holstein in favor of Austria and Prussia. Then the very sequel occurred for which Bismarck ardently hoped: a quarrel between the victors over division of the spoils. The conflict which followed in 1866, known as the Seven Weeks' War, ended in an easy triumph for Prussia. Austria was forced to give up her claims to Schleswig and Holstein, to surrender Venetia to Italy, and to acquiesce in the dissolution of the Germanic Confederation. Immediately following the war Bismarck proceeded to unite all of the German states north of the Main River into the North German Confederation.

The final step in the completion of German unity was the Franco-Prussian War. We have learned of the part played by French politicians in provoking a crisis with Prussia over the question of succession to the Spanish throne. The attitude of Bismarck was just as provocative. He knew that a war with France would be the best possible means to kindle a *German* nationalism in Bavaria and Württemberg and in the remaining states south of the Main. When he received a dispatch sent by King William I from Ems informing him that the demand of the French for perpetual exclusion of the Hohenzollern family from the Spanish throne had been refused, he decided that the time for action had come. He determined to release the telegram from Ems in such a form as to make it appear that King William had insulted the French ambassador. Bismarck's prediction that this would have the effect of "a red rag upon the Gallic bull" was speedily borne out. When the garbled report of what happened at Ems was received in France, the whole nation was immediately in an uproar. On July 15, 1870, when Napoleon's ministers requested the legislative body to approve a declaration of war, there were only ten dissenting votes. No sooner had the struggle begun than the south German states rallied to the side of Prussia in the belief that she was the victim of aggression. Such was the beginning of a war that was destined to have tremendous effects upon the subsequent history of Europe. From the start the Prussians had the advantage. The disciplined efficiency of their military machine stood out in bold contrast to the ineptitude of the French. The result could have been foretold from the beginning. After the capture of Napoleon at Sedan in September 1870 and the conquest of Paris following a desperate siege four months later, the war was officially

Meeting to Arrange Peace Terms at the End of the Franco-Prussian War. On the left is Otto von Bismarck, chancellor of the new German Empire. In the center is Jules Favre and to his right, Louis-Adolphe Thiers, both representing the provisional government set up after the overthrow of Napoleon III.

ended by the Treaty of Frankfurt. France surrendered the major portions of Alsace and Lorraine and agreed to pay an indemnity of 5 billion francs.

2. THE SPREAD OF NATIONALISM TO SOUTHERN AND EASTERN EUROPE

Events in Italy ran a course almost parallel to that which had led to the unification of Germany. Italy before 1848, it should be remembered, was a patchwork of petty states. The most important of those possessing independence were the Kingdom of Sardinia in the north, the Papal States in the central region, and the Kingdom of the Two Sicilies in the south. The former republics of Lombardy and Venetia were held by Austria, while Hapsburg dependents ruled in Tuscany, Parma, and Modena. As the revolutionary fervor of 1848 swept across the peninsula, one ruler after another granted democratic reforms. Charles Albert of Sardinia outdistanced all the others with his celebrated Fundamental Statute providing for civil liberties and a parliamentary form of government. But it soon became evident that the Italians were more interested in nationalism than in democracy. For some years romantic patriots had been dreaming of the *Risorgimento*—the resurrection of the Italian spirit—which would restore the nation to the position of glorious leadership it had held in ancient times and during the age of the Renaissance. To achieve this, it was universally agreed that Italy must be welded into a single state. But opinions differed as to the form the new government should take. Young idealists followed the leadership of Giuseppe Mazzini (1805–1872), who labored with sincere devotion for the founding of a republic. Religious-minded patriots believed that the most prac-

Giuseppe Mazzini

847

Camillo di Cavour

Giuseppe Garibaldi

ticable solution would be to federate the states of Italy under the presidency of the Pope. The majority of the more moderate nationalists advocated a constitutional monarchy built upon the foundations of the Kingdom of Sardinia. The aims of this third group gradually crystallized under the leadership of a shrewd Sardinian nobleman, Count Camillo di Cavour (1810–1861). In 1850 he was appointed Minister of Commerce and Agriculture of his native state and in 1852 Prime Minister.

The campaign for unification of the Italian peninsula began with efforts to expel the Austrians. In 1848 revolts were organized in the territories under Hapsburg domination, and an army of liberation marched from Sardinia to aid the rebels; but the movement ended in failure. It was then that Cavour, as the new leader of the campaign, turned to less heroic but more practical methods. In 1855, to attract the favorable attention of Great Britain and France, he entered the Crimean War on their side despite the fact that he had no quarrel with Russia. In 1858 he held a secret meeting with Napoleon III and prepared the stage for an Italian War of Liberation. Napoleon agreed to cooperate in driving the Austrians from Italy for the price of the cession of Savoy and Nice by Sardinia to France. A war with Austria was duly provoked in 1859, and for a time all went well for the Franco-Italian allies. But after the conquest of Lombardy, Napoleon suddenly withdrew, fearful of ultimate defeat and afraid of antagonizing the Catholics in his own country by aiding an avowedly anticlerical government. Thus deserted by her ally, Sardinia was unable to expel the Austrians from Venetia. Nevertheless, she did make some extensive gains: she annexed Lombardy, and acquired by various means the duchies of Tuscany, Parma, and Modena and the northern portion of the Papal States. Sardinia was now more than twice her original size and by far the most powerful state in Italy.

The second step in consolidating the unity of Italy was the conquest of the Kingdom of the Two Sicilies. This kingdom was ruled by a Bourbon, Francis II, who was thoroughly hated by his Italian subjects. In May 1860 a romantic free-lance adventurer by the name of Giuseppe Garibaldi set out with his famous regiment of 1000 "red shirts" to rescue his fellow Italians from oppression. Within three months he had conquered the island of Sicily and had then marched to the deliverance of Naples, where the people were already in revolt. By November the whole kingdom of Francis II had fallen to the gay buccaneer. Garibaldi at first apparently intended to convert the territory into an independent republic but was finally persuaded to surrender it to the Kingdom of Sardinia. With most of the peninsula now united under a single rule, Victor Emmanuel II, King of Sardinia, assumed the title of King of Italy (March 17, 1861). Venetia was still in the hands of the Austrians, but in 1866 they were forced by the Prussians to cede it to Italy. All that remained to complete the unification of Italy was the annexation of

SWITZERLAND

AUSTRIA

SAVOY
(To France in 1860)

LOMBARDY

VENETIA

KINGDOM OF
SARDINIA

• Milan

• Venice

Po R.

P I E D M O N T

• Turin

PARMA

FRANCE

• Genoa

MODENA

• Bologna

ROMAGNA

LUCCA

• Florence

Arno R.

TUSCANY

P A P A L   S T A T E S

A D R I A T I C   S E A

UMBRIA

Tiber R.

CORSICA
(To France)

Rome ★

K I N G D O M

★ Naples

KINGDOM
OF
SARDINIA

T Y R R H E N I A N

S E A

O F

T H E

T W O

S I C I L I E S

0   200 miles

M E D I T E R R A N E A N

• Palermo

• Messina

SICILY

S E A

THE UNIFICATION OF ITALY

Rome. The Eternal City had resisted conquest thus far largely because of the military protection accorded to the Pope by Napoleon
III. But in 1870 the outbreak of the Franco-Prussian War compelled
Napoleon to withdraw his troops. The opportunity was too good
to be overlooked. In September 1870 Italian soldiers occupied Rome,
and in July of the following year it was made the capital of the
united kingdom.

The occupation of Rome brought the kingdom of Italy into conflict with the papacy. Indeed, the whole movement for unification
had been characterized by hostility to the Church. Such was inevitably the case, with the Pope ruling in the manner of a secular prince
over the Papal States and hurling the thunders of his wrath against
those who would rob him of his domain for the sake of a united
Italy. Following the occupation of Rome in 1870 an attempt was

Anticlericalism
in Italy

849

made to solve the problem of relations between the state and the papacy. In 1871 the Italian Parliament enacted the Law of Papal Guaranties purporting to define the status of the Pope as a reigning sovereign. He was to be granted full authority over the Vatican and Lateran buildings and gardens and the right to send and receive ambassadors. In addition, he was to have free use of the Italian postal, telegraph, and railway systems and was to be paid an annual indemnity of about $645,000. This law the reigning pontiff, Pius IX, promptly denounced on the ground that issues affecting the Pope could be settled only by an international treaty to which he himself was a party. Whereupon he shut himself up in the Vatican and refused to have anything to do with a government which had so shamefully treated Christ's Vicar on earth. His successors continued this practice of voluntary imprisonment until 1929, when a series of agreements between the Fascist government and Pius XI effected what appeared to be a satisfactory settlement of the dispute.

In eastern Europe during the nineteenth century nationalism partook primarily of a liberation character. This was particularly true of the lands of the Balkans. Before 1829 the entire Balkan peninsula—bounded by the Aegean, Black, and Adriatic Seas—was controlled by the Turks. But during the next eighty-five years a gradual dismemberment of the Turkish empire occurred. In some instances the slicing away of territories was perpetrated by rival European powers, especially by Russia and Austria; but generally it was the result of nationalist revolts by the Sultan's Christian subjects. In 1829, at the conclusion of the first Russo-Turkish War, the Ottoman Empire was compelled to acknowledge the independence of Greece and to grant autonomy to Serbia and to the provinces which later became Rumania. As the years passed, resentment against Ottoman rule spread through other Balkan territories. In 1875–1876 there were uprisings in Bosnia, Herzegovina, and Bulgaria, which the Sultan suppressed with murderous vengeance. Reports of atrocities against Orthodox Christians gave Russia an excuse for renewal of her age-long struggle for domination of the Balkans. In this second Russo-Turkish War (1877–1878) the armies of the Tsar won a smashing victory. The Treaty of San Stefano, which terminated the conflict, provided that the Sultan surrender nearly all of his territory in Europe, except for a remnant around Constantinople. But at this juncture the great powers intervened. Austria and Great Britain, especially, were opposed to letting Russia assume jurisdiction over so large a portion of the Near East. In 1878 a congress of the great powers, meeting in Berlin, transferred Bessarabia to Russia, Thessaly to Greece, and Bosnia and Herzegovina to the control of Austria. Seven years later the Bulgars, who had been granted some degree of autonomy by the Treaty of Berlin, seized the province of Eastern Rumelia from Turkey and in 1908 established the independent Kingdom of Bulgaria.

In the very year when this last dismemberment occurred, Turkey herself was engulfed by the tidal wave of nationalism. For some

Nationalism in the Balkans

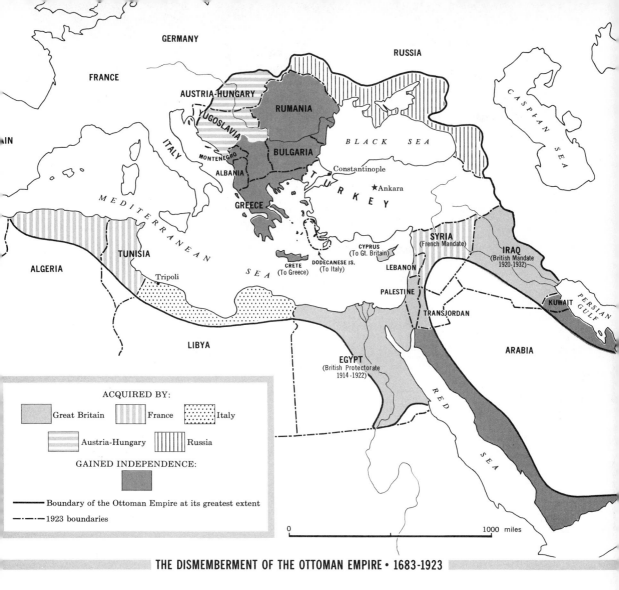

GERMANY

FRANCE

RUSSIA

AUSTRIA-HUNGARY

YUGOSLAVIA

RUMANIA

ITALY

MONTENEGRO

BULGARIA

BLACK SEA

CASPIAN SEA

ALBANIA

Constantinople

GREECE

TURKEY

★Ankara

MEDITERRANEAN

CYPRUS
(To Gt. Britain)

SYRIA
(French Mandate)

IRAQ
(British Mandate
1920-1932)

TUNISIA

CRETE
(To Greece)

DODECANESE IS.
(To Italy)

LEBANON

SEA

ALGERIA

Tripoli

PALESTINE

KUWAIT

PERSIAN GULF

TRANSJORDAN

LIBYA

EGYPT
(British Protectorate
1914-1922)

ARABIA

RED SEA

ACQUIRED BY:

Great Britain   France   Italy

Austria-Hungary   Russia

GAINED INDEPENDENCE:

Boundary of the Ottoman Empire at its greatest extent

1923 boundaries

0 _____ 1000 miles

THE DISMEMBERMENT OF THE OTTOMAN EMPIRE · 1683-1923

time her more enlightened citizens had been growing increasingly
disgusted with the weakness and incompetence of the Sultan's government. In particular, those who had been educated in the universities of England and France were becoming more and more convinced that their country should be rejuvenated by the introduction
of Western ideas of science, patriotism, and democracy. Organizing
themselves into a society known as the Young Turks, they forced
the Sultan in 1908 to establish constitutional government. The following year, when a reactionary movement set in, they deposed the
reigning Sultan, Abdul Hamid II, and placed on the throne his wit-
less brother, Mohammed V, as a titular sovereign. The real powers
of government were now entrusted to a grand vizier and ministers
responsible to an elected parliament. Unfortunately this revolution
did not mean increased liberty for the non-Turkish inhabitants of

The Young
Turk revolution

851

EUROPE AFTER THE CONGRESS OF BERLIN · 1878

the empire. Instead, the Young Turks launched a vigorous movement to Ottomanize all of the Christian subjects of the Sultan. At the same time the disturbances preceding and accompanying the revolution opened the way for still further dismemberment. In 1908 Austria annexed the provinces of Bosnia and Herzegovina, which the Treaty of Berlin had allowed her merely to administer, and in 1911–1912 Italy made war upon Turkey for the conquest of Tripoli.

Nationalism in Russia amounted to comparatively little until nearly the end of the nineteenth century. Few national minorities rose in revolt, and those that did were seldom successful. Discontented ethnic elements did not form any large proportion of the Russian nation, as was the case in Turkey, Austria, and Italy. As a consequence the Tsars did not generally find nationalist revolts a serious

Nationalism in Russia

threat within their borders. Russian nationalism moved in the direction of external goals. Its aim was to foster external greatness rather than to cultivate the domestic genius of the people. But there were a few notable exceptions.

One was the Narodnik or populist movement. Originating in the 1860's, it spread rapidly. The nationalism of the populists found expression largely in the work of the Slavophil faction which extolled the culture of the Slavs as one of the finest products of civilization. Populism, in fact, was originally an offshoot of the Slavophil movement. It did not become a radical political party until about 1870.

The most active of the Pan-Slavists, however, were not populists but nationalists committed to an aggressive foreign policy. Their program had no more to do with internal reform in Russia than the *Rule Britannia* movement or *Deutschland über alles* in their respective countries. The Pan-Slavists sought to uphold for Russia a predominant position among all of the Slavs regardless of the country in which they lived. It was held to be the duty of Great Russia to serve as the guide and protector of the Poles, Bulgars, Montenegrins, and all the subject nationalities of the Austrian and Turkish empires. Under its guise Russian imperialists interfered in the concerns of all these bordering peoples and sought to draw them into the Tsarist orbit. Russian ambitions often constituted a threat to the independence and even the existence of such border states as Austria-Hungary and Turkey.

3. NATIONALISM IN THE WESTERN HEMISPHERE

Nearly every development in American history has closely approximated the pattern adhered to by the nations of Europe. The Revolutionary War, though it involved some social issues, was mainly a struggle for independence. The War of 1812 bore little relationship to its alleged cause, the impressment of American seamen, and turned mainly into a struggle for the conquest of lands of the Indians. The Mexican War and the Spanish-American War were blatantly expansionist, the first against Mexico and the second against Spain. Except for the Louisiana Territory, the vast proportion of new lands annexed by the United States before 1900 were acquired by forcible expansion. Even the American Civil War was waged by the North primarily as a nationalist crusade. President Lincoln declared that his main purpose in continuing the war was not to destroy slavery but to preserve the Union.

Nearly thirty years before he became President, John Adams declared that he had always considered the settlement of America as "the opening of a grand scheme and design in Providence for the illumination of the ignorant and the emancipation of the slavish part of mankind." Nationalism in the United States was closely associated with ethnic chauvinism, or in some cases, racism. Throughout the

**White ethnicism
in the
United States**

Manifest Destiny

nineteenth century doctrines of race superiority were freely propagated and accepted. In the minds of many the classification of superior included only those who would now be called WASPs. The Chosen People did not embrace recent immigrants from Southern and Eastern Europe and certainly not from Asia or Africa. God had given to Anglo-Saxons a mission to organize inferior peoples and to civilize the world.

Worship of national greatness in the United States generally went hand in glove with territorial expansion. The prophets of nationalism were commonly advocates of a manifest destiny. For years they could not avert their hungry eyes from the prospect of conquering Cuba, Canada, the lands of the Indians, and Mexico. Not all of these territories were forcibly annexed, but enough were seized to whet the appetite for further conquests.

4. THE NEW IMPERIALISM OF THE NINETEENTH CENTURY

**The universality
of imperialism**

The history of nearly every outstanding nation has had its imperialist phase. Moreover, it is hardly an exaggeration to say that imperialism is the same wherever it is practiced. It is inseparable from domination and exploitation where one nation sets itself up as a superior breed and arrogates to itself the right to rule another without its consent.

**The expansion of
imperialism**

In the competition for empire among the powers of the Old World, Great Britain led the way. By the end of the nineteenth century more than half of the land area of the world had been brought under the British flag. India, Canada, Australia, New Zealand, South Africa, Burma, the Sudan, and South Africa, together with innumerable islands, made up a vast empire. France came next with possessions almost equal in area but much less thinly populated and poorer in natural wealth. Algeria, French West Africa, Equatorial Africa, and Indochina ranked as the principal stars in her imperial crown.

854

"*The Rhodes Colossus.*" The ambitions of Cecil Rhodes, the driving force behind British imperialism in South Africa, are satirized in this cartoon appearing in *Punch.*

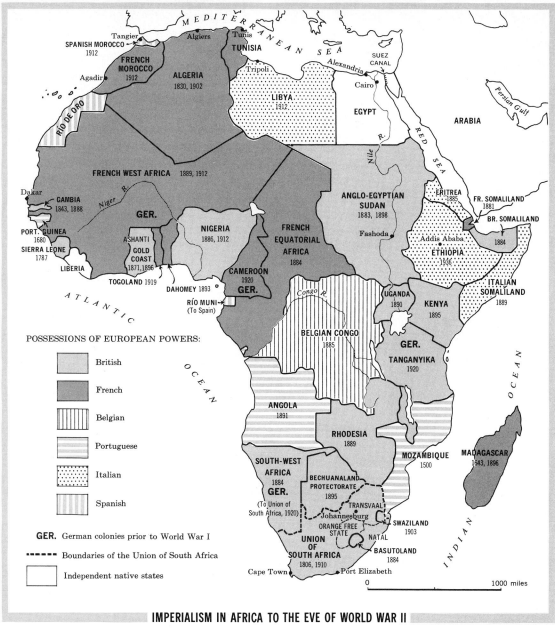

POSSESSIONS OF EUROPEAN POWERS:

British

French

Belgian

Portuguese

Italian

Spanish

GER. German colonies prior to World War I

- - - - Boundaries of the Union of South Africa

Independent native states

0   1000 miles

IMPERIALISM IN AFRICA TO THE EVE OF WORLD WAR II

Germany and Italy entered the race for colonies late. Both were preponderantly interested in such internal problems as national unification, industrial development, and quarrels between Church and state. Nevertheless, by 1880 both nations were ready to enter the imperial scramble. Though Bismarck at first had scoffed at the acquisition of colonies, he was eventually persuaded to enter the contest for an empire in Africa. Extensive areas were carved out of the southern area of the continent, although most of them proved of limited value. Italy also embarked on a quest for African colonies, but her efforts were even more discouraging than those of Germany. Italian armies were cut to pieces in 1896 when they attempted the conquest of Abyssinia (Ethiopia). The imperialist ambitions of

Late comers in the imperial scramble

855

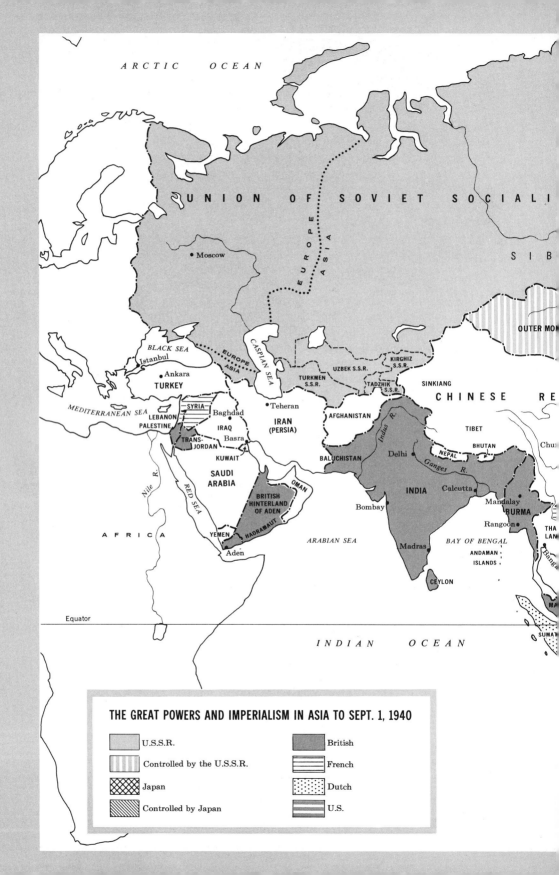

ARCTIC OCEAN

UNION OF SOVIET SOCIALI

SIB

• Moscow

EUROPE
ASIA

OUTER MON

BLACK SEA
Istanbul

EUROPE
ASIA

CASPIAN SEA

KIRGHIZ
S.S.R.

SINKIANG

• Ankara

UZBEK S.S.R.

TURKEY

TURKMEN
S.S.R.

TADZHIK
S.S.R.

CHINESE   RE

MEDITERRANEAN SEA

SYRIA

Baghdad

LEBANON
PALESTINE

IRAQ

AFGHANISTAN

Teheran

TIBET

BHUTAN

Chu

Indus R.

IRAN
(PERSIA)

NEPAL

TRANS-
JORDAN

Basra

KUWAIT

BALUCHISTAN

Delhi •

Ganges R.

Nile R.

SAUDI
ARABIA

OMAN

INDIA

Calcutta •

RED SEA

BRITISH
HINTERLAND
OF ADEN

Bombay •

Mandalay •

BURMA

Rangoon •

THA
LAN

AFRICA

YEMEN

HADRAMAUT

ARABIAN SEA

Madras •

BAY OF BENGAL

Banga

Aden •

ANDAMAN
ISLANDS

CEYLON

MA

Equator

SUMA

INDIAN   OCEAN

THE GREAT POWERS AND IMPERIALISM IN ASIA TO SEPT. 1, 1940

U.S.S.R.

British

Controlled by the U.S.S.R.

French

Japan

Dutch

Controlled by Japan

U.S.

ARCTIC OCEAN

ALASKA

BERING SEA

PUBLICS

SEA OF
OKHOTSK

Amur R.

MANCHUKUO
Harbin

Vladivostok

SEA OF JAPAN

CHOSEN
(KOREA)

JAPAN

Tokyo
Yokohama

Osaka

ng

Shanghai

ow

E. CHINA SEA

ow

Foochow

TAIWAN
(FORMOSA)

atow

Kong (Br.)

PACIFIC

OCEAN

nila

PHILIPPINE

ISLANDS

0   1000 miles along the equator

CELEBES

MOLUCCAS
(SPICE ISLANDS)

NEW GUINEA

AUSTRALIA

Tsarist Russia did not take the form of a struggle for overseas colonies. Instead, the Russians concentrated on expansion into contiguous areas. As early as 1582 they began the penetration of Siberia, and in less than a century had extended their domain to the Pacific. Finally, during the closing years of the nineteenth century imperialism blossomed in Japan. In 1894–1895 she made war upon China and forced her to cede Formosa and to grant Korea independence. It must not be thought that only the major powers of the world engaged in the quest for colonies. In 1885 Belgium acquired the Belgian Congo, a territory several times as large as the homeland itself. The Netherlands found rich prizes in the East Indies as early as 1600 and gradually transformed them into a Dutch empire.

**Causes of the
new imperialism**

The causes of the new imperialism did not differ greatly regardless of the country by whom it was practiced. A major one was nationalism. As the new imperialists saw it, the prestige of a nation was largely determined by the size of the yellow, pink, or blue patch on the map indicating the size of its territory. Outranking nationalism was a collection of economic causes. The spread of industrialization to various countries after 1870 produced an intense competition for markets and for new areas of investment of surplus capital. As production continued to grow, the belief prevailed that nothing short of external territories would suffice as dumping grounds for articles the home market could not absorb. It was dimly realized that the prosperity of all rested upon a nicely adjusted balance of imports and exports. But the trouble was that everyone wanted to export as much as possible and import as little as possible. A final cause of the new imperialism was the desire to find homes for surplus inhabitants. It was considered essential that they should not be lost as citizens and therefore potential soldiers of the fatherland.

The balance sheets of the new imperialism seldom present a very creditable record. Its aim of providing homes for the surplus population of the mother country was not often realized. More Japanese

The Transvaal Gold Fields. The combination of low-cost labor plus high-yield mines results in enormous profits for some companies and individuals.

emigrants sought homes in Hawaii and California than in Korea or Manchuria. Emigrants from Italy greatly preferred New York and Chicago to Eritrea and Somaliland. A similar story can be told regarding economic results. With the exception of some parts of the British Empire, colonial possessions did not absorb any large proportion of the surplus production of the mother country. To illustrate, less than 1 per cent of Germany's exports went to her colonies. The bulk of exports from the United States did not go to her colonies but to other independent countries such as Great Britain, Canada, and Japan. Economically developed countries preferred to trade with other developed countries where they could find the richest markets and the most eager demand for their goods. In sum, the economic advantages of colonial empires were mainly an illusion. This is not to say that no one gained from the acquisition of colonies. Individual citizens often reaped rich rewards: investors, merchants, owners of mines and railways. But nations as a whole seldom benefited. They made great sacrifices fighting and dying to conquer and hold some obscure territory in Africa or Asia and had little to show for their pains except a feeling of power and pride.

The balance sheets of imperialism

SELECTED READINGS

· *Items so designated are available in paperbound editions.*

NATIONALISM

· Binkley, R. C., *Realism and Nationalism*, New York, 1935 (Torchbook). A stimulating account of the period 1852–1871.
· Eyck, Erich, *Bismarck and the German Empire*, London, 1950 (Norton Library). The best one-volume study of the Iron Chancellor.
  Eyck, Frank, *The Frankfurt Parliament, 1848–1849*, New York, 1968.
  Gewehr, W. M., *The Rise of Nationalism in the Balkans, 1800–1930*, New York, 1931. Brief but scholarly.
  Griffith, G. O., *Mazzini, Prophet of Modern Europe*, New York, 1932.
  Guérard, A. L., *Napoleon III*, New York, 1958. A laudatory account.
  Hayes, C. J. H., *The Historical Evolution of Modern Nationalism*, New York, 1931.
· Kohn, Hans, *The Idea of Nationalism*, New York, 1944 (Macmillan). A perceptive analysis.
· ———, *Basic History of Modern Russia*, New York, 1957 (Anvil).
  Noether, E. P., *Seeds of Italian Nationalism, 1700–1815*, New York, 1951.
  Siegfried, A., *France, a Study in Nationality*, New Haven, 1930. An interesting interpretation.
  Simpson, F. A., *The Rise of Louis Napoleon*, New York, 1925.
  Snyder, L. L., *From Bismarck to Hitler*, Williamsport, Pa., 1935. A thorough and scholarly account.
· ———, *Basic History of Modern Germany*, New York, 1957 (Anvil).
· Thompson, J. M., *Napoleon and the Second Empire*, Oxford, 1954 (Norton Library).
· Whyte, A. J., *The Evolution of Modern Italy*, Oxford, 1944 (Norton Library). A good introductory study.
· Williams, Roger L., *The French Revolution of 1870–1871*, New York, 1969 (Norton).

Angell, Norman, *The Great Illusion*, New York, 1933.

· Beisner, Robert L., *Twelve against Empire: The Anti-Imperialists, 1898–1900*, New York, 1968.

Beloff, Max, *Imperial Sunset; Britain's Liberal Empire, 1897–1921*, Vol. I, New York, 1970.

· Betts, Raymond F., *Europe Overseas: Phases of Imperialism*, New York, 1968 (Basic Books).

Carroll, E. M., *Germany and the Great Powers, 1866–1914*, New York, 1938.

Chubb, O. E., *20th Century China*, New York, 1964.

Clark, Grover, *The Balance Sheets of Imperialism*, New York, 1936. A good study of results.

Elletson, D. H., *The Chamberlains*, New York, 1966.

· Feis, Herbert, *Europe, the World's Banker, 1870–1914*, New Haven, 1930 (Norton Library). An interesting economic analysis.

Fraser, H. F., *Foreign Trade and World Politics*, New York, 1926.

Graham, Gerald S., *Great Britain in the Indian Ocean*, New York, 1967.

Harris, N. D., *Europe and Africa*, New York, 1927.

——, *Europe and the East*, New York, 1926.

Hoffman, Ross, *Great Britain and the German Trade Rivalry, 1875–1914*. Philadelphia, 1933. A perceptive account.

Hoskins, H. L., *European Imperialism in Africa*, New York, 1930.

Langer, W. L., *The Diplomacy of Imperialism*, New York, 1950. A standard work.

May, Ernest R., *American Imperialism*, New York, 1968.

Moon, P. T., *Imperialism and World Politics*, New York, 1926.

Owen, D. E., *Imperialism and Nationalism in the Far East*, New York, 1929.

Platt, D. C. M., *Finance, Trade, and Politics in British Foreign Policy*, New York, 1968.

Simon, W. M., *Germany in the Age of Bismarck*, New York, 1968.

Somervell, D. C., *The British Empire*, London, 1948.

· Tan, C. C., *The Boxer Catastrophe*, New York, 1955 (Norton Library). The most recent scholarly account.

Tuveson, Ernest Lee, *Redeemer Nation: The Idea of America's Millennial Role*, Chicago, 1968.

Willcox, W. B., *Star of Empire*, New York, 1950.

SOURCE MATERIALS

Bismarck, Otto von, *Bismarck, the Man and the Statesman, Written and Dictated by Himself*, London, 1899, 2 vols.

Renan, Ernest, *What Is a Nation?*

Ruskin, John, *The Crown of Wild Olive.*

Schurz, Carl, *Reminiscences*, pp. 163–65. Failure of the Frankfort Assembly.

· Tocqueville, Alexis de, *Recollections*, pp. 79–89, February Revolution in France, New York, 1949 (Meridian).

CHAPTER 29

The Maturing of Democracy
in Europe and America (1810-1914)

The people, consequently, *may* desire to oppress a part of their number; and precautions are as much needed against this as against any other abuse of power. . . . "The tyranny of the majority" is now generally included among the evils against which society requires to be on its guard.

—John Stuart Mill, *On Liberty*

At no time, at no place . . . had the American people officially proclaimed the United States to be a democracy. The Constitution did not contain the word or any word lending countenance to it. . . . When the Constitution was proclaimed no respectable person called himself or herself a democrat.

—Charles A. and Mary R. Beard,
America in Midpassage

After the revolutions of 1830 many nations of the Western world experienced a rebirth of democracy. In Europe, Great Britain took the lead while France, Germany, and Italy lagged behind. But even Spain, Turkey, and the Balkan kingdoms ultimately adopted at least some of the forms of democratic rule. What most of these countries were interested in was governmental or political democracy, exemplified by parliaments, universal manhood suffrage, and the cabinet system. Not until after the beginning of the twentieth century was there much concern with social or economic democracy.

The rebirth of democracy

In order to understand the true meaning of democracy, we need to consider its historical origins. As a political ideal, democracy had its roots in the philosophy of Rousseau. It was Rousseau's doctrine of the absolute sovereignty of the majority, together with his and the other romanticists' deification of the common man, which more than anything else gave us our ideal of the voice of the people as the voice of God. Historically, political democracy meant, above all, that the majority of the people should be entitled to speak for the entire nation, and that in forming that majority the votes of all the citizens should be equal. The machinery of the democratic state therefore included universal suffrage and such provisions as frequent elections and adequate popular control over the officers of

The meaning of political democracy

government. In order that this machinery operate effectively, the citizens must have the right to organize political parties and to choose freely among them. Freedom of speech and freedom of the press were also considered essential components of the democratic ideal. But none of these rights was regarded as absolute and beyond the control of the majority. To be sure, if they were destroyed entirely, democracy would cease to exist; but the majority could most certainly limit them when there was a clear and immediate danger to the public safety. Historically, all that democracy has really required is that all ideas unaccompanied by threat of violence be tolerated and that *peaceful* minorities be allowed to strive to become the majority. The political ideal which affirms the *absolute* right of the citizen to write or speak or live as he pleases, so long as he does no actual harm to his neighbor, is not democracy but individualism, or, as some would call it, liberalism.

I. THE EVOLUTION OF DEMOCRACY IN GREAT BRITAIN

The evolution of democracy in Great Britain includes primarily three different stages: the extension of the suffrage, the development of the cabinet system of government, and the growth of the supremacy of the House of Commons. Prior to 1832 the system of voting and representation in England was exceedingly undemocratic. Only in a very few boroughs could the majority of the citizens vote. In the rural areas the franchise was restricted to a mere

The undemocratic character of the British government in the early 19th century

Interior of the House of Commons. The government and opposition members sit on opposite sides of this chamber. Those supporting the government, or cabinet, sit to the right of the Speaker, who occupies the canopied throne. Her Majesty's Loyal Opposition sits on the Speaker's left. The cabinet and the "shadow cabinet" of the opposition sit on the front benches.

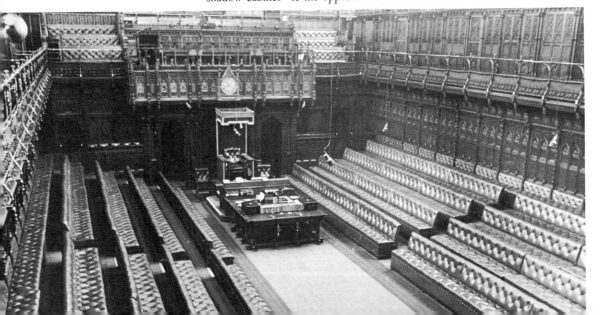

handful of the larger proprietors. Out of a total membership of
about 650 in the House of Commons no more than a third could be
said to have been elected in any proper sense. The rest were appointed by local magnates or selected by petty groups of the richest
property-holders or by members of favored guilds. In some cases
the positions were openly sold or offered for rent for a term of
years. To make matters worse, the distribution of seats had been
thrown out of balance by the shift of population to the industrial
centers of the north. While many of the new cities, such as Birmingham and Manchester, with more than 100,000 people in each,
were denied representation entirely, villages in the south which had
been almost depopulated continued to send as many as two and
three members to the House of Commons. One of these villages
(Old Sarum) was a deserted hill; another (Dunwich) had slipped
beneath the waves of the sea; yet both were still represented in Parliament, by that remarkable British capacity for preserving a fiction
long after the facts have disappeared.[1]

Despite the smug assurance of the Duke of Wellington that the
political system described above was "perfectly satisfactory," there
was much agitation against it. Not only the common people but also
members of the middle class were thoroughly dissatisfied with an arrangement which gave almost a monopoly of power to the landed
aristocracy. Emboldened by the success of the July Revolution of
1830 in France, the British Whigs under the leadership of Lord John
Russell and Earl Grey inaugurated a movement for electoral reform.
Strong opposition and vigorous agitation forced Wellington to resign as Prime Minister. Earl Grey then formed a new ministry, and
the famous Reform Bill of 1832 became a law. Though its provisions
were much more moderate than many of the radicals would have
liked, it was still a noteworthy gain. The bill enfranchised most of
the adult males of the middle class and nearly all of the smaller landholders and tenant farmers; but the great masses of agricultural laborers and industrial workers in the cities were still excluded from
the suffrage. The proportion of voters was increased from about 1
out of every 100 inhabitants to 1 out of 32. In addition, the bill provided for some sweeping reforms in representation. Villages with a
population of less than 2000 were deprived of their right to elect
representatives to the House of Commons, while towns of slightly
larger size had their representation cut in half. The seats in the
Commons thus set free were distributed among the great industrial
cities of the north.

*The movement for
political reform*

---

[1] The prize example of these "rotten boroughs" was the village of Bute in
Scotland. Here there was only one inhabitant left who was qualified to vote,
but the village retained its right to send a representative to Parliament. On
election day this solitary voter regularly appeared at the polling place, "moved
and seconded his own nomination, put the question to the vote, and was
unanimously elected" to a seat in the House of Commons.

Results of the
Reform Act of
1832

The Reform Act of 1832 definitely established the supremacy of the middle class. In the elections that followed soon afterward, the Whigs, who now began to call themselves Liberals, captured a majority of seats in the House of Commons. The Tories, henceforth more commonly known as Conservatives, also began to bid for capitalist support. The result was a wave of parliamentary enactments distinctly favorable to bourgeois interests. One appropriated money to private societies for the maintenance of schools. Another, the celebrated Poor Law of 1834, abolished "outdoor" relief, except for the sick and the aged, and provided that all able-bodied paupers be compelled to earn their keep in workhouses. This law was based upon the theory that poverty is a man's own fault, and that consequently the poor should be forced to work as a punishment for their shiftlessness. The crowning achievement of this period of bourgeois legislation was the repeal of the Corn Laws in 1846. The Corn Laws were a form of protective tariff for the benefit of the landowning class. Their effect was to give a rich bounty to the British landowners and at the same time to keep the price of bread exceedingly high. For more than twenty years industrial capitalists had clamored for repeal of these tariffs, on the double ground that they necessitated the payment of higher wages and limited the sale of British manufactures in foreign markets. It was not, however, until 1846 that their efforts were successful. The repeal of the Corn Laws started Britain on the road to her free-trade policy, which was continued in force until after World War I.

The Chartist
movement of
1838–1848

None of these results of middle-class supremacy conferred much immediate benefit upon the working class. Hours in the factories were still unconscionably long; and, despite the rapid expansion of industry, periods of hard times still punctuated the rising prosperity. Moreover, Parliament was deaf to all the pleas of the lower classes for a share in the franchise. The great Liberal statesman, Lord John Russell, flatly declared that the reforms granted in 1832 were "final." In the face of such resistance many urban workers decided that the only hope of relief was to strive for a complete democratization of the British government. Accordingly, they enlisted with great enthusiasm under the banner of Chartism, a movement organized in 1838 under the leadership of Feargus O'Connor and William Lovett. Chartism derived its name from its celebrated People's Charter, a program of six points. They included demands for universal manhood suffrage, the secret ballot, abolition of property qualifications for members of the House of Commons, and payment of salaries to members of Commons. Though some of the Chartists advocated violence, most of them confined their activities to mass demonstrations and to the drafting of petitions to be presented to Parliament. In 1848, under the stimulus of the February Revolution in France, the leaders prepared for a giant effort. A procession of 500,000 workers was to march to the Houses of Parliament for the purpose of presenting a monster petition and overawing the members into granting reforms. The ruling classes were badly frightened. The pugnacious old Duke of Wellington was again summoned to command the troops. In addition to the regular army, he was provided with a special force of 170,000 constables. But on the day scheduled for the demonstration there was a heavy downpour of rain. Instead of the 500,000 workers who were to march in the parade, only a tenth of that number appeared. When the petition was presented to Parliament, it was found to contain less than half of the vaunted 6,000,000 signatures, and some of these were fictitious.

Though Chartism ended in failure, the spirit it represented lived on. It is significant that most of the six points, with the single exception of the demand for annual Parliaments, have since been incorporated in the British constitution. In the years following the fiasco of 1848 the forces of democracy gradually recouped their strength and succeeded under the guidance of more practical leaders in achieving considerable progress. In 1858 they wrung from a Conservative government the abolition of property qualifications for members of the House of Commons. By 1866 the democratic movement had gained such headway that the leaders of both parties were ready to compete with each other for popular support. The result was the Reform Act of 1867, maneuvered through Parliament by the Conservative Benjamin Disraeli when the old generation of Liberals refused to go along with William E. Gladstone in enacting the more moderate bill of the preceding year. The Reform Act of 1867 conferred the franchise upon nearly all men in towns and cities who made up the class of industrial workers. In 1884 the Liberals had a turn at extending the franchise. The Reform Act of that year, the third in the series of great electoral reform measures, was sponsored by Gladstone. Its main provision was to extend the voting requirements hitherto adopted for the cities and towns to the counties. The result was to enfranchise nearly all the agricultural

The Reform Acts of 1867 and 1884

A Chartist Demonstration in London

The British
cabinet system

The early evolu-
tion of the
cabinet system

laborers. All that remained was to give the suffrage to women, migratory laborers, and the very poor who could not meet any of the residence or property requirements previously set up. These final concessions were not made until 1918.

The second of the chief factors in the evolution of democracy in Great Britain was the development of the cabinet system. Without the growth of this system Britain might well have remained simply a limited monarchy. It must be understood that the cabinet is not merely a council of ministers but is the supreme organ of the government. It is a committee of Parliament, responsible to the House of Commons, which exercises in the name of the crown the supreme legislative and executive authority. Not only does it decide all questions of general policy, but it originates nearly all legislation; and, as long as it remains in office, it determines what bills shall be passed. If it is defeated in the House of Commons on a fundamental issue, it must either resign forthwith or "go to the country"—that is, dissolve Parliament and order a new election to test the opinion of the voters. In other words, the cabinet has full responsibility for the management of public affairs, subject only to the will of the people and to that of their representatives in the House of Commons. When Englishmen speak of "His (or Her) Majesty's Government," it is the cabinet they have in mind. When the party in power loses an election and thereby control of the House of Commons, the leader of the opposition party immediately forms a new cabinet. While awaiting his turn to become Prime Minister he receives a salary as leader of His (or Her) Majesty's Loyal Opposition.

As almost everyone knows, the cabinet system was the product of a slow evolution of precedent. No statute or great charter brought it into being, and to this day it rests solely upon custom. Its history goes back no farther than the Glorious Revolution. Not until after the supremacy of the king had been superseded by the supremacy of Parliament was the principle established that the chief ministers of the crown should be responsible to Parliament. Upon coming to the throne in 1689, William and Mary acceded to the demand that their choice of advisers should be satisfactory to the legislature. For a time they selected their ministers from both of the major parties, but as the need for harmonious relations with Parliament grew more urgent, they gradually restricted their choice to the party which held the majority. In this way the precedent was set that all the chief ministers should possess the confidence of the dominant group in Parliament. But the cabinet was not yet a very powerful body. It did not become so until the reign of George I (1714–1727). George was a dull-witted prince from the German state of Hanover. Since he could neither speak nor understand the English language, he entrusted the whole work of governing to his ministers. He stayed away from meetings of the cabinet entirely and allowed that body to pass under the direction of Sir Robert Walpole. Though he persistently disclaimed the title, Walpole was the first Prime Minister in the modern sense. He was the first to perform the double function of head of the cabinet and leader of the majority party in the House of Commons. When in 1742 he suffered defeat in the House of Commons, he resigned immediately, notwithstanding the fact that he still possessed the full confidence of the king.

Such was the early evolution of the cabinet system. Though most of the precedents upon which it rests had already been set by the middle of the eighteenth century, it still had a rocky road to travel. Some members of Parliament disliked the system, since it appeared to involve a partial surrender of Parliamentary supremacy. Not until about the middle of the nineteenth century was the cabinet system universally accepted or fully comprehended as an integral part of the British constitution. Its operation was first clearly described by Walter Bagehot in his *English Constitution*, published in 1867. In more recent years a number of new precedents were added, the most important of them being that when the cabinet is defeated in the House of Commons, the Prime Minister and his colleagues shall have the option of resigning immediately or of dissolving Parliament and appealing to the country in a great national referendum.

Scarcely less important in the evolution of political democracy in Great Britain was the emergence of the House of Commons as the more powerful branch of Parliament. Down to the eighteenth century the House of Lords, composed of hereditary peers and the princes of the church, enjoyed much greater dignity and influence. The first step toward the supremacy of the representative chamber was the establishment of the principle, during Walpole's ministry, that the cabinet should be responsible exclusively to the Commons. In the early nineteenth century the precedent became fixed that the lower house should have final authority over matters of finance. But still the Lords had enormous power. They had a veto over general legislation, which was limited only by the fear of public resentment and by the authority of the Prime Minister in an emergency to threaten the creation of new peers.[2] Furthermore, since the upper chamber was invariably a Tory stronghold, the favorite schemes of Liberal cabinets were often balked. Matters reached a crisis in 1909 when the Lords threw out the budget prepared by David Lloyd George, Chancellor of the Exchequer, and backed by the Asquith cabinet. The Prime Minister dissolved Parliament and appealed to the voters. Though his party won but a modest victory, he was convinced that the nation was on his side and began preparation of a bill to clip the wings of the House of Lords. The measure, known as the Parliament Act of 1911, was finally passed after a threat to swamp the upper house with a majority of Liberal peers. The Parliament

The later evolution of the cabinet system

The emergence of the House of Commons as the more powerful branch of Parliament

[2] In Britain the monarch has the authority to elevate an unlimited number of men to the peerage. But since the crown acts only upon the advice of the Prime Minister, it is this official who has the actual power to create new members of the House of Lords. If necessary, he could use this power to pack the upper house with his own followers.

Act provided that money bills should become laws one month after they had been passed by the House of Commons, whether the Lords approved them or not; in the case of other legislation the House of Lords was given only a suspensive veto: if ordinary bills were passed by the Commons in three consecutive sessions, they became laws at the end of two years, despite the opposition of the upper house. It is therefore accurate to say that the popularly elected branch of Parliament was henceforth, for all practical purposes, the real legislative body in Great Britain.

2.   DEMOCRACY ON THE CONTINENT OF EUROPE

The first major country on the Continent of Europe to undergo a movement toward democracy was France. The process began during the reign of Louis Philippe (1830–1848). Louis Philippe professed to rule with the consent of the people, but he really took his cue from the bourgeoisie and systematically ignored the lower classes. However, the movement stopped short of its goal. When completed, only 200,000 Frenchmen could vote. By 1848 the king and his ministers had so aroused the disgust of a large number of their subjects that the latter were ready to incur the risks of a new revolution to overthrow the monarchy.

The insignificant progress of democracy in France before 1848

The French revolution of 1848 is known as the February Revolution. Its causes were several. One was the demand of all but a small minority of the people for more democracy. Another was disgust with the corruption of Louis Philippe and his intimate circle; convinced, like Louis XV in an earlier day, that soon would come the deluge, they strove to enrich themselves as fast as possible at public expense. A third cause was discontent of Catholics with the apparent anticlerical bias of Louis Philippe. He had appointed as his chief minister the Protestant Guizot and had allowed him to discriminate against Catholic schools. A fourth cause was the spread of socialism through the ranks of the industrial proletariat. During the lean months of the depression which began in 1847, many of the workers had been converted to the socialism of Louis Blanc, with its scheme for national workshops to give employment and prosperity to all. But the February Revolution was also a product of nationalism, and in the end this factor was destined to dwarf all the others. As "king of the bourgeoisie" Louis Philippe had placed business above everything else. His chief capitalist supporters were determined that France should not become involved in any war lest their trade and investments be imperiled. Consequently they refused to yield to the clamor for intervention on behalf of the Poles against Russia or of the Italians against Austria. This angered patriotic Frenchmen who thirsted for national glory and for the restoration of France to a position of leadership among the powers of Europe.

Causes of the Revolution of 1848

By 1847 the government of Louis Philippe had alienated the sympathies of nearly all but a wealthy minority of its subjects. However, the most defiant opposition came from patriotic republicans and monarchists and from the socialists. In 1847 these groups organized huge demonstrations designed to impress upon the king the need for reform. When the government took alarm and prohibited a demonstration scheduled for February 22, 1848, barricades were thrown up in the streets, and two days later Louis Philippe was forced to abdicate. A provisional government of republicans and socialists took over control of the state, and in April elections were held for a constituent assembly. The results of the voting were a disappointment to the socialists, for the reactionaries and middle-class parties had combined to protect the interests of private property. A revolt broke out which was finally crushed after bloody fighting in the slums of the capital. The way was now cleared for the bourgeois majority in the Constituent Assembly to complete a constitution for the Second Republic. The document as it finally emerged was copied in part from that of the United States. It contained a bill of rights and provided for universal manhood suffrage and for the separation of powers. There was to be a President elected by the people for a four-year term, and the people were also to choose a single-chambered legislative assembly. Having finished their work, the authors of the constitution set December 10, 1848, as the date for the election of the first President.

As we learned in a previous chapter, the outcome of this election was the choice of Louis Napoleon Bonaparte, nephew of Napoleon I, as President. Though he had ample powers as a constitutional executive, he was not satisfied with a less grandiose title than that of his famous uncle. Accordingly, in 1851, he made himself dictator and a year later Emperor of France. Thereafter most remnants of democracy disappeared, though following the collapse of his Mexican venture the Emperor found it expedient to restore to the Assembly the power to initiate laws and to ratify or reject the budget. Further concessions might also have been made in time had it not been for the Franco-Prussian War. Napoleon III allowed himself to be dragged into this war, with disastrous results. Following the defeat of his armies in the Battle of Sedan (September 2, 1870) and his capture soon afterward, his government was overthrown by an uprising in Paris. A National Assembly was elected and a provisional republic set up which later came to be called the Third Republic.

The constitution of the Third Republic consisted of three organic laws adopted by the National Assembly in 1875. Though amendments and precedents effected some changes, its essential form continued until the dissolution of the Third Republic on July 9, 1940. The government established by this constitution was about as

The overthrow of Louis Philippe

Drawing of a Medallion by Daumier. The inscription reads "Louis Philippe, the Last King of France." It reflects a popular sentiment of the time.

Beginning of the Third Republic

democratic as any in the world. There was a parliament, with a lower house elected by universal manhood suffrage, and a President chosen by parliament. The cardinal feature, however, was the cabinet system, copied in part from Great Britain. The most important powers of the government were exercised by a ministry responsible to parliament. The President was about the nearest approach to a nonentity that it would be possible to find among heads of state. His every official act had to be countersigned—which is to say, approved—by a member of the ministry. On the other hand, there were several important differences between the cabinet system in France and that in Great Britain. The French cabinet was responsible not only to the lower house or Chamber of Deputies but also to the Senate, which was elected indirectly by the people; the cabinet in Great Britain was responsible exclusively to the House of Commons. The most important difference consisted in the fact that the French Premier had no effective authority to dissolve parliament. This meant that members of parliament could overturn cabinets at will, with no risk of being forced to stand for reelection. If defeated on the floor of either house, the Premier and his colleagues had no alternative but to resign. With the possible exception of the multiplicity of parties, nothing contributed so much to the instability of the French system. Cabinets were sometimes unable to hold the support of a majority in parliament for more than a few weeks or even a few days. Although this instability was often deplored, it was really the product of a natural reaction of the French people against previous dictatorial regimes.

Meanwhile, as a result of the Franco-Prussian War, events were moving toward a new climax in Germany. A great outburst of patriotism across the Rhine made it possible for Bismarck to absorb the south German states into a North German Confederation. Treaties negotiated during the course of the war stipulated that all of Germany should be united into a Hohenzollern empire. These agreements were given formal effect by an impressive ceremony staged in the palace of Louis XIV at Versailles on January 18, 1871, in which King William I of Prussia was invested with the title of German Emperor. Bismarck, now raised to the dignity of prince, became the first Imperial Chancellor. The government thus created had only two features which could positively be considered democratic. First, there was universal manhood suffrage in national elections; second, there was a parliament with a lower house, or Reichstag, elected by popular vote. In other respects the system was well adapted to conservative rule. In place of the cabinet system, the Chancellor and the other ministers were responsible solely to the Emperor. The Emperor himself was no figurehead; he was vested with extensive authority over the army and navy, over foreign relations, and over the enactment and execution of the laws. Besides, he could declare war if the coasts or territory of the Empire were at-

William I of Prussia

tacked, and as King of Prussia he controlled one-third of the votes in the upper house, or Bundesrat, of the imperial parliament.

Yet the government of the German Empire was not a complete autocracy. Although the Kaiser could influence the enactment of legislation, he had no veto power. All treaties he negotiated had to be approved by the Bundesrat, and he could get no money without the consent of the Reichstag. Indeed, the latter body was far from a mere debating society, as was so often alleged by Germany's enemies during World War I. On the contrary, it had law-making powers virtually the equivalent of those of the Bundesrat, and it was strong enough to extort concessions from several Chancellors.

It should be recognized, further, that the government of the German Empire was a constitutional government and not a party dictatorship like that of the Nazis in the twentieth century. The laws were extensive and complete and, for the most part, were strictly observed. Every little bureaucrat had a code to follow, and no one, not even the Emperor, was above the law. The chief defect of the system, aside from the absence of ministerial responsibility to parliament, was the inability of the representatives of the people to originate legislation. Their power was essentially negative: they could veto proposals of the Kaiser and his ministers, but they could rarely initiate measures of their own. Finally, it should be borne in mind that the German Empire was a federal state. Though it was described by President Lowell of Harvard as a union comprising "a lion, a half-dozen foxes, and a score of mice," the division of powers made by the constitution was essentially the same as in the United States. That is, all powers not granted to the central government were reserved to the states. All of the states had control over their own forms of government, relations of church and state, public education, highways, and police. In addition, certain of the larger southern states were given special privileges when they entered the Empire. Even the enforcement of the laws was left primarily in the hands of the state governments, since the government of the Empire had no courts or police and no other machinery for applying the laws against individuals.

Like the republic of France, the new German Empire also had trouble with the Catholic Church. The motivating forces in the two countries were different. French anticlericalism was mainly a liberating movement against the government in league with the Catholic Church. The German movement was chiefly government inspired and directed against the Catholic Church. Called by the pretentious name of *Kulturkampf*, or "struggle for civilization," it was initiated by Bismarck with some help from intellectual liberals, in 1872. Bismarck's motives were almost exclusively nationalistic. He was neither a skeptic nor a materialist but a staunch Lutheran. Nevertheless, he perceived in some Catholic activities a threat to the power and stability of the Empire he had just created. He resented, first of all, the support Catholic priests continued to give to the states'-rights movement in southern Germany and to the grievances of Alsatians and Poles. He was alarmed also by recent assertions of the authority of the Pope to intervene in secular matters and by the promulgation in 1870 of the dogma of papal infallibility. For these reasons he resolved to deal such a blow to Catholic influence in Germany that it would never again be a factor in national or local politics. His weapons were a series of laws and decrees issued between 1872 and 1875. First, he induced the Reichstag to expel all the Jesuits from the country. Next, he forced through the Prussian Landtag the so-called May Laws, which placed theological seminaries under state control and permitted the government to regulate the appointment of bishops and priests. No one was allowed to be appointed to any position in the Church unless he was a German citizen and then only after a state examination. At the same time civil marriage was made compulsory, even though a religious ceremony had already been performed. In the enforcement of these measures, six of the ten Catholic bishops in Prussia were imprisoned, and hundreds of priests were driven from the country.

The failure of the *Kulturkampf*

Although Bismarck won some of the chief battles of the *Kulturkampf*, he lost the war. The causes of his failure were several. First, he antagonized his progressive followers by refusing to consider their demands for ministerial responsibility. Second, the Catholic or Center party appealed so effectively on behalf of the persecuted clergy and adopted so enlightened an economic program that it grew into the largest political party in Germany. In the elections of 1874 it captured nearly a fourth of the seats in the Reichstag. Third, Bismarck was alarmed by the growth of socialism, and he was even more dismayed when the chief sponsors of this philosophy, the Social Democrats, formed an alliance with the Centrists. At their current rate of growth these two parties would soon have a majority in the Reichstag. To prevent this Bismarck gradually relaxed his persecution of the Catholics. Between 1878 and 1886 nearly all of the obnoxious legislation was repealed, and the *Kulturkampf* passed into the limbo of statesmen's blunders. The Catholic Church was thus restored practically to its former position in Germany.

Democracy in Italy

As in Germany, the advancement of democracy in Italy was closely tied in with a nationalist movement for unification. By a series of revolutions, wars, and diplomatic maneuvers, this movement attained its goal, accomplished, as we have seen, between 1848 and 1871. As the revolutionary fervor of 1848 swept across the peninsula, one ruler after another granted reforms. Charles Albert, King of Sardinia, outdistanced all the others with his celebrated Fundamental Statute providing for civil liberties and a parliamentary form of government. Ultimately, this Statute became the constitution of a united Italy, as the various states were brought under the rule of the House of Savoy, the reigning dynasty of the Kingdom of Sardinia.

Some of the smaller states of central and west central Europe actually made more progress in democracy than did most of the
large neighbors. For example, all had the cabinet system of government by the eve of World War I. In addition, universal manho
suffrage had been adopted in Switzerland, in Belgium, and in
Scandinavian countries. Norway and Denmark had taken the
logical step of extending the franchise to women. Belgium, Swe
and Switzerland had adopted proportional representation, and
zerland had made extensive use of the initiative and referer
Proportional representation is a device for guaranteeing representation to minorities as well as to the majority. Each political party is
awarded a number of representatives in the legislative body in direct
proportion to its voting strength. The initiative and referendum are
instruments of *direct* democracy. Under the initiative a certain percentage of the voters can initiate legislation and compel a legislature
or parliament to take action upon it. The referendum is a device for
submitting legislation to the people for their final approval or rejection. With the exception of proportional representation, which was
adopted for limited use in local elections in Great Britain, none of
these devices produced much appeal in the larger countries.

3. EQUALITARIAN DEMOCRACY IN THE
UNITED STATES

The United States did not begin its history as a democracy. Although a few early leaders like Roger Williams and Samuel Adams
professed democratic ideals, these were not the doctrines of the most
prominent. The Fathers of the Constitution were definitely not interested in the rule of the masses. James Madison thought the people
were too prone to impetuous and violent impulses ever to be trusted
with unlimited power. The primary aim of the fathers of our government was not to enthrone the masses but to establish a *republic*
that would promote stability and protect the rights of property
against the leveling of tendencies of majorities. For this reason they
adopted checks and balances, devised the Electoral College for
choosing the President, created a powerful judiciary, and entrusted
the selection of Senators to the legislatures of the several states. In
spite of these features the political system the fathers created was
liberal in comparison with other governments of that time. The
President, at least, was not a monarch, nor was the Senate a chamber
of nobles.

Following the establishment of a new government in 1789, ideals
of a viable democracy began to make headway in the United States.
Until 1801 the Federalist party held the reins of power, representing
the big landowners, the money power, and the conservatives generally. In the latter year the Democratic-Republicans gained control as a result of the election of Thomas Jefferson to the Presidency

Democracy
in embryo

Thomas Jefferson. Painting by Gilbert Stuart.

in 1800. This event is often referred to as the Jeffersonian Revolution, on the supposition that Jefferson was the champion of the masses and of the political power of the underprivileged. There is danger, however, in carrying this interpretation too far. In several respects Jefferson's ideas were far removed from democracy in its historic meaning. Instead of being a follower of Rousseau, he was a disciple of Locke. He believed that that government is best which governs least, and he strenuously opposed the unlimited sovereignty of the majority. His conception of an ideal political system was an aristocracy of "virtue and talent," in which respect for personal liberty would be the guiding principle. Furthermore, he compared the mobs of great cities to sores on the human body and despised the mass of industrial workers as "panders of vice, and instruments by which the liberties of a country are generally overturned." [3]

Yet it cannot be denied that the Jeffersonian movement had a number of democratic objectives of cardinal importance. Its leaders were vigorous opponents of special privilege, whether of birth or of wealth. They worked for the repeal of primogeniture and entail and the abolition of established churches. They led the campaign for the addition of a Bill of Rights to the Federal Constitution and were almost exclusively responsible for its success. Although professing devotion to the principle of the separation of powers, they actually believed in the supremacy of the representatives of the people and viewed with abhorrence the attempts of the executive and judicial branches to increase their power. Three of the most typical ideals of Jefferson himself were decentralized government, periodic revisions of constitutions and laws, and the importance of public education. He stressed the value of local government to the extent of advocating primary assemblies similar to the New England town meetings for the exercise of a large proportion of the public powers. He urged that constitutions and laws be submitted to the people for their approval or rejection every nineteen or twenty years, on the theory that no one generation has the right to bind its successors for the indefinite future. In later life he completed plans for an elaborate system of public education. There was to be free instruction for all children in the elementary schools, and scholarships were to be provided in district colleges and in the state university for a limited number of students selected on the basis of intelligence and achievement. By this method Jefferson sought to ensure opportunity for all, not simply for the well-born and the rich. The persons thus educated would be available for selection as natural aristocrats by enlightened citizens who had received enough knowledge to recognize good men when they saw them.

By the end of the War of 1812 the force of Jeffersonian Democracy was almost entirely spent. Any democratic movement of the

[3] *Writings of Jefferson* (Washington ed.), I, 403.

future would have to proceed from different premises and rest upon new foundations. Not only did the war create new problems and divert men's interests from the need for reform, but the economic aspect of the country had undergone numerous changes. The common people in the cities had grown conscious of their political importance and had begun to demand privileges. More important, the dominance of the Old South, the stronghold of Jeffersonian Democracy, had passed into history. As a result of the Louisiana Purchase and the settlement of the Northwest Territory, a new frontier had come into existence. Life in the new areas was characterized by a rugged freedom and independence that left no room for snobbishness or class distinctions. In the struggle to survive, the things that counted most were hard work and sharp wits. Birth and education were of little value. As a consequence, a new democracy, which eventually found its leader in Andrew Jackson, rapidly crystallized around the major principle of equality. The Jacksonian Democrats considered all men politically equal, not merely in rights but in privileges. They therefore stood for universal manhood suffrage, for making all public offices elective, and for rotation in office. Since they considered one man as good as another, they rejected the idea that special knowledge or ability was required for government positions. They even threw open to ordinary citizens such offices as county surveyor and superintendent of schools. Paradoxically, the Jacksonian Democrats approved of a strong executive. They restored the veto power to the state governors, lengthened their terms of office, and acclaimed the President of the United States as the real representative of the people's will. The explanation seems to lie in the fact that they had come to regard legislative bodies as strongholds of "special interests."

The most powerful influence affecting the growth of American democracy in the nineteenth century was the Civil War, or War between the States, as it is sometimes called. The most obvious cause of the war, of course, was slavery. The first Negro slaves were brought to Virginia from Africa in 1619. Thereafter for nearly two centuries their numbers increased slowly. But in 1793, with the invention of the cotton gin, the picture was changed radically. The production of cotton was transformed from a minor activity into a tremendously profitable enterprise. Output grew from 4000 bales in 1790 to 4,000,000 in 1860. The plantation system based on slave labor became firmly fixed in the South.

Yet it would be a mistake to assume that slavery was the sole cause of the Civil War. Sentiment in favor of abolition was far from unanimous even in the North. Abolitionists were commonly regarded as fanatics and were sometimes brutally mistreated. Even lynching was not unknown. The majority of citizens in the North seemed perfectly willing to tolerate the continued existence of slavery in the South. But they opposed its extension into the Louisiana Purchase or into the regions of the Southwest conquered from Mexico in 1848. Such areas they hoped to organize into free states to be settled by land-hungry migrants from New England and the Middle Atlantic region. Leaders of the South were just as anxious to organize as much of these territories as possible into slave states, and thereby to prevent the reduction of their section to a status of permanent inferiority with the North. This conflict over the extension of slavery was probably the basic cause of the Civil War.

Consequences of the Civil War

The Civil War ushered in epochal changes in the political and social environment of the United States. By the Thirteenth Amendment slavery was legally abolished. Two succeeding amendments gave the former slaves citizenship and prohibited their disfranchisement because of race, color, or previous condition of servitude. Yet these amendments appeared to grant more than they actually accomplished. Although the former slaves were no longer the property of a master, they were often doomed to a kind of wage slavery that made a mockery of their so-called freedom. In like manner the Fifteenth Amendment gave no one the right to vote but simply prohibited denial of the vote on account of race or previous condition of servitude. The makeshift character of these arrangements was eventually ratified by the "compromise of 1877." This compromise was an understanding between Northern Republicans and Southern Democrats by which troops were to be withdrawn from the South, the seceding states were to be readmitted to the Union, and the South was to be left largely to its own devices in observing the Fourteenth and Fifteenth Amendments. Fundamentally, it was a conservative agreement, and one of its primary purposes was to enlist the cooperation of Southern agrarians with Northern businessmen in opening the South to capitalist exploitation.

Efforts for the widening of democracy

Movements toward the broadening of democracy flourished between 1880 and 1914. Again, the motivation was largely economic. Severe economic crises punctuated the 1870's, 1880's, and 1890's. Collapse of agricultural prices and shutting down of factories caused great suffering in both rural and urban areas. Political adventurers convinced many people that a restricted money supply was the root of the evil. Accordingly, demands arose for the issue of greenbacks to supplement inadequate quantities of gold and silver. In the 1890's the pressure for greenbacks was replaced by a demand for the coinage of silver in a much larger ratio to gold than had hitherto existed. Not only did the depression parties of the late nineteenth century advocate currency inflation; both the Greenback party and the Populist party urged an income tax, government ownership of railroads and telegraph and telephone lines, and direct election of United States Senators. Both parties went down to defeat in the Presidential elections, although the Populists rolled up a total of 6,500,000 votes in the election of 1896.

Theodore Roosevelt. The candidate of the Progressive party, or Bull Moose party, is shown campaigning in Vermont, 1912.

Though Populism declined with the end of the century, the movement it represented did not die. It sprang to life anew with the organization of the Progressive party in the early 1900's. In general, it had a broader appeal than either of its immediate forerunners. It was not essentially an agrarian movement but sought the support of liberal reformers from all classes. Its leaders sidetracked the currency reforms of Greenbackers and Populists and concentrated on political objectives. Among these were the initiative, referendum, and recall, the secret ballot, the direct primary, the short ballot, and proportional representation. The high-water mark of the movement was the election of 1912, when Theodore Roosevelt ran as the Progressive candidate for President against William H. Taft, the regular Republican, and Woodrow Wilson. Though Wilson himself was in many ways a Progressive, he ran under the Democratic label and was victorious in the three-cornered contest.

Populism graduates to Progressivism

Democratic evolutionary movements in the United States generally fell upon evil days before they were completely successful. They usually managed to attain some of their goals before they went down into the dust of history but none achieved its full program. Nearly all were defeated by some extrinsic factor. In the vast majority of cases that factor was war. Jeffersonian democracy was killed by the War of 1812. Jacksonian democracy came to an untimely end with the Mexican War. Any chance that the better elements of Populism might have survived was stifled by the Spanish-American War. Finally, the most promising of the democratic reform movements of the early twentieth century, the Progressive movement, received a crushing blow by the outbreak of World

The doom of Populism and Progressivism by war

877

War I. Though the United States did not enter that war immediately, the fear and suspicion engendered by the conflict in Europe fostered an environment hostile to democratic progress everywhere. As in previous instances advancement was not resumed until after hostilities had ceased.

SELECTED READINGS

· Items so designated are available in paperbound editions.

DEMOCRACY

Bernstein, Samuel, *Blanqui*, Paris, 1970.

Brogan, D. W., *France under the Republic*, New York, 1940.

· Cole, G. D. H., and Postgate, R., *The British Common People, 1746–1946*, New York, 1947 (Barnes & Noble).

· Derry, J. W., *A Short History of Nineteenth-Century England*, New York, 1963 (Mentor).

· Gordon, Donald C., *The Moment of Power: Britain's Imperial Epoch*, Englewood Cliffs, N.J., 1970 (Prentice-Hall).

Hovell, M., *The Chartist Movement*, New York, 1925.

Karpovich, M., *Imperial Russia, 1801–1917*, New York, 1932. An excellent short treatise.

Lindsay, A. D., *The Essentials of Democracy*, Philadelphia, 1929.

——, *The Modern Democratic State*, New York, 1947.

· Maynard, John, *Russia in Flux*, New York, 1948 (Collier).

· Mayo, H. B., *An Introduction to Democratic Theory*, New York, 1960 (Oxford).

Neumann, Robert G., *European and Comparative Government*, New York, 1960.

· Pares, Bernard, *A History of Russia*, New York, 1928 (Vintage). A standard work.

Postgate, Raymond, *1848: Story of a Year*, London, 1955.

Reid, J. H. S., *The Origins of the British Labour Party*, Minneapolis, 1955.

Riasanovsky, N. V., *A Short History of Russia*, New York, 1963.

Robinson, G. T., *Rural Russia under the Old Regime*, New York, 1932.

Seymour, Charles, *Electoral Reforms in England, 1832–1885*, New Haven, 1915.

· Thompson, J. M., *Louis Napoleon and the Second Empire*, New York, 1955 (Norton Library). A valuable summary based on scholarly works.

SOCIAL REFORM

· Hobsbawm, E. J., *Primitive Rebels*, London, 1959 (Norton Library).

Keep, J. L. H., *The Rise of Social Democracy in Russia*, New York, 1963.

Laski, H. J., *The Rise of Liberalism*, New York, 1936. A critical study from a Marxist viewpoint.

Pipkin, C. W., *Social Politics and Modern Democracies*, New York, 1931.

· Robertson, Priscilla, *Revolutions of 1848: A Social History*, Princeton, 1952 (Torchbook). A stimulating account written from the viewpoint of the people who lived at that time.

· Thompson, E. P., *The Making of the English Working Class*, New York, 1964 (Vintage).

Woodward, Ernest, *The Age of Reform, 1815–1870*, Oxford, 1938. Great Britain during the Age of Democracy.

CHAPTER 30

The Emergence of Latin America

> What is the oligarchy? It consists of the great landowners—the *"latifundistas"*—their political and military henchmen, and their financial allies (the bankers and the capitalists, in the old sense of the word). . . . The oligarchs form a true caste, with aristocratic impulses, racist attitudes, and a profound contempt for their own countries.
>
> —Víctor Alba, *Alliance Without Allies: The Mythology of Progress in Latin America*

I. CONQUISTADORES AND COLONISTS OF LATIN AMERICA

By far the oldest civilization in the Western Hemisphere is that of Latin America. Here the first settlements were made by the Spanish and Portuguese explorers and conquerors who followed in the path of Columbus. But centuries before any white men set foot on American soil, Indians in Guatemala, Mexico, and the Andean Highland had developed superior cultures which bore almost all the characteristics of civilizations. Had they not been conquered, they might well have provided the basis for a native cultural growth in Central and South America equal to that of any of the other continents. The reasons for this superiority appear to lie almost exclusively in geographic conditions favorable to the progress of agriculture. The lush fertility and benign climate of the valleys of Central America and the northwest portion of South America made possible the production of surplus food. As a result, population increased rapidly, a diversification of trade and industry occurred, cities and towns multiplied, and a priestly class came into existence devoted to the cultivation of sacred lore. Such developments facilitated the growth of science and other branches of learning and the invention of new crafts and skills. By contrast, the Indians of the greater part of the United States and Canada were forced to continue their existence as nomads and hunters. Their homelands were either so densely forested or so arid as to make agriculture discouraging and profitless.

Native civilizations of Latin America

879

The Public Entry of Cortes into the Aztec Capital. Hernando Cortes arrived in Mexico in 1519 and within four years had overrun the entire area of high culture in central Mexico.

Civilized Indians in Latin America: (1) the Aztecs

The principal discoverers of Latin America—Christopher Columbus, Amerigo Vespucci, Juan de Solis, and Vasco de Balboa—were quickly followed by a horde of conquerors. Best-known among them were Hernando Cortés and Francisco Pizarro. Restless, greedy, and zealous for adventure, they endured incredible hardships, dragging their men through jungles and swamps and over snow-capped mountains in quest of plunder. The former won fame of a sort as the subjugator of Mexico and the latter as the conqueror of Peru. At the time they made their conquests both countries were occupied by various peoples in advanced stages of cultural development. Mexico was inhabited by the Aztecs and Mayas, while Peru was the home of the Incas. The Aztecs were relative newcomers on the scene of civilization. They established themselves in central Mexico about the thirteenth century A.D. and founded their capital, Tenochtitlán (Mexico City), a short time later. Their achievements included a system of pictographic writing, some knowledge of astronomy and engineering, an elaborate architecture, and the building of roads and aqueducts. Their capital city had a population of some 200,000. Its streets were paved with stone and were kept scrupulously clean by an efficient public-works department. The ruler of the country was an hereditary monarch whose powers were limited to those of commander of the army and chief justice. Aztec religion can only be described as a maze of superstitions and cruel practices. Its distinguishing feature was the sacrifice of war captives and, on occasions, of Aztecs themselves on the altars of the gods. Pouring out the blood of human beings was believed to be especially effective in winning the divine favor.

Representing higher stages of cultural achievement were the Mayas and Incas. The former originated in Guatemala and Honduras and reached the climax of their progress in the eighth and

Detail of an Aztec Pyramid in Central Mexico. The serpent was an object of worship for the Aztecs.

ninth centuries A.D. About 1000 A.D. most of them migrated to Yucatán and were concentrated there when conquered by the Spaniards. Mayan culture seems to have been developed primarily by a (2) the Mayas leisure class of nobles and priests. It revealed a high level of progress in many fields. A system of writing, in which some of the symbols apparently had phonetic value, was extensively used for religious purposes. Writing materials included stone, deer skin, and a kind of paper made from the maguey plant. A calendar, with a year of 365 days, enabled the priests to determine lucky and unlucky days and the appropriate periods for planting and harvesting crops. Mathematical calculations were refined to the extent of having a vigesimal system (with twenty instead of ten as the basic unit) and a conception of zero as a device for giving different values to the same number. Notable also was progress in the arts. The Mayas excelled in making gold and silver ornaments and in the erection of truncated pyramids with temples on top. Tastes in personal adornment included the curious practice of filing and chipping teeth to give them sharp points and sometimes inlaying them with precious stones. Beards were removed by a scorching process instead of by shaving. Religion was no more highly developed than that of the Aztecs and included the same barbarities of human sacrifice.

Of more recent origin than the culture of the Mayas was that of the Incas, who were at the zenith of their progress when conquered by the Spaniards. Extending into Ecuador, Bolivia, northern Chile, (3) the Incas and northwestern Argentina, the Inca empire had its center in southeastern Peru. It was organized on the basis of collectivist paternalism. All the land belonged to the emperor, to the priests, or to the tribe, and was cultivated by males of the common classes between the ages of twenty-five and fifty. In good years the surplus production was stored by the emperor to provide for his subjects in

881

time of famine. From the produce on its lands the tribe took care of the young and the aged, the disabled and the sick. It was a paradise of security but with little freedom. In intellectual achievements the Incas did not equal the Mayas. They had no system of writing but used knotted strings of many colors to record numbers and sets of facts. On the other hand, they had an extensive knowledge of medicine and surgery and built excellent roads and suspension bridges. They understood also the principles of fertilization and irrigation and knew how to terrace hillsides to prevent erosion.

During the sixteenth and seventeenth centuries the entire area of Mexico and Central and South America passed under the domination of Spain and Portugal. Three-fifths of it was taken by Spain, and the remainder probably would have been also, had not the Pope intervened in an attempt to give equal recognition to the claims of both countries. In 1493 he issued a Bull of Demarcation drawing a line from north to south 100 leagues west of the Azores. All territory that might be discovered east of the line was to belong to Portugal, and everything west of the line to Spain. In 1494 the two countries signed a treaty relocating the line 370 leagues west of the Cape Verde Islands. Portugal thereby acquired a foothold on the eastern bulge of South America, which was later expanded into Brazil.

Division of Latin America between Spain and Portugal

The methods of colonization and colonial administration followed by both Spain and Portugal were of such a character as to influence profoundly the entire history of Latin America. This was particularly true of Spain, which also set the pattern for her neighboring state since both were united under a common sovereign between 1580 and 1640. The cardinal elements in Spanish colonial policy

Spanish colonial policy

Machu Picchu. The "Lost City of the Incas" is located in the Andes Mountains, Peru.

were despotism and paternalism. The highest authorities in the empire were the viceroys, who ruled as the personal representatives of the Spanish king. At first there were two, one in New Spain including Mexico and Central America, and the other in Peru. In the eighteenth century two additional viceroyalties were created: New Granada (Panama, Colombia, Venezuela, Ecuador) and La Plata, or Buenos Aires. The viceroys were paid magnificent salaries, amounting at one time to the equivalent of $200,000 a year. The purpose behind such generosity was to prevent corruption, an objective by no means universally attained. At the same time their royal master took precautions to prevent the viceroys from becoming too powerful. The authority they exercised was to be that of the Spanish crown, not their own. For this reason they had to tolerate the existence of an advisory council, or *audiencia*, which also served as a court of appeal against their decisions. Members of the *audiencia* had the right to communicate with the king regarding the acts of the viceroy without the latter's knowledge. At the end of his term, and occasionally during it, the viceroy must submit to a searching inquiry or investigation in which a royal judge heard the complaints of all and sundry as to official misconduct.

As an adjunct to despotic rule in the colonies, the Spanish kings made use of the Church. The priests gave valuable help in teaching the population to obey the king and his agents and in opposing new ideas and expressions of discontent. In almost any emergency the hierarchy could be counted upon to give loyal support to the government. By the middle of the sixteenth century the Inquisition had been extended to Latin America as an instrument for maintaining absolute rule. Headquarters were established in Mexico City and Lima from which inquisitors were sent out to all parts of the continent to discover and punish unorthodox belief. Public executions were occasionally staged in the principal cities to provide object lessons of the fearful punishment in store for any who might waver in the faith. To such exhibitions the public was regularly invited in the hope that the deterrent effect would be complete. That the penalties of the Inquisition were sometimes invoked for political and personal reasons goes almost without saying.

The keynote of economic administration in the colonies was paternalism. Actually, nothing else could have been expected, since, according to the theory, the land of the Americas was the personal possession of the king. It was his private estate which he could dispose of as he saw fit. But economic administration in the Spanish colonies was also shaped to a large extent by the theory of mercantilism, which was beginning to dominate the thinking of all Western nations. Mercantilism demanded that colonies should exist for the benefit of the mother country; they should bring bullion into her treasury and contribute in every way possible toward making her rich and powerful. It followed that the government of the mother

The Church as an arm of the government

Paternalism and mercantilism

883

Brazilian Colonial Church in the Portuguese Baroque Style. Baroque workmanship in colonial Latin America is thought by some authorities to be finer than that in Spain and Portugal.

country had the right to regulate and control the economic activities of the colonies in her own interest—to dictate what they should produce and from whom they should buy and to whom they should sell. In substance this meant a monopoly of colonial trade for the merchants of the mother country and a strict prohibition of manufactures.

The economic policies described had unfortunate effects upon both the Spanish colonies and the homeland. The resources of the former were poorly developed, and some lay unused or undiscovered for centuries. With attention focused upon gold and silver and with manufacturing prohibited, there was little incentive to exploit the deposits of copper, manganese, and other minerals which might well have supported a considerable industry. Some branches of agriculture were also discouraged in order that the colonies might produce vast quantities of sugar, cotton, and tobacco which would help the mother country in maintaining a favorable balance of trade, since these products would not have to be purchased for gold outside the empire. The whole system of restrictive policies was stupid and vicious and retarded the development not only of the colonies but of the country that owned them. As late as the end of the sixteenth century Spain was an economically backward nation, with a large portion of her wealth concentrated in cattle and sheep, with no powerful commercial or industrial class, and with manual labor frowned upon as unworthy of a good Spaniard.

Early in the eighteenth century the Hapsburg dynasty in Spain was supplanted by Bourbon rulers. Recognizing the corruptions and inefficiency of the system of colonial administration, the Bourbon kings initiated reforms. They were no more interested in the welfare of the colonies than their predecessors had been, but they did perceive the danger that a disgruntled colonial population might become a prey to foreign conquest. They hoped, moreover, to increase the flow of revenue into the royal treasury. With these ends in view they modified trade restrictions, encouraged industry and a more varied agriculture, and even granted commercial concessions to foreigners. The most noted of these was the *asiento* of 1701, which conferred upon France the privilege of supplying the Spanish colonies with Negro slaves. In 1713, at the end of the War of the Spanish Succession, it was transferred to Britain. By the close of the eighteenth century the Spanish-American trade as a whole was the richest in the world, and had more than tripled in fifty years.

Reforms of the Bourbon monarchs

Silver Mining at Potosi. By an unknown artist, about 1584. The discovery of silver at Potosi in the Bolivian highlands in 1545 marked the beginning of a greatly accelerated flow of bullion from the New World to Spain.

Between 1808 and 1826 Latin America was engulfed by a tidal wave of revolutions. The underlying causes did not differ greatly from the factors which had produced the North American Revolution of 1775. Pre-eminent among them was dissatisfaction with the mercantilist policies of the home government. Despite the reforms of the Bourbons, many relics of oppression and discrimination survived. A rigid censorship was imposed. Books of European and North American radicals could be obtained only by smuggling. As late as 1773 a Colombian scientist was condemned for giving lectures on the Copernican system. Taxes were numerous and excessive, and monopoly and favoritism flourished. Prosperous Creoles, or colonial whites, resented their exclusion from the highest and most lucrative positions in the government and the Church, which were reserved for Spanish-born aristocrats. The former were not starving, any more than were the members of the bourgeoisie in France on the eve of that country's revolution. What rankled in their breasts was being deprived of privileges that they believed should rightly belong to them on the basis of their wealth and intelligence.

It is possible that the discontent of Spain's colonies would never have reached revolutionary proportions had it not been for the examples already set by the revolutions in France and in North America. The colonists' grievances had abated rather than increased and probably would have lessened still further. But revolutions are contagious. An outbreak in one country is almost certain to spread to other countries where similar conditions exist even if in much smaller degree. This is especially true when a philosophy of discon-

Spanish Colonial Patio. Examples of the cultural heritage of old Spain have been adapted by the wealthier citizens of Latin America.

Portuguese Chart of the South Atlantic. Miller Atlas, 1519.

tent is propagated on an international scale. During the latter half of the eighteenth century hundreds of Creoles had imbibed revolutionary doctrines from the writings of Voltaire, Rousseau, Jefferson, and Paine. Some had been educated or had traveled in Europe or in the United States. The discovery that intellectual leaders in other countries were boldly attacking despotic government and superstitious religion made a profound impression and led Spanish colonials to ask themselves why such things should be tolerated in their own lands.

Just as in North America a period of indifference and "salutary neglect" by the British government fostered a spirit of independence in the colonies, so in Latin America a similar period weakened the ties between Spain and her possessions. Between 1803 and 1808 Spain as a satellite of France took part in the wars of Napoleon to make himself master of Europe. In 1805 the British defeated Napoleon's fleet at Trafalgar and virtually destroyed the sea power of France and her allies. Spain, in particular, experienced great difficulty in maintaining communications with her empire. As a result her colonies in Latin America acquired habits of self-reliance. More and more they depended upon their own efforts in solving political and economic problems. So great was their isolation from Spain that they cultivated a profitable trade with the British. For the mother country to have forced them back under the yoke of mercantilist restrictions would have been difficult indeed.

Spain's neglect of her colonies during the wars of Napoleon

The spark that ignited colonial unrest into actual revolution burst forth in 1808. A quarrel had developed between the weak Bourbon king of Spain, Charles IV, and his son Ferdinand. Napoleon forced both to abdicate and gave the Spanish crown to his brother Joseph. When news of these highhanded proceedings reached the colonies, there was general indignation. At first the colonies vented their wrath against the French, but gradually they came to realize that

Immediate cause of the revolutions

887

CANADA
(British)

UNITED STATES
OF AMERICA

ATLANTIC

OCEAN

GULF OF MEXICO

NEW SPAIN

Mexico City •

CUBA (Spain)

SAINT DOMINGUE (France)

BR. HONDURAS

JAMAICA (British)

SANTO DOMINGO (Spain)

CARIBBEAN SEA

Orinoco R.

Bogotá •

(British after 1803)

FRENCH GUIANA

NEW GRANADA

DUTCH GUIANA

PACIFIC

Equator

GALAPAGOS IS.

Amazon R.

OCEAN

BRAZIL

ANDES

Lima •

P E R U

MOUNTAINS

Rio de Janeiro •

BUENOS AIRES OR LA PLATA

Santiago •

Montevideo

Buenos Aires •

La Plata R.

1000   2000 miles

0

PATAGONIA

FALKLAND ISLANDS

CAPE HORN

Spanish

Portuguese

British

LATIN AMERICA ON THE EVE OF INDEPENDENCE ca. 1800

here was an opportunity to get rid of all foreign oppressors. Agitation took an anti-Spanish turn and was ultimately followed by declarations of independence and revolutionary wars. Wealthy Creoles took the lead, especially in Caracas, Buenos Aires, Quito, Bogotá, and Santiago.

The first of the larger Spanish colonies to proclaim its independence was Venezuela. Here a revolutionary pattern had been developing for a number of years. In 1806 the impetuous Creole, Francisco de Miranda, attempted with the help of foreigners to land filibustering expeditions in his native country and wrest control of it from Spain. He obtained aid from English and American sources but failed to gain more than a temporary foothold on the territory of Venezuela. Five years later representatives from a number of provinces met in a revolutionary assembly and declared Venezuela an independent republic. Learning of the revolutionists' activities, Miranda sailed from England to enlist in the cause. Appointed commander-in-chief of the patriot armies, he launched a campaign to conquer the remainder of the country. Misfortune stalked his efforts. Reverses suffered by his armies were turned into disaster when an earthquake shook the provinces controlled by the revolutionists and snuffed out the lives of 20,000. Equal to the occasion, the Spanish government sent priests with instructions to tell the people that the catastrophe was a divine punishment for their sin of rebellion. The patriot armies disintegrated, and their commander was seized and thrown into a dungeon.

With the defeat of Miranda, the revolution in Venezuela was left to be completed by his erstwhile friend, Simón Bolívar. A wealthy Creole rancher, Bolívar had finally turned against Miranda, accusing him of deserting the revolution, and had been partly responsible for his capture by the Spaniards. Concluding thereafter that the revolutionary cause in Venezuela was hopeless, he went to Colombia and joined the patriot forces there. He returned to Venezuela in 1813 and captured Caracas. In January 1814, the Second Venezuelan Republic was proclaimed with Bolívar as its head with the title of "Liberator." In six months the new government had been crushed by the Spaniards, and its founder fled to Jamaica. He did not return for three years. In 1817 he began the rebuilding of a stronger patriot force in Venezuela, and two years later, with the help of 4000 soldiers of fortune from Great Britain, completed a spectacular foray into Colombia. Inflicting a decisive defeat upon the Spaniards and their collaborators, he proclaimed the Republic of Colombia on August 10, 1819. Three months later a constitution was issued for the United States of Colombia, including Venezuela, with Bolívar as President. Thereafter the great Liberator devoted his efforts to freeing the remainder of the northern portion of the continent from Spanish rule. By 1821 he had liquidated the royalist forces in Venezuela. Meanwhile, his able lieutenant Antonio José de Sucre,

Equestrian Statue of Simón Bolívar (1783–1830), Soldier, Statesman, and Revolutionary Leader. On Plaza Bolívar, Caracas, Venezuela.

889

had begun the liberation of Ecuador, and in 1822 won a brilliant victory against the Spaniards, which assured the independence of the country. Soon afterward Bolívar arrived in Quito and persuaded the Ecuadorean revolutionists to unite with Colombia and Venezuela in a republic of Gran Colombia.

Concurrently with these events in the northern areas, an independence movement was growing apace in the south. As early as 1790 business men in the port of Buenos Aires had developed a profitable trade with Spain and an even more profitable one with Great Britain. They longed for relief of these ventures from monopolistic restrictions imposed by the Spanish government. During the Napoleonic Wars their demands were encouraged by the British government. In 1810 a band of Creoles in Buenos Aires overthrew the viceregal government of Joseph Bonaparte and appointed a supreme governing council to rule in the name of Ferdinand VII. While the urban Creoles were debating how far they should go in the direction of complete independence, and what form of government would best suit their needs, delegates from the outlying provinces assembled at Tucumán in 1816 and declared absolute independence from the mother country. Thenceforth rivalry between the capital and the rural provinces impeded the progress of the revolution.

At least one native of Argentina perceived that internal squabbles would lead to nothing but ultimate defeat. This man was José San Martín, who had served in the Spanish army from the age of eleven and had fought the French invaders in the Peninsular campaign. With Spain under the heel of Napoleon, he had returned to his native country. Ignoring local quarrels, he determined to give positive direction to the Argentine revolution by attacking the royalists in Peru, their principal stronghold on the continent. He obtained an appointment as governor of the province of Cuyo, on the eastern slope of the Andes, where he planned to organize and equip an army for an incursion into Chile, which would then be used as a base for operations against Peru. In his preparations he was assisted by Bernardo O'Higgins, a Chilean revolutionary of Irish descent. By 1817 everything was ready for the daring expedition. Scrambling over the rocky slopes of the continental divide, the invaders came down into Chile, fell upon the royalists near Santiago, and won a spectacular triumph. The grateful Chileans offered San Martín a dictatorship, which he declined, insisting that it be conferred upon his Chilean collaborator, O'Higgins. San Martín then turned his attention to completing plans for the attack on Peru. The expedition got under way in September 1820. Less than a year later the redoubtable patriot entered Lima, issued a declaration of independence from Spain, and was vested with the title of "Protector" of the new Peruvian government. Although a dictator in theory, he exercised little power. He seemed to feel that his mission as a revolutionist was now fulfilled. Moreover, he was unable to agree with

Bolívar as to the form of government to be established when the
time should come to unite the countries they had liberated from
Spanish rule. In 1822 he left Peru, sojourned briefly in Chile and
Argentina, and then left for France, where he died in 1850.

The struggle for independence in Brazil followed a less violent
course than that in most other South American countries. Revolutionary feeling was not strong, perhaps for the reason that Brazil
was more backward than most of her neighbors. Two-thirds of her
population were slaves. There was no large middle class and there
were no cities worthy of the name. Schools were few, and scarcely
more than a tenth of the people could read and write. Even more
than in the Spanish colonies, the impetus for revolution in Brazil
came from the Napoleonic Wars. When Napoleon's troops drove
the Portuguese rulers from Lisbon in 1807, they sailed to Brazil,
arriving in Rio de Janeiro in March 1808. The Regent, Prince John,
was chagrined to find his colony so backward and launched an
immediate program of reform and improvement. He established
schools, a bank, hospitals, and a library. He reorganized the administration of the colony, sponsored new methods of agriculture, and
abolished the restrictions on colonial manufacturing. He raised the
status of the colony to that of a kingdom on a par with Portugal
itself. But upon becoming king of both countries after the death of
his deranged mother in 1816, he surrounded himself with a royal
court in Brazil and gave a virtual monopoly of high offices in
Church and state to his Portuguese favorites. The effect was to
antagonize many of his Creole subjects. Although the majority confined the expression of their discontent to grumbling, a group in the
north attempted unsuccessfully to establish an independent republic
(1817).

*Portuguese rule
in Brazil*

In 1820 a liberal revolution broke out in Portugal. King John
sailed for Lisbon and left his young son Pedro as Regent in Brazil.
Scarcely had the new government gained power in Portugal than it
turned to a reactionary policy, particularly with regard to the empire. Brazil was reduced once more to a mere colony, and Pedro was
ordered to return to Portugal to "complete his political education."
The Brazilians implored him to remain as their ruler, and he agreed
to do so. When all attempts to compromise with the Portuguese
failed, a revolt broke out in Brazil. In 1822 Pedro was raised to the
status of emperor, and within a year the Portuguese troops had been
driven from the country.

*The Brazilian
revolution*

By 1826 all the South American countries had thrown off the
yoke of European rule. Uruguay remained a province of Brazil,
however, until 1828, and Argentina was unable to solve the problem
of unity between Buenos Aires and her rural provinces until 1861.
Meanwhile another section of Latin America was striving for the
goal of independence. This was the viceroyalty of New Spain,
which included Mexico, Central America, portions of the West

*The revolution
in Haiti*

891

Indies, and the Spanish territory within the present limits of the
United States. The island of Haiti was the first to raise the standard
of revolt. During the eighteenth century it had become a colony of
France—her most lucrative, by the way. It was a seething volcano
of discontent, however. Its population had a three-class structure.
At the top were a few thousand whites, mostly French planters and
officials. At the bottom were 500,000 miserably exploited Negro
slaves. A middle layer comprised the mulattoes, torn into mutually
hostile factions and despised by both blacks and whites. In 1791
Toussaint L'Ouverture, a slave but the grandson of an African king,
emerged as the leader of the Negroes. Under the influence of the
French Revolutionary policy of abolishing slavery in the colonies,
he led the Negroes in a prolonged revolt against their masters. With
some accuracy he can be regarded as a forerunner of twentieth-
century guerrilla leaders. His followers were a straggling force of
irregulars, poorly armed and equipped, who followed a tactic of
strike and run. In ten years they gained control of the entire island.
Toussaint issued a constitution and assumed dictatorial powers.

When Napoleon had established himself as master of France, he
resolved to put an end to the rule of the upstart rebel. Avowing that
he would never "leave an epaulette on the shoulder of a Negro," he
sent a huge expedition under the command of his brother-in-law,
General Le Clerc, to overthrow Toussaint's government. Nearly
two years and an act of treachery were required to accomplish the
task. Informing Toussaint that he would "not find a more sincere
friend than myself," he invited the Negro to his quarters for negotiations. He then seized him and shipped him off in chains to a
prison in France. Angered by this treachery, the slaves again rose in
rebellion and with new and equally capable leaders soon forced the
French to withdraw. In 1803 Haiti was proclaimed an independent
kingdom. Curiously, the precedent set by the Haitians seemed to
exert little influence upon the other principal islands of the West
Indies. Cuba and Puerto Rico, for example, remained under Spanish
rule until 1898.

Scarcely anywhere in Latin America did the revolution present a
more discouraging aspect than in Mexico. Here the Creoles did not
constitute so powerful a middle class as in some parts of South
America. Moreover, the antagonism of the Indians and the poorer
mestizos, or half-breeds, against the whites hindered combined
action to oust the Spaniards. A revolt was finally launched in 1810,
however, in the rural provinces. Its leader was a Creole priest,
Father Hidalgo. The son of a poor farmer, he had obtained a good
education and had become rector of the Colegio de San Nicolàs.
But he was an ardent admirer of Rousseau and was reputed to have
questioned the Virgin Birth and the authority of the Pope. His original plan was to lead the Indians in a rebellion against the Spanish-
born aristocrats, but when his scheme was exposed he turned upon

the government itself. He captured the important towns of Guanajuato and Guadalajara and then advanced with 80,000 men upon Mexico City. Ultimately defeated, he was captured, condemned by the Inquisition, and shot. One of his followers, José Morelos, continued the revolution for four more years and attempted to set up an independent government. But like Hidalgo, he eventually fell into the hands of the royalists and was condemned to death. The destinies of the revolution then passed into the hands of a crafty adventurer, Agustín de Iturbide. A soldier by profession, who had hitherto fought on the side of the royalists, Iturbide saw a chance to further his ambitions by joining the patriots. Openly espousing independence and racial equality, he attracted formidable support and in September 1821, entered Mexico City in triumph. The following year he proclaimed himself Emperor of an independent Mexican empire. But since the basic economic and social problems remained unsolved, the future of the nation continued to be fraught with anxiety and turmoil.

3. PROBLEMS OF GROWTH AND DEVELOPMENT

Following their achievement of independence, the Latin American states went through a long struggle for national maturity. It could scarcely be said that many of them attained this goal before the end of the nineteenth century. A score of difficulties beset them on every hand. To begin with, the population was heterogeneous. The former Spanish colonies were composed of 45 per cent Indians, 30 per cent *mestizos*, or half-breeds, 20 per cent whites, and 5 per cent Negroes. In Brazil half the people were Negroes, a fourth were whites, and the remainder Indians and half-breeds. Over the continent as a whole the nonwhites outnumbered the Caucasians 4 to 1; yet the latter fought tooth and nail to maintain a dominant position. The success achieved in this struggle was purchased at the price of class hatred and the perpetuation of social and economic backwardness.

Obstacles to national maturity: (1) heterogeneous population

A second obstacle, related to the first, was the wide disparity of economic condition among the classes. At the top was a tiny minority of rich Spaniards and prosperous Creoles. At the bottom was a vast multitude of half-starved peasants, eking out a precarious livelihood on lands no one wanted or compelled to become laborers on the estates of the rich. The inevitable consequence was periodic revolts of the masses to force a redistribution of the land. Since land comprised the bulk of the wealth, capital accumulated slowly. In the main, the deficiency was made up by foreign investors, who frequently demanded political concessions and were eager to fish in troubled waters for their own advantage. Few causes contributed more toward encouraging unscrupulous adventurers to overturn governments at the behest of their foreign sponsors.

(2) the gulf between rich and poor

893

Still a third difficulty was the political inexperience of the Latin American peoples. More than 90 per cent, of course, were uneducated, and consequently both ignorant and indifferent with respect to political problems. But even many of the educated ones were ill prepared to assume the tasks of governing. Their knowledge of politics came not from experience but from reading the books of theorists. Enthusiasm for this or that form of government burned with white-hot intensity, and factions vied with each other to put their ideas into effect overnight, frequently by revolutionary action. Worse yet, as a result of the long and sanguinary struggles for independence, a military tradition was firmly implanted in most of the states, and swaggering generals overshadowed civilian leaders.

Although Latin Americans are often reproached with their failure to achieve political maturity and stability as soon as did the English-speaking inhabitants of North America, such comparisons have little validity. They leave out of reckoning the fact that the United States went through a long period of sectional conflict, culminating in civil war, before its people could decide whether they were one nation or a confederation of nations. But aside from this, the circumstances affecting Latin America were so different from those obtaining in Canada and the United States that any conception of the two regions as parallel entities is bound to be inaccurate.

Perhaps the most important difference resided in the fact that Canada and the United States comprised millions of acres of practically unoccupied land. The native peoples were so few in numbers and so widely scattered that they could easily be pushed aside or exterminated. In Latin America the Indians were more numerous, in many cases more highly civilized, and therefore more successful in resisting the encroachments of the whites. The policy of the Spaniards, moreover, was to convert the natives to Christianity, not to exterminate them. It did not seem inconsistent with this that they should also be exploited and oppressed. As a consequence, there quickly developed a class system based upon race, with a prosperous minority of Spaniards and Creoles monopolizing the good things of life and a subject population composed of Indians and half-breeds living in squalor and toiling for the barest subsistence.

As a second difference, the Spanish colonies were founded by one of the most unprogressive nations in Europe. The economic system of Spain was outmoded. Her government was despotic and corrupt. Spanish Catholicism reeked with intolerance and superstition. The Church was used by the government as an instrument of repression, and the fanaticism of the Spanish Inquisition was notorious. On the eve of the discovery of America the most enterprising of Spain's inhabitants—the Moors and the Jews—had been driven from the country. England had the advantage of not beginning her colonization of the New World until the seventeenth century. By that time the power of her middle class was well-consolidated and able to set up obstacles to despotic government. Instead of one church having a monopoly of religious authority, the Christians of England were divided into competing sects, and no one of them was strong enough to impose its will upon the others. The country, moreover, had been a haven of refuge for persecuted religionists from other nations, for the Huguenots in particular. Many of these were enterprising merchants and artisans who brought their initiative and skills with them, adding no small amount to the intellectual wealth of England. Long before the end of the seventeenth century, the "tight little island" was the most progressive nation in Europe. And while the Spanish colonists brought with them the customs and institutions of the Middle Ages, those who went out from England carried the ideas of the modern world. They believed in education, in equality of opportunity, and in the application of ambition and intelligence to the solution of human problems. These viewpoints helped immensely in promoting a free and dynamic society in North America in contrast with the static, semifeudal society of Central and South America.

The last three quarters of the nineteenth century unfolded a record of developments in Latin America similar in some respects to that in the United States. There was the same feverish activity in railroad building and in the construction of telegraph and telephone lines. There was the same rapid growth of population, owing largely to the influx of immigrants from Europe. The population of Argentina, for example, grew from 2 million in 1870 to about 4 million in 1900; and more than half of this increase was the result of immigration from Italy, Spain, France, Germany, and the British Isles. In Latin America as in the United States there were bitter struggles over centralization versus states' rights. There was sharp rivalry also between liberals and conservatives over extension of the suffrage and over economic reform for the benefit of the lower classes.

Growth and development during the 19th century

But the differences were quite as significant. Nearly every country of Latin America was torn by revolutions, many of them resulting in the enthronement of military dictators. The history of Colombia was almost unique in that only twice during the century following independence was her government overthrown by violence. In neighboring Venezuela revolutions occurred with such frequency as to reduce economic development virtually to a standstill. Only the accession in 1909 of a man on horseback, Juan Vicente Gómez, who ruled for twenty-six years, brought a semblance of stability to the country. In many states of both Central and South America, religion complicated the struggle between factions. The conservatives, made up of the landholding and aristocratic elements, invariably supported the Church. The liberals, who drew their following mainly from the business classes, were anticlerical. On occasions the latter allied themselves with the landless peasants in attacks upon the extensive holdings of the clergy.

Political instability

The major difference, however, consists in the numerous wars fought by the Latin American states against each other. The longest was the struggle between Uruguay and Argentina, which lasted for fourteen years (1838–1852). The most famous was the War of the Pacific (1879–1883), in which Chile, Peru, and Bolivia fought over the desert region of Atacama. The bloodiest was the war of 1865–1870, in which the dictator of Paraguay (Francisco López) resisted the combined onslaughts of Brazil, Uruguay, and Argentina for five years. The Paraguayans fought almost literally to the last man. Only a handful of adult males survived, and more than half of the total population was wiped out. The only element of justice in the outcome was the fact that López himself was numbered among those killed. It was this dictator's imperialist ambitions which had precipitated the conflict in the first place.

Wars of the Latin American states

Two states of Latin America went through experiences during the nineteenth century in a number of respects distinctive. One was Brazil and the other was Mexico. The former was almost unique in her political stability and in her capacity for gradual and orderly change. The reasons lay not in the different character of the Brazilian people but in their stronger national consciousness and in the fact that they gained their independence quickly and easily. In the absence of a protracted military struggle, no clique of generals and colonels emerged to overawe the civil authorities, and no professional revolutionaries threw apples of discord among the masses. As the years passed Brazil made a gradual transition from an absolute to a constitutional monarchy and eventually to a republic.

The unique development of Brazil

Soon after Pedro I became Emperor of the new independent state of Brazil, he summoned a constituent assembly. The assembly met in April 1823. It was dissolved six months later, however, when disagreements developed between its leaders and the Emperor. Pedro thereupon appointed a commission of ten to complete the work of drafting a constitution under his own supervision. The constitution was submitted to local governments throughout the country and was proclaimed in effect on March 25, 1824. It was a moderately liberal document. It guaranteed freedom of speech, of the press, and of religion and provided for a legislative assembly, with an appointive Senate and an elected Chamber of Deputies. At the same time it left the Emperor above the law and exempt from responsibility for the acts of his ministers. He not only appointed the members of the Senate, but he had power to dissolve the Chamber of Deputies.

The constitution of 1824 remained in effect for sixty-five years. It covered the reigns of two emperors, Pedro I and Pedro II. By 1831 Pedro I had suffered a loss of popularity, partly because of his scandalous personal life but also because of military reverses and his practice of bullying the assembly. He gave up the throne in favor of his young son, who became Emperor as Pedro II. The latter ruled until 1889 when he too experienced a decline of prestige and was forced to abdicate. He was accused of favoring the Free Masons against the Catholic Church and of disregarding the rights of high army officers. But the factor which really led to his downfall was

Emperor Pedro II of Brazil.

the abolition of slavery. In 1887 he sailed for a vacation in Europe leaving his impetuous daughter Isabella in charge of the government. In 1888 she signed a bill emancipating all the slaves without compensation to their owners. This action deprived the empire of its remaining supporters and opened the way for revolution. An armed uprising led by General Deodoro da Fonseca forced the Emperor to abdicate. A republic was proclaimed under a provisional government headed by the victorious general.

In 1890 a committee of lawyers drafted a constitution for the Republic of Brazil, which went into effect the following year. It provided for a government almost identical with that of the United States. Significantly, it included a bill of rights guaranteeing freedom of religion and the separation of church and state. Executive power was vested in a President elected for a four-year term, and legislative power in a congress comprising a Senate and a Chamber of Deputies. The members of the former represented the states, but both the senators and the deputies were chosen by direct popular vote. The government was reorganized as a federal system with reserved powers left to the states and enumerated powers granted to the central authority. However, the central government was given powers of intervention which could easily be interpreted in such a way as to restrict the freedom of the states. With few changes the Constitution of 1891 continued in effect until the suspension of constitutional government by the Vargas dictatorship in 1930.

The Republic of Brazil

The history of Mexico in the nineteenth century resembled the history of Brazil in that both countries wavered between monarchy and republicanism and had similar conflicts over church and state. But Mexico was one of the few Latin American countries in which the *mestizos* and Indians (the former especially) played an active part in determining the course of political developments. Her first ruler after independence, Iturbide, who became Emperor Agustín I, was of mixed white and Indian parentage. As a statesman, though, he was a failure and in little more than a year was driven from the throne and forced into exile. In 1824 a republic was set up with a constitution similar to that of the United States, except that the Roman Catholic faith was made the established religion. Between 1833 and 1855 Mexico was ruled most of the time by the redoubtable Antonio Lopez de Santa Anna, famous as the opponent of the United States in the dispute over Texas and in the war that followed. Although holding the title of President, he governed as a dictator with the support of a clerico-military oligarchy. Cruel, treacherous, and greedy for power, he exemplified that *personalismo* which has been the curse of so many Latin-American countries. His downfall was achieved by a coalition of radicals and liberals led by two full-blooded Indians, Juan Álvarez and Benito Juárez, and a Creole, Ignacio Comonfort. Although Comonfort became President, the real leader of the coalition was Juárez. He and his followers

Iturbide and Juárez as rulers of Mexico

**The War of
the Reform and
the overthrow of
the republic**

inaugurated a program aimed at the destruction of clerical and military privilege, the suppression of the Church, and the distribution of Church lands to the people. These reforms were eventually incorporated in a new constitution adopted in 1857.

The clericals and conservatives did not take kindly to the Constitution of 1857. The consequence was civil war, the so-called War of the Reform, from 1858 to 1861. It ended in a complete victory for Juárez and his followers, with the result that more drastic anticlerical laws were enacted to supplement the provisions of the constitution. Religious orders were suppressed, Church property was nationalized, and civil marriage was established. But the triumph of the liberals did not obliterate the nation's troubles. The government was so desperate for money that it sold some of the confiscated Church lands to secular landlords. The peasants were merely transferred from one exploiter to another. The war disrupted economic conditions to such an extent that payments on foreign debts were suspended. This gave the wily Napoleon III an excuse to intervene. In 1862 he sent a French army to Vera Cruz, which finally battered its way to Mexico City and took possession of the government. Meanwhile an assembly of Mexican conservatives went through the sham of "offering" the Mexican throne to Archduke Maximilian of Austria, who had already been selected by Napoleon III as his puppet ruler.

As Emperor of Mexico, Maximilian was worse than a failure. Although he was kindly, idealistic, and sympathetic with the plight of most of his new subjects, he was amateurish and dominated by an overly ambitious wife. Moreover, he antagonized the conservatives by his acid criticisms of corruption and indifference in the Church and in the army. The followers of Juárez had distrusted him from the beginning. The primary cause of his downfall, however, was a shift in the power struggle in Europe. The Austro-Prussian War of 1866 put Napoleon in a position where he could no longer afford to give military support to Maximilian. As a result of her victory in that war Prussia now loomed as a dangerous rival of France. Soon afterward, therefore, the French Emperor withdrew his troops. He was impelled to take this action partly, of course, by vigorous protests from the government of the United States against French violation of the Monroe Doctrine. But even without these protests, his decision could not have been long delayed.

Maximilian, Emperor of Mexico.

**The return of
Juárez**

In the absence of French military support, Maximilian's empire in Mexico speedily collapsed. The liberal forces of Juárez closed in upon him, and he was captured, court-martialed, and executed by a firing squad. Juárez was quickly elected President and re-elected in 1871, but death overtook him the following year. He had time to accomplish only a few of his aims for making Mexico a modern, progressive state. He drastically reduced the size of the army, eliminated waste and extravagance in the government, and initiated steps for a wide extension of public education. But the troubles of the nation were far from ended. It was impossible to repair overnight the damage caused by twenty years of civil strife. The national debt continued to increase, economic activity had shrunk, and the country seemed almost on the verge of exhaustion. In 1877 the government of Juárez's successor was overthrown, and a dictatorship was established that was destined to remain in power for more than thirty years. The new ruler was Porfirio Díaz, the son of a Creole father and an Indian mother. Originally a pupil and follower of Juárez, he repudiated his master when the latter was re-elected President in 1871. Thereafter he pursued his own ambitions and strove with an iron will to mold his country in accordance with his cherished schemes.

The regime of Díaz brought Mexico prosperity but nothing that resembled democracy. For the most part he ruled benevolently but always with an eye to the perpetuation of his own power. He soon controlled the electoral machinery and used government funds to buy off potential opponents. Those who couldn't be bought he dealt with in more summary fashion. For disposing of suspected revolutionaries his general order to the army and the public was: "When caught in the act, kill in cold blood." Yet under his rule the nation made rapid progress, and the business classes at least luxuriated in dividends and profits. Foreign trade multiplied six times over, and railroad mileage increased from 400 to 16,000. Mines were brought up to unprecedented levels of production, smuggling was eliminated, the national budget was balanced, and interstate tariffs were abolished to the substantial benefit of industry and commerce. Many of these improvements were made possible, however, by the importation of foreign capital. The suppliers of these funds frequently drove unscrupulous bargains as part of the terms of the investment. They exacted concessions to buy land at ridiculous prices, including full title to all minerals beneath the surface. Prosperity at the price of so large a part of the nation's heritage eventually proved to be too much for the middle classes to endure. By 1900 the reputation of Díaz had lost its luster. By 1911 when his government collapsed and the aged dictator sailed for France, the Mexican republic was ripe for revolution to undo the evils of three decades.

The Díaz regime

Porfirio Diaz. The Diaz rule in Mexico from 1877 to 1911 was characterized by political dictatorship and economic development.

4. THE TWENTIETH-CENTURY REVOLUTIONARY ERA

It would scarcely be an exaggeration to say that Latin America witnessed more social and political changes from 1900 to 1968 than in the previous four centuries of her history. Two significant developments distinguish the record of the twentieth century thus far. The first is a phenomenal increase in population. Around 1800, Central and South America had a population of about 17 million; by 1900 this had grown to about 70 million and by 1970 to 280 million.

Phenomenal increase in population

The population of Brazil more than trebled between 1900 and 1960. Argentina surpassed even this ratio, with a growth in numbers from 4,200,000 in 1900 to 20 million sixty years later. The number of Mexicans rose from 20 million in 1940 to 47 million in 1968 and might well reach 73 million by 1980. With an average annual growth rate of about 3 per cent, the Latin American countries seem destined to more than double their present population before the year 2000 when, according to predictions, it would total 650 million. Nearly everywhere population was beginning to exert terrific pressure upon available resources. Since 1950 there has been a steady migration of people from rural districts to the cities, but the expansion of industry and commerce has been too limited to absorb them into profitable employment.

The continuing
need for economic
reform

The second outstanding development was progress—although halting and insufficient—toward solution of the age-old problems of poverty and ignorance among the masses. At the turn of the century 90 per cent of Latin Americans lived a hand-to-mouth existence of squalor and wretchedness. Most of them were peons, or laborers on large estates, doomed to a kind of slavery by debts they could never repay. Their families were crowded together in one-room shacks with no stove or fireplace, no running water, and no sanitary facilities. Wages received for a day's toil scarcely equaled the hourly pay for comparable work in the United States. Most of the fertile lands were owned by a few wealthy families, who ruled their great estates, or *haciendas*, in semifeudal fashion. Though less than 10 per cent of the population, this powerful landlord class monopolized the professions, government positions, and the officer ranks in the army. Its members sent their sons to the universities, which produced excellent lawyers, historians, poets, and essayists but neglected the sciences and engineering. The masses, of course, remained illiterate and steeped in ignorance and superstition.

The Madero
revolution in
Mexico

The country which made the most spectacular progress in solving its land problem and in conquering illiteracy was Mexico. We have seen that, as late as 1911, the so-called Republic of Mexico was still under the rule of the suave but sometimes ruthless dictator, Porfirio Díaz. In that year he was forced by open revolt to step down from his exalted position and take refuge in France. His successor as President was Francisco Madero, the intellectual leader of the anti-Díaz forces. A nervous man with a high-pitched voice, a vegetarian and a spiritualist, Madero was ill-equipped for leadership of a country in the throes of a revolution. When he failed to carry out land reform speedily enough, some of his most powerful allies withdrew their support. He seemed helpless in the face of corruption on the part of relatives and subordinates. Denouncing him as a visionary and a lunatic, the United States Ambassador schemed to bring about his overthrow. In February 1913 he was deposed by his chief rival, Victoriano Huerta, and soon afterward was murdered.

LATIN AMERICA TODAY

Dates indicate year of independence

CANADA

UNITED STATES OF AMERICA

ATLANTIC OCEAN

MEXICO (1821)

GULF OF MEXICO

Rio Grande

Havana

Mexico City ★

Nassau

BAHAMAS (Brit.)

CUBA (1898)

JAMAICA (1962)

Port au Prince

HAITI (1804)

DOMINICAN REP. (1844)

San Juan

PUERTO RICO (U.S.)

Santo Domingo

BARBADOS (1967)

TRINIDAD AND TOBAGO (1962)

Port of Spain

CARIBBEAN SEA

SEE INSET BELOW →

CENTRAL AMERICA

PACIFIC OCEAN

Equator

GALAPAGOS IS. (Ecuador)

Caracas

VENEZUELA (1811)

Bogotá

COLOMBIA (1821)

Orinoco R.

Georgetown

GUYANA (1966)

Paramaribo

SURINAM (Du.)

FRENCH GUIANA Cayenne

Quito

ECUADOR (1822)

Amazon

R.

PERU (1821)

Lima

ANDES MTS.

BRAZIL (1822)

★ Brasília

BOLIVIA (1825)

★ La Paz

Sucre

PARAGUAY (1811)

★ Asunción

Rio de Janeiro

CHILE (1818)

ANDES MOUNTAINS

URUGUAY (1828)

★ Montevideo

Santiago ★

Buenos Aires ★

La Plata R.

ARGENTINA (1816)

0   1000   2000 miles

FALKLAND ISLANDS (Br.)

CAPE HORN

CENTRAL AMERICA

JAMAICA (1962)

Kingston

Belize

BRITISH HONDURAS

GUATEMALA (1821)

Guatemala ★

HONDURAS (1821)

Tegucigalpa

CARIBBEAN SEA

Salvador

EL SALVADOR (1821)

NICARAGUA (1821)

Managua

PANAMA CANAL

Panama

San José

COSTA RICA (1821)

PANAMA (1903)

PACIFIC OCEAN

General Pancho Villa and Staff. Villa is second figure from the left.

Huerta, Villa, and Carranza

Through the next four years chaos reigned supreme in Mexico. Huerta ruled as provisional president until July 1914 when, under pressure from President Woodrow Wilson, he resigned and fled to Europe. Then ensued a long conflict between rival generals contending for power. Venustiano Carranza, although recognized as the lawful President by the United States, did not receive the universal support of his own people. Pancho Villa kept the northern part of the country in turmoil, while in the south General Zapata marshaled the landless Indians in a crusade for economic reform. In 1916 the United States government sent an expeditionary force across the border to capture Villa "dead or alive" as a punishment for his raid on Columbus, New Mexico. He managed to elude his pursuers, but he was finally revealed as little more than a daring bandit, with no large following or substantial military force. Meanwhile, President Carranza, with arms furnished by the United States, was able to solidify his own position and to improve the stability of his government. He was eventually persuaded by his liberal followers to summon a constitutional convention. The convention met early in 1917 and drafted a constitution which was put into effect in May of that year.

The Constitution of 1917 had several objectives in line with the revolutionary ideals of those who had been struggling to remake the country ever since the end of the Díaz regime: (1) to democratize the government; (2) to reduce the influence of the Church; and (3) to give to the nation control over its economic resources and to provide for the masses a more equitable share of the wealth they produced. In pursuance of the first, the Constitution bestowed the suffrage upon all male citizens twenty-one years of age and over and subjected the powers of the President to a measure of control by Congress. In keeping with the second, freedom of religion was guaranteed, the Church was forbidden to conduct primary schools, and the state legislatures were empowered to limit the number of priests in each district. But the most significant provisions of the Constitution were probably those dealing with economic reform. Peonage was abolished. An eight-hour day with one day's rest in seven was proclaimed the standard for industrial workers. The right to strike was recognized, and the government was given the authority to provide for social insurance. Mineral resources were declared to be the property of the nation. No foreigners were to be granted concessions to develop them unless they agreed to be treated as Mexican citizens. Private property of any kind might be expropriated by the government after the payment of just compensation.

Though apparently promising much, the economic provisions of the new Constitution had little immediate effect. Carranza, who was still President, was not a convinced liberal and had no enthusiasm for carrying them out. Realizing this, dissatisfied elements rallied around General Álvaro Obregón, organized a revolt, and drove Carranza from the capital. Obregón became President in December 1920. During his term and those of his successors, especially Plutarco Calles and Lázaro Cárdenas, completion of the revolutionary aims of the Constitution was vigorously pushed. Millions of acres of land were expropriated and distributed to the peasants. Teacher-training programs were instituted and new schools were built. Primary education was made free and compulsory up to the age of fifteen. Legislation was enacted guaranteeing old-age pensions and

THE
TWENTIETH-CENTURY
REVOLUTIONARY ERA

The Mexican
Constitution of
1917

Economic and
social progress
in Mexico

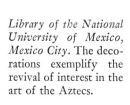

Library of the National University of Mexico, Mexico City. The decorations exemplify the revival of interest in the art of the Aztecs.

providing insurance for illness, accidents, and unemployment. The petroleum industry was nationalized, with compensation to the former owners. Under more recent Presidents the government has taken a somewhat more conservative turn. In 1965 President Diaz Ordaz pronounced a five-year development plan based on the preservation of private initiative.

In spite of her liberal Constitution and success in avoiding military dictatorships, Mexico has not yet fulfilled the promise of an equitable and democratic society. The dominance of a single political party, the Institutional Revolutionary Party (PRI), has bred corruption and complacency. The PRI chooses the presidential condidate, the legislature, the state governors, and most of the judges. The President in turn exercises practically unlimited authority over all branches of government. Although Mexico achieved one of the highest economic growth rates in the world, 40 per cent of her people have failed to benefit from it. The rural areas, lacking in schools and adequate medical care, remain neglected and exploited. In 1968 only 175,000 students were enrolled in public universities—out of a population of close to 50 million. Even agrarian reform, the core of the revolutionary program, has been limited and erratic. Repressive policies led to a student insurrection in 1968, which was brutally suppressed by President Díaz Ordaz's special troops, who massacred several hundred people in the main square of Mexico City. Luis Echeverría Alvarez, who took office as President in December 1970, promised to bring social justice and a more equitable distribution of wealth. Supported by a group of students and intellectuals, Echeverría stood firm against rightists in his own entourage who tried to sabotage his efforts at conciliating student unrest, and he dismissed several insubordinate officials.

Brazil made no advance toward democracy in government until 1934. A Constitution which went into effect in that year provided for the secret ballot and for the enfranchisement of both men and women, though a literacy qualification debarred many from voting. This Constitution continued in effect for only three years, and possibly was never intended as more than a polite gesture. Economic depression and the growth of Communism gave an excuse to the President, Dr. Getulio Vargas, to make himself a dictator. He issued a new constitution which gave him practically absolute authority to deal with national problems at his own discretion. Though his rule was comparatively mild, the rights and liberties of the people were virtually at his mercy until he was forced to resign by a bloodless revolution in 1945. Chosen President again in 1950, he was ousted by the military four years later and committed suicide. For several years a bitter struggle raged between Vargas's followers and their opponents.

In spite of factional wrangling, the later 1950's showed stirrings of progress in Brazil. President Juscelino Kubitschek planned an ambitious program of economic development, but because he avoided

Unfulfilled promises of Mexico's revolution

President Getulio Vargas of Brazil.

tax increases, his policy of government spending was highly inflationary. At the same time, volunteer reformers, supported by trade unions, political radicals, a Catholic Action Movement, and even some bishops of the Church hierarchy, brought help to the depressed rural area of northeastern Brazil, organizing peasant cooperatives, starting schools and health clinics, and offering technical assistance. Such radical activity at the grass roots, added to the mild reformism of the government, was too much for the oligarchy that controlled most of the land and the army. Kubitschek's successors had been no more successful than he in stabilizing the economy, and in April 1964 President João Goulart, a leader of the Labor party, was overthrown by a coup d'état. A military dictatorship has held Brazil in its grip ever since.

In the 1960's the country seemed to be caught in the surge of an economic boom. A resplendent new capital, Brasília, was constructed deep in the interior, and São Paulo on the coast grew from a sleepy provincial town to become the largest city in Latin America. Proponents of a trans-Amazonian highway boasted that the gigantic project would be visible to the naked eye from the moon, although ecologists warned that destruction of the Amazon rain forests would endanger the oxygen supply and lead to soil exhaustion. Industry expanded and diversified, to free the economy from dependence upon its single staple, coffee. Manufactures—including shipbuilding, automobiles, steel products, and precision instruments—increased sufficiently to contribute 20 per cent of Brazil's exports. By 1971 the overall annual growth rate approached 11 per cent. Prosperity, however, was somewhat fictitious and was obtained at the risk of eventual disaster. The nation's military rulers suppressed not only the democratic process but every vestige of civil liberty. A new constitution, promulgated in 1967 and modified a year later, retained the office of President but gave the chief executive unlimited powers. When President Costa e Silva became incapacitated by a cerebral hemorrhage in 1969, the heads of the armed services installed as his successor another general, Garrastazú Médici, then summoned a Congress to "elect" him. If President Médici had intended to restore democracy, as he declared, he soon changed his mind. Brazil has remained a police state, under tight censorship, incarcerating citizens without trial, and systematically using torture upon suspected opponents of the regime. The country's increasingly industrialized economy is precarious because it depends on outside support—chiefly from the United States, Canada, and West Germany—for 40 per cent of capital investment and 62 per cent of foreign trade. The ruling clique of landowners, capitalists, and military chiefs, fearful of any social distrubance that might frighten away foreign investors, has done almost nothing to alleviate the poverty and ignorance of the majority of people. While national income rose substantially between 1964 and 1969 and the earnings of university graduates went up by 50 per cent, real wages for the great body of workers declined by

Progress in the 1950's

Specious prosperity under a military dictatorship

El Teniente Copper Mine, Chile. El Teniente Mining Company had been jointly owned by the Kennecott Copper Corporation and the Chilean government until the Allende government expropriated it in 1971. Chile ranks third in world copper production, after the United States and Zambia.

almost 40 per cent. President Médici recently confessed, "The economy is going well; the people not so well."

The recent history of Chile contrasts sharply with that of Brazil. Chile had its "man on horseback" in the person of Carlos Ibañez, President from 1927 to 1931 and again from 1952 to 1958. Ibañez ruled most of the time on behalf of the chief landowners and foreign investors, despite the fact that 60 per cent of his people lived in cities and a quarter of the citizens were so poor that they existed almost entirely outside the money economy. Chilean politics tended to follow a moderate course, although discontent grew among the peasants and industrial workers who constituted 70 per cent of the population. In 1964 Eduardo Frei, a lawyer of German extraction, was chosen President. His party, the Christian Democrats, took a middle position between socialism and capitalism, deriving its philosophy from the encyclicals of liberal popes and the teachings of contemporary Catholic thinkers. Although Frei's government accomplished some reforms, including agreements for a gradual transfer of the copper mines from foreign to national ownership, it made little headway with the basic problem of land distribution. The presidential election of 1970, with 86 per cent of the registered voters participating, brought into office Salvador Allende, heading a Popular Unity coalition of Socialists, Communists, and other leftists. A long-time member of the Chilean Socialist party, Allende sought radical changes but was determined to achieve them by democratic methods. His government broke the control of monopolies, enacted

906

a substantial program of agrarian reform, and brought relief to the workers by reducing unemployment. Meanwhile, Allende and his program were plagued with such economic bugbears as inflation and budget deficits, and he faced vociferous opposition at home and abroad. Hostile demonstrations, riots, and widespread strikes led him to place much of the country under a state of emergency in the fall of 1972. Although conservatives denounced him as a dangerous Marxist, not all of Chile's difficulties were Allende's fault. A simultaneous rise in food costs and a drop in the price of copper, Chile's main export, had put the economy in a crunch. The Anaconda and Kennecott corporations quarreled with the government over the terms of compensation for their expropriated mining properties. The United States, while continuing its offer of military aid, cut off economic aid to the Allende regime, which turned to Russia for a loan in 1972. In spite of these hazards and setbacks, Allende defeated his opponents—a coalition of Christian Democrats and the right-wing National party—in the election of March 1973. Though he still fell short of a majority, he enlarged his support in both the Chamber of Deputies and the Senate. His troubles were by no means over; but in spite of the country's shaky economy, deep political antagonisms, and hostile demonstrations against him, Allende evinced a determination to continue to govern without forsaking the democratic process. Pressures continued to build until September 1973 when the armed forces united and executed a violent coup during which Allende allegedly committed suicide.

The richest and most highly urbanized of Latin American countries has one of the poorest records as an exemplar of political

Salvadore Allende, President of Chile, 1970–1973.

Modern Brazil. Left: A slum on the outskirts of Rio de Janeiro contrasts sharply with Brasília, Brazil's new capital, on the right.

and economic democracy. Although Argentina adopted universal manhood suffrage, the secret ballot, and minority representation in 1912, most of these provisions have had little meaning, especially in recent years. Voting has often been manipulated by powerful cliques for their own advantage, and authoritarian government has been the rule rather than the exception. The reasons for this lack of democratic progress require careful analysis. It can be traced in part to the rapid industrialization and to the fierce antagonism between urban and rural classes. More than 50 per cent of the population is employed in industry, and a wide gulf separates the interests and attitudes of Buenos Aires—where a third of the population is concentrated—from those of the outlying provinces. Industrialization and urbanization proceeded so rapidly after World War I that a precarious stability has characterized the economic system ever since. The country has been especially vulnerable to world-wide depressions. A second cause has been the ebullient nationalism of the Argentine people. Unlike most other Latin American countries, Argentina is a "white" nation. Her Indian population has always been small, and a liberal immigration policy has given her a predominantly European character. This uniqueness has imbued her citizens with an intense national pride. They believe that their country should be the leader of Latin America and particularly resent interference by the United States in the affairs of the southern continent. Devotion to the trappings of national glory has a tendency to foster autocratic government.

Much of Argentine political history in the twentieth century has revolved around a small number of dominating personalities. As early as 1905 a middle-class leader, Hipólito Irigoyen, organized a plot to seize the city of Buenos Aires. The scheme was thwarted, but Irigoyen remained to plague the conservatives and landowning classes for twenty-five years. Reserved, modest, and lacking in oratorical ability, he nevertheless inspired fanatical loyalty among his followers. In 1916 he was elected President for a six-year term and was elected again in 1928. His popularity stemmed partly from the fact that he managed, against powerful opposition, to keep Argentina neutral during World War I and to gain for her later a place of recognition in world affairs. But he ruled as an autocrat, enforcing a vicious antistrike policy against labor, and, during his second term, permitting widespread corruption. He was overthrown by a bloodless revolution in 1930 engineered by conservatives and high-ranking officers of the armed forces.

Irigoyen was succeeded by José F. Uriburu, a former inspector-general of the army. He promised to govern in accordance with the Constitution, but he immediately dissolved the Congress and filled the administrative offices with his own henchmen. When the date for the next election rolled around, Uriburu dictated the choice of his successor by declaring the opposition candidates ineligible. A period followed when conservatives and bourgeois liberals alternated in the possession of power. With the outbreak of World War II a sinister fascist movement began to develop in Argentina. Sympathy with the Axis, based in part upon fear of communism, was widely prevalent. Large numbers of the business classes were of German or Italian extraction, and many army officers were German trained. The nation was already in the throes of economic crisis. The government was almost bankrupt, and inflation and overcrowding in the cities inflicted cruel hardships on people with meager resources. Besides, the official policy of paying low wages as a means of boosting exports created a surly, rebellious class of workers ready to follow any demagogue who promised to better their condition. The first of such mountebanks to appear on the scene was Juan D. Perón. Leader of a movement to force the resignation of President Ramírez in 1943, he ran for President himself in 1946. By promising wage increases, rent controls, and partitioning of great estates, he won enough support among the *descamisados* ("shirtless ones") in addition to that of the military and business elements to ensure his election. Three years after his inauguration he changed the Constitution to make himself eligible for re-election. His methods of governing resembled closely the familiar pattern of fascist dictatorship—censorship, saber-rattling, militarism, antiforeignism, imperialism, and economic nationalism.

By June 1955, the Argentine people had had enough of Perón. He antagonized the Catholics by legalizing divorce and by attempting the separation of Church and state. And while he did little for the peasants, he incurred the enmity of the middle class by the expensive benefits he conferred upon his followers in the General Confederation of Labor and by his expansion of the national debt. Though a revolt which broke out in June was suppressed, it smoldered and flared up again in September. The rebels won the support of the navy and finally threatened to bombard the city of Buenos Aires if Perón did not surrender. A military junta persuaded him to relinquish his power and to go into exile. He fled to Paraguay and later found refuge in Madrid. In May 1956, the Constitution of 1853 was restored. The rights of the individual were reaffirmed, and the great liberal newspaper, *La Prensa*, was given back to its rightful owners.

The restoration of constitutional government did not end the threat to democracy in Argentina. It was impossible to eradicate overnight the influence of two million *peronistas* who longed for a revival of the dictatorship that had conferred so many favors upon the working classes. It was impossible also to suppress the ambitions of the generals and colonels, who demanded strong government until Peronism and communism should be completely eliminated as effective instruments of class legislation. Although free elections were held in 1958, Arturo Frondizi, the successful candidate, survived as President for only four years. He was ousted by the mili-

Juan Péron, President of Argentina.

The overthrow
of Perón

The persistence
of the Peronist
heritage

tary, who distrusted him since it was widely known that he owed his victory in the election to the votes of the *peronistas*. The new President, accepted by the military, was José María Guido. In order that the nation might continue to receive financial benefits from the United States, amounting to over $300,000,000 annually, he preserved a façade of democracy. But the economic ills dating from the Perón regime and from the depression of the 1930's and 1940's remained—the trade deficit with foreign countries, the chronic unemployment, the mountain of public debt, and the steadily advancing cost of living. In July 1963, Dr. Arturo Illia, a country physician, was chosen to succeed Guido as President of the harassed republic. Illia's rule endured but three years. Accusing him of Leftist sympathies, a military junta overthrew him and established a new dictatorship headed by General Carlos Ongania, who dissolved all political parties, purged the universities, and brought the trades unions under control.

The "Argentine Revolution" of 1966 promised stability and growth but brought instead more inflation, unemployment, and further crises. Three army generals ruled successively, the third of whom was Alejandro Lanusse, chosen by the joint chiefs of staff as head of the nation in March 1971. Abler than his predecessors, Lanusse also showed himself to be more conciliatory. He legalized political parties, restored some confiscated property, and announced his intention of holding elections for the office of President within two years. This seemed a bold plan in view of the dissensions within the country. Lanusse faced two military uprisings against him and opposition from both the right and the left, including labor unions, middle-class terrorists, and even a revolutionary faction of the Catholic clergy. Though he had himself once been imprisoned by Perón, Lanusse invited the exiled dictator to return for a month's visit, and unregenerate *peronistas* nominated their aging hero as the presidential candidate of their Justicialist Liberation Front. Perón chose not to run, but when the elections were held as scheduled in March 1973, his stand-in, Dr. Héctor Cámpora, a sixty-four year old former dentist, outdistanced his closest rival by better than two to one. Accepting the unexpected verdict, Lanusse relinquished the presidential office in May. But Cámpora's inauguration as the first civilian President in seven years did not halt the bloody violence and terrorism that racked the country, and in July Cámpora stepped down in favor of Perón.

Nearly 60 per cent of the people of Latin America live under direct military rule or under governments responsible to the military. There have been sixteen military coups since 1960. Most of these governments are both repressive and reactionary, depleting resources through excessive military budgets and employing specially trained counterinsurgency forces to destroy any opposition within their own countries. They are generally allied with local oligarchs and assisted by foreign capital. An exception is Peru, where an authoritarian regime installed by the army in October 1968 has carried out fundamental social reforms, redistributing some 8 million acres of land, setting up workers' cooperatives, and extending educational opportunities for both men and women. Under the leadership of General Juan Velasco, Peru has pursued an independent foreign policy. Velasco cultivated the friendship of Chile's Socialist President Allende, recognized Communist China and Castro's Cuba, while also trying, not very successfully, to improve relations with the United States.

Uruguay, smallest of the South American republics, has a better record of educational and political progress than many of her neighbors. She ranks next to Canada and the United States as the most literate nation in the Western Hemisphere. Since 1903 she has had only one revolution, and that a peaceful one. Her Constitution, modeled upon that of Switzerland, provides for equal suffrage, the secret ballot, and minority representation. Her greatest statesman, José Batlle y Ordóñez, President from 1903 to 1907 and again from 1911 to 1915, created a type of welfare state that won for Uruguay a reputation as the "Switzerland of South America." His reforms, which included the eight-hour day and minimum wages, old-age pensions and social insurance, benefited city workers but, unfortunately, did less for the peasants because they left the monopolistic land system unchanged. After several decades of relative prosperity and a rising standard of living, since mid-century the country has suffered economic decline, attributable partly to falling prices for its exports of wool, meat, and hides, but partly to such internal factors as a narrow concentration of wealth, inefficiency in both agriculture and industry, and bureaucratic waste in government. Demoralized by a runaway inflation, Uruguay has been torn by strikes and riots and terrorized by bands of desperate guerillas. Yielding to pressure from the army, President Juan Bordaberry, in June 1973, dissolved Congress and announced that he would govern by decree. His coup was accompanied by harsh repression and the wholesale arrest of trade union leaders. Although Uruguay's rightist military regime proclaimed the need for reforms, it seemed to mark the downfall of one of the few genuine democracies in Latin America.

Most of the small banana and sugar republics of Central America and the West Indies have been denied the advantages of progressive and orderly democracy. Guatemala, for instance, has been the victim of dictatorship and foreign intervention. When President Jacobo Arbenz of Guatemala attempted to expropriate idle lands and transfer them to landless peasants in 1954, the oligarchy of large estate owners overthrew his government by an armed invasion, staged in neighboring Honduras with the support of the United Fruit Company and the C. I. A. Despite acceptable constitutions, the Dominican and Haitian republics passed under personal dictatorships tempered by assassination or the threat thereof. The Dominican Republic suffered under the misrule of General Rafael

Political and
social progress in
Uruguay

Political turbulence
in the
West Indies

911

L. Trujillo for nearly thirty years until he was blotted out by assassins' bullets in 1961. Graft, nepotism, and police terrorism had been the instruments of his power. Elections held in 1962 resulted in the choice of Juan Bosch, a liberal intellectual, as President. After less than a year he was overthrown, and a military clique assumed power. In 1965 Bosch and his followers, including some Communists, launched a counterrevolt. Bloody strife ensued followed by prompt United States intervention. President Johnson professed an obligation to protect American lives and to save the island from communism. Eventually, upon pleas from Washington, the Organization of American States sent a joint expedition to maintain order in the Dominican Republic. In 1966 Joaquín Balaguer became President as the result of a new election.

Similar troubles beset the republic of Haiti. Beginning in 1945 a series of revolutions alternating with chaos culminated in 1957 in the dictatorship of François Duvalier. Though he ruled with the title of President, his power rested upon the armed forces. In 1964 he was made President for Life. Relying on repression as harsh as that of General Trujillo, he faced the constant possibility of revolution, for Haiti is poorer and culturally more backward than the Dominican Republic. It has the highest rate of illiteracy, the deepest poverty, and the most primitive economic development of all the countries of Latin America. Nevertheless, its government had one advantage over the governments of some neighboring states: it enjoyed the support of Washington. The State Department evidently considered Duvalier the least of a number of possible evils. When "Papa Doc" died in 1971, his twenty-year-old playboy son, Jean-Claude Duvalier, succeeded him as President for Life. Temporarily, at least, the atmosphere of terror relaxed. Haiti's tourism industry revived, and the prospects for foreign investments seemed brighter.

Among the smaller Latin American nations, Cuba occupies a unique position because of the transformation it has undergone and because of the controversy it has aroused. Freed from Spanish rule by the United States in 1898, Cuba became an independent republic four years later. But political inexperience combined with the weakness of the two-crop economy left the country a prey to disorder and the breakdown of civilian rule. Events reached a crisis during the world depression of the 1930's. In 1936 a ruthless army sergeant, Fulgencio Batista, with aid from the United States and the support of the army, gained control of the government. In 1940 he was elected President. With the titular as well as the actual authority in his hands, he maintained a dictatorial rule until 1959. In that year he was overthrown by a coterie of young revolutionists under the leadership of Fidel Castro. Castro's program was essentially a patchwork and his followers a motley assortment. Some were anti-Communists, some were democratic socialists, and several had definite commitments to communism. Calling their bid for power the

Twenty-sixth of July Movement because it had been launched on July 26, 1953, Castro and his comrades eventually demanded a complete revolution in Cuba. They would obliterate all traces of United States imperialism, expropriating American owners of banks, industries, and hotels. They would nationalize these properties and some others in order to provide jobs for the unemployed. They proposed also an extensive land reform for the benefit of the peasants. As the movement extended its power over the country and gained full control in 1959, it took on a more radical character. In 1961 Castro announced himself "a Marxist-Leninist." He proceeded also to align his country more and more closely with the Communist bloc.

The pro-Communist orientation of the Castro regime aroused antagonism in the United States. In April 1961 the United States government encouraged and assisted an invasion of Cuba by embittered exiles who had been driven from the country. An attempted landing at the Bay of Pigs was a total failure. In October 1962 the government in Washington obtained evidence of large-scale Soviet military assistance to the Castro regime. Missile bases had been established and considerable numbers of Soviet bombers had been stationed in Cuba. President Kennedy responded to these findings by ordering a naval blockade of the island republic. He informed the Soviets that the blockade would continue until the missiles and bombers were removed from Cuban soil. Premier Khrushchev took alarm at the threat of nuclear war and promised to withdraw, within a few days, both missiles and bombers. Kennedy had gambled on the chance that Khrushchev would not consider Cuba worth a war, and had won. As Secretary of State Dean Rusk is alleged to have expressed it, "We were eyeball to eyeball, and I think the other fellow just blinked."

The Communist orientation of the Castro regime

The Cuba of Castro's revolution presents strange contradictions. The revolution has accomplished many needed reforms and, in spite of erratic changes in government policy, has bettered living conditions for classes that had always been impoverished. Improved sanitation, hygiene, medical and hospital facilities raised the level of public health, as evidenced by a decline in deaths from tuberculosis, malaria, and typhoid. Illiteracy has been reduced, beaches and resorts have been opened to the public, and the administration of justice—except for political offenders—is more evenhanded than before. Although industrial development is still slight, Cuba's resources could make her one of the most prosperous agricultural countries in the world. The other side of the picture is the suppression of personal freedom, constant indoctrination—"government by oratory"—and similar dismal and familiar accompaniments of dictatorship. By 1960 Castro was holding far more political prisoners than had been jailed by Batista. Over 700,000 Cubans have left the country and other hundreds of thousands undoubtedly would do so if they could. The strong and weak points of the regime reflect the complex

The contradictions of Castro's Cuba

personality of its ruler, a man of tremendous charisma, courage, and drive but essentially an improviser, who drifted ideologically from constitutional democrat and anti-Communist "humanist" to "socialist" and then to "Marxist-Leninist" and Communist. That the revolution which began as a struggle for freedom should end in repression is explained partly by external circumstances, including the hostility of the United States, which sought to weaken Cuba economically and to isolate her diplomatically; but the outcome is also a product of the movement and its leader. In his hour of triumph in 1959 Castro spoke prophetically: "Who can be 'the enemies of the revolution'? We ourselves the revolutionaries, who might turn out to be like the many revolutionaries of the past." [1]

By the early 1970's it seemed clear that only revolutionary reforms could move the Latin American societies toward the well being enjoyed by developed nations of the Western Hemisphere, or even to enable them to keep pace with other developing areas of the world. Real economic progress could come only if joined to a transformation of the political structure, too long dominated by small and essentially parasitic minorities. In Latin America as a whole 65 per cent of the land is in large estates held by 15 per cent or less of the population. El Salvador belongs to fourteen families, the coffee oligarchy. In Ecuador compulsory servitude, virtually indistinguishable from slavery, is exacted from farm laborers. Until recently, Peru's rural population of 7.5 million, amounting to 65 per cent of the total, received only 13 per cent of the national income. Secondly, Latin America needs financial and technical assistance from outside; but to promote constructive change, any aid program must be designed to help free its recipients from a condition of subservience. The well-intentioned Alliance for Progress, initiated by President Kennedy in 1961, had the opposite effect. In contrast to the Marshall Plan for Europe, it disbursed aid chiefly in the form of loans, tied to United States exports and primarily benefiting the groups that already had a stranglehold on the Latin American economies. Designed to usher in a "Development Decade," the Alliance for Progress actually widened the gap between the rich and the poor and made governments more dependent than ever upon foreign investors. United States corporations control upwards of 75 per cent of Latin America's raw materials resources and approximately half of its modern industry, banking, and foreign trade. Finally, most observers believe that regional federations must be developed on the continent to make it possible to coordinate efforts for solving common problems. A trend in this direction is indicated by the Andean Common Market created in 1969 among Bolivia, Chile, Colombia, Ecuador, and Peru, and by moves on the part of several states to end the isolation of Cuba.

[1] Hugh Thomas, *Cuba: The Pursuit of Freedom*, p. 1034.

· *Items so designated are available in paperbound editions.*

Alexander, R. J., *The Perón Era*, New York, 1951.

———, *Prophets of the Revolution: Profiles of Latin American Leaders*, New York, 1962.

Arciniegas, Germán, *Latin America: A Cultural History*, New York, 1967.

Bailey, Helen, and Nasatir, A. P., *Latin America: The Development of Its Civilization*, 2nd ed., Englewood Cliffs, N. J., 1968.

Burnell, Elaine, ed., *One Spark from Holocaust: The Crisis in Latin America*, Santa Barbara, 1972. A valuable and provocative symposium.

· Cline, H. F., *The United States and Mexico*, Cambridge, Mass., 1953 (Atheneum).

Crawford, W. Rex, *A Century of Latin American Thought*, Cambridge, Mass., 1944.

· Cumberland, C. C., *The Meaning of the Mexican Revolution*, New York, 1967 (Heath).

· Douglas, William O., *Holocaust or Hemispheric Co-op: Cross Currents in Latin America*, New York, 1971 (Random House).

Draper, Theodore, *Castroism, Theory and Practice*, New York, 1965. Highly critical.

· González Casanova, Pablo, *Democracy in Mexico*, 2nd ed., tr. Danielle Salti, New York, 1972 (Oxford). A brief study by a distinguished Mexican scholar.

Gordon, W. C., *The Political Economy of Latin America*, New York, 1965.

Hanke, Lewis, *Contemporary Latin America: A Short History*, Princeton, 1968. Includes selected readings.

Hirschman, A. O., ed., *Latin-American Issues*, New York, 1961. An objective study emphasizing economic problems.

Lambert, Jacques, *Latin America: Social Structure and Political Institutions*, tr. Helen Katel, Berkeley, 1967.

Lockwood, Lee, *Castro's Cuba, Cuba's Fidel: An American Journalist's Inside Look at Today's Cuba in Text and Picture*, New York, 1967.

· Lynch, John, *The Spanish American Revolutions, 1808–1826*, New York, 1973 (Norton).

MacEoin, Gary, *Revolution Next Door: Latin America in the 1970s*, New York, 1971. A profoundly disturbing view of Latin American realities.

· Picón-Salas, Mariano, *A Cultural History of Spanish America: From Conquest to Independence*, tr. I. A. Leonard, Berkeley, 1962 (California).

· Pike, Frederick B., *Spanish America 1900–1970: Traditional and Social Innovation*, New York, 1973 (Norton).

Rotberg, R. I., with Clague, C. K., *Haiti: The Politics of Squalor*, Boston, 1971.

Skidmore, J. E., *Politics in Brazil*, New York, 1967.

Thomas, Hugh, *Cuba: The Pursuit of Freedom*, New York, 1971. A monumental, well-documented history of Cuba from 1762 to 1970.

· Waddell, D. A. G., *The West Indies and the Guianas*, Englewood Cliffs, N. J., 1967 (Spectrum).

Weaver, Muriel, *The Aztecs, Maya, and Their Predecessors: Archaeology of Mesoamerica*, New York, 1972.

Whitaker, A. P., and Jordan, D. C., *Nationalism in Contemporary Latin America*, New York, 1966.

Wilgus, A. C., ed., *South American Dictators during the First Century of Independence*, Washington, 1937.

915

CHAPTER 31

China, Japan, and Africa under the Impact of the West (1800-1914)

> The virtue and prestige of the Celestial Dynasty having spread far and wide, the kings of the myriad nations come by land and sea with all sorts of precious things. Consequently there is nothing we lack, as your principal envoy and others have themselves observed. We have never set much store on strange or ingenious objects, nor do we need any more of your country's manufactures.
> —Edict of the Manchu Emperor Ch'ien Lung to King George III of England, 1793

During the nineteenth century, for the first time in history the most advanced Western states, through the dynamic effects of the Industrial Revolution, became strong enough to alter the destinies of Far Eastern nations by direct intervention. Consequently, the chief problems affecting the Eastern nations in this period revolved around the readjustments necessitated by Western expansion. Cultural phenomena were subordinated to political objectives, and international relations became of crucial importance. Because China and Japan responded quite differently to the changing world conditions that confronted them, the contrasts between these two countries became greater than ever before.

I. IMPERIALISM AND REVOLUTION IN CHINA

The nineteenth century, which witnessed tremendous economic, political, and intellectual progress in the Western world, was a period of trouble for China. The central factor in China's distress was the decadence of the Manchu Dynasty and the incompetence of its administration, but all her problems were aggravated by the pressure that Western powers were now exerting in the Far East. As in the case of India the objectives of the Westerners at the outset were almost exclusively commercial, and in China as in India the British

The misfortunes of China under the impact of imperialism

917

River View of Canton. Canton was the only authorized port of exchange, other than Macao, where the Portuguese had special privileges, until the mid-nineteenth century.

played the leading role. Although China escaped complete subjugation, her institutions were greatly altered under the Western impact; she suffered the humiliation of seeing her territory and sovereignty infringed upon by Europeans; and for the first time in history Japan displaced China as the leading Asian state.

It was unfortunate that increasing interest in the China trade on the part of Western nations came at a time when the imperial government was almost moribund, undermined by corruption, and lacking in imaginative leadership. During many earlier periods of their history the Chinese had shown themselves not only enterprising traders but also capable of profiting from the stimulation offered by contacts with the outside world. By the nineteenth century the eyes of officials were closed to the desirability of any change and to the danger of having unwelcome changes forced upon them. Both the Manchu aristocracy and the Chinese class of scholar-officials that supported it were schooled in the tradition that trade was a contemptible business, unworthy of a gentleman's attention. The Westerners who came to China specifically for purposes of trade were looked down upon as a low order of humanity, and the power they were able to exert in enforcing their demands was slow

How Western traders gained a foothold

to be recognized. The policy of the Manchu government was to avoid contamination from the Western hucksters by keeping them at a safe distance and requiring them to have relations only with Chinese merchants, not with government officials. At the same time the government expected to derive profit from levying taxes on whatever trade was permitted, and members of the bureaucracy from top to bottom also exacted commissions for extending privileges to merchants.

At the opening of the nineteenth century, although Western trade had reached fairly large proportions, it was still carried on under cumbersome restrictions which in many ways were disadvantageous to the Chinese as well as to foreigners. Aside from the Portuguese settlement at Macao, the only authorized port of exchange was Canton (by an imperial edict of 1757), at the opposite extremity of the empire from Peking, the seat of government. Silk and tea, the leading Chinese exports, had to be carried overland a distance of at least 500 miles to Canton; their transportation by boat along the coast was not permitted for fear that payment of the excise tax might be evaded. The trade at Canton was under the general supervision of a Manchu official known to foreigners as the "Hoppo" and was handled through a guild of Chinese merchants called the Cohong. While the Co-hong merchants enjoyed a monopoly of foreign trade, they were taxed and "squeezed" by numerous officials and also were held personally responsible for the conduct of the foreigners with whom they dealt. Beginning about the middle of the eighteenth century a system of "security merchants" had been instituted, whereby every incoming foreign vessel was assigned to the supervision of a particular member of the Chinese guild during its entire stay in port. Foreign merchants were permitted to come to Canton only during the designated trading season (the winter

Restrictions upon
Western traders

Chinese Silk Factory, ca. 1800. (Illustration from a French treatise on the silk industry.)

months) and their acitvities were highly circumscribed. They were forbidden to bring their women or families with them, to ride in sedan chairs, or to employ Chinese servants. They were, theoretically at least, confined to the special area set aside for the "factories," and they could make no request to a government officer except through a Co-hong merchant as intermediary.

That the Canton trade was profitable both to the Chinese and to the foreigners is evidenced by the fact that it continued to grow in spite of the annoying regulations surrounding it and in spite of fluctuations in the assessments upon it. Foreigners were often kept in ignorance of the schedule of duties fixed by the Peking government. The Co-hong merchants—under pressure from the Hoppo, who in turn had to satisfy various other greedy bureaucrats and recover the expenses he had incurred in getting himself appointed to office— were inclined to charge what the traffic would bear. The foreign traders, if fleeced unduly, could of course threaten to break off intercourse altogether. Actually, remarkably stable relations were established between Chinese and foreign merchants at Canton. Large transactions were handled, sometimes on a credit basis, with only oral agreements between the two parties, and by communication through a vernacular known as "pidgin English." [1]

As the volume of Western trade increased, however, friction was bound to arise. Two fundamentally different civilizations were coming into contact with each other. There were wide gaps between the Western and the Chinese concepts of justice and legal procedure. Westerners regarded as barbarous the Chinese view of group, rather than individual, responsibility for misbehavior and the use of torture in obtaining confessions. Consequently, misunderstandings occurred over the apprehension and punishment of criminals. Perhaps even more serious was the fact that the character of the trade began to change in a direction that was disadvantageous to China. In early days Chinese exports—tea, silk, and cotton cloth in lesser quantities—had far exceeded the value of imports into China; and the difference was made up in silver payments to Chinese merchants. Western traders would have preferred to make the exchange in goods, but they had difficulty in discovering any appreciable Chinese demand for commodities which they could supply. The Chinese attitude, as expressed by the Emperor Ch'ien Lung to the British in 1793, was: "The Celestial Empire possesses all things in prolific abundance and lacks no product within its borders. There is therefore no need to import the manufactures of outside barbarians in exchange for our own products." [2]

Methods of trade

*The development
of friction
between Chinese
and Westerners*

---

[1] Some large fortunes were accumulated in the process. In 1834, one member of the Co-hong estimated his personal estate at $26,000,000. H. B. Morse and H. F. MacNair, *Far Eastern International Relations*, p. 68.

[2] C. P. Fitzgerald, *China, a Short Cultural History*, 3rd ed., pp. 557–58.

Eventually, a means of altering the balance of trade was supplied by the increase of opium consumption in China. Opium had long been used in China as a medicine and as a drug, and the practice of smoking it was introduced along with tobacco-smoking in the seventeenth century. In spite of imperial edicts against it, traffic in the drug grew steadily, with the bulk of the shipments coming from India. So ineffective was an imperial order of 1800 prohibiting this trade that by 1839 more than 4 million pounds of opium were being shipped in annually. Thoroughly aroused to the gravity of the situation, the imperial government resolved to take stronger measures, both for moral and for economic reasons. The traffic was draining specie out of China and, because it was illegal, it brought no revenue to the state while lining the pockets of smugglers and conniving officials.

Although traders of various nationalities, including Americans, participated in the China trade, the greater share had been in the hands of the British East India Company. When, in 1834, the company was divested entirely of its trading functions and the traffic was thrown open to all comers, the situation in China became more critical than ever. As British mercantile interests in the Far East continued to expand, the demand arose in England for the establishment of regular diplomatic relations with the Chinese government. In 1834 Lord Napier was sent as chief superintendent for British trade, under instructions to announce his arrival directly to the viceroy, the highest Chinese functionary at Canton. Napier was unable to carry out his instructions because the viceroy refused to see him on the ground that the "barbarian headman" must conduct his business through the Co-hong merchants, in keeping with law and custom. According to the viceroy: "The petty affairs of commerce are to be directed by the merchants themselves. The officials are not concerned with such matters. . . . To sum up the whole matter: the nation has its laws; it is so everywhere. Even England has its laws; how much more the Celestial Empire!" [3]

The vigorous attempts of a special Chinese commissioner to enforce the prohibitions against the opium traffic created a series of incidents which culminated in the Anglo-Chinese War of 1839–1842. This conflict, which was confined to the coastal regions near Canton and the lower Yangtze ports, is known as the Opium War because of the dispute that precipitated it. Actually the British objectives were broader and more ambitious than this title suggests. The real importance of the war is that it served as an entering wedge for the expansion of commercial intercourse and marked the beginning of the subjection of China to conditions imposed by the Western powers. By the treaty of Nanking in 1842 (supplemented the following year) the Chinese government ceded the island of

The opium traffic

Worsening of the conflict

The Opium War of 1839–1842 and the "unequal treaties"

---

[3] H. M. Vinacke, *A History of the Far East in Modern Times*, 5th ed., p. 40.

Hong Kong to the British, promised an indemnity and compensation for the opium chests which had been confiscated, and agreed to treat Britain as a most favored nation in any future concessions that might be made. Four ports besides Canton were opened to trade, the Co-hong monopoly was abolished, and the right of residence was granted to foreigners in the treaty ports. Other nations, which had followed the course of the war with interest, were quick to follow the example of Britain in demanding similar privileges, confirmed in separate treaties. A significant feature of the treaty negotiated by the American minister, Caleb Cushing, was that it specifically included the principle of extraterritoriality, which conceded to foreigners accused of crime the right to be tried in their own national courts rather than by Chinese tribunals. These initial treaties omitted reference to the opium traffic but provided that the Chinese tariff on exports and imports should be "uniform and moderate," a phrase interpreted as denying the Chinese government the right to raise the tariff without consent of the Western commercial powers. Thus by 1844 China was saddled with "unequal treaties," depriving her of control over her tariffs and limiting the powers of her courts over foreigners.

The results of the first Anglo-Chinese war were to intensify friction instead of removing it. Much of the fault lay with the foreigners, who took advantage of the weakness and corruption in the Chinese administration to enlarge their own interests. The privilege of extraterritoriality was abused, being extended to cover Chinese servants in the employ of foreigners, and inadequate punishment was given by the foreign powers to their own nationals who were convicted of crime. Portuguese vessels, and some others, engaged in "convoying," nominally to protect coastal shipping against piracy

*Results of the war
and the treaties*

The Emperor Tao Kuang Reviewing His Guard inside the Forbidden City of Peking at the Time of the Opium War. From a painting by Thomas Allom.

The Signing of the Treaty of Tientsin. The treaties of Tientsin and Peking (1858, 1860) formalized the Chinese government's acceptance of the demands of the Western powers trading with China.

but actually to extort tribute from legitimate traders. Another reprehensible practice, carried on by Europeans and Americans during the middle of the century, was the recruiting of Chinese contract labor for export to plantations in the New World under conditions reminiscent of the old African slave trade. On the other hand, Westerners complained that the Chinese were evading both the spirit and the letter of the treaties. The attempt to establish foreign settlements at Canton led to rioting, because the Cantonese interpreted the treaties as granting foreigners the right of residence only outside the city walls. Less trouble was encountered in the new trading ports, where local sentiment was eager to attract commerce away from Canton now that Canton's monopoly had been broken. In Shanghai, the influx of foreigners resulted in the creating of an "International Settlement"—controlled jointly by British and Americans—and a separate French Settlement in the same city.

In all disputes with China the Western powers had the advantage of superior force, which they did not hesitate to use upon occasion. For a time, pressure was applied only locally, in the particular district where an untoward incident had occurred. In 1858, however, the British and French cooperated in large-scale hostilities against the Peking government. After negotiations at Tientsin (the port of Peking), a misunderstanding arose as to the route for the foreign representatives to follow en route to Peking, whereupon the British and French forced their way up the river to the capital, drove the emperor in flight into Manchuria, and burned the beautiful summer palace of the Manchus. This war of 1858–1860 opened China more widely than ever before to Western penetration. The treaties of Tientsin and Peking added eleven ports to the list of authorized trading centers, legalized and imposed a tax upon the opium traffic, granted foreigners the right to travel in all parts of China, and promised that diplomatic representatives of the Western nations would

The war of 1858–1860

923

be received in Peking. Largely because of the interest of the French in missionary activity, the Chinese government, compelled to acknowledge that "the Christian religion inculcates the practice of virtue," undertook to protect missionaries and their property.

Although by 1860 the ineffectiveness of China as a sovereign state had been clearly demonstrated, the Manchu government showed no inclination to take a realistic view of the situation or to profit from its own mistakes. The heavily staffed bureaucracy numbered some men of genuine ability among its ranks, but it was practically paralyzed by its own inertia. Local officials had acquired the habit of minimizing or concealing problems rather than attacking them, and the top authorities provided no incentive for the drastic renovation that was needed to make the country strong enough to stop the intrusion of European powers. Unwilling to contemplate the necessity or the desirability of change, they tended to regard the Western pressure as a temporary affliction that would disappear in the course of time, as had other calamities in the past. Unable any longer to repel the ocean-borne "barbarians," the government nevertheless indulged in annoying and dilatory tactics, exhausting the patience of Westerners (not a very difficult task) without gaining any real advantage in return. The Manchu rulers were reluctant to give up the illusion that foreign emissaries were merely tribute-bearers from vassal states who should perform the *kowtow* (ceremonial prostration) before the throne. In spite of the pledges given in 1860, no imperial audience was granted to the foreign diplomatic corps at Peking before 1873, and not until twenty years later was it conducted in a manner acceptable to the Western ministers. Oddly enough, while the Manchu rulers persisted in an attitude of irresponsible and haughty superiority toward the Western nations, they were coming to rely upon these nations to carry out some of the normal functions of government within the Chinese Empire and even to protect their regime when it was menaced by rebellion.

While the Western powers were tightening their grip on China's commerce and installing their agents in her coastal cities, internal upheavals created havoc and threatened to overthrow the dynasty. The most famous example, although actually only one of a number of contemporary revolts, was the movement known as the Taiping Rebellion, which began in 1851 and was not suppressed until more than a decade later. Its originator and leader, Hung Hsiu-ch'üan, was a native of the region near Canton in Kwangtung province who had shown promise as a scholar but had thrice failed in the provincial civil-service examinations. Frustrated in office-seeking, he nourished a bitter grudge against the Manchu government (which, with some justice, was suspected of discriminating against southern Chinese), and gradually his resentment became fused with a conviction that he had a divine mission to perform. He had received instruction for a short period from a Baptist missionary in Canton and, after an illness and a series of visions which he interpreted as revelations from God Almighty, he undertook to win his countrymen to the true faith. Hung's religion was largely Christian in ideology but with peculiar variations. He recognized God the Father as supreme deity, revered Christ as Elder Brother, and described himself as "Heavenly King and Younger Brother of Jesus." He also identified God with the ancient deity Shang Ti whom the Chinese had worshiped in pre-Chou times, and therefore believed that in propagating his version of Christianity he was actually urging the Chinese to return to their own original faith. Taoism, Buddhism, and ancestor worship he regarded as idolatry, and his followers first attracted the attention of authorities by their zeal in desecrating temples. Eventually Hung conceived his destiny to be to lead the "Association for Worshiping God" in a movement to overthrow the Manchus and inaugurate the "Heavenly Kingdom of Great Peace." Thus the Taiping Rebellion was both an antidynastic revolt and a religious crusade.

Originating in the extreme south, the rebellion spread northward and in 1853 the Taiping leaders captured Nanking, which they retained as their capital for eleven years, entirely cutting off the rich Yangtze valley from the control of the Peking government. Fighting occurred in fourteen out of China's eighteen provinces, and in 1853 rebel troops came within twelve miles of Tientsin. That the Taiping regime ultimately collapsed in spite of the inability of the Manchus to suppress it was due partly to inherent limitations in the movement and partly to the attitude of the great powers. Fundamentally a peasant uprising, the rebellion failed to win the support of the Chinese intelligentsia and actually antagonized this class by repudiating not only popular religions but the whole Confucian tradition as well. In addition, the Chinese gentry realized that the Taipings would institute radical economic changes, jeopardizing private property rights. Some foreign residents, especially Protestants, were at first inclined to view the revolt with sympathy because of its association with Christian teaching, but they soon became aware that a triumph of the Taipings would not serve the interests of Christian missionaries. Hung evidently believed that all Christians in China should accept his authority because his revelations were more recent than any described in the Bible, and the rebel leaders became increasingly fanatical. Undoubtedly also, a factor influencing the decision of the Western powers not to support the Taiping movement was that these powers had already successfully pressed demands upon the imperial government and preferred a weak but compliant regime to an aggressive one founded upon revolution.

Reasons for the failure of the Taiping Rebellion

Without formal intervention in the Taiping wars, the Western powers assisted the Manchus in suppressing the rebellion—even while the British and French were conducting their own war against the Peking authorities in 1858–1860. In view of the confused state of Chinese affairs, perhaps it is not strange that one of the military heroes in the imperial service was Frederick T. Ward, a sea captain from Salem, Massachusetts, who raised a volunteer corps for the protection of Shanghai contrary to the wishes of his own government and over the protest of British naval authorities. General Ward adopted Chinese citizenship, and, in gratitude for the exploits of his "Ever-Victorious Army," the emperor commanded that altars should be erected and perpetual sacrifices offered to his spirit. Ward's most distinguished successor was an Englishman, Major Charles ("Chinese") Gordon. Meanwhile several able Chinese, from the civilian gentry rather than from the professional military clique, had come to the rescue of the hapless Manchus and earned the major credit for suppressing the rebellion. In 1864, the combined Chinese, French, and British forces captured Nanking, the last Taiping stronghold.

The liquidation of Hung's "Heavenly Peace" movement did not bring peace even of an earthly variety to China. Moslem rebellions in the southwest and the northwest remained unsubdued until considerably later. During the thirteen years of Taiping intransigence two-thirds of the provinces had been devastated, the whole country impoverished, and probably no less than twenty million people killed by battle, massacre, and famine. The Manchu Dynasty had been saved only through the efforts of its Chinese subjects and by grace of the foreign powers. Furthermore, the injury to China's intellectual heritage through the destruction of libraries and academies in the Yangtze valley was incalculable. In reaction against Taiping fanaticism the bureaucracy became more uncompromisingly conservative than ever.

The story of China from 1860 to 1911 is the depressing tale of a discredited dynasty clinging to its prerogatives while its people were oppressed and the nation's independence was being gradually whittled away. A little color was added by the career of the famous Empress Dowager, T'zu Hsi, a Manchu woman of great cunning and strong will, who dominated the Peking administration through her control of puppet emperors during much of the period between 1861 and her death in 1908. The "old Buddha," as she was nicknamed, in spite of her irregular and unscrupulous methods, somewhat recouped the prestige of the ruling house, but she neither understood nor contributed to the solution of China's basic problems. Out of the chaos of the Taiping era came a reorganization and centralization of the Chinese maritime customs service. A temporary arrangement, whereby foreigners had collected tariff duties at Shanghai while the authority of the Peking government was paralyzed, was perpetuated and extended to all the treaty ports. The higher personnel of the customs service was composed of foreigners, nominated by their consuls but appointed by Peking, with the understanding that so long as the English predominated in China's foreign trade the inspector general would always be a British subject. Thus the customs administration, while foreign-staffed, was an agency of the Chinese government, maintained its headquarters at Peking, and operated as a unit regardless of provincial divisions. The fact that the foreign inspectorate functioned efficiently emphasized all the more glaringly the general decrepitude of the Manchu administration.

In the last quarter of the nineteenth century China's weakness was further revealed in the loss of some of her outlying possessions. By 1860 she had renounced to Russia all claims to territory beyond the Amur and the Ussuri rivers, thus allowing Russia to surround Manchuria and to control the entire Asiatic seacoast north of Korea. Through a combination of diplomatic and military pressure, culminating in a small-scale war (1884–1885), France acquired a protectorate over virtually all of Indochina except the independent state of Siam. The murder of a British explorer in China's southwestern province of Yunnan led the British to demand, and China to yield, sovereignty over Upper Burma (1886). The Japanese government enforced a claim to suzerainty over the Ryukyu Islands (1881). Not to be outdone, the Portuguese, who had occupied Macao for 300 years, obtained its formal cession in 1887. The full measure of China's humiliation, however, followed the Sino-Japanese War of 1894–1895. Japan, only recently emerged from feudalism and isolation, gave the world a startling demonstration of China's impotence by defeating the Celestial Empire in the short space of eight months. Shortly afterward five great powers—Russia, Great Britain, France, Germany, and Japan—participated in a "battle for concessions," through which the major part of China proper was partitioned into "spheres of interest." The spheres of interest, somewhat vaguely defined and usually radiating from a leased port, theoretically did not impair China's sovereignty; but the concessions as a whole made her an economic dependency of the great powers.

Dividing the
Chinese melon

Before the close of the nineteenth century, conditions in China provoked a growing spirit of resentment against both the incompetence of the government and the foreign elements that had taken advantage of it. A group of educated Chinese who were sincerely interested in their country's welfare and also appreciative of Western institutions began to agitate for reform. As might be expected, the reformers were mostly from southern China, especially Kwangtung province. Their first outstanding leader was K'ang Yu-wei, who had been influenced by the Han Learning scholars and wished to utilize Confucian principles in reconstructing the government. On social questions K'ang adopted some decidedly radical views, even contemplating the abolition of the family; but he was not impetuous and set as his immediate goal the attainment of constitutional monarchy for China. For a brief period, known as the "Hundred Days

The "Hundred
Days of Reform"

CHINA AND JAPAN IN THE NINETEENTH CENTURY

of Reform" (June to September 1898), it looked as if the ideas of
K'ang would bear fruit as the young emperor, under K'ang's guidance, issued a series of edicts that indicated a break with the past.
The movement came to an unhappy end, however, when the Empress Dowager T'zu Hsi executed a *coup d'état* and forced the
emperor into retirement. K'ang Yu-wei escaped arrest and decapita-
tion by fleeing the country.

Having rebuffed the liberal reformers, the Manchu court next
gave its blessing to extreme reactionaries. The Empress Dowager
shrewdly directed the fulminations of various secret societies—which
were potentially a threat to the dynasty—into the channel of anti-

foreignism. The climax came in 1900 when the so-called Boxers ("Society of Harmonious Fists") unleashed a violent attack upon Christians and foreigners in Shantung and the adjacent northeastern provinces. In view of the fact that the movement was secretly encouraged by the Empress Dowager and was based on extreme anti-Western fanaticism, the number of lives lost was not tremendous even in the critical areas. In other parts of China the provincial authorities, disregarding T'zu Hsi's instructions, generally tried to maintain order and protect the resident foreigners. Thus the Boxer movement was neither a revolution nor an actual war against the West; but the Western powers cooperated to stifle it with promptness and vigor, allowing their troops to indulge in wanton looting in Tientsin and in Peking, where far more damage was inflicted after the allied forces occupied the capital than while it had been held by the Boxers. Instead of abolishing the Manchu Dynasty as they might easily have done, however, the Western governments decided to shore it up, extracting certain guaranties of good behavior for the future. By the terms of settlement (the Boxer Protocol of 1901) the imperial government was required to pay heavy indemnities and to mete out punishments to certain of its own officials; the civil-service

Boxer Uprising. German troops march into the Forbidden City of Peking after the rebels have been driven from the city.

Efforts to shore up
the old regime

The Revolution of
1911

examinations and the importation of arms were suspended temporarily; and the Western powers were granted permission to maintain military units in the Peking area.

In a final attempt to save the dynasty and partly in response to foreign pressure, the Manchu rulers during the period 1901–1911 projected a series of reforms, which emphasized railroad construction, modernization of the military services, public education, and liberalization of the political structure. These measures, beneficial as they appeared to be, were poorly planned and carried out only half-heartedly, and the reform program actually speeded the coming of revolution. In 1905 the ancient civil-service examinations were formally abolished, preparatory to erecting a modern educational system. But the initiative in implementing the program was left to the provincial governors, most of whom did little about it. Many ambitious Chinese youths went abroad to study, particularly to Japan, where instruction of a very superficial character was supplied to meet the sudden desire for "Western learning." A youth movement began to manifest itself in China, characterized by impatience with the old order but inadequately prepared for leadership in the creation of anything better. The government announced plans for a gradual transition to a constitutional regime with an elected parliament and, as a first step in this direction, established provincial assemblies in 1909. Although these assemblies were not democratically elected and were intended to be only debating societies, they vociferated so loudly that the government deemed it expedient to summon a National Assembly the following year. The National Assembly of 1910 was devised as a bulwark of conservatism, with half its members directly appointed by the emperor. Nevertheless, it proceeded to criticize the government and pressed the demand for more rapid reform.

Meanwhile resentment was mounting against the policy of the government in regard to railroad construction. The original plan had been to build a unified network of roads by letting the provincial authorities assume responsibility for specific sections, raising the necessary funds by stock subscriptions among the wealthy citizens of each province. It was hoped thus to stimulate national interest in the project and also to avoid recourse to foreign loans. In 1909, however, the Peking government took the whole program into its own hands, partly because it feared that decentralization was dangerous to the imperial authority and partly because mismanagement and graft in the provinces were eating up the funds. The government's decision made it necessary to borrow from foreign capitalists and offended provincial interests. Investors were angered when they learned that their stock would not be redeemed at face value, and in the fall of 1911 outbreaks of violence occurred. The railroad controversy was only one among many factors which brought anti-dynastic feeling to the point of open rebellion. A bomb explosion in

Hankow, on October 10, touched off a general uprising in the Yangtze valley cities, during which Li Yüan-hung, commander of a rebellious imperial garrison, cast in his lot with the revolutionaries.

The revolutionary elements in China, which moved into the foreground with the impromptu insurrections of 1911, were by no means in agreement as to program or tactics. A number of liberal leaders, headed by K'ang Yu-wei, clung to the ideal of a limited monarchy. They would accept the continuation of the dynasty if it was willing to renounce absolutism and promote progress. A more radical group wished to abolish the monarchy altogether and convert China into a republic. The prime figure among the radicals was Dr. Sun Yat-sen (1866–1925), born of a peasant family near Canton, in the province which had produced the leader of the Taipings and countless other opponents of the Manchu regime. At the invitation and expense of an elder brother, Sun had gone to Hawaii to obtain a Western education and had been converted to Christianity. After returning to China he studied medicine, chiefly with Protestant missionary physicians, and received a medical diploma at Hong Kong. He participated in an abortive revolt against the government in 1895, from which he barely escaped with his life. Thereafter Dr. Sun traveled widely, residing in the United States and visiting both England and Continental Europe. During these years he had studied Western institutions, which he became convinced could be successfully adopted in China, and dedicated his energies to stirring up opposition to the Manchus among Chinese at home and abroad. In China his work was carried forward by a secret "Alliance Society," which attracted various disaffected elements in the period preceding the 1911 outbreak.

Lack of coordination among reformist and revolutionary groups, the distracted and impoverished state of the country, and the persistence of strong sectional loyalties made it impossible for the revolution to follow a clear-cut pattern. Events of the next few years were confused and somewhat paradoxical. Yüan Shih-k'ai, a conservative bureaucrat who had reorganized the army in northern China, was ordered by the Manchu court to suppress the rebellion. Probably because he realized that the dynasty's days were numbered, he avoided decisive engagements with the southern insurgents, even though his army was superior to theirs. The National Assembly at Peking, while demanding immediate constitutional reforms and amnesty for the rebels, at the same time nominated Yüan Shih-k'ai—the Manchu's last hope—as prime minister. There was even more confusion in the south than in the north, although a united front was presented against the imperial government by an assembly at Nanking in which central Chinese and Cantonese cooperated. The Nanking assembly elected as president Dr. Sun, who had only recently arrived in China, and declared for a republic. Instead of puncturing this radical trial balloon with one stroke, Yüan arranged

The revolutionary elements: Dr. Sun Yat-sen

"Father of the Chinese Republic." Dr. Sun Yat-sen and his second wife, Soong Chingling (sister of Mme. Chiang Kai-shek). The widowed Mme. Sun is now a vice-chairman of the People's Republic of China.

931

with the representatives of Nanking a settlement which embodied a compromise between the northern and southern groups. As a concession to the southern (and radical) factions, China was to be designated a republic with Li Yüan-hung as vice-president and with Nanking as the capital. But to promote harmony, Dr. Sun stepped out of the limelight and recommended that Yüan Shih-k'ai, who was supported by the northern armies, be made provisional president of the republic. Although the Manchu emperor was required to abdicate, Yüan secured an extremely generous settlement for the royal family.

Thus, with comparatively little bloodshed or social upheaval and without interference by the great powers, both the Manchu Dynasty and the institution of monarchy had been overthrown. However, these events proved to be only the beginning of China's revolution; and they were a prelude to one of the most severe periods of distress in China's long history. Obviously, any regime that succeeded the Manchus was confronted with the staggering problems of administrative corruption, economic stagnation, and general demoralization which were the fruits of Manchu misrule. Furthermore, the unequal treaties and foreign spheres of interest that had been imposed upon the country made the attainment of a unified modern state doubly difficult. Progress was bound to be slow at best, but the men who attained power during this stage of the revolution seemed more bent on advancing their own interests than those of the country. Yüan Shih-k'ai, who had not the least sympathy with republican principles, maneuvered himself into the position of a dictator. He refused to transfer the seat of government to the south, and when a parliament met at Peking in 1913 to draw up a constitution he intimidated, tricked, and bribed the delegates. Dr. Sun's Alliance Society had reorganized as the Kuomintang ("Chinese Nationalist Party"), and Kuomintang elements were dominant in the parliament which was attempting to prepare a frame of government. The constitution as drafted placed limits on the executive power; but so successful was Yüan in corrupting the members of parliament that they elected him to the presidency. Yüan then contemptuously dissolved the assembly, outlawed the Kuomintang, and promulgated a "Constitutional Compact" of his own devising, retaining himself as president. From 1914 until his death two years later Yüan Shih-k'ai ruled as a military dictator, backed by the northern army which he had organized for the imperial service. The Western governments, whose attitude toward the Chinese revolution had been remarkably apathetic, were on the whole favorably disposed toward Yüan and extended loans to him through an international banking group. The powers were willing to support a "strong man" in China—so long as China herself remained weak. Russian intrigue combined with Mongol nationalist sentiment to secure autonomy for Outer Mongolia; rebellion in Tibet enabled the

*The dictatorship of
Yüan Shih-k'ai*

Yuan Shih-k'ai. Yuan, chosen provisional president of the Republic of China, ruled as dictator from 1912 until his death in 1916.

British to extend their influence in that dependency; and the Japanese were beginning to cast covetous eyes on the Shantung Peninsula.

Although reactionary, Yüan Shih-k'ai's dictatorship at least demonstrated the fact that monarchy was thoroughly discredited in China. When Yüan committed the mistake of trying to perpetuate the power of his family by ascending the Dragon Throne as the founder of a new dynasty, he met with unexpected opposition. The great powers, particularly Japan, disapproved of his scheme, and fresh rebellions broke out in the southern provinces. The sudden death of the frustrated dictator in the summer of 1916 theoretically restored the republic under its "permanent" constitution. But a clique at Peking carried on Yüan's highhanded methods, while various provincial governors and military commanders were rendering themselves independent of any central authority. China, it seemed, had gotten rid of the Manchus only to fall prey to greedy and unprincipled warlords.

2. THE TRANSFORMATION OF JAPAN INTO A MODERN STATE

Japan's policy of isolation, carefully maintained since the early seventeenth century by the Tokugawa Shoguns, was bound to give way when Western nations expanded their trading activities in the Far East. Before the middle of the nineteenth century several attempts, all unsuccessful, had been made by European powers to open Japan to trade. That the United States government finally took the initiative in forcing the issue was due partly to the fact that the British were busily engaged in China. It was also an indication that America's Far Eastern commerce had attained considerable proportions. Since about 1800, United States whaling and clipper ships had passed through Japanese waterways en route to China, and with the rise of steam navigation the need for stations where ships could be refueled and provisioned became more imperative.

When Commodore Perry's "black ships" steamed into Tokyo Bay in July 1853, Perry was under instructions from Washington to secure from the Japanese government the promise of protection for shipwrecked United States seamen, permission for merchant ships to obtain repairs and fuel, and the right to trade. Perry's gunboats were sufficiently impressive to induce the Shogun to give a favorable reply when the Commodore returned to Edo early the following year. However, the significance of the change in Japan's position was not apparent until a United States consul-general, Townsend Harris, after many vicissitudes negotiated a commercial treaty with the Shogun in 1858. Harris had no gunboats to back his arguments, but he skillfully used the object lesson of European aggression in China to convince the Japanese that they would be better off to yield peaceably to American demands. The Harris Treaty provided for the opening of several ports to traders and for the establishment of diplomatic intercourse, placed limitations on the Japanese tariff, and recognized the principle of extraterritoriality. Following the United States lead, other Western powers secured treaties granting them similar privileges, and it seemed that the pattern that was unfolding in China might be duplicated in Japan. But, as events turned out, Japan's reaction to the Western impact produced results almost the opposite of contemporary developments in China. The reason for this contrast is that the Japanese, after recovering from their initial shock, turned enthusiastically to the task of assimilating Western culture and techniques for the purpose of strengthening their state and winning equal recognition among other nations.

The first important effect of the opening of Japan was that it led to the abolition of the Shogunate, making possible a reorganization of the government along modern lines. As will be recalled, the "outer *daimyo*"—especially the heads of the great "western clans" (Choshu, Satsuma, Hizen, and Tosa)—had long been awaiting an opportunity to displace the Tokugawa family from its dominant position. The action of the Shogun in yielding to the Western powers provided just such an opportunity. Before signing the treaties the Shogun had taken the unprecedented step of going to Kyoto to consult the emperor. The clan leaders subsequently demanded that the emperor should be restored to his rightful position as ruler, denounced the Shogun for his weakness in submitting to the foreigners, and raised the cry that the "barbarians" must be expelled. The antiforeignism of the western clan leaders was broken by direct action on the part of the "barbarians." In 1863, after an Englishman had been slain by people of the Satsuma *Daimyo*, British

The abolition of the Shogunate

Commodore Perry's Landing at the Village of Kurihama in Tokyo Bay, July 14, 1853. The Japanese had erected a special building (with conical roofs) to receive the foreigners but also arranged an impressive display of troops (in the background). Perry disembarked with 110 marines (shown flanking the shore), two bands, sailors, and naval officers, while his two frigates kept their guns trained on the beach.

vessels bombarded the Satsuma capital. Duly impressed, the Satsuma leaders immediately voiced the desire to acquire a navy like that of Britain. The feudal lords of Choshu were similarly chastened and reoriented in their thinking in 1864 when British, French, Dutch and United States men-of-war unleashed a joint action upon Shimonoseki. In a remarkably short time the key men of the great feudal estates dropped their attitude of uncompromising hostility to the foreigners, meanwhile becoming more determined than ever to end the outmoded dual system of government.

In 1867 the Shogun was prevailed upon to surrender his prerogatives to the emperor. He had expected to be retained as generalissimo, and when he was ordered to lay down his military command also, he resisted. However, the principal clans, acting in concert and in the name of the emperor, quickly defeated the ex-Shogun's forces and relegated the Tokugawa family not to obscurity but to private station. Upon the abolition of the Shogunate, which had existed for almost 700 years, the imperial residence was moved from Kyoto to Edo, renamed Tokyo ("Eastern Capital"), and the old castle of the Shogun was converted into an imperial palace. This series of events constituted what is known as the Meiji Restoration.

The Meiji Restoration (1867–1868)

It so happened that the Emperor Mutsuhito, a lad of fifteen at the time of the Restoration, proved to be an extremely capable person who helped materially in the task of reorganizing Japanese institutions. The years of his reign, known as the Meiji or "Enlightened" era (1867–1912), witnessed the emergence of Japan as a modern and powerful state. Nevertheless, it would be a mistake to attribute Japan's transformation to the initiative of the emperor. As in previous periods of the country's history, effective leadership was supplied by less exalted figures, who used the throne as a symbol to promote a sentiment of national solidarity and to give the sanction of authority to their program. Quite understandably, the leaders in the political field were recruited chiefly from the ranks of feudal society, although they included some members of the old court nobility. In spite of their aristocratic backgrounds, however, the leaders were quick to perceive the necessity of breaking with the past if genuine progress along Western lines was to be achieved. Some of the western clans voluntarily liquidated feudal institutions within their own jurisdiction, urging others to follow their example, and in 1871 the emperor formally abolished the whole feudal system. The hereditary fiefs reverted to the state and by authority of the emperor were divided into prefectures for administrative purposes; the peasants were made, in theory, free landowners, paying taxes instead of feudal rents. The *daimyo* and their *samurai* retainers were granted pensions (later converted into lump-sum payments) amounting to less than the revenues they had formerly claimed.

The emergence of Japan as a modern state

It may seem strange that a feudal nobility would so readily surrender its privileges. The explanation lies partly in the genuine desire of forward-looking members of the aristocracy to strengthen Japan and partly in the fact that feudal institutions were no longer very profitable and had been largely undermined by the growth of a mercantile economy. Furthermore, able members of the *samurai* class, who had been the real managers of great domains in Tokugawa times, saw the advantages in establishing a regime in which their talents could be more fully utilized and more adequately recognized. This class did in fact supply many of the leading statesmen during Japan's period of transition. Nevertheless, the abolition of feudalism exacted a real sacrifice of the *samurai* as a whole. The *daimyo* received a fairly generous financial settlement and were assigned ranks in a newly created order of nobility. But the *samurai* found themselves deprived of their incomes while, at the same time, the government forbade them to wear any longer the traditional two swords and ordered them to merge into the ranks of the commonalty. Smoldering discontent among the *samurai* broke out into open revolt in 1877, presenting the government with a test of strength which it met with complete success. The newly organized conscript army, composed of peasants with modern weapons, quickly defeated the proud *samurai*, and the rebellion of 1877 proved to be "the last gasp of a fast dying feudal society."

The sweeping political, social, economic, and intellectual changes which took place in Japan during the Meiji era were sufficient to constitute a revolution. However, they were not the result of a mass movement or of any tumultuous upheaval from the bottom of society. The revolution was one directed and carefully controlled from above. The fact that the Tokugawa regime had already unified the country and through its discipline had instilled habits of docility in the population facilitated the work of the Restoration leaders. The majority of the population played only a passive role in the transformation, even though they were profoundly affected by it.

In carrying out their carefully channeled revolution, Japan's leaders made a painstaking study of the institutions of all the major Western nations and copied, with adaptations, what seemed to be the best features of each. In the political sphere, they reached the conclusion that the principles of constitutional monarchy should be introduced. A bold but somewhat ambiguous statement of policy, known as the Emperor's Charter Oath (1868), had hinted at the establishment of a deliberative assembly; but when plans for the drafting of a constitution were announced, it was made clear that any concessions would be in the nature of a gift from the throne rather than in recognition of inherent popular rights. A hand-picked commission drafted a constitution which, promulgated by the emperor in 1889, was patterned somewhat after the model of the German Imperial Constitution of 1871. It provided for a bicameral parliament or Diet, with a House of Peers (including some representatives of the wealthy taxpayers) and a House of Representatives chosen by an electorate of property owners. The Diet was assigned the normal legislative powers, except that its control over finance was limited, and the Constitution included a Bill of Rights. In spite of some liberal features, the conservative character of the new government was unmistakable. So high was the property qualification for voting that only about 1 per cent of the population was enfranchised. The position of the emperor was declared to be inviolable; he retained supreme command of the army and navy, directed foreign affairs, and could veto bills passed by the Diet. Notably lacking was the principle of parliamentary control over the executive; ministers were responsible not to the Diet but to the emperor. Furthermore, although there was a Cabinet of Ministers as well as a Privy Council, both these bodies were created *before* the Constitution went into effect. A peculiarity of the Japanese Cabinet (aside from the fact that it was not responsible to the Diet) was that the Army and Navy ministers could consult with the emperor directly, without the mediation of the Premier.

While the Japanese Constitution incorporated several important features and much of the nomenclature of Western political institutions, the government remained close to Japanese traditions in its spirit and functioning. These traditions (which had more in common with Confucianism than with Western political concepts) included such fundamental ideas as that men are by nature unequal and the inferior person should be subject to the superior, that society is more important than the individual, that government by man

The persistence of ancient traditions

The Opening of the First Japanese Parliament, in November, 1890. From a Japanese engraving. Note the Western-style Diet chamber, lighting, decor, and costumes.

is better than government by law, and that the patriarchal family is the ideal pattern for the state.[4] Political reforms were considered only a means to an end, which was not necessarily to produce the greatest happiness of the greatest number but to promote the efficiency, strength, and prestige of the state. The men who, in consultation with the emperor, introduced the Constitution of 1889 had no notion of relinquishing their command at the instigation of parliamentary cliques or under the pressure of public opinion. The guiding personalities were a fairly large group, numbering perhaps a hundred men, chiefly ex-*daimyo* and ex-*samurai*, who together composed a sort of oligarchy. Young men at the time of the Restoration, they retained their influence throughout the Meiji period and beyond, and eventually were referred to as the "elder statesmen" (*Genro*). Acting quietly behind the scenes, they frequently made important decisions of policy. Fortunately for Japan, these "elder statesmen" were as a whole realistic in outlook, moderate in judgment, and highminded.

Political parties

In spite of the absence of democratic traditions and in spite of the authoritarian character of the Restoration government, the granting of a constitution led, almost from the outset, to a desire for further political reforms. Members of the Diet at least had the right to criticize the ministers, and voices were raised in favor of the extension of parliamentary control over the ministry. Political parties were organized, leading to a struggle in the Diet between the defenders of bureaucratic government and the advocates of the cabinet system. The germination of political parties actually antedated the Constitution. The "Liberal" party, which appeared in 1881, was primarily an outgrowth of an "association for the study of political science" founded several years earlier by Itagaki, a *samurai* of the Tosa clan. In 1882, Count Okuma of the Hizen clan launched his "Progressive" party. These two "radical" aristocrats were doubtless motivated partly by resentment against the fact that their own clans had secured relatively few posts in the bureaucracy, most of which were filled by Choshu or Satsuma men. Nevertheless, the introduction of political parties helped to strengthen the movement for the establishment of representative government.

**Significance of
political parties**

After the Constitution went into effect, the character and the activities of political parties in Japan were peculiar and not entirely healthy. Emphasizing personalities rather than specific programs, parties came and went, fusing into one another, or changing their names in a bewildering fashion. Their effectiveness was lessened by their lack of a broad popular base, by the government's censorship of press and speech, and by the fact that when party spokesmen became too troublesome they could usually be quieted by offering them patronage or admitting them to the lower ranks of the bureau-

[4] For an illuminating discussion of these concepts, see R. K. Reischauer, *Japan: Government-Politics*, Chapter I.

cracy. But, with all their faults, the parties provided opportunities for acquiring political experience and also forced the bureaucrats to explain and defend their policies to the public. The campaign to achieve party government—that is, to make the Cabinet responsible to the Diet—gained considerable headway on the eve of World War I and was resumed vigorously during the 1920's.

Experiments with constitutional government were only one aspect of Japan's political transformation. A modern and efficient military establishment was a prime objective that was rapidly attained, with a navy modeled after Great Britain's and an army copied from that of Germany, largely because the superiority of the latter had been strikingly demonstrated in the Franco-Prussian War. The principle of universal military service, introduced in 1873, was not a Japanese invention (although conscript peasant armies had been known to both China and Japan in ancient times and had played a part in Japan's feudal wars of the sixteenth century), but was based upon the example of modern European states. The administrative system was revised, and new judiciary and legal codes were adopted which compared favorably with those of Western countries and enabled the Japanese to claim successfully that they were not behind the West in the administration of justice. In 1894 Great Britain voluntarily surrendered her extraterritorial rights in Japan, and by 1899 all the other powers had taken the same step. The abrogation of external control over the customs duties required a longer period of negotiation, but tariff autonomy was achieved in 1911. Henceforth Japan was entirely free from the humiliation of "unequal treaties."

The economic changes of the Meiji era were perhaps even more significant than the political. In Tokugawa feudal days Japan was far from being a purely agrarian nation, and before the Restoration of 1867 an urban economy, chiefly mercantile and capitalistic, had come into being. When the new regime undertook to strengthen the state and secure the benefits of Westernization, it launched an ambitious program for the development of industry and a modern system of communications. Because private capital was not available in sufficient quantities to do the job quickly and because of the fear that extensive borrowing from foreign investors would endanger Japan's economic independence, the government assumed the initiative in constructing railroads, telegraph and telephone lines, docks, shipyards, and even manufacturing plants, while it also aided private industry by loans and subsidies. There was no tradition of laissez faire in Japan to stand in the way of government participation in the economic sphere, and public officials were anxious to move ahead as rapidly as possible. However, many enterprises which had been fostered by the state were eventually transferred to private hands, although the state retained control of railways and communications for strategic and security reasons. Hence, in Japan, economic prog-

Militarism and the abolition of foreign privileges

The growth of capitalism

ress led to the growth of a capitalist class, but one which did not correspond exactly with similar classes in the Western industrial nations. The members of the new capitalist class, like the prominent political figures, were drawn largely from the old aristocracy, while not excluding men of bourgeois origin—money-lenders and rice merchants of the Tokugawa era. *Daimyo* now found a profitable field of investment for the funds they had received upon surrendering their feudal privileges, and the more nimble-witted of the *samurai* also participated in industrial development.

Mitsui
and Mitsubishi

The history of the famous house of Mitsui, which grew to be the largest combination of mercantile, financial, and industrial interests in Japan, illustrates the remarkable success of a *samurai* family that was shrewd enough to anticipate future developments. In early Tokugawa times the Mitsui, defying the prejudices of their class, had abandoned fighting in favor of the solider rewards of commerce. They opened a store in Kyoto and in its management apparently anticipated the techniques of modern scientific salesmanship, displaying advertising posters and on rainy days giving away to customers paper umbrellas printed with the Mitsui trademark. Before the close of the seventeenth century, the family had established a banking house in Edo. The Mitsui heartily welcomed the opening of Japan to foreign trade, and so confident were they of the success of the Restoration that they lent large sums of money to the emperor and his entourage while the new government was in the process of formation. The Mitsui family also formed a connection with the great Choshu clan, whose members filled important government posts, and thus were enabled to participate in various aspects of the economic program.[5] The Mitsubishi group of interests,

[5] O. D. Russell, *The House of Mitsui.*

Modern View of Mitsubishi Shipyards. A Greek tanker is under construction.

which was the greatest rival of the Mitsui and, like them, developed under *samurai* leadership, effected a similar connection with the Satsuma clan. In spite of the rapid industrialization of Japan, capitalists were relatively few, and they were generally affiliated with clan bureaucrats who dominated the government.

Industrial developments in Japan in the late nineteenth and early twentieth centuries differed in several respects from the typical pattern of economic change in the West. In the first place, they were so rapid that in one generation the country was producing a surplus of manufactured goods, and foreign markets had become essential to the national economy. Second, the Industrial Revolution was transported to Japan after it had already reached an advanced stage in the Western nations, and consequently characteristics of the First and Second Industrial Revolutions were intermingled. The employment of women in industry at low wages, the lack of organization among the laborers or of legal safeguards to protect them, and the working conditions in factories and mines were parallel to the early stages of the Industrial Revolution in the West. On the other hand, the projection of the government into the business sphere and the appearance of finance capitalism were phenomena that were only beginning to manifest themselves in Western Europe and the United States. To a considerable extent in Japan, finance capitalism preceded industrial capitalism, because there had not been time for financial reserves to accumulate from the savings effected by a gradual mechanization of industry. The wealth of the aristocracy and of merchant and banking houses—essentially unproductive classes—was drawn upon to expedite industrial progress, and the fortunate members of these groups were in a position to dominate the productive enterprises of mining, manufacturing, and distribution as these grew to maturity.

Peculiarities of Japanese capitalism

Another peculiarity of Japan's industrial development was the fact that, while total production increased rapidly and some large plants were built for heavy industries, the majority of the factories remained small. Even in the 1930's, when Japan's industrial laborers numbered six million, almost three-fourths of them worked in small establishments employing fewer than a hundred workers and about one-half of them toiled in plants employing not more than five. The small factories, however, were usually not independent but were controlled by the great financial houses, which resembled trusts in their structure and obtained monopolies of whole fields of production. Workers in the cotton and silk textile mills, for example, might be likened to workers under the domestic system in early modern Europe, even though they tended machines instead of using hand tools. The supplying of raw materials and the distribution and sale of finished products—especially in the export trades—were handled by a few centralized organizations from which a network of controls extended over hundreds of tiny workshops scattered throughout the

The Japanese trusts

Japanese Buddhists Expiate Their Sins. Japanese Buddhists, seen copying sutras in Zojoji Temple in Tokyo, reflect one of the traditional religious means of coping with the stress of modernization.

country. Naturally this system placed the worker at a great disadvantage, and his bargaining position was further weakened by the prevalence of an oversupply of cheap labor. In spite of the growth of huge cities, the larger part of the population remained on the land, which was insufficient in resources to support the peasant families. Hence these families were glad to supplement a meager income by letting some of their members, especially daughters, work in the shops for such wages as they could get. Between the depressed class of small farmers and laborers and the wealthy capitalists, the gulf was as great as that which had separated the upper and lower strata of the old feudal hierarchy.

The Japanese workers

Extensive social and cultural changes also accompanied the transformation of Japan's economic and political institutions. Some of these changes were brought about deliberately by government action; others were unintended or even unwelcome. To carry out a program of Westernization a system of public education was clearly necessary. A Ministry of Education was established in 1871, careful studies were made of the procedures of Western countries, and schools were built rapidly at state expense. Japan was the first Asian nation to introduce compulsory education and did it so successfully that illiteracy almost disappeared, even among the poorest classes of society. There was also notable progress in instructional facilities at the higher level, providing boys with opportunities for technical and professional as well as academic training, and offering separate and more limited instruction for girls. The program was extremely ambitious and the curricula of the middle and higher schools were exacting. The study of Chinese classics and Confucian philosophy was retained, and to these were added—besides Japa-

Social and cultural changes

nese language, literature, and history—Western scientific and technical subjects as well as foreign languages. Notably lacking, however, was the encouragement of original thought. The system was devised to serve the ends of the government and aimed to produce a nation of loyal, efficient, and disciplined conformists. To that end, all students were required to take so-called "morals classes," which stressed patriotism. Western science and technology were appropriated without the liberal and humanistic traditions which had engendered them; and investigation of the social sciences was almost entirely neglected. Thus, the emphasis was not upon the fullest development of the individual but upon enabling him to fit into a firmly fixed pattern of society without questioning it. The Ministry of Education exercised strict surveillance over teachers and texts, making the schools a powerful agency for indoctrination.

The creation of a wide reading public stimulated literary production, some of which was intended for mass circulation. Although Japanese writers were greatly influenced by contemporary Western literature, as reflected in their tendency toward realism, they were by no means mere imitators and produced literary work of great merit. Journalism became a flourishing occupation, and some newspapers of high caliber appeared. The Japanese press, however, labored under disadvantages, the most serious being the arbitrary and often erratic governmental censorship. Editors who dared to criticize officials, or who were merely unlucky enough to publish news which officials desired to keep from the public, were likely to be fined and imprisoned or to have their offices closed. It is significant that a considerable number of journalists, in spite of the risks involved, persisted in giving expression to independent and critical opinion.

In passing successfully through the difficult years of the Restoration period, the Japanese gave abundant evidence of vitality, courage, and versatility. In many fields they had come abreast of the Western nations, while they had also retained their own distinctive cultural heritage. At the same time, the accomplishments were not an unmixed good, and social problems had arisen which could not be easily solved. The most dubious aspect of Japan's condition, in spite of her mounting industrial strength, was in the economic sphere. Scientific knowledge, improved sanitation and medical facilities, and especially the impact of the Industrial Revolution induced a terrific increase in a population that had remained almost stationary for over a century. Between 1867 and 1913, the population grew from about 30 million to more than 50 million, and from this time on the rate of growth was still more rapid. There was hardly enough arable land in Japan to produce food for such large numbers, even under the most efficient methods of cultivation. While a brisk foreign trade could correct the deficiency, not only was a

Literary production

New social problems

sufficient volume of trade difficult to maintain but the profits from manufacturing and commerce were concentrated in the hands of a small group. The standard of living of the farmers—the great majority of the population—remained almost at a standstill while the total national income was rising. With the abolition of feudalism, the peasants had become free landed proprietors, but their economic condition was not greatly improved thereby. Taxation bore far too heavily upon them; they had to compete in a cash market dominated by large landlords and industrialists; and their individual holdings were often insufficient to support a family. Many farmers had to supplement their small plots by renting additional holdings. Tenant farming in place of independent proprietorship became a striking characteristic of Japanese agriculture. The urban laborers were even worse off than the poor farmers; and Japan lacked a strong middle class to redress the balance of society. The revolutions of the Meiji era, unlike their counterparts in the Western world, were not essentially middle-class movements and had not broken the ascendancy of leaders whose ideals and outlook had been shaped in a feudal atmosphere.

Factors
contributing to an
authoritarian
trend

The fundamental attitudes and loyalties of the old Japan passed into the new, even though they wore a somewhat different guise and were associated with more effective implements. It was not difficult for the creed of unswerving loyalty to a feudal superior to be converted into an intense patriotism, for which the emperor served as a symbol of national unity and object of common devotion. Ancient legends and the Shinto cults were refurbished to stimulate patriotic sentiments and to inspire confidence in Japan's unique destiny. As already suggested, an efficient and in many ways progressive educational system was utilized for this same end. The army, also, became an educational agency of a very potent kind. It

Japanese Religious Festival. The participants are dressed in gorgeous costumes of different epochs.

Japanese Agriculture. Left: Transplanting rice in the paddy field early in June. Right: Harvesting rice in a farm village. In the background is Mount Fuji with its eternal snow.

was made up largely of literate but unsophisticated peasants, who found membership in the military establishment more rewarding financially and more gratifying to the ego than a life of grubbing on a tiny farm. The provincialism, prejudices, and legitimate resentments of the peasant rendered him susceptible to indoctrination by fanatics who preached the superiority of Japan over other nations, the infallibility of the divine emperor, and the subordination of civilians to the military. However, the influences promoting an authoritarian or militaristic regime were never unopposed. Continuous and broadening contacts with the outside world and a gradual reaction to the disturbing consequences of rapid economic change introduced a train of liberal thought, which threatened to collide with the forces of conservatism.

Japan's external relations during the Meiji era were directly related to, and appreciably affected by, her internal development. It is not strange that Japan, in the process of becoming a modern state, adopted a policy of imperialism, in view of her agility in assimilating the techniques of Western nations and also in view of the stresses created by the industrialization of the country. As time went on, however, differences of opinion appeared among Japanese statesmen, business and financial leaders, and intellectuals as to the proper course to pursue in advancing the interests of the state. Some bureaucrats were conservative or even reactionary, generally unsympathetic to parliamentary institutions, and inclined to favor an aggressive foreign policy. Others were primarily interested in building up Japan's economic and financial strength, securing for-

Moderates vs. extremists

945

A Gate of the Toshogu Shrine, Nikko National Park. Although the Japanese have adopted Western architectural styles for their public buildings, for religious edifices they retain the native style with its curved roofs and lavish ornamentation.

eign markets by peaceful penetration, and creating a prosperous and stable society at home. While not genuinely democratic, they at least accepted the implications of constitutional government and were anxious to win an honorable position for their country within the family of nations. Fortunately for Japan, the moderate expansionists were fairly successful during this period in holding the militant faction in check, although not without making some concessions to them.

Japanese expansion in Eastern Asia would almost inevitably be at the expense of the decadent Chinese Empire. In 1876, the Japanese government took direct steps to end the isolation of Korea, a "hermit nation" which had been as tightly sealed against outside influences as Japan under the Tokugawa Shogunate. Copying a page from the Western book, the Japanese negotiated a treaty with the Seoul government which accorded them extraterritoriality and other rights, as well as opening Korea to commercial intercourse. The treaty also recognized Korea as an independent state, in total disregard of the fact that the Peking government considered the peninsula a tributary dependency of the Manchu Empire. Actually the Manchu officials had neglected to enforce their claims, and their belated attempt to recover their position by counterintrigue against the Japanese was almost certain to provoke a clash with Japan. Korea, at this time, was an ideal breeding ground for war. In spite of brilliant episodes in its past, the kingdom had degenerated into one of the most backward regions of Asia. The administration was corrupt and predatory, the peasants ignorant and wretched, and conditions in general thoroughly belied the country's poetic name—Chosen ("Land of the Morning Calm"). Japan's interest in Korea was both economic and strategic, the latter because Russia had acquired the Maritime Province on the Pacific coast directly north of the Korean border and had already attempted to intervene in Korea's troubled affairs. After a local rebellion had furnished the excuse for both China and Japan to rush troops into Korea, the Sino-Japanese war was precipitated.

It could be—and has been—argued that, beginning with her swift victory over China in 1895, Japan's policy in Asia was one of territorial aggression. In the treaty of Shimonoseki, Japan required from China not only recognition of Korean independence and the payment of an indemnity but also the cession of Formosa, the Pescadores Islands, and the southern projection of Manchuria—the Liaotung Peninsula. Japan joined in the scramble for concessions in China, acquiring a sphere of interest in Fukien province opposite Formosa. When harassed by the advance of Russian imperialism in Korea, Japan attacked Russia in 1904 and, after defeating her on land and sea, annexed the southern half of Sakhalin Island and obtained economic concessions in Manchuria. These facts, however, are only part of the story, which in its entirety indicates that the Japanese were adept in mastering the object lessons of European diplomacy and power politics. Following the Sino-Japanese war, under pressure from Russia, France, and Germany, Japan had been forced to relinquish her claim to the Liaotung Peninsula, on the

Wars with China and Russia

The Heian Jingu Shrine, Kyoto.

ground that occupation of this region by a foreign power would threaten the safety of the Peking government. Almost immediately afterward, Russia, by a treaty of alliance with China, secured control of the very region she had denied to Japan and converted practically all Manchuria into a Russian sphere of interest. Several attempts on the part of the Japanese government to reach an accommodation with Russia in regard to Korea and Manchuria were frustrated by the recklessness and duplicity of the Tsar's agents. Nevertheless, some influential Japanese considered war with Russia too dangerous an undertaking, and the government would probably not have dared to attack Russia except for the fact that the Anglo-Japanese Alliance of 1902 assured Japan of the friendly backing of the world's greatest naval power. The British welcomed Japan's accession to a position of strength as a means of checking Russian expansion in the Far East. During the Russo-Japanese war, sentiment in both Great Britain and the United States was prevailingly in favor of Japan, largely because of the devious and bullying tactics that the Russians had been pursuing. President Theodore Roosevelt's sympathy for Japan helped in terminating the hostilities, and the peace treaty was negotiated at Portsmouth, New Hampshire.

Japan's victory over Russia seemed for a time to restore a balance of power in the Far East. Russia, shaken by her Revolution of

The Sino-Japanese War. Japanese troops attack Chinese forces defending Pyongyang in Korea, September 15, 1894.

NAVAL SEE-SAW.—LI HUNG CHANG
GETS A JOLT.

JAPANESE NAVY RESCUING COREA FROM THE
CHINESE DRAGON.

*The Sino-Japanese Struggle over Korea, as
seen by a Japanese Cartoonist (1894).*

CHINA AND JAPAN WRESTLING OVER THE MAP OF COREA.

A PAGE OF CARTOONS BY A JAPANESE ARTIST.

1905, and Japan, her financial reserves drained by the war, quickly agreed on apportioning their respective spheres in Manchuria—publicly affirming, of course, that they had no intention of violating China's territorial integrity. But the balance of power proved to be unstable. The outbreak of the European war in 1914, necessitating a "retreat of the West" from Asia, provided Japan with a golden opportunity to consolidate and extend her position.

A temporary balance of power in East Asia

3. AFRICA DURING THE CENTURY OF EUROPEAN IMPERIALIST EXPANSION

By the opening of the nineteenth century, the cause for the abolition of the slave trade was winning a growing number of converts among governing circles in Denmark, England, France, and the United States. Humanitarian abolitionist sentiment was strongest among the Quakers, particularly in Great Britain. And in the economic realm, a growing chorus of British merchants and industrialists questioned mercantilism and championed the doctrines of laissez-faire and free trade. There was an increasing belief among plantation owners that free, paid labor was more efficient than slave labor. At the same time, sons of the Industrial Revolution were convinced that greater profits could be made from trade in tropical raw materials, especially mineral resources, needed to supply European industries. Moreover, British attitudes towards the establishment and maintenance of colonies had become increasingly negative since the fiasco of the American Revolution. In the first decade of the nineteenth century these sentiments prompted the abolition of the slave trade. Denmark took the lead in 1805, followed by Britain in 1807 and the United States shortly afterward. Henceforth, British naval squadrons in West African waters would protect legitimate traders and attempt to suppress the seaborne trade in slaves.

Free trade, abolitionist sentiment grows

949

In West Africa the slave trade had contributed to the growth of autocratic, militaristic institutions in those societies that had profited from it. In some forest states, power had shifted from the elders, priests, and traditional chiefs to kings and their warrior bands. From an economic point of view, the productive capacities of Africans had been severely retarded by the slave trade. Therefore, it was now incumbent upon the Europeans to encourage farming, mining, and legitimate trading, and to stimulate the cultivation of cotton, tobacco, cocoa, and other cash crops which might contribute to an improvement in African living standards while also serving as a resource for European industries. Freed slaves from the ships of illegal slavers would be westernized, Christianized, and returned to the "Dark Continent." Africa was still considered the "white man's graveyard," and humanitarians confidently assumed that repatriated blacks were better equipped to spread the fruits of western civilization to their beknighted brothers in the bush. All these assumptions, while perhaps well-meaning, were deeply rooted in a cultural chauvinism dating back to the heyday of the slave trade. Yet in response to such sentiments, colonies for freed blacks were established by the British in Sierra Leone in 1808, by the Americans in Liberia in 1821, and by the French at Libreville in Gabon in 1849.

Ironically, the outlawing of the slave trade contributed to an inflation in the price of slaves and a consequent growth in volume of the traffic. Furthermore, Eli Whitney's cotton gin, invented in 1795, created new demands for slaves on the plantations of the southern United States. The growth in illicit trade led to more stringent attempts at suppression after 1820. United States participation in the anti-slave-trade naval squadrons propelled American legitimate merchants to Africa's shores in large numbers. Between 1850 and 1862, United States merchants, mainly from Salem, Massachusetts, dominated West African trans-Atlantic commerce. From the mid-1840's the Atlantic slave trade declined steadily, and President Lincoln's Emancipation Proclamation of 1863 nearly brought it to an end.

The slave trade and the concomitant traffic in European arms contributed to the emergence of a new class of African and mulatto merchants in West African seaports. In their societies, power rested on personality and ability, not birth. A few of these merchants became extremely wealthy capitalists.

The Atlantic trade after 1800 triggered unprecedented political and economic expansion in the palm oil-rich Niger Delta. Local chiefs and affluent nonroyal entrepreneurs organized a remarkably democratic House-Canoe institution of governance, which acted as a cooperative trading unit and as an institution of local government. The old hierarchical forest empires of Benin and Oyo, unable to adjust to the challenges of legitimate trade and to the rise of this dynamic merchant class, were gradually eclipsed. Asante and Dahomey, on the other hand, survived by culturally assimilating their slaves and organizing them to perform large-scale labor in Asante gold mines or on expansive plantations in Dahomey.

Former European slaving nations also had to make painful economic readjustments to the termination of the slave trade. After 1843 it was clear to the British that chartered companies lacked the financial resources to maintain the old coastal fortresses and warehouses. Reluctantly, the Crown assumed these responsibilities. The Dutch and the Danes failed to make the adjustment to the changing nature of trade and transferred their coastal installations to the British in 1850 and 1872 respectively. British treaties with African potentates, aimed initially at restricting the slave trade, gave way in the 1830s to treaties calling for the protection of European commercial interests through the establishment of consulates. British consuls would be responsible for ensuring the free flow of goods from the interior to European warehouses in coastal ports. Because the British treasury, bending to popular opinion at home, refused to undertake the costs of maintaining such enclaves, the consuls had to finance them by levying duties. Beginning in the 1860's, ambitious consuls, on their own initiative, did not hesitate to dispatch military expeditions to inland kingdoms to punish chiefs if they hindered the free flow of trade.

Such interference in the affairs of African governments created a vicious cycle of political distintegration. Recalcitrant chiefs, humiliated and intimidated by the superior firepower of European weapons, lost their ability to hold distant provinces together. In Oyo in the 1860's and in Asante after 1874, this condition released centrifugal tendencies and contributed to a breakdown of law, order, and security. Oyo's economy, crippled from the decline of the slave trade, was further weakened by the rise of a coastal trade in palm oil. As inland states, Benin and Oyo found it impossible to compete effectively with African trading houses located among the oil-rich

African and European responses to the abolition of the slave trade

Political disintegration

Middlemen in African Slave Trade. The nineteenth century residence of a mulatto merchant who was active in the slave trade. Elmina, Gold Coast.

estuaries of the Niger Delta. From 1821 to 1893 the Oyo empire in particular was torn first by a breakdown in the constitution, then by a destructive Fulani invasion that left its magnificent capital in ruins, and finally by civil war. By 1865 refugees from the countryside had begun to stream into stockaded villages like Ibadan, which swelled into sprawling cities. The Yoruba became an urbanized people almost overnight, and leadership passed into the hands of professional military men who could offer protection.

Once the British had thrown their weight onto the balance of African rivalries, it became a matter of prestige and commitment for them to remain in Africa. In the Niger Delta in 1854 they exiled the powerful African trader king, Dappa Pepple, for cornering the lucrative palm oil trade to the detriment of British nationals. In 1861 they established a consulate at Lagos, thus opening a hundred-year chapter of direct interference in Nigerian trade and politics. In 1874 they bombarded the capital of Asante in order to punish the king for closing trade routes to the coast. And after 1874 they squelched an experiment by the Fante people in nation-building along Western democratic lines by declaring a "Gold Coast Colony" over their territory. Likewise, ambitious French governors in Senegal had, since 1854, become involved in the internal affairs of inland Moslem states.

British interfer-
ence in Nigerian
trade and politics

Significantly, these militant gestures were usually initiated not by home governments but rather by men in the field—governors, consuls, and sometimes traders. Before 1875, European powers rarely manifested an impulse to territorial empire in Africa. Nor had any of them formulated a coherent or consistent colonial African policy. The tide of public opinion, especially in Great Britain, ran against imperialist ventures, largely because they were so costly. Other than officials and entrepreneurs, those who came to Africa were usually scientists, privately financed and interested in resolving botanical, ethnographic, or geographical questions; or they were missionaries and physicians like David Livingstone, who sought to root out domestic slavery and the slave trade, introduce modern medical practice, and further Christian proselytization.

By 1875 the major geographical mysteries had been solved: the course of the Niger river (1830), the source of the Nile (1862), Mounts Kilimanjaro and Kenya (1848 and 1849, respectively) and the vast river system of the upper Congo Basin (1860's). European explorers had also made direct contact with the major inland empires: Asante (1817), Sokoto Caliphate (1824), Bunyoro (1872). In 1854 quinine proved to be an effective drug for mitigating the effects of the hitherto deadly malaria. European probes into the interior now became more frequent and less costly in human lives. Fear of malaria had previously discouraged the white man from penetrating the tropical rain forest.

Unlike West Africa, East Africa during the first three quarters of the nineteenth century witnessed a dramatic revival of trade, particu-

Indian Financiers in Zanzibar. An Indian merchant's house in Zanzibar.

larly in slaves, cloves, and ivory. By 1800 Africans in what are today Kenya and Tanzania had begun to organize long-distance caravans and trading networks. Previously, items passed haphazardly from community to community before reaching their destination. Criteria for leadership among these small-scale societies now changed from skills in hunting and expertise in rain-making to ability in organizing trade, negotiating business deals, and accumulating European manufactured weapons.

The expansion of East African trade brings social, political, economic reorientations

The Omani Arabs, preoccupied with internal strife in southern Arabia for over a century, were reunited by 1805 and determined to reassert their authority over the East African coastal towns. Under the cunning leadership of Sultan Sayyid Said, Omani hegemony was restored and the capital was transferred from Muscat in Oman to the fertile and picturesque island of Zanzibar, some twenty miles off the East African coast. On Zanzibar, Sultan Said stimulated the growth of a vast plantation economy, built upon the cultivation of cloves and coconuts and worked by African slaves imported from the mainland. Indians were attracted to the island to serve as financial advisers and moneylenders to Arab and Swahili caravan operators.

Sayyid Said and the reassertion of Omani hegemony

Slaves were readily available in the 1840's because of a severe social and demographic upheaval in what are known today as Tanzania, Malawi, and northern Mozambique. Thousands of warrior bands of Ngoni streamed into the region from South Africa. They descended upon the local populations, which had no tradition of fighting and were therefore defenseless. Entire communities were often sold into bondage to Arab, Swahili, and other African slavers.

Ngoni invasions bring social upheaval

East Africa by mid-century had become the world's most important source of ivory and the major area for illicit slaving. Dispossessed captives were forced to carry huge quantities of elephant

953

The East African
ivory and slave
trade

Arab
penetration

Growing British
influence over
the Zanzibar
Sultanate

Zanzibar: spring-
board for mission-
ary activity in
East Africa

and rhinoceros tusks to the coast. The ivory was shipped to Britain and India while the slaves were sold either to Arab plantation owners on Zanzibar, to French planters on the nearby sugar-producing islands of Mauritius and Réunion, or to sheiks in Arabia.

By the 1870's numerous East African individuals and communities had established their own trading networks and armed themselves to protect their economic spheres. The He-he, taking advantage of an unprecedented growth in the European arms traffic after the Franco-Prussian war, became highly organized warriors. Entrepreneurs like Tippu Tip and Mirambo forged their own extensive trading operations and successfully competed with the Arabs for inland resources. However, the Arabs enjoyed the financial backing of Zanzibar as well as commercial connections with Indian and Arabian overseas markets.

In 1843 Arab traders were received at the court of the king of Buganda on the northwest shore of Lake Victoria. Within another decade they extended their operations west of Lakes Victoria and Tanganyika. They were not interested in the propagation of Islam nor in territorial conquest; their sole concern was for trade. And for that reason they often found a warm reception among East African chiefs, who sought arms and imported luxury items in order to boost their own prestige.

While the East African interior sank into a condition of almost complete social disintegration, Sayyid Said continued to build a vast commercial empire in the western Indian Ocean. Nearly every important coastal town from Mombasa in Kenya to the Mozambique border fell under Said's commercial sway. Not since the fifteenth century had the Swahili city-states enjoyed such prosperity. But it was a false wealth, based on exploitation of the interior. Fortunes were made in Zanzibar on slaves, cloves, and ivory; and the economic stability and security provided by Sultan Said attracted sea-farers from Britain, Germany, France, and the United States. While these nations established consulates at Zanzibar, only the British one survived beyond 1850. Indeed, after the opening of the Suez canal in 1869, the western Indian Ocean, particularly Zanzibar, became strategically more important to British interests in India than it had ever been before.

Since 1822, the British had forced on Sultan Said a series of ordinances restricting his slave-trading activities. In return, the British navy would protect the Sultan's legitimate trade and government from foreign interference. Sayyid Said struck an excellent bargain and kept it until his death in 1856, after more than half a century in power. After his demise, the British quickly split his domain into two parts, Muscat and Zanzibar, with separate sultans over each. Henceforth, ambitious British consuls in Zanzibar used the pretense of slave-trade suppression as a cloak for the expansion of their own control over the Sultanate.

In the 1870's Zanzibar became a springboard for European missionary activity on the mainland. British, German, and French missionaries, Catholic and Protestant, followed the trails blazed only decades earlier by the caravan drivers. They found the interior of Tanzania in social and political chaos. The fabric of civilization had been almost totally destroyed. Yet along the western shores of Lake Victoria, the highly centralized kingdom of Buganda had begun to emerge as the most powerful state in East Africa. Its king, or *kabaka*, was both respected and feared by Europeans and Africans alike. Buganda itself had recently passed from a feudal to a bureaucratic stage of development and was in the process of undertaking an imperialistic policy of territorial expansion.

The nineteenth century in South Africa opened with a change of European rule at the Cape from the Dutch East India Company to the British Crown. The Dutch East India Company had established a refreshment station at Table Bay in 1652 for their ships sailing between the Netherlands and Java. By 1750 it had swelled into a large company colony, consisting not only of Dutch settlers and company employees but also of French Huguenots and Germans. Some merged into the indigenous African population to form a distinct racial group called the "Cape Colored." However, the majority of these predominantly Calvinistic settlers remained racially aloof and clung dogmatically to a fundamentalist interpretation of the Bible. Their religion became a justification for racial separation. Far removed from the European Enlightenment and liberal currents, they remained intensely provincial in outlook. The majority were illiterate farmers and cattlemen whose only socially cohesive force was the Dutch Reformed Church and its preachers, or predikants. As strong individualists, these frontiersmen resented the authority of company rule, emanating from distant Cape Town.

In 1795 the British temporarily occupied the Cape to prevent it from falling into the hands of Napoleon's navy. The Netherlands

Buganda. Kausubi tomb and former palace of Buganda's Kabakas, constructed in 1882 of wood posts, grass, and reeds.

had already been overrun by the French and were in no position to assume responsibilities for the nearly bankrupt Dutch East India Company. British occupation became permanent after 1806. Following the Napoleonic wars, Britain enjoyed mastery of the world's major sea lanes. The Cape Colony was thus taken primarily for its strategic importance in relation to India. Table Bay, at the foot of the African continent, offered one of the finest harbors en route to the Orient.

Britain's attempt to Anglicize the Cape Colony met with fierce resistance from the predominantly Dutch settlers. The settlers hated the liberal, cosmopolitan, nonracial attitudes of these newcomers, many of whom were Anglican missionaries. They also resented the substitution of English for Afrikaans as the official language and the introduction of British-staffed circuit courts, with judges who allowed slaves to testify against their masters. In 1834 the institution of slavery was abolished and Africans were henceforth equal to Europeans before the law.

The following year, several thousand Dutch settlers, called Boers, reacted to these ordinances by migrating en masse across the Orange River onto the high grassy plains known as the veld. This "Great Trek" culminated in the establishment of a series of autonomous racist republics. However, the so-called Promised Land had been inhabited by politically segmented but culturally related Bantu societies for nearly six hundred years. Their small, defenseless communities were no match for well armed, determined foreigners. The Boers, however, were not the only group in search of new pastures. Both the savanna people and the Boers had to contend with an expanding Zulu empire moving up from the southern coast. Tragically, the savanna dwellers became caught in this destructive Boer-Zulu vise.

British policy towards the Boers and Bantu had always been one of vacillation. In 1848 the British crushed the new Boer republics, only to restore their independence less than a decade later. Their policy regarding the Bantu swung from noninterference and racial separation to paternalistic cooperation and integration. The only constant elements in their policy were the prevention of Boer access to the sea and the minimization of Bantu-Boer conflicts.

Clashes between Zulu and Boer east of the Orange River brought havoc to the local Sotho, Nguni, and Ndebele populations and forced them to disperse in all directions. Some refugees coalesced and organized centralized kingdoms in parts of what are today Lesotho, Swaziland, Botswana, Zambia, and Rhodesia. Others, like the Nguni, became warriors in self defense against Zulu imperialism and moved northward across the Zambezi River into Tanzania. There these roving bands of Ngoni (as they were called in East Africa) caused the same kind of social disruption that had been inflicted upon them by the Zulu and Boers only decades earlier in their former South African homelands. In 1879, in a gesture of conciliation to the Boers, the British defeated the highly disciplined though ill-equipped Zulu and shattered their proud empire into thirteen weak chieftaincies. The Zulu empire ceased to exist, but Zulu nationalism and culture continued to flourish.

SELECTED READINGS—GENERAL

· *Items so designated are available in paperbound editions.*

Clyde, P. H., and Beers, B. F., *The Far East*, 4th ed., Englewood Cliffs, N.J., 1966.

· Griswold, A. W., *The Far Eastern Policy of the United States*, New York, 1938 (Yale).

Peffer, Nathaniel, *The Far East: A Modern History*, Ann Arbor, 1958.

Romein, Jan, *The Asian Century: A History of Modern Nationalism in Asia*, Berkeley, 1962.

Vinacke, H. M., *A History of the Far East in Modern Times*, 6th ed., New York, 1959.

CHINA (*See also Readings for Chapter 4*)

Bland, J. O. P., and Backhouse, E. T., *China under the Empress Dowager*, Philadelphia, 1910.

Chan, W. T., *Religious Trends in Modern China*, New York, 1953.

Chang Chung-li, *The Chinese Gentry*, Seattle, 1955.

Ch'èn, Jerome, *Yuan Shih-k'ai*, 2nd ed., Stanford, 1972.

· Chesneaux, Jean, *Peasant Revolts in China: 1840–1949*, New York, 1973 (Norton).

Cohen, Paul, *China and Christianity, 1860–1870*, Cambridge, Mass., 1963.

Collis, Maurice, *Foreign Mud*, London, 1964. An account of life among the English merchants at Canton.

· Fairbank, J. K., *The United States and China*, 3rd ed., Cambridge, Mass., 1971 (Compass). Brief but perceptive.

Fleming, Peter, *The Siege at Peking*, New York, 1959. The Boxer uprising and its suppression.

· Franke, Wolfgang, *A Century of Chinese Revolution 1851–1949*, New York, 1971 (Torchbooks).

Gaster, Michael, *Chinese Intellectuals and the Revolution of 1911*, Seattle, 1969.

Hsü, C. Y., *The Rise of Modern China*, New York, 1970. Especially good on the nineteenth century.

· Levenson, J. R., *Confucian China and Its Modern Fate: A Trilogy*, Berkeley, 1968 (California).

· Michael, Franz, *The Taiping Rebellion: History*, Seattle, 1972 (University of Washington).

· Schiffrin, H. Z., *Sun Yat-sen and the Origins of the Chinese Revolution*, Berkeley, 1968 (California).

· Tan, C. C., *The Boxer Catastrophe*, New York, 1955 (Norton Library).

Yeng, S. Y., *The Taiping Rebellion and the Western Powers*, New York, 1971. Comprehensive and informative.

JAPAN (*See also Readings for Chapter 4*)

Akika, George, *Foundations of Constitutional Government in Modern Japan, 1868–1900*, Cambridge, Mass., 1967.

READINGS   Allen, G. C., *A Short Economic History of Modern Japan, 1867–1937*, rev. ed., New York, 1963.

Barr, Pat, *The Coming of the Barbarians: The Opening of Japan to the West, 1853–1870*, New York, 1967.

Beckmann, G. M., *The Making of the Meiji Constitution: The Oligarchs and the Constitutional Development of Japan, 1868–1891*, Lawrence, Kan., 1957.

Borton, Hugh, *Japan's Modern Century*, 2nd ed., New York, 1970.

Brown, D. M., *Nationalism in Japan: An Introductory Historical Analysis*, Berkeley, 1955.

Craig, A. M., *Chōshū in the Meiji Restoration*, Cambridge, Mass., 1961.

Ike Nobutaka, *The Beginnings of Political Democracy in Japan*, Baltimore,

Jansen, M. B., *Sakamoto Ryōma and the Meiji Restoration*, Princeton, 1961. A penetrating study of the conflict and confusion in Japanese politics at the end of the Tokugawa period.

· Lockwood, W. W., *The Economic Development of Japan, 1868–1938*, Princeton, 1954 (Princeton University Press).

Okamoto Shumpei, *The Japanese Oligarchy and the Russo-Japanese War*, New York, 1971.

Reischauer, R. K., *Japan: Government-Politics*, New York, 1939.

Russell, O. D., *The House of Mitsui*, Boston, 1939.

Scalapino, R. A., *Democracy and the Party Movement in Prewar Japan*, Berkeley, 1953.

· Storry, Richard, *A History of Modern Japan*, Baltimore, 1960 (Penguin).

Walworth, Arthur, *Black Ships off Japan*, New York, 1946.

· Webb, H., *An Introduction to Japan*, New York, 1957 (Columbia).

Yanaga Chitoshi, *Japan Since Perry*, New York, 1949.

AFRICA

Boahen, Adu, *Topics in West African History*, New York, 1968.

Curtin, Philip D., *The Image of Africa*, Madison, Wis., 1964.

Davidson, Basil, *The African Slave Trade*, Boston, 1961.

Fage, J. D., *A History of West Africa*, New York, 1969.

Forde, D., and Kaberry, P. M., eds., *West African Kingdoms in the Nineteenth Century*, New York, 1967.

Gailey, H. A., *A History of Africa 1800 to the Present*, New York, 1972.

Ogot, B. A., and Kieran, J. A., eds., *Zamani: A Survey of East African History*, New York, 1969.

Pope-Hennessy, John, *A Study of the Atlantic Slave Traders: Sins of the Fathers*, New York, 1969.

SOURCE MATERIALS

Crowder, M., and Ade Ajayi, J. F., eds., *History of West Africa*, Vol. I.

Curtin, Philip D., ed., *Africa Remembered*.

· de Bary, W. T., ed., *Sources of Chinese Tradition*, Chaps. XXIV, XXV, XXVI (Columbia).

· ——, ed., *Sources of Japanese Tradition*, Chaps. XXIV, XXV (Columbia).

· Michael, Franz, *The Taiping Rebellion: Its Sources, Interpretations, and Influences* (University of Washington).

Emerson, Joyce, tr., *The Lotus Pool*. Autobiographical account of struggle against restrictions of the patriarchal family.

· Teng Ssu-yü, and Fairbank, J. K., *China's Response to the West: A Documentary Survey*, 2 vols. (Atheneum).

The Complete Journal of Townsend Harris.

Waley, Arthur, tr., *The Opium War through Chinese Eyes.*

CHAPTER 32

Intellect and the Arts in the Age of Democracy and Nationalism

> If a single cell, under appropriate conditions, becomes a man in the space of a few years, there can surely be no difficulty in understanding how, under appropriate conditions, a cell may, in the course of untold millions of years, give origin to the human race.
> —Herbert Spencer, *Principles of Biology*

The advancement of learning in the seventeenth and eighteenth centuries is often referred to as *the* Intellectual Revolution. It would be just as accurate to apply this term to the intellectual progress between 1830 and 1914. Never before in so short a time had the mind of man yielded discoveries and provocative ideas in such profusion. And certainly a large proportion of these were quite as revolutionary in their effects as any that had come down from the past. But in several respects the intellectual revolution from 1830 to 1914 was different from that of the seventeenth and eighteenth centuries. The deductive or rationalist tradition was now almost entirely dead, and the decay of rationalism was reflected in a marked decline in the relative importance of philosophy. Indeed, in the new age philosophy was often little more than an echo of science. It was not that the problems of the universe had finally been solved, or that men had lost the ability to think, but rather that the sciences had come to be accepted as the only worthwhile sources of knowledge. To be sure, there were some seekers of wisdom who rebelled against the new tendency; but there were few who had the hardihood to advocate a revival of pure deduction or the viewpoint of the mystic in discovering truth. In other words, the victory of empiricism, or that philosophy which derives its truths from concrete experience rather than from abstract reasoning, was almost complete.

The character of the new intellectual revolution

959

Compared with all preceding epochs, the period from 1830 to 1914 marked the zenith of scientific progress. The attainments of this period were not only more numerous, but they probed more deeply into the hidden mysteries of things. Each of the older branches of science was greatly developed, and a dozen or more new ones were added to the list. The phenomenal scientific progress of this era was the result of various factors. It was due in some measure to the stimulus of the First Industrial Revolution, to the rising standard of living, and to the desire for comfort and pleasure. But to think of modern science as essentially a species of practical knowledge is to misunderstand its import. The contemporary pure physicist or chemist is no more concerned with problems of the workaday world than was St. Thomas Aquinas or Albert the Great. In fact, pure science occupies a position in the modern age somewhat similar to that of Scholasticism in the thirteenth century. It is at once a substitute for logic as a discipline for the mind and an expression of an insatiable desire for the conquest of all knowledge, for an intellectual mastery of the universe.

The nature and causes of the tremendous scientific progress

Although none of the sciences was neglected between 1830 and 1914, it was the biological sciences and medicine which underwent the greatest development. The outstanding achievement in biology was the development of new explanations of the theory of organic evolution. We have seen that this theory was at least as old as Anaximander in the sixth century B.C., and that it was accepted by many of the great minds of antiquity. We have learned also that it was revived in the eighteenth century by the scientists Buffon and Linnaeus. But neither of these men offered much proof or explained how the process of evolution works. The first to develop a systematic hypothesis of organic evolution was the French biologist, Jean Lamarck (1744–1829). The essential principle in Lamarck's hypothesis, published in 1809, is the inheritance of acquired characteristics. He maintained that an animal, subjected to a change in environment, acquires new habits, which in turn are reflected in structural changes. These acquired characteristics of body structure, he believed, are transmissible to the offspring, with the result that after a series of generations a new species of animal is eventually produced. Lamarck's successors found little evidence to confirm this hypothesis, but it dominated biological thought for upwards of fifty years. Though still not absolutely discredited, it is admitted to have no more than a partial validity.

Explanations of organic evolution: the hypothesis of Lamarck

A much more scientific hypothesis of organic evolution was that of Charles Darwin, published in 1859. Darwin was born in 1809, the son of a small-town physician. Though he lived to be seventy-three, he was of frail constitution, and during most of his adult life he seems never to have enjoyed a day of the health of ordinary men. In

Beatrice and Dante, William Blake (1757–1827). This painting is from Blake's series for *The Divine Comedy*. (The Tate Gallery, London)

The Gleaners, Jean François Millet (1814–1875). Sensuous colors and love of natural settings typifies Millet's work. (Louvre)

Above: *The Guitarist*, Édouard Manet (1832–1883). Right: *Émile Zola*, Manet. Though Manet is called the "father of impressionism," he was also a rebel against the traditions of sweetness and artificiality that dominated the XIX cent. He liberated painting, as his friend Zola emancipated literature. (MMA) (Louvre)

Village Girls, Gustave Courbet (1819–1877). One of the first of the realists, Courbet often portrayed life in a bitter and disparaging light. He eschewed imagination and painted only what he saw. (MMA)

The Third-Class Carriage, Honoré Daumier (1808–1879). Though Daumier was noted for his realistic caricatures and satires, his attitude toward common folk was one of sympathy and understanding. (MMA)

accordance with his father's wish, he began the study of medicine at Edinburgh, but soon withdrew and entered Cambridge to prepare for the ministry. Here he gave most of his time to natural history and was graduated only tenth in his class among those not seeking honors. In 1831 he obtained an appointment as naturalist without pay on H.M.S. *Beagle*, which had been chartered for a scientific expedition around the world. The voyage lasted nearly five years and gave Darwin an unparalleled opportunity to become acquainted at first hand with the manifold variations of animal life. He noted the differences between animals inhabiting islands and related species on nearby continents and observed the resemblances between living animals and the fossilized remains of extinct species in the same locality. It was a magnificent preparation for his life's work. Upon returning from the voyage he happened to read Malthus' *Essay on Population* and was struck by the author's contention that throughout the world of nature many more individuals are born than can ever survive, and that consequently the weaker ones must perish in the struggle for food. Finally, after twenty more years of careful and extensive research he issued his *Origin of Species*, which has probably done as much to influence modern thinking as any other single book ever written.

Charles Darwin

Darwin's hypothesis as contained in his *Origin of Species* (1859) is known as the hypothesis of natural selection. This involves the idea that it is nature, or the environment, which selects those variants among the offspring that are to survive and reproduce. Darwin pointed out, first of all, that the parents of every species beget more offspring than can possibly survive. He maintained that, consequently, a struggle takes place among these offspring for food, shelter, warmth, and other conditions necessary for life. In this struggle certain individuals have the advantage because of the factor of *variation*, which means that no two of the offspring are exactly alike. Some are born strong, others weak; some have longer horns or sharper claws than their brothers and sisters or perhaps a body coloration which enables them better to blend with their surroundings and thus to elude their enemies. It is these favored members of the species that win out in the struggle for existence; the others are eliminated generally before they have lived long enough to reproduce. He regarded variation and natural selection as the primary factors in the origin of new species. In other words, he taught that individuals with favorable characteristics would transmit their inherited qualities to their descendants through countless generations, and that successive eliminations of the least fit would eventually produce a new species. Finally, it should be noted that Darwin applied his concept of evolution not only to plant and animal species but also to man. In his second great work, *The Descent of Man* (1871), he attempted to show that the human race originally sprang from some apelike ancestor, long since extinct, but probably a common forebear of the existing anthropoid apes and man.

The Darwinian hypothesis of natural selection

The Darwinian hypothesis was elaborated and improved by several later biologists. About 1890 the German August Weismann (1834–1914) flatly rejected the idea that acquired characteristics could be inherited. He conducted experiments to show that body cells and reproductive cells are entirely distinct, and that there is no way in which changes in the former can effect the latter. He concluded, therefore, that the only qualities transmissible to the offspring are those which have always been present in the germ plasm of the parents. In 1901 the Dutch botanist, Hugo De Vries (1848–1935), published his celebrated mutation hypothesis, based in large part upon laws of heredity discovered by the Austrian monk, Gregor Mendel (1822–1884). De Vries asserted that evolution results not from minor variations, as Darwin has assumed, but from radical differences or mutations, which appear in more or less definite ratio among the offspring. When any of these mutations are favorable to survival in a given environment, the individuals possessing them naturally emerge triumphant in the struggle for existence. Not only do their descendants inherit these qualities, but from time to time new mutants appear, some of which are even better adapted for survival than their parents. Thus in a limited number of generations a new species may be brought into existence. The mutation theory of De Vries corrected one of the chief weaknesses in the Darwinian hypothesis. The variations which Darwin assumed to be the source of evolutionary changes are so small that an incredibly long time would be necessary to produce a new species. De Vries made it possible to conceive of evolution as proceeding by sudden leaps. [1]

Illustrations from Darwin's First Edition of *The Descent of Man.* The drawings were used to point up the similarity between a human embryo (top) and that of a dog (bottom).

Next to the exposition and proof of organic evolution, the most important biological achievement was probably the development of the cell theory. The German biologist Theodor Schwann (1810–1882) pointed out about 1835 that not only plants but animals also are composed of cells, and that all but the simplest of living things grow and mature by the division and multiplication of these tiny structural units. A few years later it was discovered that all cells are composed of essentially the same combination of matter, to which Hugo von Mohl (1805–1872) gave the name *protoplasm*. Another of the important biological achievements of this period was the development of embryology. The father of the modern science of embryology was the German-Russian Karl Ernst von Baer (1792–1876), who, about 1830, set forth his celebrated law of recapitulation. This law, which was subsequently elaborated by Ernst Haeckel (1834–1919), states that during the embryonic period each individual recapitulates or reproduces the various important stages in the life history of the species to which it belongs.

[1] It must be understood that the hypothesis of De Vries is not complete in itself, but is based upon Darwin's main principle of natural selection.

Louis Pasteur at Work in His Laboratory

Embryology was not the only subdivision of biology to be developed during the nineteenth century. About 1865 Louis Pasteur (1822–1895) laid the basis for the science of bacteriology by his epochal attack upon the theory of spontaneous generation. Hitherto it had been commonly supposed that bacteria and other microscopic organisms originated spontaneously from water or from decaying vegetable and animal matter. Pasteur succeeded in convincing the scientific world that all existing forms of life, no matter how small, are reproduced only by living beings. This was his famous law of biogenesis (all known forms of life come from pre-existing life).

Cytology and bacteriology

Even more spectacular than the achievements in biology was the progress in medicine. Following the discovery of vaccination for smallpox by Jenner in 1796, the next great landmark in the development of modern medicine was the introduction of ether as a general anaesthetic. Credit for this achievement was formerly given to William T. G. Morton, a Boston dentist, but it is now known that a Georgia physician, Crawford W. Long, performed the earliest operation with the use of ether in 1842. This discovery not only diminished the anguish of the patient, but enabled the surgeon to take his time and thereby increased the number of successful operations. But still many people died as a consequence of the bungling practice of physicians. Mortality was especially high in obstetrical cases, until methods were discovered of controlling the possibilities of infection. In 1847 the Hungarian physician Ignaz Semmelweiss found out that by washing his hands in antiseptic solutions he could reduce the death rate in obstetrical operations by more than four-

Landmarks of progress in medicine

963

fifths. This discovery was extended to the whole field of surgical practice about 1865 by the Englishman Joseph Lister (1827–1912), who is considered the father of antiseptic surgery. Lister achieved sensational results in preventing infection by cleansing wounds and surgical instruments with carbolic acid and by introducing carbolized catgut for surgical sewings. He was rewarded by the British government with a baronetcy in 1883 and was elevated to the peerage in 1897.

The germ theory of disease

The most significant milestone of medical progress during the second half of the nineteenth century was undoubtedly the germ theory of disease. Certainly few other accomplishments have contributed so much to the conquest of the most deadly maladies which afflict mankind. The germ theory of disease was mainly the work of Louis Pasteur and Robert Koch. Pasteur had been practically certain of the germinal origin of disease ever since he had established his biogenetic law, but he was unable to convince the medical profession. Because he was a chemist, physicians were inclined to be scornful of his work. They admitted the existence of germs, but they regarded them as more probably the results of disease than the cause. The opportunity to prove the validity of the theory came with the spread of an epidemic of anthrax, a disease which was carrying off hundreds of thousands of cattle and sheep in Germany and in France. About 1875 Robert Koch (1843–1910), an obscure country physician of East Prussia, began a series of experiments to prove that anthrax was the result of the tiny rodlike organisms found in the blood of the diseased animals. He inoculated mice with this contaminated blood and noticed that they soon sickened and died. He made cultures of the germs, breeding them on potatoes, and found that the germs alone, when introduced into the bodies of animals, were just as deadly as the blood. Meanwhile Pasteur had also been engaged in researches on anthrax. In 1881 he was challenged by his medical opponents to make a public test on cattle. He divided the animals into two groups. Half of them he inoculated with weakened germs of anthrax, and the remainder he left untreated. A few days later he injected malignant germs into all of the cattle. To the discomfiture of his opponents, every one of the animals that had not been inoculated died, while all of the others survived. The theory that germs were the cause of the disease could no longer be disputed.

The conquest of diseases produced by germs

Once the germ theory was positively established, achievements in medicine multiplied rapidly. The talents of Pasteur and Koch were still by no means exhausted. The former in 1885 evolved a method of treating persons afflicted with hydrophobia, one of the most horrible diseases known to humanity. As a result of this accomplishment, the death rate from a malady hitherto almost always fatal was reduced to less than 1 per cent. In 1882–1883 Koch discovered the bacilli of tuberculosis and of Asiatic cholera. Within a few years the germs of yet other diseases were isolated—of diphtheria, of the bubonic plague, of lockjaw, and of sleeping-sickness. For the prevention and treatment of several of these diseases, antitoxins or serums were developed, the first being the diphtheria antitoxin produced in 1892 by Emil von Behring. About the end of the century effective means of combating malaria and yellow fever were made possible by the discovery that both are spread by particular varieties of mosquitoes. Much advancement was made also in the treatment of syphilis. After the germ had been identified in 1905, August von Wassermann (1866–1925) devised a test for revealing its presence in the human body. In 1910 Paul Ehrlich developed a new drug, known as salvarsan, which proved to be an efficient specific for the disease in its primary and secondary stages. Still later the Austrian pathologist Julius Wagner von Jauregg (1857–1940) found out that a fever temperature induced by malaria or by other means has remarkable effects in alleviating advanced stages of the disease, such as syphilis of the brain or paresis.

Finally, it should be noted that by the outbreak of World War I a beginning had been made in the study of the ductless glands and in the discovery of the vitamins. The first step toward an understanding of the ductless or endocrine glands was taken in 1901 when the Japanese scientist Takamine isolated adrenalin, secreted by the suprarenal glands, and showed that it was useful in regulating the action of the heart. About 1912 it was revealed that the pituitary gland yields a substance vitally necessary for regulating the other glands of the body. These discoveries paved the way for a considerable development of glandular therapy in more recent years, including methods of curing certain forms of idiocy by supplementing the hormone secretion of the thyroid gland. On the eve of World War I it was demonstrated by a British biochemist that a healthful diet requires not merely starches, fats, sugars, and proteins but "accessory factors" found only in particular foods. These factors were soon named vitamins, and research was begun to determine their character. In 1915 an American scientist at Johns Hopkins, E. V. McCollum, proved that there are at least two vitamins: Vitamin A, contained in butter, egg yolks, and fish-liver oils; and Vitamin B, which is found most abundantly in yeast, lean meats, whole cereals, and green vegetables. Later investigations have disclosed the existence of at least twenty of these mysterious substances, all of them essential to growth or repair or to the prevention of disease. The discovery of the vitamins has been especially significant in the conquest of illnesses of malnutrition, such as beriberi, scurvy, and rickets.

The discovery of hormones and vitamins

Achievements in
the physical
sciences

The record of attainment in the physical sciences is somewhat less impressive until practically the final quarter of the nineteenth century. Nevertheless, three achievements stand out in the earlier period. About 1810 the English Quaker schoolmaster, John Dalton, revived the atomic theory of matter and defended it so assiduously that it was soon adopted as a basic premise of scientific thought. In 1847 Hermann von Helmholtz formulated the principle of the conservation of energy, or the first law of thermodynamics. This law states that the total energy in the universe is constant, that it can be changed from one form into another but can neither be created nor destroyed. In 1851 came the second law of thermodynamics, or the law of the dissipation of energy. Explained systematically for the first time by William Thomson (Lord Kelvin), this law maintains that, while the total energy of the universe remains constant, the amount of *useful* energy is being steadily diminished. Few discoveries have been more fruitful in influencing the conclusions of astronomers and also of certain philosophers.

Probably it would be safe to say that the period from about 1870 to 1914 surpassed all others since the age of Copernicus in the number of revolutionary developments in the physical sciences. Indeed, it may be doubted whether there was ever a period when so many time-honored scientific conceptions were seriously challenged or overthrown. First of all, there were some extensive revisions of older theories of light, electricity, and energy. About 1865 Clerk Maxwell (1831–1879) showed that light appears to behave in much the same way as electromagnetic waves. The discovery of the X-ray by Wilhelm von Röntgen in 1895 led scientists to wonder whether similar rays might not be given off spontaneously in nature. This suspicion was confirmed by the discovery of uranium in 1896 and of the much more active element, radium, by Madame Curie two years later. About 1903 the British physicists, Ernest Rutherford and Frederick Soddy, developed their disintegration theory, explaining how various radioactive elements break down to form less complex elements, giving off at the same time emanations of electrical energy. The net result of these several discoveries was the conclusion that light, electricity, the X-ray, and all other forms of energy are essentially the same.

Madame Curie

Revisions of the
conception of
matter

From this conclusion it was a comparatively easy step to fundamental revisions of the conception of matter. As early as 1892 Hendrik Lorentz advanced the contention that matter is not composed of solid, indivisible atoms, but that the atom itself is made up of smaller units of an electrical nature. About 1910 Ernest Rutherford and the Danish scientist Niels Bohr presented a picture of the atom as a kind of miniature solar system, composed of a nucleus containing one or more positively charged *protons* around which revolve a number of negatively charged *electrons*. As we shall see, this conception has been modified in more recent years, but its main implication still stands—that electricity is the fundamental constituent of matter.

The years from 1830 to 1914 were characterized also by an extensive development of the social sciences. Most of these subjects are of comparatively recent origin. Before the nineteenth century nearly all of man's efforts to analyze his social environment were restricted to history, economics, and philosophy. The first of the new social sciences to be developed was sociology, originated by Auguste Comte (1798–1857) and elaborated by Herbert Spencer (1820–1903). Next came the founding of anthropology. Though sometimes defined very broadly as "the science of man," anthropology is more commonly restricted to such matters as man's physical evolution, the study of existing human types, and the investigation of prehistoric cultures and of primitive institutions and customs. About 1870 psychology was broken off from philosophy and cultivated as a separate science. Following its origin in Germany under the guidance of Wilhelm Wundt (1832–1920), it was given a new orientation in the 1890's by the work of the Russian Ivan Pavlov (1849–1936). By experiments with animals Pavlov discovered what is known as the conditioned reflex, a form of behavior in which natural reactions are produced by an artificial stimulus. He showed that if dogs were fed immediately following the ringing of a bell, they would eventually respond to the sound of the bell alone and secrete saliva exactly as if confronted by the sight and smell of the food. This discovery suggested the conclusion that the conditioned reflex is an important element in human behavior and encouraged psychologists to center their attention upon physiological experiment as a key to understanding the mind.

The founding of new social sciences

After the opening of the twentieth century, psychologists divided into a number of conflicting schools. A group of disciples of Pavlov inaugurated a type of physiological psychology known as behaviorism. Behaviorism is an attempt to study the human being as a purely physiological organism—to reduce all human behavior to a series of physical responses. Such concepts as *mind* and *consciousness* are relegated to the scrap heap as vague and meaningless terms. For the behaviorist nothing is important except the reactions of muscles, nerves, glands, and visceral organs. There is no such thing as an independent psychic behavior; all that man does is physical. Thinking is essentially a form of talking to oneself. Every complex emotion and idea is simply a group of physiological responses produced by some stimulus in the environment. Such was the extremely mechanistic interpretation of human actions offered by followers of Pavlov. Subject to a number of modifications, it remains the dominant approach for those who believe that psychology should be as objective a science as physics or chemistry.

New types of psychology: (1) behaviorism

967

Sigmund Freud

Herbert Spencer

The other most important school of psychology to make its appearance after the turn of the century was psychoanalysis, founded by Sigmund Freud (1856–1939), an Austrian physician. Psychoanalysis interprets human behavior mainly in terms of the subconscious or unconscious mind. Freud admitted the existence of the conscious mind, but he avowed that the subconscious is much more important in determining the actions of the individual. He considered man as exclusively an egoistic creature propelled by basic urges of power, self-preservation, and sex. These urges are much too strong to be overcome; but inasmuch as society has branded their unrestrained fulfillment as sinful, they are commonly driven into the subconscious, where they linger indefinitely as suppressed desires. Yet they are seldom completely submerged; they rise to the surface in dreams, or they manifest themselves in lapses of memory, in fears and obsessions, and in various forms of abnormal behavior. Freud believed that most cases of mental and nervous disorders result from violent conflicts between natural instincts and the restraints imposed by an unfortunate environment. His investigations and the theories he evolved from them vitally affected the treatment of mental ailments and exerted a profound influence upon literature and the arts.

2.   THE TWILIGHT OF METAPHYSICS

Most of the philosophic movements in the later decades of the nineteenth century and in the early years of the twentieth were deeply influenced by the progress of science. Characteristic examples are to be found in the evolutionary philosophies of Spencer, Huxley, and Haeckel. The first of this trio, Herbert Spencer (1820–1903), was one of the most influential figures of modern times. Born into a family of English Methodists and Quakers of modest means, he refused the offer of relatives to send him to Cambridge and determined to educate himself and live his own life. He worked for a time as a civil engineer on the London and Birmingham railway. Later he became an assistant editor of the *Economist*, but resigned that position upon inheriting $2500 from an uncle. Despite his humble background, he cared little for wealth or power. Moreover, he was inclined to be indolent, reading but haphazardly and neglecting serious books that failed to arouse his interest. For years his life was ill-planned and his ambitions erratic. He spawned ideas for inventions at every turn and cluttered his notebooks with plans for candle-extinguishers, patent saltcellars, wheel chairs, and other ingenious contraptions. His earliest writings were on political and social problems, the most important of them being his *Social Statics*, published in 1850. Not until he was about forty did he develop a serious interest in philosophy. He completed his three-volume work, *Synthetic Philosophy*, at the age of seventy-six.

The keynote of Spencer's philosophy is his idea of evolution as a universal law. He was deeply impressed by Darwin's *Origin of Species* and enriched the hypothesis of natural selection with a phrase that has clung to it ever since—"the survival of the fittest." He contended that not only species and individuals are subject to evolutionary change, but also planets, solar systems, customs, institutions, and religious and ethical ideas. Everything in the universe completes a cycle of origin, development, decay, and extinction. When the end of the cycle has been reached, the process begins once more and is repeated eternally. Strange as it may seem, Spencer was not a mechanist. He argued that back of the evolutionary process there must be some kind of supernatural Power, and he generally assumed that in the long run evolution is synonymous with progress. But he referred to this Power as the Unknowable and declared that it should be dismissed from scientific consideration. Man's capacity for knowledge is limited to matter and motion, to the facts of sensory experience; these alone should constitute the field of his speculation. As a political philosopher, Spencer was a vigorous champion of individualism. He condemned collectivism as a relic of primitive society, as a feature of the earliest stage of social evolution when individuals had not yet been separated from the undifferentiated mass. He held the state in such great abhorrence that he delivered his manuscripts to his publisher in person rather than entrust them to any such agency of tyranny as the post office.

The other philosophers of the evolutionist tradition accepted a great many of the fundamental suppositions of Spencer's theory. Thomas Henry Huxley (1825–1895) defended the doctrine of evolution, not only with logical arguments but with a convincing array of scientific facts; for he was a brilliant biologist as well as philosopher. A "square-jawed man, greedy of controversy," he gloried in the title, "Darwin's bulldog." His celebrated book, *Man's Place in Nature*, was almost as influential in converting the world to evolutionary principles as the *Origin of Species*. But Huxley had broader interests than merely defending organic evolution. Like Spencer, he proposed to extend the evolutionary concept to all of the great problems that trouble man's dreams. He argued that social institutions and moral ideals, instead of being divinely ordained, are simply products of a biological heritage. "The actions we call sinful are part and parcel of the struggle for existence." [2] While he did not reject the possibility of a supernatural power, he averred that "there is no evidence of the existence of such a being as the God of the theologians." [3] He pronounced Christianity to be "a compound of some of the best and some of the worst elements of Paganism and Judaism, moulded in practice by the innate character of certain people of the

[2] Leonard Huxley, *The Life and Letters of Thomas Henry Huxley*, II, 282.
[3] *Ibid.*, II, 162.

Western World." [4] A large part of his philosophy is embraced in his famous doctrine of *agnosticism*, a word which he invented to express his contempt for the attitude of dogmatic certainty symbolized by the beliefs of the ancient Gnostics. [5] As propounded by Huxley, agnosticism is the doctrine that neither the existence nor the nature of God nor the ultimate character of the universe is knowable. It is not atheism, but simply an affirmation that man does not know and never can know whether a God exists and whether the universe is governed by purpose or is merely a blind machine.

Ernst Haeckel

The most uncompromising of the evolutionist philosophers was Ernst Heinrich Haeckel (1834–1919). Originally a physician in Berlin, he became disgusted with crotchety patients and soon turned to the more congenial occupation of a professor of zoology. He was the first outstanding scientist on the Continent of Europe to subscribe wholeheartedly to Darwinism. At the age of sixty-five he summarized his conclusions in a book which he entitled *The Riddle of the Universe*. The philosophy of Haeckel comprises three main doctrines: atheism, materialism, and mechanism. He would have nothing to do with Huxley's agnosticism or with Spencer's assumption of an Unknowable Power; on the contrary, he dogmatically affirmed that nothing spiritual exists. The universe, he maintained, is composed of matter alone in a process of constant change from one form into another. This process is as automatic as the ebb and flow of the tides. There is no fundamental difference between living and nonliving matter, except that the former is more complex. The first life originated from the spontaneous combination of the essential elements of protoplasm. From these earliest forms of protoplasm all the complex species of the present have gradually evolved through the process of natural selection. Haeckel regarded the mind of man as just as much a product of evolution as his body. The human mind differs only in degree from the minds of the lower animals. Memory, imagination, perception, and thinking are mere functions of matter; psychology should be considered a branch of physiology. Such was the compact philosophy of materialism and determinism which appeared to Haeckel and his followers to be a logical deduction from the new biology.

Friedrich
Nietzsche

The writings of another German—Friedrich Nietzsche—also reveal a decided influence of the idea of evolution. Nietzsche was not a scientist, nor was he interested in the nature of matter or in the problem of truth. He was essentially a romantic poet glorifying the struggle for existence to compensate for his own life of weakness and misery. Born in 1844, the son of a Lutheran minister, he was educated in the classics at Leipzig and Bonn and at the age of twenty-five was made a professor of philology at the University of

---

[4] T. H. Huxley, *Collected Essays*, V, 142.
[5] See p. 77

Basel. Ten years later he was forced to retire on account of ill health. He spent the next decade of his life in agony, wandering from one resort to another in a fruitless quest for relief. If we can believe his own statement, each year was made up of 200 days of pain. In 1888 he lapsed into hopeless insanity, which continued until his death in 1900.

THE TWILIGHT OF
METAPHYSICS

Nietzsche's philosophy is contained in such works as *Thus Spake Zarathustra, A Genealogy of Morals,* and *The Will to Power.* His cardinal idea is the notion that natural selection should be permitted to operate unhindered in the case of human beings as it does with plants and animals. He believed that such a constant weeding out of the unfit would eventually produce a race of supermen—not merely a race of physical giants but men distinguished above all for their moral courage, for their strength of character. Those who should be allowed to perish in the struggle are the moral weaklings, the ineffective and craven ones, who have neither the strength nor the courage to battle nobly for a place in the sun. Before any such process of natural selection could operate, however, religious obstacles would have to be removed. Nietzsche therefore demanded that the moral supremacy of Christianity and Judaism should be overthrown. Both of these religions, he alleged, are Oriental cults glorifying the virtues of slaves and of other downtrodden folk. They exalt into virtues qualities which ought to be considered vices—humility, nonresistance, mortification of the flesh, and pity for the weak and incompetent. The enthronement of these qualities prevents the elimination of the unfit and preserves them to pour their degenerate blood into the veins of the race. Nietzsche admired the ancient Germanic virtues of bravery, strength, loyalty, honor, and cunning. He defined *good* as "all that heightens in man the feeling of power, the desire for power, power itself." *Bad* he characterized as "all that comes from weakness." [6]

Nietzsche's philosophy

Friedrich Nietzsche

Toward the end of the period we are considering, philosophy began to reflect some of the confusion creeping into the sciences. The revolution in physics accomplished by the discoveries regarding the structure of matter caused a number of thinkers to lose confidence in the optimism of Spencer and in the mechanistic universe of Haeckel. Some renounced mechanism and materialism entirely; others embraced attitudes of skepticism and hopelessness or sought refuge in the worship of beauty. Symptomatic of the new trend was a popular American philosophy known as Pragmatism. Founded by Charles Peirce (1839–1914), it was developed in comprehensive form by William James (1842–1910) and John Dewey (1859–1952). Pragmatism takes its name from its central teaching that any idea which meets the pragmatic test—that is, gives practical results—must be accepted as true, provided, of course, it does not conflict

The antimaterialist interlude

[6] Quoted by E. A. Singer, *Modern Thinkers and Present Problems,* p. 204.

with experience. In other words, if a belief in a personal God—or in a multitude of gods—gives mental peace or spiritual satisfaction to any individual, that belief is true for him. The Pragmatists scoffed at all efforts to discover absolute truth or to determine the ultimate nature of reality. They abandoned metaphysics as futile and taught that knowledge should be sought after, not as an end in itself, but as an *instrument* for improving conditions on earth. It should be mentioned also that the Pragmatists rejected all forms of determinism. They denounced interpretations of the universe that reduced man to a slave of some rigid principle or placed him at the mercy of an all-powerful fate.

A much more determined protest against the mechanism and materialism of the nineteenth century came from the New Idealists.

The New Idealism Among the leaders of this school were the Italian Benedetto Croce (1866–1952), the Englishman F. H. Bradley (1846–1924), and the American Josiah Royce (1855–1916). The New Idealism was essentially a compound of the doctrines of Hegel and of Kant. From the former came the tendency to glorify the state and to subordinate the individual to the group; from the latter was derived the idea of parallel truths in religion and science which never conflict because they belong in two separate realms. The New Idealists admitted that the universe revealed by science is a gigantic machine which grinds on relentlessly, and that man is a helpless atom. But this revelation did not trouble them, for they contended that it is only part of the picture. Science is but a feeble instrument which enables us merely to see as in a glass darkly. We have other methods of knowing which enable us to perceive not merely surface appearances but reality. If we make up our minds to follow the deepest convictions of our being, we shall see the universe as a star-domed city of God, ruled by benevolent purpose and replete with hope for bewildered man. Truths such as these gained by intuition are more valid than any discovered by the telescope of the scientist. Thus did the New Idealists manage to preserve their faith in religion and in ultimate perfection against the onslaughts of skeptics and materialists.

Certain other philosophers drew far different conclusions. A group known as the New Realists despised the tendency to seek

The New Realists refuge in faith or in any other form of retreat from reason. They conceded that the evidence from science may not be the complete or final truth; but they argued that it is the only truth substantial enough to be taken as a guide for living. They felt that the divorce of philosophy from science was an unmitigated disaster, and that a large proportion of the world's woes could be traced to the growth of mysticism. Though recognizing that science confronts man with a cold and alien universe, they saw in this no need for clinging to the skirts of faith. Even if man is no more than a bundle of atoms,

whose gift of immortality is merely to mingle with the dust of centuries, this does not prevent him from living nobly and from waging
a good fight to overcome such evils as are within his power. He can
at least preserve his self-respect by striving to direct the forces of
nature to the good of himself and his fellows, by avoiding any action which may be the cause of suffering to others, and by cherishing "the lofty thoughts that ennoble his little day; disdaining the
coward terrors of the slave of Fate, to worship at the shrine that his
own hands have built." [7] Such in particular was the philosophy of
the Englishman Bertrand Russell (1872–1970), later Lord Russell, one
of the most prominent of the New Realists and a leading philosophical writer of the twentieth century.

3. THE TRIUMPH OF REALISM IN LITERATURE

The dominant literary trend in the Western world from about
1830 to 1914 was *realism*. Classicism was now practically defunct.
Romanticism continued as a secondary trend, and even enjoyed a
revival of popularity toward the end of the nineteenth century. In
truth, realism and romanticism had elements in common. Both believed in the affirmation of human freedom, though the realists
emphasized much more than the romanticists the obstacles standing
in the way of that freedom. Both were idealistic, striving for a better world, however they might differ as to the means of attaining
their goals. Literary realism before World War I was distinguished
by a number of extraordinary qualities. First, it was a protest against
sentimentality and emotional extravagance. The realists sought to
portray life in accordance with the hard facts revealed by science
and philosophy. Second, realism was distinguished by an absorbing
interest in psychological and social problems—in analyzing in detail
the conflicting tendencies of human behavior and in depicting the
struggles of individuals to overcome the frustrations of their environment. Finally, it should be noted that realists were quite generally governed by one or another of the popular scientific or philosophic conceptions of their time. Perhaps the majority were
determinists, holding to the view that mortals are the irresponsible
victims of heredity and environment. Others were guided by the
evolutionary concept, interpreting man's nature as made up very
largely of bestial qualities inherited from his animal ancestors. Still
others were swayed by the fervor for social reform and pictured the
inequities of the human scene against a sordid background so as to
point the need for abolishing poverty, for eliminating war, or for
treating those who had broken the laws of society more justly.

The decline of
classicism and
the emergence of
realism

Realism as a distinct literary movement made its initial appearance
in France. Its leading exponents were four great novelists who ex-

[7] Bertrand Russell, "A Free Man's Worship," *Mysticism and Logic,* p. 57.

Honoré de Balzac

Gustave Flaubert

erted an influence far beyond the confines of their native land. First in order of time was Honoré de Balzac (1799–1850). In his stupendous *Human Comedy*, Balzac uncovered with brutal frankness the stupidity, greed, and baseness of men and women, chiefly of the bourgeoisie. He delighted in laying bare the hidden springs of human action and in revealing the rottenness behind the polished exterior of respectable society. An even more precise expression of the realist tradition is to be found in the work of Gustave Flaubert (1821–1880). His foremost novel, *Madame Bovary*, is a cool analysis of human degeneration. It is a study of the tragic conflict between romantic dreams and the dreary realities of ordinary existence. Though the book was condemned as salacious, and its author prosecuted for publishing an immoral work, it has been acclaimed by some critics as one of the greatest novels in modern literature.

Realistic writing of a somewhat different brand flowed from the pen of Émile Zola (1840–1902). Indeed, Zola is sometimes classified as a naturalist rather than a realist, to convey the idea that he was interested in an exact, scientific presentation of the facts of nature without any coloring of personal philosophy. But in actual truth Zola did have a definite philosophic viewpoint. His years of wretched poverty in early life imbued him with a deep sympathy for the common man and with a passion for social justice. Though he portrayed human nature as weak and prone to vice and crime, he was not without hope that a decided improvement might come from the creation of a better society. Many of his novels dealt with such social problems as alcoholism, bad heredity, poverty, and disease. He was an aggressive champion of the Third Republic and toward the end of his life took an active part in exposing the hypocrisy of the Dreyfus affair. The fourth of the great figures in French realism before World War I was Anatole France (1844–1924), who preached a gospel of wise and tolerant cynicism. Though he satirized human folly, he seldom gave vent to righteous wrath. His goddess was Irony, a gentle and kindly deity who "teaches us to laugh at rogues and fools whom, but for her, we might be so weak as to despise and·hate."[8] Yet his tolerance of evil was by no means unlimited. He joined with Zola in a vigorous attack upon the persecutors of Dreyfus and lent his support to many other unpopular causes. In his later years he became so firmly convinced of the injustice of modern society that he allied himself with the socialists. His works included a varied collection of skeptical essays, mischievous short stories, and pungent satires on religion and politics. Among them are *Penguin Island*, *The Revolt of the Angels*, and *The Garden of Epicurus*.

Realist literature in England included the writings of the vast majority of the Victorian novelists and dramatists.[9] Among the first

---

[8] Alfred Allinson (trans.), *The Garden of Epicurus*, p. 94.
[9] The Victorian period is named, of course, from the reign of Queen Victoria (1837–1901).

of the novelists to employ the methods of realism were William Makepeace Thackeray (1811–1863) and Charles Dickens (1812–1870). Thackeray was the novelist of the elegant world of the aristocracy, though he was far from admiring all of its qualities. He delighted in exposing the scandals of people in high places and in ridiculing their foibles. Like most of the early Victorians, he was inclined toward a self-satisfied moralizing on the evils of mankind. As Thackeray was the representative of the upper class, so Dickens was the spokesman for the lower. In such novels as *Oliver Twist*, *Dombey and Son*, and *David Copperfield* he wrote with poignant sympathy of the bitter lot of the poor. He denounced the horrors of the workhouses and scathingly portrayed the delays in the courts and the inhuman treatment of prisoners for debt. Though he was often swept into excesses of sentimentality, his books exerted considerable influence in hastening the progress of social reform.

The writings of Thackeray and Dickens were forerunners of the deeper realism expressed by English novelists toward the end of the Victorian Age. The most renowned of late Victorian realists was undoubtedly Thomas Hardy (1840–1928). In such well-known narratives as *The Return of the Native, Jude the Obscure,* and *Tess of the D'Urbervilles* he expressed his conception that men are the playthings of inexorable fate. The universe is beautiful, he thought, but in no sense friendly, and the struggle of individuals with nature is a pitiable battle against almost impossible odds. If any such being as God exists, He simply watches with indifference while the helpless denizens of the human ant-heap crawl toward suffering and death. It is to be noted that Hardy's attitude was essentially one of pity for his fellow creatures. He regarded man not as a depraved animal but as an atom of dust caught in the wheels of a cosmic machine.

Thackeray and Dickens

Thomas Hardy

The Title Page of *David Copperfield* by Charles Dickens

George Bernard Shaw at His Typewriter

Henrik Ibsen

With the beginning of the twentieth century, realism in English literature took a decidedly different turn. The period from 1900 to 1914 was an era of great progress in social reform and of magnificent dreams for the future. It was natural that this spirit of confidence and hope should be reflected in the leading writings. The first literary genius to sound the clarion call of the new age was George Bernard Shaw (1856–1950). Born in Dublin of Anglo-Irish parents, Shaw betook himself to London at the age of twenty, where he earned his living as a journalist-critic of art and the drama. He soon became interested in socialism and emerged as a leader of the Fabian Society dedicated to the advancement of a modified Marxism. He combined his enthusiasm for socialism with a devotion to materialistic philosophy, an abiding faith in the value of science, and an acid contempt for the artificialities of bourgeois society. By 1900 he had found his true place in literature as the author of realistic dramas. From then on he wrote an amazing number of plays, on subjects ranging from prostitution to socialism and from the Salvation Army to creative evolution. For the most part, his works were not dramas at all in the conventional sense. They were vehicles for the expression of his ideas, in which the plot was completely overshadowed by witty and incisive dialogue. Likewise didactic in tone was the realism of H. G. Wells (1866–1946). The son of a professional cricket player, Wells devoted his early career to teaching science in a private school. As in the case of Shaw, it was a mixture of socialism and faith in the beneficence of science that provided the inspiration for his work as a writer. Most of the novels he published before 1914 depicted scientific utopias, in which toil and poverty would be eliminated by marvelous improvements in technology, while superstition and war would be banished by proper education. His conception of the tragedy of life was not that of a hopeless struggle against nature but the slavery of individuals to outworn institutions and perverted ideals. Among the best-known of his earlier novels are *Tono Bungay, Anne Veronica*, and *The History of Mr. Polly*.

Realism was also a virile movement in many other countries. In Germany it was exemplified in the dramas of Gerhart Hauptmann (1862–1946) and in the first great novel of Thomas Mann (1875–1955). Hauptmann was a social dramatist who chose his main themes from the age-long struggle of the working classes against poverty and ill treatment at the hands of their masters. He also wrote satires and symbolical plays of psychological conflict. The first great novel of Thomas Mann was published in 1903. Entitled *Buddenbrooks*, it relates the story of the rise and decline of a great merchant family of Lübeck. The narrative is presented with the same lingering fondness for significant detail that distinguishes the author's later works.

Doubtless the most eminent of all the realists of Teutonic nationality was Henrik Ibsen (1828–1906). Though born in Norway,

Ibsen was descended from ancestors who were mainly Danish and German. Years of poverty and drudgery in his early life produced a lasting impression upon his mind and left him resentful and bitter. Until the age of twenty-two nearly all of his education had been acquired by assiduous reading. His early dramas were not very favorably received, and while still a young man he decided to abandon his native country. Residing first in Italy and then in Germany, he did not return permanently to Norway until 1891. His writings were characterized most of all by bitter rebellion against the tyranny and ignorance of society. In such plays as *The Wild Duck*, *Hedda Gabbler*, and *An Enemy of the People* he mercilessly satirized the conventions and institutions of respectable life. Along with this scorn for hypocrisy and social tyranny went a profound distrust of majority rule. He despised democracy as the enthronement of unprincipled leaders who would do anything for the sake of votes to perpetuate themselves in power. He makes one of his characters in *An Enemy of the People* say: "A minority may be right—a majority is always wrong."

Notwithstanding the strength of the Puritan tradition in the United States, realism as a literary movement was far from unimportant in that country. Traces of it were to be found as early as the middle of the nineteenth century in the novels of Herman Melville (1819–1891). His masterpiece, *Moby Dick*, combined marvelous descriptions of the wonders and terrors of nature with a profound searching into the mysteries of the universe and of man. But realism scarcely became a dominant force until many years later. Toward the end of the nineteenth century a group of young novelists began writing frankly of political and social abuses, often in such manner as to awaken a desire for reform. Stephen Crane described some of the less romantic aspects of war in his *Red Badge of Courage*. Mark Twain pilloried sham and hypocrisy in a series of novels, the most famous of which was *Adventures of Huckleberry Finn*. The cutthroat speculation of high financiers furnished the theme for Frank Norris's *Octopus*. But the most typical of the realists before 1914 was Theodore Dreiser (1871–1945). His first novel, *Sister Carrie*, was followed by two others of similar type—*Jennie Gerhardt* and *The Genius*. Dreiser's novels were characterized by a rigid determinism that recognized neither purpose in the universe nor meaning in life. But he suffused his writings with a quality of sympathy for his puny figures in their hopeless struggles against the forces of disaster.

Another of the great literatures which came into its own during the age of realism was that of the Russians. However, the boundaries separating particular movements in Russian literature are far from distinct. Several of the great novelists combined their realism with attitudes essentially romantic, others were incorrigible idealists. Among the names that stand out are Ivan Turgeniev (1818–1883),

Realism in American literature

Leo Tolstoi in His Study Dictating to His Secretary

Feodor Dostoievski (1821–1881), and Leo Tolstoi (1828–1910).
Turgeniev, who spent much of his life in France, was the first of the
Russian novelists to become known to western Europe. His chief
work, *Fathers and Sons*, describes in brooding and delicate gloom
the struggle between the older and younger generations. The hero is
a nihilist (a term first used by Turgeniev), who is convinced that
the whole social order has nothing in it worth preserving. Dostoievski was almost as tragic a figure as any he projected in his novels.
Condemned at the age of twenty-eight on a charge of revolutionary
activity, he was exiled to Siberia, where he endured four horrible
years. His later life was harrowed by poverty, by family troubles,
and by epileptic fits. As a novelist, he chose to write of the seamy
side, exploring the anguish of miserable creatures driven to shameful
deeds by their raw, animal emotions and by the intolerable meanness
of their lives. He was a master of psychological analysis, probing
into the motives of distorted minds with an intensity that was almost morbid. At the same time he filled his novels with a broad
sympathy and with a mystic conviction that the soul of man can be
purified only through suffering. His best-known works are *Crime
and Punishment* and *The Brothers Karamazov.*

It is generally conceded that the honor of being Russia's greatest
novelist must be divided between Dostoievski and Tolstoi. As a
communistic anarchist and an earnest champion of the simple life of
the peasant, Tolstoi was somewhat less deterministic than the author
of *Crime and Punishment.* Yet in his *War and Peace*, a majestic epic
of Russian conditions during the period of the Napoleonic invasion,
he expounds the theme that individuals are at the mercy of Fate
when powerful elemental forces are unleashed. His other most celebrated novel, *Anna Karenina*, is a study of the tragedy which lurks
in the pursuit of selfish desire. The hero, Levin, is really Tolstoi
himself, who eventually finds refuge from doubt and from the vani-

ties of worldly existence in a mystic love of humanity. As Tolstoi grew older he became more and more an evangelist preaching a social gospel. In such novels as *The Kreutzer Sonata* and *Resurrection* he condemned most of the institutions of civilized society and called upon men to renounce selfishness and greed, to earn their living by manual toil, and to cultivate the virtues of poverty, meekness, and nonresistance. He set the example by deeding his property to his wife and by adopting the dress and humble fare of the peasant. His last years were devoted mainly to attacks upon such evils as war and capital punishment and to the defense of victims of persecution.

Realism was by no means the only movement to hold the allegiance of the literary world between 1830 and 1914. Romanticism continued to be exceedingly popular, especially in the realm of poetry. Notable among the poets of this age whose attitudes were essentially romantic were Robert Browning (1812–1889) and Alfred Tennyson (1809–1892). Browning is noted for his sense of the dramatic and for his penetrating studies of human character; but, like a true Victorian, he conceived of man as a moral being and the universe as governed by benevolent purpose. His optimism stands out in bold contrast to the fatalism and pessimism of so many of the realists. He understood the baseness of human passions, but he never lost faith in the ultimate triumph of goodness and truth. A poet of much greater fame in his own lifetime was Alfred Tennyson. In 1850 he was made poet laureate, and in 1884 he became Lord Tennyson. His merit, however, consists primarily in his wizardry with words. The majority of his poems are distinguished for their pictures and music rather than for the expression of ideas. His mastery of color and rhythm enabled him to invest the most commonplace thoughts with a power and brilliance that seemed to endow them with lofty and original meaning. Though he tried hard to be a thinker, he seldom did more than reiterate some of the popular ideas of the Victorian Age. He sang the praises of virtue and of patriotism and delved into medieval legends to revive the glories of King Arthur's court. His nearest approach to profundity is *In Memoriam*, written after the death of a beloved friend. It is a series of lyrics in which the author passes from moods of doubt and despair to a final confident hope in "one far-off divine event, To which the whole creation moves."

The surviving influence of romanticism: Browning and Tennyson

The Manuscript Title Page of Tennyson's Translation of *Claudian*

Three other English authors may also be considered as representatives of the romantic tradition. The first two, Thomas Carlyle (1795–1881) and John Ruskin (1819–1900), were essayists and critics; the other, Rudyard Kipling (1865–1936), was a poet and a writer of popular stories. Thomas Carlyle is perhaps best known for his theory that heroic individuals are the makers of history and for his trenchant criticisms of nineteenth-century culture. Industrialism, democracy, materialism, science, and utilitarianism were the objects of his special fury. A victim of chronic dyspepsia, he often appeared

Work by Ford Madox Brown. Brown, a member of the pre-Raphaelite movement, often chose common people as his subjects. Notable exceptions in this grouping are Carlyle and Frederick Dennison Maurice, standing to the right.

The romanticism of Carlyle, Ruskin, and Kipling

to be crabbed and unreasonable. Yet he was not a mere pessimist and faultfinder. He had a keen perception of the real weaknesses of many modern institutions, and he anticipated some contemporary European ideas of the right of the strong to rule. Carlyle and Ruskin had several attributes in common. Both had a tendency to look back to the Middle Ages. Neither had much use for democracy. Ruskin as much as Carlyle detested the factory regime and abhorred the crude materialism of nineteenth-century science. But Ruskin's philosophy was more nearly that of the aesthete and social reformer. He was repelled not only by the poverty and degradation of the industrial system but also by its ugliness. He condemned the ferocious capitalist struggle for profits and urged that workers be treated as partners in industry, entitled to a more generous share of what they produced. The romanticism of Rudyard Kipling was of an altogether different sort. He had no interest in either the social or the artistic implications of the industrial regime. In his poetry he trumpeted the glories of British imperialism, representing the subjugation of Hindus and Africans as a glamorous missionary enterprise to rescue the heathen from darkness. His prose narratives are mainly

stories of adventure, rich in sentimental fondness for the enchant-
ments of India but not very significant from the standpoint of ideas.

4. THE BIRTH OF MODERN ART

From 1830 to about 1860 the leading trend in painting was undoubtedly romanticism. Its most significant expressions were to be
found in the work of the Pre-Raphaelites and of Jean François Millet
(1814–1875). The chief figure in the Pre-Raphaelite movement was
Dante Gabriel Rossetti (1828–1882), an Englishman of Italian ancestry who is better known as a poet than as a painter. Rossetti and
his followers aimed to restore painting to the simplicity, directness,
and naturalism which they believed it to have possessed in the Middle Ages and in the early Renaissance. All of the artificial and decorative tendencies that had appeared since the time of Raphael they
deeply deplored. Repudiating the ideal of pure beauty, they insisted
that art, in order to be worthy of the name, must be directly related
to life; it must be useful, either in ministering to the needs of man or
in conveying intellectual meaning.

A much greater painter than any of the members of the Pre-Raphaelite group was Jean François Millet. Though associated with the
Barbizon school,[10] Millet did not always follow the Barbizon tradition of romantic landscape painting. His paramount interest was in
depicting the struggles of humble toilers against poverty and the
cruel whims of nature. In *The Man with the Hoe* and *The Sower* he
interpreted the bitter life of the peasant in a manner worthy of his

> Romanticism in
> painting: the
> Pre-Raphaelites

> Millet

[10] See p. 786

The Annunciation by
Rossetti

981

realist successors, but in *The Angelus* and in *The Path through the Wheat* he betrayed the romantic fondness for sentimental piety and for intensity of color.

The development of realism in nineteenth-century painting is generally associated with the work of Gustave Courbet (1819–1877) and Honoré Daumier (1808–1879). Both were concerned with presenting the facts of life as they saw them, often in a coarse or satirical fashion. They were rebellious against classical and romantic traditions and intensely conscious of the social significance of art. Profoundly sympathetic toward the lower classes, especially the poor of the cities, they delighted in portraying scenes of squalor and misery and in pillorying the vices and foibles of the comfortable bourgeoisie. Daumier, in particular, was a powerful satirist of social and political evils. He ridiculed the corruption of petty officials, the pompous blundering of lawyers and judges, and the hypocritical piety of the rich. Courbet won great popularity by scornfully refusing the cross of the Legion of Honor offered to him by Napoleon III. Both Courbet and Daumier were zealous champions of the victims of oppression and exploitation, performing a function in art somewhat similar to that of Dickens and Zola in literature. Of course, not all of their painting took the form of social indictment. Much of it was mild and sympathetic portrayal of homely scenes from the lives of the poor. Whatever the subject, they strove to present it without the sentimental embellishments of the romantic schools.

The first completely original movement in nineteenth-century painting was *impressionism*. In a sense, the impressionist was a realist, for he was determined to paint only what he saw, and he was vitally interested in the scientific interpretation of nature. But his technique was different from that of the older realists. He did not depict scenes from the world around him as they would appear after careful study or thoughtful analysis. On the contrary, he sought to present the immediate impressions of his senses, leaving it to the mind of the observer to fill in additional details. This often resulted in a type of work appearing at first glance to be nonnaturalistic. Figures were commonly distorted; a few significant details were made to represent an entire object; and dabs of primary color were placed side by side without a trace of blending. Convinced that light is the principal factor in determining the appearance of objects, the impressionists fled from the studio to the woods and fields in an attempt to capture the fleeting alterations of a natural scene with each transitory shift of sunlight and shadow. From science they had learned that light is composed of a fusion of primary colors visible in the spectrum. Accordingly, they decided to use these colors almost exclusively. They chose, for example, to achieve the effect of the green in nature by placing daubs of pure blue and yellow side by side, allowing the eye to mix them. Some of their paintings appear at close view to be nothing but splotches of color, but if studied from across the room, they gradually reduce themselves to a natural design, in which mountains, trees, houses, and the like are more or less clearly discernible.

Like so many of the other artistic movements of modern times, impressionism originated in France. It was founded about 1870 by Édouard Manet (1832–1883), who had been deeply affected by a study of the old Spanish masters, especially Velásquez. Probably the greatest of the impressionists were Claude Monet (1840–1926) and Auguste Renoir (1841–1919). Monet was perhaps the leading exponent of the new mode of interpreting landscapes. His paintings have no structure or design in the conventional sense; they do not depict, but subtly suggest, the outlines of cliffs, trees, mountains, and fields. Intensely interested in the problem of light, he would go out at sunrise with an armful of canvases in order to paint the same subject in a dozen momentary appearances. It has been said of one of his masterpieces that "light is the only important person in the picture." The work of Renoir exhibited a greater variety than that of any of his compeers. His subjects include not only landscapes but portraits and scenes from contemporary life. He is famous most of all for his pink and ivory nudes, done in a manner reminiscent of Titian or Rubens. Renoir made use of the familiar device of spots of sunlight for the purpose of bringing certain parts of a picture into high relief, but he presented his subjects with much more solidity of form than did the other members of his group. To this day he is the most popular of the impressionists.

The impressionist painters

See color plates at page 1056

For upwards of twenty years impressionism flourished as the dominant style of painting in nearly all countries of the Western world. But in the 1890's it yielded its popularity to a new movement, which is called for want of a better name *postimpressionism*. The postimpressionists criticized the formlessness and lack of volume of their predecessors. They contended that the figures of the painter's art should be as solidly and completely molded as statues. They objected also to the impressionist's preoccupation with the casual and momentary aspects of nature, and they deplored his indifference to ideas. The expression of meaning, they argued, should be the fundamental purpose of art; form and method are not ends in themselves but are important only insofar as they contribute to the expression of meaning. Postimpressionism was not only a reaction against impressionism, but in its ultimate tendencies, at least, it was a revolt against all of the hidebound formulas of the past. It was an expression of the chaos and increasing complexity of the machine age. It symbolized the restlessness and bewilderment that accompanied the emergence of a new society during the closing years of the nineteenth century. It was the beginning of nearly all that we now understand by *modern* art.

Postimpressionism

The artist who laid the foundations of postimpressionism was Paul Cézanne (1839–1906), now recognized as one of the greatest painters who ever lived. A native of southern France, Cézanne wandered through the world of art as in a dream. Ever hopeful of reaching some higher goal of achievement, he cared little for the works he had finished. His son cut out the windows of some of his masterpieces for amusement, and his servant used others to clean the stove. Cézanne viewed these disasters quite calmly, for he was convinced that he would produce much better work in the future. His aim as a painter was to represent nature in such a way that objects on a flat canvas would appear to have the roundness and depth of sculpture. To accomplish this he practiced mild distortion, applied paint in thick layers, and modeled his figures with meticulous care. So well did he succeed that it has been said that since Cézanne there is no longer any excuse for sculpture.

Gauguin and
Van Gogh

The influence of Cézanne was reinforced and extended by two other great artists of the postimpressionist manner. One was the half-Peruvian Frenchman Paul Gauguin (1848–1903), and the other was the Dutchman Vincent Van Gogh (1853–1890). Both were revolutionary in their methods. Gauguin threw off all the restraints of conventional painting. Declaring that the artist should not be the slave either of nature or of the past, he introduced into his work an exotic symbolism and the most startling adaptations of color. His cardinal purpose was to emotionalize nature, to portray the world in accordance with his own subjective feelings. Gauguin is important also as a symbol of the disillusionment which spread through intellectual and artistic circles toward the end of the nineteenth century.

See color
plates at pages
1024, 1056

Dismayed by the complexity and artificiality of civilization, he fled to the South Sea islands and spent the last decade of his life painting the hot and luscious colors of an unspoiled, primitive society. He was the forerunner of an extensive primitivist movement in twentieth-century art. For a time Gauguin was a friend of the Netherlands painter Van Gogh, but the friendship abruptly ceased when he awoke one night to find the Dutchman advancing upon him with a knife. Van Gogh was unquestionably demented; he cut off one of his ears and carried it to a woman who had offended him, and he finally took his own life. Yet there can be no denying his genius. In order to express the intensity of his feelings, he worked with feverish haste, applying directly to his canvas little worms of violent color which he squeezed from his tubes of paint. Van Gogh has been the chief inspiration for nearly all those modern painters who see in the expression of subjective ideas the exclusive function of art.

paint. Van Gogh has been the chief inspiration for nearly all those modern painters who see in the expression of subjective ideas the exclusive function of art.

In the years between 1900 and World War I modern art underwent still further revolutionary development. First, Henri Matisse (1869–1954) greatly extended Cézanne's use of distortion and gradually evolved a type of painting that definitely repudiated fixed ideas of aesthetic merit. This tendency was carried much farther by

Nude Descending a Staircase. This painting by Marcel Duchamp was first displayed at the Armory Show in New York in 1911. The cubist-surrealist style was roundly criticized at the time.

Pablo Picasso (born 1881), a Catalan Spaniard who came to Paris in 1903 and developed *cubism*, a style that takes its name from the attempt to resolve each figure or object into its underlying geometric elements. It is based upon a doctrine once casually enunciated by Cézanne that the fundamental ideas of form could best be expressed through such shapes as cubes, cones, and cylinders. Picasso took this doctrine literally. But cubism is much more than this. It involves not only distortion but in some cases actual dismemberment. The artist may separate the various parts of a figure and rearrange them in other than their natural pattern. The purpose is partly to symbolize the chaos of modern life but also to express defiance of traditional notions of form—to repudiate the conception of art as mere prettiness. In the opinion of leading authorities cubism represented the real break with nineteenth-century art. Its influence extended beyond painting to sculpture, literature, and music.

Another of the main offshoots of postimpressionism that made its appearance before World War I was *futurism*. The spiritual father of futurism was a poet, F. T. Marinetti, who later took an active part in launching Italian Fascism. In 1910 Marinetti and a group of disciples issued a stirring manifesto calling for relentless war against the aesthetic ideals of the past. They condemned the worship of old masters, the slavish devotion to Roman ruins and to the art of the

Cubism

See color plates at page 1057

Futurism

985

Renaissance, "the erotic obsession," "purism," sentimentality, quietism, and nature-worship. As painters the futurists aspired to glorify the machine and the achievements of modern science. They regarded it as imbecilic that an artist surrounded by the wonders of the modern scientific age should spend his time mooning over pastoral landscapes or attempting to recapture the beauty of classical mythology. Taking their cue from the discovery in physics that the ultimate fact of nature is energy, they insisted that *movement* should be the principal theme of art. Accordingly, they proceeded to break up form in such a manner as to produce the illusion of shimmering and vibration. They loved to depict the motion of a racing animal, the speed of an automobile, or the power and beauty of some complicated machine in a factory. Futurism has exerted a decided influence, especially upon the interior decoration of modern skyscrapers, railroad stations, and government buildings.

Sculpture in the age of democracy and nationalism

Although sculpture flourished in abundance during the age of democracy and nationalism, there was comparatively little that could be considered significant. Most of it was an imitation of the baroque—grandiose, heavy, and exuberantly decorative. It was developed largely for patriotic purposes, to embellish monuments celebrating national greatness. But in the later years of the nineteenth century there was at least one sculptor whose work stands out as original. He was the Frenchman Auguste Rodin (1840–1917), and his achievements have been compared not unfavorably to those of Michelangelo, by whom he was strongly influenced. Rodin was preeminently a realist, but he also reflected the currents of romanticism and impressionism. He was interested in psychological analysis and in man's animal origins and his struggle against the forces of nature. His most elaborate work was *The Gate of Hell*, inspired by Dante's *Inferno*. It is a tragedy depicting the sufferings of the great mass of mankind, damned by the passions of their animal natures. Rodin is perhaps even better known for his statue, *The Thinker*, which suggests the evolution of man from lower species. Soon after the dawn of the twentieth century, sculpture began to exemplify certain traits of postimpressionist painting. It grew more and more abstract and distorted, indicating the strength of the revolt against prettiness and sentimentality.

Architecture

As in sculpture, so in architecture the influence of the past was exceedingly strong. Until nearly the end of the nineteenth century the builder's art continued to be governed by classical and medieval principles. In general, it was the classical that predominated, exemplified especially by the survival of the ponderous and ornate baroque. Monuments of this style included the National Opera in Paris

The Gate of Hell by Rodin. Incorporated in this composite sculpture are many of the artist's other figures. Prominent is *The Thinker*, top center.

The Carson Pirie Scott Building. Designed by Louis Sullivan and constructed in Chicago, it typified the purity of design resulting from the "form follows function" philosophy.

and the Reichstag building and Protestant cathedral in Berlin. Accompanying this development of the baroque, there was a vigorous revival of the Gothic. The renewal of interest in Gothic architecture was a product of the romantic tendency to glorify everything medieval. Just as old legends of knights in armor had been refurbished by poets, so there had to be a return to the building style of the thirteenth century. Consequently Gothic was adopted on a generous scale for churches, universities, and even for some parliament and office buildings.

Between 1880 and 1890 certain architects in Europe and America awoke to the fact that the prevailing styles of building construction were far out of harmony with the facts of modern civilization. The result was the launching of a new architectural movement known as *functionalism*. Its chief pioneers were Otto Wagner (1841–1918) in Germany and Louis Sullivan (1856–1924) and Frank Lloyd Wright (1869–1959) in the United States. The basic principle of functionalism is the idea that the appearance of a building shall proclaim its actual use and purpose. There must be no addition of friezes, columns, tracery, or battlements merely because some people consider such ornaments beautiful. True beauty consists in sincerity, in an honest adaptation of materials to the purpose they are intended to serve. Functionalism also includes the idea that architecture shall express either directly or symbolically the distinguishing features of contemporary culture. Ornamentation must therefore be restricted to such elements as will reflect the age of science and the

Development of functional architecture

988

machine. Modern man does not believe in the Greek ideas of harmony, balance, and restraint or in the medieval virtues of piety and chivalry, but in power, efficiency, speed, and comfort. These are the ideals which should find a place in his art.

There would seem to be little doubt that the functional style of building construction is one of the most significant architectural developments since the Renaissance. Among all of the styles which have been adopted during the last 300 years, it is the only one that is really original. Known also as *modern* architecture or the *international* style, it is the best approach that has yet been made to an efficient use of the tremendous mechanical and scientific resources of the contemporary world. It permits an honest application of new materials—chromium, glass, steel, concrete—and tempts the builder's ingenuity in devising others. Though many people dislike its stark simplicity and its angular, cubist lines, functional architecture has undoubtedly won an established place for the future. It has been adopted for countless new apartment houses, hotels, office buildings, stores, and factories not only in the United States but also in nearly every other civilized nation of the world.

The significance of functional architecture

5. MUSIC IN THE AGE OF DEMOCRACY AND NATIONALISM

Romanticism did not die out in music nearly so early as it did in literature and in the other arts. It was at its height during the middle of the nineteenth century, and it has continued as an important tendency far into the twentieth. Many of the changes in musical expression and ideals in the later nineteenth century are comparable to the trends in literature and the fine arts, but exact parallels can be drawn only with difficulty. For example, although realism asserted itself, it could not be pushed to extremes in an art which is essentially neither descriptive nor pictorial. So productive was this period

Romanticism in music

Taliesin East by Frank Lloyd Wright (1911-1925). A famous example of functional style with the pattern of the house conforming to the natural surroundings.

Schumann and
Mendelssohn

that space will permit discussion of only its most salient features and its most eminent composers.

Romanticism was emphasized in the work of the two contemporary German composers and friends, Robert Schumann (1810–1856) and Felix Mendelssohn (1809–1847). Schumann excelled in songs and in chamber and piano music, though he also composed symphonies. While he was one of the most romantic of composers, he was at the same time one of the most intellectual. As an editor and writer he urged the development of musical scholarship and an appreciation of the history of musical achievement. Among his services was the publicizing of the neglected wealth in the songs of Schubert. The insanity which darkened the last two years of Schumann's life was particularly tragic in view of the fineness of his character and influence. Felix Mendelssohn was the grandson of the Jewish philosopher, Moses Mendelssohn. Not the least among his gifts, as in the case of Schumann, were those of his personality. Mendelssohn was at home in all forms of music except opera, and all of it is informed by a classicist elegance and remarkable knowledge of the craft of composition. Mendelssohn's piano music, found too sentimental a generation or two ago, has regained a measure of esteem. His chamber music is the best of the age between Schubert and Brahms. Two of his symphonies and the violin concerto are played everywhere, as is his fine oratorio *Elijah*. The incidental music composed to Shakespeare's *A Midsummer Night's Dream* is unique in that literature.

Franz Liszt (1811–1886) spent his long life moving his place of residence from Paris, to Weimar, to Budapest, to Rome, the model of the modern international musical personality. He early distinguished himself as a concert pianist, and is commonly regarded as the greatest performer upon that instrument who ever lived. Later he turned intensively to composition, with results which were dazzling if not often of lasting import. Schumann and Mendelssohn had cultivated romanticism with restraint; Chopin brought it to the border of sentimentality; Liszt was the first of the romantic realists whose music could be bombastic and sensational but was always highly original. His flair for exotic effects is most successfully revealed in his treatment of native Hungarian themes. Liszt was acquainted with many French literary figures and showed considerable interest in the revolutionary currents of his day. His chief influence derives from his piano playing and teaching, orchestral conducting, and philanthropic activities on behalf of needy musicians. His kindly assistance to Wagner when the latter was being hounded out of Germany was an incalculable service.

Richard Wagner (1813–1883), the outstanding musical figure of the later nineteenth century, was a thoroughgoing revolutionary in the world of art. His initial interest was in the drama, and when he

Richard Wagner

turned to music it was primarily for its dramatic possibilities. His musical training came comparatively late and was largely self-administered, but was nonetheless remarkable. In his operas—which he preferred to call music-dramas—he applied a technique of blending together action, words, music, and scenic effects; his ideal was really a fusion of all the arts into an integrated whole. The result was something different from the conventional opera. Wagner dispensed with the arbitrary division of acts into scenes and discarded all artificial trappings; he took wide liberties with harmony and departed from stereotyped melodic patterns. He sought for a continuous flow of music, not subject to the tyranny of form but sensitive to every demand of expression. In several ways his operas, especially the later glorifying a cult of brutality and egoism. There is no other instance in the history of music where a man's political and aesthetic ideas as well as his music exerted such pervasive influence on generations of musicians. Wagner's operatic ideals became binding—even in France. His harmonies and his magical orchestra enslaved practically every musician, and it was with difficulty that composers were able to liberate themselves from his overwhelming personality even in. the earlier part of our century.

Such a pervasive force as nationalism could not help making its imprint upon music. In most European countries and even in the United States, folk music came under the scrutiny of scholars or found its way into the compositions of the learned. Many composers were fervent patriots. The early operas of Verdi (d. 1901), dedicated to the cause of Italian liberation, were sufficiently inflammatory to arouse the ire of the Austrian authorities. But Verdi, who lifted the opera to new artistic heights, was no narrow patriot. He drew his mature inspiration from a wide variety of sources, including the plays of Shakespeare. Nationalism is typified in the Bohemians Smetana (d. 1884) and Dvořák (d. 1904) and in the Norwegian Grieg (d. 1907). However, most of the devotees of national music did not deviate widely from accepted idioms of expression, but added their bit to the common European store. César Franck (d. 1890), a Belgian by birth and the founder of a modern French school of composers, is distinguished by a quality of otherworldly mysticism. The Finn, Jean Sibelius (1865–1957), although celebrating national sentiments in his tone poem *Finlandia*, displays in his seven symphonies capacities too universal to classify him as a mere nationalist.

One of the most remarkable of the national schools of music to appear was the Russian. Throughout the greater part of the nineteenth century Russian musicians had been content to follow the lead of the Italians, French, and Germans. Even such a brilliant composer as Tchaikovsky (1840–1893) introduced no real innovations. However, fresh paths were opened up by Borodin, Moussorg-

The revolutionary achievements of Wagner

Nationalism in music

Tchaikovsky

INTELLECT AND THE ARTS
IN THE AGE OF
DEMOCRACY AND
NATIONALISM

The Russian
school

The classicism of
Brahms and
Richard Strauss

sky, and Rimsky-Korsakov, the last of whom lived into the twentieth century. With the exception of Tchaikovsky, none was trained as a professional musician, a fact which makes their achievement all the more impressive. While they did not throw overboard the familiar European scales and harmony, they brought to composition a fresh point of view, an indifference to orthodoxy, and an enthusiastic appreciation of Slavic folk songs and dances. These qualities won a place for Russia in the very front rank of modern music.

Soon after the close of the last century several divergent tendencies had begun to assert themselves, indicating dissatisfaction with old forms which characterized all the arts. Some of these trends constituted new departures and others a return to the ideals of the past. The flowering of romanticism did not mean that the classical tradition had withered away. A classicist line runs through the romantic age to the end of the century, its most distinguished representative being Johannes Brahms (1833–1897). Though palpably a romantic, Brahms shows a discipline of mind and an understanding for the principles that actuated the old masters. These qualities, as well as his devotion to the symphonic style, made him the successor of Beethoven. Although Richard Strauss (1864–1949) began as a Wagnerian, his fondness for experiment soon became evident and was given free rein, first in his skillfully orchestrated symphonic poems and then in his music-dramas. The latter, in spite of resemblances, are essentially different from the operas of Wagner. While Wagner was romanticism incarnate, Strauss was a realist who summoned all the resources of the modern orchestra to convert music into a pictorial medium capable of evoking concrete and often commonplace images in the listener. Not content with stimulating intangible emotions, as the romanticists had done, he undertook to paint meticulous pictures, asserting that it should be quite possible to depict even a teaspoon by means of musical sounds. The content of his determined realism ranges all the way from the bleating of sheep and the whirring of windmills in *Don Quixote* to abstract philosophic ideas in *Thus Spake Zarathustra* (based on a text of Nietzsche's).

Another manifestation, perhaps of more enduring significance than Strauss's realism, was impressionism, created by the French composer, Claude Debussy (1862–1918). Like the impressionist painters, Debussy abandoned rigidity of design and intellectuality in the attempt to translate into tone the ecstasy or pathos of a particular mood or moment. Also like the impressionists of the brush he moved freely from one tone color to another without blending. Debussy was probably at his best when he applied his sensitive imagination directly to evoking the imagery implicit in the expanse of the sea, the play of moonlight, or the amorous reverie of a faun on a midsummer afternoon. Rejecting precise form and abstract beauty as artistic imperatives, he sought satisfaction not in the realism of life but in a fantastic world of dreams and shadows.

Claude Debussy

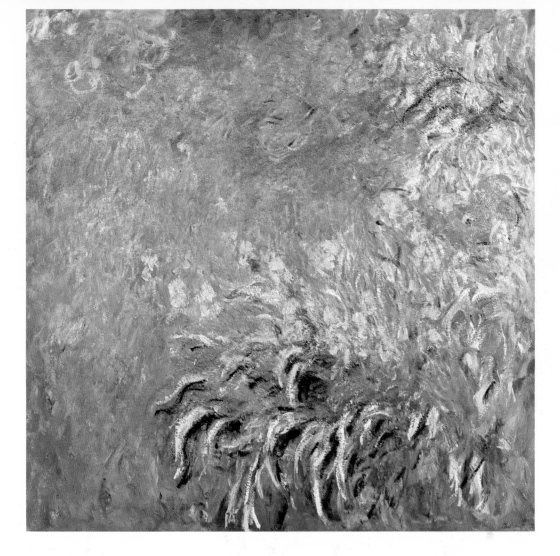

Above: *Iris beside a Pond*, Claude Monet (1840–1926). Monet called some of his paintings Impressions, and the name soon came to designate a school. (The Art Institute of Chicago) Right: *Pink and Green*, Edgar Degas (1834–1917). Degas was an impressionist to the extent of his interest in fleeting motion. But as an admirer of the classicist Ingres, he emphasized line and careful composition. (MMA)

Still Life, Cézanne. It has been said that when the impressionists painted a haystack, there was light, but there was no haystack. When Cézanne painted an apple, there was the play of light; there was also the apple. (MMA)

Montagne Sainte-Victoire with Aqueduct, Paul Cézanne (1839–1906). This landscape has been a source of inspiration for many of the tendencies of so-called "modern" art. The composition is as structurally balanced and proportioned as a Greek temple. (MMA)

The Card Players, Cézanne. Here are exemplified Cézanne's skill in composition, his discriminating sense of color, and the sculptured qualities of solidity and depth he gave to his figures. (Stephen C. Clark)

The Japanese Divan, Henri de Toulouse-Lautrec (1864–1901). Toulouse-Lautrec found his chief source of inspiration in the night life of Paris. *Divan Japonais* was a noted Paris café. (MMA)

· *Items so designated are available in paperbound editions.*

PHILOSOPHY

· Barzun, Jacques, *Darwin, Marx, Wagner*, Boston, 1941 (Anchor). Thoughtful and stimulating.
· Bober, M. M., *Karl Marx's Interpretation of History*, Cambridge, 1927, 1948 (Norton Library).
· Brinton, Crane, *English Political Thought in the Nineteenth Century*, Cambridge, Mass., 1949 (Torchbook).
———, *Ideas and Men*, Englewood Cliffs, N.J., 1950.
Burns, E. M., *Ideas in Conflict*, New York, 1960.
· Hayes, C. J. H., *A Generation of Materialism*, New York, 1941 (Torchbook).
· Hofstadter, Richard, *Social Darwinism in American Thought*, Philadelphia, 1949 (Beacon). The standard work on the subject.
Joad, C. E. M., *A Guide to Modern Thought*, New York, 1933.
Mosse, G. L., *The Culture of Western Europe: The Nineteenth and Twentieth Centuries*, Chicago, 1961.
· Perry, R. B., *The Thought and Character of William James*, Cambridge, Mass., 1948 (Torchbook, briefer version).
Randall, J. H., Jr., *The Making of the Modern Mind*, New York, 1926, Chs. XVIII–XXI. A lively summary.
· Reichenbach, Hans, *The Rise of Scientific Philosophy*, Berkeley, 1951 (University of California Press). A book for the student with some knowledge of philosophy.
· Russell, Bertrand, *History of Western Philosophy*, New York, 1945 (Simon & Shuster). Good for both summary and interpretation.
Sabine, G. H., *A History of Political Theory*, New York, 1961. Good for the first half of the nineteenth century.
· Tucker, Robert, ed., *The Marx-Engels Reader*, New York, 1972 (Norton).
· ———, *The Marxian Revolutionary Idea*, New York, 1969 (Norton Library).

SCIENCE

· Butterfield, H. B., *The Origins of Modern Science*, Glencoe, Ill., 1957 (Free Press).
Conant, J. B., *On Understanding Science: An Historical Approach*, New Haven, 1947.
· De Kruif, Paul, *Microbe Hunters*, New York, 1926 (Pocket Book).
· Eddington, A. S., *The Nature of the Physical World*, New York, 1946 (Ann Arbor).
· Himmelfarb, Gertrude, *Darwin and The Darwinian Revolution*, New York, 1959 (Norton Library).
· Jones, Ernest, *The Life and Work of Freud*, New York, 1953 (Anchor, abr.). The best biography of the founder of psychoanalysis.
McKenzie, A. E. E., *The Major Achievements of Science*, New York, 1960.
Robinson, Victor, *The Story of Medicine*, New York, 1936.
· Russell, Bertrand, *The A B C of Relativity*, New York, 1925 (Mentor).
Sears, Paul, *Charles Darwin: The Naturalist as a Cultural Force*, New York, 1950.
Singer, Charles, *A History of Biology*, New York, 1950.
Singer, Charles, and Underwood, A. E., *A Short History of Medicine*, 2d ed., New York, 1962.

993

READINGS LITERATURE

Brandes, Georg, *Main Currents in Nineteenth Century Literature*, New York, 1901–06.

· Young, G. M., *Victorian England: Portrait of an Age*, Garden City, N.Y., 1954 (Oxford).

· Wilson, Edmund, *Axel's Castle: A Study in the Imaginative Literature of 1870–1930*, New York, 1931 (Scribner Library).

ART

Faure, Elie, *History of Art*, New York, 1937, Vol. IV. A lucid and instructive account.

Gardner, Helen, *Art Through the Ages*, fourth edition, New York, 1967.

Hitchcock, H. R., *Modern Architecture*, New York, 1929.

Janson, H. W., *The History of Art*, New York, 1969.

Wright, W. H., *Modern Painting*, New York, 1927. An excellent interpretation of the leading movements.

MUSIC

Abraham, Gerald, *A Hundred Years of Music*, New York, 1938.

Einstein, Alfred, *Music in the Romantic Era*, New York, 1947.

Lang, Paul, *Music in Western Civilization*, New York, 1941.

Machlis, Joseph, *The Enjoyment of Music*, third ed., New York, 1970.

Newman, Ernest, *The Life of Richard Wagner*, New York, 1937.

SOURCE MATERIALS

· Appleman, Philip, Editor, *Darwin*, New York, 1970 (Norton).

Baumer, F. L. V., *Main Currents of Western Thought*, New York, 1952.

· Darwin, Charles, *The Origin of Species*, especially Chs. IV, XV, Cambridge, 1964 (Collier and others).

———, *The Descent of Man*, especially Ch. XXI.

Dewey, John, *Human Nature and Conduct*, New York, 1930.

· ———, *Reconstruction in Philosophy* (Beacon, 1957).

· Freud, Sigmund, *An Outline of Psychoanalysis*, New York (Norton Library).

· Huxley, T. H., *Man's Place in Nature*, Ann Arbor, 1959 (Ann Arbor).

James, William, *The Philosophy of William James*, New York, 1925.

· ———, *The Will to Believe*, Gloucester, Mass. (Dover).

· Mill, J. S., *Autobiography; Utilitarianism*, Urbana, Ill., 1961 (Library of Liberal Arts and others).

Spencer, Herbert, *Social Statics*, New York, 1954.

CHAPTER 33

Foretastes of Political and Social Revolution

> Man is stark mad; he cannot make a worm, and yet he will be making gods by dozens.
> —Montaigne, *Essays*, Book II

That a period as turbulent as the nineteenth century should have been a period of political and social upheaval was a fact unlikely to deceive many observers. Not all of the upheavals and threatened upheavals burst into full-fledged revolution. Some partook of the character of half-baked sorties against the government. Others were outbreaks against social institutions with only incidental threats against the state. Yet all reflected the growth of discontent and the inability of millions to adjust to the rapidity of social and economic change. As the century advanced, conditions paving the road for deeper rumblings of discontent quickly emerged.

Rumblings of discontent

I. THE WEAKENING OF SURVIVING ESTABLISHMENTS

It is a distressing fact of history that periods of turbulence have generally exceeded periods of tranquillity. Even the so-called Golden Ages—the Age of Pericles in Greece, the Augustan Age in Rome—were really not exceptions. Some ages, though, were more plagued by violence than others. This condition was clearly true of the nineteenth century. The century was born of violence. The Wars of Napoleon did not terminate the age of conflict that had marked their beginning. Instead, they gave rise to new antagonisms that kept the Western world in turmoil for many years. France had no fewer than three outbreaks. Belgium, Poland, and Russia had one each. Spain, Hungary, and Italy had a like number. Not all of the uprisings were successful. Several should be classified as revolts

Signs of an uneasy society

995

rather than true revolutions. Yet all were symptoms of a discontent that marked the emergence of an uneasy society.

The weakening of reigning establishments occurred partly because of economic chaos—panics and depressions, displacement of skilled workers by advances in technology, conflicts between capital and labor, and inability of the masses to keep pace with the demands of a system they could neither understand nor control. Social factors also contributed to revolutionary ferment. Rapid growth of population created problems hitherto nonexistent. Overcrowding in cities left hordes of poor people living in filth, assailed by vermin, and subject to the ravages of transmissible disease. The burden of guilt, in so far as it was recognized, was generally divided between rulers and the members of the new owning class. Not all of the impoverished, of course, languished in misery, and not all of the proprietors and bosses lived off the fat of the land, but the gulf that separated the two classes was wide enough to be a major cause of discontent.

Obviously, not to be denied as factors precipitating the disturbances of the nineteenth century were the political causes. Many of these reflected economic grievances, but others were products of the stubbornness of rulers and failure to keep pace with the needs of the times.

2. THE SPREAD OF DOMESTIC VIOLENCE

Aside from the Paris Commune, already discussed in Chapter 23, the most serious outbreaks of domestic violence in the Second In-

Tenements in Glasgow. This photo, taken during the 1860's, shows the filthy conditions in which city dwellers often lived their lives. The narrow courtyard was both the source of water (the standpipe at the lower right of the photo) and the dumping ground of garbage and sewage.

The Haymarket Square Riots. A bomb is seen exploding among the police in this illustration by a contemporary artist.

dustrial Revolution were the Haymarket Square riots of 1886 and the Russian revolutionary movement of 1905. The former grew out of an attempt by organized labor to foment a strike among the McCormick Harvester workers in Chicago. A meeting was called at which radical speakers harangued the crowd. One policeman considered the behavior of the multitude dangerous and led a detachment of armed officers against them. A bomb was thrown, no one knows by whom. Anarchists and socialists were widely blamed for the tragedy. Chicago officials rounded up eight of them and accused them of murder. Seven were condemned to death and four were actually hanged. Though the proceedings were of doubtful legality, organized labor in America received a blow from which it did not fully recover for many years.

The Russian Revolutionary Movement of 1905 had numerous forerunners. Waves of discontent broke out several times during the nineteenth century. Threatened uprisings around 1850–1860 persuaded Tsar Alexander II to grant local self-government, to reform the judicial system, and, most of all, to liberate the serfs. Yet he failed to carry through on all these reforms. A wave of reaction followed. Radicalism revived and the number of sects increased. New and well-organized revolutionary parties, Social Democrats and Social Revolutionaries, dominated the scene. The former comprised Marxists while the latter was a peasant party committed to the principle, "The whole land to the whole people." Allied with either or both parties were the nihilists who tended to condemn the whole political and social system. Nihilism originated about 1860 as a movement to solve Russian problems by spreading enlightenment among the peasants. In general it denounced everything that did not lend itself to critical and scientific analysis. Its leaders were mostly

The Haymarket Square riots

The Revolutionary Movement of 1905 in Russia

997

students and mature intellectuals who did not belong to the aristocracy. Their major prophets were Charles Darwin, Karl Marx, and some of the anarchists. Failing to win much support by propagandist methods, they turned more and more to terrorism. The culminating act of this terrorism was the assassination of the Tsar in 1881.

The years that followed the death of Alexander II marked the flood tide of reaction against the entire policy of reform. The new Tsar, Alexander III (1881–1894), governed under the theory that Russia had nothing in common with western Europe, that her people had been nurtured on despotism and mystical piety for centuries and would be utterly lost without them. Such Western ideals as rationalism and individualism would undermine the childlike faith of the Russian masses and would plunge the nation into the dark abyss of anarchy and crime. In like manner, Western institutions of trial by jury, parliamentary government, and free education could never produce other than the most hideous fruits if planted in Russian soil. With such doctrines as his guiding principles, Alexander III enforced a regime of stern and vengeful repression. He curtailed in every way possible the powers of the local assemblies, increased the authority of the secret police, and even subjected the governments of the villages to wealthy nobles selected by the state. These policies were continued, though in somewhat less rigorous form, by his son, Nicholas II, who was a very much weaker man. Both Tsars were ardent proponents of Russification and used it with a vengeance to strengthen their power. Russification was simply the more ruthless counterpart of similar nationalistic movements in various countries. Its purpose was to extend the language, religion, and culture of Great Russia, or Russia proper, over all of the subjects of the Tsar and thereby to simplify the problem of governing them. It was aimed most of all at the Poles, the Finns, and the Jews, since these were the nationalities considered most dangerous. Inevitably it resulted in some cruel oppression. The Finns were deprived of their constitution; the Poles were compelled to study their own literature in Russian translations; and high officials in the Tsar's government connived at *pogroms* against the Jews.

The immediate cause of the revolutionary movement was the calamitous outcome of Russia's war with Japan. As reports came in telling how the armies of the Tsar had been routed time after time on the fighting front in Manchuria, it was impressed upon the Russian people as never before that the system of tyranny under which they lived was rotten and incompetent. Members of the middle class who had hitherto refrained from association with the revolutionists, now joined in the clamor for change. Radical workingmen organized strikes and held demonstrations in every important city. By the autumn of 1905 nearly the whole urban population had enlisted in a strike of protest. Merchants closed their stores, factory owners shut down their plants, lawyers refused to plead

Alexander III and Nicholas II

The growth and decline of the revolutionary movement

cases in court, and even valets and cooks deserted their wealthy employers. It was soon evident to the slow-witted Tsar that the government would have to yield. On October 30, he issued his famous October Manifesto pledging guaranties of individual liberties, promising a moderately liberal franchise for the election of a Duma, or national legislature, and affirming that henceforth no law would be valid unless it had the Duma's approval. This was the high-water mark of the revolutionary movement. During the next two years Nicholas issued a series of sweeping decrees which made the October Manifesto virtually a dead letter. He deprived the Duma of most of its powers and decreed that it be elected indirectly on a class basis by a number of electoral colleges. Thereafter the legislative body was pretty well packed with obedient followers of the Tsar.

The reasons for this setback to the revolutionary movement are not hard to discover. In the first place, the army remained loyal to its commander-in-chief. Consequently, after the termination of the war with Japan in 1905, the Tsar had an enormous body of troops who could be counted upon if necessary to decimate the ranks of the revolutionists. An even more important reason was the split in the ranks of the revolutionists themselves. After the issuance of the October Manifesto, large numbers of the bourgeoisie became frightened at threats of the radicals and declared their conviction that the revolution had gone far enough. Withdrawing their support altogether, they became known henceforth as Octobrists. The more liberal merchants and professional men, under the name of Constitutional Democrats, or Cadets, maintained that opposition should continue until the Tsar had been forced to establish a government modeled after that of Great Britain. This fatal division rendered the middle class politically impotent. Finally, disaffection appeared within the ranks of the proletariat. Further attempts to employ the general strike as a weapon against the government ended in disaster.

Causes of the decline

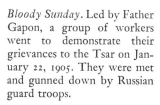

Bloody Sunday. Led by Father Gapon, a group of workers went to demonstrate their grievances to the Tsar on January 22, 1905. They were met and gunned down by Russian guard troops.

Gains from the
revolutionary
movement

But the Russian revolutionary movement of 1905 was not a total failure. The cruel vengeance taken by the bloodhounds of the Tsar convinced many people that their government was not a benevolent autocracy, as they had been led to believe, but a stubborn and brutal tyranny. The uprising revealed to the masses their principal mistakes and taught them what sources of strength they should rely upon for success in the future. Even a few of the concessions actually obtained were not completely wiped out. The Duma, for instance, was not abolished. It continued to serve as a means by which at least scattered remnants of opponents of reaction could make themselves heard. Significantly enough, the revolution of 1917 actually began in the Duma. But this was not all. The revolt of 1905 persuaded some of the more sagacious advisers of the Tsar that last-ditch conservatism was none too safe. The result was the enactment of a number of reforms designed to conciliate the troublesome classes. Among the most significant were the agrarian reforms sponsored by Premier Stolypin between 1906 and 1911. These included: (1) the transfer of 5,000,000 acres of crown lands to the peasants; (2) permission for the peasant to withdraw from the *mir* and set himself up as an independent farmer; and (3) cancellation of the remaining installments owed by the peasants for their land. Nor were the working classes altogether forgotten. Decrees were issued permitting the formation of labor unions, providing for a reduction of the working day (to not more than ten hours in most cases), and establishing sickness and accident insurance. Yet the hopes of some liberals that Russia was on the way to becoming a progressive nation on the Western model proved illusory. The Tsar remained stubbornly autocratic. Few of the peasants had enough money to buy the crown lands offered for purchase. In view of the rising cost of living, the factory workers considered their modest gains insufficient and lapsed into a sullen passivity. A new revolutionary outbreak merely awaited a convenient spark.

The Easter
Rebellion
in Ireland

Yet another outbreak of violence in this period was the Easter Rebellion in Ireland. At the beginning of World War I, Irish nationalists, who resented the rule of their country by the British, were ripe for revolt. They had actually been promised self-rule on the eve of the war, but the British later reneged on the ground that a national emergency must take preeminence over everything else. This greatly displeased the people of southern Ireland. They scheduled Easter Monday, 1916, as a day for revolt. British forces quelled the uprising, but not until after a hundred people had been killed. Sporadic outbreaks kept the island in turmoil for years thereafter but were finally brought almost to an end by an agreement constituting Southern Ireland as a Free Republic. The Northern counties, or the province of Ulster, were to continue subject to the British Crown. On the surface the revolt in Ireland was a protest against

British rule with undercurrents of religious conflict. The British Protestants in Ulster were and still are determined to maintain their sovereignty over Northern Ireland.

3. THE REVOLT IN RELIGION

Both Protestant and Catholic branches of Christianity suffered dissension within their ranks during the nineteenth and early twentieth centuries. For a time the Catholic Church was more deeply affected. The reason lay partly in sharp disagreements over Papal policy. In 1864 Pope Pius IX issued a *Syllabus of Errors* condemning what he regarded as the principal religious and philosophical "errors" of the time. Among them were materialism, free thought, anticlericalism, Freemasonry, nationalism, and "indifferentism," or the idea that one religion is as good as another. Though the *Syllabus* was generally accepted by the Church, it was condemned by some critics as a "crusade against civilization."

While heated discussions continued over the *Syllabus of Errors* Pope Pius convoked a Church Council, the first to be summoned since the Catholic Reformation. The name given to the new council was the Vatican Council, to distinguish it from Vatican II convoked by John XXIII a hundred years later. The most noted pronouncement of Vatican I (1869) was the dogma of Papal Infallibility. In the language of this dogma the Pope, when he speaks *ex cathedra*—that is in his capacity "as pastor and doctor of all Christians"—is infallible in regard to all matters of faith and morals. Though generally accepted by pious Catholics, the dogma of Papal Infallibility evoked a storm of protest in many circles. Governments of several Catholic countries denounced it, including France, Spain, and Italy. Even in Germany the enunciation of the dogma was a paramount cause, or at least an excuse, for beginning the *Kulturkampf*. The death of Pius IX in 1878 and the accession of Pope Leo XIII brought a more genial climate to the Church. The new Pope was ready to concede that there was "good" as well as "evil" in modern civilization. He added a scientific staff to the Vatican and opened archives and observatories. However, he made no concessions to "liberalism" or "anticlericalism" in the political sphere. He would go no farther than to urge capitalists and employers to be more generous in recognizing the rights of organized labor. Whatever Leo XIII's intentions may have been, they seemed to have little effect in abating the force of anticlerical opposition to the universal Church. Drastic legislation was enacted, especially in France, but also in Italy and Spain and some countries of Latin America.

Disaffection among Protestants scarcely equaled that in the Catholic Church. For one reason Protestants did not constitute a compact body with a single authority over its members. They were themselves rebels against an older establishment and later found it easy to

Pope Pius IX

Pope Leo VIII

fall into habits of dissension. Their custom of revering an "inerrant Bible" instead of an infallible Church left them a prey to shifting winds of doctrine. Defections from among their orthodox midst had been characteristic of most of the nineteenth century. The most

serious resulted from the scientific revolution. New discoveries in biology and physics provoked doubts in the minds of many Protestants who had hitherto been satisfied with a literal interpretation of the Scriptures. Foremost among these discoveries were the conclusions of Charles Darwin. Darwin was in no sense a theologian. He made no pretense of being able to interpret the divine will or purpose. He did not profess to know *why* species had appeared on the earth, but merely to discover how they had evolved and what their probable destinies would be in the future. Yet he threw most of the world of orthodox belief into a quandary. The Darwinian theory forced the faithful to abandon much of their accepted doctrine or to explain it away by a figurative interpretation. The latter alternative led to the formation of a "Modernist" wing in the leading Protestant denominations. Darwin, of course, was not alone responsible for the "culture shock" inflicted upon Protestantism. Also important were the teachings of such radical evolutionists as Thomas H. Huxley and August Weismann. Some Modernists rejected the idea of an infallible Bible and taught that the Scriptures were a product of evolution like any other religious writings. Others went so far as to question the Trinity, the Virgin Birth, and even the divinity of Christ Himself.

But challenging the validity of Protestant theology was by no means the only objective of those who sought to transform the Christian epic. Toward the end of the nineteenth century there came

into prominence a movement called the Social Gospel. Its leaders were Modernists in every sense. Needless to say, they rejected the Trinity, the Virgin Birth, the Incarnation, the miracles, but also much later excrescences as original sin, eternal punishment, and infant damnation. Love of one's neighbor as one's self was usually their highest ethical slogan. The Social Gospel derived its name from the fact that its ministers proclaimed the importance of aiding the working man in his struggles for justice. Accordingly, they defended the worker's right to organize and strike, and they urged the enactment of numerous laws for the benefit of the working classes. At the same time, they refused to endorse socialism. The most they would countenance was a limited form of government ownership together with cooperatives to keep down the cost of living and strengthen the laborer's security. "The Kingdom of God," one of them wrote, "is expressed in cooperation rather than in competition."

Most exponents of the Social Gospel were content with proclaiming a humanitarian message of benevolence and justice to the less fortunate. Such was the goal of middle-of-the-road liberals like Washington Gladden and their followers in both England and the United States. But other Social Gospelers had broader conceptions. A famous "sky pilot" and Secretary of the Home Mission Society,

Josiah Strong, published books and articles warning of the dangers of concentrated wealth and calling upon the church to recognize its responsibilities to the poor. But he was no soapbox radical. He was much more deeply concerned with issues of national and racial destiny. From some of the Aryanists of his day he had imbibed notions of ethnic superiority. The mighty Anglo-Saxon race, he taught, is destined to hold sway over all the peoples of the earth. In fulfilling this mission the people of the United States will perform the most glorious role. It is possessed of such a wealth of resources and such wondrous traditions that it can scarcely escape a glowing destiny. Moreover, the fate of its people is sealed by the fact of their Anglo-Saxon stock. This stock is destined to populate and rule the entire earth. With the Americans as their vanguard, nothing can stop them. They will spread themselves "down upon Mexico, down upon Central and South America, out upon the islands of the sea, over upon Africa and beyond." No one spoke more eloquently as the voice of racism and American imperialism. The fact that Strong's books sold so widely indicated the capacity of evangelical Protestantism to fit itself into the new pattern of aggrandizement and wealth. It was frequently not difficult to translate the Social Gospel into the Gospel of Wealth made famous by John D. Rockefeller and Andrew Carnegie.

Protestantism and Catholicism were not alone involved in the revolt in religion. Only less seriously affected was Judaism. Although the Jews had no Pope or Church councils to issue authoritarian decrees, a substantial basis of unity prevailed among them. The Old Testament, the Talmud, and the forms of synagogal worship were powerful unifying symbols. Besides, the Jews had a common heritage, veneration of scholarship, a vast array of laws and customs, and for the most part a belief in a common destiny. Yet even Judaism had not escaped the kind of conflicts that had beset the other religions. Dissension between die-hards and liberals, between conservatives and modernists, and between dogmatists and rationalists was just as rife as in any of the branches of Christianity.

A liberal wing of the Jewish faith came into prominence during the Enlightenment. Its leaders were Gotthold Lessing and Moses Mendelssohn. Renouncing many of the beliefs of their fathers, they taught all religions should be judged by their effects upon their followers. Unlike the general run of their successors, they rejected the Chosen People idea and the notion of themselves as a superior race. Gradually a body of doctrines and usages developed as a major branch of the Jewish religion. Known as Reform Judaism, it took its place beside the Orthodox and Conservative branches, which had divided the religion for more than a century. Reform Judaism was not chiefly a product of the eighteenth- and nineteenth-century awakening. Instead, it was mainly inspired by rationalist influences. Its idols were the major Prophets of ancient times, Maimonides in the Middle Ages, Spinoza, and the leaders of the Enlightenment. Reform Judaism emphasized ethical content rather than legal forms

1003

and requirements. In this it was not a defiance of the best traditions of Judaism. The Hebrew religion in its prime had always been an ethical religion.

Divisions among Hebrews in the Western World were not exclusively religious and ethical. No one could ignore the politico-religious movement known as Zionism. The most active founder of Zionism was Theodor Herzl, a native of Hungary, who lived for a time in Paris but spent most of his life in Vienna. As a journalist in Paris at the time of the Dreyfus affair, he was horrified by the persecution of the Jews and became convinced that they could find no solution for their problem except in "a land of their own." He did not insist at first that this land be Palestine; he thought that some portion of East Africa might be preferable. Later under the influence of some Eastern European followers he adopted the view that nothing less than the true Jewish homeland of their ancestors would suffice. Just as ancient Jews longed for a return to Zion and a rebuilding of the temple in Jerusalem, so their modern descendants yearned for a reconstitution of the ancient homeland. The true Zion would not be primarily political; instead it would be essentially religious, based upon Biblical prophecy and grandiose dreams for the future. By the beginning of World War I it was already one of the most vigorous movements among the Jewish people.

Zionism

4. THE REVOLT IN EDUCATION

Education has seldom been an arena of violent rebellion or even of peaceful, deep-rooted change. The reasons lie close to the surface. Educational institutions are generally pillars of the established order. They take their cue from those in positions of authority over them. Usually this means the government, although in occasional instances the Church is supreme. The nineteenth century witnessed the triumph of secular education. France took the lead during the Great Revolution and even more definitely during the time of Napoleon. Prussia joined in the movement in the regeneration following the overthrow of Napoleon. Enthusiasm spread rapidly through Germany during the upsurge of patriotism accompanying the founding of the Empire. Britain fell in arrears of most other West European states. The nation had no comprehensive system of public education until 1870. It was not made compulsory until 1880, and fees were not abolished until 1891. Developments in the United States were not much different from those in Great Britain. If anything, the greater number of churches strengthened the notion that schools should be under private control. Some states took steps to combat this notion by appointing state superintendents with powers of visitation and inspection. Still education was not free, public, or universal. Educational facilities were inadequate, and as late as 1900 only about 10 per cent of high-school-age youth were actually in school.

Education all over the world suffered grievously from barbarous practices and outworn philosophies. Nearly everywhere the time-

*The backwardness
of education*

English Schoolboys. In the early part of this century, these students of the Bluecoat School, marching through the cloisters, were regimented both in dress and action.

honored objective was to make faithful believers out of the children, or if not that, at least dutiful citizens. Little attention was given to the varying psychologies of children, or to the reasons why some children fail. The welfare of the children themselves received scant consideration. Uppermost were the interests and requirements of church and state. Yet a few bold spirits challenged this system. The most eminent among them was the French-Swiss philosopher and author of the *Social Contract*, Jean Jacques Rousseau. The educational ideas of this unusual man were contained in his novel *Émile*. They revolved around the doctrine that man is fundamentally good. This does not mean that human beings are angels. Neither are they devils. It is simply that there is no such thing as original sin. Yet men in society are bad and unhappy. What makes them so? The answer, according to Rousseau, is the whole social environment, the state, the church, and the schools. Banish the corrupting influence of these, and every individual will have an equal chance to develop in peace and happiness.

It was inevitable that other leaders should join the vanguard of educational reform after Rousseau. First in line was the Swiss Johann Pestalozzi. Unlike Rousseau, Pestalozzi was not a philosopher. Instead he devoted himself to practical efforts for the benefit of destitute and neglected children. His basic educational principle was the importance of "sense impression." He doubted the value of any learning not founded upon accurate observation of concrete objects. With this observation he exerted a deep influence upon Prussia during her period of regeneration following the defeat of Napoleon's armies. The second of the great educational reformers who followed Rousseau was the Italian Maria Montessori. Educated as a doctor of medicine, she did not attract attention as an educator until after 1900. She began her system of instruction with supposedly "de-

Maria Montessori

fective" children and showed that they could be trained in habits of alertness and persistence as well as youngsters of more gifted qualities. Lessons ranged from a quarter of an hour to an hour in length, and only so much was assigned as the child could readily master. Instruction began at an early age and continued into the high-school years. Regardless of the subject, the instruction was given almost exclusively on an individual basis. Discipline constituted no problem since each pupil moved at his own pace and not at the demands of a slave driver anxious to please his own boss.

Efforts to reform education culminated in the Progressive Education movement at the end of the nineteenth century. Its roots could

The Progressive Education movement

be traced back many years not only to Rousseau but even to Sir Francis Bacon. However, its main inspiration was the American philosopher John Dewey. Dewey sought to infuse into education the approach and methods of the pragmatist or "instrumentalist" philosophy. That is, he strove to make education yield a truth that would meet the pragmatic test and serve as an instrument for the solution of social problems. He would place the emphasis upon sciences and other utilitarian subjects and relegate ancient history and the classics to the background. The program of the school should be student-centered and not subject-centered. In so far as any approach or viewpoint should be inculcated, Dewey insisted that this should be the scientific method. Nothing else would provide the key to sound knowledge.

Progressive Education in full reign did not survive much longer than fifty years. Though it spread to England and Germany, it en-

The decline of Progressive Education

joyed great influence only in the United States. Its strength waned everywhere as the icy fingers of blood and suspicion tightened their grip upon the nations. Armaments competition, national hatreds, industrial rivalry, and wars produced an environment decidedly inhospitable to a movement that fostered freedom and exalted the individual above the state. Humanists and conservatives criticized its aversion to discipline and indifference to classical literature and ancient languages. Religionists, both Catholic and Protestant, castigated its materialism and demanded more emphasis on spiritual values. Finally, hardheaded patriots condemned its radicalism and failure to worship at the shrine of national virtue. All that was left was for the hysteria surrounding World War I and the fears that came in its wake to seal the doom of the more meaningful kinds of educational reform. And what was true of elementary and secondary schools was no less true of colleges and universities.

Higher institutions in most countries were more likely to be ossified and moth-eaten than those of lower grade. Improvements were far apart and generally of small importance. They included the admission of women to some universities in England and to a few colleges in the United States. Dozens of medieval rules and requirements were abolished all over Europe. The first state universities, mostly Western, were established in America and were paralleled by the "Redbrick" universities in Britain. Both were under the control of the state, though in Britain they were generally governed and maintained by a major industrial city. They were among the first universities to provide an exclusively secular education. In some of the "Redbrick" universities the teaching of religion was forbidden. Aside from these departures, higher education changed but little. The majority of colleges and universities continued the line of development they had followed since they were founded. In many cases, notably Great Britain, this meant loyalty to the heritage of the Renaissance. In America traditions were carried over from the colonies. The result was an educational pattern dominated by the churches. Doctors of divinity were generally the governing officials. The chief subjects of study were almost invariably Bible, ethics, the classical languages, and literature. The sciences were quite largely neglected. Where they were introduced, as in Russia under Alexander II, they were often considered dangerous to the state and to religion. Nearly everywhere the functions of higher education were "polite letters" and divinity. Until late in the nineteenth century not a single American or British university granted degrees in advanced professional work. Doctors and lawyers obtained their training by studying with some experienced practitioner or in some "fly-by-night" vocational school. About 1880 the German system of advanced professional training and graduate degrees in law, medicine, and philosophy was imported into the United States. Britain steered clear of the custom until much later.

Problems of
higher
education

5. MOODS OF OPTIMISM VERSUS DECLINE

By common supposition the period from the French Revolution to the outbreak of World War I was a period of optimism. Men were disposed to think of it as a time when God was in His Heaven, and all was right with the world. The progress in science, and perhaps most of all the progress in technology, seemed to impugn the sanity of all who questioned this belief. Pulpit orators, popular writers, lecturers, and college presidents vied with one another in acclaiming the grandeur of the new order. Optimism flowered into a national religion. Everything that happened seemed to be a herald of a glorious dawn. The growth of population, the acquisition of territory, the expansion of production, the conquest of disease, and the extension of empire into distant lands across the seas—who could deny that the Sun of Heaven conferred its smiles upon such "progress"?

Yet there were some who did deny it in no unmistakable terms. Carlyle, Ruskin, and William Morris questioned the basic assumptions of industrial civilization. Thoreau and Tolstoi went even further. Still others worked out complete philosophies of pessimism stark to the point of despair. First among this inglorious company was the German Arthur Schopenhauer. His cardinal idea was the

The prevailing
mood of
optimism

1007

notion that a single force directs all growth and movement in the universe. This force he taught is "will," a blind, unconscious craving of individuals and species to survive. Since the will to live is present in all animate forms, and since it leads the strong to devour the weak, this world is the worst of all possible worlds. Since misery and pain are inseparable from life itself, happiness for man consists in as complete a denial of life as possible. The Oriental ascetic has a better chance of finding Nirvana than has Western man of finding the mythical pot of gold at the end of a rainbow.

Equally distinguished among prophets of "doom and gloom" was another German philosopher, Friedrich Nietzsche. Educated partly in Switzerland, Nietzsche was given an appointment as professor of classical philology at the University of Basel. But with the outbreak of the Franco-German War he returned to Germany and spent the remainder of his life in that country. His philosophy in general is discussed elsewhere.[1] As a pessimist he was not so dyed-in-the-wool as Schopenhauer. He did not preach defeatism or take refuge in Oriental quietism. On the contrary, he glorified strength, bravery, courage, and the other ancient Germanic virtues which he believed should distinguish the Overman. The passive virtues of Christianity and Judaism he regarded as relics of a slave morality. Nietzsche allowed at least one element of optimism to creep into his philosophy. He believed that an unhindered natural selection would ultimately produce a race of Overmen.

Pessimistic views of life were by no means confined to German philosophers. Such conceptions were not unknown in other countries. In America the two Adams brothers, Henry and Brooks, could find little to inspire confidence and hope even in the glittering decades at the turn of the century. Both foresaw the decay of civilizations mainly as a result of depletion of energy. Nothing can save them except an infusion of "barbarian blood," or perhaps a return to the simple faith of the twelfth century. Pessimism made only a limited appeal to other philosophers in America and almost none in England and France. Yet by a curious coincidence it drew its converts by the dozens from the ranks of poets and novelists. Nathaniel Hawthorne, for example, was preoccupied with the problem of original sin and sharply critical of bigotry and intolerance. Herman Melville was concerned with the isolation of man, baffled with the search by inquiring minds, and hopeful of solving problems he could never fathom. British and French writers plumbed the depths of utter hopelessness in some of the things they wrote. James Thomson in his *City of Dreadful Night* wrote of

A mockery, a delusion: and my breath
Of noble human life upon this earth
So racks me that I sigh for senseless death.

[1] See pp. 970–71

It was, of course, not merely minor representatives of Western letters who wrote in such a doleful vein. Matthew Arnold spoke of the world as "a darkling plain" where there is "neither joy, nor love, nor light, nor certitude, nor peace, nor help for pain." Even the great Poet Laureate of the British Empire, Lord Tennyson, did not always sing of pompous generals, brave warriors, and "flowers in crannied walls." He could express poignancy and even fleeting moods of despair, as in one of his alternating sentiments in *In Memoriam:*

> O weary life! O weary death!
> O spirit and heart made desolate!
> O damned vacillating state!

SELECTED READINGS

· *Items so designated are available in paperbound editions.*

Demerath, N. J., and Peterson, Richard A., eds., *System Change and Conflict*, New York, 1961.

· Derry, J. W., *A Short History of Nineteenth-Century England*, New York, 1963 (Mentor).

De Vries, Egbert, *Man in Rapid Social Change*, New York, 1961.

· Fanon, Frantz, *The Wretched of the Earth*, New York, 1968 (Evergreen Black Cat Edition).

Graham, Stephen, *Tsar of Freedom: The Life and Reign of Alexander II*, New Haven, 1935.

· Hobsbawm, E. I., *Primitive Rebels*, London, 1959 (Norton Library).

· Horowitz, David, *Empire and Revolution: A Radical Interpretation of Contemporary History*, New York, 1970 (Vintage).

Hovell, M., *The Chartist Movement*, New York, 1925.

Hughes, H. Stuart, *The Obstructed Path: French Social Thought in the Years of Desperation, 1930–1960*, New York, 1968.

Jones, Peter d'A., *The Christian Socialist Revival, 1877–1914*, Princeton, 1968.

Karpovich, M., *Imperial Russia, 1801–1917*, New York, 1932. An excellent short treatise.

Keep, J. L. H., *The Rise of Social Democracy in Russia*, New York, 1963.

Orth, S. P., *Socialism and Democracy in Europe*, New York, 1913.

· Pares, Bernard, *A History of Russia*, New York, 1928 (Vintage). A standard work.

Pipkin, C. W., *The Idea of Social Justice*, New York, 1928.

Postgate, Raymond, *1848: The Story of a Year*, London, 1955.

· Raeff, Marc, *Origins of the Russian Intelligentsia*, New York, 1966 (Harcourt, Brace and World).

· Robertson, Priscilla, *Revolutions of 1848: A Social History*, Princeton, 1952 (Torchbook). A stimulating account written from the viewpoint of the people who lived at that time.

Robinson, G. T., *Rural Russia under the Old Regime*, New York, 1932.

· Thompson, E. P., *The Making of the English Working Class*, New York, 1964 (Vintage).

· Thompson, J. M., *Louis Napoleon and the Second Empire*, New York, 1955 (Norton Library). A valuable summary based on scholarly sources.

Wagar, W. Warren, *Good Tidings, The Belief in Progress from Darwin to Marcuse*, Bloomington, Ind., 1972.

Woodward, Ernest, *The Age of Reform, 1815–1870*, Oxford, 1938. Great Britain during the Age of Democracy.

Younger, Carlton, *Ireland's Civil War*, New York, 1969.

PART **VII**

The Contemporary World, 1914-: The Age of Deepening Conflict

From the beginning of the Renaissance to the outbreak of World War I in 1914, European culture and technology set the standards for the majority of nations in both East and West, except for the more isolated ones like China and Japan. Near the end of the nineteenth century a struggle ensued among Western European Powers for control of the outside world. But they did not have the field to themselves. They were soon confronted with formidable competition from the United States, Japan, and eventually Russia. Indeed, the history of the twentieth century thus far has been occupied largely by contentions for mastery over the hundreds of millions of people in Asia, Africa, and the islands of the Pacific. The great question has been, who shall rule the world? Before 1914 a varied collection of candidates vied for the honor—Britain, France, the Netherlands, Germany, Russia, Japan, and the United States. Between 1918 and 1933 the list was narrowed principally to Germany, Russia, the United States, and Japan. The defeat of 1945 eliminated, for the time being at least, Germany and Japan, leaving the world a bipolar structure with the Soviet Union and the United States competing for the right to rule it. After 1949 the collision course followed by these two giants was modified by the emergence of a new colossus, Communist China, with claims to inherit the remains of European empires. But the rapid emergence of newly independent African states, the irrepressible force of nationalism, and the slowly awakening sense of solidarity among peoples of the "Third World" suggested that world domination might be beyond the reach even of a superpower.

1011

A Chronological Table

INTERNATIONAL	THE AMERICAS

1900

Triple Alliance, 1882–1914
Diplomatic Revolution, 1890–1907
Berlin-to-Baghdad Railway, 1890–1914

Entente Cordiale, 1904–1923
Triple Entente, 1907–1917
Bosnian Crisis, 1908
Balkan Wars, 1912–1913
Assassination of Archduke Francis Ferdinand, 1914
World War I, 1914–1918
U.S. enters World War I, 1917

New constitution in Mexico, 1917

1919

Treaty of Versailles, 1919

League of Nations, 1920–1946

John Dewey, *Reconstruction in Philosophy*, 1920
Eugene O'Neill, *Strange Interlude*, 1920
Renaissance of painting in Mexico, *ca.* 1921
Discovery of insulin, 1922

French invasion of Ruhr Valley, 1923

Locarno Agreements, 1925

Pact of Paris, 1928

1929

Great Depression 1929–1934

Regionalism in art, U.S., ca. 1930

Japan invades Manchuria, 1931

Cancellation of German reparations, 1932'

World Economic Conference, 1933

Anglo-German naval pact, 1935
Franco-Soviet alliance, 1935
Italy conquers Ethiopia, 1935–1936
Hitler remilitarizes Rhineland, 1936
Rome-Berlin Axis, 1936
Germany absorbs Austria (*Anschluss*), 1938
Appeasement at Munich, 1938

U.S. abandons gold standard, 1933

NRA, 1933–1935
New Deal 1933–1939

INDIA, THE MIDDLE AND FAR EAST	BRITAIN AND EUROPE	AFRICA	
	Pan-Slavism, 1890–1914 Expressionism in art, 1893 Pan-Germanism, 1895–1914 Greater Serbia movement, 1900–1914 Industrial supremacy of Germany, 1900–1914	Boer War, 1899–1902	**1900**
		Union of South Africa, 1909	
Dictatorship of Yüan Shih-k'ai, 1914–1916 Era of war lords in China, 1916–1928	A. N. Whitehead, *The Organization of Thought*, 1916 Bolshevik Revolution, 1917		
Amritsar Massacre (India), 1919 Intensification of Indian nationalism, 1919–1947 Republic of Turkey proclaimed, 1923 Mustafa Kemal Atatürk, President of Turkey, 1922–1938	Impressionism in music, 1918 Expressionism in music, 1918 Surrealism, 1918 Revolution in Germany, 1918 O. Spengler, *Decline of the West*, 1918 First Communist regime in Hungary, 1919 Weimar Republic, 1919–1933 NEP in Russia 1921–1929 Fascist Revolution in Italy, 1922 Runaway inflation in Germany, 1923 First Labour Government, 1924 Death of Lenin, 1924 Dictatorship of Stalin, 1924–1953		**1919**
Nationalist regime in China (Chiang Kai-shek), 1928–1949 Japanese invasion of Manchuria, 1931 Triumph of militarists in Japan, 1936 Japan invades China, 1937	Second Labour Government, 1929–1931 First Five-year Plan in Russia, 1929–1933 Discovery of penicillin, 1930 Overthrow of monarchy in Spain, 1931 Abandonment of gold standard, 1931 Discovery of neutrons, 1932 Abandonment of free trade, 1932 Nazi Revolution in Germany, 1933 Development of sulfa drugs, 1935 Popular Front in France, 1936–1938 Civil War in Spain, 1936–1939 Existentialism, *ca.* 1938		**1929**

	INTERNATIONAL	THE AMERICAS

1940

Nazi-Soviet Pact, 1939
World War II, 1939–1945

Atlantic Charter, 1941
Attack on Pearl Harbor, 1941
Cairo Conference, 1943
Teheran Conference, 1943
Establishment of United Nations, 1945

Atomic bombs dropped on Japan, 1945
Yalta Conference, 1945
Potsdam Conference, 1945
Cold War of East and West, 1946–
Truman Doctrine, 1947

European Recovery Program (Marshall Plan), 1948

Discovery of streptomycin, *ca.* 1940

Fair Deal in the U.S., 1945–1953

Perón regime in Argentina, 1946–1955

Discovery of cortisone, 1948

1950

NATO, 1949

Korean War, 1950–1953

Schuman Plan, 1952

Summit Conference, Geneva, 1955
Bandung Conference, 1955

Hydrogen bomb, 1952
Return of Republicans to power in U.S., 1953–1961

Overthrow of Perón regime in Argentina, 1955

Establishment of Castro regime in Cuba, 1959
Election of John F. Kennedy, Democrat, as President of U.S., 1960
Cuban missile crisis, 1962
Assasination of President Kennedy and the beginning of the presidency of Lyndon B. Johnson, 1963

1960

U. S. escalates Vietnam War, 1964
Military dictatorship in Brazil, 1964–

Black revolt, 1965–

1970

Revolt of youth, 1966
First human heart transplant, 1967
Women's liberation movement, 1968–
Man lands on moon, 1969
China admitted to U.N., 1971
U.S.-Soviet trade agreements, 1972
SALT agreements, 1972
Japan and China restore diplomatic relations, 1972
Vietnam cease-fire, 1973

Assassination of Martin Luther King, 1968
Assassination of Robert F. Kennedy, 1968
Election of Richard M. Nixon, Republican, as President of U.S., 1968
Election of Salvador Allende, a Marxist, as President of Chile, 1970
Re-election of Richard M. Nixon, 1972

INDIA, THE MIDDLE AND FAR EAST	BRITAIN AND EUROPE	AFRICA	
	Franco regime in Spain, 1939– Atomic fission, 1939 Neo-Orthodoxy, *ca.* 1940		1940
Japanese conquest of Southeast Asia and South Pacific, 1941–1942			
Vietnam war: French phase, 1947–1954 Dead Sea Scrolls found, 1947 India and Pakistan achieve independence, 1947 State of Israel proclaimed, 1948 Establishment of Communist regime in China, 1949	Third Labour Government, 1945–1950 Communist coup in Hungary, 1947 Communist coup in Czechoslovakia, 1948 Division of Germany into East and West zones, 1948 Establishment of German Federal Republic and German Democratic Republic, 1949	*Apartheid* policy in South Africa, 1948– Libya gains independence, 1949 Revolts in northern and central Africa, 1950–	
Japan peace treaty, 1952 Egypt becomes republic, 1952–1953 SEATO, 1954 Suez crisis, 1956 War in Middle East, 1956 U. N. Emergency Force in Middle East, 1956 Military rule of General Ayub Khan in Pakistan, 1958–1969 Sino-Soviet rift, 1960– Military junta seizes power in Indonesia, 1965 Indira Ghandi Prime Minister of India, 1966–1969 Great Proletarian Cultural Revolution in China, 1966– 6 Day War, 1967 Communist China explodes a hydrogen bomb, 1967 ASEAN, 1967 Soviet-Chinese border clashes, 1968	Death of Stalin, 1953 Russia develops hydrogen bomb, 1953 Dictatorship of Khrushchev, 1958–1964 European Economic Community (Common Market), 1959 1963–1970 Fourth Labour Government, 1963– Breszhnev-Kosygin regime, 1964– Military coup in Greece, 1967 Protestant-Catholic civil war in Northern Ireland, 1968- Russian occupation of Czechoslovakia, 1968	Mau Mau revolt in Kenya, 1952–1958 Algerian war of independence, 1954–1962 Ghana independent republic, 1960 Jomo Kenyatta, President of Kenya, 1963– Kwame Nkrumah deposed in Ghana, 1966 Civil war in Nigeria, 1967– 1970	1950

1960 |
| India-Pakistan war, 1971 Republic of Bangladesh, 1972 | Bonn-Warsaw Pact, 1970 Massacre of Israeli Olympic team, 1972 Britain admitted to Common Market, 1973 | Indian expulsion from Uganda, 1972 | 1970 |

World War I

Victory! Victory!
 On with the dance!
Back to the jungle!
 The new beasts prance!
God, how the dead men
 Grin by the wall,
Watching the fun
 Of the Victory Ball.
   —Alfred Noyes, "A Victory Dance,"
   Collected Poems, 1919

The war that broke out in 1914 was one of the most extraordinary in history. Though it was not really the "first world war," since such conflicts as the Seven Years' War and the Napoleonic Wars had also been global in extent, it had an impact far exceeding either of these. It quickly became a "people's war" in which civilians as well as soldiers in the trenches participated in violent demands for extermination of the enemy. It bore fruit in an epidemic of revolutions and sowed the dragon's teeth of new and even more venomous conflicts in the future. In such ways it set the pattern for an age of violence that continued through the greater part of the twentieth century. Even more extraordinary was the fact that World War I marked the close of a long era of peace. For almost a century after the end of the Napoleonic Wars in 1815, Europe experienced no major conflicts. True, there were the Crimean War in 1854–1856, the Franco-Prussian War in 1870–1871, and the Russo-Turkish War in 1878–1879, but these were minor affrays compared with those that were to follow. That no more serious conflicts occurred until 1914 must be attributed chiefly to the celebrated balance of power, established by Great Britain about 1818 with the cooperation of Austria, Prussia, and France. Essentially it was a *Pax Britannica,* since it rested upon British economic supremacy and the power of the British navy. When war threatened or broke out in Europe, Britain

End of the Hundred Years' Peace

1017

generally threw her weight into the scales on the side of the weaker country, thereby restoring or redressing the balance.

1. UNDERLYING CAUSES OF THE WAR

But the balance of power was never in perfect adjustment. It was threatened by Napoleon III in mid-century, by Bismarck in 1870, and by Russia in 1878. Much more serious threats came after 1900. By that date Germany had emerged as the most powerful state on the European Continent. France was no longer a match for her, and even Russia could not hold a candle to her in military might and efficiency. The Germans cultivated grandiose schemes for enlarging their power in world affairs. Under Kaiser William II, who came to the throne in 1888, they developed ambitions for control of North Africa, for economic imperialism in Turkey, and for the building of a navy able to throw down a challenge to that of Great Britain. That they might speedily attain these goals was evidenced by their phenomenal economic growth after 1871. By 1914 Germany was producing more iron and steel than Britain and France combined. In chemicals, in aniline dyes, and in the manufacture of scientific equipment she led the world. She threw down a challenge to the supremacy of Britain in the carrying trade and produced some of the largest and fastest ships on the Seven Seas. Bursting with pride in these accomplishments, she was impatient with the refusal of other nations to accord her a dominant position on the European Continent. Indeed, many historians have drawn the conclusion that it was Germany's threat to the European balance of power that constituted the real and primary cause of the two world wars of the twentieth century.

Threats to the balance of power were implicit in the aims of a number of principal states. By 1900 six great powers in Europe—Germany, France, Russia, Italy, Austria-Hungary and Great Britain—were competing for power, security, and economic advantage. Each had specific objectives, the fulfillment of which it regarded as essential to its national interest. Germany built her ambitions around eastward expansion. After 1890 German capitalists and imperialists dreamed of a *Drang nach Osten* (Drive to the East) and planned the construction of a railway from Berlin to Baghdad to facilitate economic control of the Ottoman Empire. Austria also looked to the east, but to the Balkans rather than to any part of western Asia. Her hold on Trieste and other portions of the Adriatic coast was precarious, since much of this territory was inhabited by Italians. If she could carve a highroad through the Balkans to the Aegean, her access to the sea would be more secure. As time passed, Austria and Germany became more dependent upon each other, the former because of trouble with the Slavs both inside and outside her borders, and the latter because of a growing fear of encirclement. In 1879

The European Balance of Power

Aims of the great powers: Germany and Austria-Hungary

Bismarck entered into an alliance with Austria, which was renewed and strengthened in subsequent years. It was an alliance with a corpse, but the Germans clung to it more and more desperately as international tensions deepened.

To a large degree the objectives of France were dictated by a desire to curb or counterbalance the growing might of Germany. France hoped to recover Alsace and Lorraine, which had suddenly become very valuable as the result of a discovery by Sidney Thomas and P. C. Gilchrist in 1878 of a method of converting low-grade iron ore into steel. But recovery of the lost provinces was not the only French objective. The French were determined to add Morocco to their African empire regardless of the interests of other powers in that sadly misgoverned country. The motives of the Paris statesmen were both economic and political. Morocco contained rich mineral deposits, but it would be valuable also for strategic reasons and as a reservoir from which troops might be drawn to offset the manpower shortage at home.

A paramount ambition of Russia was to gain control of the Bosporus and the Dardanelles. She had regarded this as her "historic mission" since early in the nineteenth century. Achievement of this mission would prevent her fleet from being bottled up in the Black Sea in the event of war with some naval power or powers. Besides, it would give her unquestioned access to the Mediterranean and probably possession of Constantinople. Turkey would be eliminated from Europe, and Russia would fall heir to the Balkans. In addition, if the Tsar's agents could get to Constantinople before the Germans, they could turn the Berlin-to-Baghdad railway into an empty dream. But Imperial Russia had other ambitions. She coveted access to the Persian Gulf and Indian Ocean and tried for years to make Persia a Russian protectorate. She strove also for better outlets to the Pacific and attempted to extend her control over Manchuria. Finally, through Pan-Slavism she aspired to play the role of guide and protector of all the Slavic peoples of eastern Europe, including those who were under the rule of Austria-Hungary. That each of these ambitions constituted a threat to the status quo scarcely needs emphasis.

The power policies of Great Britain and Italy were somewhat less closely related to the specific actions of other countries. The policy of Britain, in fact, was directed against almost everyone. She was no less suspicious of the Russian ambitions at Constantinople than she was of the German. Until after the beginning of the twentieth century she distrusted France. Her cardinal aims were (1) to maintain the life lines of her empire, (2) to keep open the sea lanes to her sources of imports and her foreign markets, and (3) to preserve a balance among the nations on the European Continent so that no one of them would ever become strong enough to attack her. If the actions of any other country threatened to interfere with these car-

1019

dinal aims (as they often did), the hostility of Britain would instantly be aroused. She would seek to put the offending nation in its place by diplomatic pressure, forming an alliance against it, or by going to war, as she finally did against Germany in 1914. Italian policy was mainly based on hopes of aggrandizement at the expense of Austria and Turkey. Austria continued to hold territories which Italy regarded as rightfully hers: the so-called *Italia Irredenta* (unredeemed Italy) as late as 1915; while Turkey blocked Italy's acquisition of Tripoli and other territories in North Africa.

One of the clearest expressions of the realities of power politics before 1914 was the growth of militarism. Since the nations of the world were living in a condition of international anarchy, it was almost inevitable that their fears and suspicions should lead to competition in armaments. Europe in particular became an armed camp. After 1870 every one of its chief powers, with the exception of Great Britain, adopted conscription and universal military training. Not only that, but they adopted the belief that national security depended almost entirely upon the extent of military and naval preparedness. After every war scare the size of armies and navies increased until, by 1914, all of the important countries, and many of the smaller ones also, were staggering under a burden which, in a saner world, would have been regarded as intolerable. There were, of course, men of humanity and wisdom who recognized the danger and did all in their power to ward it off. But there were far too many others who not only denied that any danger existed but stoutly maintained that militarism was a positive benefit. Theodore Roosevelt argued that training for war was necessary to preserve the "manly and adventurous qualities" in a nation. Field Marshal von Moltke and Heinrich von Treitschke saw in military conflict one of the divine elements of the universe and a "terrible medicine" for the human race. The French philosopher, Ernest Renan, justified war as a condition of progress, "the sting which prevents a country from going to sleep." Although the propagation of such doctrines was not the chief cause of militarism, it undoubtedly strengthened the position of those who believed in armaments and war as the best methods of solving a nation's problems.

Power politics and the failure of the balance of power may be regarded as perhaps the paramount underlying causes of World War I. Prominent also among these causes was nationalism. This factor, as previously explained, had roots extending at least as far back as the French Revolution. By the early twentieth century, however, nationalism had come to assume a variety of particularly dangerous forms. Foremost among them were the Greater Serbia scheme, the Pan-Slav movement in Russia, the revenge movement in France, and the Pan-German movement. The first two were closely related. Since the beginning of the twentieth century at least, little Serbia had dreamed of extending her jurisdiction over all the peoples alleged to be similar to her own citizens in race and in culture. Some

Militarism and the armed peace

Nationalism: the Greater Serbia movement

Field Marshal von Moltke

of these peoples inhabited what were then the two Turkish provinces of Bosnia and Herzegovina. Others included Croatians and Slovenes in the southern provinces of Austria-Hungary. After 1908 when Austria suddenly annexed Bosnia and Herzegovina, the Greater Serbia scheme was directed exclusively against the Hapsburg Empire. It took the form of agitation to provoke discontent among the Slav subjects of Austria, in the hope of drawing them away and uniting the territories they inhabited with Serbia. It resulted in a series of dangerous plots against the peace and integrity of the Dual Monarchy. And the fateful climax of these plots was the murder of the heir to the Austrian throne on June 28, 1914.

In many of their activities the Serbian nationalists were aided and abetted by the Pan-Slavists in Russia. The Pan-Slav movement was founded upon the theory that all of the Slavs of eastern Europe constituted one great family. Therefore, it was argued that Russia as the most powerful Slavic state should act as the guide and protector of her little brother nations of the Balkans. The latter were to be encouraged to look to Russia whenever their interests were endangered. Serbs, Bulgarians, and Montenegrins, in their struggles with Austria or with Turkey, were to be made to understand that they always had a powerful and sympathetic friend on the other side of the Carpathians. Pan-Slavism was not merely the wishful sentiment of a few ardent nationalists, but was really a part of the official policy of the Russian government. It went far toward explaining Russia's aggressive stand in every quarrel that arose between Serbia and Austria.

The influence of Pan-Germanism as a species of nationalism before 1914 is difficult to assess. The name of the movement is generally taken to refer to the ideas of the Pan-German League, founded about 1895. Specifically, the League advocated the expansion of Germany to incorporate all of the Teutonic peoples of central Europe. The boundaries of the Empire should be extended to take in Denmark, the Netherlands, Luxemburg, Switzerland, Austria, and Poland as far east as Warsaw. A few of the leaders were not even satisfied with this but demanded a large colonial empire and a vast expansion into the Balkans and western Asia. They insisted that such peoples as the Bulgars and the Turks should at least become satellites of the German Reich. Although the Pan-German League made a great deal of noise, it could scarcely claim to represent the entire German nation. As late as 1912 it had a membership of only 17,000, and its violent criticism of the government was widely resented. Nevertheless, a large number of its doctrines had been latent in German thinking for upwards of a century. The philosopher Fichte had taught that the Germans, because of their spiritual superiority, had a mission to impose peace upon the rest of Europe. Ideas of Aryanism and of Nordic supremacy also contributed to the notion that the Germans had a divine destiny to persuade or compel "inferior races" to accept their culture. Finally, the efforts of philosophers

Pan-Slavism

The Pan-German movement

like Heinrich von Treitschke to deify the great state and to glorify power as the instrument of national policy helped to impregnate the minds of many Germans of the middle and upper classes with an intolerance of other nations and a belief in the right of Germany to dominate her weaker neighbors.

Nationalism of the types described would have been almost sufficient in itself to have plunged a considerable number of European nations into the maelstrom of war. But the conflict might well have remained limited in character had it not been for the system of entangling alliances. It was this system which transformed a local squabble between Austria and Serbia into a general war. When Russia intervened on behalf of Serbia, Germany felt obliged to come to the defense of Austria. France had close ties to Russia, and Great Britain was drawn in at least partly on account of her commitments to France.

The evolution of the system of entangling alliances goes back to the 1870's, and its original architect was Bismarck. In the main his purposes were peaceful. Prussia and her German allies had emerged victorious in their war with France, and the newly created German empire was the most powerful state on the Continent. Bismarck was anxious, above all, to preserve the fruits of this victory; there is nothing to indicate that he planned any further conquests. However, he was disturbed by fears that the French might start a war of revenge. There was little prospect that they would attempt such a thing singlehanded, but they might with the help of some other power. Therefore Bismarck determined to isolate France by attaching all of her potential friends to Germany. In 1873 he managed to form an alliance with both Austria and Russia, the so-called League of the Three Emperors. But this combination was of a precarious nature and soon went on the rocks. With the League of the Three Emperors defunct, Bismarck cemented a new and much stronger alliance with Austria. In 1882 this partnership was expanded into the celebrated Triple Alliance when Italy was added as a member. The Italians did not join out of love for either Germany or Austria but from motives of anger and fear. They resented the French occupation of Tunisia (1881), a territory which they regarded as properly theirs. Moreover, the Italian politicians were still at odds with the Church, and they feared that the clericals in France might gain the upper hand and send a French army to defend the Pope. In the meantime, the Three Emperors' League had been revived. Though it lasted for only six years (1881–1887), Germany managed to hold the friendship of Russia until 1890.

Thus after little more than a decade of diplomatic maneuvering, the Iron Chancellor had achieved his ambition. By 1882 France was cut off from nearly every possibility of obtaining aid from powerful friends. Austria and Italy were united with Germany in the Triple Alliance, and Russia after a three-year lapse was back once more in

The effects of the system of entangling alliances

The evolution of the system of alliances

the Bismarckian camp. The only conceivable quarter from which help might come was Great Britain; but, with respect to Continental affairs, the British had returned to their traditional policy of "splendid isolation." Therefore, so far as the danger of a war of revenge was concerned, Germany had little to fear. But if either Bismarck or anyone else imagined that this security would be permanent, he was headed for disillusionment. Between 1890 and 1907, Europe went through a diplomatic revolution which practically annihilated Bismarck's work. To be sure, the Germans had Austria still on their side; but they had lost the friendship of both Russia and Italy, and Britain had abandoned her isolation to enter into agreements with Russia and France. This shift in the balance of power had fateful results. It convinced the Germans that they were surrounded by a ring of enemies, and that consequently they must do everything in their power to retain the loyalty of Austria—even to the extent of supporting her reckless foreign adventures.

The first of the major results of the diplomatic revolution was the formation of the Triple Entente. This came about through a series of stages. In 1890 Russia and France began a political flirtation which gradually ripened into a binding alliance. The secret military convention signed by the two countries in 1894 provided that each should come to the aid of the other in case of an attack by Germany, or by Austria or Italy supported by Germany. This Dual Alliance of Russia and France was followed by the *Entente Cordiale* between France and Great Britain. During the last two decades of the nineteenth century the British and the French had frequently been involved in sharp altercations over colonies and trade. The two nations almost came to blows in 1898 at Fashoda in the Egyptian Sudan. But suddenly the French withdrew all of their claims to that portion of Africa and opened negotiations for a broad compromise of other disputes. The result was the conclusion in 1904 of the *Entente Cordiale*. It was not a formal alliance but a friendly agreement, covering a variety of subjects. The final step in the formation of the Triple Entente was the conclusion of a mutual understanding between Great Britain and Russia. Again there was no formal alliance. The two powers simply came to an agreement in 1907 concerning their ambitions in Asia. The core of it provided for the division of Persia into spheres of influence. To Russia was assigned the northern portion and to Great Britain the southern. A middle section was to be preserved, temporarily at least, as a neutral area under its legitimate ruler, the Shah.

Thus by 1907 the great powers of Europe had come to be arrayed in two opposing combinations, the Triple Alliance and the Triple Entente. Had these combinations remained stable and more or less evenly matched, they might well have promoted the cause of peace. But no such condition prevailed. Each grew weaker and less stable with the passage of time. The Triple Alliance declined in strength

The diplomatic revolution of 1890–1907

Results of the diplomatic revolution; formation of the Triple Entente

1023

because of a growing coolness between Italy and Austria. Moreover, Italian nationalists coveted territory in North Africa, notably Tripoli, which they believed they could obtain only by supporting French ambitions in Morocco. Meanwhile, the Triple Entente was

threatened by discord between Britain and Russia. Because their lifeline to the East might be imperiled, the British could not view with equanimity the cardinal aim of Russia to "open the Straits" and gain control of Constantinople. Disharmony in the Triple Entente also increased when Britain and France refused to support Russia in her dispute with Austria over the latter's annexation of Bosnia and Herzegovina. In short, conflicts were so numerous that the members of neither alliance could be quite sure where their opposite numbers might stand in case of a real threat of a European war.

Between 1905 and 1913 five serious international crises endangered the peace of Europe. In a sense they were not so much causes

as they were symptoms of international animosity. Yet each of them left a heritage of suspicion and bitterness that made war all the more probable. In some cases hostilities were averted only because one of the parties was too weak at the time to offer resistance. The result was a sense of humiliation, a smoldering resentment that was almost bound to burst into flame in the future. Three of the crises were generated by disputes over Morocco. Both Germany and France yearned for control of that unhappy country, mainly because of the mineral wealth and trading opportunities it was supposed to contain. In 1905, 1908, and 1911 the two powers stood on the brink of war. Each time the dispute was smoothed over but not without the usual legacy of suspicion and resentment.

In addition to the clash over Morocco, two crises occurred in the Near East. The first was the Bosnian crisis of 1908. At the Congress

The Near
Eastern Crises:
1) the annexa-
tion of Bosnia
and Herze-
govina

of Berlin in 1878 the two Turkish provinces of Bosnia and Herzegovina had been placed under the administrative control of Austria, though actual possession was still to be vested in the Ottoman Empire. Serbia also coveted the territories, since they would double her kingdom and place her within striking distance of the Adriatic. Suddenly, in October, 1908, Austria annexed the two provinces, in flat violation of the Treaty of Berlin. The Serbs were furious and appealed to Russia. The Tsar's government threatened war, until Germany addressed a sharp note to St. Petersburg announcing her firm intention to back Austria. Since Russia had not yet fully recovered from her war with Japan and was plagued by internal troubles, she finally informed the Serbs that they would have to wait until a more favorable time.

Still more bad blood between the nations of Eastern Europe was created by the Balkan Wars. In 1912 Serbia, Bulgaria, Montenegro, and Greece, with encouragement from Russia, joined in a Balkan alliance for the conquest of the Turkish province of Macedonia. The war was started in October, 1912, and in less than two months the

Above: *Portrait of the Artist,* Vincent van Gogh (1853–1890). This self-portrait shows a deep seriousness and intense concentration. (V. W. van Gogh) Right: *Ia Orana Maria,* Paul Gauguin (1848–1903). Gauguin revolted not only against the complexity and artificiality of European life, but against civilization itself. He finally fled to Tahiti to paint the lush, colorful life of an uncorrupted society. (MMA) Below: *The Starry Night,* van Gogh. This painting gives vivid expression to van Gogh's bold conceptions. (Mus. Mod. Art) Below Right: *Sunflowers in a Vase,* van Gogh. The feverish technique seems to have endowed the flowers with rhythmic motion. (V. W. van Gogh)

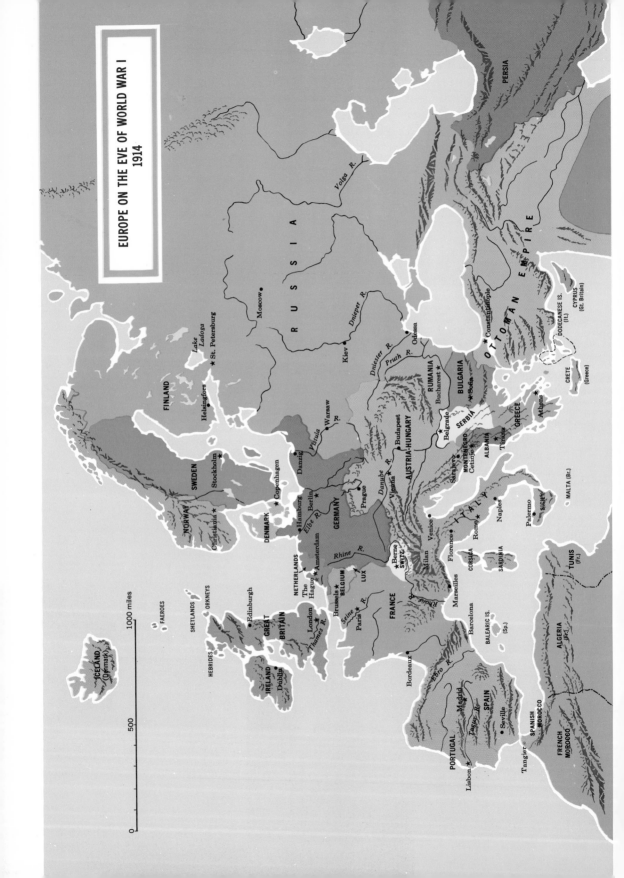

EUROPE ON THE EVE OF WORLD WAR I
1914

1000 miles

500

ICELAND
(Denmark)

FAEROES

SHETLANDS

ORKNEYS

HEBRIDES

Edinburgh ●

IRELAND
Dublin ●

GREAT
BRITAIN

London ★
Thames R.

NETHERLANDS
The Hague ★
Amsterdam ●
Brussels ★
BELGIUM
LUX.

FRANCE

Seine R.
Paris ★

Bordeaux ●

PORTUGAL
Lisbon ★

Madrid ★
Tagus R.
● Seville
SPAIN

SPANISH
MOROCCO

Tangier ●

FRENCH
MOROCCO

ALGERIA
(Fr.)

Ebro R.
Barcelona ●

BALEARIC IS.
(Sp.)

Marseilles ●

Rhone R.

Berne ★
SWITZ.
Milan ●

Venice ●

Florence ●

Rome ★

ITALY

Naples ●

CORSICA

SARDINIA

TUNIS
(Fr.)

SICILY

Palermo ●

MALTA (Br.)

NORWAY

Christiania ★

SWEDEN
Stockholm ★

DENMARK
Copenhagen ●

FINLAND

Helsingfors ●

Lake
Ladoga

St. Petersburg ★

Moscow ●

R U S S I A

Volga R.

Danzig ●

Hamburg ●

Berlin ★
Elbe R.

GERMANY

Prague ●

Vistula
R.

Warsaw ●

Rhine R.

Danube
R.

Vienna ●

Budapest ★
AUSTRIA-HUNGARY

Kiev ●

Dnieper R.

Dniester R.

Pruth R.

Odessa ●

RUMANIA
Bucharest ★

Belgrade ★
SERBIA

MONTENEGRO
Cetinje ●
Sarajevo ●

ALBANIA

Tirana ★

BULGARIA
★ Sofia

GREECE
Athens ★

O T T O M A N   E M P I R E

Constantinople ★

Odessa ●

CRETE
(Greece)

DODECANESE IS.
(It.)

CYPRUS
(Gt. Britain)

PERSIA

0

resistance of the Turks was shattered. Then came the problem of dividing the spoils. In secret treaties negotiated before hostilities began, Serbia had been promised Albania, in addition to a generous slice of Macedonia. But now Austria, fearful as always of any increase in Serbian power, intervened at the peace conference and obtained the establishment of Albania as an independent state. For the Serbs this was the last straw. It seemed that at every turn their path to western expansion was certain to be blocked by the Hapsburg government. From this time on, anti-Austrian agitation in Serbia and in the neighboring province of Bosnia became ever more venomous.

2. THE ROAD TO ARMAGEDDON

It is generally held that the immediate cause of World War I was the assassination of Archduke Francis Ferdinand on June 28, 1914. This was the match thrown into the powder-keg of accumulated suspicion and hate. Nevertheless, it was not quite so trivial an event as many people think. Francis Ferdinand was not simply a useless member of the Austrian nobility; he was soon to become Emperor. The reigning monarch, Francis Joseph, had reached his eighty-fourth year, and his death was expected momentarily. The murder of the heir to the throne was therefore considered as in a very real sense an attack upon the state.

The actual murderer of Francis Ferdinand was a Bosnian student by the name of Princip. But this does not tell half of the story. Princip was merely the tool of Serbian nationalists. The murder, though committed in Sarajevo, the capital of Bosnia, was the result of a plot hatched in Belgrade. The conspirators were members of a secret society officially known as Union or Death but commonly called the Black Hand. What were the motives of the conspirators? If there is any one answer, it would seem to lie in the plan which Francis Fer-

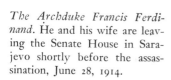

The Archduke Francis Ferdinand. He and his wife are leaving the Senate House in Sarajevo shortly before the assassination, June 28, 1914.

dinand was known to be developing for the reorganization of the Hapsburg Empire. This plan, designated as *trialism*, involved a proposal for changing the Dual Monarchy into a triple monarchy. In addition to German Austria and Magyar Hungary, already practically autonomous, there was to be a third semi-independent unit composed of the Slavs. This was exactly what the Serb nationalists did not want. They feared that if it were put into effect their Slovene and Croatian kinsmen would be content to remain under Hapsburg rule. Therefore they determined to get Francis Ferdinand out of the way before he could become Emperor of Austria-Hungary.

In the weeks immediately following the tragedy, Austrian officials conducted an investigation which confirmed their suspicions that the plot was of Serbian origin. Consequently, on July 23, they dispatched to the Serbian government a severe ultimatum consisting of eleven demands. Among other things Serbia was to suppress anti-Austrian newspapers, to crush the secret patriotic societies, to eliminate from the government and from the army all persons guilty of anti-Austrian propaganda, and to accept the collaboration of Austrian officials in stamping out the subversive movement against the Hapsburg Empire. On July 25, in accordance with the time limit of forty-eight hours, the Serbian government transmitted its reply. Of the total of eleven demands, only one was emphatically refused, and five were accepted without reservations. The German Chancellor regarded it as almost a capitulation, and the Kaiser declared that now all reason for war had fallen to the ground. The Austrians, however, pronounced it unsatisfactory, severed diplomatic relations, and mobilized parts of their army. The Serbs themselves had been under no illusions about pleasing Austria, since, three hours before transmitting their reply, they had issued an order to mobilize the troops.

The Austrian ultimatum to Serbia

At this point the attitude of other nations becomes important. In fact for some time before this, several of the rulers of the great powers had assumed very belligerent attitudes. As early as July 18 Sazonov, the Russian Foreign Minister, warned Austria that Russia would not tolerate any effort to humiliate Serbia. On July 24 Sazonov exclaimed to the German ambassador: "I do not hate Austria; I despise her. Austria is seeking a pretext to gobble up Serbia; but in that case Russia will make war on Austria."[1] In the adoption of this attitude, Russia had the support of France. About the twentieth of July, Raymond Poincaré, who was now President of the French Republic, paid a visit to St. Petersburg. He kept urging Sazonov to "be firm" and to avoid any compromise which might result in a loss of prestige for the Triple Entente. He warned the Austrian ambassador that "Serbia has very warm friends in the Russian people. And Russia has an ally, France."[2]

Russia and France assume a belligerent attitude

[1] S. B. Fay, *The Origins of the World War*, II, 300.
[2] *Ibid.*, II, 281.

The attitude of Germany in these critical days was ambiguous. Although the Kaiser was shocked and infuriated by the assassination, his government did not make any threats until after the actions of Russia gave cause for alarm. Unfortunately, both the Kaiser and the Chancellor, von Bethmann-Hollweg, adopted the premise that stern punishment must be meted out to Serbia without delay. They hoped in this way to confront the other powers with an accomplished fact. The Kaiser declared on June 30: "Now or never! Matters must be cleared up with the Serbs, *and that soon.*" On July 6 Bethmann-Hollweg gave to the Austrian Foreign Minister, Count Berchtold, a commitment which was interpreted by the latter as a blank check. The Austrian government was informed that the Kaiser would "stand true by Austria's side in accordance with his treaty obligations and old friendship." In giving this pledge Bethmann and his imperial master were gambling on the hope that Russia would not intervene for the protection of Serbia, and that therefore the quarrel would remain a mere local squabble.

Austria declared war against Serbia on July 28, 1914. For a fleeting, anxious moment there was a possibility that the conflict might be localized. But it was quickly transformed into a war of larger scope by the action of Russia. On July 29 Sazonov and the military clique persuaded the Tsar to issue an order to mobilize all of the troops, not only against Austria but against Germany as well. Their argument was a logical one. Such a vast country as Russia would require considerable time to get her military machine into operation. But before the order could be put into effect, Nicholas changed his mind, having just received an urgent appeal from the Kaiser to help in preserving peace. On July 30 Sazonov and General Tatistchev, the Chief of Staff, went to work to induce the Tsar to change his mind again. For more than an hour they sought to convince the reluctant autocrat that the entire military system should be set in motion. Finally, General Tatistchev remarked: "Yes, it is hard to decide." Nicholas retorted with a show of irritation: "I will decide," and signed an order for immediate mobilization. Sazonov hurried to the telephone to communicate the news to the Chief of Staff. The next morning in a remote Siberian village an English traveler was awakened by a commotion outside his window, followed by the query of an excited peasant: "Have you heard the news? There is war." [3]

There was now no drawing back from the abyss. The Germans were alarmed over Russian preparations for war. The latest action of the Tsar's government made the situation far more critical, since in German military circles, and also in French and Russian, general mobilization meant war. Upon learning that the Tsar's decree had gone into effect, the Kaiser's government sent an ultimatum to St. Petersburg demanding that mobilization cease within twelve hours.

The attitude of Germany

Russian mobilization

The German ultimatums to Russia and France

[3] *Ibid.,* II, 472–73.

August 1, 1914. A German officer reading the declaration of war in the streets of Berlin.

On the afternoon of August 1 the German ambassador requested an interview with the Russian Foreign Minister. He appealed to Sazonov for a favorable answer to the German ultimatum. Sazonov replied that mobilization could not be halted, but that Russia was willing to continue negotiations. The ambassador repeated his question a second and a third time, emphasizing the terrible consequences of a negative answer. Sazanov finally replied: "I have no other answer to give you." The ambassador then handed the Foreign Minister a declaration of war and, bursting into tears, left the room.[4] In the meantime, the Kaiser's ministers had also dispatched an ultimatum to France demanding that she make known her intentions. Premier Viviani replied on August 1 that France would act "in accordance with her interests," and immediately ordered a general mobilization of the army. On August 3 Germany declared war upon France.

All eyes now turned in the direction of Britain. What would she do, now that the other two members of the Triple Entente had rushed headlong into war? For some time after the situation on the Continent had become critical, Britain vacillated.

The attitude of Britain

It is difficult to believe that the British would have long remained out of the war, even if the neutrality of Belgium had never been violated. In fact, as early as July 29, Sir Edward Grey had given the German ambassador in London a "friendly and private" warning that if France were drawn into the war, Great Britain would enter also.[5] Nevertheless, it was the invasion of Belgian territory which

Britain enters the war

[4] G. P. Gooch, *Before the War: Studies in Diplomacy,* II, 368.
[5] B. E. Schmitt, "July, 1914: Thirty Years After," *Journal of Modern History,* XVI (1944), 193.

provided the immediate cause of Britain's unsheathing the sword. In 1839, along with the other great powers, she had signed a treaty guaranteeing the neutrality of Belgium. Moreover, it had been British policy for a century or more to try to prevent domination of the Low Countries, lying directly across the Channel, by any powerful Continental nation. But the famous Schlieffen Plan of the Germans provided for attacking France through Belgium. Accordingly, they demanded of the Belgian government permission to send troops across its territory, promising to respect the independence of the nation and to pay for any damage to property. When Belgium refused, the Kaiser's gray-coated legions began pouring across her frontier. The British Foreign Secretary immediately went before Parliament and presented the idea that his country should rally to the defense of international law and to the protection of small nations. He argued that peace under the circumstances would be a moral crime, and declared that if Britain should fail to uphold her obligations of honor in this matter she would forfeit the respect of the civilized world. The next day, August 4, the cabinet decided to send an ultimatum to Berlin demanding that Germany respect Belgian neutrality, and that she give a satisfactory reply by midnight. The Kaiser's ministers offered no answer save military necessity, arguing that it was a matter of life and death for Germany that her soldiers should reach France by the quickest and easiest way. As the clock struck twelve, Great Britain and Germany were at war.

Other nations were quickly drawn into the terrible vortex. On August 7 the Montenegrins joined with their kinsmen, the Serbs, in fighting Austria. Two weeks later the Japanese declared war upon Germany, partly because of their alliance with Great Britain, but mainly for the purpose of conquering the German possessions in the Far East. On August 1 Turkey negotiated an alliance with Germany and in October began the bombardment of Russian ports in the Black Sea. Thus most of the nations definitely bound by alliances entered the conflict in its early stages on one side or the other. Italy, however, though still technically a member of the Triple Alliance, proclaimed her neutrality. The Italians insisted that Germany was not fighting a defensive war, and that consequently they were not bound to go to her aid. Italy maintained her neutrality until May, 1915, when she was bribed by secret promises of Austrian and Turkish territory to engage in the war on the side of the Triple Entente.

The tumult and excitement that accompanied the beginning of the great holocaust of 1914 have long since died away. But the questions of how and why the conflagration occurred are still vital ones. Historians who have studied the evidence are generally of the opinion that no one nation was solely responsible. Perhaps none of the great powers really wanted war; they would have preferred to achieve their aims by other means. But in pursuing these aims they followed policies that made war virtually inevitable. The most dan-

The conflagration spreads

The question of war guilt

1029

gerous of national objectives were probably those of Germany. This was true not because they were more selfish than those of Russia or Austria but because they posed a more serious threat to the balance of power in Europe. Germany was attempting to achieve on the Continent of Europe objectives that Britain and France succeeded in attaining in Asia and Africa. Fritz Fischer has shown that, from the beginning of the war, some of Germany's rulers were thinking in terms of a vastly enlarged German empire that would include as satellite states, Poland, Belgium, Holland, the Balkans, and Turkey. Thus would be established a great sphere of influence comparable to that of the United States in the Western Hemisphere and of Russia in the heartland of Eurasia. How many of these territories would be annexed was not made clear; in any event they would constitute a gigantic *Mitteleuropa* dominated by Germany.[6] Fears of what this German scheme would do to the European balance of power produced nightmares in the chancelleries of London and Paris.

During the war and for years afterward there was a tendency among many historians to blame the conflict on the stupidity or criminality of rulers. The villain most commonly singled out was Kaiser Wilhelm II. Count Berchtold, Foreign Minister of Austria, and Alexander Sazonov, Foreign Minister of Russia, were also frequently named. It is doubtful, however, that any of these individuals acted with malevolent intent. For the most part, they did what they felt they had to do. They responded to pressure from various groups within their own countries—industrialists and financiers eager for new economic opportunities, and organizations of expansionists and chauvinists such as the Pan-German League and the Navy League in the Hohenzollern Empire. In some cases they feared revolution if they did not follow a bellicose foreign policy. Like numerous politicians throughout history they sensed the efficacy of a belligerent stand against foreign enemies as the best means of allaying dissension at home. Doubtless the motive that prompted most of them, though, was conformism with the prevailing system of power politics. This system involved suspicion and fear of neighboring countries. The world of nations was assumed to be a jungle, and the only way of preserving peace in that jungle was to curb the predations of warlike states with a balance of power. Whenever that balance was disturbed, it was taken for granted that the rulers of threatened nations must always be ready to throw down the gage of battle. No potential aggressor must be allowed to gain an advantage by springing a surprise of any kind. In some military circles it was argued that to preclude such a possibility launching a preventive war would be justified.

The guilt of individuals

[6] *Germany's Aims in the First World War*, pp. 348–349. Prof. Fischer is concerned primarily with German war aims formulated after the beginning of the war. He pays little regard to the fact that the objectives of a nation at war are almost invariably expanded *during* the conflict. Evidence for this can readily be found in the statement of Allied war aims contained in the notorious Secret Treaties, 1915–1917.

In the prophetic gospel known as Revelation it is related that the forces of good and evil shall be gathered together on "the great day of God" to do battle at Armageddon. The unknown author might almost have been thinking of the titanic conflict which engulfed the nations of Europe in 1914. For World War I was seldom admitted to be a struggle between rival imperialist powers or a product of nationalist jealousy. Instead, it was represented by spokesmen for both sides as a crusade against the forces of evil. No sooner had the war begun than social and political leaders in England and France pronounced it a gallant effort to safeguard the rights of the weak and to preserve the supremacy of international law and morality. Prime Minister Asquith on August 6, 1914, declared that Britain had entered the conflict to vindicate "the principle that smaller nationalities are not to be crushed by the arbitrary will of a strong and overmastering Power." Across the Channel, President Poincaré was pompously assuring his countrymen that France had no other purpose than to stand "before the universe for Liberty, Justice and Reason." Later, as a consequence of the inspiring preaching of such eloquent writers and orators as H. G. Wells, Gilbert Murray, and Woodrow Wilson, the crusade of the Entente powers became a war "to end all wars," to "make the world safe for democracy," and to redeem mankind from the curse of militarism. In the opposing camp the subordinates of the Kaiser were doing all in their power to justify Germany's military efforts. The struggle against the Allies was represented to the German people as a crusade on behalf of a superior *Kultur* and as a battle to protect the Fatherland against the wicked encirclement policy of the Entente nations.[7]

The holy war of the principal powers

World War I was unique in several respects. Not only were scores of new weapons introduced, but methods of fighting differed quite radically from those in most earlier conflicts. Open warfare disappeared from the Western Front almost at the beginning. After the first few weeks the opposing armies settled down in a vast network of trenches, from which attacks to dislodge the enemy were launched usually in the murky hours just before dawn. For the most part, the struggle was an endurance contest, in which victory depended mainly upon natural resources and upon the ability of the Entente nations to obtain almost unlimited supplies of money, food, and munitions from across the sea. Probably it is safe to say that World War I was fought with greater savagery than any preceding military engagement of modern times. The use of poison gas, of the machine gun, of liquid fire, and of explosive bullets took a toll in lives and in ghastly wounds unprecedented even in the much longer campaigns of Napoleon. It is an interesting sidelight on this savagery

Unique features of World War I

[7] The quotations in this paragraph are taken from J. S. Ewart, *The Roots and Causes of the Wars*, I, 16, 104. See also I. C. Willis, *England's Holy War*.

Modern Warfare. Top: After the first few battles, World War I on the Western Front settled into static or position warfare. During the four-year period veritable cities of mud, stone, and timber sprang up behind the trenches. Left: British armored trucks move toward the front. Above: A British tank and field ambulance.

that the number of civilians killed in air raids, in massacres, in famines, and in epidemics exceeded the number of soldiers killed in battle. Finally, the war was unique in the tremendous size of its armies. Altogether about 65,000,000 men fought for longer or shorter periods under the flags of the various belligerents. This was the climax of the steady trend toward mass warfare that had had its beginning during the French Revolution.

As the conflict dragged on through four appalling years, more and more nations threw down the gage of battle on one side or the other. We have seen that Italy postponed her entrance until the spring of 1915. Bulgaria joined the Central Powers in September, 1915, and Rumania entered on the opposite side about a year later.

But the event which finally tipped the scales in favor of an Entente victory was the declaration of war against Germany by the United States on April 6, 1917. The United States entered the war for a variety of reasons. All sorts of moral arguments were avowed by President Wilson and other high officials of the government—to "make the world safe for democracy," to banish autocracy and militarism, and to establish a league or society of nations in place of the old diplomatic maneuvering. Undoubtedly, the primary reason, though, was the concern of the American government over maintenance of the balance of power in Europe. For years it had been a cardinal doctrine in the State Department and among military and naval officers that the security of the United States depended upon a balance of forces in the Old World. No one power must be allowed to establish its supremacy over all of Europe. So long as Great Britain was strong enough to prevent that supremacy, the United States was safe. Some authorities believe that American officials had grown so accustomed to thinking of the British Navy as the shield and buckler of American security that they could hardly tolerate the thought of any different situation. Germany, however, presented not merely a challenge to British naval supremacy but threatened to starve the British nation into surrender and make herself dominant over all of Europe.

The direct cause of United States participation in World War I was the submarine warfare of the Germans. Some historians regard it as the most important of all the factors, on the ground that without it the United States would not have entered the war at all. When the war began, Germany had only a small fleet of submarines, but she rapidly increased their number. On February 4, 1915, the Kaiser's government announced that neutral vessels headed for British ports would be torpedoed without warning. President Wilson

Widening of the conflict; entrance of the United States

The submarine warfare of the Germans

Wartime Leaders. Left: Haig, Joffre, and Lloyd George discuss strategy. Right: Reviewing a map are members of the German high command, Hindenburg, William II, and Ludendorff.

The Lusitania Leaving New York Harbor. In February of 1915 the Lusitania was torpedoed and sunk by a German U-boat. Among the nearly 1200 people drowned were 119 Americans. The disaster was one step in the chain of events which led to the entry of the United States into the war on the side of Britain and France.

replied to this challenge by declaring that the United States would hold Germany to "a strict accountability" if any harm should come to American lives or property. The warning had little effect. The Germans were convinced that the U-boat was one of their most valuable weapons, and they considered themselves justified in using it as an answer to the British blockade. They violated pledges to respect American rights and continued occasional sinkings of passenger vessels, in some cases causing the deaths of American citizens. When the Kaiser's ministers announced that, on February 1, 1917, they would launch a campaign of unrestricted submarine warfare, Wilson cut off diplomatic relations with the Berlin government. On April 2 he went before a joint session of the two houses of Congress and requested a declaration of war. The declaration was approved four days later with only six negative votes in the Senate and fifty in the House of Representatives.

Peace proposals

While fighting on the several fronts raged through four horrible years, various attempts were made to bring about the negotiation of peace. In the spring of 1917 Dutch and Scandinavian socialists decided to summon an international socialist conference to meet at Stockholm in the hope of drafting plans for ending the fighting which would be acceptable to all the belligerents. The Petrograd Soviet embraced the idea and on May 15 issued an appeal to socialists of all nations to send delegates to the conference and to induce their governments to agree to a peace "without annexations and indemnities, on the basis of the self-determination of peoples." The socialist parties in all the principal countries on both sides of the war accepted this formula and were eager to send delegates to the conference; but when the British and French governments refused to permit any of their subjects to attend, the project was abandoned. That the rulers of the Entente states were not afraid of these proposals merely because they emanated from socialists is indicated by the fact that a similar formula suggested by the Pope was just as emphatically rejected. On August 1 of this same year Pope Benedict XV appealed to the various governments to agree to the renunciation of claims for indemnities, to the future settlement of international disputes by arbitration, to a reduction of armaments, to the restoration of all occupied areas, and to the holding of plebiscites to determine what should be done with such territories as Alsace-Lorraine, Poland, and the Trentino. Nowhere was there a disposition to take these proposals seriously. Woodrow Wilson, as spokesman for the Allies, declared that negotiation of peace *under any conditions* was impossible so long as Germany was ruled by the Kaiser. The Central Powers professed to regard with favor the general import of the papal suggestions, but they refused to commit themselves on indemnities and restorations especially the restoration of Belgium.

The most famous of all the peace proposals was President Wilson's program of Fourteen Points, which he incorporated in an address to Congress on January 8, 1918. Summarized as briefly as possible, this program included: (1) "open covenants openly arrived at," or the abolition of secret diplomacy; (2) freedom of the seas; (3) removal of economic barriers between nations; (4) reduction of national armaments "to the lowest point consistent with safety"; (5) impartial adjustment of colonial claims, with consideration for the interests of the peoples involved; (6) evacuation of Russia; (7) restoration of the independence of Belgium; (8) restoration of Alsace and Lorraine to France; (9) a readjustment of Italian frontiers "along clearly recognizable lines of nationality", (10) autonomous development for the peoples of Austria-Hungary; (11) restoration of Rumania, Serbia, and Montenegro, with access to the sea for Serbia; (12) autonomous development for the peoples of Turkey, with the Straits from the Black Sea to the Mediterranean "permanently opened"; (13) an independent Poland, "inhabited by indisputably Polish populations," and with access to the sea; (14) a League of Nations. On several other occasions throughout 1918 Wilson reiterated in public addresses that this program would be the basis of the peace for which he would labor. Thousands of copies of the Fourteen Points were scattered by Allied planes over the German trenches and behind the lines in an effort to convince both soldiers and people that the Entente nations were striving for a just and durable peace.

By the close of the summer of 1918 the long nightmare of carnage was approaching its end. A great offensive launched by the British, French, and United States forces in July dealt one shattering blow after another to the German battalions and forced them back almost to the Belgian frontier. By the end of September the cause of the Central Powers was hopeless. Bulgaria withdrew from the war on September 30. Early in October the new Chancellor of Germany, the liberal Prince Max of Baden, appealed to President Wilson for a negotiated peace on the basis of the Fourteen Points. But the fighting went on, for Wilson had returned to his original demand that Germany must drop the Kaiser. Soon afterward Germany's remaining allies were tottering on the verge of collapse. Turkey surrendered at the end of October. The Hapsburg Empire was being

HALT the HUN!

BUY U.S. GOVERNMENT BONDS
THIRD LIBERTY LOAN

World War I Posters Held Back Little in Their Appeal to Emotions.

The approaching end of the struggle

cracked wide open by the revolts of the Slavs. Moreover, an Austrian offensive against Italy had not only failed but had incited the Italians to a counteroffensive, with the consequent loss to Austria of the city of Trieste and 300,000 prisoners. On November 3 the Emperor Charles, who had succeeded Francis Joseph in 1916, signed an armistice which took Austria out of the war.

Germany was now left with the impossible task of carrying on the struggle alone. The morale of her troops was rapidly breaking. The blockade was causing such a shortage of food that her people were in danger of starving. The revolutionary tremors that had been felt for some time swelled into a mighty earthquake. On November 8 a republic was proclaimed in Bavaria. The next day nearly all of Germany was in the throes of revolution. A decree was published in Berlin announcing the Kaiser's abdication, and early the next morning the neurotic old gentleman was hustled across the frontier into Holland. In the meantime, the government of the nation had passed into the hands of a provisional council headed by Friedrich Ebert, leader of the socialists in the Reichstag. Ebert and his colleagues immediately took steps to conclude negotiations for an armistice. The terms as now laid down by the Allies provided for acceptance of the Fourteen Points with three amendments. First, the item on freedom of the seas was to be stricken (in accordance with the request of the British). Second, restoration of invaded areas was to be interpreted in such a way as to include *reparations*. Third, the demand for autonomy for the subject peoples of Austria-Hungary was to be changed to a demand for *independence*. In addition, troops of the Entente nations were to occupy cities in the Rhine valley; the blockade was to be continued in force; and Germany was to hand over 5000 locomotives, 150,000 railway cars, and 5000 motor trucks, all in good condition. There was nothing that the Germans could do but accept these terms. At five o'clock in the morning of November 11, two delegates of the defeated nation met with Marshal Foch in the dark Compiègne forest and signed the papers offi-

German Supplies Moving toward the Somme Front during the Last German Offensive in 1918

cially ending the war. Six hours later the order, "cease fire," was given to the troops. That night thousands of people danced through the streets of London, Paris, and Rome in the same delirium of excitement with which they had greeted the declarations of war.

Victory had been won at last, but what a grim tragedy it turned out to be. Of a total of over 42,000,000 men mobilized by the Entente allies, at least 7,000,000 had been slaughtered. Five million of these had been killed in action or had died of wounds; the remainder had been reported "missing" after the battles were over. More than 3,000,000 others had been totally disabled. Thus it will be seen that almost one out of every four of the soldiers enlisted in the Allied armies suffered a major casualty. This would have been a terrific price even if all the results which were supposed to flow from an Entente victory had really been achieved. But few indeed were the permanent gains. The war which was to "end all wars" sowed the seeds of a new and more terrible conflict in the future. The autocracy of the Kaiser was indeed destroyed, but the ground was prepared for new despotisms which made the empire of William II look like a haven of liberty. In addition, World War I did nothing to abate either militarism or nationalism. Twenty years after the fighting had ended, there were nearly twice as many men under arms as in 1913; and national rivalries and racial hatreds were as deeply ingrained as ever.

The price of victory

4. THE VICTORS' PEACE

The peace concluded at the various conferences in 1919 and 1920 resembled more closely a sentence from a court than a negotiated settlement. The explanation may be found primarily in the fact that the war became a peoples' war rather than a war of governments. Mob passions raged during the conflict and inhibited rational judgments. Politicians pandered to these passions and, in some instances, cultivated them zealously. Thus David Lloyd George campaigned during the election of 1918 on the slogan, "Hang the Kaiser!", while one of his partisans demanded "Squeeze the German lemon until the pips squeak!". In all the Allied countries nationalism and democracy combined to make compromise impossible and to interpret the war as a crusade of Good against Evil. The peace settlement drafted by the victors inevitably reflected these feelings.

Character of the Allied peace settlement

Had the Central Powers emerged victorious in the war, the world might well have seen an even harsher peace. The major examples leading to such a conclusion are the treaties of Brest-Litovsk and Bucharest. The former was concluded by Germany with Russia in March 1918. Its terms required the Russians to surrender control over Estonia, Latvia, Lithuania, and Russian Poland, to recognize the independence of Finland and the Ukraine, and to pay an indemnity of $1,500,000,000. The treaty of Bucharest, imposed upon Rumania in February 1918, provided for the cession of territory to Bulgaria

The Treaties of Brest-Litovsk and Bucharest

The Council of Four. Meeting to draft a peace treaty in Paris were Orlando of Italy, Lloyd George of Britain, Clemenceau of France, and U.S. president Wilson.

and Hungary and gave to the Central Powers such extensive control over the Danube and over the railways and oilfields that Rumania would have been placed in a condition of economic vassalage for years to come. The final defeat of Germany and her allies resulted in the abrogation of both of these treaties, though most of the territories taken from Russia were not restored to her because of antagonism in Western countries toward the new Soviet rulers.

The Paris Conference

The conference convoked in Paris [8] to draft a peace with Germany was technically in session from January until June of 1919, but only six plenary meetings were ever held. Most of the delegates might just as well have stayed at home. All of the important business of the conference was transacted by small committees. At first there was the Council of Ten, made up of the President and Secretary of State of the United States, and the premiers and foreign ministers of Great Britain, France, Italy, and Japan. By the middle of March this body had been found too unwieldy and was reduced to the Council of Four, consisting of the American President and the English, Italian, and French premiers. A month later the Council of Four became the Council of Three when Premier Orlando withdrew from the conference in a huff because Wilson refused to give Italy all she demanded.

The Big Three: Wilson and Lloyd George

The final character of the Treaty of Versailles was determined almost entirely by the so-called Big Three—Wilson, Lloyd George, and Clemenceau. These men were about as different in personality as any three rulers who could ever have been brought together for a common purpose. Wilson was an inflexible idealist, accustomed to dictating to subordinates and convinced that the hosts of righteousness were on his side. When confronted with unpleasant realities, such as the secret treaties among the Entente governments for division of the spoils, he had a habit of dismissing them as unimportant

---

[8] The conference did most of its work in Paris. The treaty of peace with Germany, however, takes its name from Versailles, the suburb of Paris in which it was signed.

and eventually forgetting that he had ever heard of them. Though he knew little of the devious trickeries of European diplomacy, his unbending temperament made it difficult for him to take advice or to adjust his views to those of his colleagues. David Lloyd George was a canny little Welsh attorney who had succeeded Asquith as Prime Minister of Britain in 1916. His cleverness and his Celtic humor enabled him to succeed, on occasions, where Wilson failed; but he was above all a politician—shifty, ignorant of European conditions, and unconcerned about even his most critical mistakes. Clemenceau said of him: "I suppose that man can read, but I doubt that he ever does."

The third member of the great triumvirate was the aged and cynical French Premier, Georges Clemenceau. Born when the nineteenth century was still young, Clemenceau had been a journalist in the United States just after the Civil War. Later he had won his nickname of "the Tiger" as a relentless foe of clericals and monarchists. He had fought for the French Republic during the stormy days of the Boulangist episode, the Dreyfus affair, and the struggle for separation of church and state. Twice in his lifetime he had seen France invaded and her existence gravely imperiled. Now the tables were turned, and the French, he believed, should take full advantage of their opportunity. Only by keeping a strict control over a prostrate Germany could the security of France be preserved.

Clemenceau

From the beginning a number of embarrassing problems confronted the chief architects of the Versailles Treaty. The most important was what to do about the Fourteen Points. There could be no doubt that they had been the basis of the German surrender on November 11. It was beyond question also that Wilson had represented them as the Entente program for a permanent peace. Consequently there was every reason for the peoples of the world to expect that the Fourteen Points would be the model for the Versailles settlement—subject only to the three amendments made before the armistice was signed. But what was the result? Not a soul among the highest dignitaries at the conference, with the exception of Wilson himself, gave more than lip service to the Fourteen Points. In the end, the American President was able to salvage, in unmodified form, only four of the parts of his famous program: point seven, requiring the restoration of Belgium; point eight, demanding the return of Alsace and Lorraine to France; point ten, providing for independence for the peoples of Austria-Hungary; and the final provision calling for a League of Nations. The others were ignored or modified to such an extent as to change their original meaning.

Emasculating the Fourteen Points

By the end of April 1919 the terms of the Versailles Treaty were ready for submission to the enemy, and Germany was ordered to send delegates to receive them. On April 29, a delegation, headed by Count von Brockdorff-Rantzau, Foreign Minister of the provisional republic, arrived in Versailles. A week later the members of the delegation were commanded to appear before the Allied representa-

Germany sentenced

tives to receive the sentence of their nation. When Brockdorff-Rantzau protested that the terms were too harsh, he was informed by Clemenceau that Germany would have exactly three weeks in which to make up her mind whether to sign or not to sign. Eventually the time had to be extended, for the heads of the German government resigned their positions rather than accept the treaty. Their attitude was summed up by Chancellor Philip Scheidemann in the pointed statement: "What hand would not wither that sought to lay itself and us in those chains?" The Big Three now made a few minor adjustments, mainly at the instance of Lloyd George, and Germany was notified that seven o'clock on the evening of June 23 would bring either acceptance or invasion. Shortly after five a new government of the provisional republic announced that it would yield to "overwhelming force" and accede to the victors' terms. On June 28, the fifth anniversary of the murder of the Austrian Archduke, representatives of the German and Allied governments assembled in the Hall of Mirrors at Versailles and affixed their signatures to the treaty.

The provisions of the Treaty of Versailles can be outlined briefly. Germany was required to surrender Alsace and Lorraine to France, northern Schleswig to Denmark, and most of Posen and West Prussia to Poland. The coal mines of the Saar Basin were to be ceded to France, to be exploited by her for fifteen years. At the end of this time the German government would have the privilege of buying them back. The Saar territory itself was to be administered by the League of Nations until 1935 when a plebiscite would be held to determine whether it should remain under the League, be returned to Germany, or be awarded to France. Germany's province of East Prussia was cut off from the rest of her territory, and her port of Danzig, almost wholly German, was subjected to the political control of the League of Nations and to the economic domination of Poland. Germany was, of course, disarmed. She gave up all of her submarines and her navy of surface vessels, with the exception of six small battleships, six light cruisers, six destroyers, and twelve torpedo boats. She was forbidden to have any airplanes, either military or naval, and her army was limited to 100,000 officers and men, to be recruited by voluntary enlistment. To make sure that she would not launch any new attack upon France or Belgium, she was forbidden to keep soldiers or maintain fortifications in the Rhine valley. Lastly, Germany and her allies were held responsible for all the loss and damage suffered by the Entente governments and their citizens, "as a consequence of the war imposed upon them by the aggression of Germany and her allies." This was the so-called war-guilt provision of the treaty (Article 231), but it was also the basis for German reparations. The exact amount that Germany should pay was left to a Reparations Commission. In 1921 the total was set at $33,000,000,000.

For the most part, the Treaty of Versailles applied only to Germany. Separate pacts were drawn up to settle accounts with

The main provisions of the Treaty of Versailles

Germany's allies—Austria, Hungary, Bulgaria, and Turkey. The final form of these minor treaties was determined primarily by a Council of Five, composed of Clemenceau as chairman and one delegate each from the United States, Great Britain, France, and Italy. The settlement with Austria, completed in September, 1919, is known as the Treaty of St. Germain. Austria was required to recognize the independence of Hungary, Czechoslovakia, Yugoslavia, and Poland and to cede to them large portions of her territory. In addition, she was compelled to surrender Trieste, the south Tyrol, and the Istrian peninsula to Italy. Altogether the Austrian portion of the Dual Monarchy was deprived of three-fourths of its area and three-fourths of its people. In several of the territories surrendered the inhabitants were largely German-speaking—for example, the Tyrol, and the region of the Sudeten Mountains awarded to Czechoslovakia. The Austrian nation itself was reduced to a small, land-locked state, with nearly one-third of its population concentrated in the city of Vienna.

The second of the minor treaties was that of Neuilly with Bulgaria, which was signed in November 1919. Bulgaria was forced to give up nearly all of the territory she had gained since the First Balkan War. The Dobrudja went back to Rumania, western Macedonia to the new kingdom of Yugoslavia, and western Thrace to Greece. All of these regions were inhabited by large Bulgarian minorities. Since Hungary was now an independent state, it was necessary that a separate treaty be imposed upon her. This was the Treaty of the Trianon Palace, signed in June 1920. It required that Slovakia should be ceded to the Republic of Czechoslovakia, Transylvania to Rumania, and Croatia-Slavonia to Yugoslavia. In few cases was the principle of self-determination of peoples more flagrantly violated. Numerous sections of Transylvania had a population that was more than half Hungarian. Included in the region of Slovakia were not only Slovaks but almost a million Magyars and about 500,000 Ruthenians. As a consequence, a fanatical irredentist movement flourished in Hungary after the war, directed toward the recovery of these lost provinces. It may be pertinent to add that the Treaty of the Trianon Palace slashed the area of Hungary from 125,000 square miles to 35,000, and her population from 22,000,000 to 8,000,000.

The settlement with Turkey was a product of unusual circumstances. The secret treaties had contemplated the transfer of Constantinople and Armenia to Russia and the division of most of the remainder of Turkey between Britain and France. But Russia's withdrawal from the war after the Bolshevik revolution, together with insistence by Italy and Greece upon fulfillment of promises made to them, necessitated considerable revision of the original scheme. Finally, in August 1920, a treaty was signed at Sèvres, near Paris, and submitted to the government of the Sultan. It provided that Armenia be organized as a Christian republic, that most of Tur-

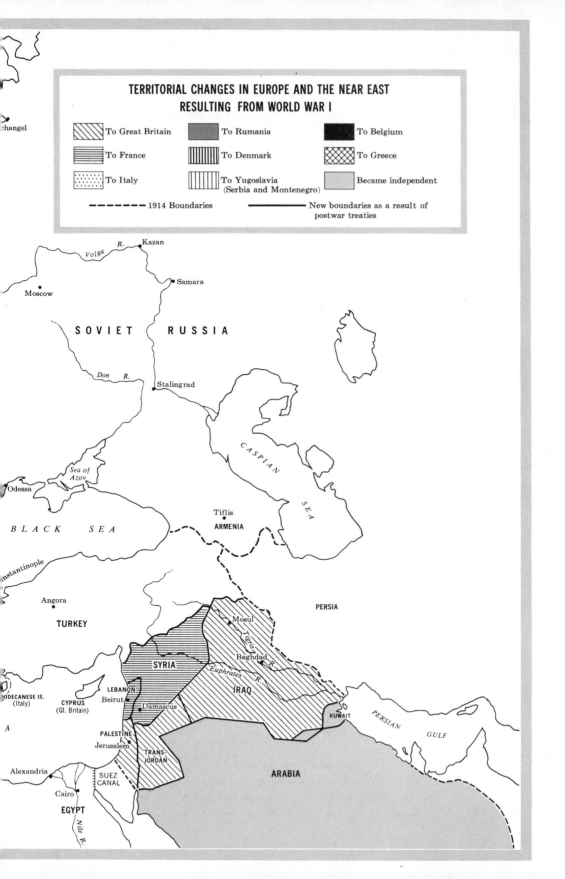

TERRITORIAL CHANGES IN EUROPE AND THE NEAR EAST RESULTING FROM WORLD WAR I

To Great Britain

To France

To Italy

To Rumania

To Denmark

To Yugoslavia
(Serbia and Montenegro)

To Belgium

To Greece

Became independent

- - - - - - 1914 Boundaries

———— New boundaries as a result of postwar treaties

Archangel

Volga R.

Kazan

Moscow

Samara

SOVIET RUSSIA

Don R.

Stalingrad

CASPIAN SEA

Sea of Azov

Odessa

BLACK SEA

Tiflis

ARMENIA

Constantinople

Angora

TURKEY

Mosul

PERSIA

Tigris R.

Baghdad

SYRIA

Euphrates R.

DODECANESE IS.
(Italy)

CYPRUS
(Gt. Britain)

LEBANON

Beirut

Damascus

IRAQ

KUWAIT

PERSIAN GULF

PALESTINE

Jerusalem

TRANS-JORDAN

Alexandria

SUEZ CANAL

ARABIA

Cairo

EGYPT

Nile R.

key in Europe be given to Greece, that Palestine and Mesopotamia become British mandates, that Syria become a mandate of France, and that southern Anatolia be set apart as a sphere of influence for Italy. About all that would be left of the Ottoman Empire would be the city of Constantinople and the northern and central portions of Asia Minor. The decrepit government of the Sultan, overawed by Allied military forces, agreed to accept this treaty. But a revolutionary government of Turkish nationalists, which had been organized at Ankara under the leadership of Mustapha Kemal (later called Ataturk), determined to prevent the settlement of Sèvres from being put into effect. The forces of Kemal obliterated the republic of Armenia, frightened the Italians into withdrawing from Anatolia, and conquered most of the territory in Europe which had been given to Greece. At last, in November 1922, they occupied Constantinople, deposed the Sultan, and proclaimed Turkey a republic. The Allies now consented to a revision of the peace. A new treaty was concluded at Lausanne in Switzerland in 1923, which permitted the Turks to retain practically all of the territory they had conquered. Though much reduced in size compared with the old Ottoman Empire, the Turkish republic still had an area of about 300,000 square miles and a population of 13,000,000.

Incorporated in each of the five treaties which liquidated the war with the Central Powers was the Covenant of the League of Nations. The establishment of a League in which the states of the world, both great and small, would cooperate for the preservation of peace had long been the cherished dream of President Wilson. Indeed, that had been one of his chief reasons for taking the United States into the war. He believed that the defeat of Germany would mean the deathblow of militarism, and that the road would thenceforth be clear for setting up the control of international relations by a *community* of power instead of by the cumbersome and ineffective balance of power. But in order to get the League accepted at all, he felt himself compelled to make numerous compromises. He permitted his original idea of providing for a reduction of armaments "to the lowest point consistent with domestic safety" to be changed into the altogether different phrasing of "consistent with *national* safety." To induce the Japanese to accept the League he allowed them to keep the former German concessions in China. To please the French he sanctioned the exclusion of both Germany and Russia from his proposed federation, despite his long insistence that it should be a combination of *all* the nations. These handicaps were serious enough. But the League received an even more deadly blow when it was repudiated by the very nation whose President had fathered it.

Established under such unfavorable auspices, the League was never a brilliant success in achieving the aims of its founder. In only a few cases did it succeed in allaying the specter of war, and in each of these the parties to the dispute were small nations. But in every

The League of Nations

League of Nations Buildings, Geneva, Switzerland. Since the dissolution of the League in 1946, its main building has been occupied by the International Labor Office.

dispute involving one or more major powers, the League failed. It did nothing about the seizure of Vilna by Poland in 1920, because Lithuania, the victimized nation, was friendless, while Poland had the powerful backing of France. When, in 1923, war threatened between Italy and Greece, the Italians refused to submit to the intervention of the League, and the dispute had to be settled by direct mediation of Great Britain and France. Thereafter, in every great crisis the League was either defied or ignored. Its authority was flouted by Japan in seizing Manchuria in 1931 and by Italy in conquering Ethiopia in 1936. By September 1938, when the Czechoslovakian crisis arose, the prestige of the League had sunk so low that scarcely anyone thought of appealing to it. On the other hand, the point must be made that Wilson's great project justified its existence in other, less spectacular, ways. It reduced the international opium traffic and aided poor and backward countries in controlling the spread of disease. Its agencies collected invaluable statistics on labor and business conditions throughout the world. It conducted plebiscites in disputed areas, supervised the administration of internationalized cities, helped in finding homes for racial and political refugees, and made a notable beginning in codifying international law. Such achievements may well be regarded as providing a substantial groundwork for a later effort at international organization, the United Nations, formed after World War II.

Successes and failures of the League

SELECTED READINGS

· *Items so designated are available in paperbound editions.*

WORLD WAR I

Chambers, Frank, *The War behind the War, 1914–1918: A History of the Political and Civilian Fronts*, London, 1939. A graphic portrayal of civilian attitudes and political and economic problems.

READINGS

· Dehio, Ludwig, *Germany and World Politics in the Twentieth Century*, London, 1959 (Norton Library).

Earle, E. M., *Turkey, the Great Powers and the Bagdad Railway*, New York, 1924.

· Fay, S. B., *The Origins of the World War*, New York, (Free Press), 2 vols.

· Feis, Herbert, *Europe: The World's Banker, 1870–1914*, New Haven, 1930 (Norton Library).

· Fischer, Fritz, *Germany's Aims in the First World War*, New York, 1967 (Norton).

· ———, *World Power or Decline: The Controversy over Germany's Aims in the First World War*, New York, 1973 (Norton).

· Gregory, Ross, *Origins of American Intervention in the First World War*, New York, 1971 (Norton).

· Lafore, Laurence, *The Long Fuse: An Interpretation of the Origins of World War I*, Philadelphia, 1965 (Lippincott). A discriminating account.

· Lee, D. E., *The First World War—Who Was Responsible?* New York, 1963 (Heath, rev. ed.).

Link, A. S., *Wilson: The Struggle for Neutrality*, Princeton, 1961. A well-balanced, scholarly account.

· Mayne, Richard, *The Community of Europe*, New York, 1963 (Norton).

Morgenthau, Hans, *Politics among Nations*, New York, 1954.

Read, J. M., *Atrocity Propaganda, 1914–1919*, New Haven, 1941.

Remak, Joachim, *Sarajevo*, New York, 1959. Fascinating and scholarly.

Tansill, C. C., *America Goes to War*, Boston, 1938. A scholarly and very critical account.

Taylor, A. J. P., *The Struggle for Mastery in Europe, 1848–1918*, New York, 1954. A well-balanced account.

Thomson, G. M., *Twelve Days, 24 July–4 August*, London, 1964. Thorough and scholarly.

· Turner, L. C. F., *Origins of the First World War*, New York, 1970 (Norton).

Vagts, Alfred, *A History of Militarism*, New York, 1937.

· Wheeler-Bennett, J. W., *Brest-Litovsk: The Forgotten Peace, March 1918*, New York, 1938 (Norton Library).

THE PEACE OF 1919–1920

· Bailey, T. A., *Woodrow Wilson and the Lost Peace*, New York, 1944 (Quadrangle).

Birdsall, Paul, *Versailles Twenty Years After*, New York, 1941.

Mayer, Arno J., *Politics and Diplomacy of Peacemaking: Containment and Counter-revolution at Versailles, 1918–1919*, New York, 1967.

Nicolson, Harold, *Peacemaking, 1919*, New York, 1946.

SOURCE MATERIALS

Baker, R. S., and Dodd, W. E., eds., *The Public Papers of Woodrow Wilson*, 6 vols.

Carnegie Endowment for International Peace, *The Treaties of Peace, 1919–1923*, 2 vols.

Gooch, G. P., and Temperley, H., eds., *British Documents on the Origins of the War, 1898–1914*.

Grey of Fallodon, Edward Grey, 1st viscount, *Twenty-five Years*, New York, 1937, 2 vols.

Hendrick, B. J., ed., *The Life and Letters of Walter Hines Page*, 2 vols.

CHAPTER 35

The Challenge of Totalitarianism

> Revolution, *n*. In politics, an abrupt change in the form of government.
> —Ambrose Bierce, *The Devil's Dictionary*
> Poverty is the parent of revolution and crime.
> —Aristotle, *Politics*, II.vi (Jowett trans.)

Though republicanism had made some progress in Europe by 1914, the same could not be said for democracy. France was a thriving republic and so was Switzerland. Moreover, quite a number of governments headed by monarchs were republics in everything but name. The list included Great Britain, Sweden, Denmark, Norway, Belgium, the Netherlands, Italy, and in some respects Germany and Austria-Hungary. Yet few of these could be considered democracies in the political sense, and almost none of them in a social and economic sense. The real issue in most parts of Continental Europe was whether control of the government and the economic system should continue in the possession of feudal aristocracies, industrialists, and financiers, or a combination of all of them. None of these elements had gone very far in providing the masses with rights and privileges. It was inevitable, therefore, that the war in many countries should have taken on the character of a "war within a war," that the masses should have seen in the emergency an opportunity to dethrone their oppressors. In some cases, the opportunity was not grasped until after the international conflict had ended. But in Russia the bourgeoisie overturned the autocracy in March 1917, and were themselves overturned by the Bolsheviks later in the same year. Socialists in Germany overthrew the Kaiser in early November 1918. The British and French governments had serious trouble with striking workmen, and Britain passed under control of the Labour party a few years after the conflict had ended. Nearly everywhere the right

Struggles of the masses

1047

of the old ruling classes to govern became a major issue. The gravest challenge to that right after the war was thrown down by Italy and Germany. Each adopted compulsory military training openly or in secret, and Germany began a program of naval expansion in 1935. Perverted though their fascist regimes were, they had many of the characteristics of mass movements.

I. THE EMERGENCE OF FASCISM

The first of the nations of Western Europe to turn its back on the old ruling class was Italy. This may seem strange in view of the fact that the Italians emerged from World War I on the winning side. But the point must be kept in mind that Italy had been the victim of frustrated nationalism for many years. Time after time her aspirations for power and for empire had been shattered. The effect was to produce a sense of humiliation and shame, especially in the minds of the younger generation, and to foster an attitude of contempt for the existing political regime. Members of the old ruling class were held up to scorn as cynical, vacillating, defeatist, and corrupt. Even before World War I there was talk of revolution, of the need for a drastic housecleaning that would deliver the country from its incompetent rulers.

*Frustrated
nationalism
in Italy*

But the establishment of a Fascist dictatorship in Italy would never have been possible without the demoralizing and humiliating effects of World War I. The chief business of the Italian armies had been to keep the Austrians occupied on the Southern Front while the British, French, and Americans hammered Germany into submission along the battle lines in Flanders. To accomplish her purpose Italy had to mobilize more than 5,500,000 men, and of these nearly 700,000 were killed. The direct financial cost of her participation in the struggle was over $15,000,000,000. These sacrifices, of course, were no greater than those made by the British and the French; but Italy was a poor country. Moreover, in the division of the spoils after the fighting was over, the Italians got less than they expected. While Italy did receive most of the Austrian territories promised her in the secret treaties, she maintained that these were inadequate rewards for her sacrifices and for her valuable contribution to an Entente victory. At first the nationalists vented their spleen for the "humiliation of Versailles" upon President Wilson, but after a short time they returned to their old habit of castigating Italy's rulers. They alleged that such men as Premier Orlando had been so cravenly weak and inept that they had allowed their own country to be cheated.

*The demoralizing
and humiliating
effects of the war*

The war contributed to the revolution in a multitude of other ways. It resulted in inflation of the currency, with consequent high prices, speculation, and profiteering. Normally wages would have risen also, but the labor market was glutted on account of the return to civilian life of millions of soldiers. Furthermore, business was demoralized, owing to extensive and frequent strikes and to the closing of foreign markets. Perhaps the most serious consequence of the war, to the upper and middle classes at least, was the growth of socialism. As hardship and chaos increased, the socialists embraced a philosophy akin to Bolshevism. In 1918 they voted as a party to join the Moscow International. In the elections of November 1919, they won about a third of the seats in the Chamber of Deputies. During the following winter socialist workers took over about a hundred factories and attempted to run them for the benefit of the proletariat. Radicalism also spread through the rural areas, where the so-called Red Leagues were organized to break up large estates and to force landlords to reduce their rents. The owning classes were badly frightened and were therefore ready to accept Fascism as a less dangerous form of radicalism that might save at least part of their property from confiscation.

How much the Fascist movement depended for its success upon the leadership of Mussolini is impossible to say. Benito Mussolini was born in 1883, the son of a socialist blacksmith. His mother was a schoolteacher, and in deference to her wishes he entered a normal school and eventually became a teacher. But he was restless and dissatisfied and soon left Italy for further study in Switzerland. Here he gave part of his time to his books and the rest of it to begging his bread and writing articles for socialist newspapers. He was finally expelled from the country for fomenting strikes in factories. Upon returning to Italy he took up journalism as a definite career and eventually became editor of *Avanti*, the leading socialist daily. His ideas at this time were a mixture of contradictory forms of radicalism. He professed to be a Marxian socialist, but he mingled his socialism with doctrines taken from the syndicalists. In fact, the great syndicalist leader Sorel once referred to him as his most promising disciple.

Rather than a thinker or a sincere believer, Mussolini was essentially a rebel against the status quo. No man with a definite philosophy could have reversed himself so often. He not only condemned the imperialism which he later practiced so zealously, but at one time or another before the war he defamed the Church, vilified the king, and called the Italian flag "a rag to be planted on a dung hill." [1] When World War I broke out in August 1914, Mussolini insisted that Italy should remain neutral. But he had scarcely adopted this position when he began urging participation on the Entente side. As early as October 1914, he had gone over bag and baggage to the interventionist camp. Deprived of his position as editor of *Avanti*, he founded a new paper, *Il Popolo d'Italia*, and dedicated its columns to whipping up enthusiasm for war. The decision of the government

[1] For these and other contradictions between his earlier and later teachings, see Gaudens Megaro, *Mussolini in the Making*.

the following spring to go in on the side of the Entente allies he regarded as a personal victory.

The word Fascism had a dual origin. It derives in part from the Latin *fasces*, the ax surrounded by a bundle of rods representing the authority of the Roman state; it comes also from the Italian *fascio*, meaning group or band. *Fasci* were organized as early as October 1914, as units of agitation to swing Italy over to the Entente cause. Their membership was made up of young idealists, futurists, fanatical nationalists, bored white-collar workers, and misfits of every description. The original platform of the Fascist movement was prepared by Mussolini in 1919. It was a surprisingly radical document, which demanded, among other things, universal suffrage; abolition of the Senate; the establishment by law of an eight-hour day; a heavy capital levy; a heavy tax on inheritances; confiscation of 85 per cent of war profits; acceptance of the League of Nations; and "opposition to all imperialisms." This platform was accepted more or less officially until May 1920, when it was supplanted by another of a more conservative character. Indeed, the new program omitted all reference to economic reform. On neither of these platforms did the Fascists achieve much political success. Even after the elections of 1921 they had only thirty-five representatives in the Chamber of Deputies.

The Fascists made up for their lack of numbers by disciplined aggressiveness and strong determination. And when the old regime became so decrepit that it practically abdicated its functions, they prepared to take over the government. In September 1922, Mussolini began to talk openly of revolution and raised the cry, "On to Rome." On October 28 an army of about 50,000 Fascist militia occupied the capital. The Premier resigned, and the following day Victor Emmanuel III invited Mussolini to form a cabinet. Thus without firing a shot the blackshirted legions had gained control of the Italian government. The explanation is to be found, not in the strength of Fascism, but in the chaos created by the war and in the weakness and irresolution of the old ruling classes. By the end of the next three years Mussolini's revolution was virtually complete. He had abolished the cabinet system, made the political system a one-party system, and reduced the functions of the parliament to ratifying decrees. The leading doctrines of Fascism may be summarized as follows:

(1) Totalitarianism. The state incorporates every interest and every loyalty of its members. There must be "nothing above the state, nothing outside the state, nothing against the state."

(2) Nationalism. The nation is the highest form of society ever evolved by the human race. It has a life and a soul of its own apart from the lives and souls of the individuals who compose it. There can never be a real harmony of interests between two or more distinct peoples. Internationalism is therefore a perversion of human progress.

The evolution of Fascism

The march on Rome

Major doctrines of Fascism

Left: *"On to Rome."* Mussolini (wearing a suit) and uniformed Fascists march into Rome in October 1922. Right: *Mussolini Addressing a Crowd of His Followers from the Balcony of the Palazzo Venezia in Rome*

(3) Authoritarianism. The sovereignty of the state is absolute. The citizen has no rights but simply duties. What nations need is not liberty, but work, order, prosperity. Liberty is "a putrefying corpse," an outworn dogma of the French Revolution.

(4) Militarism. Strife is the origin of all things. Nations which do not expand eventually wither and die. War exalts and ennobles man and regenerates sluggish and decadent peoples.

Germany succumbed to fascism much later than Italy, mainly for the reason that the forces of nationalism and militarism were temporarily discredited as a result of her defeat in World War I. From 1918 to 1933 Germany was a republic. The revolution which overthrew the Kaiser in November 1918, brought into power a coalition of Socialists, Centrists, and Democrats. In 1919 the leaders of these parties drafted the Weimar Constitution, an instrument of government remarkable for its progressive features. It provided for universal suffrage; the cabinet system of government; and for a bill of rights, guaranteeing not only civil liberties but the right of the citizen to employment, to an education, and to protection against the hazards of an industrial society. But the republic set up under this constitution was beset with troubles from the start. Reactionaries and other extremists plotted against it. Moreover, the German people had had little experience with democratic government. The Weimar Republic did not spring from the desires of a majority of the nation. It was born of a revolution forced upon Germany in her hour of defeat.

The era of the republic in Germany

The factors which led to the eventual triumph of German fascism were many and various. First was the sense of humiliation arising from defeat in the war. Between 1871 and 1914 Germany had risen to lofty heights of political and cultural prestige. Until 1900, at least,

1051

Depression in Germany. Following the defeat in World War I, inflation was rampant and food in short supply. Here a fallen horse is torn to shreds by hungry citizens.

she was the leading power on the European Continent. Her universities, her science, her philosophy, and her music were known and admired all over the world. She had likewise attained a fabulous prosperity, and by 1914 she had surpassed even Britain and the United States in several fields of industrial production. Then came the crushing blow of 1918. She was toppled from her pinnacle and left at the mercy of her powerful enemies. It was too much for the German people to understand. They could not believe that their invincible armies had really been worsted in battle. Quickly the legend grew that the nation had been "stabbed in the back" by Socialists and Jews in the government. There was, of course, little truth in this charge, but it helped to salve the wounded pride of German patriots.

A few other causes of the rise and growth of National Socialism may also be mentioned. There was the fact that Germany had always been a military state, imbued with traditions of discipline and order. To many of the people the army was the symbol not merely of security but of national greatness. The qualities of obedience and regimentation, which the military life represented, were virtues most dear to the German heart. As a consequence, many patriotic citizens were seriously disturbed by the laxity and irresponsibility that appeared to distinguish the republican regime. It was alleged that Berlin had displaced Paris as the most frivolous and immoral city of Europe. A cause of more than minor importance was the fear of Bolshevism. The followers of this philosophy in Germany originally called themselves Spartacists. Subsequently they changed their name to Communists. In the Presidential election of 1932 the Communist party polled about 6,000,000 votes, or over one-seventh of the total. As had happened in Italy, a number of capitalists and property owners took alarm at what they regarded as a growing danger of Bolshevik revolution and secretly gave their support to the triumph of fascism as the lesser of two evils.

Yet the factor that gave the Nazi movement the proportions of an avalanche was the Great Depression. This conclusion is

Causes of the triumph of German fascism: (1) defeat in the war

(2) militarism and fear of Bolshevism

1052

supported by the fact that the party was never able to win more than 32 seats (barely 1/20) in the Reichstag prior to the election of 1930. In the early days the movement had drawn its converts chiefly from dissatisfied and uprooted members of the lower middle class and from former army officers unable to adjust to civilian life. After 1929 it received much broader support from a large segment of the German people who felt themselves disinherited and at odds with the ruling elements. Some were farmers angered by the collapse of agricultural prices and by their crushing burdens of debt and taxes. Others were university students who saw little prospect of gaining a place in the overcrowded professions. Undoubtedly the most numerous of all were the unemployed, whose ranks had swelled to 6,000,000 by 1932. Members of all these classes were groping in bewilderment and terror. By no means were they all Nazis, but their despair was so great as to induce them to accept almost any demagogue who promised to deliver them from confusion and fear. Never in the history of the nation had the future appeared so dark.

The origins of German fascism go back to 1919 when a little group of seven men met in a beer hall in Munich and founded the National Socialist German Workers' party.[2] Presently the most obscure of the seven emerged as their leader. His name was Adolf Hitler, born in 1889, the son of a petty customs official in the Austrian civil service. His early life was unhappy and maladjusted. Rebellious and undisciplined from childhood, he seems always to have been burdened with a sense of frustration. He wasted his time at school drawing pictures and finally decided that he would become an artist. With this purpose in view he went to Vienna in 1909, hoping to enter the Academy. But he failed the required examinations, and for the next four years he was compelled to eke out a dismal existence as a casual laborer and a painter of little sketches and watercolors which he sometimes managed to sell to the humbler art shops. Meanwhile he developed some violent political prejudices. He became an ardent admirer of certain Jew-baiting politicians in Vienna; and since he associated Judaism with Marxism, he hated that philosophy also. When World War I broke out, Hitler was living in Munich, and though an Austrian citizen, he immediately enlisted in the Bavarian army.

The Nazi revolution began in what appeared to be a quite harmless fashion. During the summer of 1932 the parliamentary system broke down. No Chancellor could retain a majority in the Reichstag; for the Nazis declined to support any cabinet not headed by Hitler, and the Communists refused to collaborate with the Socialists. In January 1933, a group of reactionaries—industrialists, bankers, and Junkers—prevailed upon President von Hindenburg to designate Hitler as Chancellor, evidently in the belief that they

[2] The name of the party was soon abbreviated in popular usage to Nazi.

One Step Away from Power. President von Hindenburg followed by Hitler, Göring on the extreme right, and other Nazi party members.

could control him. It was arranged that there should be only three Nazis in the cabinet, and that Franz von Papen, a Catholic aristocrat, should hold the position of Vice Chancellor. But the sponsors of this plan failed to appreciate the tremendous resurgence of mass feeling back of the Nazi movement. Hitler was not slow in making the most of his new opportunity. He persuaded von Hindenburg to dissolve the Reichstag and to order a new election on March 5. When the new Reichstag assembled, it voted to confer upon Hitler practically unlimited powers. Soon afterward the flag of the Weimar Republic was hauled down and replaced by the swastika banner of National Socialism. The new Germany was proclaimed to be the Third Reich, the successor of the Hohenstaufen Empire of the Middle Ages and of the Hohenzollern Empire of the Kaisers.

Of course, these events marked only the initial stage of the Nazi revolution. Within a few months, other and more sweeping changes were added. Germany was converted into a highly centralized state with the destruction of the federal principle. All political parties except the Nazi party were declared illegal. Totalitarian control was extended over the press, over education, the theater, the cinema, radio, and many branches of production and trade. Drastic penalties were imposed upon the Jews: they were eliminated from government positions, deprived of citizenship, and practically excluded from the universities. With the passing of the years, the entire regime seemed to shift more and more in a radical direction. The new tendency approached its climax in 1938 with the extension of party control over the army and with the institution of a fanatical crusade against the Jews to expel them from the Reich or to annihilate them entirely.

So far as its ideology was concerned, German fascism resembled in a great many of its essentials the Italian variety. Both were collectivistic, authoritarian, nationalistic, militaristic, and romantic (in the sense of being anti-intellectual). Yet there were some outstanding differences. Italian Fascism never had a racial basis. True, after the formation of the Rome-Berlin Axis, Mussolini issued some anti-Jewish decrees; but most of them appear not to have been enforced very strictly. By contrast, National Socialism made the factor of race a central pillar of its theory. The Nazis argued that the so-called Aryan race, which was supposed to include the Nordics as its most perfect specimens, was the only one ever to have made any notable contributions to human progress. They contended further that the accomplishments and mental qualities of a people were actually determined by blood. Thus the achievements of the Jew forever remained Jewish, or Oriental, no matter how long he might live in a Western country. It followed that no Jewish science or Jewish literature or Jewish music could ever truly represent the German nation. Obviously, most of this racial doctrine was mere rationalization. The real reason why the Nazis persecuted the Jews seems to have been that they needed a scapegoat upon whom they could place the blame for the nation's troubles. Before this extremism had run its course millions of Jews had been exterminated by brutal SS men and Gauleiters.

There were also other differences, both in theory and in practice. Despite the fact that Germany was one of the most highly industrialized countries in the world, National Socialism had a peculiar peasant flavor which Italian Fascism did not possess. The key to Nazi theory was contained in the phrase *Blut und Boden* (blood and soil). The word *soil* typified not only a deep reverence for the beautiful homeland but an abiding affection for the peasants, who were considered to embody the finest qualities of the German race. No class

Blood and soil; the state and the economy

A Nazi Party Rally. Hitler at the height of his power, followed by other Nazi party officials.

of the population was more generously treated by the Nazi government. This high regard for country folk came partly no doubt from the circumstance that they were the most prolific of the nation's citizens and therefore the most valuable for military reasons. It was explainable also by the reaction of the Nazi leaders against everything that the city stood for—not only intellectualism and radicalism but high finance and the complicated problems of industrial society. As upstarts of obscure origin, the Nazis strove to compensate for their sense of inferiority by glorifying the simple life. Finally, it may be said that National Socialism was more frenzied and fanatical than Italian Fascism. It was comparable to a new religion, not only in its dogmatism and its ritual, but in its fierce intolerance and its zeal for expansion.

The significance of fascism, whether German or Italian, is still a subject of controversy among students of modern history. Some argue that it was simply the enthronement of force by big capitalists in an effort to save their dying system from destruction. It is true that the success of both movements in gaining control of the government depended in some measure upon support from great landowners and captains of industry. A second interpretation of fascism would explain it as a reaction of debtors aaginst creditors, of farmers against bankers and manufacturers, and of small businessmen against high finance and monopolistic practices. Still other students of the movement interpret it as a revolt against communism, a reversion to primitivism, a result of the despair of the masses, a protest against the weaknesses of democracy, or a supreme manifestation of chauvinism. Undoubtedly fascism was all of these things combined and a great many others besides. An increasingly popular view in recent years holds that fascism was simply an extreme expression of tendencies prevalent in all industrialized countries. Though most of these tendencies were minority movements, they nevertheless exerted a wide influence. Indeed, official policies in most Western countries in the 1930's took on more and more of a fascist semblance—a tightly controlled economy, limitation of production to maintain prices, and expansion of armaments to promote prosperity. In brief, nearly all nations in that period were beset with similar problems. Had it not been for the expansionist dynamics of the German Reich and its threat to the balance of power, perhaps little opposition would have developed, in the outside world, to Nazi policies.

The complex significance of fascism

2. THE COMMUNIST UTOPIA (?) IN RUSSIA

Although Russia fought in World War I on the side of the powers that eventually triumphed, she was the first of the belligerent nations to be engulfed by revolution. The reasons for the initial explosion, at least, seem fairly obvious. The Russian government's conduct of the war was not distinguished for brilliance. The weak-

Balzac, Auguste Rodin (1840–1917). Rodin was the great realist of XIX-cent. sculpture. He concentrated most of his attention upon facial detail, no matter how unflattering the result might be. (MMA)

Above: *A Young Woman in the Sun*, Auguste Renoir (1841–1919). Though Renoir used impressionist techniques, the results sometimes bore little resemblance to the work of other impressionists. He believed that "a picture ought to be a lovable thing, joyous and pretty." (Jeu de Paume) Right: *Luncheon of the Boating Party*, Renoir. (Phillips Memorial Gallery)

The Piano Lesson, Henri Matisse (1869–1954). Matisse conveyed a freshness of approach and a vitality of line and color. (Mus. Mod. Art)

Portrait of Gertrude Stein, Pablo Picasso (1881–). Picasso seems to have given this portrait of the great experimenter in poetry some elements of the distortion of form characteristic of the work of both. (MMA)

Three Musicians, Pablo Picasso. Th painting, regarded by many as th masterpiece of cubism, sums up th final stage of the movement. (Mu Mod. Art)

Left: *Tsar Nicholas II and His Family on the Eve of the Revolution*. Right: *An Open-Air Market in Petrograd*. In the foreground for sale are items taken from the home of the Russian aristocracy.

willed Tsar came more and more under the influence of the superstitious Tsarina, who was putty in the hands of an infamous "holy man," Gregory Rasputin. In some instances soldiers were sent to the front without rifles and were inadequately supplied with suitable clothing. There were seldom enough surgeons or hospital facilities to take care of the wounded. The Russian railway system broke down, producing a shortage of food not only in the army but in the congested cities as well. Added to these troubles was a series of crushing defeats by the Germans. Though Russia mobilized 15,000,-000 men, she was unable to hold up her end of the fight on the Eastern Front. By the end of 1916 her power of resistance had practically collapsed.

Effects of the war in causing the initial outbreak of revolution

The revolution in Russia followed a succession of stages somewhat similar to those of the great French Revolution of 1789. The first of these stages began in March 1917 with the forced abdication of the Tsar. For this the principal cause was disgust with the conduct of the war. But there were also many other factors—the inflation and consequent high prices, and the scarcity of food and of coal in urban areas. With the overthrow of the Tsar, the authority of the government passed into the hands of a provisional ministry organized by leaders in the Duma in conjunction with representatives of the Petrograd workers. With the exception of Alexander Kerensky, who was a Social Revolutionary, nearly all of the ministers were bourgeois liberals. Their conception of the revolution was mainly to transform the autocracy into a constitutional monarchy modeled after that of Great Britain. In accordance with this aim they issued a proclamation of civil liberties, released thousands of prisoners, and made plans for the election of a constituent assembly.

The overthrow of the Tsar

The downfall of
Milyukov and the
accession of
Kerensky

The provisional government proved itself inadequate to deal with its problems. Its leaders did not seem to understand the new conditions created by the war or even some of those arising in the prewar period. Among them were congestion in the cities, the emergence of a proletariat, and the inevitable harshness of the class conflict in the initial stages of industrialization. Further, the heads of this provisional government made the mistake of attempting to continue the war on the old basis of 1914–1917. They were just as imperialistic as the Tsar and his minions. They hoped to get Constantinople and everything else that had been promised in the secret treaties. But the masses of the people were desperately weary of the years of hardship and struggle. What they wanted was peace and a chance to return to a normal life. Consequently, in May, when the leaders renewed their pledge of support for the Allies, criticism was so strong that they were forced to resign. A new government was organized which managed to stay in power until September. Its head was Alexander Kerensky, and it consisted primarily of moderate socialists. The ultimate failure of this regime may be ascribed chiefly to the insignificant role played by the middle class in Russia at that time. In no sense can it be compared as a revolutionary force with the bourgeoisie in France in 1789. It was much smaller in size and lacked the prestige and wealth of the elements that destroyed the absolute monarchy of Louis XVI. Moreover, it had little support from the masses.

The downfall of Kerensky's regime marked the end of the first stage of the Russian revolution. The second began immediately after with the accession of the Bolsheviks to power on November 7, 1917. The Bolsheviks were originally members of the Social Democratic party, but in 1903 this party had split into two factions: a majority or Bolshevik faction of Marxist revolutionists and a minority faction of Mensheviks, who contended that the time for revolution was not yet ripe. Soon after the overthrow of the Tsar the Bolsheviks began laying plans for a socialist revolution. They worked their way into the Petrograd Soviet, or Council of Workers' and Soldiers' Deputies, and quickly gained control of it from the Mensheviks and Social Revolutionaries. They organized an armed Red Guard and took possession of strategic points throughout the city. By November 7 everything was ready for the grand *coup*. Red Guards occupied nearly all the public buildings and finally arrested the members of the government, though Kerensky himself escaped. Thus the Bolsheviks climbed to power with scarcely a struggle. Their slogan of "Peace, Land, and Bread" made them heroes to the soldiers disgusted with the war, to the peasants hungry for land, and to the poor of the cities suffering from the shortage of food.

The chief actor in the Bolshevik drama was Vladimir Lenin, whose real name was Vladimir Ulianov (1870–1924). His father was an inspector of schools and a state counsellor and therefore entitled to rank in the petty nobility. An older son, Alexander, was

Lenin Speaking to Crowds in Moscow. At the right of the platform, in uniform, is Trotsky.

hanged for participating in a plot to assassinate the Tsar. In the very same year Vladimir was admitted to the University of Kazan. However, he was soon afterward expelled for engaging in radical activity. Later he was admitted to the University of St. Petersburg and in 1891 obtained a degree in law. From then on he devoted his entire life to the cause of socialist revolution. From 1900 to 1917 he lived principally in Germany and England, acting much of the time as editor of the Bolshevik journal *Iskra* (*The Spark*). Like most of the Russian revolutionists, he wrote under a pseudonym, signing his articles N. Lenin.[3] When the revolution broke out in March 1917, he was living in Switzerland. With the aid of the Germans he made his way back to Russia and immediately assumed leadership of the Bolshevik movement. Lenin had all of the qualities necessary for success as a revolutionary figure. He was an able politician and an exceedingly effective orator. Absolutely convinced of the righteousness of his cause, he could strike down his opponents with the zeal and savagery of a Robespierre. On the other hand, he cared nothing for the fleshpots of wealth or of personal glory. He lived in two rooms in the Kremlin and dressed little better than an ordinary workman.

The most prominent of Lenin's lieutenants was the brilliant but erratic Leon Trotsky. Originally named Lev Bronstein, he was born in 1879 of middle-class Jewish parents in Ukrainia. He seems to have been the stormy petrel of revolutionary politics during most of his life. Before the revolution he refused to identify himself with any particular faction, preferring to remain an independent Marxist. For his part in the revolutionary movement of 1905 he was exiled to Siberia; but he escaped, and then for some years led a roving existence in various European capitals. He was expelled from Paris in 1916

Vladimir Lenin

Leon Trotsky

[3] The "N." did not stand for anything in particular, though many people have assumed that it was a symbol for Nikolai.

1059

for pacifist activity and took refuge in the United States. Upon learning of the overthrow of the Tsar, he attempted to return to Russia. Captured by British agents at Halifax, he was eventually released upon the plea of Kerensky. He arrived in Russia in April and immediately began plotting for the overthrow of the provisional government and later of Kerensky himself. He became Minister of Foreign Affairs in the government headed by Lenin and later Commissar for War.

Revolutionary political and economic changes

No sooner had the Bolsheviks come to power than they proceeded to effect some drastic alterations in the political and economic system. On November 8 Lenin decreed nationalization of the land and gave the peasants the exclusive right to use it. On November 29 control of the factories was transferred to the workers, and a month later it was announced that all except the smallest industrial establishments would be taken over by the government. Banks also were nationalized soon after the Bolshevik victory. But the problem of greatest urgency was termination of the war. After vain attempts to induce the Allies to consent to a peace without annexations or indemnities, Trotsky signed an armistice with Germany on December 15. This was followed by the peace of Brest-Litovsk in March 1918, which officially ended the war so far as Russia was concerned.

The civil war between Whites and Reds

Scarcely had the Bolsheviks concluded the war with the Central Powers than they were confronted with a desperate civil war at home. Landlords and capitalists did not take kindly to the loss of their property. Besides, the Allies were determined to punish the Russian government and accordingly sent troops into the country to support the armies of reactionary generals. The result was a prolonged and bloody combat between the Reds, or Bolsheviks, on the one side, and the Whites, or reactionaries, and their foreign allies on the other. Both sides were guilty of horrible brutality. At times the government resorted to mass executions, as was done in August 1918,

The Red Army, 1919. This scene near the south front was the celebration of the victory over the counterrevolutionary forces.

after a Social Revolutionary had attempted to assassinate Lenin. But at length the terror abated. By the end of 1920 the civil war was practically over. The Bolsheviks had driven nearly all of the foreign soldiers from the country and had forced the reactionary generals to abandon the struggle.

The civil war was accompanied by an appalling economic breakdown. In 1920 the total industrial production was only 13 per cent of what it had been in 1913. To make up for the shortage of goods the government abolished the payment of wages and distributed supplies among the workers in the cities in proportion to their need. All private trade was prohibited, and everything produced by the peasants above what they required to keep from starving was requisitioned by the state. This system was not pure communism, as is often alleged, but was mainly an expedient to crush the bourgeoisie and to obtain as much food as possible for the army in the field. It was soon abandoned after the war had ended. In 1921 it was superseded by the New Economic Policy (NEP), which Lenin described as "one step backward in order to take two steps forward." The NEP authorized private manufacturing and private trade on a small scale, reintroduced the payment of wages, and permitted the peasants to sell their grain in the open market. The new policy continued in force until 1929 when the first of the famous Five-Year Plans was adopted. It was succeeded by a series of others all designed to make Russia a great industrial country, and to further the evolution of a classless, communist society.

Economic breakdown and the NEP

In the meantime, the death of Lenin in January 1924 precipitated a titanic struggle between two of his lieutenants to inherit his mantle of power. Outside of Russia it was generally assumed that Trotsky would be the man to succeed the fallen leader. But soon it was revealed that the fiery commander of the Red Army had a formidable rival in the shaggy and mysterious Joseph Stalin (1879–1953). The son of a peasant shoemaker in the province of Georgia, Stalin received part of his education in a theological seminary. But he was expelled at the age of seventeen for "lack of religious vocation" and thereafter dedicated his career to revolutionary activity. In 1917 he became Secretary-General of the Communist party, a position through which he was able to build up a party machine. The battle between Stalin and Trotsky was not simply a struggle for personal power; fundamental issues of political policy were also involved. Trotsky maintained that socialism in Russia could never be entirely successful until capitalism was overthrown in surrounding countries. Therefore he insisted upon a continuous crusade for world revolution. Stalin was willing to abandon the program of world revolution, for the time being, in order to concentrate on building socialism in Russia itself. His strategy for the immediate future was essentially nationalist. The outcome of the duel was a complete triumph for Stalin. In 1927 Trotsky was expelled from the Communist party, and two years later he was driven from the country. In 1940

The struggle between Trotsky and Stalin

Left: *Lenin's Casket Is Carried through the Streets of Moscow.* It was not known with certainty until 1956 that, prior to his death, Lenin had discredited Stalin. Right: *Stalin in the Early 1920's*

he was murdered in Mexico City by Stalinist agents. It is interesting to note that Lenin did not hold either of the two rivals in lofty esteem. In a "testament" written shortly before his death, he criticized Trotsky for "far-reaching self-confidence" and for being too much preoccupied with administrative detail. But he dealt far less gently with Stalin, condemning him as "too rough" and "capricious" and urging that the comrades "find a way" to remove him from his position at the head of the party.[6]

The third stage of the Russian revolution

About 1934 the Bolshevik regime entered a new and in some ways more conservative phase, which should perhaps be considered as the third stage of the Russian revolution. It was characterized by a number of significant developments. For one thing, there was a revival of militarism, of nationalism, and of an interest in playing the game of power politics. The army was more than doubled in size and was reorganized in accordance with the Western model. Patriotism, which the older strict Marxists despised as a form of capitalist propaganda, was exalted into a Soviet virtue. In like manner, there was a growing tendency to discard the internationalism of Marx, to strive to make Russia self-sufficient, and to play an active part in old-fashioned diplomacy. With Nazism firmly established in Germany, the rulers of the Kremlin seemed to have decided that Russia needed friends. Along with their efforts to build up a great army and to make their own country self-sufficient, they adopted a policy of cooperation with the Western powers. In 1934 they entered the League of Nations, and in 1935 they exchanged ratifications of a military alliance with France. It is apparent, however, that the real purpose of these moves was to drive a wedge between Germany on the one side and Britain and France on the other. At any rate, when the Soviet leaders became suspicious in 1938–1939 that Britain and France were encouraging Hitler to expand eastward, they did not

See color map at page 1216

hesitate to conclude a nonaggression pact with the Nazi government.[4]

The original philosophy of Bolshevism, now more popularly known as communism, was developed primarily by Lenin. It was not supposed to be a new body of thought but a strict interpretation of the gospel of Marx. Nevertheless, from the beginning there were various departures from the master's teachings. Whereas Marx had assumed that a capitalist stage must prepare the way for socialism, Lenin denied that this was necessary and insisted that Russia could leap directly from a feudal to a socialist economy. In the second place, Lenin emphasized the revolutionary character of socialism much more than did its original founder. Marx did believe that in most cases revolution would be necessary, but he was inclined to deplore the fact rather than to welcome it. Further, in his Amsterdam speech of 1872 he had stated that "there are certain countries such as England and the United States in which the workers may hope to secure their ends by peaceful means." Last of all, Bolshevism differed from Marxism in its conception of proletarian rule. There is nothing to indicate that Marx ever envisaged a totalitarian workers' state as arbitrary and oppressive in its methods of governing as fascism. True, he did speak of the "dictatorship of the proletariat"; but he meant by this a dictatorship of the whole working class over the remnants of the bourgeoisie. Within the ranks of this class, democratic forms would prevail. Lenin, however, set up the ideal of the dictatorship of an *élite*, a select minority, wielding supremacy not only over the bourgeoisie but over the bulk of the proletarians themselves. In Russia this *élite* is the Communist party, whose membership has varied from 1,500,000 to 13,000,000.

In 1936, eighteen years after coming to power, the rulers of Communist Russia drafted a new constitution for the entire country to replace earlier ones that had proved inadequate. It was adopted by popular vote and went into effect January 1, 1938. The official name retained for the state was the Union of Soviet Socialist Republics. It provided for a union of eleven (later fifteen) republics, each supposedly autonomous and free to secede if it chose. The constitution established universal suffrage for all citizens eighteen years of age and over. They were to vote not only for the local soviets but for members of a national parliament. The highest organ of state power was declared to be the Supreme Soviet of the U.S.S.R., composed of two chambers—the Soviet of the Union and the Soviet of Nationalities. The former was to have 600 members elected by the people for four-year terms. The Soviet of Nationalities was to consist of 400 members chosen for similar terms by the governments of the several republics. Both chambers were given equal legislative powers. To represent it between sessions, the Supreme Soviet was to elect a committee of thirty-seven members known as the Presidium. This

The philosophy of Bolshevism

The constitution of 1936

[4] See p. 1205

body also was empowered to issue decrees, to declare war, and to annul the acts of administrative officials which did not conform to law. The highest executive and administrative agency was to be the Council of Ministers, likewise elected by the Supreme Soviet. Each Minister was to be head of a department, such as War, Foreign Affairs, Railways, Heavy Industry, Light Industry, and so forth. Finally, the constitution of 1936 contained a bill of rights. Citizens were guaranteed the right to employment, the right to leisure, the right to maintenance in case of old age or disability, and even the traditional privileges of freedom of speech, of the press, of assemblage, and of religion.

The party the
real power in
the U.S.S.R.

The constitution of 1936 was, and still is, more of a sham than a reality. Its provisions for universal suffrage, for the secret ballot, and for a bill of rights looked good on paper but had little meaning. The explanation lies in the fact that the real power in the Soviet Union rests with the Communist party, the only party allowed to exist. The organs of the government are little more than the vocal mechanisms through which the party expresses its will. It is noteworthy that the very period in which the constitution was being put into effect witnessed an eruption of mass arrests and executions of persons alleged to be "Trotskyists, spies, and wreckers." Nearly all the old war-horses who had worked with Lenin to make the revolution a success, with the exception of Stalin, fell victims in the frenzied purges. Altogether at least fifty prominent theoreticians and party leaders were put to death, in most cases with little evidence except the accused's own confessions. In addition, about 9,000,000 other persons were arrested and imprisoned or sent to Siberia.

Economic and
social results of
the Soviet
upheaval

Perhaps enough has been said to indicate that the Soviet upheaval was not merely political in character but had profound economic and social results. By 1939 private manufacturing and private trade had been almost entirely abolished. Factories, mines, railroads, and public utilities were exclusively owned by the state. Stores were either government enterprises or producers' and consumers' cooperatives. Agriculture also had been almost completely socialized. State farms included about 10 per cent of the land; collective farms, organized on a cooperative basis, occupied nearly all of the remainder. No less revolutionary were the developments in the social sphere. Religion as a factor in the lives of the people declined to a place of small importance. To be sure, Christianity was still tolerated; but churches were reduced in number, and were not permitted to engage in any charitable or educational activities. Furthermore, members of the Communist party were required to be atheists. Communism not only renounces all belief in the supernatural but attempts to cultivate a new ethics. The primary aim is to create a *positive* morality, based upon duty to society, in place of the old negative morality, founded upon a notion of personal sin. The cardinal virtues in this positive morality are industry, respect for public property, willingness to sacrifice individual interests for the good of society, and loyalty to the Soviet fatherland and to the socialist ideal at all times.

By the outbreak of World War II the Soviet regime had undeniable accomplishments to its credit. Among the principal ones may be mentioned the following: (1) the reduction of illiteracy from a proportion of at least 50 per cent to less than 20 per cent; (2) a notable expansion of industrialization; (3) the establishment of a planned economy, which at least operated successfully enough to prevent unemployment; (4) the opening of educational and cultural opportunities to larger numbers of the common people; and (5) the establishment of a system of government assistance for working mothers and their infants and free medical care and hospitalization for most of the citizens.

Accomplishments of the Bolshevik regime

But these accomplishments were purchased at a very high price. The program of socialization and industrialization was pushed at so dizzy a pace that the good of individual citizens was almost overlooked. It must not be forgotten either that the Soviet regime fastened upon Russia a tyranny just as extreme as that of the Tsar. Indeed, the number of its victims sentenced to slave-labor camps probably exceeded the number consigned by the Tsars to exile in Siberia. This tyranny, it may be noted, was relaxed considerably in later years. Under the co-dictatorship of Leonid Brezhnev and Aleksei Kosygin labor camps as agencies of punishment were largely abolished (1964).

The price of revolution

3.   THE DEMOCRACIES BETWEEN TWO WARS

By 1939 only three of the chief powers—Great Britain, France, and the United States—remained in the list of democratic countries. Among the lesser states democracy survived in Switzerland, the Netherlands, Belgium, the Scandinavian countries, a few republics of Latin America, and the self-governing dominions of the British Commonwealth. Nearly all of the rest of the world had succumbed to despotism of one form or another. Italy, Germany, and Spain were fascist; Russia was communist; Hungary was dominated by a landowning oligarchy; Poland, Turkey, China, and Japan were essentially military dictatorships. For the most part, this cleavage represented a division between the so-called Have and Have-not nations—the former including the democracies, and the latter the dictatorships. Great Britain, France, and the United States were sated countries, comparatively rich in territorial empire and in mineral resources. Italy, Germany, and Japan were "hungry nations," coveting more lands in the belief that greater amounts of soil and other natural resources would solve their economic problems. They were disgruntled also with their power status, considering it inferior to that of other nations with large empires. Evidence is far from convincing that the citizens of the so-called Have-not coun-

Division of the world into democracies and dictatorships

tries were really worse off than the inhabitants of states with more extensive territory. But politicians greedy for power used this alleged inequality for propaganda purposes. They overlooked the fact that standards of living bear little relation to extent of territory. The average citizen of Sweden or Switzerland was just as prosperous as the citizens of France or Great Britain notwithstanding his country's total lack of imperial possessions.

The struggle of classes in Britain, France, and the U.S.A.

It will be impossible to describe minutely internal developments in all the democracies. In general, events in the principal states ran closely parallel. Preeminent among them was a struggle between wealthy bankers and industrial monopolists, on the one side, and organized labor and the lower middle class, on the other. In some countries members of the old order were able to hold their supremacy until after the onslaught of the Great Depression in 1929. In the United States and France, for example, there was little difference between the type of rule in the 1920's and that which had prevailed before the war. Great Britain, however, experienced the triumph of a Labour government as early as 1924. Its tenure was brief and its accomplishments few, but two years later the strength of the working class was sufficient to tie the whole national economy in knots by a general strike, which lasted for nine days. During most of the 1920's France was firmly under the thumb of such arch-conservatives as Georges Clemenceau and Raymond Poincaré. The years 1924–1926, though, witnessed a brief tenure of power by the Radical Socialists under the leadership of Édouard Herriot; better than any other party they represented the interests of small business and the lower middle class. The United States was undoubtedly the most impregnable fortress of conservative power among the democracies. The Presidents elected during the 1920's—Warren G. Harding, Calvin Coolidge, and Herbert Hoover—upheld a social philosophy formulated by the barons of big business in the nineteenth century, and the Supreme Court used its power of judicial review to nullify progressive legislation enacted by state governments and occasionally by Congress.

Labor Troubles in Britain. Mounted police escorting delivery wagons through a mob of angry strikers during the general strike of 1926.

The Stock Market Crash, October 24, 1929. Crowds milling outside the New York Stock Exchange the day of the big crash.

The depression that began in 1929 was one of the most shattering experiences in the economic history of the modern world. It was not limited to any one country, nor can the policies of any one nation be blamed for its origin. Nevertheless, the role of the United States in bringing it on cannot be discounted. At the end of World War I America was the richest nation in the world. While the states of Europe had been mauling each other on the battlefield, Americans had been capturing their markets, penetrating their fields of investment, and expanding their own industry and agriculture enormously. Yet much of the prosperity stimulated by these practices rested upon foundations of sand. It had been fostered in the beginning by the high prices of the war era. Farmers in the mid-West had plunged head over heels into debt to buy land in the arid regions of western Nebraska, eastern Colorado, and western Oklahoma, in the expectation that wheat would always be selling for more than $2.00 a bushel. When the price dropped to 93 cents in 1923, they found themselves stuck with their mortgages. But farmers were not the only ones who had been tempted into overexpansion by fantastic prices; many more coal mines and factories were opened than were necessary to supply the normal demand. A second weakness in American prosperity was the fact that it·was based quite largely upon foreign loans. By 1930 American private loans in foreign countries amounted to about $16,000,000,000. Many of these were founded upon inadequate security or mere promises to pay. As a consequence, defaults were widespread. Nor should it be forgotten that United States tariff policy made it difficult for foreign nations to sell their products in American markets and thus to acquire the resources with which to pay their debts. Even as late as 1930 President Hoover, against the advice of more than 1000 economists, signed the Hawley-Smoot bill, which raised the duties on many commodities to the highest levels in the nation's history. Since this was followed by retaliatory tariffs elsewhere, the effect was virtually to strangle international trade.

The depression of 1929

Results of the
depression

Leon Blum

The severity of
the depression in
the United States

The results of the depression took varied forms in different countries. In 1931 Great Britain abandoned the gold standard, and the government of the United States followed suit in 1933. This action was the forerunner of a broad program of currency management, which became an important element in a general policy of economic nationalism. By way of illustration, President Franklin D. Roosevelt informed the London Economic Conference of 1933 that "the sound internal economic system of a nation is a greater factor in its well-being than the price of its currency in changing terms of the currencies of other nations." As early as 1932 Great Britain abandoned completely her time-honored policy of free trade. Protective tariffs were raised in some instances as high as 100 per cent. Of the European democracies France went farthest in the direction of a controlled economy, though little change occurred until 1936. In that year the nation came under the rule of the so-called Popular Front, headed by Leon Blum, and composed of Radical Socialists, Socialists, and Communists. The Popular Front nationalized the munitions industry and reorganized the Bank of France so as to deprive the 200 largest stockholders of their monopolistic control over credit. In addition, it decreed a 40-hour week for all urban workers and initiated a program of public works. For the benefit of the farmers it established a Wheat Office to fix the price and regulate the distribution of grain.

The most spectacular changes in policy after the depression occurred, not in Europe, but in the United States. The explanation was twofold. The United States had clung longer to the economic philosophy of the nineteenth century. Prior to the depression the business classes had adhered firmly to the dogma of freedom of contract and insisted upon their right to form monopolies and to use the government as their agent in frustrating the demands of both workers and consumers. The depression in the United States was also more severe than in the European democracies. Industrial production shrank by about two-thirds. The structure of agricultural prices and of common stocks collapsed. Thousands of banks were forced to close their doors. Unemployment rose to 15,000,000, or to approximately one-third of the total labor force. Had it not been for widespread feelings of hopelessness and despair, revolution might well have swept the country. Millions were deterred by fear from taking any action that might jeopardize what little security they already had. Rescue from disaster was finally provided by a program of reform and reconstruction known as the New Deal. The chief architect and motivator of this program was Franklin D. Roosevelt, who succeeded Herbert Hoover in the Presidency on March 4, 1933.

Few historians would deny that the New Deal was one of the most significant events in the history of modern nations. Since its results were mainly in the direction of preserving rather than destroying capitalism, it can scarcely be called a revolution. Nevertheless, it probably did more for the farmer and the wage earner than any of the so-called revolutions in American history. Under the New Deal the incomes of these classes increased nearly 100 per cent compared with their level during the depression. Perhaps more important, these classes gained a degree of economic security they had never known before. On the other hand, a number of crucial problems remained unsolved. The most serious was unemployment. In 1939, after six years of the New Deal, the United States still had more than 9,000,000 jobless workers—a figure which exceeded the combined unemployment of the rest of the world. Ironically, it seemed that only the outbreak of a new world war, with its wholesale destruction of wealth and consumption of manpower, could provide the full recovery and full employment that the New Deal had failed to assure. In other words, the New Deal was hardly more than a stop-gap solution that would sooner or later break down under the strain of crucial events.

SELECTED READINGS

· *Items so designated are available in paperbound editions.*

FASCIST ITALY

Ebenstein, William, *Fascist Italy*, New York, 1939.

Schneider, H. W., *Making the Fascist State*, New York, 1928. A penetrating analysis.

NAZI GERMANY

· Bullock, A. L. C., *Hitler: A Study in Tyranny*, London, 1952 (Bantam). A good biography.

Carr, E. H., *German-Soviet Relations Between the Two World Wars, 1919–1939*, Baltimore, 1951.

Deutsch, Harold C., *The Conspiracy against Hitler in the Twilight War*, Minneapolis, 1968.

· Halperin, S. W., *Germany Tried Democracy, 1918–1933*, New York, 1946 (Norton Library). A dependable history of the Weimar Republic.

Neumann, Franz *Behemoth, The Structure and Practice of National Socialism*, New York, 1942.

Orlow, Dietrich, *The History of the Nazi Party*, Pittsburgh, 1969.

Rothfels, H., *The German Opposition to Hitler*, Hinsdale, Ill., 1948.

Scheele, Godfrey, *The Weimar Republic: Overture to the Third Reich*, London, 1946.

Schweitzer, Arthur, *Big Business in the Third Reich*, Bloomington, Ind., 1964. Contends that big business held Nazi regime in check in early days.

· Waite, Robert G. L., *Vanguard of Nazism: The Free Corps Movement in Postwar Germany, 1918–1923*, Cambridge, 1952 (Norton Library).

SOVIET RUSSIA

· Brinton, Crane, *The Anatomy of Revolution*, New York, 1952 (Vintage, rev. ed.). Includes a suggestive comparison of the Russian Revolution with earlier revolutions in Western Europe.

READINGS

· Curtiss, J. S., *The Russian Revolution of 1917.* (Anvil).

· Daniels, R. V., *The Nature of Communism*, New York, 1962 (Vintage). An objective study.

· ———, *Russia*, Englewood Cliffs, N. J., 1964 (Spectrum). Emphasizes period of the U.S.S.R.

· Hunt, R. N. Carew, *The Theory and Practice of Communism*, New York, 1951 (Penguin). A splendid introductory study.

· Pares, Sir Bernard, *A History of Russia*, New York, 1953 (Vintage). One of the best short histories.

· Shub, David, *Lenin*, New York, 1948 (Mentor, abr.). Perhaps the best biography.

Shukman, Harold, *Lenin and the Russian Revolution*, New York, 1967.

· Von Laue, T. W., *Why Lenin? Why Stalin? A Reappraisal of the Russian Revolution, 1900–1930*, Philadelphia, 1964 (Preceptor).

· Wolfe, B. D., *Three Who Made a Revolution*, New York, 1948 (Beacon). A penetrating study of Lenin, Trotsky, and Stalin.

THE DEMOCRACIES

· Burns, J. M., *Roosevelt: The Lion and the Fox*, New York, 1956 (Harvest). A thoughtful interpretation.

· Feis, Herbert, *The Diplomacy of the Dollar, 1919–1932*, Baltimore, 1950 (Norton Library).

Friedel, Frank, *Franklin D. Roosevelt: The Triumph*, Boston, 1956. A stimulating and scholarly account.

Fusfield, D. R., *The Economic Thought of Franklin D. Roosevelt and the Origins of the New Deal*, New York, 1956.

· Graves, Robert and Alan Hodge, *The Long Weekend: A Social History of Great Britain, 1918–1939*, London, 1940 (Norton Library).

Gregg, Pauline, *The Welfare State: An Economic and Social History of Great Britain, 1945 to the Present Day*, Amherst, Mass., 1969.

· Hofstadter, Richard, *The American Political Tradition: and the Men Who Made It*, New York, 1948 (Vintage).

Mitchell, Broadus, *Depression Decade; from New Era through New Deal, 1929 to 1941*, New York, 1947.

Nevins, Allan, *The United States in a Chaotic World*, New Haven, 1950.

Schlesinger, A. M., Jr., *The Age of Roosevelt: The Crisis of the Old Order, 1919–1933*, Boston, 1957.

Warren, Sidney, *Battle for the Presidency*, Philadelphia, 1968.

SOURCE MATERIALS

Columbia University, *Introduction to Contemporary Civilization in the West*, Vol. II, pp. 1062–66, 1077–86, Soviet Constitution of 1936 and Weimar Constitution.

· Hitler, Adolf, *Mein Kampf*, especially Vol. I, Chs. II, IV, XI; Vol. II, Chs. II, XIII, XIV, New York, 1962 (Sentry).

· Lenin, Vladimir, *The State and Revolution* (International Publishers).

Stalin, Joseph, *Leninism*, 2 vols.

———, *Problems of Leninism*.

Trotsky, Leon, *History of the Russian Revolution*, Ann Arbor, 1957, 3 vols.

von Mohrenshildt, Dimitri, ed., *The Russian Revolution of 1917; Contemporary Accounts*, New York, 1970.

1070

CHAPTER 36

The Commonwealth of Nations

We have, then, if I may sum up, two duties in the West, first to protect our institutions within the city walls from deterioration and decay, and then to defend the walls themselves. There is, however, a third and even more important duty: to bring about a state of affairs in the world where no one will wish to attack us at all—or we, them; where eventually walls themselves will be as much of an anachronism as trenches, barbed wire, and forts on the United States-Canadian border.
—Lester B. Pearson, *Where Do We Go From Here?*

One of the most significant developments in the history of democracy in the modern world has been the evolution of the Commonwealth of Nations. Originally called the British Commonwealth of Nations, it now includes a number of states which repudiate any suggestion of allegiance to Britain. All members of the Commonwealth are self-governing, but many of them recognize the British monarch, represented by a governor-general, as their head of state. This group includes—in addition to the United Kingdom—the large Dominions of Canada, Australia, and New Zealand, and such small ones as Barbados, Jamaica, Malta, Mauritius, Sierra Leone, and Trinidad and Tobago. Political changes within the last few years have resulted in the creation within the Commonwealth of many republics, with no ties to the British Crown. The most conspicuous example is India, but the Commonwealth embraces more than a dozen republics, ranging in size from medium to tiny: Bangladesh, Botswana, Cyprus, Sri Lanka (Ceylon), Fiji, Gambia, Ghana, Guyana, Kenya, Malawi, Malaysia, Nigeria, Singapore, Tanzania, Uganda, and Zambia. The little African state of Lesotho (an enclave within the Republic of South Africa) has the distinction of being a separate kingdom within the Commonwealth, under the headship of its Paramount Chief. Evidently the only requisite for membership in the Commonwealth is the desire to belong. Because members may secede at any time and

The Commonwealth defined

1071

new states may join, the Commonwealth is an evolving organization. Ireland withdrew in 1949 and South Africa in 1961. Pakistan—shaken by a disastrous war with India and angered by the recognition accorded to Bangladesh—terminated its membership in the Commonwealth in 1972. The newly independent republic of Bangladesh joined the next year. There has been a difference of opinion between the British government and southern Rhodesia over the status of this former colony ever since 1965, when the dominant white minority led by Ian Smith issued a declaration of independence for Rhodesia. Britain is no longer the focal point of the Commonwealth, whose membership is spread around the globe. Since 1965 the organization has had its own Secretariat headed by a Secretary-General.

The history of the United Kingdom and of the principal African states is discussed elsewhere. The purpose of this chapter is to give an account of the major Asian republics that arose within the Commonwealth and of the self-governing dominions settled primarily by emigrants from Britain.[1]

The Commonwealth of Nations as an association of independent or virtually independent states has a history of about seven decades. At an Imperial Conference in 1887, attended by prime ministers of the principal British possessions, suggestions were made that the colonies farthest advanced ought to have the right to participate in the government of the Empire. The idea was revived at subsequent Imperial Conferences, in 1897, in 1902, and in 1907. It was not, however, until World War I that the proposal gave much promise of becoming a reality. The free and liberal assistance given to the Mother Country by the dominions in that struggle fortified their claims not only to a direct voice in imperial affairs but to a more definite recognition of their own independence. The Imperial Conference of 1921 agreed that the events of the war had clearly established the right of the self-governing dominions to be considered coequals with the Mother Country in foreign affairs. The Conference of 1926 adopted a report prepared by Arthur James Balfour, former Prime Minister of Great Britain. The report described the self-governing areas under the British flag (including the United Kingdom) as "autonomous communities within the British Empire, equal in status, in no way subordinate one to another in any aspect of their domestic or external affairs, though united by a common allegiance to the crown, and freely associated as members of the British Commonwealth of Nations." In 1931 the substance of the Balfour Report was enacted by Parliament in a memorable law known as the Statute of Westminster.

The growth of the Commonwealth

[1] The Commonwealth of Nations must be distinguished clearly from the British Empire. The latter consists of two parts: the independent empire and the dependent empire. The independent empire includes those members of the Commonwealth of Nations which still render some tenuous allegiance to Great Britain. The dependent empire comprises more than thirty colonies scattered all over the globe and ruled directly from London.

Since the enactment of the Statute of Westminster the several states of the Commonwealth of Nations have functioned as practically independent republics. No longer may any law passed by a dominion parliament be disallowed by the Parliament in London or vetoed by the British Cabinet, and no law of the British Parliament may be applied to any dominion unless its government specifically requests that this be done. The prime minister of each dominion has an equal right with the Prime Minister of Britain to "advise" the king directly. The king himself serves as a mere symbol of the unity of the Commonwealth. Although he is represented in each dominion (but not in the Republics) by a governor-general, the latter has no real authority. His primary function is to receive the resignation of an outgoing prime minister and to designate the leader of the opposition party as his successor. This involves no more freedom of choice than is exercised by the monarch himself when the head of the British Cabinet loses the support of the majority in the House of Commons and gives way to the leader of His (Her) Majesty's Loyal Opposition.

The Commonwealth is no longer the boon to Great Britain that it formerly was. Even those members that acknowledge allegiance to the British monarch have shown an increasing spirit of economic independence and indifference to the welfare of the United Kingdom. It has been said that most of the Old-World members are about as beneficial to the former Mother Country as "poor relations on pay day." Though they continue to look for generous contributions of British aid, they show little disposition to confer any benefits in return. Ghana, for example, grants no preference to British goods. While Australian industrial products enter New Zealand duty free, British goods are subject to tariffs. Not only do Air India and Pakistan International Airways compete with BOAC, but they equip their fleets with Boeings and DC-8's purchased from the United States. In 1965 British auto shipments to Australia declined by 38 per cent. During the same year Britain had a total trade deficit with the Commonwealth nations of over 1 billion dollars. Meanwhile, because of squabbles within several of the Commonwealth countries, or threats from neighboring states, Britain must maintain a costly military force that places a heavy burden on her domestic economy.

I. THE DOMINION OF CANADA

The recorded history of Canada dates from 1608 when Samuel Champlain, a French naval officer with an interest in the fur trade, founded a settlement at Quebec. For thirty years thereafter he continued his activities in the St. Lawrence valley, staking claims for the French king as far west as Lake Huron. Later in the seventeenth century the French government granted monopolies to trading companies to colonize and develop "New France." Although

1073

the companies ultimately failed, they did establish a few forts and trading posts and brought over a few thousand of their countrymen as permanent settlers. Finally, Jesuit missionaries contributed their part toward opening up the country and enlarging knowledge of its resources and attractions. By the middle of the eighteenth century the population of Canada included about 60,000 Frenchmen.

France lost Canada to Great Britain in the French and Indian War, but for some years thereafter the British continued to assume that their newly acquired possession would remain French. When the British Parliament passed the Quebec Act in 1774 to correct certain defects in the organization of the Empire, Canada was not given a representative assembly, since it was taken for granted that the people could neither understand nor be loyal to British institutions. But after the American War for Independence so many Loyalist refugees from the United States, together with immigrants from Great Britain, settled in Ontario that William Pitt thought it advisable to have Parliament enact a law in 1791 separating Upper Canada (Ontario), which was almost entirely British, from Lower Canada (Quebec), which was overwhelmingly French, and providing for an elective assembly in each of the two provinces. The scheme ended in failure. The French and British distrusted each other, and conflicts soon arose between the elective assemblies and the royal governors sent out from London. In 1837 the antagonism flared into an open rebellion. Although quickly suppressed, it called attention to Canada's grievances and impressed upon the British government the necessity of doing something about them. The result was the appointment of a High Commissioner, Lord Durham, with authority to investigate conditions and to institute reforms. When he proceeded to act in too arbitrary a fashion, the government in London withdrew its support and revoked some of his decrees. Durham resigned in anger and returned to England, but subsequently published a report which was destined to become famous in the history of dominion government.

The Durham Report enunciated two principles, which may be regarded as the cornerstone of the dominion system. First, its author declared that colonies already possessing representative institutions should be granted "responsible government." This meant that they should be permitted to manage their local affairs through cabinets or ministries responsible to their own legislatures. In the second place, Lord Durham urged the principle that similar colonies in the same geographic area should be federated into one large unit. Applying this to Canada, he pleaded for the unification of the British and French portions into a single dominion. In accordance with this recommendation Upper and Lower Canada were presently united. In 1847 Lord Durham's son-in-law, Lord Elgin, became governor of Canada and put into effect the principle of

The Fathers of Confederation. By R. Harris.

choosing his cabinet from the party that controlled a majority of seats in the assembly. He allowed it to be inferred that the cabinet would remain in office only so long as it received the support of the majority party. In addition he signed bills sponsored by the cabinet, despite the fact that they conflicted with the interests of the Mother Country. By these means he conferred upon Canada for all practical purposes a system of responsible government similar to that of Great Britain.

But the dominion government as we now know it dates only from 1867. In that year the hitherto separate colonies of New Brunswick and Nova Scotia united with Quebec and Ontario to form a confederation under the name of the Dominion of Canada. A frame of government was provided for them by the British North America Act passed by the London Parliament in the same year. This Act embodied a constitution which the Canadians themselves had adopted in 1864. It established a federal system with a division of powers between the central government and the governments of the provinces. All powers not delegated to the governments of the provinces were declared to be reserved to the central government. This departure from the federal pattern in the United States was inspired in part by the fact that the claims of the seceding Southern states to full sovereignty had helped to bring on the American War between the States.

The British North America Act confirmed the principle of responsible government. A Governor-General, appointed technically

Establishment of the Dominion of Canada

1075

by the king but actually by the British Cabinet, was made the nominal head of the Dominion. The real power over local affairs was placed in the hands of a Dominion cabinet, nominally appointed by the Governor-General but actually responsible to the lower house of the legislature for its official acts and its tenure of office. Legislative power was vested in a Parliament of two houses, a Senate appointed by the Governor-General for life, and a House of Commons elected by the people. Except for the fact that cabinet responsibility was to be enforced by the House of Commons exclusively and that money bills must originate therein, both houses were given equal powers. In practice, however, the Senate has retired into a kind of dignified obsolescence, performing no functions except those of an unambitious revising chamber. The Canadian constitution also provided for responsible government in the provinces. The nominal head of each province is a Lieutenant-Governor appointed by the Dominion cabinet. The effective authority is exercised by a cabinet responsible to the provincial legislature. Except in Quebec the legislative bodies in the provinces have only one house.

Since 1867 the growth of Canada has roughly paralleled that of the United States. When the British North America Act was passed, Canada had a population of 3½ million. By 1966 it had grown to 20 million. During the same period the population of the United States increased from 38 million to 196 million. The growth in area of the Dominion of Canada was equally phenomenal. In 1869 the province of Manitoba was carved out of territory purchased from the Hudson's Bay Company. In 1871–1873 British Columbia and Prince Edward Island were added to the Dominion. By 1905 the completion of the Canadian Pacific Railway made possible the creation of two new prairie provinces, Alberta and Saskatchewan. But the growth of Canada cannot be measured in terms of area and population alone. The latter half of the nineteenth century and the early years of the twentieth witnessed the establishment of a sound banking and currency system, a civil service, and a protective tariff for the benefit of Canadian industry. Marked progress occurred also in the exploitation of mineral and forest resources. Canada became the chief supplier of nickel, asbestos, cobalt, and wood pulp to the United States.

But the Dominion had not yet attained national maturity. It could not amend its own constitution, which in form was an act of the British Parliament, and it was dependent upon the Mother Country for the conduct of its foreign relations. Perhaps more significant, its population was not being welded into homogeneity. With the opening up of the West, thousands of Ruthenians, Russians, Poles, Scandinavians, and Germans flooded the prairie provinces. Between 1903 and 1914 nearly 2,700,000 such immigrants made their way into Canada. As late as 1941 more than 40 per cent of the population of the prairie provinces was of Central or East European origin. But by far the largest minority population was to be found in Quebec. It comprised the French Canadians, whose settlement in the country went back to the earliest beginnings. At the present time they constitute about 30 per cent of the total population, and with the high birth rate that prevails among them, the percentage is likely to increase. Fearful of domination by the English-speaking majority, they have resisted assimilation and have clung to ancient customs in defiance of innovations. The ideal which many of them strive to uphold seems to be: "In this land of Quebec naught shall die and naught shall suffer change."

For a long time the French Canadians were the chief impediment to the attainment of full independence by the Dominion of Canada. They preferred to perpetuate the ties with Britain, not because of affection for the British but as the lesser of two evils. They looked with disfavor upon full independence lest it give new opportunities to the English-speaking majority for monopolizing control of the country. Their attitude was exemplified dramatically in the defeat of the Reciprocity Agreement between Canada and the United States in 1911. For some time Canadian agricultural and mining interests had longed to expand their markets in the United States. Accordingly, in 1910, the Dominion Prime Minister, Sir Wilfrid Laurier, entered into an agreement with the Taft Administration in Washington providing for reciprocal tariff concessions on a wide list of natural products and a few manufactured articles. The agreement was to be put into effect by concurrent legislation in the two countries. The scheme precipitated a furious controversy in Canada. Manufacturers portrayed it as a Yankee plot to annex the Dominion to the United States. Unfortunately, some weight was given to their denunciations by reckless utterances south of the border. Champ Clark, Speaker of the House of Representatives, proclaimed his desire to see the American flag wave over the whole expanse of territory to the North Pole. It is doubtful, though, that the industrialists would have succeeded had they not been able to enlist the support of ultranationalists in Quebec. To these die-hards among the French minority reciprocity looked like a scheme to destroy the unique way of life of Canada and harness the country to the ambitions of American imperialists.

Fears of the French Canadians

It is generally asserted that Canada achieved maturity as a nation during World War I. Although interested but little in the tortuous diplomacy leading up to the conflict, the Ottawa government accepted Britain's declaration as an automatic commitment for the whole Empire. The Dominion pledged itself to unlimited support and made sacrifices proportionately equal to those of the Mother Country itself. Out of a population of only 9 million at the time, 600,000 joined the armed forces, and more than 50,000 gave up their lives on the fighting front. Proud of their efforts in what was

Effects of World War I in welding Canada into a nation

generally regarded as a noble cause, Canadians lost their sense of
colonial inferiority and came forth as leading champions of Western ideals of democracy and peace. After 1917 the Canadian Prime
Minister sat in the Imperial War Cabinet as an equal of the Prime
Minister of Great Britain in formulating policy. When the war
ended, Canada demanded and received a seat at the Peace Conference and subsequently was admitted to the League of Nations. In
the years that followed, the Dominion asserted its independence in
foreign policy by refusing to accept commitments under the
Locarno Agreements and other treaties negotiated by the British
without Canadian participation. Nevertheless, when World War II
broke out, Canada plunged into the fray with hardly a moment's
hesitation. The threat to the survival of Britain was almost universally regarded as a threat to the interests of Canada. Although she
might legally have remained neutral, she pledged her wealth and
the lives of her youth in the same unstinted measure as had characterized her action in World War I.

Victory for the Allies in World War II did not free Canada
from uncertainties and troubles. Many of her old problems remained unsolved. As a nation she was still underpopulated. With an
area almost equal to that of Europe, she had fewer inhabitants than
New York State. Forty-five per cent of her people dwelt in the St.
Lawrence valley in an area covering but 2 per cent of the country.
Her Yukon and Northwest territories, equal in size to half of the
United States, contained only 14,000 inhabitants. At least 50 per
cent of the land of the Dominion remained unsuitable for agriculture or for almost any other occupation except fur trading and
mining. Worse still, the population was sharply divided on the basis
of sectional and ethnic interests. Ontario was dominated by industrial and financial ambitions, which gave to the province a conservative outlook in economic affairs and at the same time a determination to achieve independence from British and American influences. The prairie provinces, inhabited largely by immigrants from
the United States and from Continental European countries, were
the stronghold of agrarian collectivism and of radical innovations
for currency inflation and cheap credit. French Canada, embraced
by the province of Quebec, continued its devotion to the culture
and religion of its ancestors and its resistance to domination from
Ottawa. Disaffection in the French-speaking areas sometimes erupted
in acts of violence, and provoked among some extremists the demand
for a separate state. This was the case in the 1970 kidnapping and
assassination of a government minister by a revolutionary terrorist
group.

The geographic position of Canada was also a source of uneasi-
ness. She had the misfortune to lie directly athwart the air routes
between Russia and the United States. As the Cold War between
these two giants waxed in intensity, Canada had reason to fear that

*Old problems
remaining un-
solved*

the United States might attempt to dictate an increasing number of her military and economic policies. Many Canadian businessmen disliked the influx of capital investment from the United States, the control of branch factories by American head offices, and the excess of American imports over Canadian exports purchased by the United States. So strong was the ill feeling that President Eisenhower paid a visit to Ottawa in 1958 and arranged for the setting up of a joint committee of the Canadian and American governments to promote cooperation and a better understanding between the two countries. Any results the committee may have achieved were nullified by sharp criticism by the United States government, early in 1963, of Canada's unwillingness to equip her armed forces with nuclear weapons from the United States. In the ensuing controversy Prime Minister Diefenbaker lost the support of a majority in the House of Commons. Instead of resigning forthwith he exercised his option of dissolving Parliament and ordering a general election for April 9. The result was the failure of any one party to gain a majority. But since the Liberals emerged with a plurality, Diefenbaker soon announced his resignation in order to make way for the Liberal leader, Lester B. Pearson, to succeed him as Prime Minister. The Liberals were returned to power in 1965 with Pearson as their leader. Three years later Pearson resigned on account of ill health and was succeeded by Pierre Trudeau.

By 1970 United States-Canadian relations had been further strained by economic developments. American investments in Canada stood at about $35 billion. With American capital controlling 85 per cent of the rubber industry and 75 per cent of petroleum and transportation, and with the United States absorbing 68 per cent of the Dominion's exports and supplying 75 per cent of her imports, Canadians feared the nation's economy would be swallowed by their great neighbor to the south. At the same time American officials were disturbed to find that, beginning in 1968, the balance of trade between the two countries had shifted in Canada's favor. The fact that Canada was the United States' primary trading partner, and that for 23 years the exchange of goods had yielded a dollar surplus to the United States, did not win preferential treatment for Canada when, in the summer of 1971, the Nixon administration imposed a surtax on foreign imports. Rather than making concessions, Secretary of the Treasury John Connally urged the Canadian government to revalue its currency upward, in order to make Canadian manufactures less competitive with American. In April 1972 President Nixon paid a conciliatory visit to Prime Minister Trudeau, and, while in Ottawa, assured Parliament that the United States was fully aware of Canada's "separate identity" and desire for economic independence. Aside from economic friction, political issues, especially the Vietnam war, aroused anti-American feelings. Canada has provided a refuge for hundreds of war resisters from across the border.

THE DOMINION OF CANADA

Canada's crucial position

Prime Minister Pierre Trudeau of Canada.

1079

The Landing of Captain Cook at Botany Bay, 1770. This painting by E. Phillips Fox depicts the first landing by Englishmen on the east coast of the Australian continent.

Promise for the future

With full allowance for all of Canada's difficulties, there seems little doubt that her future is bright with promise. She is one of the most richly endowed countries in the world in natural resources. Although her population is only one-tenth that of the United States, her total foreign trade is almost one-third as large. She leads the world in the production of asbestos, nickel, platinum, zinc, and wood pulp. She ranks second in the production of aluminum, cobalt, and uranium, third in the production of gold and titanium, and fourth in the production of wheat. Recently, extensive deposits of iron ore have been discovered in Labrador and oil in the prairie provinces and in British Columbia. The development of atomic fission has made the uranium resources in the vicinity of Great Bear Lake immensely valuable. She is rapidly developing a national culture and an independent foreign policy. Perhaps the prediction of Sir Wilfrid Laurier fifty years ago that "the twentieth century is Canada's" is not mere empty rhetoric.

2. THE COMMONWEALTH OF AUSTRALIA

Australia as a penal colony

The second largest island[2] in the world and the smallest of the continents, Australia began its recorded history under inauspicious circumstances. Discovered by the Dutch in the seventeenth century and rediscovered and claimed for England by Captain James Cook in 1770, it was too remote from the homeland to offer attractions for settlement. When the American Revolution elimi-

[2] Australia has an area of 2,967,000 square miles. Antarctica, also an island and a continent, has an estimated area of 6,000,000 square miles.

nated the thirteen colonies in the Western Hemisphere as dumping grounds for British convicts, the government in London turned to Australia. The first convict ship sailed for the island continent in 1787, and Australia remained a penal colony for fifty years. It should be noted, however, that not all the prisoners transported were burglars and cutthroats. The criminal laws of England at that time provided drastic penalties for trivial offenses, such as petty larceny or hunting partridges on some noble's estate. We can reasonably assume, therefore, that many of the original colonists in Australia were far from being what we would now call hardened criminals.

The first settlers were convicts exclusively, except for 200 soldiers sent to guard them. This continued to be the case for some time. Gradually a few adventurous free citizens learned of the possibilities of sheep-raising and filtered into the colony to establish ranches or "stations." Convicts were released to them as shepherds, with the provision that after the expiration of their terms of sentence they would continue to live in Australia. By 1830 the wool industry had become the backbone of the Australian economy. Ten years later the number of free settlers had grown sufficiently large to justify a decision by the British government to abandon the practice of dumping prisoners in most parts of the continent.

In 1848 the trend of Australian development was abruptly changed by the discovery of gold in New South Wales and Victoria. Fortune-hunters and adventurers from all over the world followed the magic lure of the yellow metal. Between 1850 and 1860 the population of the continent almost trebled. Inevitably more people came than could find a livelihood in prospecting and mining. When the excitement died away, and the hills and streams no longer yielded gold in easy abundance, the problem arose of what

Convicts and settlers

The discovery of gold

Commissioner Hardy Collecting License fees in Victoria Gold Fields in the 1850's. Diggers scatter in order to evade paying the fees.

to do with the surplus population. The logical solution seemed to be to encourage them to become farmers. Efforts to establish themselves in this occupation involved a desperate struggle. Scanty rainfall, inadequate transportation facilities, and refusal of the woolgrowers to "unlock" their vast estates dogged the footsteps of all but the most fortunate farmers with disaster. Not until the building of railways to the ports, the perfection of dry-farming techniques, the development of suitable strains of wheat, and the improvement of chemical fertilizers was agriculture in Australia placed on a sound foundation.

Effects of the
gold rushes

A considerable number of the basic political and social policies of Australia as a nation can be traced to the gold rushes of the 1850's and their aftermath. First was the White Australia policy, designed to exclude black, brown, and yellow races from settlement on the continent. This policy was an outgrowth of conflicts between Chinese and Caucasian miners in the gold fields. A second was the attempt to build up a manufacturing industry through the use of protective tariffs. Originally adopted by the colony of Victoria in the 1860's, tariffs were later extended to the Commonwealth as a whole. Their use was motivated in part at least by the need for domestic industry to absorb the surplus miners. A third policy was the adoption of heavy governmental borrowing for the construction of public works. Obviously, the need for public-works construction could be justified for many reasons: to provide irrigation projects for the benefit of farmers in arid regions; to speed up the development of transportation facilities; to furnish employment opportunities for the influx of immigrants brought in by the discovery of gold.

The growth of
democracy in the
Australian states

The Australian Commonwealth as an organized state did not come into existence until 1901. Prior to that time the continent was divided into separate colonies, most of which had split off from the original colony of New South Wales. Movements to federate them made slow progress, mainly because the weak feared domination by the strong and prosperous. But such fears did not prevent a rapid growth of local democracy. By 1850 each of the colonies had its legislative council as a check upon the Governor, and had obtained the right to alter its own constitution. Soon afterward the eastern colonies achieved responsible government. Universal manhood suffrage was introduced in South Australia in 1855, in Victoria in 1857, and in New South Wales a year later. About the same time the secret ballot was adopted in Victoria, South Australia, New South Wales, and Queensland. Before 1900 two colonies had begun payment of salaries to members of their legislatures, and several had given women the privilege of voting.

The stage was eventually reached where the arguments for federation outweighed the objections. Foremost among them was the need for a common defense against the militant imperialism of the

Establishment of Seat of Government at Canberra. The Duke and Duchess of York in the Senate at the official opening of the Federal Parliament House in Canberra on May 9, 1927. The Duke reads King George V's commission for the establishment of the seat of government at Canberra.

Great Powers. Important also was the growing inconvenience of tariffs levied by the various colonies against each other. The first step for a union of the continent was taken in 1885 with the establishment of the Australasian Federal Council. Possessing only legislative power with no executive or financial authority, this agency was reduced to impotence by the non-cooperation of New South Wales. Its chief significance lay in the renewed impetus it gave to the demand for effective union. In 1897–1898 a series of conferences resulted in the drafting of a plan of federation which in 1901 was approved by the British Parliament and became the Constitution of the Commonwealth of Australia. The Commonwealth was organized as a federal union comprising the six states of New South Wales, Victoria, Queensland, South Australia, Western Australia, and Tasmania. The capital was temporarily established at Melbourne, but the Constitution contained a provision that a permanent capital should be built in the state of New South Wales, not less than 100 miles from Sydney. In the course of a decade the government invited city planners from all over the world to submit blueprints for a garden municipality to be known as Canberra. The award was given to W. B. Griffin of Chicago, an associate of Frank Lloyd Wright. In 1927 the seat of government of the Commonwealth was formally transferred to the new federal city.

The government of Australia bears a closer resemblance to that of the United States than does the government of Canada. Such a development was rendered inevitable by the spirit of independence existing within the states of Australia and by their distrust of each other. Consequently, when the division of powers was made by the Constitution, it was logical that the government of the Common-

Establishment of the Commonwealth of Australia

The government of Australia

wealth should be given only specified powers, and that all powers
not thus delegated should be reserved to the states. In some other
respects also the Australian system resembles, superficially at least,
the American. The Australian Parliament consists of two houses, a
Senate and a House of Representatives. The former is composed of
six members from each state, elected directly by the people for six
years. Membership in the House is proportionate to population. Like
several other members of the Commonwealth, Australia has a
Governor-General representing the British Crown, but his powers
are insignificant. As in all of the dominions, executive authority as
well as the primary control over legislation is vested in the cabinet
headed by the Prime Minister.

One of the most interesting facts of Australian history is the extent to which the country has pursued a policy of social and economic planning. Even during the nineteenth century when the
Mother Country was worshiping the slogans of free competition
and free trade, Australia was steadily enlarging the sphere of governmental action to promote social cohesion and maintain a high
standard of living. The reasons for this policy are numerous and
varied. Geography alone provides a large part of the explanation.
One-third of the continent has an average annual rainfall of less
than 10 inches, and most of the remainder has less than 20. But
even these averages do not reflect the poor distribution of the rain
that does fall. In many areas the precipitation may be concentrated
within a short period of the year, with months or years of subsequent drought. As a result, only about 8 per cent of the total area
can be utilized for farming or orchard purposes. About 40 per cent
is waste, and 50 per cent is used for pasture. Under such conditions, it has been impossible for Australia to develop into a nation
of independent proprietors cultivating small plots as family farms.
In the pasture areas rainfall is so scanty or unreliable that sheep and
cattle must be grazed over thousands of acres. This has necessitated
the development of vast estates or pastoral "stations" established by
owners with considerable capital. They provide employment for
what is essentially an agricultural proletariat: shepherds, shearers,
and "boundary riders," who have no hope of ever becoming proprietors. Conscious of their grievances, they have been drawn since
the later nineteenth century into militant trade unions to struggle
for old-age pensions, unemployment insurance, and minimum wages.
They have been among the most consistent supporters of government intervention in economic affairs.

A second factor contributing to governmental control and regulation was the gold rushes of the 1850's. As previously noted,
these produced a surplus of prospectors and miners who had to be
channeled into new occupations. The result was positive action by
the colonial governments to promote the development of industry
and to extend agriculture into all parts of the limited area where

*Factors
contributing to
social and eco-
nomic planning:
(1) scanty rainfall*

rainfall would permit. The discovery of gold also gave rise to racial problems. In the 1850's thousands of Chinese poured into Victoria and New South Wales and threatened the wage scales and living standards of the white miners. Rapidly the Australians became obsessed with the idea that their country was a "white island in a vast colored ocean." Having already expropriated and partially exterminated the native black population, they pointed to the hundreds of millions of dark-skinned inhabitants of India, the Netherlands Indies, China, and Japan as a flood-tide which would overwhelm them unless they built dikes in the form of rigid exclusion laws. Even the tropical regions of northern Australia were to be kept uncontaminated by Oriental labor. Queensland, for example, has taken pride in recent years in the ability of its white inhabitants to cultivate its sugar plantations without being defeated by the moral and physical diseases that have commonly wreaked such havoc upon Caucasians in the tropics.[3] We can say, therefore, that the White Australian policy has been motivated both by feelings of race superiority and by fear of economic competition. Some of its sponsors argue that it is essential to democracy. Racial divisions, they say, would create tensions and conflicts and destroy the spirit of compromise which can exist only in a community of equals. After World War II immigration policy was modified somewhat. Yet as late as 1960 only 5 per cent of Australians were of non-British origin. A few of these were Asians, but most had migrated from European countries other than Britain.

Still another influence promoting intervention by the government for social and economic purposes has been the peculiar nationalism of the Australians. Since the 1880's their statesmen and poets have extolled the nation as the bearer of a grandiose destiny. Its mission was to reclaim a vast continent from savagery. While Britain and other European countries were engrossed in militarism and in the sordid disputes of power politics, Australia was building a humanitarian democracy. Here, if anywhere, men would be equal and free, and no one would suffer want or be left unprotected against the slings and arrows of evil fortune. Whatever government might do to give such protection would be considered within its province, and no "natural economic laws" or dogmas of individualism would be allowed to stand in the way.

One of the earliest forms of government intervention in Australia was control of international trade. The methods employed have included tariffs, bounties, quotas, and marketing restrictions. From the middle of the nineteenth century the several Australian colonies imposed protective tariffs on intercolonial trade. They did so not merely for the benefit of the business classes but to provide

(2) the gold rushes of the 1850's

(3) nationalism

Protectionism

[3] It is an ironical fact, however, that in the nineteenth century thousands of Melanesians and Polynesians were brought in from the Pacific islands and shamelessly exploited. They were deported in 1906.

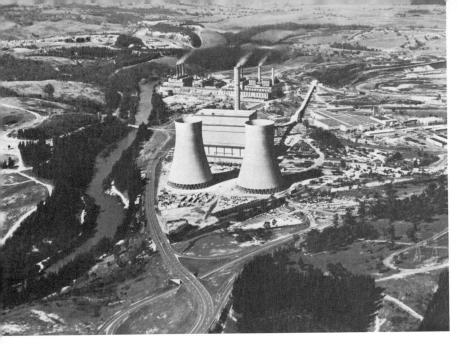

Australia's New Power Project. A new 350 megawatt turbo-generator was commissioned in August 1973 at Yallourn, 90 miles east of Melbourne. The Yallourn complex is the main source of power for the highly industrialized state of Victoria. The new plant, built by a Japanese firm, is dominated by the two giant cooling towers. In the background are the old Yallourn power station and an open cut coal field.

employment and to maintain as high a standard of living as possible for farmers and workers. When the Commonwealth was established in 1901, the tariff policy was continued, and the rates have been steadily increased. Sentiment in favor of protection is almost universal. Labor as well as capital insists upon the importance of controlling economic forces for the general welfare. Neither has any respect for the laissez-faire philosophy or is willing to trust the fate of Australia to the shifting trends of the international market.

Government ownership

A second form of government intervention for which Australia has been particularly noted is public ownership of a wide variety of economic enterprises. Ventures brought under government ownership include railways, shipping lines, power plants, hotels, banks, insurance companies, lumber mills, and coal mines. Because of the federal structure of the government, most of such enterprises are conducted by the states rather than by the Commonwealth. Government ownership in Australia is the result in part of the strong influence which labor wields in both state and national politics. Owing to a rigid control of immigration, the supply of labor has been kept from exceeding the demand. This has fostered the growth of a unionism surpassing in strength that of most other countries. In Australia at the present time about 40 per cent of all wage earners are enrolled in labor unions, compared with little more than 25 per cent in the United States. But organized labor has not been the only force supporting state ownership. The geography of Australia has impelled many capitalists and landowners to look with favor upon government operation of railways and public utilities, at least. Scanty rainfall over most of the continent has limited the growth of cities and towns in the hinterland. But the construction of railroads to bring out the grain, wool, meat, and minerals has been none the less important. With few private corporations bold enough to incur the risks involved, there was no alternative but for governments to shoulder the burden. As a consequence, in these and in some other lines, public ownership of economic ventures has been welcomed as an aid and support of private business.

In social-welfare legislation Australian achievements have been little more distinctive than those of most other democracies. In a number of cases Australia (together with New Zealand) pioneered in this type of regulation. In other cases she merely duplicated the pattern of Great Britain. Old-age pensions, widows' allowances, unemployment and health insurance, slum clearance, and child subsidies stand out as the principal examples. A bonus is paid for every infant born in Australia, and an endowment is provided for every child under 16. A National Health System furnishes free drugs, subsidizes hospital and medical expenses, and provides pensions for the blind and victims of tuberculosis. One other element of Australian collectivism, however, has had no counterpart in the Mother Country. This is a system of compulsory arbitration and wage-fixing, designed to maintain industrial peace and safeguard standards of living for industrial workers. In sharp contrast with the attitude of organized labor in most countries, Australian workers have accepted, and for the most part actually welcomed, compulsory arbitration. They regard it as a means to security and as a source of strength for the labor movement, since it tends to bring more members into the union. Moreover, the political strength of the workers is so great that they look upon the government as an agency they can hope to control. Therefore, they do not fear compulsory arbitration as a device which anti-labor elements might use against them.

For more than two decades following World War II Australian politics were dominated by a coalition of two parties, the Liberal party and the Country party, each of which was actually conservative. The Labor party, weakened by a split in its ranks, could not win a majority at the polls, even though it retained the support of the powerful labor unions. Apprehension over national security, aggravated by the Cold War and the fear of Communism, helped give the conservatives their long tenure of power. During this era the government generally followed the lead of the United States in foreign affairs. It sent troops to fight in Korea and in the war in Vietnam, and permitted the United States to install defense bases on Australian soil. By the early 1970's dissatisfaction with these commitments had become widespread, and it grew sharper in 1971 following the United States overtures to Communist China. President Nixon's sudden reversal of policy jarred the Liberal-Country coalition and proved an asset to the Labor party, which had long advocated recognition of the People's Republic of China. Inflation

Other forms of collectivism

Prime Minister E. Gough Whitlam of Australia. Mr. Whitlam's Labor Party returned to power in December 1972, ending a long era of conservative administrations.

and the threat of rising unemployment also undermined the popularity of Prime Minister William McMahon, who was accused of having no plan of attack on such problems. Australia's economy had been changing over the years and seemed to call for basic policy changes. Although Australia was a member of the Sterling Bloc and in 1960 had sent Great Britain 27 per cent of her exports and received in return 36 per cent of her imports, her chief market now was Japan. By 1971 30 per cent of her total exports went to Japan and more than 60 per cent of her mineral exports. For coking coal the figure was close to 100 per cent. Furthermore, while Australia had become Japan's chief supplier of raw materials, she might expect to develop a profitable market in China, especially for Australian wheat, if political conditions were favorable. In the national election of December 1972 the Labor party returned to power with a majority in the House of Representatives, and Gough Whitlam, the new Prime Minister, began positive action in a number of areas. Long a critic of the Vietnam war, he ended the military draft and freed draft resisters who had been imprisoned. He established diplomatic relations with the Peking government and severed ties with the Chinese Nationalists. On the domestic front he announced a new reform program, including one long overdue—humane treatment of the black aborigines who had been oppressed, neglected, and forced to live in the desolate "Outback" or in city slums. He promised to transfer to them ownership of tribal lands, to provide better schools, and to encourage preservation of their indigenous culture and languages. Equally startling was a government announcement that it would modify Australia's immigration regulations to end discrimination against non-whites.

Sydney, Australia. In the foreground are road and rail approaches to the Harbour Bridge, linking the northern suburbs with the inner city area. Sydney has a population of about 2,500,000 and is the largest city in Australia.

Located about 1100 miles southeast of Australia, New Zealand was also discovered by the Dutch but explored and claimed for the British by Captain James Cook. At the time of discovery (1769) it was inhabited exclusively by Maoris, an intelligent but warlike people of Polynesian stock. For three-quarters of a century thereafter the only white settlers were missionaries, who labored with modest success to convert the Maoris to Christianity. In 1840 the first boatload of British colonists entered the harbor of what is now Wellington. They had been sent out by the New Zealand Company, founded by Edward Gibbon Wakefield, leader of the new British school of systematic colonizers. While completing a prison term for abducting a schoolgirl heiress, Wakefield came to the conclusion that Britain would be engulfed by civil war unless new economic opportunities could be found for the distressed population of her industrial cities. Caught in the maelstrom of depression and unemployment, workers by the thousands were turning to Chartism and sundry varieties of socialism. A conflict with the privileged classes was inevitable. Eventually Wakefield hit upon the idea that colonization would banish the specter of civil war. The company he founded would transport selected colonists to New Zealand. They would be provided with land at prices sufficiently high to discourage easy accumulation. Only the more prosperous and enterprising colonists would attain the status of owners. The others would have to content themselves for years with jobs as farm laborers. In time they too would buy land, and the proceeds from the sale would be used to finance further immigration.[4]

Discovery and settlement

Wakefield's scheme attracted so much attention that the British government decided to take action. A governor was appointed, and the islands were formally annexed to the British Empire. The announced purpose was to protect the Maoris against unscrupulous white settlers. A week after the first colonists landed at Wellington the newly appointed governor arrived. He proceeded to negotiate a treaty with the native chiefs recognizing the sovereignty of the British Crown over all New Zealand. In return the British guaranteed to the Maoris full possession of their lands, "except as the Crown might wish to purchase them," and granted to the natives the rights and privileges of British subjects. Perhaps it was well that the government acted as it did, for a broadening stream of colonists continued to flow to the islands. By 1856 New Zealand had a white population of 45,000.

Annexation to the British Empire

In 1852 the British Government endowed New Zealand with a constitution. It conferred the executive power upon a Governor-

---

[4] The scheme had already been tried in South Australia, but with limited success. Wakefield subsequently turned to New Zealand in the hope that his theories would be vindicated.

General representing the King, and acting with the advice of an Executive Council. Legislative authority was vested in a House of Representatives elected by the people and a Legislative Council appointed by the Governor-General. In 1856 the Executive Council was formally recognized as a cabinet, exercising its functions under the principle of responsible government, and in 1951 the appointive upper house was abolished. Other steps in the direction of political democracy came easily. In 1879 universal manhood suffrage was adopted, and a few years later plural voting was abolished. In 1893 New Zealand led the Commonwealth of Nations in bestowing the suffrage upon women in national elections.

The development of political democracy

Economic reform followed in the wake of political democracy. When the Liberals came into power in 1891 they dedicated their efforts to making New Zealand a nation of small, independent farmers and herdsmen. Measures were adopted to break up large holdings, the formation of which had previously been encouraged by the sale of Maori lands to wealthy individuals. To combat the power of the big landowners required the support not only of landless agriculturists but also of workers in the cities. The Liberals therefore espoused a program of combined agrarian and labor reform which won the allegiance of both classes. The agrarian measures took the form primarily of special taxes on land held for speculative purposes and limitation of the size of holdings in the future. For the benefit of the workers the Liberals provided old-age pensions, factory inspection, regulation of working hours, and compulsory arbitration of industrial disputes. The accession of the Labor party to power in 1935 brought an extension of these measures, with increased benefits to the urban workers.

Economic reform

New Zealand has followed policies of collectivization quite similar to those of Australia. The reasons also have been similar. Lacking the capital to take advantage of new inventions, especially the railroad and the telegraph, the Dominion turned to foreign sources. Money proved to be more easily obtainable when the government itself was the borrower. Moreover, there was a deeply rooted fear among the colonists themselves of private monopoly. The beginning of collectivism occurred about 1870, when the Dominion Government entered the London capital market for funds to construct roads, trunk railways, and telegraph lines. About the same time a state life-insurance system was established, and later state fire and accident insurance. A few coal mines also were added to the list of public enterprises, and finally a Bank of New Zealand. Important as a principle of collectivization has been the use of state-owned enterprises for "yardstick" purposes. Government purchase of coal mines, for example, was dictated by the theory that private companies needed the restraint of state competition to keep them from charging excessive prices.

Collectivism

It is not an exaggeration to say that New Zealand enjoys all the advantages for future progress possessed by Australia with none of Australia's disadvantages. The two dominions have homogeneous populations overwhelmingly British in origin. In Australia 99.2 per cent of the people are of European extraction, and 97 per cent of these are of British ancestry. In New Zealand the percentages are 93 and 96, respectively. In both dominions systematic efforts have been made to preserve perpetually the British character of the nation. The early emigrants to New Zealand brought with them not merely the social customs and political institutions but the flowers, trees, birds, and even animal pests of their native England. New Zealand, like Australia, was populated in considerable measure by people of liberal and even radical tendencies. Both dominions received inundations of immigrants attracted thither by the discovery of gold. Coming from the landless and unemployed elements of Britain, many were infected with Chartism and even traces of socialism. As a consequence, they developed in the colonies institutions of political and economic democracy surpassing those of the Mother Country.

But with respect to one political and social policy New Zealand has had an advantage over Australia. She has not been under the same pressure to embrace an extreme nationalism. Her problem of providing employment opportunities for displaced gold miners was not so acute as Australia's, and therefore the necessity of developing industry was not so imperious. More important, New Zealanders exported some 80 per cent of what they produced, and consequently recognized the need of continuing to purchase imports. Both factors militated against economic nationalism as a dominion policy. In addition, New Zealand has never been threatened with incursions of Oriental immigrants to the same extent as Australia. One reason is the greater distance from the chief centers of Asian congestion. Another is the fact that she has no vast areas of sparsely populated territory inviting occupation. Nevertheless, immigration is not left unrestricted. Barriers have been erected against the influx of laborers allegedly a menace to the white man's standard of living. Though it has never been propagated with the emotional fervor behind its Australian equivalent, a "White New Zealand policy" does exist.

Geographically, also, New Zealand has a wide margin of superiority over Australia. Although a mountainous region, with peaks that rise to 12,000 feet, extends the entire length of the southern island, there are no deserts and few areas unsuited to agriculture or grazing. Almost everywhere rainfall is adequate and permits an intensive use of the land. North Island, which contains over 60 per cent of the population, has an average of about 50 inches of rain annually. Throughout the Dominion temperatures fluctuate within

1091

Upper Takaka Valley, Nelson, New Zealand. New Zealand enjoys the advantages of beautiful scenery, an ideal climate, and an abundance of space for its population.

a comparatively narrow range. Extremes of over 100 degrees or below zero have never been recorded, and in both islands 75 degrees is considered unpleasantly high and 40 degrees uncomfortably low. Such favorable geographic conditions have given to New Zealand a character quite different from that of Australia. For one thing, the distribution of population is much more even. Instead of a few large cities along the seacoast and an almost unoccupied hinterland, there are hundreds of towns of moderate size and not a single city exceeding 400,000. The mean density of population is slightly over 15 persons per square mile compared with 2 for Australia. Geography, more than anything else, has made New Zealand a democracy of small, independent agrarians.

New Zealand has remained more closely connected with her British antecedents than has Australia. For one reason, the British and New Zealand economies are complementary rather than competitive. New Zealand is predominantly agricultural. Two-thirds of her land is suitable for farming and grazing. Her only important manufactures are meat and dairy products, fertilizer, pulp and paper. Two-thirds of New Zealand's exports are sold to Great Britain, and half of her imports come from British sources. Unlike Australia, New Zealand has not faced any dangerous threat of aggression. She has therefore not felt the necessity of developing an independent foreign policy. She has generally been content to walk in the shadow of Great Britain, with occasional glances in the direction of Australia and the United States. However, with the recent British trend toward withdrawal from responsibilities east of Suez, New Zealand's ties with Great Britain appear to be loosening. Also Britain's entry into the European Common Market

Close ties with Britain

in 1973—ending the protected market in the Mother Country for New Zealand's butter, cheese, and lamb—affected her more seriously than it did Australia.

4. INDIA UNDER COMPANY AND CROWN

In securing outposts in India, the British were motivated solely by an interest in trade and had no intention either of colonizing or of ruling territories. Gradually and quite unsystematically, their trading posts were transformed into centers of political administration. The absorption or conquest of native states, even though it ultimately involved large-scale military operations, was carried out not by the British Government but by the British East India Company—a privately owned joint-stock corporation, chartered by the Crown and increasingly subjected to control by Parliament. When finally, in 1858, the Company was dissolved and the British Government assumed full responsibility for Indian affairs, the administrative and financial system developed by the Company was continued in essential features. Another distinctive aspect of the British position in India was the fact that the country was never conquered in its entirety. The British seized strategic regions until their possessions formed a ring around the whole subcontinent (and included substantial portions of the interior as well), but they left hundreds of native states nominally independent. Nevertheless, although Britain's control over India was acquired piecemeal and indirectly, it became as thorough as if it had been imposed by a conquering horde capable of beating down all resistance.

As the trading posts of the East India Company expanded, they gradually took on the nature of colonies. This process had begun even before the close of the seventeenth century and increased rapidly during the eighteenth century. The assumption by

Foundations of The British East India Company

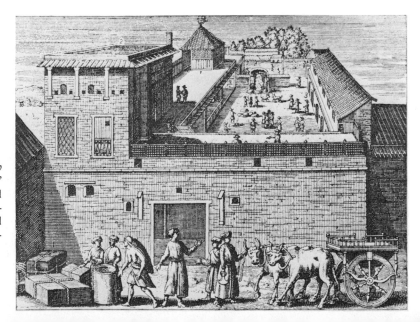

The Modest Beginning of British Rule in India. An early "factory" or trading station, with walled enclosure containing a warehouse, promenade area, and church. From a copper engraving.

Homage to Governor Warren Hastings. Chait Singh, Raja of Benares, was induced to transfer his allegiance from the Mogul's representative to the British East India Company in 1775. (Later Hastings deposed the Raja and transferred his dominions to Chait's nephew at double the previous assessment.)

The British East India Company as sovereign

the Company of sovereign power over various territories created a need for efficient administration, a need which was not met promptly or adequately. In the early days Company agents had been selected without regard to their knowledge of Indian affairs (proficiency in Latin and Greek literature was considered much more important), and most of the agents did not remain in India long enough to become well-acquainted with the country or its people. There was little integration between the administration of the separate British holdings, although the acquisition of the great province of Bengal (by Robert Clive, in 1757) made Calcutta eventually the Company's most important center of administration. Furthermore, the governing body of the Company, the Court of Directors in London, was so far away that its members could not be adequately informed as to what was going on in India. The governors, sent out as servants of the Company, in practice often modified or even formulated its policies. They negotiated treaties with native rulers, fought wars, and annexed territories.

Changes in the status of the Company

An act of Parliament in 1814, which renewed the Company's charter for twenty years, threw open the commerce of India to all British subjects but allowed the Company to retain its monopoly in China and the Far East. By 1834 free-trade sentiment had become so influential in England that the Charter Act of that year deprived the Company of all its trading privileges, in China as well as in India. Since it had originally been founded for the purpose of engaging in trade and had now lost that function altogether, the British East India Company might logically have expired in 1834. Instead of doing so, it was permitted to continue administering patronage in the British portions of India, serving as a governmental agency although ultimately subject to parliamentary check. Furthermore, to satisfy the English stockholders, dividends of the Company were fixed by law at 10½ per cent annually, to be derived no longer from the profits of commerce but levied as a permanent charge upon the revenues of India.

British territorial expansion inevitably led to conflicts with states beyond the Indian borders. Two Burmese wars made possible the annexation of Lower Burma (1852) and gave the British control of the Bay of Bengal. Less fortunate in sequel was an intervention in the independent state of Afghanistan in 1838–1839, a project unjustified in the first place and so thoroughly bungled that out of an invading force of 16,000 troops only one man escaped death or capture. The fiasco of the Afghan war, however, was a prelude to one of the boldest strokes in the history of British imperialism—the conquest and annexation of Sind. In violation of a signed treaty, the British, during the Afghan war, marched their troops through this independent and neutral state and used the country as a military base. Shortly afterward the British government sent Sir Charles Napier with an army into Sind to impose new demands upon the ruling princes. Without even a declaration of war Napier razed a fortress, exiled the rulers, and transferred their sovereignty to the Company (1843). Apparently Sir Charles, whose share of the plunder was £70,000, believed that the benefits of British rule outweighed any irregularities in the methods used to establish it. He referred to his own conduct in Sind as "a very advantageous, useful, humane piece of rascality." [5] After two wars against the Sikhs in the Punjab, the Governor-General, acting on his own responsibility, annexed the Punjab in 1849. Thus, by the middle of the century, most of the sovereign units in India capable of offer-

Expansion and conquest

[5] P. E. Roberts, *History of British India*, p. 330.

Tipu's Tiger. Wooden model of a tiger mauling a British East India Company Officer. This monstrosity (fitted inside with a bellows and miniature organ pipes to simulate groans) was made for Sultan Tipu, ruler of Mysore. Tipu was defeated and killed by Governor Wellesley's troops in 1799.

ing a serious military threat to the British position had been neutralized or brought under the jurisdiction of the Company.

In 1857 an armed uprising, known as the Great Mutiny, produced a crisis in Anglo-Indian relations and necessitated significant changes in British policy. Although the revolt was technically a mutiny because it originated among the native troops (sepoys) employed by the British, it received some popular support and it reflected the political aspirations both of Moslem and of Hindu elements. The underlying causes of the Mutiny lay in general discontent and in suspicions which British policies had aroused. The immediate cause can be attributed to carelessness and gross errors of judgment on the part of the military commanders. The British officials were caught quite unprepared for the revolt, which began near Delhi in May 1857, raged intensively for a few months in parts of northern and central India, and was not entirely suppressed until the following year. Many Europeans were slaughtered indiscriminately by the rebel troops, and sickening atrocities were committed on both sides, but the uprising never assumed the character of a mass movement or a genuine revolution. Its leaders were divided in purpose from the beginning. While Moslems dreamed of rehabilitating the Mogul Empire, the Marathas hoped to recover their ascendancy as a powerful Hindu state. The great majority of native princes remained aloof from the rebellion, probably because they recognized the superiority of British military resources.

The most important political result of the Mutiny was the termination of the East India Company and the transfer of full responsibility for the government of India to the British Crown and

Indian mutineers surprised by the Ninth Lancers Unit. A drawing from the book *Campaign in India, 1857–1858.*

Parliament.[6] The Government of India Act of 1858 created a Secretary of State for India with an advisory council to assist him and bestowed upon the Governor-General the title of Viceroy. There was no immediate change in the details of the administrative system, but a royal proclamation issued by Queen Victoria offered conciliatory assurances in regard to religious toleration, material improvements, and the admission of native Indians to government service.

After 1858, in contrast to the earlier period, the policy of the British government in India was one of caution and conservatism. To minimize the danger of rebellion in the future, the bulk of the people were disarmed and the army was reorganized. The recruited troops were carefully trained, instilled with pride in the service, and grouped in accordance with sectarian, tribal, or local divisions so that there would be little feeling of common interest among the different units. Although Europeans formed a minority of the military personnel, they monopolized the ranks of commissioned officers and retained possession of the heavy artillery. At the same time the government sought to avoid antagonizing any powerful element or prejudice within the population. Notably, the British authorities refrained from further territorial aggression. By treaties with the remaining native princes, the British government guaranteed to these rulers their hereditary rights and possessions but required them to relinquish all control over external affairs. Henceforth a clear division was maintained between the five or six hundred native states and the British provinces. The states ranged in size from Hyderabad—with an area almost equal to that of Great Britain—to tiny principalities, and included altogether about 40 per cent of the land area of India. A few of the rulers were more progressive than the British, but most of them were uninspiring survivals from an age of despotism, quite content to enjoy the protection of the "paramount" power, Great Britain.

The government's policy of conservatism and caution

The several changes introduced into the government of British India between 1858 and 1919 were more in form than in substance. While the Governor-General retained full authority, the door was gradually opened for Indian participation in the administrative machinery by the development of the Indian Civil Service. From the 1880's on, Indians were allowed to compete in examinations for the selection of civil servants, and they eventually came to supply most of the personnel for the lower and intermediate positions. The Indian Civil Service grew to be one of the most remarkable institutions of its kind in the world and a

The Indian Civil Service

[6] The Company stockholders were still treated with tender consideration. The guaranteed annual dividends of 10½ per cent continued to be paid until 1874, at which time the stock was redeemed by a government purchase in the amount of £12,000,000.

source of great pride to the British because of the integrity, efficiency, and loyalty of its members. It exhibited, however, the typical faults of a bureaucracy—inflexibility, conservatism, and lack of imagination. Because there was always an oversupply of educated Indians seeking government posts, and the lucky ones who obtained appointments found their modest salaries considerably above the average income of their countrymen, the civil servants usually developed an attitude of subservience to their superiors. In spite of its beneficent aspects, the Indian Civil Service became—like the native states—a bulwark of English supremacy and of the *status quo*.

Widely divergent views have been expressed concerning the over-all effects which British administration had upon India and her people, particularly in the nineteenth century. The British themselves do not agree on this question. Some of the harshest criticisms of British imperialism and its fruits in India have been voiced by Englishmen. Indisputably, a number of material benefits resulted from British rule. English authorities were generally effective in checking the more violent types of crime, suppressing organized bands of marauders, reducing the hazards of travel, and protecting property. They also attempted to eliminate such cruel customs as suttee, which was outlawed in 1829, and infanticide. Under British rule the population of India expanded greatly, rising from 150 million in 1850 to 250 million in 1881. By 1921 it exceeded 300 million, and another 100 million was added by 1945. This impressive increase is attributable largely to the curbing of internal warfare and to improvements in sanitation and medical facilities under British auspices. Irrigation works were constructed sufficient to provide for 30 million acres of land. Modern communications were introduced, including an extensive network of railroads totaling eventually more than 40,000 miles, a figure far in excess of the railroad mileage of any other Asian country.

Almost all the improvements, however, had their darker side. The rapid increase in population depressed the living conditions of large numbers of the people, and the problem of an adequate food supply was never solved. Severe famines had been known in India long before the British arrived, but some of the worst occurred during the period of British control. Ironically, the proclamation of Queen Victoria as Empress of India in 1877 coincided with the greatest famine in India's history, which took a toll of 5 million lives. It is estimated that between 1877 and 1900 no fewer than 15 million people died of famine. A basic cause of these disasters was the fact that a majority of the population lived close to the starvation level even in normal times and had no savings and no reserves of physical stamina to carry them through an emergency.

Although British rule did not introduce poverty into India, it did little to alleviate it and in some areas intensified it. The taxation system contributed heavily to the poverty of India's population.

The principle generally followed by the government was to demand *one-half* the rental value of the land. British officials pointed to the fact that the tax schedules were somewhat less extortionate than those of earlier autocratic regimes. An important difference, however, was that the British assessments were not theoretical; they were actually collected. Also, in contrast to the situation under earlier empires, much of the revenue raised was drained out of India—in salaries to the higher administrative officials and to European army officers, in dividends to the East India Company stockholders, and in interest on the public debt, most of which was held by Englishmen. Not only did taxation bear too heavily upon the poorest classes but only a small fraction of the government's budget was allotted to relief, social welfare, or education. The major portion was expended on the police, the courts, and especially the Indian army, a professional body which was sometimes used in imperial wars outside of India—in Afghanistan, Burma, or China. In spite of the introduction of sanitation measures, the Indian death rate remained appallingly high, augmented by such diseases as cholera, malaria, and bubonic plague, which can be controlled by modern medical science and have been almost eliminated in Western countries.

Probably the aspect of British rule in India most open to criticism was its economic policy. In the early days of the East India Company there had been a great demand for Indian handmade goods of superior quality, especially silks, cottons, and muslins, which were generally paid for in specie. With the coming of the Industrial Revolution in England, the character of Far Eastern commerce changed. The British became interested in India as a source of raw materials and, even more, as a market for manufactured goods. The Indians were forced to accept "free trade" as applied to British manufactures but were effectively denied the right to export their own manufactures either to England or other countries. An inevitable result of this policy was the decline of village handicrafts which had for centuries constituted a vital element in the whole Indian economy. During the period of British rule, in spite of the growth of some large cities, the proportion of India's population dependent on the land for sustenance actually increased, until by the opening of the twentieth century it constituted more than 80 per cent of the total. Excessive ruralization, small tenant holdings, oppressive taxes, and the unchecked extortions of moneylenders go far to explain why India remained a land of poverty and famine. The introduction of factory industries in the late nineteenth century offered a new source of employment, but only for a tiny fraction of the population. An oversupply of labor kept wages extremely low, and the sordid conditions of English mill towns during the early Industrial Revolution were repeated and far exceeded in India.

Inequities in the system of taxation

Other evils of economic policy

Social and cultural
effects of British
rule

*Burmese Royal Headdress
(Nineteenth Century).* Of gold
openwork on a cloth base, or-
namented with gold, beetles'
wings, and precious stones.

Somewhat more difficult to assess are the effects of the British occupation upon Indian society, culture, and mentality. Quite early the English rulers recognized an obligation to promote educational facilities. Several European scholars became intensely interested in the study of Sanskrit and the related ancient languages and advocated the promotion of a fuller knowledge of India's intellectual heritage. The printing press, introduced by missionaries, was utilized for works in the vernacular. The first newspaper, published in the Bengali dialect, appeared in 1818. A fundamental change in English educational policy in India came in 1833 with the decision to devote all educational funds henceforth to instruction solely in the English language. Lord Macaulay, the famous essayist and historian, who was a member of the Governor's council at this time and was primarily responsible for the decision, regarded Hindu literature as nothing but "false history, false astronomy, false metaphysics, false religion." [7] As a matter of fact, the government did very little to carry out the educational plans which had been announced, and it is probable that, with the economic and political decline of the formerly autonomous villages, instructional facilities in India actually deteriorated. Some village schools were still flourishing in the early nineteenth century, but with the decay of village life education gradually fell into neglect and illiteracy increased accordingly. Nevertheless, the official emphasis upon Western studies familiarized Indian intellectuals with nineteenth-century liberal traditions and in the long run intensified their desire for self-government.

Toward the close of the nineteenth century the growth of an Indian nationalist sentiment manifested itself in various ways. The event of greatest import for the future was the formation of the Indian National Congress in 1885 under the initiative of educated Hindus and English sympathizers. The objectives of the organization were ambitious if somewhat vague, and embodied the hope that it would "form the germ of a Native Parliament and . . . constitute in a few years an unanswerable reply to the assertion that India is still wholly unfit for any form of representative institutions." The Congress was never exclusively a Hindu body. It attracted a number of Moslems, and during the first thirty years of its existence five Englishmen were elected to its presidency.

Government officials had at first looked upon the Indian National Congress with benevolence, regarding it as a harmless debating society or as a safety valve for upper-class discontent. However, as the Congress—which met every December in a different Indian city—pressed more insistently for reform measures, the official attitude became cool or hostile. The result was that the nationalist movement entered a more radical phase about the turn of the cen-

Factors
accounting for the
growth of Indian
nationalism

[7] H. G. Rawlinson, *India, a Short Cultural History*, p. 409.

tury. A contributing factor to this trend was the shattering of the myth of European invincibility by the Italian defeat in Ethiopia in 1896, by the difficulty which Britain encountered in subduing the small Boer states of South Africa, and by Japan's dramatic victory over the great Russian empire in 1905. Incensed by the dictatorial policy of the Viceroy, Lord Curzon, some Indian patriots began to demand *swaraj* (independence) and also launched a *swadeshi* campaign, which was an attempt to injure Britain economically by boycotting the sale of British goods and reviving native industries. Outbreaks of violence in western Bengal and in the Punjab merely strengthened the determination of the government to stand firm. The vernacular press was muzzled; agitators were arrested and some of them were deported.

The growth of a militant opposition to British rule led to dissension within the Indian National Congress and to a cleavage between the moderates and the extremists. The 1907 meeting of the Indian Congress was disrupted by rioting, but the moderate faction succeeded in retaining control of the organization. The nationalist movement, hampered by disagreement among the Hindu leaders, was also weakened somewhat by the establishment of a Moslem organization which stood in rivalry to the Indian National Congress. The Moslem League, founded in 1905, was inspired partly by the fear of the Moslem minority that they might be subjected to Hindu domination if popular government was established in India—a fear heightened by the truculence and the appeal to religious prejudice which some radical Hindu nationalists had displayed. The League also reflected an attempt to reawaken interest in the whole community of Islam, which seemed to be jeopardized by the decline of the Ottoman Empire. In contrast to the Indian Congress the Moslem League was a communal (sectarian) organization; further, it was founded under conservative rather than liberal auspices.

During World War I only minor disturbances occurred in India. Representatives of all important organizations expressed their sympathy for the British cause and offered assistance. Indian contributions in behalf of Britain and her allies were tremendous. Indian troops fought on the Western front, in East Africa, in the Middle East, and in the Far East; and the country furnished vast supplies of raw materials, foodstuffs, and even manufactures, as cotton, jute and steel production was intensified. The cooperative attitude of the Indian people during the war was induced by the belief that a victory for Britain and her allies would bring benefits to the world's colonial areas. Woodrow Wilson's utterances on war aims and peace objectives aroused enthusiasm in India as elsewhere, and from the beginning of the war British spokesmen had intimated that generous reforms would be forthcoming in recognition of Indian loyalty. In 1917 Edwin Montagu, Secretary of State for India, announced in the

The conflicts between moderates and extremists and the rise of the Moslem League

Indian cooperation during World War I, in hope of reward from a grateful Britain

1101

House of Commons that England's policy toward India was: "the increasing association of Indians in every branch of the administration and the gradual development of self-governing institutions with a view to . . . responsible government as an integral part of the British Empire."

Although the close of the war found India in a state of high expectancy, the prevailing mood quickly changed to disappointment for several reasons. First, the period was one of widespread suffering, caused by inflated prices, a severe famine, and the ravages of disease, including an influenza epidemic which wiped out 13 million people in 1918–1919. Second, the political reforms embodied in the Government of India Act of 1919 fell far short of responsible government. The franchise was still restricted to a tiny minority of property owners numbering about 3 per cent of the population of British India. In addition, the electorate was split up into communal groups, with separate constituencies for Hindus, Moslems, Sikhs, landholders, and other special interests. To Indian nationalists, the constitution of 1919 appeared to be a breach of promise on England's part.

Probably an even greater factor than the Act of 1919 in arousing resentment was the repressive policy which the British Government of India adopted at the close of the war. Punitive measures against rioting led to angry protests and to open violence, climaxed by one of the most shocking affairs in the annals of British rule in India—the Amritsar massacre of 1919. To check a series of outrages in the Punjab, the government had sent troops into the province under the command of Brigadier-General Dyer. At Amritsar on April 13, learning that a large crowd of people was assembling for a public demonstration, General Dyer took a detachment of soldiers to the meeting place and immediately ordered his men to open fire. The crowd, which was listening to speeches and was unarmed, had gathered in an enclosed space, of which Dyer blocked the exit. After ten minutes of steady rifle fire, almost 400 people were killed and more than a thousand wounded. News of this cold-blooded butchery—perpetrated in the name of upholding the "rule of law"—inflamed public indignation throughout India and elsewhere. General Dyer was deprived of his commission but received no other punishment, and English admirers raised a purse in his behalf. The Amritsar massacre, and the indulgent attitude of the government toward those responsible for it, antagonized many Indian leaders who had previously been consistent defenders of Britain. The great poet and educator, Rabindranath Tagore, returned the commission of knighthood with which he had been honored. Another Hindu and friend of Tagore who now became the enemy of British rule and threw himself into the nationalist cause was Mohandas K. Gandhi.

The bitter fruit of disillusionment

British repression; the Amritsar massacre

Leaders of Indian Nationalism— Nehru and Ghandi. Ghandi was assassinated in 1948. Nehru served as Prime Minister of India from 1947 to his death in 1964.

The man who was destined to make the greatest single contribution to the movement for Indian independence gave little evidence in his early life that such would be his role. Gandhi was born in 1869 in a small native state on the western coast of India. He came from a middle-class family which had supplied prime ministers to the prince, and his mother, a pious Hindu, endeavored to instill in him fidelity to the traditions of their caste. His family sent him to England to study law, and after his return home he was offered a position with an Indian firm in South Africa, where he spent some twenty years and had a successful legal practice. His chief interest in South Africa, however, became a deep concern for the unfair treatment to which his countrymen were subjected in that color-conscious region. At the risk of his life and in disregard of insults and humiliation, he campaigned continually against economic and social discrimination, encouraging the timid Indian laborers to organize and calling upon the government to remove flagrant injustices. In this campaign he eventually met with considerable success, but even more important to his later career was his discovery of a technique of mass action that could be effectively employed in defending a moral principle against superior physical force. Gandhi called this technique *satyagraha*, which is loosely translated as "nonviolent resistance" but which means literally "soul force" or "the power of truth." With a keen sensitivity to social injustice, he also became convinced that social and political evils could never be eliminated through violence. He believed these evils should be fought against, but with such weapons as refusal to cooperate with oppressors, no matter what the price; attempting to change the evil-doer by force of example; and, above all, developing in oneself the

The emergence of Gandhi

1103

attitudes and the disciplines which are essential to an improved social order. While arriving at these ideas by the route of religion, Gandhi also applied them to the political sphere.

Returning to India in 1914, Gandhi warmly endorsed the cause of Britain in the war against the Central Powers, even putting aside his pacifist principles to urge people to enlist, so confident was he that the struggle was against autocracy and militarism. But disillusioned by the government's behavior and shocked by the Amritsar massacre, he repudiated the new Indian Constitution of 1919 and persuaded the Indian National Congress to adopt a program of noncooperation with the government. In 1922, he launched his first mass campaign of nonviolent resistance or "civil disobedience," but suspended the movement after a few weeks when he found that it was being used by terrorists to injure life and property. The program of the Indian National Congress and of the associated Gandhian movement already had begun to attract wide support and cut across sectarian lines. The Moslem League supported it for a while, partly because Gandhi had endorsed the so-called Khilafat (Caliphate) movement—a protest of Indian Moslems against the imminent dismemberment of Turkey, which they regarded as a threat to the head of Islam (the Sultan-Caliph). This particular issue was short-lived, but Gandhi was unswerving in his insistence upon Hindu-Moslem cooperation.

During the 1920's, as the nationalist movement acquired momentum, a number of new personalities came to the fore, of whom the

most prominent was Jawaharlal Nehru. The Nehrus were a distinguished Brahman family, wealthy and influential. They had everything to lose, from the purely material standpoint, by casting their lot with a revolutionary movement; but such was the choice they made. Both father and son, and other members of the family, became admirers of Gandhi and joined the National Congress. The father adhered generally to the moderate faction, while his son, who was elected president of the Congress several times, became a leader of the militant and radical wing. The son, Jawaharlal (1889–1964), was educated at the best English schools, taking a B.A. degree at Cambridge University, and became thoroughly Westernized in his tastes and personal interests. Unlike Gandhi, he was by temperament rational and scientific and approached India's problems from a secular standpoint, welcoming industrial development and material progress. While he revered India's cultural heritage, he was emancipated from the dogmas and taboos of traditional Hinduism and—like most of the educated nationalist reformers—opposed the institution of caste. Nehru also became intensely concerned with the need for social reform. He did not embrace Marxism, but he advocated government intervention to alleviate poverty, rehabilitate the peasants, and protect industrial workers. Under Nehru's influence a substantial segment of the National Congress adopted as its two major objectives the winning of complete independence for India and the establishment of a democratic and moderately socialistic regime.

The Indian National Congress at its 1928 session had adopted a resolution demanding that Britain grant Dominion status within one year. At a lively and unusually large conclave of the Congress in December 1929, the dynamic triumvirate of Gandhi and the two Nehrus persuaded members to take the pledge of *Purna Swaraj* ("Complete Independence"). They announced that January 26 would be celebrated as "Independence Day," reinforced by the threat of civil disobedience. Accordingly, Gandhi's second mass campaign of civil disobedience was launched in the spring of 1930. Indians resigned from public office, stopped buying foreign goods, picketed shops and courts, and even refused to pay taxes. The most dramatic event was Gandhi's famous "march to the sea," in which he led a large body of followers on foot through village after village until they reached the coast. There they filled pans with sea water and let it evaporate to make salt, breaking the law by evading the salt tax and defying a government monopoly. In the salt episode as in the boycotting of state liquor shops, Gandhi shrewdly combined a political issue with a moral principle, thus putting his opponents in an embarrassing position. Widespread arrests accompanied the disobedience campaign. Gandhi was imprisoned in May, and the total number of Congress members jailed at this time has been estimated as high as 60,000.

Civil disobedience

Modifying his strategy but not his objectives, Gandhi next attempted to reach an understanding with the British authorities. He had been released from prison early in 1931 and obtained a series of interviews with the Viceroy, Lord Irwin (much to the disgust of Winston Churchill, who was "nauseated" at the thought of "a seditious fakir striding half-naked up the steps of the Viceregal Palace").[8] Gandhi agreed to suspend the civil-disobedience campaign and to participate in the second Round Table Conference in London. At this time Gandhi's chief concern was the problem of the Untouchables (outcastes). In disagreement with the representative of the Untouchables (Dr. Ambedkar), Gandhi firmly opposed the idea of placing them in a special electorate, so convinced was he that these depressed classes should be treated as an integral part of the Hindu community and freed from all discrimination.

Gandhi en route to Meetings with Viceroy Lord Irwin in March 1931. Gandhi had recently been released from prison, where he had been interned after his dramatic "march to the sea" in 1930.

At the close of the civil-disobedience campaign of 1931–1934, Gandhi retired temporarily from politics. He had proved to be the most powerful political figure in the Congress; he was a factor to reckon with at Whitehall and Westminster as well as at Delhi, and he had thousands of followers who would carry out his will almost blindly. Furthermore, he had developed, in the technique of non-

[8] Quoted in T. W. Wallbank, *India in the New Era*, p. 128.

violent resistance, an instrument of mass action of immeasurable potency. In stepping out of the political arena Gandhi was not unaware of the effectiveness of the political weapons he had forged. He recognized, however, the dangers in any form of mass action, and he believed that the Indian people, including himself, needed to perfect their self-control. He said openly that he would prefer for India to remain subject to Britain than for her to attain freedom through a violent revolution. At the opposite pole from Machiavelli, Lenin, and many others, Gandhi denied that the end justifies the means. He believed instead that the means largely determine what the end will be.

The religious
motivation of
Gandhi's
philosophy

Another factor which influenced Gandhi to disassociate himself from the Congress temporarily was that he did not consider himself primarily as a political leader. He disavowed the title of Mahatma ("Great Soul") by which he was known and strenuously discouraged the tendency of ignorant admirers to deify him. Still, he was essentially a religious figure in his personal convictions and in his world view. His beliefs were derived partly from the *Bhagavad-Gita* (which he first read in London in an English translation), partly from the writings of Tolstoi and Ruskin, and partly from the New Testament. He considered himself a Hindu and retained many traditional notions, but he embraced much of the spirit of Christianity, and his real interest lay in the development of religious and ethical values in human society. He had no faith in any political or economic formula and believed that the only real hope for India—or for the world—lay in the cultivation of spiritual resources.

Gandhi's
economic and
social views

Finally, Gandhi wished to devote the remaining years of his life to helping the downtrodden peasants. He established his *ashram* (hermitage) in one of the poorest regions of Central India and attempted to educate the villagers in better methods of cultivation and sanitation and in the use of subsidiary industries, especially home spinning and weaving, to improve their living standards. He gave impetus to a widespread movement to rehabilitate the ancient village economy which had long been in decay. At one time he repudiated the entire Industrial Revolution and even Western science. However, he came to recognize that industrialization was inevitable; and under Nehru's influence he was converted, not to socialism, but to the necessity of government intervention to promote land reform and a more equitable distribution of wealth. He became the particular champion of the Untouchables, declaring that if the stigma of untouchability did not disappear, then Hinduism would have to disappear. He named his weekly newspaper *Harijan,* which was the term he coined for the Untouchables and which means "Children of God."

A new constitution embodied in the Government of India Act of 1935 disappointed Indian nationalists, both radicals and moderates.

It made provincial ministries responsible to elected assemblies which could discuss and act upon any matter not reserved to the central authority. But the provincial governor retained "special responsibilities" and "discretionary powers," which raised doubts as to whether the new system would be much different from the old. The franchise was considerably extended to include about 30 million voters, roughly one-fourth of the adult population of British India, but the device of communal electorates was carried to an excess. Not only religious groups but also special economic classes were given separate representation, and the constitution seemed to be weighted in favor of religious minorities and the propertied interests. The Act also provided for letting the native states enter a federation with the central government under terms which would have given the states (most of which were autocracies) an excessive representation.

The Indian National Congress strongly condemned the new constitution, but decided to run candidates in elections, first with the intention of obstructing the processes of government, and later, as the Congress party gained sweeping victories at the polls, with the idea of forming ministries and enacting legislation. By 1937, the Indian Congress had working majorities in seven of the eleven provinces of British India, and during the next two years these provinces enjoyed a taste of responsible parliamentary government. Most remarkable was the novel sight of English civil servants dutifully executing the policies of Indian ministers.

In spite of the good omen of Anglo-Indian cooperation, there were signs of trouble in the offing. A cleavage was growing between the moderate and radical wings of the National Congress, and even more serious was the increased friction between the Congress and the Moslem League. The Hindu-Moslem tension was caused partly by occasional outbreaks of violence incited by religious fanatics; partly by a fear among Moslems that if India became self-governing they would be at a disadvantage as a minority group; and partly by the fact that the Moslem League had come under the aggressive leadership of Mohammed Ali Jinnah and began to revive as a definite political force.

That M. A. Jinnah (1876–1948) should become the guiding figure of a militant sectarian organization was somewhat ironic. Jinnah, a successful lawyer, had received a Western education and was decidedly secular in temperament. He did not observe the code of pious Moslems, and he had married a Parsee. Jinnah joined the Indian National Congress, in which he took an active part, but he resigned when Gandhi began to come into ascendancy. After withdrawing from political activity for a while, Jinnah undertook to vitalize the Moslem League and succeeded in making it, for the first time, the mouthpiece of the majority of Indian Moslems and a political party which would have to be bargained with in the future. Jinnah insisted that special guaranties were necessary to pro-

INDIA UNDER
COMPANY AND CROWN

Disappointment
with the Government of India Act
of 1935

The ascendancy
of the Congress
party

Mohammed Ali Jinnah, President of the Moslem League.

Indian Railway Workshop Producing Munitions during World War II.

tect the Moslem minority, and finally, by 1940, went so far as to claim that the Indian Moslems were not merely a minority or a religious community but a distinct nation. The claim was dubious. Most Moslems in India were the descendants of natives who had been converted to Islam (Jinnah's family belonged to a group of recent converts) and were as truly Indian as the Hindus. If religious affiliation were to be made the basis of nationhood, then India would have to be split into many fragments and a united state would be impossible. The championing by the Moslem League of the interests of the Islamic community finally culminated in the demand for a separate state—Pakistan—an idea not original with Jinnah but which he at last adopted.

India and World War II

The outbreak of World War II brought matters to a critical juncture in India. The Congress took the blunt position that India would fight only as a free nation and demanded self-government with permission to draw up a new constitution. The Viceroy could only promise that the 1935 Constitution would be reconsidered after the war and that, for the time being, he would welcome greater "consultation" with representative groups. In October 1940, the Congress authorized the Mahatma to inaugurate a nonviolent civil-disobedience campaign, which began at once. It was not a mass movement, though, and took the form of having individuals make speeches against the war. In each instance the authorities were duly notified in advance, the speaker was arrested quietly, and the jails began to swell again. There was no active interference with the civil or military administration. Actually, Indian contributions to the war against the Axis were enormous—far greater than in World War I—because Indian manufactures had now become important. Two million men were recruited for the Indian army and many Indian officers were commissioned.

With the Japanese invasion of Malaya and Burma, the British government determined on a new effort to rally Indian public opinion to its support and sent Sir Stafford Cripps to India in March 1942 to present a proposal. The "Cripps Offer" was in many ways a generous one, promising (after the war) full Dominion status for India under a constitution drafted by Indians, including representatives of the native states. Practically all the articulate Indian groups rejected the proposal for several reasons. First, although Cripps was looked upon as a sincere friend of India, there was hesitancy in accepting at face value an offer from the Churchill government. Churchill had previously declared that the Atlantic Charter did not apply to Britain's colonial areas and he was remembered for strong denunciations of the Congress leaders. Second, the plan gave permission for any province to refuse to join the proposed federation and retain a separate connection with Britain, a provision which the nationalists feared might lead to the "Balkanization" of the Indian subcontinent. Finally, the Indian demand for immediate transfer of responsibility to Indians in the Viceroy's Council was rejected.

The failure of the Cripps Offer of 1942 revealed that Indian nationalist sentiment had reached such a degree of agitation that it could no longer be easily smoothed over. As the war neared its close, it became evident that the British government would renew or even go beyond the Cripps proposal. Events moved

The "Cripps Offer"

Riot in Calcutta, 1946. A dead Hindu surrounded by Moslems armed with lathis. Such scenes were not uncommon on the eve of Indian independence, when extreme tension developed between Hindu and Moslem segments of the population.

rapidly when the Churchill government was replaced by a Labor cabinet under Clement Attlee. In March 1946 Attlee announced that the choice of a new constitution would be India's alone and that, while he hoped the Indian people would remain within the Commonwealth, this must be by their own free will. A Cabinet Mission accordingly was sent to India to work with Indian leaders in arranging the transfer of authority.

The Hindu-Moslem controversy and the decision for partition

Now that the British government was prepared to grant independence, the chief stumbling block was found to lie in the Hindu-Moslem controversy, which had grown to large proportions as a political issue only during the preceding decade. For a while it looked as if the partition of India could be avoided. The Cabinet Mission drafted a scheme for a federal union with safeguards to protect minorities and with provisions for considerable regional autonomy. Both the Congress and the League at first accepted this general plan, but in July 1946 Jinnah, reversing his earlier position, rejected the Mission proposal, demanded a separate Moslem state, and summoned his followers to engage in "direct action." The consequence was bloody communal rioting in which about 12,000 lives were lost. When a Constituent Assembly met in December to draft a constitution, the Moslem League sent no representatives, nor could it be persuaded to do so. Although Jinnah's intransigence was evident, some of the blame must rest with Congress members, who made it clear that they would not be bound by any pledges emanating from the British Cabinet Mission. So much ill will had been aroused on both sides that compromise was very difficult. A few extreme Hindu nationalists viewed the prospect of partition with indifference, rashly assuming that a separate Moslem state would sooner or later have to seek reunion with India on India's terms. The British government's determination to relinquish its responsibilities as quickly as possible—in striking contrast to the cautious and dilatory policy of the preceding 90 years—doubtless also lessened the chances of resolving the deadlock between the Hindu and Moslem communities. Attlee had served notice that England would leave India by June of 1948. Seeing no other alternative, the new Viceroy (Lord Mountbatten) prepared to transfer British authority to two governments instead of one, a delicate and difficult operation. Not only were the Hindu and Moslem provinces separated, but three provinces—Bengal, the Punjab, and Assam—had to be split in order to prevent large Hindu minorities from being assigned to Pakistan. Although Pakistan did not include all the areas demanded by the Moslem League, the division was accepted by both sides in the controversy. Indian independence was formally granted by act of Parliament in July 1947, and in August all authority was surrendered to the two new Dominions.

The end of British Raj

It was a tragic circumstance that the Indian struggle for independence, characterized more by patience than by slaughter, should conclude with the country divided and in an atmosphere of hostility. The partition of India, from the standpoints of geography and economics, was highly artificial. Pakistan included the areas producing jute, cotton, and rice. India, with an insufficient food supply, has the factories needed to process Pakistan's raw materials. Important canals and river systems were bisected by the political boundaries. Nor did partition solve the minority problem. Approximately 15 per cent of Pakistan's inhabitants are non-Moslems, chiefly Hindus. The Republic of India has a Moslem minority of approximately 10 per cent. Even before partition was completed, refugees began to stream across the borders—Hindus and Sikhs fleeing from Moslem domination and Moslems fearing Hindu persecution. More than 10 million people were involved in the mass exodus during the latter part of 1947, and their suffering was indescribable. The governments of India and Pakistan could not prevent the outrages committed by frenzied fanatics on both sides. It was in connection with this religious strife that Gandhi, a frail old man in his late seventies, performed his last service to India. By appealing to the Hindus and by threatening to fast, he stopped riots in Calcutta. Early in 1948 he went to Delhi and began a fast which ended when the key spokesmen for the Congress pledged protection for the lives and property of Moslems. On January 30, on his way to evening prayers, Gandhi was shot to death by a member of a chauvinistic Hindu society. He was mourned all over India and in Pakistan, and the shock of his assassination had at least a temporarily sobering effect upon the public temper.

The tragic division of India; the assassination of Gandhi

A prime source of controversy between India and Pakistan was the disposition of the native states. Since the states were no longer protected by the British Raj, it was assumed that they would voluntarily join either India or Pakistan. Most of them did so, the greater number of course going to India, but in a few instances there was trouble. Hyderabad in the Deccan, the largest state in India, had a Hindu population ruled over by a Moslem prince, the Nizam. The Indian government refused to let the Nizam remain independent, as he apparently planned to do. It dispatched an army into Hyderabad and quickly took over the administration (September 1948). In this instance the Indian government claimed to be acting on behalf of the Nizam's Hindu subjects, but it had already taken a somewhat different position in the Kashmir dispute. In this northern state a Hindu prince ruled over subjects who were predominantly Moslems. In 1947 the New Delhi government announced that Kashmir had acceded to the Indian Union at the re-

The native states; the Kashmir conflict

Republic of India Declared. Prime Minister Jawaharlal Nehru moves resolution for an independent sovereign republic before the constituent assembly in New Delhi in 1950.

quest of the Maharaja, who, it was argued, had the legal right to transfer his sovereignty. The Maharaja, faced with an invasion of Moslem tribesmen, had appealed to India for military support, and the Indian government had insisted upon the accession of Kashmir to India as a prior condition to granting his request. Fighting between Indian and Pakistani troops was halted in 1949 by a cease-fire agreement arranged through a United Nations commission. The cease-fire, however, proved to be only a truce and left Kashmir divided into two parts, occupied respectively by Pakistan and India, with the larger portion under Indian control.

India retained the status of a Dominion only until 1950, when a new constitution made it an independent republic, replacing the Governor-General by an elected President and severing all ties with the British crown. Nevertheless, India voluntarily remained within the Commonwealth of Nations (with the term "British" deleted) and thus became the first completely independent republic to hold membership in the association. India has an independent judiciary and a President chosen by an electoral college, but follows the English system of parliamentary government, with the chief power vested in a Prime Minister responsible to the lower house of the central legislature. The subordinate states, with unicameral legislatures, have the same type of ministerial government. Both the state and national legislative bodies are elected by universal adult suffrage for five-year terms. The Constitution includes a comprehensive Bill of Rights, outlawing untouchability and discrimination based on caste, and providing for legal equality of the sexes. Although federal in structure, the government has been handicapped by a distribution of power between the center and the states which is both rigid and ambiguous. The Constitution gives the

President power to suspend a state government in an emergency, but some very critical areas of jurisdiction are reposed in the states, including education, agriculture, and taxes on land.

Many difficulties confronted the Republic of India from the very beginning. The absorption of more than 500 princely states into the new political structure, a formidable task in itself, was handled with relative dispatch. Some of the dethroned rajas were retained as governors for a time, but by 1957 all of them were removed from office. They were compensated for their loss of power by the award of generous pensions which continued until 1971, when a constitutional amendment reduced the maharajas to the rank of commoners. Other problems proved more obstinate, revealing dangerous sectional and social cleavages. One of them had to do with linguistic rivalries. In the interest of promoting national unity, the government announced that Hindi, the principal tongue of northern India but spoken by only about one-third of the total population, was to become the official language of the country by 1965. Resistance on the part of other regional linguistic groups proved so strong, however, that on the date when the change was to go into effect, in January 1965, bloody riots broke out in the south, two cabinet ministers resigned, and the government felt constrained to announce that English would remain an "associate official language" as long as non-Hindi-speaking Indians desired.

Within the framework of democratic institutions India, during her first quarter century of independence, operated under what was in effect a one-party system. The Congress party, instead of dissolving as Gandhi had recommended, dominated all branches of the government, and Jawaharlal Nehru served continuously as Prime Minister until his death in May 1964. This long tenure of power was not an unmixed blessing either for the party or for the country. Once the focal point of an indomitable struggle for freedom, the Congress developed into an Establishment, entrenched behind its monopoly of patronage and the Administrative Services (vastly larger than the old British Indian Civil Service), and its vigor and integrity became corroded. Even the luster of Nehru—generally revered as a revolutionary hero and Gandhi's heir—dimmed in later years. Endowed with qualities of mind and heart that entitle him to high rank among popular leaders of this century, Nehru was not entirely successful as a statesman. His own idealism was unquestionable but fuzzy in application, his policies vacillating and impulsive. As an avowed enemy of colonialism, in 1961 he authorized the forcible occupation of Goa, Diu, and Damão, the last remnants of Portugal's empire on the subcontinent; but the next year he blundered into a border clash with Communist China with humiliating results. In the long controversy with Pakistan over Kashmir he was both unyielding and inconsistent. Although publicly admitting the right of the Kashmiris to determine their own destiny, he deposed and imprisoned without trial Sheik Abdullah, the Premier of Kashmir,

Obstacles to Indian unity: linguistic differences

Preponderance of the Congress party under Nehru

when Abdullah advocated independence for the country. In 1957 he announced the formal annexation of Kashmir to India and subsequently took the position that Kashmir was a domestic issue not subject to mediation by any outside agency. Nehru appeared blind to the corruption and incompetence of his trusted associates, and he neglected to press for the reform program that he himself recognized as essential to India's welfare. His chief asset as a leader was his personality, which combined intellectual faculties of a high order with a charisma that won and held the allegiance even of the unlettered masses.

Nehru's death left the party with no leader of sufficient stature to hold its dissident factions together; rivalries broke out into the open, while India's internal condition deteriorated. In 1966 the party chiefs picked as Prime Minister Nehru's daughter, Mrs. Indira Gandhi, hoping that the prestige of the family name would restore public confidence. Disenchantment with the administration was amply demonstrated in India's fourth general election (February 1967), the first one to be marred by tumult and violence. Although the Congress party retained a slim majority in the central parliament, it lost control in half of the state governments. Threatened by opposition from elements of both the extreme Right and the extreme Left, the Congress party in 1969 split into two factions, and a struggle for power ensued between established leaders of the "old Congress" and Mrs. Gandhi's "new Congress party." Squarely accepting the challenge, Nehru's daughter exhibited a tenacity equal to her father's and a superior talent for practical policies. Defining the issue as an ideological conflict "between those who are for Socialism, for change and for the fullest internal democracy and those who are for the status quo," she battled openly against recalcitrant party members and against "powerful economic interests." She took the daring step of calling for general elections in March 1971—a year ahead of schedule—and she campaigned throughout the country, traveling by car, helicopter, and jet plane, and sometimes making fourteen speeches in a single day. The result of the fifth general election was a personal triumph for Indira Gandhi and a landslide victory for her party, which won a two-thirds majority in the national legislature (Lok Sabha). Not only the old Congress faction but also extreme Rightist parties—notably the militant Hindu Jan Sangh—lost ground, while the Communists gained only a few seats. The two Indian Communist parties—CPI "Marxist" (pro-Peking) and CPI "Marxist-Leninist" (pro-Moscow) —have never attained national influence, although they have shown significant strength in a few of the states. The general election of 1971 undoubtedly represented a popular mandate for social and economic reform and also confidence in the ability of a democratically elected government to achieve it, in spite of its mediocre performance heretofore.

Difficulties following Nehru's death; Indira Gandhi's new Congress party

Prime Minister Nehru with His Daughter, Mrs. Indira Gandhi, in 1956.

INDIA TODAY

The independent states of India and Pakistan were bequeathed many things of value by the British: the rudiments of parliamentary government, trained civil servants, an excellent network of railroads, the nuclei of effective military forces, and an educated elite versed in Western institutions and practices. The new states also inherited the unsolved problems of the era of colonial rule, chief of which is the backwardness and crushing poverty of most of the population. Steady and substantial economic progress is necessary if India and Pakistan are to make their way as successful modern states—or even to survive as political entities. The Indian government, committed to material progress, created a Planning

Economic problems; the Five-Year Plans

1115

Commission and launched a series of Five-Year Plans, beginning in 1951. In many fields impressive results were achieved. Food production has grown by almost 90 per cent; power generation increased sevenfold in less than a decade, while irrigation facilities doubled. By 1970 India was exporting heavy machinery and manufacturing 85,000 motor vehicles a year. Two nuclear power plants were in operation by August 1972. But even in the vital area of agriculture, improvements did not suffice to offset an inexorable growth in the numbers of people. Widely publicized campaigns in support of birth control have failed to check the rate of increase, which has actually doubled since independence. By 1970 India's population of about 550 million was receiving an increment of 13 million each year and was expected to approach 695 million within the next decade. Consequently, per capita annual income has remained below a level of $100, and the majority face a life of desperate poverty. India is not yet able to feed her own people. Even in good years large quantities of food grains must be imported, and occasional droughts bring severe crises. Social services, even necessities are lacking for the bulk of the population, 75 per cent of whom are still illiterate.

Deficiencies
in the Plans

The Five-Year Plans fell short of their objectives for a variety of reasons. An overgrown and inept bureaucracy mangled well-intentioned projects, but considerable blame must be placed on the Congress party and its leader Nehru for failure to press vigorously for necessary changes. Long on rhetoric but short on performance, they continually postponed action or compromised with vested interests. Under a government that adheres to the formulas of democracy and offers the remarkable spectacle of the world's largest free electorate—with no restrictions based on property, sex, or literacy—India's society remains undemocratic. Caste is still a potent factor, intensifying linguistic jealousies, class conflicts, and political divisions. The Constitutional provision outlawing untouchability has not improved the lot of or removed the stigma from the Harijans, who suffer from discrimination and segregation. Even in the cities their acceptance has amounted to little more than tokenism.

The need for
basic reforms

While India is predominantly a country of landowners and cultivators, the poor peasants at the bottom have not shared in agricultural progress as have the upper strata of large landowners who control the farm cooperatives and wield a disproportionate influence over the state and national legislatures. This fortunate minority, possessing considerable capital, has almost entirely escaped taxation. Consequently the government has lacked funds to implement its ambitious development and welfare programs. Even scientifically designed projects for the modernization of agriculture through mechanization, intensive fertilization, and diversified cropping have thus far proved disappointing. The widely acclaimed "green revolution," launched in the late 1960's with the help of international experts, brought a spectacular increase in the per-acre yield of grains,

Coke Ovens at the Tata Iron and Steel Company, Jamshedpur, Behar. Tata is the largest steel producer in India. India has the world's largest iron ore reserves.

particularly wheat. But the benefits accrued to relatively prosperous landowners, rather than to small farmers, tenants, and laborers unable to afford the new techniques. With 5 per cent of rural householders possessing 35 per cent of the cultivable land and about half of all agricultural families owning no land at all, the basic need is for a thorough reorganization of land ownership, something the government has never undertaken in spite of its promises. Oddly, in the one state where significant land reforms have been accomplished (Uttar Pradesh), they were begun under British rule.

Nature has not condemned India to be a land of poverty forever. The country holds extensive resources—the world's largest iron ore reserves, estimated at nearly 22 billion tons, manganese and other valuable minerals, substantial deposits of coal and probably of oil, and great potential for hydroelectric development. Under effective leadership India could probably support a prosperous, industrialized, and educated society. Her Fourth Five-Year Plan, begun in 1969, calls for an expenditure of funds six times as large as the First Plan and stresses the vital goals of population control, reduction of unemployment, and attainment of self-sufficiency in foodstuffs. A gigantic twenty-five-year project for an irrigation and canal network reaching from the Ganges valley to the Deccan has been announced. Prime Minister Indira Gandhi, pledged to extensive reform, received an overwhelming mandate from the people in the election of 1971, partly because the peasantry in greater numbers than ever before defied the dictates of local landowners, to whom they have traditionally been subservient, and voted for her party.

India's great potential

Under Nehru's guidance India's foreign policy initially was one of neutralism or nonalignment, stemming from a distaste for military alliances and from a desire to cultivate a spirit of friendship with other Asian countries, including the Communist. Sino-Indian relations, which had been marked by expressions of cordiality on both sides, suffered a rude shock following China's provocative action in Tibet. The New Delhi government gave asylum to the Dalai Lama, who escaped from his country while Chinese troops were suppressing a Tibetan rebellion in 1959. A brief border war between India and China in 1962, although accompanied by acrimonious debate, apparently stemmed more from the absence of clearly defined geographical boundaries in the snowcapped Himalayas than from planned aggression by either party. The abrupt rout of ill-equipped Indian troops induced the government to upgrade and expand its military forces, which proved more effective in a three weeks' war against Pakistan in 1965. These summer hostilities, provoked by friction over Kashmir, accomplished nothing except to aggravate bad feelings between the two nations and to draw India away from the United States—whose arms the Pakistanis were using against her—and into the orbit of the Soviet Union, with whom she signed a twenty-year treaty of friendship and cooperation in August 1971. India relied on Moscow's backing during her two weeks' war with Pakistan the following December, when both China and the United States supported Pakistan and refused to denounce the brutalities committed by Pakistani troops in East Bengal. It should not be concluded that India has abandoned her attempt to maintain an independent international posture. If the conflict over Bangladesh was something less than the "holy war for democracy and human rights" acclaimed by a Calcutta journalist, India's smashing victory at least heightened her national self-confidence. India had attained an identity—not as the exemplar of nonviolence that Gandhi envisioned—but as a military power.

The problems confronting Pakistan have been similar to India's and even more acute. Pakistan began not as a nation but as a collection of heterogeneous racial and linguistic communities dominated by the Urdu-speaking Punjabis. The country's West and East wings —separated geographically by 1000 miles—were equally far apart in terms of economics, language, and cultural traditions, with religion serving as the only common bond. Separatist movements within a state which was itself the fruit of separatism threatened to disrupt it and finally succeeded, with the secession of East Pakistan in 1971.

Political democracy has been almost nonexistent in Pakistan, where the creation of any kind of viable government proved an arduous task. Against a background of dissension and without effective leadership (M. A. Jinnah died in 1948 and the Moslem League gradually disintegrated) two successive constituent assemblies struggled with the drafting of a constitution, which was declared in effect in March 1956. Pakistan, while remaining a member of the Commonwealth, was defined as an "Islamic Republic" under a President who was required to be a Moslem. Elections were never held under this constitution. The ensuing period was one of unbridled political bickering, racketeering, and corruption, terminated only when General (later Field Marshal) M. Ayub Khan in October 1958 seized control of the government and imposed martial law. Although Ayub had acted at the instigation of the President, he soon removed him from office along with other prominent party officials, offering them a choice between jail sentences or retirement from politics (most of them chose the latter). Ayub's avowed purpose was to "clean up the mess," and in this he temporarily succeeded, by direct and peremptory measures.

Not a stereotype of the military dictator but a "strong man" reminiscent in some ways of Turkey's Kemal Ataturk, Ayub Khan won considerable respect among his own countrymen and among foreign observers. His regime brought some improvement over the conditions prevalent during the politicians' paradise of the preceding decade. Inflation was halted, a few modest reforms were enacted, and a new capital was built at Rawalpindi near the Northwest Frontier. Most impressive was the economic development of West Pakistan, whose economy during the 1960's seemed to be booming. Agricultural expansion exceeded the rise in population, and manufactures showed one of the highest growth rates in the world. But rapid industrialization, producing a prosperity more apparent than real, was accompanied by questionable and potentially damaging policies. It depended on heavy doses of foreign aid, both economic and military, from the United States. To a large extent it was accomplished at the expense of the peasants. Wages and food prices were kept low while the profits from manufacture soared, creating capital to provide a high rate of reinvestment for further growth but widening the gap between the upper and lower segments of society. Most of the wealth remained concentrated in a plutocracy of "twenty-two families," which controlled 65 per cent of Pakistan's industry and 80 per cent of her banking assets, as well as the best farmland. Finally, the progress of West Pakistan rested on the exploitation of the eastern wing, which the Rawalpindi government treated like a colony. East Pakistan (formerly East Bengal and now Bangladesh) with only one-sixth of the nation's area contained more than half of the population. Its jute industry earned most of Pakistan's foreign exchange, but the larger share of this was diverted to development in the West. While contributing substantially to the nation's expanding economy, East Pakistan was denied its fair share of the benefits, and the disparity in per capita income between the two sections increased steadily. Economic oppression—coupled with political discrimination, social neglect, and undisguised contempt for Bengalis—prepared the ground for revolt in East Pakistan.

Although President Ayub gave the country the appearance of stability, public confidence in his rule deteriorated, especially after his futile war with India in 1965. Widespread poverty and the

General Ayub Khan's regime: basic defects

General Mohammed Ayub Khan, Pakistan's Head of State, 1958–1969.

1119

General Yahya
Khan: disaffection
and revolt in
East Pakistan

*Sheik Mujibur Rahman, Prime
Minister of Bangladesh.*

The India-Pakistan
war of 1971

government's suppression of civil rights fostered opposition. Ayub had introduced a new constitution in 1962 incorporating what he called "Basic Democracy," but its operation was strictly authoritarian. The regime that had justified its seizure of power in 1958 as an attack on corruption became itself riddled with corruption from top to bottom. Demonstrations by workers and students erupted into bloody riots, and when the army refused any longer to support him, Ayub resigned in March 1969. His successor was another general, Yahya Khan, who proclaimed martial law, rooted out corruption, and restored order, filling much the same role as had his ousted predecessor a decade earlier. But he was no more able than Ayub to resolve the country's troubles, which centered more and more insistently in the rebellious mood of the East Pakistanis. Seemingly inclined to a policy of reconciliation, President Yahya Khan agreed to hold general elections for a national assembly to draft a new constitution as a step toward parliamentary government resting on universal suffrage. The elections, held in December 1970, brought a resounding victory in East Pakistan to Sheik Mujibur Rahman and his Awami League, a party demanding regional autonomy. Even with no support in the West, Mujibur had won the largest representation in the national assembly and was acknowledged by President Yahya as "the next prime minister of Pakistan." But the hard liner Z. Ali Bhutto, whose Pakistan People's Party had gained a majority of West Pakistan's seats, obstructed attempts to work out a settlement. President Yahya postponed the opening of the assembly; yet he agreed to negotiate with Sheik Mujibur and, accompanied by Bhutto, went to Dacca in March 1971. Apparently the talks served to screen more drastic action. Yahya's troops, with reinforcements secretly flown in, suddenly struck in Bengal, and Mujibur was imprisoned.

The murderous events in East Bengal from March to December 1971, resulting in a full-scale war between India and Pakistan, were among the most horrible in a century of unprecedented horrors. Atrocities may have been initiated by the Bengalis, and were perpetrated by them on the Bihari minority after the war had ended; but the most revolting excesses were committed by government troops. West Pakistani soldiers, who began their attack by shooting helpless university students, raped some 200,000 women and slaughtered whole communities of civilians. Their program of genocide was apparently aimed at exterminating every potential leader among the population they despised as rebels and racial inferiors. The government of India admitted 10 million refugees into West Bengal, assisted East Pakistani guerrillas, and early in December entered the war as an active belligerent. The brief combat, conducted on western and eastern fronts, demonstrated India's decisive military superiority over her rival, whose forces surrendered on December 16.

Bangladesh ("Bengal Nation") was born from the ashes of victory as an independent state, but whether its 74 million people could survive as a political entity—or survive at all—was a difficult question to determine. With a population density of 1200 per square mile, it is a land of poverty, and one frequently subject to disastrous storms and floods. To the normal level of misery was now added the problems of repairing the ravages of war, finding food and shelter for returning refugees, disarming guerrilla bands that still roamed the countryside, and creating a government out of chaos. Sheik Mujibur Rahman, given a hero's welcome when he entered Dacca in January 1972 after nine months in West Pakistani jails, plunged into the task. He set up a provisional government with himself as Prime Minister and vowed that Bangladesh would be "a secular, democratic socialist state." Desperately in need of foreign aid, he found Russia most responsive.

Pakistan, reduced in territory and resources, was left with 60 million people, mostly illiterate and increasing their numbers at the alarming rate of 3 per cent a year. Humiliated by defeat, the mood of the nation was resentment against the leaders responsible for a policy of disaster. Yahya Khan resigned the presidency in December 1971, and for the first time in thirteen years Pakistan had a civilian head of state when Z. Ali Bhutto took the oath as President and immediately assumed most of the other important Cabinet posts as well. A graduate of the University of California and of Oxford, Bhutto was both a capable and a colorful figure, but he had been belligerently nationalistic, anti-India, and anti-Bangladesh—seemingly an unlikely choice for binding up the nation's wounds. He soberly announced, however, "We are going to have to build a new

Victims of the Indian-Pakistani War of 1971. Left: Refugees from East Bengal seeking sanctuary in India. Right: Prime Minister Indira Gandhi of India visiting a refugee camp in West Bengal, offering reassurance to homeless East Bengalis.

world, a new country again." Gradually relations with India returned to normal. Bhutto and Mrs. Gandhi signed a peace agreement in July 1972 and began a mutual withdrawal of their armed forces. By the year's end prospects appeared brighter than ever before for a permanent settlement of the Kashmir territorial dispute. On the domestic front Bhutto ended martial law, introduced an interim constitution with popular elections, and drafted plans for a permanent constitution. His Pakistan People's Party is committed to a socialistic reform program, including land reform, which may be difficult to accomplish.

Pakistan's international position has been materially affected by her disillusioning experience with alliances. While India was pursuing the path of neutralism, Pakistan became a member both of SEATO and of CENTO, thus identifying herself with the Western power bloc. Under a military aid pact of 1954, the United States agreed to provide supersonic aircraft and other modern weapons, and in turn received permission to use Pakistan territory for strategic intelligence activities. This military partnership intensified India's mistrust and hostility but did nothing to mitigate Pakistan's disastrous defeat in the Bangladesh war. In 1972 President Bhutto announced his country's withdrawal from the Commonwealth of Nations and also from SEATO. In seeking closer associations Pakistan may turn to such neighbors as Iran and Turkey and especially Afghanistan, which has always been friendly and has a long record of strict neutrality in world politics. Afghanistan's iron ore could be profitably exchanged for Pakistan's coal, and Pakistan could offer rail and port facilities for Afghan exports.

Changes in Pakistan's foreign policy

SELECTED READINGS—THE BRITISH COMMONWEALTH

· *Items so designated are available in paperbound editions.*

Belshaw, Horace, *New Zealand*, United Nations Series, Berkeley, 1947.

Brady, Alexander, *Democracy in the Dominions*, Toronto, 1958.

Cameron, Roderick, *Australia: History and Horizons*, New York, 1971.

Creighton, Donald G., *Dominion of the North, A History of Canada*, Boston, 1944.

Dawson, R. M., *The Government of Canada*, Toronto, 1963.

Fitzpatrick, Brian, *The Australian People, 1788–1945*, Melbourne, 1946. An analytical and revealing account.

Grattan, C. H., *Australia*, Berkeley, 1947.

Lipson, Leslie, *The Politics of Equality; New Zealand's Adventures in Democracy*, Chicago, 1948.

MacInnes, Colin, *Australia and New Zealand*, New York, 1966.

McInnis, E. W., *Canada; a Political and Social History*, New York, 1959.

Shaw, A. G. L., *Convicts and the Colonies*, New York, 1966.

· Siegfried, André, *The Race Question in Canada*, New York, 1907 (McClelland & Stuart). A perceptive study.

Wade, Mason, *The French Canadians*, New York, 1955.

Anstey, Vera, *The Economic Development of India*, rev. ed., London, 1952.

Bhatia, Krishan, *The Ordeal of Nationhood: A Social Study of India since Independence, 1947–1970*, New York, 1971. Informed and objective account of India's problems.

Bonarjee, N. B., *Under Two Masters*, New York, 1970. By a former civil servant; highly critical.

• Bondurant, Joan, *Conquest of Violence: The Gandhian Philosophy of Conflict*, rev. ed., Berkeley, 1965 (California).

Brecher, Michael, *Nehru: A Political Biography*, New York, 1959.

• Brown, D. M., *The Nationalist Movement: Indian Political Thought from Ranade to Bhave*, Berkeley, 1961 (California).

Dean, Vera M., *New Patterns of Democracy in India*, 2nd ed., Cambridge, Mass., 1969.

Edwardes, Michael, *Nehru: A Political Biography*, New York, 1972.

Embree, A. T., *India's Search for National Identity*, New York, 1972. An analysis of Indian nationalism to 1947.

• Erikson, E. H., *Gandhi's Truth: On the Origins of Militant Nonviolence*, New York, 1969 (Norton).

• Fischer, Louis, *The Life of Mahatma Gandhi*, New York, 1950 (Collier). An admirable biography.

Frankel, Francine, *India's Green Revolution: Economic Gains and Political Costs*, Princeton, 1971. A significant and challenging study.

Griffiths, Percival, *Modern India*, 4th ed., London, 1965.

Hardgrave, R. L., Jr., *India: Government and Politics in a Developing Nation*, New York, 1970. Well balanced and clear.

Harrison, S. S., *India: The Most Dangerous Decades*, Princeton, 1960. A vigorous study of the disruptive elements in Indian society and politics.

Heimsath, C. H., *Indian Nationalism and Hindu Social Reform*, Princeton, 1964.

Hodson, H. V., *The Great Divide: India-Britain-Pakistan*, New York, 1971. An examination of events leading to Partition.

Ikram, S., and Spear, P., eds., *The Cultural Heritage of Pakistan*, London, 1956.

Kochanek, S. A., *The Congress Party of India: The Dynamics of a One-Party Democracy*, Princeton, 1968.

Kothari, Rajni, *Politics in India*, Boston, 1970. Throws light on relationship between caste and politics.

Malik, Hafeez, *Moslem Nationalism in India and Pakistan*, Washington, 1963.

• Maxwell, Neville, *India's China War*, Garden City, N. Y., 1972 (Anchor). Scathingly critical of India's role in the 1962 clash.

Menon, V. P., *The Transfer of Power in India*, Princeton, 1957.

Metcalf, T. R., *The Aftermath of Revolt: India, 1857–1870*, Princeton, 1964.

• Morris-Jones, W. H., *The Government and Politics of India*, London, 1964 (Anchor).

• Nehru, Jawaharlal, *The Discovery of India*, New York, 1946 (Anchor).

• Palmer, N. D., *The Indian Political System*, Boston, 1961 (Houghton Mifflin).

Roberts, P. E., *History of British India under the Company and the Crown*, 3rd ed., New York, 1952. An excellent political text.

Sayeed, K. B., *Pakistan: The Formative Phase, 1857–1948*, 2nd ed., New York, 1968.

• Sen Gupta, Bhabani, *Communism in Indian Politics*, New York, 1972 (Columbia).

Siddiqui, Kalim, *Conflict, Crisis, and War in Pakistan*, New York, 1972. An indictment of Pakistan's civilian and military elites.

1123

READINGS
· Spear, Percival, *India, Pakistan, and the West*, 4th ed., New York, 1967 (Oxford).
· Srinivas, M. N., *Social Change in Modern India*, Berkeley, 1966 (California).
· Tinker, Hugh, *India and Pakistan: A Political Analysis*, New York, 1962 (Praeger). By a former member of the Indian Civil Service.
  von Vorys, Karl, *Political Development in Pakistan*, Princeton, 1965. Pessimistic.
· Wallbank, T. W., *India in the New Era*, Chicago, 1951 (Mentor).
  Weekes, R. V., *Pakistan: Birth and Growth of a Muslim Nation*, Princeton, 1964.
· Woodruff, Philip, *The Men Who Ruled India*, 2 vols., New York, 1954 (Schocken).
  Ziring, Lawrence, *The Ayub Khan Era: Politics in Pakistan 1958–1969*, Syracuse, N. Y., 1971. Generally favorable to Ayub.

SOURCE MATERIALS

Birla, G. D., *In the Shadow of the Mahatma: A Personal Memoir*. Selections from Gandhi's correspondence, interviews and conversations.
Chakravarty, A., ed., *A Tagore Reader*.
· Gandhi, M. K., *The Story of My Experiments with Truth* (Beacon). Autobiography.
· Jack, H. A., ed., *The Gandhi Reader: A Source Book of His Life and Writings* (Evergreen).
McLane, J. R., ed., *The Political Awakening in India*.
· Nehru, Jawaharlal, *Toward Freedom* (Beacon). Autobiography.
———, *Independence and After* (Speeches, 1946–1949).
———, *Jawaharlal Nehru's Speeches, 1949–1953*.
Philips, C. H., *The Evolution of India and Pakistan, 1858 to 1947: Select Documents*.
Russell, W. H., *My India Mutiny Diary*. Contemporary account by the London *Times* correspondent.
Tagore, Rabindranath, *My Reminiscences*.

CHAPTER 37

The Middle East and Africa
(1800-1973)

Civilization is based more on the village and on God's earth than
on the town, however attractive certain features of our town life
may be. It is in the quiet nooks and corners of the village that the
language, the poetry and literature of a country are enriched. The
stability of the country does not depend so much on the towns as
on the rural population. The more numerous and the more settled
the latter, the wider and more solid is the basis of the state. . . .
—Chaim Weizmann, *Trial and Error*

1. THE MIDDLE EAST

Few areas of the earth have witnessed more turbulence and rapidity of change than have the countries of the Middle East in recent times. The pattern of their history has been much the same.
Before World War I most of them stagnated and slumbered under
the rule of the Ottoman Turks. With the breakup of the Ottoman
Empire they saw visions of independence and a chance to throw
off all traces of foreign domination. Nationalist movements sprang
up to prod governments into vigorous action. In many instances
they gained control of governments, often in defiance of the religious authorities. They proceeded then with attempts to launch
programs of modernization, for building highways, railroads, and
schools, subsidizing industries, and sponsoring scientific agriculture
and land reform. The problems they encountered, however, in the
form of ignorance, corruption, vested interests, and foreign meddling were often too great to be overcome. To this day illiteracy,
disease, and high death rates persist in many parts of the Middle
East, and poverty is all but universal.

A survey of the Middle East may properly begin with Turkey,
since it ranks first in population and since nearly the whole region
at one time was subject to Turkish rule. We have already seen that
the dismemberment of the Turkish Empire began as early as 1829
when the Sultan's government was forced to acknowledge the in-

*The pattern of
Middle Eastern
history*

1125

dependence of Greece. Thenceforth one after another of the European provinces broke away. By 1914 Turkey in Europe had been reduced to nothing but Istanbul (Constantinople) and a corner of eastern Thrace. But Turkey in Asia still included a vast area from the western border of Persia to the Mediterranean Sea. At the end of World War I, the Turkish government, which had fought on the losing side, accepted a treaty depriving the Empire of virtually everything except Istanbul and the northern and central portions of Asia Minor. But before this treaty could be put into effect a group of nationalists, under the leadership of Mustafa Kemal, reconquered much of the lost territory. In 1922 they marched on Istanbul, deposed the Sultan, and in 1923 proclaimed Turkey a republic. The Allies, in the meantime, consented to the making of a new treaty at Lausanne, Switzerland, which permitted the Turks to retain practically all the lands they had reconquered. The new state included Anatolia, Armenia, and eastern Thrace, but none of the outlying territories of Mesopotamia, Arabia, Palestine, or Syria.

For two decades the history of the Turkish republic was almost synonymous with the personal history of Mustafa Kemal. It was his imagination and determination that made the country over from a corrupt and somnolent Oriental despotism into a modern, progressive state with most of the forms if not the substance of democratic government. He began by abolishing the Caliphate and secularizing the state. Under the Sultan religion and the state were intertwined. The Sultan himself was the Caliph, or "Successor of the Prophet," and therefore the spiritual ruler of all Moslems. The law was religious law, and the only officially recognized schools were those attached to the mosques. Kemal's decree abolishing the Caliphate declared that the antiquated religious courts and codes must be replaced by "modern scientific civil codes," and that the schools of the mosques must give way to government schools, which all children between the ages of six and sixteen would be required to attend. But before much progress could be made in educational reform, it was necessary to take one further step, and that was to adopt a new system of writing. The Turkish language was still written in Arabic script, which Kemal regarded as an impossible medium for the expression of Western ideas. In 1928 he had a commission prepare an alphabet using the Roman letters, and this was done so successfully that modern Turkish spelling is consistently phonetic. When he had taught himself the new alphabet, Kemal proceeded to teach others, traveling throughout the country with his blackboard, lecturing audiences on how the characters should be formed. Soon he issued a decree forbidding the holding of public office by anyone who was not adept in the new writing.

The achievements of Kemal also included a social and economic revolution. He issued decrees abolishing the fez, discouraging polygamy, and encouraging women to appear unveiled and both sexes to wear Western clothes. He established schools for girls and made women eligible for business careers and for the professions. In 1929 he gave women the suffrage in local elections and five years later in national elections. Equally significant were his economic reforms. He endowed agricultural colleges, established model farms, and founded banks to lend money to farmers. He freed the peasant from the tithe and set up agencies to distribute seed and farm machinery to almost anyone who could offer a guaranty to use them effectively. Although he undoubtedly had the power to do so, he refrained from instituting measures of forced collectivization such as those of the Russians. He chose rather to adhere to the tradition of Mohammed in encouraging small holdings, in helping the farmer to buy his land, and in teaching him to work it profitably. At the same time he recognized the importance of promoting industrialization. Agriculture alone could not provide the people with a high standard of living or enable the country to make the best use of all its resources. He therefore built thousands of miles of railways and established state monopolies for the manufacture of tobacco, matches, munitions, salt, alcohol, and sugar. Despite the fact that Turkey has abundant resources of coal, iron, copper, and petroleum, and is the world's largest producer of chrome, three-fourths of its nearly 40 million inhabitants still derive their living from agriculture.

Mustafa Kemal (later called Kemal Atatürk) ruled over Turkey from 1922 until his death in 1938. Whether he was simply another twentieth-century dictator, somewhat more benevolent than his compeers, is a question for debate. Legally, his position was that of an elective President, chosen by the Assembly for a four-year term and indefinitely re-eligible. But he himself was president of the Assembly, and, except for a brief period in 1930, he permitted no opposition party to exist. On the other hand, he always described his regime as temporary and transitional. After ten years he still maintained that the people were not yet ready for self-government. He must continue to rule for another decade or so until the citizens grew in wisdom and a sense of responsibility and liberated themselves from the habits and prejudices of the past. To his credit it can be said that he did not involve his country in war and that he never sought the extermination of racial minorities. Although he suppressed a revolt of the Kurds in 1930 with merciless severity, executing twenty-nine of the leaders, he never maintained a Gestapo or Cheka or any similar agency of irresponsible tyranny.

Mustafa Kemal Atatürk.

Under Kemal Ataturk's successors, Ismet Inonu and Celal Bayar, Turkey took steps toward supplanting her benevolent dictatorship with a democratic republic. But after World War II, severe economic difficulties, resulting mainly from extravagant spending and inflation, led the government of Premier Adnan Menderes to impose restrictions. Freedom of the press was abolished, and members of

Parliament opposing the government were arrested. Successive student demonstrations against these repressive measures triggered a revolt in 1960 by army officers, who seized control and, under Lieutenant-General Cemal Gürsel, established a provisional government. Nearly 600 members of the previous regime were tried on charges of corruption and subversion of the Constitution. Of those convicted by the court, three were executed, including the deposed prime minister Adnan Menderes. In 1961 a new constitution was adopted proclaiming the Second Turkish Republic. It provided for a President elected by a Grand National Assembly (parliament) for a seven-year term and ineligible for re-election, and for a Prime Minister designated by the President on the basis of party representation in the parliament. It included also guaranties of civil liberties, clauses for the protection of workers' rights, and safeguards against abuse of executive power. When elections were held in October 1961, no party gained a majority. A coalition government was formed with the seventy-seven-year-old Ismet Inönü as Prime Minister. Faced with vexing difficulties and lacking adequate support in the National Assembly, he resigned in 1965.

During the 1960's Turkey made considerable economic progress, accompanied by political instability and ominous social unrest. Although inflation continued at a galloping rate, industry expanded steadily and a third Five-Year Plan for economic development was scheduled to begin in 1973. By 1971 Turkish oil production had grown sufficiently to meet domestic needs. A huge dam constructed on the Euphrates River promised electric power to transform the primitive rural area of eastern Anatolia. But while foundations were being laid for a modern industrialized society, both the economy and democratic institutions were threatened by bitter factional strife; and in dealing with disorders the government moved in an authoritarian direction. Strikes, riots, and outbreaks of violence among university students led in 1971 to the imposition of martial law, wholesale arrests, and the suspension of prominent newspapers. The Republican People's party, custodian of Atatürk's reforms but now split into two factions, seemed powerless to halt reactionary elements that Atatürk had stifled. The Turkish army, which by tradition was nonpolitical but had intervened on the liberal side in the 1960 revolution, by the early 1970's was backing ultraconservatives, and in the guise of a "government of national union" imposed a quasi-dictatorship. In a wave of repression the Turkish Labor party was outlawed and its head—a woman graduate of the University of Michigan—arrested. Also arrested was the famous Turkish novelist Yaşar Kemal, who had translated a book on Marxism and was charged with spreading "Communist propaganda."

Second in population among nations of the Middle East is the Arab Republic of Egypt. Although technically a part of the Ottoman Empire until 1914, Egypt was for all practical purposes a dependency of Great Britain after 1882. The British kept up the

Suez Canal at the Onset of World War I. Britain's concern for the Suez Canal as a lifeline to the Empire was one of the primary factors behind the establishment of a protectorate over Egypt in 1914 and the "reservations" linked to the proclamation of independence in 1922.

pretense of acknowledging the sovereignty of the Khedive and his overlord the Sultan, but when Turkey joined the Central Powers in 1914 the London government issued a proclamation that Egypt would henceforth constitute a protectorate of the British Empire. When the war ended, the London authorities refused to allow Egypt to send a delegation to Paris to lay her case before the peace conference. The upshot was the emergence of an Egyptian nationalist movement known as the *Wafd*. The name means literally "delegation," and the movement had been organized originally to present Egypt's demands and grievances at the peace conference. When the British attempted suppression and deported its leader to Malta, the *Wafd* came forth with an insistence upon nothing less than complete independence.

The beginning of nationalism in Egypt; the rise of the *Wafd*

Following a campaign of sabotage and terrorism waged by the *Wafd*, the British decided to abolish the protectorate and in 1922 proclaimed Egypt an independent and sovereign state. But "independence" was made subject to four reservations, to be left absolutely to the discretion of the British pending adjustment by mutual agreement. The first was the protection of the Suez Canal and other vital links in the lifeline of the British Empire. The second was the defense of Egypt itself against foreign encroachments or interference. The third was the protection of foreign interests and minorities in Egypt. The fourth was the maintenance of the dependent status of the Sudan under the joint rule of Britain and Egypt. For the next three decades the history of Egypt was largely occupied by controversy and conflict over these four points or reservations.

Abolition of the British protectorate

Although the majority of Egyptians resented the attempts of the British to keep the country in a state of vassalage, they were alarmed by Mussolini's invasion of Ethiopia in 1935, and in 1936 accepted an

1129

The revival of
nationalism after
World War II

Anglo-Egyptian Treaty of Friendship and Alliance. Egypt agreed to coordinate her foreign policy with that of Britain in return for British assistance in gaining admission to the League of Nations. Before all the terms of the Anglo-Egyptian Treaty could be put into effect, World War II broke out. The British were reluctant to take any steps that might threaten their communications with the East, and the Egyptians did not press the issue of the removal of British troops from their soil. But when the war ended, the flames of nationalist aspirations were kindled anew. The Egyptians now demanded that the British withdraw entirely from both the Suez Canal area and the Sudan. In 1951 the Egyptian government announced that it was abrogating the Treaty of 1936 and also the condominium or joint rule in the Sudan. In July 1954 Britain agreed to the removal of all British troops from Egyptian territory.

Proclamation of
a republic in
Egypt

In July 1952, Major General Mohammed Naguib seized control of the Egyptian government and the army. The pleasure-loving King Farouk I, alleged to be subservient to the British, was deposed. The constitution was suspended, political parties were abolished, and a provisional government was brought into existence. A year later Egypt was proclaimed a republic, with General Naguib as its first President and Premier. The new ruler announced a program of sweeping economic and social reforms. Compulsory education was ordered for all children between the ages of seven and twelve. Provisions for land reform were also enacted. Holdings were limited to 200 acres, and large estates were to be broken up and redistributed. They were to be made available to landless peasants on a plan of 30-year payments. But before these reforms could be fully effected, conflict developed within the military junta which had overthrown the monarchy. Naguib was temporarily deposed in February 1954. Though he was restored to the Presidency a few days later, the Premiership was retained by his rival, Lieutenant-Colonel Gamal Abdel Nasser. In June 1956, by a carefully managed election in which he was the only candidate, Nasser was chosen President. He received 99.9 per cent of the votes cast. Ironically, in the same election the Egyptian voters adopted a new constitution proclaiming the country an Islamic-Arab state with a democratic form of government.

Gamal Abdul Nasser, Dynamic Arab Nationalist and President of Egypt, 1956–1970.

The Suez crisis

Nasser resolved to continue and enlarge the program of economic and social reform. In particular, he was determined to relieve the condition of the impoverished masses. He proceeded with plans to distribute 750,000 acres of land, giving farms to 250,000 landless peasants. He soon realized, however, that on account of Egypt's rapid growth in population, more productive land must be made available. To accomplish this purpose he decided upon the construction of the Aswan High Dam, a gigantic reservoir to back up the waters of the Upper Nile and provide irrigation for 2 million acres of arable land. Since the cost ($1.3 billion) would be more than Egypt could stand, he hoped to borrow large sums of money

Aswan High Dam. The Dam was designed to serve a two-fold purpose: to facilitate the irrigation of vast areas of arid land and to generate electrical power.

from the World Bank and from the United States and British governments. Alarmed by the Egyptian purchases of arms from Czechoslovakia (a Communist source), the United States suddenly withdrew its offer of a loan to Nasser, and great Britain did likewise soon after. Nasser retaliated by expropriating the owners of the Suez Canal, who were chiefly British and French, and declared that he would use the revenues of the Canal to build the dam. After months of fruitless negotiation, the British and French encouraged an invasion of Egyptian territory by the Republic of Israel. The Israelis had plenty of grievances, since they had been the victims of border raids from the Sinai Peninsula for many years. The invasion began on October 29, 1956, and the British and French intervened soon afterward. The affair precipitated a crisis which threatened for a time to engulf the world. The Soviet rulers warned Israel that its very existence was in danger and darkly hinted their intention of joining forces with Egypt. The United Nations finally arranged a cease-fire, and in March 1957 the Nasser government reopened the Canal, under its own terms of national ownership, to all users except Israel. In 1958 Nasser established the United Arab Republic with Syria as the Northern Region, Egypt as the Southern Region, and Yemen as a federated member. Three years later Syria seceded. The name—which implied more unity in the Arab world than in fact existed—was changed to the Arab Republic of Egypt in 1971, when Egypt, Syria, and Libya agreed to form a loose federation.

Following Nasser's death in 1970, Anwar Sadat, a relatively obscure member of the group that had overthrown the monarchy in

1131

President Anwar Sadat of Egypt.

The formation of Saudi Arabia

Progress under ibn Saud

1952, became President of Egypt. Confronted with problems at home and abroad, he attempted to continue Nasser's policies while moderating their harshness. A new constitution enacted in 1971 contained democratic features, but political power remained with the one and only legal party, the Arab Socialist Union, which had become bureaucratic and unprogressive. As in most Middle Eastern countries, the bulk of the population are poverty stricken and upwards of 65 per cent are illiterate. Economic development is slow. The Aswan Dam, completed in 1970 and hailed as the most impressive structure built in the Middle East since the pyramids, has been less successful in desert reclamation than was hoped and, by enormously increasing the flow of water, has upset the ecological balance in the lower Nile. Egypt's substantial petroleum reserves are not yet fully exploited. Her government depends on annual cash subsidies from her oil-rich neighbors Saudi Arabia and Libya. Egypt's foreign policy has been based upon an aspiration for pre-eminence in the Arab world and upon enmity with Israel, which impelled her to close relations with the Soviet Union. The U.S.S.R. supplied both economic and military aid, and in 1971 the two governments signed a fifteen-year treaty of mutual friendship and cooperation. This association, however, has proved troublesome to both parties. Russia sought to restrain the belligerence of her ally, while Egyptians complained they were not receiving the weapons they needed. In July 1972 President Sadat expelled the Soviet experts and military advisers, but after a visit to Moscow the following spring, he claimed to have received a guarantee of sufficient power "to liberate our land."

Until recently, the most barren and backward of the countries formerly included in the Ottoman Empire was that which is now called Saudi Arabia. Covering an area more than one-fourth that of the United States, Arabia is almost 100 per cent desert. Not a single river or lake exists to relieve the monotonous aridity. Inhabited to this day by only 8½ million people, the country did not become a united state until 1927. Previous to that time it was divided into the two main areas of the Hejaz and Nejd. The king of the Hejaz was Sherif Hussein, Protector of the Holy Cities of Mecca and Medina and, after 1924, self-appointed Caliph of Islam. Hussein was driven from his kingdom by the ruler of Nejd, Abdul ibn Saud (1880–1953), who in January 1926 had himself proclaimed King of the Hejaz in the Great Mosque of Mecca. Soon afterward he united his two kingdoms of Hejaz and Nejd into a theocratic state which he named Saudi Arabia.

Such progress as has occurred in Saudi Arabia can be credited in part to the shrewdness of ibn Saud. He realized that the Moslem world could not hold its own against Western encroachments without adopting Western improvements. Accordingly, he allowed a few railways to be built and imported motor vehicles for his own court and for the transportation of pilgrims to the Holy Cities. He instituted plans for free education for the children of his subjects and made provision, on paper at least, for free medical attention. But by far the greatest impetus to advancement was the discovery, in the early 1930's, that eastern Arabia contained undreamed-of riches in the form of petroleum deposits, amounting to the world's largest known reserves. King ibn Saud granted concessions for the exploitation of this wealth to the Arabian-American Oil Company (Aramco), owned jointly by Texaco and the Standard Oil Company of California. Royalties paid by Aramco have provided the funds for electrification of cities and the construction of highways, railroads, and airports, to say nothing of aid to agriculture, education, and public health.

Abdul ibn Saud's successor—a son bearing the same name but a wildly reckless spendthrift—was deposed in 1964 by his half brother Faisal. King Faisal, who also assumed the prime ministership, has proved to be the most enlightened and statesmanlike of the dynasty. Although he has not ended the abject poverty still prevalent outside the few rapidly modernizing cities, he commands resources more than ample to provide for the needs of the country's inhabitants. Oil revenues, which in 1971 rose by 68 per cent to a total of nearly $2 billion, enable his government to contribute substantial annual subsidies to Egypt, Jordan, and Syria.

When World War I ended, the country now known as Israel was a province of Turkey. Its population was about 70 per cent Arab and 30 per cent Jewish and Christian. By the defeat of Turkey in 1918, it was made a mandate of the League of Nations under the guardianship of Great Britain. In the meantime, Zionists in Britain and the United States worked zealously to convert Palestine into a national home for the Jewish people. In return for their labors the British

Kuwait, an Arab Sheikdom on the Persian Gulf. Oil resources, exploited by the Kuwait Oil Company, jointly owned by Gulf Oil and Anglo-Iranian Oil, give Kuwait one of the highest per capita incomes in the world.

government issued the famous Balfour Declaration promising to view with favor the establishment in Palestine of a national home for Jewish people. At the same time provision would be made for safeguarding the rights of non-Jewish communities in Palestine.

On the basis of the Balfour Declaration, Britain accepted the mandate for Palestine. She promised as she did so not merely to establish a Jewish National Home, but "to secure the preservation of an Arab National Home and to apprentice the people of Palestine as a whole in the art of self-government." It was an optimistic ambition, but at the time optimism seemed justified. In fact, for a period of ten years there was every reason to expect that the undertaking would be successful. Palestine prospered as never before in its history. Factories were built, land was reclaimed, irrigation works were constructed, the Jordan River was harnessed for electric power, and unemployment disappeared from the face of the land. Except for rioting in Jaffa in 1921, no incident of violence occurred to disturb the general tranquillity. The aspect of the country was so peaceful that in 1926 the British reduced their armed forces to a single RAF squadron and two companies with armored cars.

By 1929, however, evidences of disharmony had begun to appear in the land that was holy to three great religions. The Jews were too prosperous and well-educated and were arousing the envy and fears of the Arabs by their high standard of living and their more strenuous competition. Their purchases of land, in many cases from absentee owners, had resulted in the displacement of thousands of Arab cultivators and had thrown them into the cities at a time when the Great Depression was beginning to make unemployment a serious problem. But the major cause of Arab foreboding was the steady increase in the Jewish population. The opportunity to emigrate to Palestine had offered a greater temptation than the Arabs had expected. As a consequence, some of them foresaw a relentless advance and expansion of Europeans and Americans, backed by foreign capital and flaunting a culture that was alien to the ways of the Arab majority. In 1929, 1930, and 1931 armed attacks were waged upon Jewish settlements followed by terrorist murders.

But these episodes paled into insignificance when compared with the bloody violence that followed. When the mandate was established, no one could have foreseen the desperate plight that was to overtake the European Jews with the accession of the Nazis to power in Germany. As news of the persecutions spread, it was inevitable that pressure should be brought upon the British government to relax the barriers against immigration into Palestine. During the period 1933–1935 the admission of more than 130,000 Jewish immigrants was authorized, and uncounted thousands more came in illicitly. From this time on Palestine was a seething caldron of violence and warfare. The Arabs rose in open rebellion against the mandate. Organized terrorism swept the country. Guerrilla at-

The bright prospects of the early years

The development of conflicts between Jews and Arabs

Rebellion of the Arabs against the mandate

Immigration to Palestine. Left: British soldiers guard the shore as a ship loaded with unauthorized refugees attempts to land in 1947. Right: A view of the unbearably crowded conditions aboard ships bringing refugees to Palestine.

tacks in the rural areas and looting, burning, and sabotage in the towns and cities kept the whole population in turmoil. By 1938 Britain had 20,000 troops in Palestine, and even these were unable to maintain order.

The early years of World War II were characterized by relative quiet in Palestine. Both sides were subdued in some measure by fears that the war would spread, but the primary reason was the White Paper of 1939, which the British government issued a few months before the conflict began. In this document Britain envisioned the "establishment within ten years of an independent Palestine State," with protection for the "essential interests" of both Jews and Arabs, and a government in which both peoples would share. Meanwhile, land purchases from Arabs were to be restricted, and the number of Jews admitted to Palestine was to be limited to 75,000. Though the plan was unfavorably received by the Mandates Commission of the League of Nations, it seemed to allay the fears of the Arabs and to give them a ray of hope that their interests would be protected. But trouble broke out anew when a conference of American Zionists at the Biltmore Hotel in New York, in May 1942, adopted the so-called Biltmore Program, repudiating the White Paper of 1939 and demanding the establishment of a Jewish state and a Jewish army in Palestine. Soon afterward both Jews and Arabs prepared for war to the hilt. Fanatical Zionists, as well as Arabs, resorted to the use of terrorist methods. Illegal military organizations sprang up on both sides and devoted their energies to raiding, burning, and assassination.

In April 1947 the British government referred the Palestine problem to the United Nations and announced that a year later it would terminate the mandate and withdraw all its troops from the coun-

Renewal of the conflict after World War II

1135

Termination of the
mandate and
establishment of
the State of Israel

try. On May 15, 1948, the British mandate came to an end, and on the same day a Jewish provisional government proclaimed the establishment of an independent State of Israel. Elections were held for a Constituent Assembly, which met in February of the following year and adopted a temporary constitution for a democratic republic. Its chief features were a weak president, a strong cabinet, and a powerful parliament. It was clearly intended that the last two agencies should really govern the country. The cabinet was vested with general direction of the legislative process as well as with executive authority. But the parliament, or Knesset, would exercise independent legislative power, and could overturn cabinets which no longer enjoyed its confidence. The constitution also provided for proportional representation, a unicameral parliament, and universal suffrage for Jews and Arabs alike. A unique element in the system was the close association of religion with the state. Marriage and divorce were placed under the exclusive jurisdiction of religious courts—Jewish, Christian, or Moslem as the affiliation of the parties might require.

Meanwhile, from the day of proclaimed independence until the spring of 1949, Israel and its Arab neighbor countries were at war. United Nations efforts brought about truces several times, but nothing lasting was achieved until Israel and Egypt signed a general armistice agreement in February 1949; Jordan and Syria also signed armistices in April. The United Nations peace effort was at first under the direction of Count Folke Bernadotte of Sweden; when he was assassinated in September 1948, by Israeli extremists in Jerusalem, it was continued by Dr. Ralph Bunche of the United States. The status at the cease-fire was regarded as a victory for Israel and a defeat for the Arab powers; neither, however, accepted it as final. Violent incidents continued to occur, including retaliatory massacres.

Israeli Tanks Move into Jerusalem. A scene during the second Arab-Israeli War, June 1967.

Despite her troubles with the Arabs, Israel strengthened her economy, and many new industries were created. Large sums of money flowed into the country as a result of West German restitution for the outrages of Nazism. Agriculture advanced to a stage sufficient to supply the needs of the home market while export crops such as olives, melons, and citrus fruits were rapidly developed. Land under cultivation more than doubled between 1955 and 1967. The index of industrial production increased from 100 in 1963 to 185 in 1969. The nation had seven universities, two with more than 10,000 students each. Total enrollment in all state schools had increased from 130,000 in 1948 to approximately 800,000 in 1970.

Yet the fate of Israel was not a happy one. Trouble brewed in Sinai in 1967 until President Nasser resolved to teach the Jewish nation a lesson. He formed alliances with Jordan and Syria and vowed that Israel must be wiped from the map. Nasser closed Aqaba, Israel's only direct outlet to the Red Sea. The Israelis responded with a lightning war against Egypt and her Arab allies. The Egyptian and Syrian forces were routed in six days, and the Syrians accepted a cease-fire a short time later. But cease-fire did not spell peace, and Israel's smashing victory did not bring her the security she had hoped for. In some ways it augmented her difficulties—requiring the defense of frontiers deep in hostile territory and saddling her with responsibility for the fate of more than a million Arabs, concentrated chiefly in the Jordan West Bank and the Gaza Strip adjoining the Sinai peninsula. Efforts by the great powers and the United Nations to end the Israeli-Arab feud were stalemated by Israel's insistence that the Arab states grant her formal recognition and by their demand that she must first withdraw to the pre-June 1967 boundaries. Violence erupted again in October 1973 when Egypt and Syria launched a surprise offensive in the Sinai and Golan Heights areas respectively. After seventeen days of fierce fighting a cease-fire was established under pressure from the United States and the U.S.S.R. The cease-fire lines left Israeli troops in possession of more Syrian territory than before and a small area west of the Suez Canal. The Egyptians retained a foothold on the east side of the canal. In the wake of this latest war the search for an enduring solution to this long-term feud continued.

Internal problems also confronted the Israelis as they prepared to celebrate in May 1973 the twenty-fifth anniversary of their nation's birth. The economy appeared still vigorous and bustling; industrial output had doubled in the five years since 1967. But inflation had not been halted nor poverty conquered. Defense spending, four times as large as in 1967, consumed half the national budget. Armed to the teeth, Israel was now exporting armaments to some fifty other countries. And contrary to the hopes of many Zionists, Israel had become not a haven for small farmers or a community of agricultural cooperatives but a land of teeming cities, with a society 82 per cent urban.

The only country of the Middle East which was not under the rule of Turkey at one time or another before 1918 was Persia. But this did not mean freedom from foreign domination. Remote, steeped in languor, and rich in resources, Persia was a constant temptation to ambitious imperialists. In 1907 Great Britain and Russia signed an agreement providing for the division of the country into spheres of influence. The northern sphere was assigned to Russia and the southern to Great Britain. A middle zone was to be left, temporarily at least, under the control of the native Shah. The overthrow of the Tsar in 1917 filled the minds of British imperialists with hopes that all Persia might be theirs. By 1919 Lord Curzon had extorted from the Shah an agreement transferring to Great Britain political and military control of the entire country. But the plans of the British were frustrated by Riza Khan, a young army officer who essayed for himself a role somewhat similar to that of Mustafa Kemal in Turkey. With no more than 3000 troops at his back he forced the Shah to appoint him Minister of War and commander-in-chief of the army. In 1923 he became Premier and two years later Shah with the title Riza Pahlavi. He took steps to reduce foreign influences, and forbade his own officials to associate with Europeans. In 1932 he canceled the concession of the powerful Anglo-Persian Oil Company and obtained a new contract with terms more advantageous to his own government. In 1935 he changed the name of his country from Persia to Iran, or land of the Aryans.

World War II brought almost as much turmoil and anguish to Iran as if she had been one of the belligerents. Riza Shah abdicated in 1941 and was succeeded by his son Mohammed Riza Pahlavi. Because of its strategic importance, Iran's territory was occupied by the British, Russians, and Americans under pledges to respect her sovereignty and independence and to render economic assistance during and after the war. Despite these pledges, unrest and inflation plagued the country. Communism flourished under the aegis of the Tudeh (Masses) party, and conflicts developed between the Shah and political leaders. In 1951 antiforeign extremists in the Iranian Parliament voted to nationalize the oil industry, and the Premier, Dr. Mohammed Mossadegh, rejected all proposals for arbitration. The result was the closing down of the Anglo-Iranian oil refinery at Abadan, the largest in the world, which employed over 55,000 persons at an annual wage total of $67,000,000. Since the company also paid over $38,000,000 in taxes, the shutdown meant virtual bankruptcy for the Iranian government. No signs of a possible compromise appeared until after the Premier was seized and imprisoned by supporters of the Shah during a civilian and military uprising in August 1953. A year later his successor signed an agreement with a consortium of eight foreign oil companies which provided that the consortium should extract, refine, and market the

Mohammed Riza Pahlavi, Shah of Iran.

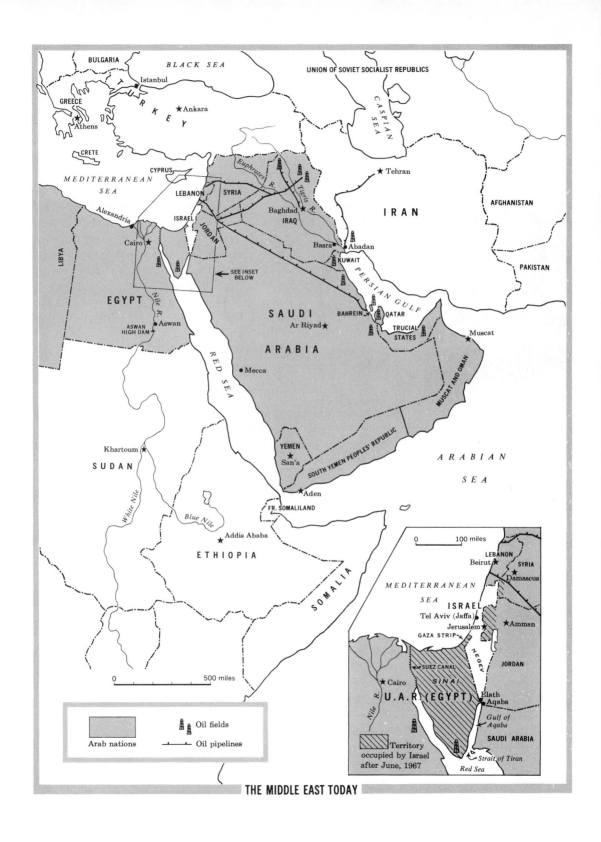

THE MIDDLE EAST TODAY

The Shah's
benevolent
despotism

President Paul Kruger of the Transvaal

products of Iran's nationalized oil industry and turn over to the government approximately one-half of the net profits.

Under Mohammed Riza Pahlavi, who cast off his youthful role of self-indulgent playboy to become an energetic ruler, Iran has made appreciable strides toward ending its condition of primitive squalor. During the 1960's the country achieved an annual economic growth rate of 9 per cent and doubled its gross national product. Revenues from oil, the chief natural resource, have been utilized for highway construction, power generating dams, and the beginnings of a system of public education. The Shah introduced social and economic reforms, distributing thousands of acres of land to peasants who had been virtually serfs and enabling workers in government-owned industries to share in the profits. But his benevolent paternalism— anathema to radical critics—has made few concessions to democracy. His one-man rule employs a cumbersome and corrupt bureaucracy and ruthlessly suppresses all opposition. Since 1968, in response to Britain's announced intention of withdrawing from the Persian Gulf, the Shah has evinced a determination to make Iran the dominant military power in that vital area.

The troubles of the Middle East arise from the poverty and ignorance of the masses, the conflicting national ambitions of small but militant states, and competing ideologies. At the same time, the vast energy potential of an area so rich in oil, together with converging strategic interests of rival great powers, has made it a likely tinder box for world conflagration. One tragic circumstance—the fruit of conflict and a cause of its continuance—is the presence of more than a million Palestinian refugees, bereft of a homeland ever since the Jewish-Arab war of 1948. A United Nations Assembly resolution called for their repatriation, but they have remained in refugee camps in the Arab states, a burden to their hosts and an obstacle to reconciliation between Arabs and Jews. Organizations dedicated to the "liberation" of Palestine—notably Fatah and its secret "Black September" corps—perpetrated acts of savage barbarity. Their activities not only provoked fierce and swift reprisals from Israel but also led to armed clashes between Palestinian guerrillas and the governments of Jordan and Lebanon, which were accused of willingness to compromise with Israel. Various attempts to promote unity among the countries of the Middle East have met with limited success. In 1945 an Arab League was formed, with Egypt, Saudi Arabia, Jordan, Iraq, Syria, Lebanon, and Yemen as the original members. The League was weakened by a tendency of its members to align themselves in conservative and progressive blocs and by resentment against Egypt's President Nasser, who aspired to dominate the Arab community. Cleavages reflected Cold War rivalry, especially as the United States and the Soviet Union became chief armorers for Israel and the Arab states, respectively. Common economic interests present the most likely basis for cooperation. The Organization of Petroleum Exporting Countries, whose members supply 90 per cent of the world's oil, can exert leverage on the great powers. The petroleum concessions of major Western companies are being nationalized, even in such tiny Persian Gulf states as Qatar, Kuwait, and Abu Dhabi. With oil the potentially dangerous political weapon that it is, all parties might profitably heed the temperate counsel of Saudi Arabia's oil minister, Sheik Ahmed Yamani, who in 1972 addressed a conference of the Organization of Petroleum Exporting Countries: "We believe that being aware of one's power is the basis of being aware of one's responsibility. The world needs oil and we, in turn, need the world."

2. THE REPUBLIC OF SOUTH AFRICA

Perhaps in no other African state have the problems of nation-building, tribalism, and racial cooperation proved more difficult than in the Republic of South Africa. Conflicts between Boer, Bantu, and Briton have punctuated the history of South Africa for generations. Each group almost fanatically adheres to its own traditions and conceptions of how society should be organized.

The problems of South Africa

Before the 1870's Great Britain had followed a colonial policy of benign neglect toward South Africa. The interior, long considered barren in natural resources, was of little importance to the British. Indeed, their prime concern lay in protecting the vital sea route to India by controlling the strategically-important harbors along the South African coast. But in 1870 diamonds were discovered at Kimberley, and fifteen years later the fabulous gold fields of the Witwatersrand became a mecca for prospectors and adventurers from all over the world. Between 1872 and 1902 the white population of South Africa quadrupled. Congested cities such as Johannesburg and Bloemfontein mushroomed on the veldt. The simple pastoral economy of the old-fashioned Boers had come to an end.

Prime Minister Cecil Rhodes of the Cape Colony.

The discovery of diamonds and gold multiplied the political difficulties of the Boer republics. Britishers and other foreigners swarmed in in such numbers that they threatened to overwhelm the white Afrikaner settlers. The latter retaliated by branding the immigrants as outlanders and denying them political privileges except under the most rigorous conditions. The suffrage was refused, the press censored, and public meetings practically forbidden. In desperation the British organized a conspiracy to overthrow the most obstinate of the Boer governments, that of Paul Kruger, President of the Transvaal. Ammunition was collected, with the connivance of Cecil Rhodes, Prime Minister of the Cape Colony; and on December 29, 1895, 600 Britons and their armed retainers, under the leadership of Rhodes's friend, Dr. Leander Jameson, raided the Transvaal. The invaders were quickly surrounded and captured, but their act greatly magnified the tension between British and Boers.

The Afrikaner governments increased the restrictions against foreigners and accumulated arms in preparation for a showdown. In October 1899, war broke out between these republics and the colonies predominantly British.

The Boer War (1899–1902)

The Boer War dragged its length through three bloody years. Not until Britain sent sizeable reinforcements under the leadership of her best generals was she able to snatch victory from the jaws of defeat. Finally, outnumbered seven to one, the Boers yielded and signed the Treaty of Vereeniging. In return for submitting to British rule, they were exempted from indemnities, promised representative institutions at an early date, and permitted to retain their own language in the courts and schools. The British government provided $15,000,000 to accelerate the process of reconstruction. It was one of the most generous peace settlements in history. At this time, the victorious British were in the position to impose on South Africa a universal, nonracial franchise. Tragically, the plight of the African majority was ignored. The question of racial justice was avoided in the name of Boer-British reconciliation.

The Union of South Africa

In 1909 Cape Colony, Natal, the Orange Free State, and the Transvaal were merged into the Union of South Africa. The National Convention that drafted the Constitution provided for a unitary instead of a federal state. The reasons were several. The need for railway construction and for solving the problems of a large native population seemed to demand unification. More important was the fact that the two white nationalities did not occupy separate provinces as in Canada. In most states the rural population was Afrikaner or Boer, the urban population British. In some additional respects also the government of South Africa differed from that of the other dominions. The Cabinet did not stand or fall as a unit, but, theoretically at least, disagreements were permitted among the members. Its control over the upper house of Parliament was more effective. In case of a conflict between the Cabinet and the Assembly, or lower house, both houses might be dissolved and their members compelled to stand for re-election. South Africa had a much more conservative attitude toward the suffrage than did the other dominions. Universal manhood suffrage for whites was not adopted until 1930. Woman suffrage was also adopted in the same year, but in the face of stiff opposition. The Minister of Justice, for example, declared that the female franchise conflicted "with the intentions that the Creator had for women." As for the natives, who constitute more than 75 per cent of the population, all were disfranchised except in the southernmost Cape Province, where Negro and Asian citizens vote under limited conditions.

The sharpest controversies in South African politics since the formation of the Union have been those relating to nationality and race. Although the British made repeated efforts at reconciliation

General James B. M. Hertzog, Leader of Afrikaner Nationalist Party.

following the Boer War, the old hatreds died hard. In 1912 a faction of extremist Boers broke away from their kinsmen and formed the Nationalist party. Under the leadership of General Hertzog, they strove to preserve the cultural independence of the Afrikaners and to tolerate no fusion with the British. They resented British aggressiveness and regarded it as synonymous with an imperialism which threatened to obliterate the customs and institutions of their revered ancestors. They eventually came to advocate the severance of all ties with the British and the transformation of the Dominion into an Afrikaner republic. Anti-Semitism also emerged as a cardinal policy in the minds of the most fanatical. The finance capitalists who controlled the gold and diamond mines of the Rand[1] were alleged to be mostly Jews who were lightly taxed by the British-dominated government. By 1938 the Nationalists seemed almost as greatly disturbed by the "Jewish Menace" as they were by the "Black Peril" and were demanding the exclusion of all Jewish immigrants.

The two world wars of 1914 and 1939 contributed to the strength of the Nationalist movement. The followers of General Hertzog were determined that South Africa should not be dragged into war at the behest of the London government. The right to remain neutral they considered an indispensable badge of their nation's sovereignty. In 1914 some of them organized a rebellion as an armed protest against enslavement to British objectives. But the policy of their opponent, General Jan Christiaan Smuts, prevailed, and South Africa contributed its share toward winning the war. Eight years after the Armistice the Nationalists, supported by Labor, gained control of the government, but with a watered-down program that did not demand complete independence. When Britain again went to war in 1939, the South African government split. Six Cabinet ministers supported the war, five opposed. In the Assembly the vote was 80 in favor of the war to 67 against. It was obvious that the termination of hostilities would leave the country torn asunder and that the difficulties and tensions growing out of the war would widen the cleavage still further. Military production brought thousands of natives into the towns and created fears of Communist uprisings or some other form of social revolution. As a party of the extreme right, the Nationalists played upon these fears and gained control of Parliament in 1948. They not only espoused the idea of a republic but demanded a policy of *apartheid*, or strict separation of races. Raising the cry of "a white civilization in peril," they clamored for curtailment of the natives' privileges and denounced the citizens of British extraction for fostering the amal-

The rise
of Afrikaner
nationalism

Growth of the
nationalist
movement

General Jan Christian Smuts, Spokesman of South African Moderates.

---

[1] The Rand, or Witwatersrand, is a 60-mile ridge which constitutes a watershed between the Vaal and Limpopo Rivers.

Prime Minister Hendrik Verwoerd of South Africa. Verwoerd after leading South Africa out of the commonwealth in March 1961.

gamation of races through the promotion of industrialism.[2] Indeed, the program of the new Nationalists was almost as anti-British as it was anti-Negro. They longed for a republic completely purged of British influence. Its children would learn but one language, Afrikaans, a colloquial form of Dutch, and venerate the life of their grandfathers on the lonely veldt. It would be a republic founded upon the ideals of Paul Kruger, not upon those of Cecil Rhodes.

In 1961 Prime Minister Hendrik Verwoerd took steps toward implementing these ideals when he ordered the withdrawal of South Africa from the Commonwealth of Nations and proclaimed the country an independent republic. For the time being there would be two capitals, Cape Town and Pretoria, and two languages, English and Afrikaans. It was clear, however, that the ultimate objective was an Afrikaner nation thoroughly purged of British influences. In 1960 the attempted assassination of Verwoerd had already led to severe restrictions on the Negro population. They were forced to live in "reserved" areas, subjected to a rigid curfew, and deprived of all rights to freedom of assemblage, speech, and press. In 1967 a severe Terrorism Act was passed presuming the guilt of everyone accused of terrorism until he could prove himself innocent.

In common with Australia and New Zealand, South Africa has embraced an extensive policy of government control over economic affairs. The reasons have been partly geographic. The severe droughts, the frequent visitations of locusts, the perennial struggle to keep the topsoil from being washed into the sea—all make farm-

[2] It should be emphasized that *apartheid* is merely an extreme form of the racial philosophy accepted almost universally by South Africans of European extraction. Only a negligible minority believes that Negroes can be given political and social equality with whites in the foreseeable future.

Apartheid in South Africa. Among the restrictions imposed upon the black natives is the requirement that they carry passports. Here a policeman and an interpreter check the papers of a native bound for Johannesburg to work in the mines.

Diamond Mining in Southwest Africa. To make the diamond-bearing gravels accessible, vast quantities of sand must be removed. Diamonds are sometimes buried 70 feet beneath the surface.

ing a desperate gamble against odds that are often too great for an individual to withstand. But in South Africa the additional objective of protecting the white man against the competition of the natives has fostered economic collectivism. Agrarian leaders have believed for some time that nothing short of tariffs, bounties, and subsidies will enable the Caucasian farmer to stay on the land and save him from becoming a "poor white." Only with the help of such forms of government intervention can he maintain his standard of living and not be driven into bankruptcy by low-cost production.

Collectivism in South Africa has assumed an even greater variety of forms than in most other countries. A Land and Agricultural Bank, deriving its capital from the government, lends money to farmers to buy land, to prevent foreclosures, and for such special purposes as the construction of fences and silos. Imports of wheat have been prohibited at times for the purpose of promoting self-sufficiency. Sugar production is carefully fostered by tariffs, price controls, and crop limitation. But the policy of collectivism is not restricted to agriculture. Public utilities and railroads are government-owned. More unusual is the South African Iron and Steel Industrial Corporation, established by the government in 1928 because of a belief that private companies were unable to raise sufficient capital to expand their capacity. The government corporation currently supplies about half of the country's steel requirements. Finally, it should be noted that South Africa has an extensive program of welfare and labor legislation for the white population. It includes old-age pensions, unemployment insurance, maximum-hour and minimum-wage laws, and compulsory arbitration of industrial disputes.

Forms
of collectivism

1145

3. THE UPSURGE OF AFRICA

Early African
nationalism and
pan-Africanism

Modern African nationalism and pan-African sentiment are not post-World War II phenomena. Their roots go back to 1847 with the establishment of the independent Republic of Liberia. Liberia was the first independent state in Africa to support Western-style institutions and to prove that black men were capable of governing themselves along so-called modern lines. Edward Blyden, a leading Liberian intellectual (born in the West Indies), called in the 1860's for racial integrity and solidarity and coined the phrase "Africa for Africans." He exhorted black men to preserve the African essence of their civilizations and to resist Westernization at the hands of European imperialists. Native-born, Western-educated intellectuals on the Gold Coast (now Ghana) and Nigeria were to take up this call in the two decades prior to the first World War. Nevertheless, these protonationalists represented but a thin veneer and were predominantly drawn from among second sons of wealthy traditional nobility. Many of them were torn between their rich African heritage and that of Western civilization and found it difficult to identify with their peasant brethren in the bush. They were willing to work within the colonial framework and to pursue a moderate, gradualist course. After World War II, these early elites were eclipsed by impatient youthful nonaristocratic intellectuals who returned to Africa after many years abroad. Armed with the techniques of political party organization, they reached out to the masses, particularly the urban unemployed.

The 1950's and 1960's witnessed a groundswell of colonial revolts in northern and central Africa. For the most part, they were directed against Great Britain and France, though Belgium, Italy, and

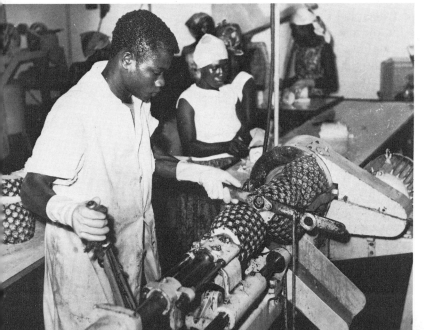

A Pineapple Processing Plant in Ghana. The new African states, rich in natural resources, are now attempting to meet the challenge of industrialization.

Algeria, 1962. After nearly eight years of strife and terror, Algeria was on the threshold of independence.

Portugal were also involved. The first of the former colonies to gain independence was Libya. Taken by Italy from Turkey in 1912, Libya passed under the control of the United Nations at the end of World War II. In 1949 the U.N. recognized the Libyan demand for freedom, and two years later independence was formally proclaimed.

The most violent of the colonial revolts in northern Africa occurred in Algeria. Algeria had been a part of the French Empire since the middle years of the nineteenth century. The French poured millions of dollars of capital into their colony, and thousands of French nationals came there to settle. Many people of other nationalities, especially Spaniards, also emigrated to Algeria, with the result that by 1960 the European inhabitants numbered about 1 million in a total population of 10,300,000. These Europeans, inaccurately referred to as the "French" population, monopolized not only the government positions but also the best economic opportunities in industry, agriculture, trade, and finance. The Arab and Berber inhabitants were chiefly peasants and laborers, though some, of course, maintained their own shops in the *casbah,* or native quarter, of each of the large cities. In 1954 Arab and Berber (Moslem) nationalists rose in revolt when their demand for equal status with the European population was denied by the French government. The revolt continued its bloody course for seven years. It was complicated by the fact that many of the European settlers (*colons*) hated the government in Paris almost as much as they did the Algerian nationalists. They were determined to keep Algeria "French" and feared a sell-out by President Charles de Gaulle that would make the former colony

1147

independent and subject the *colons* to the rule of the Arab and Berber majority. In April 1961, the announcement of a plan by de Gaulle to negotiate a settlement in Algeria that would pave the way for eventual independence led to a revolt in the territory by four French generals. They seized government buildings, arrested loyal French officials, and threatened to invade France. De Gaulle proclaimed a state of emergency and ordered a total blockade of Algeria. In the face of such determined opposition the revolt collapsed. The war of the nationalists, however, continued for another year. On a promise of immediate self-government and eventual independence the nationalists laid down their arms in March 1962. Three months later Algeria entered the ranks of independent states and was admitted to the United Nations. The war had cost the lives of about 40,000 soldiers and civilians and had left a heritage of bitterness that would probably linger for years.

If any one country could be considered the leader of the African colonial revolt, it was Ghana, formerly called the Gold Coast, a colony of Great Britain. In 1954 Britain granted self-government, and in 1960 Ghana became a republic. Leadership of the Ghana independence movement was at that time supplied by Kwame Nkrumah. The son of an illiterate goldsmith, he obtained an education in the United States and in England. He returned to his homeland in 1948 and became a nationalist agitator. Though he classified himself as a Marxist, he denied being a Communist. Yet he admired Lenin and generally looked to Moscow for support of his policies rather than to London or Washington. Apparently the key to his thinking was opposition to imperialism. He considered it preposterous that the Negroes of Central Africa, with their proud traditions of an ancient culture, should be ruled by Europeans. He regaled his followers with stories of a Golden Age in Africa, whose cultural center was in Timbuctoo, with a great university manned by distinguished scholars. For a time Nkrumah ruled benevolently even after converting the nation into a one-party state. He established hospitals and schools and raised the literacy standards. Accused of extravagance and corruption, he was deposed by a revolt of army officers in 1966. He was driven from his homeland and forced to take refuge in Guinea where he died in 1972. Nevertheless, Nkrumah's writings on neocolonialism and his pan-African ideas are still widely read by African intellectuals.

Kwame Nkrumah (center, seated) and Members of His Government in Ghana

The revolt in
the Congo

The most violent of the revolts in Central Africa occurred in the Congo, where there was not simply one previous colony but two. The smaller is now the People's Republic of the Congo. Though granted nominal independence in 1960, it is still under the influence of France and the People's Republic of China. Conditions in the larger Congo, now called Zaire, which was at one time a colony of Belgium, have been more serious. Fearing an outbreak of violence among her disaffected colonial subjects, Belgium, in 1960,

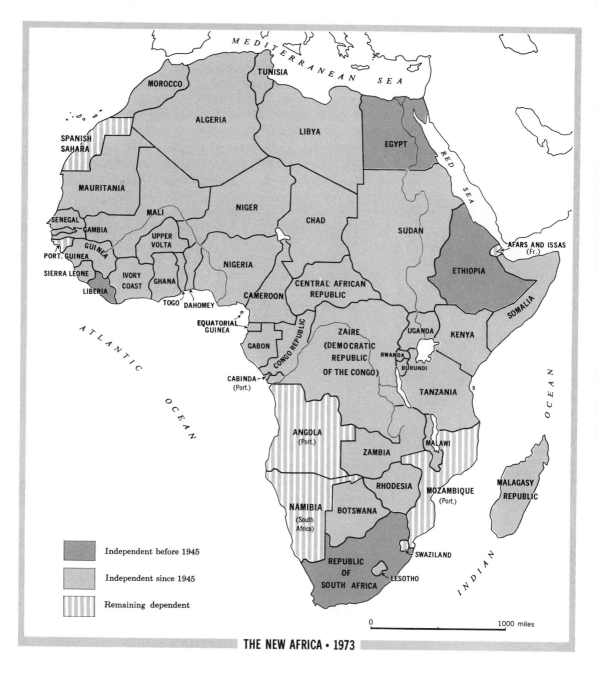

THE NEW AFRICA · 1973

Legend:
- Independent before 1945
- Independent since 1945
- Remaining dependent

granted them independence. This was the signal for the beginning
of a series of rebellions and assassinations that raged for more than
five years. A chief cause of the flaming disorders centered in the
southeastern province of Katanga. Here were located rich copper
resources controlled by Belgian capitalists. At one time the copper
mines of Katanga had produced revenues sufficient to defray one-
half the costs of the colonial government. In July 1960, Katanga

1149

seceded and attempted to gain control of the entire country. In the revolt several former premiers and other high officers were murdered. The U.N. Security Council sent a contingent to guard against revival of civil war. Strong-man rule was revived by President Mobutu, and a degree of stability was ultimately restored.

In most other sections of Central and Eastern Africa there was at least the illusion of tranquillity. Such countries as Nigeria and Kenya seemed like good examples. Both were former British colonies. Some authorities held that British colonial administration was wiser than that of most other European empires. Whereas the French and Belgians withheld self-government as long as they could, and then granted it suddenly, the British brought their colonies to independence more gradually. Many local leaders were trained in administration and knew how to deal with intricate problems before they actually arose. Yet even in Nigeria the familiar charges of corruption and inefficiency led to the murder of the Premier and the overthrow of the government in 1966. After more assassinations a military government seized control. Within a year the Eastern Region seceded and proclaimed itself the Republic of Biafra. Civil war followed and harassed the country for three years. The total of casualties was enormous. More than 1,000,000 people lost their lives. Thousands were killed in battle, but many more died of starvation. The rebels capitulated in 1970. From every standpoint the war was a tragedy. Nigeria is one of the most richly endowed of African countries. Its natural resources include oil and natural gas, coal, and the world's greatest abundance of columbium (used in steel manufacturing).

Also hovering on the verge of tragedy has been the recent history of Kenya, a country of East Africa lying athwart the Equator. Unlike Nigeria, Kenya is a poor country. The whole northern three-fifths of the territory is barren and almost waterless. Sections can be found in which there is no rainfall whatever for years at a time. The only well-watered sections are in the south and along the coast. It follows that agricultural resources are limited. The staple crops include coffee, sisal, tea, and wheat. Sugar cane, maize, tobacco, and cotton are also grown. Most of the farms are small. The construction of the railroad from the Kenya coast to Uganda at the turn of the century brought in thousands of Indian settlers. They did not become farmers or artisans, but settled in the cities and towns as petty traders. Despite their low standard of living and their meager profits they encouraged the indifferent Negroes to substitute a money economy for the age-old system of barter. Nevertheless, many Indians in Uganda and Kenya remained aloof, choosing not to become citizens or to allow Africans to enter their trades. This caused serious friction between the two races, and in 1972 led to the mass expulsion of Indians from Uganda.

The population of Kenya has never been closely unified. Tribal jealousies are rampant and sometimes break into open conflict. These jealousies seem not to be based on economic competition or greed.

Civil War in Nigeria

Conditions in Kenya

They appear rather to spring from ancient differences rooted in cultural characteristics and hatreds from the past. The most serious of these conflicts broke into the open in 1952 when the Mau Mau rebellion occurred. The Mau Mau were an offshoot of the Kikuyu tribe, who had been forcibly removed from their ancestral lands by European settlers at the turn of the century. By the close of the Second World War, the Kikuyu were experiencing a population explosion and sought to regain their lost territory. They instituted a reign of terror in some parts of the colony against the white settlers and all their kinsmen who sympathized with the colonial government. By 1958 the revolt was suppressed, and five years later the country obtained independence. Basically, Mau Mau was a Kikuyu-inspired nationalist movement aimed at achieving African self-determination over questions of land and governance.

Jomo Kenyatta Addressing an All-Africa Congress in London

The native leader who has done most to promote the growth and progress of Kenya has been Jomo Kenyatta, President of his country since 1963. Now over eighty years of age, he has devoted a long career to the defense of his homeland against the white man's exploitation. In 1952 he was thrown into prison for seven years, accused as a Mau Mau leader and a dangerous enemy of the state. His imprisonment seems to have done more to educate him in the realities of politics than to imbue him with hatred of his captors. While in prison he developed his philosophy of African socialism. Although for a time Kenyatta had studied at Moscow University, he adopted almost none of the trappings of Soviet communism. Instead his socialism bore a closer resemblance to that of the British or the Scandinavian countries. He urged his followers to forget the wrongs of the past and to concentrate on building a better world for the future. This future would be found in avoiding affiliations with either the East or the West. The African way has little in common with either capitalism or communism. The sharp antagonisms of class that exist in Europe and America have not been conspicuous elements in the African tradition. African socialism, according to Kenyatta, cannot be based on a dictatorship of the proletariat or any other form of class rule. Rather, its aim should be to prevent the seizure of power by individuals or groups armed with economic power. Its aim should be to enable every mature citizen to participate fully and equally in political affairs. Such is the essence of democracy and also of African socialism, according to Kenyatta's conception.

What will happen to Kenya when the aging Kenyatta passes from the scene, no one can predict. He is undoubtedly one of the greatest statesmen East Africa has produced. In his attitude toward guns and swords as the foundation of power, he resembles no one so much as the late Indian statesman Jawaharlal Nehru. Yet Kenyatta has not been able to solve the problem of tribalism in his own country. He has preached that every man has the right to take pride in the culture and customs of his tribe. But apparently this sentiment must not be carried so far as to endanger the unity of the state. In 1969 his gov-

The uncertain future of Kenya

1151

ernment was forced to deal with a violent revolt by the Kikuyu representing the impoverished North. After threats to disrupt national unity, their political party, the KPU, was banned and a number of its leaders confined in prison. More recently, disgruntled politicians are accused of plotting to seize Kenyatta's mantle of power whenever he is forced to surrender it by death or disability.

One of the most successful experiments in African nation-building has occurred in Tanzania under its President, Julius Nyerere. Unlike neighboring Kenya, Tanzania is not plagued by tribalism. There are not two or three major tribes maneuvering for power. Rather, Tanzania embraces a multitude of small tribes none of which is strong enough to dominate the political system. Tanzania itself is the result of the merging of two British-administered colonial units: the United Nations Trust Territory of Tanganyika and the Protectorate of Zanzibar. Since their union in 1964, Nyerere has gradually decreased his dependence on British trade and is relying more heavily on foreign assistance from the Communist world, particularly the People's Republic of China, which is completing a rail link between land-locked, copper-rich Zambia and Tanzania's port of Dar es Salaam on the Indian Ocean. Nevertheless, under Nyerere's able and democratic leadership, Tanzania is pursuing a policy of nonalignment. Nyerere, a noted Third World political theorist, has developed a unique brand of African socialism called *Ujamaa* ("familyhood" in Swahili) which is rooted in the traditional com-

Tanzania and experiments in African socialism

President Julius Nyerere of Tanzania. Nyerere, accompanied by a group of Chinese officials, lays the foundation stone of the New Chinese-Tanzanian Friendship Textile Mill in Dar es Salaam.

munalistic, extended family form of social organization. Yet it also draws heavily upon the experimental Chinese communes and the Israeli kibbutzim. The accent of Nyerere's socialism is upon the dignity of work, and national self-reliance. While Nyerere, a practicing Catholic, claims to be a socialist, he is opposed to Marxist doctrinaire socialism. According to Nyerere, modern African socialism "can draw from its traditional heritage the recognition of 'society' as an extension of the basic family unit." While it is still too early to predict the success of Tanzania's model Ujamaa villages, Nyerere's influence is strongly felt throughout Africa south of the Sahara.

SELECTED READINGS

THE MIDDLE EAST

· *Items so designated are available in paperbound editions.*

Ahmed, J. M., *The Intellectual Origins of Egyptian Nationalism*, New York, 1960. Informative and well-documented account.

Ben-Gurion, David, *Israel: A Personal History*, New York, 1971.

Bose, T. C., *The Superpowers and the Middle East*, New York, 1972.

· Chaliand, Gérard, *The Palestinian Resistance*, Baltimore, 1972 (Penguin).

Halpern, Manfred, *The Politics of Social Change in the Middle East and North Africa*, Princeton, 1967.

Harris, C. P., *Nationalism and Revolution in Egypt*, Stanford, 1967.

· Hitti, Philip K., *History of the Arabs*, New York, 1940 (St. Martin's).

Hoskins, H. L., *The Middle East*, New York, 1954. A careful, judicious study.

Issawi, Charles, *Egypt in Revolution: An Economic Analysis*, New York, 1963.

Karpat, Kemal, *Turkey's Politics: The Transition to a Multi-Party System*, Princeton, 1959. Sophisticated account by a Turkish political scientist.

Khouri, Fred J., *The Arab-Israeli Dilemma*, Syracuse, N. Y., 1968.

· Kirk, George E., *A Short History of the Middle East*, London, 1948 (Praeger).

· Laqueur, Jacques, *The Struggle for the Middle East*, Baltimore, 1972 (Penguin).

Lenczowski, George, *The Middle East in World Affairs*, 3rd ed., Ithaca, 1962.

———, *Oil and State in the Middle East*, Ithaca, 1960.

Lewis, Bernard, *The Emergence of Modern Turkey*, New York, 1961.

Lewis, Geoffrey, *Turkey*, 3rd ed., London, 1965.

Nolte, R. H., *The Modern Middle East*, New York, 1963.

· Prittie, Terence, *Israel: Miracle in the Desert*, rev. ed., Baltimore, 1968 (Penguin).

· Quandt, W. B., Jabber, F., and Lesch, A. M., *The Politics of Palestinian Nationalism*, Berkeley, 1973 (California).

· Rodinson, Maxime, *Israel and the Arabs*, Baltimore, 1970 (Penguin).

Segre, V. D., *Israel: A Society in Transition*, New York, 1971.

Twitchell, K. S., *Saudi Arabia*, Princeton, 1958.

Bartlett, Vernon, *Struggle for Africa*, New York, 1953.

Carter, G. M., *The Politics of Inequality*, New York 1958. A penetrating study of South Africa.

Clark, M. K., *Algeria in Turmoil*, New York, 1959.

· Macmillan, W. M., *Africa Emergent*, 1949 (Penguin).

· Marquard, L., *The Peoples and Policies of South Africa*, New York, 1952 (Oxford).

Nyerere, Julius, *Ujamaa: Essays on Socialism*, New York, 1971.

· Oliver, Roland, and Atmore, Anthony, *Africa since 1800*, New York, 1967 (Cambridge).

Pannikkar, K. M., *The Afro-Asian States and Their Problems*, New York, 1959. Brief but discerning.

Ranger, T. O., ed., *Aspects of Central African History*, London, 1969.

Thompson, L. M., *Politics in the Republic of South Africa*, Boston, 1966.

Wilson, M., and Thompson, L. M. eds., *The Oxford History of South Africa*, 2 vols., New York, 1971.

SOURCE MATERIALS

Apartheid: Its Effects on Education, Science, Culture and Information (UNESCO).

CHAPTER 38

Eruption in the Far East

How can a government be made all-powerful? Once the government is all-powerful, how can it be made responsive to the will of the people?

—Dr. Sun Yat-sen

The democratic system is to be carried out within the ranks of the people, giving them freedom of speech, assembly, and association. The right to vote is given only to the people and not to the reactionaries. These two aspects, namely democracy among the people and dictatorship over the reactionaries, combine to form the people's democratic dictatorship.

—Chairman Mao Tse-tung

The contemporary era of the Far Eastern countries began under the stimulation provided by the impact of Western explorers and merchants. By the middle of the twentieth century profound changes had taken place not only within the Eastern countries but also in their relationship to the West. No longer merely peripheral to the main fields of interest of the Western nations, they had become in some measure the pivotal center of world affairs. Japan seized upon a large empire in Asia and the Pacific, which she retained until defeated in a long struggle against the most powerful of the Western states. China, after almost disintegrating and after passing through a cycle of revolution, emerged with radically altered institutions but, once again, as one of the strongest states of Asia. Moreover, China for the first time in her history was in a position to assume a major role in world politics.

I. NATIONALISM AND COMMUNISM IN CHINA

The overthrow of the Manchu Dynasty, accomplished with comparatively little effort in 1911, marked the beginning in China of a long period of instability and disorder that has witnessed a wide displacement of China's traditional institutions and culture.

1155

Perhaps never before in the country's history has there occurred such a transformation as during her modern revolutionary era. The Chinese Revolution falls roughly into four overlapping stages: (1) the pseudo-republic of Yüan Shih-k'ai, 1912–1916; (2) the rule of warlords and the weakening of the central government, 1916–1928; (3) the Nationalist revolution, 1923–1949; and (4) the Communist revolution, which gained momentum in the 1930's and triumphed in 1949. The second period, almost purely negative, was the natural result of the decadence that had preceded the downfall of the Manchu Dynasty. The third and fourth stages had some objectives in common and were combined for a time, although they finally came to be directly opposed to each other.

Yüan Shih-k'ai, the first President of the Republic, who tried unsuccessfully to restore the monarchy, maintained at least a semblance of unity in the state. After his death in 1916, much of China passed under the rule of independent military commanders, although a group at Peking preserved the fiction of a republican government. Some of these militarists had been officials under the Manchus; others were ex-soldiers or ex-bandits who had collected an army and taken over the administration of one or more provinces. Most of them were extortionate, and the common people of China suffered deplorably from their tyranny. China's participation in World War I at a time when the central government was unable even to put its own house in order was a factor contributing to internal confusion. At the urging of the Allied powers, the Peking government declared war on Germany in 1917, hoping to gain advantages at the peace settlement. During the war, however, Japan seized the opportunity to "assist" her weak ally, selling war materials and extending loans to China and securing economic concessions within the country. At the Paris Peace Conference the requests of the Chinese delegation were almost completely disregarded, and Japan refused to restore the Shantung Peninsula, which she had taken over from Germany.

The third stage of the Revolution is associated with the personality and program of Sun Yat-sen. Dr. Sun's part in the inauguration of the Republic in 1912 had been a brief one, but after returning to Canton, where his following was strongest, he directed a barrage of criticism against the Peking military government. The rise of warlords was not confined to the north, and Sun actually was dependent for support upon militarists in control of the Kwangtung-Kwangsi area. His party, the Kuomintang, was a small faction, and its professed principles of parliamentary democracy seemed utterly unrealistic in a "phantom Republic" ravaged by irresponsible military bands. But with remarkable swiftness the Kuomintang changed into a dynamic organization capable of making a bid for control of the state. The initiative and organizing skill for accomplishing this transformation were largely supplied from outside China, by agents of the revolutionary Communist regime in Russia.

Understandably, the Bolshevik leaders, faced with the task of consolidating their power in Russia and confronted by the hostility of the Great Powers, were eager to win support in revolutionary China. Rebuffed by the Peking government, they turned to Dr. Sun in Canton. The Third (Communist) International had organized a Far Eastern division and established at Moscow a university named after Sun Yat-sen to train Chinese revolutionaries, some of whom joined the Communist party. Although Dr. Sun rejected communism, he had hoped for the support of Western nations and welcomed the offer of Russian cooperation. In 1923 Sun and the Russian emissaries arrived at a working agreement which provided for Russian assistance and for the admission of Chinese Communists to the Kuomintang but left Sun the undisputed head of the Kuomintang party. Acknowledging that China's immediate task was to achieve national unity and free herself from the yoke of foreign imperialism, the Soviet government sent military and political advisers to Canton.

During the Moscow-Canton entente of 1923–1927, the Chinese nationalist movement acquired a disciplined leadership, clear-cut objectives, and considerable popular support. A general dissatisfaction with the dreary and corrupt rule of the military cliques, the humiliation of China at the Paris Peace Conference, and the entrenched position of the Great Powers in their spheres of interest all helped to intensify nationalist sentiment. Disillusionment following the war stimulated a spirit of revolt among young intellectuals and among the lower classes, as evidenced by the growth of labor unions in the Yangtze valley industrial cities, peasant movements, youth movements, and movements for the emancipation of women. The various dissident elements needed only effective leadership to be enlisted in a campaign for the regeneration and strengthening of China under a truly national government. Soviet advisers taught Sun Yat-sen and his associates how to supply this leadership. Under the direction of Michael Borodin, a seasoned revolutionary who had worked as an agitator in Turkey and Mexico, the Kuomintang was revamped on the model of the Russian Communist party. On the propaganda front, posters, pictures, and slogans dramatized the Kuomintang program, which was to unseat the warlords, introduce honest and democratic government, stamp out the opium habit, and promote other reforms.

By 1925 Canton had become the center of a small but effective government, which collected taxes, regulated commerce, and was developing its own "new model" army, officered by men trained at the Whampoa Academy (near Canton) under supervision of European military experts, and indoctrinated with loyalty to Sun Yat-sen and to his party. This Canton government was actually a Soviet regime without being Communist. Controlled by the high command of the Kuomintang, it provided the first example of a party dictatorship in China. Although the Canton government showed

Russian aid to the Kuomintang under Dr. Sun

Consolidation of power by the Kuomintang at Canton

Character of the Canton government

1157

vigor, it was not recognized by foreign powers, not even by Soviet Russia. Russia maintained correct relations with the Peking government, and restored some Russian concessions to its jurisdiction after Peking recognized the Soviet Union in 1924. At the same time, Russian agents were assisting Sun Yat-sen's group in preparations to overthrow the Peking regime.

The doctrines
of Sun Yat-sen

Dr. Sun did not live to see the phenomenal success of the organization that he had founded, but he left a body of doctrines as a heritage of the Kuomintang party. His most important writings were put together rather hastily during the period of Communist-Kuomintang collaboration and partly at the urging of Borodin, who recognized their value for propaganda purposes. The gist of Sun's program and political philosophy is contained in the famous *San Min Chu I* ("Three Principles of the People"), which became a sort of Bible for the Kuomintang. The Three Principles, usually translated as "Nationalism," "Democracy," and "Livelihood," have been likened to Abraham Lincoln's "government of the people, by the people, and for the people"; but there is considerable difference between the American and the Chinese interpretations of the terms. By *nationalism* Sun meant, first, the freeing of China from foreign interference and, second, the development of loyalty among the people to the state instead of to the family or the province. In his second Principle, Sun was concerned with popular sovereignty and the ideal of representative government. Recognizing that people are unequal in capacity, he believed that the chief political problem, in both China and the West, was to discover how popular sovereignty could be combined with direction by experts. The Principle of Livelihood referred to the necessity for material progress and also to social reform, rejecting Marxism but failing to outline any specific program. Sun's ideas as a whole were neither very original nor very radical nor even very clear. Democracy appeared in his conception as a rather remote goal, to be attained at the end of the revolutionary struggle. The three stages of revolution, according to Sun, would be: (1) the military stage, necessary to establish order, (2) the "tutelage" stage, devoted to training the people and with power restricted to the revolutionary leaders (the Kuomintang party), and (3) the constitutional stage, embodying representative popular government.

The death and
increased venera-
tion of Dr. Sun

In view of Dr. Sun's limitations both as a leader and as a thinker, it is remarkable that he came to be revered as the Father of the Revolution. His life ended, characteristically, on a note of futility. He had gone north in the latter part of 1924 to arrange an alliance with two of the warlords against a third, but arrived in Peking to find that a settlement had been made without his knowledge. Already in poor health, he died the following March. But when finally removed from the scene, Sun became a legendary figure to

Dr. Sun Yat-sen Surrounded by His Military Staff.

his followers, and "Sunyatsenism" proved to be a far more potent force than Dr. Sun had ever been. He left behind him a legacy of hope, and he had stirred the imagination of Chinese all over the world with the vision of a strong and free China under a republican constitution which would combine the best thought of ancient sages with modern scientific techniques. By the Kuomintang his writings and speeches were treasured as unalloyed wisdom, while their vagueness made it possible to invoke the master's authority for contradictory policies.

By 1926, when the Canton government had become strong enough to challenge the northern militarists, the Nationalist revolution entered its active phase. Kuomintang forces under command of the young general Chiang Kai-shek swept rapidly northward into the Yangtze valley and in less than six months overran half the provinces of China. The success of this "punitive expedition," however, brought to the surface a dissension that had been stirring for some time within the party. A conservative faction distrusted the Communist connection and wanted to oust Communists entirely. The radical wing, hoping to base the organization upon the support of the peasant and working classes, stressed the desirability of a concrete reform program and of continued association with the Russian advisers. Temporarily the radicals seemed to have won. Chiang Kai-shek, whose sympathies were conservative and who had suppressed radical demonstrations at Shanghai and executed Communists and suspected Communists when Kuomintang troops occupied this important city, was temporarily deprived of his command. But by midsummer of 1927 the picture had com-

Chiang Kai-shek and the triumph of conservatism

1159

pletely changed. Borodin and the other Russian advisers were dismissed; trade unionists and radicals were disciplined or driven out of the party, and some party members went into voluntary exile in Russia.

Although the reversal of direction in 1927 was startling and decisive, actually there had been little likelihood that the radicals could maintain their ascendancy. The Chinese Communists at this time numbered only about 50,000. While there were plenty of discontented peasants and a Chinese Federation of Labor claimed two and a half million members, these groups were not capable of carrying to successful conclusion the fight against the northern militarists. And the Kuomintang army was far from being a radical body. Kuomintang leaders had welcomed and benefited from Russian assistance, but now that they felt strong enough to stand alone they had no desire to serve the interests of a foreign power. There were grounds for suspecting that the Russians intended to convert the Chinese revolution into an outpost of Soviet Communism, and the discovery of a Soviet plot at Peking prompted the northern government to break off relations with Russia. In supporting the Moscow-Canton entente of 1923–1927, the Soviet leaders, hoping for the speedy coming of world revolution, had gambled and lost. But they had provided the spark without which the Kuomintang might never have been fired into action.

After the purge of the radical wing, the Kuomintang leaders proceeded rapidly with their plan to extend their authority throughout the country. From this time forward the dominant figure of the party was Chiang Kai-shek, whose return to a position of influence was automatic with the triumph of the conservatives. In addition to his repute as a military commander, Chiang enjoyed the prestige of belonging to the "ruling family" of the Revolution, through his marriage to the American-educated Soong Mei-ling, a sister of Madame Sun Yat-sen. Kuomintang forces pushed on, without too much difficulty, through the territories of discredited military governors, and occupied Peking in 1928. The Nationalists renamed the city *Pei-p'ing* ("Northern Peace") and moved their capital to Nanking, in keeping with pledges made in the early period of the Revolution.

The task of national reconstruction confronting the Kuomintang leaders was a far more difficult undertaking than the seizure of power had been. Even the maintenance of power was not easy, as remnants of the warlord regimes lingered on in various parts of China. Although Kuomintang supremacy still depended upon military support, the party claimed that it had completed the first, or military, stage of Dr. Sun's formula of revolution and had inaugurated the second stage—that of political "tutelage." In spite of its anti-Communist orientation, the structure both of the Kuomintang and of the government which it set up at Nanking followed closely the Soviet pattern. The party was a hierarchy, reaching from the smallest units, or cells, through district and provincial bodies up to the Central Executive Committee at the top. The President of the National Government and the members of his Council of State were selected by the Central Executive Committee of the Kuomintang, of which the key member was Chiang Kai-shek. At the central, provincial, and local levels the government embodied, not democracy, but a party dictatorship.

A number of important accomplishments can be credited to the Nationalist regime at Nanking. The portions of China which were brought under its jurisdiction became more unified than at any time since the eighteenth century, and China's prestige in the eyes of the world was enhanced. The Nationalists promptly secured diplomatic recognition and financial assistance from abroad, and they made progress, although slowly, toward revision of the unequal treaties. Following the lead of the United States, the Great Powers agreed to relinquish their control over customs duties, granting tariff autonomy to China by 1929. Nationalist forces had occupied foreign concessions in several of the Yangtze valley cities, and a few of the ports that had been leased to foreign powers were voluntarily returned to China soon after the Nanking government was established. It was more difficult to persuade the Great Powers to surrender their privileges of extraterritoriality, a step not taken by the United States and Great Britain until 1943.

Accomplishments
of the Nationalist
regime

While progress undeniably occurred during the era of Nationalist rule, the defects of the regime became more and more serious. Radical elements had been expelled before the triumph of the Kuomintang, and even moderate liberals were given scant encouragement. Originating as a party of revolution, the Kuomintang when in power neglected to carry out the social reforms that were necessary to relieve the suffering and win the allegiance of the common people. Very little was done to improve the condition of poor tenants and farm laborers, even though Sun Yat-sen had specified that assistance to these classes was a primary objective of the "Principle of Livelihood." In command of a one-party government and eager to perpetuate its own authority, the Kuomintang employed coercive measures against those who opposed it. It maintained secret police, disguised under the title of "Bureau of Investigation and Statistics." To indoctrinate potential party members it organized a tightly disciplined Youth Corps (ironically named the *San Min Chu I* after Sun's "Three Principles"). The Nationalist regime seemed to be preparing the Chinese people less for constitutional democracy than for a permanent condition of tutelage.

Defects of the
Nationalist regime

The downfall of the Kuomintang in China after a rule of twenty years was caused by three factors: (1) failure of the Kuomintang regime to solve the problems of Chinese society, (2) unrelenting opposition from the Chinese Communists, who ultimately set up a

1161

rival government, and (3) the long war beginning with the Japanese invasion of 1937, which drained the country's resources, demoralized the people, and promoted the chaotic conditions so favorable to the spread of communism. The struggle against the Communists began almost as soon as the Kuomintang had established its government at Nanking and was a continuous process even during the most successful years of the Nationalist period. Following the rupture with the Kuomintang in 1927, the Communist party had been driven underground but extended its activities in both rural and urban areas of central and southern China, and in Kiangsi province it organized a rival government in the form of a Soviet Republic. Almost annihilated by Kuomintang forces in a series of military campaigns, the Communist leaders turned the desperate struggle to their advantage by inciting revolutionary aspirations among the depressed peasantry and by developing the technique of guerrilla warfare into a fine art. Mao Tse-tung was the key personality behind both of these policies.

The son of a relatively well-to-do peasant, Mao Tse-tung as a youth had rebelled against landlordism and the tyranny of parental authority. One of a dozen men who founded the Chinese Communist Party in 1921, he became a deputy member of the Central Executive Committee of the Kuomintang and was entrusted by the Communists with the task of peasant organization. A report prepared for the Chinese Communist Party in 1927 on peasant revolutionary activity in Hunan (south central China) provides the clue to Mao's strategy of revolution and is prophetic of his ultimate program for China. Already he was instigating direct action among the lowliest tenants: (1) forming village co-operative associations, (2) smashing temples and burning the wooden idols for fuel, (3) intimidating and assaulting "bad gentry." "A revolution is not the same as inviting people to dinner," he wrote. "A rural revolution is a revolution by which the peasantry overthrows the authority of the feudal landlord class." "In a very short time . . . several hundred million peasants will rise like a tornado or tempest, a force so extraordinarily swift and violent that no power, however great, will be able to suppress it." In sharp disagreement with both the Chinese and Russian party leaders, Mao was convinced that whoever won the peasants would win China.

Threatened with extinction by Chiang's superior troops, Mao Tse-tung conceived and executed the famous "Long March" of October 1934 to October 1935—a mass migration across 6,000 miles of difficult terrain and one of the most amazing exploits in military history. Of the 90,000 men who slipped through Chiang's lines in southwestern China, not more than 20,000 reached Yenan, in northern Shensi Province, which was to be the Communists' headquarters until their final victory in the civil war. Shattering as the experience had been, it served to weld the survivors into a solid group of tested loyalty and toughness, relying upon their own ingenuity rather than upon directives from Moscow, and it established Mao Tse-tung as undisputed leader of the party. He had demonstrated his tactics of "retreat in order to advance" and his ability to sustain and renew his forces directly from the countryside while the cities and economic apparatus of the state were in the hands of his enemies. Gradually the Communist region of the northwest acquired the attributes of a separate state, with a fluid political structure and well-organized military units. In expanding the area of their influence, the Communists' chief asset was their introduction of reforms which the Nanking government had promised but never fulfilled. They tackled the land problem directly, breaking up great estates, forcing rent reductions, establishing land banks and cooperative societies, building irrigation works, and educating ignorant peasants in better methods of cultivation and crop control. Their immediate and practical assistance to farmers who had been oppressed by high rents and high taxes and their success in eliminating graft in the region under their administration enabled them to compete successfully with the Kuomintang regime for popular favor. The Communists also strengthened their position by calling for national resistance against Japanese aggression, to which Chiang Kai-shek, intent upon crushing Communism, had offered only half-hearted opposition.

When, in line with the Soviet strategy of fostering antifascist "popular fronts," the Chinese Communists appeared cooperative, pressure within the Kuomintang induced Chiang Kai-shek to enter into an alliance with them to halt the common enemy, Japan. But this had the unfortunate effect of encouraging the Japanese militarists to make war. Faced with the prospect of a united China, they

War with Japan

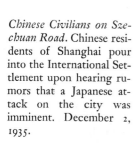

Chinese Civilians on Szechuan Road. Chinese residents of Shanghai pour into the International Settlement upon hearing rumors that a Japanese attack on the city was imminent. December 2, 1935.

goaded their government into launching an attack in the Peiping area (July 7, 1937). This was the beginning of a fateful conflict which soon expanded into World War II.

The course of the war revealed that China was a far stronger nation than she had been forty years earlier. Even though the mighty Japanese military machine eventually occupied the coastal cities and almost all of eastern China and forced the Nationalist government to move its capital far inland to Chungking, it was never able to conquer the entire country. Actually, after the United States entered the war against Japan and began to supply China with substantial military aid, the Nationalist government contributed little to the war effort. Chiang Kai-shek, unsure of the loyalty of his own staff and determined to hoard his military resources, ignored the American advisers who tried to prod him into action. While doing little against the Japanese, he kept an army of half a million men in the northwest to isolate the Communist "Border Region" government at Yenan. American negotiations attempting to bring the Yenan and Chungking regimes into a coalition government failed because Chiang insisted that the Communists give up their separate command and put all military forces at his disposal, a condition they regarded as equivalent to a death sentence. Without the advantage of foreign aid or help from Chungking, Communist guerrillas successfully penetrated Japanese lines and gradually secured control of much of northern China. At the close of the war when the Nationalists, assisted by an American airlift, occupied the principal cities, Communist units held the countryside, and they seized stores of Japanese arms and ammunition that Russian troops withdrawing from Manchuria had conveniently left behind. After the Japanese surrender, China's international conflict gradually turned into a civil war.

The Nationalists had formulated plans for reform and promised to replace the party dictatorship with a democratic representative

Chinese Communist Artillery Units in Action near Peking.

government. They drafted a constitution and early in 1947 conducted elections for a National Assembly, which dutifully chose Chiang Kai-shek as President of the Republic. But while the Nationalists were inaugurating a democratic constitution for China, they were rapidly being dispossessed from the country by the advance of Communist armies. In 1949 the southerly retreat of Nationalist forces turned into a rout that ended with all the mainland in the hands of the Communists. By 1950 the jurisdiction of President Chiang's government was confined to the island of Taiwan (Formosa).

Although the conquest of China by the Communists represented a military victory, it was greatly facilitated by the failure of the Nationalists to win the confidence of any substantial segment of the population. The promise of democratic constitutionalism was too little and too late, and the long anticipated social and economic reforms were not forthcoming at all. They were vitiated by inefficiency and corruption within the Kuomintang party. Hoarding, profiteering, and a runaway inflation added to the impoverishment of the very groups that were most in need of help. The impression spread rapidly that many of the Kuomintang leaders were primarily interested in feathering their own nests and were no better than the old warlords of the 1920's. So low had the prestige of the party fallen that it could summon very little assistance in its hour of peril. From the purely military standpoint, the Nationalists committed the grave mistake of attempting to recover the north and even to drive the Communists out of Manchuria before the Nanking government had consolidated its hold upon central and southern China. By extending their lines too far they weakened their position and made its collapse the more catastrophic.

After their victory over the Nationalists, the Communist leaders moved rapidly to secure their hold upon the vast territory of China. In October 1949 they proclaimed The People's Republic of China with its capital in Peking. On Organic Law, promulgated as a temporary frame of government, was replaced by a formal constitution in 1954. The Constitution of The People's Republic, like that of Soviet Russia, combines the language and forms of parliamentary democracy with the principle of domination by the Communist party. Nominally, supreme authority is vested in an All-China People's Congress, which meets annually and which, in addition to enacting laws, elects the major officials, including the President (Chairman of the Republic). The Constitution contains a Bill of Rights which covers the whole field of individual liberties, recognizes equality of the sexes, declares all persons over 18 years of age eligible to vote and to hold office, and even guarantees the ownership of private property. However, it leaves the application of these rights very tentative by giving the government power to punish "traitors, counterrevolutionaries, and bureaucratic capitalists."

Generalissimo Chiang Kai-shek.

The People's Republic of China; the Constitution of 1954

Mao Tse-tung at a Desk in His Cave Headquarters during the Communist Advances in 1948.

The "Democratic Dictatorship"

The Communist regime in China is defined officially not as a dictatorship of the proletariat but as a "People's Democratic Dictatorship." Allegedly it came into existence as the result of a coalition of classes, namely peasants, workers, petty bourgeoisie, and "national bourgeoisie." The inclusion of the last two classes marked a departure from orthodox Marxism and an attempt to win the support of financial and industrial elements whose cooperation was essential to bolstering the economy. Businessmen who qualified as "Communist" or "national" capitalists by being willing to work with the new government were allowed to retain their properties temporarily, but found their affairs subjected to rigid control, and in 1956 the national bourgeoisie were formally expropriated. The Central Committee of the Communist party or Chairman Mao himself has determined public policies, the permissible limits of debate, and the operation of organs of government.

Unique features of the Chinese Communist revolution

The Chinese Communist revolution has proved to be one of the most far-reaching and dynamic in history. Adapting theoretical Marxism to immediate problems and blending it with elements of China's traditional culture pattern, the revolution reflects the dominating personality of Party Chairman Mao Tse-tung. Throughout his turbulent career Mao's policies have varied, sometimes appearing to shift erratically, after his accession to power no less than before. In defying the Kuomintang, Russian advisers, Japan, and doubters within his own party he displayed a fixity of purpose combined with versatility and flexibility in tactics that enabled him to outmaneuver his opponents. China's is the first large-scale and successful revolution to be founded on peasant support and directed by a leader from the peasant class. In this respect it contrasts with the revolution of Lenin and Stalin, which entailed expropriation and forcible suppression of the peasants. No less than the Soviet revolu-

1166

tion it aimed at creating a new society and, again in contrast to the Russian, after 25 years it had not yet subsided into a conservative stage.

The economic transformation of China since 1949 is an impressive aspect of the Communist revolution, all the more remarkable when viewed against the previous retarded condition of the country. As in India, industrialization was given high priority and—in contrast to India—the government possessed sufficient coercive power to effect rapid change. Geological surveys have revealed mineral resources far in excess of previous estimates: gigantic deposits of iron ore and coal, the indispensable ingredients of heavy industrial growth; oil reserves of more than 2 billion tons; and adequate supplies of manganese, tungsten, antimony, tin, copper, and aluminum. By 1960 China's furnaces were producing almost as much steel as was made in France; her pig iron production exceeded West Germany's as well as Great Britain's. Also by 1960 the output of electric power had been increased ten times, even though many hydroelectric projects were still in the planning stage. The acreage of irrigated land more than doubled between 1949 and 1960, and the same period witnessed an extensive forestation program highly significant for soil and water conservation. A complex system of dams and reservoirs in the Yellow River valley was designed to end the danger of flooding in this region and to provide a larger and surer crop yield—of rice as well as wheat. These ambitious projects have not been entirely completed. Railroad mileage has doubled but is still far from adequate, especially since the objective is a wide dispersion of industry hitherto concentrated in Manchuria and the eastern seaboard. With Soviet technical assistance the Chinese trained their own engineers capable of designing precision tools. Their manufactures include such items as cars, trucks, and jet planes; also electronic, surgical, and scientific instruments.

More profound than the changes in the scope and tempo of industrialization has been the agrarian revolution. The character of agriculture and of the society engaged in it has been altered radically, through successive stages. The first phase of land reform was simply expropriation of the landlords, many of whom were killed. Then, the newly created peasant proprietors were urged to form cooperatives, pooling the resources of one or more villages. The next step was a drive for collective farms, communally owned and directed by party members or supporters. This was accomplished with remarkable swiftness, between 1955 and 1957, by which time more than 90 per cent of the family holdings had been collectivized. Although Chinese farmers undoubtedly "volunteered" to join cooperatives because they were given little choice, the government relied primarily upon psychological and social pressure, employing what Mao has described as "persuasive reasoning," and there was no liquidation of resisting peasants. But without waiting for the collec-

Economic objectives and prospects

The agrarian revolution and the "Great Leap Forward"

tives to prove themselves, the party leaders in 1958 announced a third stage of the Communist agrarian pattern. It called for the merging of rural co-operatives and collective farms into large communes, which, it was claimed, embodied the principle of ownership by the whole people rather than by a single community. The purpose of the communes was to provide a mobile labor force to implement an overly ambitious program of rapid industrialization advertised as the "Great Leap Forward" and to increase food production. For a variety of reasons—including the callousness and ineptitude of local directors and a prolonged drought in the Yellow River valley that brought poor harvests in 1959 and 1960—the Great Leap Forward turned out to be a disaster. Food shortages necessitated the importation of grain; the demoralization of labor and the drainage of capital resources caused a severe industrial depression; and the Second Five-Year Plan, scheduled for the period 1958–1962, had to be abandoned. Forced to revise its tactics drastically, the government in 1962 announced its intention to give agriculture top priority for the immediate future. While the communes were retained and their number increased, they were reduced in size, a degree of ownership and management was restored to local production teams, and farmers were permitted to cultivate small private plots and sell on the open market. By 1965 the danger of famine had passed, and a Third Five-Year Plan, emphasizing both the expansion of heavy industry and the development and modernization of agriculture, was launched in 1966.

It is still difficult to assess the character of Chinese society and culture under the Communists. Probably never before in history have so many people been changed so much in so short a time. Intensive efforts to provide medical facilities, improve standards of hygiene and sanitation in the cities and villages, stamp out opium addiction, and eliminate prostitution have raised the level of public

Workers' School. Railway workers in Northern China attend classes as part of the state's attempt to extend education.

health. China is still poor in comparison with developed Western countries. Per capita income scarcely exceeds that of India, but a significant difference is that instead of being concentrated at the top, it is fairly evenly distributed. There is no doubt that the bulk of the Chinese people are better off in basic material necessities than they have been for many centuries. A huge and steadily expanding population heightened the difficulty of fulfilling these needs, but through vigorous campaigns for birth control the rate of increase has been reduced to an acceptable level—about 1½ per cent a year. A government report released in Peking in 1972 listed China's population as slightly less than 700 million. Chinese officials, however, admit that they do not have reliable statistics. Some estimates place the total population as high as 850 million.

A significant aspect of social change is the demise of the centuries-old patriarchal family structure, which had already begun to disintegrate. A marriage law of 1950 gave women equal rights with men in respect to choice of spouse, conjugal privileges and obligations, and divorce. Legal equality between the sexes led not to the disappearance of the family as an institution but to enhanced status for the single-unit monogamous family. Although women have probably not attained complete liberation even in China, they have been admitted to most occupations and professions that formerly were man's preserve. Abolition of the double standard, emphasis upon productive labor, and attachment of social stigma to extramarital sexual relations have brought a stricter adherence to conventional morality in the society of Communist China than is found in the bourgeois societies of Europe and America.

Changes in the family and the position of women

To refashion and extend education, the government established not only full-time day schools but also "half-study half-work" schools, evening and correspondence schools, factory schools, and others. An attempt to romanize the complex Chinese written char-

Education and social services

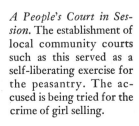

A People's Court in Session. The establishment of local community courts such as this served as a self-liberating exercise for the peasantry. The accused is being tried for the crime of girl selling.

acters was abandoned, but the characters have been simplified to make them easier to learn. Officials claim that less than 10 per cent of the population is now illiterate. A prime objective of educational reform was to combine theory with practice and study with physical activity, for teachers as well as students. Insisting that intellectuals can learn from peasants and workers and that the purpose of education is to prepare one to serve society, the Communists repudiated completely the classical Chinese tradition of a scholarly elite. Also, by supplementing a scarce supply of skilled professionals with semiskilled trainees, they have been able to expand the country's social services, which include child day-care centers, homes for the aged, hospitals and mobile clinics employing both up-to-date Western and traditional Chinese medicines and techniques.

Of course there is a darker side to the picture of China's changing society, and a high price has been paid for rapid material progress. The party chiefs used ruthless means to seize power and to keep it. Violence and terror, however, have not been the typical weapons either of party discipline or of popular coercion. There has been no mass liquidation of "kulaks" or of bourgeoisie. Psychological pressure, "thought control," and "reform through labor" have been employed regularly in the effort to remold recalcitrants. Political indoctrination is effected through the mass communication media, entirely controlled by the government, and is a primary aim of education. In conformity with the slogan, "Let politics take command," schools were required to base their curricula on "the thought of Mao Tse-tung." Undoubtedly intellectual freedom has been restricted; but the common people, though constantly exposed to indoctrination, are encouraged to participate in discussion and policy formation at the local level, and they seem to be less intimidated or inhibited than under previous regimes. At the same time, the growth of a huge body of government and party functionaries—evolving into a new elite with its own stratified hierarchy and set apart from the ordinary citizens—jeopardized the Communist ideal of a classless society. Attempting to check the drift toward bureaucracy, party leaders subjected their agents and state officials to corrective discipline—requiring them to attend study sessions and "struggle meetings," periodically assessing their performance and fitness, and, through a program of "downward transfer," assigning them to work as manual laborers at the lowliest tasks.

Chinese Communist ideology has evolved some distinctive characteristics of its own. Mao's disciples acclaim him as the greatest living exponent of Marxism-Leninism, and they affirm that the Chinese Communist revolution—stemming from the peasants and gaining momentum through guerrilla warfare—is the exemplar to be followed by other peoples of Asia and Africa. Like most Marxists, Chinese Communists defend their program as the logical culmination of historic forces. Mao Tse-tung's interpretation of Chinese history is vivid and pointed, though boldly oversimplified. A period of some

Suppression of individualism and the bureaucratization of society

Ideology; Mao's interpretation of history

Left: *The Cultural Revolution at the Grass Roots.* Agricultural workers have erected red painted signs with quotations from Chairman Mao and carry copies of his "Quotations" into the fields with them. Right: *A Reservoir and Irrigation Project in Chekiang Province, eastern China.* Labor-saving machinery is still in short supply.

3000 years, reaching to the middle of the nineteenth century, he designates as "feudal," referring to the dominance of the scholar-gentry elite. He identifies the class struggle with recurring though unsuccessful peasant uprisings, including the nineteenth-century Taiping rebellion. There is a strong flavor of nationalism in Mao's ideology. He invokes reverence for China's "splendid historical heritage" and "glorious revolutionary tradition," and pays tribute to some pre-Communist reformers and to Sun Yat-sen, whose widow—Chiang Kai-shek's sister-in-law—holds one of the two vice chairmanships of the People's Republic. Another distinctive feature of Mao's teaching is his rejection of the historical determinism implicit in orthodox Marxism. He stresses the importance of ideas and of human will and resolution in shaping events, holding that these nonmaterial factors can themselves become an objective force in history.[1]

The rapid unification of China under a totalitarian regime has drastically altered the power relationships in Asia and the Far East. With a powerful army at their disposal, the Communists re-established Chinese jurisdiction over important areas that had been lost during the decline of the Manchu Dynasty. They took possession of Manchuria, retained Sinkiang in the far west, and installed their forces in Tibet. And while augmenting China's national prestige they posed as the champions of Asian peoples against Western imperialism, assisting revolutionary movements against the British in Malaya and against the French in Indochina.

China's internal developments and policies have been affected by her relations with other countries. At the outset the greatest threat

China's foreign relations

[1] H. L. Boorman, "Mao Tse-tung as Historian," *The China Quarterly*, Oct.-Dec., 1966, pp. 82–105.

Blast Furnaces at Anshan. The major steel producing center in southern Manchuria, it is a testament to China's growing industrial strength.

to the Communist regime seemed to lie with the United States, which had supported Chiang Kai-shek throughout the war, continued its alliance with him, and financed his military establishment of 600,000 troops on the island of Taiwan—within 100 miles of the mainland and regarded by both the Nationalists and the Communists as an integral part of China. When the Chinese intervened in the Korean war in 1950, the United States government employed remnants of Kuomintang armies in Burma in an attempt to invade China's adjacent Yunnan Province. Under successive administrations Washington's policy seemed to be compounded of two contradictory assumptions: (1) that the Communists were fanatical bunglers who could not retain control of their own country, and (2) that they were superdemons who threatened to conquer the world. The United States withheld diplomatic recognition from Peking, blocked its admission to the United Nations, embargoed American trade with the mainland, and installed a ring of military bases around East Asia. Through its "containment" policy, implemented by a network of defensive alliances, the United States sought to isolate China, and effectively isolated its own citizens from contact with an important area of the world.

The simultaneous isolation of China and Russia—as the Cold War alienated the U.S.S.R. from her erstwhile Western allies—at first strengthened the fraternal and ideological bonds between the two large Communist states. In 1950 their representatives signed a thirty-year treaty of "friendship, alliance, and mutual assistance," which invalidated the 1945 treaty between the U.S.S.R. and the Chinese Nationalists. The preamble of China's 1954 Constitution reaffirms "indestructible friendship" with the Soviet Union. China relied heavily upon Russia for technical assistance in economic development. Between 1950 and 1955 China's exchange with the Soviet-bloc countries increased from 26 per cent to 75 per cent of her total foreign trade. By the late 1950's, however, there was evidence of disaffection between the two Communist giants. Differences flared into the open at the Moscow international conference of Communist parties in 1960 and led swiftly to deterioration in both diplomatic and economic relations. By 1962, 61 per cent of China's foreign trade had shifted to countries outside the Communist bloc. The Sino-Soviet rift is attributable to a number of causes. The Chinese resented the Russians' failure to fulfill their aid agreements, including the promise of help in developing atomic weapons. Other factors were the inevitable rivalries of great-power politics and conflicting national territorial ambitions. The Chinese hinted at the eventual rectification of their frontiers at Russia's expense, and both China and the Soviet Union deployed large numbers of troops along their common border from Central Asia to Manchuria. In 1969 violent clashes occurred between Russian and Chinese troops in Sinkiang in the far west and along the Ussuri River in the northeast. By the next year tension had eased somewhat, and a new trade agreement was signed in November 1970. Probably the most fundamental source of disagreement between the two countries is ideological. Peking accused the Russians of abandoning the cause of world revolution against imperialism, condemned Khrushchev's policy of peaceful coexistence and the test ban treaty of 1963, claimed that Moscow had joined a counterrevolutionary "Holy Alliance" with the United States, India, Yugoslavia, and others to encircle China, and even charged that Soviet leaders were working "hand in glove" with American imperialists in the Vietnam war. The breach between Peking and Moscow reflected the differences in outlook between the heirs of an old revolution and the directors of one still comparatively young. In Mao Tse-tung's view Soviet Russia, now a have nation, had succumbed to revisionism and was taking the primrose path to accommodation with the capitalist powers for the sake of security and the gratification of consumer demands.

Mao Tse-tung and his associates have striven to avoid close dependence on any other state, Communist or not. Although they have broken decisively with much of China's past, they adhere to the ancient tradition that viewed China as a unique and indestructible community, proudly self-sustaining. The aid China received from Russia during the 1950's came chiefly in the form of loans rather than gifts, and in spite of slim capital reserves the loans were repaid, sometimes ahead of schedule. Mao's determination to preserve an independent stance in the face of external dangers is also illustrated by the widely acclaimed Great Proletarian Cultural Revolution of 1966–1969, the most severe upheaval that China has experienced since the Communist seizure of power.

Before 1965 the Communist movement in China had presented the appearance of remarkable harmony within the party and solidarity among its leadership, dominated by Mao Tse-tung but including members who, like him, were veterans of the Long March and had grown old together in the revolutionary cause. Now, an increasingly bitter struggle within the party and state structure re-

China's determination to remain independent

vealed the existence of serious cleavages. Under a barrage of charges ranging from "hedonism" to "revisionism," "anti-party activity," and "taking the road to capitalism," scores of officials were demoted, consigned to obscurity, or forced to make public confession of their "crimes." The purge, which shook the party hierarchy severely, numbered among its targets such prominent figures as Liu Shao-ch'i, President of the Republic since 1959 and long regarded as Mao's heir apparent, the Secretary General of the Party, and the Army Chief of Staff. Into the spotlight as Mao's most trusted comrade stepped Marshal Lin Piao, Defense Minister and Commander of the People's Liberation Army, a man noted for his industry and integrity and also for his austere fanaticism. As the stepped-up purification campaign met with stubborn resistance, Mao closed the schools and urged students to organize themselves into units of Red Guards (formally inaugurated at Peking in August 1966) and devote their energies to ferreting out enemies of the revolution. China was treated to the unprecedented spectacle of mobs of teen-age youths denouncing their elders, smashing ancient monuments, invading private homes, and noisily demanding unswerving devotion to the thought of Mao Tse-tung.

Origins of the
Cultural Revolu-
tion: Mao vs. Liu

Although the violent eruption took most observers by surprise, it is clear that a struggle between rival factions within the party had been in progress ever since the controversy over the Great Leap Forward of 1958 and its subsequent failure. Liu Shao-ch'i, an opponent of radical experimentation, in 1959 replaced Mao as President of the Republic and worked assiduously during the next six years to restore the country's shaken economy. Meanwhile Mao sought to strengthen his own position by an intensive campaign of political indoctrination carried out among the masses and, with the help of the fanatical Defense Minister Lin Piao, within the army. The breach be-

A Red Guard Demonstration in Peking. Middle school students display their solidarity with the Cultural Revolution by waving copies of the book of quotations from Chairman Mao. The slogan painted on the wall proclaims: "We are not only able to destroy the old world, we are able to build a new world instead—Mao Tse-tung."

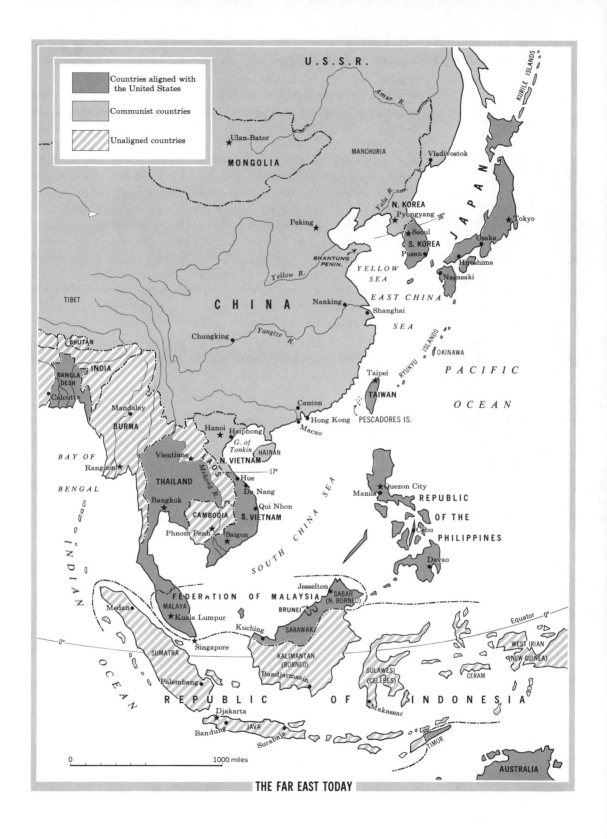

THE FAR EAST TODAY

tween Party Chairman Mao and State Chairman Liu was brought to a climax by Chinese reaction to American expansion of the Vietnam war in 1965. Liu Shao-ch'i, viewing escalation as a prelude to an attack on China, called for united action by Socialist countries, necessarily including the Soviet Union, to intervene in defense of North Vietnam. Mao, backed by Commander Lin Piao, rejected any suggestion of collaboration with Soviet "revisionists." Arguing that a people's "war of liberation" like that in Vietnam must be fought by the people directly involved, he insisted that China should not permit herself to be drawn into the conflict unless attacked and that she should concentrate on her own internal development. He was determined to "bypass the Soviet Union on its way to Communism" and apparently felt that the time was ripe for another "leap forward." By August 1966 the Mao-Lin faction, supported by Premier Chou En-lai, had attained dominance in the Central Committee of the party, although it by no means controlled the entire party hierarchy, the state apparatus, or even all units of the army.

While Mao's firm hand undoubtedly played a significant part in averting a direct military confrontation with the United States, he had several objectives in precipitating the Cultural Revolution. Desiring to reform the party both in personnel and in structure, he temporarily disrupted it completely. He aimed at smashing the bureaucracy emerging in both the state and the party. He viewed with misgivings the tendency of a bureaucracy to become rigid and complacent, creating its own managerial class more "expert" than "red." He feared that the prospect of material success had brought a relaxation of effort, which China could ill afford in view of her still unrealized potential and her weak military position. Seeing China as "poor and blank," he warned that decades of austerity and sacrifice on the part of the people would be necessary. Above all he was determined to keep the revolution from losing its fervor, and to this end was willing to sacrifice immediate material benefits. Meeting resistance within the bureaucracy and from party members, he turned to the nation's youth, who were exhorted by slogans to undertake their own Long March and to "learn revolution-making by making revolution." Apparently Mao's ultimate objective was to create a direct and permanent working relationship between the party's top leadership and the masses, eliminating as far as possible the middle levels of authority. To promote an "open party consolidation movement" he encouraged the formation of Revolutionary Committees combining party and nonparty members, and put them in charge of factories, local and provincial governments, and even important departments of the central government. He hoped to replace the Soviet's dual system of parallel state and party structures that was developing in China with a flexible but unified system.

Chairman Mao Tse-tung. Shown here with his then "closest comrade" Marshal Lin Piao (Defense Minister and Vice Chairman of the Republic who was purged in 1971). Premier Chou En-lai stands behind them.

The attempt to achieve such radical goals brought not only resistance but a condition of chaos bordering on anarchy. Strikes in major industrial centers, disruption of the transport system, and widespread disorders in rural areas placed China's economic gains in jeopardy. At the same time the Chinese found themselves isolated diplomatically, even in the Communist world. Excesses committed by Red Guards and bands of "Revolutionary Rebels," leading to the outbreak of civil war in some provinces in 1968, made it imperative for Mao and Chou En-lai to stem the revolutionary tide. They called on the People's Liberation Army to restore order, and the party line shifted to a denunciation of extremists. Lin Piao, a prime instrument of the Cultural Revolution and named as Mao's successor in a new party constitution of 1969, fell into disgrace. Reportedly he was killed in an airplane crash while attempting to defect to Siberia in September 1971.

In spite of its ugly aspects, its toll of lives and property, the Proletarian Cultural Revolution accomplished some of its objectives. At the top level the struggle was political, psychological, and ideological rather than lethal. Unlike most revolutions that have witnessed intense convulsions, the Cultural Revolution did not destroy its protagonists, nor many of its antagonists. Testifying to rapid economic recovery was a record high output of food grains in 1970–1972, an annual industrial growth rate of about 10 per cent, and the launching of a Fifth Five-Year Plan in January 1971. In the midst of her domestic crisis China succeeded in producing a hydrogen bomb (June 1967), far earlier than Western experts had thought possible. There is no doubt that Mao had succeeded in inspiring enthusiasm for his leadership and for his policies. More dubious is his belief in the possibility of a permanent revolution. China, now about 20 per cent urban, has begun to create her own bourgeois class, and it is unlikely that a Chinese bourgeoisie will differ fundamentally from its counterpart in other countries.

The Peking government restored diplomatic relations ruptured during the Cultural Revolution and proceeded to win recognition from a rapidly growing number of states. The end of China's isolation was dramatically demonstrated by her rapprochement with the United States and by her admission to the United Nations in 1971 on her own terms—the simultaneous expulsion of the Chinese Nationalists. President Nixon's decision to cultivate cordial relations with his inveterate ideological enemies and hold summit meetings with them in Peking in February 1972 was prompted by several considerations, aside from the inescapable fact that the People's Republic of China had become a military power, equipped with nuclear bombs and missiles. By offering trade concessions to both China and Russia he hoped to play one against the other and perhaps also to induce them to put pressure on Hanoi for a settlement of the Indochina war on American terms. His hopes rested on slender

1177

foundations. The Sino-Soviet split was never irreparable, and acquiescence by China in a policy of coexistence with "imperialists" would remove one bone of contention between her and the Soviets. China still needed Russian assistance to speed her technological development, and neither of the great Communist states was willing to see its North Vietnam ally destroyed. One reason why the Chinese leaders had agreed to a summit meeting with Mr. Nixon was his previous announcement that he planned a gradual withdrawal of American forces from Asia. Also, both Russia and China had become concerned over the growing military potential of Japan, presently allied with the United States.

2. THE CLIMAX OF IMPERIALISM AND THE BEGINNING OF A NEW ERA IN JAPAN

While China was in the throes of revolutionary struggle, Japan was enjoying relative stability and increasing prosperity. The transformations which characterized the Meiji Restoration had been accomplished without seriously disturbing the structure of Japanese society. Before 1914 Japan had enlarged her territories, acquired the basis for a strong industrial economy, and finally found herself in a position to seek hegemony in the Far East.

The ascendancy of Japan by 1914

The Japanese government entered the war against Germany in 1914, nominally out of regard for the Anglo-Japanese alliance but actually from a desire to secure Kiaochow Bay and the German concessions in the Shantung Peninsula. The Japanese also seized the German outposts in the Pacific north of the equator—the Marshall, Caroline, and Mariana Islands. Japan showed little interest in the Western phases of the war, but utilized to the utmost the opportunities presented by China's weakness and by the involvement of the Western powers in the titanic struggle in Europe. Japan obtained Peking's permission to extend her economic interests in Manchuria and Inner Mongolia and to provide capital for industrial development in the Yangtze valley, and secured further guaranties of her interests by secret treaties with her Western allies.

Results of participation in World War I

The success of Japan's policy of exerting diplomatic and economic pressure was demonstrated at the Peace Conference of 1919. The Chinese delegation naturally demanded the restoration of Shantung, a request entirely consonant with Wilsonian principles. The Japanese, however, refused to comply, and Wilson did not press the matter vigorously, partly because another Japanese objective of a less questionable character had been defeated. The Japanese had asked for a declaration endorsing the principle of "the equality of nations and the just treatment of their nationals." On this issue the Chinese and Japanese stood together, supported also by the representatives of several European states. But the fear that such a declaration would conflict with the policy of limiting Orien-

Japan's victories and defeats at the Peace Conference

tal immigration led the Americans and British to oppose it when the matter was put to a vote in the League of Nations Commission. The Western statesmen rebuffed Japan when she was supporting a moral issue entirely consistent with the ideals for which the war had been fought, but they yielded to her on the Shantung question where her claims had no moral justification whatever. Japan was allowed to retain, as mandates under the League of Nations, the North Pacific islands that she had taken from Germany.

In spite of having plucked the fruits of imperialism, Japan after World War I seemed to be moving in a liberal direction, both in domestic affairs and in her international relations. The antiwar sentiment which became prevalent for a short time in much of the Western world was manifest, to a lesser degree, in Japan and provoked a revulsion against military leadership. Japan had been associated with the foremost Western democracies during the war; she had been one of the "Big Five" at the Paris Peace Conference; and—in contrast to Wilson's own United States—she had signed the Versailles Treaty and joined the League of Nations. Twice before in their history the Japanese had revealed a capacity for adopting what seemed to be the most effective and up-to-date institutions in the world as they knew it, and many of their leaders were persuaded that democracy was essential for progress in the twentieth century. Even purely from the standpoint of strengthening Japan as a state, there was much to be said for the democratic thesis. Japanese statesmen were impressed by the fact that autocratic and militaristic Germany had been defeated and autocratic Russia had collapsed in revolution, while the apparently weaker democratic nations had been victorious. And, although few of these statesmen were convinced democrats in the full sense of the term, they were at least desirous of retaining the good will of the democratic powers which seemed to be in command of the world's destiny at the moment.

During much of the 1920's Japan's international policy was on the whole conciliatory, amounting to a partial reversal of her earlier aggressiveness. This is illustrated by her part in the Washington Conference of 1921–1922, which produced a Naval Arms Limitation Agreement, a Nine-Power "Open Door" Treaty concerning China, and a Four-Power Pacific Pact. The Conference had been summoned by the United States largely because of American fear that Japan, with the increased industrial and military potential she had acquired during the war, was endangering the balance of power in the Far East. The Japanese accepted a limitation of Japan's battleship tonnage to a figure three-fifths that of the United States and of Britain, and agreed to terminate their alliance of twenty years' standing with Great Britain. The Four-Power Pact which replaced the alliance was based on nothing more substantial than the promise of friendly consultation on problems of the Pacific and

1179

pledges to maintain the *status quo* in regard to fortifications in this area. The Nine-Power Treaty affirmed the principle of the Open Door in China, giving the term a somewhat broader definition than it had had before, and assured China that the signatory powers would seek no further spheres of interest in her dominions. The treaty actually restored nothing to China, but the Japanese delegates, in private conferences with the Chinese, promised that their government would withdraw its troops from Shantung and return the administration of the province to China, leaving Japanese interests represented only in the form of private capital investments. This action was carried out as promised before the close of 1922.

Economic bases
of Japan's
moderation

The reasonable attitude displayed by Japan at the Washington Conference, particularly in the attempt to conciliate China on the Shantung question, was based to some extent upon economic considerations. China, only slightly developed industrially, represented an enormous potential market for Japanese goods and a valuable source of raw materials. Many Japanese businessmen were convinced that the cultivation of friendly relations with the sprawling mainland state would pay far bigger dividends than would the seizure of territory by force and at the risk of inviting a boycott of Japanese trade.

The counter
influence of
nationalism

Promising as the liberal-democratic trends in Japan were, they did not become vigorous enough to extinguish the deeply entrenched reactionary forces which eventually led the country to disaster. The failure of the liberal elements must be attributed in part to external factors. The disillusionment and cynicism that became general in the postwar years throughout the West had their counterpart in Japan. Contrary to the optimistic predictions of liberal statesmen in Japan and other countries, the trends of international politics did not indicate a substantial gain for democratic processes. The rise of fascism in Europe demonstrated a powerful movement in the opposite direction. Almost everywhere, virulent nationalism seemed to be in the ascendancy, obscuring the hope of a cooperative world order. With democracy on the defensive or in retreat in the countries of the West, where it was indigenous, it could scarcely be expected to triumph easily in such a nation as Japan, where it was a recent innovation with no cultural or institutional roots.

Discriminatory
policies of
Western
nations

The sensibilities of the Japanese were irritated by the discrimination they encountered in the form of tariffs against their goods and immigration laws against their citizens. In 1924 the United States Congress passed an Oriental Exclusion law, placing Asians in a category inferior to that of the most backward Europeans. The United States was not alone in such a policy, and many Japanese began to feel that the great white nations were determined never to treat them as equals. The high tariff policies of the United States and other Western powers were another disturbing factor, producing psychological as well as economic repercussions. By 1930 the larger share of Japan's foreign trade, both export and import, was with the United States, with a trade balance decidedly favorable to the latter country. Protectionists in the United States alleged that American standards were threatened by competition from "cheap" Japanese labor. Yet the chief Japanese import was raw cotton and Japan's leading export to the United States was raw silk, an item hardly competitive with American industry.

In the last analysis, the defeat of liberal forces was due to deficiencies in the structure of Japanese society and in the economic system. The fundamental problem of creating a stable economy and satisfactory living standards for the majority of the people was never solved, and the problem became steadily more acute as the population continued to increase at the rate of one million a year. In spite of the expansion of commerce and manufacture, Japan's per capita income by 1928 was equal only to about one-eighth of that of the United States. Japan's prosperity, such as it was, depended upon participation in a world market that was subjected to more and more intense competition. Her foreign trade received a severe blow when the price of silk, her leading article of export, declined about 75 per cent between 1925 and 1934. To compensate for the collapse of the silk market, Japanese manufacturers stepped up the production of cotton cloth, but in this field they were bucking old and strongly established competitors. The Great Depression struck Japan just when the country seemed to be pulling out of a slump. Between 1929 and 1931 Japan's foreign commerce fell off by one-half, while rural and industrial indebtedness swelled to a figure in excess of the national income.

Fatal defects in the economic system

The highly inequitable distribution of wealth within Japan made for an artificial stratification of classes and interests that was unfavorable to the development of a democratic society. The middle class was too small and insecure to be a very effective liberal force. The great body of farmers and laborers had been ushered out of the discipline of Tokugawa feudalism into the discipline of an efficient centralized bureaucracy, without ever being emancipated from their traditions of docility and the acceptance of direction from above. Aspects of a feudal mentality persisted within the nation after feudalism had been replaced by a modern capitalist order. Industry, commerce, and finance were concentrated in the hands of a few huge trusts, known collectively as the *Zaibatsu*, each controlled by a closely integrated family group and almost beyond the reach of public supervision. The *Zaibatsu* not only dominated the economic picture but also were affiliated with bureaucrats in the government and deeply influenced political parties.

The persistence of a feudal mentality

The flimsy foundations of Japanese liberalism are revealed in the history and character of political parties during the 1920's and early 1930's, by which time two competing parties had risen to promi-

The illiberal
character of
Japanese parties:
the *Seiyukai*

The *Minseito*

The failure of
moderation; the
Manchuria
incident

nence. About 1900 the *Seiyukai* party had been organized under
the auspices of one of the most influential clan bureaucrats. The
Seiyukai was a descendant of the old Liberal party of Itagaki, but it
exemplified a metamorphosis of liberalism into something almost its
opposite. Itagaki's party, largely agrarian from the beginning, had
passed under the domination of great landlords in place of the small
tenants. To this conservative agrarian element was added the leading representative of big business, the house of Mitsui. Thus the
Seiyukai constituted an alliance of landlords, monopoly capitalists,
and bureaucrats, and it had connections also with the armed services. While the party favored constitutional methods, it was extremely conservative on domestic issues and rabidly expansionist on
foreign policy, advocating forceful measures to improve Japan's
economic position.

In 1927 an opposition party to the *Seiyukai* was formed, incorporating remnants of the old Progressive party of Count Okuma.
This new party, the *Minseito*, was backed primarily by industrial
rather than agrarian interests, and favored policies conducive to
the health of the business community, including social welfare measures to relieve working-class discontent. The *Minseito* frowned on
a policy of territorial aggression and deplored the reckless brag-
gadocio of chauvinistic nationalists. But while it was progressive in
comparison with the *Seiyukai*, it could hardly be considered truly
liberal in composition or principles. It was supported by one of the
great *Zaibatsu* houses (the Mitsubishi) and was as intensely nationalistic as the *Seiyukai*, differing from the latter chiefly on the question of which methods would best advance the country's interests.

A hopeful interlude, of brief duration, began when a *Minseito*
cabinet came into office in 1929 and attempted to reverse the
"strong" policy of the previous ministry, which had thrown troops
into Shantung province as the Chinese Nationalist forces advanced
toward Peking. The impact of the world depression upon Japan's
economy, however, jeopardized the position of the moderate *Minseito* cabinet, and the assassination of the premier by a fanatic not
only weakened the cabinet but also gave ominous warning of the
length to which intransigent nationalist groups would go in promoting their own cause. Then, in September 1931, the Japanese
army stationed in Manchuria took matters into its own hands by
attacking Chinese troops. By the following February, Manchuria
had become the "independent" state of Manchukuo under Japanese
auspices, and in 1933 Japan, branded publicly as an aggressor, de-
fiantly withdrew from the League of Nations.

Throughout the 1930's liberal elements in Japan never entirely
abandoned their struggle to hold back the tide of militant nationalism. But when the issues became international, as in the struggle
over Manchuria and, later, in the war against China, patriotic sentiments blunted the edge of popular opposition. The only groups

strong enough to challenge the militarists were the financial and business interests, and these were easily seduced by the promise of profits in the offing. Most of the business leaders had come to regard expansion as essential to Japan's economy. They hoped it could be carried out peacefully and painlessly, but they had helped to build, and had profited from building, a war machine that would be extremely difficult to hold within bounds.

IMPERIALISM AND A NEW ERA IN JAPAN

The omnipotence of nationalism

Of course, the primary center of aggressive truculence lay in the military services themselves, particularly the army. As previously pointed out, the Japanese army was composed largely of peasants, an unfortunate class, whose legitimate discontents were, under skillful direction, sublimated into an unreasoned and frenzied patriotism. After the Meiji period the army officers also were drawn chiefly from small towns and rural communities, and they lacked the temperate and relatively broad-minded attitude that had distinguished the *samurai* leaders. Gradually a "young officer" group developed an ideology of its own, which began to permeate the rank and file. Idealists in the worst sense of the term, these soldier fanatics preached absolute loyalty to the emperor and affirmed that Japan, of divine origin and superior to other nations, had the right to extend her rule over other parts of the world. At the same time, reflecting their peasant affinities, they demanded agrarian reforms or even nationalization of the land and castigated both capitalists and politicians as selfish and corrupt. Their program, a medley of radical and reactionary principles, aimed to make Japan an invincible state, solidly unified under the imperial will, which they claimed to represent most faithfully. Although it has been likened to fascism, the "Imperial Way" proclaimed by the ultranationalists undoubtedly had more in common with the ancient Japanese concepts of the state as a patriarchal society and of the superiority of government by men to government by law.

The rise of fanatical militarism

The creation of the puppet state of Manchukuo in 1932 and its development under Japanese management did not yield the substantial benefits to Japan's economy that had been anticipated. To exploit the coal, iron, and oil resources of Manchuria required an extensive outlay of capital, and Japanese capital was not readily forthcoming, partly because of the fear that industry in Manchukuo would compete with Japan's and partly because of the rigid governmental controls imposed upon capital and industry in the puppet state. Reflecting the antifree-enterprise bias of the army nationalists, the government attempted to create in Manchukuo a type of state-directed economy; and, when the *Zaibatsu* houses seemed reluctant to participate, an independent group of Japanese investors was recruited to support the new "capitalism of the people." As plans matured for making Manchuria not simply a source of raw materials for Japan but a center of heavy industry for Asia, it became apparent that the assurance of access to a wide market

The conquest of Manchuria as a prelude to war against China

Japanese Troops in Walled City of Mukden, Manchukuo (Manchuria).

area was imperative. Hence, Japanese expansionists attempted to convert China's northeastern provinces into an "autonomous" region, linked economically with Manchukuo. Finally they enlarged their objectives to encompass the creation of a "Greater East Asia Co-Prosperity Sphere." Instead of alleviating Japan's economy, her leaders had saddled it with additional burdens, entailing larger and larger expenditures for armaments in support of a program that had no foreseeable limits and was bound to meet with resistance at every point.

The role of Japan in World War II, into which her conflict with China was merged, is discussed elsewhere in this volume. Japan's surrender in 1945 was the prelude to a new phase of her history, in many ways different from anything she had experienced in the past. Never before had the Japanese nation been defeated in war and never before had the country been occupied by a foreign power. The occupation of a conquered country was also a new experience for the United States. At the very least it can be said that both the Japanese and the Americans conducted themselves in such a way as to produce a minimum of friction in relationships which were necessarily difficult.

For six and a half years the real authority in Japan was nominally held by the Far Eastern Commission in Washington and the advisory Allied Council for Japan in Tokyo, with General of the Army Douglas MacArthur as Supreme Commander for the Allied Powers; actually it was held by General MacArthur, under orders from Washington, and by the Japanese government. From beginning to end the Japanese Occupation was an undertaking and a responsibility of the United States. Military rule was indirect, however, and was exercised through the regular Japanese government, which had not disintegrated with Japan's military defeat. The emperor accepted the surrender terms, called upon his subjects to cooperate

The defeat of
Japan in World
War II

The American
Occupation

1184

with the occupying forces, and served as the connecting link between the old order and the new. In spite of the relative unimportance of the emperor politically in modern times, his role was of great value psychologically in providing a symbol of continuity when so much of the past seemed to have been destroyed forever.

One of the first major tasks of the Occupation authorities was to furnish Japan with a new constitution grounded in democratic principles. A draft prepared by a group of Japanese consultants was replaced by an American document, which was approved by the emperor and formally promulgated by him in the Diet in November 1946. It went into effect in May of the following year. The Japanese Constitution of 1946 is one of the most remarkable documents of its kind ever issued. It has been aptly described as "the world's outstanding model of the conveying of political rights by constitutional fiat." [2] Breaking cleanly with tradition and with the Constitution of 1889, it declared that sovereignty lay with the Japanese people and left the emperor with only formal powers like those of the British monarch. The new Constitution contained an elaborate Bill of Rights, in which to the normal civil liberties were added such benefits as the right to work and to bargain collectively, social equality, and equality of the sexes. Universal adult suffrage was established, with a bicameral Diet, and a cabinet responsible to the House of Representatives. The Constitution also incorporated the American principles of separation of church and state and judicial review of acts of the legislature. Particularly arresting was Article 9, which declared that "the Japanese people forever renounce war as a sovereign right of the nation" and that "land, sea, and air forces, as well as other war potential, will never be maintained." Altogether, the new Constitution had a highly utopian flavor. If its principles could have been carried into active and complete realization, they would have made Japan a more advanced democratic nation than the United States.

While introducing political changes the Occupation authorities projected a reform program which, on the directive level at least, was far-reaching. In conformity with the policy of demilitarization, an extensive purge was conducted to remove from office and from teaching positions all persons suspected of ultranationalist proclivities. A direct attack was launched against the *Zaibatsu* groups with the passage of an Antimonopoly Law and the creation of a Fair Trade Commission. General MacArthur, who claimed complete success for the campaign, appeared to be a greater trust buster than even Theodore Roosevelt. Pursuant to the liberal economic provisions of the new Constitution, labor organizations were encouraged. Between 1945 and 1950 membership in labor unions increased from 5000 to more than 6,000,000 and the government enacted a

The Constitution of 1946

The reform program

[2] Linebarger, Djang, and Burks, *Far Eastern Governments and Politics: China and Japan*, p. 479.

comprehensive labor welfare code. Perhaps most significant among the reforms was that which dealt with the long-neglected problem of land ownership. An agrarian law of 1946, providing for government purchase of tracts from absentee landlords and for the sale of these tracts to tenant farmers at moderate prices, led to a sweeping transformation of agricultural land ownership. Comprehensive and rigorous as it was, Japan's "New Deal" could not of course remake the whole fabric of society in a few years. All of the reforms were initiated by the Occupation authorities rather than by the Japanese themselves. Furthermore, the experience of the Occupation illustrates how difficult it is to couple reform with coercion, no matter how benevolent the administration. For example, the purge directed against militarists and ultranationalists caught some liberals whose only fault seemed to be their adherence to the ideals which were boldly announced in the new Constitution. Labor was prodded into organizing and collective bargaining, but strikes were restricted by the Occupation government. Also, beginning in 1947, Occupation policy, reflecting the pressures of global power politics, shifted from reform to retrenchment and recovery. The program of decentralizing industry, which perhaps would have proved temporary in any case, halted with the realization that if Japan's industrial strength were preserved it could be an asset to the West in the Cold War with the Communist powers.

A peace treaty between the United States and Japan was negotiated at San Francisco in September 1951, and ratified the following April. It was also signed by 48 other states, not including the Soviet Union, however, which remained technically in a state of war with Japan until 1956. The peace settlement, although it ended the

The Beginning of the Occupation in Japan. American troops entering Tokyo, September 8, 1945. The devastating effects of bombing raids are plainly evident.

Destruction of Japanese Naval Weapons. Miniature submarines at the naval base at Kure are being destroyed. In its new constitution, Japan renounced the right to make war.

Occupation and restored formal independence to Japan, was very drastic territorially. Depriving the nation of all its empire, the treaty reduced Japan to the same area it had held at the time of Commodore Perry's visit in 1853, although its population was now three times as great. The peace treaty, supplemented by a security treaty, acknowledged Japan's right to arm for "self-defense" and authorized the stationing of foreign troops (meaning American) in Japan for the defense of the country.

The Peace of 1951 and end of the Occupation

Encouraged by a democratic constitution, numerous political parties sprang into being, but the persisting tradition of loyalty to personalities, kinship groups, or local interests made it difficult to establish them on a nationwide basis with broad popular support. In 1955 two major organizations, successors respectively of prewar *Seiyukai* and *Minseito*, merged to form the Liberal Democratic party, which has held a predominant position ever since. In spite of its name the party is conservative, and its continual success reflects the conservative bias of the majority of voters. Deriving support from the business community, old-line bureaucrats, rural constituents—which are overrepresented in the Diet—and civil service officials, it has operated as a coalition of factions without a clear program or well-organized and active membership. In power for almost two decades, the party became in effect the Japanese Establishment, nourishing the country's expanding economy and maintaining its ties with the United States. Unpopular government policies and even scandals in high places have not sufficed to dislodge the LDP, largely because unprecedented material prosperity came about under a succession of conservative administrations.

Political trends in postwar Japan: The Liberal Democratic party

The principal, though not very effective, opposition is offered by the Japanese Socialist party, backed by large labor federations.

Vehement antimilitarists, the Socialists call for disbanding Japan's Defense Forces and replacing the Security Treaty by nonaggression pacts with China, the U.S.S.R., and the United States. They have never commanded more than a third of the votes in national elections and suffered a party split in 1966, but showed appreciable strength in the 1972 parliamentary elections. Second among the opposition parties but far behind the Socialists is the Japanese Communist party, which dwindled to insignificance in the 1950's but succeeded in winning 10½ per cent of the popular vote in 1972. Aligned neither with Moscow nor with Peking, the Communists minimize radical ideology, endorse parliamentary procedures, and attempt to woo the electorate with such innocuous slogans as "Cover drainage ditches" and "Build more day nurseries." At the extreme right is the Clean Government Party, political arm of a militant Buddhist sect. Advocating a vaguely defined moral rearmanent and promising a "new society of peace and plenty by following the middle way," it has appealed particularly to middle- and lower-income groups. Although the LDP retained a majority of seats in the House of Representatives, the 1972 elections showed that it was losing popular support, especially in urban areas.

The economic difficulties confronting Japan immediately after her surrender seemed practically insurmountable. Before the close of hostilities almost one-third of the homes in Japan's urban areas were destroyed by air attacks, and the direct economic loss caused by the war was staggering. Japan was shorn of her empire, her industrial production had fallen 80 per cent below the 1937 level, her foreign trade stood at zero, and she was dependent upon imports even for foodstuffs. Viewed against this dismal background, Japan's economic recovery and advance have been spectacular. By 1953 the index of production was 50 per cent above the level of the mid-1930's, and it continued upward, with textiles, metal goods, and machinery leading the way. During the 1950's economic productivity doubled; in the next decade it overtook that of England, France, and West Germany to become the third largest in the world. Per capita income by 1970 was still less than half that of the United States, but Japan's gross national product of about $200 billion was expected to double before 1980. A remarkable aspect of this economic expansion was that Japan both competed successfully in long-established industries and also pioneered in new fields. She became the world's largest shipbuilder, exported steel, light and heavy machinery, and gained a commanding position in such areas as chemicals, synthetics, optics, electronics, and computer technology. Although the farm population declined to about 18 per cent of the total, through the application of scientific methods Japan was able to increase agricultural output by 50 per cent.

Several factors explain Japan's seemingly miraculous rise from a condition of prostration to one of dizzying prosperity. First, in spite of devastating losses from the war, the Japanese retained their technical proficiency, labor force, and traditions of hard work. A determination to recover lost ground and to overtake and surpass the West became a national obsession, eliciting self-sacrifice and mitigating disputes between management and underpaid labor. Employees of large corporations served them with a loyalty like that of the old feudal *samurai* to his lord. Statistics reporting the growth of the GNP were scanned with the avidity devoted in more leisurely societies to the sports pages. Postwar Japan achieved an extremely high ratio of savings to earnings, in some years amounting to 30 per cent. A second factor helping to stimulate recovery was American financial aid, not only during the Occupation but especially by the purchase of goods and services for the Korean conflict. A third factor was the initiative of the government in stimulating and guiding the growth of an essentially private-enterprise economy. The government encouraged capital investment by incentive tax and loan policies, deliberately slowed down the economy when the trade balance threatened to become too unfavorable, spent generously to offset the effects of recessions, and operated an Economic Planning Agency to compile data, predict market trends, and set production targets. But perhaps the most important asset of all was —paradoxically—the defeat and elimination of Japan's military establishment, which had systematically drained the country's re-

Explanation of Japan's rise to prosperity

Electronics Industry of Japan. Mass production lines of TV sets at Matsushita Electric Industrial Company plant in Ibaragi. At least 90 percent of Japanese families own TV sets.

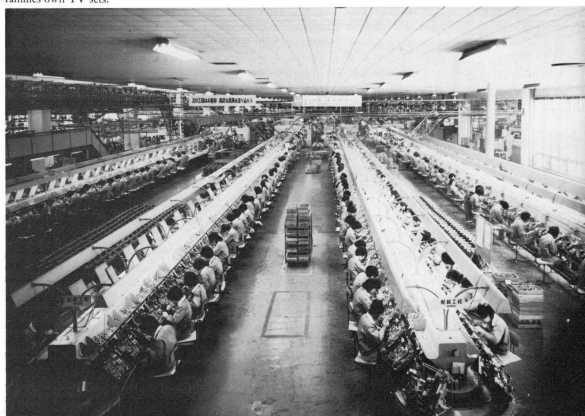

Pollution in Industrial Japan. Kawasaki is a heavily industrialized city in the Tokyo-Yokohama Industrial Zone. The works of numerous heavy and chemical industry companies are located here.

sources. During a crucial period Japan enjoyed the distinction of being the only great industrial nation operating on a peace economy instead of a war economy. Her armed forces of 300,000 men will undoubtedly be enlarged, but thus far the Defense Agency has consumed less than 1 per cent of the GNP and less than 8 per cent of the national budget—amounting to $13 per capita. Comparable figures on per capita defense spending are, for West Genmany $90, for the U.S.S.R. $164, for the United States $393. In 1969 Japan allotted more than three times as much to social security, education, and the promotion of science as to defense.

Japanese society has been profoundly affected by the tremendous expansion of the nation's economy. A continual rise in the standard of living—the highest in Asia and approaching that of Western Europe—is illustrated by successive changes reported in the traditional Japanese conception of the "three sacred treasures" desired by every household. The mirror, jewel, and sword of ancient times gave way to the electric refrigerator, washing machine, and television set. By 1970, 90 per cent of the families possessed these items, and they aspired to a color TV, "room cooler," and motor car; or even to the luxury of central heating, an electric cooking range, and a vacation cottage. Far from solving all of Japan's problems, prosperity has augmented some of them. A staggering rate of population increase, which brought the total to 106 million, has apparently been successfully halted, as it has in China. But half the inhabitants are concentrated on 2 per cent of the land, the bulk of them in an urban belt stretching from Tokyo to Osaka. Tokyo, with nearly 9 million people, became the largest city in the world—although it recently yielded this dubious honor to Shanghai. Tokyo is still one of the dirtiest, noisiest, and most congested of cities. With population density in urban areas three times as great as in the United States, Japan faces a major problem of air and water pollution. While industrial progress has created large fortunes, it has done little to raise wages in the small shops and home factories that still employ a majority of the working force. One precarious element in Japan's prosperity is her dependence on external markets. Although foreign trade represents a smaller proportion of her total economy than before World War II, it is still significant, and she must import many essential raw materials, including coal, copper, iron and other ores, gas and oil. A nuclear reactor with high potential for generating electric power is expected to supplement her energy sources in the 1970's. The Japanese have begun to experience the problems and anxieties common to affluent societies, notably a tendency—especially among the young—to question the validity of materialistic standards and a relentless drive for a bigger GNP.

Since World War II Japan's foreign policy has been conditioned by two main factors: a struggle for economic recovery and ascendancy, and—until recently—a close and dependent relationship with the United States. Striving to dispel the hostility and distrust remaining as a legacy from her imperialist era, Japan made generous reparations settlements with the small states of Southeast Asia that her armies had overrun. She contributed substantially to various development programs, including a multinational project for irrigation, power, flood control, and navigation in the Mekong River basin. When the Asian Development Bank was inaugurated in 1966, a Japanese became the first president of this regional organization. Japan's foreign aid, however, although extensive, has been criticized for being geared more to her own economic needs than to those of the recipient countries. Most of it has been in the form of loans, under terms profitable to Japanese investors and traders. Japan's successful penetration of the market in Indonesia, Malaysia, Singapore, the Philippines, and Thailand has aroused resentment throughout Southeast Asia. The image of the "ugly American" gave way to one inspired by Japanese businessmen, bankers, and technicians, disparagingly referred to as "honorary whites" or "Yellow Yankees." Some observers predict that Japan through her economic superiority will come to dominate Southeast Asia as completely as she once did through military conquest. One American futurologist contemplates with approval the establishment of a Japanese-American Co-Prosperity Sphere embracing the whole Pacific area.[3] Such predictions are dubious, partly because the Japanese are sensitive to accusations of neocolonialism and, more importantly, because the Southeast

Japan's economic ascendancy in Southeast Asia

[3] Herman Kahn, *The Emerging Japanese Superstate*, p. 172.

Asia market is not adequate to fulfill their needs. To reap full benefit from their specialized and advanced technology they must have access to high-income areas, such as Australia, western Europe, and North America. In 1965 Japan's share of the Asian market was only 17 per cent. It will undoubtedly grow larger, especially as Chinese-Japanese trade increases. Meanwhile the Japanese are seeking other areas for investment and are already active in Latin America.

Relations with the Soviet Union

Japan found it more difficult to reach an understanding with the Soviet Union than with any other of her former enemies. An agreement signed by the two countries in October 1956 restored diplomatic relations and paved the way for Japan's entrance into the United Nations, but it was not a formal treaty of peace. There have been frequent disputes—over Japanese prisoners of war never accounted for by Russia, fishing rights, and Japanese claims in the Kuril Islands, all of which are held by Russia. Japan's bargaining position seemed to improve in the early 1970's when Russia sought her assistance in a plan to develop Siberian reserves of oil and gas.

Japanese-American relations

The American presence continued to be felt in Japan by virtue of the Security Treaty of 1951, which pledged the two countries to mutual consultation and allowed the United States to retain military bases in Japan. Successive Japanese administrations followed Washington's lead in international diplomacy so dutifully that some critics accused the Foreign Ministry of being "the Asian Department of the United States State Department." Mounting popular resentment led to riotous demonstrations against renewal of the Security Treaty in 1960 and again in 1970. Anti-American sentiment was further aroused by the escalating war in Indochina, toward which the Japanese shared the feelings of most Asians. Pride in Japan's economic upsurge stimulated dissatisfaction with a condition of dependence, the more so as the character of trade between the United States and Japan changed. By the late 1960's the trade balance had shifted in Japan's favor; in 1971 the value of her exports to the United States exceeded the value of American goods imported by $3.2 billion. Moreover, in the exchange of commodities the United States had begun to look more like a junior partner or a colony than a highly developed nation—selling agricultural products and raw materials to Japan and receiving in return steel, machinery, electrical appliances, and such specialized articles as pianos and barber chairs. American automobile sales in Japan matched only a small fraction of Japanese car sales in the United States, and while Detroit manufacturers were protesting their inability to meet designated pollution control standards by 1975, their Japanese competitors were already meeting them in 1973. Evidencing a more independent stand, the Japanese government in 1970 refused Washington's request to extend for three more years "voluntary" quotas on textile exports to the United States.

One lingering source of friction between Japan and her Western ally has finally been alleviated. The Bonin and Ryukyu Islands,

Automobile Assembly Line, Toyota Motor Company. In 1967 the Japanese automobile industry became the second largest in the world after the United States.

occupied by the United States under terms which recognized Japan's "residual sovereignty," were heavily fortified, stocked with nuclear weapons, and used as bomber bases in the Korean and Vietnam wars. In June 1968 Japan recovered jurisdiction over the Bonin Islands and in May 1972 the Ryukyus, including the key island of Okinawa, returned to Japanese rule after 27 years of military occupation. The terms of the transfer agreement called for the removal of nuclear weapons but left the United States the right to continue to use the bases.

Japan's recovery of the Bonin and Ryukyu Islands

A decided turn in United States-Japanese relations followed President Nixon's announcement in the summer of 1971 of his intention to visit Peking the following year. The surprise announcement angered the Japanese because the United States had pressured them into close ties with the Nationalist regime in Taiwan and had stressed the necessity of consultation and joint action in dealing with mainland China, and yet had not informed them in advance of Washington's dramatic reversal of policy. Beyond suffering a temporary loss of face, they now felt impelled to mend their own diplomatic fences. Prime Minister Kakuei Tanaka, who in July 1972 was chosen as head of the Liberal Democratic party, appeared more dynamic and aggressive than the retiring Prime Minister Eisaku Sato. Tanaka had worked his way to success from a background of poverty and without benefit of an education, in contrast to most of the other political figures, who were graduates of prestigious Tokyo University. In September 1972 Tanaka made his pilgrimage to a summit meeting in Peking, offered an apology to the Chinese people for Japan's past misconduct, and—in advance of the United States—established formal diplomatic relations between Japan and the

Prime Minister Kakuei Tanaka of Japan.

1193

People's Republic of China. The inevitable rupture with the Nationalist Chinese government posed problems for both Japan and Taiwan because Taiwan's economy depended heavily on Japanese investments and trade connections.

The question of what course Japan would pursue in the 1970's aroused considerable speculation and some apprehensions. After the

Whither Japan?

December 1972 elections Tanaka formed a cabinet dominated by conservative nationalists. The government's Fourth Defense Build-up Plan (1972–1976) calls for doubling the military budget and would make Japan the seventh largest national defense spender in the world. Her strength in conventional weapons is already greater than it was at the peak of World War II, and although Japan is a signatory to the nuclear nonproliferation treaty, she has the potential to become a nuclear power. As in most other highly developed states, a military-industrial complex advocates and stands to profit from armaments expansion. Still, a restraining factor is the antimilitarist sentiment of the majority of Japanese people, evident throughout the postwar era. The Self-Defense Forces, despite skillful public relations campaigns and inducements to encourage enlistment, have never been popular with the public. In a speech in 1970 the Director General of the Defense Agency asserted that Japan had rejected "the outdated concept that economic great powers must necessarily become great military powers." Indisputable was the fact that worsening conditions of overcrowding, inadequate sanitation, and pollution would require more attention and a larger share of the national income if Japan were to become the "ideal community living in a garden" projected by some planners.

SELECTED READINGS

—(*See also Readings for Chapters 4 and 12*)

· *Items so designated are available in paperbound editions.*

CHINA

· Barnett, A. Doak, *Communist China, the Early Years, 1949–1955*, New York, 1964 (Praeger).
· Barrett, David, *Dixie Mission: The United States Army Observer Group in Yenan, 1944*, Berkeley, 1970 (California). A firsthand account.
· Baum, Richard, ed., *China in Ferment: Perspectives on the Cultural Revolution*, Englewood Cliffs, N. J., 1971 (Spectrum). A stimulating symposium.
Bianco, Lucien, *Origins of the Chinese Revolution, 1915–1949*, tr. Muriel Bell, Stanford, 1971. A brilliant interpretive summary.
· Ch'en, Jerome, *Mao and the Chinese Revolution*, New York, 1965 (Galaxy).
· Chesneaux, Jean, *Peasant Revolts in China 1840–1849*, New York, 1973 (Norton).
· Clubb, O. E., *Twentieth-Century China*, 2nd ed., New York, 1972 (Columbia). One of the best surveys of recent Chinese history.
· Cohen, A. A., *The Communism of Mao Tse-tung*, Chicago, 1964 (Phoenix).
Davies, J. P., Jr., *Dragon by the Tail: American, British, Japanese, and Russian Encounters with China and One Another*, New York, 1972. An

American diplomat's jolting account of bungling and intrigue in the Asian theater of World War II.

Dulles, F. R., *American Policy toward Communist China. The Historical Record: 1949–1969*, New York, 1972.

· Floyd, David, *Mao Against Khrushchev: A Short History of the Sino-Soviet Conflict*, New York, 1964 (Praeger). A readable account.

· Griffith, W. E., *The Sino-Soviet Rift*, Cambridge, Mass., 1964 (M. I. T.). An analysis with pertinent documents.

· Hinton, H. C., *China's Turbulent Quest: An Analysis of China's Foreign Relations since 1949*, Bloomington, Ind., 1972 (Indiana). Accurate; coldly objective.

Hsiung, J. C., *Ideology and Practice: The Evolution of Chinese Communism*, New York, 1970. Valuable for an understanding of the Cultural Revolution.

· Hsu Kai-yu, *Chou En-lai: China's Gray Eminence*, Garden City, N. Y., 1969 (Anchor).

· Isaacs, H. R., *The Tragedy of the Chinese Revolution*, Stanford, 1964 (Atheneum).

· Larkin, B. D., *China and Africa, 1949–1970: The Foreign Policy of the People's Republic of China*, Berkeley, 1973.

· Lifton, R. J., *Thought Reform and the Psychology of Totalism*, New York, 1961 (Norton). A psychiatrist's analysis.

Mehnert, Klaus, *China Returns*, New York, 1972. A sympathetic, restrained appraisal by a West German journalist.

· Prybyla, Jan S., *The Political Economy of Communist China*, Scranton, Pa., 1970 (International Textbook Company).

Robinson, T. W., ed., *The Cultural Revolution in China*, Berkeley, 1971.

Selden, Mark, *The Yenan Way in Revolutionary China*, Cambridge, Mass., 1971. Scholarly treatment of the "Border Region," 1935–1947.

Sharmon, Lyon, *Sun Yat-sen: His Life and Its Meaning*, New York, 1934. A critical biography.

· Snow, Edgar, *Red China Today: The Other Side of the River*, New York, 1970 (Random House). An informative account, based largely on personal observations.

· ———, *Red Star over China*, New York, 1938 (Black Cat). A classic account of the Communists' early years of struggle.

· Solomon, R. H., *Mao's Revolution and the Chinese Political Culture*, Berkeley, 1971 (California).

· Terrill, Ross, *800,000,000: The Real China*, New York, 1972 (Delta). A vivid and discriminating account by an Australian journalist-scholar.

· Tuchman, Barbara, *Stilwell and the American Experience in China, 1911–1945*, New York, 1972 (Bantam).

· Waller, D. J., *The Government and Politics of Communist China*, Garden City, N. Y., 1971 (Anchor). Concise and informative.

Wilson, Dick, *The Long March: The Epic of Chinese Communist Survival*, New York, 1971.

JAPAN

Allen, G. C., *Japan's Economic Expansion*, New York, 1965.

Axelbank, Albert, *Black Star over Japan: Rising Forces of Militarism*, New York, 1972. An alarming prognosis.

· Benedict, Ruth, *The Chrysanthemum and the Sword*, New York, 1967 (Meridian). A classic analysis of prewar Japanese society.

Brzezinski, Z. K., *The Fragile Blossom: Crisis and Change in Japan*, New York, 1972. A timely analysis of Japan's economic, political, and strategic position.

Buck, Pearl, *The People of Japan*, New York, 1966. A personal account.

· Burks, A. W., *The Government of Japan*, 2nd ed., New York, 1964 (Crowell).

READINGS

Butow, R. J. C., *Japan's Decision to Surrender*, Stanford, 1954.

———, *Tojo and the Coming of the War*, Princeton, 1961.

Emmerson, J. K., *Arms, Yen and Power: The Japanese Dilemma*, New York, 1971. Balanced, informative, optimistic.

· Ishida Takeshi, *Japanese Society*, New York, 1971 (Random House).

Kahn, Herman, *The Emerging Japanese Superstate: Challenge and Response*, Englewood Cliffs, N. J., 1970.

Kawai Kazuo, *Japan's American Interlude*, Chicago, 1960.

· Maki, J. M., *Government and Politics in Japan: The Road to Democracy*, New York, 1962 (Praeger).

Minear, R. H., *Victors' Justice: The Tokyo War Crimes Trial*, Princeton, 1972. Challenges the moral and legal validity of the trials.

Morris, Ivan, *Nationalism and the Right Wing in Japan: A Study of Post-War Trends*, London, 1960. A clear and forceful study.

· Nakane Chie, *Japanese Society*, Berkeley, 1972 (California). A social anthropologist's analysis.

Packard, G. R., *Protest in Tokyo: The Security Treaty Crisis of 1960*, Princeton, 1966.

Reischauer, E. O., *The United States and Japan*, 3rd ed., New York, 1965.

· Scalapino, R. A., and Masumi, J., *Parties and Politics in Contemporary Japan*, Berkeley, 1962.

Thayer, N. B., *How the Conservatives Rule Japan*, Princeton, 1969.

Tsuneishi, W. M., *Japanese Political Style: An Introduction to the Government and Politics of Modern Japan*, New York, 1966. An excellent brief study.

· Van Alstyne, Richard W., *The United States and East Asia*, New York, (Norton).

Yanaga Chitoshi, *Big Business in Japanese Politics*, New Haven, 1968.

SOURCE MATERIALS

· Brandt, C., Schwartz, B. F., and Fairbank, J. K., *A Documentary History of Chinese Communism* (Atheneum).

· Chai, Winberg, ed., *The Essential Works of Chinese Communism* (Bantam).

Chiang Kai-shek, *China's Destiny*.

· de Bary, W. T., ed., *Sources of Chinese Tradition*, Chaps. XXVII, XXVIII, XXIX (Columbia).

· ———, ed., *Sources of Japanese Tradition*, Chaps. XXVI, XXVII, XXVIII, XXIX (Columbia).

· Fraser, S., *Chinese Communist Education* (Science Editions). A collection of documents for the period 1944–1960.

Grew, Ambassador Joseph C., *Ten Years in Japan*.

· Li, Dun J., ed., *The Road to Communism: China Since 1912* (Van Nostrand Reinhold).

· *Quotations from Chairman Mao Tse-tung* (Bantam).

CHAPTER 39

The Origins and Legacy of World War II

The President [Roosevelt] and the Prime Minister [Churchill], after a complete survey of the world situation, are more than ever determined that peace can come to the world only by a total elimination of German and Japanese war power. This involves the simple formula of placing the objective of this war in terms of an unconditional surrender by Germany, Italy, and Japan.
—Franklin D. Roosevelt, Casablanca, January 24, 1943

In September 1939, Europe plunged again over the rim of the abyss. The peace of 1919–1920 had turned out to be only an armistice, and millions of people were now locked in a conflict that surpassed in frightfulness any that had occurred heretofore. As had happened in 1914–1918, the new struggle soon became worldwide. Of course, World War II was not merely a continuation of, or a sequel to, World War I. Yet the similarity in causes and characteristics was more than superficial. Both were precipitated by threats to the balance of power. Both sprang in some measure out of rivalry between the sated and the dynamic nations—the first resolved to keep what they had already gained, and the others determined to conquer living space for their burgeoning populations and to gain new sources of wealth and power. Both were conflicts between peoples, whole nations, rather than between governments. The lineup of the two sides, in the beginning, was similar, with Great Britain and France opposing Germany, and with Italy remaining temporarily neutral. On the other hand, there were notable differences. Japan aligned herself with Germany instead of with the Western powers,

A comparison of the two world wars

1197

and Russia did not enter the conflict until two years after it began. The methods of warfare in World War II had little in common with those of the earlier conflict. Trench warfare was largely superseded by aerial bombing and by blitzkrieg attacks with highly mobile armies. It seems safe to say that the distinction between soldiers and civilians was more completely obliterated in the second conflict than it had been in the first.

I. UNDERLYING AND IMMEDIATE CAUSES

Defects of the peace of 1919–1920

The causes of World War II went back a great many years. To some extent they were related to the failure of the peace of 1919–1920. That peace, while perhaps as good as could be expected in view of the passions and hatreds engendered by the war, created almost as many problems as it solved. By yielding to the demands of the victors for annexation of territory and the creation of satellite states, the peacemakers sowed new seeds of bitterness and conflict. Had the League of Nations they set up been better organized, it might have relieved some of the tensions and prevented clashes between nations still unwilling to relinquish their absolute sovereignty. Moreover, it was not a league of all nations. Both Germany and Russia were excluded, thereby pushing them into the role of outcasts.

Threats to the balance of power

Although President Wilson and other sponsors of the League acclaimed it as a means of eliminating the balance of power, it did nothing of the sort. It merely substituted a new and more precarious balance for the old. The signatures on the peace treaties had scarcely dried when the victors began the construction of new alliances to maintain their supremacy. A *cordon sanitaire* consisting of the Baltic states, Poland, and Rumania was created as a buffer against Soviet Russia. A Little Entente composed of Czechoslovakia, Yugoslavia, and Rumania was established to prevent a revival of Austrian power. These combinations, together with a Franco-Belgian alliance and a Franco-Polish alliance would also serve to isolate Germany. Thus the old system of power politics was reconstituted along essentially the same lines it had had before World War I. Even the League itself was fundamentally an alliance of the victors against the vanquished. That there would be fears and anxieties over a disturbance of the new power arrangement could hardly be unexpected. The first sign of such a disturbance appeared in 1922 when Germany and Russia negotiated the Treaty of Rapallo. Though disguised as a mere trade agreement, it opened the way for political and, according to some accounts, even military collaboration between the two states. In 1935 the German government under the direction of Hitler tore up the disarmament provisions of the Treaty of Versailles. It announced the revival of conscription and the return to universal military training. By threatening the creation

The Krupp Shipworks in Germany. Seen here are German submarines in the final stages of assembly.

of a huge air force Hitler hoodwinked the British into signing a naval agreement permitting Germany to build war vessels up to 35 per cent of the strength of Britain's navy. Finally, in 1936, he flouted the peace settlement by sending troops into the Rhineland to occupy the area of Germany demilitarized by the Treaty of Versailles.

Apostles of peace made various attempts to preserve or restore international amity during the 1920's and 1930's. Some saw in disarmament the most promising means of achieving their purpose. Accordingly, a succession of conferences was called in the hope of limiting at least the competition in armaments. The results were negligible. In 1925 representatives of the chief European powers met at Locarno and acted on the suggestion of the German Foreign Minister, Gustav Stresemann, that Germany and France pledge themselves to respect the Rhine frontiers as established in the Versailles Treaty. They agreed also that they would never go to war against each other except in "legitimate defense." More widely celebrated than the Locarno Agreements was the Pact of Paris, or Kellogg-Briand Pact, of 1928. Its purpose was to outlaw war as an international crime. Eventually nearly all the nations of the world signed an agreement renouncing war as "an instrument of national policy" and providing that the settlement of international disputes "of whatever nature or of whatever origin" should never be sought "except by peaceful means." Neither the Locarno Agreements nor the Pact of Paris was much more than a pious gesture. The signatory nations adopted them with so many reservations and exceptions in favor of "vital interests" that they could never be effective instruments for preserving peace.

As Germany recovered strength during the 1930's, the victorious powers adopted varying attitudes. France, for a time, remained inflexible in her determination to hold Germany down. Her government, however, tolerated Japan's invasion of Manchuria in 1931 and even encouraged Italy's conquest of Ethiopia in 1936. As a trading

Attempts to preserve international amity

1199

Members of the Council of the League of Nations. In the front row from the right are Chamberlain of Great Britain, Vandervelde of Belgium, Stresemann of Germany, and Briand of France.

nation anxious to rebuild her markets in central Europe, Britain favored a policy of leniency toward Germany. Although she had a good legal case for doing so, she refused to take any action against the military occupation of the Rhineland. She was tolerant also toward the Japanese invasion of Manchuria and the Italian conquest of Ethiopia. Like France, she declined to take positive steps to assist the Spanish Republic when Germany and Italy intervened in the Spanish Civil War to guarantee a victory of the Spanish fascists under General Franco. Not until Germany revealed, in 1939, that she had definite ambitions for conquests in Eastern Europe did Britain and France show serious concern over enforcing the balance of power. Their action came too late, for the balance had already been badly upset by the gains Germany and Italy had made through their aggressive policies.

If we look for economic causes of World War II, we can consider, first of all, division of the world into Have and Have-not powers. The former included Great Britain, the United States, France, and Russia. Britain had the smallest homeland, but her empire extended over 13,000,000 square miles, one-fourth of the land area of the earth, and was inhabited by 500,000,000 people, or one-fifth of the population of the globe. France had a total empire of 4,000,000 square miles and 100,000,000 inhabitants. Neither the United States nor Russia owned vast overseas possessions, but both had extensive home areas rich in natural resources. The former ruled over 3,735,000 square miles with a population of 130,000,000. The Union of Soviet Socialist Republics extended over an area of 8,000,000 square miles and was inhabited by no fewer than 170,000,000 people. The position of the Have-not powers—Germany, Italy, and Japan—seemed poor indeed by comparison. The three of them combined had an area of less than 1,500,000 square miles, to accommodate a home population that exceeded the total for Great Britain and the United States. German patriots could point out that the average German citizen had only .004 of a square mile of living space at his disposal, whereas the average Briton could draw upon

Varying attitudes of the Western powers

The revolt of the Have-not powers

1200

the wealth and economic opportunities of almost three square miles of imperial territory.

The fallacies in this view of the matter were seldom noticed. It seemed sufficient for the German nationalist to reflect upon the fact that standards of living in Britain were higher than in his own country to prove to him that the existing division of the earth's surface was unjust. He was therefore ready to disrupt the status quo by any means in his power. Perhaps diplomatic cunning would be sufficient, but if not, he would resort to war. Italians and Japanese seemed to have even weightier evidence of the injustice of the existing order, since standards of living in their countries were lower than in Germany. None of them appeared to recognize the fact that living standards in some small European countries, totally or almost completely lacking colonial empires, were just about equal to the average in Britain. But Germany, Italy, and Japan had a sense of grievance for a number of reasons, and presenting themselves before the world as Have-not nations helped to justify their bellicose foreign policies.

Perhaps the most serious economic cause of World War II was the Great Depression. The depression contributed to the coming of the war in several ways. First and foremost, it intensified economic nationalism. Baffled by problems of unemployment and business stagnation, governments resorted to high tariffs in a frenzied attempt to preserve the home market for their own producers.

The depression also had other effects perhaps more difficult to assay. For one thing, it was responsible for a marked increase in armaments. Armaments expansion, on a large scale, was first undertaken by Germany about 1935. The results in a few years were such as to dazzle the rest of the world. Unemployment disappeared and business boomed. It would have been too much to expect that other dissatisfied nations would not copy the German example. Similarly, the depression resulted in a new wave of militant expansionism directed toward the conquest of neighboring territories as a means of solving economic problems. Japan took the lead in 1931 with the invasion of Manchuria. A primary cause was the decline of Japanese exports of raw silk and cotton cloth. Since the nation as a consequence was unable to pay for needed imports of coal, iron, and other minerals, Japanese militarists were furnished with a convenient pretext for seizing Manchuria, where supplies of these commodities could then be purchased for Japanese currency.

Most important of all, the depression was primarily responsible for the triumph of Nazism in Germany. The Nazi party would probably have remained weak and ineffectual had it not been for the influx of millions of followers from the ranks of the farmers and the unemployed and from frightened members of the white-collar classes. The whirling spiral of economic decline had overwhelmed these people with a sense of despair. Convinced that capitalism, socialism, and democracy had all failed, they were ready to grasp at

Power politics
as a cause of
wars

almost any straw that would save them from sinking deeper into the quicksands of depression.

It may be well before leaving this subject of underlying causes to look at the matter from the standpoint of a different interpretation. According to an important school of thought, which may be called the power-politics school, only a few of the factors mentioned above deserve more than slight consideration. Doubtless leaders of this school would accept the economic causes, but most of the others they would dismiss as inconsequential. They place nearly all of the emphasis upon power politics. They maintain that power rivalries and power struggles have been the real causes of international wars since the beginning of modern history. Such forces as nationalism, militarism, and imperialism have simply been instruments for achieving the ends of a quest for power. The seventeenth century, they point out, was marked by a great power struggle between France and Austria, in which France was victorious. During the eighteenth century a primary struggle raged between Britain and France and culminated in the Seven Years' War, with a decisive victory for Britain. The French attempted to recover their power during the wars of the Revolution and under Napoleon, but the effort failed, and Britain gradually emerged as the dominant nation on the earth. Toward the end of the nineteenth century, however, Germany rose to challenge British supremacy, and the result was World War I. After the war conflicting ambitions among the victors permitted a revival of Teutonic power, with the consequence that, by 1939, Germany was ready to challenge again the ability of the dominant nations to continue ruling the world. The fact that Germany and her allies had fascist governments had little to do with the case. According to the power-politics theorists, fascism was simply a by-product of an age-old struggle among nations to gain advantages at their neighbors' expense.

Evidence for the
power-politics
hypothesis

That there is much truth in the foregoing hypothesis seems almost indisputable. The existence of the modern state system practically guarantees that nations shall be engaged in either cold or hot wars nearly all of the time. Under it the relation among states is the same as that among individuals in the supposed state of nature, which philosophers like Locke and Rousseau believed to have existed before the formation of political society. In other words, there is no law or order except that which results from agreements between sovereign units. In making these agreements, the units retain their full sovereignty, and therefore may repudiate them whenever they choose. Another element in the hypothesis which is difficult to refute is the contention that ideologies are not fundamental causes of wars. If British politicians had been gravely concerned about the evils of fascism they could never have pursued their policy of appeasement, for they must have known that its effect would be to strengthen Italy and Germany. Indeed, there is evidence that Neville Chamberlain was perfectly willing to collaborate with

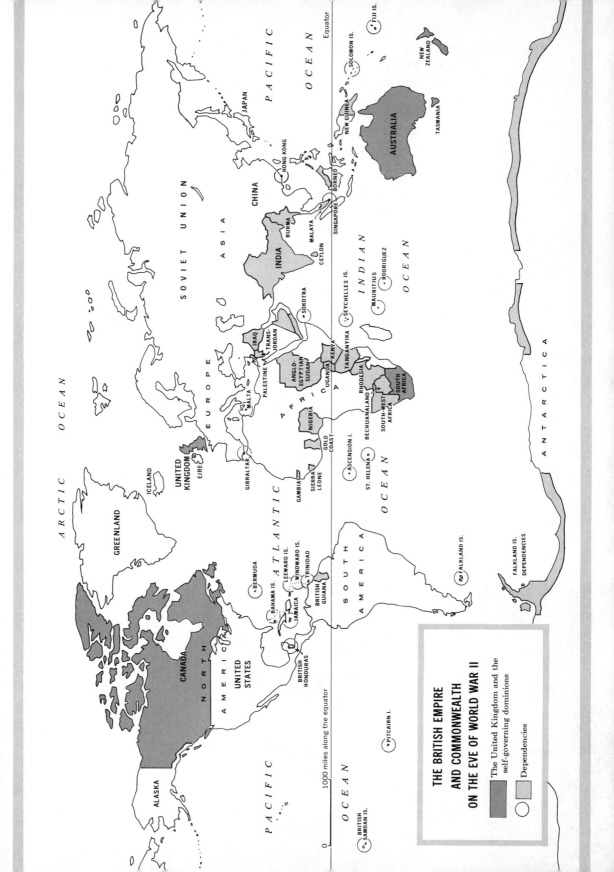

THE BRITISH EMPIRE
AND COMMONWEALTH
ON THE EVE OF WORLD WAR II

The United Kingdom and the
self-governing dominions

○ Dependencies

1000 miles along the equator

fascist governments for his own purposes. One of his chief reasons for going to Munich was to bring Germany, Italy, France, and Britain into a four-power alliance to determine the destinies of Europe. It is significant also that Germany and the Soviet Union became allies in 1939, despite the fact that, shortly before, Hitler had described the Bolsheviks as "scum of the earth," while Stalin had referred to the Nazis as "bloody assassins of the workers." The power-politics hypothesis would appear to suffer, not from inaccuracy, but, like most specialized theories, from a failure to give proper recognition to all of the factors. If nationalism and militarism are not originally primary causes of wars, they often become so as international tension increases.

If there was any one immediate cause of World War II, it could doubtless be found in the appeasement policy of Britain and France. Appeasement may be defined as a policy of granting concessions to an aggressive and unscrupulous nation from motives of fear or indolence. Invariably, the concessions are made at the expense of a weaker country. Appeasement has nothing to do with either benevolence or justice. Appeasement was used several times during the 1930's. It characterized the policy of Britain with regard to Japan in 1931 when the Japanese invaded Manchuria, technically a part of China. Though China appealed to the League of Nations, the British would allow nothing to be done since they feared retaliation against their own interests in the Far East and hoped to use Japan in the future as a counterweight against Russia.

The classic example of appeasement, however, was the Munich Agreement of 1938. By September of that year Hitler had pushed

The appeasement
policy

The Munich Conference, 1938. Left: Hitler, Chamberlain, partially hidden behind Hitler, Mussolini with his back to the camera, and Daladier on the far right. Right: Prime Minister Chamberlain addressing a crowd on his return from the Munich conference. In this speech, September 30, 1938, he proclaimed that "peace in our time" would result from the agreement.

German Troops Entering Prague, April 2, 1939. While Nazi motorized units passed by, some Czechs sang "Where Is My Home" and others wept.

his drive to the East so far that only one obstacle, Czechoslovakia, stood in his way. Earlier in the year he had annexed Austria, which left Czechoslovakia almost surrounded by German territory. From that point on he exerted relentless pressure against the Slav republic. Convinced of the imminent danger of war, the British Prime Minister, Neville Chamberlain, determined to leave nothing undone to pacify the German dictator. Frantic appeals came also from other sources, including France, Italy, and the United States. Finally, on September 28, the Fuehrer agreed to meet with Chamberlain, Premier Daladier of France, and Mussolini in a four-power conference in Munich. The result was a complete surrender to the violent, browbeating Chancellor. During the next few months Hitler not only annexed the Sudetenland, or western portion of Czechoslovakia (as the Munich Agreement had permitted him to do), but he annihilated the entire Czech republic. Instead of bringing peace to a frightened Europe, this action intensified the crisis. The Soviet government was convinced that the Munich settlement was a diabolical plot by Britain and France to save their own skins by diverting Nazi expansion eastward. In August 1939, Stalin and his colleagues entered into a pact of their own with the Nazi government. Its effect was to give Hitler the green light for an attack on Poland. Apparently, there was an understanding that the two dictators would divide Poland between them. In going to Munich, Britain and France had thought of nothing but their own interests; Russia would now look to hers.

The Munich Agreement

2. THE OUTBREAK OF HOSTILITIES

Following the extinction of Czechoslovakia, Hitler turned his aggressive designs against Poland. He demanded the abolition of the Polish Corridor and the return of Danzig to Germany. Convinced finally that the Fuehrer's appetite for power was insatiable, Chamberlain announced that Britain would give Poland armed assistance. Soon afterward he declared that his government would come to the aid of *any* country that felt itself menaced by Hitler's ambitions. In

The beginning of World War II

The Beginning of World War II. A long line of German tanks speeding into Poland.

the weeks that followed, both Britain and France gave definite guaranties not only to Poland but to Greece, Rumania, and Turkey. Hitler apparently believed that these pledges were worthless. With the Soviets drawn into his camp, he probably thought that Poland would quickly capitulate, and that the Western allies would back down once more as they had done at Munich. When Poland stood firm, the Fuehrer decided to attack. On September 1, 1939, a long column of German tanks crossed the Polish border. Upon learning of the attack, Britain and France sent a joint warning to Germany that she must cease her aggression. To this there was no reply. September 3 brought a radio announcement by Neville Chamberlain that Britain was at war with Germany. He spoke of the "bitter blow" it was to him that his "long struggle for peace" had failed. He asserted that it was evil the British nation would be fighting against —"brute force, bad faith, injustice, oppression, and persecution." Later the same day France also entered the war.

Stages of the war

World War II passed through several stages. The conflict with Poland proved to be a brief encounter. In less than three weeks the Polish armies had been routed, Warsaw had been captured, and the chiefs of the Polish government had fled to Rumania. For some months after that the war resolved itself into a kind of siege, a "phony war" or "sitzkrieg," as it was sometimes called. Such fighting as did occur was largely confined to submarine warfare, aerial raids on naval bases, and occasional battles between naval vessels. In the spring of 1940 the sitzkrieg was suddenly transformed into a Blitzkrieg. The Germans struck lightning blows at Norway, Denmark, Belgium, the Netherlands, and France, conquering them one after another. Following these disasters the war entered a new stage, the so-called Battle of Britain. Instead of launching an invasion across the Channel, the Nazis decided to attempt the reduction of Britain to submission by air raids. From August 1940 to June 1941 thousands of planes smashed at British ports, industrial centers, and air defenses throughout the country. Despite the fact that whole sections of cities were laid in ruins and more than 40,000 citizens killed, the British held firm and finally were able to retaliate by even more devastating attacks upon German cities.

Frustrated in his attempt to subjugate Britain, Hitler turned eastward, on June 22, 1941, with a massive invasion of Russia. Before the end of the year his armies had smashed their way to the very gates of Moscow but never succeeded in capturing it. Meanwhile, the war was converted into a global war when Japan struck a deadly blow at Pearl Harbor on December 7 of the same year. The Japanese were already involved in a costly war with China. To wage it successfully they needed the oil, rubber, and extensive food resources of the Netherlands Indies, the Malay Peninsula, and Indochina. Before attacking these areas they apparently considered it necessary to lock the back door by crushing American naval and air power on the great base of Pearl Harbor. The next day the United States Congress recognized a state of war with Japan, and on December 11 Germany and her fascist allies declared war upon the United States.

The course of the war was marked by several turning points. The first was the stubborn defense of Moscow by Stalin's armies in November and December, 1941. The second was the defeat of the Germans in North Africa, which opened the way for the Allied invasion of Italy and the overthrow of Mussolini. The third was the Battle of Stalingrad in 1943, when the Germans failed in their attempt to cut northern Russia off from the food-producing region of the Ukraine and from the oil resources north and south of the Caucasus. The turning points in the Pacific war came during the

A German V-2 Rocket. Used in the latter years of the war, it was the forerunner of the early space launch vehicles.

Below: *French Refugees Driven from Their Home during the Early Years of the Nazi Occupation.* Right: *London during the Blitz.* This picture gives a vivid impression of the agony which the British capital suffered during the Battle of Britain from August 1940 to June 1941. In back of the tumbling ruins brought down by fire bombs is St. Paul's Cathedral.

Pearl Harbor, December 7, 1941. This photo shows American battleships sunk at their moorings following the Japanese raid on what President Franklin D. Roosevelt declared was "the day that will live in infamy."

spring of 1942 with the defeat by the United States Navy of Japanese forces in the battles of the Coral Sea and of Midway. These defeats spelled the doom of Japanese attempts to capture Australia and the Hawaiian Islands and thereby deprive the United States of advance bases for a counteroffensive against Japan.

End of the war in Europe

By the winter of 1944–1945 World War II was nearing its end. On June 6, 1944 (D-Day), American forces had crossed the English Channel and landed successfully in northern France. On August 25 they liberated Paris. In September advance detachments drove to the Rhine, and eventually whole armies penetrated to the heart of Germany. Meantime, Soviet troops were approaching from the east. On April 21 they hammered their way into the suburbs of Berlin. During the next ten days a savage battle raged amid the ruins and heaps of rubble. On May 2 the heart of the city was captured, and the Soviet red banner flew from the Brandenburg Gate. A few hours earlier Adolf Hitler killed himself in the bomb-proof shelter of the Chancellery. On May 7 representatives of the German High Command signed a document of unconditional surrender. Peace had come at last to an exhausted Europe after five years and eight months of slaughter and barbarism.

V-J Day

The end of the war in the Pacific was delayed for another four months. Victory over the Japanese empire had to be achieved by savage naval battles and by bloody assaults upon almost impregnable islands. In June 1945, Okinawa was taken, after eighty-two days of desperate fighting. The Americans now had footholds less than 500 miles from the Japanese homeland. The government in Tokyo was nervously anticipating an invasion and calling upon the citizens for supreme endeavors to meet the crisis. On July 26 the heads of the United States, British, and Chinese governments issued a joint proclamation calling upon Japan to surrender or be destroyed. In the absence of a reply the highest officials of the United States government resolved to make use of a new and revolutionary weapon to end the war quickly. This weapon was the atomic bomb recently devel-

1208

oped in great secrecy by American scientists. Though many high military and naval officers contended that use of the bomb was not necessary, on the assumption that Japan was already beaten, President Harry S. Truman decided otherwise. On August 6 a single atomic bomb was dropped on Hiroshima, completely obliterating about 60 per cent of the city. Three days later a second bomb was dropped, this time on Nagasaki. That night President Truman warned that the United States would continue to use the deadly new weapon as long as might be necessary to bring Japan to her knees. On August 14 Tokyo transmitted to Washington an unconditional acceptance of the Allied demands. As the news spread through the victorious nations millions of people danced and cheered and paraded in the streets amid the screaming of horns and the shrieking of sirens. Some of the more thoughtful assembled in churches the following day to give thanks that the terrible ordeal was over.

3. THE PEACE SETTLEMENT

The peace settlement at the end of World War II, if such it can be called, was a fragmentary accomplishment. The first statement of Allied objectives in the event of victory was the Atlantic Charter, issued by President Roosevelt and Prime Minister Winston Churchill on August 14, 1941. Its essential principles were as follows:

The Atlantic Charter and the United Nations Declaration

(1) No territorial changes that do not accord with the wishes of the people concerned.

(2) The right of all peoples to choose the form of government under which they will live.

Below: *D-Day*. Cargo ships are seen pouring supplies ashore during the invasion of France. Balloon barrages float overhead to protect the ships from low-flying enemy strifers. Right: *Signing the German Surrender, May 7, 1945*

View of Hiroshima after First Atom Bomb Was Dropped, August 6, 1945. This photo, taken one month later, shows the utter devastation of the city. Only a few steel and concrete buildings remained intact.

(3) All states to enjoy access, on equal terms, to the trade and raw materials of the world.

(4) Freedom to traverse the seas without hindrance.

(5) Disarmament of all nations that threaten aggression.

The Atlantic Charter acquired a broad significance when it was re-affirmed by the United Nations Declaration on January 2, 1942. Twenty-six nations signed this Declaration, including Great Britain, the United States, the Soviet Union, and the Republic of China. Subsequently about fourteen others added their signatures.

As the war progressed, high officials of the leading United Nations met in various conferences for the purpose of determining the conditions of peace. The first of outstanding importance was the conference that met in Cairo in November 1943, to discuss the fate of the Japanese empire. The participants were President Roosevelt, Prime Minister Churchill, and Generalissimo Chiang Kai-shek. They agreed that all of the territories taken by Japan from China, with the exception of Korea, were to be restored to the Chinese Republic. Korea was to become free and independent. They agreed, further, that Japan was to be stripped of all the islands in the Pacific which she had seized or occupied since 1914, and of "all other territories which she had taken by violence or greed." What disposition was to be made of these islands and territories was not specified.

The second important conference to determine the conditions of peace met in Yalta, in the Crimea, in February 1945. This time the chief participants were Roosevelt, Churchill, and Stalin. A formal report issued at the close of the conference declared that the Big Three had agreed upon plans for the unconditional surrender of Germany, upon methods of controlling Germany and her allies after the war, and upon the establishment of a United Nations

The Cairo Declaration

The Yalta Agreement

1210

Organization to keep the peace. In addition, it was announced that Poland would surrender her eastern provinces to Russia and be compensated by "substantial accessions of territory" in the north and west—to be taken, of course, from Germany. The existing government of Poland, set up under Soviet auspices, was to be reorganized with the inclusion of democratic leaders from among the Poles. The government of Yugoslavia was also to be broadened in similar fashion. Regarding the Far East, it was agreed that Russia should enter the war against Japan and receive as her reward all the territories taken from her by Japan in the war of 1904–1905.

The surrender of Germany on May 8, 1945 seemed to require yet another conference of the victorious powers. On July 17 Joseph Stalin, Winston Churchill, and Harry S. Truman, who had succeeded Franklin D. Roosevelt as President of the United States on April 12, met in Potsdam, a suburb of Berlin. Before the conference had finished its work, Churchill was replaced by Clement Attlee, the new Labour Prime Minister of Great Britain. The most important provisions of the formal Declaration, issued on August 2, were 1) East Prussia to be divided into two parts, the northern part to go to the Soviet Union, and the southern part to be assigned to Poland; 2) Poland to receive the former free city of Danzig; 3) all German territory east of the Oder and Neisse rivers to be administered by Poland, pending a final settlement; 4) the military power of Germany to be totally destroyed; and 5) Germany to be divided into four occupation zones to be governed, respectively, by the U.S.S.R., Great Britain, the United States, and France.

The Potsdam Declaration

After the end of the war the victorious states drafted peace treaties with Japan and with Germany's satellites. The treaty with Japan deprived her of all the territory she had acquired since 1854—in other words, her entire overseas empire. She gave up the southern half of Sakhalin Island and the Kuril Islands to Soviet Russia, and the Bonins and Ryukyus to control by the United

The Treaty with Japan

The Yalta Conference. Below: Roosevelt at the airport. Right: Churchill, Molotov, Secretary of State Stettinius (left), and Stalin (center) with glasses raised in a toast. To Stalin's left, Roosevelt, Churchill, and Molotov.

The Potsdam Conference. Two of the Big Three had changed: Clement Atlee had replaced Churchill as British prime minister, and Harry Truman had succeeded U.S. president Roosevelt.

States. She also renounced all rights to Formosa, which was left in a status still undefined. She yielded to the United States the right to continue maintaining military installations in Japan until the latter was able to defend herself. The treaty went into effect in April 1952, against the opposition of the Russians, who had hoped that Japan would be crippled by drastic punishments and thereby left an easy prey to communism.

As in the case of the Versailles Treaty one of the most significant elements in the World War II settlement was its provision for international organization. The old League of Nations had failed to avert the outbreak of war in 1939, and in April 1946, it was formally dissolved. Allied statesmen had long recognized the need for a new organization. In February 1945, they agreed at Yalta that a conference to implement that need should be convoked for April 25 in San Francisco. Despite the tragic death of President Roosevelt two weeks earlier, the conference met as scheduled. A charter was adopted on June 26, providing for a world organization to be known as the United Nations and to be founded upon the principle of "the sovereign equality of all peace-loving states." Its important agencies were to be 1) a General Assembly composed of representatives of all the member states; 2) a Security Council composed of representatives of the United States, Great Britain, the U.S.S.R., the Republic of China, and France, with permanent seats, and of six other states chosen by the General Assembly to fill the nonpermanent seats; 3) a Secretariat consisting of a Secretary-General and a staff of subordinates; 4) an Economic and Social Council composed of eighteen members chosen by the General Assembly; 5) a Trusteeship Council; and 6) an International Court of Justice.

By far the most important functions of the new organization were assigned by the Charter to the Security Council. This agency has the "primary responsibility for the maintenance of international peace and security." It has authority to investigate any dispute be-

Establishment of the United Nations

tween nations, to recommend methods for settlement, and, if necessary to preserve the peace, to employ diplomatic or economic measures against an aggressor. If, in its judgment, these have proved, or are likely to prove, inadequate, it may "take such action by air, naval, or land forces" as may be required to maintain or restore international order. The member states are required by the Charter to make available to the Security Council, on its call, armed forces for the maintenance of peace.

The Security Council

The Security Council was so organized as to give almost a monopoly of authority to its permanent members. It was the belief of the Big Three who assembled at Yalta, and of President Roosevelt especially, that the peace of the world depended upon harmony among the states primarily responsible for winning the war. Accordingly, they agreed that when the Security Council should be set up, no action of any kind could be taken without the unanimous consent of Great Britain, France, the United States, the Republic of China, the Soviet Union, and two other members besides. This absolute veto given to each of the principal states had none of the hoped-for effects. Instead of bolstering the peace of the world, its chief result was to cripple the Council and to render it helpless in the face of emergencies. The primary cause was the growth of distrust between Soviet Russia and the West. Each has opposed most of the demands of the other with respect to disarmament, the control of nuclear weapons, and the admission of new states.

The veto power of the Big Five

The remaining agencies of the U.N. were given a wide variety of functions. The Secretariat, composed of a Secretary-General and a numerous staff, is chiefly an administrative authority. Its duties, though, are by no means routine, for the Secretary-General may bring to the attention of the Security Council any matter which, in his opinion, may threaten international peace. The functions of the Economic and Social Council are the most varied of all. Composed of eighteen members elected by the General Assembly, it has au-

Other agencies of the U.N.

The United Nations. Buildings of the permanent headquarters in New York are the General Assembly building (foreground) and behind it the thirty-eight-story Secretariat.

ARCTIC OCEAN

GREENLAND

ICELAND

ALASKA

CANADA

IRELAND

KIN

FR

PORT.

SPAI

UNITED STATES

PACIFIC

ATLANTIC

MOROCCO

SP. SAHARA

BAHAMAS (adm. since 1945)

MAURITANIA

MEXICO

CUBA

HAITI

DOMINICAN REP.

JAMAICA

GUATEMALA

HONDURAS

EL SALVADOR

NICARAGUA

COSTA RICA

PANAMA

BARBADOS

TRINIDAD AND TOBAGO

VENE-
ZUELA

GUYANA

SURINAM

FR. GUIANA

MAL

SENEGAL

GAMBIA

PORT. GUINEA

GUINEA

SIERRA LEONE

LIBERIA

IVORY COAST

UPPER
VOLT

GHANA

TOG

DAH

COLOMBIA

ECUADOR

0   2000 miles at the equator

OCEAN

PERU

BRAZIL

OCEAN

BOLIVIA

PARAGUAY

CHILE

URUGUAY

ARGENTINA

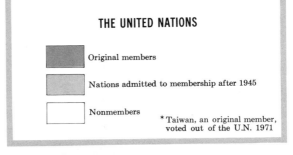

THE UNITED NATIONS

Original members

Nations admitted to membership after 1945

Nonmembers

*Taiwan, an original member,
voted out of the U.N. 1971

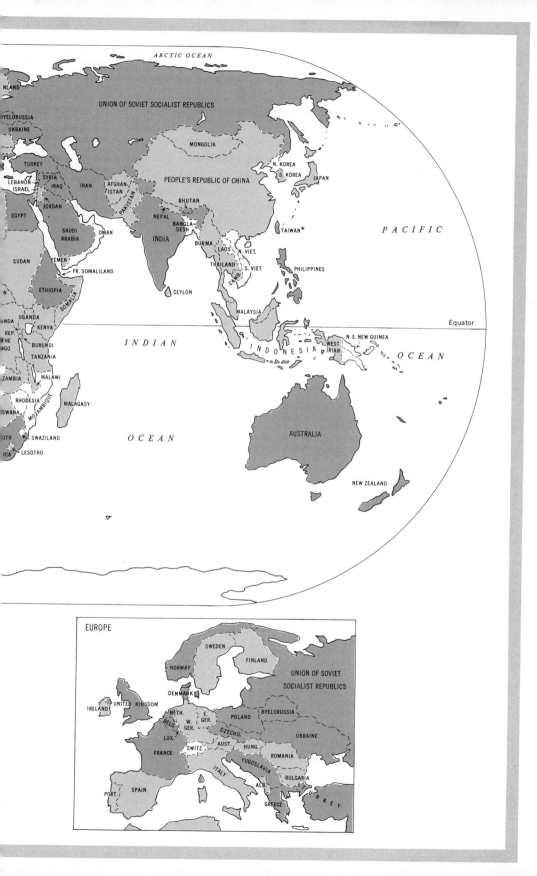

thority to initiate studies and make recommendations with respect to international social, economic, health, educational, cultural, and related matters, and may perform services within such fields at the request of U.N. members. Under its jurisdiction are such specialized agencies as: the World Health Organization (WHO), which works to control epidemics and to assist backward nations in stamping out cholera, typhus, and venereal disease and in raising standards of health and sanitation; and the Food and Agriculture Organization (FAO), which seeks to promote increases in food production by finding remedies for agricultural depressions, for plant and animal diseases and insect pests, and by projecting plans for mechanizing small farms and for the more efficient distribution of food.

Achievements
of the U.N.

During the first three decades of its history the achievements of the U.N. constituted a modestly impressive record. It induced Soviet Russia to withdraw her troops from Iran, and Britain and France to take their forces out of Syria and Lebanon. It appointed a commission to investigate the infiltration of foreign Communists into Greece. It terminated a bloody war between Dutch and native forces in Indonesia. It induced the British to agree to the partition of Palestine, and it persuaded the warring Jews and Arabs to conclude a truce. It assisted in arranging a cease-fire agreement between India and Pakistan, which temporarily prevented war from inundating some 400 million people. But against these accomplishments must be recorded several failures. It failed in its efforts to establish control of nuclear weapons. Despite the specific requirements of Article 26 of the Charter, it did nothing to provide for a general reduction of armaments. It failed also to curb the increasing friction between the U.S.S.R. and the United States, which was certainly a threat to international peace. It was powerless in the face of Soviet suppression of the Hungarian revolt in 1956. It has been argued, however, that one of the main contributions of the U.N. was the prevention of a direct clash between the U.S. and the U.S.S.R. By providing makeshift solutions as well as a forum for the discussion of grievances, the U.N. helped to keep the two giants from a head-on collision. As a consequence, crises mounted to a crescendo of bitterness without resulting in a holocaust that would destroy the world.

Other forms of
internationalism:
(1) the movement
for a world
republic

In the light of conditions obtaining after World War II, it was perhaps inevitable that internationalism should assume a number of forms. Some thoughtful observers criticized the United Nations as a mere replica of the old League of Nations. Both, it was said, were leagues of governments, not federations of peoples. Those who felt this way argued for nothing less than a world federal republic similar in structure to the United States, with an actual transfer of sovereign powers to a central government. They believed that the government of this republic should include not merely a court to hear disputes and a world executive with police authority, but,

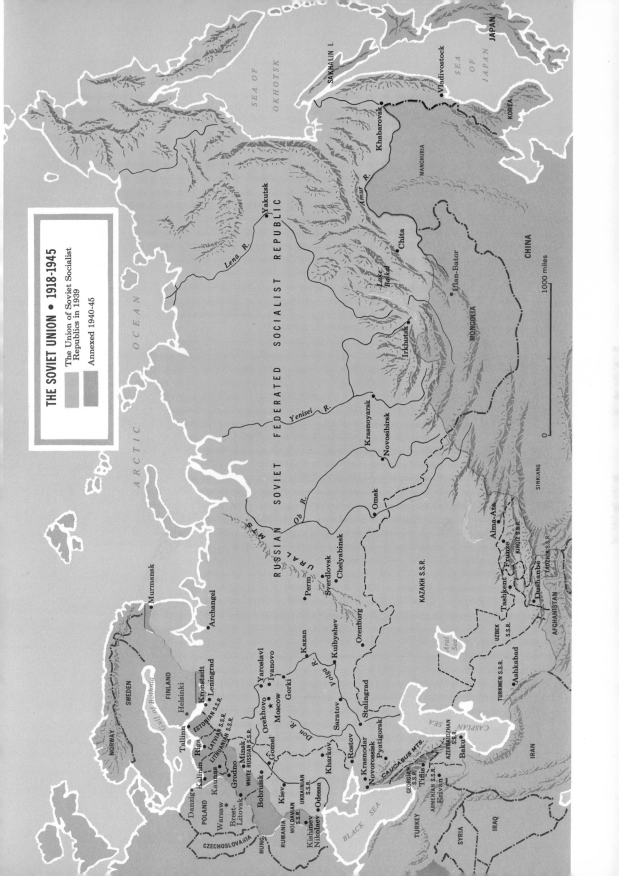

THE SOVIET UNION • 1918-1945

The Union of Soviet Socialist
Republics in 1939

Annexed 1940-45

1000 miles

ARCTIC OCEAN

SEA OF OKHOTSK

SAKHALIN I.

JAPAN

Vladivostock

SEA OF JAPAN

KOREA

MANCHURIA

Khabarovsk

Amur R.

Yakutsk

Chita

Lena R.

Lake Baikal

CHINA

Irkutsk

Ulan-Bator

MONGOLIA

SOVIET FEDERATED SOCIALIST REPUBLIC

Yenisei R.

Krasnoyarsk

Novosibirsk

Omsk

SINKIANG

Ob R.

RUSSIAN

URAL MTS.

Sverdlovsk

Chelyabinsk

Perm

KAZAKH S.S.R.

Alma-Ata

Frunze

KIRGIZ S.S.R.

Tashkent

Dushanbe

TADZHIK S.S.R.

Orenburg

Kuibyshev

Aral Sea

UZBEK S.S.R.

AFGHANISTAN

Ashkabad

TURKMEN S.S.R.

Murmansk

Archangel

Kazan

Volga R.

Saratov

Stalingrad

IRAN

CASPIAN SEA

Yaroslavl

Ivanovo

Orekhovo

Moscow

Gorki

Don R.

Rostov

Pyatigorsk

CAUCASUS MTS.

Novorossisk

Krasnodar

Baku

AZERBAIDZHAN S.S.R.

Tiflis

GEORGIAN S.S.R.

ARMENIAN S.S.R.

Erivan

TURKEY

SYRIA

IRAQ

SWEDEN

FINLAND

Helsinki

Kronstadt

Leningrad

Tallinn

ESTONIAN S.S.R.

Riga

LATVIAN S.S.R.

Kalinin

Kaunas

LITHUANIAN S.S.R.

Grodno

Minsk

WHITE RUSSIAN S.S.R.

Gomel

Bobruisk

Kiev

UKRAINIAN S.S.R.

Kharkov

Odessa

Nikolaev

Kishinev

MOLDAVIAN S.S.R.

RUMANIA

HUNG.

CZECHOSLOVAKIA

Danzig

POLAND

Warsaw

Brest-Litovsk

NORWAY

Gulf of Bothnia

BLACK SEA

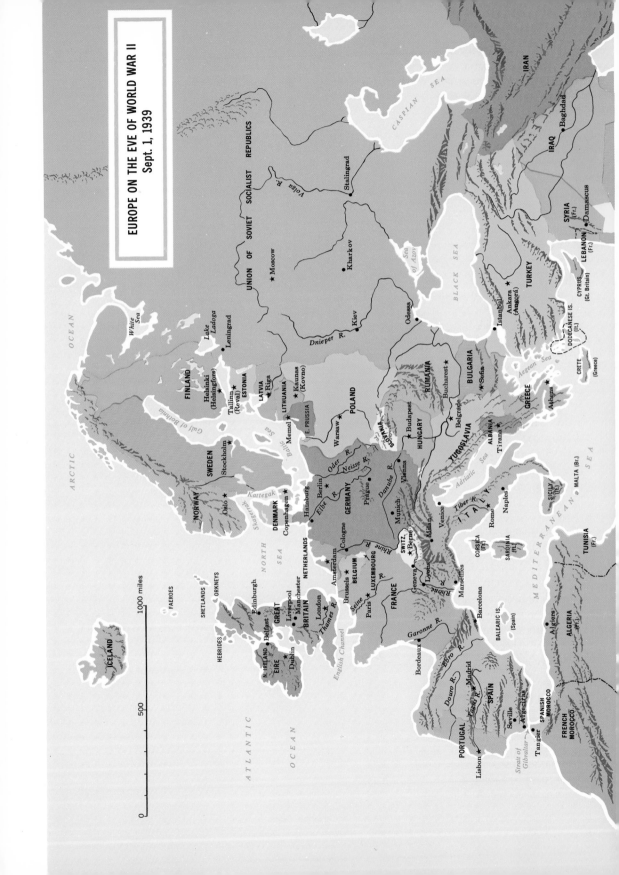

EUROPE ON THE EVE OF WORLD WAR II
Sept. 1, 1939

0   500   1000 miles

ICELAND

ATLANTIC
OCEAN

ARCTIC
OCEAN

White
Sea

OCEAN

FAEROES

SHETLANDS

ORKNEYS

HEBRIDES

N. IRELAND
Belfast ★
EIRE
Dublin ★

Edinburgh ★
GREAT
Liverpool • Manchester •
BRITAIN
London ★
Thames R.

English Channel

NORTH
SEA

NORWAY
Oslo ★

SWEDEN
Stockholm ★

FINLAND
Helsinki
(Helsingfors) ★
Tallinn
(Reval) ★
ESTONIA
LATVIA
Riga ★
LITHUANIA
Kaunas
(Kovno) ★
Memel •
E. PRUSSIA

Lake
Ladoga
Leningrad •

UNION OF SOVIET SOCIALIST REPUBLICS

Moscow ★

Volga R.

Stalingrad •

Kharkov •

Dnieper R.

Kiev •

Odessa •

Sea
of Azov

BLACK SEA

CASPIAN
SEA

Gulf of Bothnia

Baltic Sea

Kattegat

Skagerrak

DENMARK
Copenhagen ★

Hamburg •
Elbe R.
Berlin ★
GERMANY
Cologne •
Rhine R.

Oder R.
Neisse R.

POLAND
Warsaw ★

SUDETENLAND
Prague ★
Danube R.
Vienna ★
Munich •

CZECHOSLOVAKIA

HUNGARY
Budapest ★

RUMANIA
Bucharest ★

BULGARIA
Sofia ★

GREECE
Athens ★

Belgrade ★
YUGOSLAVIA

ALBANIA
Tirana ★

Adriatic Sea

Aegean Sea

CRETE
(Greece)

DODECANESE IS.
(It.)

CYPRUS
(Gt. Britain)

TURKEY
Ankara
(Angora) ★
Istanbul •

SYRIA
(Fr.)
Damascus •
LEBANON
(Fr.)

IRAN

IRAQ
Baghdad •

NETHERLANDS
Amsterdam •
BELGIUM
Brussels •
LUXEMBOURG
Seine R.
Paris ★
FRANCE

SWITZ.
Berne ★
Geneva •
Lyon •
Rhône R.
Marseilles •

Milan •
Venice •
I T A L Y
Tiber R.
Rome ★
Naples •

CORSICA
(Fr.)

SARDINIA
(It.)

SICILY
(It.)
• MALTA (Br.)

MEDITERRANEAN   SEA

Bordeaux •
Garonne R.

Barcelona •

BALEARIC IS.
(Spain)

Algiers •

ALGERIA
(Fr.)

TUNISIA
(Fr.)

Douro R.
Tagus R.
Madrid ★
SPAIN
Seville •
Algeciras •
Ebro R.

PORTUGAL
Lisbon ★

Tangier •
SPANISH
MOROCCO
FRENCH
MOROCCO

Strait of
Gibraltar

above all, a world parliament representing peoples rather than governments and capable of enacting laws which would apply directly to individuals. It was not argued that the functions of the world state should entirely supersede those of national governments. On the contrary, only such sovereign powers as control over armaments, tariffs, and colonial areas should be transferred to the central authority; the rest would be reserved to the national units.

Less idealistic statesmen and publicists held to the belief that the U.N. should be supplemented by military and political alliances. Convinced that the U.S.S.R. was bent upon world conquest, they could think only in terms of a combination of force for the "containment" of Soviet power. Such was the opinion of President Truman and his advisers in the United States, and they seem to have converted to similar views most of the governments of the Atlantic region. In April 1949, a group of representatives of North Atlantic states together with Canada and the United States signed an agreement providing for the establishment of the North Atlantic Treaty Organization (NATO). Subsequently Greece, Turkey, and West Germany were added as members. The treaty declared that an armed attack against any one of the signatory parties would be regarded as an attack against all, and that they would combine their armed strength to whatever extent necessary to repel the aggressor. It was decided also that the joint military command, or NATO army established in 1950, should be increased from thirty to fifty divisions in 1953, and that West Germany should be rearmed and invited to contribute twelve of the divisions. It was thereby hoped that NATO would be ready for any emergency that might arise as a consequence of the expansionist policies of Soviet Russia. By 1966, however the status of the alliance had been compromised by disharmony between France, on the one side, and Great Britain and the United States on the other. Whereas Britain generally supported the policies of the United States, France under de Gaulle aspired to organize Western Europe as an independent entity opposing the threat of communist expansion. He seemed anxious to exclude the United States from a dominant role in European affairs. Western European nations, he believed, were capable of saving themselves and taking care of their own future. To accomplish his aims he was ready for a reconciliation with Germany and practically forced the withdrawal of NATO troops from French soil.

(2) NATO

SELECTED READINGS

· *Items so designated are available in paperbound editions.*

· Aron, Raymond, *The Century of Total War*, Boston, 1955 (Beacon).
· Bailey, T. A., *Woodrow Wilson and the Lost Peace*, New York, 1944 (Quadrangle).
· Carr, E. H., *The Twenty Years' Crisis*, London, 1946 (Torchbook). Stimulating but somewhat dogmatic.

READINGS
· Chadwin, Mark Lincoln, *The Warhawks: American Interventionists before Pearl Harbor*, Chapel Hill, 1968 (Norton Library).

Coox, A. D., *Year of the Tiger*, Tokyo, 1964. A study of the beginning of the Sino-Japanese War in 1937–1938.

Divine, Robert A., *Roosevelt and World War II*, Baltimore, 1969.

· Eyck, F. Gunther, *The Benelux Countries: An Historical Survey*, Princeton, 1959 (Anvil).

· Feis, Herbert, *The Road to Pearl Harbor*, Princeton, 1950 (Atheneum).

· ———, *Churchill-Roosevelt-Stalin: The War They Waged and the Peace They Sought*, Princeton, 1957 (Princeton).

Finer, Herman, *America's Destiny*, New York, 1947.

Gay, Peter, *Weimar Culture: The Outsider as Insider*, New York, 1968.

Géraud, André, *The Gravediggers of France*, New York, 1944. A critical and impassioned account.

Holbòrn, Hajo, *The Political Collapse of Europe*, New York, 1951. A penetrating analysis.

Lafore, Laurence, *The End of Glory: An Interpretation of the Origins of World War II*, Philadelphia, 1970. Asserts that that war resulted from efforts of European powers to run affairs with institutions and ideas made obsolete by World War I.

· Langer, William L., *Our Vichy Gamble*, New York, 1947 (Norton Library).

Lifton, Robert J., *Death in Life: The Survivors of Hiroshima*, New York, 1967.

Morgenthau, H. J., *Politics among Nations: The Struggle for Power and Peace*, New York, 1948. A provocative analysis from the viewpoint of a realist.

Neumann, William L., *After Victory: Churchill, Roosevelt, Stalin and the Making of the Peace*, New York, 1967.

· O'Connor, Raymond G., *Diplomacy for Victory: FDR and Unconditional Surrender*, New York, 1971 (Norton).

· Reves, Emery, *The Anatomy of Peace*, New York, 1945 (Compass). An eloquent plea for a world federal republic.

Robertson, E. M., ed., *Origins of the Second World War*, New York, 1970.

· Rowse, A. L., *Appeasement: A Study in Political Decline, 1933–1939*, New York, 1961 (Norton Library).

· Taylor, A. J. P., *The Origins of the Second World War*, New York, 1961 (Fawcett).

· Trevor-Roper, H. R., *The Last Days of Hitler*, New York, 1947 (Collier).

Viorst, Milton, *Hostile Allies: FDR and Charles de Gaulle*, New York, 1965.

Wittner, Lawrence S., *Rebels against War*, New York, 1969.

· Wolfers, Arnold, *Britain and France between Two Wars*, New York, 1940 (Norton Library).

SOURCE MATERIALS

· Churchill, W. S., *Blood, Sweat, and Tears*. Also available in paperback under the title *The Years of Greatness* (Capricorn).

· ———, *The Second World War*, New York, 1960, 6 vols. (Bantam, 1962, 6 vols.).

· Eisenhower, D. D., *Crusade in Europe*, New York, 1948 (Dolphin).

Grew, J. C., *Report from Tokyo*, New York, 1942.

Liebling, A. J., ed., *The Republic of Silence*, New York, 1947. A collection of materials on the French Resistance movement.

Maurois, André, *Tragedy in France: An Eyewitness Account*.

U.N. Dept. of Public Information, *Yearbook of the United Nations*.

CHAPTER 40

New Power Relationships

> If we don't have peace and the nuclear bombs start to fall, what difference will it make whether we are Communists or Catholics or capitalists or Chinese or Russians or Americans? Who will be left to tell us apart?
>
> —Nikita Khrushchev in interview with Norman Cousins, January 1963

> Mankind must put an end to war—or war will put an end to mankind. . . . Let us call a truce to terror. Let us invoke the blessings of peace. And as we build an international capacity to keep peace, let us join in dismantling the national capacity to wage war.
>
> —President John F. Kennedy, September 25, 1961, Address to the General Assembly of the United Nations

World War II left the political world of Europe, Asia, and the United States in a state of disorder. Of course, no such result was intended by those who fought to destroy fascism and to reorganize **The new world** the world under a new system to take the place of the League of **of disorder** Nations. However, their calculations went awry. The new United Nations proved to be no more effective than the old League. The war itself spawned nationalist revolts all over the world. As victory approached, wartime allies buried their hatchets in each other's backs. With the conclusion of peace, wars broke out on three continents. Some were nationalist struggles to gain independence for former colonies of dying empires. The success of some of these struggles seldom brought peace but merely a continuation of strife in new forms. Still other clashes took the form of conflict between the superstates or some of their satellites. These were among the bloodiest and most destructive of all the outbursts of savagery that marked the period after World War II. Several eclipsed the savagery of that war itself and did much to brand our own age as one of the most barbarous in history.

An outstanding phenomenon of the period that followed World War II was the decline of Europe. Ever since the last centuries of

1219

the pre-Christian era, a small peninsula of Eurasia—for that is what Europe is—had dominated the civilized world. This limited area had most of the technological advances, the bulk of the wealth, and most of the science, philosophy, literature, music, art, and other embellishments that go to make up the total of civilization. Many of these achievements were based on a hard-driving expenditure of energy that had its origin in religion. Many others sprang from conquest of less enterprising peoples and from enslavement of the least fortunate.

I.   THE SECOND HUNDRED YEARS' WAR

The years 1337–1453 marked the period of the so-called Hundred Years' War. The name leaves much to be said from the standpoint of accuracy. In the first place it suggests a continuous conflict, which did not prevail. Instead, there were numerous truces or suspensions of hostilities while the two sides jockeyed for position or bargained for advantages. A similar period in world history began in 1870 and has continued, with interruptions, until the present day. Some observers think it will not terminate before the end of the twentieth century. It began with the Franco-German War in 1870 and continued with the Sino-Japanese War in 1895, and the Russo-Japanese War in 1904–1905. It reached its first great climax in the two World Wars of 1914 and 1939. But destructive though these conflicts were, they did not bring peace to an exhausted world. Instead, they spawned new violence on a more limited scale but with steadily increasing brutality.

The initial armed clash of the post–World War period was the Korean War of 1950–1953. To most people in the West this seemed an obvious attempt of the Russians to use their allies, the North Koreans, as agents for extending Soviet power in the Far East. Most of them were unaware of the conflicting ambitions of North and South Korea. The South Korean President, Syngman Rhee, openly proclaimed his ambition to unite the whole country, by force if necessary. Open warfare began on June 25, 1950 when troops from North Korea crossed the 38th parallel to attack the non-communist republic of South Korea. Soon afterward President Truman sent armed assistance to the South Koreans. Theoretically, the United States forces were fighting merely as representatives of the United Nations. Actually, they were waging an old-fashioned power struggle not essentially different from that between Russia and Japan in 1904–1905. By 1951 the Korean War had reached a stalemate, and two years later a *pro forma* peace settlement was concluded.

The second major example of international violence in the wake of World War II has been the Indochina conflict. This subject will be discussed in full in the next chapter. Suffice it to emphasize now that the Indochina War grew out of a kind of last gasp of nineteenth-century imperialism. The peninsula of Indochina had been

War in Korea. U.S. Marines firing into a bleak hillside.

organized as a French colony in the time of Napoleon III. Over the years it became one of the most valuable of French possessions. When, in 1941, the Japanese extended their aggressions into Southeast Asia, the made Indochina a major target of attack. They set up puppet rulers and governed the peninsula as a colony of Japan. With the defeat of Japan and the end of the war, native nationalists sought to prevent their country from falling into the grasp of the imperialists. Foremost among the native nationalists was a Vietnamese party known as Viet Minh. Their leader was a Moscow-trained Communist, Ho Chi Minh. The rebels resorted to guerrilla warfare and inflicted such costly defeats upon the French that they were forced to abandon the struggle in 1954.

2. THE DECLINE AND REVIVAL OF IDEOLOGY

Despite all the talk about the threat of world communism and the imminence of ideological conquest, the danger of either seems clearly to have diminished in the past decade. Most Communist haters of a bygone age have mellowed and bent over backward to give their blessings to the Soviet Union. Some did this during World War II when Russia was an ally of Britain and the United States. The most famous were Franklin D. Roosevelt and Winston Churchill. In the honeymoon that followed briefly the defeat of Germany, President Truman confessed that he "rather liked Old Joe." Most interesting of all the reversals of attitudes toward communism was that of Richard M. Nixon. Foremost among leaders of anticommunism in the United States during the Cold War, he had gained national fame by goading the prosecution of such Russian sympathizers as Alger Hiss. He referred to the State Department scornfully as Dean Acheson's College of Cowardly Communist Containment. As President, however, Mr. Nixon set himself up as a champion of Communist China, forgetting all the harsh comments

1221

he and his subordinates had been making in the recent past regarding Peking as the regal propagator of the Indochina War. He visited China in 1972 and pushed for its membership in the United Nations. This was to be done, he asserted, without sacrificing the interests of "our old friends," the Nationalist Chinese on the island of Taiwan. His motives are not entirely clear. While probably political, they may also have been to develop Red China as a counterpoise against Russia, and perhaps even against Japan for the long pull.

But America was not the only nation to substitute a shrewd political realism for the Communist-baiting of the past. Orthodox gospels of Marxism have almost disappeared from the scene all over the world. A few proponents can still be found in Russia and Albania and doubtless also in Mainland China. Communist parties exist under compulsion in Poland, Czechoslovakia, and Yugoslavia, but few could vouch for the sincerity of what they believe. Several of their leaders have adopted so many elements of production for profit and for the satisfaction of consumer demands that they have drifted far from the orthodox teachings of Marx and Lenin. A Polish wit has distinguished thus between capitalism and communism: "Capitalism is a system wherein man exploits man. And communism is vice versa."[1] The story of international communism seems little different from that within the several countries. No world communism has swept the globe, despite the dire prediction of many conservatives. In every country west of the Iron Curtain Communist parties have shrunk to insignificance. Italy is an exception, where the Communists constitute the second largest party with a third of the votes cast. In the new states of Africa, which seemed for a time to be such a fertile ground for both Russian and Red Chinese agents, the movement has lost ground. Even in Egypt many of the Kremlin's representatives have been thrown into jail in defiance of whatever dreams they may have had of using the land of the pyramids as a fulcrum of Soviet power in the Middle East. What is true of communism in most countries of the world seems scarcely less true of socialism. Socialists no longer advocate collective ownership of the means of production; they have faded into exponents of the welfare state. It is not uncommon to hear from them slighting references to "baggy-pants Marxism." Defenders of capitalism still exist in theory but few would recognize it if they saw it in full swing. For capitalist economies are no longer free enterprise systems but "mixed" economies, involving government controls, managed currencies, and forced distribution of profits. The small-time capitalist, at least, is permitted to gloat over his gains for a period before turning them over to the government to finance its wars and armaments and public relief.

The causes of the decline of ideology have been several. Many of the architects of utopias were naïve. They believed in the

[1] Daniel Bell, *The End of Ideology*, p. 16.

inherent goodness of human nature and assumed that new and better institutions would provide the open sesame to a perfect society. Rising incomes and the increasing availability of luxuries for members of the lower middle class fostered a disinterest in reform movements. Instead, workers and their families began dreaming of houses in the suburbs, luxury automobiles, and expensive vacations. Even in the Soviet Union, according to Nikita Khrushchev, near the end of his regime, what the Russian masses wanted was not more doctrine but "better goulash." The decline of ideology can also be illustrated by the history of the Socialist party in the United States since World War I. In the Presidential election of 1920 the party polled about 1 million votes. By 1928 the vote had dwindled to 267,000. By 1960 the fortunes of the party were at so low an ebb that it did not even nominate a candidate for President. A final cause of the diminishing importance of ideology was disillusionment with radicalism itself, especially in Western countries. Socialists failed to present a united front against World War I. Though a few remained steadfast in opposing the conflict, most of them were nationalists first and socialists second. Even more disenchanting were the attitudes of Communists in the years that followed. In Germany members of the party collaborated with the Nazis to assist the latter's accession to power. They more or less openly mouthed the slogan, "After Hitler, Our Turn." Communist rulers of the Soviet Union entered into a virtual alliance with Nazi Germany in 1939 which practically assured that Hitler would attack Poland and plunge Europe into World War II.

No account of the decline of ideology would be complete without some further mention of what has been happening in the Soviet Union. Roughly, a situation has developed not unlike that which characterized the intelligentsia in the nineteenth century. A considerable number of writers, scholars, scientists, and artists have emerged who have no sympathy whatever with the Soviet government. The major change came in 1953 with the "timely" death of Stalin. His tyranny had been so deadly and irksome that intellectuals continued to hate it even after he was gone. Among the leaders of the reaction have been Andrei Amalrik, Aleksandr Solzhenitsyn, and Boris Pasternak. Their methods have consisted in staging protests against such events as the occupation of Czechoslovakia and the publication abroad of anti-Soviet books. Although their movement is called a "democratic movement," its aims so far have not gone beyond insistence that government officials adhere strictly to Soviet law.

Ideology experienced a partial revival in the sixties and seventies. Its scope and duration, however, were impossible to predict. It found voices in the writings and speeches of Fidel Castro, his disciple Ernesto Guevara, Herbert Marcuse, Frantz Fanon, and the Weathermen. Although the philosophies of most of these leaders

Causes of the decline of ideology

Fidel Castro

1223

Latter-day
radicals: Castro,
Guevara, and
Marcuse

"Che" Guevara

were heavily tinctured with communism, they bordered more closely upon anarchism. Such was true of Fidel Castro and even more true of Ernesto "Che" Guevara, who fled from Cuba to the mainland of South America in the hope of fomenting revolutions against militarists and exploiters. He was killed in 1967 by Bolivian soldiers. Most popular of the radicals, among intellectuals at least, is the German-American philosopher Herbert Marcuse. His philosophy is a compound of Marxism and Freudianism with an apparent predominance of the latter. He is so far removed from Marx that he condemns modern technological society as "tyrannical." Despite threats on his life by the Ku Klux Klan, he is not in all cases an advocate of violence. He believes in "subverting" the social order because of its "tyranny," but he has opposed campus demonstrations because he thinks of the universities as oases of freedom and critical thinking.

What Herbert Marcuse has been to radical intellectuals of the present generation, Frantz Fanon has been to the helpless and disinherited of the Third World. As Fanon used the term, the Third World comprised the victims of capitalist dominance wherever they might live. They were inhabitants of the developing nations of Africa, Asia, and the Pacific islands. But others lived in independent countries of the Western Hemisphere where forms of enslavement were just as rife though under different names. Fanon himself was a black, born on the French island of Martinique, though he did not confine his sympathies to his own race. He championed the cause of the downtrodden everywhere, and at one time numbered as many Arabs among his followers as he did blacks. He served in the Algerian war for liberation from France as a psychiatrist from 1954 to 1960, and as a guerrilla fighter by night. As he saw the modern world, imperialism or colonialism was its most glaring evil. He would take all measures possible to accomplish its overthrow. Methods he would employ include revolutionary violence, demand for reparations, and measures to effect the rebirth of the native cultures. On the other hand, he was not a nihilist. Though he recognized the necessity of abrupt and violent change, he was more interested in building a better world than he was in destroying. Fanon's influence has grown by many cubits since his death from leukemia in 1961. He was deified by some of the more violent upheavals in Europe and the United States in the 1960's, especially by those in Paris and at Columbia. The most lasting influence has been that of the Black Panthers. They gave him a place among their saints and heroes soon after publication of the American edition of his *Wretched of the Earth* in 1963.

3. THE THREAT TO WESTERN HEGEMONY

Prior to 1914 the list of world powers included no fewer than eight states. Of these, Great Britain, France, Germany, Austria-Hungary, Russia, and Italy were generally the real arbiters of world affairs. The United States and Japan were sometimes accorded a grudging position but they generally did not weigh very heavily in the international scale. After World War I the number of powers shrank to five. Austria-Hungary was eliminated permanently and Germany and Russia for a period of years. On the other hand, the United States and Japan rose to positions much higher than they had previously occupied, while Britain and France sank a bit lower. The effects of World War II upon power relationships were far more upsetting. Germany, Italy, and Japan were defeated so overwhelmingly that they seemed destined to be relegated permanently to the background. They recovered more quickly than expected, however, and regained positions nearly comparable to those they had occupied before the war. Officially, the list of great powers included five states—the U.S.S.R., the United States, Great Britain, France, and the Republic of China. These were the famous Big Five that seemed fated to rule the world. However, China was soon overwhelmed by Communist revolution, while Britain and France became increasingly dependent upon the United States. As a consequence, the world of nations took on a bipolar character, with the United States and the U.S.S.R. contesting for supremacy and striving to draw the remaining states into their orbits.

As had happened several times in the afterglow of victorious wars, America, in the 1950's and 1960's, basked in a kind of Golden Age unparalleled in history. From the standpoint of economic power she had far outdistanced the rest of the nations. Since 1939 her people had doubled their national income and quadrupled their savings. Though they constituted only 7 per cent of the world's population, Americans enjoyed over 30 per cent of the world's estimated income. For the first time in her history the United States was in a position to be the arbiter of the destinies of at least half of the earth. Japan was virtually her colony; she controlled both the Atlantic and Pacific Oceans, policed the Mediterranean, and shaped the development of international policy in Western Europe. But it must not be imagined that her people had found for themselves an earthly paradise. The national debt in 1945 stood at $260,000,000,000, and it has since risen to over $370,000,000,000. More money was required to pay the interest on this debt than had been necessary to defray the entire cost of government before the war. By 1948 the cost of living had risen to 172 per cent of the 1935–1939 average, and one family out of every four was spending in excess of its earnings. Moreover, despite her sacrifice of billions of dollars and 350,000 lives, the United States had not gained security. For years after the war, her citizens lived in as much dread of a new attack as they had felt at almost any time while the war was in progress. Without exception they embraced a policy of success through superior strength. They believed that the United States should never suffer a diminution of this strength which she had inherited from World War II. Moreover, her rulers

Changing status of the great powers

The illusion of American power and prosperity

did not seem to believe that such a diminution would ever be likely. America had a perpetual monopoly of death-dealing atomic weapons, and she could use them in accordance with what she conceived as her noble purposes. When the Soviet Union cracked this monopoly in 1949, it might well have plunged America's rulers into a slough of despair. They remained convinced, however, that the policy of superior strength was still completely valid. All that was now necessary was to add new and more deadly weapons and thereby to make sure that no rival could successfully challenge the United States. A chip-on-the-shoulder attitude dominated American policy thenceforth.

Containment

The foreign policy of the United States followed a remarkable consistency throughout the 1950's and 1960's. Regardless of the party in power, the cornerstone of that policy was really the "containment" of communism. At least, it was called that in polite diplomatic circles. Its actual purpose may have been a bit more cynical. It apparently included the protection of American business in Western Europe, the extension of trade with all countries of the "free" world, and the safeguarding of American oil interests in the Middle East and in the dying empires of Asia and Africa.

*Origin of
containment
policy*

The containment policy actually originated during the Presidency of Harry S. Truman. It was first formulated by a State Department official, George F. Kennan, in 1947. According to Kennan, the U.S.S.R. under Stalin did not rightfully belong in the family of nations. Her national system was not a state in the proper meaning of the term but a religion stamped with demonology and Oriental mysticism. The adoption of this viewpoint by President Truman and his subordinates marked the beginning of the so-called Cold War. Its aim was to isolate the Soviet Union and render it harmless against the West. Soon afterward he decided to speed the development of a hydrogen bomb and recommended increasing "defense" expenditures to $20 billion.[2] The containment policy has continued under Truman's successors.

*Kennedy's action
against Cuba*

In April 1961 John F. Kennedy approved a plan for the invasion of Cuba to overthrow the government of Fidel Castro. The plan, conceived under Eisenhower by the CIA, called for the training of Cuban exiles and refugees in Florida and Guatemala followed by a secret landing on the Bay of Pigs. The attempted execution of the plot ended in disaster. Few of the participants escaped death or capture. In October 1962 Kennedy aspired to set Russia back on her heels when he instituted a naval blockade of Cuba in order to prevent the Soviet government from supplying "offensive" weapons to that country. The Soviet government took alarm at the threat of a new world war and agreed to remove their missiles and bombers from Cuban soil. The full story of this affair is still locked in the archives of the State Department in Washington.

[2] See George F. Kennan, "The Sources of Soviet Conduct," *Foreign Affairs,* vol. XXV, no. 4 (July 1947), 576.

President Kennedy also applied his vigorous containment policy to other areas. He served notice on the Soviet government that it must respect the rights of the United States in its treaty rights in West Berlin, and that the American stand with regard to those rights was not "negotiable." In 1961 he went so far as to announce that "in some circumstances we might have to take the initiative" in using nuclear weapons against our enemies. His successors chose to accent Kennedy's policy rather than to tone it down. Lyndon Johnson proceeded to "escalate" the Indochina War whenever he thought that increased pressure might bring the enemy to heel. Richard Nixon professed a determination to "wind down" this war, but it was not clear whether he meant a real change or merely a redirection that would give the appearance of victory.

Soviet Russia emerged from World War II as the second strongest power on earth. Though her navy was small, her land army and possibly her air force by 1948 were the largest in the world. Her population was climbing rapidly toward 200,000,000, and this in spite of the loss of 7,000,000 soldiers and about 8,000,000 civilians during the war. In mineral wealth her position compared favorably with that of the richest countries. After 1946 she claimed a large percentage of the world supply of petroleum. On the other hand, there can be no doubt that her industrial machine had been badly crippled by the war. No fewer than 1700 of her cities and towns had been totally destroyed and about 40,000 miles of railway and 31,000 factories. Stalin declared in 1946 that it would probably require at least six years to repair the damage and rebuild the devastated areas.

It seems reasonable to suppose that much of the hostility displayed by the U.S.S.R. in her dealings with other nations was attributable in some measure to the losses she sustained during the war. Resentful of the fact that she had been compelled to make such sacrifices, she became obsessed with security as a goal that must be attained regardless of the cost to her neighbors. Fearful that poverty and hardship might make her own people rebellious, her rulers adopted a chip-on-the-shoulder attitude in their foreign policy. Soviet citizens must be led to think that their country was in imminent danger of attack by capitalist powers. For similar reasons they must be induced to believe that their rulers were entitled to a kind of worship hitherto reserved for divine-right monarchs. In accordance with a new nationalism designed to bolster the people's courage, the Russians laid claim to a majority of the inventions and scientific discoveries of modern times—from the electric light and wireless telegraphy to penicillin.

The tenseness of Soviet attitudes seemed to relax a bit after the death of Joseph Stalin in March 1953. Stalin was succeeded within twenty-four hours by Georgi M. Malenkov, a dominant figure in the party apparatus. Soon after his elevation to power he declared that there was no dispute or unresolved question between the Soviet

Other uses of the containment policy

The U.S.S.R. after World War II

Explanation of Russian attitudes

Union and any other nation which could not be settled by "mutual agreement of the interested countries." Prospects for better relations between the Soviet Union and the West were further enhanced in 1955 when Malenkov resigned and the supreme power passed into the hands of Nikita S. Khrushchev. Though he did not immediately become Premier, he held the all-important position of Secretary of the Communist party. Khrushchev seemed more anxious than his predecessor to create the impression that the Soviet government was ready to repent of the error of its ways. He denounced Stalin for his paranoid suspicions of everyone around him and for his brutal tyranny. He and his colleagues announced their approval of the doctrine of "more than one road to socialism." They concluded peace with Austria and withdrew their occupying troops. In 1955 they agreed to a "conference at the summit" with the chiefs of government of Great Britain, France, the United States, and the U.S.S.R. as the participants. The conference was held in Geneva, and the utmost cordiality prevailed. Repeated pledges of trust and friendship were given by both sides.

This policy of the "Great Thaw," as it was called, was undoubtedly prompted by discontent within the country. The Russian masses had no zest for another war, and they were weary of the restrictions and rigidities imposed by the Stalin regime. They believed that the time had come for less emphasis on the production of munitions and capital goods and more on providing the amenities of life. The most genial of Soviet dictators, Khrushchev was disposed to sympathize with these demands. The new policy, however, soon ran into heavy weather. The first sign of change was the suppression of revolts in Poland and Hungary in 1956. The Poles were let off rather lightly when they promised to remain within the Soviet orbit in return for permission to make various modifications in their socialist system. The Hungarians were repressed with bloody violence when they attempted not merely to change the economic system but to break all ties with the Soviet

*Nikita Khrushchev Visiting
East Berlin Accompanied by
Walter Ulbricht*

Revolt in Hungary. By 1956 discontent with Soviet domination manifested itself in several of the satellite states. Violent revolt broke out in Poland and Hungary. Left: The photograph indicates the extent of the violence in Budapest. Right: A group of Hungarian freedom fighters

Union. At the beginning of another "summit" conference in Paris in May 1960, Premier Khrushchev erupted violently when he learned that the United States was sending U-2 planes far over Soviet territory to discover the location of bases and other military installations. Though at first Washington officials denied these flights, they later admitted them and sought to justify them as necessary for the military security of the United States. The summit conference terminated immediately, with nothing but a poisoned atmosphere to mark its effects, despite the subsequent suspension of U-2 flights. Yet Khrushchev was not ready to abandon completely his policy of conciliation. Later in 1960 he enunciated his principle of "peaceful coexistence." Though he did not renounce the ultimate triumph of communism, insisting that "we will bury you," he refused to admit that this triumph must be accomplished by force of arms.

With respect to Germany, until recently the Soviet leaders remained unyielding. They nurtured the fear that Germany might launch a new war, aided and abetted by her capitalist allies. For this reason they staunchly opposed unification of the country and insisted upon recognizing East Germany as one of their satellites. In 1961 they ordered the East German government to build a high wall separating the two sectors of Berlin, in order to cut off the escape of thousands of East Germans to West Berlin and then to western Germany. Many did make their escape, but the wall remained as a symbol of Soviet determination to prevent the formation of a united Germany. The development of nuclear weapons fixed in the minds of the Soviet leaders another obsession regarding Germany. They feared that West Germany might be given a finger on the trigger of some project that could be used to destroy the Soviet Union.

The genial Khrushchev did not survive as Soviet dictator indefinitely. In 1964 he was deposed and reduced to the level of an "unperson." The reins of power then passed into the hands of a joint

Intransigent attitude toward the problem of Germany

1229

The Occupation of Czechoslovakia. In 1968 the liberalized regime of Alexander Dubcek was suppressed by the Soviets. The violent response by the citizens was put down by military force.

dictatorship of Aleksei Kosygin as Premier and Leonid Brezhnev as Secretary of the Communist Party. The government did not return to Stalinist policy, but some of the new trends moved noticeably in that direction. A cardinal example was the occupation of Czechoslovakia in 1968. The Soviet dictators accused the Czechs of flirtation with West Germany to such an extent as to threaten the Soviet system and weaken its ties over Eastern Europe. In particular, they resented the economic and social privileges allowed by the Czech government to its own citizens. Accordingly, they sent in armored troops and puppet rulers to take over the country. They followed this action by issuance of the Brezhnev Doctrine, which asserted the right of Moscow to interfere in the affairs of any satellite that strayed from the path of Soviet leadership.

The downfall of Khrushchev and the accession of a new regime in Russia

4.   THE IMPOTENCE OF POWER

One of the amazing assumptions of our contemporary age is the doctrine that "God is for the big battalions," as Voltaire expressed it; or in the words of Mao Tse-tung, "Power proceeds from the muzzle of a gun." No doubt, these are keen observations, but they are not universally true. In the past ten to fifteen years they have been much less true than they were in the bloody afterglow of World War II. It did not take long for some of the world's discontented to demonstrate the hollowness of Allied victory.

The emptiness of great power supremacy

By 1970 the one-time great powers had been reduced to pale imitations of their former selves. On the surface this was not true. States that belonged to the "Nuclear Club" seemed to have acquired a weapon that would enable them to impose their will on their neighbors for an indefinite time to come. But this was as empty as any imaginable illusion. A balance of terror canceled their power to wage war against each other. They could not even dictate to their satellites or to any two-bit nation that wished to defy them.

How have the mighty fallen

The United States, theoretically the greatest military power the world had ever seen, found itself stymied by a primitive nation of peasants in North Vietnam. Such fourth-rate powers as North Korea (backed by Soviet threats) and Peru have also made the giant United States military and diplomatic machinery look ridiculous by their defiance. The status of the U.S.S.R. does not benefit by comparison. The Soviets have not been able to control absolutely their own satellites. Poles, Czechs, and Rumanians have managed to gain considerable independence in following their own devices by secret or open defiance of Moscow's authority. An eminent American journalist has said that the world has had only two great powers for the past decade—Israel and South Vietnam. They have wielded more influence in determining the course of recent history than any other nations regardless of size or deadliness of weapons.

THE IMPOTENCE OF POWER

Thus it may be noted that attempts to maximize power have in nearly every instance been marked by its concomitant of impotence. States both great and small have yielded to superior force and sometimes almost no force at all in the domain of external relations. But there has been one outstanding exception. At the end of World War II the victorious states bound themselves to unprecedented legal and moral restraints and then proceeded to ignore or flout them completely. These restraints are known as the Nuremberg Principles, unanimously endorsed by the General Assembly of the United Nations in 1946. Embodied in these principles was the Nuremberg Judgment, which condemned all those wars undertaken except in strict self-defense. All wars in this category were classified as wars of aggression and therefore the supreme international crime. Few except legal hairsplitters could exclude from the ban of the Nuremberg Judgment Ho Chi Minh's slaughter of his enemies in North Vietnam, the murder of hundreds of Indian nationalists by the British at Amritsar in 1947, the massacre of guerrilla fighters by the French in Algeria in 1957–1958, and the indiscriminate B-52 bombings by the United States in the Indochina War.

The Nuremberg Judgment

Characteristic examples of the impotence of power have not been rare in modern history. We shall see in other connections how it was illustrated by the struggle against the British in India, the revolt in Algeria, and the war in Indochina. Conspicuous also has been strife in Ireland. We have noted already that violence against British oppression flared at intervals during the eighteenth and nineteenth centuries and reached its climax in the Easter Rebellion of 1916. It died down after the war when the British agreed to the establishment of an Irish Free State.

The beginnings of strife in Ireland

It would be a mistake to consider the roots of conflict in Ireland as entirely religious. In a broader sense they are political and social. The majority of the Irish still consider the British intrusion into their land as a form of invasion and occupation. Such feelings, moreover, are heightened by social cleavage. The workers, especially in the large cities, whether Catholic or not, are mostly im-

Social and economic cleavage

poverished and insecure. Their willingness to work for starvation wages has made them targets of fear and hatred as despised classes invariably are. The wealthy, who are mainly Protestant, strive to keep their status as overlords of a privileged society. Even if religion were not a divisive influence, economics and politics would keep the two classes bitterly antagonistic.

The most deadly polarization in Ireland began in 1968, that year of bitter turmoil all over the world. The major arena of conflict has been Ulster, especially the cities of Londonderry and Belfast. Ulster was established in the seventeenth century originally as a kind of British Colony. The Irish natives were driven back into the hills while their lands were absorbed by English invaders. Monopolization of economic advantages by these invaders and their descendants gave rise to a series of violent altercations. The first in our own time occurred when a march of demonstrators was stopped by a line of police supported by an angry horde of Protestants armed with clubs and sticks. Insulting taunts and threats were exchanged by both sides. Although there was no bloodshed, passions smoldered for another time.

The recent polarization

The attitude of the British throughout the United Kingdom seems to have been one of general sympathy with their kinsmen in Ulster. When the Free State was formed, Ulster remained part of the United Kingdom. The final authority over it was the Home Secretary in London. British policy toward malcontents in Ulster was sometimes conciliatory, but there was usually a gloved hand concealing a mailed fist. New confrontations were not long delayed. The first involving serious violence started on New Year's Day, 1969. A march protesting official tyranny was ambushed by Protestant extremists on the road from Belfast to Londonderry. Scores of men, women, and girls, many of them students at Queen's University, were brutally clubbed, while the police pursued a hands-off policy. Catholic workers shut themselves into their Bogside ghetto and prepared for revenge. New ruptures of the peace

Later confrontations in Ulster

Strife in Ireland, 1916. British troops raiding the office of a Dublin printer who supported the rebellion.

A Renewal of "The Troubles" in Ireland. British soldiers congregate near the ruins of a bar which was blasted by terrorists in August of 1972. As in other parts of the world, bombing had become one of the chief instruments of political terrorism and rebellion.

were inevitable. The next major battle began in the summer of 1969 when extremists of both sides engaged in savage violence. In three nights of rioting five persons were killed and more than 200 injured. The British seemed unable to think of any means of control except to send in more troops. By February 1972 at least 15,000 British soldiers with armored vehicles were stationed in Ireland. The interval of peace came to an end when some of these soldiers fired into a demonstration of Irish civilians, killing thirteen of them. Radicalism took on new life as defiant parades and a general strike spread through Ulster. Government buildings were destroyed in Belfast, the British embassy in Dublin was burned, and mobs stormed the Prime Minister's residence in London. The regime of violence continued through most of 1972. Even the establishment of direct rule from London did not terminate the disorders. Sporadic attacks from both sides continued. The violence of the Irish Republican Army was invariably matched by the fanaticism of the Protestants, who generally controlled the government in Belfast even after the transfer of authority to representatives of the British Crown.

SELECTED READINGS

· *Items so designated are available in paperbound editions.*

· Acheson, Dean, *The Korean War*, New York, 1971 (Norton).
———, *The Struggle for a Free Europe*, New York, 1971 (Norton).
· Almond, G. A., *The Appeals of Communism*, Princeton, 1954 (Princeton University Press).
· Aron, Raymond, *The Century of Total War*, Boston, 1955 (Beacon). The world today in historical perspective.
Barghorn, F. C., *Soviet Russian Nationalism*, New York, 1956.

READINGS Barnett, A. Doak, *A New U.S. Policy toward China*, Brookings Institution, 1971.

Berger, Earl, *The Covenant and the Sword: Arab-Israeli Relations, 1948–1956*, Toronto, 1965. Impartial.

Cady, J. F., *Southeast Asia: Its Historical Development*, New York, 1964.

Drucker, P. F., *The End of Economic Man*, New York, 1939. A really profound study of modern man's predicament.

Fairbank, J. K., *The United States and China*, Cambridge, Mass., 1971. A revised and updated edition.

· Fanon, Frantz, *The Wretched of the Earth*, New York, 1968 (Evergreen).

Fleming, D. F., *The Cold War and Its Origins, 1917–1960*, Garden City, N.Y., 1961, 2 vols. A radical interpretation. Places the blame for the Cold War on the Western allies.

· Gatzke, H. W., *The Present in Perspective*, 3d ed., New Haven, 1965 (Rand McNally).

Gregg, Pauline, *The Welfare State: An Economic and Social History of Great Britain, 1945 to the Present Day*, Amherst, Mass., 1969.

· Halpern, Manfred, *The Politics of Social Change in the Middle East and North Africa*, Princeton, 1963 (Princeton University Press).

Issawi, Charles, *Egypt in Revolution: An Economic Analysis*, New York, 1963.

· Kolko, Gabriel, *The Politics of War*, New York, 1970 (Vintage).

Laski, H. J., *Reflections on the Revolution of Our Time*, New York, 1943. A discerning analysis not seriously marred by a Marxist viewpoint.

· Leckie, Robert, *Conflict: The History of the Korean War*, New York, 1962 (Avon). Emphasizes military history.

Lenczowski, George, *The Middle East in World Affairs*, Ithaca, N.Y., 1956.

Lyon, Peter, *Neutralism*, New York, 1963.

McCune, Shannon, *Korea's Heritage: A Regional and Social Geography*, Tokyo, 1956.

Macmillan, W. M., *Bantu, Boer, and Briton*, New York, 1963.

Mannheim, Karl, *Diagnosis of Our Time*, New York, 1944. A thoughtful study.

Marcuse, Herbert, *Counterrevolution and Revolt*, Boston, 1972.

· Mosely, Philip, *The Kremlin and World Politics*, New York, 1961 (Vintage).

· Popper, K. R., *The Open Society and Its Enemies*, New York, 1962 (Torchbook). A vigorous comparison of the totalitarian and democratic philosophies.

· Reves, Emery, *The Anatomy of Peace*, New York, 1945 (Compass). The most eloquent of pleas for a world republic.

Robinson, R. D., *The First Turkish Republic*, Cambridge, Mass., 1963.

· Seton-Watson, Hugh, *Neither War nor Peace: The Struggle for Power in the Post-War World*, London, 1960 (Frederick A. Praeger, rev. ed.).

· Spanier, John W., *The Truman-MacArthur Controversy and the Korean War*, Cambridge, 1959 (Norton Library).

Warth, R. D., *Soviet Russia in World Politics*, New York, 1963.

Wilmot, Chester, *The Struggle for Europe*, New York, 1952.

Young, Crawford, *Politics in the Congo: Decolonization and Independence*, Princeton, 1965.

SOURCE MATERIALS

Roosevelt, F. D., "The Four Freedoms," *Congressional Record*, Vol. 87, pp. 46–47.

U.N. Dept. of Public Information, *Yearbook of the United Nations*.

CHAPTER 41

New Nations and Forces

There are some defeats more triumphant than victories.
—Montaigne, *Essays*, Chapter 30

Africa, all I ask from you is the courage to know: to look about you and see what is happening in this old and tired world; to realize the extent and depth of its rebirth and the promise which glows on your hills.
—W. E. B. Du Bois, *Autobiography*

It is a truism that the essence of the contemporary world is change. In a sense this has been true of all ages. But except for the Protestant Revolution and the French Revolution, few ages have witnessed so many drastic and sweeping changes as the time in which we now live. Few people in the present age can remember anything other than turbulence and confusion. And though they may glamorize the past as a time of tranquillity, a knowledge of recent history soon convicts them of self-deception.

Protracted change

1. THE ANTICOLONIAL REVOLT

One of the most conspicuous areas of change in recent times has been the revolt of colonies against their former rulers. Again, as it must be emphasized repeatedly in history, this development is nothing new. Colonies have rebelled against their mother countries since the American Revolution. The Irish revolt of 1798, though unsuccessful, was another example. So were the Greek revolt in 1821 and the Belgian revolt against the Dutch in 1830. This is not to forget the numerous revolutions in Latin America against both Spain and Portugal or the rebellion of the Southern states against the North in the 1860's. Yet numerous though these uprisings were, they did not match in intensity the revolutions of our time. Moreover, many of them were unsuccessful.

The early revolutions for independence

1235

The Early Stirrings of Anticolonial Revolt. At first defeated in their efforts to subdue the Boer Republic, British might eventually won out in 1902 but not without considerable loss of prestige. The photo shows a line of Boer commandos.

Multifaceted revolts of the present age

The anticolonial revolt in the present age has taken the form in some cases of wars for independence, and in other cases of struggles within a country by discontented elements against a dominant group. Examples of the latter would include the revolts of the Czechs, Hungarians, and Poles against Soviet oppression in 1956, and the recent Irish revolt against British rule, which has raged from 1910 to the present. A number of revolts in our time have had a double character. The Algerian revolution affords an example. It began as an outbreak against greedy and domineering landlords in 1954. When the French came to the rescue of their kinsmen as a beleaguered master class, the rebels turned their revolt against the French government. The result was an independent Algeria in 1961.

2. THE DESTRUCTION OF THE BRITISH, DUTCH, AND FRENCH EMPIRES

The liquidation of old empires

From the standpoint of the old ruling classes the most serious of the upheavals after World War II was the liquidation of the British, Dutch, and French empires. This event was often regarded as a greater catastrophe than the threat of world communism. In fact, it was commonly thought of as a mere prelude to such a disaster. World communism, it was supposed, provided the drive and inspiration for most of the local revolutions. They could not have succeeded, it was argued, without generous external support.

Agitation to break up the old empires actually began before Russian communism cut much of a figure in world politics. Nationalism as far back as World War I was its genesis. The Allied doctrine of "self-determination" produced an upsurge that eventually sealed the doom of most world empires. The peace conferences added encouragement to this upsurge when they granted independence to Czechs, Slovaks, Yugoslavs, and Poles. World War II provided an even stronger influence. Winston Churchill and Franklin D. Roosevelt parroted the Wilsonian doctrine when they drafted the Atlantic Charter. It was not strange that many a struggling "half-naked" and half-starved colony should have come to envisage itself as a full-fledged member of the family of nations.

The first empire to undergo liquidation in the anticolonial struggle was the British. Its main problem child was India. Rebel movements had harassed the representatives of British *raj* in that country throughout the nineteenth century. The successful dénoument of this revolutionary struggle is recounted in Chapter 17. By 1947 British rule had ended throughout the entire Indian subcontinent, including Burma. In the meantime Great Britain had been constrained to give up most of the remaining portions of her empire. Over a period of years she liberated Ceylon, Malaysia, Mauritius, Fiji, Singapore, and Nauru, together with the New World territories of Guyana, Trinidad and Tobago, and Antigua. More significant was her forced withdrawal from Egypt. In 1952 a clique of Egyptian nationalist army officers seized control of the government. They deposed the playboy King Farouk, alleged to be subservient to the British, and in 1953 proclaimed Egypt a republic. With the collapse of the British power in India and Egypt, to say nothing of the long chain of smaller dependencies, little was left of the grand empire on which "the sun never set" except Hong Kong, British Honduras, Gibraltar, Aden, and Southern Rhodesia—and even the status of some of these was uncertain.

The second of the European colonial empires to go down the drain was Indonesia. Known for more than two centuries as the Netherlands Indies, it was the most valuable jewel of the Dutch imperial crown. Indeed, it was one of the richest countries in the world in natural resources. When Japan extended her aggressions to Southeast Asia in 1941, the empire of the Dutch was one of her prize conquests. But toward the end of the war, nationalists, under the leadership of Sukarno, a one-time architect and flamboyant politician, rebelled and proclaimed Indonesia an independent republic. Although the Dutch attempted for four years to regain their sovereignty, the opposition of the natives proved too strong. In 1949 the kingdom of the Netherlands recognized the independence of their former colony.

During the nineteenth century France put forth a strenuous effort to keep up with the British and the Dutch in building an overseas empire. On the whole she was successful. By exploiting the wealth and labor of her conquered possessions she managed to acquire and hold rich portions of Western and Central Africa and Southeast Asia. But her good fortune could not have been expected to last. Two of her richest colonies rebelled almost simultaneously: Algeria and Indochina. Algeria was inhabited by about 1,000,000 immigrants, mainly Frenchmen, in a total population of 10,300,000. These immigrants monopolized not only the government positions but also the best economic opportunities in industry, trade, and finance. The Arab and Berber inhabitants were chiefly peasants and laborers, though some, of course, maintained small shops in the native quarters of the large cities. In 1954 Arab and Berber nationalists rose in revolt when their demand for equal status with the French was denied by the government. The revolt continued its bloody course for seven years. It was complicated by the fact that many of the European settlers hated the French government almost as much as they did the Algerian nationalists. They were determined to keep Algeria "French" and feared a sellout by President Charles de Gaulle that would make the former colony independent and subject the immigrant governing class to the rule of the Arabs and Berbers. The upshot was a revolt by four French generals. They seized government buildings, arrested French officials, and threatened to invade France. De Gaulle proclaimed a state of emergency and ordered a total blockade of Algeria. In the face of such determined opposition the revolt collapsed. On a promise of self-government the nationalists laid down their arms in 1962. Additional sections of the French empire in North Africa were also whittled away after World War II. In 1955 the French gave up their protectorate over Morocco and allowed it to be organized as an independent kingdom. A short time afterward they renounced their protectorate over Tunisia, except for a naval and air base at Bizerte. The Tunisian government resisted and after a brief interval the U.N. commanded the French to give up the Bizerte base.

The struggle over Indochina was the most dramatic episode in the extinction of the French empire. We have noted before that Indochina was a casualty of Japanese conquests during World War II.

Anti-imperialist Revolt in Algeria, 1960. At Dar-es-Saada, Moslems take furniture from the homes of Europeans and burn it in the streets.

After the defeat of Japan in 1945 France sought to recover her lost empire. Her efforts ended in failure. She was immediately confronted by a rebellion of Vietnamese nationalists under the leadership of Ho Chi Minh. The rebels resorted to guerrilla warfare and inflicted such costly defeats upon the French that the latter decided to abandon the struggle. An agreement was signed at Geneva in 1954 providing for the division of Vietnam into two zones, pending elections to determine the future government of the entire country. Ho Chi Minh became President of North Vietnam and established his capital at Hanoi. His followers, who came to be called Viet Cong, were numerous in both halves of the country. Had elections been held as provided by the Geneva Agreement, Ho Chi Minh would probably have been elected President of all of Vietnam. But the government of South Vietnam, backed by the United States, refused to permit the elections to be held.

From this point on, involvement by the United States in the Vietnamese civil war steadily increased. President Kennedy seemed to be convinced that the Chinese Communist juggernaut would soon roll over all of Southeast Asia. The first victims would be Vietnam, Laos, Cambodia, Malaysia, and Singapore. Then would come Thailand, Burma, and India. How far Kennedy would have gone in his crusade against communism had he escaped the assassin's bullet in 1963 is impossible to say with certainty. Kennedy's successor, Lyndon B. Johnson, seemed to think that a relatively small force of perhaps 100,000 men would be sufficient to defeat the enemies of the South Vietnamese and drive them back into their own country. No consideration was given to the fact that these enemies were solidly entrenched in both states of Vietnam, and that they had been waging a bitter national struggle for upwards of eighteen years. They had succeeded in driving out the French in 1954 and were not likely to surrender to a new invader, as they conceived the Americans to be. The Viet Cong and the North Vietnam regulars were poorly armed and poorly equipped. They had no air force or navy and little or no artillery. Nevertheless, they fought the South Vietnamese and their American allies to a standstill on several occasions. During the Tet offensive of 1968 they came close to capturing Saigon, the South Vietnamese capital.

Exasperated by failure to win an easy victory in South Vietnam, the American civilian and military chiefs determined upon aerial bombing. A series of incidents in 1964 provided the justification. Reports, of doubtful veracity, indicated that North Vietnamese ships had attacked American naval vessels in Tonkin Gulf. President Johnson pronounced these incidents acts of war and immediately obtained from Congress authorization to use whatever measures necessary to repel Communist aggression. Soon afterward the first American bombers unloaded their first cargoes upon towns and villages occupied by the North Vietnamese and the Viet Cong. Although evidence increased casting doubt on the efficacy of these raids, they

The war in Vietnam

Ho Chi Minh, Vietnamese Nationalist Leader in Struggle for Independence and President of North Vietnam.

President Johnson escalates the war

1239

THE DECLINE OF COLONIALISM AFTER WORLD WAR II

Territories gaining independence during postwar period

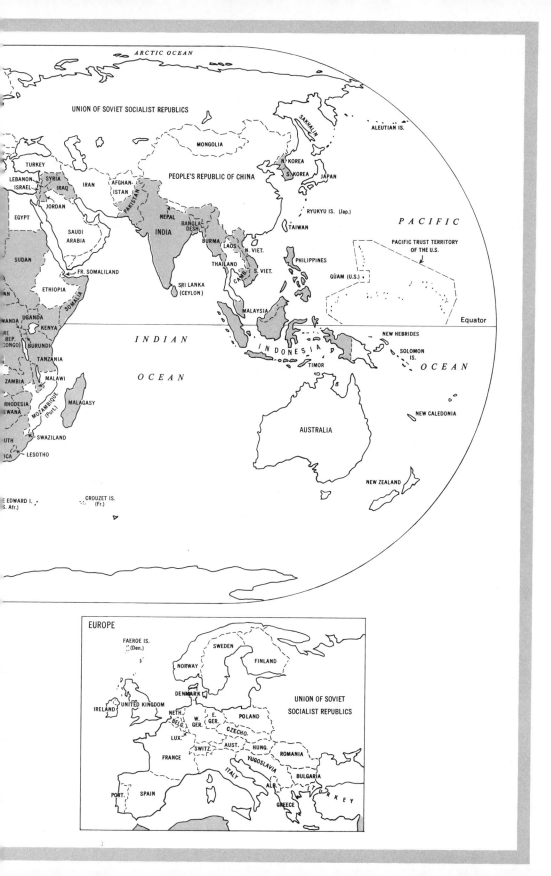

continued to be used. It has been estimated that at least as much tonnage in bombs was dropped on tiny Vietnam as was unloaded by the Allied forces on all of Germany in World War II. But still the deadly onslaught continued. The only answer of those responsible for strategy in Washington and Saigon seems to have been "Cover up the failure by escalating the war." As the struggle entered its fifth year, with no end in sight, disillusionment spread throughout the United States. Criticism of President Johnson was so harsh in 1968 that he was forced to abandon his plans to run for a second term.

The Nixon policies

Johnson's successor, Richard M. Nixon, was elected on the strength of promises to end the war. But this turned out to be a shadowy promise. While ground troops were being withdrawn from Vietnam, in May 1970, the United States invaded Cambodia and a few months later the kingdom of Laos. In April 1972, the North Vietnamese, with massive aid from Russia and China, launched a powerful counteroffensive with the apparent objective of conquering South Vietnam and driving all foreign armies out of the country. A number of South Vietnamese strongholds were captured and the offensive seemed more dangerous than the famous Tet offensive of 1968. Nixon countered with increased bombing of North Vietnam's factories and railroads and by mining its harbors. The stalemate continued until a few weeks before the United States presidential election in November 1972, when Nixon's adviser, Henry Kissinger, was sent to hold secret negotiations with North Vietnamese officials. A few days before the election, Nixon was able to declare that "peace was at hand." After his landslide re-election the negotiations bogged down. Alleging that the North Vietnamese had stiffened their terms, the President during the Christmas season ordered a bombing attack on the heavily populated areas of Hanoi and Haiphong, which destroyed, among other things, the largest hospital in North Vietnam. The long anticipated cease-fire agreements, signed in Paris in January 1973, were hailed by President Nixon as the achievement of "peace with honor." But although they brought the release of American prisoners of war, they did not halt the civil wars in Indochina, which continued, not only in South Vietnam but in Cambodia and Laos as well. More than half of Cambodia was controlled by insurgents loyal to the exiled ruler, Prince Sihanouk, who was eager to negotiate a settlement; but the American representatives in Paris refused to meet with him. The United States continued heavy bombing in Cambodia, in support of a "government" whose authority extended hardly beyond the capital city, Phnom Penh.

3. THE THIRD WORLD

Closely related to the extinction of the old empires has been the growth of what is often called the Third World. The expression

"Third World" was originally popularized by Charles de Gaulle, who used it around 1949 to designate his followers who opposed the Fourth Republic. When he came to power a short time later, he endowed the expression with a broader meaning. The expression has since come to be restricted to the emergent, underdeveloped countries of the world, especially of Africa and Asia. Examples would include India, Pakistan, Bangladesh, and Indonesia. Most countries of the Third World have been products of the revolutionary conditions that followed World War II. For this reason many were inclined for a time to throw in their lot with the Communist half of the postwar world. Latterly, however, most of these attitudes have faded, leaving each state with discretion to go its own way.

Origin of the term "Third World"

Standards of living and stages of economic development are by no means uniform throughout the world. This has been notoriously true since the end of World War II. A relatively small number of nations, mostly in Europe and the Western Hemisphere but also including Japan, sit on top of the world and enjoy the fruits of modern science and technology. Their wealth enables them to command the resources of the earth whether the tin of Bolivia, the fruits of the tropics, or the oil of Arabia and Indonesia. Illustrations can be found in the Gross National Product and the literacy figures for various nations. At the end of the 1960's Great Britain and West Germany each had a GNP of $1500 per capita. The less developed countries for the same period had an average per capita GNP of about $200. Comparative literacy figures for developed and underdeveloped countries also have significant meaning. Percentages of literacy for such countries as Denmark, the Netherlands, and the United States were 100 per cent or slightly lower. For such underdeveloped nations as India it was 30 per cent, for the Sudan 19 per cent, and for Pakistan 16 per cent. Obviously these percentages must be qualified by the effects of immigration and emigration and in some cases by the tyranny and neglect of former rulers. Yet poverty has doubtless been the major influence holding back economic and cultural progress.

Comparison of developed and underdeveloped nations

The new states of Southeast Asia have some apparent natural advantages. Besides containing great stores of strategic raw materials, they normally produce a surplus of foodstuffs and—in comparison with India, China, and Japan—are under-populated. However, their progress toward political stability and economic development has been hampered by the fact that they were catapulted from the age of colonialism into that of Cold War rivalries. Billions of dollars' worth of "aid" poured into this region has gone mostly to feed military establishments. Indonesia, with a population in excess of 100 million, is the largest and potentially richest state of Southeast Asia. Under the colorful but erratic leadership of President Sukarno, a hero of the struggle for independence against the Dutch, Indonesia assumed an aggressive role in Asian politics, but his reckless policies

The new states of Southeast Asia

The tragic fate
of Indochina

*Prince Norodom Sihanouk of
Cambodia.* Since his expulsion
by a military coup in 1970 he
has maintained a government-
in-exile at Peking.

Resistance to
pressure from the
world's superstates

brought both economic disaster and internal discord. An abortive
coup on September 30, 1965, attributed to the Communists, led to
the imposition of a military regime which gradually stripped Sukarno
of all his powers. The Indonesian Communist party—the third
largest such party in the world—was shattered, but at the price of
a reign of terror lasting several months and a bloodbath that took
the lives of at least half a million people.

Indochina, a focal point in the East-West power struggle, has remained the most distressed area in all of Southeast Asia. The Vietnam
war foreshadowed the possibility of the total annihilation of a country by the technology of modern warfare. In South Vietnam alone,
besides those killed and wounded, at least 8 million people were
turned into homeless refugees. Damage to the land, through bombing, defoliation of forests, and destruction of crops, is incalculable.
Incidental to the confrontation in Vietnam the United States military
conducted a secret war in Laos, where the C.I.A. trained and
equipped a native mercenary force and where bombing sorties wiped
out a community of 50,000 people in the Plain of Jars. Another
casualty of the Indochina conflict was the downfall of Prince
Norodom Sihanouk's government in Cambodia, the only state that
had managed to remain neutral. A military coup in March 1970 replaced Sihanouk by Marshal Lon Nol, who has set a record among
heads of state for corruption and incompetence, and whose only
claim to rule is American military support. Prince Sihanouk, under
pressure from both sides, had held Communist influence in Cambodia
to a minimum. Within the space of two years Lon Nol, assisted by
South Vietnamese and United States troops, reduced his country to
a shambles and lost three-fourths of it to the Communists. It is
doubtful that the military dictatorships entrenched in Thailand,
South Vietnam, and Cambodia can last indefinitely, even with B-52
bombers on call. In attempting to use these dictatorships to stem the
tide of social revolution, the United States provided a costly demonstration of the arrogance, and the impotence, of power.

If the Southeast Asian states have failed to establish a common
identity, they have resisted being drawn into the power blocs of
the world's superstates. A Southeast Asia Defense Treaty
(SEATO), organized by the United States in 1954 as a counterpart
of NATO, proved to be neither popular nor effective. Only three
of the eight members of SEATO were Asian states (Thailand, Pakistan, and the Philippines); by 1967 France had virtually withdrawn
from the alliance, and Pakistan left in 1972. Nor have the attempts of
Moscow and Peking to shape the political destinies of Asian countries been any more successful than those of the Western powers.
China's prestige among the peripheral states of the continent declined after the Sino-Indian border war of 1962 and reached a nadir
during the chaotic period of China's proletarian cultural revolution.
While the intervention of outside powers may have momentous
consequences for the peoples of Southeast Asia, its ability to effect

ideological change seems negligible. The destruction of the Indonesian Communist party—a significant rebuff to Peking—was an internal affair, accomplished without any assistance from the West. And the United States' enormous military expenditure in Vietnam neither restricted communism nor advanced democracy in any part of Indochina. The most potent ideology among the states of Southeast Asia, as among those of Africa and the Middle East, is nationalism. Ho Chi Minh rose to prominence not as a Communist but as a leader of the movement for national independence; in his struggle against the French he received help from many non-Communists, including Nationalist Chinese.

The ideal of solidarity among nations of the Third World was given its most dramatic expression by the Asian-African Conference held at Bandung, Indonesia, in 1955. Twenty-nine states joined in a display of friendship and dedication to humane objectives. While the internationalism envisioned by the Bandung Conference has failed to materialize, some progress has been made toward economic cooperation. The so-called Colombo Plan, originated in 1950, arranges loans and technical assistance for underdeveloped areas. In addition to the Commonwealth countries and the United States, most of the non-Communist states of Asia have participated in the Plan, either as donors or as recipients. An Asian Development Bank, capitalized at $1 billion, was formally inaugurated in August 1966 with headquarters in Manila. Perhaps bearing most promise for the future is the Association of Southeast Asian Nations (ASEAN), established in 1967 among Indonesia, Singapore, Malaysia, Thailand, and the Philippines. In contrast to SEATO, the Association aims to mobilize not military but economic power. In 1971 its spokesmen called for the recognition of the whole of Southeast Asia as a "zone of peace, freedom, and neutrality." If ASEAN should succeed in forging a link between Communist-oriented Indochina and anti-Marxist Indonesia, it could prove to be an effective counterbalance to the superpowers of East and West.

Efforts toward Third World solidarity

4· THE GROWTH OF BLACK MILITANCY

The growth of insurgency among blacks has been predominantly an American movement. Through most of the years from the Civil War to 1900 Negroes were an abject and docile race. Emancipation and the Thirteenth and Fourteenth Amendments brought little change in this attitude. Such changes might have been postponed indefinitely had it not been for the migration of Southern Negroes northward in search of more freedom and better employment opportunities. Thousands came around 1910 and many more thousands during World War I. For the most part, their fate was deplorable. During the war years they benefited from the shortage of labor in

Negro migrations northward

Marcus Garvey

Martin Luther King, Jr.

industrial cities, but during the postwar depression they were the first to be trampled underfoot.

The year 1919 saw the rise to prominence of the first Negro Messiah. He was Marcus Garvey, a native of Jamaica. Toward the end of the war he made his way to New York City and gained fame among the downcast members of his race for his torrential eloquence. His philosophy had a broad appeal, especially to those outside the "mulatto aristocracy." He fought to gain for the depressed masses a resplendent place in the sun. He rejected the very term "Negro" and taught his followers to refer to themselves as "blacks." He claimed that they were descendants of the "greatest and proudest race who ever peopled the earth." He whipped up enthusiasm for a vast empire in Africa to which Negroes would emigrate. But he closed his career under a cloud. He was convicted of using the mails to defraud, spent two years in the Atlanta penitentiary, and was deported.

Yet Garvey's life was not a failure. He encouraged the Negro Renaissance, or Harlem Renaissance, in the 1920's. Several of its leaders derived inspiration from him, notably Langston Hughes and Countee Cullen. Garvey's philosophy also extended indirectly to the Black Muslim movement through his influence on the father of its most vigorous proselytizer, Malcolm X. Malcolm X was converted in prison by his brother to the religion of Islam. After his release he became a spokesman for Elijah Muhammad, founder of the movement. Most of his followers were people of the same background who had flocked to Garvey's standard—recent migrants from the Deep South who now lived in hopeless poverty in the black ghettos of Northern cities. Malcolm X attempted to overcome their feeling of helplessness by giving them a new religion to take the place of the white man's Christianity and by restoring black pride. This new religion was Islam, which Malcolm X described as the true faith of Africans. Though he and his followers were firm believers, they were not generally fanatics. They did not renounce worldliness as a life of sin. They urged Negroes to pool their resources and establish black-owned businesses. This would help them to overcome their weakness and lack of status. They taught their adherents to avoid aggression and to fight only when attacked. Their charismatic minister broke with the Black Muslims in 1964. In February 1965 he was shot and killed as he started to speak at a rally in Harlem. The Black Muslim movement rapidly declined.

In the meantime black militancy branched out into new forms. One was the Congress of Racial Equality (CORE) founded by James Farmer, a leader of the Fellowship of Reconciliation, in 1942. His announced aim was to translate "love of God and man" into specific crusades against injustice. By 1950 it began to combine its efforts with those of other protest organizations seeking to end discrimination against Negroes. It helped in promoting "Freedom Rides" for civil rights and boycotts against stubborn whites. After 1955 Farmer often collaborated with Martin Luther King, Jr., a young Baptist minister with a Ph.D. from Harvard. Like Farmer, King also embraced the Gandhian philosophy of nonviolence. For more than ten years he was widely regarded—and feared—as the most effective defender of Negro rights. However, his career was brought to an end by an assassin's bullet as he stood on the balcony of a motel in Memphis in 1968.

Important successors to King, Farmer, and in a sense the Black Muslims, were the Black Panthers. Their story is not simple, mainly because they have been the product of varying influences. The movement began during the civil rights confrontations of the 1950's and 1960's in Alabama and Mississippi. From there it rapidly spread northward and about 1968 established its headquarters in Oakland, California. Its leaders—such men as Huey Newton, Bobby Seale, and Eldridge Cleaver—adopted for their party the name of Black Panthers. They saw in the panther an animal slow to take the aggressive but fierce in retaliation when attacked by its enemies.

The Black Panthers differed from other Negro militants in a number of ways. First of all, they were frankly revolutionary. They believed that only by seizing power could they redress society's wrongs. They adopted Mao Tse-tung's slogan that "All power comes from the mouth of a gun." Second, the Black Panthers, unlike so many of their forerunners, are not pro-African. They struggle for a free America, not for some mythical empire in Africa. Finally, the Black Panthers profess a kind of internationalism similar to that of other revolutionaries. They will not fight for any white empire, regardless of how benevolent it may claim to be. In connection with the United States draft, they seem to have originated the slogan "Hell no, we won't go!"

The chief factor in the growing dynamism of the Black Panthers was disillusionment with the failures of conciliation and nonviolence. Other leaders had attempted, during the 1950's, to gain rights for the Negroes, and even the privilege of registering to vote in Southern states, by peaceful means; and to what avail? Scores of marchers and demonstrators were beaten and murdered. Neither the age nor the sex of the victims mattered. Four small girls were killed when a segregationist mob bombed a Negro church in Birmingham. No effective attempt was made by law enforcement authorities to bring the murderers to justice. But while disillusionment helped add to the Black Panthers' ranks, the movement has not been an unqualified success. It has suffered from constant harassment from the police, and as a revolutionary organization it has been torn by conflicts over methods and objectives. Several of its leaders have been caught in the bloody crossfire of internal warfare and by the savage persecution of external opponents. Recently many Panthers have turned their attention to self-improvement and raising the social and intellectual status of their own members.

Rise of the Black Panthers

Other doctrines of the Black Panthers

Factors explaining the rise of the Black Panthers

1247

· *Items so designated are available in paperbound editions.*

Cady, J. F., *Southeast Asia: Its Historical Development*, New York, 1964.

Duncanson, Dennis J., *Government and Revolution in Vietnam*, New York, 1968.

· Fontaine, Andre, *History of the Cold War*, New York, 1970–1971 (Vintage), 2 vols.

· Gettleman, Marvin E., ed., *Viet Nam: History, Documents, and Opinions on a Major World Crisis*, New York, 1965 (Fawcett).

Hammer, E. J., *The Struggle for Indochina*, Stanford, 1954.

· Kahin, George M., and Lewis, John W., *The United States in Vietnam*, New York, 1967 (Delta).

Low, Francis, *The Struggle for Asia*, New York, 1956.

McCune, Shannon, *Korea's Heritage: A Regional and Social Geography*, Tokyo, 1956.

Myrdal, Gunnar, *The Challenge of World Poverty: A World Anti-Poverty Program in Outline*, New York, 1970.

Nogueira, Franco, *The Third World*, London, 1968.

Rossi, Mario, *The Third World*, New York, 1963.

· Ward, Barbara, *The Rich Nations and the Poor Nations*, New York, 1962 (Norton).

Weisbord, Robert G., *African Zion. The Attempt to Establish a Jewish Colony in the East Africa Protectorate*, Philadelphia, 1968.

Worsley, Peter, *The Third World*, 2d ed., Chicago, 1970.

Young, Crawford, *Politics in the Congo: Decolonization and Independence*, Princeton, 1965.

· Zinn, Howard, *Vietnam: The Logic of Withdrawal*, Boston, 1967.

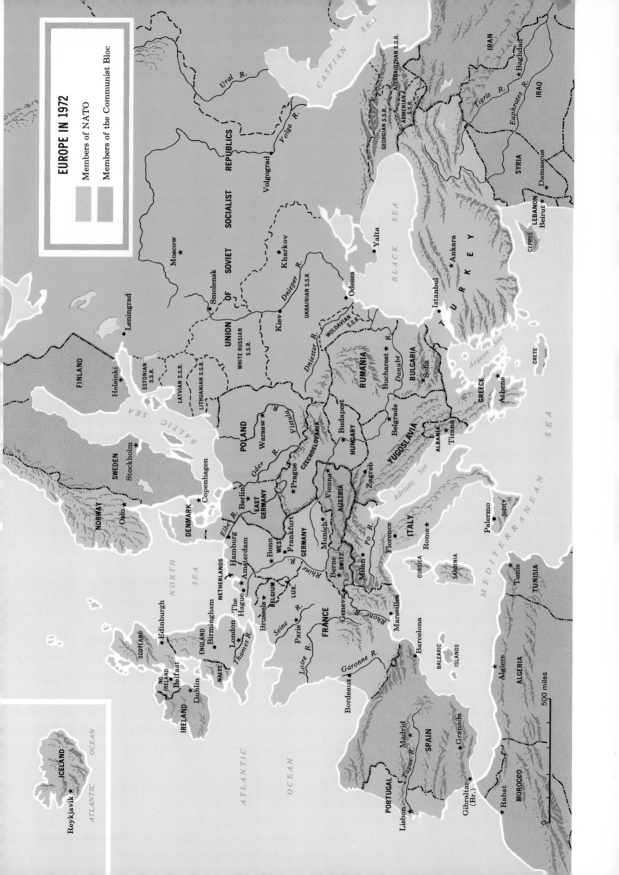

EUROPE IN 1972

Members of NATO

Members of the Communist Bloc

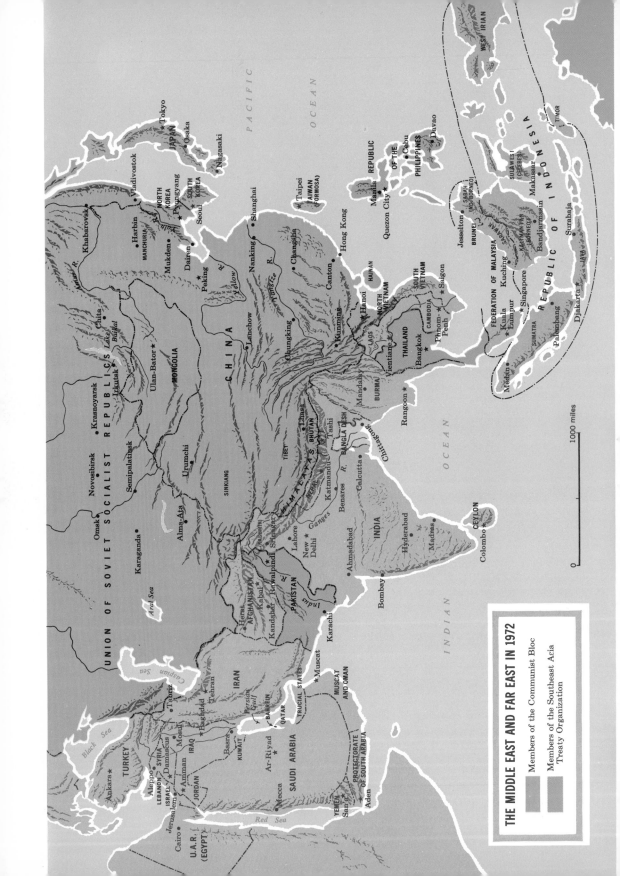

THE MIDDLE EAST AND FAR EAST IN 1972

Members of the Communist Bloc

Members of the Southeast Asia
Treaty Organization

PACIFIC   OCEAN

UNION OF SOVIET SOCIALIST REPUBLICS

Amur R.

Khabarovsk

Vladivostok

Chita

Lake Baikal

Irkutsk

Krasnoyarsk

Novosibirsk

Semipalatinsk

Omsk

Ulan-Bator ★

MONGOLIA

Karaganda

Alma-Ata

Urumchi

Aral Sea

Caspian Sea

Black Sea

TURKEY

Ankara ★

Aleppo

LEBANON   SYRIA

Damascus ★

ISRAEL

Jerusalem ★   Amman ★

JORDAN

Cairo

U.A.R.
(EGYPT)

Red Sea

Mecca

SAUDI ARABIA

Ar-Riyad ★

YEMEN
San'a

PROTECTORATE
OF SOUTH ARABIA

Aden

Mosul

Baghdad ★

IRAQ

Basra

KUWAIT

Tehran ★

IRAN

Tabriz

BAHREIN

QATAR

TRUCIAL STATES

Muscat ★

MUSCAT
AND OMAN

Persian Gulf

AFGHANISTAN

Herat

Kabul ★

Kandahar

Rawalpindi

KASHMIR

Srinagar

Lahore

New ★
Delhi

PAKISTAN

Indus R.

Karachi

Ahmedabad

Bombay

SINKIANG

TIBET

Lhasa

HIMALAYAS

NEPAL

Katmandu ★

BHUTAN

Tashi

BANGLA DESH

Chittagong

Benares

Ganges R.

Calcutta

INDIA

Hyderabad

Madras

Bombay

CHINA

Lanchow

Chungking

Kunming

Yellow R.

Yangtze R.

Peking ★

Nanking

Shanghai

Changsha

Canton

Hong Kong

Hainan

NORTH
VIETNAM

Hanoi

LAOS

Vientiane ★

THAILAND

Bangkok ★

BURMA

Mandalay

Rangoon ★

CAMBODIA

Phnom-
Penh ★

SOUTH
VIETNAM

Saigon ★

Harbin

Mukden

Dairen

MANCHURIA

NORTH
KOREA

Pyongyang ★

SOUTH
KOREA

Seoul ★

JAPAN

Tokyo ★

Osaka

Nagasaki

Taipei

TAIWAN
(FORMOSA)

REPUBLIC   OF THE

Cebu

Davao

PHILIPPINES

Manila ★

Quezon City

INDIAN   OCEAN

CEYLON

Colombo

FEDERATION OF MALAYSIA

Kuala
Lumpur

Singapore

SARAWAK

SABAH
(NORTH BORNEO)

BRUNEI

Jesselton

Kuching

KALIMANTAN
(BORNEO)

Bandjarmasin

SUMATRA

Medan

Palembang

Djakarta

JAVA

REPUBLIC OF INDONESIA

SULAWESI
(CELEBES)

Makassar

Surabaja

TIMOR

WEST IRIAN

1000 miles

0

CHAPTER 42

The Revolution of Our Age

The love of money as a possession . . . will be recognized for what it is, a somewhat disgusting morbidity, one of those semi-criminal, semi-pathological propensities which one hands over with a shudder to the specialists in mental disease.
—John Maynard Keynes, *Essays in Persuasion*, Part V

Revolutions have never lightened the burden of tyranny; they have only shifted it to another shoulder.
—George Bernard Shaw, *Revolutionist's Handbook*

When World War I broke out Sir Edward Grey, British Foreign Secretary, stood at the window of his office in Whitehall and commented sadly to a friend, "The lamps are going out all over Europe." Sir Edward Grey, later Viscount Grey, lived until 1933. Had he survived a few more decades, he might well have considered his early comment increasingly appropriate. The lamps have been going out not only all over Europe but all over the world. Revolutions, violent uprisings, degradation of long-standing customs and institutions, and frightening rivalries between superstates all emphasize the prevailing uncertainty and confusion. Even as late as the 1970's fears and anxieties had little abated. To a host of questions no one knew the answers. Would economic stability eventually be restored? Or was it merely a flimsy product of war and armaments expansion? Would the balance of terror postpone indefinitely World War III, or, as more and more countries crashed their way into the "Nuclear Club," would some power-hungry dictator precipitate a conflict that would engulf the globe? These and many similar issues tormented the minds of a whole generation, especially those who distrusted the past and doubted the possibilities of the future.

The world of uncertainty and discouragement

I. POLITICAL REVOLUTION

The political world of the 1970's bore only a faint resemblance to that which had existed in the nineteenth century, or even to that before World War II. It was sometimes assumed that the only

1249

The world of the
forgotten past

The replacement
of trust and
confidence by
suspicion and fear

Executive
despotism

essential difference was a change in the relationships among the great powers. A mere handful of powerful nations, under the leadership of Great Britain, had kept the world in order and dictated the terms of existence to the non-Caucasian peoples. But this system began to break down with the two world wars of the twentieth century. By 1970 it was little more than a memory. Britain's empire was gone, and so were the empires of France, Belgium, and the Netherlands. Some Americans think that *their* country should take over the one-time role of Great Britain as arbiter of the destinies of the globe, but they fail to realize that the role is extinct, and that no one nation or small group of nations is capable of reviving it. The spread of nuclear weapons and the fact of mutual destructiveness have put an effective end to that.

Before 1914 a balance of power among the strongest nations was, as we have seen, the world's chief reliance for preserving the peace. World Wars I and II substituted international organization for the balance of power. Now for all practical purposes both are gone. Attitudes of distrust have poisoned the relations of those formerly embarked on similar aims. The revival of a nationalism based on suspicion and hatred and motives of aggrandizement have precluded more than minimal cooperation in raising standards of living and educational advancement. The new attitude of the chief nations was illustrated by what happened on the twenty-fifth anniversary of the United Nations. The day was signalized by the resumption of massive nuclear testing by the United States, the U.S.S.R., and the People's Republic of China. The event was probably a coincidence but a most unfortunate one. It symbolized not only the preoccupation of the chief powers with military strength but also their "indifference to the principles of the United Nations." [1]

By an interesting paradox governments of recent times with the strongest commitments to democracy have often been just as autocratic in their actual operation as governments making no pretense to popular rule. The government of the Third Republic in France was no more wise and temperate in dealing with its enemies, whom it sent to Devil's Island, than was the Tsar of Russia in exiling political prisoners to Siberia. The government of Imperial Germany was hardly much more autocratic than some of the governments of its wartime opponents. Though far removed from democracy, it was preserved from rank autocracy by the rule that every German official must exercise his powers in conformity with definite codes of law. But the zenith of arbitrary rule by so-called civilized governments has been reached in the years since World War II.[2] Most governments have been offenders and the gravity of the offenses has usually varied in direct proportion to the wealth and population of the nation committing them. To illustrate, the occupation of Czecho-

[1] James Reston, *New York Times*, Oct. 16, 1970.
[2] Mr. Justice Douglas has described today's Establishment as "the new George III." *Points of Rebellion*, New York, 1971, p. 85.

slovakia by the Soviets in 1968 had no more legal justification than did the similar actions committed by the Nazis in 1938–1939. In like manner the practice of waging war without the formality of a declaration by the legislative body, as was done by the United States in Korea, Vietnam, Cambodia, and Laos, exemplifies the growing extreme of usurpation. Wars can be conducted not only without legislative authorization but even without the knowledge of the legislators or the citizens. For fourteen months prior to the May 1970 invasion of Cambodia, United States planes subjected that country to continuous bombing, while President Nixon declared emphatically that his government was scrupulously respecting Cambodian neutrality. When the truth emerged, some three years later, spokesmen for the administration and for the Pentagon openly defended the right of the executive to conceal facts from the American public "in the national interest." Both the President of the United States and the Prime Minister of Great Britain can rule virtually in defiance of Congress and Parliament. The latter have become mere ratifying bodies, with power over both the making and execution of laws concentrated in the hands of the executive.

A challenge to unlimited executive power was presented by the revelation, during 1972 and 1973, of various clandestine activities that had accompanied the campaign for the re-election of President Nixon. The "Watergate" hearings, conducted publicly by a special Senate investigating committee during the summer of 1973, uncovered startling evidence of espionage, bribery, burglary, and the invasion of civil rights by employees or agents of the White House, and finally led to a direct confrontation between the executive and the legislature when the President refused to release the tapes of telephone conversations he had secretly recorded. Although the recriminations, the court battles, and the severe blow to the President's credibility produced by Watergate threatened the government with temporary paralysis, they did not necessarily herald a real change in the balance of power. President Nixon, confident that he would not be impeached, vetoed bills passed by Congress, including one to end military involvement in Indochina. He accepted a compromise permitting the bombing of Cambodia to continue until August 15.

A challenge to executive power: the Watergate hearings

Executives have undergone accretions of power in a number of ways. Presidents of the United States, for instance, assumed the sponsorship, each in his turn, of some broad and colorful program for the national welfare. For John F. Kennedy it was the New Frontier, for Lyndon B. Johnson, the Great Society, and for Richard M. Nixon, the New Federalism. Regardless of its label, a President's program covers almost everything he might want the government to adopt during his term of office. It would include his tariff and internal revenue policies, his plans for the national budget and for increasing or reducing the public debt, his hopes for dealing with relief and unemployment and his schemes for subsidizing agriculture and crippled industries. In recent years, however, the majority of

The increase of executive power

1251

these programs have been tied in closely with the military, and their nature has been conditioned by the needs of rearmament and hostile combat.

None but extremists woud agree with Tolstoi that the modern state is nothing but "Genghis Khan with the telegraph." For the rulers of nearly every government now in existence profess to be ruling with an eye to the welfare of their subjects. The impression is carefully cultivated that without the fostering care of the government, prosperity would be impossible, education and health would suffer neglect, science and the arts would languish, and crime would run riot in the streets. How much of this doleful picture is true is difficult to determine. Since World War II the welfare state all over the globe has become a cliché. Capitalists vie with Communists and even military dictators in claiming the beneficence of their purposes. Such claims may serve to disguise the destruction of citizens' rights by a General Franco in Spain or the ironclad Colonels of Greece. They make further invasions of civil liberties easy to accomplish and increase the worship of the rulers' own majestic presence.

A good measure of the capacity of modern governments to fulfill their functions is their ability to provide for the requirements of the welfare state. These include provisions for the health, safety, and a reasonable prosperity for the citizens. Under the subject of health would come protection from sickness and disability in places of employment and in traveling to and from work. The prevalence of "black lung" among the coal miners of Appalachia would not fit in with a decent compliance with such a standard. Neither would the construction of elaborate freeways leading to excessive speed and reckless driving. Of course, some of the high-speed traveling is done by travelers over long distances, but statistics show that most of the fatal accidents occur within twenty-five miles of the victim's home. Contrary to general opinion, the rate in the United States is not the highest in the world. Some West European countries have a better claim to that "honor." Of course, the replanning and reconstruction of a national highway system would be tremendously expensive, but it would hardly equal more than two days' cost of the Indochina War or a single year of space exploration. It must be granted, of course, that significant accomplishments have occurred in medicine and public health in recent years. In the United States, for example, the death rate declined to 7.3 per thousand in 1967 from 9.0 per thousand twenty years earlier. Even more dramatic was the decline in the infant mortality rate in Sweden of more than 20 per cent.

The majority of American citizens would almost certainly classify crime as the most dangerous menace threatening the dissolution of our civilization. But few topics in the annals of modern states are more loaded with misapprehension. Crime may be taken to include every kind of social maladjustment from premeditated murder to possession of marijuana or even marijuana paraphernalia. Ordinarily in the infliction of penalties distinctions are made on the basis of the gravity or supposed gravity of the offense. But the distinction is often artificial. An offense involving bodily harm to another individual may not draw any stiffer penalty than nude bathing or the sale of an indecent postcard. Persons are sometimes held indefinitely for minor crimes when often it is their politics which threaten the Establishment. Most modern nations still have a distance to go before giving full recognition to the special category of "victimless" crimes. Meanwhile, our judicial machinery is clogged with miscellaneous offenses that never come to trial. It has been estimated that more than half of the alleged criminals in the United States have never laid a hand on any victim or stolen any other citizen's property. What they have done in many cases is to drink in public, engage in illicit sex, take part in the numbers racket, or to be caught in homosexuality. No doubt some of these acts deserve punishment, or at least condemnation, but no police authority can cover the entire waterfront and rake in every loafer or vagrant whom someone might consider a dangerous character. No modern state has the prison facilities to accommodate these hordes of minor offenders. As it is, the State of California spends $100 million a year rounding up its marijuana users. Penal laws are weird and often grotesque. In some states parole cannot be granted for certain violations until after thirty years, while in others murderers are eligible for parole after seven years. The Chief of Police of Washington, D.C., has said, "It's simply not worth arresting the street peddler of narcotics or the petty gambler. We should be going after the top men in the organization." [3]

Weird classification of crime

2. THE THIRD INDUSTRIAL REVOLUTION

Each economic revolution in modern history has been marked by cataclysmic changes through prosperity and panic and back again. The revolution that began about 1914 has been no exception. The years of the 1920's completed a fabulous cycle in 1929. Never had the prospects appeared more rosy. Prosperity seemed to have established a permanent base in the years that followed. A short time after the great stock market crash of 1929 President Hoover declared that the fundamental business of the country was "on a sound and prosperous basis." Informed economists knew better.

The distinguishing feature of the Third Industrial Revolution has been the substitution of synthetic products for natural ones in many processes of manufacturing. The production of synthetics actually began at the end of the First Revolution when William H. Perkin discovered that coal tar could be converted into an infinite variety of

The initial phase of prosperity

[3] *Wall Street Journal*, Aug. 25, 1971.

products. The process continued apace during the Second Revolution, but it did not reach its full potential until about 1940. Today it is probably safe to say that the number of goods produced synthetically exceeds the number derived from natural materials. Most automobile tires, for instance, are made from petrochemicals. Rubies, sapphires, and other gems can be produced so perfectly in factories as to be scarcely distinguishable from the genuine precious stones. Even many foods, such as whipped cream, salad oil, coffee "cream," butter substitutes, flavoring, and preservatives consist wholly or partially of synthetic substitutes. A reflective Chinese woman said recently: "When I was a little girl in China, I ate dirt; now that I am a grown-up woman in America, I eat chemicals." Yet, the results have not been a total loss. Margarine can be made to look and taste like butter but without the high cholesterol content of the natural product. The same can be said of salad oils made from peanuts or soybeans, which contain only vegetable fat. On the other hand, the use of chemicals to fatten poultry and cattle may be a detriment to the health of the ultimate consumer.

Electronics

The electronics industry has been one of the economic miracles of the Third Industrial Revolution. Electronics derives from that branch of physics which deals with the behavior and effects of electrons, or negative constituents within the atom. Electronic devices have multiplied in staggering profusion since World War II. Among them are devices to measure the trajectory of missiles, to give warnings of approaching missiles or aircraft, to make possible "blind" landings of airplanes, to store and release electrical signals, to amplify and regulate the transmission of light and sound images, and to provide the power for photoelectric cells that open doors and operate various automatic machines. The spacecraft industry,

The Age of Television. Left: The first working television pickup camera, 1929. Right: The Telstar communications satellite. Weighing only 170 pounds, and measuring 34 inches in diameter, it is powered by 3600 solar cells. It circles the earth at a speed of 1600 miles per hour at a height of from 500 to 3000 nautical miles.

which has made possible the exploration of outer space, including voyages to the moon, is closely dependent upon electronics.

Scarcely any two developments in modern industry could be more closely related than electronics and automation. Indeed, it was the use of electronic devices for radio reception that led to the initial progress in automation. Automation should not be confused with mechanization, though it may be considered the logical extreme of that process. More correctly conceived, automation means a close integration of four elements: (1) a processing system; (2) a mechanical handling system; (3) sensing equipment; and (4) a control system. Though all of these elements are necessary, the last two are the most significant. Sensing equipment performs a function similar to that of the human senses. It observes and measures what is happening and sends the information thus gained to the control unit. It employs such devices as photoelectric cells, infra-red cells, high-frequency devices, and devices making use of X-rays, isotopes, and resonance. It operates without fatigue and much faster and more accurately than do the human senses. Moreover, its observations can be made in places unsafe for, or inaccessible to, human beings. A control system receives information from a sensing element, compares this information with that required by the "program," and then makes the necessary adjustments. This series of operations is continuous, so that a desired state is constantly maintained without any human intervention, except for that initially involved in "programming." This revolution has been greatly extended by the invention of lasers. A laser is a device for amplifying the focus and intensity of light. High energy atoms are stimulated by light to amplify a beam of light. Lasers have demonstrated their value recently in medicine. They have been used effectively in arresting hemorrhaging of the retina in eye afflictions. Through automation expensive and complicated machines are constantly taking the place of much human labor. Data processing machines and electronic computers are employed to control switching operations in railroad yards, to operate assembly lines, to operate machines that control other machines, and even to maintain blood pressure during critical operations in hospitals.

The Third Industrial Revolution has gone beyond the Second in the adoption of new materials in the manufacturing process. Foremost among them have been plastics, manufactured from various substances, such as casein, phenol, and coal and petroleum derivatives. Plastic steering wheels, plastic machinery housings, and plastic bottles are only a few of them. To a considerable extent aluminum is taking the place of steel and copper, and in some instances where an even lighter material is required, as in airplane construction, magnesium is being substituted for aluminum. Other new metals have been adopted, not principally as substitutes for older metals, but to give toughness and strength or rust-proof qualities to steel. Notable

Automation

New materials

1255

among these are the ferro-alloys, which include tungsten, manga-nese, nickel, molybdenum, and chromium. Found largely in such countries as Turkey, Russia, China, India, Canada, and Rhodesia, they are indispensable to modern industry. Together with other widely scattered critical materials, they furnish excellent examples of the economic interdependence of the contemporary world.

Problems affect-
ing labor

That the Third Industrial Revolution would germinate problems affecting labor was a foregone conclusion. The most obvious was technological unemployment. Though new industries absorbed many workers, others were bound to be displaced by automation. In the mid-1960's no one could be quite sure of the extent of this dis-placement. Apparently, most of those whose jobs were taken found new opportunities with the development of new industries. In any case unemployment, in the United States, had declined by February 1966, to 3.7 per cent of the labor force. But this was a condition of a war economy. What would happen when peace returned, no one could say. Moreover, it was a fact that while the demand for skilled labor remained high, the so-called "entry jobs" as helpers, sweepers, and miscellaneous unskilled workers were fast disappearing. They were being eliminated not by computers so much as by fork-lift trucks and motorized conveyors and sweepers. Mechanization of agriculture also knocked out thousands of jobs for unskilled and un-educated workers. The mechanical cotton picker in the South and Southwest and the combine on the great wheat farms of the West displaced innumerable field hands who fled to the cities to lead lives of misery and despair in the slums. The problem of the future seemed to be not so much a repetition of the mass unemployment of the 1930's as a dearth of jobs at the bottom, and a surplus of engineers and technical workers.

Changes in the
nature of
capitalism:
(1) consolidation
and diversification

That the Third Revolution would involve further changes in the nature of capitalism goes almost without saying. Though holding companies had been largely eliminated in the public utility industry by New Deal legislation in the United States, in other industries they continued and even proliferated. They usually took the form, not of trusts but of mergers, composed of dozens of subsidiaries, more or less closely related, and formerly independent companies. The object usually was to strive for product diversification and thereby guard the parent company against shifting patterns of con-sumer demand. Thus Eastman Kodak continued to manufacture cameras and photographic materials but also acquired subsidiaries ex-tensively engaged in the production of plastics, chemicals, and syn-thetic fibers. A trend toward consolidation characterized the railroad industry, merchandising, and even banking. The largest bank in New York City, the Chase Manhattan—itself the result of a merger of two giant banks—acquired 130 branches in the Greater New York area, to say nothing of 33 overseas branches throughout the free world.

Along with this trend toward consolidation has gone, strange as it may seem, a diffusion of ownership. In 1970 it was estimated that 1 out of every 6 of the people of the United States was a shareholder in one or more American corporations. This was true despite the bear market of 1968–1970. The amount they owned was usually an infinitesimal fraction of the total shares outstanding and therefore precluded any control over the affairs of the companies. The bulk of the stock in large corporations generally came into the possession of investment trusts, insurance companies, and pension funds, colleges and universities, and foundations. Yet another characteristic of ownership in the Third Revolution has been the virtual disappearance of the old "dynastic" capitalism. The DuPont and Ford families are among the few exceptions. The name Rockefeller is no longer synonymous with oil or the name Carnegie with steel. Management has become increasingly separate from ownership. Presidents and board chairmen of modern corporations are not proprietors but financiers and bureaucrats who made their way up as lawyers or bankers or as successful heads of smaller companies. In some cases they have little direct knowledge of the basic operations of the firms over which they preside. It has been said that a recent chairman of the board of one of our largest steel corporations never saw a blast furnace until "after he died."

3. KEYNES AND THE NEW ECONOMICS

It would be difficult to exaggerate the influence of John Maynard Keynes (later Lord Keynes) in shaping the theory that has underlain the economic programs of modern states. Keynes was born in 1883 and died in 1946. He was thoroughly educated in mathematics and the classics before being sent to Cambridge University. When only twenty-three he passed the British Civil Service examination with the second highest honors. He would have ranked first except for a low grade in economics. At the Paris Peace Conference of 1919 he was the chief economic adviser of the British delegation. He spent a good part of his time castigating the ignorance and indifference of the chief delegates, including Woodrow Wilson. After the war he devoted his talents to lecturing and also to a business career. He became manager of an investment company, chairman of an insurance company, and Director of the Bank of England. He amassed a large fortune, evidently with some qualms, if we can judge from his later writings.

But Keynes was far from being a socialist. He wondered how any doctrine so "illogical and so dull" could have exercised so powerful and lasting an influence over the minds of men. Moreover, he believed that capitalism with its inner faults corrected could provide all the justice and efficiency reasonable men could expect. Capital-

John Maynard Keynes

1257

ism, though, would require a "face-lifting" that some of its old-time defenders would consider drastic. First, the idea of a perpetually balanced budget would need to be abandoned. Keynes never advocated continuous deficit financing. He would have the government deliberately operate in the red whenever private investment was too scanty to provide for the needs of the country. But when depression gave way to recovery, private financing could take the place for most purposes of deficit spending. He is supposed to have urged the "euthanasia of the rentier," or the extinction of the no-risk investor. This would leave the road clear for venture capital, which is the only socially productive form of capital. Finally, Keynes recommended monetary control as a means of promoting prosperity and full employment. He would establish what is commonly called a "managed currency," regulating its value by a process of contraction or expansion in accordance with the needs of the economy. Prosperity would thus be assured in terms of the condition of the home market, and no nation would be tempted to "beggar its neighbor" in the foolish pursuit of a favorable balance of trade.

The influence
of Keynes

Though he numbered his critics in the thousands, Keynes was an enthusiastic proponent of much of what is generally accepted today as the new economics. He was strongly convinced, especially in his later years, that an economic system could not be grounded on the gold-standard, laissez-faire principles of the nineteenth century. He held that full employment could be achieved only if governments deliberately encouraged investment in new capital goods, and he sponsored cheap money as one of the best means of accomplishing this. He had no patience with the old negative conception which required the state to spend as little as possible lest businessmen be frightened into a loss of confidence. In his opinion it was better that a moderate number of men be put to work digging holes and filling them up again than that a large number should be unemployed. Although Keynes did not have a high opinion of the economic literacy of some of his followers, many of his doctrines were idolized by statesmen and others of fiscal authority. In the 1930's they strongly influenced the policies of President Franklin D. Roosevelt and formed a major ingredient of his recovery program. Since the beginning of World War II nearly all Western nations, the United States and Britain in the vanguard, have paid homage to Keynesian economics in one form or another.

4. THE CRISIS OF ECOLOGY AND
THE POPULATION EXPLOSION

Ecology is the science which concerns the interrelationships of organisms and their environments. The word is often used primarily to refer to man and his environment, but it is much broader than that. Ecologists think of man as a link in a vast chain of life which

Industrial Pollution. The photo shows the Bethlehem Steel Company's plant at Sparrow Point, Maryland. While polluting gases and particular matter are released into the air, industrial wastes, both thermal and chemical, are released into the water.

extends all the way back through mammals, amphibians, invertebrates, and the simplest microorganisms which may be either plants or animals. In popular usage ecology may be synonymous with pollution problems. Again this is an oversimplification. The causes and prevention of pollution make up important elements in the study of ecology, but they are not the whole subject. Equally important is man's use of his environment in ways that will safeguard his heritage of fertile soil, pure air, fresh water, and forests for those who come after him.

The meaning of ecology

Ecological violations consist not merely of poisoning the atmosphere and contaminating oceans, rivers, and lakes by dumping wastes into them but by any assault upon them that makes them less valuable for human survival. The excessive construction of dams, for example, causes the silting of rivers and the accumulating of nitrates at a faster rate than the surrounding soil can absorb. The use of insecticides, especially those containing DDT, may result in upsetting the balance of nature. An example in the recent history of Malaysia illustrates such an occurrence. The Malaysian government resorted to extensive spraying of remote areas with DDT in the hope of stamping out malaria. The DDT killed the mosquitoes but also poisoned the flourishing cockroaches. The cockroaches in turn were eaten by the village cats. The net result was a multiplication of rats formerly kept from a population explosion by their natural enemies, the cats. So badly disturbed was the balance of nature that a fresh supply of cats had to be airlifted from more settled regions. Other assaults upon the balance of nature have been even more serious. The Aswan High Dam of Egypt, undoubtedly valuable for increasing the water supply of that country, has at the same time cut

Other assaults upon nature

1259

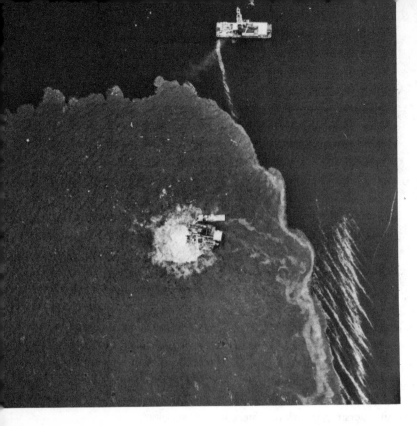

An Oil Spill off the Coast of Santa Barbara, California, 1969. Offshore oil drilling has been responsible for numerous spills. Here, at a view from 1800 feet, spreading oil can be seen moving from the offshore rig to pollute the nearby shores.

down the flow of algal nutrients to the Mediterranean with damaging effects on the fishing industry of various countries. From the ecological standpoint the fantastic development of industry in modern times is almost an unmitigated disaster. For thousands of years the human race introduced into the environment no more waste substances than could easily be absorbed by the environment. But modern technological man has introduced into nature a variety of wastes never abundant before. Among them are carbon monoxide, sulfur dioxide, and nitrogen oxides. And this is to say nothing of the discharge into nature of pesticides, the great host of synthetic products that are not biologically degradable, and the fruits of nuclear weapons testing.

It is not simply the destruction of our environment by the dumping of harmful and nondegradable products but it is also the wastage

of land as our most valuable natural resource. In many parts of the world rivers run brown because they are filled with earth washed from the fields bordering them. In some of the largest American cities two-thirds to three-quarters of the land area is paved with streets and parking lots. Meanwhile, the nation's crop land is shrinking at an alarming rate. Ecologists say that much of this land will probably have to be abandoned. Yet the mad race continues, and optimists stumble over each other in their worship of progress. Growth, speed, ingenuity, mobility have become fetishes in a nation that does not know what to do with these ends when it has achieved them. President Eisenhower hailed the $41 billion highway project launched during his administration as the greatest public welfare undertaking in history. The President made no justification of his project in terms of what it might mean for the public good. Nor did he raise any questions as to ultimate costs in case the passion for growth mounted still higher, as it almost certainly would.

A close link exists between the problems of ecology and the population explosion. Indeed, if population control had remained a reality, the problems of ecology might well have passed unnoticed for many years. For example, New York City on the eve of the Civil War had a total population of 700,000. The area was not essentially different from what it is now. Yet the inhabitants of the five boroughs constituting the city have multiplied ten times over. This increase has been accompanied by physical transformations that have facilitated crowded living by masses of people. Oil lamps were replaced by gas light and then by electricity, horse-drawn wagons and carriages by trolley cars and "gas buggies." While some of these contraptions eliminated a few forms of pollution, the general effect was to multiply sources of contamination and abuse of the natural environment. The example of New York City can be duplicated in many other overcrowded areas, not only in America but especially in Asia. Calcutta now has a population of 5 million compared with 3 million in 1961. Tokyo has grown from 9 million to over 11 million in little more than ten years. In some cities of the Orient, though not in Japan, thousands of the inhabitants sleep in the streets, and children compete with dogs and rats for scraps of refuse thrown into the discard by more "affluent" citizens.

Ecology and the population explosion

Radical environmentalists teach that unless we stop the population from growing and start its eventual decline, we haven't a chance to solve our ecological problems. As the population increases, man creates more and more problems and the damage done by each person escalates rapidly. Conditions in Los Angeles illustrate the danger. Despite excellent laws the city makes little progress in carrying them out. Increases in the number of smog-producers nullify every victory the control experts succeed in gaining. The worst offenders in vitiating ecological progress are the big industrial powers. For one thing they combine exhaustion of natural resources with contamination of the environment by nuclear poisons and their by-products. But aside from their quest of military superiority, the industrial powers consume hundreds of times more natural products than do most of the inhabitants of the Third World. An American, for instance, will consume 300 times as much steel per capita as a native of Indonesia. Paul Ehrlich, the renowned population authority at Stanford, claims that every American baby born is 50 times more of a disaster than an Indian baby because of the vast difference in standards of consumption.

Effects of population explosion

All nations of the contemporary world are in danger of being overwhelmed by a population explosion. Its major cause has been what the experts call the demographic revolution. By this is meant an overturning of the ancient balance between births and deaths, which formerly kept the population on a stationary or slowly rising level. This balance is a biological condition common to nearly all species. For thousands of years of his history man was no exception. It is estimated, for example, that the total population of the earth at the beginning of the Christian era was about 250 million. More than sixteen centuries passed before another quarter billion had been added to the total. Not until 1860 did the population of the globe approximate 1 billion. From then on the increase was vastly more rapid. The sixth half billion, added about 1960, required scarcely more than ten years.[4] According to United Nations projections, the total population of the world by 1975 will be 4 billion. To add the last half billion will require only seven or eight years.

What have been the causes of this radical imbalance known as the demographic revolution? Fundamentally, what has happened has been the achievement of a twentieth-century death rate alongside a medieval birthrate. Medicine and the other health sciences have made such rapid strides that the span of life has been substantially lengthened all over the world. Infant mortality rates have markedly declined. Deaths of mothers in childbirth have also diminished. The great plagues, such as cholera, typhus, and tuberculosis, take a much smaller toll than they did in earlier centuries. Wars and famines still number their victims by the millions, yet such factors are insufficient to counteract an uncurbed rate of reproduction. Though the practice of contraception has been approved by the governments of such nations as India, China, and Japan, only in the last have the effects been worthy of notice. In some countries the desire of adults to have numerous offspring to care for them in old age has stood as an obstacle. In others poverty, religion, and abysmal ignorance have made the widespread use of contraceptives impossible.

Of course, the demographic revolution has not affected all countries uniformly. Its incidence has been most conspicuous in the underdeveloped nations of Central and South America, Africa, and Asia. Whereas the population of the world as a whole will double, at present rates of increase, in thirty-five years, that of Central and South America will multiply twofold in only twenty-six years. An outstanding example is that of Brazil. In 1900 its population was estimated to be 17 million. By 1970 this total had grown to 94 million, more than a fivefold increase. Mexico and Venezuela have two of the highest birthrates in the world. The population of Asia (excluding the U.S.S.R. and Japan) grew from 813 million in 1900 to approximately 2 billion in 1970. By way of summary, at midcentury, the population of the underdeveloped portions of the globe was more than twice that of the developed portions. Their total land areas were about equal.

⁴ P. M. Hauser (ed.), *The Population Dilemma*, pp. 8–11.

Some would-be authorities contend that the population explosion, though a crucial problem for underdeveloped countries, is not a matter of serious moment to the United States. True, the rate of growth in America is only half as fast as the world average and only one-third as great as many underdeveloped countries. Yet America with less than 6 per cent of the world's population consumes 40 per cent of its wood pulp, 36 per cent of its fossil fuels, 20 per cent of its cotton, and 10 per cent of the world's food products. Few other industrialized nations lag far behind. As a consequence, according to Gerald Leach in the *London Observer*, most talk about the developing nations catching up with the advanced nations of the West is a "gigantic swindle." Wherein lies the remedy? Correcting or eliminating pollution is not enough. No underdeveloped nation is going to refrain from building factories to abate the smog nuisance for the benefit of nations already wallowing in luxurious living. Nor are they interested in protecting their own rivers and lakes in order to enable rich exploiters to hog the last scenery for themselves. Indeed, it often seems that environmentalism standing alone is really a kind of class warfare. Rich nations show no signs of a willingness to share the resources in their possession. Moreover, it is the well-heeled nations that have led in recent years the strongest campaigns for population control. Not a few leaders of the non-Caucasian peoples have denounced these campaigns as efforts to promote white supremacy.

Despite these criticisms most environmentalists continue to advocate population control as one of the two indispensable means of saving our planet. Paul Ehrlich thinks almost exclusively of limitation of offspring. He believes that that is the goal toward which every family should strive, with zero population growth the aim for as many as possible. He admits that stopping population growth will not necessarily solve all our problems, but unless we stop the growth and start the decline in the very near future, it may already be too late. We cannot wait for the underdeveloped countries to take the lead. They are too undernourished, too afflicted by disease, and too harassed by wars and exploitation to do much of anything to save themselves. If they go down, however, they will not perish alone. Other environmentalists go even beyond the population factor. They contend that the ecology of the world can be cleared up only by radical changes in every economic, social, and political sphere that seems to the existing power structure as important. The conception of unlimited profit and material success, and, above all, growth and expansion as national fetishes must go by the board. Robert Heilbroner of The New School for Social Research has described our dilemma as tantamount to asking the world's privileged classes to "agree to euthanasia." But what other way of escape is there? The hopes of some optimists that a Green Revolution involving the introduction and cultivation of new and better crops is only a possible answer. After four years of improved grains, better fertilizers and farming techniques, food production in the Third World is still lag-

THE CRISIS OF ECOLOGY AND THE POPULATION EXPLOSION

Margaret Sanger, a Leader in the Movement to Awaken the World to the Necessity of Birth Control

The need for drastic remedies

1263

ging. Primary reasons are the conversion of valuable lands into dust bowls by overuse of fertilizers and excessive grazing, and destruction of water resources.

Recent statistics provide a slender reed of encouragement on which to lean. The United States Census Bureau has published figures showing a record decline in births in the past decade. One might assume that these figures would be a universal cause of rejoicing. But not so. Manufacturers of toys, clothes, automobiles, motorcycles, and even builders feel themselves threatened. Other observers seem deeply disturbed because the decline did not occur in one of the crowded and unprogressive countries of the Orient instead of in a nation as industrially advanced as the United States. Their attitude was reminiscent of that of Secretary of Commerce Sinclair Weeks, who rejoiced when the population of America hit 170 million in 1957. He was "happy to welcome this vast throng of new customers for America's goods and services." They would "help insure a rising standard of living. . . ." [5] Eleven years later the population hit the fantastic total of 205 million. Obviously, an end would be reached sometime. But what fantastic "boon" would bring it to pass? Some new version of the Black Death, perhaps, or some weird and unanticipated misuse of nuclear energy.

[5] David Lyle, "The Human Race Has, Maybe, Thirty-five Years Left," *Esquire Magazine*, Sept. 1967.

Urban Congestion. A traffic jam of major proportions in the market district of London during the early part of the twentieth century.

5. GALLOPING URBANIZATION

Closely allied to the population explosion has been the rapid growth of urban areas in nearly all countries. Though the highest birthrates are generally found in agricultural nations, the pressure of increased numbers and falling incomes forced thousands to flee from the land to the cities. The core population of many American cities is already made up of refugees from the cotton fields of the South or from the sugar plantations of West Indian islands. The urban explosion has been much more rapid than the population explosion in general. The population of the United States in 1920 was slightly less than 106 million, with only a little more than half of this total living in urban centers. By 1970 the total had grown to 200 million, with 68 per cent living in other than rural communities. Urbanization, of course, was not confined to the United States. During the first half of the twentieth century, as world population increased by 49 per cent, the inhabitants of cities increased by over 200 per cent. The increase in urban living

Concentration of population in large cities has been almost an unmitigated disaster. Most of the influx crowds into the core cities where welfare is available and a life of profitable crime is at least a possibility. The more prosperous and better educated inhabitants then leave the older sections and flee to the suburbs. The whole character of a city may thus be changed with radical transformations of its social and economic life. Studies made of social conditions in the "Inner City" of Washington reveal incredible truths. The area is a center of unemployment, infant mortality, and venereal disease. Thirty-six per cent of all young men between twenty and twenty-four years of age are heroin addicts, and 24 per cent of those between nineteen and twenty-four. Ramsey Clark emphasized the point graphically: "In any city when you put poor education, poor employment, poor housing, and probably poor health on the map, you have marked the same place every time." [6]

Consequences of population congestion

In some respects it would be more accurate to speak of galloping "metropolitanization" instead of an urban explosion. Actually, the so-called growth of cities, especially in the United States, has consisted of the growth of large urban areas, each comprising a central city and surrounding suburbs. In a few instances the central city and its suburbs sprawl over so large an area that it is difficult to tell where one metropolis ends and another begins. Some observers predict the development, in the United States, of the "megalopolis," a huge aggregation of cities and suburbs formerly maintaining independent existences. One such megalopolis would be an area extending from Boston to Washington, taking in Providence, New Haven, New York, Philadelphia, and Baltimore. A second would be the Milwaukee–Chicago–South Bend area. Still another would stretch all the way from San Francisco to Los Angeles and San Diego.

Metropolitanization

[6] *New York Times*, Feb. 7, 1971.

Urban Congestion. One of the many curses of urbanization is the automobile. Its use is perpetuated at the expense of sensible mass transit systems as a result of spreading affluence and the feeling that each individual must be able to move about where and when he or she pleases.

The impact of urbanization

Rapid urbanization has had a profound impact upon contemporary society. As in past ages, cities have been the principal means of fostering cultural growth. They provide the art museums, centers of learning, scientific institutes, the great libraries, and other cultural and educational facilities. It is almost a commonplace that without cities civilization can neither grow nor flourish. At the same time, it appears also to be true that metropolitan cities pose a threat to the very existence of civilization. In recent times, particularly, they present problems that almost defy solution. Made possible originally by the automobile, such cities today face strangulation by traffic congestion. Overcrowding combined with industrialization results in smog and miscellaneous pollution and in an environment favorable to the spread of disease. Blight and decay in the older areas magnify the problem of finding sufficient revenue to provide for essential services. These must be constantly expanded because of the increasing numbers of indigent, unemployed, and ignorant who populate the widening slums. So grave were these problems that, in the 1970's, most municipal rulers were urgently pleading with Washington to come to their rescue.

6. THE REVOLT OF YOUTH

Origins of the youth revolt

The years from 1964 onward through 1970 were marked by protest and upheaval by the younger generation more rampant than the world had witnessed in many decades. The agitation was not confined to any one country. It was most far-reaching in the United States, but it did not begin there. Disturbances were common in Japan, France, Italy, and Latin America. About the only nations to escape were those under communism or under the iron heel of dictatorship like Greece and Spain. In the opinion of some observers the youth revolution was nothing new. Attempts have been made to see the current movement as a mere replica of the Beat Generation of Jack Kerouac and Allen Ginsberg. Their predecessors were the Bohemians and anti-Babbitts, who fulminated against the conformists and lame brains of the 1920's. Even long in advance of them were the Thoreaus and Whitmans of the nineteenth century. Such modern exponents of the anti-youth movement as Bruce Cook, Book Editor of the *National Observer*, presents the "hippies as just second-generation Beats." [7] Although the author has a good understanding of background, he seems only dimly aware of the full significance of the current movement. He appears to classify every youth in revolt as a hippie, a confusion which no informed critic would be likely to commit.

The violent phase of the youth revolt

The youth revolt of the past few years has often been associated with vandalism and violence. Few newspaper readers have forgotten the uprisings at the University of Paris in 1968, the violence at Columbia, Berkeley, and San Francisco State, and the wild disorders at the Democratic National Convention at Chicago in the same year.

[7] *The Beat Generation*, New York, 1971, p. 205.

Students of the University of Paris during the Uprisings of 1968. Of interest is the student in the center who with his right hand throws a paving brick and in his left clutches a camera to record the event.

Some commentators portray participants in the youth rebellion as engaged in a deadly war with the adult world. *Adult* repression they consider as the primary cause of the violence that accompanies this war. Most of this violence, at least when it takes the form of bloodshed, they credit to overzealous police action. They point out that none of the participants in the outbreaks at Kent State, Jackson (Miss.) State, and Orangeburg, S.C., was armed. Young rebels are sometimes portrayed as unwitting belligerents in an uneven war. Governments marshal against them many of the weapons and techniques used by armed forces against guerrilla fighters in Vietnam. Helicopters, gas warfare, search-and-destroy operations, hit-and-run bombings, and mass arrests are only a few of them.[8] Emphasis by the news media on these picturesque and sometimes tragic clashes between the generations gives a distorted view of the violence and disorder. Many adults have gained the impression of a mass uprising in which only small minorities of students have remained passive or neutral. Undoubtedly some rebellions have reached such a crescendo of frenzy that they have drawn the majority of the student body into their orbit. More often it is clear that the fire-eating dissenters have remained a minority with the body of students intent upon other things or giving no more than verbal support. Competent observers have recently estimated that only about 1 per cent of college and university students have ever engaged in violence.[9]

But the real youth revolution does not consist in the violent upheaval of rock throwing, window-smashing attacks upon venerable institutions and the men who run them. Rather it is in the minds and hearts of its authors who renounce the values of conventional society but do not advocate wrecking its institutions. Instead of activists, most of them are quietists living their own lives as individuals or as members of primitive groups. Most of them are strongly apolitical. They consider politics to be self-defeating. It merely substitutes one form of authoritarian domination for another. In particular, they decry political revolutions. Political revolutions even more than shifts of parties result in changes of masters—Napoleon and later the restored Bourbons for the First Republic in France; the Bolsheviks for the Romanoffs in Russia. Human aggrandizement "is a determining factor in human behavior. . . ."[10] Youth leaders believe that this evil must be annihilated and new goals substituted for it.

It is easy to fault the youth movement of our time. Its most obvious deficiency is indifference to creative achievement. Only in music and to a limited extent in art do its leaders show much interest in equaling or surpassing the accomplishments of the past. Science leaves them cold or even antagonistic because of its association with

The apolitical or quietist revolution

Achievements of the youth rebellion

[8] John R. Seeley, "Youth in Revolt," Special Report, *Britannica Book of the Year,* 1969.

[9] Charles A. Wells, *Between the Lines,* Sept. 15, 1971.

[10] Jean-François Revel, "Without Marx or Jesus," *Saturday Review,* July 24, 1971.

war-making activities. Literature has little appeal except for caustic novels and dramas and satiric poetry. Social sciences, by contrast, evoke a more positive response. Sociology, anthropology, and environmental studies seem more relevant to a threatened world than ancient history, languages, and advanced mathematics. Yet against these generally negative attitudes must be ranked some outstanding achievements. One of these is a more constructive view of race relations. Young people, with few exceptions, regard notions of racial superiority and inferiority as a mass of baseless prejudice. Many have suited their actions to their principles by campaigning for desegregation and civil rights, by free racial association, and sometimes by intermarriage. Finally, it is not too much to credit the youth rebellion with frustrating the designs of certain great powers in many parts of the Third World. It was this rebellion that exposed the inhumanity and hypocrisy of the American adventure in Southeast Asia. Long before adult liberals lifted a finger against the bombing raids and body counts of that war, students in colleges and universities stormed the institutions of the Establishment in angry protest. Although they did not stop the war, they brought the Johnson administration to its downfall in March 1968. Their compeers in France a year later contributed much to bringing about the defeat of President Charles de Gaulle.

7. EDUCATION IN TRAVAIL

The education system as a whole did not escape the tribulations of students and administrators. All was tranquil enough until 1957. That was the year of Sputnik, when Soviet scientists became the first to place an artificial satellite in orbit around the earth. The unexpected Russian triumph shocked Western educators out of their complacency. Soon everyone was asking how the West could have been brought so low as to suffer defeat by a nation whose mathematicians are still using the abacus. What had gone wrong with Western systems of education? Had they failed because of an excess of "permissiveness," too many frills? These and many other questions were symptomatic of the anxieties of the generation caught up in the Cold War.

It was probably inevitable that the first reaction to the perplexities raised by Sputnik should be a demand for stiffer requirements in secondary schools and colleges, more emphasis on mathematics, languages, and the sciences. But this did not last. The world of the educational conservatives was thrown into confusion by the introduction of the "New Math," which seemed to call into question the convenient assumption that mathematics was the basis of all reasoning. "Relevant" subjects like sociology, ecology, and political science attracted larger enrollments than literature, philosophy, and the physical sciences. More significant was the revival of democratization in the schools. This trend had already begun in the early part of the

The year of Sputnik

Modifications of requirements in the schools

1269

century. In England and America it was symbolized, as we have learned, by the Progressive Education movement under the leadership of John Dewey. The movement evoked a great deal of criticism from educational traditionalists, and it fell into such disrepute that it almost died out. Now in spite of Communist scares and threats of war it was revived. Western European countries took the lead, although even some Eastern ones did not lag far behind. In 1967–1968 Denmark removed the last traces of corporal punishment from its schools, thus making the prohibition of physical penalties complete throughout Scandinavia. Surprising as it may seem, the Greek government in 1968 declared corporal punishment an anachronism and banned it from its schools. Similar efforts were made in Great Britain, but teacher opposition prevented them from being completely successful. Further efforts at democratization included dilution of educational authoritarianism and movements for the Open University. France was the pioneer in the former. In 1968 Edgar Faure, Minister of Education, promulgated a new system of governance for the schools of the nation. Each would be under the control of a council made up of representatives of three groups approximately equal in size. The groups would be (1) the administration of the school with a contingent of distinguished citizens; (2) teachers and other employees of the school; and (3) pupils and parents.

The first Open University to be established was set up in England in 1962. Its founder was Jennie Lee (now Lady Lee), wife of Aneurin Beven, sometime Minister of Health in the Labour Cabinet after the war. Its purpose was to combat élitism in higher education. Nearly all the previous requirements for university admission were abolished. The Open University is free to all. The course of study, however, is not unlimited. The object is the training of "generalists" rather than specialists. About 1969 the City University of New York began a transformation into an open university. As in England nearly all the old requirements for admission were broken down. About all that was left was the single condition that the aspiring student live within the boundaries of the city.

The Open University in England and America

Students at Work at the Lenin State Library, Moscow

Many of the new developments, including the one just mentioned, were products of agitation by racial minorities. Blacks in the Northern cities of the United States were the most active. For years they contended that they had been deprived of privileges rightfully theirs on the basis of their numbers and contributions to the national life. Some, of course, did meet the standards of white colleges and succeeded in graduating, in a few instances with brilliant records. The majority, however, were relegated to Negro colleges of indifferent quality maintained by churches in the Southern states. Often these were the only colleges the black students were qualified to enter. Black leaders admitted that this was true, although they contended that in many cases exclusion from the better institutions was likely to be founded on race. Spokesmen for the blacks insisted that in either case their kinsmen were almost certainly being penalized for lack of opportunity—for being born black or for being deprived of the chance to get the rudiments of an education in their very early lives. They therefore urged that colleges admit black students under provisions that would equalize this disparity of opportunity. In response to these demands many colleges adopted relaxed admission standards for the benefit of minorities. Curricula were changed also to provide for new courses on Afro-American Studies, African History, Swahili, and more emphasis on such "relevant" subjects as ecology and sociology.

However the winds of change buffeted the educational systems of most countries, one nation stood as a bulwark against them. This was the Soviet Union. Leonid Brezhnev, General Secretary of the Communist Party, made the official position of the Soviet regime startlingly clear. The revolutionary disturbances in the West he characterized as signs of the deepening crisis of capitalism. He commanded Soviet students to maintain firm discipline and to remember Lenin's advice: "Firstly to study, secondly to study, and thirdly to study." But he rejected all conceptions of objectivity in education. He would not have the schools follow the path of truth wherever it might lead. It was the duty of the Soviet teacher to produce "ideologically convinced fighters for the Communist cause." Could anyone doubt that this was a march backward straight into the arms of Stalin?

SELECTED READINGS

· *Items so designated are available in paperbound editions.*

Banfield, Edward C., *The Unheavenly City*, Boston, 1970.
· Bell, Daniel, *The End of Ideology*, Glencoe, Ill., 1960 (Free Press).
· Brodine, Virginia, and Selden, Mark, eds., *Open Secret: The Kissinger-Nixon Doctrine in Asia*, New York, 1972.
Crowe, F. E., ed., *Collection: Papers by Bernard Lonergan*, New York, 1967.

READINGS   Drucker, P. F., *The End of Economic Man*, New York, 1939. A really profound study of modern man's predicament.

· Ehrlich, Paul R., *The Population Bomb*, New York, 1968.

Galbraith, John, *The Liberal Hour*, New York, 1960.

——, *The New Industrial State*, Boston, 1967.

· Harrington, Michael, *The Other America: Poverty in the U.S.*, New York, 1962 (Penguin).

——, *Socialism*, New York, 1972. A penetrating recent analysis.

· Hauser, P. M., ed., *The Population Dilemma*, Englewood Cliffs, N.J., 1963 (Spectrum).

——, *Population Perspectives*, New Brunswick, N.J., 1960.

Laski, H. J., *Reflections on the Revolution of Our Time*, New York, 1943. A discerning analysis not seriously marred by a Marxist viewpoint.

Mannheim, Karl, *Diagnosis of Our Time*, New York, 1944. A thoughtful study.

Neumann, Sigmund, *The Future in Perspective*, New York, 1943.

Schapiro, J. S., *The World in Crisis*, New York, 1950.

Snow, C. P., *The Two Cultures and A Second Look*, Cambridge, 1965.

· Toffler, Alvin, *Future Shock*, New York, 1971 (Random House).

· Tugwell, Rexford G., *Constitution for a United Republics of America*, Santa Barbara, Calif., 1970 (Center for the Study of Democratic Institutions).

· Ward, Barbara, *The Rich Nations and the Poor Nations*, New York, 1962 (Norton).

· ——, *Nationalism and Ideology*, New York, 1966 (Norton).

——, *The West at Bay*, New York, 1948.

· Wheeler, Harvey, *Democracy in a Revolutionary Era*, Santa Barbara, Calif., 1970 (Center for the Study of Democratic Institutions).

Wingo, Lowden, Jr., ed., *Cities and Space*, Baltimore, 1963.

SOURCE MATERIALS

Dolivet, Louis, *Handbook of the United Nations*, Charter of the United Nations.

Proposed Constitution for a World Republic, *Saturday Review of Literature*, Vol. 31 (April 3, 1948).

CHAPTER 43

Twentieth-Century Culture

I believe that man will not merely endure: he will prevail.
—William Faulkner, Speech upon
receiving the Nobel Prize, Stockholm, December 10, 1950

Occident, *n.* The part of the world lying west (or east) of the
Orient. It is largely inhabited by Christians, a powerful tribe of
the Hypocrites, whose principal industries are murder and cheating, which they are pleased to call "war" and "commerce." They
also are the principal industries of the Orient.
—Ambrose Bierce, *The Devil's Dictionary*

The twentieth century thus far has constituted one of the most critical periods of modern history. It has been an age of wars and upheavals that have threatened the destruction of some of our most
basic ideals and institutions. Some, in fact, did virtually go under in
the devastating flood of barbarism and unreason that have characterized much of the period so far. The early years of the century saw
a continuation of many of the trends begun during the late decades of the nineteenth century. Perhaps one can say that this
was true of ideals such as optimism, confidence in reason as an
instrument of knowledge, and faith in the beneficience of science. To be sure, philosophies such as Pragmatism had attacked the old metaphysics hallowed from the time of Aristotle,
and had cast doubt on the ability of the human mind to discover
ultimate truth. Yet philosophers like F. H. Bradley could still write
of the universe as a "star-domed city of God ruled by benevolent
purpose," if only bewildered man would follow the proper methods
of apprehending its reality. The novelist H. G. Wells and the playwright George Bernard Shaw exuded a sublime confidence in science and in social reform to reshape man's environment and to
enable him quickly to solve his most serious problems. But there
were rumblings of a distant thunder which forced men to question
their views along many of these lines. As time went on, issues of the
most fundamental kind were examined and challenged. Nothing

Trends in the early twentieth century

1273

escaped, and often the conclusions drawn were profoundly disturbing in nature. No one could accuse contemporary man of being
naïve. At least, he himself would be the last to admit it.

I. THE DECLINE OF PHILOSOPHY

The history of philosophy since early in the twentieth century presents in large part a record of pessimism and confusion.

Characteristics
of contemporary
philosophy
To the majority of thinkers who have lived during this period
the events taking place around them justified the deepest anxiety.
World War I seemed the beginning of a new dark age. Later
the onrush of fascism and the plunge into a second world conflict appeared to leave little hope that civilization would ever
recover. To be sure, few of the philosophers gave way to despair, but an increasingly large number lost confidence in the ability of man to save himself without the support of authority or the
aid of supernatural powers. George Santayana fled from the materialist world in disgust and established himself for his declining years
in the Convent of the Blue Nuns in Rome. An even more spectacular change of views was accomplished by the English philosopher
C. E. M. Joad. Agnostic, advocate of polygamy and euthanasia, and
author of the Oxford Oath, which pledged its signers never to fight
for king and country, he turned before his death in 1953 into a
staunch upholder of original sin and a defender of the Christian
faith as a light to live by in a darkening world.

One of the most important of the philosophies that tended to give
a pessimistic view of man and his world was the Protestant conserv-

Protestant
Conservatism
atism of the Swiss-German theologian Karl Barth and the American
Reinhold Niebuhr. In form a system of theology, it presented profound philosophical conclusions concerning the nature of life and the
destiny of man. Barth and Niebuhr discussed the universe and
its problems in something approaching Calvinist terms. They
believed the world to be governed by an all-powerful Diety, who
controls all things for His own purposes. They considered man to
be a moral being, created in the divine image, and responsible to
God for the use that he makes of this life. Above all, they emphasized what they regarded as the fundamental fact of sin in the
world. Although man is capable of sympathy and benevolence, his
nature is sadly corrupted by pride and self-love. These commonly
take the form of a will to power, which is the primary source of
war, race conflict, tyranny, and exploitation. Sin can be conquered
only as men humble themselves before God, acknowledge the evil in
their own natures, and accept the redeeming power of the Christian
religion. By such means alone can they achieve that love and respect
for others which are the essence of democracy. The fatherhood of
God is the essential foundation of the brotherhood of man.

In the view of some contemporary philosophers, a more satisfying
concept of the nature of man and the problems of the world is being

expressed in the work of some twentieth-century Jesuit thinkers. Their foremost leader is the French Canadian Bernard Lonergan (born 1904). Lonergan is not a philosopher in a really broad sense of the term. He has devoted most of his life thus far to building and defending a system of theology. He has shown little interest in such topics as freedom versus authority, the primacy of faith over knowledge, and the supposedly sinful nature of man. From time to time he has touched upon such doctrines as the Assumption of Mary in an unusually broad and suggestive fashion. He has incorporated with the Assumption doctrine such concepts as the role of suffering, death, and resurrection in the total scheme of the universe. But here he has stopped short of any broad speculation. He seems never satisfied with partial answers and would rather wait for complete solutions no matter how long they must be delayed.

Jean-Paul Sartre in Front of His Portrait by Picasso

The depths of pessimism in philosophy were reached by a movement known as Existentialism, the most popular form of which originated in France about 1938. Founded by Jean-Paul Sartre, a teacher of philosophy in a Paris *lycée* and subsequently a leader of the Resistance against the Germans, it takes its name from its doctrine that the *existence* of man as a free individual is the fundamental fact of life. But this freedom is of no help to man; instead, it is a source of anguish and terror. Realizing, however vaguely, that he is a free agent, morally responsible for all his acts, the individual feels himself a stranger in an alien world. He can have no confidence in a benevolent God or in a universe guided by purpose, for, according to Sartre, all such ideas have been reduced to fictions by modern science. His only way of escape from forlornness and despair is the path of "involvement," or active participation in human affairs. It should be noted that in addition to the atheistic Existentialism of Sartre, there was also an older, Christian form, which had its origin in the teachings of Sören Kierkegaard, a Danish theologian of the middle nineteenth century. Like its atheistic counterpart, Christian Existentialism also teaches that the chief cause of man's agony and terror is freedom, but it finds the source of this freedom in original sin. It is not difficult to detect the influence of Kierkegaard and his followers upon the Neo-Orthodoxy of Karl Barth and Reinhold Niebuhr. Since 1930 the leading exponent of Christian Existentialism has been Karl Jaspers, philosophy professor at the University of Heidelberg.

At least two philosophers of the contemporary age retained their optimism amid the welter of gloom and uncertainty. One was Alfred North Whitehead. Born in England, the son of a clergyman of the Church of England, he spent the most fruitful years of his life as Professor of Philosophy at Harvard. Originally a mathematician, he turned to philosophy in an effort to harmonize modern thinking with the revolutionary discoveries of the new age of science. The system of thought he rapidly developed owed much to Plato, Kant, and Einstein. Like the first two, at least, he regarded intuition as just

The optimistic philosophy of Whitehead

as valid a method of knowing as reason or sensory experience. He rebuked the hardheaded positivists who heaped scorn upon the mystic, the artist, and the romantic poet. A liberal in politics and in social theory, he had a firm belief in the certainty of progress. He had an abiding faith also in a benevolent God. But Whitehead refused to think of this God as a divine autocrat handing down tables of laws and punishing men eternally for trespassing against them. Instead, he conceived of Him as a God of love, as "the poet of the world, with tender patience, leading it by his vision of truth, beauty, and goodness." [1] The defect of most religions, Christianity included, has been to represent God as a God of power. God is not omnipotent, else He would be the author of evil. His primary function is to save human beings from the evil which necessarily arises in connection with their struggle for the good. Such was Whitehead's conception of a friendly universe in which God and man are partners in striving toward perfection.

The second of the philosophers whose thinking was basically optimistic was the American John Dewey. Born in 1859, Dewey had already achieved renown before 1918 as a philosopher of Pragmatism. He never abandoned his allegiance to that movement, but after World War I he gave more and more attention to specific human problems. In his celebrated *Reconstruction in Philosophy*, published in 1920, he urged that philosophy should abandon its dealings "with Ultimate and Absolute Reality" and "find compensation in enlightening the moral forces that move mankind." [2] Unlike most of his contemporaries, he retained a healthy confidence in the powers of the human intellect. He believed that man, making use of the resources acquired by reason and experience, could solve his own problems without any assistance from the supernatural. In common with the Humanists of the past, he considered human beings to be the most important creatures in the universe, and he refused to concede that their nature was corrupt or depraved. Amid the rising tide of totalitarian oppression in the 1930's, he stressed increasingly the importance of freedom. This, together with a belief in equality and in the capacity of men to form intelligent judgments when guided by experience and education, he held to be the essence of democracy.

The Pragmatism of John Dewey was one of the first of modern philosophies that can be classified as antimetaphysical. By some it has been called anti-intellectual, for it denies the possibility of finding conclusive answers to any of the great questions of life—the nature of the universe, the meaning of life, the possibility of a God as the source of the moral law and the architect of human destiny. Dewey had an able ally in Bertrand, Lord Russell, who continued the development of his New Realism into the twentieth century. One of Russell's disciples, Ludwig Wittgenstein, participated in the founding of Logical Positivism, the most extreme of all the antimetaphysi-

John Dewey

Bertrand Russell

[1] *Process and Reality*, p. 526.
[2] Pp. 26–27.

cal philosophies. Developed further by the so-called Vienna Circle, whose leader was Rudolf Carnap, Logical Positivism emerged as an uncompromisingly scientific philosophy. It is not concerned with values or ideals except to the extent that they may be demonstrable by mathematics or physics. In general, the Logical Positivists reject as "meaningless" everything that cannot be reduced to a "one-to-one correspondence" with something in the physical universe. In other words, they reduce philosophy to a mere instrument for the discovery of truth in harmony with the facts of the physical environment. They divest it almost entirely of its traditional content and use it as a medium for answering questions and solving problems. They are concerned especially with political theory, for they regard that subject as particularly burdened with unproved assumptions and questionable dogmas.

Included among the social and political philosophies after 1918 were the theories of some who despised democracy and therefore contributed to the deepening crisis. Foremost among them were the Italian Vilfredo Pareto and the German Oswald Spengler. Their forerunner was the Frenchman Georges Sorel, who has already been discussed as the founder of Syndicalism. For the most part, all of them agreed in their contempt for the masses, in their belief that democracy was impossible, in their anti-intellectual viewpoint, and in their admiration for strong and aggressive leaders. Spengler was, in many respects, more extreme than Pareto. Although he completed about 1918 an erudite and in some respects brilliant philosophy of history, which he entitled *The Decline of the West*, his later writings were as full of prejudice as the books of the Nazis. In his *Hour of Decision*, published in 1933, he fulminated against democracy, pacifism, internationalism, the lower classes, and the colored races. He sang the praises of those "who feel themselves born and called to be masters," of "healthy instincts, race, the will to possession and power." He despised the cold, analytical reasoning of urban intellectuals and called upon men to admire the "deep wisdom of old peasant families." Human beings, he maintained, are "beasts of prey," and those who deny this conclusion are simply "beasts of prey with broken teeth."

Antirationalist and antidemocratic philosophies

The years following World War II witnessed an increasing popularity of conservative political and social philosophy. The creeping shadow of communism was undoubtedly largely responsible, but the trend had been initiated while the U.S.S.R. was still an ally of the West. The paternity of the new movement should perhaps be ascribed to Frederick A. Hayek, an Austrian political economist who had taken up residence in London. In *The Road to Serfdom*, Hayek condemned all forms of collectivist interference with capitalism, on the ground that they would lead to socialism and eventually to communism or fascism. Destruction of economic freedom, he contended, must surely lead to the destruction of all freedoms, for the right of the individual to unhampered choice in the pursuit of

The New Conservatism

1277

tastes and interests is the very essence of freedom. A more strictly political variety of the new conservatism is exemplified by the work of Peter Viereck, Eric Voegelin, and Russell Kirk. All three espouse a philosophy essentially reactionary and antirational. Viereck, for example, describes himself as one who "distrusts human nature and believes (politically speaking) in Original Sin which must be restrained by the ethical traffic lights of traditionalism." According to Voegelin, Western society can be saved by venerating its tradition-rooted institutions and by abandoning the belief that knowledge, rather than faith, is the greatest good. Russell Kirk demands a revival of family piety, the defense of property, and recognition that a "divine intent rules society" and that "Providence is the proper instrument for change."

2. THE CHANGING FACE OF RELIGION

In the early twentieth century religion seemed the most solidly entrenched of institutions. Scarcely anyone appeared to challenge its authority or to question its right to prescribe public and private morality and what should be taught in the schools. As late as 1925 a teacher in Tennessee was convicted and sentenced to a $100 fine for teaching the theory of evolution to his high school class in biology. Although he won an appeal two years later, the law was not overturned until 1967. Bible-reading and public prayers were not only universal requirements in Western schools, but courses in religion were quite often mandatory even in nondenominational colleges and universities. In the United States the typical college president was a Doctor of Divinity. He might also be a professor—of philosophy in the larger institutions, or of something called Christian Evidences in the smaller ones.

The dominance of religion

For the most part religion followed a straight and narrow path until well into the twentieth century. To be sure, as we have seen, factional movements sprang up in both the Catholic and Protestant churches. Each had its modernist revolt fostered by the growth of science and the new emphasis on that subject as the key to human welfare. Dissension mounted within the economic system involving conflicts between capital and labor and between rich and poor. But none of these dissensions continued long in full swing. All gave way in time to more conservative tendencies. The succession of Popes illustrated the trend in the Catholic Church. The liberal Pope Leo XIII was followed in turn by a series of moderately conservative successors. Then came the reign of the tolerant peasant, John XXIII, who presided over the Church from 1958 to 1963. Although seventy-seven years old at the beginning of his reign, he proved himself one of the most vigorous leaders of the Church in modern times. Just before he mounted the throne he announced that he would summon a great Church council to be called Vatican II to revise and update the decrees of an earlier council that had met 100 years before. It was

The reign of Pope John XXIII

Pope John XXIII

arranged that the new council should open in October 1962 and that it should be the most representative since the Fourth Lateran Council in 1215. Vatican II marked a milestone in the liberalization of the Church. Pope John urged the fathers to practice freedom of discussion and to find new means of making the fath live in the minds and hearts of the people. He insisted that the present-day Church in opposing errors should use compassion instead of harshness. Pope John XXIII left much of his work unfinished when death overtook him at the age of eighty-one. His successor, Paul VI, announced that meetings of the Council would be resumed in September 1963.

Pope Paul VI has seemed anxious to return to the conservative paths marked out by his earlier predecessors of the twentieth century. Though he has initiated changes, he has confined these to liturgical and formal matters. At his instigation the Vatican Council has authorized the use of vernacular languages instead of Latin exclusively in the services of the Church. He has provided for changes in the Roman Curia, limiting the terms of its members and authorizing early retirement. On the other hand, he has refused to modify the Church's position on birth control and on celibacy of the clergy, except in some cases to permit deacons to marry. But modifications of the Catholic religion outside the central hierarchy have been more important than those made by Popes and Church Councils. In France forty-four priests left the ministry in 1970 declaring that they could no longer accept the rule forbidding priests to marry. Later the same year an international assemblage of clerics dissatisfied on the same

Pope Paul VI

1279

subject convened in Amsterdam. In some Latin American countries and in parts of Spain the Church ran into heavy weather because of its tendency to support military regimes and semifascist governments.

As for the United States, disaffection among Catholics has developed peculiar characteristics. Much of it has grown out of a rigorous dogmatism handed down from the past and solidified by a dominant clergy. A good portion was politically motivated. The tendency of some members of the higher clergy to endorse the foreign adventures of the United States government, as illustrated by Cardinal Spellman's blessing of the Vietnam War, annoyed liberal Catholics. The action of the two Berrigan brothers and their associates in burning draft records evoked considerable applause, even though they went to prison for their deeds. Most other deviations from the official Catholic position have been the work of laymen rather than members of the clergy. A poll conducted by *Newsweek* in the early 1970's indicated social and moral heresies among Catholics that a few years ago would have been considered scandalous. Sixty-three per cent had not gone to confession in the past eight weeks. Sixty per cent did not regard a divorced Catholic who remarries as living in sin. Fifty-three per cent believed that priests should be permitted to marry. Doubtless similar questionnaires given to adherents of other religions would bring out answers not greatly different.

Despite the tendencies of organized churches to resist change, they have not been wholly successful in doing so. Protest denominations have generally been less successful than the Church of Rome. Methodists, Baptists, Presbyterians have suffered heavy losses by the growth of Pentecostal movements within their borders. The aim of these movements has been to encourage emotional, revivalistic religion for the poorer classes. In many cases new denominations readily took shape in response to the emotional environment. Many bore unusual names: Church of God, Church of God in Christ, Assembly of God, Church of the Open Bible, Church of the Nazarene, Four Square Gospel Church, and many others. Nearly all appealed to the poor and disinherited classes, and some made a special bid for the support of blacks.

Similar to the Pentecostal movements are the religions associated with contemporary youth. The new religions resemble the Pentecostal movements in rejecting the stiffness and formality of the Establishment churches. There are significant differences, however. The campus religions do not represent the poor and downtrodden; many of their members are affluent and could easily find "spiritual" homes in the rich denominations of their parents. More significant, the campus groups have no ecclesiastical affiliations or membership requirements. Anyone may join who wishes to take part in the kind of "celebrations" they regard as important. The participants may be Catholics, Methodists, Presbyterians, Hindus, Buddhists, or atheists. "Worship" may consist of a small group sitting on the floor with legs crossed and attempting to probe the mysteries of life through won-

Catholic disaffection in the United States

Pentecostal movements

Campus religions

I and the Village, Marc Chagall (1889–). The subject refers to the artist's childhood and youth in Vitebsk, Russia. The profile on the right is probably that of the artist himself. (Mus. Mod. Art)

The Table, Georges Braque (1881–). An example of later cubism showing the predominance of curvilinear form and line instead of geometric structure. (Mus. Mod. Art)

The Persistence of Memory, Salvador Dali (1904–). The Spaniard Dali is the outstanding representative of the surrealist school. Many objects in his paintings are Freudian images. (Mus. Mod. Art)

Sea and Gulls, John Marin (1870–1953). A native of New Jersey, Marin was a gifted abstract painter. His objects are sometimes recognizable, sometimes not. He painted not the likeness of nature, but *about* nature. (MMA)

Barricade, José Clemente Orozco (1883–1949). The Mexican muralist Orozco was one of the most celebrated of contemporary painters with a social message. His themes were revolutionary fervor, satire of aristocracy and the Church, and deification of the common man. (Mus. Mod. Art)

Around the Fish, Paul Klee (1879–1940). Klee is recognized as the most subtle humorist of XX-cent. art. The central motif of a fish on a platter suggests a banquet, but many of the surrounding objects appear to be products of fantasy. (Mus. Mod. Art)

Above: *Little Big Painting*, Roy Lichtenstein (born 1923). Oil on canvas. (The Whitney Museum of American Art). In the 1960's and early 1970's, American artists dominated the new movements, particularly "Pop," "Op," and "the New Realism." The works on this and the following page are by some of the best-known contemporary artists. Below: *Summer Rental No. 2*, Robert Rauschenberg (born 1925). Oil on canvas. (Collection Whitney Museum of American Art). Gift of the Friends of the Whitney Museum of American Art.

Top Left: *Girl in Doorway*, George Segal (born 1924). A life-size construction in plaster, wood, glass, and aluminum paint. (Collection Whitney Museum of American Art). Top Right: *Green Coca Cola Bottles*, Andy Warhol (born 1931). Oil on canvas. (Collection Whitney Museum of American Art). Gift of the Friends of the Whitney Museum of American Art. Left: *Gran Cairo*, Frank Stella (born 1936). Synthetic polymer paint on canvas. (Collection Whitney Museum of American Art). Gift of the Friends of the Whitney Museum of American Art.

der and awe. Chants may be repeated for hours at a stretch while the aid of rock music, psychedelic lights, and even drugs may be invoked. Obviously, the forms and ceremonies of the new youth religions bear little resemblance to those of the Establishment churches. Their origin and significance are quite different. Their values, also, have little in common with the religions of the past generation. Although they consider themselves Christians, they do not think of this in any official sense. Jesus to them is a man with a perfect understanding and rapport with God. Rather than his being a "King of Kings" or a "Son of God who goes forth to war," they think of him as an unconventional rebel like themselves.

3. SCIENCE —THE HOPE OF THE WORLD?

For much of the twentieth century thus far science has proved to be the savior of mankind. Although its practitioners did not generally turn their backs on religion, they no longer placed their trust in faith or miracles to give them the answers. Science had its own miracles and solutions that made many Biblical legends seem childish. The prestige of science, however, did not continue untarnished. Too many research institutes and the men who worked within them were devoting their careers to the production of weapons of death to arouse much sympathy. Science and technology were made to shoulder the blame for air and water pollution, for the destruction of forests, for the devastation of the land and exhaustion of irreplaceable mineral resources like the fossil fuels. Of course, scientific progress has helped in the conquest of disease, enlarging food supplies, and in maximizing comfort and pleasure; however, in the opinion of many contemporary citizens these effects are counterbalanced by the ambition and greed of the rich and powerful.

The tarnished reputation of science

The most significant climax in the physical sciences in the twentieth century was reached with the publication of the Einstein theories. Originally issued in limited form in 1905, they were expanded with a more general application ten years later. Einstein challenged not merely the older conceptions of matter but practically the entire structure of traditional physics. The doctrine for which he is most noted is his principle of relativity. During the greater part of the nineteenth century, physicists had assumed that space and motion were absolute. Space was supposed to be filled with an intangible substance known as *ether*, which provided the medium for the undulations of light. The planets also moved in it like ships sailing in definite courses over the bounding main. The motion of the heavenly bodies was therefore to be measured by reference to this more or less static ether, just as the speed of a vehicle could be measured in terms of the distance traveled on a highway. But elaborate experiments performed by English and American physicists near the end of the century virtually exploded the ether hypothesis. Einstein then set to work to reconstruct the scheme

Albert Einstein

of the universe in accordance with a different pattern. He maintained that space and motion, instead of being absolute, are relative to each other. Objects have not merely three dimensions but four. To the familiar length, breadth, and thickness, Einstein added a new dimension of *time* and represented all four as fused in a synthesis which he called the *space-time continuum*. In this way he sought to explain the idea that mass is dependent upon motion. Bodies traveling at high velocity have different proportions of extension and mass from what they would have at rest. Included also in the Einstein physics is the conception of a finite universe—that is, finite in space. The region of matter does not extend into infinity, but the universe has limits. While these are by no means definite boundaries, there is at least a region beyond which nothing exists. Space curves back upon itself so as to make of the universe a gigantic sphere within which are contained galaxies, solar systems, stars, and planets.

The Einstein theories had a major influence in precipitating other revolutionary developments in physics. By 1960 it had been discovered that the conception of the subatomic world as a miniature solar system was much too simple. The atom was found to contain not only positively charged protons and negatively charged electrons, but *positrons*, or positively charged electrons; *neutrons*, which carry no electric charges; and *mesons*, which may be either negative or positive. Mesons, it was discovered, exist not only within the atom (for about two millionths of a second) but are major components of the cosmic rays that are constantly bombarding the earth from somewhere in outer space. A recent hypothesis assumes the existence of a *neutral* meson that has a "life" of only one one-hundredth of a sextillionth of a second, but which, in disintegrating, is converted into the energy that holds the universe together.

Several of the developments in physics outlined above helped to make possible one of the most spectacular achievements in the history of science, the splitting of the atom to release the energy contained within it. Ever since it became known that the atom is composed primarily of electrical energy, physicists had dreamed of unlocking this source of tremendous power and making it available for man. As early as 1905 Einstein became convinced of the equivalence of mass and energy and worked out a formula for the conversion of one into the other, which he expressed as follows: $E = mc^2$. E represents the energy in ergs, m the mass in grams, and c the velocity of light in centimeters per second. In other words, the amount of energy locked within the atom is equal to the mass multiplied by the square of the velocity of light. But no practical application of this formula was possible until after the discovery of the neutron by Sir James Chadwick in 1932. Since the neutron carries no charge of electricity, it is an ideal weapon for bombarding the atom. It is neither repulsed by the positively charged protons nor absorbed by the negatively charged electrons. Moreover, in the process of bombardment it produces more neutrons, which hit other atoms and cause them in turn to split and create neutrons. In this way the original reaction is repeated in an almost unending series.

In 1939 two German physicists, Otto Hahn and Fritz Strassman, succeeded in splitting atoms of uranium by bombarding them with neutrons. The initial reaction produced a chain of reactions, in much the same way that a fire burning at the edge of a piece of paper raises the temperature of adjoining portions of the paper high enough to cause them to ignite. The potential of the neutrons employed in the splitting was only one-thirtieth of a volt, but the potential released was 200,000,000 volts. It was soon revealed that not all forms of uranium are equally valuable for the production of energy. Only the isotope 235, which forms only a tiny fraction of natural uranium, will split when bombarded with neutrons. Uranium 238, which constitutes over 99 per cent of the world supply, absorbs the neutrons and transmutes itself into neptunium and plutonium. The latter, however, behaves very much like uranium 235. That is, it does split and release great quantities of energy. More recently, the practice has developed of manufacturing plutonium in a structure known as an atomic pile, in which large quantities of uranium 238 are exposed to neutrons from uranium 235.

It is a sad commentary on modern civilization that the first use made of the knowledge of atomic fission was in the preparation of an atomic bomb. The devastating weapon was the achievement of a galaxy of scientists working for the War Department of the United States. Some were physicists who had been exiled by Nazi or Fascist oppression. By 1945 their work was completed, and in July of that year the first atomic bomb was exploded in a test conducted in the New Mexican desert near the War Department laboratory at Los Alamos. On August 6 the first atomic bomb used in warfare was dropped on the Japanese city of Hiroshima. A second bomb was unloaded on Nagasaki on August 9. The deadly effects of the new weapon almost passed belief. It was estimated that a single bomb had the explosive force of 20,000 tons of TNT. More than 100,000 people were killed in the two cities, large portions of which were literally wiped from the map. Man had at last acquired control over the basic forces of the universe, but whether he had created a Frankenstein's monster which might ultimately destroy him, no one could predict. Doleful queries were raised about what would happen in the future when the ability to produce atomic weapons would be no longer a monopoly of Anglo-Americans. This monopoly was brought to an end in the fall of 1949, when the U.S.S.R. exploded an atomic bomb. Since then Great Britain and France have acquired atomic weapons, and so has Communist China.

Even more disturbing were the first tests of a hydrogen bomb by the United States Atomic Energy Commission in November 1952. The tests were conducted at Eniwetok Atoll in the South Pacific,

Atomic fission

Atomic weapons

An H-Bomb Mushrooms. The cloud spreads into a huge mushroom following a 1952 explosion of a hydrogen bomb in the Marshall Islands of the Pacific. The photo was made 50 miles from detonation site at about 12,000 feet. The cloud rose to 40,000 feet two minutes after the explosion. Ten minutes later the cloud stem had pushed about 25 miles. The mushroom portion went up to 10 miles and spread 100 miles.

and according to reports an entire island disappeared after burning brightly for several hours. The hydrogen bomb, or H-bomb, is based upon fusion of hydrogen atoms, a process which requires the enormous heat generated by the splitting of uranium atoms to start the reaction. The fusion results in the creation of a new element, helium, which actually weighs less than the sum of the hydrogen atoms. The "free" energy left over provides the tremendous explosive power of the H-bomb. The force of hydrogen bombs is measured in *megatons*, each of which represents 1,000,000 tons of TNT. Thus a 5-megaton H-bomb would equal 250 times the power of the A-bombs dropped on Hiroshima and Nagasaki. By 1962 both the Soviet Union and the United States were conducting experimental tests, including high-altitude explosions and devices of unparalleled destructive force. In 1966 China produced her fourth atomic bomb, this time in the form of a nuclear missile that flew 400 miles to its target.

> The hydrogen bomb

On October 4, 1957, the government of the Soviet Union inaugurated a new stage in man's control of his physical environment by rocketing into space the first artificial satellite, which began circling the earth at a speed of about 18,000 miles an hour. Though it weighed nearly 200 pounds, it was propelled upward higher than 500 miles. This Russian achievement gave the English language a new word—*Sputnik*, the Russian for *satellite* or *fellow traveler*. A month later the Soviet scientists surpassed their first success by sending a new and much larger Sputnik to an altitude of approximately 1000 miles. Sputnik II weighed more than half a ton and contained elaborate scientific instruments and even a live dog.

> The exploration of space

These Sputniks were simply the forerunners of others of greater significance. In April 1961, the Russians succeeded in sending the first man into orbit around the earth. Four months later the Soviets achieved an even greater triumph when they sent another of their army officers in a space capsule around the earth. He remained in orbit 25 hours and encircled the earth 17½ times. Meanwhile, scientists and military specialists in the United States had been working hard on the problem of space satellites. After a number of successes with animals and "uninhabited" capsules, they finally succeeded, on February 20, 1962, in launching the first American manned spaceship into orbit around the earth. The successful astronaut was Lieutenant-Colonel John H. Glenn, Jr., and he encircled the globe three times at a top speed of over 17,000 miles per hour. In 1966 a United States Navy officer left the cabin of his spacecraft and walked in space for forty-four minutes, hundreds of miles above the earth. His feat was surpassed in 1969, when Neil Armstrong left his lunar landing module and walked a measurable distance on the moon's surface. All over the world these successful voyages were hailed as events of capital importance. They at least promised an extension of our knowledge of outer space and would doubtless prepare the way for exploration of the moon and eventually of distant planets. But they also had sinister aspects. In addition to depriving possible social welfare programs of billions of dollars, the purpose that inspired them was almost exclusively to gain military advantage. It was assumed, for example, that giant spaceships or artificial satellites hurled into orbit might enable the nation that controlled them to dominate the earth. A disturbing factor for the United States and its allies was thus added to the armament race between East and West. Although space activity continued into the 1970's, emphasis was reduced.

SCIENCE—THE HOPE OF THE WORLD?

Moon exploration

Space aeronautics

Calder Hall. Built in 1956 in England, this is the world's first large-scale atomic power station. The two towers on the left are for cooling.

The Earth. This view taken from the moon by astronauts John W. Young and Charles M. Duke, Jr., of the Apollo 16 mission, shows the west coast of the North American continent, the Gulf of Mexico, Florida, and, below it, Cuba.

Notable advances in the biological sciences also occurred after World War I. An outstanding one was the discovery of the viruses.

Advances in biology

Viruses are organisms so small that they pass through ordinary filters. Only by means of special filters made of collodion films, or by the use of ultraviolet or electron microscopes, can their presence be detected. They are the cause of a multitude of dread diseases, including smallpox, measles, infantile paralysis, influenza, rabies, yellow fever, and the common cold. No one has yet been able to say whether they should be classified as animate or inanimate objects. In some ways they appear to have the properties of living creatures, including the capacity to reproduce. But they are closely dependent upon their living host, and remain completely dormant except when they come into contact with living tissue. They seem to occupy a kind of intermediate stage between the inorganic and organic worlds, and are sometimes referred to as "the bridge between Life and Death." Perhaps Aristotle was right more than twenty-two centuries ago when he wrote: "Nature makes so gradual a transition from the inanimate to the animate kingdom that the boundary lines which separate them are indistinct and doubtful."

From time to time during the history of medicine, discoveries have been made which can justifiably be described as epochal, in the

Antibiotics

sense that they open up new and much greater possibilities for the conquest of disease. One example was the discovery of vaccination for smallpox by Sir Edward Jenner in 1796. Another was the development and proof of the germ theory of disease by Louis Pasteur and Robert Koch about 1881. After 1918 a series of such epochal discoveries laid the foundations for another new era of medical progress. In 1935 a German named Gerhard Domagk discovered the first of the sulfa drugs, which he called sulfanilamide. Soon others were added to the list. Each was found to be marvelously effective in curing or checking such diseases as rheumatic fever, gonorrhea, scarlet fever, and meningitis. About 1930 Sir Alexander Fleming described the first of the antibiotics, which came to be known as penicillin. Antibiotics are chemical agents produced by living organisms and possessing the power to check or kill bacteria. Many have their origin in molds, fungi, algae, and in simple organisms living in the soil. Penicillin was eventually found to be a kind of miracle drug producing spectacular results in the treatment of pneumonia, syphilis, peritonitis, tetanus, and numerous other maladies hitherto frequently fatal. About 1940 the second most famous of the antibiotics —streptomycin—was discovered by Dr. Selman A. Waksman. Streptomycin seems to hold its greatest promise in the treatment of tuberculosis, though it has been used for numerous other infections that do not yield to penicillin. Still other antibiotics are neomycin, also discovered by Dr. Waksman; aureomycin, effective against Rocky Mountain fever; and chloromycetin, valuable in the treatment of typhus and typhoid fever. Many antibiotics are now used in powerful combinations against a wide variety of human ailments. Yet another category of so-called "miracle drugs" were the tranquilizers. Introduced in 1955, they came to be used in the treatment of mental disorders and achieved success in making violent patients more tractable. They thus eliminated to some extent the "snake pits," the old-fashioned mental institutions with barred windows and locked doors. Although these drugs do not themselves effect cures, they help make the patient more accessible to other forms of therapy. Tranquilizers, of course, also gained comparatively widespread usage among the population at large as antidepressants and tension relievers. Indiscriminate use by the ill-informed led to some glaring evils.

Of almost equal importance with the discovery of new drugs has been the development of means of preventing disease. For the most part these have taken the form of vaccination. A characteristic example has been the development of two types of vaccination against poliomyelitis, or infantile paralysis. The first type was discovered by Dr. Jonas Salk of the Salk Institute for Biological Studies at San Diego. Salk used "killed" viruses of the disease to assist the bodies of human beings to build up immunity against infection. About five years later Dr. Albert B. Sabin of the University of Cincinnati developed a second type of vaccination using "live" but weakened viruses administered orally. The respective advantages of the two types of vaccination continued for some time to be a matter of controversy. During World War II a remarkable insecticide was perfected which gave promise of the ultimate elimination of two of the most ancient ene-

Dr. Jonas Salk in His Laboratory

mies of mankind, malaria and typhus. Popularly known as DDT, it destroys the lice and mosquitoes that transmit these diseases. Recent years have witnessed also the development and wide though not universal acceptance of the fluoridation process for preventing tooth decay in young people. It consists of the simple expedient of adding sodium fluoride to the water supply of municipalities. So impressive was the progress in these and other aspects of preventive medicine that some scientists incautiously predicted that in the comparatively near future every infectious disease known to man would be finally and completely conquered. Their optimism received a shock, however, about 1960, when it was discovered that "new" bacteria, resistant to antibiotics, were making their appearance. Whether they were mutants or older organisms formerly held in check by the balance of nature and now released through the destruction of their natural "enemies" by antibiotics, their menace was serious. This destruction of the balance of nature has recently become the source of great alarm among conservationists. They have procured the enactment of laws prohibiting the use of DDT and other pesticides by farmers and horticulturists in all developed countries. Farm bloc leaders took a different view. Banning of powerful insecticides like DDT and dieldrin would boost the cost of agricultural production almost to prohibitive levels.

Other medical achievements

No account of medical achievements since 1914 would be complete without mention at least of the following: the development of insulin by the Canadian scientist Frederick Banting for the treatment of diabetes; the perfection of radiation treatments for cancer; the discovery that malignant tumors develop their own fluids essential for growth, and that when these fluids are inhibited, tumors fail to grow and soon actually die or become harmless; the discovery of new methods of detecting cancer and other diseases by the use of radioactive isotopes as "tracers"; the development of techniques for storing blood and blood plasma for transfusions; the discovery of the hormone ACTH and its application to asthma and to inflammatory diseases of the eye; the development of artificial kidneys and mechanical hearts to assist and even partially to supplant natural organs weakened by injury or disease; the discovery of atabrine as a substitute for quinine in the treatment of malaria; and the development of psychosomatic medicine based upon a recognition of the importance of anxiety, fear, and other psychological factors in causing ulcers, asthma, high blood pressure, and diseases of the heart. By 1970 the people of the world ought to have enjoyed the most abundant health since the dawn of medicine. Statistically, perhaps they did, taken as a whole. But many parts of the world still suffered from the health problems associated with war, social upheaval, poverty, and famine. Depressing reports of understaffed hospitals, or even hospitals with no staff at all in certain departments, made a mockery of high standards of medical practice even in advanced countries.

In the great majority of the "advanced" nations the issue was one of priorities. Nearly everywhere the military budget took the lion's share of public appropriations. In Soviet Russia expenditures for defense amounted to 8.5 per cent of the Gross National Product. In the United States 8.6 is the percentage. Only in France do expenditures for education exceed those for national defense. In smaller countries the fraction of expenditures to the Gross National Product is 4.0 for Sweden, 2.2 for Switzerland, 2.6 for Denmark.[3]

Overemphasis upon military expenditures

The record of scientific development in the twentieth century requires consideration of the social sciences. Most of these disciplines were already in existence when the century began, but new interpretations were added and some of the older conceptions were reversed. The two sciences most susceptible to radical change were anthropology and sociology. Originally a study of races and the physical characteristics of man, anthropology was broadened later into a science of "cultures." The pioneers in promoting this transformation were Franz Boas and Bronislaw Malinowski. Both were born and educated in Europe, and both died after years of lecturing in the United States. Their contributions lay principally in the advancement of racial equality. Boas denied the alleged superiority of the Caucasians on the ground of the proved inability of the colored races to resist the white man's diseases. Some of Boas' disciples went even farther than their master in repudiating notions of the inequality of races. A notable example was Ruth Benedict, who taught in the 1940's that the assumed superiority of races by nature was largely a myth. She showed that during World War II Negro children transferred from the Southern states to the North soon revealed themselves the equal of their Northern classmates under conditions of approximately equal opportunity. Malinowski was mainly interested in the emancipation of primitive man from the stigma of brutality and tyranny that rested upon him. He did not describe the "noble savage" as an angel in disguise, but neither did he regard him as "to his fellow man a wolf." Rather he thought of the earliest societies as founded on a basis of need and convenience in getting things done. Such considerations he found among the extremely primitive Trobriand Islanders in the South Pacific, and he assumed them to have been typical of all peoples only remotely touched by civilization.

Anthropology

The great names in sociology were borne by men who began their careers early in the twentieth century, although some have lived to our day. The pioneer among them was Max Weber. Born in Germany before World War I, he served as a professor of law and society at the University of Munich. After Germany became a republic in 1918 he was appointed a member of the commission that drafted

Sociology: Max Weber

[3] *The Military Balance*, Institute for Strategic Studies, London, 1970–1971.

the Weimar Constitution. As a sociologist Weber won fame for a book entitled *The Protestant Ethic and the Spirit of Capitalism*. In it he placed a heavy burden of guilt upon Protestantism for alienating man from a benevolent God and a kindly universe. It made work a cardinal virtue and idleness a supreme vice. After the Protestant Revolution man could gain happiness only by driving himself with the fury of the damned. A distressing product of the Protestant Revolution, according to Weber, was revival of the doctrines of original sin and total depravity. He found such doctrines as lingering remnants in the writings of Soren Kierkegaard, Karl Barth, and Reinhold Niebuhr. One of their forerunners, Joseph deMaistre, taught that "men cannot help killing each other."

Sociology in our time has made a special appeal to blacks, both in the United States and abroad. Quite a number of their scholars who began their careers in other fields have switched to sociology because of the opportunities it provides for the study and analysis of racial problems. The greatest expounder of black racial attitudes in the twentieth century was probably William E. B. Du Bois. Though proud of his French and Dutch ancestry, he identified himself with the black race. He gloried in the name of Negro and was "proud of the black blood that flowed in his veins." He attended Fisk University and graduated with second honors. In 1895 he became the first Negro to win a Ph.D. from Harvard. For many years he was head of the Department of Sociology at Atlanta University. Toward the end of his life, however, he devoted himself largely to Pan-African unity. In 1961 he applied for membership in the Communist Party and left the United States to live in Ghana. From his early years Du Bois ranked as a strong advocate of the uniqueness of the black man and his culture. He rejected the approach of Booker T. Washington and his advocacy of industrial education. He believed the Negro to be the intellectual equal of the white man, and he would accept no inferior position for black culture. He held that the Talented Tenth, regardless of race, must always provide the vanguard of every new civilization. Throughout his life he was subject to rising and falling tides of vilification. At fifty he wrote that the occurrence of his death would have been hailed with approval; at seventy-five his "death was practically requested." [4]

William E. B. Du Bois

Another black sociologist of recent times was Martin Luther King, Jr. Better known for his defense of civil rights than for his scholarship, King was the most active spokesman in the cause of desegregation in both North and South. Although he was educated for the ministry, his interests gravitated principally to sociology. He led marches and demonstrations and made countless speeches in behalf of racial justice. For years he was the foremost exponent of nonviolent resistance in the United States. In 1964 he was awarded a

**Martin Luther
King, Jr.**

[4] *Autobiography of W. E. B. Du Bois*, New York, published posthumously in 1968, p. 414.

Nobel Peace Prize. It was one of the last great triumphs of his career. Already he had begun to divert his attention from Negro rights to crusading against the Vietnam War. On April 4, 1968 he was assassinated outside his motel room in Memphis, Tennessee.

4. CONTEMPORARY MAN AND HIS WORLD AS REFLECTED THROUGH LITERATURE

Literary movements during the period of the depression and the two world wars showed tendencies similar to those in philosophy. Indeed, in many instances, it was difficult to tell where philosophy ended and literature began. The major novelists, poets, and dramatists were deeply concerned about social and political problems and about the hope and destiny of man. Like the philosophers, they were disillusioned by the brute facts of World War I and by the failure of victory to fulfill its promises. Many were profoundly affected also by the revolutionary developments in science and especially by the probings of the new psychology into the hidden secrets of the mind. Instead of a being created by God just "a little lower than the angels," man seemed now to be a creature just a bit higher than the apes. Finally, of course, literary men were influenced by the Great Depression and by the return to war in 1939. Both these developments led to a searching of methods and, among many writers, to a partial revision of objectives.

Major tendencies in literature

Much of the literature of the interwar period revolved around themes of frustration, cynicism, and disenchantment. It was the era of the "lost generation," of young men whose ideals had been shattered by the brutal events of their time. Its mood was set by the early novels of Ernest Hemingway, by the poetry of T. S. Eliot, and by the dramas of Eugene O'Neill. In *A Farewell to Arms* Hemingway gave to the public one of its first insights into the folly and meanness of war and set a pattern which other writers were soon to follow. T. S. Eliot in his poem, *The Waste Land* (1922), presented a philosophy that was close to despair. Once you are born, he seemed to be saying, life is a living death to be ground out in boredom and frustration. The pessimism of Eugene O'Neill appeared to be somewhat different from that of his contemporaries. His tragedies depicted man not so much as a victim of society but rather as the pitiable slave of his own abnormal nature. Most critics would probably agree that O'Neill's greatest dramas were *Strange Interlude* (1927) and *Mourning Becomes Electra* (1931). His own story of his tortured life, *Long Day's Journey into Night*, was not published until after his death. By general consent O'Neill is regarded as America's greatest playwright. By conviction he was a dyed-in-the-wool pessimist. All the old gods were dead, and no new ones were likely to appear. There was no salvation except resignation to a stoic fate no one could explain or understand. Other tendencies manifest-

T. S. Eliot (1888–1965). Noted author of *The Waste Land* and *Murder in the Cathedral* in his London study. He was awarded the Nobel Prize for Literature in 1948. American born, he had been a citizen of Great Britain since 1927.

1291

*Noel Coward and Ernest
Hemingway in Havana*

ing themselves during this era were determinism and stream-of-consciousness writing. Theodore Dreiser brought determinism to a climax in *An American Tragedy* (1925). Deeply influenced by psychoanalysis, James Joyce became the leading exponent of stream-of-consciousness writing. His greatest novel, *Ulysses* (1922), was essentially a study of reverie rather than action.

The Great Depression of the 1930's forced a reexamination of the methods and purposes of literature. In the midst of economic stagnation and threats of fascism and war, the theory evolved that literature must have a serious purpose, that it should indict meanness, cruelty, and barbarism and point the way to a society more just. The new trend was reflected in the works of a diversity of writers. John Steinbeck depicted the sorry plight of impoverished farmers fleeing from the "dust bowl" to California only to find that all the good earth had been monopolized by big land companies that exploited their workers. Pervading some of the plays of Robert Sherwood and the novels of André Malraux was the strong suggestion that man's struggle against tyranny and injustice is the chief thing that gives meaning and value to life. A similar theme may be said to have characterized Ernest Hemingway's *For Whom the Bell Tolls* (1940). Here also was the strong implication that the individual, in sacrificing himself for the cause of the people, gives a meaning and dignity to life that can be achieved in no other way.

Literature with a serious purpose tended later to emphasize the lonely and tragic life of the common man and to protest ever more

Influence of the Depression: literature with a serious purpose

strongly against cruelty and injustice. A warm affinity for the plain folk of rural New England was expressed by Robert Frost, greatly beloved American poet. Nobel-prize winner William Faulkner devoted superb artistic talents to portrayals of crude elemental behavior in backward areas of the Deep South. The tragedy of World War II brought a series of novels dealing with the conflict itself, with the heroism of those who resisted Nazi tyranny, or with the brutality and inefficiency of military systems. Foremost among such writings were Norman Mailer's *The Naked and the Dead* and James Jones' *From Here to Eternity*. Both portrayed the coarseness and cruelty of military life with a ruthless realism. But along with these trends toward warm sympathy and stark realism as means of conveying hatred of injustice and oppression, there were also some new manifestations. One was a turning to religion to compensate for a sense of overwhelming tragedy or to prevent calamities which seemed certain to flow from allowing science to get out of control. T. S. Eliot, who in the 1920's had found the universe a barren wasteland with no fruits but boredom and despair, now discovered that life could be meaningful when ennobled by the ageless truths of the Church. His new mood was exemplified by *Murder in the Cathedral* and *The Cocktail Party*. In spite of the different directions of their thinking, most of the postwar writers seemed to have much in common. They were expressing with one voice their concern over the loneliness of man. They saw human beings in an age of mass thinking and mass actions as helpless and pitiable creatures, craving assistance from whatever source it might seem available.

Most of the literary moods of midcentury continued into the 1960's and 1970's. Especially marked was the revolt against the complexities of modern life. There was the same protest against injustice and maltreatment of the weak and unfortunate. Significantly, some of these trends made themselves evident in the Soviet Union, especially after the death of Stalin in 1953. Soon after that date a novel written by Boris Pasternak and bearing the title *Dr. Zhivago* was promptly acclaimed as one of the best to be written in modern times. Though it was allowed to be published only in Italian and English translations, there could be no question of the author's understanding of Russian life and Russian culture. He wrote a burning indictment of the Stalinist campaign to pour every citizen into the same mold. Interesting parallels to the life of Pasternak are to be found in the career of Aleksandr Solzhenitsyn. Both were novelists entitled to rank with the world's greatest. Each was awarded the Nobel Prize for Literature, Pasternak in 1958 and Solzhenitsyn in 1970. Both were blacklisted in their own country and neither considered it wise to go to Stockholm to receive the Nobel award. Each produced at least one novel of outstanding merit—Pasternak's *Dr. Zhivago* and Solzhenitsyn's *The First Circle*. The two works defended the right of the individual to live his own life and threw much

Aleksandr Solzhenitsyn

1293

light on internal conditions in the Soviet Union. Interestingly enough Solzhenitsyn's works have not been popular among the workers of the Soviet Union. They seem to be regarded with much the same attitude that "hard hats" in most countries take toward the achievements of intellectuals.

As one would expect, the literature of protest has been more conspicuous in Western countries than in Soviet Russia. It has often involved not simply a castigation of human baseness but an indictment of the whole scheme of the universe. The foremost exponent of bitter discontent in the literature of the early twentieth century was the German novelist Franz Kafka. Educated in the German schools of Prague, he fought the stubborn tyranny of a violent father in striving to gain a foothold as a writer. To his other sufferings was added a raging lung disease which brought an end to his life at the age of forty. Kafka's novels present a vision of man in a hostile universe hopelessly striving to come to terms with a remote and unknown power. It is not so much a dream as it is a nightmare composed of weird, fantastic details brought together in a terrifying pattern. His best-known work, *The Castle*, is at once a satire on bureaucracy and a philosophical representation of the isolation of man in the universe.

The plight of Western man in a hostile world

Yet another movement has distinguished the literary developments of our age. This is the movement known as the Literature of the Absurd. It is so called from the fact that its authors see individuals as trapped in a nonsense world which moves with its own mad logic. The movement has been inspired by the plays of the German Bertolt Brecht, and the Rumanian Eugène Ionesco. The great master of the movement, however, is Samuel Beckett. Born in Ireland but removing as a young man to Paris, he lived almost entirely as a recluse. Though he recognized the hopelessness of man's condition, he contended that the human animal must go on striving after rays of light that might have the faintest chance of penetrating the dusk and gloom. In 1969 he was awarded the Nobel Prize in Literature but like several others who had been similarly honored, he refused to travel to Stockholm to receive the award. His best-known play is *Waiting for Godot*, published in 1952.

The Literature of the Absurd

A principal forerunner of the literature of the absurd was the French-Algerian Albert Camus. Though enough of an idealist to participate in the Resistance during World War II, he really had no faith in anything. He sought for some years to work out the tenets of an atheistic humanism; yet in his books he stressed the irrational nature of the universe, even to the extent of its irrationality and proneness to suicide. His death in an auto accident in 1963 brought an end to his stormy but brilliant career.

Albert Camus

Most black literature is American largely because in America blacks have been most conscious of their race and most sensitive to the ebb and flow of their racial hopes. It had its origin primarily in the 1920's, in a movement known as the Harlem Renaissance. Such writers as Countee Cullen sought to invest the Negro with a culture at least equal to that of the white man. Their poetry did not generally foreshadow the fiery wrath of their later protagonists but sought to idealize the Negro's past and portray his dreams of equality with whites. The Great Depression brought an end to the dreams of the Harlem Renaissance. In the 1930's Langston Hughes gave a high place to themes of working-class life in his poetry and lauded the spirit of protest in his "Brass Spitoons," a bitter account of a hotel porter's daily rounds.

The major disenchantments and searing indictments in black literature did not begin until the revolutionary era that followed in the wake of the Depression and World War II. The initiator of the new trend was Richard Wright, a product of the misery and squalor of rural Mississippi. As a youth he drifted to Chicago and became a resident of and spokesman for the black ghetto. In his *Native Son* and in his autobiography, *Black Boy*, he portrayed with scathing realism the oppression of working-class Negroes. Despite the pretensions of the New Deal he found that the burdens of that class had not been appreciably lightened. As a novelist Wright has been compared with Dostoievski, but in his social and psychological determinism he bore a closer kinship with Theodore Dreiser. He seems to have been the first American black to preach the liberating effect of killing an enemy. In *Black Boy* the hero (Wright himself) experienced a sense of freedom because he "had done something the white man would notice." He seemed to be saying, though, that a youth reared in the ghetto is almost doomed to ruin. The frenzied pursuit of money and sex, and the wretchedness of poverty, combined with "neurosis-producing" racial suppression, can be guaranteed to accomplish that result.

The most talented black writers of the postwar generation have probably been James Baldwin and Lorraine Hansberry. James Baldwin was born in Harlem, the son of a clergyman, a rigid and embittered man with few gifts of leadership. At the age of fourteen James became a Pentecostal preacher. But his heart was not in it. He left home and drifted into whatever odd employments he could find. After World War II he lived for ten years in Paris. Perhaps his greatest work was *Go Tell It on the Mountain*, which he published in 1953. The dominant theme of his novels was whatever demeans the black man by its very nature demeans the white man who is the author of it. Baldwin was an articulate spokesman of the black American revolution, but he wrote also in defense of deviants and nonconformists generally. Such was true especially of *Another Country* and *Nobody Knows My Name*. One of the most sensitive contemporary black writers was Lorraine Hansberry. She was not primarily a novelist but essentially a poet and dramatist. She won distinction in her brief lifetime for her play *Raisin in the Sun*. Her dramatic talent was shown even more clearly in *To Be Young, Gifted and Black*, presented on the New York stage four years after her death. Unlike

American leadership in black literature

Complete disenchantment and furious indictment

James Baldwin

many of her contemporaries, she was not an exponent of black revolution. Nevertheless, she could write in defiance, and sometimes in
bitterness, when the delight she saw in life was swallowed up by
bigotry and repression. In common with scores of great artists, she
was torn between hope and despair. But she never lost faith in the
greatness of the human spirit. She believed that the human race does
command its own destiny, and that that destiny can "eventually embrace the stars." Her own destiny was to die of cancer at the age of
thirty-four.

5.   THE FULFILLMENT OF TRENDS
IN ART AND MUSIC

As in literature, so in art the twentieth century was marked by
revolt against exquisiteness and artificiality. In the closing decades of
the preceding century this revolt had taken the form of a reaction
against impressionism. Cézanne and Van Gogh criticized the formlessness and insubstantiality of the work of the impressionists and
held that the figures of the painter's art should be as solidly and completely molded as statues.

The revolt against impressionism

The work of Cézanne and Van Gogh, we have noted, led directly
to *cubism*, the most revolutionary art of the twentieth century. It
was developed about 1905 by Pablo Picasso, and continues to
be a popular mode of artistic expression. Cubism began as an art of
realism *par excellence*. It endeavors to present life, not in accordance with a nicely adorned conventional pattern, but as a jumble of
arms, legs, heads, and bodies caught in motion and having no arrangement among themselves except that given by the observer. But
disorder and disorganization are not for the cubist ends in themselves. They are intended partly to reflect notions of form—to
repudiate the conception of art as mere prettiness.

Cubism

An even more violent movement of rebellion against traditional
standards of art and of life was *surrealism*, whose high priest since
1929 has been the Spaniard Salvador Dali. Originating about 1918
under the combined influence of the war and psychoanalysis,
surrealism flourished during the age of nihilism that followed that
war. The aim of its followers was not to represent the world of
nature but to portray the reactions of the human mind. For this
purpose they delved into the subconscious and attempted to depict
the content of dreams and the weird impressions of reverie. This
commonly resulted in a technique quite different from that of traditional art. In general, the surrealists paid little attention to the conventional standards of beauty and form. They argued that, in the
light of the new psychology, naturalism was impossible if art were
to have any value as an accurate expression of meaning.

Surrealism

For a time after 1930 the bizarre and anarchic painting of the extreme modernist schools went into a partial eclipse. Its place

was taken to an extent by a virile and popular art of the common man.[5] Among the chief representatives of the new movement were the Mexicans, Diego Rivera and José Clemente Orozco, and the United States painters Thomas Benton, Adolph Dehn, William Gropper, and Grant Wood. The fundamental aim of these artists was to depict the social conditions of the modern world and to present in graphic detail the hopes and struggles of peasants and toilers. While they scarcely adhered to any of the conventions of the past, there was nothing unintelligible about their work; it was intended to be art that anyone could understand. At the same time, much of it bore the sting or thrust of social satire. Orozco, in particular, delighted in pillorying the hypocrisy of the Church and the greed and cruelty of plutocrats and plunderers.

Around 1950 another innovating movement in painting began to attract considerable attention. Known by different names, it is perhaps most accurately called *abstract expressionism*. Thus far its chief exponents have been Jackson Pollock, Willem de Kooning, and Franz Kline. So far as the past is concerned it owes most to cubism and surrealism. But the abstract expressionists prefer to repudiate nearly all the traditions of the past. They believe in innovation, experimentation, and the use of bold and startling devices to achieve effects. Some of the work of their minor disciples hardly appears to be painting at all, but seems rather a hodgepodge of daubs of paint interspersed with scraps of metal, bits of cloth and paper, and similar objects. Some who cannot draw achieve interesting results with coffee grounds and bread crumbs.

[5] The art of the common man is also called regional art, especially in the forms developed in the United States.

The new art of the common man

Abstract expressionism

See color plates at pages 1280, 1281

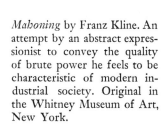

Mahoning by Franz Kline. An attempt by an abstract expressionist to convey the quality of brute power he feels to be characteristic of modern industrial society. Original in the Whitney Museum of Art, New York.

**The chief trends
in contemporary
music**

It was inevitable that music should reflect the spirit of disillusionment that reached a climax following World War I. The more original developments were closely parallel to those in painting. Most fundamental of all was the revolt against the romantic tradition, especially as it had culminated in Wagner. Many, although by no means all, composers went so far as to repudiate the aesthetic ideal entirely, relying upon complexity and novelty of structure or on a sheer display of energy to supply interest to their works.

Impressionism

Deviations from the classical and romantic formulas have been generally of two types, designated broadly as impressionism and expressionism. The former seeks to exploit the qualities of musical sound to suggest feelings or images. The latter is concerned more with form than with sensuous effects and tends toward abstraction. The most perfect exponent of impressionism was Claude Debussy, its originator, whose work was described in an earlier chapter. Even in France impressionism did not prove to be an enduring school. With Maurice Ravel (1875–1937), most celebrated of the composers who reflected Debussy's influence, it became less poetic and picturesque and acquired a degree of cold impassivity together with greater firmness of texture.

Igor Stravinsky

Expressionism, more radical and more influential than impressionism, comprises two main schools: *atonality*, founded by the Viennese Arnold Schoenberg (1874–1951), and *polytonality*, best typified by the Russian Igor Stravinsky (1882–1971). Atonality implies the repudiation of the concept of fixed tonal relationships; it abolishes *key*. In this type of music, dissonances are the rule rather than the exception, and the melodic line commonly alternates between chromatic manipulation and strange unsingable leaps. In short, the ordinary principles of composition are reversed. However, emancipation from the bonds of tradition has enabled the atonalists to give undivided attention to the development of their own subjective ideas with the utmost originality. They attempt, with some success, to let musical sound become a vehicle for expressing the inner meaning and elemental structure of things. Odd as it may appear, some atonal works are deeply emotional in effect. They betray a kinship with symbolism and also show the influence of the theories of the subconscious derived from psychoanalysis. Most of the distinctive features of the atonal school are vividly incorporated in Schoenberg's *Pierrot Lunaire*. This fantasy, in which the singer intones her part in a special "song-speech," somewhat between singing and reciting, has been described as creating "a whole world of strange fascination and enchantment, of nameless horrors and terrible imaginings, of perverse and poisonous beauty." [6]

**Expressionism:
atonality**

Polytonality, of which Stravinsky is the most famous exponent, is essentially a radical kind of counterpoint, deriving its inspiration

[6] Cecil Gray, *A Survey of Contemporary Music*, p. 176.

partly from baroque practices of counterpoint that were placed in the service of new ideas. However, it is not content simply to interweave independent melodies which together form concord, but undertakes to combine separate keys and unrelated harmonic systems, with results that are highly discordant. It is thus another example of revolt against the European harmonic heritage and differs from atonality more in technique than in ultimate aim. But while the atonalists have retained elements of romanticism, the polytonalists have tried to resurrect the architectural qualities of pure form, movement, and rhythm, stripping away all sentimentality and sensuous connotations. Stravinsky affirmed that his intention was to produce music in which acoustic properties were the only consideration and which would appeal to the physical ear alone. His coldly detached, anti-aesthetic experiments have much in common with cubism and similar tendencies in modern painting. The application of his theories to such purposes conveys the sardonic impression of human beings who are mere automatons, manipulated by their own physical urges or by the grim hand of a mechanical fate. Stravinsky's style and interests have undergone successive changes; in recent years he has turned from the theater to more distinctly concert forms. Without sacrificing his intense individuality, he has achieved an increasing clarity of expression and an almost classical integration of structural design.

Polytonality

The twentieth century produced other great composers who, though touched by neoclassicism and the other prevailing trends, went their own individual ways. Mention should be made of the Hungarian Béla Bartók (1881–1945), the German Paul Hindemith (1895–1963), and the Russian Serge Prokofiev (1891–1953). In the meantime American music also came of age. After a period largely dominated by German romanticism, in the third decade of the twentieth century there emerged a "school" of music which, though representing various shades of modernism, can rightfully be called American. Aaron Copland (born 1900), Roger Sessions (born 1896), and William Schuman (born 1910), as examples, can take their place among the best composers active in Europe.

Other twentieth-century composers

6. EPILOGUE

No one can do more than strike a tentative balance of good and evil in the long record of human history. The clouds of ignorance and mystery hang so low as to be almost impenetrable. Time was when the skies were brighter. John Milton wrote of *Paradise Lost*, and then perhaps with slightly more confidence sang of the delights of *Paradise Regained*. The socialists of the nineteenth century, from Owen to Marx, recognized man as a victim of oppression and poverty, but believed that a golden day would dawn with a new freedom from exploitation.

The balance of good and evil

1299

The remaining years of the nineteenth century did not greatly alter the scene. A few outbursts of sadness and dejection punctuated the general environment, but the prevailing atmosphere was suffused with confidence and hope. World War I, however, brought signs of a bitter reaction. The cruelty and waste of that war, to say nothing of its egregious folly, persuaded young men who were its actual or probable victims to view it with nothing but disgust and horror.

Many young people today have only a limited sense of history. The great events of the past seem too remote to bear much significance. In like manner the future is too uncertain to be a guide to hapless man. The consequence, then, has been a revival of some of the caustic views of history popular in the eighteenth century. History in those days had almost no standing as a scientific appraisal of the past or a possible guide to the future. For Herbert Spencer history was "worthless gossip." To Napoleon it was a "fable agreed upon." To Edward Gibbon it appeared to be "little more than a register of the crimes, follies, and misfortunes of mankind." The German philosopher Hegel maintained in one of his darker moments that "the only thing that peoples and governments learn from the study of history is that they learn nothing from the study of history."

Does history repeat itself sufficiently to enable us to predict the future? A large proportion of the philosophers of history have conceived of a uniform pattern characterizing the growth and decline of civilizations over thousands of years. Toynbee attributes the growth primarily to a condition of adversity and the decline to such factors as militarism and war, barbarization from within, and the rise of an "internal proletariat." By the last term he means a class like the city mob of ancient Rome who are "in" but not "of" a given society. Despised and disinherited, they nurse grievances against the society and gradually undermine it. Oswald Spengler saw the growth and decay of civilizations, or cultures as he called them, paralleling the four seasons or the life of an organism. Each had its spring or youth phase, its summer or early maturity phase, its autumn or late maturity phase, and its winter or senility phase.

Even in periods of the brightest optimism writers who have done much thinking about the meaning of history have generally assumed that decay and disintegration will follow prosperity and progress. For example, the Founding Fathers in the United States viewed the future of their own country with grave misgivings. So long as the nation remained predominantly agricultural, with an abundance of cheap land, all would be well. But increasing population in a few generations would result in the growth of large cities, with their slums, corrupt politicians, and a dependent mob ready to sell its votes to the highest bidder. The ultimate outcome would be the rise of Catilines and Caesars, who would seek, with the support of the proletariat, to overthrow the republic. In the late nineteenth century, when the age of science and industry in the United States was still facing the rising sun, Brooks Adams and his brother Henry described with accents of gloom the ultimate decay of Western culture. Henry Adams sought to interpret civilization in terms of a scientific law—the second law of thermodynamics, or the law of the dissipation of energy. He predicted that the civilization of Western man would expend its vital force and die of exhaustion by 1932.

There seems little doubt that civilizations do grow old and die from a number of causes. A major one apparently is urbanization, carried to the point where a large proportion of the population is crowded into huge metropolitan areas. This condition adds so much to the complexity of social problems that human intelligence is unable to solve them. Crime, disease, boredom, insanity, corruption, poverty in the midst of plenty are only a few of these critical problems. Pollution of water and air threaten to make large portions of the earth uninhabitable. Excessive concentration of industry results in overproduction and leads to depressions and to exhaustion of natural resources. Whether our own civilization has reached this stage is a question impossible to answer. There are, of course, many ominous portents tempered by a few rays of hope. Disease in the form of several of the great pestilences seems on the way toward extinction. Cholera is largely confined to the Third World and to a few other areas where standards of sanitation are low. Smallpox in advanced countries is becoming so rare that health departments no longer insist upon wholesale vaccinations. Tuberculosis also is nearing extinction as a major disease. On the other hand, much work remains to be done to advance medical progress in other fields. Cardiac and circulatory ailments continue as the principal killers of human beings despite all the recent progress in open heart surgery, "pacers," and transplants. Cancer, emphysema, and venereal diseases continue as troublesome maladies even in countries most widely known for medical advancement. We can only conjecture what may be happening in those parts of the world where famine stalks the land and overpopulation and erosion rule out most chances of a better day.

Despite all the efforts of world leaders, the ghastly threat of annihilation still hangs over the human race. No one can gauge the extent of this threat. It may take the form of defense against a nuclear attack, or more probably the use of a nuclear threat as a means of intimidation. In either case the effect is almost certain to be catastrophic war. Through the entire course of history war has been the chief enemy of civilization. Its principal fruits have been inflation, impoverishment, revolution, and chaos. It has destroyed the best blood of nation after nation and left the weaklings to become the fathers of the new generation.

War, of course, should not be regarded as an insoluble problem. Other evils in the past have been corrected or eliminated even

The fate of our own civilization

Signs of hope tempered by darker shadows

The most ghastly threat of all

1301

though long established or deeply entrenched. Few reformers would have foreseen the abolition of slavery in the early nineteenth century in the British Empire and the United States or the emancipation of the serfs in Russia in 1861. But none of these evils had the powerful backing of governments themselves in keeping them alive.

SELECTED READINGS

· *Items so designated are available in paperbound editions.*

Barzun, Jacques, *Romanticism and the Modern Ego,* Boston, 1945. A discerning interpretation.

Boulding, Kenneth, *The Meaning of the 20th Century,* New York, 1964.

· Bracey, John H., Jr., Meier, August, and Rudwick, Elliot M., *Black Nationalism in America,* New York, 1970 (Bobbs Merrill).

Brisbane, Robert H., *The Black Vanguard,* Valley Forge, Pa., 1970. Scholarly but skimpy for the period since 1960.

Burns, E. M., *Ideas in Conflict,* New York, 1960. A survey of contemporary thought.

· Copland, Aaron, *The New Music,* New York, 1968 (Norton Library).

· Hecht, Selig, *Explaining the Atom,* New York, 1947 (Compass, rev.).

Heilbroner, Robert, *The Future as History,* New York, 1959.

· Jeans, Sir James, *The Universe Around Us,* New York, 1944 (Cambridge University Press).

Lang, Paul, *Music in Western Civilization,* New York, 1941. An excellent, inclusive account.

Logan, Rayford W., ed., *W. E. B. Du Bois, A Profile,* New York, 1971.

Machlis, Joseph, *The Enjoyment of Music,* third ed., New York, 1970.

Mead, Margaret, *Continuities in Cultural Evolution,* New Haven, 1964.

Moore, Wilbert E., *Social Change,* Englewood Cliffs, N.J., 1964.

· Muller, H. J., *The Uses of the Past,* New York, 1952 (Mentor).

Peeks, Edward, *The Long Struggle for Black Power,* New York, 1970. An excellent account by a black liberal.

Singer, Charles, *A History of Biology,* New York, 1950.

· Slochower, Harry, *No Voice Is Wholly Lost,* New York, 1945. Also available in paperback under the title *Literature and Philosophy between Two World Wars* (Citadel, 1964).

· Snow, C. P., *The Two Cultures and A Second Look,* Cambridge, 1965 (Mentor).

· Storing, Herbert, J., ed., *What Country Have I? Political Writings by Black Americans,* New York, 1970 (St. Martin's).

· Wilson, Edmund, *Axel's Castle,* New York, 1958 (Scribner Library). An interpretative study of recent trends in literature.

· Wittels, Fritz, *Freud and His Time,* New York, 1948 (Universal Library).

SOURCE MATERIALS

Baumer, F. L. V., *Main Currents of Western Thought,* New York, 1952.

· Dewey, John, *Reconstruction in Philosophy* (Beacon, 1957).

· ———, *Liberalism and Social Action* (Capricorn, 1963).

· Niebuhr, Reinhold, *The Children of Light and the Children of Darkness,* New York, 1960 (Scribner Library).

Spengler, Oswald, *The Decline of the West,* Introduction, New York, 1945, 2 vols.

Rulers of Principal European States since 700 A.D.

———— *The Carolingian Dynasty* ————

Pepin, Mayor of the Palace, 714
Charles Martel, Mayor of the Palace, 715–741
Pepin I, Mayor of the Palace, 741; King, 751–768
Charlemagne, King, 768–814; Emperor, 800–814
Louis the Pious, Emperor, 814–840

WEST FRANCIA
Charles the Bald, King, 840–877; Emperor, 875
Louis II, King, 877–879
Louis III, King, 879–882
Carloman, King, 879–884

MIDDLE KINGDOMS
Lothair, Emperor, 840–855
Louis (Italy), Emperor, 855–875
Charles (Provence), King, 855–863
Lothair II (Lorraine), King, 855–869

EAST FRANCIA
Ludwig, King, 840–876
Carloman, King, 876–880
Ludwig, King, 876–882
Charles the Fat, Emperor, 876–887

———— *Holy Roman Emperors* ————

SAXON DYNASTY
Otto I, 962–973
Otto II, 973–983
Otto III, 983–1002
Henry II, 1002–1024

FRANCONIAN DYNASTY
Conrad II, 1024–1039
Henry III, 1039–1056
Henry IV, 1056–1106
Henry V, 1106–1125
Lothair II (of Saxony), King, 1125–1133; Emperor, 1133–1137

1303

—————— Rulers of France from Hugh Capet ——————

Philip I, 1060–1108
Louis VI, 1108–1137
Louis VII, 1137–1180
Philip II (Augustus), 1180–1223
Louis VIII, 1223–1226
Louis IX, 1226–1270
Philip III, 1270–1285
Philip IV, 1285–1314
Louis X, 1314–1316
Philip V, 1316–1322
Charles IV, 1322–1328

House of Valois

Philip VI, 1328–1350
John, 1350–1364
Charles V, 1364–1380
Charles VI, 1380–1422
Charles VII, 1422–1461
Louis XI, 1461–1483
Charles VIII, 1483–1498
Louis XII, 1498–1515
Francis I, 1515–1547
Henry II, 1547–1559
Francis II, 1559–1560
Charles IX, 1560–1574
Henry III, 1574–1589

Bourbon Dynasty

Henry IV, 1589–1610
Louis XIII, 1610–1643
Louis XIV, 1643–1715
Louis XV, 1715–1774
Louis XVI, 1774–1792
First Republic, 1792–1799
Napoleon Bonaparte, First Consul, 1799–1804
Napoleon I, Emperor, 1804–1814
Louis XVIII (Bourbon Dynasty), 1814–1824
Charles X (Bourbon Dynasty), 1824–1830
Louis Philippe, 1830–1848

—————— *Rulers of France* ——————

Second Republic, 1848–1852
Napoleon III, Emperor, 1852–1870

Third Republic, 1870–1940
Pétain regime, 1940–1944
Provisional government, 1944–1946
Fourth Republic, 1946–1958
Fifth Republic, 1958–

Rulers of England

ANGLO-SAXON KINGS

Egbert, 802–839
Ethelwulf, 839–858
Ethelbald, 858–860
Ethelbert, 860–866
Ethelred, 866–871
Alfred the Great, 871–900
Edward the Elder, 900–924
Ethelstan, 924–940
Edmund I, 940–946
Edred, 946–955
Edwy, 955–959
Edgar, 959–975
Edward the Martyr, 975–978
Ethelred the Unready, 978–1016
Canute, 1016–1035 (Danish Nationality)
Harold I, 1035–1040
Hardicanute, 1040–1042
Edward the Confessor, 1042–1066
Harold II, 1066

ANGLO-NORMAN KINGS

William I (the Conqueror), 1066–1087
William II, 1087–1100
Henry I, 1100–1135
Stephen, 1135–1154

ANGEVIN KINGS

Henry II, 1154–1189
Richard I, 1189–1199
John, 1199–1216
Henry III, 1216–1272
Edward I, 1272–1307
Edward II, 1307–1327
Edward III, 1327–1377
Richard II, 1377–1399

HOUSE OF LANCASTER

Henry IV, 1399–1413
Henry V, 1413–1422
Henry VI, 1422–1461

House of York

Edward IV, 1461–1483
Edward V, 1483
Richard III, 1483–1485

Tudor Sovereigns

Henry VII, 1485–1509
Henry VIII, 1509–1547
Edward VI, 1547–1553
Mary, 1553–1558
Elizabeth I, 1558–1603

Stuart Kings

James I, 1603–1625
Charles I, 1625–1649

Later Stuart Monarchs

Charles II, 1660–1685
James II, 1685–1688
William III and Mary II, 1689–1694
William III alone, 1694–1702
Anne, 1702–1714

House of Hanover

George I, 1714–1727
George II, 1727–1760
George III, 1760–1820
George IV, 1820–1830
William IV, 1830–1837
Victoria, 1837–1901

House of Saxe-Coburg-Gotha

Edward VII, 1901–1910
George V, 1910–1917

House of Windsor

George V, 1917–1936
Edward VIII, 1936
George VI, 1936–1952
Elizabeth II, 1952–

Prominent Popes

Silvester I, 314–335
Leo I, 440–461
Gelasius I, 492–496

Gregory I, 590–604
Nicholas I, 858–867
Silvester II, 999–1003
Leo IX, 1049–1054
Nicholas II, 1058–1061
Gregory VII, 1073–1085
Urban II, 1088–1099
Paschal II, 1099–1118
Alexander III, 1159–1181
Innocent III, 1198–1216
Gregory IX, 1227–1241
Boniface VIII, 1294–1303
John XXII, 1316–1334
Nicholas V, 1447–1455
Pius II, 1458–1464
Alexander VI, 1492–1503
Julius II, 1503–1513
Leo X, 1513–1521
Adrian VI, 1522–1523
Clement VII, 1523–1534
Paul III, 1534–1549
Paul IV, 1555–1559
Gregory XIII, 1572–1585
Gregory XVI, 1831–1846
Pius IX, 1846–1878
Leo XIII, 1878–1903
Pius X, 1903–1914
Benedict XV, 1914–1922
Pius XI, 1922–1939
Pius XII, 1939–1958
John XXIII, 1958–1963
Paul VI, 1963–

Rulers of Austria and Austria-Hungary

*Maximilian I (Archduke), 1493–1519
*Charles I (Charles V in the Holy Roman Empire), 1519–1556
*Ferdinand I, 1556–1564
*Maximilian II, 1564–1576
*Rudolph II, 1576–1612
*Matthias, 1612–1619
*Ferdinand II, 1619–1637
*Ferdinand III, 1637–1657
*Leopold I, 1658–1705
*Joseph I, 1705–1711
*Charles VI, 1711–1740
  Maria Theresa, 1740–1780
*Joseph II, 1780–1790
*Leopold II, 1790–1792

*Francis II, 1792–1835 (Emperor of Austria as Francis I after 1804)
Ferdinand I, 1835–1848
Francis Joseph, 1848–1916 (after 1867 Emperor of Austria and King of Hungary)
Charles I, 1916–1918 (Emperor of Austria and King of Hungary)
Republic of Austria, 1918–1938 (dictatorship after 1934)
Republic restored, under Allied occupation, 1945–1956
Free Republic, 1956–

* Also bore title of Holy Roman Emperor.

Rulers of Prussia and Germany

*Frederick I, 1701–1713
*Frederick William I, 1713–1740
*Frederick II (the Great), 1740–1786
*Frederick William II, 1786–1797
*Frederick William III, 1797–1840
*Frederick William IV, 1840–1861
*William I, 1861–1888 (German Emperor after 1871)
Frederick III, 1888
William II, 1888–1918
Weimar Republic, 1918–1933
Third Reich (Nazi Dictatorship), 1933–1945
Allied occupation, 1945–1952
Division into Federal Republic of Germany in west and German
  Democratic Republic in east, 1949–

* Kings of Prussia.

Rulers of Russia

Ivan III, 1462–1505
Basil III, 1505–1533
Ivan IV, 1533–1584
Theodore I, 1584–1598
Boris Godunov, 1598–1605
Theodore II, 1605
Basil IV, 1606–1610
Michael, 1613–1645
Alexius, 1645–1676
Theodore III, 1676–1682
Ivan V and Peter I, 1682–1689
Peter I (the Great), 1689–1725
Catherine I, 1725–1727
Peter II, 1727–1730
Anna, 1730–1740
Ivan VI, 1740–1741
Elizabeth, 1741–1762

1309

Peter III, 1762
Catherine II (the Great), 1762–1796
Paul, 1796–1801
Alexander I, 1801–1825
Nicholas I, 1825–1855
Alexander II, 1855–1881
Alexander III, 1881–1894
Nicholas II, 1894–1917
Soviet Republic, 1917–

——————Rulers of Italy——————————————

Victor Emmanuel II, 1861–1878
Humbert I, 1878–1900
Victor Emmanuel III, 1900–1946
Fascist Dictatorship, 1922–1943 (maintained in northern Italy until 1945)
Humbert II, May 9–June 13, 1946
Republic, 1946–

——————— Rulers of Spain ———————————

Ferdinand ⎧ and Isabella, 1479–1504
　　　　　⎨ and Philip I, 1504–1506
　　　　　⎩ and Charles I, 1506–1516
Charles I (Holy Roman Emperor Charles V), 1516–1556
Philip II, 1556–1598
Philip III, 1598–1621
Philip IV, 1621–1665
Charles II, 1665–1700
Philip V, 1700–1746
Ferdinand VI, 1746–1759
Charles III, 1759–1788
Charles IV, 1788–1808
Ferdinand VII, 1808
Joseph Bonaparte, 1808–1813
Ferdinand VII (restored), 1814–1833
Isabella II, 1833–1868
Republic, 1868–1870
Amadeo, 1870–1873
Republic, 1873–1874
Alfonso XII, 1874–1885
Alfonso XIII, 1886–1931
Republic, 1931–1939
Fascist Dictatorship, 1939–

Principal Rulers of India

Chandragupta (Maurya Dynasty), *ca.* 322–298 B.C.
Asoka (Maurya Dynasty), *ca.* 273–232 B.C.
Vikramaditya (Gupta Dynasty), 375–413 A.D..
Harsha (Vardhana Dynasty), 606–648
Babur (Mogul Dynasty), 1526–1530
Akbar (Mogul Dynasty), 1556–1605
Shah Jahan (Mogul Dynasty), 1627–1658
Aurangzeb (Mogul Dynasty), 1658–1707
Regime of British East India Company, 1757–1858
British *raj*, 1858–1947
Division into self-governing dominions of India and Pakistan, 1947
Republic of India, 1950–
Republic of Pakistan, 1956–

Dynasties of China

Hsia, *ca.* 2205–1766 B.C. (?)
Shang (Yin), *ca.* 1766 (?)–1027 B.C. (or *ca.* 1523–1027 B.C.)
Chou, *ca.* 1027–249 B.C.
Ch'in, 221–207 B.C.
Han (Former), 206 B.C.–8 A.D.
Interregnum (Wang Mang, usurper), 8– 23A.D.
Han (Later), 25–220
Wei, 220–265
Tsin (Chin), 265–420
Southern Dynasties: Sung (Liu Sung), Ch'i, Liang, Ch'ên, 420–589
Northern Dynasties: Northern Wei, Western Wei, Eastern Wei, Northern Ch'i, Northern Chou, 386–581
Sui, 589–618
T'ang, 618–907
Five Dynasties: Later Liang, Later T'ang, Later Tsin, Later Han, Later Chou, 907–960
Sung, 960–1279
Yüan (Mongol), 1279–1368
Ming, 1368–1644
Ch'ing (Manchu) Dynasty, 1644–1912

Periods of Chinese Rule

Chinese Republic, 1912–1949
Communist Regime, 1949–

Periods of Japanese Rule

Legendary Period, *ca.* 660 B.C.–530 A.D.
Foundation Period, 530–709 A.D.
Taika (Great Reform) Period, 645–654
Nara Period, 710–793
Heian Period, 794–1192
Kamakura Period, 1192–1333
Namboku-cho ("Northern and Southern Dynasties") Period, 1336–1392
Muromachi (Ashikaga) Period, 1392–1568
Sengoku ("Country at War") Period, *ca.* 1500–1600
Sengoku Period, *ca.* 1500–1600
Edo (Tokugawa) Period, 1603–1867
Meiji Period (Mutsuhito), 1868–1912
Taisho Period (Yoshihito), 1912–1926
Showa Period (Hirohito), 1926–

Rulers of Principal African States

Mansa Musa, ruler of Mali empire, 1312–1337
Ewaure the Great, Oba of Benin, 1440–1473
Muhammad Runfa, King of Kano, 1463–1499
Afonso I, King of Kongo, 1506–1543
Ibrahim Maje, King of Katsina, 1549–1567
Idris Alooma, Mai of Bornu, 1569–ca. 1619
Osei Tutu, King of Asante, ca. 1670–1717
Agaja, King of Dahomey, 1708–1740
Sayyid Said, ruler of Zanzibar and Muscat, 1804–1856
Shaka, King of the Zulu, 1818–1828
Moshesh, King of Basutoland, 1824–1868
Menelik, King of Shoa, 1865–1889; Emperor of Ethiopia, 1889–1913

Illustrations in Color

(page numbers refer to facing pages)

Illustrations in the Text

1317

1319

Index

A

B

C

D

E

F

G

H

I

J

K

L

M

N

O

P

Q

R

S

T

U

W